Fodor's
Touring USA:
Eastern
Edition

Fodor's Travel Publications, Inc.
New York • London • Toronto

The tours in this book have been adapted from material that appears in the following other Fodor's guidebooks:

Fodor's Chicago
Fodor's Florida
Fodor's New England
Fodor's New York State
Fodor's Philadelphia
Fodor's The South
Fodor's The Upper Great Lakes Region
Fodor's Washington, D.C.

Fodor's Touring USA

Editor: Holly Hughes
Editorial Contributors: Susan Bain, Bob Blake, Don Davenport, Jeffrey Obser, Patricia Preston, Marcy Pritchard
Art Director: Fabrizio LaRocca
Cartographer: David Lindroth
Illustrator: Karl Tanner
Cover Photograph: Del Mulkey/Photo Researchers

Design: Vignelli Associates

Special Sales

Contents

Foreword *vii*

Essential Information *1*

Before You Go *2*

Visitor Information *2*
Tour Groups *2*
Package Deals for Independent Travelers *2*
Insurance *2*
Tips for British Travelers *2*
Traveling with Children *4*
Hints for Disabled Travelers *4*
Hints for Older Travelers *5*
Home Exchange *6*

Arriving and Departing *6*

Traveling by Plane *6*
Traveling by Car *9*
Traveling by Train *10*
Traveling by Bus *10*

On the Road *11*

Emergencies *11*
Cash Machines *11*
Dining *11*
Lodging *11*
Credit Cards *12*

Tour 1: Boston to Bar Harbor *13*

Tour 2: New York City to Boston *110*

Tour 3: New York to the Cape *196*

Tour 4: Philadelphia and Historic Pennsylvania *269*

Tour 5: Washington, D.C., and Historic Virginia *332*

Tour 6: The Southeast Coast to Orlando *411*

Tour 7: Nashville to New Orleans *523*

Tour 8: New Orleans to Orlando *593*

Tour 9: Chicago and the Upper Great Lakes *639*

Index *751*

Maps

Touring USA *viii–ix*
Boston *20–21*
Boston Dining and Lodging *38–39*
The North Shore *51*
New Hampshire Coast *63*
Southern Maine Coast *73*
Portland *81*
Penobscot Bay *94*
Acadia *104*
New York City (Uptown) *118*
New York City (Downtown) *127*
New York City Dining and Lodging (Uptown) *136*
New York City Dining and Lodging (Downtown) *137*
Hudson Valley *154*
The Berkshires *171*
The Pioneer Valley *186*
Southwestern Connecticut *201*
Southeastern Connecticut *216*
Rhode Island Coast *227*
Newport *238*
Cape Cod *252–253*
Philadelphia *276–277*
Valley Forge *305*
Lancaster County *309*
Gettysburg *327*
Washington, D.C. *342–343*
Washington, D.C., Dining and Lodging *366–367*
Northern Virginia *381*
The Piedmont *389*
Richmond *390*
Williamsburg and Environs *397*
Shenandoah Valley and the Highlands *402*
South Carolina Coast *417*
Charleston *427*
Savannah Historic District *453*
Golden Isles *469*
Northeast Florida *476*
St. Augustine *479*
Central Florida *484*
Walt Disney World *499*
Orlando Area *503*
Downtown Nashville *529*
Nashville *529*
Natchez Trace *543*
Baton Rouge and Plantation Country *561*
New Orleans *572–573*
New Orleans Dining and Lodging *582–583*
Mississippi Coast *599*
Mobile and the Gulf Coast *606*
The Panhandle *616*
Northeast Florida *631*

Chicago Downtown *647*
Hyde Park and Kenwood *654*
River North and Lincoln Park *659*
Chicago Dining and Lodging (North) *670*
Chicago Dining and Lodging (Downtown) *671*
Northeastern Illinois *686*
Milwaukee *690–691*
Eastern Wisconsin *703*
Northern Wisconsin *717*
Arrowhead Minnesota *725*
Northwestern Michigan and Upper Peninsula *733*
Southwestern Michigan *745*

Foreword

While every care has been taken to ensure the accuracy of the information in this guide, the passage of time will always bring change, and consequently the publisher cannot accept responsibility for errors that may occur.

All prices and opening times quoted here are based on information supplied to us at press time. Hours and admission fees may change, however, and the prudent traveler will avoid inconvenience by calling ahead.

Fodor's wants to hear about your travel experiences, both pleasant and unpleasant. When a hotel or restaurant fails to live up to its billing, let us know and we will investigate the complaint and revise our entries where the facts warrant it.

Send your letters to the editors of Fodor's Travel Publications, 201 E. 50th Street, New York, NY 10022.

Touring USA: The East *(Boxes refer to detail maps of regional tours)*

NORTH DAKOTA
★ Bismarck

SOUTH DAKOTA
★ Pierre

MINNESOTA

Lake Superior

MICHIGAN

St. Paul ★

WISCONSIN

Lake Michigan

Milwaukee ○

Lansi

Madison ★

Chicago ○

IOWA

NEBRASKA

Lincoln ★

Des Moines ★

ILLINOIS

INDIA

Springfield ★ Indianapolis ★

Topeka ★

Jefferson City ★

KANSAS

MISSOURI

Tour 7

Nashville ★

TENNESSEE

OKLAHOMA

Little Rock ★

Oklahoma City ★

ARKANSAS

MISSISSIPPI

Jackson ★

TEXAS

LOUISIANA

Mobi ○

Austin ★

Baton Rouge ○
★
New Orleans ○

Essential Information

Before You Go

Visitor Information

State tourism offices, city tourist bureaus, and local chambers of commerce are listed at the beginning of each tour chapter in this book. British visitors seeking general information about the United States may want to contact the U.S. Travel and Tourism Administration (22 Sackville St., London W1X 2EA, tel. 071/439–7433).

For information on national parks, battlefields, and recreational areas, write to the National Park Service (Department of the Interior, Washington, DC 20240).

Tour Groups

Although the tours outlined in this book are designed for use by independent travelers, some people prefer the security (and, in many cases, the savings) offered by escorted tours. Some prominent operators include Casser Tours (46 W. 43rd St., New York, NY 10036, tel. 212/840–6500 or 800/251–1411); Domenico Tours (751 Broadway, Bayonne, NJ 07002, tel. 201/823–8687 or 800/554–TOUR); Globus Gateway/Cosmos (9525 Queens Blvd., Rego Park, NY 11374, tel. 718/268–7000 or 800/556–5454); Maupintour (Box 807, Lawrence, KS 66044, tel. 913/843–1211 or 800/255–4266); and Tauck Tours (Box 5027, Westport, CT 06880, tel. 203/226–6911 or 800/468–2825).

Package Deals for Independent Travelers

Organizations offering transportation/hotel packages include American Express (Box 5014, Atlanta, GA 30302, tel. 800/241–1700 or 800/282–0800 INGA); American FlyAAway Vacations (tel. 800/321–2121); Continental Airlines (tel. 800/634–5555); Delta Air Lines (tel. 800/872–7786); TWA Getaway Vacations (tel. 800/GETAWAY); and United Airlines (tel. 800/328–6877).

Insurance

Comprehensive travel insurance packages usually include personal, accident, trip cancellation, and sometimes default and bankruptcy insurance. Several companies offer comprehensive policies:

Access America, Inc. (a subsidiary of Blue Cross/Blue Shield; Box 11188, Richmond, VA 23230, tel. 800/334–7525 or 800/284–8300).
Carefree Travel Insurance (Box 310, 120 Mineola Blvd., Mineola, NY 11501, tel. 516/294–0220 or 800/323–3149).
Near Services (450 Prairie Ave., Suite 101, Calumet City, IL 60409, tel. 708/868–6700 or 800/654–6700).
Travel Guard International (underwritten by Transamerica Occidental Life Companies; 1145 Clark St., Stevens Point, WI 54481, tel. 715/345–0505 or 800/782–5151).

Tips for British Travelers

Passports and Visas British visitors need a valid 10-year passport to enter the United States (cost £15 for a standard 32-page passport, £30 for a 94-page passport). Application forms are available from most travel agents and major post offices and from the **Passport Office** (Clive House, 70 Petty France, London SW1H 9HD, tel. 071/279–3434 for recorded information or 071/279–4000). You do not need a visa if you are visiting either on business or pleasure, are staying less than 90 days, have a return ticket, are traveling with a major airline (in effect, any airline that flies from the United Kingdom to the United States), and complete visa waiver form I791, which is supplied either at the airport of departure or on the plane. If you fail to comply with any one of these requirements or are entering the United States by land, you will need a visa. Apply to a travel agent or the **United States Embassy** (Visa and Immigration Department, 5 Upper Grosvenor St., London W1A 2JB, tel. 071/499–3443 for a recorded message or 071/499–7010). Visa applications to the U.S. Embassy must be made by mail, not in person. Visas can be given only to holders of 10-year passports, although visas in expired passports remain valid.

Customs Entering the United States, a visitor 21 or over can bring in 200 cigarettes or 50 cigars or 2 kilograms of tobacco; 1 U.S. liter of alcohol; duty-free gifts to a value of $100. You may not bring in meat or meat products, seeds, plants, or fruit. Absolutely avoid carrying illegal drugs.

Returning to the United Kingdom, a traveler 17 or over can take home (1) 200 cigarettes or 100 cigarillos or 50 cigars or 250 grams of tobacco; (2) two liters of still table wine; (3) one liter of alcoholic drink over 22% volume *or* two liters of alcoholic drink under 22% volume *or* two liters of fortified or sparkling wine or two more liters of still table wine; (4) 60 ml of perfume and 250 ml of toilet water; (5) other goods to a value of £32, but no more than 50 liters of beer or 25 lighters.

Insurance We recommend that you take out insurance to guard against health problems, motoring mishaps, theft, flight cancellation, and loss of luggage. Most major tour operators offer holiday insurance, and details are given in brochures. For free general advice on all aspects of holiday insurance, contact the **Association of British Insurers** (Aldermary House, 10–15 Queen St., London EC4N 1TT, tel. 071/248–4477). A proven leader in the holiday insurance field is **Europ Assistance** (252 High St., Croydon, Surrey CR0 1NF, tel. 081/680–1234).

Airlines Airlines flying from the U.K. to the United States include **Air India** (tel. 071/491–7979); **American Airlines** (tel. 071/629–8817); **British Airways** (tel. 081/897–4000); **Continental** (tel. 0293/567–955); **Delta Airlines** (tel. 0800/414767); **El Al** (tel. 071/437–9255); **Northwest** (tel. 0293/28822); **TWA** (tel. 071/439–0707); and **Virgin Atlantic** (tel. 0293/567711). Airfares vary enormously, depending on the type of ticket you buy and the time of year you travel. The small ads in the daily and Sunday papers are a good source for low-cost flight offers.

Tour Operators The following is a selection of companies that offer tour packages to the eastern United States. For details of these and other resources, consult a travel agent.

Albany Travel (Manchester) Ltd. (Central Buildings, 211 Deansgate, Manchester M2 5QR, tel. 061/833–0202); **American Airplan** (Airplan House, Churchfield Rd., Walton-on-Thames, Surrey KT12 2TZ, tel. 0932/231322); **Cosmos** (ground floor, Dale House, Tiviot Dale, Stockport, Cheshire SK1 1TB, tel.

061/480–5799); **North American Vacations** (Acorn House, 172/
174 Albert Rd., Jarrow, Tyne & Wear NE32 5JA, tel. 091/483–
6226); **Poundstretcher** (Atlantic House, Hazelwick Ave., Three
Bridges, Crawley, W. Sussex RH10 1NP, tel. 0293/518022);
Premier Holidays (Premier Travel Center, Westbrook, Milton
Rd., Cambridge CB4 1YQ, tel. 0223/355977).

Traveling with Children

Family Travel Times is a newsletter published 10 times a year
by Travel with Your Children (TWYCH, 80 8th Ave., New
York, NY 10011, tel. 212/206–0688). A one-year subscription
for $35 includes access to back issues and twice-weekly oppor-
tunities to call for specific advice.

Great Vacations with Your Kids, by Dorothy Jordan (founder of
TWYCH) and Marjorie Cohen, offers complete advice on planning a trip with children (toddlers to teens) and reports on special travel accommodations available to families (E. P. Dutton,
2 Park Ave., New York, NY 10016, tel. 212/725–1818; $12.95
paperback).

Family Travel Guides (Carousel Press, Box 6061, Albany, CA
94706, tel. 415/527–5849) is a catalog offering guidebooks,
games, diaries, and magazine articles geared to traveling with
children. To receive the catalog, send $1 for postage and han-
dling or a business-size SASE with 45¢ postage.

Hints for Disabled Travelers

The **Information Center for Individuals with Disabilities** (Fort
Point Pl., 27–43 Wormwood St., Boston, MA 02210, tel. 617/
727–5540; TDD 617/727–5236) offers useful problem-solving
assistance, including lists of travel agents who specialize in
tours for the disabled.

Moss Rehabilitation Hospital Travel Information Service (1200
W. Tabor Rd., Philadelphia, PA 19141, tel. 215/456–9600; TDD
215/456–9602) provides information on tourist sites, transportation, and accommodations in destinations around the world
for a small fee.

Travel Industry and Disabled Exchange (TIDE, 5435 Donna
Ave., Tarzana, CA 91356, tel. 818/368–5648), for a $15 (per per-
son) annual membership fee, provides a quarterly newsletter
and a directory of travel agencies that specialize in service to
the disabled.

Mobility International USA (Box 3551, Eugene, OR 97403, tel.
503/343–1284) is an internationally affiliated organization with
500 members. For a $20 annual fee, it coordinates exchange
programs for disabled people in the United States and around
the world and offers information on accommodations and organized study programs.

Twin Peaks Press publishes three useful resources: *Travel for
the Disabled* ($9.95), *Directory of Travel Agencies for the Dis-
abled* ($12.95), and *Wheelchair Vagabond* ($9.95). Order
through a bookstore or from the publisher, Twin Peaks Press
(Box 129, Vancouver, WA 98666, tel. 206/694–2462). When ordering by mail, add $2 postage for one book, $1 for each additional book.

Access to the World: A Travel Guide for the Handicapped, by
Louise Weiss, offers tips on travel and accessibility around the
world. It is available from Henry Holt & Co. for $12.95 (tel.
800/247–3912; order number 0805001417).

***Access America: An Atlas and Guide to the National Parks for
Visitors with Disabilities,*** published by Northern Cartograph-
ic (Box 133, Burlington, VT 05402, tel. 802/655–4321), contains
detailed information on access for the 37 largest and most visited national parks in the United States. Available directly
from the publisher, the award-winning book costs $44.95 plus
$5 shipping.

Hints for Older Travelers

The **American Association of Retired Persons** (AARP, 1909 K
St. NW, Washington, DC 20049, tel. 202/662–4850) has two
programs for independent travelers: (1) the **Purchase Privilege
Program,** which offers discounts on hotels, airfare, car rentals,
RV rentals, and sightseeing; and (2) the **AARP Motoring Plan,**
provided by Amoco, which furnishes emergency aid (road service) and trip-routing information for an annual fee of $33.95
per person or couple. (Both programs include the member and
member's spouse or the member and another person who
shares the household.) **AARP Travel Experience** (tel. 800/927–
0111) also arranges group tours at reduced rates through
American Express. AARP members must be 50 years or older;
annual dues are $5 per person or per couple.

Elderhostel (75 Federal St., 3rd fl., Boston, MA 02110, tel. 617/
426–7788) is an innovative educational program for people 60
and older. Participants live in dorms on some 1,200 campuses
around the world. Mornings are devoted to lectures and semi-
nars, afternoons to sightseeing and field trips. Fees for two- to
three-week trips, including room, board, tuition, and round-
trip transportation, range from $1,800 to $4,500. The catalog is
free for the first year (and if you participate in a program); after that it costs $10.

National Council of Senior Citizens (925 15th St. NW, Washington, DC 20005, tel. 202/347–8800) is a nonprofit advocacy group
with some 5,000 local clubs across the country. Annual membership ($12 per person or per couple) brings you a monthly
newspaper with travel information and an ID card for reduced
rates on hotels and car rentals.

Mature Outlook (6001 N. Clark St., Chicago, IL 60660, tel. 800/
336–6330), a subsidiary of Sears Roebuck & Co., is a travel club
for people over 50, with hotel and motel discounts and a bi-
monthly newsletter. Annual membership is $9.95, and there
are 800,000 members currently. Instant membership is available at Sears stores and participating Holiday Inns.

Golden Age Passport is a free lifetime pass to all parks, monuments, and recreation areas run by the federal government.
People over age 61 can pick one up at any national park that
charges admission. The passport also provides a 50% discount
on camping, boat launching, and parking (lodging is not included). A driver's license or other proof of age is required.

Saga International Holidays (120 Boylston St., Boston, MA
02116, tel. 800/343–0273) specializes in group travel for people
over 60 and offers a variety of tour packages at various prices.

September Days Club (tel. 800/241–5050) is run by the moderately priced Days Inns of America. The $12 annual membership fee for individuals or couples over 50 entitles them to reduced car-rental rates and reductions of 15%–50% at most of the chain's 350 motels.

When using an AARP or other discount identification card, ask for reduced hotel rates when you make your reservation, not when you check out. At participating restaurants, show your card to the maitre d' before you're seated, since discounts may be limited to certain set menus, days, or hours. When renting a car, remember that economy cars, priced at promotional rates, may cost less than cars available with your discount ID card.

The International Health Guide for Senior Citizen Travelers, by W. Robert Lange, M.D., is available for $4.95 plus $1 shipping, and *The Senior Citizens Guide to Budget Travel in the United States and Canada,* by Paige Palmer, is available for $3.95 plus $1 shipping, both from Pilot Books (103 Cooper St., Babylon, NY 11702, tel. 516/422–2225).

The Discount Guide for Travelers Over 55, by Caroline and Walter Weintz, lists helpful addresses, package tours, and reduced-rate car rentals in the United States and abroad. To order, send $7.95 plus $1.50 shipping to Penguin USA/NAL (120 Woodbine St., Bergenfield, NJ 07621, tel. 800/526–0275; order number ISBN 0–525–483–58–6).

Home Exchange

Vacation Exchange Club (Box 820, Haleiwa, HI 96712, tel. 800/638–3841) specializes in domestic home exchanges. The club publishes an annual directory in August. Membership, at $50 per year, entitles you to one listing and all directories; photos cost another $12, listing a second home costs $10.

Loan-a-Home (2 Park La., Apt. 6E, Mount Vernon, NY 10552, tel. 914/664–7640) is popular with the academic community on sabbatical and with businesspeople on temporary assignment. There's no annual membership fee or charge for listing your home, but one directory and a supplement costs $35.

Arriving and Departing

Traveling by Plane

When booking a flight, travelers will want to keep in mind the distinction between *nonstop flights* (your destination is the only scheduled stop), *direct flights* (one or more stops are scheduled before you reach your destination), and *connecting flights* (you'll stop and change planes before you reach your final destination).

Here are the toll-free reservations numbers for the major airlines serving this region:

Air Canada (tel. 800/776–3000)
American (tel. 800/433–7300)
British Airways (tel. 800/247–9297)
Continental (tel. 800/525–0280)
Delta (tel. 800/221–1212)

Midwest (tel. 800/452–2022)
Northwest (tel. 800/225–2525)
Pan American (tel. 800/221–1111)
Trump Shuttle (tel. 800/247–8786)
TWA (tel. 800/221–2000)
United (tel. 800/241–6522)
USAir (tel. 800/428–4322)

Smoking The Federal Aviation Administration has banned smoking on all scheduled flights within the 48 contiguous states; within the states of Alaska and Hawaii; to and from the U.S. Virgin Islands and Puerto Rico; and on flights of under six hours to and from Alaska and Hawaii. The rules apply to both domestic and foreign carriers, but only to the domestic legs of foreign routes (they do not affect international flights). When necessary, a request for a seat in a no-smoking section should be made at the time you make your reservation.

If the airline tells you there are no seats available in the no-smoking section on the day of the flight, insist on one: Department of Transportation regulations require U.S. carriers to find seats for all nonsmokers, provided they meet check-in time restrictions.

Carry-on Luggage Passengers aboard major U.S. carriers are usually limited to two carry-on bags. Bags stored under the seat must not exceed $9'' \times 14'' \times 22''$. Bags hung in a closet can be no larger than $4'' \times 23'' \times 45''$. The maximum dimensions for bags stored in an overhead bin are $10'' \times 14'' \times 36''$. Any item that exceeds the specified dimensions will generally be rejected as a carryon and handled as checked baggage. Keep in mind that an airline can adapt these rules to circumstances; on a crowded flight, you may be allowed to take only one carry-on bag aboard.

In addition to the two carryons, passengers may bring aboard: a handbag; an overcoat or wrap; an umbrella; a camera; a reasonable amount of reading material; an infant bag; and crutches, braces, a cane, or other prosthetic device upon which the passenger is dependent. Infant/child safety seats can also be brought aboard if parents have purchased a ticket for the child or if there is space in the cabin. (Rules on safety seats are in the process of changing, so check with your airline before leaving.)

Note that these regulations are for U.S. airlines only. Foreign airlines generally allow only one piece of carry-on luggage in tourist class, in addition to handbags and bags filled with duty-free goods. Passengers in first and business class are also allowed to carry on one garment bag. It is best to call your airline in advance to learn its rules regarding carry-on luggage.

Checked Luggage Luggage allowances vary slightly among airlines. Many carriers allow three checked pieces; some allow only two. It is best to consult with the airline before you go. In all cases, checked luggage cannot weigh more than 70 pounds per piece or be larger than 62 inches (length + width + height). Rules governing foreign airlines vary from airline to airline, so check with your travel agent or the airline itself before you go.

Lost Luggage On domestic flights, airlines are responsible for up to $1,250 per passenger in lost or damaged property. Airlines are responsible for up to $9.07 per pound ($20 per kilo) for checked baggage on international flights, and up to $400 per passenger for unchecked baggage on international flights. If you're carrying valuables, either take them with you on the plane or purchase additional insurance for lost luggage. Some airlines will issue luggage insurance when you check in, but many do not. Rates are generally $1 for every $100 valuation, with a maximum of $25,000 valuation per passenger. Hand luggage is not included.

Insurance for lost, damaged, or stolen luggage is available through travel agents or directly through insurance companies. (Coverage for lost luggage may also be part of a comprehensive travel-insurance package that includes insurance against personal accident, trip cancellation, and sometimes default and bankruptcy; *see* Insurance, *above*.) Two companies that issue luggage insurance are **Tele-Trip** (Box 31685, 3201 Farnam St., Omaha, NE 68131, tel. 800/228–9792), a subsidiary of Mutual of Omaha, and **The Travelers Corporation** (Ticket and Travel Dept., 1 Tower Sq., Hartford, CT 06183, tel. 203/277–0111 or 800/243–3174). Tele-Trip operates sales booths at airports and issues insurance through travel agents. Tele-Trip will insure checked or hand luggage through its travel insurance packages. Rates vary according to the length of the trip. The Travelers Corporation will insure checked or hand luggage with a valuation of $500–$2,000 per person for up to 180 days. Rates for $500 valuation are $10 for 1–5 days, $85 for 180 days.

Before you go, itemize the contents of each bag in case you need to file an insurance claim. Be certain to put your address on each piece of luggage, including carry-on bags. If your luggage is stolen and later recovered, the airline will deliver it to your home free of charge.

Flying with Children
On domestic flights, children under 2 not occupying a seat travel free. Various discounts apply to children age 2–12. If possible, reserve a seat behind the bulkhead of the plane; these offer more legroom and usually enough space to fit a bassinet (supplied by the airlines). Regulations governing infant travel on airplanes are in the process of being changed. Until they do, however, if you want to be sure your infant is secured in his/her own safety seat, you must buy a separate ticket and bring your own infant car seat. (Check with the airline in advance; certain seats aren't allowed. Or write for the booklet "Child/Infant Safety Seats Acceptable for Use in Aircraft," from the Federal Aviation Administration, APA–200, 800 Independence Ave. SW, Washington, DC 20591, tel. 202/267–3479.) Some airlines allow babies to travel in their own safety seats at no charge if there's a spare seat available on the plane; otherwise safety seats are stored and the child must be held by a parent. If you opt to hold your baby on your lap, do so with the infant outside the seat belt so he or she isn't crushed in case of a sudden stop.

When making reservations, inquire about special children's meals or snacks, which are also offered by most airlines. (For a rundown on children's services offered by 46 airlines, see "TWYCH's Airline Guide," in the February 1990 and 1992 issues of *Family Travel Times*, published by Travel With Your Children (80 8th Ave., New York, NY 10011, tel. 212/206–0688).

Kids and Teens in Flight is a brochure developed by the Department of Transportation on children traveling alone. To order a free copy, call 202/366–2220.

Disabled Passengers   *Fly Rights,* a free brochure available on request from the U.S. Department of Transportation (tel. 202/366–2220), gives airline access information for the disabled.

Traveling by Car

Rules of the Road   Highway speed limits are 55 miles per hour (some states have raised the limit to 65, but this part of the country, as a rule, hasn't). Watch for lower speed limits posted in towns and on smaller back roads. Most states require front-seat passengers to wear seat belts, and children under 4 must ride in approved child safety seats or be buckled into seat belts.

In some communities, it is permissible to make a right turn at a red light, once the car has come to a full stop and there is no oncoming traffic. When in doubt about local laws, however, wait until the green light.

The fastest routes are usually the interstate highways, each numbered with an prefix "I–". Even numbers (I–80, I–40, etc.) are east–west roads, odd numbers (I–91, I–55, etc.) run north–south. These are fully signposted, limited-access highways with at least two lanes in each direction. In some cases they are toll roads (the Pennsylvania Turnpike is I–76; the Massachusetts Turnpike is I–90). Near large cities, interstates usually intersect with a circumferential loop highway (I–295, etc.) that carries through traffic around the city.

The next level of highway—not limited access, but well-paved and usually multilane—is the U.S. highways (designated U.S. 1, etc.). State highways are also well-paved and often have more than one lane in each direction.

Car Rentals   **Avis** (tel. 800/331–1212), **Budget** (tel. 800/527–0700), **Dollar** (tel. 800/800–4000), **Hertz** (tel. 800/654–3131), **National** (tel. 800/328–4567), **Sears** (tel. 800/527–0770), and **Thrifty** (tel. 800/367–2277) maintain airport and city locations throughout the United States. Other national companies, which may offer lower rates, include **American International** (tel. 800/225–2529), **Alamo** (tel. 800/327–9633), **General** (tel. 800/327–7607), and **Rent-A-Wreck** (tel. 800/221–8282).

Make your car arrangements before you leave home, and do some comparison shopping before making a reservation. Costs vary greatly among companies, depending on the number of days you expect to need the car, whether you need it for weekend or weekday use, and whether you expect to do a lot of driving or a little. Car rental advertisements can be misleading. Be sure to ask about add-on charges for insurance coverage (collision, personal injury), gasoline (some companies include gas in their daily rate, others in their mileage fees, others make a separate charge for gas, and still others leave the gas up to you), and drop-off at a location other than the one where you picked up the car (subcharges here can be substantial).

Find out what the collision damage waiver (CDW), usually an $8–$12 daily surcharge, covers and whether your corporate or personal insurance already covers damage to a rental car (if so, bring a photocopy of the benefits section along). More and more companies are now holding renters responsible for theft and vandalism damages if they don't buy the CDW; in response, some credit card and insurance companies are extending their coverage to rental cars. These include **Access America** (tel. 800/

851–2800), **Chase Manhattan Bank Visa Cards** (tel. 800/645–7352), and **Dreyfus Consumer Bank Gold and Silver Master-Cards** (tel. 800/847–9700).

When you've decided on the company and reserved a car, *be sure to get a reservation number*. Remember, if the company doesn't have the car you reserved when you arrive to pick it up, the company must provide a comparable or better car at the price you reserved.

Auto Clubs   The **American Automobile Association (AAA)** (12600 Fair Lakes Circle, Fairfax, VA 22033, tel. 703/222–6000 or 800/763–6600) offers maps, route planning, and emergency road service to its members. Look in local telephone directories for the AAA Emergency Road service number, or call 800/336–HELP.

Two other helpful auto clubs are **Allstate Motor Club** (Allstate Pl., Northbrook, IL 60062, tel. 312/402–5461) and **AMOCO Motor Club** (Box 9014, Des Moines, IA 50306, tel. 800/334–3300).

Traveling by Train

Amtrak (tel. 800/872–7245; TDD 800/523–6590) is the national passenger rail service. The tours described in this book cannot be made entirely by train, but each tour chapter provides information on the location of Amtrak stations en route.

Some trains travel overnight, and you can sleep in your seat or book a berth at additional cost. Most trains have attractive diner cars with acceptable food, but you may prefer to bring your own. Excursion fares, when available, may save you nearly half the round-trip fare.

Amtrak requests advance notice to provide redcap service, special seats, or wheelchair assistance at stations equipped to provide these services. All elderly and disabled passengers are entitled to a 25% discount on regular coach fares. A special children's disabled fare is also available, offering qualified children age 2–12 a 50% discount on already discounted children's fares. However, it is wise to check the price of excursion tickets first. These often work out much cheaper than disabled discounts on regular tickets. For a free copy of *Access Amtrak*, which outlines all its services for the elderly and disabled, contact Amtrak (National Railroad Corp., 400 N. Capitol St. NW, Washington, DC 20001).

Traveling by Bus

Various regional bus companies serve their areas of the country; the most extensive long-haul service is provided by **Greyhound/Trailway Lines,** which can be reached by calling local numbers listed in the tour chapters. Call Greyhound/Trailways (tel. 800/752–4841; TDD 800/345–3109) for special fares for disabled passengers and their companions. Greyhound/Trailways also offers special fares for senior citizens, subject to date and destination restrictions; call local numbers.

On the Road

Emergencies

In most local communities, you can call police, fire, or ambulance by dialing 911.

Cash Machines

Virtually all U.S. banks belong to a network of ATMs (Automated Teller Machines) that dispense cash 24 hours a day in cities throughout the country. There are some eight major networks in the United States, the largest of which are Cirrus, owned by MasterCard, and Plus, affiliated with Visa. Some banks belong to more than one network. To receive a card for one of these systems, you must apply for it. Cards issued by Visa and MasterCard also may be used in the ATMs, but the fees are usually higher than the fees on bank cards. There is also a daily interest charge on credit card "loans," even if monthly bills are paid on time. Each network has a toll-free number you can call to locate machines in a given city. The Cirrus number is 800/424–7787; the Plus number is 800/843–7587. Check with your bank for information on fees and on the amount of cash you can withdraw on any given day.

Express Cash allows American Express cardholders to withdraw up to $1,000 in a seven-day period (21 days overseas) from their personal checking accounts at ATMs worldwide. Gold-cardholders can receive up to $2,500 in a seven-day period (21 days overseas). Express Cash is not a cash-advance service; only money already in the linked checking account can be withdrawn. Every transaction carries a 2% fee with a minimum charge of $2 and a maximum of $6. Apply for a PIN (Personal Identification Number) and to link your accounts at least two–three weeks before departure. Call 800/CASH–NOW to receive an application or to locate the nearest Express Cash machine.

Dining

The restaurants listed in this guide are grouped by price categories. Because prices may vary greatly from region to region, or between a city and the surrounding countryside, categories have been defined for each leg of the tour at the beginning of that region's dining list. These categories are based on the average cost of a three-course dinner, per person, excluding drinks, tips, and local taxes. Highly recommended restaurants are indicated by a star (★).

Lodging

The hotels, motels, inns, and resorts listed in this guide are grouped by price category. Because prices may vary greatly from region to region, or between a city and the surrounding countryside, price categories have been defined for each leg of the tour at the beginning of that region's lodging list. These categories are based on the average cost of a standard double room in high season, not including local taxes or gratuities. Highly recommended lodgings are indicated by a star (★).

Credit Cards

The following credit card abbreviations are used in this guide:
AE, American Express; D, Discover; DC, Diners Club; MC,
MasterCard; V, Visa. It's always a good idea to call ahead and
confirm an establishment's credit card policy.

Tour 1:
Boston to
Bar Harbor

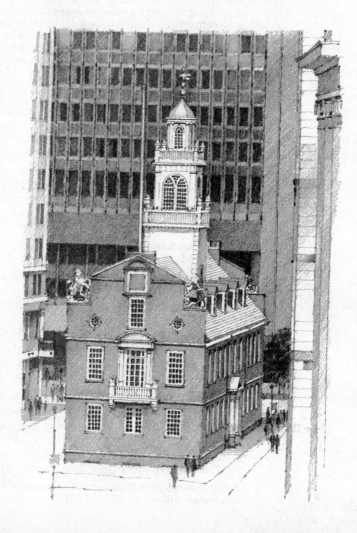

This stretch of Atlantic coastline is classic New England. The tour begins in Boston, cradle of the American Revolution and the unofficial capital of New England; it moves up the North Shore of Massachusetts to picturesque Cape Ann, swings through New Hampshire's few miles of bustling beach towns, and then traces the jagged Maine coastline, with its succession of salty harbor towns. This area of the country really comes alive in summer, when the beaches are busy and excursion boats prowl the coastline, but late spring and early fall are excellent times to visit, especially if you believe that a little fog is atmospheric.

There's good shopping here, whether you like browsing through musty antiques shops or prowling for bargains in outlet stores; for luxury items, of course, you'll want to indulge yourself while you're still in Boston.

The trip from Boston to Bar Harbor could be made in a couple of days driving straight through, but once you get off I–95 and begin stopping off along the way, you should allow at least a week. Even better would be to choose one or two of the resort towns en route where you'd like to stay put for three or four days before completing the circuit. Loll on a beach, take a sailboat cruise, pedal a bike along flat, sandy shore roads, and fill your lungs with the tang of salt air.

If you're starting from New York City, you can combine this tour with either Tour 2, which ends up in Boston, or Tour 3, which ends in Cape Cod (the drive from Cape Cod to Boston takes only an hour and a half, provided you don't get stuck in the weekend exodus in summer).

Visitor Information

Massachusetts **Massachusetts Office of Travel and Tourism** (100 Cambridge St., Boston 02202, tel. 617/727–3201).

Boston Common Information Kiosk (Tremont St., where the Freedom Trail begins, tel. 617/536–4100).

National Park Service Visitor Center (15 State St., Boston, tel. 617/242–5642).

North of Boston Visitors and Convention Bureau (Box 3031, Peabody 01961, tel. 508/532–1449).

Cape Ann Chamber of Commerce (33 Commercial St., Gloucester 01930, tel. 508/283–1601).

Essex North Chamber of Commerce (29 State St., Newburyport 01950, tel. 508/462–6680).

Rockport Chamber of Commerce Visitor's Booth (Box 67, Upper Main St., Rockport 01966, tel. 508/546–6575).

Salem Chamber of Commerce and Visitor Information (32 Derby Sq., Salem 01970, tel. 508/744–0004).

New Hampshire **New Hampshire Office of Vacation Travel** (Box 856, Concord 03301, tel. 603/271–2665 or 800/678–5040).

Seacoast Council on Tourism (1000 Market St., Portsmouth 03801, tel. 603/436–7678 or 800/221–5623 outside NH).

Hampton Beach Area Chamber of Commerce (836 Lafayette Rd., Hampton 03842, tel. 603/926–8717).

Greater Portsmouth Chamber of Commerce (500 Market St., Portsmouth 03801, tel. 603/436–1118).

Dover Chamber of Commerce (299 Central Ave., Dover 03820, tel. 603/742–2218).

Exeter Area Chamber of Commerce (120 Water St., Exeter 03833, tel. 603/772–2411).

Maine **Kennebunk-Kennebunkport Chamber of Commerce** (Cooper's Corner, Rtes. 9 and 35, tel. 207/967–0857).

Kittery Tourist Information Center (Rte. 1 and I–95, tel. 207/439–1319).

Convention and Visitors Bureau of Greater Portland (142 Free St., tel. 207/772–4994).

Boothbay Harbor Region Chamber of Commerce (Box 356, Boothbay Harbor, tel. 207/633–2353).

Acadia National Park (Box 177, Bar Harbor 04609, tel. 207/288–3338).

Bar Harbor Chamber of Commerce (Box BC, Cottage St., Bar Harbor 04609, tel. 207/288–3393 or 207/288–5103).

Festivals and Seasonal Events

Mid-Apr.: Reenactments of **Paul Revere's ride** and the **Battle of Lexington and Concord** take place on site the Sunday before Patriot's Day. Tel. 617/862–1450.

Mid-June: Market Square Day Weekend features a street fair with some 300 exhibitors, a road race, a concert, historic-house tours, and fireworks in Portsmouth, New Hampshire. Tel. 603/431–5388.

Mid-June: Old Port Festival sees street performers and sales at the Old Port in Portland, Maine, on the second Saturday. Tel. 207/772–6828.

July 4–mid-Aug.: Prescott Park Arts Festival provides art, music, theater, and dance on the waterfront in Portsmouth, New Hampshire. Tel. 603/436–2848.

July–Aug.: Bar Harbor Music Festival hosts classical and popular music concerts in Bar Harbor, Maine. Tel. 212/222–1026.

Early Aug.: The Maine Festival, Portland's premier fair, brings together musicians, artists, dancers, and farmers. Tel. 207/772–9012.

Mid-Dec.: Reenactment of the Boston Tea Party takes place on the *Tea Party Ship* in Boston Harbor. Tel. 617/338–1773.

What to See and Do with Children

Most attractions described below are described fully in the tour that follows.

Boston is a great city to visit with kids of any age. The **Freedom Trail** sights bring history to life, especially the **Paul Revere House** and the USS *Constitution.* The Boston Children's Museum has lots of interactive exhibits, and older junior scientists will also enjoy the **Computer Museum** at the same location, as well as the **Museum of Science,** with its planetarium and Omni

Theater. The **New England Aquarium** is a fantastic experience, and it's right across the street from the lively shops at **Quincy Market.** Rides on the swan boats at the **Public Gardens,** featured in the children's book *Make Way For Ducklings,* are usually a hit with the younger set. The ***Boston Parents Paper*** (tel. 617/522–1515), published monthly and distributed free throughout the city, is an excellent resource for finding out what's happening.

On the **North Shore,** the witch-related Colonial history of **Salem** intrigues youngsters.

Summertime is the time to visit such beach towns as **Salisbury,** Massachusetts, with its amusement parks, water slides, food stalls, and arcades, and **Hampton Beach,** New Hampshire, with its 3-mile boardwalk, water slide, casino, and amphitheater. **Old Orchard Beach,** Maine, a few miles north of Biddeford on Route 9, features an amusement park, Palace Playland.

Portsmouth, New Hampshire, has a **Children's Museum** (280 Marcy St., tel. 603/436–3853; open Tues.–Sun.) with hands-on exhibits for every age from toddlers to young teens. **Saco,** Maine, offers the **Maine Aquarium** (Rte. 1, tel. 207/284–4511; open daily). Also in Maine, **Boothbay** offers the **Boothbay Railway Village,** and **Portland** has the **Children's Museum of Maine** (746 Stevens Ave. at Westbrook College, tel. 207/797–5483; open Mon.–Sat.). In **Trenton,** you can visit the 100-acre **Acadia Zoological Park,** which has a petting zoo (Rte. 3, tel. 207/667–3244; open May–Columbus Day), and **Southwest Harbor** has the **Mount Desert Oceanarium** (Clark Point Rd., tel. 207/244–7330; open mid-May–mid-Oct.) with its hands-on "touch tank."

Arriving and Departing

By Plane   Boston's **Logan International Airport,** the largest airport in New England, has scheduled flights by most major domestic and foreign carriers. To get from the airport to downtown Boston, you can hire a cab outside each terminal (fares to downtown should be around $15), take the **Airport Water Shuttle** (tel. 800/235–6426) to Rowes Wharf, or ride the **MBTA Blue Line** into town (free shuttle buses connect all terminals to the airport subway station; call 617/561–1800 or 800/235–6426 for Logan Airport Public Information).

Maine's major airports are **Portland International Jetport** (tel. 207/774–7301) and **Bangor International Airport** (tel. 207/947–0384); each has scheduled daily flights by major U.S. carriers. **Bar Harbor Airport** (tel. 207/667–7329), 8 miles northwest of the city, is served by Continental Express (tel. 800/525–0280) and Northeast Express Regional (tel. 800/322–1008).

By Car   The major highway running up the New England coast is I–95, but the more scenic and leisurely roads are Route 1 and Route 1A. If you plan to circumvent any section of this tour, you may want to switch over to I–95 to make up some time, then return to the scenic highways when you're ready for more sightseeing. I–95 turns inland at Brunswick, Maine, heading north to Bangor and the Canadian border; Route 1 continues to trace the coast all the way.

By Train   Amtrak's **Northeast Corridor** service (tel. 800/872–7245) links Boston with Washington, DC, and principal cities in between.

The *Lake Shore Limited*, which stops at Springfield and the Berkshires, carries passengers from Chicago to Boston.

Rail service does not operate all the way up the coast, but **Massachusetts Bay Transportation Authority (MBTA)** (tel. 617/227–5070) trains leaving North Station, Boston, go as far as Salem, Beverly, Gloucester, Rockport, and Ipswich.

By Boat **A.C. Cruise Lines** (28 Northern Ave. Bridge, Pier 1, Boston, tel. 617/426–8419 or 800/422–8419) operates a daily 3-hour excursion in the summer from Boston to Gloucester, Massachusetts.

Casco Bay Lines (tel. 207/774–7871) provides ferry service from Portland, Maine, to the islands of Casco Bay, and **Maine State Ferry Service** (tel. 207/594–5543) provides ferry service from Rockland to Penobscot Bay.

If you'd like to continue on up into Canada at the end of this tour, you can take the ferry operated by **Marine Atlantic** (tel. 800/341–7981) between Yarmouth, Nova Scotia, and Bar Harbor; **Prince of Fundy Cruises** (tel. 800/341–7540) operates ferry service between Yarmouth and Portland (May–October only).

By Bus **Greyhound/Trailways** (tel. 617/423–5810 or 603/436–0163), **Vermont Transit Lines** (tel. 800/451–3292), and **Peter Pan Bus Lines** (tel. 800/237–8747) connect Boston and other major cities in New England with cities throughout the United States. **Bonanza** (tel. 800/556–3815) serves Boston and eastern Massachusetts from Providence with connecting service to New York.

The Coach Company Bus Lines (tel. 800/874–3377) operates an express commuter service between Boston and Newburyport, and **Hudson Bus Lines** (tel. 617/395–8080) provides a limited North Shore link.

Boston

New England's largest and most important city, the cradle of American independence, Boston is 360 years old, far older than the republic it helped to create. Its most famous buildings are not merely civic landmarks but national icons; its great citizens are the Adamses, Reveres, and Hancocks who live at the crossroads of history and myth. At the same time, Boston is a contemporary center of high finance and higher technology, a place of granite and glass towers rising along what once were rutted village lanes. Its enormous population of students, artists, academics, and young professionals have made the town a haven for foreign movies, late-night bookstores, racquetball, sushi restaurants, New Wave music, and unconventional politics.

Best of all, Boston is meant for walking. Most of its historical and architectural attractions can be found in compact areas, and its varied and distinctive neighborhoods reveal their character and design to visitors who take the time to stroll through them.

Getting Around The MBTA, or T, operates subways, elevated trains, and trolleys along four connecting lines. Park Street Station (on the Common) is the major downtown transfer point for Red and Green Line trains; the Orange and Blue Lines cross at State
Boston
By Subway
and Trolley

Street. Trains operate from about 5:30 AM to about 12:30 AM. Current fares on subways and trolleys are 75¢ adults, 35¢ children 5–11, free under 5. An extra fare is required for the distant Green Line stops. Tourist passes are available for $8 (3 days) and $16 (7 days). The MBTA (tel. 617/722–3200 or 617/722–5657) has details.

By Car Boston drivers are notoriously aggressive and unpredictable, traffic patterns can be bewildering, and rush hours are a nightmare, especially at the two tunnels that link Boston to the North Shore. If you can avoid bringing a car into Boston, do so. Otherwise, minimize your frustration by keeping to the main thoroughfares and by parking in lots—no matter how expensive—rather than on the street. Major public parking lots are at Government Center and Quincy Market; beneath Boston Common (entrance on Charles Street); beneath Post Office Square; at the Prudential Center; at Copley Place; and off Clarendon Street near the John Hancock Tower.

By Taxi Cabs are not easily hailed on the street, except at the airport; if you're in a hurry, use a hotel taxi stand or telephone for a cab. Companies offering 24-hour service include **Checker** (tel. 617/536–7000), **Independent Taxi Operators Association,** or ITOA (tel. 617/426–8700), and, in Cambridge, **Cambridge Taxi** (tel. 617/876–5000).

Guided Tours **Brush Hill Transportation Company** (439 High St., Randolph, tel. 617/986–6100 or 800/343–1328) departs from several downtown hotels daily for 3½-hour "Boston Adventure" tours of Boston and Cambridge.

Gray Line (275 Tremont St., tel. 617/426–8805) buses offer a three-hour tour of Greater Boston, April through October.

Bay State Cruise Co., Inc. (ticket office at 67 Long Wharf, tel. 617/723–7800), runs a three-hour (each way) excursion to the tip of Cape Cod aboard the *Provincetown II*, which departs from Commonwealth Pier. There are daily sailings from Memorial Day to Labor Day. Harbor trips to Georges Island depart three times daily on weekdays, four times daily on weekends; whale-watch cruises run weekends from late April to mid-June.

Walking Tours **Freedom Trail.** The 1½-mile Freedom Trail is marked on the sidewalk by a red line that winds its way past 16 of Boston's most important historic sites. The walk begins at the Freedom Trail Information Center on the Tremont Street side of Boston Common, not far from the MBTA Park Street station. Sites along the Freedom Trail include the State House, Park Street Church, Old Granary Burial Ground, King's Chapel and burying ground, Globe Corner Bookstore, Old State House, Boston Massacre Site, Faneuil Hall, Paul Revere House, Old North Church, Copp's Hill Burying Ground, and the USS *Constitution*, with a side trip to the Bunker Hill Monument.

Harborwalk. Maps are available at the Boston Common Information kiosk for a self-guided tour that traces Boston's maritime history. The walk begins at the Old State House (206 Washington St.) and ends on the Congress Street Bridge near the Boston Tea Party ship and museum.

Boston Common and Beacon Hill

Numbers in the margin correspond to points of interest on the Boston map.

❶ Nothing is more central to Boston than its **Common,** the oldest public park in the United States and undoubtedly the largest and most famous of the town commons around which all New England settlements were once arranged.

Start your walk at the **Park Street Station,** on the common on the corner of Park and Tremont streets. This is the original eastern terminus of the first subway in America, opened in 1897 against the warnings of those who believed it would make the buildings along Tremont Street collapse. The copper-roof kiosks are National Historic Landmarks. A well-equipped **visitor information booth** is less than 100 yards from here. It serves as the starting point for the Freedom Trail; guide booklets are available at no charge.

❷ The Congregationalist **Park Street Church,** designed by Peter Banner and erected in 1809–1810, occupies the corner of Tremont and Park streets. Here, on July 4, 1831, Samuel Smith's hymn "America" was first sung, and here in 1829 William Lloyd Garrison began his long public campaign for the abolition of slavery. *Open to visitors last week in June–third week in Aug., Tues.–Sat. 9–3:30. Year-round Sun. services 10:30 and 6. Closed July 4.*

❸ Next to the church is the **Old Granary Burial Ground.** The most famous individuals interred here are heroes of the Revolution: Samuel Adams, John Hancock (the precise location of his grave is not certain), James Otis, and Paul Revere. Here, too, are the graves of the philanthropist Peter Faneuil, Benjamin Franklin's parents (Franklin is buried in Philadelphia), and the victims of the Boston Massacre. *Open daily 8–4:30.*

❹ At the corner of Park and Beacon streets, at the summit of Beacon Hill, stands Charles Bulfinch's magnificent **State House,** arguably the most architecturally distinguished of American seats of state government. The design is neoclassical, poised between Georgian and Federal; its finest features are the delicate Corinthian columns of the portico, the graceful pediment and window arches, and the vast yet visually weightless golden dome. The dome is sheathed in copper from the foundry of Paul Revere. During World War II, the entire dome was painted gray so that it would not reflect moonlight during blackouts. *Tel. 617/727–3676. Admission free. Open weekdays 10–4. Research library (free) open weekdays 9–5.*

Beacon Hill is the area bounded by Cambridge Street on the north, Beacon Street on the south, the Charles River Esplanade on the west, and Bowdoin Street on the east. The highest of three summits, Beacon Hill was named for the warning light (at first an iron skillet filled with tallow and suspended from a mast) set on its peak in 1634.

No sooner do you put the State House behind you than you encounter the classic face of Beacon Hill: brick row houses, nearly all built between 1800 and 1850 in a style never far divergent from the early Federal norm. Even the sidewalks are brick, and they shall remain so; in the 1940s residents staged a sit-in to prevent conventional paving. Since then, public law, the Bea-

African Meeting House, **6**

Beaver II, **22**

Boston Children's Museum, **23**

Boston Common, **1**

Bunker Hill Monument, **15**

Christian Science Church, **29**

Computer Museum, **24**

Copley Place, **28**

Copp's Hill Burying Ground, **13**

Esplanade, **8**

Faneuil Hall, **19**

Fenway Park, **35**

Gibson House, **26**

Harvard Square, **36**

Isabella Stewart Gardner Museum, **34**

John Hancock Tower, **27**

King's Chapel, **16**

Louisburg Square, **5**

Massachusetts Institute of Technology, **37**

Museum of Afro-American History, **7**

Museum of Fine Arts, **33**

Museum of Science, **9**

New England Aquarium, **21**

Old Granary Burial Ground, **3**

Old North Church, **12**

Old South Meeting House, **17**

Old State House, **18**

Park Street Church, **2**

Paul Revere House, **11**

Public Garden, **25**

Quincy Market, **20**

Rutland Square, **31**

State House, **4**

Symphony Hall, **30**

Union Oyster House, **10**

Union Park, **32**

USS *Constitution*, **14**

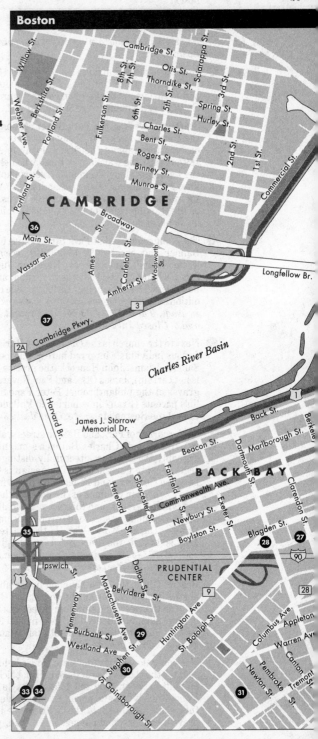

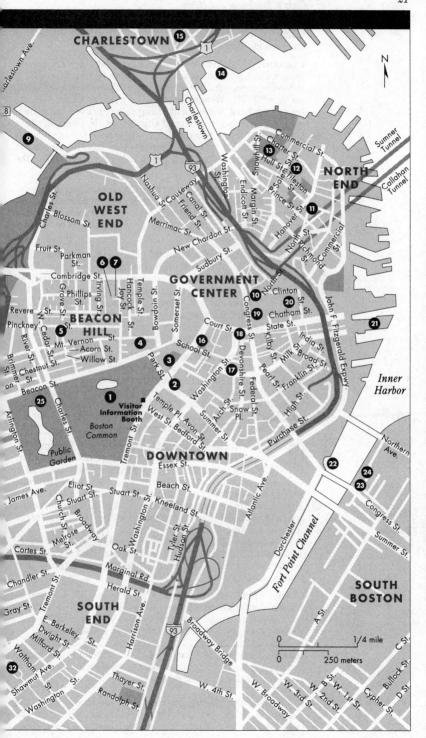

con Hill Civic Association, and the Beacon Hill Architectural Commission have maintained tight controls over everything from the gas lamps to the color of front doors.

Chestnut and **Mt. Vernon,** two of the loveliest streets in America, are distinguished not only for the history and style of their individual houses but for their general atmosphere and character as well. **Mt. Vernon Street** is the grander of the two, its houses set back farther and rising taller; it even has a free-standing mansion, the Second Otis House. Mt. Vernon opens
❺ out on **Louisburg Square,** an 1840s model for town-house development that was never repeated on the Hill because of space restrictions. The little green belongs collectively to the owners of the homes facing it.

Chestnut Street is more modest than Mt. Vernon, yet in its trimness and minuteness of detail it is perhaps even more fine. Delicacy and grace characterize virtually every structure, from the fanlights above the entryways to the wrought-iron boot scrapers on the steps.

Running parallel to Chestnut and Mt. Vernon streets, half a block down Willow Street from Louisburg Square, is **Acorn Street,** a narrow span of cobblestones lined on one side with almost toylike row houses and on the other with the doors to Mt. Vernon's hidden gardens. These were once the houses of artisans and small tradesmen; today they are every bit as prestigious as their larger neighbors. Acorn Street may be the most photographed street of its size in Boston.

❻ On the north slope of Beacon Hill is the **African Meeting House** at 8 Smith Court (near Joy and Myrtle), built in 1806, the oldest black church building still standing in the United States. It was constructed almost entirely with black labor, using funds raised in both the white and the black communities. In 1832 the New England Anti-Slavery Society was formed here under the leadership of William Lloyd Garrison.

Opposite the Meeting House is the home (1799) of **William Nell,** a black crusader for school integration active in Garrison's circle. These sites and others are part of a **Black Heritage Trail,** a walking tour that explores the history of the city's black community during the 19th century. The recently established
❼ **Museum of Afro-American History** provides information on the trail and on black history throughout Boston. Daily tours of the African Meeting House begin here. *46 Joy St., tel. 617/742-1854. Admission free. Open weekdays 9–5. Information on the Trail can also be obtained from the National Park Service Visitor Center, 15 State St., tel. 617/742–5415. Admission free. Open weekdays 9–5.*

Charles Street, on the flat part of Beacon Hill, is home to Boston's antiques district and an assortment of bookstores, leather stores, small restaurants, and vintage-clothing boutiques. Stroll along the romantically lit street after dusk.

Time Out   **Il Dolce Momento** (30 Charles St.), with its homemade gelato and pastries and freshly made gourmet sandwiches, is a perfect stop for a meal, a light snack, or a late-night espresso.

If you head east toward the river, you can cross over to the
❽ **Esplanade** on the Arthur Fiedler Footbridge, named for the late maestro who conducted the Boston Pops for 50 years. Many

of his concerts were given right here, in the **Hatch Memorial Shell,** where the Pops plays each summer. The Esplanade is one of the nicest places in the city for jogging, picnicking, and watching the sailboats along the Charles River.

Across the Charles River, and a short walk away, Boston's **Museum of Science** has more than 400 exhibits covering astronomy, anthropology, progress in medicine, computers, the organic and inorganic earth sciences, and much more. Many exhibits invite the participation of children and adults. The Transparent Woman's organs light up as their functions are described, newborn chicks hatch in an incubator, and a powerful generator produces controlled indoor lightning flashes. The museum has three restaurants and a gift shop. *Tel. 617/723–2500 (for recorded information, tel. 617/523–6664). Admission: $6 adults, $4.50 children 4–14 and students, free under 4, senior citizens, and Wed. 1–5. Open Tues.–Sun. 9–5, Fri., until 9. Closed Thanksgiving, Christmas, and Mon. except May 1–Labor Day and Mon. holidays.*

The **Hayden Planetarium,** located in the Museum of Science, features a planetarium projector and sophisticated multi-image system that combine to produce exciting programs on astronomical discoveries. Laser-light shows, using a new visual technology complete with brilliant laser graphics and computer animation, are scheduled Friday–Sunday evenings. *Tel. 617/589–0270. Admission for each show: $6 adults, $4.50 children and senior citizens.*

The **Mugar Omni Theater** in the Museum of Science features a 76-foot, four-story domed screen, which wraps around and over you; 27,000 watts of power drive the sound system's 84 loudspeakers. *Tel. 617/523–6664. Admission: $6 adults, $4.50 senior citizens and children 4–14, under 4 not admitted. Afternoon shows weekdays, evening shows Tues.–Sun. Reduced-price combination tickets are available for the museum, planetarium, and Omni Theater.*

The North End and Charlestown

From **Government Center** walk northeast toward the raised central artery (the Fitzgerald Expressway) and you'll soon come upon the oldest commercial block in Boston, the Blackstone Block. In this block Boston's oldest restaurant, the **Union Oyster House,** has been operating since 1826. Around the corner on Friday and Saturday, come rain or sleet, Haymarket vendors hawk fruit, vegetables, meat, and fish.

Opposite the pedestrian tunnel beneath the expressway is the oldest neighborhood in Boston and one of the oldest in the New World. Men and women walked the narrow streets of the **North End** when Shakespeare was not yet 20 years dead and Louis XIV was new to the throne of France. In the 17th century the North End *was* Boston, for much of the rest of the peninsula was still under water or had yet to be cleared of brush.

The North End visible to us today is almost entirely a creature of the late 19th century, when brick tenements began to fill with European immigrants. The Irish and the Jews both had their day here, but the Italians, more recent arrivals, have stayed. For more than 60 years the North End has been Italian Boston. This is not only a district of Italian restaurants (there are dozens) but of Italian groceries, bakeries, churches, social clubs, cafés, festivals honoring saints and food, street-corner debates over soccer games, and encroaching gentrification.

⑪ Hanover Street is the main thoroughfare dividing the North End. Off Hanover Street is North Square, home to the **Paul Revere House**—the oldest house in Boston—built nearly a hundred years before Revere's 1775 midnight ride through Middlesex County. Revere owned it from 1770 until 1800, although he and his wife Rachel rented it out during the later part of that period. Attendants are available to answer questions. *19 North Sq., tel. 617/523–1676. Admission: $2 adults, 75¢ children 5–17, $1.50 senior citizens and college students. Open Apr. 15–Oct. 31, daily 9:30–5:15; other times until 4:15. Closed holidays and Mon. Jan.–Mar.*

Time Out The **Caffe Vittoria** (296 Hanover St.) serves cappuccino and special coffee drinks in an Old World café ambience. Next door, **Mike's Pastry** (300 Hanover St.) is the place for ricotta cannoli.

Past North Square on Hanover Street is **St. Stephen's,** the only one of architect Charles Bulfinch's churches still standing in Boston. At Hanover and Tileston streets, the **Prado,** or **Paul Revere Mall,** is lined with bronze plaques that tell the stories of famous North Enders. The centerpiece is Cyrus Dallin's equestrian statue of Paul Revere.

⑫ Continue on Tileston Street to Salem Street to see the church steeple where the two lanterns were hung as a signal to Paul Revere on the night of April 18, 1775. Christ Church, the **Old North Church** (1723), the oldest church building in Boston, was designed by William Price from a study of Christopher Wren's London churches. *Tel. 617/523–6676. Open daily 9–5. Sun. services at 9, 11, and 4. Closed Thanksgiving.*

⑬ Walk uphill on Hull Street to reach the **Copp's Hill Burying Ground,** which incorporates four cemeteries established between 1660 and 1819. Many headstones were chipped by practice shots fired by British soldiers during the occupation of Boston, and a number of the musketball pockmarks can still be seen. Of all Boston's early cemeteries, Copp's Hill seems most to preserve an ancient and melancholic air. *Open daily 9–4.*

The view from Copp's Hill to the north encompasses the mouth of the Charles and much of Charlestown. The USS *Constitution* can be reached via the Charlestown Bridge, which is visible to the northwest.

The USS *Constitution,* nicknamed Old Ironsides for the strength of its oaken hull, not because of any iron plating, is the oldest commissioned ship in the U.S. Navy. She is moored at a national historic site, the **Charlestown Navy Yard,** one of six established to build warships.

⑭ The USS *Constitution* was launched in 1797 in Boston, where Constitution Wharf now stands. During her principal service in Thomas Jefferson's campaign against the Barbary pirates, off the coast of North Africa, and in the War of 1812, she never lost an engagement. Sailors show visitors around the ship, taking them below decks to see the impossibly cramped living quarters as well as the guns where the desperate and difficult work of naval warfare under sail was carried out. *Tel. 617/426–1812. Admission to the Constitution free. Admission to the museum:*

$2.50 adults, $1.50 senior citizens and children 6–16. The ship will go into dry dock for repairs in September 1992, but parts of the ship will remain open as other parts are repaired. Open daily 9:30–3:50.

The phrase "Battle of Bunker Hill" is one of America's most famous misnomers. The battle was fought on Breed's Hill, and that is where Solomon Willard's 220-foot shaft of Quincy granite stands. The monument, for which the Marquis de Lafayette laid the cornerstone in 1825, rises from the spot where, on June 17, 1775, a citizen's militia, commanded not to fire "till you see the whites of their eyes," inflicted more than 1,100 casualties on the British regulars (who eventually seized the hill).

15 Ascend the **Bunker Hill Monument** (Main Street to Monument Street, then straight uphill) by a flight of 295 steps. There is no elevator, but the views from the observatory are worth the climb. At the base, four dioramas tell the story of the battle; ranger programs are given hourly. If you are in Boston on June 17, go to the hill to see a full-scale historical demonstration. *Admission free. Lodge open daily 9–5, monument until 4:30. Closed Thanksgiving, Christmas, New Year's Day.*

Downtown Boston

The financial district—what Bostonians usually refer to as "downtown"—is off the beaten track for visitors who are concentrating on following the Freedom Trail, yet there is much to see in a walk of an hour or two. There is little logic to the streets here; they were, after all, village lanes that only now happen to be lined with 40-story office towers. The area may be confusing, but it is mercifully small.

16 Just south of Government Center, at the corner of Tremont and School streets, stands **King's Chapel,** built in 1754 and never topped with the steeple that the architect Peter Harrison had planned. It took five years to build the solid Quincy granite structure. As construction proceeded, the old church continued to stand within the walls of the new, to be removed in pieces when the stone chapel was completed. The chapel's bell is Paul Revere's largest and, in his opinion, his sweetest-sounding. *Open Tues.–Sat. 10–4, Sun. 1–4. Sun. service at 11. Music program Tues. 12:15–12:45.*

The adjacent **King's Chapel Burying Ground,** the oldest in the city, contains the remains of the first Massachusetts governor, John Winthrop, and several generations of his descendants. Here, too, are many other tombs of Boston worthies of three centuries ago.

Follow School Street down from King's Chapel and pass the **old City Hall,** with Richard S. Greenough's bronze statue of **Benjamin Franklin** (1855), which was Boston's first portrait sculpture. Franklin was born (1706) a few blocks from here on Milk Street and attended the Boston Latin School.

At the Washington Street corner of School Street stands the **Globe Corner Bookstore,** until recently a museum of old editions and now once again a working bookstore, thanks to the good offices of the *Boston Globe.* It was built in 1718, and throughout most of the 19th century it counted among its clientele the leading lights of literary society—Emerson, Holmes, Longfellow, Lowell.

Time Out **Rebecca's Cafe** (56 High St.), with an array of fresh salads, sandwiches, and homemade pastries, is a comfortable place to stop for a casual lunch.

⑰ The **Old South Meeting House** is a short block away, at the corner of Washington and Milk streets. Built in 1729, it is Boston's second oldest church. Unlike the older Old North, the Old South is no longer the seat of an active congregation. (Its principal associations have always been more secular than religious.) Some of the fieriest of the town meetings that led to the Revolution were held here, including the one Samuel Adams called concerning some dutiable tea that activists wanted returned to England.

Washington Street is the main commercial street of downtown Boston. You'll pass many of the area's major retail establishments (don't overlook the side streets) and the two venerable anchors of Boston's mercantile district, Filene's and Jordan Marsh.

The **Combat Zone,** off lower Washington Street, a two-block area of nude-dancing bars, peep shows, "adult" bookstores, and "adult" movie houses, occasionally lives up to its name. While it is not particularly dangerous during the daytime, it is not recommended to the casual stroller at night.

Retracing your steps on Washington Street to its intersection with Court Street, you'll come to a brightly colored lion and unicorn, symbols of British imperial power, on the facade of the

⑱ **Old State House.** The Old State House was the seat of the Colonial government from 1713 until the Revolution, and after the evacuation of the British from Boston in 1776 it served the independent Commonwealth until the new State House on Beacon Hill was completed. John Hancock was inaugurated here as the first governor under the new state constitution. The Old State House will reopen in the spring of 1992, following more than a year's worth of structural renovations. *206 Washington St., tel. 617/720–3290. Admission: $1.25 adults, 50¢ children 6–16, 75¢ senior students and college students, free to Massachusetts schoolchildren. Open Apr. 1–Nov. 1, daily 9:30–5; Nov. 1–Mar. 31, daily 10–4.*

Turning left onto Congress Street, we encounter, first, an historic marketplace of ideas and, second, an old provisions market reborn as the emblem of downtown revitalization. Faneuil Hall ("the Cradle of Liberty") and the Quincy Market (also known as Faneuil Hall Marketplace) face each other across a small square thronged with people at all but the smallest hours.

⑲ **Faneuil Hall** (pronounced "Fan'l") was erected in 1742 to serve as both a place for town meetings and a public market. Though it has been rebuilt, enlarged, and remodeled over the years, the great balconied hall is still made available to citizen's groups.

⑳ **Quincy Market** consists of three structures and has served its purpose as a retail and wholesale distribution center for meat and produce for a century and a half. By the 1970s, though, the market area had become seedy. Some of the old tenants—the famous Durgin Park restaurant and a few butchers and grocers in the central building—had hung on through the years, but the old vitality had disappeared.

Thanks to a creative and tasteful urban-renewal project, the north and south market buildings, separated from the central market by attractive pedestrian malls with trees and benches, house retail establishments, offices, and restaurants. There may be more restaurants in Quincy Market than existed in all of downtown Boston before World War II. Abundance and variety, albeit of an ephemeral sort, have been the watchwords of Quincy Market since its reopening in 1976. Some people consider it all hopelessly trendy; but another 50,000 or so visitors a day rather enjoy the extravaganza. You'll want to decide for yourself. *Open Mon.–Sat. 10–9, Sun. noon–6. Restaurants and bars generally open daily 11 AM–2 AM.*

At the end of Quincy Market opposite Faneuil Hall is Columbus Park, bordering the harbor and several of Boston's restored wharves. **Central Wharf,** immediately to the right of Long Wharf as you face the harbor, is the home of one of Boston's most popular attractions, the **New England Aquarium.** Here you'll find seals, penguins, a variety of sharks and other sea creatures—more than 2,000 species in all, some of which make their home in the aquarium's four-story, 187,000-gallon observation tank. *Tel. 617/973–5200 (whale-watch information, 617/973–5277). Admission: $7 adults, $3.50 children 3–15, $6 senior citizens; free Oct.–Apr., Thurs. after 4. Open Mon., Wed., Fri. 9–5, Thurs. until 8, weekends and holidays until 6. Closed Thanksgiving, Christmas, New Year's Day.*

Along Atlantic Avenue, at the foot of Pearl Street, a plaque set into the wall of a commercial building marks the site of the **Boston Tea Party.** When you cross Fort Point Channel on the Congress Street Bridge, you encounter the ***Beaver II,*** a faithful replica of one of the Tea Party ships that was forcibly boarded and unloaded on the night Boston Harbor became a teapot. Visitors receive a complimentary cup of tea. *Admission: $5 adults, $3 children 5–14, 20% discount senior citizens and college students. Open daily 9–5. Sometimes closed in Jan. for repairs.*

At the opposite end of the bridge is Museum Wharf, home of the popular **Boston Children's Museum.** The multitude of hands-on exhibits includes computers, video cameras, and exhibits designed to help children understand cultural diversity, their bodies, and disabilities. *300 Congress St., tel. 617/426–6500 (617/426–8855 for recorded information). Admission: $6 adults, $5 children 2–15 and senior citizens, free under 1; $1 Fri. 5–9. Open Tues.–Sun. 10–5, Fri. until 9. Closed Mon. except during Boston school vacations and holidays.*

Museum Wharf is also the home of the world's only **Computer Museum,** housing exhibits chronicling the spectacular development of machines that calculate and process information. The more than 75 exhibits include a two-story walk-through model of a desktop computer. *300 Congress St., tel. 617/426–2800. Admission: $6 adults, $5 children, senior citizens, and students; free under 5; half price Sat. until noon. Open Tues.–Sun. 10–5, Fri. until 9. Closed Mon. except during school vacations; closed Fri. evening in winter.*

Back across the channel and south along Atlantic Avenue brings you to Boston's **Chinatown,** with one of the larger concentrations of Chinese-Americans in the United States. Most Chinese restaurants, food stores, and retail businesses are located along Beach and Tyler streets and Harrison Avenue. The area around the intersection of Kneeland Street and Harrison Avenue is the center of Boston's textile and garment industry.

Time Out It's a special treat to sample the Chinese baked goods in shops along Beach Street. Many visitors familiar with Cantonese and even Szechuan cookery will still be surprised and delighted with moon cakes, steamed cakes made with rice flour, and other sweets that seldom turn up on restaurant menus.

The Back Bay and the South End

The Back Bay once was truly a bay, a tidal flat that formed the south bank of a distended Charles River in the 1850s. Beacon Street was built in 1814 to separate the Back Bay from the Charles River. At the rate of 3,500 railroad carloads of gravel a day, it took 30 years to complete the filling as far as the Fens. When the work was finished, the 783-acre peninsula of Boston had been expanded by approximately 450 acres. By 1900 the area was the smartest and most desirable in all Boston.

25 A walk through the Back Bay properly begins with the **Public Garden,** the oldest botanical garden in the United States. Its establishment marked the first phase of the Back Bay reclamation project, occupying what had been salt marshes on the edge of the Common's dry land. Its pond has been famous since 1877 for its **swan boats,** which make leisurely cruises during the warm months of the year.

The best place to begin exploring the streets of the Back Bay is at the corner of Commonwealth Avenue and Arlington Street, with a statue of Washington and his horse looking over your shoulder. The planners of the Back Bay were able to do something that had never before been possible in Boston: to lay out an entire neighborhood of arrow-straight streets. While other parts of Boston may be reminiscent of the mews and squares of London, the main thoroughfares of the Back Bay (especially Commonwealth Avenue) resemble nothing so much as they do Parisian boulevards.

Beginning at the Charles River, the main east–west streets are bisected by eight streets named in alphabetical order from Arlington to Hereford, with three-syllable street names alternating with two-syllable names. Service alleys run behind the main streets; they were built so that delivery wagons could be driven up to basement kitchens. That's how thorough the planning was.

26 Back Bay is a living museum of urban Victorian residential architecture. The **Gibson House** offers a representative look at how life was arranged in—and by—these tall, narrow, formal buildings. One of the first Back Bay residences (1859), the Gibson House is relatively modest in comparison with some of the grand mansions built during the decades that followed. Unlike other Back Bay houses, the Gibson family home has been preserved with all its Victorian fixtures and furniture intact—not restored, but preserved: A conservative family scion lived here until the 1950s and left things as they were. Here you will understand why a squad of servants was a necessity in the old Back Bay. *137 Beacon St., tel. 617/267–6338. Admission: $3. Tours May 1–Nov. 1, Wed.–Sun. at 1, 2, and 3.*

The Great Depression brought an end to the old Back Bay style of living, and today only a few of the houses serve as single-family residences. Most have been cut up into apartments and expensive condominiums.

Newbury Street is Boston's Fifth Avenue, with dozens of up-scale specialty shops offering clothing, china, antiques, and art. It is also a street of beauty salons and sidewalk cafés. Boylston Street, similarly busy but a little less posh, boasts elegant apparel shops.

Time Out The **Harvard Book Store Café** (190 Newbury St.) serves meals or coffee and pastry—outdoors in nice weather. Since it's a real bookstore, you can browse to your heart's content.

Boylston Street, the southern commercial spine of the Back Bay, separates the sedate old district (some say not effectively enough) from the most ambitious developments this side of downtown. One block south of Boylston, on the corner of St. James Avenue and Clarendon Street, stands the tallest building in New England: the 62-story **John Hancock Tower,** built in the early 1970s and notorious in its early years as the building whose windows fell out. The 60th-floor observatory is one of the three best vantage points in the city, and the "Boston 1775" exhibit shows what the city looked like before the great hill-leveling and landfill operations commenced. *Observatory ticket office, Trinity Pl. and St. James Ave., tel. 617/247–1977. Admission: $2.75 adults, $2 children 5–15 and senior citizens. Open Mon.–Sat. 9 AM–10:15 PM, Sun. noon–10:15. Closed Thanksgiving, Christmas.*

The Hancock Tower stands at the edge of **Copley Square,** a civic space that is defined by three monumental older buildings. One is the stately, bowfronted **Copley Plaza Hotel,** which faces the square on St. James Avenue and serves as a dignified foil to two of the most important works of architecture in Boston, if not in the United States. At the left is **Trinity Church,** Henry Hobson Richardson's masterwork of 1877. In this church Richardson brought his Romanesque Revival to maturity.

Across the street from Copley Square stands the **Boston Public Library.** When this building was opened in 1895, it confirmed the status of McKim, Mead, and White as apostles of the Renaissance Revival and reinforced a Boston commitment to the enlightenment of the citizenry that goes back 350 years to the founding of the Public Latin School. In the older part of the building is a quiet courtyard with chairs around a flower garden, and a sumptuous main reference reading room. *Tel. 617/536–5400. Open Mon.–Thurs. 9–9, Fri.–Sat. 9–5.*

With a modern assertive presence, **Copley Place** comprises two major hotels (the high-rise Westin and the Marriott) and dozens of shops and restaurants, attractively grouped on several levels around bright, open indoor spaces. The scale of the project bothers some people, as does the fact that so vast a complex of buildings effectively isolates the South End from the Back Bay. *Shopping galleries generally open weekdays 10–7, Sat. 10–6, Sun. noon–5.*

Down Huntington Avenue is the headquarters complex of the **Christian Science Church.** Mary Baker Eddy's original granite First Church of Christ, Scientist (1894), has since been enveloped by the domed Renaissance basilica added to the site in 1906, and both church buildings are now surrounded by the offices of the *Christian Science Monitor* and by I. M. Pei's complex of church administration structures completed in 1973. The 670-foot reflecting pool is a pleasant spot to stroll around. *175 Huntington Ave., tel. 617/450–3790. Open Mon.–Sat. 9:30–4, Sun. 11:15–2. Free tours on the hour in the church and every 10 minutes in the maparium. Services Sun. at 10 and 7, Wed. at 7:30 PM.*

The best views of the pool and the precise, abstract geometry of the entire complex are from the **Prudential Center Skywalk,** a 52nd-floor observatory that offers fine views of Boston, Cambridge, and the suburbs to the west and south. *800 Boylston St., tel. 617/236–3318. Admission: $2.75 adults, $1.75 children 5–15, students, and senior citizens. Skywalk open Mon.–Sat. 10–10, Sun. noon–10.*

㉚ **Symphony Hall,** since 1900 the home of the Boston Symphony Orchestra, stands at the corner of Huntington and Massachusetts avenues, another contribution of McKim, Mead, and White to the Boston landscape. Acoustics, rather than exterior design, make this a special place. Not one of the 2,500 seats is a bad one. *Tel. 617/266–1492. Tours by appointment with the volunteer office.*

From here you can walk southeast on Massachusetts Avenue to explore the South End or southwest on Huntington Avenue to the Fens and the Museum of Fine Arts. This tour finishes with a visit to the **South End,** a neighborhood eclipsed by the Back Bay more than a century ago but now solidly back in fashion, with upscale galleries and restaurants on Tremont Street catering to young urban professionals. The observation is usually made that while the Back Bay is French-inspired, the South End is English. The houses, too, are different. In one sense they continue the pattern established on Beacon Hill (in a uniformly bowfront style), yet they also aspire to a much more florid standard of decoration. Although it would take years to understand the place fully, you can capture something of the flavor of the South End with a short walk. To see elegant house **㉛** restorations, go to **Rutland Square** (between Columbus Avenue **㉜** and Tremont Street) or **Union Park** (between Tremont Street and Shawmut Avenue). These oases seem miles from the city around them.

There is a substantial black presence in the South End, particularly along Columbus Avenue and Massachusetts Avenue, which marks the beginning of the predominantly black neighborhood of Roxbury. The early integration of the South End set the stage for its eventual transformation into a remarkable polyglot of ethnic groups. You are likely to hear Spanish spoken along Tremont Street, and there are Middle Eastern groceries along Shawmut Avenue. At the northeastern extreme of the South End, Harrison Avenue and Washington Street connect the area with Chinatown, and consequently there is a growing Asian influence. Still another minority presence among the neighborhood's ethnic groups, and sometimes belonging to one or more of them, is Boston's largest gay population.

Time Out   **St. Botolph's on Tremont** (569 Tremont St.) serves gourmet Italian cuisine in light and airy surroundings. The café atmos-

phere is achieved through the black, white, and red decor.
Dishes range from $6 to $12.

The Fens

The Back Bay Fens mark the beginning of Boston's Emerald
Necklace, a loosely connected chain of parks designed by Frederick Law Olmsted that extends along the Fenway, Riverway,
and Jamaicaway to Jamaica Pond, the 265-acre Arnold Arboretum, and the zoo at Franklin Park. The Fens park consists of
still, irregular reedbound pools surrounded by broad meadows, trees, and flower gardens.

33 The **Museum of Fine Arts,** the MFA, between Huntington Avenue and the Fenway, has holdings of American art that surpass
those of all but two or three U.S. museums. The MFA boasts
the most extensive collection of Asiatic art gathered under one
roof, and European art is represented by works from the 11th
through the 20th centuries. It has strong collections of textiles
and costumes and an impressive collection of antique musical
instruments. The museum's new West Wing, designed by I. M.
Pei, is used primarily for traveling exhibitions and special
showings of the museum's permanent collection. On the
Fenway Park side of the Museum of Fine Arts, the newly constructed **Tenshin Garden,** the "garden at the heart of heaven,"
allows visitors to experience landscape as a work of art. The
museum has a good restaurant and a less formal cafeteria serving light snacks; both are in the West Wing. *465 Huntington
Ave., tel. 617/267-9300 (617/267-9377 for recorded schedule
and events information). Admission: $6 adults, $5 senior citizens, $3 children 6-17, free under 6; free to all Wed. 4-6. Open
Tues.–Sun. 10-4:45, Wed. until 9:45. West Wing open Thurs.
and Fri. until 9:45. 1-hr tours available.*

Two blocks west of the MFA, on the Fenway, stands the
34 **Isabella Stewart Gardner Museum,** a monument to one woman's
taste—and, despite the loss of a few masterpieces in a daring
1990 robbery, still a trove of spectacular paintings, sculpture,
furniture, and textiles. There is much to see: *The Rape of
Europa,* the most important of Titian's works in an American
collection; paintings and drawings by Matisse, Whistler, Bellini, Van Dyck, Botticelli, and Rubens; John Singer Sargent's oil
portrait of Mrs. Gardner herself, in the Gothic Room. At the
center of the building is the magnificent courtyard, fully enclosed beneath a glass roof. *280 The Fenway, tel. 617/566-1401
(617/734-1359 for recorded concert information). Admission:
$5 adults, $2.50 children over 12, students, and senior citizens.
Open Tues.–Sun. noon–5. Concerts Sept.–June.*

The Boston shrine known as **Fenway Park** is one of the smallest
and oldest baseball parks in the major leagues. It was built in
1912, when the grass on the field was real—and it still is today.
Babe Ruth pitched here when the place was new; Ted Williams
and Carl Yastrzemski slugged out their entire careers here.

35 **Kenmore Square,** home to fast-food parlors, new-wave rock
clubs, an abundance of university students, and an enormous
neon sign advertising gasoline, is two blocks north of Fenway
Park. The neon sign is so thoroughly identified with the area
that historic preservationists have fought successfully to save
it—proof that Bostonians are an open-minded lot who do not

require that their landmarks be identified with the American Revolution.

Cambridge

Cambridge is an independent city faced with the difficult task of living in the shadow of its larger neighbor, Boston, while being overshadowed as well by the giant educational institutions within its own borders. It provides the brains and the technical know-how that, combined with Boston's financial prowess, has created the vibrant high-tech economy of which Massachusetts is so proud. Cambridge also continues to function as the conscience of the greater Boston area; when a new social experiment or progressive legislation appears on the local scene, chances are it came out of the crucible of Cambridge political activism.

Cambridge, just minutes from Boston by MBTA, is easily reached on the Red Line train to **Harvard Square.**

A good place to begin a tour is the **Cambridge Discovery** information booth near the MBTA station entrance, where you will find maps, brochures, and information about the entire city. The walking tour brochures cover Old Cambridge, East Cambridge, and Revolutionary Cambridge. Cambridge Discovery also gives a rewarding tour of Old Cambridge conducted by a corps of well-trained high school students. *Cambridge Discovery, Inc., Box 1987, Cambridge 02238, tel. 617/497–1630. Open in winter, Mon.–Sat. 9–5, Sun. 1–5; in summer, Mon.–Sat. 9–6, Sun. 1–5.*

In 1636 the country's first college was established here. Named in 1638 for a young Charlestown clergyman who died that year, leaving the college his entire library and half his estate, Harvard remained the only college in the New World until 1693, by which time it was firmly established as a respected center of learning.

The Harvard University information office on the ground floor of Holyoke Center (1350 Massachusetts Ave.), run by students, offers a free hour-long tour (once a day Mon.–Sat.) of Harvard Yard and maps of the university area. The tour does not include visits to museums, but it provides a fine orientation and will give you ideas for further sightseeing.

Harvard has two celebrated art museums, each a treasure in itself. The most famous is the **Fogg Art Museum,** behind Harvard Yard on Quincy Street, between Broadway and Harvard Street. Founded in 1895, it now owns 80,000 works of art from every major period and from every corner of the world. Its focus is primarily on European, American, and Far Eastern works; it has notable collections of 19th-century French Impressionist and medieval Italian paintings. Special exhibits change monthly. *32 Quincy St., tel. 617/495–5573. Admission: $4 adults, $2.50 senior citizens and students, free under 18; free to all Sat. 10–noon. Open Tues.–Sun. 10–5.*

A ticket to the Fogg will gain you admission to the noted **Busch-Reisinger Museum** (Werner Otto Hall, tel. 617/495–4544), entered via the Fogg. In its new building as of fall 1991, the museum hosts collections specializing in Central and Northern European art. Hours are the same as the Fogg.

When you purchase a ticket to the Fogg, you are also entitled to tour the **Arthur M. Sackler Museum** (tel. 617/495–9400) across the street. It exhibits Chinese, Japanese, ancient Greek, Egyptian, Roman, Buddhist, and Islamic works. The Sackler keeps the same hours as the Fogg.

Harvard also maintains the **Harvard University Museums of Natural History,** north of the main campus on Oxford Street. It contains four distinct collections: comparative zoology, archaeology, botany, and minerals. The most famous exhibit here is the display of glass flowers in the **Botanical Museum.** The **Peabody Museum of Archaeology and Ethnology** holds one of the world's outstanding anthropological collections; exhibits focus on Native American and Central and South American cultures. *26 Oxford St., tel. 617/495–3045 for general information. Admission: $3 adults, $1 children 5–15, $2 students and senior citizens; free to all Sat. 9–11. Open Mon.–Sat. 9–4:30, Sun. 1–4:30. Closed major holidays.*

Across Massachusetts Avenue, at the north end of the Cambridge Common, go down Appian Way through a small garden to the heart of **Radcliffe College.** Founded in 1897 "to furnish instruction and the opportunities of collegiate life to women and to promote their higher education," Radcliffe is an independent corporation within Harvard University.

From Harvard Square, follow elegant **Brattle Street** out to the **Longfellow National Historic Site.** George Washington lived here throughout the siege of Boston. The poet Henry Wadsworth Longfellow received the house in 1843 as a wedding gift and filled it with the exuberant spirit of his own work and that of his literary circle, which included Emerson, Thoreau, Holmes, Dana, and Parkman. *105 Brattle St., tel. 617/876–4491. Admission: $2 adults, free under 16 and over 62. Open daily 10–4:30; last tour departs at 4.*

37 An exploration of Cambridge would not be complete without a visit to the **Massachusetts Institute of Technology.** The 135-acre campus of MIT borders the Charles River, 1½ miles south of Harvard Square. Obviously designed by and for scientists, the MIT campus is divided by Massachusetts Avenue into the West Campus, which is devoted to student leisure life, and the East Campus, where the heavy work is done. The West Campus has some extraordinary buildings. The **Kresge Auditorium,** designed by Eero Saarinen with a curving roof and unusual thrust, rests on three instead of four points. The **MIT Chapel,** another Saarinen design, is lit primarily by a roof oculus that focuses light on the altar, as well as by reflections from the water in a small moat surrounding it, and it is topped by an aluminum sculpture by Theodore Roszak. **Baker House** was designed in 1947 by the Finnish architect Alvar Aaltoa in such a way as to give every room a view of the Charles River. MIT's East Campus buildings are connected by a 5-mile "infinite corridor," touted as the second-longest corridor in the country.

The Institute maintains an Information Center and offers free tours of the campus Monday–Friday at 10 and 2. *Building Seven, 77 Massachusetts Ave., tel. 617/253–4795. Open weekdays 9–5.*

Shopping

Boston's shops and stores are generally open Monday through
Saturday from 9 or 9:30 until 6 or 7; many stay open until 8 late
in the week. Some stores, particularly those in malls or tourist
areas, are open Sunday from noon until 5. Boston's two daily
newspapers, the *Globe* and the *Herald,* are the best places to
learn about sales; Sunday's *Globe* often announces sales for later in the week.

Shopping Districts Most of Boston's stores and shops are located in an area
bounded by Quincy Market, the Back Bay, downtown, and
Copley Square. There are few outlet stores in the area, but
there are plenty of bargains, particularly in the world-famous
Filene's Basement and Chinatown's fabric district.

Cambridgeside Galleria, a new three-story mall that opened in
September 1990, has more than 60 shops including the larger
anchor stores of Filene's, Lechmere, and Sears. The indoor
shopping area is located between Kendall Square and the Museum of Science in Cambridge.

Copley Place, an indoor shopping mall connecting the Westin
and Marriott hotels, has 87 stores, restaurants, and cinemas
that blend the elegant, the glitzy, and the overpriced.

Downtown Crossing, Boston's traditional downtown shopping
area at Summer and Washington streets, has been spruced up:
It's now a pedestrian mall with outdoor food and merchandise
kiosks, street performers, and benches for people-watchers.
Here are the city's two largest department stores, Jordan
Marsh and Filene's.

Faneuil Hall Marketplace has small shops, kiosks of every description, street performers, and one of the great food experiences, Quincy Market. The intrepid shopper must cope with
crowds of people, particularly on weekends. Nearby Dock
Square is a great place to hunt for bargains in restaurant supply houses.

Harvard Square in Cambridge has more than 150 stores within
a few blocks. In addition to the surprising range of items sold in
the square, Cambridge is a book-lover's paradise.

Newbury Street is Boston's version of New York's Fifth Avenue, where the trendy gives way to the chic and the expensive.

Department Stores **Filene's** (426 Washington St., tel. 617/357–2100). This full-
service department store's most outstanding feature is its two-
level bargain basement, where items are automatically reduced
in price according to the number of days they've been on the
rack. The competition can be stiff for the great values on discontinued, overstocked, or slightly irregular items.

Harvard Coop Society (1400 Massachusetts Ave., tel. 617/492–
1000; at MIT, 3 Cambridge Center, tel. 617/491–4230). Begun
in 1882 as a nonprofit service for students and faculty, the Coop
is now a full department store known for its extensive selection
of records and books.

Food Markets Every Friday and Saturday, **Haymarket** (near Faneuil Hall
Marketplace) is a crowded jumble of outdoor fruit and vegetable vendors, meat markets, and fishmongers. The fruit sold
here is often very ripe, and you may have to discard some of it,
but you will still end up with more for your money. If you dare

to choose your own fruit, be prepared to suffer the wrath of the vendors!

Antiques **Charles Street** in Beacon Hill is a mecca for antiques lovers from all over the country.

Clothing **Ann Taylor** (18 Newbury St., tel. 617/262–0763, and Faneuil Hall Marketplace, tel. 617/742–0031) stocks high-quality fashions for both classic and trendy dressers along with shoes and accessories.

Louis (234 Berkeley St., tel. 617/965–6100). Now located in the former Bonwit Teller building, Louis carries elegantly tailored designs and a wide selection of imported clothing and accessories, including many of the more daring Italian styles. It also has subtly updated classics in everything from linen to tweed.

Jewelry **Shreve, Crump & Low** (330 Boylston St., tel. 617/267–9100) has a complete line of the finest jewelry, china, crystal, and silver. A beautiful collection of Steuben glass is on the second floor as well as an extensive collection of clocks and watches. Shreve's, one of Boston's oldest and most respected stores, is where generations of Brahmin brides have registered their china selections.

Sports Equipment **Eastern Mountain Sports** (1041 Commonwealth Ave., Brighton, tel. 617/254–4250) has New England's best selection of gear for the backpacker, camper, climber, skier, or all-round outdoors person.

Participant Sports and Fitness

Bicycling A free pamphlet showing the bike route from Boston Common to Franklin Park is available from the Park Rangers (tel. 617/522–2639). The **Dr. Paul Dudley White Bikeway**, approximately 18 miles long, runs along both sides of the Charles River.

Jogging Both sides of the Charles River are popular with joggers. Many hotels have printed maps of nearby routes.

Physical Fitness The **Westin Hotel** (Copley Place, Back Bay, tel. 617/262–9600) has complete health club facilities. Nonguests are welcome to use the facilities for a $7 fee.

Spectator Sports

Baseball The **Boston Red Sox,** American League (tel. 617/267–8661 or 617/267–1700 for tickets), play at Fenway Park.

Basketball The **Boston Celtics,** NBA (tel. 617/523–3030 or 617/720–3434 for tickets), shoot hoops at Boston Garden on Causeway Street.

Football The **New England Patriots,** NFL (tel. 800/543–1776), play football at Sullivan Stadium in Foxboro, 45 minutes south of the city.

Hockey The **Boston Bruins,** NHL (tel. 617/227–3223), are on the ice (the ice is under the Celtics' parquet) at Boston Garden.

Dining

The main ingredient in Boston restaurant fare is still the bounty of the North Atlantic, the daily catch of fish and shellfish that appears somewhere on virtually every menu, whether the cuisine be new French, traditional American, Oriental, or simply seafood.

Seafood or no, the choice of dining experience in Boston is unusually wide. At one extreme, respected young chefs emphasize the freshest ingredients and the menu reflects the morning's shopping; at the other, the tradition of decades mandates recipes older than the nation and the menu seems forever unchanged. Between the extremes lies an extensive range of American, French, Italian, and other national and ethnic cuisines, their variety ample enough to create difficult decisions at mealtime.

Bostonians are not traditionally late diners. Many of the city's finest restaurants are busy by 7 PM, and those near the theater district begin filling up earlier. (Advise your waiter when you sit down if you plan to attend an after-dinner performance.)

The following dining price categories have been used: *Very Expensive*, over $40; *Expensive*, $25–$40; *Moderate*, $12–$25; *Inexpensive*, under $12. As a general rule, you can expect to tip about 15% on a check of less than $60, about 20% on a check larger than $60.

Back Bay **Le Marquis de Lafayette.** One of the city's newest hotel dining
★ rooms is also one of its grandest, with candlelight dining accompanied by harp music. In this French restaurant, the execution of the menu by chef Jacky Pluton approaches perfection in dish after dish. Dining is on the highest, most creative level, yet the food doesn't sacrifice flavor for mere innovation. This is a classically based kitchen at the cutting edge of what is new. The menu changes seasonally. *Lafayette Hotel, 1 Ave. de Lafayette, tel. 617/451–2600. Reservations required, especially for weekend. Jacket and tie advised. Valet parking after 5 PM. AE, DC, MC, V. No lunch. Sun. brunch 11:30–2:30. Very Expensive.*

★ **L'Espalier.** The simpler, lighter preparations and larger portions that characterize contemporary French and American cuisine are created here by chef/owner Frank McClelland. The fixed-price, three-course dinner might include roast native partridge with chanterelles, salmon steak with mint and wild onion butter and a salad of peas and radishes, and for dessert a luscious but low-calorie arrangement of figs and peaches with wild strawberry sauce and mascarpone cheese. A seven-course *menu dégustation*, which provides a sampling of many items, is available on request Monday through Friday. There is an excellent wine list of 150 choices and the decor of the three dining rooms is intimate but elegant. *30 Gloucester St., tel. 617/262–3023. Reservations required. Jacket and tie advised. Dinner only. AE, MC, V. Closed Sun. Very Expensive.*

Rarities. If you're looking for posh dining plus a view of a corner of Harvard Square, this dining room in the Charles Hotel is the place. The black-lacquer chairs upholstered in gray create a cool, contemporary air, and the floor-to-ceiling windows offer a view of the passing parade. The menu is New American: chive pasta with lobster and lemon, honey-roasted duck with thyme and shallots. The adjacent Quiet Bar is a serene oasis for those tired of the square's bustle. *1 Bennett St., tel. 617/661–5050. Reservations advised. Jacket advised. AE, DC, MC, V. Very Expensive.*

Suntory. Opened by the giant Japanese distillery Suntory, this elegant new Japanese restaurant offers a variety of dining experiences—all of them first class—in three dining rooms. A bustling sushi bar dominates the first floor; *shabu shabu* (Japanese hot pot) is served on the second floor; and steaks are cooked on your table by swashbuckling chefs at the *teppan yaki* steak house on the third floor. *212 Stuart St., tel. 617/338–2111. Reservations advised. Dress: casual. AE, DC, MC, V. No lunch weekends. Expensive–Very Expensive.*

Boodle's. This London-style chophouse is one of the Back Bay's best-kept restaurant secrets. Bible-thick steaks and fresh local fish, along with a variety of vegetables, are expertly grilled over hickory, cherry, and other woods. There are dozens of sauces to choose from, and guests are encouraged to share larger cuts of meat. The split-level bar and dining room is furnished like a 19th-century club. *40 Dalton St. in the Back Bay Hilton, tel. 617/236–1100. Reservations advised on weekends. Jacket advised on weekends. AE, DC, MC, V. Expensive.*

Bnu. This small café is a slick, set-designer's version of Tuscany. Thin-crust designer pizzettas, no-red-sauce pastas, and frescoes that make the walls look the perfect degree of ancient, all create the feeling that you're sitting on the piazza sipping Chianti, even when it's snowing outside. Try to visit sometime other than when everyone is rushing to catch a show at one of the nearby theaters. *123 Stuart St., Transportation Bldg., tel. 617/367–8405. Reservations accepted only for 5:45 and 6 PM pre-theater seatings. Dress: casual. MC, V. No lunch weekends. Moderate–Expensive.*

Legal Sea Foods. What began as a tiny adjunct to a fish market has grown to important status, with additional locations in Cambridge, Chestnut Hill, and Worcester. Always busy, Legal still does things its own way. Dishes are not allowed to stand until the orders for a table are completed but are brought individually to insure freshness. The style of food preparation is, as always, simple: Seafood is raw, broiled, fried, steamed, or baked; fancy sauces and elaborate presentations are eschewed. You can have a baked stuffed lobster or mussels au gratin, but otherwise your choice lies among the range of sea creatures available that day. The wine list is carefully selected, the house wine equally so. *64 Arlington St., Park Sq., in the Boston Park Plaza Hotel, tel. 617/426–4444. No reservations for dinner or weekend lunch; expect to wait. Dress: casual but neat. AE, DC, MC, V. Moderate.*

Joyce Chen Restaurant. Joyce Chen offers a gracious setting and an extensive menu of Mandarin, Shanghai, and Szechuan food. Specialties include hot and cold soups, Szechuan scallops, and moo shu dishes. The lunch buffet on weekdays is a real value. *115 Stuart St., tel. 617/720–1331. Reservations suggested for large parties. Dress: informal. AE, MC, V. Moderate.*

Thai Cuisine. Thai restaurants have become known as some of the city's best bets for inexpensive, good food. This 50-seat place is convenient to Symphony Hall and the Back Bay. The food can be spicy, but since everything is prepared to order, you can request some modification of the heat on many dishes. The duck and green-curry dishes are favorites. The decor is a mixture of cool postmodern salmons and grays with carved Thai masks. *14A Westland Ave., tel. 617/262–1485. No reservations. Dress: informal. AE, DC, MC, V. No lunch Sun. Inexpensive–Moderate.*

Cambridge **The Harvest.** This is the sort of place where junior Harvard
★ faculty might come to celebrate getting a fellowship. It adopted

Boston Dining and Lodging

Dining

Bartley's Burger Cottage, **8**

Blue Diner, **30**

Bnu, **27**

Boodle's, **16**

Daily Catch, **41**

Durgin-Park, **38**

East Coast Grill, **2**

Grendel's Den, **12**

Hamersley's Bistro, **22**

The Harvest, **6**

Ho Yuen Ting, **29**

Iruna, **7**

Jimmy's Harborside, **31**

Joyce Chen Restaurant, **3**

Legal Sea Foods, **24**

Le Marquis de Lafayette, **32**

L'Espalier, **15**

Michela's, **13**

Rarities, **11**

Restaurant Jasper, **40**

Ristorante Lucia, **42**

Seasons, **39**

Suntory, **25**

Thai Cuisine, **17**

Union Oyster House, **36**

Lodging

Boston Harbor Hotel at Rowes Wharf, **35**

Boston International Hostel, **18**

Boston Park Plaza Hotel & Towers, **24**

Bostonian, **37**

Cambridge House, **10**

The Charles Hotel, **4**

Copley Plaza, **21**

Copley Square Hotel, **20**

Eliot Hotel, **14**

Four Seasons, **26**

Harvard Motor House, **9**

Hilton (at Logan Airport), **43**

Hotel Meridien, **34**

Lenox Hotel, **19**

Omni Parker House, **33**

Ritz-Carlton, **23**

Sheraton Commander, **5**

Susse Chalet Inn, **1**

Tremont House, **28**

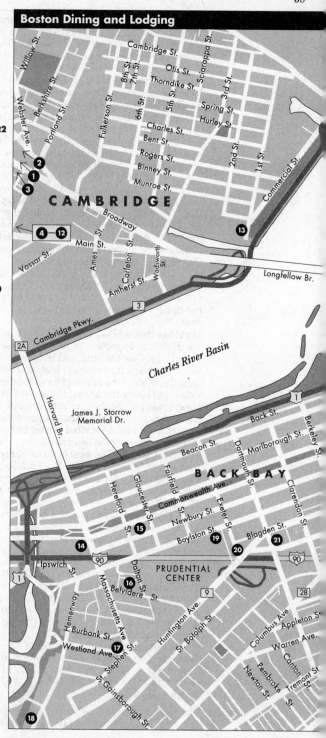

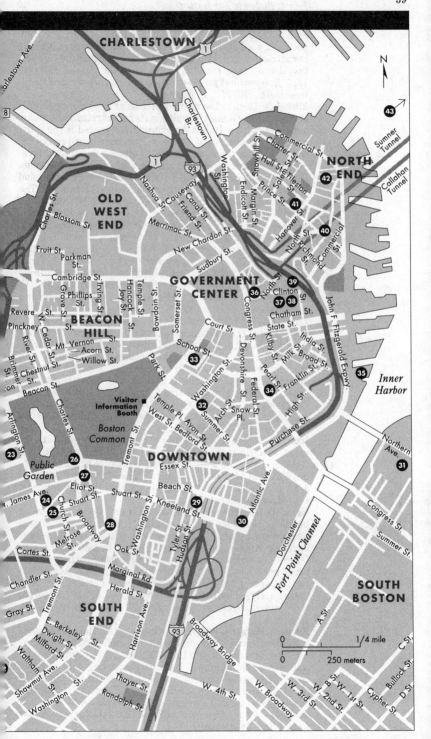

CHARLESTOWN

N

NORTH
END

OLD
WEST
END

Sumner
Tunnel

Callahan
Tunnel

43

42

41

40

Commercial St.
Charter St.
Snow Hill St.
Hull St.
Tileston
Prince St.
Endicott St.
Margin St.
Hanover St.
North St.
Richmond
Commercial St.
John F. Fitzgerald Expwy.

Charlestown Br.

Washington St.

Nashua St.
Causeway St.
Canal St.
Friend St.
Merrimac St.
New Chardon St.
Sudbury St.

GOVERNMENT
CENTER

Clinton St.
39
37 38
Chatham St.

36

State St.
Kilby St.
Milk St.
Broad St.
India St.
Franklin St.
High St.

35

Inner
Harbor

Court St.

Congress St.

Devonshire St.

Federal St.

Pearl St.

Purchase St.

Charles St.
Blossom St.

Fruit St.
Parkman St.
Cambridge St.
Grove St.
Phillips St.
Irving St.
Temple St.
Hancock St.
Joy St.
Bowdoin St.
Somerset St.
School St.

Revere St.
Pinckney St.
N. Cedar St.
River St.
Mt. Vernon St.
Acorn St.
Willow St.
Chestnut St.
Brimmer St.
Beacon St.

BEACON HILL

33

Park St.

Washington St.
Arch St.
Summer St.
Avon St.
West St.
Bedford St.
Snow Pl.

32

34

Visitor
Information
Booth

Boston
Common

Temple Pl.

DOWNTOWN

Essex St.

Northern
Ave.

31

23

Public
Garden

26

27

Arlington St.

Eliot St.
Stuart St.
St. James Ave.

24
25

Church St.
Melrose St.
Broadway

28

Stuart St.
Kneeland St.

Beach St.

29

30

Atlantic Ave.

Congress St.

Summer St.

Fort Point Channel

Dorchester

SOUTH
BOSTON

Washington St.
Tyler St.
Hudson St.

Oak St.

Cortes St.

Chandler St.
Gray St.

Tremont St.
E. Berkeley St.
Dwight St.
Milford St.
Waltham St.
Shawmut Ave.
Washington St.

SOUTH
END

Marginal Rd.
Herald St.
Harrison Ave.

93

Broadway Bridge

Thayer St.
Randolph St.

W. 4th St.

W. Broadway
W. 3rd St.
W. 2nd St.
W. 1st St.

A St.
B St.
C St.
Bullock St.
Cypher St.
D St.

0   1/4 mile
0   250 meters

nouvelle American cuisine early on, hosting a game festival each fall that features the likes of elk and antelope. The leafy patio is a good choice for an outdoor meal in summer, and the bar attracts young, brainy singles. The less expensive café section doesn't take reservations. *44 Brattle St., tel. 617/492–1115. Reservations for the dining room only. Jacket and tie optional. AE, DC, MC, V. Expensive.*

Michela's. Deep in the heart of Artificial Intelligence Alley is one of the city's most popular restaurant/trattoria/bar/takeout spots. Classy Italian fare superbly prepared is the spirit here. Bright splashes of intense yellow, purple, and red on the walls showcase the clientele, which often includes head-turning local celebrities as well as lovers of imaginative cuisine. Dinner might include grilled Italian sausage with lentils and braised fennel, or polenta with artichokes and black olives. The café in the atrium of the office building where Michela's is located serves a more casual menu; diners sit beneath gigantic canvas umbrellas. The seasonal menus, which change every couple of weeks in the café and every couple of months in the dining room, often focus on the food of a particular region. *1 Athenaeum St., (lobby of former Carter Ink Bldg.), Cambridge, tel. 617/225–2121. Reservations advised in dining room. Jacket and tie advised in dining room. AE, DC, MC, V. No lunch Sat. Closed Sun. Dinner only in dining room and café. Moderate–Expensive.*

East Coast Grill. The chef calls his food "equatorial cuisine" to acknowledge the hot pepper and spices. The specialty is New American and American (in particular, North Carolina) barbecue, with a number of such ethnic dishes as grilled tuna with West Indies *sofrito*, grilled sweetbreads, jerk chicken, and "pasta from Hell"—a pasta livened with inner-beauty hot sauce. The dining room is small, bright, and very busy. *1271 Cambridge St., tel. 617/491–6568. No reservations; go early or late to avoid a long wait. Dress: informal. Takeout only for lunch. AE, MC, V. Moderate.*

Iruna. This Spanish restaurant, popular with students for years, specializes in paellas and seafoods and has great salads. Outdoor dining, on a private patio, is possible in warm weather. Wine and beer only. *56 John F. Kennedy St., tel. 617/868–5633. Reservations accepted. Dress: informal. No credit cards. Closed Sun. Moderate.*

Grendel's Den. Housed in a former Harvard College fraternity building, Grendel's has an unusually warm, clubby atmosphere, a downstairs bar, and an eclectic assortment of cuisines, including Middle Eastern, Greek, Indian, Italian, and French. Diners are welcome to mix and match small-portion dishes, which generally include such diverse items as shish kebab, fettuccine, spareribs, moussaka, hummus, and broiled fish. And there's a large salad bar. *89 Winthrop St., tel. 617/491–1160. No reservations. Dress: informal. AE, DC, MC, V. Inexpensive–Moderate.*

Bartley's Burger Cottage. Stepping into this Harvard Square institution you're confronted with the smell of 20 years of frying. The main concessions to the '90s are frozen yogurt and the waitresses' black tights. This is bargain eating with a vengeance; most entrées are less than $5. Besides the 42 varieties of burgers, there are daily specials, such as baked meat loaf with mashed potatoes and a veggie. *1246 Massachusetts Ave., tel. 617/354–6559. No reservations. Dress: casual. No credit cards. Closed Sun. Inexpensive.*

Downtown **Blue Diner.** Among the '50s icons revived in the last few years are guilt-ridden sex, boomerang Formica, and the chrome-side corner diner. With its tableside jukeboxes and Monday meatloaf special, this vest-pocket nook combines authentic with arch. At the counter, traditional diner customers elbow architects and artists from the burgeoning offices and galleries nearby. The menu includes a few concessions to the passage of time, such as grilled fish, but concentrates on such diner staples as a roast-turkey plate and macaroni and cheese. On weekends the diner serves breakfast 24 hours a day. Try the chocolate layer cake. *178 Kneeland St., tel. 617/338–4639. No reservations. Dress: informal. AE, DC, MC, V. Inexpensive–Moderate.*

★ **Ho Yuen Ting.** Every night a waiting line forms outside this Chinatown hole-in-the-wall. The reason is simple: Ho Yuen Ting serves some of the best seafood in town. The house specialty is a sole-and-vegetable stir-fry served in a spectacular whole, crisply fried fish. Come with friends so you can also enjoy the clams with black bean sauce, lobster with ginger and scallion, and whole steamed bass. *13A Hudson St., tel. 617/426–2316. No reservations. Dress: informal. No credit cards. Inexpensive–Moderate.*

Faneuil Hall **Seasons.** At this solarium-like restaurant overlooking Faneuil
★ Hall, the cuisine of chef Labri Dahrouch is eclectic American with international influences and changes seasonally. Selections from a summer menu included grilled lamb sausage with feta and calamata olives as an appetizer; veal ribeye with avocado, crab cakes, and lime; and, for dessert, poppy Madeira cake with fresh peaches and cream. The wine list is exclusively American, with the notable exception of champagne. *Bostonian Hotel, North and Blackstone Sts., tel. 617/523–3600. Reservations suggested. Jacket required. AE, DC, MC, V. Expensive–Very Expensive.*

Union Oyster House. It's Boston's oldest restaurant, and few people seeing Boston for the first time can resist the temptation to slip down a bowl of oyster stew or a dozen chilled cherrystones on the half-shell at the bar where Daniel Webster used to devour dozens at one sitting. The upstairs rooms at the top of the narrow staircase are dark, low-ceilinged, and Ye-Olde-New-Englandy; a more recent bar addition has a lighter feel. The food here tends to be broiled, fried, or heavy on the cream sauce, and topped with breadcrumbs. Stick to the simpler items and absorb the atmosphere. There's a $10 minimum per person. *41 Union St., tel. 617/227–2750. Reservations accepted. Dress: informal. AE, DC, MC, V. No lunch Sun. Moderate–Expensive.*

Durgin Park. When it opened in the 1830s, Durgin Park was a simple upstairs dining hall with a bar on the first floor that catered to the wholesale meat and produce district. Today the main reason for going to this legendary eatery is its rough-and-ready atmosphere. Here you still sit family style, elbow to elbow with your neighbor—friend or stranger. The floor is worn plank, the waitresses act tough and gruff, the ceiling is still embossed tin, and red-checkered cloths cover the long tables. The prime rib, pot roast, and baked beans are traditional New England fare served in generous portions; the strawberry shortcake (in season) is mountainous; the fish chowder and broiled scallops are good buys. *340 Faneuil Hall Marketplace (North Market Bldg.), tel. 617/227–2038. No reservations; expect to* *wait at prime dining hours. Dress: informal. AE, MC, V. Inexpensive–Moderate.*

North End **Restaurant Jasper.** Jasper White, a young chef with an impres-
★ sive record in the establishments of others, opened his own restaurant on the city's waterfront and soon acquired a national
reputation for his stunning new American cuisine. Low-key decor, spacious seating, and good service complement a respect-
able wine list and superb food. There is adequate choice of
seafood, meat, and fowl. *240 Commercial St., tel. 617/523–
1126. Reservations advised, required on weekends. Jacket and
tie optional. AE, DC, MC, V. Lunch Fri. only. Closed Sun.
and Mon. Expensive.*

Ristorante Lucia. Some aficionados consider Lucia's the best
Italian restaurant in the North End. Its specialties from the
Abruzzi region include batter-fried artichoke hearts or mozzarella in carrozza as appetizer and the chicken alla Lucia or *pollo
arrabiatta*. Check out the upstairs bar, with its pink marble
and its takeoff on the Sistine Chapel ceiling. *415 Hanover St.,
tel. 617/523–9148. Reservations advised; a limited number of
reservations accepted on Sat. Dress: casual. AE, MC, V. No
lunch Mon.–Thurs. Moderate–Expensive.*

Daily Catch. Shoulder-crowding small, with an informal oyster
bar, this storefront restaurant specializes in calamari dishes,
lobster *fra diavolo*, linguine with clam sauce—and extremely
low prices. A second restaurant has opened at 261 Northern
Avenue, across from Jimmy's Harborside, and a third just
opened in Davis Square in Somerville. Hours of operation vary
greatly; call for times. *323 Hanover St., tel. 617/523–8567. No
reservations. Dress: informal. No credit cards. Inexpensive.*

South End **Hamersley's Bistro.** Fiona and Gordon Hamersley opened their
★ French-American bistro in July 1987 and have gotten rave reviews. The black-and-white decor in both dining rooms is accented by a fire-engine-red bar and maître d' station.
Specialties that have a permanent place on the daily menu include a garlic-and-mushroom sandwich served as an appetizer
(the mushrooms change seasonally); a fish stew (whose ingredients change with the season); and roast chicken with garlic,
lemon, and parsley. *578 Tremont St., tel. 617/267–6068. Reservations advised. Dress: informal. MC, V. Expensive.*

Waterfront **Jimmy's Harborside.** This exceedingly popular seafood establishment enjoys a solid reputation. The bright, three-tier main
dining room was designed to ensure that every table has an unobstructed view of the harbor. In addition to the many fresh
seafood preparations that have long been standard fare, the
menu now offers such specials as pasta primavera with a medley of sautéed shrimp, veal, and pork tenderloin. As a change
from chowder or traditional bouillabaisse, try the scampi Luc-
iano, a bouillabaisse made with white wine, cream, and a variety of fresh fish and shrimp. The wine list showcases American
wines. The Boat Bar, the scene of high-spirited camaraderie, is
a favorite watering hole of politicians, among them Tip O'Neill.
*242 Northern Ave., tel. 617/423–1000. Limited reservations for
the 6:30 and 8:30 seatings Mon.–Sat. Jacket preferred after 6
PM. AE, DC, MC, V. Closed Sun. Moderate–Expensive.*

Lodging

Many of the city's most costly lodging places offer attractively priced weekend packages. These weekend rates (and their availability) will vary; for a free copy of the *Boston Travel Planner*, contact the **Greater Boston Convention and Visitors Bureau** (Box 490, Boston 02199, tel. 617/536–4100).

Although Boston does not have a large number of bed-and-breakfasts, there are several, and they are usually very reasonable, with daily rates in the $55–$120 per-room range. Reservations may be made through **Bed and Breakfast Associates Bay Colony** (Box 57166, Babson Park Branch, Boston 02157, tel. 617/449–5302).

The following lodging price categories have been used: *Very Expensive*, over $150, *Expensive*, $95–$150; *Moderate*, $70–$95; *Inexpensive*, under $70.

Back Bay

★ **Copley Plaza.** The stately, bowfronted classic among Boston hotels, built in 1912, was completely refurbished in 1989. Guest rooms have carpeting from England, customized furniture from Italy, and new bathroom fixtures surrounded by marble tile. The Plaza Bar has seating to accommodate piano bar performances; Copley's Bar has just been renovated. A separate concierge area has been created. The hotel staff is multilingual, children under 18 stay free in their parents' room, and pets are welcome. *138 St. James Ave., 02116, tel. 617/267–5300 or 800/826–7539. 396 rooms, 49 suites. Facilities: 2 restaurants, 2 bars, beauty and barber salons. AE, DC, MC, V. Very Expensive.*

★ **Four Seasons.** The only hotel (other than the Ritz) to overlook the Public Garden, the newer 15-story Four Seasons specializes in luxurious personal service, Old World elegance, and comfort. The rooms have king-size beds, individual climate control, minibars, fresh flowers daily, cable movies, and 24-hour room service. A room overlooking the Garden is worth the extra money. The antique-filled public rooms include a relaxed piano lounge, and Aujourd'hui, a fine restaurant serving American cuisine. Small pets are welcome. *200 Boylston St., 02116, tel. 617/338–4400 or 800/332–3442. 288 rooms and suites. Facilities: lounge, concierge, heated indoor pool, sauna, exercise machines, whirlpool, valet parking. AE, DC, MC, V. Very Expensive.*

★ **Ritz-Carlton.** Since 1927 this hotel overlooking the Public Garden has been one of the most luxurious and elegant places to stay in Boston, and many people consider it the only place in town. Its reputation for quality and service (there are two staff members for every guest) continues. All the rooms are traditionally furnished and equipped with bathroom phones, and some rooms have refrigerators. The most coveted rooms remain the suites in the older section, which have working fireplaces and the best views of the Public Garden. Public rooms include the elegant café, with a window on chic Newbury Street; the sumptuous second-floor main dining room; the sedate Street Bar; and The Lounge. Small pets welcome. *Arlington and Newbury Sts., tel. 617/536–5700 or 800/241–3333. 278 rooms, 48 suites. Facilities: affiliated with a spa a block away, exercise room, valet parking, concierge, 24-hr room service, laundry service, beauty and barber salons, multilingual staff, baby-sitting. AE, DC, MC, V. Very Expensive.*

Boston Park Plaza Hotel & Towers. Built in 1927 as flagship for
the Statler hotels, the Plaza has had extensive renovations and
is an excellent choice for those who want to be at the heart of
the action. The hotel is just a block away from the Public Garden (of which some rooms on the top floor have a fine view) and a
short walk from Newbury and Boylston streets, Copley
Square, and downtown. The rooms vary in size, but all are
equipped with direct-dial phones, air-conditioning, and in-
room movies. Unless you want to look out on a brick courtyard,
ask for an outside room. The lobby is spacious, elegant, and
welcoming, with plants, crystal chandeliers, and comfortable
couches. High tea is served weekdays and Saturday afternoon.
The popular Legal Sea Foods is one of three restaurants; there
are two lounges, and the Terrace Room has live shows and entertainment. Children stay free in their parents' room. *One
Park Plaza at Arlington St., 02117, tel. 617/426–2000 or 800/
225–2008. 966 rooms and suites. Facilities: health club, 24-hr
room service, overnight laundry and dry-cleaning, foreign
currency exchange, specialty shops, garage parking available,
travel agency, hairstylist, all major airline ticket offices. AE,
DC, MC, V. Expensive.*

Copley Square Hotel. One of Boston's oldest hotels (1891), the
Copley Square is still one of the best values in the city. The hotel is popular with Europeans and is European in flavor. The
rooms, which are set off long, circuitous hallways, vary tremendously in size from very small to spacious. All rooms have
direct-dial phones, air-conditioners, windows you can open,
color TV, and automatic coffee makers with the necessary materials. If you want a quiet room, ask for one on the courtyard.
The popular Café Budapest is downstairs. Children under 12
stay free in their parents' room. *47 Huntington Ave., 02116,
tel. 617/536–9000 or 800/225–7062. 150 rooms. Facilities: use of
Westin Hotel's Health Club for a small fee, family suites, airport limousine service, coffee shop, overnight parking across
the street. AE, DC, MC, V. Expensive.*

Lenox Hotel. Constructed in 1900, the Lenox has long been a
comfortable—if unexciting—hotel, but extensive renovations
have given it a low-key elegance. The soundproof guest rooms
have spacious walk-in closets, color TV, AM/FM radio, and air-
conditioning. Bathrooms come equipped with hair dryers,
shaving mirrors, and amenities. The decor is Early American
or Chinese on the lower floors, French Provincial on the top
floor. The lobby is ornate and handsome, trimmed in blues and
golds and set off by a large, welcoming fireplace that evokes the
ambience of a country inn. The recently remodeled Diamond
Jim's Piano Bar, with its loyal local clientele, is a popular spot
for joining in on sing-alongs. Children under 18 stay free in
their parents' room. *710 Boylston St., 02116, tel. 617/536–5300
or 800/225–7676. 222 rooms. Facilities: 2 restaurants, valet
service, valet pay parking, baby-sitting service. AE, DC, MC,
V. Expensive.*

Eliot Hotel. An ambitious renovation brought a new elegance
and lots of marble to a formerly modest nine-floor, European-
style, family-run hotel. The upper four floors, all suites, got
marble baths and new period furnishings in 1990, and lower five
floors along with the marble-clad lobby, were redone in 1991.
One-bedroom and two-bedroom suites are available. The quietest rooms are those that do not face Commonwealth Avenue
and those on the higher floors. All rooms have air-conditioning
and color cable TV. There is no restaurant; the popular bar

next door is not owned by the hotel; parking is at a nearby garage. *370 Commonwealth Ave., 02215, tel. 617/267–1607. 12 rooms, 81 suites. Facilities: valet laundry, Continental breakfast in the lobby. AE, DC, MC, V. Rates include Continental breakfast. Moderate.*

Boston International Hostel is a youth-oriented hostel near the Museum of Fine Arts and Symphony Hall. Guests sleep in dormitories accommodating four to six persons and must provide their own linens or sleep sacks (sleeping bags are not permitted). The maximum stay is three nights in summer, six nights off-season. Reservations are highly recommended. Doors close at midnight. Preference is given to members of the American Youth Hostel network during the high season; to become a member, write to The Greater Boston Council of American Youth Hostels (1020 Commonwealth Ave., Boston 02215, tel. 617/731–5430). *12 Hemenway St., 02115, tel. 617/536–9455. Capacity: 220 in summer, 100 in winter. Cash or traveler's check with proper ID. Inexpensive.*

Cambridge **The Charles Hotel.** The 296-room Charles anchors one end of
★ the Charles Square development, which is set around a brick plaza facing the Charles River. The architecture is sparse and modern, softened by New England antiques and paintings by local artists. Guest rooms have quilts, TV in the bathroom, and an honor bar. Despite being a new hotel, furniture and carpeting at the Charles were entirely refurbished in 1991. The dining room, Rarities, serves New American cuisine. A Sunday buffet brunch is served in the Bennett Street Cafe. The Regattabar is one of the city's hottest spots for jazz. Children under 18 stay free in their parents' room. Small pets allowed. *1 Bennett St., 02138, tel. 617/864–1200 or 800/882–1818. 296 rooms. Facilities: full spa services, indoor pool, 24 shops, 24-hr room service, paid parking. AE, DC, MC, V. Very Expensive.*

★ **Sheraton Commander.** A nicely maintained older hotel on Cambridge Common, its rooms are furnished with Boston rockers and four-poster beds. All rooms have color TV and air-conditioning, and some have kitchenettes. *16 Garden St., 02138, tel. 617/547–4800 or 800/325–3535. 175 rooms and suites. Facilities: restaurant, lounge, fitness room with rowing machines and exercise cycles, multilingual staff, valet service, free parking. AE, DC, MC, V. Expensive.*

Cambridge House Bed and Breakfast. A gracious old home listed on the National Register of Historic Places, Cambridge House offers seven antique-filled guest rooms and five more in its Carriage House. The site is convenient to the T and buses; there is also a reservations center here for host homes in the metropolitan Boston area. Rates include a full gourmet breakfast and afternoon tea and sherry. *2218 Massachusetts Ave., 02140, tel. 617/491–6300 or 800/232–9989. Facilities: free parking. MC, V. Moderate.*

★ **Harvard Manor House.** This modern five-story motel in Brattle Square is the nearest lodging to Harvard Square shops, restaurants, and tourist sites. All rooms have color TV and air-conditioning, and the rate includes a complimentary Continental breakfast. Children under 16 stay free in their parents' room. *110 Mt. Auburn St., 02138, tel. 617/864–5200 or 800/458–5886. 72 rooms. Facilities: free parking. AE, DC, MC, V. Moderate.*

Susse Chalet Inn. This is a typical Susse Chalet: clean, economical, and sparse. It's isolated from most shopping or sites, a 10-

minute drive from Harvard Square, but it is within walking distance of the Red Line terminus, offering T access to Boston and Harvard Square. All rooms have color TV, air-conditioning, and direct-dial phones. *211 Concord Tpke., 02140, tel. 617/661–7800 or 800/258–1980. 79 rooms. Facilities: free parking. AE, DC, MC, V. Inexpensive.*

Downtown **Boston Harbor Hotel at Rowes Wharf.** Boston's newest and one
★ of its most elegant luxury hotels has opened right on the water, providing a dramatic new entryway to the city for travelers arriving from Logan Airport via the water shuttle that docks at the hotel. The hotel is within walking distance of Faneuil Hall, downtown, the New England Aquarium, and the North End. The guest rooms begin on the eighth floor, and each has either a city view or a water view; the decor has hints of mauve or green and cream, and the traditional furnishings include a king-size bed, sitting area, minibar, and remote control TV. The bathrooms have phones, guest bathrobes, hair dryers, and amenity kits. Some rooms have balconies. The elegant and comfortable Rowes Wharf Restaurant offers seafood and American regional cuisine as well as sweeping harbor views. The spectacular Sunday buffet is expensive at $32 per person but worthwhile for those with healthy appetites. There are also an outdoor café and a bar. Small pets accepted. *70 Rowes Wharf, 02110, tel. 617/439–7000 or 800/752–7077. 230 rooms, including 26 suites. Facilities: concierge, health club and spa with 60-foot lap pool, whirlpool, sauna, steam and massage rooms; gift shop, marina, commuter boat to the South Shore, water shuttle, valet parking. AE, DC, MC, V. Very Expensive.*

Bostonian. One of the city's smallest hotels and one of its most charming, the Bostonian epitomizes European-style elegance in the fresh flowers in its rooms, the private balconies, and the French windows. The Harkness Wing, constructed originally in 1824, has rooms with working fireplaces, exposed beam ceilings, and brick walls. The rooms tend to be a bit small but are extremely comfortable. The service is attentive, and the highly regarded Seasons Restaurant has a glass-enclosed rooftop overlooking the marketplace. Children under 12 stay free in their parents' room. *Faneuil Hall Marketplace, 02109, tel. 617/523–3600 or 800/343–0922. 152 rooms. Facilities: concierge, Jacuzzi in some suites, 24-hr room service, valet parking. AE, DC, MC, V. Very Expensive.*

★ **Hotel Meridien.** The respected French chain refurbished the old downtown Federal Reserve Building, a landmark Renaissance-Revival building erected in 1922. The rooms, including some cleverly designed loft suites, are airy and naturally lighted, and all have been redecorated recently. Most rooms have queen- or king-size beds; all rooms have a small sitting area with a writing desk, a minibar, modern furnishings, in-room movies, and two phones, one of them in the bathroom. Julien, one of the city's finest restaurants, is here, as is the Café Fleuri, which serves an elegant, award-winning Sunday brunch. There are two lounges. Teddy bears and crayons are presented to children upon arrival. Some pets permitted. *250 Franklin St., 02110, tel. 617/451–1900 or 800/543–4300. 326 rooms, including several bilevel suites. Facilities: health club with whirlpool, dry sauna, and exercise equipment; indoor pool, concierge, 24-hr room service, no-smoking floor, valet parking. AE, DC, MC, V. Very Expensive.*

Omni Parker House. Said to be the oldest continuously operating hotel in America, though its present building dates only from 1927 (and has had extensive renovations), the Parker House is centrally located, one block from the Common and practically in the central business district. All rooms have color TV, some have refrigerators; some rooms have showers only. Parker House rolls, invented here, are still a feature in the main dining room, where Sunday brunch is an extravaganza. Children under 16 stay free in their parents' room. There are special rates for students. *60 School St., 02108, tel. 617/227–8600 or 800/843–6664. 546 rooms. Facilities: 2 restaurants, 2 bars, complimentary use of nearby Fitcorp Health and Fitness Center, concierge, valet and room service, barber and beauty salons, multilingual staff, baby-sitting service. AE, DC, MC, V. Very Expensive.*

Logan Airport **Hilton.** The Hilton is the only hotel at the airport (though a Ramada Inn is just 1½ miles down the road), and the airport's proximity to downtown means that the Hilton is close to the action, too. The rooms, all refurbished in 1990, are modern, soundproof, air-conditioned; each has color TV with in-room movies. There's a restaurant and lounge, and pets are allowed. Children stay free in their parents' room. *75 Service Rd., Logan International Airport, East Boston 02128, tel. 617/569–9300 or 800/445–8667. 542 rooms. Facilities: outdoor pool, free parking, valet, baby-sitting service, free 24-hr shuttle service to airlines. AE, DC, MC, V. Expensive.*

Theater District **Tremont House.** Because the Tremont House was built as national headquarters for the Elks Club in 1925, when things were done on a grand scale, its spacious lobby has high ceilings, marble columns, a marble stairway, lots of gold leaf and a 16-foot, four-tier crystal chandelier. The guest rooms tend to be small; they are furnished in 18th-century Thomasville reproductions and decorated with prints from the Museum of Fine Arts. The double rooms have queen-size beds, but two double beds are available. The bathrooms also tend to be small; all have tub-and-shower combinations. All rooms have color cable TV. The Roxy, a dance club, is popular, as are the New York City Juke Box and the Stage Delicatessen. *275 Tremont St., 02116, tel. 617/426–1400 or 800/331–9998. 281 rooms. Facilities: room and laundry service, concierge, no-smoking floor, handicapped accessible, valet parking. AE, DC, MC, V. Expensive.*

The Arts

Boston is a paradise for patrons of all the arts, from the symphony orchestra to experimental theater and dance to Orson Welles film festivals. Thursday's *Boston Globe* Calendar and the weekly *Boston Phoenix* provide comprehensive listings of events for the coming week.

Bostix is Boston's official entertainment information center and the largest ticket agency in the city. Half-price tickets are sold here for the same day's performances. *Faneuil Hall Marketplace, tel. 617/723–5181. Open Tues.–Sat. 11–6, Sun. 11–4. Cash only for same-day ticket purchases. Closed major holidays.*

Concert Charge (tel. 617/497–1118) and **Ticketron** (tel. 800/382–8080) are ticket brokers for telephone purchases.

Theater First-rate Broadway tryout theaters are clustered in the theater district (near the intersection of Tremont and Stuart streets) and include the Colonial, the Shubert, the Wang Center, and the Wilbur. Local theater companies all over the city thrive as well.

American Repertory Theatre (Loeb Drama Center, Harvard University, 64 Brattle St., Cambridge, tel. 617/547–8300), associated with Harvard University, produces both classic and experimental works.

The Huntington Theatre Company (264 Huntington Ave., tel. 617/266–3913), under the auspices of Boston University, is Boston's largest professional resident theater company, performing a mix of established 20th-century plays and classics.

New Ehrlich Theater (539 Tremont St., tel. 617/482–6316) originates its own productions—classic and modern plays and new works.

Music For its size, Boston is the most musical city in America, unsurpassed in the variety and caliber of its musical life. Of the many contributing factors, perhaps the most significant is the abundance of universities and other institutions of learning. Boston's churches also offer outstanding, often free, music programs; check the Saturday listings in the *Boston Globe*. Early music, choral groups, and chamber music also thrive.

Symphony Hall (301 Massachusetts Ave., tel. 617/266–1492), one of the world's most perfect acoustical settings, is home to the Boston Symphony Orchestra and the Boston Pops.

Dance **Dance Umbrella** (tel. 617/492–7578) is one of New England's largest presenters of contemporary dance. Performances are scheduled in theaters throughout Boston. The Umbrella also offers information on all dance performances in the Boston area.

Boston Ballet (42 Vernon St., Newton, tel. 617/964–4070 or 617/931–2000 for tickets), the city's premier dance company, performs at the Wang Center for the Performing Arts.

Film Cambridge is the best place in New England for finding classic, foreign, and nostalgia films.

The Brattle Theater (40 Brattle St., Cambridge, tel. 617/876–6837) is a recently restored landmark cinema for classic-movie buffs.

Nickelodeon Cinema (606 Commonwealth Ave., tel. 617/424–1500) is one of the few theaters in the city that shows first-run independent and foreign films as well as revivals.

Opera **Opera Company of Boston** (539 Washington St., tel. 617/426–5300), under the brilliant direction of Sarah Caldwell, has established itself as a world force in opera.

Nightlife

Boston restaurants, clubs, and bars, often clustered in distinct areas in various parts of the city, offer a broad spectrum of evening and late-night entertainment.

The Quincy Market area may be the center of the city's nightlife; it has been thronged with visitors from the day the restoration opened in 1976. Here in the shadow of historic

Faneuil Hall you'll find international cuisine and singles bars among the specialty shops and boutiques.

Copley Square is the hub of another major entertainment area, and Kenmore Square, near the Boston University campus, has clubs and discos devoted to rock and new-wave groups.

The most breathtaking views of the city at night are from the Top of the Hub Restaurant, 60 stories up atop the Prudential Center, and the Bay Tower Room at 60 State Street. Both have convivial bars and live music.

Thursday's *Boston Globe* Calendar, a schedule of events for the upcoming week, includes an extensive listing of live entertainment in the *Nightlife* section. The weekly *Boston Phoenix* is another excellent source for entertainment.

Bar and Lounge **Bull and Finch Pub** (84 Beacon St., tel. 617/227–9605) claims to be the inspiration for the TV series *Cheers*.

Cafés and **Au Bon Pain** (1360 Massachusetts Ave., Cambridge, tel. 617/
Coffeehouses 497–9797), is a true café, handily located in Harvard Square. Some tables are reserved for chess players who challenge all comers.
Passim's (47 Palmer St., Cambridge, tel. 617/492–7679) is one of the country's first and most famous venues for live folk music, a nightly gathering place for folk and bluegrass music or poetry readings.

Comedy **Comedy Connection** (Charles Playhouse, 76 Warrenton St., tel. 617/426–6339) is a popular cabaret-style club in the heart of the theater district.

Disco **Rachel's** (in the Boston Marriott, Long Wharf, 296 State St., tel. 617/227–0800) features video monitors set up all around the dance floor and 99¢ appetizers, weekdays 5–7.

Jazz **Regattabar** (Bennett & Eliot Sts., tel. 617/864–1200) is a spacious and elegant club in the Charles Hotel.
The **Boston Jazz Line** (tel. 617/262–1300) reports jazz happenings.

Rock **The Channel** (25 Necco St., tel. 617/451–1050 or 617/451–1905) is a huge, noisy club with two dance floors, four bars, and a game room. Rock, reggae, and new-wave music is performed by local as well as national and international bands; the crowd is mostly in their early 20s.

Singles **Cityside Bar** (262 Faneuil Hall Marketplace, tel. 617/742–7390) offers live entertainment nightly by local rock groups. It's a good spot, but it can be crowded and noisy.

The North Shore

The slice of Atlantic coast known as the North Shore extends from Boston's well-to-do northern suburbs, past grimy docklands to the picturesque Cape Ann region, and beyond the Cape to Newburyport, just south of the New Hampshire border. It takes in historic Salem, which thrives on a history of witches, millionaires, and maritime trade; quaint little Rockport, crammed with crafts shops and artists' studios; Gloucester, the oldest seaport in America; and Newburyport, with its redbrick center and rows of clapboard Federal mansions. Bright and busy in the short summer season, the North

Shore is a tranquil area between November and June, when the holiday-making facilities have closed down.

Leaving Boston, you can take the Callahan Tunnel to get onto Route 1A, although this is not a particularly scenic drive until you get to Marblehead. A faster alternative may be to take I–93 out of Boston across the Tobin Bridge and continue north to Route 128, which will lead you east toward the North Shore.

Numbers in the margin correspond to points of interest on the North Shore map.

① Not exactly on the North Shore but north of Boston (take Route 1) and inland from Lynn, **Saugus** is worth a visit because of the **Saugus Iron Works** National Historic Site. The foundry on the Saugus River was the first in America when it was begun in 1646 by John Winthrop, son of the governor of Massachusetts. Reconstruction of the site began in the 1950s, and today the restored ironworks has all the appearance of a country village, with stone buildings, waterwheels, and the nearby river. The furnace and the rolling and slitting mills operate by water power, and blacksmiths hammer nails in the forge fires. *224 Central St., tel. 617/233–0050. Admission free. Open Apr. 1–Nov. 1, daily 9–5; Nov. 1–Apr. 1, daily 9–4. Closed Thanksgiving, Christmas, New Year's Day.*

② Head north on Route 1A, and then branch off onto scenic Route 129 to reach **Marblehead.** Founded by fishermen from Cornwall in 1629, the town is reminiscent of Cornish fishing villages. Now it's also one of the major yachting centers on the East Coast, and Marblehead's Race Week, usually the last week of July, attracts participants from all over the eastern seaboard.

Time Out To experience the fisherman's Marblehead, visit the **Driftwood** (tel. 617/631–1145), a simple, red-clapboard restaurant by the harbor on Front Street. Fishnets hang from the ceiling and excellent, inexpensive breakfasts and lunches are served from 5:30 AM until 2 PM.

The patriotic work of art *The Spirit of '76,* painted by A. M. Willard to celebrate the nation's centenary in 1876, hangs in Marblehead's redbrick town hall. *Washington St., Marblehead, tel. 617/631–0528. Admission free. Open weekday business hours; Memorial Day–Nov., Sat. 9–6, Sun. 11–6.*

③ Follow Route 114 out of Marblehead, turn right onto Route 1A, and drive the short distance to **Salem,** the most compelling town on the North Shore. Park in the central car park at Riley Plaza by the visitor information booth, and begin your exploration by following the Heritage Trail (painted on the sidewalk) around the town. If you prefer not to walk, the **Sightseeing Trolley and Shuttle Service** (tel. 617/744–5463) leaves from the same booth on narrated tours of the city, every hour 10–4, April through November.

Salem unabashedly calls itself "Witch City." Witches astride broomsticks enhance the police cars; witchcraft shops, a local witch, and more recall the city's infamous connection with the witchcraft trials of 1692. Sites commemorating the witch hysteria, which resulted in the hangings of 19 innocent people, are numerous. The **Salem Witch Museum** offers a multisensory presentation re-creating the events with 13 stage sets and life-size models. *Washington Square N, Salem, tel. 508/744–1692.*

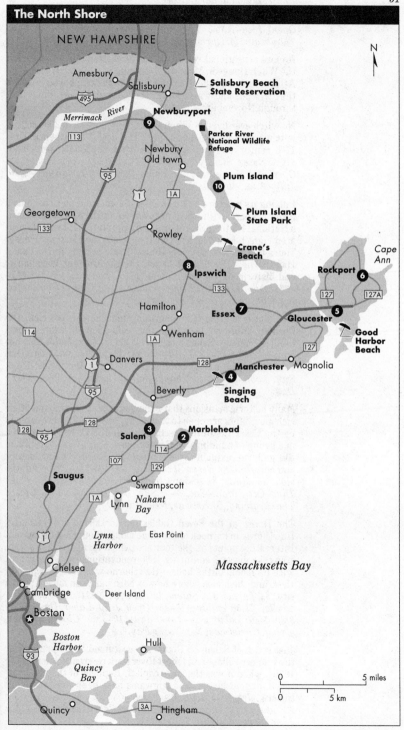

The North Shore

NEW HAMPSHIRE

Amesbury

Salisbury

495

Merrimack River

Salisbury Beach State Reservation

113

Newburyport ❾

Newbury
Old town

95

1

1A

Parker River National Wildlife Refuge

Plum Island

❿

Plum Island State Park

Georgetown

133

Rowley

Crane's Beach

Cape Ann

❽ **Ipswich**

Rockport ❻

133

127

127A

Hamilton

❼ **Essex**

❺

114

Wenham

1A

Gloucester

Good Harbor Beach

Danvers

128

Manchester

127

Magnolia

95

Beverly

❹

Singing Beach

128

128

95

❸ **Salem**

❷ **Marblehead**

114

1

129

Saugus ❶

107

Swampscott

1A

Lynn

Nahant Bay

East Point

Lynn Harbor

Massachusetts Bay

Chelsea

Cambridge

Deer Island

Boston ★

93

Boston Harbor

Hull

Quincy Bay

Quincy

3A

Hingham

0   5 miles
0   5 km

*Admission: $3.50 adults, $2 children 6–14, $3 senior citizens.
Open July–Aug., 10–7, Sept.–June, daily 10–5. Closed
Thanksgiving, Christmas, New Year's Day.*

A more sensational version of the same events is presented at
the **Witch Dungeon Museum** (16 Lynde St., tel. 508/744–9812).
After witnessing the live re-creation of the trials, you can visit
the "witches and warlocks" in the dungeon below, daily May
through November.

No witch ever lived at **Witch House,** but more than 200 accused
witches were questioned there. The decor is authentic late-
17th century, reflecting the era when the trials were held.
*310½ Essex St., Salem, tel. 508/744–0180. Admission: $3.
Open mid-Mar.–June and Labor Day–Dec. 1, daily 10–4:30;
July–Aug., daily 10–6.*

Putting its macabre past behind it, Salem went on to become a
major seaport, with a thriving overseas trade. **Salem Maritime,**
a National Historic Site operated by the National Trust, is situated right beside Derby Wharf, opposite the Customs House.
Tours take in the Customs House, made famous in Nathaniel
Hawthorne's *The Scarlet Letter;* the Government Warehouse;
and historic shipowners' homes. *174 Derby Rd., tel. 508/744–
4323. Admission free. Open daily 8:30–5. Closed Thanksgiving, Christmas, New Year's Day.*

The oldest continuously operating museum in America, the
Peabody Museum houses a fine collection of exotic items
brought back by Salem's merchant ships. *East India Sq., Salem, tel. 508/745–1876. Admission: $5 adults, $2.50 children
6–16, $4 senior citizens and students. Open Mon.–Sat. 10–5,
Sun. noon–5. Closed Thanksgiving, Christmas, New Year's
Day.*

Many historic mansions that belonged to shipowners and other
rich merchants are open to the public, several of them overseen
by the **Essex Institute Museum Neighborhood,** headquartered
in a group of buildings on Essex Street. Additional exhibits in
five galleries explain three centuries of Essex County history
and culture. *132 Essex St., Salem, tel. 508/744–3390. Admission: $5 adults, $4 senior citizens, $2.50 children 6–16. Open
June–Oct., Mon.–Sat. 9–5, Sun. and holidays 1–5. Closed
Thanksgiving, Christmas, New Year's Day.*

The **House of the Seven Gables,** immortalized by Nathaniel
Hawthorne in his book of the same name, should not be missed.
Interesting points on the tour are period furnishings, a secret
staircase discovered during 1886 renovations, and the garret
with its model of the house. Hawthorne was born in Salem in
1804, and the house where he was born has been moved to this
site. *54 Turner St., Salem, tel. 508/744–0991. Admission: $6
adults, $2.50 children 6–16. Open July–Labor Day, daily
9:30–5:30; Labor Day–June, daily 10–4:30. Closed Thanksgiving, Christmas, New Year's Day.*

Just south of Salem on Route 1A, costumed "interpreters" at
the **Pioneer Village and Forest River Park** re-create Salem of the
1630s, when it was the state capital. Replicas of thatched cottages, dugout homes, and wigwams have been constructed at
the site. *Jct. Rtes. 1A and 129, tel. 508/745–0525. Admission:
$3 adults, $2 senior citizens and children under 12. Open
June–Sept., daily 10–5.*

North of Salem, pass through Beverly on Route 127 and on to
④ the small seaside town of **Manchester,** with its excellent Singing
Beach, so-called because of the noise of the wind against the
sand. Head down Hesperus Avenue in the village of Magnolia
to see "Norman's Woe Rock," made famous by Longfellow in his
poem *The Wreck of the Hesperus*.

The rock can also be viewed from **Hammond Castle Museum,** a
stone building inspired by the castles of the Middle Ages and
built in 1926 by the inventor John Hays Hammond Jr. It contains medieval furnishings and paintings, and the Great Hall
houses an impressive organ with 8,600 pipes and 126 stops. *80
Hesperus Ave., tel. 508/283–2080. Admission: $5 adults, $3
children 6–12, $4 senior citizens and students. Open Tues.–
Sun. 9–5. Open Mon. on national holidays. Closed Thanksgiving, Christmas, New Year's Day.*

⑤ As the road continues along the coast, you enter **Gloucester**
along a fine seaside promenade. The first sight you'll see is the
famous statue of a man at a ship's wheel, eyes on the horizon,
dedicated to those "who go down to the sea in ships." Gloucester, the oldest seaport in the nation, is still a major fishing port.
Another personality of the town is illustrated by **Rocky Neck,**
the oldest working artists' colony in America.

⑥ **Rockport,** at the very tip of Cape Ann, is reached via the scenic
coastal Route 127A, or more quickly by cutting inland on Route
127. Originally a fishing port that developed into an artists'
colony in the 1920s, it's a cultured if touristy town that holds
firmly to its refined character. Along **Bearskin Neck,** a promontory in the town center, is a concentration of art galleries,
crafts stores, and cafés. Walk out to the end for an excellent
view of the Atlantic and the red lobster shack affectionately
known as Motif #1 because of its favor as a subject for amateur
artists. A curious site to visit is **Paper House,** its walls and furnishings constructed almost entirely of rolled-up newspapers.
*Pigeon Hill, Rockport, tel. 508/546–2629. Admission: $1
adults, 50¢ children. Open July 4–Labor Day, daily 10–5, and
by appointment.*

Head west out of Cape Ann on Route 128 and then turn north on
⑦ Route 133 for the village of **Essex.** Surrounded by salt marshes,
the town has more than 15 seafood restaurants. The **Essex
Shipbuilding Museum** displays exhibits from the 19th century,
when the town was an important shipbuilding center. *Rte. 133,
Essex, tel. 508/768–7541. Admission: $2. Open May–Oct.,
Thurs.–Sun 11–4.*

Time Out | **Woodman's of Essex** (Rte. 133, tel. 508/768–6451) claims to
have fried the first clams in town back in 1916. Today, this large
wood shack with unpretentious booths is *the* place for "seafood
in the rough," and the menu includes lobster, a raw bar, clam
chowder, and, of course, fried clams.

⑧ Four miles north of Essex, **Ipswich** is a small historic town with
a few mills beside the river. Its best feature is nearby **Crane's
Beach** (off Argilla Rd., tel. 508/356–4354), part of the privately
owned Crane Reservation, where upkeep costs mean a hefty
$6–$10 parking fee in summer. The white-sand beach is more
than 5 miles long; the refuge covers 735 acres.

⑨ Route 1A continues north and eventually becomes the main street through historic **Newburyport,** lined with some of the finest Federal mansions in New England. The granite **Customs House** on the waterfront has been restored, and houses the **Maritime Museum** with shipbuilding and Coast Guard exhibits. *25 Water St., Newburyport, tel. 508/462–8681. Admission: $2 adults, $1 children 6–16, $1.50 senior citizens. Open Apr.– Dec., Mon.–Sat. 10–4; Jan.–Mar., weekdays 10–4.*

⑩ A causeway connects Newburyport with **Plum Island,** which has a long, broad, sandy beach and a wildlife refuge at one end. The beaches are open to swimmers and anglers; self-guided trails provide excellent bird-watching opportunities. *Plum Island, tel. 508/462–4481. Admission free. Open daily dawn– dusk.*

Shopping

The greatest concentration of antiques stores on the North Shore is around Essex, but there are plenty sprinkled throughout Salem and Cape Ann as well. As an artist's colony, Rockport has several artists' studios and galleries selling work by local painters; most are located on Main Street near the harbor, and on Bearskin Neck.

Antiques Try the **Pickering Wharf Antique Gallery** in Salem, where five shops house 50 dealers.

Crystals and Magic **Pyramid Books** (214 Derby St., Salem, tel. 508/745–7171) stocks New Age books and music, tarot decks, incense, quartz crystals, and healing stones, as well as "power wands" and "metaphysical jewelry." **Gornigo** (Pickering Wharf, Salem, tel. 508/745–0552), complete with a black shop cat, sells a marvelous array of scented herbs, herbal teas, potion perfumes, runes, spirit lamps, and crystals. Crystals are a specialty at **The Crystal Chamber** (1 Hawthorne Blvd., Salem, tel. 508/745–9400).

Sports and Outdoor Activities

Canoeing The best areas are on the Ipswich and Parker rivers. For salt-water canoeing and kayaking, the waters of the Essex River Estuary are generally calm and protected. The **Harold Parker State Forest** in North Andover and the **Willowdale State Forest** in Ipswich also permit canoeing.

Fishing In Gloucester try **Captain Bill's Deep Sea Fishing** (9 Traverse St., tel. 508/283–6995), and in Newburyport try **Captain's Fishing Parties** (Plum Island Point, tel. 508/462–3141).

Surf casting is even more popular—bluefish, pollock, and striped bass can be taken from the ocean shores of Plum Island; permits to remain on the beach after dark are obtainable free of charge by anyone entering the refuge with fishing equipment in the daylight. You don't need a permit to fish from the public beach at Plum Island, and the best spot to choose is around the mouth of the Merrimac River.

For freshwater fishing, the Parker and Ipswich rivers are both stocked with trout each spring, and many state parks permit fishing.

Sailing Marblehead is the pleasure-sailing capital of the North Shore, but here and elsewhere it's not easy to find mooring space for your private yacht; many towns have waiting lists of several years. Town harbormasters will be able to inform you of nightly fees at public docks, when space is available.

Whale-watching Four breeds of whale feed in the area between May and October, and whales are so thick in the sea that you're practically guaranteed to see at least half a dozen—on "good" days you may see 40 or more. Some of the more reputable whale-watch operations include **Cape Ann Whale Watch** (415 Main St., Gloucester, tel. 508/283–5110), **Captain Bill's Whale Watch** (9 Traverse St., Gloucester, tel. 508/283–6995), **New England Whale Watch** (54 Merrimac St., Newburyport, tel. 508/465–9885 or 800/848–1111), and **Yankee Fleet/Gloucester Whale Watch** (75 Essex Ave., Gloucester, tel. 508/283–0313).

Camping

Cape Ann Campsite (80 Atlantic St., West Gloucester, tel. 508/283–8683) is open May through October. The **Black Bear Campground** (116 Main St., Salisbury, tel. 508/462–3183) and the **Rusnik Campground** (Box 5441, Newburyport, tel. 508/462–9551) are both open May 15 through October 1. Just two of the region's state parks permit camping—**Harold Parker State Forest** and the **Salisbury Beach State Reservation** (*see* National and State Parks, *below*).

Beaches

Here are some of the best beaches on the North Shore: **Crane's Beach** (Ipswich), **Parker River Refuge** (Newbury), **Plum Island** (Newburyport), **Salisbury State Reservation** (Salisbury), **Singing Beach** (Manchester), and **Wingaersheek Beach** and **Good Harbor Beach** (Gloucester).

National and State Parks

Of the numerous parks in the area, the following have particularly varied facilities: **Halibut Point State Park** (Rte. 127 to Gott Ave., Rockport, tel. 508/546–2997), the 3,000-acre **Harold Parker State Forest** (Rte. 114, North Andover, tel. 508/686–3391), **Plum Island State Reservation** (off Rte. 1A, Newburyport, tel. 508/462–4481), **Salisbury Beach State Reservation** (Rte. 1A, Salisbury, tel. 508/462–4481), and the **Willowdale State Forest** (Linebrook Rd., Ipswich, tel. 508/887–5931).

Dining and Lodging

Massachusetts claims fame for inventing the fried clam, a revolutionary event that apparently took place in Essex. Fried clams, therefore, appear on many North Shore menus, especially around the salt marshes of Essex and Ipswich. Eating seafood "in the rough" (from paper plates in shacklike wooden buildings dominated by deep-fryers) is a revered local custom. Rockport is a "dry" town, though you can almost always take your own alcohol into restaurants; most places charge a nominal corking fee. This law leads to early closing hours—many Rockport dining establishments are shut by 9 PM. Unless otherwise noted, reservations are not necessary for North Shore restaurants.

The following dining price categories have been used: *Very Expensive*, over $40; *Expensive*, $25–$40; *Moderate*, $12–$25; *Inexpensive*, under $12.

The following lodging price categories have been used: *Very Expensive*, over $100, *Expensive*, $70–$100; *Moderate*, $40–$70; *Inexpensive*, under $40.

Danvers   **Quality Inn King's Grant.** This modern building has tastefully
Lodging   appointed guest rooms with some reproduction antiques. Live entertainment is provided Friday and Saturday nights in the British Colony lounge, and the dining room re-creates 19th-century England. There's also an atrium with fish in the "brook," parrots in the air, and paths among the palms. *Box 274 (Rte. 128, exit 21N), 01923, tel. 508/774–6800. 125 rooms, 2 suites. Facilities: restaurant, lounge, indoor pool, Jacuzzi. AE, D, DC, MC, V. Expensive.*

Essex   **Dexter's Hearthside.** This 250-year-old converted farmhouse is
Dining   the epitome of coziness. Four small dining rooms have open fireplaces and exposed beams: The first is low-ceilinged with stencils on the walls; the others have cathedral ceilings with rough-panel walls and small windows. The newest eating area is in the loft. Entrées include baked stuffed haddock, seafood casserole, sirloin steak, lobster, and chicken. *Rte. 133, tel. 508/ 768–6002 or 508/768–6003. Dress: casual. AE, MC, V. Moderate.*

Tom Shea's. Picture windows in this single-story, cedar-shingled restaurant overlook the salt marsh. Inside, walls are white, and the room has mismatched wooden furniture, with many hanging plants. Seafood is the main fare, including shrimp in coconut beer batter, scallop-stuffed sole, Boston scrod, lobster, and, of course, the fried clams for which Essex is famous. *122 Main St., Rte. 133, tel. 508/768–6931. Dress: casual. AE, DC, MC, V. Moderate.*

Gloucester   **White Rainbow.** This excellent restaurant is in the basement of
Dining   a west-end store downtown, and candlelight gives a romantic
★   atmosphere. Specialties include Maui onion soup, grilled beef with a Zinfandel wine sauce, lobster *estancia* (lobster sautéed with tomatoes, artichoke hearts, olives, scallions, wine, and herb butter), and fresh fish of the day. *65 Main St., tel. 508/ 281–0017. Dress: casual. AE, D, DC, MC, V. Closed lunch; Mon. Expensive.*

★   **The Rhumb Line.** Despite its unimpressive location, this restaurant is worth the three-minute drive from the town center. The skillful decoration of the upstairs dining room gives customers the impression of sitting on a ship's deck, with the wheel and compass at one end, rigging overhead, captain's chairs at the tables, and seascapes on the walls. The selections include seafood casserole of shrimp, crabmeat, and scallops in garlic-lemon butter and white wine; roast duckling glazed with Grand Marnier, honey, and marmalade sauce; and charbroiled steaks. *Railroad Ave., tel. 508/283–9732. Dress: casual. AE, MC, V. Moderate–Expensive.*

Captain Courageous. The most recent owner of this ideally situated restaurant has created a seafaring atmosphere with nets, rigging, and paintings of old ships. In summer dining is on the outside deck above the water. Seafood is the main fare, and daily specials include sautéed scallops, lobster, and scrod. *25 Rogers St., tel. 508/283–0007. Reservations advised. Dress: casual. AE, D, DC, MC, V. Moderate.*

Gloucester House. The large white-clapboard building is located on the historic Seven Seas Wharf, which has been in continuous use for more than 350 years. Inside it's simply furnished with imitation leather booth seating and wood-panel walls decorated with fishing boat paraphernalia. Lobster is the specialty; the menu also offers fisherman's stew, seafood cakes, shrimp casserole, and chowders. *Seven Seas Wharf, off Rte. 127, tel. 508/283–1812. Dress: casual. AE, D, DC, MC, V. Moderate.*

Lodging **Best Western Twin Light Manor.** This is not your characteristic chain hotel—it was a manor first, a Best Western second. The English Tudor mansion was built in 1905 as a private home, complete with elevator, children's playhouse, and seven-car garage equipped with a turntable! Newer buildings nearby offer different styles of accommodations, and the complex is set on 7 acres of ground, overlooking the ocean. The most interesting guest rooms are those in the manor itself; some are enormous and have nonworking fireplaces. Guests have golf privileges on a local course, and the hotel is affiliated with a Gloucester health club. *Atlantic Rd., 01930, tel. 508/283–7500 or 800/528–1234. 63 rooms. Facilities: dining room, golf, health club, 2 outdoor pools, games room, bicycles, badminton, volleyball, croquet, shuffleboard, baby-sitters, gardens. AE, D, DC, MC, V. Very Expensive.*

Vista Motel. The name describes it well, because every room in this excellently situated motel overlooks the sea and Good Harbor Beach, just a few minutes' walk away. The rooms, perched atop a small, steep hill, vary in quality depending on price, but all are basically well furnished and spacious. Some have decks, and some have refrigerators. *22 Thatcher Rd., 01930, tel. 508/ 281–3410. 40 rooms. Facilities: outdoor pool. AE, MC, V. Expensive.*

Back Shore Motor Lodge. This lodge in East Gloucester overlooks the ocean from a rocky headland. All guest rooms have sea views, and some have sliding doors onto decks at the front of the building. Furnishings are good-quality motor-lodge style, with some reproductions, and the color scheme is sea green. Breakfast, lunch, and dinner are served in summer. *85 Atlantic Rd., 01930, tel. 508/283–1198. 23 rooms. Facilities: dining room, outdoor pool. No credit cards. Moderate–Expensive.*

Marblehead **The Landing.** Right on the Marblehead harbor and still in the
Dining historic district, this pleasant, small restaurant offers outdoor dining on a balcony over the sea. Inside are wood chairs and tables, with lots of hanging plants. The chef prepares lobster, swordfish provençale, Oriental red snapper in soy-ginger-lime marinade, Atlantic sole florentine, Ipswich clams, and seafood kabob. A limited choice of steak and chicken are also available. *Clark's Landing off Front St., tel. 617/631–6268. Dress: casual. AE, D, DC, MC, V. Expensive.*

Lodging **Harbor Light Inn.** This is the best place to stay in Marblehead
★ and competes with the Clark Currier Inn in Newburyport as one of the most comfortable and authentic inns on the North Shore. Special features include some in-room Jacuzzis, skylights, rooftop decks, and spacious, modern bathrooms; tradi-

tional touches are found in the four-poster and canopy beds, carved arched doorways, sliding (original) Indian shutters, wide-board floors, and antique mahogany furnishings. A generous Continental breakfast is served daily in the first-floor guest parlor with its wingback chairs and fireplace. *58 Washington St., tel. 617/631–2186. 12 rooms, 1 suite. Facilities: lounge. No pets. AE, MC, V. Rates include Continental breakfast. Expensive–Very Expensive.*

10 Mugford St. This large bed-and-breakfast in the historic old town is just one block from the harbor. Rooms of varying sizes are furnished with antiques and four-poster beds, and suites with private porches and a yard are available in a recently renovated house across the street. *10 Mugford St., 01945, tel. 617/639–0343. 4 rooms share 3 baths, 5 suites with bath. Facilities: dining room, garden. No pets. AE, MC, V. Rates include Continental breakfast. Moderate–Expensive.*

Newburyport
Dining
★

Scandia. The restaurant is well known locally for its fine cuisine, and house specialties are veal and lobster sauté, and seafood linguine. The dining room is small and narrow, and dimly lighted with candles on the tables and "candle" chandeliers. *25 State St., tel. 508/462–6271. Reservations advised. Dress: casual. D, DC, MC, V. Expensive.*

David's. The restaurant on the first floor of the Garrison Inn changed management in late 1990, and the dining room and the menu were both revitalized. The decor is bright and light, with white cloths, and crystal on the tables, and damask chairs and drapes. Specialties include sautéed lobster with roasted red pepper, snowpeas, and sherry; duck with dried fruit compote and wild rice pancakes; and lamb casserole. The basement offers lighter, less expensive meals. *Brown Sq., tel. 508/462–8077. Reservations advised. Dress: casual. AE, DC, MC, V. Moderate.*

East End Seafood Restaurant. For a true dining "in the rough" experience, visit this restaurant just south of Newburyport in the village of Rowley. The exterior is somewhat shabby, but inside, the shedlike building is pleasantly airy, with wood paneling, cathedral ceilings, and rustic beams. Dining is at wooden picnic tables, and the fare is deep-fried seafood. Note that the place closes at about 8 PM. *Corner Rte. 1A and Railroad Ave., Rowley, tel. 508/948–7227. No reservations. Dress: casual. No credit cards. Closed Mon. Nov.–April. Inexpensive.*

Lodging

Garrison Inn. This four-story Georgian redbrick building is set back from the main road on a small square. Inside, the atmosphere is impersonal. An elegant lounge and a formal dining room are furnished with smart reproductions; the basement tavern is more casual, with exposed brick arches and wood stoves in open fireplaces. Guest rooms vary in size; all have handsome replicas. The best rooms are definitely the top-floor suites, set on two levels: Spiral or Colonial staircases lead up from the sitting room to the sleeping area above. *11 Brown Sq., 01950, tel. 508/465–0910. 18 rooms, 6 suites. Facilities: dining room, lounge, tavern, room service. No pets. AE, DC, MC, V. Expensive.*

★ **Clark Currier Inn.** Opened in 1989, this is one of the newest inns in town, and perhaps the best. The innkeepers have renovated this 1803 Federal mansion with care, taste, imagination, and enthusiasm. Guest rooms are spacious and furnished with antiques: Some have pencil four-poster beds, one has a reproduction sea captain's bed complete with drawers below, and another contains a glorious sleigh bed dating from the late 19th century. Rooms also have fireplaces, but they are not useable. There's a Federalist "good morning" staircase (so-called because two small staircases join at the head of a large one, permitting family members to greet each other on their way down to breakfast). *45 Green St., 01950, tel. 508/465–8363. 8 rooms. Facilities: TV lounge. AE, MC, V. Moderate–Expensive.*

Rockport
Dining
★

The Hungry Wolf. This inconspicuous restaurant outside the town center has been receiving rave reviews ever since the owners (Charlie and Laura Wolf) moved here from Gloucester's Rocky Neck in 1988. The small, rather cutesy dining room has no views—the windows are high up on the clapboard walls—and some may wonder why the "candles" on the tables are electric. But few will question the quality of the food, which is first class. Specialties include French onion soup gratinée and scrod. Steak and chicken are also available, and meals come with large salads topped by homemade dressing. *43 South St., tel. 508/546–2100. Reservations advised. Dress: casual. D, MC, V. BYOB. Closed lunch; Sun.; Mon. Oct.–Apr. Moderate.*

My Place by the Sea. By the sea it is—this tiny restaurant is perched at the very end of Bearskin Neck. Inside, the small dining area has white wicker chairs and rustic beams; outside, the lower deck has tables overlooking the ocean. The restaurant serves mainly seafood, including baked scrod, swordfish steak, seafood fettuccine, and sandwiches. *Bearskin Neck, tel. 508/546–9667. Dress: casual. AE, DC, MC, V. BYOB. Closed Jan.–mid May. Moderate.*

Lodging
★

Yankee Clipper Inn. The imposing Georgian mansion that forms the main part of this impressive, perfectly located inn sits surrounded by gardens on a rocky point jutting into the sea. It was built as a private home in the 1930s, but has been managed as an inn by one family for more than 40 years. Guest rooms vary in size, but most are spacious. Furnished with antiques, they contain four-poster or canopy beds, and all but one has an ocean view. In the Quarterdeck, a newer building across the lawn, all rooms have fabulous sea views; the decor here is more modern, and rooms are again spacious with big picture windows. The Bullfinch House across the street is an 1840 Greek Revival house, appointed with tasteful antique furnishings, but with less of a view. *96 Granite St., 01966, tel. 508/546–3407. 27 rooms, 6 suites. Facilities: restaurant, lounge, outdoor pool, gardens. No pets. AE, D, MC, V. Rates include full breakfast. Very Expensive.*

Eden Pines Inn. A five-minute drive from the center of Rockport, Eden Pines is right on the ocean; five of its six rooms have balconies hanging over the waves, with a great view of the twin lights of Thatcher's Island. Large bedrooms are furnished with a mixture of modern rattan and wicker, with a few wood antiques. Walls are a fresh blue or sea-green with white moldings, and furnishings are in modern floral fabrics which match the pastel-tone carpets. The innkeepers own another property down the street; Eden Point House sits on a jutting rock, hugged by the sea on three sides, with an enormous semicircular lounge and floor-to-ceiling picture windows. *Eden Rd., 01966, tel. 508/546–2505. 6 rooms. Facilities: breakfast room, lounge, dip pool, private decks, croquet lawn. No pets. MC, V. Rates include Continental breakfast. Expensive–Very Expensive.*

Addison Choate Inn. This lovely, white clapboard inn sits inconspicuously among private homes, just a minute's walk from the center of Rockport. The spacious rooms, with large hand-tiled bathrooms, are beautifully decorated; the navy and white captain's room contains a dark-wood four-poster bed with a net canopy, handmade quilts, rag rugs, and models of ships. Other rooms—all with polished pine floors—have Hitchcock rockers and headboards, spool or filigree brass beds, local seascape paintings, and unfinished wood antiques. The two luxuriously appointed duplex carriage house suites have skylights, cathedral ceilings, and exposed wood beams. *49 Broadway, 01966, tel. 508/546–7543. 7 rooms, 2 suites. Facilities: breakfast room, lounge, outdoor pool. No smoking; no pets. MC, V. Closed Jan. 15–31. Expensive.*

Seacrest Manor. The distinctive inn, surrounded by large gardens, sits on top of a hill overlooking the sea. Two elegant sitting rooms with floral-print wallpaper have antiques and leather chairs. The hall and staircase are hung with paintings—some of which depict the inn—by local artists. Guest rooms vary in size and character: In the new wing they have more modern furnishings; upstairs, two have large private decks with sea views. Special touches are everywhere: complimentary morning newspapers, shoe shining, custom soap and shampoos, a nightly turndown service, and mints on the pillow accompanied by a Shakespearean motto. *131 Marmion Way, 01966, tel. 508/546–2211. 8 rooms, 2 with shared bath. Facilities: dining room, 2 lounges, gardens. No pets. No credit cards. Rates include full breakfast. 2-night minimum stay weekends. Closed mid-Dec.–mid-Feb. Expensive.*

Seaward Inn. This cedar-shingled inn is situated on a quiet promontory less than a mile south of Rockport, right across a narrow lane from the sea. Rooms in the inn have Colonial furnishings; those at the front with an ocean view are the best. Clothespins are used as napkin holders in the dining room, and guests write their names on the peg—when they return to the inn at a later date, their clothespin will be waiting for them on a string alongside thousands of others. Cottages with wood paneling and working fireplaces are available. *62 Marmion Way, 01966, tel. 508/546–3471. 38 rooms, 10 suites, 7 cottages. Facilities: 3 dining rooms, lounge, outdoor pool, gardens, putting green, bicycles, playground. No pets. No credit cards. Closed mid Oct.–mid May. Expensive.*

Bearskin Neck Motor Lodge. Set almost at the end of Bearskin Neck, the guest-room balconies here overhang the water. From the windows all you see is sea, and at night you can hear it lapping—or thundering—against the rocks below. Rooms are simply appointed with white and wood furniture and paneled walls. The exterior is gray cedar shingles, and a large deck over the sea at one end of the building can also be used by guests. *Bearskin Neck, 01966, tel. 508/546–6677. 8 rooms. No pets. No credit cards. Closed Dec. 30–Mar. 30. Moderate–Expensive.*

Inn on Cove Hill. This Federal building on a picturesque hillside dates back to 1792, when it was reportedly constructed with money from a cache of pirates' gold. Some guest rooms are small, but all are cheerful, pretty, and carefully appointed with bright, flowery print paper, patchwork quilts, and old-fashioned beds—some are brass, others are canopy four-posters. Rooms have polished wideboard floors, iron latches, wood bathroom fixtures, and pastel-tone Oriental rugs. *37 Mt. Pleasant St., 01966, tel. 508/546–2701. 11 rooms, 9 with bath.*

*No smoking; no pets. No credit cards. Rates include Continen-
tal breakfast. Closed mid Oct.–mid Mar. Moderate.*

Sally Webster Inn. Sally Webster was a member of Hannah
Jumper's so-called "hatchet gang," which smashed up the
town's liquor stores in 1856 and turned Rockport into the dry
town it remains today. Sally lived in this house for much of her
life, and the guest rooms are named for members of her family.
They contain rocking chairs; non-working brick fireplaces;
pineapple four-poster, brass, canopy, or spool beds; and pine
wideboard floors with Oriental rugs. Bonnets and wickerwork
hang on the walls; all rooms have candle-lanterns that can be lit
in the evening. *34 Mt. Pleasant St., 01966, tel. 508/546–9251. 6
rooms. Facilities: dining room, lounge. No pets. MC, V. Rates
include Continental breakfast. Closed Dec.–Jan; weekends
only, Feb.–Apr. Moderate.*

Salem
Dining

Nathaniel's. This formal restaurant at the Hawthorne Hotel on
Salem Common is hung with chandeliers. The menu includes
lobster, swordfish in mustard cream, prime rib, and poached
sole on spinach with champagne cream sauce. *On-the-Common, tel. 508/744–4080. Dress: casual. AE, D, DC, MC, V. Expensive.*

Chase House. This restaurant is extremely busy in summer,
ideally located as it is on Pickering Wharf, overlooking the harbor. A giant swordfish hangs beside the chimney in the saloon,
and the main dining room has low ceilings and walls of exposed
brick. The menu offers steak, squid, flounder, and "old-fashioned seafood dinners" of clams, scallops, shrimp, fish, and lobster with onion rings. *Pickering Wharf, tel. 508/744–0000.
Dress: casual. AE, D, DC, MC, V. Moderate.*

Lyceum. The Lyceum's great claim to fame is that Alexander
Graham Bell made his first public phone call from this building
in 1877. The decor connotes the '40s, with paneled ceilings,
wood bar, fans, and old photographs. Entrées include chicken
cutlets with lemon-cucumber sauce; swordfish steak; and black
angus sirloin stuffed with spinach, garlic, and pignola nuts. *43
Church St., tel. 508/745–7665. Reservations advised. Dress:
casual. AE, MC, V. Moderate.*

Victoria Station. This restaurant creates the atmosphere of an
English railway station, from the red telephone kiosk to the authentic metal signposts; walls are exposed brick, with lots of
beams and woodwork. Despite the attractive decor, most summertime visitors prefer to sit outside at tables beside the harbor, overlooking the historic maritime site. The restaurant
may look English, but the food is all-American and includes
steak, seafood, chicken, and burgers. The unlimited salad bar
is a great value. *Pickering Wharf, tel. 508/745–3400. Reservations advised. AE, DC, MC, V. Closed Dec. 25. Moderate.*

Oh Calcutta! This Indian restaurant, part of a Boston-based
chain, opened in Salem in 1989. The decor is, of course, Indian,
and the spicy menu includes a large variety of lamb, chicken,
beef, shrimp, and vegetarian dishes. *6 Hawthorne Blvd. (Rte.
1A), tel. 508/744–6570. Dress: casual. MC, V. Inexpensive.*

Lodging

Hawthorne Hotel. The former Hawthorn Inn changed its name
and its character after a $4 million restoration project back in
1986. The imposing redbrick structure is now the only full-
service hotel in Salem—conveniently situated on the green
just a short walk from the commercial center and most attractions. Guest rooms in brown and beige are appointed with reproduction antiques, armchairs, and desks (because business

clients are numerous). *On-the-Common, 01970, tel. 508/744–4080. 83 rooms, 6 suites. Facilities: restaurant, lounge, tavern, exercise room, meeting rooms, ballroom. AE, D, DC, MC, V. Expensive.*

The Arts

The **North Shore Music Theatre** (62 Dunham Rd., Beverly, tel. 508/922–8500) is a professional company that, from April through December, performs popular and modern musicals as well as children's theater. On Cape Ann the **Gloucester Stage Company** (267 E. Main St., Gloucester, tel. 508/281–4099) is a nonprofit professional group staging new plays and revivals year-round.

Nightlife

The Grog (13 Middle St., Newburyport, tel. 508/465–8008) hosts live entertainment downstairs Thursday–Sunday nights and features a wide variety of blues and rock bands.

Blue Star Lounge (Rtes. 1/99, Saugus, tel. 617/233–8027), a rockabilly roadhouse on a busy strip, plays country music Wednesday–Sunday evenings.

New Hampshire

In 1603 the first English explorer sailed into the mouth of the Piscataqua River, and in 1623 the first colonists settled at Odiorne's Point. Yet the New Hampshire coast today is more than 18 miles of Early Americana. Six state parks and beaches provide picnicking space, walking trails, swimming, boating, fishing, and water sports. Hampton Beach has a boardwalk right out of the 1940s—and the coastal area includes a scramble of patchy retail and housing development. Portsmouth's restaurants, galleries, special events, historic houses, and an outdoor museum at Strawbery Banke attract a trendsetting Boston crowd. Inland, Exeter is an important Colonial capital with 18th- and early 19th-century homes clustered around Phillips Exeter Academy. The crowds are heaviest on summer weekends; weekdays in summer and weekends in June or September are more likely to provide quiet times along the dunes and salt marshes.

Route 1 leads from Newburyport, Massachusetts, 6 miles across the state line to Seabrook, the starting point of this leg of the tour. If you've driving on I–95, Seabrook is the first New Hampshire exit; the town itself is a couple of miles east of the interstate. **Seacoast Trolley** (tel. 207/439–1941) operates a trolley that connects New Hampshire's beaches in summer.

Numbers in the margin correspond to points of interest on the New Hampshire Coast map.

❶ Our tour of the coast begins at **Seabrook,** an old town where whaling boats were once built and residents were known for their Yorkshire accents. Today Seabrook is virtually a one-industry town, and the nuclear power plant, finally granted an operating license early in 1990, is visible from the road.

Two miles farther north, where Route 1 meets Route 88,
❷ **Hampton Falls** offers a jogging trail, cross-country skiing in

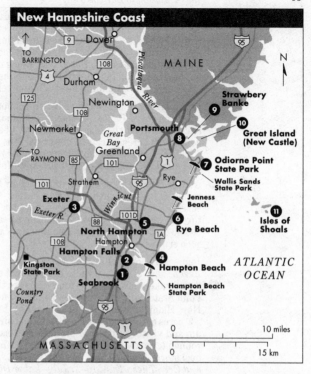

New Hampshire Coast

63

winter, and the **Applecrest Farm Orchards**, a pick-your-own apple grove and berry patch, with a picnic ground, shop, and bakery where you can put together a bread-and-cheese lunch or add fresh fruit and farm apple cider to the contents of your own picnic basket. *Rte. 88, Hampton Falls, tel. 603/926–3721. Open daily 10–dusk.*

3 Route 88 at Hampton Falls affords the opportunity to visit **Exeter,** the state's Revolutionary capital, 8 miles to the northwest. Today the town is known best for **Phillips Exeter Academy,** one of the nation's oldest prep schools and an assembly of Georgian architecture on a verdant campus. Settled in 1638, Exeter was a radical and revolutionary counterpoint to Tory Portsmouth in 1776. Among the handsome Colonial homes is the **Gilman Garrison House** (Water St., Exeter, tel. 603/227–3956), where settlers once fortified themselves against Native Americans and the Governor's Council met during the American Revolution.

Time Out The **Loaf and Ladle,** at 9 Water Street in Exeter, is a bistro where the chowders, soups, and stews are homemade and even the sandwiches come on homebaked bread. Overlooking the river, the Loaf and Ladle is handy to shops, galleries, and historic houses.

4 Return to (or continue on) Route 1 at Hampton Falls; it's 2 miles north to the junction with Route 101, where we turn east to the coastal Route 1A and **Hampton Beach.** Sometimes bawdy, never boring, the two-beach and 3-mile-boardwalk complex has the look of a location for a movie taking place in the 1940s and 1950s. This is an area of pizza and cotton candy, palm readers and performers, fireworks and fast-talking pitchmen. Young people swarm across Ocean Boulevard, oblivious to honking cars and blaring radios. Bands play swing in the amphitheater on the beach, and big names perform in the club of the 7-acre, multiple-arcade Hampton Beach Casino (tel. 603/926–4541).

5 Route 1A continues north to North Hampton (west on Route 101D) and Rye Beach. In **North Hampton,** Millionaires' Row sits just beyond the blare of Hampton Beach. At Fuller Gardens are 2 acres of estate flower gardens, circa 1939, where 1,500 rose bushes bloom all summer. *10 Willow Ave., North Hampton, tel. 603/964–5414. Open mid-May–Oct., daily 10–6.*

6 At **Rye Beach** the petrified stumps of an Ice Age forest protrude at low tide, and from Rye harbor one can embark on coastline cruises, whale watches, and one-hour lobster trips through the agency of New Hampshire Seacoast Cruises (tel. 603/964–5545); though Portsmouth offers a larger selection of such cruises.

Jenness Beach and Wallis Sands State Park, north of Rye Beach, have attractive white beaches that can be readily seen; **7** it will take a few hours or more to make the most of **Odiorne Point State Park** and Audubon Nature Center, site of the first New Hampshire settlement (Pannaway Plantation) and now 230 acres of tide pools, nature trails, and bird walks. The museum and visitor center has programs on ecology and the environment, and one can find further information in the bookstore. *Rte. 1A, Rye, tel. 603/436–8043. Open June, Sept., and Oct., Tues.–Sun. 10–4; July–Labor Day, weekends 10–4.*

8 Routes 1, 1A, and 1B all converge on **Portsmouth,** the state's principal coastal city, the conclusion of the 18-mile New Hampshire coast, and the beginning launch of I–95 and Route 1 on their long journeys up the coast of Maine. **Portsmouth Livery Company** (tel. 603/427–0044) provides horse-and-carriage tours of the Portsmouth area.

The shops, galleries, restaurants, and historic houses of Portsmouth recall Colonial times. On entering the city from the south, turn right on Little Harbor Road to visit the **Wentworth-Coolidge Mansion** (tel. 603/446–6607), once the official residence of the Royal Governor. No furnishings are original to the house, but all are of the period. What is said to be the oldest lilac bush in New Hampshire still blooms in the garden.

Time Out **Ceres Bakery,** at 51 Penhallow, is a bright, simple place to go for an apricot brioche and coffee mid-morning; homemade soup and quiche at lunch; tea and an almond torte mid-afternoon.

The **Portsmouth Historical Society** is located in the **John Paul Jones House** (Middle and State Sts., tel. 603/436–8420), which has been restored and furnished as it might have been when it was the boardinghouse residence of the naval hero. It is now one of six historic houses on the Portsmouth Trail, a historic walking tour. Tickets good for one or all may be purchased at each house and at the Chamber of Commerce (500 Market St., tel. 603/436–1118). Candles light the way on the Portsmouth Trail on evenings in late August.

Along the waterfront, Prescott Park is an ever-blooming re-treat between Strawbery Banke and the river, with a fishing pier and two historic warehouses. One of them contains the **Folk Art Museum** (tel. 603/431–8748), with its carved mast-heads and ship models.

The **Port of Portsmouth Maritime Museum,** in Albacore Park, has the USS *Albacore,* built here in 1953 as a prototype and testing submarine for the U.S. Navy. A film, followed by a tour, shows visitors how the 55-man crew lived and worked aboard the vessel. A section of Albacore Park has been dedicated as a memorial to submariners. *500 Market St., tel. 603/ 436–3680. Admission: $4.50 adults, $3.50 senior citizens, $2 children over 8, $12 family. Open daily 9:30–5:30. Closed Dec. 1–Feb. 28.*

❾ Portsmouth's ever-changing major attraction is **Strawbery Banke,** a 10-acre outdoor museum with period gardens, month-ly activities, and more than 40 original buildings that date from the years 1695 to 1820. The Candlelight Tours in early Decem-ber are downright romantic. The boyhood home of Thomas Bai-ley Aldrich (author of *The Story of a Bad Boy*) is the **Nutter House.** The **Wheelwright House** affords a daily demonstration of 18th-century cooking. Snacks and lunch are served in the museum restaurant, the Washington Street Eatery. *Marcy St., tel. 603/433–1100. Admission: $10 adults, $8 senior citi-zens, $5 children under 17, $25 family. Open May–Oct., daily 10–5; early Dec., weekends 4:30–8:30.*

❿ **Great Island,** commonly called New Castle, just east of Ports-mouth and overlooking the Piscataqua River, is reached by Route 1B (New Castle Avenue) from Portsmouth. Its attrac-tions are New Castle Path and **Fort Constitution.** The fort, then a British bastion, was raided by rebel patriots in 1774 and the stolen munitions used against the British at the Battle of Bunk-er Hill four months later. Take the paved walking trail from the fort through the 18th-century town for a close-up look at the former Colonial residences that are now private homes. *Fort Constitution, Great Island. Open mid-June–Labor Day, daily 9–5; Labor Day–mid-June, weekends 9–5.*

⓫ **Isles of Shoals** is an archipelago of nine islands (eight at high tide) in the Atlantic, one hour from Portsmouth, that was one of the region's major attractions for settlers. The islands were named for the shoals (schools) of fish that supposedly jumped into the nets of fishermen. A dispute between Maine and New Hampshire over the ownership of the islands caused them to be divided between the two states, but the invisible boundary is only of academic interest. In the 19th century the islands were an offshore retreat for the literary and art circle of the poet Celia Thaxter, whose Appledore Island is now used by the Ma-rine Laboratory of Cornell University; Star Island houses a conference center for Unitarian, Universalist, and Congrega-tional church organizations. In summer scheduled cruises take visitors to Star in the morning, leave them long enough for a nonalcoholic picnic and a hike, and return them to the mainland in mid-afternoon (only conference attendees may stay over-night in the rambling hotel and cottages). The Isles of Shoals Steamship Company also runs whale-watch expeditions, and its M/V *Thomas Leighton,* a Victorian-era steamship replica, schedules minivoyages on which ghost and pirate stories—the islands have them in abundance—are told; other excursions include some meals. Light snacks are available on board, or you can bring your own. *Isles of Shoals Steamship Company, Barker Wharf, 315 Market St., Portsmouth, tel. 603/431–5500 or 800/441–4620. Reservations advised. Cruises mid-June–Labor Day; foliage cruises Oct. Christmas cruises.*

Shopping

Portsmouth's harborside district has unusual and high-quality gift and clothing specialty shops, though you will find art and crafts galleries of particular note in the towns of Dover and Exeter as well. Newington has two large shopping malls: **Fox Run Mall** (Fox Run Rd., Newington, tel. 603/431–5911) and **Newington Mall** (45 Gosling Rd., Newington, tel. 603/431–4104).

From May to October, street fairs, yard sales, and flea markets may be found all along the seacoast. Look for posted notices and in the classified section of the newspapers. There is a regular Sunday **flea market** in the Star Center (25 Fox Run Rd., Newington, tel. 603/431–9403).

Antiques In Portsmouth, look on Chapel and Market streets. Along Route 4 between Portsmouth and Durham is an antiques row of barns and overflowing shops.

Galleries and Craft Shops **A Pictures Worth a Thousand Words** (65 Water St., Exeter, tel. 603/778–1991) offers two showrooms of pictures (antique and contemporary prints, old maps) and rare books.

Country Curtains (2299 Woodbury Ave., Newington, tel. 603/431–2315), located on the Old Beane Farm, has fabrics, ready-made as well as custom curtains, bedding, furniture, gifts, and folk art.

Exeter League of New Hampshire Craftsmen (61 Water St., Exeter, tel. 603/778–8282) is the seacoast shop for originals by select, juried members of L.N.H.C. Exhibits feature a different local craftsperson each month.

Guild of Strawbery Banke, Inc.–Kingsbury House (93 State St., Portsmouth, tel. 603/436–8004) stocks books, fine handcrafts, needlework, reproductions, and gifts in an 1815 town house.

Salamandra Glass Studio/Gallery (133 Market St., Portsmouth, tel. 603/431–4511) gives new meaning as well as form to hand-blown glass. Also shown are jewelry and gifts.

Salmon Falls Stoneware (The Engine House on Oak St., Dover, tel. 603/749–1467 or 800/621–2030) is handmade, American salt-glaze ware decorated with traditional, country, and whimsical designs. Potters are on hand if you want to place a special order.

The Square Rigger (143 Market St., Portsmouth, tel. 603/433–2422) sells everything from scrimshaw to sculpture, decoys to foul-weather gear. There is also a children's corner.

Tulips (19 Market St., Portsmouth, tel. 603/431–9445) was Portsmouth's first craft gallery and is still the city's leading venue for both local and national craftspeople. Wood crafts and quilts are specialties.

Outlet Shopping Outlet shopping mavens may want to stop at **Artisan Outlet Village** (72 Mirona Rd., Portsmouth, tel. 603/436–0022) or **North**

Hampton Factory Outlet Center (Rte. 1, Lafayette Rd., North Hampton, tel. 603/595–9000).

Roadside Stands   Country and farm products such as homemade jams and pickles are available at Applecrest Farm and Raspberry Farm, Hampton Falls; Emery Farm, Durham; and Thornwood Farm, Dover.

Sports and Outdoor Activities

Audubon Society of New Hampshire (Box 528B, Concord 03301, tel. 603/224–9909) conducts field trips of the coast.

Bird-watching   The magnificent **Great Bay** estuary, 4 miles west of Portsmouth, is the haunt of seabirds, migrating land birds, herons, and harbor seals. Every species of regional aquatic fowl may be seen here and, in Great Bay Access on the southeastern shore, every species of indigenous animal except moose and bear. Great Bay Access is reached by taking Route 101 to Greenland and turning north on the unmarked road near Winnicut River; leave your car at the railway track and walk in. The University of New Hampshire maintains the Jackson Estuan Laboratory on the western shore, an area that can be toured on Durham Point Road, which loops east from Route 108 at points south of Durham and north of Newmarket.

Biking   The Durham-to-Exeter route is a flat, pleasant round-trip of about 30 miles. Start off on Route 108/85 and return by crossing Route 101 and taking back roads along and across the Piscassic and Lamprey rivers. Avoid Route 1. A bike trail runs along part of Route 1A, and you can take a break at Odiorne Point. For **group rides** in various locations from April to October, call 603/898–9926.

Boating   There are rentals aplenty, along with deep-sea fishing charters, at Hampton, Portsmouth, Rye, and Seabrook piers, available from **Eastman Fishing & Marine** (Seabrook 03874, tel. 603/474–3461), **Atlantic Fishing Fleet** (Rye Harbor 03870, tel. 603/964–5220), **Al Gauron Deep Sea Fishing** (Hampton Beach 03842, tel. 603/926–2469), and **Smith & Gilmore** (Hampton Beach 03842, tel. 603/926–3503).

Hiking   There are good short hikes at **Blue Job Mountain** (Crown Point Rd. off Rte. 202A, 1 mi from Rochester) and at the Urban Forestry Center, Portsmouth. Serious hikers should move on to the White Mountains.

Beaches

Swimming beaches on the New Hampshire shore and one inland freshwater pond are maintained and supervised by the Division of Parks and Recreation. You will usually find Jenness, Rye, and Wallis Sands less congested than Hampton, but you can view them and take your choice as you cruise Route 1A. For freshwater swimming, try Kingston State Park at Kingston on Great Pond (not to be confused with Great Bay). In summer a trolley connects the ocean beaches. Beaches outside the state park system include Foss Beach, Rye; New Castle Common, New Castle; and Four Tree Island, Portsmouth.

Dining and Lodging

Portsmouth has a reputation throughout New England for dining excellence. Because many of its most highly regarded restaurants are small and prepare all dishes to order, reservations are imperative and in some cases should be made several days ahead.

The following dining price categories have been used: *Very Expensive*, over $35; *Expensive*, $25–$35; *Moderate*, $15–$25; *Inexpensive*, under $15.

All the lodgings described here are convenient to both town and shore, and all require advance reservations, at least during the period from mid-June to mid-October.

The following lodging price categories have been used: *Very Expensive*, over $150, *Expensive*, $100–$150; *Moderate*, $60–$100; *Inexpensive*, under $60.

Dover
Dining
★

Newick's Lobster House. This is a regular stop for many who travel the coast, and, until foul weather drives everyone inside, the dining is outdoors. It's an informal place, with paper napkins and plastic plates and the owner in rubber boots keeping an eye on things. The principal fare is lobster, clams, and oyster stew; slaw and chewy bread are the natural accompaniments. *431 Dover Point Rd. (Rte. 16), tel. 603/742–3205. No reservations. Dress: casual. MC, V. Closed Mon. and Thanksgiving, Dec. 25. Inexpensive–Moderate.*

Durham
Dining

The Woods. On-campus dining at the restaurant of the New England Center Hotel at the University of New Hampshire is a pleasing mix of American and Continental cuisine served by a congenial student staff. Chicken and veal are lightly sauced; beef comes done to order; and there are vegetarian and low-calorie dishes. The attractiveness is enhanced by the pine woods outside and an art gallery upstairs. *15 Strafford Ave., tel. 603/862–2815. Reservations advised. Dress: neat but casual. MC, V. Closed Dec. 20–Jan. 3. Moderate.*

Lodging

New England Center Hotel. Set in a pine grove on the campus of the University of New Hampshire, this is a quiet spot. The rooms are larger in the new wing. *15 Strafford Ave., 03824, tel. 603/862–2800. 115 rooms with bath. Facilities: restaurant, lounge, cable TV. No pets. AE, MC, V. Moderate.*
Country House Inn. A farmhouse in the 1800s and an inn since 1985, this inn is up-to-date and unusual. How many country inns offer sculling packages, even if they are located near the water? Great Bay and the University of New Hampshire campus are close at hand. The suite has its own wood stove and a private deck. *Stagecoach Rd. and Rte. 108, 03824, tel. 603/659–6565. 20 rooms, 18 with bath. Facilities: restaurant (closed dinner), some cable TV, cross-country skiing, sculling. MC, V. Inexpensive–Moderate.*

Exeter
Dining

Exeter Inn Dining Room. The restaurant on the Phillips Exeter Academy campus serves chateaubriand on a plank that goes miles beyond any student's dream night out with Mom and Dad. On Friday and Saturday night, look for cherries flambé or some equally spectacular flaming dessert. Sunday brunch, with at least 60 savory items, including a variety of omelets, provides a bright start to the day, for the dining room is a circle of windows with a fig tree growing in the center. *90 Front St., tel.*

603/772–5901. Reservations advised; not accepted for Sunday brunch. Dress: neat but casual. AE, D, DC, MC, V. Moderate–Expensive.

Lodging **Best Western Hearthside.** Although a designated business-person's place, the motor inn's well-furnished rooms and good management (the manager has been with the inn in various capacities since high school) recommend it to family travelers as well. *Portsmouth Ave. (Rte. 108), 03833, tel. 603/772–3794 or 800/528–1234. 33 rooms. Facilities: restaurant, lounge, pool. No pets. AE, D, DC, MC, V. Moderate.*

Exeter Inn. A three-story, Georgian-style inn with handsomely appointed guest rooms is properly set on the campus of the Phillips Exeter Academy, in the heart of Exeter's historic district. This is understated elegance, New England–preppie style. *90 Front St., 03833, tel. 603/772–5901 or 800/782–8444; fax 603/778–8757. 50 rooms. Facilities: restaurant, cable TV, fitness room. No pets. AE, D, DC, MC, V. Moderate.*

Hampton **Ron's Beach House.** Cioppino, pasta with white clam sauce, and
Dining a fish chowder with Cajun-style mushroom caps lead a menu of imaginative specialties that has made an overnight success of this family-run restaurant. In the Plaice Cove section of Hampton, Ron's occupies a restored house on the waterfront, 3 miles north of the boardwalk. *965 Ocean Blvd., tel. 603/926–1870. Reservations advised. Dress: casual. AE, MC, V. Moderate–Expensive.*

Lamie's Tavern. The terrace is open for dining when the weather allows, and the New England cookery has been lightened: Bean soup has fresh tomatoes; lobster comes sautéed as well as stuffed. This is a good place to wind down from the Hampton Beach action. *490 Lafayette Rd. (junction Rtes. 1 and 101C), tel. 603/926–0330. Reservations advised. Dress: neat but casual. AE, MC, V. Moderate.*

Hampton Beach **Ashworth by the Sea.** Since this centrally located hotel opened
Lodging in 1912, it has been renovated, rebuilt, and renovated again and is familiar to generations of beachgoers. Most rooms have decks, and the furnishings are either period or contemporary, depending on the room. Be sure to specify whether you want sea view or quiet, because you can't have it both ways. *295 Ocean Blvd., 03842, tel. 603/926–6762. 105 rooms. Facilities: 3 restaurants, pool, room service. AE, MC, V. Moderate.*

Hampton Falls **Luka's Greenhouse Restaurant.** A big, fresh, greenery-filled
Dining restaurant where, in addition to steak, seafood, and lamb, there are such traditional Greek specialties as moussaka and spinach pie. The contemporary cooking matches the setting. *12 Lafayette Rd., tel. 603/926–2107. Reservations advised in summer. Dress: casual. AE, MC, V. Closed Thanksgiving, Dec. 25. Moderate.*

Portsmouth **The Blue Strawbery Restaurant.** The label "American Cuisine"
Dining understates the inventiveness of this menu that changes every night according to what is freshest in the local market that morning. The prix-fixe, reservations-only policy of this small waterfront restaurant never deters diners; in fact, some drive hours to get here. *29 Ceres St., tel. 603/431–6420. Reservations required. Dress: neat but casual. No credit cards. Dinner only. Closed Oct. 15–July 3, Mon.–Wed. Very Expensive.*

★ **L'Auberge.** Classic French versions of duck à l'orange, frogs' legs, veal, and escargots are prepared by the owner and chef.

The tarte of the evening is always a surprise. Reserve as far in advance as possible. *96 Bridge St., tel. 603/436–2377. Reservations required. Jacket advised. AE, DC, MC, V. Dinner only. Very Expensive.*

Strawbery Court Restaurant Français. In spite of the proximity of Strawbery Banke, the cuisine here is classic and nouvelle French, not Early American. The tiny Federal brick town house has been lovingly restored, its twin front rooms each holding a handful of tables. Oyster bisque, white asparagus, and escargots may be on the prix-fixe menu. *20 Atkinson St., tel. 603/431–7722. Reservations required. Dress: neat but casual. AE, MC, V. Closed Sun., Mon., Thanksgiving, Dec. 25, Jan. 1. Very Expensive.*

Seventy-Two. Getting to church on time has culinary overtones here, for this popular restaurant is located in the shell of a 19th-century Free Will Baptist church. The French chef prepares asparagus and broccoli bisques as well as lobster. Desserts include a chocolate truffle cake. *45 Pearl St., tel. 603/436–5666. Reservations advised. Dress: neat but casual. MC, V. Expensive.*

Anthony's Al Dente. A busy, noisy restaurant with a loyal following is located in what was once a customs-house cellar on the harbor. Among the attractions of the kitchen are fresh tomato marinara over homemade pasta; a peppery anchovy sauce; and clams served simply with chopped parsley and garlic. A long wine list features hard-to-find Italian vintages. *59 Penhallow, tel. 603/436–2527. Reservations advised. Dress: casual. DC, MC, V. Closed Mon. Moderate–Expensive.*

The Dolphin Striker. The locals hang out here, but they have to squeeze in past the tourists in high season. Seafood is the specialty (mariner's pie is a fisherman's platter in a crust) but not the only choice; steaks, chops, chicken, and vegetarian selections are on the menu, too. The ambience is what you would expect in a restored warehouse: original beams, low ceilings, a stone-wall tavern downstairs. *15 Bow St., tel. 603/431–5222. Reservations advised. Dress: casual. AE, DC, MC, V. Closed Thanksgiving, Dec. 25. Moderate.*

★ **State Street Saloon.** It's new on the block, but this small Italian restaurant in the harbor district is known by the line of prospective diners waiting outside every night. An imaginative chef is one reason; another is the price. Consider pork tenderloin Marsala; chicken breasts and artichokes over fettuccine; and a true *bruschetta* (toasted bread prepared with garlic and olive oil). With its corrugated-tin ceiling and the black-and-white color scheme, only the bill will convince you you're not in Boston's North End. *268 State St., tel. 603/431–4357. Dress: casual. MC, V. Inexpensive–Moderate.*

Lodging **Sheraton Portsmouth Hotel.** This five-story redbrick Sheraton blends nicely with the 19th-century architecture of the historic district. Despite its harbor views and central location, it's more of a conference center than a cozy inn. *250 Market St., 03801, tel. 603/431–2300 or 800/325–3535. 148 rooms, 20 apartments. Facilities: restaurant, lounge, nightclub, room service, cable TV, health spa, indoor pool. No pets. AE, D, DC, MC, V. Expensive.*

★ **Sise Inn.** With silks and polished chintz, rubbed woods and armoires, this inn re-creates the lifestyle of the affluent of the 1880s. The Queen Anne town house is in Portsmouth's historic district and is ideally located for waterfront strolling and dining. No two rooms are alike. *40 Court St., 03801, tel. 603/433–1200 or 800/232–4667. 34 rooms. Facilities: cable TV, VCR, fitness room, some whirlpool tubs, morning newspaper. No pets. AE, MC, V. Rates include breakfast. Expensive.*

Inn at Christian Shore. The inn is owned—and decorated—by former antiques dealers who came to B&B innkeeping after restoring and furnishing houses elsewhere. It is a 10-minute walk from the historic district, the harbor, and shops; and you'll need the walk after breakfasting on fruit, eggs, a meat dish, vegetables, and homemade muffins. *335 Maplewood Ave., 03801, tel. 603/431–6770. 6 rooms, 3 with bath. Facilities: cable TV. No credit cards. Rates include full breakfast. Inexpensive–Moderate.*

Rye
Lodging
★

Rock Ledge Manor. This B&B was once part of a late-19th-century resort colony, and its sun room and white wicker are signs of its past. The owners speak French, and you may well find crepes served one morning in the sunny dining room overlooking the Atlantic. All the bedrooms have sea views. *1413 Ocean Blvd. (Rte. 1A), 03870, tel. 603/431–1413. 4 rooms, 2 with bath. No pets. No smoking. No credit cards. Rates include full breakfast. Moderate.*

The Arts

Strawbery Banke Chamber Music Festival (Box 1529, Portsmouth, tel. 603/436–3110) schedules performances from October to June.

Hampton Playhouse (357 Winnacunnet Rd., Rte. 101E, Hampton, tel. 603/926–3073) has children's theater and professional summer theater from July to September. Tickets are available at the box office or at the Chamber of Commerce Sea Shell office on Ocean Boulevard.

Theatre by the Sea (125 Bow St., Portsmouth, tel. 603/433–4472) operates year-round professional theater.

Nightlife

Club Casino (Ocean Beach Blvd., Hampton Beach, tel. 603/926–4541) gets as many as 2,500 people crowding the floor on a summer night, and all generations are well represented. Nightly shows feature nationally known music and comedy stars. *Open Apr.–Oct.*

The Press Room (77 Daniels St., Portsmouth, tel. 603/431–5186) is an old three-story, five-fireplace brick building with a variety of shows: jazz and folk music nightly 5 PM to 9 PM; variety shows on Tuesday night; sea shanties, pre-1850 Celtic ballads, or maybe just open jams on Fridays.

North from Kittery

Maine's southernmost coastal towns won't give you the rugged, wind-bitten "downeast" experience, but they offer all the amenities, they are easy to drive to from the south, and most have the sand beaches that all but vanish beyond Portland.

Kittery, which lacks a large sand beach, hosts a complex of factory outlets. North of Kittery the Maine coast has long stretches of hard-packed white-sand beach, closely crowded by nearly unbroken ranks of beach cottages, motels, and ocean-front restaurants. The summer colonies of York Beach, Ogunquit, and Wells Beach have the crowds and the ticky-tacky shorefront overdevelopment. Farther inland, York's historic district is on the National Register.

More than any other region south of Portland, the Kenne-bunks—and especially Kennebunkport—offer the complete Maine coast experience: classic townscapes where perfectly proportioned white-clapboard houses rise from manicured lawns and gardens; rocky shorelines punctuated by sandy beaches, beach motels, and cottages; quaint downtown districts packed with gift shops, ice-cream stands, and tourists; harbors where lobster boats bob alongside yachts; lobster pounds and well-appointed dining rooms. The range of accommodations includes rambling Victorian-era hotels, beachside family motels, and inns.

Numbers in the margin correspond to points of interest on the Southern Maine Coast map.

❶ **Kittery,** which is just east of I–95 on Route 1, three miles north of Portsmouth, New Hampshire, will be of most interest to shoppers headed for its factory outlet stores. Beyond Kittery,
❷ Route 1 heads north to **the Yorks.** A right onto Route 1A (York Street) leads to the **York Village Historic District,** where a number of 18th- and 19th-century buildings have been restored and maintained by the Old York Historical Society. Most of the buildings are clustered along York Street and Lindsay Road, and you can buy an admission ticket for all the buildings at the Jefferds Tavern (Rte. 1A and Lindsay Rd.), a restored late-18th-century inn. Other historic buildings open to the public include the Old York Gaol (1720), once the King's Prison for the Province of Maine, which has dungeons, cells, and jailer's quarters; and the Elizabeth Perkins House (1731), with Victorian-era furniture that reflects the style of its last occupants, the prominent Perkins family. The district offers tours with guides in period costumes, crafts workshops, and special programs in summer. *Tel. 207/363–4974. Admission: $6 adults, $2.50 children 6–16, $16 family. Open mid-June–Sept., Tues.–Sat. 10–4.*

Complete your tour of the Yorks by driving down Nubble Road (turn right off Route 1A) to the end of Cape Neddick, where you can park and gaze out at the Nubble Light (1879), which sits on a tiny island just offshore. The keeper's house is a tidy Victorian cottage with pretty gingerbread woodwork and red shutters.

Shore Road to Ogunquit passes the 100-foot Bald Head Cliff, which allows a view up and down the coast; on a stormy day the surf can be quite wild here. Shore Road will take you right into
❸ **Ogunquit,** a coastal village that became a resort in the 1880s and gained fame as an artist's colony, though few artists or actors can afford the condos and seaside cottages that now dominate the Ogunquit seascape.

On Shore Road, the **Museum of Art of Ogunquit,** a low-lying concrete building overlooking the ocean and set amid a 3-acre sculpture garden, shows works by Henry Strater, Marsden Hartley, William Bailey, Gaston Lachaise, Walt Kuhn, and Reginald Marsh. The huge windows of the sculpture court command a view of cliffs and ocean. *Shore Rd., tel. 207/646–4909.*

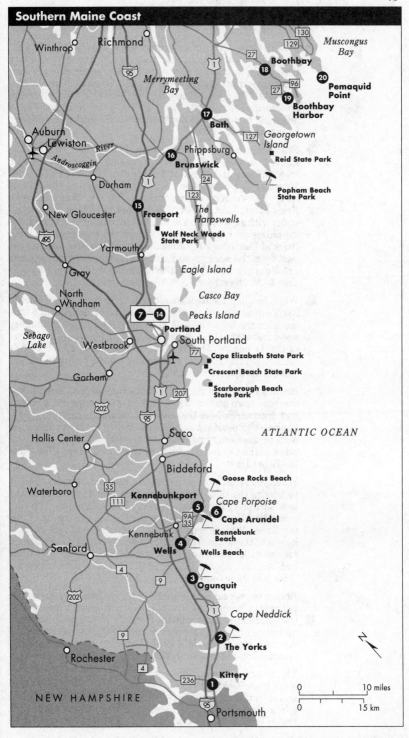

*Admission free. Open June–Labor Day, Mon.–Sat. 10:30–5,
Sun. 1:30–5.*

Perkins Cove, a neck of land connected to the mainland by a pedestrian drawbridge as well as a narrows, is ½ mile from the art
museum. Quaint is the only word for this jumble of sea-beaten
fish houses transformed by the tide of tourism to shops and restaurants. When you've had your fill of browsing and jostling the
crowds at Perkins Cove, stroll out along the Marginal Way, a
mile-long footpath that hugs the shore of a rocky promontory
known as Israel's Head.

4 Follow Route 1 north through **Wells.** Five miles north of Wells,
Route 1 becomes Main Street in Kennebunk. For a sense of the
area's history and architecture, begin here at the **Brick Store
Museum.** The cornerstone of this block-long preservation of
early 19th-century commercial buildings is William Lord's
Brick Store, built as a dry-goods store in 1825 in the Federal
style, with an open-work balustrade across the roof line, granite lintels over the windows, and paired chimneys. Walking
tours of Kennebunk's National Historic Register District depart from the museum on Friday at 2, June through October.
*117 Main St., tel. 207/985–4802. Admission: $2 adults, $1 chil-
dren 6–16. Open Tues.–Sat. 10–4:30.*

5 While heading for **Kennebunkport** on Summer Street (Route
35), keep an eye out for the **Wedding Cake House** about a mile
along on the left. The legend behind this confection in fancy
wood fretwork is that its sea-captain builder was forced to set
sail in the middle of his wedding, and the house was his bride's
consolation for the lack of a wedding cake. The home, built in
1826, is not open to the public.

Route 35 takes you right into Kennebunkport's **Dock Square,**
the busy town center, which is lined with shops and galleries
and draws crowds in the summer. Parking is tight in Kennebunkport in peak season. One possibility is the municipal lot
next to the Congregational Church ($2/hour, May–Oct.); an-
other is the Consolidated School on School Street (free, June
25–Labor Day).

When you stroll around the square, walk onto the drawbridge
to admire the tidal Kennebunk River. Then turn around and
head up Spring Street two blocks to Maine Street and the very
grand **Nott House,** known also as the White Columns, an imposing Greek Revival mansion with Doric columns that rise the
height of the house. The Nott House is the gathering place for
village walking tours on Tuesday and Friday mornings in July
and August. *Maine St., tel. 207/967–2751. Admission: $2.
Open mid-June–mid-Oct., Tues., Fri., Sat. 1–4.*

Return to your car for a leisurely drive on Ocean Avenue, which
follows the Kennebunk River to the sea and then winds around
6 the peninsula of **Cape Arundel.** Parson's Way, a small and tranquil stretch of rocky shoreline, is open to all. As you round Cape
Arundel, look to the right for the entrance to President Bush's
summer home at Walker's Point.

The **Seashore Trolley Museum,** on Log Cabin Road about 3
miles from Dock Square, shows transport from classic Victorian-era horsecars to vintage 1960s streetcars and includes exhibits about the Atlantic Shore Railway, which once ran a
trolley from Boston to Dock Square. Best of all, you can take a

trolley ride for nearly 2 miles through woods and fields and past
the museum restoration shop. *Log Cabin Rd., tel. 207/967–
2712. Admission: $5.50 adults, $4.50 senior citizens, $3.50
children 6–16. Open mid-June–Labor Day, daily 10–5:30; late
Apr.–mid-June, weekends for a trolley ride at 1:30; Labor
Day–Oct., weekends noon–5, weekdays for a trolley ride at
1:30.*

Shopping

Several factory outlet stores along Route 1 in Kittery and Wells
offer clothing, shoes, glassware, and other products from top-
of-the-line manufacturers. As an outgrowth of its long-estab-
lished art community, Ogunquit has numerous galleries, many
on Shore Road. Perkins Cove in Ogunquit and Dock Square in
Kennebunkport have seasonal gift shops, boutiques, and galleries.

Antiques **J. J. Keating** (Rte. 1, Kennebunk, tel. 207/985–2097) deals in
antiques, reproductions, and auctions.

Old Fort Inn and Antiques (Old Fort Ave., Kennebunkport, tel.
207/967–5353) stocks a small but choice selection of primitives,
china, and country furniture in a converted barn adjoining an
inn.

Saml's Stairs Antiques (27 Western Ave., Kennebunkport, tel.
207/967–2850) has American furniture of the 18th and early
19th centuries, specializing in tiger maple, and a good selection
of Staffordshire.

Douglas N. Harding Rare Books (Rte. 1, Wells, tel. 207/646–
8785) has a huge stock of old books, maps, and prints.

Kenneth & Ida Manko (Seabreeze St., Wells, tel. 207/646–2595)
shows folk art, primitives, paintings, and a large selection of
19th-century weathervanes. (Turn right on Eldridge Rd. off
Rte. 1, and after ½ mi turn left on Seabreeze St.)

Crafts **Marlows Artisans Gallery** (109 Lafayette Center, Kennebunk,
tel. 207/985–2931) features wood, glass, weaving, and pottery
crafts.

Pascos (Ocean Ave., Kennebunkport, tel. 207/967–4722) focuses on handweaving and knitting.

Sports and Outdoor Activities

Biking **Cape-Able Bike Shop** (Townhouse Corners, Kennebunkport,
tel. 207/967–4382) has bicycles for rent.

Bird-Watching **Biddeford Pool East Sanctuary** (Rte. 9, Biddeford) is a nature
preserve where shorebirds congregate.

Rachel Carson National Wildlife Refuge (Rte. 9, Wells) is a
mile-long loop through a salt marsh bordering the Little River
and a white pine forest.

Boat Trips **Finestkind** (Perkins Cove, Ogunquit, tel. 207/646–5227) has
cruises to Nubble Lighthouse and lobstering trips.

Sail Me (Perkins Cove, Ogunquit, tel. 207/646–2457) tours the
area on the 35-foot sloop *Airborne.*

Deep-sea Fishing *Porpoise III* (York Harbor, tel. 207/363–5106) is available for
full-day or half-day trips.

Elizabeth II (Arundel Shipyard, Kennebunkport, tel. 207/967–5595) carries passengers on 1½-hour narrated cruises down the Kennebunk River and out to Cape Porpoise. The *Nautilus,* run by the same outfit, goes on whale-watching cruises from May through October, daily at 10 AM.

Beaches

Maine's sand beaches tend to be rather hard-packed and built up with beach cottages and motels. Yet the water is clean (and cold), the surf usually gentle, and the crowds manageable except on the hottest summer weekends.

Kennebunk Beach. Gooch's Beach, Middle Beach, and Kennebunk Beach (also called Mother's Beach) are the three areas of Kennebunk Beach. Beach Road with its cottages and old Victorian boardinghouses runs right behind them. For parking permits, go to the Kennebunk Town Office (1 Summer St., tel. 207/985–3675). Gooch's and Middle beaches attract lots of teenagers; Mother's Beach, which has a small playground and tidal puddles for splashing, is popular with moms and kids.

Kennebunkport. Goose Rocks, a few minutes' drive north of town, is the largest in the Kennebunk area and the favorite of families with small children. For a parking permit, go to the Kennebunkport Town Office (Elm St., tel. 207/967–4244).

Ogunquit. The 3 miles of sand beach have snack bars, boardwalk, rest rooms, and changing areas at the Beach Street entrance. The section to the north that is accessible by footbridge has rest rooms and is less crowded. The ocean beach is backed by the Ogunquit River, which is ideal for children because it is sheltered and waveless. There is a parking fee.

York. York's Long Sands Beach has free parking and Route 1A running right behind it; the smaller Short Sands beach has meter parking. Both beaches have commercial development.

Dining and Lodging

Lobster can be found on the menus of a majority of Maine restaurants; as a general rule, the closer you are to a working harbor, the fresher your lobster will be. Shrimp and crab are also caught in the cold waters off this coast. Blueberries are grown commercially in Maine, and Maine cooks use them generously in pancakes, muffins, pies, and cobblers. In the summer, expect popular restaurants in beach areas to be crowded—if no reservations are accepted, go early or plan to wait for a table.

The following dining price categories have been used: *Very Expensive,* over $35; *Expensive,* $25–$35; *Moderate,* $15–$25; *Inexpensive,* under $15.

Full country breakfasts of fruit, eggs, breakfast meats, pancakes, and muffins are commonly served at inns and bed-and-breakfasts. At many of Maine's larger hotels and inns with restaurants, Modified American Plan (includes breakfast and dinner) is either an option or required during the peak summer season. In general, when MAP is optional, hotels give dinner credits of $20 per guest.

The following lodging price categories have been used: *Very Expensive*, over $100, *Expensive*, $80–$100; *Moderate*, $60–$80; *Inexpensive*, under $60.

The Kennebunks

Dining

★ **Cape Arundel Inn.** Were it not for the rocky shore beyond the picture windows, the pillared porch with wicker chairs, and the cozy parlor, with fireplace and backgammon boards, which you just passed through, you might well think you were dining at a major Boston restaurant. The lobster bisque is creamy, with just a bit of cognac. Entrées include marlin with sorrel butter; coho salmon with mushrooms, white wine, and lemon; rack of lamb; and pecan chicken with peaches and crème fraîche. The inn has 13 guest rooms, seven in the Victorian-era converted "cottage" and six in a motel facility adjoining. *Ocean Ave., tel. 207/967–2125. Reservations advised. Dress: neat but casual. AE, MC, V. Closed mid-Oct.–mid-May. No lunch. Expensive.*

Olde Grist Mill. The bar and lounge area occupy a restored grist mill, with original equipment and fixtures intact; the dining room is a spare, modern space with white linen, china, and picture windows on the Kennebunk River. The Continental menu features sole in *papillote* with seafood stuffing; sirloin steak *au poivre;* and a classic shore dinner. The baked Indian pudding is a local legend. *1 Mill La., Kennebunkport, tel. 207/967–4781. Reservations accepted. Dress: neat but casual. AE, DC, MC, V. Closed Mon. Apr.–Oct. No lunch. Expensive.*

Breakwater Inn. The restaurant of this inn serves baked stuffed scrod; grilled game hen with basil pesto; poached salmon with orange and leeks; and spice-crusted pork tenderloin. The lobster clambake is popular. The intimate dining room has picture windows on the water. *Ocean Ave., tel. 207/967–3118. Reservations advised. Dress: neat but casual. AE, MC, V. Closed Jan.–Apr. Moderate–Expensive.*

★ **Mabel's Lobster Claw.** George and Barbara Bush have been eating here for years; his favorite is said to be the baked lobster stuffed with scallops, hers the eggplant parmigiana. The fisherman's platter includes fried haddock, scallops, shrimp, and onion rings. Mabel's is a homey, birch-paneled, family-style restaurant. *425 Ocean Ave., tel. 207/967–2562. Reservations required in summer. Dress: casual. No credit cards. Closed mid-Oct.–mid-Apr. Moderate.*

Lodging **Breakwater Inn.** Kennebunkport has few accommodations that are elegantly old-fashioned in decor, located right on the water, and well suited to families with young children, and this inn is all three. Overlooking Kennebunk Beach from the breakwater, rooms have stained-pine four-poster beds and hand-stenciling or wallpaper. The Riverside building next door offers spacious, airy rooms with sliding glass doors facing the water. *Ocean Ave., Box 1160, Kennebunkport 04046, tel. 207/967–3118. 20 rooms, 2 suites. Facilities: dining room, small playground. AE, MC, V. Closed Dec. 15–Jan. 15. Expensive–Very Expensive.*

The Captain Lord Mansion. A long and distinguished history, a three-story elliptical staircase, and a cupola with widow's walk make this something more than the standard bed-and-breakfast. The rooms, named for clipper ships, are mostly large and stately—11 have a fireplace—though the style relaxes as one ascends from the ground floor rooms (damask and mahogany) to the country-style third floor accommodations (pine furniture and leafy views). *Box 800, Kennebunkport 04046, tel. 207/967–3141. 16 rooms. D, MC, V. Expensive–Very Expensive.*

Inn at Harbor Head. The 100-year-old shingled farmhouse on the harbor at Cape Porpoise has become a tiny bed-and-breakfast full of antiques, paintings, and heirlooms. The Harbor Room upstairs has the best water view and murals; the Greenery downstairs boasts a whirlpool tub and a garden view. The grounds are bright with flower beds. *RR 2, Box 1180, Kennebunkport 04046, tel. 207/967-4873. 4 rooms, 1 suite. Facilities: private dock. No smoking. D, MC, V. Expensive–Very Expensive.*

The Seaside. The modern motel units, all with sliding glass doors opening onto private decks or patios, half of them with ocean views, are appropriate for families; so are the cottages, which have from one to four bedrooms, and where well-behaved pets are accepted. The four bedrooms in the inn, furnished with antiques, are more suitable for adults. A small breakfast is included in the room price. *Gooch's Beach, Kennebunkport 04046, tel. 207/967-4461 or 207/967-4282. 26 rooms, 10 cottages. Facilities: private beach, laundry, playground. No credit cards. Inn rooms closed Labor Day–June; cottages closed Nov.–Apr. Expensive–Very Expensive.*

Captain Jefferds Inn. The three-story white-clapboard sea captain's home with black shutters, built in 1804, has been restored and filled with the innkeeper's collections of majolica, American art pottery, Venetian glass, and Sienese pottery. Most rooms are done in Laura Ashley fabrics and wallpapers, and many have been furnished with English curly maple chests, marbletop dressers, old books, and paintings. Pets are welcome. A hearty breakfast is included. *Pearl St., Box 691, Kennebunkport 04046, tel. 207/967-2311. 12 rooms, 3 suites in the carriage house. Facilities: croquet. No credit cards. Closed Jan.–Mar., Nov. Moderate–Very Expensive.*

Bufflehead Cove. Situated on the Kennebunk River at the end of a winding dirt road, the friendly gray-shingle bed-and-breakfast affords the quiet of country fields and apple trees only five minutes from Dock Square. The small guest rooms are dollhouse pretty, with white wicker and flowers painted on the walls. *Box 499, 04046, tel. 207/967-3879. 6 rooms, 1 suite, 1 apartment. Facilities: canoe, private dock. No smoking. No credit cards. Closed Mar.–Apr. Moderate–Expensive.*

Beachwood Motel. This motel a mile from Goose Rocks Beach has farm animals, swings and sandbox, indoor and outdoor kiddie pools, basketball and racquetball courts, free portable cribs, and lots of land. The standard motel rooms have two double beds; half the rooms have kitchenettes. Off-season rates are much lower. *Rte. 9, 04046, tel. 207/967-2483. 112 rooms with bath. Facilities: tennis court; basketball court; indoor, outdoor, and kiddie pools; hot tub. MC, V. Moderate.*

Ogunquit
Dining

Old Village Inn. Each of the five dining rooms has a different character—a mock English pub, a greenhouse dense with foliage, etc.—yet the menu throughout is consistently rich: duck flambéed at tableside; prime rib; shrimp and filet mignon teriyaki kebab. Peach walnut crisp has been a favorite dessert. *30 Main St., tel. 207/646-7088. Reservations advised. Dress: neat but casual. AE, MC, V. Closed Sun. and Mon. Nov.–Mar. No lunch. Expensive.*

Tavern at Clay Hill Farm. The three softly lit dining rooms of the white-clapboard farmhouse seat 200; entrées on recent menus have included sliced breast of duck with orange horseradish sauce; poached salmon with dill hollandaise; halibut broiled in pecan lobster butter. Cajun crab cakes and stuffed mushrooms are starters. *Agamenticus Rd., tel. 207/646–2272. Reservations advised. Dress: casual. AE, MC, V. No lunch. Expensive.*

Ogunquit Lobster Pound. Select your lobster live, then dine under the trees or in the rustic dining room of the log cabin. The menu includes steamed clams, steak, and chicken; and there is a special children's menu. *Rte. 1, tel. 207/646–2516. No reservations. Dress: casual. AE, MC, V. Closed late Oct.–mid-May. Moderate.*

Lodging   **Colonial Inn.** This complex of accommodations in the middle of Ogunquit includes a large white Victorian inn building, modern motel units, and efficiency apartments. Inn rooms have flowered wallpaper, Colonial reproduction furniture, and white ruffle curtains. Efficiencies are popular with families. Two-thirds of the rooms have water views. *Shore Rd., Box 895, 03907, tel. 207/646–5191. 80 units, 78 with bath; 13 suites. Facilities: heated outdoor pool, laundromat, grills, Jacuzzi, playground, shuffleboard. AE, D, MC, V. Closed Nov.–Apr. Moderate–Very Expensive.*

Seafair Inn. A century-old white-clapboard house set back behind shrubs and lawn in the center of town, the Seafair has a homey atmosphere and proximity to the beach. Rooms are furnished with odds and ends of country furniture; the Continental breakfast is served on an enclosed sun porch. *Box 1221, 03907, tel. 207/646–2181. 18 units, 14 with bath; 4 efficiency suites. MC, V. Closed Nov.–Mar. Moderate–Expensive.*

The Yorks   **Cape Neddick Inn.** This restaurant and art gallery has an airy
Dining   ambience, with tables set well apart, lots of windows, and art everywhere. The New American menu has offered lobster macadamia tart (shelled lobster sautéed with shallots, macadamia nuts, sherry, and cream and served in pastry); breaded pork tenderloin; and such appetizers as spicy sesame chicken dumplings and gravlax with Russian pepper vodka. Duckling flamed in brandy is always on the menu. *Rte. 1, Cape Neddick, tel. 207/363–2899. Reservations advised. Dress: casual. MC, V. Closed Mon.–Tues. Columbus Day–May 31. No lunch. Expensive.*

Dockside Dining Room. The seclusion, the gardens, and the water views are the attractions of the inn dining room on a private island in York Harbor. Entrées may include scallop-stuffed shrimp Casino; broiled Boston scrod; steak au poivre with brandied mushroom sauce; and roast stuffed duckling. *York Harbor off Rte. 103, tel. 207/363–4800. Reservations advised on weekends. Dress: neat but casual. MC, V. Closed Mon. Closed late-Oct.–Memorial Day. Moderate.*

Lodging   **Dockside Guest Quarters.** Situated on a private island 8 acres large in the middle of York Harbor, the Dockside promises water views, seclusion, and quiet. Rooms in the Maine house, the oldest structure on the site, are furnished with early American antiques, marine artifacts, and nautical paintings and prints. Four modern cottages tucked among the trees have less character but bigger windows on the water, and many have kitchenettes. *Box 205, York 03909, tel. 207/363–2868. 22 rooms, 20 with bath; 5 suites. Facilities: private dock, dining rooms, small motorboat, croquet, badminton. MC, V (limit $100). Closed late Oct.–Apr. Moderate–Very Expensive.*

The Arts

Ogunquit Playhouse (Rte. 1, tel. 207/646–5511), one of America's oldest summer theaters, mounts plays and musicals from late June to Labor Day.

Portland to Pemaquid Point

Maine's largest city, yet small enough to be seen with ease in a day or two, Portland is undergoing a cultural and economic renaissance. New hotels and a bright new performing arts center have joined the neighborhoods of historic homes; the Old Port Exchange, perhaps the finest urban renovation project on the East Coast, balances modern commercial enterprise with a salty waterfront character in an area bustling with restaurants, shops, and galleries. The piers of Commercial Street abound with opportunities for water tours of the harbor and excursions to the Calendar Islands.

Freeport, north of Portland, is a town made famous by the L. L. Bean store, whose success led to the opening of scores of other clothing stores and outlets. Brunswick is best known for Bowdoin College; Bath has been a shipbuilding center since 1607, and the Maine Maritime Museum preserves its history.

The Boothbays—the coastal areas of Boothbay Harbor, East Boothbay, Linekin Neck, Southport Island, and the inland town of Boothbay—attract hordes of vacationing families and flotillas of pleasure craft. The Pemaquid peninsula juts into the Atlantic south of Damariscotta and just east of the Boothbays, and near Pemaquid Beach one can view the objects unearthed at the Colonial Pemaquid Restoration.

From Cape Arundel, it's about 20 miles to Portland, where this segment begins. You may want to pick up speed by getting onto I–95; get onto the Portland bypass, I–295, and take the Congress Street exit to get into the heart of the city. Route 1 also leads directly to Portland; you'll cross the Veterans Memorial Bridge coming into downtown.

Numbers in the margin correspond to points of interest on the Portland map.

7 Congress Street, **Portland's** main street, runs the length of the peninsular city from the Western Promenade in the southwest to the Eastern Promenade in the northeast, passing through the small downtown area. A few blocks southeast of downtown, the bustling Old Port Exchange sprawls along the waterfront.

Time Out Those who are making an early start and are ready for a meal will welcome the **Good Egg Cafe** at 705 Congress Street, where imaginative and hearty breakfasts are prepared from 6 AM weekdays, 7 AM Saturday, and 8 AM Sunday. The restaurant closes at lunchtime.

8 One of the notable homes on Congress Street is the **Neal Dow Memorial**, a gray brick mansion built in 1829 in the late Federal style by General Neal Dow, a zealous abolitionist and prohibitionist. The library has fine ornamental ironwork, and the fur-

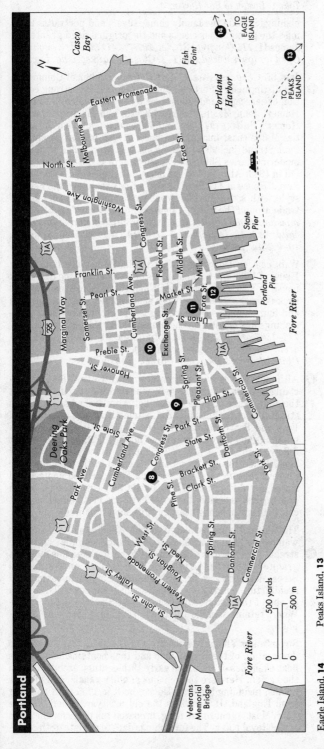

Portland

Eagle Island, **14**
Mariner's Church, **12**
Neal Dow Memorial, **8**
Old Port Exchange, **11**

Peaks Island, **13**
Portland Museum of
  Art, **9**
Wadsworth Longfellow
  House, **10**

81

nishings include the family china, silver, and portraits. Don't
miss the grandfather clocks and the original deed granted by
James II. *714 Congress St., tel. 207/773–7773. Admission free.
Open for tours weekdays 11–4. Closed Thanksgiving, Dec. 25.*

9 Just off Congress Street, next to the Chamber of Commerce,
the distinguished **Portland Museum of Art** has a strong collection of seascapes and landscapes by such masters as Winslow
Homer, John Marin, Andrew Wyeth, and Marsden Hartley.
Homer's *Pulling the Dory* and *Weatherbeaten,* two quintessential Maine coast images, are here. A wall of photographs by
Paul Strand includes some of his best work. The strikingly
modern Charles Shipman Payson wing was designed by I. M.
Pei in 1983. Also part of the museum complex is the McLellan
Sweat House at 111 High Street, a fine example of the Federal
style with a semicircular front portico and openwork balustrade around the roof. *7 Congress Sq., tel. 207/775–6148. Admission: $3.50 adults, $2.50 senior citizens and students, $1
children 6–18, free Thurs. 5–9. Open Tues.–Sat. 10–5, Thurs.
10–9, Sun. noon–5.*

10 Walk east on Congress Street to the **Wadsworth Longfellow
House** of 1785, the boyhood home of the poet and the first brick
house in Portland. The late Colonial-style structure sits well
back from the street and has a small portico over its entrance
and four chimneys surmounting the hip roof. Most of the furnishings are original to the house. *485 Congress St., tel. 207/
772–1807 or 207/774–1822. Admission: $2.50 adults, $1 children. Open June–Columbus Day weekend, Tues.–Sat. 10–4.
Closed July 4, Labor Day. Garden open daily 9–5.*

11 Although you can walk from downtown to the **Old Port Exchange,** you're better off driving and parking your car either at
the city garage on Fore Street (between Exchange and Union
streets) or opposite the U.S. Customs House at the corner of
Fore and Pearl streets. Like the Customs House, the brick
buildings and warehouses of the Old Port Exchange were built
following the Great Fire of 1866 and were intended to last for
ages. When the city's economy slumped in the middle of the
present century, however, the Old Port declined and seemed
slated for demolition. Then artists and craftspeople began
opening shops here in the late 1960s, and in time restaurants,
chic boutiques, bookstores, and gift shops followed.

The Old Port is best explored on foot. Allow a couple of hours to
wander at leisure on Market, Exchange, Middle, and Fore
12 streets. The **Mariner's Church** (376 Fore St.) has a fine facade of
granite columns, and the Elias Thomas Block on Commercial
Street demonstrates the graceful use of bricks in commercial
architecture. Inevitably the salt smell of the sea will draw you
to one of the wharves off Commercial Street; Custom House
Wharf retains some of the older, rougher waterfront atmosphere.

Stroudwater Village, 3 miles west of Portland, was spared the
devastation of the fire of 1866 and thus contains some of the
best examples of 18th- and early 19th-century architecture in
the region. Here are the remains of mills, canals, and historic
homes, including the Tate House, built in 1755 with paneling
from England. It overlooks the old mastyard where George
Tate, Mast Agent to the King, prepared tall pines for the ships
of the Royal Navy. The furnishings date to the late-18th centu-

ry. Tate House, *1270 Westbrook St., tel. 207/774–9781. Admission: $2.50 adults, $1 children. Open June–Sept. 15, Tues.– Sat. 11–5, Sun. 1:30–5.*

Sailing out of Portland harbor, the brightly painted ferries of **Casco Bay Lines** (tel. 207/774–7871) are the lifeline to the Calendar Islands of Casco Bay, which number about 136, depending on the tides and how one defines an island.

🌑 **Peaks Island,** nearest Portland, is the most developed, and some residents commute to work in Portland. Yet you can still commune with the wind and the sea on Peaks, explore an old fort, and ramble along the alternately rocky and sandy shore. A bed-and-breakfast has overnight accommodations (*see* Peaks Island Lodging, *below*).

🌑 The 17-acre **Eagle Island,** owned by the state of Maine and open to the public for day trips in summer, was the home of Admiral Robert E. Peary, the American explorer of the North Pole. Peary built a stone and wood house on the island as a summer retreat in 1904, then made it his permanent residence. The house remains as it was when Peary was here with his stuffed Arctic birds and the quartz he brought home set into the fieldstone fireplace. The *Kristy K.*, departing from Long Wharf, makes a four-hour narrated tour. *Long Wharf, tel. 207/774– 6498. Excursion tour: $15 adults, $12 senior citizens, $9 children 5–9. Departures late May–mid-Sept., daily 10, 2.*

Numbers in the margin correspond to points of interest on the Southern Maine Coast map.

🌑 **Freeport,** on Route 1, 15 miles northeast of Portland, has charming back streets lined with old clapboard houses and even a small harbor on the Harraseeket River, but the overwhelming majority of visitors come to shop, and **L. L. Bean** is the store that put Freeport on the map. Founded in 1912 as a small mail order merchandiser of products for hunters, guides, and fisherfolk, L. L. Bean now attracts some 3.5 million shoppers a year to its giant store in the heart of Freeport's shopping district on Route 1. Here you can still find the original hunting boots, along with cotton, wool, and silk sweaters; camping and ski equipment; comforters; and hundreds of other items for the home, car, boat, or campsite. Across the street from the main store, a Bean factory outlet has seconds and discontinued merchandise at marked-down prices. *Rte. 1, Freeport, tel. 800/341– 4341. Open 24 hrs.*

All around L. L. Bean, like seedlings under a mighty spruce, some 85 outlets have sprouted, offering designer clothes, shoes, housewares, and toys at marked-down prices (*see* Shopping, *below*).

🌑 It's 9 miles northeast on Route 1 from Freeport to **Brunswick.** Follow the signs to the Brunswick business district, Pleasant Street, and—at the end of Pleasant Street—Maine Street, which claims to be the widest (198 feet across) in the state. Friday from May to October sees a fine farmer's market on the town mall, between Maine Street and Park Row.

Maine Street takes you to the 110-acre campus of **Bowdoin College,** an enclave of distinguished architecture, gardens, and grassy quadrangles in the middle of the city. Campus tours (tel. 207/725–3000) depart weekdays from Moulton Union. Among the historic buildings are Massachusetts Hall, a stout, sober, hip-roofed brick structure that dates from 1802, and Hubbard Hall, an imposing 1902 neo-Gothic building that houses the **Peary-MacMillan Arctic Museum.** The museum contains photographs, navigational instruments, and artifacts from the first successful expedition to the North Pole in 1909 by two of Bowdoin's most famous alumni, Admiral Robert E. Peary and Donald B. MacMillan. *Admission free. Open Tues.–Sat 10–5; Sun. 2–5.*

Don't miss the **Bowdoin College Museum of Art,** a splendid limestone, brick, and granite structure in a Renaissance Revival style, with three galleries radiating from a central rotunda. Designed in 1894 by Charles F. McKim, the building stands on a rise, its facade adorned with classical statues and the entrance set off by a triumphal arch. The collections encompass Assyrian and Classical art and Dutch and Italian Old Masters, including Pieter Brueghel's *Alpine Landscape;* a superb gathering of Colonial and Federal paintings, notably the Gilbert Stuart portraits of Madison and Jefferson; and paintings and drawings by Winslow Homer, Mary Cassatt, John Sloan, Rockwell Kent, Jim Dine, and Robert Rauschenberg. *Walker Art Bldg., tel. 207/725-3275. Admission free. Open Tues.–Sat. 10–5. Closed holidays.*

Before going on to Bath, you may elect to drive down Route 123 or Route 24 to the peninsulas and islands known collectively as the **Harpswells.** The numerous small coves along Harpswell Neck shelter the boats of local lobstermen, and summer cottages are tucked away amid the birch and spruce trees.

⓱ Bath, 7 miles east of Brunswick on Route 1, has been a shipbuilding center since 1607. Today the Bath Iron Works turns out guided-missile frigates for the U.S. Navy and merchant container ships.

The **Maine Maritime Museum** in Bath (take the Bath Business District exit from Route 1, turn right on Washington Street, and follow the signs) has ship models, journals, photographs, and other artifacts to stir the nautical dreams of old salts and young. The 142-foot Grand Banks fishing schooner *Sherman Zwicker,* one of the last of its kind, is on display when in port. You can watch apprentice boatbuilders wield their tools on classic Maine boats at the restored Percy & Small Shipyard and Apprentice Shop. The outdoor shipyard is closed in winter, but the indoor exhibits, videos, and activities are enhanced. *243 Washington St., tel. 207/443-1316. Admission: $5 adults, $4.50 senior citizens, $2.50 children 6–15. Open daily 9:30–5. Closed Thanksgiving, Dec. 25, Jan. 1.*

From Bath it's 10 miles northeast on Route 1 to Wiscasset, where the huge rotting hulls of the schooners *Hester* and *Luther Little* rest, testaments to the town's once-busy harbor. **⓲** Across the river, drive south on Route 27 to reach the **Boothbay Railway Village,** about a mile north of **Boothbay,** where you can ride 1½ miles on a narrow-gauge steam train through a re-creation of a turn-of-the-century New England village. Among the 24 village buildings is a museum with more than 50 antique automobiles and trucks. *Rte. 27, Boothbay, tel. 207/633-4727. Admission: $5 adults, $2.50 children 2–12. Open mid-June–mid-Oct., daily 9:30–5.*

The **Boothbay Theater Museum,** opposite the post office, contains two centuries of theatrical memorabilia: stage jewelry, costumes, portraits, set models, toy theaters, playbills, photos. *Corey La., Boothbay, tel. 207/633–4536. Admission: $4. Open mid-June–mid-Sept., Mon.–Sat. by appointment only.*

Continue south on Route 27 into Boothbay Harbor, bear right on Oak Street, and follow it to the waterfront parking lots. **⑲ Boothbay Harbor** is a town to wander through: Commercial Street, Wharf Street, the By-Way, and Townsend Avenue are lined with shops, galleries, and ice-cream parlors. Excursion boats (*see* Sports and Outdoor Activities, *below*) leave from the piers off Commercial Street.

Time Out The **P&P Pastry Shoppe** (6 McKown St.) is a welcome stop for a sandwich or a pastry.

Huge tanks hold lobsters and fish, and harbor seals flop around in the outdoor saltwater pools of the **Marine Aquarium** maintained by the Maine Department of Marine Resources at McKown Point. Outdoor tables permit picnicking by the shore. *West Boothbay Harbor, tel. 207/633–5572. Open Memorial Day–Columbus Day, weekdays 8–5, weekends 9–5.*

Having explored Boothbay Harbor, return to Route 27 and head north again to Route 1. Proceed north to Business Route 1, and follow it through Damariscotta, an appealing shipbuilding town on the Damariscotta River. Bear right on the Bristol Road (Route 129/130), and when the highway splits, stay on **⑳** Route 130, which leads to Bristol and terminates at **Pemaquid Point.**

About 5 miles south of Bristol you'll come to New Harbor, where a right turn will take you to Pemaquid Beach and the **Colonial Pemaquid Restoration.** Here, on a small peninsula jutting into the Pemaquid River, English mariners established a fishing and trading settlement in the early 17th century. The excavations at Pemaquid Beach, begun in the mid-1960s, have turned up thousands of artifacts from the Colonial settlement, including the remains of an old customs house, tavern, jail, forge, and homes, and from even earlier Native American settlements. The State of Maine operates a museum displaying many of the artifacts. *Rte. 130, Pemaquid Point, tel. 207/677–2423. Admission: $1.50 adults, 50¢ children 6–12. Open Memorial Day–Labor Day, daily 9:30–5.*

Route 130 terminates at the **Pemaquid Point Light,** which looks as though it sprouted from the ragged, tilted chunk of granite that it commands. The former lighthouse keeper's cottage is now the **Fishermen's Museum,** with photos, models, and artifacts that explore commercial fishing in Maine. Here, too, is the Pemaquid Art Gallery, which mounts changing exhibitions from July 1 through Labor Day. *Rte. 130, tel. 207/677–2494. Museum admission by contribution. Open Memorial Day–Columbus Day, Mon.–Sat. 10–5, Sun. 11–5.*

From Pemaquid Point, it's less than 15 miles across Muscongus Bay to Port Clyde, but it's 50 miles for the motorist who must return north to Route 1 to circle the shore. Route 32 will lead you back from Pemaquid Point to Route 1.

Shopping

The best and most unusual shopping in Portland is at the Old Port Exchange, where many shops are concentrated along Fore and Exchange streets. Freeport's name is almost synonymous with shopping, and shopping in Freeport means **L. L. Bean** and the 85 factory outlets that opened during the 1980s. Outlet stores are located in the Fashion Outlet Mall (2 Depot St.) and the Freeport Crossing (200 Lower Main St.), and many others crowd Main Street and Bow Street. *The Freeport Visitors Guide* (Freeport Merchants Association, Box 452, Freeport 04032) has a complete listing.

Antiques **F. O. Bailey Antiquarians** (141 Middle St., Portland, tel. 207/774–1479), Portland's largest retail showroom, features antique and reproduction furniture; jewelry, paintings, rugs, and china.

The **Freeport Antique Mall** (Rte. 1, tel. 207/865–0607), five minutes south of downtown Freeport, brings together 65 antiques dealers and their goods.

Harrington House Gallery Store (45 Main St., Freeport, tel. 207/865–0477) is a restored 19th-century merchant's home owned by the Freeport Historical Society; all the period reproductions that furnish the rooms are for sale. In addition, you can buy wallpaper, crafts, Shaker items, toys, and kitchen utensils.

Galleries **Abacus** (44 Exchange St., Portland, tel. 207/772–4880) has unusual gift items in glass, wood, and textiles, plus fine modern jewelry.

Barridoff Galleries (26 Free St., Portland, tel. 207/772–5011) buys and sells 19th- and 20th-century American paintings; changing shows feature regional painters.

Stein Glass Gallery (20 Milk St., Portland, tel. 207/772–9072) specializes in contemporary glass, both decorative and utilitarian.

Hobe Sound Galleries North (58 Main St., Brunswick, tel. 207/725–4191) features contemporary and vintage 20th-century American fine art. Shows change monthly.

Sports and Outdoor Activities

Boat Trips For tours of the Portland harbor, Casco Bay, and the nearby islands, try **Bay View Cruises** (Fisherman's Wharf, tel. 207/883–5456), **The Buccaneer** (Long Wharf, tel. 207/799–8188), **Casco Bay Lines** (Maine State Pier, tel. 207/774–7871), **Eagle Tours** (Long Wharf, tel. 207/774–6498), **Longfellow Cruise Line** (Long Wharf, tel. 207/774–3578), or **Old Port Mariner Fleet** (Long Wharf, tel. 207/775–0727).

Sailing from Boothbay Harbor, *Appledore* (tel. 207/633–6598), an 85-foot windjammer, departs from Pier 6 for voyages to the outer islands. **Argo Cruises** (tel. 207/633–4925) runs the *Argo III* for morning cruises, Bath Hellgate cruises, supper sails, and whale-watching; the *Linekin II* for 1½-hour trips to Seal Rocks; the *Miss Boothbay*, a licensed lobster boat, for lobster-trap hauling trips. Departures are from Pier 6. *Balmy Days II* (tel. 207/633–2284) leaves from Pier 8 for its day trips to Monhegan Island; the *Maranbo II,* operated by the same company, tours the harbor and nearby lighthouses. **Cap'n Fish's Boat Trips** (tel. 207/633–3244) offers sightseeing cruises throughout the region, including puffin cruises, trips to Damariscove Harbor, Pemaquid Point, and up the Kennebec River to Bath, departing from Pier 1 in Boothbay Harbor.

Deep-sea Fishing Half-day and full-day fishing charter boats operating out of Portland include *Anjin-San* (tel. 207/772–7168), *Devils Den* (DeMillo's Marina, tel. 207/761–4466), and *Lazy Day* (tel. 207/883–3430).

Operating out of Boothbay Harbor, **Cap'n Fish's Deep Sea Fishing** (tel. 207/633–3244) schedules daylong and half-day trips, departing from Pier 1, and **Lucky Star Charters** (tel. 207/633–4624) runs full-day and half-day charters for up to six people, with departures from Pier 8.

Spectator Sports

Hockey The **Maine Mariners** (tel. 207/775–3411) play professional hockey at the Cumberland County Civic Center, 1 Civic Center Square, October through April.

State Parks

Wolfe's Neck Woods State Park has self-guided trails along Casco Bay, the Harraseeket River, and a fringe salt marsh, as well as walks led by naturalists. Picnic tables and grills are available, but there's no camping. Follow Bow Street opposite L. L. Bean off Route 1. *Wolfe's Neck Rd., tel. 207/865–4465. Open Memorial Day–Labor Day.*

Crescent Beach State Park (Rte. 77, Cape Elizabeth, tel. 207/767–3625), about 8 miles from Portland, has a sand beach, picnic tables, seasonal snack bar, and bathhouse.

Scarborough Beach State Park (Rte. 207, off Rte. 1 in Scarborough, tel. 207/883–2416) has a small sand beach with dunes and marshes. Parking is limited.

Popham Beach State Park, at the end of Route 209, south of Bath, has a good sand beach, tidal pools, rocky outcrops, a nature area, and picnic tables. *Phippsburg, tel. 207/389–2303. Admission: $1 per person, late Apr.–mid-Oct.*

Reid State Park, on Georgetown Island, off Route 127, has 1½ miles of sand on three beaches. Facilities include bathhouses, picnic tables, fireplaces, and snack bar. Parking lots fill by 11 AM on summer Sundays and holidays. *Georgetown, tel. 207/371–2303. Admission: $1.50 per person, late Apr.–mid-Oct.*

Dining and Lodging

Many of Portland's best restaurants are in the Old Port Exchange district. Casual dress is the rule in restaurants throughout the area except where noted; reservations are not necessary unless otherwise noted. The following dining price categories have been used: *Very Expensive,* over $35; *Expensive,* $25–$35; *Moderate,* $15–$25; *Inexpensive,* under $15.

The following lodging price categories have been used: *Very Expensive,* over $100, *Expensive,* $80–$100; *Moderate,* $60–$80; *Inexpensive,* under $60.

Bath **Kristina's Restaurant & Bakery.** This frame house turned res-
Dining taurant, with a front deck built around a huge oak tree, turns
out some of the finest pies, pastries, and cakes on the coast. A
satisfying dinner menu features New American cuisine, including fresh seafood and grilled meats. Pastries can be packed to
go. *160 Centre St., tel. 207/442–8577. Reservations advised. D,
MC, V. Closed Mon. No dinner Sun. Inexpensive–Moderate.*

Lodging **Fairhaven Inn.** This cedar-shingle house built in 1790 is set on
27 acres of pine woods and meadows sloping down to the Kennebec River. Guest rooms are furnished with handmade quilts
and mahogany pineapple four-poster beds. The home-cooked
breakfast offers such treats as peach soup, blintzes, and apple
upside-down French toast. *RR 2, Box 85, N. Bath 04530, tel.
207/443–4391. 6 rooms, 4 with bath. Facilities: hiking and
cross-country ski trails. Children welcome by prior arrangement. MC, V. Rates include breakfast. Inexpensive–Moderate.*

Boothbay **Kenniston Hill Inn.** The white-clapboard house with columned
Lodging porch offers comfortably old-fashioned accommodations in a
country setting only minutes from Boothbay Harbor. Four
guest rooms have fireplaces, some have four-poster beds, rocking chairs, and gilt mirrors. Full breakfasts are served family
style at a large wood table. *Box 125, 04537, tel. 207/633–2159.
10 rooms. No pets. No smoking. MC, V. Moderate–Expensive.*

Boothbay Harbor **Black Orchid.** The classic Italian fare includes fettuccine Al-
Dining fredo with fresh lobster and mushrooms, and *petit filet à la
diabolo* (fillets of Angus steak with Marsala sauce). The upstairs and downstairs dining rooms sport a Roman-trattoria
ambience, with frilly leaves and fruit hanging from the rafters
and little else in the way of decor. Summertime allows dining
outdoors. *5 By-Way, tel. 207/633–6659. AE, MC, V. No lunch.
Closed Nov.–Apr. Expensive.*
Andrew's Harborside. The seafood menu is typical of the area—
lobster, fried clams and oysters, haddock with seafood stuffing—but the harbor view makes it memorable. Lunch features
lobster and crab rolls; children's and seniors' menus are available. You can dine outdoors on a harborside deck during the
summer. *8 Bridge St., tel. 207/633–4074. Reservations for 4 or
more only. AE, DC, MC, V. Closed mid-Oct.–mid-May. Moderate.*

Lodging **Fisherman's Wharf Inn.** All rooms overlook the water at this
modern motel-style facility built 200 feet out over the harbor.
The large dining room has floor-to-ceiling windows, and several
day-trip cruises leave from this location. *40 Commercial St.,
04538, tel. 207/633–5090 or 800/628–6872. 54 rooms. Facilities:
restaurant. AE, D, DC, MC, V. Rates include Continental
breakfast. Closed Nov.–mid-May. Moderate–Very Expensive.*
The Pines. Families seeking a secluded setting with lots of
room for little ones to run will be interested in this motel on a
hillside a mile from town. Rooms have sliding glass doors opening onto private decks, two double beds, and small refrigerators. Cribs are free. *Sunset Rd., Box 693, 04538, tel. 207/633–
4555. 29 rooms. Facilities: all-weather tennis court, heated
outdoor pool, playground. MC, V. Closed late Oct.–late Apr.
Inexpensive–Moderate.*

Brunswick
Dining
★

Twenty-two Lincoln. The fare is rich: Maine pheasant with chanterelles and Calvados; lobster with basil and vanilla beans; Atlantic salmon with mustard mousseline. The furnishings of this gourmet restaurant in a Victorian town house in downtown Brunswick include antique oak chairs, white lace curtains, and works by local artists. The Side Door Cafe, under the same roof and using the same kitchen, serves less elaborate dishes— Maine crab cakes with sweet and piquant peppers; a vegetarian Mexican dish known as *flauta*—in a friendly, publike atmosphere. The award-winning wine list is particularly strong in California wines. *22 Lincoln St., tel. 207/725–5893. Reservations accepted. MC, V. Dinner only. Closed Sun. and Mon. in summer. Call for winter hours. Moderate–Expensive.*

Freeport
Dining

Harraseeket Inn. The formal dining room upstairs is a simply appointed, light and airy space with picture windows facing the inn's garden courtyard. Specialties include roast duckling with peach glaze; and a Maine seafood medley glacé with lobster, shrimp, crab, and scallops. Waiters prepare fettuccine Alfredo and flaming desserts tableside. Downstairs, the Broad Arrow Tavern appears to have been furnished by L. L. Bean, with fly rods, snowshoes, moose heads, and other hunting-lodge trappings. The fare is hearty, with less formal lunches and snacks and dinners of charbroiled skewered shrimp and scallops, ribs, burgers, pasta, or lobster. *162 Main St., tel. 207/865–9377. Reservations advised. No shorts at dinner. AE, D, DC, MC, V. Expensive.*

Harraseeket Lunch. This no-frills, bare-bones, genuine lobster pound and fried seafood place is located beside the town landing in South Freeport. Seafood baskets and lobster dinners are what it's all about; there are picnic tables outside, a few more tables inside. *Main St., South Freeport, tel. 207/865–4888. No reservations. No credit cards. Inexpensive.*

Lodging

Harraseeket Inn. When two white-clapboard houses, one a fine Greek Revival home of 1850, found themselves two blocks from the biggest retailing explosion ever to hit Maine, the innkeepers added a four-story building that looks like an old New England inn—white clapboard with green shutters—and is in fact a steel and concrete structure with elevators and Jacuzzis. The Harraseeket strives to achieve the country inn experience, with afternoon tea in the mahogany drawing room and fireplaces throughout. Guest rooms (vintage 1989) have reproductions of Federal-period canopy beds and bright, coordinated fabrics. The full breakfast is served buffet style in an airy upstairs formal dining room facing the garden. *162 Main St., 04032, tel. 207/865–9377 or 800/342–6423. 54 rooms, including 6 suites. Facilities: restaurant, tavern, room service until 11 PM, croquet, some rooms have a working fireplace. AE, D, DC, MC, V. Very Expensive.*

Georgetown
Dining

The Osprey. Located in a marina on the way to Reid State Park, this gourmet restaurant may be reached both by land and sea. The appetizers alone are worth the stop: homemade garlic and Sicilian sausages; artichoke strudel with three cheeses; and warm braised duck salad with oriental vegetables in rice paper. Entrées might include such classics as saltimbocca or such originals as salmon en papillote with julienne leeks, carrots, and fresh herbs. The wine list is excellent. The glassed-in porch offers water views and breezes. *6 mi. down Rte. 127, turn left at restaurant sign on Robinhood Rd., tel. 207/371–2530. Res-*

ervations advised. MC, V. Closed Jan.–Feb. Moderate–Expensive.

Newcastle
Lodging
★

Newcastle Inn. The white-clapboard house, vintage mid-19th century, has a homey living room with a red velvet sofa, books, family photos on the mantel, and a sun porch with white wicker furniture and ice-cream parlor chairs. Guest rooms are not large, but they have been carefully appointed with old spool beds, toys, and Victorian velvet sofas, minimizing clutter and maximizing the light and the river views. Guests choose between bed-and-breakfast (a full gourmet meal, perhaps scrambled eggs with caviar in puff pastry, ricotta cheese pie, or frittata) and Modified American Plan. *River Rd., 04553, tel. 207/563–5685. 15 rooms. Facilities: dining room. No smoking. MC, V. Expensive.*

Peaks Island
Lodging

The Moonshell Inn. This bed-and-breakfast has six simple, sunny rooms with wood floors, finished pine furniture, and white walls; most rooms have water views. The hearty Continental breakfast menu includes muffins, toast, and cereal. *Peaks Island 04108, tel. 207/766–2331. 6 rooms. No credit cards. Closed Columbus Day–Thanksgiving, Jan.–Apr. Moderate–Inexpensive.*

Portland
Dining

Raphael's. The delicate Northern Italian cooking is presented in an airy and stylish dining room done in subdued grays and blues with pale wood accents. Tables set well apart and soft music (often light jazz) allow you to concentrate on such specialties as fettuccine with parsley walnut pesto; medallions of veal with sun-dried tomatoes; and *fritto misto di mare* (fried squid, shrimp, and whitefish). The less formal downstairs room, Little Willie's, has a good selection of *crostini* (grilled breads with a variety of toppings). *36 Market St., tel. 207/773–4500. Reservations advised. Dress: neat but casual. AE, D, DC, MC, V. Expensive.*

★

Alberta's. Small, bright, casual, and friendly, Alberta's specializes in what one waiter described as "electric American" cuisine: dishes like London broil spiced with garlic, cumin, and lime; pan-blackened rib-eye steak with sour cream and scallions; and Atlantic salmon fillet with orange-ginger sauce, grilled red cabbage, and apple salad. The two-tier dining room has photos mounted on salmon-hued walls, and the music ranges from country to classical. *21 Pleasant St., tel. 207/774–0016. No reservations. AE, DC, MC, V. Beer and wine only. No lunch weekends. Closed Thanksgiving, Dec. 25. Moderate–Expensive.*

Baker's Table. You descend a short flight of stairs and walk through the kitchen area to arrive at a cheerful, lively, informal dining room with oak beam ceilings, hanging plants, and original art work. The bistro-style cuisine features grilled king salmon; sautéed veal medallions with *pleurrot* mushrooms and shallots; black bean chili; and seafood chowders. *434 Fore St., tel. 207/775–0303. Reservations advised on weekends. Jacket advised. AE, MC, V. Moderate–Expensive.*

F. Parker Reidy's. An old standby in the Old Port, this popular restaurant in a former bank building serves broiled scallops, sirloin and teriyaki steaks, chowders, and sandwiches in a Victorian atmosphere of exposed brick, mahogany, and brass. It's an invigorating place for Sunday brunch and late (for Portland) suppers. *83 Exchange St., tel. 207/773–4731. No reservations. AE, V. Moderate.*

Hu-Shang Exchange. An extensive Chinese menu includes Hunan chicken, lamb with ginger and scallions, and Mandarin moo shu shrimp. The three dining rooms with exposed brick walls, hanging plants, and soft lighting are far more soothing than a standard storefront Chinese restaurant. *29–33 Exchange St., tel. 207/773–0300. Reservations accepted. AE, MC, V. Moderate.*

J's Oyster Bar. Right on the waterfront, J's preserves some of the roughness and grit that renovation has smoothed out elsewhere in the Old Port. Patrons ranging from tourists to blue-collar types to local office workers sit around the central bar and wash down scallops, shrimp, and oysters (raw and nude) with free-flowing beer. *5 Portland Pier, tel. 207/772–4828. No reservations. MC, V. Inexpensive.*

Lodging **Pomegranate Inn.** Clever touches like faux marbling on the moldings and mustard-colored rag-rolling in the hallways give this bed-and-breakfast a bright, postmodern air. Most guest rooms are spacious and bright, accented with original paintings on floral and tropical motifs; the location on a quiet street in the city's Victorian Western Promenade district ensures serenity. Telephones and televisions, rare in an inn, make this a good choice for businesspeople. *49 Neal St., 04102, tel. 207/ 772–1006 or 800/356–0408. 6 rooms. AE, DC, MC, V. Expensive.*

Portland Regency Inn. The only major hotel in the center of the Old Port Exchange, the Regency building was Portland's armory in the late 19th century. While leaving intact the exterior and the windows, renovation in 1987 transformed the interior into the city's most luxurious, most distinctive hotel. The bright, plush, airy rooms have four-poster beds, tall standing mirrors, floral curtains, and loveseats. The health club, the best in the city, offers massage and has an aerobics studio, free weights, Nautilus equipment, a large Jacuzzi, dry sauna, and steam room. *20 Milk St., 04101, tel. 207/774–4200 or 800/727– 3436. 95 rooms, 8 suites. Facilities: restaurant, health club, nightclub, banquet and convention rooms. AE, D, DC, MC, V. Expensive.*

Sonesta Hotel. Across the street from the art museum and in the heart of the downtown business district, the 12-story brick building, vintage 1927, looks a bit dowdy today. Rooms in the tower section (added in 1961) have floor-to-ceiling windows, and the higher floors have harbor views. The small health club offers Universal gym equipment, rowing machines, stationary bikes, and a sauna. *157 High St., 04101, tel. 207/775–5411 or 800/343–7170. 184 rooms, 6 suites. Facilities: 2 restaurants, 2 bars, health club, banquet and convention facilities. AE, D, DC, MC, V. Moderate–Expensive.*

Prouts Neck **Black Point Inn.** At the tip of the peninsula that juts into the
Lodging ocean at Prouts Neck, 12 miles south of Portland, stands one of the great old-time resorts of Maine. The sun porch has wicker and plants, the music room—in the English country house style—has wing chairs, silk flowers, Chinese prints, and a grand piano. In the guest rooms are rock maple bedsteads, Martha Washington bedspreads, and white-ruffle Priscilla curtains. Older guests prefer the main inn; families choose from the three cottages. The extensive grounds offer beaches, hiking, a bird sanctuary, and sports. The dining room, done in pale Renaissance-style wallpaper and water-stained pine paneling, has a menu strong in seafood. *510 Black Point Rd., Scarbor-*

*ough 04074, tel. 207/883-4126, fax 207/883-9976. 80 rooms with
bath, 6 suites. Facilities: restaurant, bar, entertainment; 14
tennis courts, 18-hole golf course, outdoor saltwater pool and
Jacuzzi, indoor freshwater pool and Jacuzzi, volleyball, putting green, bicycles, sailboats, fishing boats. AE, MC, V.
Closed Nov.-Apr. Very Expensive.*

The Arts

Portland Performing Arts Center (25A Forest Ave., Portland,
tel. 207/761-0591) hosts music, dance, and theater performances, including theatrical productions by the Portland Stage
Company. **Cumberland County Civic Center** (1 Civic Center
Sq., Portland, tel. 207/775-3458) hosts touring rock groups in a
9,000-seat auditorium. The **Portland Symphony Orchestra** (30
Myrtle St., Portland, tel. 207/773-8191) gives annual seasons
of concerts. **Mad Horse Theatre Company** (955 Forest Ave.,
Portland, tel. 207/797-3398) performs contemporary and original works.

Maine State Music Theater (Packard Theater, Bowdoin College, Brunswick, tel. 207/725-8769) stages musicals from the
end of June through August. **Theater Project of Brunswick** (14
School St., Brunswick, tel. 207/729-8584) performs from late
June through August.

Nightlife

Gritty McDuff's Brew Pub (396 Fore St., Portland, tel. 207/772-
2739) attracts the young, the lively, and connoisseurs of the
ales and bitters brewed on the premises. Steak and kidney pie
and fish-and-chips are served.

Top of the East (Sonesta Hotel, 157 High St., Portland, tel. 207/
775-5411) has a view of the city and live entertainment—jazz,
piano, and comedy.

Raoul's Roadside Attraction (865 Forest Ave., Portland, tel.
207/775-2494), southern Maine's hippest nightclub/restaurant,
books both local and name bands, especially R&B, jazz, and
Reggae groups.

McSeagull's Gulf Dock (Boothbay Harbor, tel. 207/633-4041)
draws young singles with live music and a loud bar scene.

Penobscot Bay

Purists hold that the Maine coast begins at Penobscot Bay,
where the vistas over the water are wider and bluer, the shore
a jumble of broken granite boulders, cobblestones, and gravel
punctuated by small sand beaches, and the water numbingly
cold. Port Clyde in the southwest and Stonington in the southeast are the outer limits of Maine's largest bay, 35 miles apart
across the bay waters but separated by a drive of almost 100
miles on scenic but slow two-lane highways.

Rockland, the largest town on the bay, is Maine's major lobster
distribution center and the port of departure to several bay islands. The Camden Hills, looming green over Camden's fashionable waterfront, turn bluer and fainter as one moves on to
Castine, the elegant small town across the bay. Deer Isle is connected to the mainland by a slender, high-arching bridge, but

Isle au Haut, accessible from Deer Isle's fishing town of Stonington, may be reached by passenger ferry only: More than half of this steep, wooded island is wilderness, the most remote section of Acadia National Park.

Route 1 is the fastest through highway for the remainder of this tour, and from Rockland all the way to Bucksport it's a particularly scenic stretch of road. At Thomaston, turn right onto Route 131 and follow the winding road 7 miles past waterside fields, spruce woods, ramshackle barns, and trim houses to get to Tenants Harbor, the starting point for this segment. While this is an easy detour, travelers in more of a hurry may want to stay on Route 1 for 5 miles and pick up the tour at Rockland.

Numbers in the margin correspond to points of interest on the Penobscot Bay map.

① **Tenants Harbor** is a quintessential Maine fishing town, its harbor dominated by squat, serviceable lobster boats, its shores rocky and slippery, its town a scattering of clapboard houses, a church, a general store. The fictional Dunnet Landing of Sarah Orne Jewett's classic sketches of Maine coastal life, *The Country of the Pointed Firs*, is based on this region.

Route 131 ends at **Port Clyde,** a fishing town that is the point of departure for the *Laura B.* (tel. 207/372–8848 for schedules), the mailboat that serves Monhegan Island. Tiny, remote
② **Monhegan Island** with its high cliffs fronting the open sea was known to Basque, Portuguese, and Breton fishermen well before Columbus "discovered" America. About a century ago Monhegan was discovered again by some of America's finest painters, including Rockwell Kent, Robert Henri, and Edward Hopper, who sailed out to paint the savage cliffs, the meadows, the wild ocean views, and the shacks of fisherfolk. Tourists followed, and today Monhegan is overrun with visitors in summer.

Returning north to Route 1, you have less than 5 miles to go to
③ **Rockland** on Penobscot Bay. This large fishing port is the commercial hub of the coast, with working boats moored alongside a growing flotilla of cruise schooners. Although a number of boutiques and restaurants have emerged in recent years, the town has retained its working-class flavor—you are more likely to find rusting hardware than ice-cream shops at the water's edge.

The outer harbor is bisected by a nearly mile-long breakwater, which begins on Waldo Avenue and ends with a lighthouse that was built in 1888. Next to the breakwater is **The Samoset Resort** (Warrenton St., tel. 207/594–2511 or 800/341–1650), a sprawling oceanside resort featuring an 18-hole golf course, indoor and outdoor tennis and swimming, racquetball, restaurant, and a health club.

Also in Rockland is the **William A. Farnsworth Library and Art Museum.** Here are oil and watercolor landscapes of the coastal lands you have just seen, among them Andrew Wyeth's *Eight Bells* and *Her Room.* Other Wyeths (N. C. and Jamie) are represented in the collections, as are Winslow Homer, Rockwell Kent, and the sculptor Louise Nevelson. *19 Elm St., tel. 207/ 596–6457. Admission: $3 adults, $2 senior citizens. Open Mon.–Sat. 10–5, Sun. 1–5. Closed Mon. Oct.–May.*

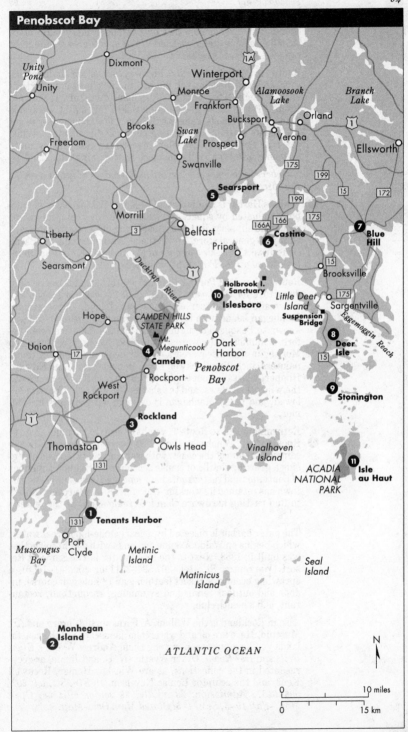

Penobscot Bay

Unity Pond
Unity
Dixmont
Winterport
1A
Monroe
Frankfort
Alamoosook Lake
Branch Lake
Bucksport
Orland
1
Brooks
Swan Lake
Prospect
Verona
Ellsworth
Freedom
Swanville
175
199
5 Searsport
199
15
172
Morrill
Belfast
166A
166
175
6 Castine
7 Blue Hill
Liberty
3
Pripet
15
Searsmont
Brooksville
Ducktrap River
1
Holbrook I. Sanctuary
Little Deer Island
175
Sargentville
Hope
CAMDEN HILLS STATE PARK
10 Islesboro
Suspension Bridge
Eggemoggin Reach
Union
17
Mt. Megunticook
Dark Harbor
8 Deer Isle
1
4 Camden
15
West Rockport
Rockport
Penobscot Bay
9 Stonington
3 Rockland
Thomaston
Owls Head
Vinalhaven Island
131
ACADIA NATIONAL PARK
11 Isle au Haut
1
1 Tenants Harbor
131
Port Clyde
Muscongus Bay
Metinic Island
Seal Island
Matinicus Island

2 Monhegan Island
ATLANTIC OCEAN

N

0   10 miles
0   15 km

Shore Village Museum exhibits U.S. Coast Guard memorabilia and artifacts, including lighthouse lenses, lifesaving gear, ship models, Civil War uniforms, and dolls. *104 Limerock St., Rockland, tel. 207/594–4950. Open June–mid-Oct., daily 10–4.*

❹ From Rockland it's 8 miles north on Route 1 to **Camden,** "Where the mountains meet the sea"—an apt description, as you will discover when you step out of your car and look up from the harbor. Camden is famous not only for geography but for the nation's largest windjammer fleet; at just about any hour during the warmer months you're likely to see at least one windjammer tied up in the harbor, and windjammer cruises are a superb way to explore the ports and islands of Penobscot Bay.

Time Out   **Ayer's Fish Market** on Main Street has the best fish chowder in town; take a cup to the pleasant park at the head of the harbor when you're ready for a break from the shops on Bayview and Main streets.

The entrance to the 6,000-acre **Camden Hills State Park** (tel. 207/236–3109) is 2 miles north of Camden on Route 1. If you're accustomed to the Rockies or the Alps, you may not be impressed with heights of not much more than 1,000 feet, yet the Camden Hills are landmarks for miles along the vast, flat reaches of the Maine coast. The park contains 25 miles of trails, including an easy trail up Mount Megunticook, the highest of the group. The 112-site camping area, open mid-May to mid-October, has flush toilets and hot showers. Park admission is $1 per person.

❺ Farther north on Route 1, **Searsport**—Maine's second largest deepwater port (after Portland)—claims to be the antiques capital of Maine. The town's stretch of Route 1 hosts a seasonal weekend flea market in addition to its antiques shops.

Searsport preserves a rich nautical history at the **Penobscot Marine Museum,** whose seven buildings display portraits of 284 sea captains, artifacts of the whaling industry (lots of scrimshaw), paintings and models of famous ships, navigational instruments, and treasures that seafarers collected. *Church St., tel. 207/548–6634. Admission: $3 adults, $2.50 senior citizens, $1 children 7–15. Open June–mid-Oct., Mon.–Sat. 9:30–5, Sun. 1–5.*

For a short cut, you may want to stay on Route 1 past Bucksport to Ellsworth, where you can pick up Route 3 to Bar Harbor. To explore more of the Penobscot Bay area, however, turn off on Route 175 just past Bucksport to reach historic ❻ **Castine,** over which the French, the British, and the Americans fought from the 17th century to the War of 1812. The town has two museums and the ruins of a British fort, but the finest thing about Castine is the town itself: the lively, welcoming town landing, the serene Federal and Greek Revival houses, and the town common. Castine invites strolling, and you would do well to start at the town landing, where you can park your car, and walk up Main Street past the two inns and on to the white Trinitarian Federated Church with its tapering spire.

Turn right on Court Street and walk to the town common, which is ringed by a collection of white-clapboard buildings that includes the Ives House (once the summer home of the poet

Robert Lowell), the Abbott School, and the Unitarian Church, capped by a whimsical belfry that suggests a gazebo.

From Castine, take Route 166 north to Route 199 and follow the signs to **Blue Hill.** Castine may have the edge over Blue Hill in charm, for Castine's Main Street is not a major thoroughfare and it claims a more dramatic perch over its harbor, yet Blue Hill is certainly appealing and boasts a better selection of shops and galleries. Blue Hill is renowned for its pottery, and two good shops are right in town.

The scenic Route 15 south from Blue Hill passes through Brooksville and on to the graceful suspension bridge that crosses Eggemoggin Reach to **Deer Isle.** The turnout and picnic area at Caterpillar Hill, 1 mile south of the junction of Routes 15 and 175, commands a fabulous view of Penobscot Bay, the hundreds of dark green islands, and the Camden Hills across the bay, which from this perspective look like a range of mountains dwarfed and faded by an immense distance—yet they are less than 25 miles away.

Route 15 continues the length of Deer Isle—a sparsely settled landscape of thick woods opening to tidal coves, shingled houses with lobster traps stacked in the yards, and dirt roads that lead to summer cottages—to **Stonington,** an emphatically ungentrified community that tolerates summer visitors but makes no effort to cater to them. Main Street has gift shops and galleries, but this is a working port town, and the principal activity is at the waterfront, where fishing boats arrive with the day's catch. The high, sloped island that rises beyond the archipelago of Merchants Row is Isle au Haut, accessible by mailboat from Stonington, which contains sections of Acadia National Park.

The island of **Islesboro,** accessible by car-and-passenger ferry from Lincolnville Beach north of Rockland (Maine State Ferry Service, tel. 207/789–5611), has been a retreat of wealthy, very private families for more than a century. The long, narrow, mostly wooded island has no real town to speak of; there are scatterings of mansions as well as humbler homes at Dark Harbor and at Pripet near the north end. A good plan is to leave your car on the mainland and bring your bike for a day of cycling the narrow roads that wind past the compounds of the summer folk. Since the amenities on Islesboro are quite spread out, you don't want to come on foot. If you plan to spend the night on Islesboro, you should make a reservation well in advance (*see* Islesboro Lodging, *below*).

Time Out   **Dark Harbor Shop** (tel. 207/734–8878) on Islesboro is an old-fashioned ice-cream parlor where tourists, locals, and summer folk gather for sandwiches, newspapers, gossip, and gifts. Open July through August.

Isle au Haut thrusts its steeply ridged back out of the sea 7 miles south of Stonington. Accessible only by passenger ferry (tel. 207/367–5193), the island is worth visiting for the ferry ride alone, a half-hour cruise amid the tiny, pink-shore islands of Merchants Row, where you may see terns, guillemots, and harbor seals. More than half the island is part of Acadia National Park; 17½ miles of trails extend through quiet spruce and birch woods, along cobble beaches and seaside cliffs, and over the spine of the central mountain ridge. From late June to mid-

September, the mailboat docks at Duck Harbor within the park. The small campground there, with five Adirondack-type lean-tos (open mid-May to mid-October), fills up quickly; reservations are essential, and they can be made only by writing to Acadia National Park (Box 177, Bar Harbor 04609).

Shopping

The most promising shopping streets are Main and Bayview streets in Camden and Main Street in Stonington. Antiques shops are scattered around the outskirts of villages, in farmhouses and barns; yard sales abound in summertime. Billing itself the antiques capital of Maine, Searsport hosts a massive weekend flea market on Route 1 during the summer months.

Antiques **Creative Antiques** (Rte. 175, Brooklin, tel. 207/359–8525) features painted furniture, hooked rugs, and prints.

Oakum Bay Ltd. (Main St., Castine, tel. 207/326–9690) carries a good selection of New England antique furniture and accessories, as well as handcrafted pewter, pottery, baskets, quilts, and paintings.

Lavender & Old Lace (Main St., Stonington, tel. 207/359–2188) offers vintage clothing, linens, glass, china, and small furniture.

Art Galleries **Gallery 68** (68 Main St., Belfast, tel. 207/338–1558) carries prints by well-known and local printmakers.

Leighton Gallery (Parker Point Rd., Blue Hill, tel. 207/374–5001) shows oil paintings, lithographs, watercolors, and other contemporary art in the gallery, and sculpture in its garden.

Deer Isle Artist Association (Rte. 15, Deer Isle Village, tel. 207/348–6864) has group exhibits of prints, drawings, and sculpture from mid-June through September.

Eastern Bay Cooperative Gallery (Main St., Stonington, tel. 207/367–5006) shows arts and crafts by numerous area artists.

Crafts and Pottery **Rackliffe Pottery** (Rte. 172, Blue Hill, tel. 207/374–2297) is famous for its vivid blue pottery, including plates, tea and coffee sets, casseroles, canisters.

Rowantrees Pottery (Union St., Blue Hill, tel. 207/374–5535) has an extensive selection of styles and patterns in dinnerware, tea sets, vases, and decorative items.

North Country Textiles (Rte. 175, South Penobscot, tel. 207/326–4131) is worth the detour for fine woven shawls, placemats, throws, and pillows in subtle patterns and color schemes.

Herbs **Meadow House** (Old Cart Rd., Blue Hill, tel. 207/374–5043) is a gorgeous herb garden worth visiting for the aromas and colors alone, and you can buy living and dried herbs and related gift items.

Sports and Outdoor Activities

Biking **Maine Sport** (Main Street, Camden, tel. 207/236–8797) rents bikes, canoes, and kayaks.

Boat Trips Windjammers create a stir whenever they sail into Camden harbor, and a voyage around the bay on one of them, whether for an afternoon or a week, is unforgettable. The season for the excursions is June through September.

Sailing out of Camden, the *Angelique* (Yankee Packet Co., Box 736, tel. 207/236–8873) makes weekly trips; **Maine Windjammer Cruises** (Box 617CC, tel. 207/236–2938) has three two-masted schooners making weekly trips along the coast and to the islands; *Mary Day* (Coastal Cruises, Box 798C, tel. 207/236–2750) offers weekly cruises departing Monday; the **Schooner *Roseway*** (Box 696, tel. 207/236–4449) takes three-day and six-day cruises.

From Rockland, the **Vessels of Windjammer Wharf** (Box 1050, tel. 207/236–3520 or 800/999–7352) organizes three- and six-day cruises on its four ships.

Timberwind (Box 247, tel. 207/236–9063) sails out of Rockport harbor.

Palmer Day IV (Stonington Harbor, tel. 207/367–2207) cruises Penobscot Bay in July and August, stopping at North Haven and Vinalhaven.

Deep-sea Fishing   **Bay Island Yacht Charters** (Box 639, Camden, tel. 207/236–2776) has charters by the day, week, and month; *Henrietta* (Rockland Public Landing, tel. 207/594–5411) takes 30 passengers for fishing and sightseeing on Penobscot Bay; *Union Jack* (Box 842, Camden, tel. 207/785–3521) goes out on fishing charters.

Water Sports   Eggemoggin Reach is a famous cruising ground for yachts, as are the coves and inlets around Deer Isle and the Penobscot Bay waters between Castine and Islesboro. For sailboat, kayak, and canoe rentals, try **Eaton's Boatyard** (Sea St., Castine, tel. 207/326–8579), **Indian Island Kayak** (Rockport, tel. 207/236–4088), **Maine Sport** (Main St., Camden, tel. 207/236–8797), or **Sailways** (Goose Cove Lodge, Deer Isle, tel. 207/348–2279).

State Parks

Camden Hills State Park (*see above*).

Holbrook Island Sanctuary (on Penobscot Bay in Brooksville, tel. 207/326–4012) has a gravelly beach with a splendid view; hiking trails through meadow and forest; no camping facilities.

Dining and Lodging

The following dining price categories have been used: *Very Expensive*, over $35; *Expensive*, $25–$35; *Moderate*, $15–$25; *Inexpensive*, under $15.

The following lodging price categories have been used: *Very Expensive*, over $100, *Expensive*, $80–$100; *Moderate*, $60–$80; *Inexpensive*, under $60.

Blue Hill   **Jonathan's.** The older downstairs room has captain's chairs,
Dining   blue tablecloths, and local art; in the post-and-beam upstairs, there's wood everywhere, candles with hurricane globes, and high-back chairs. The menu may include chicken breast in a fennel sauce with peppers, garlic, rosemary, and shallots; shrimp scorpio (shrimp served on linguine with a touch of ouzo and feta cheese); and grilled strip steak. Chocolate bourbon pecan cake makes a compelling finale. The wine list has 250 selec-

tions from French and California vineyards. *Main St., tel. 207/
374-5226. Reservations advised in summer. Dress: casual.
AE, MC, V. Dinner only. Closed Mon. Jan.-Apr. Moderate-
Expensive.*

Lodging **Blue Hill Inn.** The dignified white-clapboard building in Blue
Hill's historic district celebrated its 150th anniversary as an inn
in 1990. Five guest rooms have working fireplaces; all are decorated with Empire or early Victorian pieces, including marble-
topped walnut dressers, Oriental rugs on painted wood or
pumpkin pine floors, and wing chairs. Guests dine beneath a
Persian candle chandelier on elaborate six-course meals that
might include lobster bisque, rosemary sorbet, rack of lamb,
honey-roasted duck, cod with pecans and black beans, and
chocolate mousse with pecan bourbon. Dinner is open to the
public on a limited basis by reservation only, and jackets are
encouraged. You choose between Modified American Plan and
bed-and-breakfast. *Box 403, 04614, tel. 207/374-2844. 11
rooms. MC, V. Expensive-Very Expensive.*

Camden **The Belmont.** Round tables are set well apart in this dining
Dining room with smoke-colored walls and soft classical music or jazz.
★ The changing menu of New American cuisine might include
sautéed scallops with Pernod leek cream; grilled pheasant with
cranberry; chicken with a tomato coconut curry; or braised
lamb shanks. *6 Belmont Ave., tel. 207/236-8053. Reservations
advised. Dress: casual. MC, V. Dinner only. Closed Jan.-
Apr. Closed Mon. May-Columbus Day, closed Mon.-Wed.
Columbus Day-Dec. Expensive.*

The Waterfront Restaurant. A ringside seat on Camden Harbor
can be had here; the best view is from the outdoor deck, open in
warm weather. The fare is seafood: boiled lobster, scallops,
bouillabaisse, steamed mussels, Cajun barbecued shrimp.
Lunchtime features are lobster salad, crabmeat salad, lobster
and crab rolls, tuna niçoise, turkey melt, and burgers. *Bayview
St., tel. 207/236-3747. No reservations. Dress: casual. AE,
MC, V. Closed Jan.-mid-Feb. Moderate-Expensive.*

Village Restaurant. This restaurant recalls the days before gift
shops and condos came to Camden. The large, no-frills dining
room has windows on the water and nautical pictures; the substantial old-fashioned fare includes New England boiled dinner, chicken pie, steaks, and lobster in summer. Strawberry
angel pie heads the dessert menu. *7 Main St., tel. 207/236-
3232. No reservations. Dress: casual. MC, V. Closed Tues. Inexpensive-Moderate.*

Lodging **Norumbega.** The stone castle amid Camden's elegant clapboard
houses, built in 1886 by Joseph B. Stearns, the inventor of duplex telegraphy, was obviously the fulfillment of a fantasy. The
public rooms boast gleaming parquet floors, oak and mahogany
paneling, richly carved wood mantels over four fireplaces on
the first floor alone, gilt mirrors, and Empire furnishings. At
the back of the house, several decks and balconies overlook the
garden, the gazebo, and the bay. The view improves as you ascend; the newly completed penthouse suite features a small
deck, private bar, and a skylight in the bedroom. *61 High St.,
04843, tel. 207/236-4646. 12 rooms. AE, MC, V. Very Expensive.*

Whitehall Inn. Camden's best-known inn, just north of town on
Route 1, boasts a central white-clapboard, wide-porch ship
captain's home of 1843 connected to a turn-of-the-century

wing. Just off the comfortable main lobby with its faded Oriental rugs, the Millay Room preserves memorabilia of the poet Edna St. Vincent Millay, who grew up in Rockland. Rooms are sparsely furnished, with dark wood bedsteads, white bedspreads, and clawfoot bathtubs. Rooms in the Victorian Maine and Wicker houses across Route 1 offer quiet and king-size beds. The dining room is open to the public for dinner and breakfast, offering traditional and creative American cuisine. Dinner entrées include Eastern salmon in puff pastry, swordfish grilled with roast red pepper sauce, and lamb tenderloin. *Box 558, 04843, tel. 207/236–3391. 50 rooms, 42 with bath. Facilities: restaurants, all-weather tennis court, shuffleboard, motorboat, golf privileges. MC, V. Closed mid-Oct.–mid-May. Rates are MAP. Expensive–Very Expensive.*

Windward House. A choice bed-and-breakfast, this Greek Revival house of 1854, situated at the edge of town, features rooms furnished with fishnet lace canopy beds, cherry highboys, curly maple bedsteads, and clawfoot mahogany dressers. Guests are welcome to use any of three sitting rooms, including the Wicker Room with its glass-topped white wicker table where morning coffee is served. A small deck overlooks the back garden. Breakfasts may include quiche, apple puff pancakes, peaches-and-cream French toast, or soufflés. *6 High St., 04843, tel. 207/236–9656. 5 rooms, 1 efficiency. MC, V. Moderate–Expensive.*

Castine
Dining and Lodging

The Pentagoet. A recent renovation of the rambling, pale yellow Pentagoet gave each room a bath, enlarged the dining room, and opened up the public rooms. The porch wraps around three sides of the inn. Guest rooms are warmer, more flowery, more feminine than those of the Castine Inn across the street; they have hooked rugs, a mix of Victorian antiques, and floral wallpapers. Dinner in the deep rose and cream formal dining room (open to the public on a limited basis) is an elaborate affair; you might find such dishes as mushroom strudel, lemon egg drop soup, lobster pie, tournedos of beef, and broiled haddock. *Main St., 04421, tel. 207/326–8616. 17 rooms. MC, V. Closed Dec.–Apr. Rates are MAP. Very Expensive.*

★ **The Castine Inn.** Dark wood pineapple four-poster beds, white upholstered easy chairs, and oil paintings are typical of the room furnishings here. The newly renovated third floor has the best views: the harbor over the back garden on one side, Main Street on the other. The dining room, decorated with whimsical murals, is open to the public for breakfast and dinner; the menu features traditional New England fare—Maine lobster, crabmeat cakes with mustard sauce, roast leg of lamb, and chicken and leek pot pie. A snug, old-fashioned pub off the lobby has small tables and antique spirit jars over the mantel. *Main St., 04421, tel. 207/326–4365. 20 rooms, 2 suites. Facilities: restaurant, pub. MC, V. Closed Nov.–mid-Apr. Rates include full breakfast. Moderate–Expensive.*

Deer Isle
Lodging

Goose Cove Lodge. The heavily wooded property at the end of a back road has 2,500 feet of ocean frontage, two sandy beaches, a long sandbar that leads to the Barred Island nature preserve, nature trails, and sailboats for rent nearby. Some cottages and suites are in secluded woodlands, some on the shore, some attached, some with a single large room, others with one or two bedrooms. All but two units have fireplaces. In July and August the minimum stay is one week. *Sunset 04683, tel. 207/348–2508 (summer) or 207/767–3003 (winter). 11 cottages, 10* suites, 1 apartment. *Facilities: rowboat, canoe, volleyball, horseshoes. No credit cards. Closed mid-Oct.–Apr. Rates are MAP. Expensive–Very Expensive.*

Pilgrim's Inn. The bright red, four-story, gambrel-roof house dating from about 1793 overlooks a mill pond and harbor at the center of Deer Isle. The library has wing chairs and Oriental rugs; a downstairs taproom has pine furniture, braided rugs, and parson's benches. Guest rooms, each with its own character, sport Laura Ashley fabrics and select antiques. The dining room in the attached barn, an open space both rustic and elegant, has farm implements, French oil lamps, and tiny windows. The single-entrée menu changes nightly; it might include rack of lamb or fresh local seafood; scallop bisque; asparagus and smoked salmon; and poached pear tart for dessert. *Deer Isle 04627, tel. 207/348–6615. 13 rooms, 8 with bath, 1 cottage. Facilities: restaurant. No credit cards. Closed mid-Oct.–mid.–May. Expensive–Very Expensive.*

Isle au Haut
Lodging

Keeper's House. The converted lighthouse-keeper's house, set on a rock ledge surrounded by thick spruce forest, has no electricity and no access by road; guests dine by candlelight on seafood or chicken and read in the evening by kerosene lantern. Trails link the inn with the park trail network, and you can walk to the village, a collection of simple houses, a church, a tiny school, and a general store. The four guest rooms are spacious, airy, and simply decorated with painted wood furniture and local crafts. A separate cottage, the Oil House, has no indoor plumbing. *Isle au Haut 04645, tel. 207/367–2261. 4 rooms with bath, 1 cottage. Facilities: dock. No credit cards. Closed Nov.–Apr. Rates include 3 meals. Expensive.*

Islesboro
Dining
★

The Blue Heron. The only act in town and a wonderful find in the village of Dark Harbor, this airy, popular restaurant offers the best of New American cuisine. Changing entrées might include chicken sate in Thai peanut sauce; mussels steamed in wine, garlic, and herbs; and veal scaloppine sauteed with shiitake mushrooms and sun-dried tomatoes in a Marsala cream sauce. There's also an excellent wine list, full bar, and rich desserts. *Dark Harbor, Box 47, Islesboro 04848, tel. 207/734–6611. Reservations advised. Dress: casual. MC, V. Closed Mon. Closed Oct.–Memorial Day. No lunch. Moderate.*

Lodging

Dark Harbor House. The yellow-clapboard, neo-Georgian summer "cottage" of 1896 has a stately portico and a hilltop setting. Inside, an elegant double staircase curves from the ground floor to the bedrooms, which are spacious, some with balconies, one with an 18th-century four-poster bed. The dining room, open to the public for prix-fixe dinners, features seafood with a West Indian accent. *Box 185, 04848, tel. 207/734–6669. 12 rooms, 4 with bath. Facilities: restaurant. Closed Nov.–Memorial Day. Very Expensive.*

Lincolnville
Lodging

Sunrise Motor Court. Set on a hill a few miles north of Camden with views of a working saltwater farm and the islands of Penobscot Bay beyond, these plain, cozy cabins offer a no-frills alternative to coastal congestion. All cabins have double beds, color TVs, and bathrooms with small showers. Continental breakfast is included and usually consists of home-baked cinnamon rolls, which can be enjoyed on the small front deck. *Rte. 1, Box 545, tel. 207/236–3191. 13 cabins. D, MC, V. Closed Oct.–May. Inexpensive.*

North Brooklin **The Lookout.** The stately white-clapboard building stands in a
Dining and wide field at the tip of Flyc Point, with a superb view of the wa-
Lodging ter and the mountains of Mount Desert Island. Rustic rooms
have country antiques original to the house and newer matching pieces, though the floors show a tendency to slope, and a
century of damp has left a certain mustiness. The larger south-
facing rooms command the view. Seven cottages have from one
to four bedrooms each. With the dining room expanded onto the
porch, seven tables enjoy a view of the outdoors. Entrées could
include filet mignon, grilled salmon, and shrimp and scallops
provençale; the lobster cookout is Wednesday night. *North
Brooklin, 04616, tel. 207/359-2188. 6 rooms, 7 cottages. Facilities: restaurant. MC, V. Closed mid-Oct.-Memorial Day. Inexpensive-Moderate.*

Spruce Head **The Craignair Inn.** Built in the 1930s as a boardinghouse for
Dining and stonecutters and converted to an inn a decade later, the
Lodging Craignair commands a coastal view of rocky shore and lobster
boats. Inside the three-story gambrel-roof house you'll find
country clutter, books, and cut glass in the parlor; braided
rugs, brass beds, and dowdy dressers in the guest rooms. A few
years ago the owners converted a church dating from the 1890s
into another accommodation with six rooms—each with bath—
that have a more modern feel. The waterside dining room, decorated with Delft and Staffordshire plates, serves such fare as
bouillabaisse; lemon pepper seafood kebab; rabbit with tarragon and wine; and those New England standards: shore dinner,
prime rib, and scampi. A bourbon pecan tart and crème brûlée
are the dessert headliners. *Clark Island Rd., 04859, tel. 207/
594-7644. 21 rooms, 6 with bath. Facilities: restaurant. D, MC,
V. Closed Feb. Moderate.*

Stonington **Fisherman's Friend Restaurant.** Fresh salmon, halibut,
Dining monkfish, lobster, and even prime rib and chicken are on the
★ menu here. Friday is fish-fry day: free seconds on fried haddock, french fries, and cole slaw for $5.99. *School St., tel. 207/
367-2442. Reservations advised. Dress: casual. No credit
cards. BYOB. Closed Mon. Closed mid-Nov.-mid-Mar. Inexpensive.*

Lodging **Captain's Quarters Inn and Motel.** Accommodations, as plain
and unadorned as Stonington itself, are in the middle of town, a
two-minute walk from the Isle au Haut mailboat. You have your
choice of motel-type rooms and suites or efficiencies, and you
can take your breakfast muffins and coffee to the sunny deck on
the water. *Main St., Box 83, 04681, tel. 207/367-2420. 13 units,
11 with bath. AE, MC, V. Inexpensive-Moderate.*

Tenants Harbor **East Wind Inn & Meeting House.** On Route 131, 10 miles off
Dining and Route 1 and set on a knob of land overlooking the harbor and the
Lodging islands, the inn offers simple hospitality, a wraparound porch,
and unadorned but comfortable guest rooms furnished with an
iron bedstead, flowered wallpaper, and heritage bedspread.
The dining room has a rustic decor; the dinner menu features
duck with black currant sauce; seafood stew with scallops,
shrimp, mussels, and grilled sausage; boiled lobster; and baked
stuffed haddock. *Box 149, 04860, tel. 207/372-6366. 26 rooms,
12 with bath. Facilities: sailboat cruises in season. AE, MC, V.
No dinner Sun. Inexpensive-Moderate.*

The Arts

Bay Chamber Concerts (Rockport Opera House, Rockport, tel. 207/236–2823) offers chamber music Thursday and Friday nights during July and August; concerts are given once a month October through May.

Kneisel Hall Chamber Music Festival (Box 648, Blue Hill, tel. 207/374–2811) has concerts Sunday and Friday in summer.

Camden Civic Theatre (Camden Opera House, Elm St., tel. 207/594–4982) stages theatrical productions throughout the year.

Camden Shakespeare Company (Bok Amphitheater, Atlantic Ave., tel. 207/236–8011) produces plays, musicals, and concerts from July to Labor Day.

Nightlife

Bennett's Wharf (Sea St., Castine, tel. 207/326–4861) has a long bar that can become rowdy after dark.

Peter Ott's Tavern (Bayview St., Camden, tel. 207/236–4032) is a steakhouse with a lively bar scene.

Thirsty Whale Tavern (Camden Harbour Inn, 83 Bayview St., Camden, tel. 207/236–4200) is a popular local drinking spot.

Acadia

East of Penobscot Bay, Acadia is the informal name for the area that includes Mount Desert Island (pronounced like *dessert*) and its surroundings: Blue Hill Bay; Frenchman Bay; and Ellsworth, Hancock, and other mainland towns. Mount Desert, 13 miles across, is Maine's largest island, and it harbors most of Acadia National Park, Maine's principal tourist attraction with more than 4 million visitors a year (another section of the park occupies part of the island of Isle au Haut—*see* the Penobscot Bay section of this tour, *above*). The 34,000 acres of woods and mountains, lake and shore, footpaths, carriage paths, and hiking trails that make up the park extend as well to other islands and some of the mainland. Outside the park, on Mount Desert's east shore, an upper-class resort town of the 19th century has become a busy tourist town of the 20th century in Bar Harbor, which services the park with a variety of inns, motels, and restaurants.

From Isle au Haut or Stonington, take Route 15 inland to Route 172, which connects with Route 1 in Ellsworth. Route 3 turns south from there to Mount Desert Island and Bar Harbor.

Numbers in the margin correspond to points of interest on the Acadia map.

Mount Desert Island's center of attraction is the busy town of **Bar Harbor.** Although most of Bar Harbor's grand mansions were destroyed in the fire of 1947 and replaced by modern motels, the town retains the beauty of a commanding location on Frenchman Bay. Shops, restaurants, and hotels are clustered along Main, Mount Desert, and Cottage streets. **Bar Harbor Historical Society Museum** displays photos of Bar Harbor from the days when it catered to the very rich. Other exhibits document the great fire of 1947, in which many of the Gilded Age

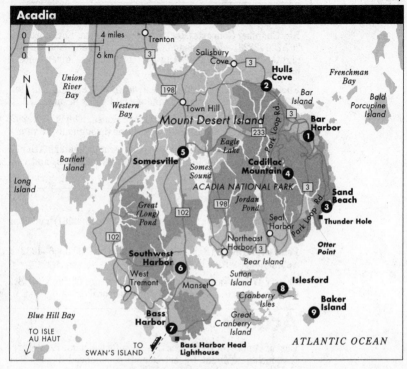

Acadia

cottages were destroyed. *34 Mt. Desert St., tel. 207/288–3838. Admission free. Open mid-June–Oct., Mon.–Sat. 1–4; by appointment in other seasons.*

Several tours of the park can be taken from Bar Harbor, including **National Park Tours** (tel. 207/288–3327), 2½-hour bus tours narrated by a park naturalist, and **Bar Harbor Trolley** tours (tel. 207/288–5741), which encompass Bar Harbor and the park.

2 All of the island's main roads—Route 3, Park Loop Road, Route 102, Route 198, and Route 233—pass in, out, and through the precincts of Acadia National Park. The **Hulls Cove** approach to Acadia National Park is 4 miles northwest of Bar Harbor on Route 3. Even though it is often clogged with traffic in summer, the scenic 27-mile Park Loop Road provides the best introduction to Acadia National Park. At the start of the loop at Hulls Cove, the visitor center shows a free 15-minute orientation film and has maps of the hiking trails and carriage paths in the park.

3 Follow the road to the parking area for **Sand Beach,** a small stretch of pink sand backed by the mountains of Acadia and the odd lump of rock known as the Beehive. The Ocean Trail, which parallels the Park Loop Road from Sand Beach to the Otter Point parking area, is a popular and easily accessible walk with some of the most spectacular scenery in Maine: huge slabs of pink granite heaped at the ocean's edge, ocean views unobstructed to the horizon, and Thunder Hole, a natural seaside cave in which the ocean rushes and roars.

4 Those who want a mountaintop experience without the effort of hiking can drive to the summit of **Cadillac Mountain,** at 1,523 feet the highest point along the eastern coast. From the smooth, bald summit you have a 360-degree view of the ocean, the islands, the jagged coast, and the woods and lakes of Acadia and its surroundings.

On completing the 27-mile Park Loop, you can continue your auto tour of the island by heading west on Route 233 for the villages on Somes Sound, a true fjord—the only one on the East **5** Coast—which almost bisects Mount Desert Island. **Somesville,** the oldest settlement on the island (1621), is a carefully preserved New England village of white-clapboard houses and churches, neat green lawns, and bits of blue water visible behind them.

6 Route 102 south from Somesville takes you to **Southwest Harbor,** which combines the rough, salty character of a working port with the refinements of a summer resort community. From the town's Main Street along Route 102, turn left onto Clark Point Road to reach the harbor.

Time Out At the end of Clark Point Road in Somesville, **Beal's Lobster Pier** serves lobsters, clams, and crab rolls in season at dockside picnic tables.

Those who want to tour more of the island will continue south on Route 102, following Route 102A where the road forks, and passing through the communities of Manset and Seawall. The Bass Harbor Head lighthouse, which clings to a cliff at the eastern entrance to Blue Hill Bay, was built in 1858. The tiny lobstering village of **Bass Harbor** has cottages for rent, a gift shop, **7** and a car and passenger ferry to Swans Island.

Situated off the southeast shore of Mount Desert Island at the entrance to Somes Sound, the five **Cranberry Isles**—Great Cranberry, Islesford (or Little Cranberry), Baker Island, Sutton Island, and Bear Island—escape the hubbub that engulfs Acadia National Park in summer. Great Cranberry and Islesford are served by the Beal & Bunker passenger ferry (tel. 207/244–3575) from Northeast Harbor; Baker Island is reached by the summer cruise boats of the Islesford Ferry Company (tel. 207/276–3717); Sutton and Bear islands are privately owned.

8 **Islesford** comes closest to having a village: a collection of houses, a church, a fishermen's co-op, a market, and a post office near the ferry dock. The Islesford Historical Museum, run by the national park, has displays of tools, documents relating to the island's history, and books and manuscripts of the writer Rachel Field (1894–1942), who summered on Sutton Island. Island Bed and Breakfast (tel. 207/244–9283), a short walk from the ferry landing, offers overnight accommodations from mid-June through September. The Islesford Dock restaurant (tel. 207/244–3177) serves three meals a day from June to September.

9 The 123-acre **Baker Island,** the most remote of the group, looks almost black from a distance because of its thick spruce forest. The cruise boat from Northeast Harbor makes a 4½-hour narrated tour, in the course of which you are likely to see ospreys nesting on a sea stack off Sutton Island, harbor seals hauled out on ledges, and cormorants flying low over the water. Because Baker Island has no natural harbor, the tour boat ties up offshore and you take a fishing dory to reach the island.

Shopping

Bar Harbor in the summer is a good place for browsing for gifts, T-shirts, and novelty items; for bargains, head for the outlets that line Route 3 in Ellsworth, which have good discounts on shoes.

Antiques **1895 Shop** (1 Steamboat Wharf Rd., Bernard, tel. 207/244–7039) has china, glassware, jewelry, postcards, and curios. The detour to Bernard—off Route 102 on Mount Desert Island—is worth making.

Acadia Mews Antique Center (Bar Harbor Rd., tel. 207/667–7323) is three shops offering folk art and country and formal furniture in mahogany and wicker.

West Tremont Antiques & Art (Rte. 102, West Tremont, tel. 207/244–3528) carries antiques and art, glassware, kitchenware, and collectibles from the 1950s and before.

Crafts **Acadia Shops** (inside the park at Cadillac Mountain summit; Thunder Hole on Ocean Dr.; Jordan Pond House on Park Loop Rd.; and 85 Main St., Bar Harbor) sell crafts and Maine foods.

Island Artisans (99 Main St., Bar Harbor, tel. 207/288–4214) is a crafts cooperative that shows work in various media and styles.

Sports and Outdoor Activities

Biking, Jogging, The network of carriage paths that wind through the woods
Cross-country and the fields of Acadia National Park is ideal for biking and jog-
Skiing ging when the ground is dry and for cross-country skiing in winter. Hulls Cove visitor center has a carriage paths map.

Bikes for hire can be found at **Acadia Bike & Canoe** (48 Cottage St., Bar Harbor, tel. 207/288–5483) and **Bar Harbor Bicycle Shop** (141 Cottage St., tel. 207/288–3886).

Boat Trips Out of Bar Harbor, **Acadia Boat Tours & Charters** (West St., tel. 207/288–9505) embarks on 1½-hour lobster fishing trips in summer; **Acadian Whale Watcher** (Golden Anchor Pier, tel. 207/288–9794) runs 2½-hour whale-watching cruises in summer; **Natalie Todd** (Inn Pier, tel. 207/288–4585) offers weekend windjammer cruises from July through September.

From Northeast Harbor, **Blackjack** (Town Dock, tel. 207/276–5043 or 207/288–3056), a 33-foot Friendship sloop, makes five trips daily, May through October, Monday through Saturday; **Sunrise** (Sea St. Pier, tel. 207/276–5352) does lobster fishing tours in the summer months.

Canoeing and For canoe and kayak rentals, see **Acadia Bike & Canoe, Life**
Kayaking **Sports** (34 High St., Ellsworth, tel. 207/667–7819), or **National Park Canoe Rentals** (Rte. 102, 2 mi west of Somesville, at the head of Long Pond, tel. 207/244–5854).

Deep-sea Fishing **Dolphin** (Frenchman Bay Co., 1 West St., Bar Harbor, tel. 207/288–3322) is available for charter from Memorial Day to Columbus Day.

Masako Queen (Clark Point Rd., Southwest Harbor, tel. 207/ 667–3281) offers fishing trips three times daily during the summer.

Hiking   Acadia National Park maintains nearly 200 miles of foot and carriage paths, ranging from easy strolls along flatlands to rigorous climbs that involve ladders and handholds on rock faces. Among the more rewarding hikes are the Precipice Trail to Champlain Mountain, the Great Head Loop, the Gorham Mountain Trail, and the path around Eagle Lake. The National Park visitor center has a trail guide and map.

Sailing   **Harbor Boat Rentals** (Harbor Pl., 1 West St., Bar Harbor, tel. 207/288–3757) has 13-foot and 17-foot Boston whalers and some sailboats.

Manset Boat Rental (Manset Boatyard, just south of Southwest Harbor, tel. 207/244–9233) rents sailboats.

Camping

The two campgrounds in Acadia National Park—**Blackwoods** (tel. 207/288–3274), open year-round, and **Seawall** (tel. 207/ 244–3600), open late May to late September—fill up quickly during the summer season. Off Mount Desert Island, but convenient to it, the campground at **Lamoine State Park** (tel. 207/ 667–4778) is open mid-May to mid-October; the 55-acre park has a great location on Frenchman Bay.

Dining and Lodging

The following dining price categories have been used: *Very Expensive*, over $35; *Expensive*, $25–$35; *Moderate*, $15–$25; *Inexpensive*, under $15.

Bar Harbor has the greatest concentration of accommodations on Mount Desert Island, much of it converted from elaborate 19th-century summer cottages.

The following lodging price categories have been used: *Very Expensive*, over $100, *Expensive*, $80–$100; *Moderate*, $60–$80; *Inexpensive*, under $60.

Bar Harbor   **George's.** Candles, flowers, and linens grace the tables in four
Dining   small dining rooms in an old house. The menu shows a distinct
★   Mediterranean influence in the lobster streudel wrapped in phyllo, and in the sautéed veal; fresh char-grilled salmon and swordfish stand on their own. Couples tend to linger in the romantic setting. *7 Stephen's La., tel. 207/288–4505. Reservations advised. Dress: casual. AE, DC, MC, V. Dinner only. Closed late Oct.–mid-June. Moderate–Expensive.*

Jordan Pond House. Oversize popovers and tea are a warm tradition at this rustic restaurant in the park, where in fine weather you can sit on the terrace or the lawn and admire the views of Jordan Pond and the mountains. The dinner menu offers lobster stew, seafood thermidor, and fisherman's stew. *Park Loop Rd., tel. 207/276–3316. Reservations one day in advance advised in summer. Dress: casual. AE, D, MC, V. Closed late Oct.–late May. Moderate.*

★   **124 Cottage Street.** The four dining rooms of the cheerful, flower-filled restaurant have the feel of a country inn, and the back room has an extra treat—a sliding glass door to a small garden and woods. The fare is seafood and pasta dishes with an Oriental twist: Szechuan shrimp; pasta primavera with pea pods and broccoli; seafood pasta with mussels, shrimp, and scallops in tomato sauce; broiled swordfish, salmon, haddock. *124 Cottage St., tel. 207/288–4383. Reservations advised. Dress: casual. MC, V. Dinner only. Closed late Oct.–mid-June. Moderate.*

Lodging **Inn at Canoe Point.** Seclusion and privacy are bywords of this snug, 100-year-old Tudor-style house on the water at Hulls Cove, 2 miles from Bar Harbor. The Master Suite, a large room with a fireplace, is a favorite for its size and the French doors opening onto a waterside deck. The inn's large living room has huge windows on the water, a fieldstone fireplace, and, just outside, a deck that hangs over the water. *216 Hulls Cove Rd., 04644, tel. 207/288–9511. 6 rooms, 5 with bath. No credit cards. Expensive–Very Expensive.*

Mira Monte. Built as a summer home in 1864, the Mira Monte bespeaks Victorian leisure, with columned verandas, latticed bay windows, and landscaped grounds for strolling and sunning; and the inn is set back far enough from the road to assure quiet and seclusion. The guest rooms have brass or four-poster beds, white wicker, hooked rugs, lace curtains, and oil paintings in gilt frames. The quieter, rear-facing rooms offer sunny garden views. Some rooms have porches, fireplaces, and separate entrances. *69 Mt. Desert St., 04609, tel. 207/288–4263 or 800/553–5109. 11 rooms. AE, MC, V. Closed late Oct.–early May. Moderate–Very Expensive.*

Wonder View Motor Lodge. While the rooms are standard motel accommodations, with two double beds and nondescript furniture, this establishment is distinguished by its extensive grounds, the view of Frenchman Bay, and a location opposite the Bluenose ferry terminal. The woods muffle the sounds of traffic on Route 3. Pets are accepted, and the dining room has picture windows. *Rte. 3, Box 25, 04609, tel. 207/288–3358 or 800/341–1553. 82 rooms. Facilities: dining room, outdoor pool. AE, MC, V. Closed late Oct.–mid-May. Inexpensive–Expensive.*

Hancock **Le Domaine.** On a rural stretch of Route 1, 9 miles east of
Dining Ellsworth, a French chef prepares *lapin pruneaux* (rabbit in a
★ rich brown sauce); sweetbreads with lemon and capers; and coquilles St. Jacques. The elegant but not intimidating dining room has polished wood floors, copper pots hanging from the mantel, and silver, crystal, and linen on the tables. *Rte. 1, Hancock, tel. 207/422–3395. Reservations advised. Dress: neat but casual. Dinner only. Closed Nov.–Apr. Expensive.*

Lodging **Le Domaine.** The seven smallish rooms in the inn are done in French country style, with chintz and wicker, simple desks, and sofas near the windows. Four rooms have balconies or porches over the gardens. The 100-acre property offers paths for walking and badminton on the lawn. *Box 496, 04640, tel. 207/422–3395. 7 rooms. Facilities: restaurant. AE, MC, V. Closed Nov.–Apr. Rates are MAP. Very Expensive.*

Northeast Harbor **Asticou Inn.** At night guests of the inn trade topsiders and polo
Dining shirts for jackets and ties to dine in the stately formal dining room, which is open to the public for a prix-fixe dinner by reservation only. A recent menu featured swordfish with orange mustard glaze; lobster; seared catfish; and chicken in a lemon cream and mushroom sauce. *Tel. 207/276–3344. Reservations required. Jacket and tie required. Closed mid-Sept.–mid-June. Expensive.*

Lodging **Asticou Inn.** This grand turn-of-the-century inn at the head of exclusive Northeast Harbor serves a loyal clientele. Guest rooms in the main building have a country feel, with bright fabrics, white lace curtains, and white painted furniture. The more modern cottages scattered around the grounds afford greater privacy; among them, the decks and picture windows make the Topsider Cottages particularly attractive. A stay at the inn includes breakfast and dinner, but the cottages and the Victorian-style Cranberry Lodge across the street operate on a bed-and-breakfast policy from mid-May to mid-June and from mid-September to January 1. *Northeast Harbor 04662, tel. 207/ 276–3344. 50 rooms, 23 suites, 6 cottages. Facilities: clay tennis court, heated pool. MC, V. Inn closed mid-Sept.–mid-June; cottages, lodge closed Jan.–Mar. Rates are MAP in summer. Very Expensive (lodge, Moderate–Expensive).*

Southwest Harbor

Dining **Claremont Hotel.** The large, airy dining room of the inn, open to the public for dinner only, is awash in light streaming through the picture windows. The atmosphere is on the formal side, with crystal, silver, and china service. Rack of lamb, baked stuffed shrimp, coquilles St. Jacques, and tournedos au poivre are specialties. *Tel. 207/244–5036. Reservations required. Jacket required. No credit cards. Closed for lunch mid-Aug.– mid-July, closed mid-Sept.–mid-June. Moderate.*

Lodging **Claremont Hotel.** Built in 1884 and operated continuously as an inn, the Claremont calls up memories of long, leisurely vacations of days gone by. The yellow-clapboard structure commands a view of Somes Sound, croquet is played on the lawn, and cocktails are served at the boathouse from mid-July to the end of August. Guest rooms are bright, white, and quite plain; cottages and two guest houses on the grounds are homier and woodsier. Modified American Plan is in effect from mid-June to mid-September. *Box 137, 04679, tel. 207/244–5036. 22 rooms, 20 with bath; 3 suites, 11 cottages, 2 guest houses. Facilities: clay tennis court, croquet, bicycles, private dock and moorings. No credit cards. Hotel closed mid-Sept.–mid-June. Cottages closed mid-Oct.–mid-May. Rates are MAP. Expensive– Very Expensive.*

The Arts

Acadia Repertory Company (Masonic Hall, Rte. 102, Somesville, tel. 207/244–7260) mounts plays in July and August.

Arcady Music Festival (tel. 207/288–3151) schedules concerts around Mount Desert Island from late July through August.

Bar Harbor Festival (36 Mt. Desert St., Bar Harbor, tel. 207/ 288–5744; 510 5th Ave., New York, NY 10036, tel. 212/222– 1026) programs recitals, jazz, chamber music, and pops concerts from mid-July to mid-August.

Nightlife

Acadia has little nighttime activity. The lounge at the **Moorings Restaurant** (Manset, tel. 207/244–7070), accessible by boat and car, is open until midnight from May to October, and the company is a lively boating crowd.

Tour 2:
New York
City
to Boston

It's easy to whiz from New York City to Boston on the train (four and a half hours) or the air shuttle (one hour); the journey gives a traveler barely enough time to make the psychological transition from New York's heady go-go-go to Boston's quaintly clubby charm. But even if your goal is to spend three or four days exploring each of these delightful cities (and three or four days is barely enough time to crack their secrets), taking the time to explore the towns and countryside that lie in between is a great way to understand why New York is the way it is and Boston is the way *it* is.

Wending your way up the Hudson Valley, you'll encounter the homesteads of early Dutch settlers, farmers who prospered in this fertile agricultural area, as well as the later mansions of the rich and powerful whose fortunes were made, and whose power was wielded, largely downriver in New York City. Swing east and you'll plunge into the Berkshire hills, the buffer that divides New York from Massachusetts, where woods and steep slopes isolate each picturesque village. As you move east through the so-called Pioneer Valley, along the Connecticut River, and on toward Sturbridge, history harks back to Puritans and pilgrims, as well as to the hard-headed Yankee peddler.

If all you want to do is to get from New York to Boston (or vice versa), it would be more logical to follow I–95 along the coast. But for a full vacation, spend a week moseying along this route. Along the way, there are constant invitations to dawdle, at a restored home here, a quaint shopping street there, and everywhere hillsides with panoramic views of river or mountains.

Visitor Information

New York   The **New York Convention and Visitors Bureau** (2 Columbus Circle [58th St. and Eighth Ave.], tel. 212/397–8222).

Columbia County Chamber of Commerce (401 State St., Hudson 12534, tel. 518/828–3375 or 800/777–9247).

Dutchess County Tourism Promotion Agency (532 Albany Post Rd., Box 2025, Hyde Park 12538, tel. 914/229–0033 or 800/445–3131).

Hudson River Valley Association (McCabe Carriage House, 42 Catharine St., Poughkeepsie 12601, tel. 914/452–4910 or 800/232–4782).

Putnam County Tourism (76 Main St., Cold Spring-on-Hudson 10516, tel. 914/265–3066).

Westchester Tourism Council (148 Martine Ave., White Plains 10610, tel. 914/285–2941).

Massachusetts   **Massachusetts Office of Travel and Tourism** (100 Cambridge St., Boston 02202, tel. 617/727–3201).

Berkshire Visitor's Bureau (Box SGB, Berkshire Common, Pittsfield 01201, tel. 413/443–9186 or 800/237–5747).

Lenox Chamber of Commerce (Lenox Academy Building, 75 Main St., 01240, tel. 413/637–3646).

Mohawk Trail Association (Box 7, North Adams 01247, tel. 413/664–6256).

Greater Springfield Convention and Visitors Bureau (34 Boland
Way, Springfield 01103, tel. 413/787–1548).

Festivals and Seasonal Events

Feb.: Chinese New Year Celebrations crackle with fireworks in
Chinatown, New York City.

June–July: Metropolitan Opera performs free starlit concerts
in parks in all five New York City boroughs. Tel. 212/362–6000.

June–Sept.: Jacob's Pillow Dance Festival at Becket in the Berkshires hosts performers from various dance traditions. Tel.
413/243–0745.

July–Aug.: New York Philharmonic's free summer concert series takes place in parks throughout New York City, and in Suf-
folk, Nassau, and Westchester counties. Tel. 212/360–1333.

July–Aug.: Shakespeare in the Park produces two free plays,
usually by the Bard, at the Delacorte Theater in New York
City's Central Park. Tel. 212/598–7100.

July–Aug.: Tanglewood Music Festival at Lenox, Massachusetts, the summer home of the Boston Symphony Orchestra,
schedules other top performers as well. Tel. 413/637–1600 or
617/266–1492.

Nov. 26: Macy's Thanksgiving Day Parade, the world's largest,
starts at 9 AM in New York City; no tickets are necessary. Tel.
212/560–4661.

Early Dec.: Christmas Tree Lighting at Rockefeller Center,
New York City, is a highlight of the city's holiday season.

Dec. 31: New Year's Eve celebration in Times Square is legendary. Fireworks go off in Central Park.

What to See and Do With Children

*Most attractions described below are described more fully in
the tour that follows.*

Despite the crowds, noise, and crime fears, **New York City** is a
magical place to visit with children. Many of its landmarks—
especially the **Statue of Liberty, Rockefeller Center, South
Street Seaport, Central Park,** and **F.A.O. Schwarz** toy store (767
5th Ave. at 58th St., tel. 212/644–9400)—make unforgettable
visits for kids who've seen them often on movies and TV. The
American Museum of Natural History is one of the world's
greatest museums for kids, with its dinosaurs, dioramas,
asteroids, and planetarium. The **Bronx Zoo** (Bronx Park, tel.
212/367–1010), the nation's largest urban zoo, is home to more
than 4,000 animals. The **Children's Museum of Manhattan** (212
W. 83rd St., tel., 212/721–1223; open Tues.–Sun.), designed
for children ages 2–12, offers interactive exhibits and activities
that amuse children for hours on end. The **Intrepid Sea-Air-
Space Museum** (Pier 86 at W. 46th St., tel. 212/245–0072; open
Wed.–Sun.), housed in a famous World War II aircraft carrier,
displays aircraft, rockets, and space vehicles.

Traveling through the **Hudson Valley** and the **Berkshires,** families may want to skip the many historic homes and go straight
for the parks, such as **Bear Mountain State Park** in New York,
which has a zoo, beaver lodge, and reptile house, and **Mount**

Greylock State Reservation in Massachusetts. **Jiminy Peak** (tel. 413/738–5500), a ski resort at Hancock, Massachusetts, offers an alpine slide, putting course, and trout fishing in summer. **Forest Park** (tel. 413/733–2251), in Springfield, Massachusetts, has many recreational facilities, including a children's zoo. **Riverside Park** (1623 Main St., Agawam, Massachusetts, tel. 413/786–9300 or 800/992–7488; open Apr.–Sept.), the largest amusement park in New England, features a giant roller coaster and many other rides.

Just outside of Pittsfield, Massachusetts, **Hancock Shaker Village** organizes special programs for children. Holyoke, Massachusetts, has a **Children's Musuem.** Also in Massachusetts, the **Berkshire Scenic Railway** in Lenox and the **Heritage State Railway** in Holyoke make fun outings for kids. Young sports fans should enjoy the **Naismith Memorial Basketball Hall of Fame** in Springfield, the town where the sport was invented. **Old Sturbridge Village,** in Sturbridge, Massachusetts, is a superb re-creation of a 19th-century village that brings history vividly alive for kids.

For attractions in **Boston,** *see* Tour 1.

Arriving and Departing

By Plane
The Airlines
Virtually every major U.S. and foreign airline serves one or more of New York's three airports: **LaGuardia Airport, John F. Kennedy International Airport,** and **Newark International Airport.** To get into Manhattan, a **taxi** will cost $15–$20 from LaGuardia (20–40 minutes), $25–$30 from JFK (35–60 minutes), or $28–30 from Newark (20–45 minutes). From LaGuardia or JFK, which are in the borough of Queens, you can get into Manhattan by **Carey Airport Express** bus (tel. 718/632–0500; fare $8.50 from LaGuardia, $11 from JFK; drop-off point 42nd St. and Park Ave. across from Grand Central Terminal). The **Gray Line Air Shuttle Minibus** (tel. 212/757–6840) drops off at major Manhattan hotels; the cost is $11 from LaGuardia, $14 from JFK. From Newark, which is west of the city, in New Jersey, you can take **NJ Transit Airport Express** buses (tel. 201/460–8444; fare $7, drop-off at Port Authority terminal, 42nd St. and 8th Ave.), the **Olympia Airport Express Bus** (fare $7, drop-off at the World Trade Center and Grand Central Terminal), or the **Gray Line Air Shuttle Minibus** (tel. 212/757-6840; fare $16, drops off at major Manhattan hotels).

Boston's **Logan International Airport,** the largest airport in New England, has scheduled flights by most major domestic and foreign carriers. To get from the airport to downtown Boston, you can hire a cab outside each terminal (fares to downtown should be around $15), take the **Airport Water Shuttle** (tel. 800/235–6426) to Rowes Wharf, or ride the **MBTA Blue Line** into town (free shuttle buses connect all terminals to the Airport subway station; call 617/561–1800 or 800/235–6426 for Logan Airport Public Information).

By Car
The **Lincoln Tunnel** (I–495), **Holland Tunnel,** and **George Washington Bridge** (I–95) connect to the New Jersey Turnpike system and points west. The Lincoln Tunnel leads to midtown Manhattan, the Holland Tunnel to lower Manhattan, the George Washington Bridge to northern Manhattan. Each of the three arteries requires a toll ($4 for cars) eastbound into New York, but no toll westbound.

From Long Island, the **Midtown Tunnel** (I–495) and **Triborough Bridge** (I–278) are the most direct arteries to Manhattan. Both require tolls ($2.50 for cars) in both directions.

From upstate New York, the city is accessible via the **New York (Dewey) Thruway** (I–87) (toll) to the **Major Deegan Expressway** through the Bronx and across the **Triborough Bridge** (toll).

From New England, the **Connecticut Turnpike** (I–95) connects to the **New England Thruway** (I–95), the **Bruckner Expressway** (I–278), and the **Triborough Bridge** (toll) to upper Manhattan.

Leaving New York City, take the Henry Hudson Parkway from the West Side up to the Sawmill River Parkway. From there, you can pick up Route 9, the main scenic road through the Hudson Valley, or the speedier but also scenic limited-access Taconic State Parkway. Both eventually intersect with I–90, which heads east to become the Massachusetts Turnpike to Boston. Within the Berkshires the main north–south road is Route 7. The scenic Mohawk Trail (Route 2) runs from the northern Berkshires to Greenfield at the head of the Pioneer Valley; I–91 runs south through the Pioneer Valley, from Greenfield to Springfield, where it links up with I–90 (the Mass Pike) heading east to Boston, about a 90-minute drive.

By Train **Amtrak** (tel. 800/872–7245) offers frequent service within the Northeast Corridor, between Boston and New York City, with a spur that travels up the Hudson Valley and another up to Springfield, Massachusetts, from New Haven, Connecticut. Trains arrive and depart from New York's Pennsylvania Station (31st to 33rd Sts., between Seventh and Eighth Aves.) and Boston's South Station (Atlantic Ave. and Sumner St., tel. 617/482–3660). Amtrak trains also serve New York's Penn Station from the Southeast, Midwest, and Far West. The *Lake Shore Limited* between Boston and Chicago calls at Springfield, Massachusetts, once daily in each direction, and two more trains run between Boston and Springfield every day.

Metro-North Commuter Railroad (tel. 212/532–4900) serves Grand Central Terminal (42nd St. and Park Ave.) from the northern suburbs and Connecticut as far east as New Haven. The **Long Island Railroad** (tel. 718/217–5477) has service from all over Long Island to Penn Station. Also at Penn Station, **New Jersey Transit** (tel. 201/460–8444) offers frequent service from the north and central regions of the state.

By Bus All long-haul and commuter bus lines to New York City feed into the **Port Authority Terminal** (tel. 212/564–8484), between 40th and 42nd streets and Eighth and Ninth avenues. Though it's recently modernized and fairly clean, the large number of vagrants make the terminal an uncomfortable place to spend much time. Bus lines serving New York include **Greyhound-Trailways** (consult local information for a number in your area), **Adirondack** and **Pine Hill Trailways** from upstate New York (tel. 914/339–4230 or 212/947–5300); **Bonanza Bus Lines** from New England (tel. 800/556–3815); **Martz Trailways** from northeastern Pennsylvania (tel. 800/233–8604);**Peter Pan Bus Lines** from New England (tel. 800/237–8747); and **Vermont Transit** from New England (tel. 800/451–3292).

Greyhound Lines' Boston terminus is on St. James St., Park Square (tel. 617/423–5810) and **Peter Pan Bus Lines'** terminus is opposite South Station, on Atlantic Avenue (tel. 617/426–7838).

By Boat   **Hudson River Day Line** (Pier 81, west end of 42nd St., New York 10036, tel. 212/279–5151) runs monthly minicruises to Bear Mountain and West Point from Manhattan.

New York City

Whatever you're looking for in a big-city vacation, you'll find in New York. The city has history: You can trace the life of the early Dutch settlers, see the spot where George Washington was sworn in as first U.S. president, and stroll around the restored site of America's greatest 19th-century seaport. The city has architecture: a succession of buildings that, in their time, ranked as the world's tallest structures (the Flatiron, Woolworth, Chrysler, and Empire State buildings, and the World Trade Center Towers), as well as contemporary architectural treasures ranging from the bizarre (Guggenheim Museum) to the sublime (Trump Tower) to the perplexingly postmodern (AT&T Building).

In show-biz terms, the Big Apple is top banana, and it has 16,000 restaurants, some of them world-famous institutions. Its ethnic neighborhoods, such as Little Italy and Chinatown, are not theme parks but vibrant, ever-changing areas that remain magnets for Old Country settlers.

Some New York attractions occupy a class by themselves. The Statue of Liberty, the Brooklyn Bridge, the Empire State Building, Times Square, and Central Park may be situated in New York City, but all belong to the world.

Above and beyond the laundry list of sights and activities, New York has an undefinable aura that exists nowhere else. It's a kind of energy level that has something to do with being in the big league, where everybody's watching and keeping score. Walking down a New York street, you might pass Henry Kissinger (with a bodyguard or two). You could go into a restaurant and get a table across from Robert DeNiro. You are very likely to turn a corner and see a feature film or TV series being filmed. And even if you don't see someone you recognize, you always feel that you just *might*.

You may already have heard that New York can be an expensive place to visit. And there is crime, which can occur in the most unexpected places. (The only reasonable precautions anyone can take are to keep jewelry and valuables out of sight on the street and to walk generally on the main thoroughfares, with the crowds.) New Yorkers themselves often appear to be brusque, haughty, cold, even rude in their manner, although when you have the opportunity to talk for a bit with New Yorkers, you'll find that they often go out of their way to be helpful. Many are the tales of visitors lost on the subway who are shepherded to safety by a Good Samaritan from Canarsie (Brooklyn).

America's greatest metropolis presents the visitor with a superfluity of opportunity. You can't do it all; you don't have the time, and nobody has the money. So you will have to make decisions, and the big one will probably be whether you see what

New York does best or you do the things that you like best. On the whole, that's a great choice to have.

Getting Around   Manhattan has a Jekyll-and-Hyde personality: Above 14th Street, the streets form a regular grid pattern, with avenues running north (uptown) and south (downtown) and numbered streets running east and west (crosstown), but below 14th Street, the map takes on a disordered personality, with streets that either angle to align with the shorelines or twist along the route of an ancient cow path. Logic won't help you below 14th Street; only a street map and good directions will.

Other important points of reference are Broadway, which cuts a westward diagonal the length of Manhattan island, and Fifth Avenue, which is the east-west dividing line for street addresses. (Avenue addresses, however, follow no such logic, so always find out what the nearest numbered cross street is.) Between 59th and 110th street, Central Park separates the East Side from the West Side, with transverse roads crossing it only at 66th, 72nd, 79th, 86th, and 96th streets.

By Subway   The 244-mile subway system is the fastest and cheapest way to get around the city. It operates 24 hours a day. You must use a token to enter; tokens cost $1.15 and are sold at token booths that are *usually* open at each station. A token permits unlimited transfers within the subway system.

A few words on safety: Most of the stops in Midtown are crowded with riders all hours of the day or night. Stay among those crowds—there's safety in numbers. At off-peak hours, try to ride in the same car as the conductor; it will stop near a line of light bulbs above the edge of the platform.

By Bus   Most buses follow easy-to-understand routes along the Manhattan grid. Routes go up or down the north-south avenues, east and west on the major two-way crosstown streets. Most bus routes operate 24 hours, but service is infrequent late at night. Bus fare is $1.15 in change only (exact change, no pennies) or a subway token. When you get on the bus you can get a free transfer good for one change to an intersecting route. Legal transfer points are listed on the back of the transfer. Transfers have time limits of at least two hours, often longer. You cannot use the transfer to enter the subway system.

By Taxi   Taxis are usually easy to hail on the street or from a line in front of major hotels. Taxis cost $1.50 for the first ⅕ mile, 25¢ for each ⅕ mile thereafter, and 25¢ for 75 seconds not in motion. A 50¢ surcharge is added to rides begun between 8 PM and 6 AM. There is no charge for extra passengers. Taxi drivers also expect a 15% tip.

By Car   Driving within Manhattan can be a nightmare of gridlocked streets and predatory fellow motorists. Free parking is almost impossible to find in Midtown, and parking lots are exorbitant. If you do drive, don't plan to use your car much for driving within Manhattan.

Guided Tours   **Circle Line Cruises** (Pier 83, west end of 42nd St., tel. 212/563-
Orientation Tours   3200) take a three-hour, 35-mile circumnavigation of Manhattan, with lively narrations, daily early March–December.

Gray Line (900 Eighth Ave. at 53rd St., tel. 212/397-2600) offers a number of different city bus tours, as does **Short Line Tours** (166 W. 46th St., tel 212/354-5122).

Special-Interest **Backstage on Broadway** (tel. 212/575–8065) puts you in a
Tours Broadway theater setting and lets you mingle with show people. Reservations are mandatory. **Art Tours of Manhattan** (tel.
609/921–2647) provides an inside view of museum and gallery
exhibits. **Gallery Passports** (tel. 212/288–3578) takes you to galleries and museums as well as admits you to artists' studios and
lofts in Manhattan. **Soho Art Experience** (tel. 212/219–0810) offers tours of Soho's architecture, galleries, shops, and artists'
lofts. **Doorway to Design** (tel. 212/221–1111) tours fashion and
interior design showrooms as well as artists' private studios.
Harlem Your Way! (tel. 212/690–1687) offers tours of New
York's historic black neighborhood, including Sunday gospel
tours.

Midtown: Rockefeller Center to 57th Street

*Numbers in the margin correspond to points of interest on the
New York City (Uptown) map.*

❶ The heart of midtown Manhattan is **Rockefeller Center,** a complex of 19 buildings occupying nearly 22 acres of prime real estate between Fifth and Seventh avenues and 47th and 52nd
streets. Built during the Great Depression of the 1930s by John
D. Rockefeller, Jr., this city-within-a-city is the capital of the
communications industry, with the headquarters for a TV network (NBC), major publishing companies (Time–Warner Inc.,
McGraw-Hill, Simon & Schuster), and the world's largest
news-gathering organization, the Associated Press. It is an international center housing the consulates of many foreign nations, the U.S. passport office, and ticket offices for numerous
airlines. Most human needs—restaurants, shoe repair, doctors, barbers, banks, post office, bookstores, clothing, variety
stores—can be accommodated within the center, and all parts
of the complex are linked by underground passageways.

Begin a tour at the ice rink on **Lower Plaza** along a little street
called Rockefeller Plaza between 49th and 50th streets.
Crowned by a gold-leaf statue of Prometheus stealing the sa-
cred fire for mankind, this famous New York attraction is an ice
rink from late September through April and an outdoor café
the rest of the year.

Just east of Lower Plaza are the **Channel Gardens,** a promenade
with six pools surrounded by flower beds filled with seasonal
plantings, conceived by artists, floral designers, and sculptors—10 shows a season. They are called Channel Gardens because they separate the British building (to the north) and the
French building (to the south). A huge statue of Atlas supporting the world stands sentry before the **International Building**
on Fifth Avenue between 50th and 51st streets, with its lobby
inspired by ancient Greece and fitted with Grecian marble from
the island of Tenos.

❷ Across Fifth Avenue stands the Gothic-style **St. Patrick's,** the
Roman Catholic cathedral of New York. Dedicated to the patron saint of the Irish—then and now one of New York's principal ethnic groups—the white marble and stone structure was
begun in 1858, consecrated in 1879, and completed in 1906.
Among the statues in the alcoves around the nave is a striking
modern rendering of the American saint, Mother Seton.

New York City (Uptown)

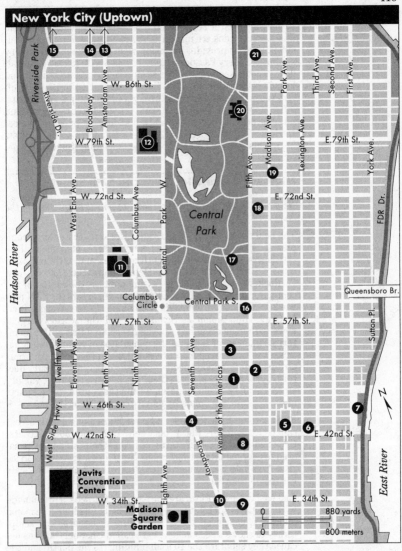

American Museum of
Natural History, **12**

Cathedral of St. John
the Divine, **13**

Central Park, **17**

Chrysler Building, **6**

Columbia
University, **14**

Empire State
Building, **9**

Frick Collection, **18**

Grand Army Plaza, **16**

Grand Central
Terminal, **5**

Grant's Tomb, **15**

Guggenheim
Museum, **21**

Herald Square, **10**

Lincoln Center, **11**

Metropolitan Museum
of Art, **20**

Museum of
Modern Art, **3**

New York Public
Library, **8**

Rockefeller Center, **1**

St. Patrick's, **2**

Times Square, **4**

United Nations
Headquarters, **7**

Whitney Museum of
American Art, **19**

One of Rockefeller Center's main attractions is the **GE Building** (formerly the RCA Building, until GE acquired RCA in 1986), the 70-story tower that occupies the block bounded by Rockefeller Plaza, Avenue of the Americas (which New Yorkers call Sixth Avenue), and 49th and 50th streets. The building is headquarters for the NBC television network. You can take a tour of the NBC studios: One leaves every 15 minutes, 9:30–4, Monday through Saturday, and Sundays during the summer; Thursdays 9:30–8 (cost: $7.25).

NBC isn't the only network headquartered in Manhattan. CBS is located in a black monolith, popularly called Black Rock, at Sixth Avenue and 53rd Street. ABC, once a close neighbor, has now moved its main office to 66th Street on the West Side.

Across 50th Street from the GE Building is America's largest indoor theater, the 6,000-seat **Radio City Music Hall.** Home of the fabulous Rockettes chorus line (which actually started out in St. Louis in 1925), Radio City was built as a movie theater with live shows; today it produces concerts, Christmas and Easter extravaganzas, awards presentations, and other special events. On most days you can tour the premises (tel. 212/632–4041 for prices and availability).

Time Out   For supercasual eating when the weather is good, the **Sixth Avenue food vendors** near Rockefeller Center offer the best selection in the city. À la "cart" diners can have tacos, falafel, souvlaki, tempura, Indian curry, Afghani kofta kebabs, or Caribbean beef jerky. Locations change periodically, so look around until you find what you like. No dish is more than $5, and most cost much less. For seating, perch on the benches and low walls in the plazas beside the massive Sixth Avenue office towers.

Two blocks north, the **Museum of Television and Radio** (formerly the Museum of Broadcasting) presents special screenings, usually retrospectives of the work of a particular radio or TV star or of an era in broadcasting history. The museum also offers its stupendous collection of more than 25,000 TV shows, 10,000 commercials, and 15,000 radio programs for individual screening. *25 W. 52nd St., tel. 212/752–7684. Suggested contribution: $4 adults, $3 students, $2 senior citizens and children under 13. Open Tues. noon–8, Wed.–Sat. noon–5.*

❸ On 53rd Street is the famous **Museum of Modern Art** (MOMA), a bright and airy four-story structure built around a secluded sculpture garden. All the important movements of modern art are represented here: Cubism, Surrealism, Abstract Expressionism, Minimalism, and Postmodernism. Some of the world's most famous paintings are hung on the second floor, including Van Gogh's *Starry Night*, Picasso's *Les Demoiselles d'Avignon*, Matisse's *Dance*. The superstars of American art appear on the third floor: Andrew Wyeth, Andy Warhol, Jackson Pollock, Frank Stella, Mark Rothko—to name a few. Afternoon and evening film showings, mostly foreign films and classics, are free with the price of admission; tickets are distributed in the lobby, and on some days they go fast. *11 W. 53rd St., tel. 212/708–9400. Admission: $7 adults, $4 students and senior citizens, children under 16 free. Pay what you wish Thurs. 5–9. Open daily 11–6, Thurs. 11–9; closed Wed.*

The stretch of Fifth Avenue between Rockefeller Center and 57th Street glitters with world-famous shops, including **Saks Fifth Avenue** (Fifth Ave. at 50th St.), **Gucci** (actually two Guccis, on adjacent corners of Fifth Avenue and 54th Street), and **Tiffany & Co.** (727 Fifth Ave., at 57thSt.). Between 56th and 57th Street is the grand Fifth Avenue entrance of **Trump Tower,** an exclusive 68-story, dark-glass apartment house built by the notorious developer Donald Trump. Its six-story shopping atrium, paneled in pinkish-orange marble and trimmed with high-gloss brass, has a fountain cascading against one wall, drowning out the clamor of the city. Shops are chic and tony, among them Cartier, Bucellati, and Abercrombie & Fitch, and the public restrooms in the basement are invitingly clean and spacious.

Midtown: 42nd Street

Crossroads of the World, Great White Way, the New Year's Eve Capital of America, **Times Square** remains one of New York's principal energy centers. Like most New York City "squares," Times Square is a triangle, this one formed by Broadway, Seventh Avenue, and 42nd Street. The square itself is occupied by the former Times Tower, now simply **One Times Square Plaza.** On its roof, workmen still lower the 200-pound New Year's Eve ball down the flagpole by hand, just as they have since 1908. The current offices of *The New York Times* occupy much of the block between Seventh and Eighth avenues.

At Duffy Square, on 47th Street between Broadway and Seventh Avenue, the **TKTS booth** of the Theater Development Fund sells half-price day-of-performance tickets to Broadway and Off-Broadway shows (*see* The Arts, *below*). Most Broadway theaters are located on the streets west of Broadway from 52nd Street to 44th Street. Today a group of thriving Off-Broadway playhouses west of Ninth Avenue are the only live theater on 42nd Street; the block between Seventh and Eighth avenues that was once the heart of the theater district is now a disreputable strip of porno shops, movie houses, and loiterers, all marking time while the city assembles the pieces of a redevelopment project that will transform the area.

Bryant Park and the **New York Public Library** (*see* Midtown: South of 42nd Street, *below*) occupy the entire block bounded by 42nd Street, Fifth Avenue, 40th Street, and Sixth Avenue. Named for the poet and editor William Cullen Bryant (1794–1878), Bryant Park was the site of America's first World's Fair, the Crystal Palace Exhibition of 1853–1854. For a while the park was getting rather shaggy, but an elaborate landscape and restoration program should be completed by the time you read this. Inside the park, along 42nd Street, **Bryant Park Half-Price Tickets** sells same-day tickets for music and dance performances throughout the city (*see* The Arts, *below*).

Continue east on 42nd Street to **Grand Central Terminal** (never "station," since all runs begin or end here). Constructed between 1903 and 1913, this Manhattan landmark was originally designed by a Minnesota architectural firm and later gussied up with Beaux Arts ornamentation. Make sure you notice the three huge windows separated by columns, and the Beaux Arts clock and sculpture on the facade above 42nd Street. The 12-story ceiling of the cavernous Main Concourse displays the constellations of the Zodiac. *Tel. 212/935–3960. Free tours Wed. at 12:30 PM.*

Ask New Yorkers to name their favorite skyscraper, and the response you'll hear most often will be the **Chrysler Building** at 42nd Street and Lexington Avenue. The Chrysler Corporation itself is long gone, yet the graceful shaft that culminates in a stainless steel point still captivates the eye and the imagination. The building has no observation deck, but you can examine the elegant dark lobby faced with African marble and covered with a ceiling mural that honors transportation and human endeavor.

For a tranquil spot to sit and rest your feet, step inside the 12-story atrium of **Ford Foundation Building** (320 E. 43rd St.), a one-third-acre greenhouse containing a terraced garden, a still pool, and a couple dozen full-grown trees (open weekdays 9–5).

The **United Nations Headquarters** complex occupies a lushly landscaped riverside tract along First Avenue between 42nd and 48th streets. A line of flagpoles with banners representing the current roster of 159 member nations stands before the striking 550-foot slab of the Secretariat Building. The interior corridors overflow with imaginatively diverse artwork donated by member nations. Free tickets to most sessions are available on a first-come, first-served basis 15 minutes before sessions begin; pick them up in the General Assembly lobby. Visitors can take early luncheon in the Delegates Dining Room or eat anytime in a public coffee shop. *Tel. 212/963–7713. Admission: $5.50 adults, $3.50 students. Children under 5 not permitted. One-hour tours leave the General Assembly lobby every 15–20 minutes, daily 9:15–4:45.*

Midtown: South of 42nd Street

At 42nd Street and Fifth Avenue stands the central research building of the **New York Public Library,** one of the largest research libraries in the world. Ascend the sweeping staircase between the two crouching Tennessee marble lions—dubbed "Patience" and "Fortitude" by Mayor Fiorello La Guardia, who visited the facility to "read between the lions." Periodic exhibitions focus on literary matters. Free one-hour tours, each as different as the library volunteer who leads it, are given Monday through Saturday at 11 AM and 2 PM. *Tel. 212/930–0800. Open Mon.–Wed. 10–8:45, Thurs.–Sat. 10–5:45.*

Head down Fifth Avenue, passing **Lord & Taylor** (424 Fifth Ave. at 38th St.) department store, a relatively uncrowded establishment that emphasizes well-made clothing by American designers. At 34th Street, the **Empire State Building** may no longer be the world's tallest, but it is certainly the world's best-loved skyscraper. The Art Deco playground for King Kong opened in 1931 after only about a year of construction. More than 16,000 people work in the building, and more than 2.5 million people a year visit the 86th-floor and 102nd-floor observatories. At night the top 30 stories are illuminated with colors appropriate to the season (red and green around Christmas; orange and brown for Halloween). *Fifth Ave. at 34th St., tel. 212/736–3100. Admission: $3.50 adults, $1.75 children under 12. Open daily 9:30 AM–midnight.*

⑩ Go west on 34th Street to **Herald Square,** a focal shopping district that's somewhat less upscale than 57th Street and Fifth Avenue. Its centerpiece is **Macy's,** the world's largest department store under one roof (between Broadway and Seventh Avenue on 34th Street). On the south side of 34th Street is **Herald Center,** a vertical shopping mall; a block south is the nine-story **A&S Plaza,** a mall containing 120 shops and restaurants. Head north on Seventh Avenue, and you enter New York's tumultuous **Garment District:** Street signs declare the stretch of Seventh Avenue between 31st and 41st streets "Fashion Avenue." The Garment District teems with warehouses, workshops, and showrooms that manufacture and finish mostly women's and children's clothing. On weekdays the streets are crowded with trucks and the sidewalks swarm with daredevil deliverymen hauling garment racks between factories and subcontractors.

Upper West Side

The West Side story begins at **Columbus Circle,** where a statue of Christopher himself crowns a stately pillar at the intersection of Broadway, Eighth Avenue, Central Park West, and Central Park South. Columbus Circle is a good place to begin any tour of New York, for it is the location of the **New York Convention and Visitors Bureau.** *2 Columbus Circle, tel. 212/397-8222. Open weekdays 9–6.*

Covering an eight-block area west of Broadway between 62nd
⑪ and 66th streets, **Lincoln Center** is New York's major-league performing arts complex, with several institutions clustered around the grand fountain in a central plaza. **Avery Fisher Hall,** named after the founder of Fisher Radio, hosts the New York Philharmonic Orchestra. The Metropolitan Opera and American Ballet Theatre perform at the **Metropolitan Opera House.** The **New York State Theater** is home to the New York City Ballet and the New York City Opera. The **Guggenheim Bandshell,** south of the Met, has free open-air concerts in summer. A single structure devoted to drama includes the **Vivian Beaumont** and **Mitzi E. Newhouse** theaters. Across 65th Street lies the world-renowned **Juilliard School,** which houses **Alice Tully Hall,** home of the Chamber Music Society of Lincoln Center, and the New York Film Festival. A one-hour guided "Take-the-Tour" covers all the grand theaters. *Tel. 212/877–1800, ext. 512, for schedule. Admission: $6.25 adults, $5.25 students and senior citizens, $3.50 children.*

Walk one block east on 67th Street to the edge of Central Park. Just inside the park, at 66th Street, is **Tavern on the Green,** a landmark spot for romantic indoor and outdoor dining. The stretch of Central Park roadway between the restaurant and the verdant Sheep Meadow is the finish line for the New York Marathon (the first Sunday in November). The stately **Dakota** presides at the corner of Central Park West and 72nd Street. One of the first fashionable West Side apartment buildings, this powerful, relatively squat structure is now better known as the place where *Rosemary's Baby* was filmed and John Lennon was shot. Directly across Central Park West, a hilly stretch of parkland has been designated **Strawberry Fields** in Lennon's memory. The city's oldest museum, the **New-York Historical Society** displays original Audubon watercolors, Early American toys, Tiffany lamps, antique vehicles, and Hudson River School landscapes. *170 Central Park West at 77th*

St., tel. 212/873–3400. Admission: $3 adults, $2 senior citizens, $1 children under 12; pay what you wish Tues. Open Tues.–Sun. 10–5.

12 The **American Museum of Natural History,** the adjacent **Hayden Planetarium,** and the surrounding grounds take up a four-block tract bounded by Central Park West, Columbus Avenue, and 77th and 81st streets. With a collection of more than 36 million items, the museum certainly has something for every taste, from a 94-foot blue whale to the 563-carat Star of India sapphire. The Naturemax Theater projects films on a giant screen. The Hayden Planetarium (on 81st Street) has two stories of exhibits and Sky Shows projected on 22 wraparound screens. *Museum: tel. 212/769–5100. Suggested contribution: $5 adults, $2.50 children. Open Sun.–Tues. and Thurs. 10–5:45; Wed., Fri., and Sat. 10–9. Planetarium: tel. 212/769–5920. Admission: $4 adults, $3 senior citizens, members, and students, $2 children; $7 for laser show. Open weekdays 12:30–4:45, Sat. 10–5:45, Sun. noon–5:45. Naturemax Theater admission: $5–$7 adults, $2.50–$3.50 children.*

From here, you may want to take a taxi or the bus up Amsterdam Avenue to an impressive trio of institutions on the Upper
13 Upper West Side. Your first stop is the **Cathedral of St. John the Divine** (Amsterdam Ave. at 112th St. tel. 212/316–7400), New York's major Episcopal church and the largest Gothic cathedral in the world (St. Peter's Basilica in Rome is the largest church of any kind). The vast 600-foot nave can seat 5,000 worshipers, and small, uniquely outfitted chapels border the nave. It's still perhaps 100 years from completion, and master craftsmen are instructing neighborhood youth in the traditional methods of
14 stonecutting and carving. The main campus of **Columbia University** (founded 1754), a large and wealthy private institution, occupies an area bounded by 114th and 121st streets, Broadway, and Amsterdam Avenue. Enter from either direction on 116th Street: The buildings so effectively wall off the city that it's easy to believe you've been transported to a more rustic Ivy League campus. The central campus has the rotunda-topped Low Memorial Library to the north and the massive Butler Library to the south. Riverside Church (Riverside Dr. at 122nd St., tel. 212/222–5900) is nondenominational, interracial, international, extremely political, and socially conscious. Its massive mock-Gothic structure is topped by a 356-foot observation tower (admission: $1) and a 74-bell carillon, the largest in the world, whose bells range in weight from 10 pounds to 20 tons. Across Riverside Drive, in Riverside Park, stands the General Grant National Memorial Monument, commonly
15 known as **Grant's Tomb,** where the Civil War general and two-term president and his wife rest. In addition to the sarcophagi, the white granite mausoleum contains photographs and Grant memorabilia. *Riverside Dr. at 122nd St., tel. 212/666–1640. Admission free. Open Wed.–Sun. 9–4:30.*

Central Park and the Upper East Side

Begin a tour of the Upper East Side, long the city's most expen-
16 sive and desirable residential area, at **Grand Army Plaza,** an open space along Fifth Avenue between 58th and 60th streets. Grand Army Plaza is flanked by a brightly gilded equestrian statue of William Tecumseh Sherman on the north and the Pulitzer (of Pulitzer Prize fame) Fountain to the south. At the

western border of that space, shaped like the token for a hotel in Monopoly, stands the **Plaza Hotel,** a registered historical landmark that has been in fashion for upper-crust transients, charity balls, coming-out parties, and romantic rendezvous since 1907.

At Grand Army Plaza, or all along Central Park South, look for horse-drawn carriage offering rides through the park. The city sets the official rates ($34 for the first 20 minutes, $10 for each additional 15 minutes), but drivers will often try to get more. Be sure to agree on a price in advance.

At Fifth Avenue and 58th Street, on the ground floor of the General Motors Building, is the flagship of the legendary **F.A.O. Schwarz** toy store. A vast selection, good lighting, and gorgeous displays make this a pleasant place to shop—and somewhat compensate for the lofty price tags.

17 **Central Park** is the 843-acre space bounded by 59th Street and 110th Street, Fifth Avenue and Central Park West (Eighth Avenue). Central Park was designed by Frederick Law Olmsted and Calvert Vaux and constructed by a crew of 3,000 mainly Irish workmen and 400 horses. Today Central Park hosts just about any activity a city dweller might engage in out of doors: jogging, cycling, horseback riding, softball, ice skating, croquet, tennis, bird-watching, boating, chess, checkers, theater, concerts, skateboarding, and break dancing. Central Park is reasonably safe during the day, though the frightening attack on a jogger in 1989 has reminded New Yorkers to stay out of it at night. *Tel. 212/397–3156 for general information, 212/360–1333 for a recorded message on city park events, 212/427–4040 for information on weekend walks and talks led by Urban Park Rangers. Bus tours are offered on Tues. and Thurs.*

Stroll north along East Drive and follow the path on your right to visit the **Central Park Zoo,** a compact wildlife showcase that recreates a polar, temperate, and tropical climate habitats; polar bears and penguins are among the most popular attractions. Admission to the adjacent children's zoo, which at press time was closed for renovations, is granted to adults only when accompanied by a child. *Central Park at E. 64th St., tel. 212/439–6500. Admission: $2.50 adults, 50¢ children 3–12, $1.25 senior citizens. Open Apr.–Oct., weekdays 10–4:30 (May–Sept., Tues. 10–7), weekends and holidays 10–5; Nov.–Mar., daily 10–4. Children under 16 not admitted without an adult.*

East Drive loops around to **The Mall,** a broad walkway lined with stately elms and busts of famous men. Just north of the mall, the handsome **Bethesda Fountain** and the graceful iron bridge over **the Lake** often model for "Sunday in New York" postcard pictures. To the west is **Strawberry Fields,** a cunningly landscaped garden dedicated to the memory of John Lennon. East of the Lake, at the **Loeb Boathouse,** you can rent a rowboat to cruise the lake or a bike for a spin around the park. You can also buy a fast-food snack or a sit-down lunch.

The 72nd Street transverse drive leads east out of the park to Fifth Avenue, where, in the last decade of the 19th century, the Astors, the Carnegies, the Vanderbilts, and the Whitneys moved into palatial stone mansions overlooking newly fashionable Central Park. Few of the residential mansions remain. Some were supplanted by high-rise apartments, others were transformed into museums or foundation headquarters, giving this stretch of Fifth Avenue the nickname "Museum Mile."

⑱ Backtrack a couple of blocks to 70th Street, to the **Frick Collection,** housed in the mansion built by the Pittsburgh coke and steel baron Henry Clay Frick to display his private collection of art. A bona fide masterpiece graces almost every room: Rembrandt's *The Polish Rider,* Fragonard's series *The Progress of Love,* Jan Van Ecyk's *Virgin and Child with Saints and Donor,* and distinguished works by Bellini, Vermeer, Titian, El Greco, Turner, Whistler, and Gainsborough. Even the rest area is a masterpiece: a tranquil indoor court with a fountain and glass ceiling. *1 E. 70th St., tel. 212/288–0700. Admission: $3 adults, $1.50 students and senior citizens. Open Tues.–Sat. 10–6, Sun. 1–6, closed holidays.*

One block east of Fifth Avenue, on Madison Avenue at 75th
⑲ Street, the **Whitney Museum of American Art** is a gray granite vault devoted exclusively to 20th-century American work, from naturalism and impressionism to pop art, abstractionism, and whatever comes next. *945 Madison Ave. at 75th St., tel. 212/ 570–3676. Admission: $5 adults, $3 senior citizens; free for students with school ID and children at all times and for everyone Tues. 6–8. Open Tues. 1–8, Wed.–Sat. 11–5, Sun. noon–6.*

⑳ Back on Fifth Avenue, the **Metropolitan Museum of Art** is the largest art museum in the Western Hemisphere (1.6 million square feet), and its permanent collection of some 3 million works of art includes items from prehistoric to modern times from all areas of the world. Its 19 curatorial departments include the world's most comprehensive collection of American art, and its holdings of European art are unequaled outside Europe. The museum also has one of the world's best collections of ancient Greek, Roman, and Egyptian art. Walking tours and lectures are free with your admission contribution. *Fifth Ave. at 82nd St., tel. 212/535–7710. Suggested contribution: $5 adults, $2.50 senior citizens and students, children free. Open Fri. and Sat. 9:30–8:45, Tues.–Thurs. and Sun. 9:30–5:15.*

㉑ Frank Lloyd Wright's **Guggenheim Museum** is a six-story spiral rotunda through which you wind down past mobiles, stabiles, and other exemplars of modern art. Displays alternate new artists and modern masters; the permanent collection includes more than 20 Picassos. A newly expanded and fully restored Guggenheim Museum reopened in the fall of 1991 after being closed for a half-year. A new tower and expanded gallery space display the newly acquired Panza Collection of minimalist art, among other works. *1071 Fifth Ave. at 89th St., tel. 212/360–3513. Admission: $4.50 adults, $2.50 students and senior citizens; free Tues. 5–7:45. Open Tues. 11–7:45, Wed.– Sun. 11–4:45.*

On up Fifth Avenue, you can visit **The National Academy of Design** (1083 Fifth Ave. at 89th St., tel. 212/369–4880), which exhibits fine art by little-known American and European artists of the past; the **Cooper-Hewitt Museum** (2 E. 91st St., tel. 212/ 860–6868), a museum of American Design housed in Andrew Carnegie's former home; the extensive collection of Judaica at the **Jewish Museum** (1109 Fifth Ave. at 92nd St., tel. 212/860– 1889); the photography exhibits at the **International Center of Photography** (1130 Fifth Ave., tel. 212/860–1777); the **Museum of the City of New York** (Fifth Ave. at 103rd St., tel. 212/534– 1672), with its fascinating exhibits on the city's past; and **El Museo del Barrio** (1230 Fifth Ave. at 104th St., tel. 212/831–

7272) which concentrates on Latin culture in general, with a particular emphasis on Puerto Rican art. Most Museum Mile institutions are closed on Mondays and open late on Tuesdays.

Time Out **Jackson Hole** (Madison Ave. at 91st St.) is a cheerful spot that serves the great American hamburger, sandwiches, omelets, chicken, and salads. Ski posters evoke the mood of the eponymous Wyoming resort.

Greenwich Village

Numbers in the margin correspond to points of interest on the New York City (Downtown) map.

Once the raffish haunt of writers and artists, today Greenwich Village—New Yorkers almost invariably speak of it simply as "the Village"—is inhabited principally by affluent professionals, students, and others aspiring to blend the flavor of small-town life with the bright lights of the big city. The heart of the **22** Village is **Washington Square** at the foot of Fifth Avenue. Its centerpiece is Washington Arch, built in 1892 to commemorate the 100th anniversary of George Washington's presidential inauguration. Washington Square started out as a cemetery; in the early 1800s it was a parade ground and the site of public executions; later it became the focus of a fashionable residential neighborhood. By the early 1980s, Washington Square had deteriorated into a tawdry place only a drug dealer could love. Then community activism motivated a police crackdown that sent the drug traffic elsewhere and made Washington Square comfortable again for Frisbee players, street musicians, skateboarders, jugglers, stand-up comics, sitters, strollers, and the twice-a-year art fair. Most of the buildings bordering Washington Square belong to New York University. The row of redbrick federal town houses along Washington Square North, between Fifth Avenue and University Place, includes **20 Washington Square North,** the oldest building (1820) on the block.

Turn north on MacDougal Street and walk a half-block to **MacDougal Alley,** a private (fenced with locked gate) cobblestone street where stables and carriage houses have been converted into charming homes adorned with gas lamps.

Eighth Street, the main commercial strip of the Village, is not the "real" Greenwich Village but a collection of fast-food purveyors, poster and record shops, and trendy clothing stores. Follow it west to Sixth Avenue and turn right. The triangle formed by West 10th Street, Sixth Avenue, and Greenwich Avenue originally held a greenmarket, a jail, and the magnificent red Gothic-style courthouse that is now the **Jefferson Market Library.** Over the years the structure has housed a number of government agencies (public works, civil defense, census bureau, police academy) but was on the verge of demolition when public-spirited citizens saved it and turned it into a public library in 1967. Go inside to look at the handsome interior doorways and climb the graceful circular stairway.

Take Christopher Street, which veers off from the southern end of the library triangle, a few steps to **Gay Street.** A bending lane lined with small row houses circa 1810, Gay Street was originally a black neighborhood and later a strip of speakeas-
23 ies. At **Sheridan Square,** Christopher Street becomes the heart

New York City (Downtown)

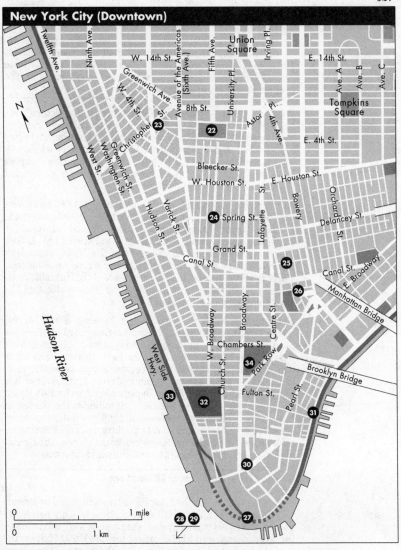

City Hall, **34**
Ellis Island, **29**
Mott Street, **26**
Mulberry Street, **25**
Sheridan Square, **23**
South Street Seaport
Historic District, **31**
Staten Island Ferry
Terminal, **27**
Statue of Liberty, **28**

Wall Street, **30**
Washington
Square, **22**
West Broadway, **24**
World Trade
Center, **32**
World Financial
Center, **33**

of New York's gay community and the location of many intriguing boutiques.

Time Out Where Christopher meets Grove Street and Waverly Place, **Pierre's** (170 Waverly Pl., tel. 212/929–7194) is a friendly little French corner bistro. The sumptuous couscous and the profiterole are two specialties.

West of Seventh Avenue, the Village turns into a picture-book town of twisting, tree-lined streets, quaint houses, and tiny restaurants. Follow Grove Street from Sheridan Square to corner of Grove and Bedford streets for a glimpse of what New York looked like in the early 19th century. Grove Street curves before the iron gate of **Grove Court,** an enclave of brick-fronted town houses of the middle 1800s.

At the end of Grove Street, on Hudson Street, is **St. Luke's-in-the-Fields,** a simple country church whose grounds are made available to church members and neighborhood residents for gardening space. Head south on Hudson Street to **St. Luke's Place,** a row of classic town houses of the 1860s, shaded by graceful ginkgo trees. Theodore Dreiser wrote *An American Tragedy* at No. 16. No. 12 is the residence of the Huxtable family depicted in the credits of *The Cosby Show*—although the Huxtables purportedly live in Brooklyn.

Heading back east, St. Luke's Place becomes Leroy Street, which terminates in an old Italian neighborhood at Bleecker Street. Amazingly unchanged amid all the Village gentrification, Bleecker between Sixth and Seventh avenues abounds with fragrant Italian bakeries, butcher shops, vegetable markets, pizza stands, and restaurants. Across Sixth Avenue lies the stretch of Bleecker Street depicted in songs by Bob Dylan and other folk singers of the 1960s. Standing in the shadow of New York University, the area around the intersection of Bleecker and MacDougal streets attracts a young crowd to its cafés, bars, jazz clubs, coffeehouses, pizza stands, Off-Broadway theaters, cabarets, and unpretentious restaurants.

SoHo, Little Italy, and Chinatown

SoHo (the district **S**outh of **Ho**uston Street, bounded by Broadway, Canal Street, and Sixth Avenue) became a hip neighborhood in the 1970s when impoverished artists were attracted to the large, cheap, well-lighted spaces provided in its 19th-century cast-iron factories and warehouses. Today, rising rents have forced out all but the most successful artists, but SoHo offers architecture and art, highstyle shopping, and plenty of intriguing places to eat and drink. **West Broadway** (which runs parallel to and four blocks west of Broadway) is SoHo's main drag and the location of many shops and galleries (*see* Shopping, *below*). SoHo's finest cast-iron architecture lies east of West Broadway, on Wooster and Greene streets. (Note the old-fashioned pavements of Belgian blocks, a smoother successor to the traditional cobblestone.) Because cast-iron walls were lighter and less expensive than stone, they were produced from standardized molds to mimic any architectural style: Italianate, Victorian Gothic, and neo-Greek facades sprout along the streets of SoHo. A classic of the cast-iron genre is the 1857 **Haughwout Building** at 488 Broadway, inspired by a Venetian palace,

24

which contained the world's first commercial passenger elevator, a steam-powered device invented by Elisha Graves Otis.

㉕ Walk east to **Mulberry Street,** and you enter **Little Italy.** Look south on Mulberry Street: Most of its buildings are of the late 19th-century New York tenement style known as railroad flats, predominant in densely populated lower Manhattan until 1901, when the city passed an ordinance requiring air shafts in the interior of buildings. Today Mulberry Street between Broome and Canal consists entirely of restaurants, cafés, bakeries, imported food shops, and souvenir stores. Former residents keep returning to Little Italy's venerable institutions.

Time Out *Ferrara's* (195 Grand St.) is a 100-year-old pastry shop that ships its creations—cannoli, peasant pie, Italian rum cake—all over the world.

Umberto's Clam House (129 Mulberry St., tel. 212/431–7545), where mobster Joey Gallo munched his last scungili in 1973, occupies the northwest corner of Mulberry and Hester streets. Around the corner on Baxter Street stands the **San Gennaro Church** (officially, Most Precious Blood Church, National Shrine of San Gennaro), which sponsors Little Italy's annual keynote event, the Feast of San Gennaro. When it happens each September, the streets become a bright and turbulent Italian kitchen.

In theory, Little Italy and Chinatown are divided by Canal Street, the bustling artery that links the Holland Tunnel (to New Jersey) and the Manhattan Bridge (to Brooklyn). However, in recent years Chinatown has gained an influx of immigrants from the People's Republic of China, Taiwan, and especially Hong Kong, and Chinatown has expanded beyond its traditional borders into Little Italy to the north and the formerly Jewish Lower East Side to the east. Canal Street itself abounds with crowded markets bursting with mounds of fresh seafood and strangely shaped vegetables in extraterrestrial
㉖ shades of green. **Mott Street** is the principal business street of the neighborhood. Narrow and twisting, crammed with souvenir shops and restaurants, and crowded with pedestrians at all hours of the day or night, Mott Street looks the way you might expect Chinatown to look. The **New York Chinatown History Project** (70 Mulberry St., corner of Bayard and Mulberry, tel. 212/619–4785) shows interactive photographic exhibitions, has a bookstore, and offers a walking tour of Chinatown. Double back to Pell Street, a narrow lane of wall-to-wall restaurants whose neon signs stretch halfway across the thoroughfare. Turn onto **Doyers Street,** a twisty little byway of storefront barber shops and restaurants, and then duck into Wing Fat, a new multilevel shopping mall. Exit onto **Chatham Square,** where 10 converging streets create pandemonium for autos and a nightmare for pedestrians. A Chinese arch honoring Chinese casualties in American wars stands on an island in the eye of the storm. Go back past Chatham Square and up the Bowery to **Confucius Plaza,** the open area monitored by a statue of Confucius and a high-rise apartment complex named for him. Head up the Bowery toward the grand arch and colonnade entrance to the Manhattan Bridge, and you'll soon return to Canal Street.

Lower Manhattan

Lower Manhattan is relatively small in area yet dense with attractions. The New Amsterdam colony was established here by
the Dutch in 1625, and the first capital of the United States was
located in the area. Wall Street is here, which means the New
York and American stock exchanges plus innumerable banks
and other financial institutions. The South Street Seaport Museum project recreates the New York's past history as a major
port.

27 The **Staten Island Ferry Terminal,** at the southernmost tip of
Manhattan, is the starting point for a 20-to-30-minute ride
across New York harbor. For only 50¢ *round-trip* you can take
in great views of the Manhattan skyline, the Statue of Liberty,
and the Verrazano Narrows Bridge between Brooklyn and
Staten Island, the world's longest suspension bridge.

To the west of South Ferry lies **Battery Park,** a verdant landfill
loaded with monuments and sculpture at Manhattan's green
toe. At **Castle Clinton,** a circular brick fortress originally built
28 as a harbor defense, you can buy a ticket to visit the **Statue of**
29 **Liberty** (tel. 212/363-3200) and **Ellis Island** (tel. 212/883-1986).
New York's trademark statue stands tall on Liberty Island,
guarding the mouth of New York Harbor; you can take an elevator 10 stories to the top of the pedestal, and the strong of heart
and limb can climb another 12 stories to the crown. Ellis Island,
now a national monument, won its fame as a federal immigration facility that processed 17 million men, women, and children between 1892 and 1954—the ancestors of more than 40%
of the Americans living today. *Round-trip fare: $6 adults, $3
children 3–17. Daily departures 9–3; extended hours in summer.*

Follow Pearl Street east from Battery Park two blocks to reach
Fraunces Tavern, a combination restaurant, bar, and museum
that occupies a Colonial (brick exterior, cream-colored portico
and balcony) tavern built in 1719 and restored in 1907. Best remembered as the site of George Washington's farewell address
to his officers celebrating the British evacuation of New York in
1783, Fraunces Tavern contains two fully furnished period
rooms and other displays of 18th- and 19th-century American
history. *Broad and Pearl Sts., tel. 212/425-1778. Admission:
$2.50 adults, $1 students, senior citizens, and children. Restaurant open weekdays. Museum open weekdays 10–4.*

30 From Battery Park, walk up Broadway to **Wall Street,** where on
your left you'll see **Trinity Church,** established as an Anglican
parish in 1697. The present structure (1846) ranked as the
city's tallest building for most of the last half of the 19th century. Once completely jet black from decades of pollutants, the
exterior sandstone is being restored to its original pink color.
Alexander Hamilton is buried beneath a white stone pyramid
in Trinity's south-side graveyard; Robert Fulton, the inventor
of the steamboat, lies nearby. *Tours daily at 2; free 40-min concerts, Tues. 12:45.*

Arguably the most famous thoroughfare in the world, **Wall**
Street was where stock traders used to conduct business along
the sidewalks or at tables beneath a sheltering buttonwood
tree. Wall Street's principal facility today is the **New York**
Stock Exchange, which has its august Corinthian main en-

trance around the corner on Broad Street. Enter at 20 Broad Street and, after what may be a lengthy wait, take an elevator to the third-floor visitor center. A self-guided tour, informative slide shows, video displays, and guides may help you interpret the chaos that seems to be transpiring down on the trading floor. *Tel. 212/656–5167. Free tickets available at 20 Broad St. at 9:30. Open weekdays 9:20–3:30.*

Across the street, a regal statue of George Washington stands at the spot where he was sworn in as the first U.S. president in 1789. The Federal Hall of that day was demolished when the capital moved to Philadelphia. The current **Federal Hall National Memorial** is a stately period structure containing exhibits on New York and Wall Street.

Go north on Broadway to Fulton Street, where you have two choices. If you turn right and go down to the East River, you'll find the **South Street Seaport Historic District.** A reminder of Manhattan's role as a great seaport, this reconstructed 19th-century marketplace, within view of Wall Street's ultramodern skyscrapers, is home to innumerable shops and restaurants, art galleries, old clipper ships, and cruise boats. Cross South Street to Pier 16 to view the historic ships: the second-largest sailing ship in existence, *Peking;* the full-rigged *Wavertree;* and the lightship *Ambrose.* Pier 16 is the departure point for the 90-minute **Seaport Harbor Line Cruise** (tel. 212/385–0791; fare $12 adults, $6 children). *Admission to ships, galleries, walking tours, Maritime Crafts Center, films, and other Seaport events: $6 adults, $5 senior citizens, $4 students, $3 children. Open daily 10–5, longer hours in summer.*

Time Out   At the dockside shopping mall Pier 17, stop by the third-floor **Promenade Food Court** for a casual lunch with a spectacular view of the East River, Brooklyn Bridge, and Brooklyn Heights.

If instead you head west on Fulton Street, on the northwest corner of Broadway and Fulton Street you'll find **St. Paul's Chapel**, the second-oldest structure (1766) in Manhattan and the only surviving example of Colonial architecture. St. Paul's displays George Washington's pew and is open throughout the day for prayer, rest, and meditation. Right behind the chapel looms the **World Trade Center,** a 16-acre complex that contains New York's two tallest buildings, a hotel, a shopping center, a huge main plaza, and, somewhat incongruously, a farmers' market on Tuesday and Thursday in a parking area along Church Street. The Observation Deck is located on the 107th floor of 2 World Trade Center, yet the ride up takes only 58 seconds. The view is potentially 55 miles, but signs at the ticket window (admission: $3.50 adults, $1.75 children and senior citizens, children under 6 free; open daily 9:30 AM–11:30 PM) disclose how far you can see that day and whether the outdoor deck is open. You get the same view with a costly meal at **Windows on the World** atop 1 World Trade Center; prices are somewhat lower for breakfast or for drinks and "grazing" at the **Hors d'Oeuvrerie** (tel. 212/938–1111; jacket required).

The rock and soil excavated for the World Trade Center begat **Battery Park City,** a hundred new acres of Manhattan reached by a pedestrian overpass above West Street on the western border of the center. Battery Park City is a complete neighborhood built from scratch, with office buildings, high-rise apartment houses, low-rise old-looking town houses, and a charming promenade overlooking the Hudson River. The **World Financial Center,** a mammoth granite-and-glass commercial complex, is the centerpeice of the development, featuring upscale shops clustered around a palatial public space called the Winter Garden, which has become a popular venue for free performances by top–flight musicians and dancers (tel. 212/945–0505). The room, adorned by a vaulted-glass roof, an immense stairway, and 16 palm trees (carefully transplanted from Borrigo Springs, California), hosts an array of performances through the center's Arts and Events program.

Return to Broadway and head north to the so-called Cathedral of Commerce, the ornate **Woolworth Building** (Park Pl. at Broadway), once the world's tallest building at 792 feet. Sculptures set into arches in the lobby ceiling represent old man Woolworth pinching his pennies and the architect Cass Gilbert contemplating a model of his creation. Across the street is triangular **City Hall Park,** which in its day has hosted hangings, riots, meetings, and demonstrations; much of the time now it accommodates brown-baggers and pigeon feeders. **City Hall,** built between 1803 and 1811, is unexpectedly elegant, sedate, graceful, small-scale, and charming. Its exterior columns reflect the classical influence of Greece and Rome, and the handsome cast-iron cupola is crowned with the statue of lady Justice. The major interior feature is a sweeping marble double staircase. The wood-paneled City Council Chamber in the east wing is small and clubby; the Board of Estimate chamber to the west has Colonial paintings and seating in the church pew manner.

Directly east of City Hall is the **Brooklyn Bridge,** New York's oldest and best known span. When built in 1883 it was the world's longest suspension bridge and, like so many others in turn, the tallest structure in the city. Walking across the Brooklyn Bridge is a peak New York experience. The walkway covers just over a mile, passing beneath the towers and through the filigree. Take the first exit to Brooklyn Heights, a charming neighborhood of brownstones, and head back toward the river to the Promenade for an exciting view of Lower Manhattan.

Other Attractions

AT&T World Headquarters (Madison Ave. and 55th Street), a postmodern skyscraper of rose granite with a peculiar "Chippendale" roof, is not only a distinctive shape on the Manhattan skyline but also the home of the **AT&T Infoquest Center,** where interactive displays explore communications technology. *Madison Ave. at 55th St., tel. 212/605–5555. Admission free. Open Wed.–Sun. 10–6, Tues. 10–9.*

CitiCorp Center (Lexington Ave. at 53rd St.), a soaring white shaft of a skyscraper rising to a sheer angled peak, has a pleasant mall of restaurants and shops on its street level.

The Cloisters, perched atop a wooded hill near Manhattan's northernmost tip, houses part of the Metropolitan Museum of Art's medieval collection in the style of a medieval monastery. Five cloisters connected by colonnaded walks transport you back 700 years. The view of the Hudson and the New Jersey

Palisades enhances the experience. The No. 4 "Cloisters-Fort Tryon Park" bus provides a lengthy but scenic ride up there; catch it along Madison Avenue below 110th Street; or take the A subway to the 190th Street station. *Fort Tryon Park, tel. 212/923–3700. Suggested admission: $6 adults, $3 senior citizens and students, children 12 and under free. Open Nov.–Mar., Tues.–Sun. 9:30–4:45; Apr.–Oct., Tues.–Sun. 9:30–5:15.*

Gracie Mansion, at the north end of Carl Schurz Park (East End Ave. at 86th St), is the official home of the Mayor of New York. Built in 1779, this Federal-style yellow frame house still feels like a country manor house.

IBM Building, across 55th Street from the AT&T building, has an inviting public atrium and the **IBM Gallery of Science and Art** located off the main lobby. *Madison Ave. at 55th St., tel. 212/745–3500. Admission free. Open Tues.–Sat. 11–6.*

Pierpont Morgan Library contains a gallery, where rotating exhibits are unfailingly fascinating, and the beautifully furnished study and library of the famous banker. *29 E. 36th St. (off Madison Ave.), tel. 212/685–0610. Suggested donation: $3 adults, $1 students and senior citizens. Open Tues.–Sat. 10:30–5, Sun. 1–5.*

Roosevelt Island Aerial Tramway (Second Ave. and 60th St.) leads to Roosevelt Island, a residential complex in the East River. It is a slightly terrifying fun ride that gives you a great view of the city. The one-way fare is $1.25.

Shopping

In general, major department stores and other shops are open every day and keep late hours on Thursday. Many of the upper-crust shops along Upper Fifth Avenue and the Madison Mile close on Sunday. Stores in such nightlife areas as SoHo and Columbus Avenue are usually open in the evenings. The bargain shops along Orchard Street on the Lower East Side close on Friday afternoon and all day Saturday for the Jewish Sabbath but keep normal hours on Sunday. Sales tax in New York City is 8¼%.

Shopping Districts **Upper Fifth Avenue.** Fifth Avenue from 49th to 58th streets, and 57th Street between Sixth and Third avenues, contains many of the most famous stores in the world, among them Saks Fifth Avenue, Bergdorf Goodman, Henri Bendel, Tiffany & Co., Cartier, and the exclusive shops in Trump Tower.

Herald Square. The area extending from Herald Square (Sixth Ave. and 34th St.) along 34th Street and up Fifth Avenue to 40th Street includes several major stores (Macy's, A&S, Lord & Taylor) and a host of lower-price clothing stores.

Madison Mile. The 20-block span along Madison Avenue between 59th and 79th streets consists of mainly low-rise brownstone buildings housing the exclusive boutiques of American and overseas designers.

SoHo. Along West Broadway between Houston ("How-ston") and Canal Streets you'll find galleries, boutiques, avant-garde housewares shops, and shops that defy categorization.

Columbus Avenue. This shopping area between 66th and 86th streets features far-out European and down-home preppie fashions, some antiques and vintage stores, and outlets for adult toys.

Lower East Side. The intersection of Orchard and Delancey streets is the axis of bargains on women's and men's fashions, children's clothing, shoes, accessories, linens. Closed on Saturday; mobbed on Sunday.

Department Stores **A&S** (Sixth Ave. at 33rd St., tel. 212/594–8500). The old Gimbel's, a block south of Macy's, lives again as home to A&S Plaza, whose 120 shops and restaurants on nine floors are anchored by Abraham & Straus, well established in the outer boroughs.

Barneys New York (106 Seventh Ave. at 17th St., tel. 212/929–9000). Famous for its menswear, this retailer has become the place to see what's hot in women's clothing and linens as well. Prices are high, but so are quality and style.

Bergdorf Goodman (754 Fifth Ave., between 57th and 58th Sts., tel. 212/753–7300). A chic and very New York place to shop for women's designer clothes. Head across the street to the new **Men's Store** (745 Fifth Ave.), which opened in August 1990.

Bloomingdale's (Lexington Ave. at 59th St., tel. 212/705–2000). The quintessence of New York style—busy, noisy, crowded, and thoroughly up-to-date.

Henri Bendel (712–716 5th Ave., between 55th and 56th Sts., tel. 212/247–1100). A specialty store made up of many classy boutiques. Prices are not necessarily stratospheric.

Lord & Taylor (424 Fifth Ave. at 38th St., tel. 212/391–3344). Not flashy but a relatively uncrowded establishment that emphasizes well-made clothing by American designers.

Macy's (34th St. and Broadway, tel. 212/695–4400). The country's largest retail store occupies 10 stories (nine above ground, one below) and an entire block. Always comprehensive and competitive, Macy's has become quite fashionable as well.

Saks Fifth Avenue (611 Fifth Ave. at 50th St., tel. 212/753–4000). The flagship store of a nationwide chain has an outstanding selection of women's and men's designer outfits.

Specialty Shops **Manhattan Art & Antiques Center** (1050 2nd Ave., between *Antiques* 55th and 56th Sts., tel. 212/355–4400). More than 100 dealers stock three floors with antiques from around the world.

Place des Antiquaires (125 E. 57th St., tel. 212/758–2900). Two elegant subterranean levels of high-ticket antiques and art dealers.

Books **Gotham Book Mart** (41 W. 47th St., tel. 212/719–4448). A browser's paradise of books on literature and the performing arts.

Rizzoli (31 W. 57th St., tel. 212/759–2424; and two other locations). This elegant shop specializes in the arts.

Strand Book Store (828 Broadway at 12th St., tel. 212/473–1452). The biggest of Manhattan's used bookstores.

Food **Zabar's** (2245 Broadway at 80th St., tel. 212/787–2000). From jams, cheeses, spices, and smoked fish to a superb selection of kitchenwares, this store has long been a favorite with New York food lovers.

Jewelry Every store is a jewelry shop in the **Diamond District** (47th St. between Fifth and Sixth Aves.). Shop around—and be ready to haggle.

Menswear **Brooks Brothers** (346 Madison Ave. at 44th St., tel. 212/682–8800). An institution in American menswear, with conservative styles and quality tailoring.

Paul Stuart (Madison Ave. at 45th St., tel. 212/682–0320). At this celebrated, pricy store, the look is traditional without being stodgy.

Saint Laurie, Ltd. (897 Broadway, between 19th and 20th Sts., tel. 212/473–0100). Traditional suits made on the premises at this family-run establishment sell for less than they would uptown.

Syms (42 Trinity Pl., tel. 212/797–1199). Designer labels at bargain basement prices. The store also carries women's clothing.

Souvenirs of New York City City souvenirs are widely available, but for something more unusual in tie tacks and T-shirts, try the city-run **Citybooks** (61 Chambers St., tel. 212/669–8245), or stop in at the **New York Bound Bookshop** (50 Rockefeller Plaza, tel. 212/245–8503) for old or rare New York books and prints.

Women's Clothing **Canal Jean** (504 Broadway, between Spring and Broome Sts., tel. 212/226–1130). Casual funk draws hip shoppers.

Charivari (2315 Broadway between 83rd and 84th Sts., tel. 212/873–1424). High style, at prices to match, with branches all over the West Side.

Harriet Love (412 W. Broadway, between Prince and Spring Sts., tel. 212/966–2280). This is the doyenne of the vintage-clothing scene.

Ms., Miss, or Mrs. (462 Seventh Ave. at 35th St., tel. 212/736–0557). A Garment District establishment with new designer fashions at 30%–60% off.

Patricia Field (10 E. 8th St., tel. 212/254–1699). The place to acquire the "downtown" look.

Polo/Ralph Lauren (867 Madison Ave. at 72nd St., tel. 212/606–2100). All the essentials for the Ralph Lauren wardrobe can be found in this grand turn-of-the-century town house.

Dining

Name any country, name any city or province in any country, and New York will probably have a *selection* of restaurants specializing in the cuisine of that area.

New York restaurants are expensive, yet savvy diners learn how to keep their costs within reason. Since most restaurants post menus in their front windows or lobbies, at least you will have a general idea of what you're getting into. But they don't post drink prices, and these can be high: $3.50 and up for a beer or a glass of wine; $4 and up for mixed drinks (some places

Manhattan Dining and Lodging (Uptown)

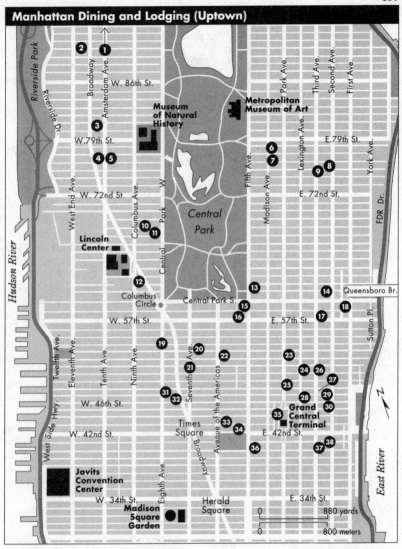

Dining

Acme Bar and Grill, **43**
Alcala, **4**
Amsterdam's, **3**
Arizona 206, **14**
Bangkok Cuisine, **19**
Café des Artistes, **11**
China Grill, **22**
Dawat, **17**
Dock's, **2, 37**
Extra! Extra!, **38**

Four Seasons, **23**
Gotham Bar and Grill, **41**
Grand Central Oyster Bar, **35**
Il Cortile, **47**
J. G. Melon's, **3, 9**
Katz's Delicatessen, **46**
La Colombe D'Or, **39**
Le Bernardin, **21**

Lutèce, **26**
Odeon, **50**
Omen, **45**
Remi, **20**
Rosa Mexicano, **18**
Silver Palace, **49**
Siracusa Gourmet Café, **42**
Smith & Wollensky, **27**
Sparks Steak House, **30**

Union Square Café, **40**
Vasata, **8**
Villa Mosconi, **44**
Vince & Eddie's, **10**
Tommy Tang, **51**
Wong Kee, **48**

Manhattan Dining and Lodging (Downtown)

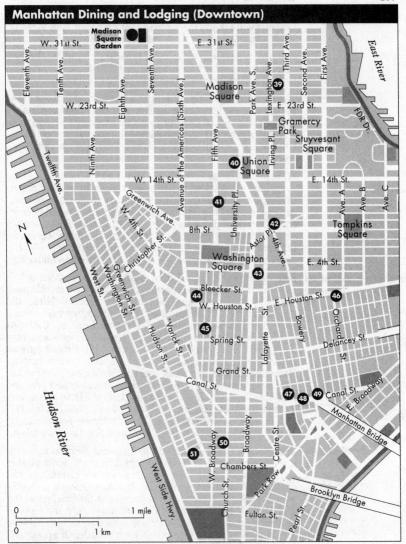

Lodging

The Algonquin, **33**

The Carlyle, **7**

Hotel Edison, **32**

Journey's End, **36**

The Mark, **6**

New York International Youth Hostel, **1**

The Pierre, **13**

The Plaza, **15**

Radisson Empire Hotel, **12**

Ramada Inn, **31**

Roger Smith Winthrop, **28**

The Royalton, **34**

The Summit, **24**

Vanderbilt YMCA, **29**

The Waldorf-Astoria, **25**

The Wyndham, **16**

charge *considerably* more). To run up your drink bill, many restaurants will ask you to wait in the bar until your table is ready. While you may have to wait, you don't have to buy a drink.

One way to save money and still experience a top-echelon restaurant is to go there for lunch rather than dinner. It may also be easier to get lunch reservations on short notice.

The slumping economy of the 1990s has worked in favor of the person who wants to eat out in New York. Many restaurants are now offering special fixed-price menus at bargain prices inconceivable a year or two ago. Although reservations are somewhat easier to come by these days, still be sure to make a reservation for any restaurant on a weekend.

What follows is a selective list of New York restaurants serving a variety of cuisines in all price ranges in neighborhoods throughout Manhattan. As the list can by no means be comprehensive, some of the city's classic restaurants have not been included. In their place, however, you'll find some lesser-known eateries that are frequented by locals. The following dining price categories have been used: *Very Expensive*, over $60; *Expensive*, $40–$60; *Moderate*, $20–$40; *Inexpensive*, under $20.

American–Continental
Very Expensive
★

Four Seasons. Menus and decor shift with the seasons in this class act. The bright and spacious Pool Room has a marble pool, changing floral displays, paintings by Picasso, Miró, and Rauschenberg. It's the rosewood Grill Room, however, where movers and shakers rendezvous for Power Lunches. Both settings have wide open spaces, impeccable service—and very high prices. An imaginative and unpredictable menu puts an Oriental spin on traditional American and French cuisine. Roast duck and pepper steak are reliable choices. The Spa Cuisine menu appeals to weight-watchers; lower-priced pre- and post-theater menus (5–6:15 and 10–11:15) at $41.50 please wallet-watchers. *The Seagram Building, 99 E. 52nd St., tel. 212/ 754–9494. Reservations required, in advance for weekends. Jacket required. AE, DC, MC, V. Closed Sat. lunch and Sun.*

Expensive

Arizona 206. The ambience of the American Southwest is captured a block away from Bloomingdale's: stark white plaster walls, wood-burning fireplace, raw timber trimming, and piped-in Willie Nelson records. The New American-Southwestern cuisine stresses chili peppers, and the brief menu (by chef Beth Valley) offers nothing ordinary, only the likes of smoked sturgeon quesadilla; grilled salmon steak with *poblano* corn custard; and black-bean cakes with dandelion greens and Cajun crawfish. Desserts are just as unusual, and the service staff is downright perky. *206 E. 60th St., tel. 212/838–0440. Reservations advised. Dress: casual. AE, DC, MC, V. No lunch Sun.*

Gotham Bar and Grill. A place with a name like Gotham better be huge, crowded, the quintessence of sophistication—and that's what this is. Owned by a former New York City commissioner, the Gotham Bar and Grill has a postmodern decor with a striking pink-green-black color scheme. The menu is eclectic and surprising: Try veal carpaccio or roasted quail salad. *12 E. 12th St., tel. 212/620–4020. Reservations advised. Dress: casual. AE, DC, MC, V. No lunch weekends.*

Moderate

Amsterdam's Bar & Rotisserie. The name tells most of the story: It's basically a bar on the Upper West Side's Amsterdam Avenue where most of the food is prepared on an open rotisserie. Low prices for roasted poultry (chicken and duck are tops) and beef dishes accompanied by a vegetable and an ambitious house salad elicit standing-room crowds late into the night. *428 Amsterdam Ave. between 80th and 81st Sts., tel. 212/874–1377. No reservations. Dress: casual. AE, DC, MC, V.*

Odeon. A converted Art Deco cafeteria in the TriBeCa neighborhood south of SoHo and north of the Financial District, it's a popular hangout with the Soho art set. The menu mingles French brasserie-style dishes with purely American fare. Steak and *frites* or poached lotte in fennel–saffron broth are good choices. *145 West Broadway at Thomas St., tel. 212/233–0507. Reservations advised. Dress: casual. AE, DC, MC, V. No lunch Sat.*

★ **Union Square Café.** A young, monied crowd frequents this site, mere feet from the greenery of renovated Union Square. Light-wood floors and cream-colored walls splashed with Chagallesque murals lend a bit of airiness to the awkward layout of the three dining areas. Executive chef Michael Romano uses rustic touches in such appetizers as fried calamari in anchovy mayonnaise and entrées like grilled marinated fillet mignon of tuna and lemon–pepper duck. Some diners choose to make a meal from the extensive selection of vegetables, which includes mashed turnips with fried shallot crisps and hot garlic potato chips. Recommended desserts include the warm banana tart or chocolate–stuffed souffle cupcake with espresso custard sauce. *21 E. 16th St., tel. 212/243–4020. Reservations advised. Jacket advised. AE, DC, MC, V. Closed Sun.*

Inexpensive **J.G. Melon.** A real "neighborhood" pub, with locations on both the East and West sides, Melon's consistently makes people feel at home. Decorated with countless paintings, and prints of (what else?) melons, the bar/restaurant is a good spot in which to meet people or have a laid-back American meal. The burgers and club sandwiches are always a good choice, accompanied by crispy cottage fries. *1291 3rd Ave. at 74th St., tel. 212/744–0585; 340 Amsterdam Ave., tel. 212/877–2220. No reservations. Dress: casual. No credit cards.*

Vince & Eddie's. In a neighborhood sorely lacking in inexpensive eating spots, this recent arrival to the Lincoln Center area offers hearty American fare at reasonable prices. Low, beamed ceilings, sturdy oak furniture, and rough whitewashed walls lend Vince & Eddie's a country-inn flavor, though the intimate atmosphere can turn intrusive when the restaurant is busy. Service is friendly but brusque; best to dine after 8 PM, when you can savor at leisure such dishes as baked mussels in extra-virgin olive oil, a moist red snapper with pecans, and succulent duck with bourbon sauce. Try at least one of the imaginative vegetable side dishes, but be forewarned: These are à la carte and can inflate your bill. In warm weather, you can dine in the garden patio beneath a 150-year-old tree. *70 W. 68th St. (between Central Park West and Columbus Ave.), tel. 212/721–0068. Reservations required. Dress: casual. AE, DC, MC, V.*

Cajun
Inexpensive **Acme Bar and Grill.** From the outside, you might mistake this restaurant for a warehouse and never discover the narrow, noisy dining area opening up to a bar behind its large metal doors. This is not the place for delicate dining—from its mismatched chairs with ripped upholstery to its ample portions of down-home southern cooking, there's nothing pretentious about a meal here. The kitchen serves up plenty of seafood, including plump fried oysters and farm-raised catfish, but it also

produces delicious corn fritters, a wonderful Cajun peanut soup, Cajun chicken, and an incredibly rich chocolate mud pie. *9 Great Jones St. (near Broadway), tel. 212/420–1934. No reservations. Dress: casual. No credit cards.*

Chinese

Note: Chinese food is a staple of the New York diet. Most restaurants serve interchangeable menus that combine dishes from various areas of China and use a star or red lettering to indicate spicy dishes. With few exceptions the food is good and truly inexpensive (less than $12 per person). Chinese restaurants typically offer low-priced lunch specials—soup, egg roll, main dish, tea—for between $5 and $7. Restaurants listed here offer something more than the typical neighborhood Chinese place.

Inexpensive

Silver Palace. The draw here on weekends is dim sum, a parade of dishes wheeled around on carts that stop at each table for diners to sample from at random. The steamed dumplings contain tasty fillings (the shrimp is particularly good), and the fried dumplings are light and delicately flavored. Portions are small, but you'll fill up fast. The tables are large, and no chair goes unused for long, so you'll probably join a meal that's already in progress. *52 Bowery, tel. 212/964–1204. Reservations not accepted for dim sum. Dress: casual. AE, DC, MC, V (no cards accepted before 6 PM). Dim sum served weekends 8–4 only.*

Wong Kee Restaurant. Diners gather behind the columned, brushed metal facade for the renowned barbecued pork, or the spiced beef chow fun (wide rice noodles), or maybe the sweet and pungent chicken (a refinement of sweet-and-sour), all highlights on this reliable Cantonese menu. Service is swift, but expect to wait for a table on weekends. *113 Mott St. (north of Canal St.), tel. 212/226–9018. Reservations advised on weekends. Dress: casual. No credit cards. BYOB.*

Czechoslovak
Moderate

Vašata. A cozy Czech restaurant that has been serving hearty food since 1952, Vašata is a survivor in a neighborhood once full of East European places. It has the look of a homey Old World wine cellar—lanterns and colorful ceramic dishes decorate pale-yellow brick walls–and it's still very popular with émigrés, who come for the goulash, schnitzel, roast duck, dumplings, and genuine Pilsner Urquell beer. Don't leave without sampling the *palačinky*, delicate dessert crepes with fruit or chocolate filling, doused in orange liqueur and flambéed at the table. *339 E. 75th St. (near 1st Ave.), tel. 212/988–7166. Reservations advised. Dress: casual. AE, MC, V. No lunch except Sun. Closed Mon.*

Deli
Inexpensive

Katz's Delicatessen. This Kosher-style New York delicatessen in the heart of the Lower East Side can get a bit chaotic at times. There is a method to the madness, however: grab a ticket when you enter, give it to the counterman as you shout your order, and hold on to it to pay the bill when you leave. You might recognize your surroundings—walls and ceilings hung with war memorabilia and hanging salamis—from the film *When Harry Met Sally.* The noise level can be a bit much, but so are the portions, so come hungry. Classics from knishes, pastrami, and brisket to the neighborhood's famous pickles—are all here, and if you like corned beef, it's a must. *205 E. Houston St. (near Orchard St.), tel. 212/254–2246. No reservations. Dress: casual. AE.*

French
Very Expensive
★

Lutèce. There isn't anyone who doesn't adore Lutèce, a temple of classic French gastronomy for over 25 years. The intimate and understated midtown town house has seating around an enclosed garden or in two more formal upstairs chambers. The regular menu is varied and specials change daily; grilled trout and pheasant are always fine choices. The impeccable service is invariably attentive and helpful, to first-time and hundredth-time diners alike. *249 E. 50th St., tel. 212/752–2225. Reservations required 2 weeks or more in advance. Jacket and tie required. AE, DC, MC, V. No lunch Sat.; closed Sun. and Aug.*

Expensive

Café des Artistes. This romantic and extremely popular Lincoln Center area institution sports famous murals of nudes cavorting in a sylvan glade and sparkling mirrors. Food is country French, and includes *confit* of duck with *flageolet* beans and herb-crusted tuna steak—both are recommended specialties. *1 W. 67th St. at Central Park West, tel. 212/877–3500. Reservations required. Jacket required at dinner. AE, DC, MC, V.*

Moderate
★

La Colombe D'Or. Pots of geraniums by the front door, lace curtains at the windows, and interior walls of rough white plaster and exposed brick set a cozy bistro atmosphere, carried out by friendly, unfawning service. The food, however, goes well beyond standard bistro fare, with creative combinations such as seared sea scallops with broccoli rabe and brazed endives, grilled salmon with chanterelle mushrooms and lettuce, or a surprisingly succulent calves' liver with carrots and grilled sweet onions. The wine list is long, decidedly French, and well priced. *134 E. 26th St. (near Lexington Ave.), tel. 212/689–0666. Reservations advised. Dress: casual. AE, DC, MC, V. Closed Sat. lunch and Sun.*

Indian
Moderate

Dawat. A sophisticated note is struck at once by softly lit, simple decor, colored in peach and aqua and accented by gleaming copper serving dishes. Classic Indian food, following the recipes of actress-author Madhur Jaffrey, carries out the promise with savory and often spicy dishes, including several vegetarian specialties and robust breads. Try the tandoori mixed grill, baked in its clay oven, the *rogan josh* (baby goat in cardamom sauce), or the *farasvi bhaji* (green beans in coconut). Lunch specials are an excellent value. *210 E. 58th St. (near 3rd Ave.), tel. 212/355–7555. Reservations advised. Dress: casual. AE, DC, MC, V.*

Italian
Moderate
★

Il Cortile. This classy establishment is one of the brightest spots in the sea of restaurants for which Little Italy is famous. Dark colors and exposed brick set a warm, intimate tone in the front dining room (try for a table by the window), while the back rooms of the restaurant are brightened by a skylight and an abundance of greenery. Dishes are well prepared and presented—try the simple *Scaloppine di Vitello al Cognac* (tender slices of veal smothered in mushrooms and a cognac gravy) or any of the fresh seafood dishes. For desserts, however, diners would do better to venture into one of the neighborhood's numerous pastry shops. *125 Mulberry St. (near Hester St.), tel. 212/226–6060. Reservations advised. Dress: casual. AE, DC, MC, V.*

★

Remi. This chic and sophisticated Italian restaurant offers consistently wonderful food, a festive atmosphere, and stunning interior design. A huge mural of the Grand Canal in Venice is a dramatic backdrop for the elegant blue and white upholstery, the Venetian glass chandeliers, the inlaid wood floor, and the well-dressed waiters. The creative menu featuring Northern Italian cuisine is enticing; especially delicious is the daily risotto special (whatever it is, it's always fabulous), *fegato alla Veneziana* (calf's liver with carmelized onions) served with fresh hen polenta, and *galetto al forno* (grilled free-range Cornish hen). *145 W. 53rd St. (near 7th Ave.), tel. 212/581-4242. Reservations advised. Jacket advised. AE, DC, MC, V. Closed lunch weekends.*

Siracusa Gourmet Café. A rather eclectic decor—clean-lined Art Deco combined with Italian folk art—sets the tone for this charming Italian eatery, where country-style Sicilian recipes are geared toward sophisticated palates. Some of the excellent pastas are **pasticciotto** (pasta stuffed with zucchini, ricotta, mushrooms, and pignoli nuts) and tagliarini **campagna** with sausage and tomato. The desserts are what really stand out here, however; if you don't feel like coming for a meal, stop by the **gelateria** next door and enjoy such flavors as ricotta, cappuccino, or chocolate—all made on the premises and wonderfully creamy. *65 4th Ave. (near 10th St.), tel. 212/254-1940. Reservations advised. Dress: casual. AE. Closed Sat. lunch and Sun.*

Inexpensive **Villa Mosconi.** In the heart of Greenwich Village, this authentic trattoria spins you back to a simpler time. Genial chef and proprietor Pietro Mosconi takes special care of the diners who nightly crowd the cozy dining room, decorated with Old World paintings. Seafood comes straight from the stalls of the Fulton fish market and all pastas are made on the premises. The menu includes dishes such as tortellini with four cheeses, veal bolognese with prosciutto and cheese in wine sauce, and shrimp scampi alla Mosconi. *69 MacDougal St. (between Houston and Bleecker Sts.), tel. 212/673-0390. Reservations advised. Dress: casual. AE, DC, MC, V. Closed Sun.*

Japanese **Omen.** Old brick, hardwood floors, timber ceilings, and Orien-
Moderate tal lanterns create the relaxing ambience of a Japanese country inn. *Omen* is the name of an opening dish almost everybody orders, a dark hot broth served with half-cooked exotic vegetables, sesame seeds, and noodles. Other favorites include a boned chicken dish called *sansho*, scallops and spinach with sesame cream, and avocado with shrimp in miso sauce. *113 Thompson St. between Spring and Prince Sts., tel. 212/925-8923. Reservations advised. Dress: casual. AE, DC. Closed lunch and Mon.*

Mexican **Rosa Mexicano.** This is a crowded midtown hangout for young
Moderate professionals. Serious dining takes place amid subdued pink
★ stucco walls and lush horticulture. Two standard Mexican items are exceptional here: chunky *guacamole* prepared at your table and margaritas blended with pomegranate. Grilled versions of shell steak, chicken, and snapper; pork *carnitas;* and skinned breast of duck are other house specialties. *1063 First Ave. at 58th St., tel. 212/753-7407. Reservations advised. Dress: casual. AE, DC, MC, V.*

Mixed Menu **China Grill.** This stark restaurant, located in the CBS building,
Moderate has endured in atmosphere and quality since its opening in 1987. The sleek orange-and-slate-gray dining room is spacious but tends to get noisy quickly. Described as French-American with oriental accents, the menu is an assortment of grilled dishes, with an emphasis on fish. Start the meal with the Pe-

king duck salad; for an entrée, try the grilled dry aged Szechuan beef with shredded potatoes or the stir-fried sea scallops with Chinese noodles make a nice combination. On the side, and not to be missed, is the crispy spinach, which literally melts in your mouth. To top off the meal indulge in the chocolate-and-amaretto parfait. *52 W. 53rd St. (off 6th Ave.), tel. 212/333–7788. Reservations advised. Jacket advised. AE, DC, MC, V. Closed Sun.*

Inexpensive **Extra! Extra!** Black and white walls peppered with giant newsprint seem appropriate for this fun spot, located in the Daily News building. Diners feast on pasta (in full or half portions), salads, sandwiches, and pizzas. The eclectic menu includes such appetizers as Louisiana fresh-grilled alligator sausage and fresh-fried *calamari*, as well as popular entrées such as crab cakes and chicken *fajitas*. It's an especially lively locale for lunch. *767 2nd Ave. at 41st St., tel. 212/490–2900. Reservations advised. Dress: casual. AE, DC, MC, V. Closed Sun.*

Seafood **Le Bernardin.** The New York branch of an illustrious Paris sea-
Very Expensive food establishment occupies the ground floor of the midtown
★ Equitable Assurance Tower; the elegant corporate decor was reportedly inspired by the Equitable boardroom. The all-seafood menu teems with rare treasures. For starters, try black bass flecked with coriander or sea urchins baked in their shell. Go on to *rouelle* of salmon sautéed with fennel julienne or any of the fresh, artfully arranged fillets. *155 W. 51st St., tel. 212/489–1515. Reservations required. Jacket and tie required. AE, DC, MC, V. Closed Sun.*

Expensive **Grand Central Oyster Bar and Restaurant.** Down in the cata-
★ combs beneath Grand Central Terminal, the Oyster Bar has a reputation for serving ultrafresh seafood. The vast main room has a vaulted tile ceiling, and lots of noise and tumult. Solos may prefer to sit at the wide white counter. By contrast, the wood-paneled Saloon feels downright clubby. More than a dozen varieties of oysters may be on hand. Pan-roasted shellfish, a kind of stew, is a house specialty. Broiled fillets change with the daily catch. *Lower level Grand Central Terminal, 42nd St. at Vanderbilt Ave., tel. 212/490–6650. Reservations advised, required for lunch. Dress: casual. AE, DC, MC, V. Closed Sat. and Sun.*

Moderate– **Dock's.** The fresh fish in this natty Upper West Side bistro
Expensive serves as a delicious reminder that New York is, after all, a seaport. Classy and unpretentious, Docks has earned a loyal clientele at both this and its east side location (633 Third Ave. at 40th St.). The crab cakes here are the best in town, the salmon and tuna dishes are excellent, and the shellfish is consistently pleasing. There is an extensive selection of beers, and the wine list is tailored to complement seafood. Try to leave room for the chocolate mud cake or the Key lime pie. *2427 Broadway at 90th St., tel. 212/724–5588; 633 Third Ave. at 40th St., tel. 212/986–8080. Reservations advised. Dress: casual. AE, DC, MC, V.*

Spanish **Alcala.** Visit this Spanish restaurant and tapas bar for the tran-
Moderate quil atmosphere and the varied menu. The large, exposed brick-walled room gives diners an opportunity to relax over a wide variety of seafood, fish, chicken, and beef dishes. Appetizers such as fried calamari and cream of cauliflower soup far surpass the entrées. Try the ice cream and sherbets for dessert. *349 Amsterdam Ave. (near 76th St.), tel. 212/769–9600.*

Reservations advised. Dress: casual. AE, DC, MC, V. Dinner only.

Steaks
Expensive
★ **Smith & Wollensky.** This midtown steak house has an authentic look, with plank floors, bent-wood chairs, and walls decked with classic sporting prints. Steak is the main draw—big blackened sirloins and filets mignon with a pepper sauce. Huge lobsters, veal chops, and terrific onion rings round out the menu. *201 E. 49th St. at 3rd Ave., tel. 212/753–1530. Reservations advised. Jacket advised. AE, DC, MC, V.*

★ **Sparks Steak House.** Steaks and male camaraderie are the specialties here, and the tender prime sirloin is the most popular selection. Filets are unusually juicy and flavorful; lobsters cruise the three- to five-pound range. Although most of the ex-athlete-size customers seem to go for beer or whiskey, Sparks boasts an award-winning wine list. *210 E. 46th St., tel. 212/687–4855. Reservations required. Jacket and tie advised. AE, DC, MC, V. Closed Sun.*

Thai
Moderate
Tommy Tang. This exuberant TriBeCa Thai restaurant, set in a bright, high-ceilinged long room with Art Deco-ish decor of turquoise and beige, draws a mixed crowd of professionals, artists, and local residents who continue to return for the consistently fine food. If possible, come with a group so you can sample a range of dishes on the imaginative menu. For starters, try the "naked" shrimp, grilled and spiced with roasted curry paste, mint, and lime juice. Entrées include the luscious Malaysian clams, sautéed with Thai basil and garlic; the ever-popular boneless Original Tommy Duck with grilled vegetables. *323 Greenwich St. (near Reade St.), tel. 212/334–9190. Reservations advised. Dress: casual chic. AE, DC, MC, V. Closed Sat. lunch and Sun.*

Inexpensive
Bangkok Cuisine. New York's oldest Thai restaurant is located just north of the Theater District. Some of the specialties include *tod mun pla* (deep-fried fish patties dipped in a sweet sauce), *pad thai* (a peanut-and-noodle dish), and whole fish dinners. *885 Eighth Ave. at 53rd St., tel. 212/581–6370. Reservations advised. Dress: casual. AE, MC, V. No lunch Sun.*

Lodging

If any single element of your trip to New York City is going to cost you a lot of money, it'll be your hotel bill. Real estate is at a premium here, labor costs are high, and market forces are not likely to drive current prices down. We have noted a few budget properties, but on the sliding scale of Manhattan prices even our "Inexpensive" category includes hotels that run as high as $125 for one night's stay in a double room. Exact prices could be misleading, though: Properties change their so-called "rack rates" seasonally, and most hotels offer savings in the form of weekend packages; look for advertisements in travel magazines or the Sunday travel sections of major newspapers such as the *New York Times*, the *Washington Post*, or the *Los Angeles Times*.

Once you've accepted that you must pay the going price, you'll have plenty of choices. Most Manhattan hotels are in the midtown area, so we have categorized them by price range rather than location. The following lodging price categories have been used: *Very Expensive*, over $260; *Expensive*, $180–$260; *Moderate*, $130–$180; *Inexpensive*, under $125.

Very Expensive **The Carlyle.** Located in one of the city's finest residential areas, this beautifully appointed traditional hotel is considered one of New York's finest. The mood is English manor house; larger rooms and suites, many of them decorated by the famous interior designer Mark Hampton, have terraces, pantries, and antique furnishings. Most visitors have heard about the famous Café Carlyle, where performers such as Bobby Short entertain. But the hotel also contains the charming Bemelman's Bar, with whimsical animal murals on the walls and live piano music at night, and the formal Carlyle Restaurant, with French cuisine and old-fashioned courtly service. *35 E. 76th St. at Madison Ave., 10021, tel. 212/744–1600. 185 rooms. Facilities: restaurant, café, bar, lounge, fitness center, VCRs and stereos, fax machines, kitchenettes and pantries in larger units, meeting rooms. AE, DC, MC, V.*

The Mark. Just one block north of the Carlyle, the former Madison Avenue Hotel has prospered under its new owner, Rafael Hotels. Even the least expensive rooms have high-quality TVs and VCRs, and its bathrooms feature Art Deco tiles or marble, deep tubs, *and* separate stall showers. Most rooms have pantries, too. Color schemes are warm to reflect the neoclassical Italian motif. *25 E. 77th St., 10021, tel. 212/744–4300 or 800/THE–MARK. 185 rooms. Facilities: restaurant, café, lounge, meeting rooms, VIP suites with terraces. AE, DC, MC, V.*

★ **The Pierre.** One might expect haughtiness along with the creamy, oriental-carpeted halls and bright chandeliers, but you won't find that here: The staff has a sense of fun about working in these posh surroundings. Rooms, most of which have been recently refurbished, are traditionally decorated in soft florals with quilted bedspreads. Formal afternoon tea is served under the blue cherubim-filled dome of the Rotunda. *5th Ave. at 61st St., 10021, tel. 212/838–8000 or 800/332–3442. 204 rooms. Facilities: restaurant, bar, tearoom, meeting rooms, manned elevators, packing service upon request, hand-laundry service. AE, DC, MC, V.*

The Plaza. When real-estate developer and casino operator Donald Trump purchased this National Historic Landmark in 1988, locals shuddered a bit, but so far misgivings have been unfounded. New color schemes are in burgundy or teal blue; fresh, floral-patterned quilted spreads grace the large beds. Furnishings, though still "hotel-like" in most units, are of high quality. Bathrooms, even those not yet fully redone, have fluffy new towels and French toiletries. One real advantage here is the size of guest rooms—only a handful of other classic properties can offer similar spaciousness in nearly all accommodations. *5th Ave. at 59th St., 10019, tel. 212/759–3000 or 800/228–3000. 807 rooms. Facilities: 2 restaurants, 2 bars, café, art gallery, handicapped-guest rooms, meeting rooms, packing service upon request, large concierge staff. AE, DC, MC, V.*

Expensive **The Royalton.** Former Studio 54 disco kings Ian Schrager and the late Steve Rubell, in their quest for a second career as New York hotel moguls, completely rehabilitated this once-shabby property directly across from the Algonquin. The Royalton, with its witty "art moderne" design by French decorator Philippe Starck, has a plush but slightly spooky atmosphere: The halls are narrow and dark, as are some of the strangely shaped rooms. Still, the beds and other furnishings are quite comfy, and the bathrooms are decidedly fun—they all have either oversize slate shower stalls or giant circular tubs (a few have both). *44 W. 44th St., 10036, tel. 212/869–4400 or 800/635–9013. 205 rooms. Facilities: restaurant with bar, meeting rooms, game and library areas, VCRs, stereos. AE, DC, MC, V.*

The Waldorf-Astoria. This Art Deco landmark, now owned by Hilton, personifies New York at its most lavish and powerful, with its carefully preserved murals and mosaics, elaborate plaster ornamentation, and fine old-wood walls and doors. Bathrooms throughout are old but beautifully kept up and rather spacious by today's standards. The hotel's richly tinted, hushed lobby serves as an interior centerpoint of city life. *301 Park Ave., 10022, tel. 212/355–3000 or 800/HILTONS. 1,692 rooms. Facilities: 3 restaurants, coffee shop, tearoom, lounge, ballroom, meeting rooms. AE, DC, MC, V.*

Moderate **The Algonquin.** This much-beloved hotel, where the Round Table group of writers and wits once met for lunch, still shelters many a celebrity, particularly literary types. While the English-drawing-room atmosphere and burnished-wood lobby have been kept intact, its working parts (the plumbing, for instance) are being improved under new Japanese owners. Bathrooms and sleeping quarters retain Victorian-style fixtures and furnishings, only now there are larger, firmer beds, modern TVs, VCRs (upon request), computerized phones, and Caswell-Massey toiletries. Personal service, especially for repeat customers, continues to be excellent. *59 W. 44th St., 10036, tel. 212/840–6800 or 800/548–0345. 165 rooms. Facilities: restaurant, 2 lounges, meeting rooms, complimentary parking on weekends, business center. AE, DC, MC, V.*

Journey's End. This Canadian chain's first Manhattan property is what the demanding bargain hunter has been waiting for. No-nonsense, clean, attractive rooms and baths are at one fixed price. Most accommodations come with queen-size beds; all have modern TVs and telephones with long cords. Guests can use a small lounge area for complimentary coffee and newspapers. There were plans at press time for an independently owned Italian restaurant to open on the premises. At night, this part of midtown is somewhat quiet and therefore prone to street crime; however, security at the hotel appears to be superior. Another plus—it's just a few blocks away from the airport bus departure area on Park Avenue near Grand Central Terminal. *3 E. 40th St., 10016, tel. 212/447-4200. 189 rooms. Facilities: lounge, restaurant, business services on request. AE, DC, MC, V.*

Loews Summit, *see* The Summit, *below.*

Radisson Empire Hotel. This old hotel recently changed ownership, but so far the changes have been promising. The lobby is warm and inviting; halls are decorated in soft gray with elegant lamps. Rooms and suites are a bit like small boxes, but nicely furnished; bathrooms are immaculate if on the small side. The restaurant is new, and the neighborhood is loaded with all-hours dining options. *Broadway at 63rd St., 10023, tel. 212/265-7400, 800/221-6509, or 800/223-9868. 368 rooms. Facilities: restaurant, coffee shop. AE, DC, MC, V.*

The Roger Smith Winthrop. Currently in the process of a gradual redecoration, in which the lobby and public areas have already been remodeled, this hotel offers guest rooms that are clean, well decorated, and spacious. Special units have small but luxurious marble baths with Jacuzzis. All rooms have pantries, and there's a complimentary Continental breakfast. *501*

Lexington Ave., 10017, tel. 212/755-1400 or 800/241-3848. 200 rooms. Facilities: restaurant, meeting room. AE, DC, MC, V.

The Summit. Loews' moderate-price New York property has an impersonal style, but most of its regulars—business travelers—don't mind because the hotel generally runs quite well. Rooms, most of them recently refurbished, are standard fare. The new Lexington Avenue Grill is a good on-site restaurant; the striking new maroon art deco carpeting and wood-tone lobby is an improvement over the old lobby. Loews takes care of its properties, so the Summit can more than hold its own with some of its neighbors. *Lexington Ave. at 51st St., 10022, tel. 212/752-7000. 766 rooms. Facilities: restaurant, lounge, meeting rooms, fitness center. AE, DC, MC, V.*

★ **The Wyndham.** This genteel treasure sits across from The Plaza and adjacent to the Helmsley Park Lane. The savvy, independent traveler who cares more about gracious rooms and a friendly atmosphere than about imposing lobbies and hand-to-mouth service might well choose this spot over its neighbors. Even the least expensive double room has fresh floral-print bedspreads, comfortable chairs, and decorator wall coverings. The small lobby is unusually secure—a doorman controls the "in" buzzer 24 hours a day. This hotel is a favorite of stars such as Carol Burnett and media personalities Leonard Maltin and Barbara Walters. *42 W. 58th St., 10019, tel. 212/753-3500. 201 rooms. Facilities: restaurant. AE, DC, MC, V.*

Inexpensive **Hotel Edison.** A popular budget stop for tour groups from here and abroad, this offbeat old hotel is getting a face-lift. The pink plaster coffee shop has become a hot place to eavesdrop on show-business gossip thanks to such celebrity regulars as Jackie Mason. Guest rooms are brighter and fresher than the dark corridors seem to hint. There's no room service, but this part of the theater district has so many restaurants and delis that it doesn't matter much. *228 W. 47th St., 10036, tel. 212/840-5000. 1,000 rooms. Facilities: restaurant, coffee shop, bar. AE, DC, MC, V.*

New York International Youth Hostel. American Youth Hostels recently opened this ambitious facility on Manhattan's Upper West Side. Here, in a renovated 19th-century Gothic-style building, you'll find dormitory accommodations at rock-bottom prices. There are no private baths; rooms hold up to six beds; and guests can rent their own sheets. All ages are welcome, but there is a limit of one week per stay. Although the immediate neighborhood is still a bit rough, the location is convenient to Columbia University, Harlem, and new stores and eating spots on upper Broadway and Columbus and Amsterdam avenues. Call in advance about exact prices and available amenities. *891 Amsterdam Ave., 10025, tel. 212/932-2300. 90 rooms. Facilities: dining area, patio, kitchen, self-service laundry, travel service desk, conference rooms for nonprofit groups. AE, DC, MC, V.*

Ramada Inn. Another of Loews' budget properties, this motel-style building has an outdoor rooftop swimming pool and lounge area with snack bar. Rooms and suites were recently upgraded. Daily garage rates are reasonable. This is a good bet for theater-bound families during the summer months. *48th St. at 8th Ave., 10019, tel. 212/581-7000 or 800/2-RAMADA. 366 rooms. Facilities: restaurant, lounge, pool, meeting room. AE, DC, MC, V.*

Vanderbilt YMCA. Of the various Manhattan Ys offering accommodations, this is the best as far as location and facilities are concerned. Although rooms hold up to four people, they are little more than dormitory-style cells—each room does have a late-model TV, however. There are no private baths; communal showers and toilets are clean. Guests are provided with basics such as towels and soap. Besides the low price, this Y offers instant free membership to its on-premises pool, gym, running track, exercise rooms, and sauna. Many of the athletic and public areas, including the pool, have been remodeled. The Turtle Bay neighborhood is safe, convenient, and interesting (the United Nations is a few short blocks away). Other YMCAs in town include the 561-room **West Side Y** (5 W. 63rd St., 10023, tel. 212/787–4400), which may be hard to get into but is in the desirable Lincoln Center area; and the 1,490-room **Sloane House YMCA** (356 W. 34th St., 10001, tel. 212/760–5860), which is in a gritty and somewhat unsafe neighborhood. *224 E. 47th St., 10017, tel. 212/755–2410. 430 rooms. Facilities: cafeteria, meeting rooms, self-service laundry, gift shop, luggage storage, pool, fitness center. No credit cards.*

Bed-and-Breakfasts Hundreds of rooms are available on a bed-and-breakfast basis in Manhattan and the outer boroughs, principally Brooklyn. B&Bs almost always cost well below $100 a night; some singles are available for under $50.

New York B&Bs fall into two categories: (1) *hosted apartments,* a bedroom in an apartment where the host is present; (2) *unhosted apartments,* entire apartments that are temporarily vacant. The unhosted option is scarcer and somewhat more expensive.

Along with saving money, B&Bs permit you to stay in "real" neighborhoods rather than in tourist enclaves. The disadvantages are that accommodations, amenities, service, and privacy fall far short of what you get in hotels. Sometimes you really do get breakfast and sometimes you don't. And you usually can't pay by credit card.

Here are a few reservation agencies that book B&B accommodations in and near Manhattan.

Bed and Breakfast Network of New York (134 W. 32nd St., Suite 602, 10001, tel. 212/645–8134).
City Lights Bed and Breakfast, Ltd. (Box 20355, Cherokee Station, 10028, tel. 212/737–7049).
New World Bed and Breakfast (150 5th Ave., Suite 711, 10011, tel. 212/675–5600 or 800/443–3800).
Urban Ventures (306 W. 38th St., 10018, tel. 212/594–5650).

The Arts

Full listings of weekly entertainment and cultural events appear in *New York* magazine. The Arts & Leisure section of the Sunday *New York Times* lists events; the Theater Directory in the daily *New York Times* advertises ticket information for Broadway and Off-Broadway shows. Listings of arts events appear weekly in *The New Yorker* and *Village Voice.*

Theater New York theater is the benchmark for quality and variety. Generally, Broadway productions are the most extravagant and expensive, while the more daring, if less polished, shows are found Off and Off-Off Broadway.

Broadway theaters are located in the Theater District, most of which lies between Broadway and Eighth Avenue, from 43rd to 52nd streets. Ticket prices range from $22.50 to as much as $100, depending on the show, the time of performance, and the location of the seat. Generally, plays are less expensive than musicals; and matinees (Wednesday, Saturday, and sometimes Sunday) and weeknight performances cost less than shows on Friday and Saturday nights. Most Broadway theaters are "dark" (closed) on Monday, although some are dark on other days.

Off-Broadway theater has professional performers but generally less elaborate productions. The theaters are located all over town. Many can be found along Theater Row, a strip of 42nd Street between Ninth and Tenth avenues; others are located in Greenwich Village, and some are on the Upper West Side. Ticket prices range from $15 to $75, with most falling into the $20–$25 range.

Off-Off-Broadway theater is alternative theater. Although you won't find lavish sets and plush seating, plays can be highly professional, with performances of everything from Shakespeare to mixed-media performance art. Off-Off-Broadway houses are located in all kinds of spaces—lofts, church basements, converted storefronts—all over town. Tickets rarely exceed $15.

Tickets All Broadway show tickets are available by phone from either **Tele-Charge** (tel. 212/239–6200) or **Ticketron** (tel. 212/246–0102), both of which operate 24 hours a day, seven days a week. You can also buy Broadway tickets at the box offices, which are open most of the day and evening. Tickets for the hottest shows—recently, *Miss Saigon* and *The Will Rogers Follies*—may be available only through ticket brokers; look in the Manhattan Yellow Pages under "Ticket Sales—Entertainment & Sports."

Off-Broadway tickets can be bought through **HIT–TIX** (tel. 212/564–8038), **Ticketmaster** (tel. 212/307–7171), or individual theaters. Tickets for many Off-Broadway shows are available at **Ticket Central** (416 W. 42nd St., tel. 212/279–4200).

For discounts of nearly 50% on Broadway and Off-Broadway shows, you can try your luck at **TKTS**, a nonprofit service that sells any remaining tickets on the day of performance for half the regular price, plus a $2 surcharge per ticket. The main TKTS booth is located in the Theater District on Duffy Square (Broadway and 47th Street, tel. 212/354–5800), open 3–8 daily for evening performances, 10–2 for Wednesday and Saturday matinees, and noon–8 for Sunday matinee and evening performances. The lines are long but congenial and they move surprisingly fast. There are shorter lines at the TKTS booth at 2 World Trade Center, open weekdays 11–5:30, Saturday 11–1. Another TKTS booth in front of Borough Hall in Brooklyn (tel. 718/625–5015) operates Tuesday–Friday 11–5:30 and Saturday 11–3:30 for evening performances only. TKTS accepts only cash or traveler's checks—no checks or credit cards.

Concerts Much of New York's serious music scene clusters around the magnificent concert halls and theaters of Lincoln Center (Broadway and 65th St., tel. 212/877–2011). **Avery Fisher Hall** (tel. 212/874–2424) is the home of the New York Philharmonic Orchestra, the American Philharmonic, the Mostly Mozart fes-

tival, and visiting orchestras and soloists. Smaller **Alice Tully
Hall** (tel. 212/362–1911), in the Juilliard School of Music building, features chamber music and jazz performances. Although
most tickets are sold on a subscription basis, individual seats
may be available at the box office in advance or through
Centercharge (tel. 212/874–6770).

Since 1891, **Carnegie Hall** (W. 57th St. at 7th Ave., tel. 212/
247–7800) has presented visiting orchestras, recitals, chamber
music, and pop concerts. The **Weill Recital Hall** features lesser-
known artists at lower prices.

A TKTS-like operation called **Bryant Park Music and Dance
Ticket Booth** sells discount day-of-performance tickets for music and dance concerts all over the city—including Lincoln Center and Carnegie Hall. Tickets cost half the regular price plus a
$2 service charge. *42nd St. just east of Sixth Ave., tel. 212/382–
2323. Open Tues., Thurs., Fri., noon–2 and 3–7; Wed. and Sat.
11–2 and 3–7; Sun. noon–6. Cash or traveler's checks only.*

Opera The **Metropolitan Opera** (Broadway at 65th St., tel. 212/362–
6000), at Lincoln Center, is a sublime setting for mostly classic
operas performed by world-class stars. Tickets can be expensive—up to $115—and hard to get, but low-price standing-room tickets may be available.

New York City Opera (Broadway at 65th St., tel. 212/870–5570),
at the State Theater, Lincoln Center, is a first-class opera company with lower ticket prices—under $50—and an innovative
and unpredictable schedule.

Dance The **American Ballet Theatre** (Broadway at 65th St., tel. 212/
362–6000), formerly under the direction of Mikhail Baryshnikov, is the resident company of the Metropolitan Opera House
in Lincoln Center. ABT is noted for its lyrical renditions of story
ballets during the spring (April–June) season. Ticket prices
start low, around $8 for standing room, and rise to over $60.

The renowned **New York City Ballet** (Broadway at 65th St., tel.
212/870–5570), a resident of Lincoln Center's New York State
Theater, reached world-class prominence under the direction
of George Balanchine. NYCB performs a spring season in May
and June, and a winter program from November through February. Tickets range from $7 to $50.

Other venues for dance (mostly modern dance) are **City Center**
(131 W. 55th St., tel. 212/581–7907), the **Joyce Theater** (175
Eighth Ave., tel. 212/242–0800), the **Dance Theater Workshop**
(219 W. 19th St., tel. 212/691–6500), and the **Brooklyn Academy of Music** (BAM, 30 Lafayette Ave., Brooklyn, tel. 718/636–
4100). Half-price day-of-performance tickets are available at
Bryant Park Music and Dance Discount Ticket Booth (*see* Concerts, *above, for details*).

Film Few cities rival New York's selection of films. Along with all the
first-run Hollywood features, an incomparable selection of foreign films, classics, documentaries, and experimental works
are playing all over town. The daily *New York Daily News* and
New York Newsday, the Friday *New York Times*, and the weekly *Village Voice* publish schedules and show times for Manhattan movies. *New York* magazine and *The New Yorker* publish
programs and capsule reviews but no schedules.

The vast majority of Manhattan theaters are first-run houses. Most charge $7.50 a ticket for adults.

Lincoln Plaza (Broadway between 62nd and 63rd Sts., tel. 212/757–2280) has three subterranean screens playing long-run foreign hits. **Quad Cinema** (13th St. between 5th and 6th Aves., tel. 212/255–8800) specializes in foreign films and interesting American independent movies. The **Film Forum 2** (209 W. Houston St., tel. 212/431–1590) in SoHo features contemporary foreign films, documentaries, and other unusual work. The **Collective for Living Cinema** (41 White St., tel. 212/505–5181) in TriBeCa has an ambitious, constantly changing program of experimental films. The **Public Theater** (425 Lafayette St., tel. 212/598–7171) concentrates on retrospectives and documentaries.

Revival Houses The **Biograph Cinema** (225 W. 57th St., tel. 212/582–4582) is a fine revival house with double-feature bills changing every couple of days. **Cinema Village** (3rd Ave. between 12th and 13th Sts., tel. 212/505–7320) often offers as many as three double-feature revivals a week. **Theatre 80 St. Mark's** (80 St. Marks Pl., tel. 212/254–7400) in the East Village has different double-feature revival programs nearly every day. The **Museum of Modern Art** (11 W. 53rd St., tel. 212/708–9490) shows film classics every day in two theaters; movies are free with museum admission.

Nightlife

Cabaret The **Ballroom** (253 W. 28th St., tel. 212/244–3005) in Chelsea combines a tapas (Spanish appetizers) bar with top-name cabaret acts and outrageous revues. **Catch A Rising Star** (1487 First Ave., near 78th St., tel. 212/794–1906) features continuous comedy by performers on their way up—or down. **Don't Tell Mama** (343 W. 46th St., tel. 212/757–0788) is a lively piano bar up front; cabaret performers work the back room. **The Duplex** (61 Christopher St., tel. 212/255–5438), a bilevel Village club, presents nightly shows with torch singers and hot comics. **The Improvisation** (358 W. 44th St., tel. 212/765–8268), New York's original comedy showcase, is where all the big-name yucksters (Rodney Dangerfield, Richard Pryor, Robert Klein) earned their first giggles. **Steve McGraw's** (158 W. 72nd St., tel. 212/595–7400) is a West Side showroom presenting scathingly irreverent satirical revues and cabaret shows.

Jazz Clubs Most jazz clubs have substantial cover charges and a drink minimum for table service. You can usually save one or both of these charges by sitting at or standing around the bar.

In Greenwich Village, the **Village Vanguard** (178 Seventh Ave. S, tel. 212/255–4037) is a basement joint that has ridden the crest of every new wave in jazz for over 50 years. The **Village Gate** (Bleecker and Thompson Sts., tel. 212/475–5120) can present different jazz-related acts and shows simultaneously in three places. No cover on the Village Gate terrace. Go to **Sweet Basil** (88 Seventh Ave. S, near Bleecker St., tel. 212/242–1785) for a roomful of jazz memorabilia and top-name groups. **The Blue Note** (131 W. Third St., tel. 212/475–8592) is a new incarnation of a legendary jazz club. **The Knitting Factory** (47 E. Houston St., tel. 212/219–3055), a hot new place on the frontier of SoHo, features avant-garde groups. At cozy **Fat Tuesday's** (190 Third Ave., at 17th St., tel. 212/533–7902), two sets are played every night but Monday. **Michael's Pub** (211 E. 55th St., tel. 212/758–2272) has mainstream jazz, top vocalists, jazz-based revues—and Woody Allen's Dixieland band most Mondays.

Pop and Rock Clubs The *Village Voice* carries the best listings of who's playing where on the pop and rock scene.

In Greenwich Village, folk headliners usually dominate the bill at **The Bottom Line** (15 W. Fourth St., off Mercer St., tel. 212/228–6300). Past performers include everyone from Stevie Wonder to Suzanne Vega. For more than 25 years **The Bitter End** (147 Bleecker St., tel. 212/673–7030) has been giving a break to folk, rock, jazz, comedy, and country acts. A low-key Irish pub, the **Eagle Tavern** (355 W. 14th St., tel. 212/924–0275) presents traditional Irish music, with bluegrass and comedy thrown in for variety.

CBGB & OMFUG (315 Bowery, tel. 212/982–4052) still blasts eardrums with the hard rock sound of heavy metal. **Wetlands Preserve** (161 Hudson St., tel 212/966–4225) is billed as "a watering hole for activists"; the music is big on psychedelic rock.

Farther uptown, dance at **The Ritz** (254 W. 54th St., tel. 212/541–8900), a restored Art Deco ballroom that hosts the newest rock groups. **The Lone Star Roadhouse** (240 W. 52nd St., tel. 212/245–2950) offers big names in country swing and big city blues.

Discos and Dance Clubs While club-hopping don't miss New York's largest, the **Palladium** (126 E. 14th St., tel. 212/473–7171). Practically an institution by now with Club MTV, it is no longer the hot ticket it was a few years ago; still, this place is to the club scene what Macy's is to shopping.

For "touch dancing" the way they used to do it, 70-year-old **Roseland** (239 W. 52nd St., tel. 212/247–0200) has two orchestras Thursday through Sunday nights and matinees from 2:30 PM. Whoosh through the revolving door at **Café Society** (915 Broadway at 21st St., tel. 212/529–8282) to find soaring ceilings, pink art deco decor, a long, inviting bar, and dinner and dancing. Most spectacular of all, the newly remodeled **Rainbow Room** atop the 65-floor RCA Building (30 Rockefeller Center, tel. 212/632–5100) gives you a dance floor straight out of the Hollywood classics.

Bars for Singles (Under 30) Downtown, there's no dearth of drinking opportunities at **South Street Seaport** (Water and Fulton Sts., tel. 212/732–7678). Bars at this major New York attraction include Roebling's, Jeremy's, the Fulton Street Café, and McDuffy's Irish Coffee House, to name a few. On warm Friday evenings Wall Street types raise a glass with young professionals from around the city. Young people throng to **McSorley's Old Ale House** (15 E. 7th St., tel. 212/473–9148), one of the oldest and most crowded bars in the city. **Downtown Beirut I** (158 First Ave., tel. 212/777–9011) is an off-beat East Village hangout that attracts artists and student types.

Farther uptown, lines are usually waiting outside the **Hard Rock Café** (221 W. 57th St., tel. 212/459–9320), a shrine to rock 'n' roll. On the Upper East Side, **T.G.I. Friday's** (1152 First Ave. at 63rd St., tel. 212/832–8512) has a long tradition as a congenial gathering place. On the Upper West Side, young crowds congregate at **Lucy's Restaurant** (503 Columbus Ave., tel. 212/787–3009).

Clubs and Bars for Singles (Over 30) **Pete's Tavern** (129 E. 18th St., tel. 212/473–7676), a crowded, friendly saloon, is famous as the place where O. Henry wrote "The Gift of the Magi." The **White Horse Tavern** (567 Hudson St. at 11th St., tel. 212/243–9260), which figures prominently in the legend and lore of Dylan Thomas, now has outdoor seating during summer. The **Cedar Tavern** (82 University Pl., tel. 212/243–9355) was a haunt of beatnik writers and abstract expressionist painters.

Farther uptown, **Jim McMullen's** (1341 Third Ave., tel. 212/861–4700) is a young, upscale, Upper East Side watering hole with a large, busy bar decked with bouquets of fresh flowers. The **Ginger Man** (51 W. 64th St., tel. 212/399–2358) is a reliable Lincoln Center area establishment.

The Hudson Valley

The Hudson River, in the stretch that links the fresh waters of Troy, Schenectady, and Albany to the salt waters of the Atlantic, is one of the busiest and most beautiful waterways in America. Its lush, dramatic valley is graced with dozens of stately mansions on magnificent estates, and the landscape is so beautiful—with its towering palisades, pine-scented forests, cool mountain lakes and streams—that it inspired an entire art movement, the Hudson River School, in the 19th century. Several Revolutionary War sites have been preserved here, and scores of orchards, vineyards, and farm markets along country roads attest to the region's agricultural richness.

Boat Tours **Hudson Highland Cruises & Tours, Inc.** (Box 265, Highland Falls 10928, tel. 914/446–7171) sails May–October from West Point, West Haverstraw, and Peekskill with daytime narrated sightseeing cruises.

Hudson River Cruises (Box 333, Rifton 12471, tel. 914/255–6515) operates narrated cruises from Kingston and West Point aboard *M/V Rip Van Winkle*, May–October.

Riverboat Tours (310 Mill St., Poughkeepsie 12601, tel. 914/473–5211) runs sightseeing cruises from Poughkeepsie, May–October.

Numbers in the margin correspond to points of interest on the Hudson Valley map.

❶ Just north of the New York City line, in **Yonkers,** is the magnificent 1876 Trevor Mansion, where the collections of the **Hudson River Museum** includes impressive paintings from the Hudson River School of artists, such as Jasper Cropsey and Albert Bierstadt. Many of the art, history, and science exhibits focus on the work of local artists. Furnishings of the Victorian era and personal objects of the Trevor family, including huge Persian carpets, are shown in the main building where the family lived. Also part of the museum is the Andrus Planetarium, which offers simulated space travel as well as an awesome look at the stars. The museum hosts a series of chamber music concerts Oct.–Apr. *511 Warburton Ave. (off Rte. 9), Yonkers, tel. 914/963–4550. Museum admission: $3 adults, $1.50 children under 12 and senior citizens. Planetarium admission: $4 adults, $2 children under 12 and senior citizens. Combination*

Hudson Valley

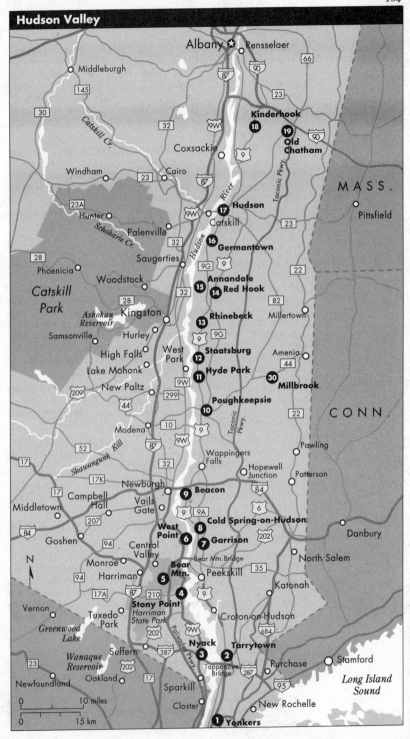

Albany ★ · Rensselaer

66

87 · 90

Middleburgh

145

32 · 9W

Coxsackie

9

Kinderhook
18 · 19
Old Chatham

90

23

M A S S.

30

Windham

23

Cairo

87

Catskill Cr.

9W · **17** **Hudson**

Catskill

Pittsfield

23A

Hunter

Palenville

32

Schoharie Cr.

Saugerties

28

Phoenicia

Woodstock

16 **Germantown**

9G · 9

23

22

Catskill Park

28

Ashokan Reservoir

Kingston

15 **Annandale**
14 **Red Hook**

Millerton

82

Samsonville

Hurley

13 **Rhinebeck**

High Falls

West Park

9 · 9G

Amenia

Lake Mohonk

12 **Staatsburg**

44

New Paltz

11 **Hyde Park**

30 **Millbrook**

209

44

9W

C O N N.

299

10 **Poughkeepsie**

Modena

10

22

52

9W

Pawling

17

Shawangunk Kill

32

Wappingers Falls

Patterson

17K

Hopewell Junction

Newburgh

84

17

Campbell Hall

Vails Gate

9 **Beacon**

Middletown

207

9 · 9A

6

Danbury

84

Goshen

94

Central Valley

West Point
6 **8** **Cold Spring-on-Hudson**
7 **Garrison**

202

North Salem

Monroe

94

Bear Mtn. Bridge

35

Harriman

Bear Mtn.
5

Peekskill

Katonah

17A

87 · 210

4

9

Vernon

Stony Point
Harriman State Park

Croton-on-Hudson

684

Tuxedo Park

202

Greenwood Lake

9W

Wanaque Reservoir

287

Nyack
3

Tarrytown

Purchase

Stamford

23

Suffern

202

17

Tappan Zee Bridge

287

Long Island Sound

Newfoundland

Oakland

Palisades Pkwy.

Sparkill

95

Closter

New Rochelle

0 — 10 miles
0 — 15 km

1 **Yonkers**

ticket: $6 adults, $2.50 children under 12 and senior citizens. Open Wed.–Sat. 10–5, Sun. noon–5 (later hours on Thurs. in summer).

Less than a mile south on Warburton Avenue is the **Philipse Manor Hall State Historic Site,** a history and art museum in a mansion once owned by the wealthy proprietors of the manor of Philipsburg. The loyalist Philipse family lost its mansion and vast land holdings during the American Revolution. The house, a fine example of 18th-century Georgian architecture, has ornate interiors, including a rare Rococo-style ceiling, and contains an extraordinary collection of portraits of American presidents. The house has recently been closed but is scheduled to reopen in April 1992. *Warburton Ave. and Dock St., Yonkers, tel. 914/965–4027. Admission free. Open late-May–late-Oct., Wed.–Sun. noon–5.*

❷ Head north on Route 9 several miles to **Tarrytown** and follow signs to **Sunnyside.** The romantic estate on the banks of the Hudson belonged to Washington Irving. The author of *The Legend of Sleepy Hollow* and *Rip Van Winkle* purchased the home in 1835. The 17 rooms, including Irving's library, contain many of his original furnishings. A stream flows through the landscape from a pond Irving called his "little Mediterranean." Sunnyside is a Registered National Historic Landmark and one of several Historic Hudson Valley Restorations. Special events are organized, and picnicking is encouraged. *Rte. 9, Tarrytown, tel. 914/631–8200. Admission: $6 adults, $5 senior citizens, $3 students. Open Apr.–Oct., Wed.–Mon. 10–5; Mar. and Nov.–Dec., Wed.–Mon. 10–4; and Jan.–Feb., weekends 10–4.*

Heading north of Tarrytown, follow signs on Route 9 to **Lyndhurst,** a castlelike Gothic Revival home set on a bluff overlooking the Hudson. Designed in 1838 by Alexander Jackson Davis, Lyndhurst has had a noteworthy list of occupants—from former New York City mayor William Paulding to merchant George Merritt and railroad magnate Jay Gould. The house is filled with an impressive collection of decorative Victorian furniture and art, and the 67-acre estate includes sweeping lawns and lovely gardens. *635 S. Broadway, Tarrytown, tel. 914/631–0046. Admission: $6 adults, $5 senior citizens, $3 students. Open May–Oct. and Dec., Tues.–Sun. 10–5; Jan.–Apr. and Nov., Sat.–Sun. 10–5.*

Farther north on Route 9 is another Historic Hudson Valley Restoration, the **Philipsburg Manor Upper Mills,** an 18th-century Dutch Colonial site that served as a trading center and the country home of the wealthy merchant Frederik Philipse. This 90,000-acre estate was the center of a bustling commercial empire that included milling and trading operations. Tours visit the stone manor house, a gristmill still run by water power (you can purchase at the gift shop the flour that's ground here), and the farm's animals and gardens. *Rte. 9, North Tarrytown, tel. 914/631–8200. Admission to house: $6 adults, $5 senior citizens, $3 students. Admission to grounds only: $3. Open Mar., Sat.–Sun. 10–5; Apr.–Dec., daily (except Tues.) 10–5.*

Near the Philipsburg Manor in North Tarrytown is the **Old Dutch Church of Sleepy Hollow,** one of the oldest churches in the Hudson Valley. Made famous in Washington Irving's *Legend of Sleepy Hollow,* the church is the only remaining example of 17th-century Dutch religious architecture in the United

States. Stone walls surround furnishings typical of 17th- and 18th-century Netherlands. The grave of Washington Irving, a National Historic Landmark, is located on the grounds. *Rte. 9, North Tarrytown, tel. 914/631–1123 or write Friends of the Old Dutch Burying Ground, 35 South Broadway, Tarrytown 10591. Admission free.*

❸ Head back to I–287 and go west straight onto the Tappan Zee Bridge. Take the **Nyack** exit for that quaint village in Rockland County. The Dutch originally farmed this region, but when the steamboats arrived Nyack became a shipping and boat-building center. The town is now an antiques and arts center, and the village sponsors many special events and street fairs. Take a walking tour to see Nyack's architectural history in its public library, the Couch Court, the Presbyterian Church, the Tappan Zee Theatre, the Reformed Church, and the Congregation of the Sons of Israel; along with numerous shops, galleries, and antiques shops. *For more information and walking-tour maps, contact The Friends of the Nyacks, Box 384, Nyack 10960, tel. 914/353–0586, or Chamber of Commerce of the Nyacks, Box 677, Nyack 10960, tel. 914/353–2221. Most stores closed Mon.*

While in Nyack, be sure to visit the **Edward Hopper House,** also known as the Hopper House Art Center. This was the birthplace and home of the American realist painter from 1882 until his death in 1967. One room is devoted to Hopper-related displays and several of his paintings, featuring local landmarks. Hopper posters, books, and postcards are available for purchase. Exhibits by outstanding local artists are held year-round. Concerts and special events are held in the gardens. *82 N. Broadway, tel. 914/358–0774. Suggested contribution: $1. Open Sat. and Sun. 1–5.*

❹ Route 9W north will tale you to the **Stony Point Battlefield Historic Site,** where George Washington demonstrated that American troops could stand up to superior British forces in the Hudson Highlands. In July 1779 General "Mad" Anthony Wayne led the elite Corps of Light Infantry in a daring midnight raid against the British. The British fortifications in the battlefield are still standing. At the museum, a slide show depicts the events that led up to the battle, and there are memorabilia explaining the tactics and strategies that led to the American victory. *Park Rd., off Rte. 9W, Stony Point, tel. 914/ 786-2521. Admission free. Open May–Oct., Wed.–Sun. 10:30–5 (museum open 11–4).*

❺ Take Route 210 west to the Palisades Interstate Parkway, where you go north to the entrances for **Bear Mountain** and **Harriman State Parks,** the most famous parks of the vast Palisades Interstate system. The two parks share 54,000 acres and both offer plenty of outdoor activity year-round. Facilities exist for boating, roller skating, picnicking, swimming, hiking, and fishing, and there are rest rooms, a bookshop, and a restaurant. At the Trailside Museum in Bear Mountain Park, exhibits and programs describe Native American history as well as the natural history of the area. Children can enjoy the zoo, beaver lodge, and reptile house. A drive, bike ride, or even a hike along the Seven Lakes Drive, and especially Lake Welch Drive, can be breathtaking in the fall and winter. Paddleboats and rowboats can be rented on the lakes. In January and February professional ski-jumping competitions and a juried crafts fair are held in the park, and in December there is a Christmas festival. *Entrance off the Palisades Interstate Pkwy., tel. 914/786–2701. Admission free; parking $3 May–Sept. Open daily dawn–dusk.*

Continue on the Palisades Parkway to the intersection with Route 9W, where you have two choices. You can head north on 9W to visit America's oldest and most distinguished military academy, West Point, or you can take the Bear Mountain Bridge across the Hudson and head north on 9D to Garrison and Cold Spring, charming historic towns with some fine inns. Either way, you'll be driving on a wonderfully scenic stretch of road. If you choose the West Point route, you can cross the river a few miles farther north at the Newburgh Bridge (I–84).

Situated on bluffs overlooking the Hudson River from the west, **West Point** has been the training ground for U.S. Army officers since 1802. Distinguished graduates include Robert E. Lee, Ulysses S. Grant, and Douglas MacArthur. There is a visitor center that shows an orientation movie. A museum at Thayer Hall houses one of the world's foremost collections of military memorabilia and equipment. Uniforms, weapons, field equipment, flags, and American military art are on display. There are also new galleries depicting the history of West Point. On the grounds there are memorials, cannons, and restored forts, such as Fort Putnam. *Rte. 9W, West Point, tel. 914/938–2638 or 914/938–5261. Admission free, but tours cost $3.50 adults, $2 children under 12. Visitor center open daily except major holidays 9–4:45; museum open daily 10:30–4:15.*

Constitution Island, a small island off the east shore of the Hudson, is separated from the mainland by marshes and can only be reached via a boat ride that leaves from West Point. The island played a critical role in General George Washington's strategy to keep the British naval traffic out of the Hudson River. During the Revolutionary War, the island had switched hands from American to British and then back to American. The British ships were stopped by an enormous iron chain that was stretched across the river from West Point to the island. When the war ended in 1783, the barracks were decommissioned and the island returned to civilian control. However, the fort structure remains intact. Part of the present tour of the island includes a visit to the home of Susan and Anna Warner, sisters and prolific writers who wrote under pseudonyms. The house has 15 rooms, all furnished in Victorian style. *Boats leave West Point's South Dock, Peekskill, tel. 914/446–8676. Cost: $6 adults, $4 senior citizens and students, $2 children under 5. Advance reservations required. Tours depart Wed. and Thurs. 1 and 2 PM.*

Across the bridge on the eastern bank of the river, it's about 10 miles north on Route 9D to **Garrison.** The **Garrison Art Center** is housed in a turn-of-the-century building facing the Hudson River, opposite the Garrison train station. The center's programs include an annual arts and crafts fair in August, as well as changing exhibits. Spring and fall auctions are held and there is a fully equipped pottery studio on the premises. *Depot Square, Garrison's Landing, Garrison, tel. 914/424–3960. Admission to center free; $2 or more donation usually requested for fair. Open weekdays 10–5, Sat. noon–5; shorter hours mid-Dec.–Mar.*

Follow Route 9D north to visit **Boscobel,** an early 19th-century
mansion that has been fully restored and furnished with the
decorative arts of the Federal period (1800–1820), including elegant carpets, fine porcelains, and hand-carved furniture.
Standing on a bluff surrounded by beautiful gardens with thousands of flowers that bloom in the spring, Boscobel affords a
breathtaking view of the Hudson River. Concerts are held on
the lawn throughout the summer. In the fall, apples from
Boscobel's orchards go on sale. *Rte. 9D, Garrison, tel. 914/265–
3638. Admission: $5 adults, $4 senior citizens, $2.50 children
under 14. Open Apr.–Oct. 9:30–5; Mar., Nov., and Dec.
9:30–4. Closed Tues.*

❽ Just north of Garrison on Route 9D is **Cold Spring-on-Hudson,** a
small 19th-century village in the heart of the Hudson Highlands. You can stroll in its quiet streets and visit its antiques
and crafts shops on your own, or join a guided walking tour of
the historic district. Tours depart from the Hudson Valley Gift
Gallery and Information Center, also a good source for free
maps and brochures about the local area. *76 Main St., or write
Box 71, Cold Spring-on-Hudson 10516, tel. 914/265–3066. Donations accepted. Tours May–Nov., Sun. 2 PM.*

❾ About 12 miles north on Route 9D in the town of **Beacon** is the
Madam Brett Homestead, a Dutch dwelling built in 1709 and
visited by Washington, Lafayette, and Baron von Steuben. The
furnishings reflect the lifestyles of the seven generations of the
Brett family through 1954, when the Daughters of the American Revolution purchased the house. The 28,000-acre estate
and gristmill were used to store military supplies during the
Revolutionary War. There is original period furniture, Canton
china, paintings, and a formal garden. The homestead is on the
National Register of Historic Places. *50 Van Nydeck Ave., Beacon, tel. 914/831–6533 or 896–6897. Admission: $3 adults, $2
children 13–18, $1 children under 12. Open May–Oct., week-
ends 1–4.*

A short distance away, **Howland Center,** a community arts center, is housed in an 1872 building designed by American architect Richard Morris Hunt. The center has a gallery for exhibits
on art and history, a performance hall for concerts, dramatic
productions, and dance, and a lecture hall. *477 Main St., Beacon, tel. 914/831–4988. Donations accepted. Gallery hours:
Wed. and Sun. 1–5 and by appointment. Call for performance
schedule.*

Past the Newburgh Bridge (I–84), drive north on Route 9D to
Route 9, which heads on up to Poughkeepsie, in the heart of
Dutchess County. Two miles south of Poughkeepsie on Route 9
is **Locust Grove,** the home of Samuel F. B. Morse, the inventor
of the telegraph. A National Historic Landmark, the house was
designed by Alexander Jackson Davis and is a classic example
of mid-19th-century Italian villa-style architecture. It sits on a
bluff overlooking the Hudson amid 150 acres of gardens and
woodland. Memorabilia on display—in addition to a model of
Morse's original telegraph—includes an extensive collection of
furniture, china, and art. *Admission: $4 adults, $3.50 senior
citizens, $1 children 7–16. Open lat May–late Sept., Wed.–
Sun. 10–4; Oct., weekends 10–4; Nov.–Dec., Apr.–May by appointment. Closed Jan.–Mar.*

10 **Poughkeepsie** is the home of Vassar College and the largest city in this part of the state. The Dutchess County Historical Society houses its collection in the **Clinton House** and the nearby **Glebe House,** two 18th-century buildings that served New York's fledgling government when it operated here in 1777. Three centuries of Hudson Valley history are documented by manuscripts, books, maps, photographs, art objects, and furnishings on display in these two historic houses. *Corner of Main and North White Sts., Poughkeepsie, tel. 914/471–1630. Admission to Clinton House free (donations accepted). Open weekdays 10–4. Admission to Glebe House by appointment only; donation requested.*

Just down the road on Main Street in the Old City Hall is the **Mid Hudson Arts and Science Center (MASC),** a multiarts service organization that organizes exhibitions and art shows throughout the year. The main floor contains two showcase galleries and the offices of the Summergroup Cooperative, a professional visual-arts group that maintains a small gallery in the rear. The second floor is used by local theater and performing-arts groups. *228 Main St., Poughkeepsie, tel. 914/471–1155. Donation: $1. Open Tues.–Fri. 11–4, Sat. noon–4 and by appointment. Galleries closed Aug.*

Head three miles west of Main Street on Route 44 to Raymond Avenue and turn south to reach **Vassar College.** Matthew Vassar not only broke new ground when he founded Vassar as a women's college in 1861, but he also was the first to include an art gallery and museum as part of an American college. The gallery owns 8,000 works of art, many of them Hudson River landscapes. There are also prints by Rembrandt and Whistler. After visiting the art museum, stop at the college's chapel to see the rare Tiffany glass windows. *Raymond Ave., Poughkeepsie, tel. 914/437–5235 or 914/437–5241. Admission free. Open Wed.–Sat. 10–5, Sun. noon–5.*

The next several miles of the Hudson river road is particularly rich in great estates. Ten miles north of Poughkeepsie on Route **11** 9, in **Hyde Park,** is the **Franklin Delano Roosevelt National Historic Site.** The library and museum contain collections of manuscripts and personal documents displaying FDR's extensive career. Family photographs, gifts he received as president of the United States, his desk from the Oval Office, items dating from the period of his service in the U.S. Navy, letters, speeches, state documents, and official correspondence are on display. The large Roosevelt family house contains original furnishings. The rose gardens surrounding the gravesites of both Franklin and Eleanor Roosevelt are serene. The library is open only for research. *519 Albany Post Rd. (Rte. 9), Hyde Park, tel. 914/229–9115. Admission: $4 adults; senior citizens over 62, school groups, and children under 12 free. Open Apr.–Oct., daily 9–5; Nov.–Mar., Thurs.–Mon. 9–5, except major holidays.*

The only historic site in the nation devoted to a first lady is the **Eleanor Roosevelt National Historic Site** at nearby Val-Kill, two miles to the east. Amid 172 acres of woods, the restored home of Eleanor Roosevelt is open for guided tours. Begin your visit by viewing the film biography, "First Lady of the World," followed by a tour of the Val-Kill cottage where Eleanor Roosevelt lived from 1945 to 1962. *Rte. 9G, Hyde Park, tel. 914/229–9115.*

Admission free. Open May–Oct., daily 9–5; Nov.–Dec. and
Mar.–Apr., weekends 9–5. Closed Jan.–Feb.

Two miles north of the Roosevelt historic sites along the river is
the 54-room **Vanderbilt Mansion,** the former spring and fall
home of Frederick and Louise Vanderbilt. Built in 1896–98, it is
a splendid example of the Beaux Arts style of architecture and
a fitting symbol of the Gilded Age. The decor includes elaborate gold-leaf trim, mahogany paneling, and many original furnishings such as marble mantels, throne-type chairs, Venetian
lanterns, beaded crystal chandeliers, Persian rugs, Flemish
tapestries, and hand-painted silk lampshades. The grounds offer panoramic views of the Hudson and acres of gardens. *Rte. 9,*
Hyde Park, tel. 914/229–9115. Admission: $2 adults; senior
citizens over 62 and children 16 and under free. Open Apr.–
Oct., daily 9–5; Nov.–Mar., Thurs.–Mon. 9–5, except major
holidays.

A short distance away on Route 9 in Hyde Park is the most respected cooking school in the United States, **The Culinary In-**
stitute of America, founded in 1946. Located on an 80-acre
campus overlooking the Hudson River, the institute is home to
1,850 students enrolled in the college's 21-month culinary arts,
baking, or pastry arts program. More than 100 chefs and
instructors from 20 countries conduct courses in the fun-
damentals of cooking, charcuterie, American, Oriental, and
international cuisines, with related courses in wines, table
service, purchasing, stewarding, beverage control, and nutri-
tion. The facilities include 35 commercially equipped production kitchens and bakeshops, a 38,000-volume library, and four
student-staffed restaurants that are open to the public by reservation (*see* Dining and Lodging, *below*). Tours are available,
by appointment, to small groups of 25 or more who have made
reservations to dine at one of the school's restaurants; the cost
for group tours is $2 per person. The institute's bookstore car-
ries hundreds of titles of interest to both amateur and professional cooks, and is also a good source for kitchen accessories
and baking aids. *For more information, contact The Culinary*
Institute of America, 651 S. Albany Post Rd. (Rte. 9), Hyde
Park 12538, tel. 914/452–9600. Bookstore open weekdays 10–
7:45, Sat. 11–3:45.

12 Head north on Route 9 for five miles to the town of **Staatsburg**
and follow signs for **The Mills Mansion,** the opulent country estate of Ogden and Ruth Livingston Mills, graced with original
furnishings of the Louis XV and Louis XVI periods. Flemish
tapestries and Oriental porcelains embellish the oversize
rooms of this 1895 Beaux Arts mansion, which has panoramic
views of the Hudson River valley and the vast manicured acre-
age bordering the shoreline. Guided tours are available and
hiking, picnicking, and cross-country skiing are encouraged.
Special lawn concerts and workshops are held during the summer. *Old Post Rd., Staatsburg, tel. 914/889–4100. Admission*
free. Open May–Labor Day, Wed.–Sat. 10–5 and Sun. 1–5; La-
bor Day–Oct., Wed.–Sat. noon–5 and Sun. 1–5. Also special
tours at Christmastime; call for schedule.

Continue north on Route 9 for three miles and enter one of the
13 oldest villages in the country, **Rhinebeck,** founded in 1688. The
Beekman Arms (*see* Dining and Lodging, *below*), located here,
is purported to be the oldest inn in America (1766) and was a
meeting place for such famous people as George Washington

and Franklin Roosevelt. Rhinebeck contains a charming state historic district, White's Corner, full of Victorian-style buildings, antiques shops, boutiques, and galleries.

The **Old Rhinebeck Aerodrome,** three miles outside Rhinebeck Village (follow the signs on Route 9) is a museum housing a large collection of antique airplanes dating from 1900 through 1937. Many of these historic wonders are still flown in weekend air shows. Adventurous visitors can experience barn-storming rides in open-cockpit biplanes, such as a 1929 New Standard D-25, which carries up to four passengers. These 15-minute flights cost $25 per person. Rides book up early, so call first thing in the morning. *42 Stone Church Rd., Rhinebeck, tel. 914/ 758–8610. Admission weekdays: $4 adults, $2 children under 10; weekends (includes an airshow): $8 adults, $4 children under 10. Open mid-May–Oct., daily 10–5; air shows at 2:30 weekends.*

⑭ Continue north on Route 9 to **Red Hook,** a village with many Federal- and Victorian-style homes and a number of fine antiques and crafts shops. A slight detour north of the village leads to one of the county's largest pick-your-own farms. Follow Rte. 9 for three miles, then turn left at Pitcher Lane for the **Greig Farm Market** (tel. 914/758–1234, open May–Dec. daily 8–6).

In the center of the village, turn left at the traffic light onto Route 199 and continue in a westward direction for approximately three miles to Route 9G. Turn right (north) and go three
⑮ miles to **Annandale.** Take a left on Annandale Road and follow the signs to **Montgomery Place,** a great home situated on a 400-acre riverside estate. This 23-room classical-revival mansion was built in 1802–05 by Janet Livingston Montgomery, widow of the Revolutionary War hero General Richard Montgomery. The interior, which is in the process of being restored, holds two centuries worth of family memorabilia as well as exquisite French china, chandeliers, leatherbound books, hand-carved furniture, ancestral portraits, and kitchen utensils. Tours are conducted regularly by uniformed docents. In addition, the sign-posted grounds offer views of the Hudson River and the Catskill Mountains, walking trails, gardens, woodlands, waterfalls, and an orchard of 5,000 fruit trees. (You can pick your own fruit in the autumn.) *River Rd. (Rte. 103), Annandale-on-Hudson, tel. 914/758–5461. Admission: $6 adults, $5 senior citizens, $3 students under 18, children under 6 free. Open Apr.–Oct., daily 10–5 (except Tues.); Nov., Dec., and Mar., weekends only 10–5. Closed Jan.–Feb.*

⑯ Continue north on Route 9G to **Germantown,** where you can visit **Clermont,** an estate that was home to seven generations of prominent Livingston families between 1728 and 1962. The historic house, gardens, and estate grounds have been restored to their 1930s appearance, and the setting offers magnificent views of the Hudson River. Special celebrations, including a sheep-shearing festival, a croquet day, a pumpkin festival, and a Hudson River steamboat festival, are held here throughout the year. *Off Rte. 9G, Germantown, tel. 518/537–4240. Admission free. The mansion is open May–Oct., Wed.–Sat. 10–5, Sun. 1–5. The grounds are open year-round, 8:30–sunset.*

⑰ Take Route 9G north on a scenic ride to **Hudson** to view the Moorish-style castle created by artist Frederic Church, the

foremost painter of the 19th-century Hudson River School.
Church and his wife, Isabel, returned from Europe and the
Middle East to build **Olana,** or "our place on high." Picturesque
grounds surrounding the villa offer panoramic vistas of the
Hudson River valley. The 37-room mansion features hand-
painted tiles on the roof, turrets, and garden paths; rich Persian rugs; and hundreds of pieces of pottery and china as well as
Egyptian wall paintings. *Rte. 9G, Hudson, tel. 518/828-0135.
Admission: $1 adults, 50¢ children under 12. Reservations rec-
ommended. Open Memorial Day–Labor Day, Wed.–Sun.
12–4; Sept.–Oct., Wed.–Sat. noon–4, Sun. 1–4.*

From Hudson you can take a short cut to the Berkshires on
Route 23 east across Columbia County, passing through Hillsdale. If you'd like to visit a bit more of historic Hudson Valley,
however, continue up Route 9 another 15 miles or so to
⑱ Kinderhook, where you'll find **Lindenwald,** the retirement
home of Martin Van Buren, the eighth president of the United
States. Van Buren was born in Kinderhook and returned here
to purchase Lindenwald in 1839. The Federal-style house was
built in 1797, and the mansion has been restored to reflect the
original furnishings and architecture, complete with shutters,
double chimneys, and arched windows. Today it is a National
Historic Site. The house contains a fine collection of Van Buren
memorabilia. *Rte. 9H, Kinderhook, tel. 518/758-9689. Admission: $1 adults, senior citizens over 62 and children under 12
free. Open Apr.–Dec., daily 9–4:30; Nov., Tues.–Sun. hours
vary.*

Also in Kinderhook is the **James Vanderpoel House,** an 1820
Federal-period house of the former prominent attorney, assem-
blyman, and judge. On display are early 19th-century furniture and decorative arts, including a fine selection of paintings
by local artists that depict Columbia County life. *16 Broad St.,
Kinderhook, tel. 518/758-9265. Admission: $3 adults, $2 senior citizens and children 12–18, children under 12 free. Open
Memorial Day–Labor Day, Mon. and Wed.–Sat. 11–5, Sun.
1–5.*

Columbia County Museum and Library is a complex established
by the Columbia County Historical Society to interpret the
300-year history of the county. There is a gallery offering
changing exhibits of paintings, costumes, photographs, and artifacts illuminating the county's cultural and historic heritage.
*5 Albany Ave., Kinderhook, tel. 518/758-9265. Admission
free. Open weekdays 10–4, Sat. 11–5, Sun. 1–5.*

⑲ West of Kinderhook, on Route 66, in **Old Chatham,** is **The Shaker Museum,** dedicated to members of the sect of English men
and women who immigrated to America in the late 18th century in order to practice their communal religion. Called "Shakers" because they danced and moved during worship services,
the group established settlements throughout the new country. The Shakers were known for being industrious, thrifty,
and plain—attributes that are reflected in the artifacts and objects on display: chairs, seed packets, tin milk pails, brooms,
clothing, cloaks, and another Shaker enterprise—pharmaceu-
ticals. *Shaker Museum Rd., Old Chatham, tel. 518/794-9100.
Admission: $6 adults, $5 senior citizens, $3 children 8–17,
children under 8 free. Open May–Oct., daily 10–5.*

Just north of Old Chatham is I–90, the highway that takes you east to the Berkshires, the next leg of this tour.

Dining and Lodging

The following dining price categories have been used: *Expensive*, over $40; *Moderate*, $20–$40; *Inexpensive*, under $20.

The following lodging price categories have been used: *Very Expensive*, over $150; *Expensive*, $100–$150; *Moderate*, $60–$100; *Inexpensive*, under $60.

Bear Mountain
Dining and Lodging

Bear Mountain Inn. For more than 50 years, this chalet-style resort has been known for both its bucolic location (in the Bear Mountain State Park on the shores of Hessian Lake) and its warm hospitality. There are rooms in the main inn and units in five different lodges on the opposite side of the lake. A two-night minimum is often imposed on weekends. *Rte. 9W, 10911, tel. 914/786–2731. 60 rooms. Facilities: restaurant, lounge, outdoor pool, picnic grounds, hiking trails, and access to ice skating, ski jumping, sledding, cross-country skiing. AE, MC, V. Moderate–Expensive.*

Canaan
Lodging

Queechy Lake Motel. Nestled on Queechy Lake in a quiet, tree-shaded setting, this contemporary two-story lodging in northeastern Columbia County is close to the Massachusetts border, less than 10 miles from Tanglewood and the Berkshire ski resorts. The guest units are furnished in a country style, but the biggest attraction is the sylvan lake view from each window. Continental breakfast included on weekdays; coffee shop operates on weekends. *Queechy Lake Dr. (Rte. 30), Box 106, 12029, tel. 518/781–4615. 18 rooms. Facilities: outdoor heated pool, lake beach passes provided to guests. MC, V. Moderate.*

Cold Spring
Dining
★

Plumbush Inn. Dating to 1867, this lovely inn is furnished in an opulent Victorian style. It offers dining by candlelight amid a decor of rose-patterned wallpaper, dark oak paneling, paintings by local artists, and the warmth of wood-burning fireplaces. In summer there is also outdoor dining on a porch overlooking the gardens. The menu ranges from fresh seafood and veal to Swiss specialties, with both fixed-price and à la carte services. The inn also has three guest rooms with bath upstairs if you want to plan an overnight. *Rte. 9D, tel. 914/265–3904. Jacket required in evening. Reservations suggested. AE, DC, MC, V. Closed Mon. and Tues. Expensive.*

Breakneck Lodge. A restaurant for more than 50 years, this cozy Old World Swiss-Tudor lodge overlooks the Hudson River and Storm King Mountain. The menu features fresh seafood, beef, veal, and game, plus Austrian, Swiss, and German dishes. *Rte. 9D, Old River Rd., tel. 914/265–9669. Dress: neatly casual. Reservations suggested, especially on weekends. AE, DC, MC, V. Moderate.*

Lodging
★

Hudson House. Formerly known as the Hudson View Inn, this is a restored historic landmark (circa 1831) on the banks of the Hudson River. Several guest rooms have balconies with views of the Hudson, West Point, or the village. The furnishings include antiques and curios such as Shaker-style sconces, lamps made from French wine decanters, and wall decorations fashioned from cookie cutters. Continental breakfast is included. *2 Main St., 10516, tel. 914/265–9355. 15 rooms with bath, 2 with* shared bath. *Facilities: restaurant, lounge, bicycle rentals. AE, MC, V. Closed Jan. Expensive.*

Olde Post Inn. This restored inn, dating from 1820, offers bed-and-breakfast in an Old World setting with such modern amenities as air-conditioning. The on-premises stone tavern features jazz entertainment on Friday and Saturday nights. Innkeepers are Barbara and Jim Ryan. *43 Main St., 10516, tel. 914/265–2510. 5 rooms share 2 bathrooms. Facilities: tavern, patio, garden. No credit cards. Moderate.*

Garrison
Dining
★

Xavier's at Garrison. This elegant French restaurant sits in a country setting, surrounded by the Highland Golf Course. Fresh flowers, crystal, and silver adorn each table, and on weekends there is background music by a harpist or pianist. In the summer, outdoor dining is also available on a covered terrace overlooking the putting greens. The menu changes often, but top entrees are grilled quail over pasta, medallions of rabbit with white grapes, and grilled Norwegian salmon basted with honey and Chinese mustard. *Rte. 9D, tel. 914/424–4228. Jacket required. Reservations required. No credit cards. Closed Mon., dinner only Tues.–Sat. Expensive.*

Dining and Lodging
★

The Bird and Bottle Inn. Dating to 1761, this one-time stagecoach stop on the Albany Post Road is still primarily known for its award-winning restaurant. Today it has three dining rooms, all with wood-burning fireplaces and a Colonial ambience enhanced by antiques, beamed ceilings, and wideplank floors. Menu choices include roast pheasant, rack of lamb, salmon Wellington, and fillet of sole poached in wine; be sure to sample the special pumpkin bread. Desserts are also very tempting, from butter pecan soufflés to chocolate rum tortes. It's open only for dinners, Wednesday through Sunday, and Sunday brunch; all meals are prix-fixe. Overnight accommodations with a Colonial ambience are available on the second floor of the inn and in an adjoining cottage. The guest rooms have four-poster or canopy beds, antique furnishings, and working fireplaces. Breakfast and dinner are included. *Old Albany Post Rd. (Rte. 9), Nelson's Corners, 10524, tel. 914/424–3000. 4 rooms. Jacket required in restaurant; reservations advised. AE, MC, V. Very Expensive.*

Hillsdale
Dining

L'Hostellerie Bressane. Transplanted from the Rhone Valley, Jean and Madeline Morel have graciously transformed an 18th-century Hudson Valley home into a French country inn. There are three cozy dining rooms, with brick walls, wood paneling, open fireplaces, and tables meticulously set with white linens, fine china and flatware, and fresh flowers and candles. The entrées, all artfully presented with colorful arrays of seasonal vegetables, include local trout, veal chop, roast duck, fillet of beef, rack of lamb, braised chicken breast, and poached king salmon. For dessert, the hot soufflés are hard to resist. *Rtes. 23 and 22, 518/325-3412. Jacket suggested. Reservations suggested. No credit cards. Closed Mon. and Tues. (closed Mon. only Aug.), dinner only. Expensive.*

Hyde Park
Dining
★

The Culinary Institute of America has four restaurants serving lunch and dinner to the public. **The Escoffier** is an award-winning restaurant where students in their final semester at the school practice the preparation and serving of classical French haute cuisine. The menus are fixed-price or à la carte and the standards are impeccable—so much so that it's often fully booked a month or more in advance. **American Bounty** focuses on an à la carte service of American regional fare, including such southern specialties as crawfish pie or shrimp etoufée and midwestern game dishes. **Caterina de Medici** serves regional Italian cuisine—both modern and traditional. This is the smallest of the four dining rooms, so space is very limited and the menu is fixed-price. There is one seating for lunch at 11:30, one seating for dinner at 6:30. **St. Andrew's Cafe,** the most informal of the four restaurants, offers à la carte service of well-balanced meals prepared according to sound nutritional guidelines. *651 S. Albany Post Rd., tel. 914/471-6608 weekdays 8:30-5. Jacket and reservations required (except dress casual at St. Andrew's Cafe). AE, DC, MC, V. Escoffier and American Bounty closed Sun., Mon.; Caterina de Medici and St. Andrew's Cafe closed weekends; all four closed school holidays and first 2 wks July. Escoffier and American Bounty Expensive; Caterina de Medici and St. Andrew's Cafe Moderate.*

Lodging **The Roosevelt Inn.** This relatively new Colonial-style motel is set back from the main road in a tree-shaded setting one mile north of the Franklin D. Roosevelt National Historic Site. *38 Albany Post Rd. (Rte. 9), 12538, tel. 914/229-2443. 25 rooms with bath or shower. Facilities: coffee shop (breakfast only), nearby dining, tennis, golf, and cross-country skiing. AE, MC, V. Closed Jan. and Feb. Inexpensive–Moderate.*
Dutch Patroon. This handy, well-kept motel is right on the main north–south route through western Dutchess County. About one quarter of the units have kitchenettes. Complimentary Continental breakfast. *Rte. 9, 12538, tel. 914/229-7141. 33 rooms. Facilities: restaurant, outdoor pool. AE, MC, V. Inexpensive.*

Kinderhook **Old Dutch Inn.** Set in the heart of the village and overlooking
Dining the green, this restaurant provides a look at Columbia County of yesteryear. The decor includes country-style furnishings, a brick hearth, and a wood stove. Featured dishes include marinated lamb roast and grilled seafood. *8 Broad St., tel. 518/758-1676. Dress: casual. Reservations suggested. MC, V. Closed Mon. Moderate.*

Poughkeepsie **Caesar's Ristorante.** As might be expected, the Caesar salads at
Dining this fine, northern Italian restaurant are exceptional, as is the antipasto. There are also many fine pasta, beef, chicken, and veal dishes on the menu. You'll find this restaurant in the heart of the historic district, directly under the Poughkeepsie Railroad Bridge. *2 Delafield St., tel. 914/471-4857. Dress: casual. Reservations not accepted. AE, DC, MC, V. Dinner only. Moderate.*
River Station. "Down by the riverside" dining is the theme of this informal restaurant overlooking the Hudson. You can enjoy river views either from the inside dining room or the outdoor deck. Specialties include seafood, veal, steak, and pasta. *25 Main St., tel. 914/452-9207. Dress: casual. Reservations not accepted on weekends. MC, V. Moderate.*

Lodging **Inn at the Falls.** Operating as a bed-and-breakfast, this rela-
★ tively new inn combines the amenities of a modern hotel with the ambience and personal attention of a country home. Situated in a residential area beside a rushing waterfall about two miles southeast of the city, the inn has an arched courtyard that joins two wings of guest rooms. The public areas are bright and airy, with pastel-toned furnishings, floor-to-ceiling paned windows, brass chandeliers, marble floors, and an abundance of

leafy plants. The guest rooms, all accessible by computer-card keys, vary in decor from English-mansion style to American country, Art Deco, or Oriental. Many bedrooms have four-poster, wrought-iron, or canopied beds, brass headboards, armoires, rolltop desks, crystal and china lamps. Continental breakfast, delivered to each guest room on a silver tray, is included. *50 Red Oaks Mill Rd., 12603, tel. 914/462–5770. 22 rooms and 14 suites, all with private bath. AE, DC, MC. Expensive.*

Edison Motor Inn. Situated four miles east of the city, this dependable motel has equipped about one-third of its units with kitchenettes, ideal for family travelers. *313 Manchester Rd. (Rte. 55), 12603, tel. 914/454-3080. 138 rooms. Facilities: restaurant, lounge, 2 tennis courts, outdoor pool, shuffleboard, playground. AE, DC,MC, V. Moderate.*

Red Hook
Dining

Greene & Bresler Ltd. This contemporary shopfront restaurant in the heart of town serves creative American and European cuisines, with such dishes as apple-smoked turkey and brie, smoked fish, charcoal-grilled fillet of beef, Norwegian salmon, pastas, and a wide variety of colorful salads. In summer, tables are set up on an outside deck. *29 W. Market St., tel. 914/758–5992. Dress: casual. Reservations suggested. AE, MC, V. Lunch daily except Wed., dinner Fri.–Sat. only. Moderate.*

Savoy. Located across from the entrance to Bard College and northwest of town, this relatively new restaurant features a blend of American and Continental cuisines, with such dishes as steak au poivre, veal champignon, vegetable crêpes, and sautéed sweetbreads, as well as fillet of salmon, lobster, and (on weekends) prime rib. *Rte. 9G, tel. 914/876–1200. Dress: neatly casual. Reservations suggested. AE, DC, MC, V. Closed Mon., dinner only. Moderate.*

Somethin' Fishy. Seafood lovers flock to this unpretentious restaurant-cum-fish market, located about 1 mile south of town on Route 9. Emphasis is on fresh fillets and shellfish cut and baked, fried, or broiled to order. Chicken and steak are also available for landlubbers. *124 S. Broadway, tel. 914/758-3474. Dress: casual. Reservations not accepted. No credit cards. BYOB. Closed Sun. and Mon. Inexpensive–Moderate.*

Lodging

Red Hook Inn. In the heart of the village, this small inn dates back to 1882, but was restored and reopened in the 1980s, with new management taking it over in 1991. The decor combines exposed brick walls, country furnishings, and local antiques (many of which are for sale). Guest rooms have air-conditioning and ceiling fans. *31 S. Broadway (Rte. 9), 12571, tel. 914/758-8445. 3 rooms, 2 suites. Facilities: restaurant, lounge, bakery. MC, V. Moderate–Expensive.*

★ **Gaslight Motel.** Located three miles north of Red Hook and set back from the main road in a tree-shaded setting, Gaslight has a Colonial-style motif and country furnishings; about half of the units have kitchenettes. There are also views of the Catskill Mountains in the distance. *Rte. 9 (R.D. 3, Box 491), 12571, tel. 914/758-1571. 12 rooms. Facilities: private gardens, patio, barbecue. MC, V. Inexpensive.*

★ **Hearthstone Motel.** This is a basic one-story motel, situated on a hillside about three miles north of the village. The guest rooms have views of the Catskill Mountains to the west. *Rte. 9 (R.D. 3, Box 51), 12571, tel. 914/758-1811. 8 rooms. AE, MC, V. Inexpensive.*

Rhinebeck
Dining
★

Le Petit Bistro. Situated in the heart of Rhinebeck less than a block from the Beekman Arms, this is a small and intimate restaurant with a French ambience, artfully prepared food, and enthusiastic service. It is run by Yvonne and Jean-Paul Croizer, previously associated with the catering department of Air France and leading restaurants in New York City and the Hudson Valley. Featured dishes include duck with fruits, Dover sole, seafood crepes, coquilles St. Jacques, coq au vin, steak au poivre, and sautéed softshell crab in season. Desserts range from feather-light meringues to velvety fondues or *crème brûlées*. The crusty breads and rich ice creams are made locally. *8 E. Market St., tel. 914/876-7400. Dress: neatly casual. Reservations suggested. AE, DC, MC, V. Closed Tues. and Wed., dinner only. Moderate-Expensive.*

Chez Marcel. Located less than two miles north of Rhinebeck, this French country inn is the domain of Renee and Marcel Disch (formerly of Chez Renee in Manhattan). Everything is cooked to order, and the menu includes such choices as sole *bonne femme*, chicken almondine, veal *cordon bleu*, and a delicately seasoned rack of lamb. *Rte. 9, tel. 914/876-8189. Dress: neatly casual. Reservations suggested. AE, DC. Closed Mon., dinner only. Moderate.*

Fox Hollow Inn. Freshly made pasta and other Italian dishes are the specialties at this rustic restaurant, located in a converted country inn about two miles south of the village. Owned and operated by the LaRocca family for 35 years, this spot is also known for veal, steaks, shellfish, and thick cuts of prime ribs. *Rte. 9, tel. 914/876-4696. Dress: casual. Reservations usually not necessary, except weekends. MC, V. Closed Tues. Inexpensive-Moderate.*

Rolling Rock Cafe. Located one mile north of town across from the Duchess County Fairgrounds, this busy eating spot has an American bistro theme, decor, and menu. Seating is available in booths or at tables, and a laser juke box provides background music. Entrees range from salmon wrapped in pastry leaves to steak Rolling Rock (with black peppercorns). *Rte. 9, tel. 914/876-7655. Dress: casual. Reservations not accepted for parties less than four. AE, MC, V. Inexpensive-Moderate.*

Foster's Coach House. The site of this restaurant-pub was once the home of a Revolutionary War drillmaster who so loved his horse that he gave the animal a proper funeral when it died. You'll not only see hitching posts on the sidewalk outside and horse prints and racing scenes on the walls within, but you can also sit at a table in a horse stall or place a call from a phone booth fashioned from a horse-drawn carriage. The atmosphere is informal and the menu concentrates on burgers, steaks, and salads. It's in the heart of town, one block north of the Beekman Arms and adjacent to Upstate Films. *22 Montgomery St., tel. 914/876-8052. Dress: casual. No credit cards. Reservations not accepted. Closed Mon. Inexpensive.*

Schemmy's. For a light snack, lunch, or coffee, don't miss this old-fashioned ice-cream parlor (with a wrought-iron ice-cream cone hanging over the front door). Situated in the center of the village, it is a real Rhinebeck institution that used to be Schermerhorn's Drug Store. You'll see a wall lined with original medicine drawers, apothecary jars, and other local memorabilia. The menu features sandwiches, burgers, quiches, soups, salads, and homemade ice cream in assorted flavors. *19*

E. Market St., tel. 914/876–6215. Dress: casual. No credit cards. Open daily 7 AM–5 PM. Inexpensive.

Lodging **Village Victorian Inn.** Located on a quiet residential street, this two-story Italianate home (circa 1860) is a quintessential bed-and-breakfast inn, with well-tended gardens, white picket fence, and front-porch rockers. The owners, Judy and Richard Kohler, have decorated the interior with area antiques, French Victorian fabrics, and Oriental rugs. Each guest room has a brass or canopy bed (king- or queen-size) adorned with a country quilt or comforter, a ceiling fan, books, and other homey touches. A gourmet breakfast (such as eggs Benedict, pecan French toast, or quiches) is included. *31 Center St., 12572, tel. 914/876–8345. 5 rooms. AE, MC, V. Expensive.*

Whistlewood Farm. For a more rural ambience, you can enjoy bed-and-breakfast at this 13-acre horse farm, located three miles east of Rhinebeck village, off Route 308. The grounds offer lovely gardens and views of the countryside, and the interior of the house is full of beamed ceilings and antique furnishings. Innkeeper Maggie Myer is well known for her hearty breakfasts (included in the rates) of fresh local fruits, cheese-filled omelets, sour-cream coffee cake, blackberry or apple crumb pie, and blueberry-banana muffins. Rates are slightly higher on weekends. *11 Pells Rd., 12572, tel. 914/876–6838. 3 rooms with private bath, 2 rooms with shared bath. Facilities: pets can be accommodated in house or in adjacent kennels. No credit cards. Moderate–Expensive.*

Rhinebeck Village Inn. Owned and operated by the Behrens family, this one-story motel, about a mile south of the village in a tree-shaded setting, has country-house charm. The spacious guest rooms are very homey, with handcrafted local furnishings and wall hangings. Continental breakfast is included in the room charge. Weekend rates are slightly higher. *Rte. 9, Box 491, 12572, tel. 914/876–7000. 16 rooms. Facilities: cable TV, refrigerators available on request. AE, DC, MC, V. Inexpensive–Moderate.*

Dining and Lodging **Beekman Arms.** One of America's oldest inns (dating to 1766),
★ this hotel has welcomed such historic guests as George Washington, Thomas Jefferson, and Franklin Roosevelt. A variety of accommodations are available, including 13 smallish antique-furnished rooms in the original building and four motel-style rooms at the rear of the inn. About a block away, there are seven rooms in Delamater House (circa 1844), a delightful two-story, American Gothic residence furnished with wicker furniture, huge armoires, and Victorian touches. There are also 30 new rooms located behind Delamater in a surrounding courtyard, carriage house, and restored town house; all have airconditioning and some have working fireplaces. A room at the Delamater House comes with complimentary Continental breakfast. The restaurant offers four different dining rooms, but all serve the same menu, with its emphasis on American regional fare. The restaurant kitchen is now operated by the management of New York City's trendy An American Place; the menu features creative regional fare such as Hudson Valley brook trout, free-range duck glazed with wildflower honey, Atlantic salmon, lobster and wild mushroom ravioli, and Black Angus steaks. *4 Mill St. (Rte. 9), 12572, tel. 914/876–7077. 59 rooms. Facilities: 4 dining rooms, tavern. Dress: casual but neat. Reservations suggested. AE, DC, MC, V. Moderate–Expensive.*

Tarrytown **Horsefeathers.** Dark-paneled walls and an antique bar distin-
Dining guish this restaurant, which features great hamburgers and
steaks, pastas, shepherd's pies, overstuffed sandwiches, and
rich New England clam chowder. The atmosphere is casual
and comfortable. *94 N. Broadway, tel. 914/631–6606. Dress:
casual. Reservations recommended, especially on weekends.
AE, MC, V. Lunch and dinner Mon.–Sat., dinner only Sun.
Moderate.*

Lodging **Tarrytown Hilton.** In a 10-acre garden setting, this multi-
winged low-rise hotel makes an ideal base for exploring the
Sleepy Hollow region. Although the architecture is modern,
the decor emphasizes Colonial and country styles, and there
are cozy touches in the public rooms, such as beamed ceilings,
wood-paneled walls, wood-burning fireplaces, Oriental rugs,
antique furnishings, and crystal chandeliers. Most guest rooms
have individual patios or terraces. *455 S. Broadway, 10591, tel.
914/631–5700 or 800/HILTONS. 249 rooms. Facilities: restaurant, coffee shop, entertainment lounge, indoor and outdoor
pools, 2 tennis courts, exercise room, jogging trail, airport
shuttle, baby-sitter service. AE, DC, MC, V. Expensive–Very
Expensive.*

West Point **Hotel Thayer.** On the grounds of the U.S. Military Academy,
Lodging this stately brick hotel steeped in history and tradition has
been welcoming military and civilian guests for more than 60
years. The hotel's public rooms are highlighted by marble
floors, iron chandeliers, military portraits, and leather furnishings. The guest rooms have standard appointments, but
many have views of the river and the West Point grounds. *Rte.
9W, 10996, tel. 914/446–4731 or 800/247–5047. 197 rooms. Facilities: restaurant, lounge, tennis court, gift shop. AE, DC,
MC, V. Moderate–Expensive.*

The Arts

Upstate Films (26 Montgomery St., Rhinebeck, tel. 914/876–
2515) is a repertory movie theater showing international and
American classics, art films, and some new or experimental
works.

The Bardavon 1869 Opera House (35 Market St., Poughkeepsie,
tel. 914/473–2072), a year-round venue for all types of performing arts, is one of the oldest theaters in the country and is listed
on the National Register.

MacHaydn Theater (Rte. 203, Chatham, tel. 518/392–9292) is
one of New York State's foremost summer-stock playhouses,
open late May–end of September.

Nightlife

Rhinebeck Tavern (19–21 W. Market St., Rhinebeck, tel. 914/
876–3059) is an informal spot featuring live rock, country-west-
ern, and pop music, especially on weekends.

Rhinecliff Hotel (Schatzell Ave., Rhinecliff, tel. 914/876–8688),
a 19th-century inn beside the Hudson, offers afternoon and
evening musical programs ranging from hard rock to jazz, bluegrass to Irish traditional music.

The Berkshires

More than a century ago, wealthy families from New York and Boston built "summer cottages" in western Massachusetts' Berkshire hills—great country estates that earned Berkshire County the nickname "inland Newport." Although most of those grand houses have since been converted into schools or hotels, the region is still popular, for obvious reasons. Occupying the entire far western end of the state, it lives up to the storybook image of rural New England, with its wooded hills, narrow winding roads, and compact charming villages. Summer offers an astonishing variety of cultural events, not the least of which is the Tanglewood festival in Lenox; fall brings a blaze of brilliant foliage; in winter, it's a popular ski area; and springtime visitors can enjoy maple-sugaring. Keep in mind, however, that the Berkshire's popularity often goes hand-in-hand with high prices and crowds, especially on weekends.

If you're entering the Berkshires from the west on I–90, the first Massachusetts exit is at West Stockbridge; go south on Route 41 to Great Barrington, or else pick up this tour in West Stockbridge. If you enter the Berkshires via Route 23 from New York state, you'll drive into Great Barrington about 12 miles past the state border.

Numbers in the margin correspond to points of interest on the Berkshires map.

① **Great Barrington** is the largest town in the southern Berkshires and a mecca for antiques hunters, as are the nearby vil-
② lages of **South Egremont** (5 miles south on Route 41) and
③ **Sheffield** (7 miles south on Route 7). Those in search of nature may want to make two excursions in this southernmost corner of the Berkshires: to **Bash Bish Falls** (Rte. 23 southwest of South Egremont, tel. 413/528–0330), where Bash Bish brook flows through a gorge and over a 50-foot waterfall into a clear natural pool; and to **Bartholomew's Cobble** (Rte. 7A south of Sheffield, tel. 413/229–8600), a natural rock garden beside the Housatonic River. The 277-acre reservation is filled with trees, ferns, wildflowers, and hiking trails.

North of Great Barrington, Route 7 takes you past **Monument Mountain;** two trails here lead to the summit at Squaw Peak, named for a Native American maiden, suffering from unrequited love, who hurled herself to her death. Route 7 then ar-
④ rives in the archetypal New England small town of **Stockbridge**, with its history of literary and artistic inhabitants. The painter Norman Rockwell, the sculptor Daniel Chester French, and the writers Norman Mailer and Robert Sherwood lived here. For the moment the **Norman Rockwell Museum** stands in the center of town, but a larger museum being constructed on Route 183 has a proposed opening date of 1993. Rockwell lived in Stockbridge between 1953 and his death in 1978; the museum owns the largest collection of Rockwell originals in the world. *Main St., tel. 413/298–3822. Admission: $5 adults, $1 children 6–18. Open May 1–Oct. 31, daily 10–5; Nov. 1–Apr. 30, weekdays 11–4, weekends 10–5. Closed Jan. 22–31, Thanksgiving, Christmas, New Year's Day.*

Time Out   **Chez Vous** (tel. 413/298–4278), signposted off Main Street in the town center, was originally Alice's Restaurant, made fa-

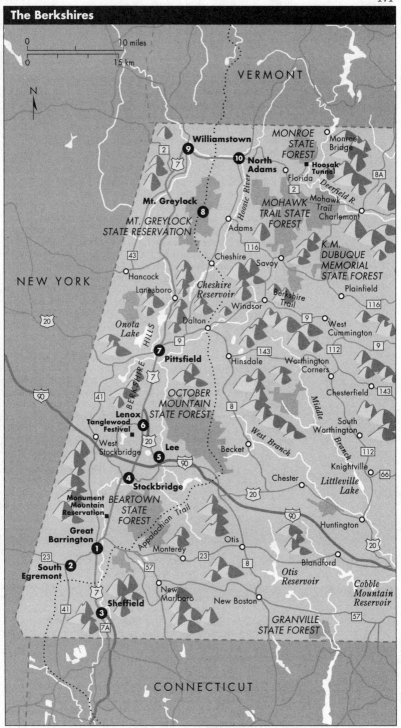

The Berkshires

VERMONT

NEW YORK

0   10 miles
0   15 km

N

Williamstown **9**

10 North Adams

MONROE STATE FOREST

Monroe Bridge

Hoosak Tunnel

Florida

Mt. Greylock **8**

MT. GREYLOCK STATE RESERVATION

Adams

MOHAWK TRAIL STATE FOREST

Mohawk Trail

Charlemont

Deerfield R.

8A

Hancock

Lanesboro

Cheshire

Savoy

K.M. DUBUQUE MEMORIAL STATE FOREST

Plainfield

43

116

Cheshire Reservoir

Onota Lake

BERKSHIRE HILLS

Dalton

Windsor

Berkshire Trail

West Cummington

116

9

9

7 Pittsfield

7

Hinsdale

143

Worthington Corners

112

Chesterfield

143

41

OCTOBER MOUNTAIN STATE FOREST

8

South Worthington

Middle Branch

112

Lenox

Tanglewood Festival

6

5 Lee

West Stockbridge

20

West Branch

Becket

Knightville

Littleville Lake

66

4 Stockbridge

Monument Mountain Reservation

BEARTOWN STATE FOREST

Appalachian Trail

Chester

20

Huntington

20

Great Barrington 1

23

South Egremont 2

Monterey

23

Otis

8

Blandford

Otis Reservoir

Cobble Mountain Reservoir

41

7

Sheffield

3

57

New Marlboro

New Boston

GRANVILLE STATE FOREST

57

7A

CONNECTICUT

Hoosic River

mous by Arlo Guthrie's comic protest song of the same name. This quirky establishment serves gourmet food to stay or to go; try the baby eggplant stuffed with curried lamb or feast on sinful chocolate cake and coffee.

Several historic houses in this area are worth seeing, especially **Chesterwood,** for 33 years the summer home of Daniel Chester French, best known for his statues of the Minute Man in Concord and of Abraham Lincoln at the Lincoln Memorial in Washington, DC. *Williamsville Rd. (off Rte. 183), tel. 413/298–3579. Admission: $5 adults, $1 children 7–18. Open May 1–Oct. 31, daily 10–5.*

❺ From Stockbridge, take Route 102 east 5 miles to Route 20 to reach **Lee,** where there are many dining and lodging opportunities. Travelers in a hurry to get on to Boston after this quick taste of the Berkshires can pick up the Massachusetts Turnpike (I–90) here; it's about a two-hour drive east to Boston. Those who wish to linger for more Berkshires charm can continue
❻ north of Stockbridge on Route 7A to the village of **Lenox,** which epitomizes the Berkshires for many visitors. In the thick of the "summer cottage" region, it's rich with old inns and majestic buildings. **Berkshire Cottage Tours** runs a 3½-hour tour that covers 20 of the summer mansions constructed at the end of the last century in the Lenox-Stockbridge region. *Edith Wharton Restoration, Box 974, Lenox 01240, tel. 413/637–1899. Operates late-July–early Sept., Thurs.–Sun.; mid-Sept.–mid-Oct., weekends.*

One of the most interesting cottages to visit is **The Mount,** former summer home of novelist Edith Wharton. The house and grounds were designed and built under Wharton's direction in 1901 and 1902. An expert in the field of design, Wharton used the principles set forth in her book *The Decoration of Houses* (1897) to plan The Mount for a calm, well-ordered lifestyle. *Plunkett St., tel. 413/637–1899. Admission: $4 adults, $2 children 13–18, $3 senior citizens. Open late May–early Sept., Tues.–Sun. 10–5; early Sept.–late Oct., Thurs.–Sun. 10–5.*

Lenox is the nearest Berkshire village to **Tanglewood,** summer home of the Boston Symphony. The 200-acre estate attracts thousands every summer to hear concerts featuring world-famous performers. One of the most popular ways to experience Tanglewood is to take a blanket and picnic on the grounds and listen to the performance from the lawn. (*See* The Arts, b*elow, for information.*)

In the village center Lenox Station is the starting point for the **Berkshire Scenic Railway,** which operates vintage railroad cars over a portion of the historic New Haven Railway's Housatonic Valley Line. The route takes in Lee and Stockbridge, and an open ticket allows passengers to alight at different stations and rejoin a later train. The **Railway Museum** is a restoration of the 1902 Lenox station, containing period exhibits and a large working model railway. *Willow Creek Rd., tel. 413/637–2210. Fares vary according to destination. Open late May–late Oct., weekends and holidays only.*

❼ Continuing north 6 miles on Route 7 will bring you to the busy town of **Pittsfield,** county seat and geographic center of the region. Though not particularly attractive, the town has a lively small-town atmosphere. The **Berkshire Museum** especially appeals to children, with its aquarium, animal exhibits, and glowing rocks. A local repository with a "bit of everything," the museum also contains works of art and historical relics. *39 South St., tel. 413/443–7171. Admission free. Open Tues.–Sat. 10–5, Sun. 1–5. Closed Thanksgiving, Christmas, New Year's Day.*

At the **Berkshire Athenaeum** (Berkshire Public Library, 1 Wendell Ave.), the **Herman Melville Memorial Room** (tel. 413/499–9486) houses a collection of books, letters, and memorabilia of the author of *Moby-Dick*. **Arrowhead,** the house Melville purchased in 1850, is just outside Pittsfield; tours include the study in which *Moby-Dick* was written. *780 Holmes Rd., tel. 413/442–1793. Admission: $3.50 adults, $2 children 6–16, $3 senior citizens. Open Memorial Day–Labor Day, Mon.–Sat. 10–4:15, Sun. 11–3:15; Labor Day–late-Oct., Thurs.–Mon. 10–4:15, Sun. 11–3.*

Take Route 20 west out of the center of Pittsfield to discover the town's star attraction—**Hancock Shaker Village.** Founded in the 1790s, Hancock was the third Shaker community in America. At its peak in the 1840s, the village had almost 300 inhabitants, who made their living from farming, selling seeds and herbs, making medicines, and producing crafts. The religious community officially closed in 1960; in 1961 the site opened as a museum. Many examples of the famous Shaker ingenuity are visible at Hancock today: the **Round Stone Barn** with its labor-saving devices and the **Laundry and Machine Shop** with its water-powered instruments are two of the best buildings to visit. *Rte. 20, 5 mi west of Pittsfield, tel. 413/443–0188. Admission: $8 adults, $4 children 6–16, $7.25 senior citizens and students. Open late-May–late-Oct., daily 9:30–5; Apr. 1–late May and Nov. 1–30, daily 10–3.*

8 The next town north on Route 7 is the pretty lakeside village of Lanesborough. Signs will direct you to the top of **Mt. Greylock,** at 3,491 feet the highest point in Massachusetts. The 10,327-acre **Mount Greylock State Reservation** (Rockwell Rd., Lanesborough, tel. 413/499–4262/3) provides facilities for cycling, fishing, hiking, horseback riding, hunting, and snowmobiling.

9 **Williamstown** is the northernmost Berkshire town, at the junction of Routes 2 and 7. When Col. Ephraim Williams left money to found a free school in what was then known as West Hooskuk, he stipulated that the name be changed to Williamstown. Williams College opened in 1793, and even today the town revolves around it. Gracious campus buildings line the wide main street and are open to visitors. Highlights include the **Gothic cathedral,** built in 1904, and the **Williams College Museum of Art,** with works emphasizing American, modern, and contemporary art. *Main St., tel. 413/597–2429. Admission free. Open Mon.–Sat. 10–5, Sun. 1–5.*

Formerly a private collection, the **Sterling and Francine Clark Art Institute** is now one of the nation's outstanding small art museums. Its famous works include paintings by Renoir, Monet, Pissaro, and Degas. *225 South St., tel. 413/458–9545. Admission free. Open Tues.–Sun. 10–5. Closed Thanksgiving, Christmas, New Year's Day.*

The **Chapin Library of Rare Books and Manuscripts** at Williams College contains the Four Founding Documents of the United

States, as well as 35,000 other books, manuscripts, and illustrations dating from the 9th to the 20th centuries. In 1983 it purchased a recently discovered copy of the Declaration of Independence that had been owned by one of the signers. *Stetson Hall, Main St., Williamstown, tel. 413/597-2462. Admission free. Open weekdays 9–noon and 1–5.*

Travelers looking for a fine scenic drive may head east on the **Mohawk Trail**, a 67-mile stretch of Route 2 that follows a former Native American path from Williamstown. The first stop is ⑩ **North Adams.** Despite the proximity of the two towns, they are utterly different in character. North Adams, once a railroad boomtown and a thriving industrial city, is still industrial but no longer thriving—the dilapidated mills and row houses are reminiscent of northern industrial England. The **Western Gateway Heritage State Park** (tel. 413/663–6312), housed in the restored freight-yard district, is open daily and tells the story of the town's past successes. The freight-yard district also contains a number of specialty stores and restaurants.

The only natural bridge in North America caused by water erosion is the marble arch at **Natural Bridge State Park**. It stands above a narrow 500-foot chasm; look for the numerous potholes, faults, and fractures in its walls. *Rte. 8 N, North Adams, tel. 413/663–6392. Admission: $3 per car. Open May–Oct., Mon.–Fri. 10–6, weekends 10–8.*

From North Adams the road begins a steep ascent, complete with hairpin turns, to the Western Summit, with excellent views of North Adams and Williamstown. It continues to Whitcomb Summit, the highest point on the trail, with more spectacular views.

Heading downhill, you can reach the entrance to the **Hoosac Tunnel** by turning left off Route 2 beyond Florida, on the road toward Monroe Bridge. The 4.7-mile tunnel took 24 years to build and was the longest in the nation when it was completed in 1875.

Back on the Mohawk Trail, just before the town of Charlemont, off to the right stands **Hail to the Sunrise,** a monument to the Native American. This 900-pound bronze statue facing east, with arms uplifted, is dedicated to the five Native American nations who lived along the Mohawk Trail. A handful of somewhat kitschy "Indian trading posts" along this highway carry out the Mohawk theme.

Shopping

The only enclosed shopping mall in the region is the **Berkshire Mall,** on Route 8 east of Lanesborough. The mall consists of 65 specialty stores and contains Hill's, JC Penney, Sears, Steiger's, several food stores, and a cinema complex.

Along Route 7 just north of Lenox are two factory-outlet malls, **Lenox House Country Shops** and **Brushwood Farms.** A number of outlet stores are concentrated at **The Buggy Whip Factory,** some distance from the main tourist routes in Southfield (Main St., Rte. 272, tel. 413/229–8280); stores include Dudley's Clothing Factory Outlet (shirts, sweaters, and jackets for men); Devoted to Children (children's toys and clothing); and the Neuma Sweater Factory Outlet (New England–made cotton sweaters). The building also contains 58 **antiques dealers** and 15 **craft stalls.**

Antiques   There are hundreds of antiques stores throughout the Berkshires, but the greatest concentration is around Great Barrington, South Egremont, and Sheffield. For a list of storekeepers who belong to the **Berkshire County Antiques Dealers Association** and guarantee the authenticity of their merchandise, send a self-addressed, stamped envelope to RD 1, Box 1, Sheffield 01257.

Great Barrington   **Corashire Antiques** (Rtes. 23 and 7 at Belcher Square, tel. 413/528–0014), a shop in a red barn, carries American country furniture and accessories, including the occasional rare Shaker piece.

Mullin-Jones Antiquities (525 S. Main St., Rte. 7, tel. 413/528–4871) has 18th- and 19th-century country French antiques: armoires, buffets, tables, chairs, architectural elements, fabrics, and lace.

Lanesborough   **Amber Springs Antiques** (29 S. Main St., Rte. 7, tel. 413/442–1237), in a shop behind a fine old white-clapboard house, shows an eclectic assortment of American furnishings from the late-18th to mid-20th centuries. Tools, pottery, and country store items are the house specialties.

Sheffield   **Bradford Galleries** (Rte. 7, tel. 413/229–6667) holds monthly auctions of furniture, paintings and prints, china, glass, silver, and Oriental rugs. A tag sale of household items is open daily.

Darr Antiques and Interiors (S. Main St., Rte. 7, tel. 413/229–7773) displays elegant 18th- and 19th-century American, English, Continental, and Oriental furniture and accessories in impressive, formal room settings in a fine Colonial house. A new second store houses another 1,600 square feet of antiques.

Dovetail Antiques (Rte. 7, tel. 413/229–2628) shows American clocks and country furniture in a small, friendly shop.

Good & Hutchinson Associates (Rte. 7, tel. 413/229–8832) specializes in American, English, and Continental furniture, paintings, fine pottery, and china "for museums and antiquarians."

South Egremont   **Red Barn Antiques** (Rte. 23, tel. 413/528–3230) has a wide selection of antique lamps and 19th-century American furniture, glass, and accessories.

The Splendid Peasant (Rte. 23 and Old Sheffield Rd., tel. 413/528–5755) concentrates on 18th- and 19th-century American and European country-primitive furnishings, including painted chests and other notable folk art.

West Stockbridge   **Sawyer Antiques** (Depot St., tel. 413/232–7062) offers early American furniture and accessories in a large, spare, clapboard structure that was once a Shaker mill.

Sports and Outdoor Activities

Boating and Canoeing   The **Housatonic River** (the Native American name means "river beyond the mountains") flows south from Pittsfield between the Berkshire Hills and the Taconic Range toward Connecticut. Suggested canoe trips in the Berkshires include Dalton–Lenox (19 miles), Lenox–Stockbridge (12 miles), Stockbridge–Great

Barrington (13 miles) and, for the experts, Great Barrington–Falls Village—a total of 25 miles. Information about these and other trips can be found in the **AMC River Guide–Central/Southern New England** (AMC, 5 Joy St., Boston 02198). Canoes, rowboats, and small motorboats can be rented from the **Onota Boat Livery** (455 Pecks Rd., Pittsfield, tel. 413/442-1724) on Onota Lake.

Fishing The rivers, lakes, and streams of Berkshire County abound with fish—bass, pike, and perch, to name but a few. Stocked trout waters include the Hoosic River (south branch) near Cheshire; Green River, Great Barrington; Notch Brook and Hoosic River (north branch), North Adams; Goose Pond and Hop Brook, Lee; and Williams River, West Stockbridge. **Points North Fishing and Hunting Outfitters** (Rte. 8, Adams, tel. 413/743-4030) organizes fly-fishing schools May through September at Jiminy Peak, which include instruction in knot tying, fly casting, and fishing in a trout pond. **Onota Boat Livery** (455 Pecks Rd., Pittsfield, tel. 413/442-1724) sells fishing tackle and live bait.

Hiking **New England Hiking Holidays** organizes guided hiking vacations through the Berkshires, with overnight stays at a country inn. Hikes vary from 5 to 9 miles per day. *Box 1648, North Conway, NH 03860, tel. 603/356-9696.*

The **Appalachian Trail** goes right through Berkshire County, and attracts many walkers. Hiking is encouraged in most state parks, and is particularly rewarding in the higher elevations of the Mount Greylock State Reservation, where the views are excellent.

Rafting Rafting takes place at just one location in the Berkshires—along the Deerfield River at Charlemont, on the Mohawk Trail. One-day raft tours over 10 miles of Classes II–III rapids take place daily April through October. *Zoar Outdoor, Mohawk Trail, Charlemont 01339, tel. 413/339-4010.*

Dining and Lodging

Expensive restaurants in the Berkshires may require formal dress at dinner. The following dining price categories have been used: *Very Expensive,* over $40; *Expensive,* $25–$40; *Moderate,* $12–$25; *Inexpensive,* under $12.

The following lodging price categories have been used: *Very Expensive,* over $100; *Expensive,* $70–$100; *Moderate,* $40–$70; *Inexpensive,* under $40.

Great Barrington **Whole Wheat 'N Wild Berries.** The original branch of this res-
Dining taurant is in Greenwich Village, New York City. This one opened in 1988, specializing in gourmet natural foods, and vegetarian and fish dishes, such as sautéed tofu, ratatouille, and fresh tuna. The setting is "country-kitchen," with flowered curtains and pine tables and chairs. *293 Main St., tel. 413/528-1586. Dress: casual. No credit cards. Closed Mon.; Tues. Nov.–Apr. Moderate.*
20 Railroad St. The exposed brick and subdued lighting lend atmosphere to this bustling restaurant, which features a 28-foot mahogany bar taken from the Commodore Hotel in New York City in 1919. Small wood tables are packed together in the long, narrow room, but despite the crowd, service is speedy. Special-

ties include sausage pie, burgers, and sandwiches. *20 Railroad St., tel. 413/528–9345. Dress: casual. MC, V. Inexpensive.*

Lodging **Windflower Inn.** A comfortable, casual atmosphere prevails at the family-run Windflower. Everything is homemade, and many vegetables and herbs come from the inn garden. The dining room is sunny, and in summer food is served on the screened porch. Bedrooms of varying sizes—mostly spacious—have four-poster beds and are filled with antiques. Several rooms contain working fireplaces: The most impressive has a stone surround that covers most of the wall. *Rte. 23 (Egremont Star Rte., Box 25), 01230, tel. 413/528–2720. 13 rooms. Facilities: restaurant, outdoor pool, gardens. No pets. No credit cards. Rates include full breakfast, dinner. Very Expensive.*

Dining and Lodging **The Egremont Inn.** The public rooms in this 1780 inn are enormous—the main lounge, with its vast open fireplace and coffee table made from an old door, is worth a visit in itself. The bedrooms, by contrast, are small, with wide-board floors, uneven ceilings, four-poster beds, and clawfoot baths. A wraparound porch is furnished with white wicker chairs. The sunny blue-and-white dining room, with its open fireplace and uneven floor, serves such entrées as sautéed trout; sole with pecan butter; smoked pork chop; and chicken breast with goat cheese and herbs. *Old Sheffield Rd. (Box 418), South Egremont 01258, tel. 413/528–2111. 22 rooms. Facilities: dining room (dress casual; reservations required weekends), lounge, bar, outdoor pool, 2 tennis courts. AE, D, DC, MC, V. Rates include Continental breakfast. Expensive.*

Hancock **Drummond's Restaurant.** At the Jiminy Peak ski resort, this
Dining restaurant is designed like a ski lodge, with cathedral ceilings, lots of wood, and a stone chimney with wood-burning stove. Tables at the back overlook the slopes, which are lit for night skiing in season. Entrées include fresh salmon, roast duck, and pasta Jericho, with scallops, shrimp, crabmeat, and clams in sherry-cream sauce. *Corey Rd., tel. 413/738–5500. Reservations advised. Dress: casual. AE, D, DC, MC, V. Moderate.*

The Springs. This restaurant sits in the shadow of Brodie Mountain and its ski resort. A fireplace in the lobby, exposed-brick walls, and wood ceiling (from which hangs the biggest chandelier in the Berkshires) make for a country-lodge atmosphere. The menu offers lobster blended with mushrooms in cream sauce, duckling flambé in cherry sauce, steak Diane, and veal dishes. *Rte. 7, New Ashford, tel. 413/458–3465. Dress: casual. AE, D, DC, MC, V. Moderate.*

Lee **Cork 'n Hearth.** A large stone fireplace separates the long din-
Dining ing room into two: On one side wood beams show off all kinds of brassware; on the other, they are hung with bundles of dried herbs. Picture windows look onto Laurel Lake, which practically laps against the side of the building. The menu is traditional, offering steak, seafood, chicken Kiev, and veal cordon bleu. *Rte. 20, tel. 413/243–0535. Reservations advised. Dress: casual. AE, D, DC, MC, V. Closed lunch; Mon. Labor Day–Memorial Day. Expensive.*

Lodging **Oak n' Spruce Resort.** Rooms in the main lodge are like high-quality motel rooms; large rooms in the building next door have modern furniture, kitchen units, and sliding doors onto the spacious grounds surrounding this former farm. The lodge lounge is a converted cow barn built around the original brick silo. An excellent children's program makes this a great place for kids. *Meadow St. (Box 237), South Lee 01260, tel. 413/243–3500. 17 rooms, 26 suites, 107 condos. Facilities: restaurant, lounge, live entertainment, indoor and outdoor pool, Jacuzzi, sauna, health club, cross-country ski trails, shuffleboard, basketball, 2 tennis courts, badminton, horseshoes, volleyball, central VCR, children's program, hiking trails. AE, MC, V. Moderate.*

The Pilgrim Motel. This motel is well furnished with gleaming reproduction antiques and color coordinated drapes, but even so the rates during the Tanglewood season are high. The location in the very center of Lee is busy but convenient. *127 Housatonic St., tel. 413/243–1328. 24 rooms. Facilities: outdoor pool, laundry, in-room coffee, Jacuzzi. AE, DC, MC, V. Moderate (Very Expensive in Tanglewood season).*

The Morgan House. Most guest rooms in this inn, which dates to 1817, are small, but the rates reflect that. Some are so narrow they resemble servants' quarters, with their scrubbed boards and brightly painted wood furniture; others have four-poster beds, stenciled walls, and well-used antiques. The lobby is papered with the pages from old guest registers; among the signatures are those of George Bernard Shaw and Ulysses S. Grant. Mrs. Nat King Cole owned the inn until 1981. *31 Main St., 01238, tel. 413/243–0181. 14 rooms, 12 with bath. Facilities: 3 dining rooms, bar. AE, D, DC, MC, V. Rates include Continental breakfast. Inexpensive (Moderate–Expensive in Tanglewood season).*

Lenox
Dining

Church St. Cafe. A well-established, popular Lenox restaurant, the stylish café serves excellent food at reasonable prices. The walls are covered with original artwork, tables are surrounded by ficus trees, and classical music plays in the background. Specialties include Louisiana gumbo, pecan breaded chicken, and crab cakes. *69 Church St., tel. 413/637–2745. Dress: casual. MC, V. Closed Nov.–Apr., Sun.–Mon. Moderate.*

Sophia's Restaurant and Pizza. This unpretentious establishment serves up pizza, generous Greek salads, pasta dishes, and grinders (the Massachusetts equivalent of a submarine sandwich). Seating is in booths with imitation-leather seats. *Rtes. 7/20, tel. 413/499–1101. Dress: casual. AE, MC, V. Closed Mon. Inexpensive.*

Lodging

Blantyre. The competition in Lenox is tough, but Blantyre has to be the best inn in town. If its unique, castlelike Tudor architecture, the sheer size of its public rooms, and its 85 acres of beautifully maintained grounds are not impressive enough, guest rooms in the main house are also fabulous: huge and lavishly decorated, with hand-carved four-poster beds, overstuffed chaise longues, chintz chairs, boudoirs, walk-in closets, and Victorian bathrooms. The $500-a-night Paterson suite has two bathrooms, a fireplace, and bay windows with wonderful views. Keep in mind that although rooms in the carriage house and the cottages are well appointed, they can't compete with the formal grandeur of the main house. Extras abound (robes, wine, fruit, newspapers), and the service is superb, but costly—a 17½% service charge is added to the bill. The stylishly prepared, five-course evening meal is wonderful. *Off Rte. 7, 01240, tel. 413/637–3556 or 413/298–3806. 13 rooms, 10 suites. Facilities: restaurant, lounge, outdoor pool, Jacuzzi, sauna, 4 tennis courts, 2 croquet lawns, room service, working fire-*

places. No pets. *AE, DC, MC, V. Rates include Continental breakfast. Very Expensive.*

Wheatleigh. One of the most expensive Berkshire inns, the Wheatleigh has a mixed reputation. The building, constructed in 1893 as a wedding present for an heiress who married a Spanish count, is based on a 16th-century Florentine palace, and it's undeniably grand. The modern furnishings, though, aren't to everyone's liking, and the service is not as lavish as one might expect for the price. Guest rooms range from medium-size to enormous, and have elegant furnishings, high ceilings, and some working fireplaces. The inn has an excellent, expensive restaurant. *W. Hawthorne Rd., 02140, tel. 413/637–0610. 17 rooms. Facilities: dining room, lounge, outdoor pool, tennis court, steam room, exercise room. AE, DC, MC, V. Closed Nov.–mid May. Very Expensive.*

★ **Rookwood Inn.** This "painted lady" was restored to her original grandeur in 1985, exactly 100 years after being built as a summer cottage for a wealthy New York family. Guest rooms are generally roomy and some have working fireplaces; the Victorian era is perfectly re-created with period wallpapers, matching linen, and English and American antiques. Some rooms have balconies. The elegant lounge has reading material, an open fire, and a screened porch with wicker furniture. The inn is on a quiet street, two minutes' walk from the center of Lenox. *19 Old Stockbridge Rd. (Box 1717), 01240, tel. 413/637–9750. 15 rooms. Facilities: breakfast room, lounge. No smoking. No pets. AE. Rates include full breakfast, afternoon tea. Expensive–Very Expensive.*

★ **Whistler's Inn.** The antiques decorating the parlor of this English Tudor mansion are ornate with a touch of the exotic—some are in the Louis XVI style, others the innkeepers brought back from various travels abroad. Bedrooms are more conventionally decorated with Laura Ashley drapes and bedspreads. Some rooms have working fireplaces, and most have great views across the valley. *5 Greenwood St., 01240, tel. 413/637–0975. 11 rooms. Facilities: lounge, library, badminton, croquet, 7 acres of gardens. AE, MC, V. Rates include full breakfast. Expensive–Very Expensive.*

Apple Tree Inn. Perched on a hillside across the street from Tanglewood's main gate, the Apple Tree Inn is perfect for summer concertgoers. You don't even need a ticket—the music wafts right across the front lawn! The parlor contains a grand piano, velvet couches, hanging plants, and German nutcracker decorations. Guest rooms have four-poster or brass beds, Victorian washstands, and lots of wicker; some rooms have working fireplaces. The 20 rooms in the lodge next door have more modern, motel-style furnishings. *224 West St., 01240, tel. 413/637–1477. 29 rooms, 27 with bath; 2 suites. Facilities: restaurant, bar, outdoor pool, gardens, fireplaces. No pets. AE, DC, MC, V. Closed Jan.–mid Apr. Expensive.*

The Candlelight Inn. Attractive, spacious bedrooms have floral-print wallpapers and antiques; those on the top floor are especially charming, with sloping ceilings and skylights. The inn is located right in the middle of Lenox village and has a popular Continental restaurant. Although elegant, this inn is less formal than the nearby Gateways. *53 Walker St., 01240, tel. 413/637–1555. 8 rooms. Facilities: 4 dining rooms, bar. No pets. AE, MC, V. Rates include Continental breakfast. Expensive (Very Expensive in Tanglewood season).*

Eastover. An antidote to the posh atmosphere prevailing in most of Lenox, this resort was opened by an ex-circus roustabout, and the tradition of noisy fun and informality continues with gusto. Guest rooms are functional and vary from dormitory to motel-style: Although the period wallpapers are stylish, some rooms with four or more beds resemble hospital wards with their metal rails and white bedspreads. Dining rooms are vast and very noisy, but period decor and furnishings temper the absolute informality to some extent. The grounds are huge, and wandered by buffalo; facilities are extensive. *East St. (off Rte. 7), Box 2160, 01240, tel. 413/637-0625. 195 rooms, 120 with bath. Facilities: 6 tennis courts, indoor and outdoor pools, golf driving range, softball, volleyball, archery, skeet shooting, cross-country and downhill skiing, tobogganing, exercise room, sauna, ice-skating, canoeing, shuffleboard, badminton, live music, dancing, free local transport, horseback riding. AE, DC, MC, V. Rates include tax, service charges, three meals a day, and most facilities. Moderate.*

Dining and Lodging **Gateways Inn.** This formal and elegant mansion was built as a summer home in 1912 by Harley Proctor of Proctor and Gamble. From the large entrance hall, a grand open staircase lit by a skylight leads to the second-floor guest rooms. The huge Fiedler Suite (Tanglewood conductor Arthur Fiedler stayed here and gave his name to it) has two working fireplaces and a dressing room. All rooms have light, period wallpapers; antiques; and Oriental rugs. The four dining rooms, hung with chandeliers and tapestries, serve Continental and American cuisine includings veal, pheasant, salmon, and rack of lamb. *71 Walker St., 01240, tel. 413/637-2532. 8 rooms. Facilities: 4 dining rooms, TV lounge. No pets. AE, DC, MC, V. Rates include Continental breakfast. Very Expensive.*

Pittsfield **Dakota.** Moose and elk heads watch over diners at this large
Dining restaurant decorated like a rustic hunting lodge. A canoe swings overhead, and Native American artifacts hang on the walls. A broiler stocked with Texan mesquite wood is used for specialties, which include swordfish steaks, shrimp, sirloin, and grilled chicken. *Rtes. 7 and 20, tel. 413/499-7900. Dress: casual. AE, DC, MC, V. Closed lunch Mon.-Sat. Moderate.*
La Cocina. This restaurant offers a selection of typical Mexican dishes, such as burritos, flautas, and fajitas. The decor is exposed brick with Mexican rug hangings; seating is at dimly lit booths. Live guitar music adds to a cozy atmosphere. *140 Wahconah St., tel. 413/499-4027. No reservations. Dress: casual. AE, DC, MC, V. Closed lunch Sun. Moderate.*

Lodging **Berkshire Hilton Inn.** This is a typically comfortable, sophisticated Hilton with a spacious hall featuring wing chairs, glass, and brass. Guest rooms have new reproductions and floral-print drapes. Upgraded rooms on the two top floors have the best views over the town and surrounding mountains. *Berkshire Common, South St., 01201, tel. 413/499-2000 or 800/445-8667. 175 rooms. Facilities: restaurant, lounge, bar, live entertainment, indoor pool, sauna, Jacuzzi, meeting rooms. AE, DC, MC, V. Very Expensive.*
Dalton House. This bed-and-breakfast enterprise has expanded over the years to include a sunny breakfast room with pine chairs and tables at the front of the 170-year-old house, and deluxe rooms in the carriage house. Guests share a split-level sitting room; the average size bedrooms in the main house are cheerful, with floral print drapes and wallpaper and rock-

ing chairs. The spacious carriage house rooms are more impressive, with exposed beams, period furnishings, and quilts. Ski packages including dinner are offered in season. *955 Main St., Dalton, 01226, tel. 413/684–3854. 9 rooms, 2 suites. Facilities: outdoor pool, lounge. AE, MC, V. Rates include breakfast. Moderate–Expensive.*

Sheffield
Dining

Stagecoach Hill Inn. Constructed in the early 1800s as a stagecoach stop, the restaurant offers a character inspired by England—there are numerous pictures of the British royal family and several hunting scenes, as well as steak and kidney pie, roast beef and Yorkshire pudding, and British ale on tap. Other menu items include pasta dishes, steak au poivre, and chicken al forno. *Rte. 41, tel. 413/229–8585. Dress: casual. AE, DC, MC, V. Closed Wed. and Mar. Expensive.*

Lodging

Ivanhoe Country House. The Appalachian Trail runs right across the property of this bed-and-breakfast. The house was originally built in 1780, but various wings were added later. The antique-furnished guest rooms are generally spacious; several have private porches or balconies, and all have excellent country views. The large sitting room has antique desks, a piano, and comfortable couches. *Undermountain Rd., Rte. 41, 01257, tel. 413/229–2143. 9 rooms, 1 suite with kitchen. Facilities: lounge, outdoor pool, refrigerators. $10 fee for dogs. No credit cards. Rates include Continental breakfast. Expensive.*

Stockbridge
Dining

Hoplands. Located about a mile north of Stockbridge center, this restaurant has two dining rooms—downstairs around the bar or upstairs in a simply furnished room with polished wood floors and no tablecloths (somewhat reminiscent of an old-fashioned schoolroom). The menu features chicken pie, stir-fry, burgers, and sandwiches. *Rte. 102, tel. 413/243–4414. Reservations required for parties of more than 6. Dress: casual. AE, MC, V. Closed Mon.; Tues. Nov.–May. Moderate.*

Lodging

The Golden Goose. This friendly, informal place 5 miles south of Lee is cluttered with antiques, bric-a-brac, and dozens of geese in various shapes and sizes (many were donated by guests). Bedrooms are Victorian in style; some have brass beds and quilts, and the walls are stenciled. Guests' names are chalked up on the little welcome board on each door. *Main Rd. (Box 336), Tyringham 01264, tel. 413/243–3008. 6 rooms, 4 with bath. Facilities: dining room, lounge. No smoking. No pets. AE. Rates include Continental breakfast. Moderate–Expensive.*

★ **Merrell Tavern Inn.** If you are looking for a genuine old New England inn, this is it. It was built in 1800, and is listed in the National Register of Historic Places; despite its age, it has good-size bedrooms, several with working fireplaces. The style is simple: polished wide-board floors, cream-painted plaster walls with Shaker pegs, and plain wood antiques. Guest rooms have pencil four-poster beds with unfussy canopies. The breakfast room has an open fireplace and contains the only complete "birdcage" Colonial bar in America. *Rte. 102, South Lee 01260, tel. 413/243–1794. 10 rooms. Facilities: breakfast room, lounge, gardens. No pets. AE, MC, V. Rates include full breakfast. Moderate–Expensive.*

Dining and Lodging

The Red Lion Inn. An inn since 1773, and rebuilt after a fire in 1896, the Red Lion is now a massive place, with guest rooms situated both in the main building and in several annexes on the property. It's a well-known landmark, but it *is* old, and many of the guest rooms are small. In general, the annex houses are more appealing. Rooms are individually decorated with floral-print wallpapers and country curtains (from the mail-order store Country Curtains owned by the innkeepers and operated out of the inn). All are furnished with antiques, and hung with Rockwell prints; some have Oriental rugs. The dining rooms are filled with antiques, and tables are set with pewter plates; New England specialties include oyster pie, broiled scallops prepared with sherry, lemon, and paprika, and steamed or stuffed lobster. *Main St., 02162, tel. 413/298–5545. 108 rooms, 75 with bath, 10 suites. Facilities: dining room, lounge, bar, outdoor pool, exercise room, meeting rooms. Restaurant: reservations advised, jacket and tie advised. AE, D, DC, MC, V. Expensive (Very Expensive in Tanglewood season).*

West Stockbridge
Dining

Shaker Mill Tavern. The only concession to Shakers here is a row of Shaker pegs on the wall, but the restaurant is located just down the street from the Shaker mill, hence its name. In summer dining can be outside on the "deck café," otherwise it's in the large modern dining room with wood floors and ceilings and lots of plants. American dishes include burgers, fried chicken, buffalo wings, pizza, and pasta dishes. *Rte. 102, tel. 413/232–8565. Dress: casual. AE, MC, V. Moderate.*

Dining and Lodging

The Williamsville Inn. A couple of miles south of West Stockbridge, this inn has been carefully renovated to re-create the late 1700s, when it was built. Guest rooms have wide-board floors, embroidered chairs, four-poster and canopy beds; several have working fireplaces, and four rooms in the converted barn have woodstoves. The halls and the bar are decorated with stencils, and four dining rooms with fireplaces look onto the woods. Entrées include broiled yellowfin tuna marinated in soy sauce, lime juice, and sesame oil; pan-seared loin veal chop with Dijon mustard and tarragon glaze; and roast duckling with brandied apricot sauce. *Rte. 41, Williamsville 01266, tel. 413/ 274–6118. 12 rooms, 1 suite, 2 cottages. Facilities: 4 dining rooms, bar, croquet, outdoor pool, tennis court, horseshoes, badminton, volleyball. Restaurant: reservations advised, Expensive. No pets. MC, V. Rates include Continental breakfast. Very Expensive.*

Williamstown
Dining

Le Jardin. Set on a hillock above the road just west of Williamstown, this French restaurant has the feel of a small inn (there are guest rooms on the upper floor). The two dining rooms are paneled and candlelit, and a fire burns in the hall in season. The menu offers snails in garlic butter, oysters baked with spinach and Pernod, sole florentine, filet mignon, and rack of lamb. *777 Cold Spring Rd. (Rte. 7), tel. 413/458–8032. Reservations advised. Dress: casual. AE, MC, V. Closed Tues.; Dec.–Apr. Expensive.*

Four Acres. Located on the commercial strip of Route 2 just east of Williamstown, this pleasant restaurant has two dining rooms: One is casual, decorated with street signs, paneling, and mirrors; the other is more formal, with collegiate insignia and modern paintings on the walls. American and Continental cuisine includes sautéed calf's liver glazed in applejack; veal cutlet sautéed in butter and topped with a Newburg of lobster and asparagus; and pork tenderloin with cognac and walnut sauce. *Rte. 2, tel. 413/458–5436. Reservations advised. Dress: casual. AE, MC, V. Closed Sun. Moderate.*

Lodging   **The Orchards.** After seeing the pale-orange stucco exterior,
and perhaps wondering about the location on a commercial
strip of Route 2 east of town, it's a pleasant surprise to enter
the quiet, tasteful interior of this small luxury hotel built in
1985. Church pews and a heavy pulpit adorn the corridors, the
cozy lounge has wall cases of silverware and an open fireplace,
and guest rooms are furnished with elegant four-poster beds,
antiques, and reproductions. Ask for a room with a view of the
hills or the small modern courtyard and its lily pond. *Main St.
(Rte. 2), tel. 413/458-9611. 49 rooms. Facilities: restaurant,
lounge, tavern, outdoor pool, sauna, Jacuzzi, room service.
AE, DC, MC, V. Very Expensive.*

Williams Inn. The spacious guest rooms in this new inn have
good-quality, modern furnishings, with floral-print drapes and
bedspreads. The lounge has an open fireplace and is comfortable—the atmosphere is collegiate. The inn allows pets for a $5
fee; children under 14 stay free in their parents' room. *On-the-
Green at Williams College, 01267, tel. 413/458-9371. 105
rooms. Facilities: dining room, lounge, coffee shop, live entertainment, indoor pool, sauna, Jacuzzi. AE, D, DC, MC, V.
Very Expensive.*

Berkshire Hills Motel. This excellent motel is housed in a two-
story brick-and-clapboard building about 3 miles south of
Williamstown. All guest rooms were recently refurbished in
Colonial style—each with a rocking chair and good-quality reproduction furniture. The lounge, complete with a teddy-bear
collection, has an open fireplace and a piano. Outside, the pool
is located across a brook amid 2½ acres of woodland and landscaped garden. *Rte. 7, 01267, tel. 413/458-3950. 20 rooms. Facilities: lounge, outdoor pool. AE, MC, V. Rates include
Continental breakfast. Moderate.*

River Bend Farm. Listed on the National Historic Register, the
Farm, constructed in 1770 by one of the founders of Williamstown, has been restored with complete authenticity by
old house–enthusiasts David and Judy Loomis. Guests enter
through a kitchen with an open range stove and bake oven hung
with dried herbs. Upstairs some bedrooms have wide-plank
walls, curtains of unbleached muslin, and four-poster beds
with canopies or rope beds with feather mattresses. Some
rooms have non-working brick fireplaces, and all are sprinkled
with antique pieces—chamberpots, washstands, wingback
chairs, and spinning wheels. For visitors in search of another
era, River Bend Farm is the perfect spot. *643 Simonds Rd.,
01267, tel. 413/458-3121. 5 rooms share 2 baths. Facilities:
kitchen, lounge, swimming in river. No pets. No credit cards.
Rates include Continental breakfast. Moderate.*

The Arts

Listings are published weekly in the *Williamstown Advocate;*
major concert listings are published Thursday in the *Boston
Globe.* The quarterly *Berkshire Magazine* contains "The Berkshire Guide," a comprehensive listing of local events ranging
from theater to sports.

Jacob's Pillow Dance Festival, the oldest in the nation, mounts a
10-week summer program every year. Performers vary from
well-known classical ballet companies to Native American
dance groups and contemporary choreographers. Before the
main events, free showings of works-in-progress are staged

outdoors. Visitors can picnic on the grounds or eat at the Pillow Café. *Rte. 20, Becket (mailing address: Box 287, Lee, 01238), tel. 413/243–0745. Open June–Sept.*

The best-known music festival in New England is the **Tanglewood** concert series near Lenox between June and September. The main shed seats 6,000; the Chamber Music Hall holds 300 for smaller concerts. *Lenox, tel. 617/266–1492 Oct.–June; 413/ 637–1940 June–Sept. Ticket prices $10–$50.*

The **Berkshire Performing Arts Center** (Kemble St., Lenox, tel. 413/637–4088), the newest arts center in the county, attracts top-name artists in jazz, folk, rock, and blues. The **Berkshire Theatre Festival** stages nightly performances in summer at the century-old theater in Stockbridge. A series of children's plays, usually written by local schoolchildren, are performed weekends during the day. *Box 797 (Rte. 102), Stockbridge, tel. 413/298–5576 or 413/298–5536.*

The **Williamstown Theatre Festival** presents well-known theatrical works on the Main Stage, and contemporary works on the Other Stage. *Adams Memorial Theatre, Williams College Campus, tel. 413/458–9545 or 413/597–3400. July–Aug.*

The **Music-Theatre** (tel. 413/298–5122 or 212/924–3108) at Lenox Arts Center presents new music-theater works, July–August.

Shakespeare and Company (tel. 413/637–3353) performs Shakespeare and Edith Wharton's works throughout the summer at The Mount (Plunkett St., Lenox).

Nightlife

The emphasis in the Berkshires is definitely on classical entertainment. However, the most popular local nightspot is **The Lion's Den** (tel. 413/298–5545) downstairs at the Red Lion Inn in Stockbridge, with nightly folk music and some contemporary local bands every evening throughout the year.

The Pioneer Valley

The Pioneer Valley, a string of historic settlements along the Connecticut River from Springfield in the south up to the Vermont border, formed the western frontier of New England from the early 1600s until the late 18th century. The fertile banks of the river (called Quinnitukut, or "long tidal river," by Native Americans) first attracted farmers and traders; later it became a source of power and transport for the earliest industrial cities in America. Educational pioneers came to this region as well—to form America's first college for women and four other major colleges, as well as several well-known prep schools.

Today, the northern regions of the Pioneer Valley remain rural and tranquil, supporting farms and small towns with typical New England architecture. Farther south, the cities of Holyoke and Springfield are more industrial.

This leg of the tour connects with the Berkshires tour segment at the end of the Mohawk Trail (Route 2), in Shelburne Falls.

*Numbers in the margin correspond to points of interest on the
Pioneer Valley map.*

Off scenic Route 2 (the Mohawk Trail) 10 miles west of Deerfield, the village of **Shelburne Falls,** a nearly perfect example of
small-town Americana, straddles the Deerfield River. The
Bridge of Flowers (tel. 413/773–5463), a 40-foot former trolley
bridge that was taken over by the Shelburne Women's Club in
1929, has been covered with plants to produce a riot of color
in spring, summer, and early fall, when you can walk across it.
In the riverbed just downstream are 50 immense **glacial potholes** ground out of the granite during the last ice age.

Once a hardy pioneer outpost and the site of a bloody massacre,
Historic Deerfield now basks in a far more genteel aura as the
site of the prestigious Deerfield Academy preparatory school.
Half the village is in fact a museum site, consisting of 13 18th-
century houses along "The Street." Some, as period homes,
contain antique furnishings and decorative arts; others exhibit
collections of textiles, silver, pewter, or ceramics. The **Barnard
Tavern** has a ballroom with fiddlers' gallery and several hands-
on displays. The whole village is an impressive historical site.
*The Street, tel. 413/774–5581. Two-day admission: $7.50
adults, $4 children 6–17. Open daily 9:30–4:30. Closed
Thanksgiving, Christmas Eve, Christmas Day.*

Head south of Deerfield on Route 5, then southeast along Route
116, to come upon the college town of **Amherst.** Three of the valley's five major colleges—the University of Massachusetts
(UMass), Amherst College, and Hampshire College—are
here. Not surprisingly, the area has a youthful bias, reflected
in its numerous bookstores, bars, and cafés.

The poet Emily Dickinson was born and spent most of her life
here, and the **Emily Dickinson Homestead** (280 Main St., tel.
413/542–8161), now owned by Amherst College, offers afternoon guided tours by appointment.

Eight miles west on Route 9 is **Northampton,** home of Smith
College, founded in 1871; it currently enrolls almost 3,000 wom-
en undergraduates. Visit the Lyman Plant House and botanic
gardens. The **College Art Museum** (Rte. 9, tel. 413/584–2700),
has more than 18,000 paintings and is open afternoons, Tuesday through Saturday.

Time Out   The **Albion Bookshop Café** (68 Green St., beside Smith College)
is a pleasant spot to relax with coffee and homemade cookies,
cakes, or brownies. Tables and chairs of various shapes and
sizes are set among the bookshelves.

Northampton was also the Massachusetts home of the 30th
U.S. President, Calvin Coolidge. He practiced law here,
served as mayor from 1910–1911, and returned to town after
his presidential term. The **Coolidge Room** at the Forbes Library (20 West St., tel. 413/586–2954) contains a collection of
papers and memorabilia.

South Hadley is a small village best known for its college,
Mount Holyoke, founded in 1837 as the first women's college in
the United States. Among its famous alumnae is Emily Dickinson. The handsome wooded campus was landscaped by Frederick Law Olmsted. The **College Art Museum** (tel. 413/538–2245)
has exhibits of Asian, Egyptian, and classical art.

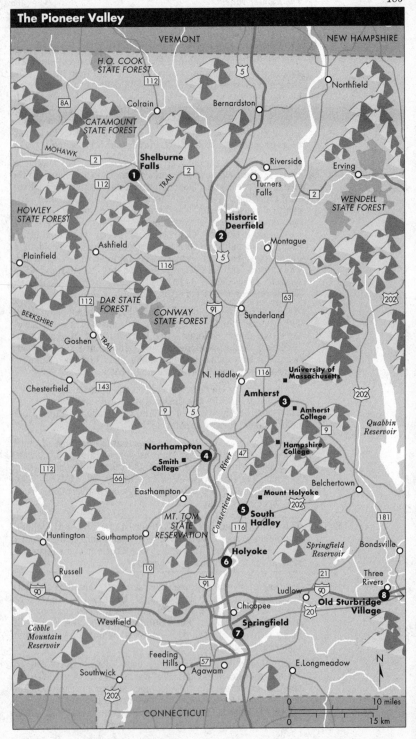

Time Out **Woodbridge's** (tel. 413/536–7341), on the common at South Hadley, was the village meetinghouse between 1733 and 1764. Now it is a restaurant that serves sandwiches, burgers, and more all day long.

❻ Head south on I–91 for **Holyoke,** a city of redbrick factories and canals. The **Wistariahurst Museum** (238 Cabot St., tel. 413/534–2216) shows how wealthy manufacturers lived; **Heritage State Park** tells the story of this so-called "Paper City" and is the starting point for the **Heritage Park Railroad** (weekends, June–Aug.)—three antique railroad cars that take visitors on one- and two-hour journeys through the valley. *221 Appleton St., tel. 413/534–1723. Admission free. Train ride: $6 adults, $4 children, $6 senior citizens. Open Wed., Thurs., Sun. noon–4:30.*

Right beside Heritage Park is the **Children's Museum,** housed in a converted mill by the canal. Packed with hands-on games and educational toys, the museum features a TV weather station, water guns, and a sand pendulum. *444 Dwight St., tel. 413/536–5437. Admission: $3. Open Tues.–Sat. 10–4:30, Sun. noon–5.*

The **Volleyball Hall of Fame** is a one-room tribute to the sport and to William Morgan, who invented it here in 1895. *444 Dwight St., tel. 413/536–0926. Admission free. Open Tues.–Fri. 10–5, weekends noon–5.*

❼ South of Holyoke is **Springfield,** the largest city in the Pioneer Valley—a sprawling industrial town where modern skyscrapers rise between grand historic buildings. The city owed much of its early development to the establishment in 1794 of the **Springfield Armory,** which made small arms for the U.S. military until it closed in 1968. It still holds one of the most extensive firearms collections in the world. *1 Armory Sq. (off State St.), tel. 413/734–8551. Admission free. Open daily 9–5. Closed Thanksgiving, Christmas, New Year's Day.*

Perhaps the city's greatest claim to fame, however, is that Dr. James Naismith invented basketball here in 1891. The **Naismith Memorial Basketball Hall of Fame** features a cinema, basketball fountain, and a moving walkway from which visitors can shoot baskets. *W. Columbus Ave. at Union St., tel. 413/781–6500. Admission: $5 adults, $3 senior citizens and children 9–15. Open July–Labor Day, daily 9–6; Sept.–June, daily 9–5. Closed Thanksgiving, Christmas, New Year's Day.*

Four more conventional museums are situated at the museum quadrangle near downtown. The **Connecticut Valley Historical Museum** (tel. 413/732–3080) commemorates the history of the Pioneer Valley. The **George Walter Vincent Smith Art Museum** (tel. 413/733–4214) contains a private collection of Japanese armor, ceramics, and textiles. The **Museum of Fine Arts** (tel. 413/732–6092) has paintings by Gauguin, Renoir, Degas, and Monet. The **Springfield Science Museum** (tel. 413/733–1194) contains an "Exploration Center" of touchable displays, a planetarium, and dinosaur exhibits. All four museums have free admission.

If you drive about 30 miles east out of Springfield, on either scenic Route 20 or the faster I–90, you'll reach the star attraction ❽ of central Massachusetts—**Old Sturbridge Village,** one of the country's finest period restorations. Though technically out of the Pioneer Valley, Old Sturbridge is worth the detour. The village is a living, working model of an early 1800s New England town with more than 40 buildings on a 200-acre site. Working exhibits include a 200-year-old newspaper printing press, a blacksmith and forge, and a sawmill. Inside the houses, interpreters in period costume demonstrate such home-based crafts as spinning, weaving, and cooking. *1 Old Sturbridge Village Rd., 01566, tel. 508/347-3362. Admission (valid for two consecutive days): $14 adults, $6 children 6-15. Open late-Apr.-late-Oct., daily 9-5; off-season, Tues.-Sun. 10-4. Closed Christmas, New Year's Day.*

From Sturbridge, go north on I-84 two exits to I-90, and head east to Boston, less than an hour's drive away. For information on sights, restaurants, hotels, and other activities in Boston, *see* Chapter 1, Boston to Bar Harbor.

Shopping

Outlet Stores Factory stores and mill shops are concentrated in Holyoke. The **Becker Jean Factory** (323 Main St., tel. 413/532-5797) carries Becker as well as Lee and Levi jeans for men, women, and children. The **Ekco Factory Store** (191½ Appleton St., tel. 413/532-3219) sells seconds, overruns, and closeouts of cookware, cutlery, and kitchen gadgets. Paper products and furniture are widely available: The **City Paper Co.** (390-394 Main St., tel. 413/532-1352) offers wholesale and retail paper and plastic disposables; **Deerfield Woodworking** (420 Dwight St., tel. 413/532-2377) and **Riverbends Woodworks** (110 Lyman St., tel. 413/532-3227) sell firsts and seconds of wood furnishings.

Specialty Stores For a list of members of the **Pioneer Valley Antique Dealers Association**, which guarantees the honest representation of merchandise, write to Maggie Herbert (Secretary), 201 N. Elm St., Northampton 01060. The **Antique Center of Northampton** (9½ Market St.) covers 8,000 square feet and houses a number of dealers; the **Hadley Antique Center** (Rte. 9, tel. 413/586-4093) contains more than 50 different stores.

Books Amherst has dozens of bookstores, as do the other collegiate centers. The **Odyssey Bookstore** (29 College St., South Hadley) is outstanding. **L.B.C. Books** (185 Main St., Holyoke) specializes in children's and discount books.

Crafts Among the larger, permanent crafts stores are the **Leverette Crafts and Arts Center** (Montague Rd., Leverett, tel. 413/548-9070), housing 15 resident artists in jewelry, ceramics, glass and fibers; the **Salmon Falls Artisans Showroom** (Ashfield St., tel. 413/625-9833) at Shelburne Falls; the **Ferrin Gallery at Pinch Pottery** (179 Main St., Northampton, tel. 413/586-4509) with exhibits of contemporary ceramics, jewelry, glass and wood; and the **Avis Neigher Gallery** (Baystate West, Springfield, tel. 413/734-1844).

Sports and Outdoor Activities

Boating and Canoeing The Connecticut River is navigable by all types of craft between the Turners Falls Dam, just north of Greenfield, and the Holyoke Dam. Canoes can also travel north of Turners Falls to beyond the Vermont border. The large dams control the water level daily, so you will notice a tidal effect, and those with larger craft should beware of sandbanks.

Canoes can be rented during summer and early fall from **Sportsman's Marina** (Rte. 9, Hadley, tel. 413/584–7141). The **Northfield Mountain Recreation Center** (RR2, Box 117, Northfield, tel. 413/659–3714) rents out canoes and rowboats at Barton Cove, from where you can paddle to the Munn's Ferry campground, accessible only by canoe.

Further south at the wide place in the river known as The Oxbow, the Massachusetts Audubon Society's **Arcadia Wildlife Sanctuary** (Fort Hill Rd., Easthampton, tel. 413/584–3009) organizes canoe trips and maintains hiking and nature trails.

Fishing   A massive cleanup program of the Connecticut River has resulted in the return of shad and even salmon to the purer waters, and in fact the river now supports 63 species of fish.

The privately owned **Red-Wing Meadow Farm** raises trout; for a fee visitors may fish in the ponds, paying for fish they catch. *500 Sunderland Rd., Amherst 01002, tel. 413/549–4118. Admission: $2, $5 family.*

Hiking   The abundance of state parks and forests in this region makes for an equal abundance of well-maintained hiking trails. Recommended parks include **D.A.R. State Forest** (Rte. 9, Goshen), **Erving State Forest** (Rte. 2A, Erving), and **Mount Tom State Reservation** (Rte. 5, Holyoke). The Audubon Society's **Arcadia Wildlife Sanctuary** also encompasses nature trails around The Oxbow; **Northfield Mountain Recreation Center** (RR 2, Northfield, tel. 413/659–3714) has 29 miles of hiking trails.

Dining and Lodging

Amherst   **Judie's.** A glassed-in porch where students crowd around small
Dining   round tables creates the atmosphere of a cheerful street café. Cuisine is Continental and imaginative American; specialties are paella and a selection of gourmet chocolate cakes. Judie's sells cookery books as well as apple butter and bottles of house dressing. *51 N. Pleasant St., tel. 413/253–3491. No reservations. Dress: casual. AE, D, MC, V. Moderate.*

Lodging   **Campus Center Hotel.** Literally on top of the UMass campus, the spacious rooms of this modern hotel have large windows with excellent views over campus and countryside. The decor is exposed cinderblock, with simple, convenient furnishings. Guests can use university exercise facilities with prior reservation, and the campus status means no tax is charged for accommodations. *Murray D. Lincoln Tower, Univ. of Mass., 01003, tel. 413/549–6000. 116 rooms, 6 suites. Facilities: 2 indoor pools, 3 tennis courts, gym. AE, MC, V. Moderate.*

Dining and Lodging   **Lord Jeffrey Inn.** This gabled brick inn with green shutters sits right on the green between the town center and the Amherst College campus. Colonial furnishings and the lounge's open fire make for an innlike atmosphere, although the smart reproduction antiques and light, floral decor in the bedrooms breathe formality more than real character. The best rooms either open onto the garden courtyard or have a balcony that overlooks it. The large, elegant dining room has an open fireplace, chandeliers, heavy drapes, and white-painted wood beams; its menu offers such fish dishes as seafood ravioli (shrimp and scallops in pasta with lobster sauce) as well as chicken and steaks. *30 Boltwood Ave., 01002, tel. 413/253–2576. 49 rooms, 6 suites. Facilities: restaurant, lounge, tavern, garden courtyard. Res-*

taurant reservations advised; dress neat but casual. AE, DC, MC, V. Expensive.

Deerfield
Lodging

Sunnyside Farm Bed and Breakfast. Country-style guest rooms of varying sizes are appointed with maple antiques and family heirlooms. All rooms, which are hung with fine art reproductions, have views across the fields, and some overlook the large strawberry farm next door. Guests share a small library. Breakfast is served family-style in the dining room, which has a wood-burning stove. The farm is about 8 miles south of Deerfield. *11 River Rd., Whately (Box 486, S. Deerfield 01373), tel. 413/665–3113. 5 rooms share 2 baths. Facilities: outdoor pool. No pets. No credit cards. Rates include full breakfast. Moderate.*

Dining and Lodging
★

Deerfield Inn. Perfectly located in the center of Historic Deerfield, this inn is superbly run by friendly, helpful owner-managers. Guest rooms have recently been redecorated with period wallpapers designed for the inn, which was built in 1884 and substantially modernized after a fire in 1981. Rooms have antiques and replicas, sofas and bureaus; some have four-poster or canopy beds. One bed is so high that a ladder is provided! The porch has rocking chairs, and it is said a ghost wanders the hallways. The large, sunny, antique-filled dining room features such specialties as saddle of venison sautéed with chestnuts in black currant sauce, rack of lamb with Dijon mustard and garlic, and *gravlox* (cured salmon with salt, herbs, and honey mustard sauce). Many recipes are taken from old cookery books in the village museum. *The Street, 01342, tel. 413/774–5587. 23 rooms. Facilities: dining room, lounge, coffee shop. Restaurant: reservations advised, jacket and tie advised, expensive. AE, DC, MC, V. Hotel rates include full breakfast. Very Expensive.*

The Whately Inn. Guest rooms with sloping old wood floors are furnished simply with antiques and four-poster beds. Two are located over the dining room, which is very busy on weekends and hence noisy. Roast duck, baked lobster with shrimp stuffing, and crabmeat casserole all come with salad, appetizer, and dessert. *Chestnut Plain Rd., Whately Center 01093, tel. 413/665–3044 or 800/635–3055. 4 rooms. Restaurant: reservations advised (closed lunch Mon.–Sat.), dress casual. MC, V. Moderate.*

Greenfield
Dining

Brickers. Right beside Route 91, this restaurant is set in a converted ice-cream factory. Decor is country style, in a large room with exposed brick walls and a high ceiling supported by metal beams and pillars. The sunny porch at one end is a pleasant place to eat lunch. Entrées include Cajun chicken, pan-fried sole, and pasta dishes; burgers and sandwiches are also available. *Shelburne Rd., tel. 413/774–2857. Dress: casual. D, MC, V. Moderate.*

Riverside. The restaurant is perched between the Bridge of Flowers, which it overlooks, and Shelburne Falls's main street. Long tables, square tables, benches, chairs, and customers are crammed into a small, bright room, and there is often a wait. The menu includes Cornish game hen with fresh cranberry and chestnut sauce; cauliflower crêpes Florentine; and "Udon, the floating meal"—tofu, scallions, and stir-fry vegetables in tamari-ginger broth. Riverside also serves soups, sandwiches, and home-baked pies. *4 State St., Shelburne Falls, tel. 413/*

625–2570. No reservations. Dress: casual. MC, V. Closed Mon. Moderate.

Lodging   **Northfield Country House.** Truly remote, this big English man-
★   or house is set amid thick woodlands on a small hill that overlooks Northfield's Main Street. A wide staircase leads to the
bedrooms, some of which have working fireplaces. The smallest rooms are in the former servants' quarters; larger rooms
are furnished with antiques, and several have brass beds. The
present owner has considerably renovated this 100-year-old
house, and has planted hundreds of tulip and daffodil bulbs in
the gardens. *School St., RR 1, Box 617, Northfield 01360, tel.
413/498–2692. 7 rooms share 4 baths. Facilities: lounge, outdoor pool. No pets. MC, V. Rates include full breakfast. Moderate.*

1797 House. Built almost 200 years ago, this white clapboard
house stands on the green in tiny, quiet Buckland Village.
Guest rooms are furnished with antiques, and the beds—one
brass, one iron, and one four-poster—have quilts. In summer,
breakfast is served on the large screened porch overlooking the
woods; in winter it's in the dining room with an open fireplace.
*Charlemont Rd., Buckland 01338, tel. 413/625–2975. 3 rooms.
Facilities: TV lounge. No credit cards. Rates include full
breakfast. Moderate.*

Holyoke   **Yankee Pedlar Inn.** In 1990, new owners took over this attrac-
Dining and Lodging   tive, sprawling inn that stands at a busy crossroads near I–91.
★   After a much-needed paint-and-paper job in early 1991, a successful redecoration of the main building has been followed by
work on individual rooms, most of which are now superbly furnished with antiques and four-poster or canopy beds. Victorian
guest rooms are elaborate and heavily curtained, with lots of
lace, while the carriage house has beams and rustic furnishings, with simple canopy beds. Suites are spacious and definitely worth the small price difference. The dining room has
exposed beams and antique wood paneling, much of it taken
from a nearby castle that was demolished; "candle" chandeliers
provide the lighting. In summer the herb garden—with its orange trees, herbs, fountain, and gazebo—is a lovely spot to
dine. The new owners have upgraded the menu to include lobster Savannah (lobster in Newburg sauce with mushrooms and
green peppers); beef Wellington; New England boiled dinner;
and Cornish game hen. *1866 Northampton St., 01040, tel. 413/
532–9494. 30 rooms, 12 suites. Facilities: 4 dining rooms, 4
banquet rooms, oyster bar, live entertainment. Dining room
reservations required for Sun. brunch, advised other times.
Dress: casual. AE, D, DC, MC, V. Hotel rates include Continental breakfast. Moderate–Expensive.*

Northampton   **Beardsley's.** The intimate aura of the first- and second-floor
Dining   dining rooms in this fine French restaurant is created by dark
wood paneling, candlelight, and shining silverware. Windows
overlooking the street make the second floor a little lighter.
The menu includes chicken roulade stuffed with spinach and
proscuitto mousse; sirloin steak; and pheasant roasted with
hazelnuts. *140 Main St., tel. 413/586–2699. Reservations advised. Dress: casual. AE, DC, MC, V. Expensive.*

Wiggins Tavern. Part of the Hotel Northampton, the Tavern
specializes in such New England dishes as Yankee cider pot
roast, chicken potpie, and Boston scrod; Indian pudding, pep-
permint-stick ice cream, and apple pie follow. Open fires burn

in three dimly lighted, "olde worlde" dining rooms, where heavy exposed beams support low ceilings and antique kitchen appliances decorate every available space. Eleanor Roosevelt and John F. Kennedy ate here. *36 King St., tel. 413/584–3100. Reservations advised. Dress: casual. AE, D, DC, MC, V. Closed lunch; closed dinner Mon., Tues. Expensive.*

Paul and Elizabeth's. This natural-foods restaurant serves such seasonal specials as butternut-squash soup, home-baked corn muffins, and Indian pudding. The restaurant is airy with lots of plants and trellis work, and fans hang from the high ceiling. *150 Main St., tel. 413/584–4832. Reservations advised. Dress: casual. MC, V. Closed Sun. Moderate.*

Lodging **Hotel Northampton.** Located in the town center, the hotel was built in 1927 and completely refurbished in 1987. Antique and reproduction furnishings combine with open fires in the parlor, lounge, and dining rooms to give the atmosphere of a cozy inn. The porch has a piano and wicker chairs. Guest rooms are appointed with Colonial reproductions, heavy curtains, and four-poster beds. Some rooms come with balconies that overlook a busy street. *36 King St., 01060, tel. 413/584–3100. 72 rooms, 5 suites. Facilities: restaurant, café, bar, lounge, ballroom, room service. AE, D, DC, MC, V. Very Expensive.*

The Knoll Bed and Breakfast. A spacious private home, this B&B sits well away from the busy road and backs onto steep woodlands. There's a sweeping staircase and Oriental rugs on polished wood floors; guest rooms are furnished with a mixture of antiques and hand-me-downs, and some have high four-poster beds. *230 N. Main St., Florence 01060, tel. 413/584–8164. 5 rooms share 2 baths. Facilities: lounge, library. No smoking. No pets. No credit cards. Rates include full breakfast. Moderate.*

Twin Maples Bed and Breakfast. Seven miles northwest of Northampton near the village of Williamsburg, this 200-year-old, fully restored farmhouse is surrounded by fields and woods. Inside are exposed beams, wide brick fireplaces, and wood stoves. Colonial-style antique and reproduction furnishings decorate the rather small guest rooms, which have restored brass beds and quilts. *106 South St., Williamsburg 01096, tel. 413/268–7925. 3 rooms share one bath. Facilities: TV lounge. No smoking. No pets. No credit cards. Rates include full breakfast. Moderate.*

Springfield **Johann's.** This stylish, well-established Dutch restaurant is lo-
Dining cated in the Marketplace shopping area in the heart of Springfield. Blue-and-white Dutch plates and reproduction Dutch masters decorate the walls, and brass chandeliers hang from the ceilings. The menu features Dutch, French, and Indonesian entrées, such as hot gouda bread, *hachee* (Dutch beef goulash), chateaubriand, and *djahe oedgang* (gingery shrimp with ginger brandy). *73 Market St., tel. 413/737–7979. Reservations advised. Dress: casual. AE, D, DC, MC, V. Closed Sun. Expensive.*

Theodore's. There's saloon-style dining at booths near the bar or in a small adjacent dining room. The 1930s are re-created with period furniture and framed advertisements for such curious products as foot soap. Brass lights date from 1897. Theodore's serves burgers, sandwiches, some Mexican dishes, chicken, and seafood. Thursday through Saturday, there is live entertainment in the evenings. *201 Worthington St., tel. 413/739–7637. Dress: casual. AE, DC, MC, V. Moderate.*

Tilly's Restaurant. Tilly's is a cheerful spot for such lighter meals as salads, burgers, and sandwiches, but the restaurant also serves full dinner entrées Wednesday through Saturday nights. The interiors feature carved ceilings, lots of pine woodwork and exposed brick, and seating is at wood booths. *1390 Main St., tel. 413/732–3613. No reservations. Dress: casual. AE, MC, V. Closed Sun. dinner. Inexpensive.*

Lodging **Marriott Hotel.** Conveniently located in the middle of downtown, this newly renovated hotel opens onto the large Baystate West shopping mall. The lobby features green marble, brass chandeliers, and Oriental rugs. Rooms at the front overlook the river, and all are comfortably decorated with oak furniture, Impressionist prints, and mauve or sea-foam green color schemes. *1500 Main St., 01115, tel. 413/781–7111 or 800/228–9290. 264 rooms, 1 suite. Facilities: restaurant, lounge, bar, indoor-outdoor pool, 2 saunas, whirlpool, fitness center, room service, meeting rooms. AE, D, DC, MC, V. Very Expensive.*

Sheraton Tara. This hotel, in the middle of downtown, was built in 1987. Guest rooms have reproduction antiques and are plush, with heavy drapes and thick carpets; they surround an impressive 14-story atrium. Hotel staff wear the distinctive red-and-gold Beefeater costume. *1 Monarch Pl., 01144, tel. 413/781–1010 or 800/325–3535. 303 rooms, 7 suites. Facilities: 2 restaurants, lounge, health club, exercise room, 4 racquetball courts, 2 saunas, steam room, whirlpool, indoor pool, room service, conference rooms, ballroom. AE, D, DC, MC, V. Very Expensive.*

Holiday Inn. Half a mile north of downtown, beside I–91, this hotel offers a relaxed atmosphere and a touch of old New England in the reproduction antique furnishings of the bedrooms (some have four-poster beds). All rooms were renovated in 1987; the Presidential Suite is enormous. Upper stories and the top-floor bar-lounge afford panoramic views of Springfield, the river, and the surrounding countryside. *711 Dwight St., 01104, tel. 413/781–0900 or 800/465–4329. 250 rooms, 12 suites. Facilities: restaurant, lounge, bar, indoor pool, whirlpool, room service, meeting rooms. AE, D, DC, MC, V. Expensive.*

Cityspace. In 1989 the Springfield YMCA renovated its standard accommodations into small, attractive pastel-tone rooms with gray cinderblock walls, modern paintings, large lamps, and large windows. Each has a private bath. The big advantage over other budget motels is that visitors can use all the sports and fitness facilities at the Y for free. Cityspace is close to I–91, near downtown, and a five-minute walk from the Amtrak station. *275 Chestnut St., 01104, tel. 413/739–6951. 124 rooms. Facilities: restaurant, indoor pool, 4 racquetball courts, 2 squash courts, 2 tracks, fitness center, gym, whirlpool, steam room, sauna, massage. MC, V. Inexpensive.*

Sturbridge **The Whistling Swan.** There are two separate eating areas here;
Dining The Ugly Duckling Loft upstairs serves lighter meals than the main dining room. The ambience in both is fairly formal, with matching floral-print drapes and wallpaper and pink tablecloths. Specialties include rack of lamb, veal, Madeira chicken, and catch of the day. *502 Main St., tel. 508/347–2321. Reservations advised. Dress: casual. AE, DC, MC, V. Closed Mon., Easter, Mother's Day, Thanksgiving, Christmas, New Year's Day. Moderate–Expensive.*

Rom's. This has become something of a local institution—after humble beginnings as a sandwich stand, the restaurant was extended to seat about 700 people. The six dining rooms have an Early American decor, with wood paneling and beam ceilings. Now serving Italian and American cuisine ranging from pizza to roast beef, Rom's attracts the crowds with a classic formula: good food at low prices. The veal parmesan is very popular. *Rte. 131, tel. 508/347–3349. Dress: casual. AE. Inexpensive.*

Lodging **Sheraton Sturbridge Inn.** The Sheraton is ideally located just across the street from Old Sturbridge Village on Cedar Lake. Luxuriously appointed bedrooms have Colonial decor and reproduction furnishings, and the lakeside location enhances the recreational offerings. *Rte. 20, 01566, tel. 508/347–7393. 241 rooms, 9 suites. Facilities: 2 dining rooms, 2 lounges, indoor pool, health club, exercise room, minigolf, 2 tennis courts, racquetball, basketball, sauna, canoes, rowboats, fishing, room service, meeting rooms. AE, D, DC, MC, V. Very Expensive.*

★ **Sturbridge Country Inn.** This imposing Greek Revival–facade inn on Sturbridge's busy Main Street was once a farmhouse. After a period as an apartment building, it reopened in 1989 as a luxury accommodation—with an atmosphere somewhere between an inn and a plush business hotel—offering lots of extras. Guest rooms—all have working gas fireplaces—are superbly furnished, with reproduction antiques and a Jacuzzi in every room. The best is the top floor suite, with a cathedral ceiling, a large Jacuzzi in the living room, and big windows. Try to avoid the first-floor rooms—they're comparably priced but small and noisy (with gurgles from the upstairs plumbing!). Service is efficient and friendly, but the Continental breakfast is rather meager. The public TV lounge, with roaring fire, also manages to mix old furnishings with modern comforts. *530 Main St. (Box 60), 01566, tel. 508/347–5503. 9 rooms, 1 suite. Facilities: lounge, in-room Jacuzzi. AE, D, MC, V. Rates include Continental breakfast. Expensive–Very Expensive.*

Dining and Lodging **Publick House and Col. Ebenezer Crafts Inn.** The Publick
★ House dates to 1771 and is now surrounded by a "complex" of different styles of lodging. Rooms in the Publick House itself are Colonial in design, with uneven wide-board floors; some have canopy beds. The neighboring Chamberlain House consists of larger suites, and the Country Motor Lodge has more modern appointments with comfortable, updated rooms. The Col. Ebenezer Crafts Inn, named for the man who built the Publick House, is the most tranquil alternative, a restored Colonial farmhouse dating from 1786 and decorated with poster beds, old desks, painted paneling, and lots of character. The main restaurant is big, bustling, and very busy during weekends. Its menu advertises "hearty gourmet meals and hefty desserts," which translates into individually baked lobster pies, double-thick loin lamb chops, duckling, and a turkey dinner served on Sunday. Desserts include Indian pudding, pecan bread pudding, and apple pie. *Rte. 131, On-the-Common, 01566, tel. 508/347–3313. 118 rooms, 12 suites. Facilities: 2 dining rooms, bar, outdoor pool, tennis court, track, shuffleboard, playground, conference rooms. Restaurant: reservations advised, dress casual. AE, D, DC, MC, V. Rates include Continental breakfast. Moderate–Expensive.*

The Arts

The **Springfield Symphony Orchestra** performs October through May at Symphony Hall, and mounts a summer program of concerts in Springfield's parks. *1391 Main St., Suite 1006, 01103, tel. 413/733-2291.*

Springfield is the home of **StageWest,** the only resident professional theater company in western Massachusetts. The schedule includes a series of plays and musicals October through May. *1 Columbus Ctr., 01103, tel. 413/781-2340.*

Nightlife

The collegiate population ensures a lively club and nightlife scene in the valley. Popular spots include **Iron Horse** (20 Center St., Northampton, tel. 413/584-0610) with a variety of folk, blues, jazz, Celtic, and new-wave music seven nights a week; **Pazzazz** (406 Dwight St., Springfield, tel. 413/732-4606) presenting comedy acts, live disco dance bands, youth nights, and college nights; **Katina's** (Rte. 9, Hadley, tel. 413/586-4463) specializing in rock and blues; **Sheehan's Café** (24 Pleasant St., Northampton, tel. 413/586-4258) featuring rock 'n' roll and blues six nights a week; and **Theodore's** (201 Worthington St., Springfield, tel. 413/739-7637), with comedians and live music Thursday through Saturday evenings.

Tour 3:
New York
to the Cape

Although the starting point of this tour is New York City (*see* Tour 2: New York City to Boston), once the metropolis has been left behind you'll discover a string of towns that make perfect refuges from city life. We'll travel along the coast of the Long Island Sound through Connecticut and Rhode Island all the way to the Cape Cod peninsula, which curls into the Atlantic Ocean from Massachusetts's eastern shore. This is not quite so much the classic New England landscape as the Atlantic coastline encountered in Tour 1, but what it lacks in picturesque oceanfront scenery it more than makes up for with cultural amenities: the campus of Yale University in New Haven, the restored seaport and aquarium in Mystic, and imposing Gilded Age mansions (built as summer "cottages") in Newport.

Of equal attraction are half a dozen lovely small towns along the way, places like Westport, Old Saybrook, Old Lyme, and Watch Hill, where the most exciting thing to do is to stroll along the main street with an ice-cream cone and peer past shade trees and shrubbery at the vintage vacation homes of the well-to-do. The final destination, of course, is the Cape, with its succession of cheerful beach towns that have been popular with summer vacationers for almost a century.

It's a long day's drive from New York City to the Cape if you don't get off the highway, but leisurely stops en route are the whole point of this tour. Mystic makes a good overnight stop; Newport is another town with plenty of hotels, restaurants, shops, and sights. Once you've reached Cape Cod, it would be a good idea to settle down in one town for at least few days (be sure to reserve ahead if you're traveling between July 4 and Labor Day). Outside of the busy summer months, sights may be closed and beaches deserted, yet the Cape exerts its particular fascination even then—some say *especially* then.

At the end of this tour, or after the Rhode Island leg, you may want to drive up to Boston, where you can pick up Tour 1.

Visitor Information

Connecticut **Greater Stamford Convention and Visitors Bureau** (2 Landmark Sq., Stamford 06901, tel. 203/359–3305).

New Haven Convention and Visitors Bureau (900 Chapel St., Suite 344, New Haven 06510, tel. 203/787–8822).

Yankee Heritage District (297 West Ave., The Gate-Lodge, Matthews Park, Norwalk 06850, tel. 203/854–7825).

Shoreline Visitors Bureau (115 State Sq., Guilford 06437, tel. 203/397–5250).

Southeastern Connecticut Tourism District (27 Masonic St., Box 89, New London 06320, tel. 203/444–2206 or 800/222–6783 outside CT).

Rhode Island **Rhode Island Department of Economic Development, Tourism Division** (7 Jackson Walkway, Providence 02903, tel. 401/277–2601 or 800/556–2484).

South County Tourism Council (Box 651, Narragansett 02882, tel. 401/789–4422 or 800/548–4662).

Newport County Convention and Visitors Bureau (23 America's Cup Ave., tel. 401/849–8048 or 800/326–6030).

Massachusetts   **Massachusetts Office of Travel and Tourism** (100 Cambridge St., Boston 02202, tel. 617/727–3201).

Cape Cod Chamber of Commerce (Jct. Rtes. 6 and 132, Hyannis 02601, tel. 508/362–3225).

Festivals and Seasonal Events

Mid-July: Newport Music Festival brings together celebrated classical musicians for a two-week schedule of morning, afternoon, and evening concerts in Newport, Rhode Island. Tel. 401/846–1133.

Mid-July: Volvo Tennis Hall of Fame Championship matches take place on grass courts at Newport Casino; **Virginia Slims of Newport** is a tournament for professional women players. Tel. 401/849–3990.

Late July: Newport Folk Festival, at Ft. Adams State Park in Newport, is the nation's premier folk festival. Box 605, Newport 02840, tel. 401/847–3709.

Late July: Barnstable County Fair in Hatchville, Cape Cod's biggest event, is six days of livestock and food judgings, arts and crafts demonstrations, entertainment, rides, and edibles. Tel. 508/563–3200.

Mid-Aug.: The JVC Jazz Festival brings renowned performers to Ft. Adams State Park in Newport. Tel. 401/847–3700.

Labor Day Weekend: Cajun & Bluegrass Music-Dance-Food Festival in Escoheag, Rhode Island, presents nationally known performers, as well as workshops, dancing, and food. Tel. 401/351–6312.

Mid-Sept.: The Harwich Cranberry Festival on Cape Cod runs for 10 days; festivities include a country-and-western jamboree, parade, fireworks, pancake breakfast, and regatta. Tel. 508/543–0100.

Dec.: Christmas in Newport celebrations include crafts fairs, holiday concerts, and candlelight tours of Colonial homes; several Bellevue Avenue mansions open for the holidays. Tel. 401/849–6454.

What to See and Do with Children

Most attractions described below are described more fully in the tour that follows.

For attractions in **New York City**, *see* Tour 2.

Connecticut offers several attractions for youngsters, including the **Barnum Museum** in Bridgeport, the **Peabody Museum of Natural History** in New Haven, and the **Thames Science Center** in New London. Mystic is the best place to visit with children, since it offers both the educational **Mystic Seaport** and the popular **Mystic Marinelife Aquarium.**

In **Rhode Island,** the pleasures are more outdoorsy. Children can ride in the **Flying Horse Carousel** in Watch Hill, play miniature golf and bumper boats at **Adventureland** (Rte. 108, Narragansett, tel. 401/789–0030; open Apr. 15–Oct.), and tour the **Norman Bird Sanctuary** (583 Third Beach Rd., Middletown, tel. 401/846–2577).

Southeastern Massachusetts, which many travelers skip on their way to Cape Cod, is worth a stop for families. There's the **Battleship Cove** in Fall River, the **Whaling Museum** in New Bedford, the interactive **Children's Museum** (276 Gulf Rd., tel. 508/993–3361) in South Dartmouth, and the antique steam **Edaville Railroad** (Rte. 58, one exit north of I–95 off I–495, tel. 508/866–4526; open Apr.–Dec.) coursing through the cranberry bogs in South Carver.

Cape Cod is a family-oriented destination par excellence. Besides the eternal allure of the beach, children can be amused at the **Aqua Circus of Cape Cod** (Rte. 28, West Yarmouth, tel. 508/775–8883; open mid-Feb.–late Nov.), with its dolphin and sealion shows, petting zoo, and aquariums; **Cape Cod Aquarium** (Rte. 6A, West Brewster, tel. 508/385–9252); **Pirate's Cove** miniature golf (728 Main St. [Rte. 28], South Yarmouth, tel. 508/394–6200); or **Water Wizz Water Park** (Rtes. 6 and 28, Wareham, tel. 508/295–3255; open Memorial Day–Labor Day).

Arriving and Departing

By Plane   Virtually every major U.S. and foreign airline serves one or more of New York's three airports: LaGuardia Airport, John F. Kennedy International Airport, and Newark International Airport. To get into Manhattan, a taxi will cost $15–$20 from LaGuardia (20–40 minutes), $25–$30 from JFK (35–60 minutes), or $28–$30 from Newark (20–45 minutes). From LaGuardia or JFK, which are in the borough of Queens, you can get into Manhattan by Carey Airport Express bus (tel. 718/632–0500; fare $8.50 from LaGuardia, $11 from JFK; drop-off point 42nd St. and Park Ave. across from Grand Central Terminal). The Gray Line Air Shuttle Minibus (tel. 212/581–3929) drops off at major Manhattan hotels; the cost is $11 from LaGuardia, $14 from JFK. From Newark, which is west of the city, in New Jersey, you can take NJ Transit Airport Express buses (tel. 201/460–8444, fare $7, drop-off at Port Authority terminal, 42nd St. and 8th Ave.), the Olympia Airport Express Bus (fare $7, drop-off at the World Trade Center and Grand Central Terminal), or the Gray Line Air Shuttle Minibus (fare $16, drops off at major Manhattan hotels).

Boston's **Logan International Airport,** the largest airport in New England, has scheduled flights by most major domestic and foreign carriers. To get from the airport to downtown Boston, you can hire a cab outside each terminal (fares to downtown should be around $15), take the **Airport Water Shuttle** (tel. 800/235–6426) to Rowes Wharf, or ride the **MBTA Blue Line** into town (free shuttle buses connect all terminals to the Airport subway station; call 617/561–1800 or 800/235–6426 for Logan Airport Public Information).

Provincetown Municipal Airport, on Cape Cod, is served by Cape Air (tel. 800/352–0714).

By Car   Leave New York City via the Triborough Bridge to pick up I–95, which runs along the coast through Connecticut and Rhode Island. The older state highways—the Merritt Parkway and the northern sections of Route 7—are scenic drives, but traffic can become heavy on the narrow roads. Leave I–95 at Pawcatuck, Connecticut, to pick up coastal Route 1 through Rhode Island. While Routes 1 and 1A may be a little bumpy in places, they are the principal routes for seeing the coastline of the state. Just past Saunderstown, turn onto Route 138, which will take you across the bridge to Newport. Either Route 138 or 114 will take you north from Newport to Route 24, which connects in Massachusetts with I–195, the road to Cape Cod.

By Train **Amtrak** (tel. 800/872–7245) service between New York's Penn Station and Boston's South Station stops at Stamford, Bridgeport, New Haven, Old Saybrook, New London, Mystic, Westerly, Kingston, and Providence.

Metro North (tel. 800/522–5624) leaves New York's Grand Central Terminal for stops along the coast from Greenwich to New Haven.

Amtrak (tel. 800/872–7245) offers three-day "Cape Escape" packages that include hotels and transfers and a four-day Boston and New England package with full-day and half-day tours.

By Bus **Greyhound Lines** (tel. 203/722–2470, 401/454–0790, or 617/423–5810) and **Bonanza Bus Lines** (tel. 800/556–3815) make stops in New York City, Stamford, Bridgeport, New Haven, New London, Providence, and Boston.

Southwestern Connecticut

The Connecticut coast west of New Haven continues the metropolitan sprawl that fans out from New York City, though most residents of Fairfield County claim that the atmosphere is distinctive here. Because so much of this suburban territory (primarily Fairfield County) lies within a commuter's reach of New York City, it has become common for residents of New England's more distant corners to suggest that Connecticut really shouldn't be considered part of New England at all—as though the state could be blackballed from the club for the offense of consorting too freely with Gotham. Whether or not this is fair, time-pressed travelers who want to get on to the "real" New England may want to stick to I–95 as far as New Haven and bypass this area.

Numbers in the margin correspond to points of interest on the Southwestern Connecticut map.

Leaving New York City, the first town you reach in Connecticut is Greenwich, 5 miles inside the state line. In **❶** north **Greenwich** the 485-acre **Audubon Center** offers 8 miles of secluded hiking trails, exhibits about the local environment, a gift shop, and a bookshop. *613 Riversville Rd. (Rte. 15, Exit 28), tel. 203/869–5272. Admission: $2 adults, $1 children and senior citizens. Open Tues.–Sun. 9–5.*

The **Bruce Museum** looks a little like a smaller version of the Bates house in *Psycho*, with a concrete-block addition. It has wildlife dioramas, a worthwhile small collection of American Impressionist paintings, and many exhibits on the area. *1 Museum Dr. (I–95, Exit 3), tel. 203/869–0376. Suggested donation: $3 adults, $1.50 senior citizens, $1 children. Open Tues.–Sat. 10–5, Sun. 2–5.*

Follow the signs to Route 1, also known as Putnam Avenue and Boston Post Road, then turn and head east on Route 1. A little more than a mile ahead, on your left, you'll see a small, barn-red cottage with strangely scalloped shingles and a small stone appendage on its eastern side. This is **Putnam Cottage,** built

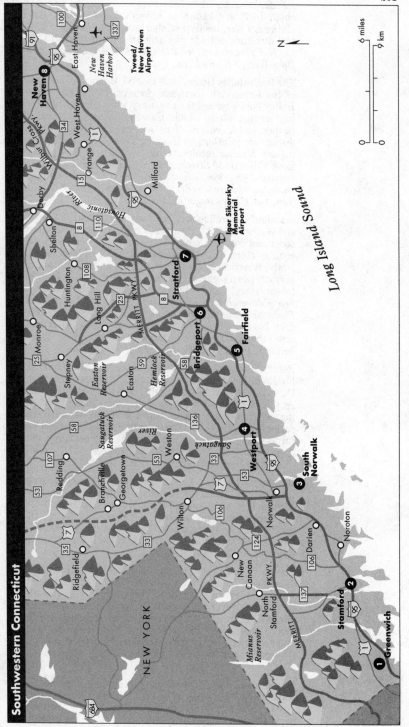

Southwestern Connecticut

New Haven **8**

East Haven

Tweed/
New Haven Airport

New Haven Harbor

West Haven

Wilbur Cross Pkwy.

Orange

Milford

Derby

Housatonic River

Shelton

Huntington

Long Hill

Monroe

Stepney

Easton Reservoir

Hemlock Reservoir

Stratford **7**

Igor Sikorsky Memorial Airport

Merritt Pkwy.

Easton

Bridgeport **6**

Fairfield **5**

Redding

Saugatuck Reservoir

Branchville

Georgetown

Weston

Saugatuck River

Westport **4**

Long Island Sound

Ridgefield

Wilton

Norwalk

South Norwalk **3**

New Canaan

North Stamford

Mianus Reservoir

Darien

Noroton

Stamford **2**

Merritt Pkwy.

Greenwich **1**

NEW YORK

N

0 miles 6

0 km 6

about 1690, and known as Knapp's Tavern during the Revolutionary War. Inside is an enormous stone fireplace and Colonial furniture; outside, the original herb garden still blooms. *243 E. Putnam Ave., tel. 203/869–9697. Admission: $2 adults. Open Wed., Fri., and Sun. 1–4.*

The **Bush-Holley House,** built in 1685, is now the headquarters of the Greenwich Historical Society. In the late 1800s the Holley family turned the two-story white-clapboard structure into an inn, where Childe Hassam, John Twachtman, Willa Cather, and Lincoln Steffens later congregated. Currently on display are paintings by Hassam, Twachtman, and Elmer Livingston MacRae, sculpture by John Rogers, and pottery by Leon Volkmar. *39 Strickland Rd., Cos Cob (I–95, Exit 4), tel. 203/869–6899. Admission: $3 adults, $1.50 senior citizens and students, children under 12 free. Open Tues.–Fri. noon–4, Sun. 1–4. Closed major holidays.*

② **Stamford**'s shoreline may be given over primarily to industry and commerce, but to the north is the 118-acre **Stamford Museum and Nature Center,** a 19th-century working farm and country store. It has permanent exhibits of farm tools, local Native American life, and early American artifacts, and an observatory and planetarium with shows on Friday from 8 to 10 (observatory) and Sunday at 3:30 (planetarium). *39 Scofieldtown Rd. (Merritt Pkwy., Exit 35), tel. 203/322–1646. Planetarium admission: $3 adults, $2 senior citizens and children 5–14; observatory admission: $2 adults, $1 senior citizens and children 5–14. Open Mon.–Sat. 9–5, Sun. and holidays 1–5. Closed Thanksgiving, Dec. 25, Jan. 1.*

Return to the Merritt Parkway and travel north to Exit 36. Follow Route 106 south to the first traffic light and turn right onto Camp Avenue. At the next light, take a left onto Hope Street. At the fourth traffic light you'll discover **United House Wrecking,** where acres of architectural artifacts, decorative accessories, antiques, collectibles, nautical items, lawn and garden furnishings, and other less valuable but certainly unusual items await you. *535 Hope St., tel. 203/348–5371. Admission free. Open Mon.–Sat. 9:30–5:30, Sun. noon–5.*

On your way back into town, take a look at the **First Presbyterian Church** of 1958. The fish-shape structure was designed by Wallace Harrison, and its famous stained-glass windows catch the light from many angles. Inside you may feel as though you're in the belly of a whale. The 56-bell carillon was added a decade later. *1101 Bedford St., tel. 203/324–9522. Open weekdays 9–5, weekends 9–1.*

The Fairfield County branch of New York's venerable **Whitney Museum of American Art** is located on the street level of the Champion International Corporation building, in the heart of downtown. Works range from George Bellows's *Dempsey and Firpo* (1924) to Roy Lichtenstein's *Little Big Painting* (1965), and there are recent acquisitions as well. Sculpture, folk art, and furniture are also displayed here. *Atlantic St. and Tresser Blvd., tel. 203/358–7630. Admission free. Open Tues.–Sat. 11–5.*

③ The new **Maritime Center** is the cornerstone of the **South Norwalk** (SoNo) redevelopment. Built around a restored 19th-century redbrick factory on the west bank of the Norwalk River, the 5-acre waterfront center brings to life the ecology and history of Long Island Sound through state-of-the-art technology. A huge aquarium competes for attention with actual marine vessels, such as the 30-foot steam tender *Glory Days* and the 56-foot oyster sloop *Hope*, both of which may be boarded in the comfort of an indoor display hall. A 340-seat Image Maximum (IMAX) theater is exactly that—an immense curving screen rising six stories and extending 80 feet, beyond the edges of peripheral vision. Special activities include scuba diving and the tracking and tagging of lobsters. *10 N. Water St. (I–95, Exit 14N or 15S), tel. 203/852–0700 or 800/243–2280. Admission: aquarium and marine hall combined, $7.50 adults, $6.50 senior citizens and children; IMAX theater, $5.50 adults, $4.50 senior citizens and children; aquarium, marine hall, and IMAX theater combined, $11.50 adults, $9.50 senior citizens and children. Open daily 10–5. Closed Dec. 25 and Jan. 1.*

Steps away from the Maritime Center, the thriving **SoNo commercial district** teems with art galleries, restaurants, and trendy boutiques.

A monument to a different time is found in the **Lockwood-Matthews Mansion Museum,** to the north on West Avenue. The vast display of Victorian decorative art is almost overwhelming to the 20th-century eye—it's hard not to be impressed by the octagonal rotunda and 50 rooms of gilt, fresco, marble, ornate woodwork, and etched glass. *295 West Ave. (I–95, Exit 14S or 15N), tel. 203/838–1434. Admission: $3 adults, $2 senior citizens. Open Tues.–Fri. 11–3, Sun. 1–4. Closed mid-Dec.–Feb.*

At the intersection of Smith and East Wall streets you'll find a cluster of reconstructed 18th- and 19th-century buildings that comprise **Mill Hill Historic Park** (tel. 203/846–0525). A one-room schoolhouse, jail, and the Fitch House law office are among them.

4 In the northern section of **Westport** you'll find the **Nature Center for Environmental Activities,** a 62-acre wildlife sanctuary containing several carefully designed trails through woods, fields, and streams. A Sensitivity Trail for the visually handicapped gets you as close as possible to flora and fauna in their natural habitat. *10 Woodside Ave. (Merritt Pkwy., Exit 41), tel. 203/227–7253. Admission: $1 adults, 50¢ children. Open Mon.–Sat. 9–5, Sun. 1–4.*

During the summer months, visitors to Westport congregate at **Sherwood Island State Park.** In addition to its long sweep of sandy beach, it boasts two picnic groves on the water and several food concessions. Sunbathing, swimming, and fishing are the chief attractions at the only truly public beach between Greenwich and New Haven. *I–95, Exit 18, tel. 203/226–6983. Open Memorial Day–Sept.*

5 The headquarters of the **Connecticut Audubon Society** maintains a 160-acre wildlife sanctuary in **Fairfield** that includes 6 miles of rugged hiking trails and special walks for the visually handicapped, disabled, and elderly. There's also a well-stocked gift shop and reference library. *2325 Burr St. (I–95, Exit 21), tel. 203/259–6305. Admission: building free; sanctuary, $1 adults, 50¢ children. Building open Tues.–Sat. 9–4:30; sanctuary open daily dawn–dusk.*

The society operates a smaller sanctuary and **Birdcraft Museum** that features a children's activity corner, along with 6 acres of trails and a pond that attracts seasonal waterfowl. *314 Unquowa (I-95, Exit 21), tel. 203/259-0416. Admission: $1 adults, 50¢ children. Open weekends noon-5.*

Time Out **Rawley's,** the ramshackle red-shingle structure at 1886 Post Road in Fairfield, has a few parking slots outside, a small counter inside, and a firm local reputation for serving the best hot dog in the world. Hot dogs, fixings, and cold soft drinks are the entire bill of fare.

6 **Bridgeport** is making strides in urban renewal, drawing on every possible resource. One of its chief assets is the **Barnum Museum,** associated with a past resident and mayor, the entrepreneur Phineas T. Barnum, who was one of the great showmen of his day. Barnum's will provided for the establishment of an Institute of Science and Industry in the city he loved, and the early original building has been incorporated into the present museum, which was renovated and reopened in 1989. The fun here is in the permanent exhibits associated with Barnum's show-business career, which feature such characters as General Tom Thumb and Jenny Lind, the Swedish Nightingale. You can tour a scaled-down model of Barnum's famous creation, the three-ring circus. The great canvas tent may be gone now, but the spirit of the Big Top lives on at the Barnum Museum. *820 Main St. (I-95, Exit 27), tel. 203/331-1104. Admission: $5 adults, $4 senior citizens, $2 children 4-18. Open Tues.-Sat. 10-4:30, Sun. noon-4:30. Closed major holidays.*

Formerly the Museum of Art, Science and Industry, the spruced up **Discovery Museum** touches all bases with an eclectic collection of art from Renaissance to contemporary, a planetarium, several hands-on science exhibits, and a children's museum. It also offers demonstrations, lectures, and workshops. *4450 Park Ave. (Merritt Pkwy., Exit 47), tel. 203/372-3521. Admission: $4.50 adults, $3.50 senior citizens and children 4-18. Open Tues.-Fri. 10-5, Sun. noon-5.*

Beardsley Zoological Gardens is Connecticut's largest zoo. The 30-acre site houses more than 200 animals, ranging from North American mammals, such as the mountain lion, elk, and bison, to the exotic Siberian tiger. A smaller children's zoo (in a farmlike setting) offers pony rides. *Noble Ave., Beardsley Park (I-95, Exit 27A), tel. 203/576-8082. Admission: $2 adults, $1 children 5-12, $1 senior citizens. Parking: $1 CT residents, $5 out-of-state cars. Open daily 9-4. Closed Thanksgiving, Dec. 25, Jan. 1.*

At the foot of Bostwick Avenue, at **Captain's Cove Seaport,** a replica of the British warship HMS *Rose* is berthed. Before boarding the Revolutionary War ship, check out the craft shops and restaurants in the area. *1 Bostwick Ave. (I-95, Exit 26), tel. 203/335-1433. Admission to HMS* Rose*: $3 adults, $2 children. Open Mar.-Oct.*

7 In northern **Stratford, Boothe Memorial Park** contains a number of unusual buildings, including a blacksmith shop, carriage and tool barns, and a museum that includes a history of the trolley among its displays. There's also a children's playground. *Main St. (Merritt Pkwy., Exit 53), tel. 203/378-9895. Ad-*

mission free. Park open 9–5; museum open Tues.–Fri. 11–1, weekends 1–4. Closed Nov.–May.

8 While **New Haven** enjoys a reputation as a manufacturing center dating back to Eli Whitney's 19th-century development of the principle of interchangeable parts, its greater fame rests on an earlier "Eli." In 1718, a donation by wealthy resident Elihu Yale enabled the Collegiate School, founded in 1701, to settle in New Haven, where it changed its name to **Yale University** to honor its benefactor. The university provides knowledgeable guides for one-hour walking tours that include Connecticut Hall in the Old Campus, which housed the young Nathan Hale, William Howard Taft, and Noah Webster during their student days. *344 College St., Phelps Gateway (I–95, Exit 47), tel. 203/432–2300. Tours free. Tours leave weekdays at 10:30 and 2, weekends at 1:30.*

Sterling Memorial Library and the **Beinecke Rare Book Library** house major collections, a Gutenberg Bible, illuminated manuscripts, and original Audubon bird prints. *Beinecke: 121 Wall St., tel. 203/432–2977. Beinecke open weekdays 8:30–5, Sat. 10–5. Closed Sat. June–Aug., major holidays. Sterling: 120 High St., tel. 203/432–1775. Sterling open Mon.–Sat. 8:30–5. Closed Sat. in Aug., major holidays.*

The **Yale Art Gallery,** the country's oldest college art museum, contains Renaissance paintings, American, African, Near and Far Eastern art, and European art of the 20th century. Don't miss the remarkable reconstruction of a Mithraic shrine. *1111 Chapel St., tel. 203/432–0600. Admission free. Open Tues.– Sat. 10–5, Sun. 2–5. Closed major holidays.*

The **Peabody Museum of Natural History** is the largest of its kind in New England. Along with exhibits of dinosaur fossils and meteorites, emphasis is placed on Connecticut's environment, including early Native American life and birds. *170 Whitney Ave., tel. 203/432–5050 or 203/432–5799 (recorded announcement). Admission: $2 adults, $1.50 senior citizens, $1 children 5–15; Tues. free. Open Mon.–Sat. 9–4:45, Sun. 1– 4:45.*

More than 850 instruments, some dating to the 16th century, make up the university's **Collection of Musical Instruments.** An annual concert series is given using some of these instruments. *15 Hillhouse Ave., tel. 203/432–0822. Admission free. Open Tues.–Thurs. 1–4. Closed Aug., university recesses.*

The **Yale Center for British Art** has a sizeable collection of British paintings, drawings, prints, sculpture, and rare books from the Elizabethan period to the present. Anglophiles will enjoy the well-stocked gift shop. *1080 Chapel St., tel. 203/432–2800. Admission free. Open Tues.–Sat. 10–5, Sun. 2–5. Closed major holidays.*

Time Out   At the bright, contemporary **Atticus Bookstore-Cafe** (1082 Chapel St.), next to the Yale Center for British Art, one can sit at the counter or at a tiny table, sip tea or freshly brewed coffee, munch on a croissant or muffin, and read. It's the kind of place where spontaneous conversations become prolonged discussions.

The most notable example of the campus's collegiate-Gothic architecture is the **Harkness Tower,** with its famous motto, sometimes described as the world's greatest anticlimax: "For God, for country, and for Yale."

Across from the old campus, the **New Haven Green** offers impressive architecture as well as a superb example of urban planning. As early as 1638, village elders set aside the 16-acre plot as a town common. Three churches, added from 1812 to 1814— the Gothic-style Trinity Episcopal Church, the Georgian-style Center Congregational Church, and the predominantly Federalist United Church—contribute to its present appeal.

At opposite ends of New Haven, two popular outdoor attractions are **East Rock Park** (East Rock Rd., tel. 203/787–8021) and **West Rock Nature Center** (Wintergreen Ave., tel. 203/787–8016). East Rock is a large municipal park, complete with picnic and recreation facilities, playgrounds, a bird sanctuary, and nature trails. West Rock is more a zoo with live animals in outdoor settings and reptiles and smaller creatures indoors. There are also picnic and hiking facilities. Follow the Regicides Trail to the infamous Judges' Cave—two of the men who signed the warrant for the execution of England's Charles I fled to the cave after the Restoration.

Black Rock Fort and **Ft. Nathan Hale** are reconstructions of forts from the Revolutionary and Civil wars, and they present a spectacular view of New Haven Harbor. *Woodward Ave., tel. 203/787–8790. Open Memorial Day–Labor Day, daily; weekends in the fall.*

To get to the city's southeastern tip, take Exit 50 off I–95 and follow Lighthouse Road. The **Pardee-Morris House,** built in 1750, was burned by the Redcoats in 1779, then rebuilt in 1780 on the original foundation. Furnishings from its earliest days to those used during the early part of the 19th century give a picture of life in those times. *325 Lighthouse Rd., tel. 203/562–4183. Admission: $2 adults, $1 senior citizens and children 6–18. Open June–Aug. 11:30–4. Closed Mon., holidays.*

Lighthouse Point (tel. 203/787–8005), at the end of the road, is an 82-acre park with a public beach, nature trails, a picnic grove, and an antique carousel set in a turn-of-the-century beach pavilion. *Open Memorial Day–Labor Day.*

Shopping

The Stamford Town Center (100 Greyrock Pl., tel. 203/356–9700), a multistory mall, has 130 shops and a parking garage.Shops on Westport's Main Street lean toward the cute and the expensive. Opposite the green in New Haven, the Chapel Square Mall (900 Chapel St., tel. 203/777–6661) has 63 shops and a parking garage.

Antiques To follow Norwalk's Antique Trail, pick up brochures and map at 140 Main Street (tel. 203/846–1242). In Westport, antiques seekers will discover "finds" rather than genuine bargains in the shops near the meeting of Riverside Avenue and Post Road West.

Books The **Yale Co-op** (77 Broadway, New Haven, tel. 203/772–2200) carries Yale-emblem goods from T-shirts to tennis togs, bar glasses to wall pennants, and a vast stock of books and records.

True bibliophiles will head for the **Arethusa Book Shop** (87 Audubon St., New Haven, tel. 203/624–1848) and its large selection of out-of-print, used, early, and first-edition volumes.

Discount Outlets Norwalk's outlets range from **Decker's** (666 West Ave., tel. 203/ 866–5593), with clothing for the family, to **The Royal Doulton Shoppe** (11 Rowan St., tel. 203/838–7859), which has china, crystal, porcelain, and gifts at reduced prices.

Supermarkets **Stew Leonard's Dairy** (100 Westport Ave., Rte. 1, Norwalk, tel. 203/847–7213) boldly proclaims itself "The Disneyland of Supermarkets." You never know what's going to be on sale in the main store, but just as much fun is the children's animal farm where the youngsters get to touch the sources of some of the amazing bargains.

Sports and Outdoor Activities

Fishing **Open boats** are provided by **Yacht Haven** (Washington Blvd., Stamford, tel. 203/359–4500), **Stratford Marina** (Broad St., Stratford, tel. 203/377–4477), and **Caswell Cove Marina** (231 Pope Island Rd., Milford, tel. 203/878–1780).

Fishing boats can be chartered from **Yacht Haven East** (Stamford, tel. 203/348–3386), **Norwalk Cove Marina** (Norwalk, tel. 203/853–2522 or 203/259–7719), and **Bridge Square** (Westport, tel. 203/255–5653).

Water Sports **Longshore Sailing School** (Cove Island Park, Stamford, tel. 203/348–6100) rents small boats; **Rick's Surf City** (570 Boston Post Rd., Milford, tel. 203/877–4257) rents sailboards and surfboards; and **Sail New Haven** (2 Lighthouse Rd., New Haven, tel. 203/469–6754) rents sailboards and sailboats, and offers lessons.

Dining and Lodging

The following dining price categories have been used: *Very Expensive*, over $25; *Expensive*, $20–$25; *Moderate*, $12–$20; and *Inexpensive*, under $12.

The following lodging price categories have been used: *Very Expensive*, over $100; *Expensive*, $75–$100; *Moderate*, $50–$75; *Inexpensive*, under $50.

Bridgeport **Ocean Sea Grill.** You'll have to make your way through derelict
Dining surroundings to reach this Art Deco fortress, a survivor of urban blight. Inside all is pleasant, uncluttered, and reassuringly contemporary-cum-deco. For more than 50 years the restaurant has served fresh seafood with an Italian influence— and chocolate mousse cake to follow. *1328 Main St., tel. 203/ 336–2132. Reservations advised. Dress: casual. AE, DC, MC, V. Closed Sun., Thanksgiving, Dec. 25. Moderate–Expensive.*
Tumbleweed's. Tex-Mex has come to Bridgeport's north end, at the Brookside Center shopping mall. Beneath a sign proclaiming "Home Sweet Home" and amid a clutter of cactus, Southwestern and international concoctions are served, among them sirloin teriyaki and Mississippi mud pie. *4485 Main St., tel. 203/374–0234. Reservations advised. Dress: casual. AE, DC, MC, V. Closed major holidays. Inexpensive.*

Lodging **Bridgeport Hilton.** Smack in the middle of downtown, this member of the Hilton chain offers comfortable lodging with particular appeal to the business trade. Rooms have modern furniture in soft color combinations of rose and off-white. The best accommodations are the named suites on the top floor; the lower floors, although well-insulated from noise, may be penetrated by city sounds from below. The bar and lounge off the lobby draw a convivial crowd. *1070 Main St., 06604, tel. 203/ 334–1234 or 800/445–8667. 224 rooms, 10 suites. Facilities: restaurant, lounge, health club, indoor pool, sauna. AE, DC, MC, V. Expensive.*

Fairfield
Lodging

Fairfield Motor Inn. The light-brick hotel with the white pillars offers attractively furnished modern bedrooms and large, full baths. The lobby, the small breakfast room, and the lounge (with a working fireplace) all have a light decor that suggests a Scandinavian influence. *417 Post Rd., 06430, tel. 203/255–0491. 80 rooms. Facilities: restaurant, outdoor pool. AE, DC, MC, V. Rates include breakfast. Moderate.*

Greenwich
Dining
★

Bertrand. The spectacular brick-vault interior of this mainstreet restaurant provides a classic setting of small, candlelit tables for a menu of classic and nouvelle French cuisine. The confit of duck with sorrel sauce, and salmon in a pastry crust, seem more at home in this onetime bank than stacks of money bags. Financial matters pale beside the nougat ice cream—until the check comes. *253 Greenwich Ave., tel. 203/869–4459. Reservations advised. Jacket and tie required. AE, DC, MC, V. No lunch Sat., Sun. Closed Jan. 1, Dec. 25. Very Expensive.*

★

Homestead Inn. This restaurant provides the perfect setting for Jacques Thiebeult's imaginative variations on classic French cuisine. In any of the cozy nooks that comprise the dining area, all-agleam with sparkling silver and crystal, you might opt for the perennial favorite Billi Bi, mussel soup, or the veal sweetbreads with chanterelles. For dessert, try the triple chocolate cake. *420 Field Point Rd., tel. 203/869–7500. Reservations advised. Jacket required. AE, MC, V. Very Expensive.*

★

Restaurant Jean Louis. The roses in silver bud-vases, the Villeroy & Boch china, and the crisp, white cloths with lace underskirts are complemented by careful service of extraordinary food. A few of Jean Louis's specialties are the quail-and-vegetable ragout with foie gras sauce; scallopine of salmon on a bed of leeks with fresh herb sauce; and for dessert lemon-and-pear gratin. *61 Lewis St., tel. 203/622–8450. Reservations advised. Jacket and tie required. AE, DC, MC, V. Lunch Sat. only. Closed Sun. Very Expensive.*

Manero's. The sign outside exhorts you to "bring the kids," and most patrons do: The place echoes with renditions of "Happy Birthday" at every meal. However, the beef aged on the premises is deservedly famous, so ignore the hokey surroundings and treat yourself to chateaubriand. An adjacent retail meat market offers the same beef for domestic consumption. *559 Steamboat Rd. (I–95, Exit 3), tel. 230/869–0049. No reservations. Dress: casual. AE, DC, MC, V. Moderate.*

Pasta Vera. The tiny, plain white dining space of this shop-cum-restaurant belies the splendor of its many variations on simple pasta, from wild mushroom ravioli to *pesto torte* (layers of zucchini pesto in puff pastry topped with tomato sauce). Full-scale entrees include lemony veal piccante with fettuccine and garlicky *calamari fra diavolo* (squid with a spicy tomato sauce). *88 E. Putnam Ave., tel. 203/661–9705. No reser-*

vations. Dress: casual. No credit cards. Closed Sun. Inexpensive–Moderate.

Lodging **Hyatt Regency Greenwich.** Once upon a time the Condé Nast
★ publishing empire was ruled from the four-story turreted tower and spire of this modern edifice. Inside, a vast but comfortable atrium boasts its own flourishing lawn and abundant flora. Spacious rooms offer all the amenities, including telephones that are modem-compatible for laptop-computer users. *1800 E. Putnam Ave. (I–95, Exit 5), 06870, tel. 203/637–1234 or 800/233–1234. 353 rooms. Facilities: 2 restaurants, jazz bar, atrium lounge, valet parking, indoor pool, health club, sauna, steam room, open-air sun court. AE, D, DC, MC, V. Very Expensive.*

★ **Homestead Inn.** Those interested in the art of hospitality should visit this inn for a graduate course. In the last decade, since its total renovation, the Homestead has achieved well-deserved renown for the superiority of its restaurant and accommodations. Each individually designed bedroom is decorated with attractive period furniture and reproductions arranged to provide respite for the weary and allure for the romantic. Clock radios and electric blankets, one firm pillow and one soft for each guest, and good reading lights are standard equipment, along with plush robes and a bouquet of bathroom goodies. *420 Field Point Rd., 06830, tel. 203/869–7500. 23 rooms. Facilities: dining room. AE, DC, MC, V. Rates include Continental breakfast. Expensive.*

Stanton House Inn. This large, Federal-period mansion within walking distance of downtown underwent considerable redesign by the noted architect Stanford White in 1900. It has been carefully refurbished and redecorated in traditional style, with a mixture of antiques and tasteful reproductions. *76 Maple Ave., 06830, tel. 203/869–2110. 26 rooms. AE, MC, V. Rates include Continental breakfast. Moderate–Expensive.*

New Haven **Robert Henry's.** From the quiet comfort of the main dining
Dining room, with its huge stone fireplace, you can gaze out the win-
★ dows at the bustle of Chapel Street. The slightly smaller but equally embracing Club Room features fine china and crystal on crisp tablecloths. Traditional and contemporary French cuisine and seasonal treats make up the menu, which includes medallions of venison, warm truffled pheasant sausage, and the restaurant's signature duck-leg confit. You may have trouble resisting the *chocolate plaisir*, a cake with bittersweet chocolate and vanilla mousse served with a chocolate sauce. *1032 Chapel St., tel. 203/789–1010. Reservations required. Jacket required. AE, DC, MC, V. No lunch. Closed Sun., July 4, Labor Day, Dec. 25. Expensive.*

★ **Azteca's.** This restaurant draws a crowd of aficionados who appreciate its elegant presentation of Mexican and Southwestern dishes in a modern, appropriately subdued setting. The artwork on the walls changes monthly; the innovative menu changes somewhat less frequently. Among the favorites are black buck-antelope tenderloin; broiled Norwegian salmon with Texas ruby-red grapefruit sauce; and chicken mole with a rich and spicy sauce. *14 Mechanic St., tel. 203/624–2454. Reservations advised. Dress: neat but casual. MC, V. No lunch. Closed Sun., major holidays. Moderate–Expensive.*

Bruxelles. In the heart of New Haven's theater district, this elegant, modern brasserie has a cosmopolitan menu that ranges from selections prepared on an open rotisserie to *pasta* *raccio*—tricolor tortellini with slivers of duck, fresh tomatoes, watercress, mushrooms, and a light Parmesan cream. The second-floor dining room is at once formal and madcap, with starched cloth napkins standing at attention in stemmed glasses on top of tablecloths covered with butcher's paper for doodling with the crayons provided. *220 College St., tel. 203/777–7752. No reservations. Dress: neat but casual. AE, MC, V. Closed Dec. 25. Moderate–Expensive.*

Carbone's. Under the pressed-tin ceiling of this restaurant, diners at green-cloth-covered tables dig into such traditional Italian favorites as the *zuppa di pesce* (shellfish and saltwater fish in tomato or cream sauce, served over linguine) and veal *paggliacei* (veal parmigiana with escarole and eggplant). Somewhat incongruous but luxurious is the California mud pie, a chocolate mousse pie with Oreo cookies and fudge topping. *100 Wooster St., tel. 203/773–1866. Reservations advised. Dress: casual. AE, MC, V. No lunch on weekends. Closed Mon., Thanksgiving, Dec. 25. Moderate–Expensive.*

Christopher Martins. This neighborhood bistro offers a long, informal bar with a few tables and a more formal dining room with cloth-covered tables and soft, indirect lighting. The Continental menu changes often, but there's sure to be a featured veal dish, such as the veal Christopher, with port wine, pignoli nuts, and mushrooms. Chances are there will also be a devastating white-chocolate mousse. *860 State St., tel. 203/772–3613. Reservations advised. Dress: casual. AE, DC, MC, V. No lunch weekends. Closed Thanksgiving, Dec. 25. Moderate–Expensive.*

Frank Pepe's. One of the major combatants in the pizza wars of Wooster Street, this contender has served pies since 1925. The big ovens on the back wall bake pizzas that are served by smart-mouthed waitresses who could teach bad manners to the legendary waiters at Lindy's in New York. On weekend evenings the wait for a table can be more than an hour, but the pizza, the sole item on the menu, is worth it. *157 Wooster St., tel. 203/865–5762. No reservations. Dress: casual. No credit cards. No lunch Mon., Wed., Thurs. Closed Tues. Inexpensive.*

Sally's. The loyal clientele of this small pizza restaurant continues to line up outdoors in all weather, having seen no change in quality since the owner and founder of the family-operated eatery died a few years ago. *237 Wooster St., tel. 203/624–5271. No reservations. Dress: casual. No credit cards. Closed Thanksgiving, Dec. 25. Inexpensive.*

Lodging **The Inn at Chapel West.** Technically a bed-and-breakfast, this inn in a restored Victorian mansion provides comfortable lodging in a big-city environment. Ten guest rooms, some with fireplaces, are furnished with a mix of antiques and modern conveniences, and breakfast is served in the dining room downstairs. *1201 Chapel St., 06511, tel. 203/777–1201. 10 rooms with bath. Facilities: concierge services, conference facilities, afternoon refreshments. AE, DC, MC, V. Rates include Continental breakfast. Very Expensive.*

Colony Inn. Set in the center of the Chapel Street hotel district, the inn offers sidewalk dining in its glass-enclosed Greenhouse Restaurant. The eclectic lobby, with an ornate chandelier, appears to be a mix of grand Baroque and Victorian. Guest rooms were refurbished in 1987, and the Colonial-reproduction furnishings and modern baths are still attractive. Some rooms on the higher floors have excellent views of the Yale campus. *1157 Chapel St., 06511, tel. 203/776–1234 or 800/458–8810 outside CT, fax 203/772–3929. 80 rooms, 6 suites. Facilities: restaurant, lounge. AE, DC, MC, V. Expensive.*

Holiday Inn Downtown. A renovation completed in 1988 left a comfortable modern decor with soft, restful colors. The best rooms in this hotel on the edge of the Yale campus are on the eighth floor, high above the traffic outside. *31 Whalley Ave., 06511, tel. 203/777–6221 or 800/465–4329, fax 203/772–1089. 154 rooms, 6 suites. Facilities: restaurant, lounge, health club, outdoor pool, free parking. AE, DC, MC, V. Moderate–Expensive.*

Park Plaza Hotel. This contemporary downtown hotel, slightly overlit, is a hub of activity near the theater district, with access to an adjacent shopping mall and parking garage. But the graffiti-scarred elevator doors suggest that the hotel, built in 1966 and since refurbished, has seen better days. Rooms are attractively furnished and modern-looking. *155 Temple St., 06510, tel. 203/772–1700 or 800/243–4221 outside CT, fax 203/624–2683. 295 rooms, 5 suites. Facilities: outdoor pool. AE, DC, MC, V. Moderate–Expensive.*

Regal Inn. Formerly the Royal Inn, there's still no majesty to this unpretentious motel in the bustling northern part of town. But the simply furnished rooms are clean and well-maintained by the present management, and the lack of frills is balanced by low rates. *1605 Whalley Ave., 06515, tel. 203/389–9504. 85 rooms. AE, DC, MC, V. Inexpensive.*

Norwalk
Dining
★

Silvermine Tavern. The dining area is enormous, but a low ceiling, Colonial decor, and many windows make this landmark restaurant an intimate setting for hearty meals. Glowing candles and gleaming silver add to the romantic atmosphere. Traditional New England favorites, such as crisp roast duckling with apple-cider sauce, are the order of the day. Chocolate silk pie is the outstanding dessert. *194 Perry Ave. (Merritt Pkwy., Exit 39), tel. 203/847–4558. Reservations advised. Dress: casual. AE, DC, MC, V. Closed Tues. (Sept.–May). Moderate–Expensive.*

Lodging

Courtyard by Marriott. A new addition to the fast-growing corporate strip north of the Merritt Parkway, this Marriott features all the state-of-the art comforts of a modern hotel—from security cards instead of room keys to coffee makers in each room and comfortable, modern furniture. Within the courtyard, a gazebo is surrounded by a perfectly groomed lawn, and a pool so serene it almost defies trespass. *474 Main Ave. (Rte. 7N), 06851, tel. 203/849–9111 or 800/321–2211, fax 203/849–8144. 133 rooms, 12 suites. Facilities: restaurant, lounge, health club, whirlpool, indoor pool. AE, DC, MC, V. Expensive.*

★ **Silvermine Tavern.** Best known for its extraordinary restaurant, the lodgings, parts of which date back to 1642, are equally attractive. Each room has a different configuration and is furnished with a variety of antiques and period pieces, as well as some modern touches. Idiosyncracies abound: Room T-8 is entered through its bathroom but is particularly cozy. Some rooms have tubs but no showers because of the slanted ceilings. All of the accommodations share the ambience of the remarkable main-floor lobby and lounges. *194 Perry Ave. (Merritt Pkwy., Exit 39), 06850, tel. 203/847–4558. 10 rooms.*

Facilities: restaurant. AE, DC, MC, V. Rates include Continental breakfast. Expensive.

Day's Inn. Built in 1988, this hotel retains its freshly minted atmosphere by attention to maintenance. The small lobby is efficient, if not cheery, and rooms contain modern furnishings in soft colors. A top-floor room will protect you from traffic noise, but none of the views is particularly interesting. *426 Main Ave. (Rte. 7N), 06851, tel. 203/849–9828 or 800/325–2525. 119 rooms. Facilities: restaurant, lounge, health club. AE, DC, MC, V. Moderate–Expensive.*

South Norwalk   **Coyote Cafe & Saloon.** Tex-Mex favorites are served here, in a
Dining   setting of bare floors, exposed brick, and bright oilcloth-covered tables. In addition to taquitos, burritos, and fajitas there are such specialties as chicken and shrimp *Tchopatoulis* (sautéed with pimientos, mild green chilies, artichoke hearts, mushrooms), and andouille sausage with linguine. If these dishes don't raise your temperature, a display of more than 100 bottled hot-sauces that lines the walls might do the trick. *50 Water St., tel. 203/854–9630. Reservations advised. Dress: casual. AE, DC, MC, V. No lunch Sat. No dinner Mon. Closed major holidays. Moderate.*

★ **SoNo's Little Kitchen.** A simple storefront turned into kitchen and dining room, this restaurant seduces you with aromas the minute you cross the threshold. You also get to watch the owner and chef Jeanette Hart prepare her specialty: Jamaican cuisine at its finest. Nibble on some Jamaican CoCo bread while you contemplate the curried goat or the jerk chicken or pork— meat that's been marinated with pimento, cloves, nutmeg, cinnamon, and peppers and is then barbecued. Hart smokes her own bluefish and serves it with sweet pepper or tomato-basil sauce. For dessert, the coconut pastry *gazada* deserves a try. *49 S. Main St., tel. 203/855–8515. Reservations advised. Dress: casual. No credit cards. No dinner Mon.–Wed. Closed Sun., Jan. 1, Thanksgiving, Dec. 25. Inexpensive.*

Stamford   **Pellicci's.** Fifties glitz, complete with fake stained-glass ceil-
Dining   ing, provides the setting for traditional Italian and Continental favorites at this large, longtime favorite in a neighborhood that is undergoing rapid change. Corporate execs mingle with the local folk over such specialties as veal marsala, shrimp marinara, and baked ziti. *96 Stillwater Ave., tel. 203/323–2542. Reservations advised. Dress: casual. AE, DC, MC, V. Closed Mon., Easter, Dec. 25. Moderate.*

Lodging   **Radisson Tara Hotel.** Formerly the Westin, this cavernous, modern, five-story hotel became the Radisson Tara in November 1990. Geared to serve the corporate community, the hotel, with its glass-covered atrium lacking in floral relief, sacrifices some intimacy to high-tech efficiency. Rooms, however, are spacious and tastefully decorated. *2701 Summer St., 06905, tel. 203/359–1300 or 800/321–2042. 457 rooms, 35 suites. Facilities: restaurant, lounge, 2 lighted tennis courts, health club, saunas, indoor pool, 23,000-square-foot meeting space, free parking, airport limo service. AE, D, DC, MC, V. Expensive.*

Sheraton Stamford Hotel and Towers. The drive leading to the ultramodern entrance of this downtown luxury hotel should prepare you for the dramatic atrium lobby inside, with its brass-and-glass-enclosed gazebo. High-tech haywire to some, the lobby is actually the well-organized axis from which the hotel's services flow. Attractive, contemporary furnishings in the rooms are complemented by such amenities as massaging showerheads in the spacious bathrooms. The Towers section contains accommodations for the carriage trade and has its own lounge and concierge service. Topping everything off is an awe-inspiring skylit swimming pool. *1 First Stamford Pl. (I–95, Exit 7N or 6S), 06901, tel. 203/967–2222 or 800/325–3535. 471 rooms, 34 suites. Facilities: 2 restaurants, lounge, health club, sauna, indoor pool. AE, DC, MC, V. Expensive.*

Stamford Marriott. One of the first of the downtown hotels built to accommodate Stamford's growth as a corporate hub, the Marriott stands out for its convenience to transportation and its up-to-date facilities. Modern and comfortable, if unmemorable, furnishings are found throughout. The large, busy lobby is a favorite meeting place for the city's movers and shakers, who frequently head for one of several meeting rooms or to Le Carrousel, which is at press time the only revolving rooftop restaurant in the state. *2 Stamford Forum (I–95, Exit 8), 06901, tel. 203/357–9555 or 800/228–9290. 500 rooms, 7 suites. Facilities: 2 restaurants, 2 lounges, health club, sauna, rooftop jogging track, indoor and outdoor pools, 2 racquetball courts, games room, valet, laundry service, free parking, airport limousine. AE, DC, MC, V. Expensive.*

Stamford Super 8 Motel. Standard modern furnishings are found in this link of the national hotel chain. It's clean and convenient to all local attractions. *32 Grenhart Rd. (I–95, Exit 6), 06902, tel. 203/324–8887 or 800/843–1991. 92 rooms, 7 suites. Facilities: coffee shop. AE, DC, MC, V. Inexpensive–Moderate.*

Westport
Dining

Le Chambord. Tiny oil lamps set on each pale-almond-colored tablecloth cast a romantic glow on gleaming silver and crystal, and quiet, attentive service accompanies such trusted classic French favorites as *canard à l'orange* (duckling with orange sauce) and baby rack of lamb with tiny vegetables. The arrival of the Grand Marnier soufflé inevitably draws sighs of pleasure. *1572 Post Rd. E, tel. 203/255–2654. Reservations advised. Dress: casual. AE, DC, MC, V. No lunch Sat. Closed Sun. and Mon., all major holidays. Very Expensive.*

Nistico's Red Barn. Under the aged beams and wagon-wheel chandeliers, tables here are decorated with crisp white cloths, pink napkins, and candle lamps. An enormous stone fireplace divides the main dining areas and provides warmth in blustery weather. Particularly cozy is the "Louis Room," to the right of the entrance, with its low ceiling and fireplace. Specialties include enormous Maine lobsters and a 32-ounce porterhouse steak. For the less ambitious, there's the 24-ounce New York strip sirloin or the 12-ounce filet mignon. *292 Wilton Rd. (Merritt Pkwy., Exit 41), tel. 203/222–9549. Reservations advised. Dress: casual. AE, DC, MC, V. Closed Dec. 25. Expensive.*

Tanglewoods. The country-modern decor in this restaurant includes ceiling fans, Tiffany-style lamps, and bentwood and rattan chairs placed around tile-topped tables. An international menu ranges from seafood scampi (scallops, crabmeat, and shrimp in a garlic-butter sauce) to grilled 8-oz. filet mignon. There's also a bread pudding in bourbon sauce, made on the premises. *833 Post Rd. E, tel. 203/226–2880. Reservations advised. Dress: casual. AE, DC, MC, V. Sun. brunch. Closed Thanksgiving, Dec. 25. Inexpensive–Moderate.*

★ **International Deli & Restaurant.** Despite the modern, Scandinavian-influenced decor, the zesty scent of corned beef and kosher pickles tells you you're in a bona fide deli. Whether you stop at the voluminous counter to buy some takeout, or settle down at a table, you'll find all the traditional deli favorites— potato pancakes, cheese blintzes, borscht, and brisket, to mention a few. The creamy New York-style cheesecake is irresistible. *1385 Post Rd. E, tel. 203/255–7900. Reservations advised for 4 or more. Dress: casual. AE, MC, V. Closed Jan. 1, Dec. 25. Inexpensive.*

Mario's. Directly opposite the southbound side of the Westport train station, this restaurant serves Italian-American food to devotees who have come here for nearly a quarter of a century. Stop off for a drink at the long bar, swap a few stories, then stick around for the seafood platter served with linguine or the veal parmigiana with spaghetti. *36 Station Pl., tel. 203/227– 9217. Reservations advised. Dress: casual. AE, DC, MC, V. Closed Easter, Thanksgiving, Dec. 25. Inexpensive.*

Lodging
★ **The Inn at Longshore.** There are very few grand hotels in the Nutmeg State, but Longshore makes a strong claim for that distinction. Although small, this late-19th-century mansion is located on one of the most beautiful sites on the Connecticut shore. As you drive up the entranceway's long alley of stately oaks, you know you're in for a treat. And the inn itself, after being taken over by private management five years ago, has been renovated and refurbished with tasteful, traditional reproductions. All rooms have a view of the water or the park. Even Room 217, rented only when there isn't a bit of space left, looks beyond an exhaust vent to the water. *260 S. Compo Rd., 06880, tel. 203/226–3316. 12 rooms, 3 suites. Facilities: restaurant, guest privileges at tennis courts, handball courts, 18- hole golf course, Olympic-size adult and children's outdoor pools, sailing, windsurfing. AE, DC, MC, V. Very Expensive.*

The Westport Inn. Vigorous new management has taken this veteran inn of two decades in hand and shaken it up, all to the good. Bedrooms have been refurbished with attractive contemporary furniture; a new restaurant has recently opened; and even the apples on the front counter are polished. Rooms surrounding the large indoor pool are set back nicely and are slightly larger than those in the nonpoolside section. *1595 Post Rd. E (Rte. 1), 06880, tel. 203/259–5236 or 800/446–8997. 112 rooms, 2 suites. Facilities: restaurant, health club, sauna, indoor pool, airport-limo stop, room service. AE, DC, MC, V. Expensive.*

Southeastern Connecticut

The urban buildup that characterizes the Connecticut coast west of New Haven appears to dissipate as you drive east from the New Haven hub on I–95; there are long stretches here where you won't see even a single man-made interruption. Activities along the eastern shore center on Long Island Sound, which opens to the Atlantic Ocean in the northeast, and where saltwater anglers go after the big ones.

Numbers in the margin correspond to points of interest on the Southeastern Connecticut map.

Just south of I–95, 3 miles east of New Haven, is the town of
❶ **East Haven,** with its principal attraction the **Shore Line Trolley
Museum,** which houses more than 100 classic trolleys, among
them the oldest rapid transit car and the world's first electric
freight locomotive. Admission includes unlimited rides aboard
a vintage trolley on a 3-mile track. *17 River St. (Exits 51N, 52S
from I–95), East Haven, tel. 203/467–6927. Admission: $4
adults, $3 senior citizens, $2 children 2–11. Open June–Aug.,
daily 11–5; May, Sept., Oct., Dec., weekends 11–5; Apr., Nov.,
Sun. 11–5. Closed Dec. 25.*

❷ **Branford** is 4 miles east of East Haven on Route 1, which becomes Main Street in Branford. Here, the restored two-story
clapboard **Harrison House,** built in 1774, has a fine collection of
late 18th- and early 19th-century furnishings and a Colonial
herb garden. *124 Main St., Branford, tel. 203/488–4828.
Admission free. Open June–Sept., Wed.–Sat. 2–5.*

Continue down the road and you'll come upon **Bittersweet Farm,**
where the **Branford Craft Village** is located. These 85 acres
have been a working farm for over 150 years, though the sale of
a wide variety of crafts made on the premises predominates today. There's a small play area on the grounds, and a café serves
refreshments. *779 E. Main St., Branford, tel. 203/488–4689.
Admission free. Open Tues.–Sat. 11–5, Sun. noon–5.*

Leave I–95 at Exit 56 and follow Leetes Island Road south to
the village of Stony Creek, the departure point for cruises to
❸ the **Thimble Islands.** This group of 365 tiny islands was named
for their abundance of thimbleberries, which are similar to
gooseberries. Legend has it that Captain Kidd buried pirate
gold on one island. Two sightseeing vessels vie for your patron-
age, the *Volsunga III* (tel. 203/481–2234 or 203/488–9978) and
the *Sea Mist* (tel. 203/481–4841). Both offer daily trips from
early May through Columbus Day, departing from the Town
Dock at the end of Thimble Island Road.

❹ **Guilford** is the next stop off I–95, at Exit 58. Among the well-
preserved houses surrounding the village green is New England's oldest stone house, built by Reverend Henry Whitfield,
an English vicar who settled here in 1639. The **Whitfield House
Museum** was originally a village stronghold and meeting hall as
well as the minister's home. The late-medieval-style building
houses a collection of 17th-century furnishings. *Old Whitfield
St., Guilford, tel. 203/453–2457 or 203/566–3005. Admission:
$3 adults, $1.50 senior citizens and children. Open Apr.–Oct.,
Wed.–Sun. 10–5; Nov.–Mar., Wed.–Sun. 10–4. Closed
Thanksgiving, Dec. 15–Jan. 15.*

In the same neighborhood, on Boston Street, is the **Hyland
House,** a Colonial saltbox built in 1666, with five fireplaces and
hand-hewn floorboards, still held together by the original
handwrought nails and bolts. A 1720 addition contains a
sophisticated Bolection molding around the fireplace. *84 Boston St., Guilford, tel. 203/453–9477. Admission: $1.50. Open
June–Sept., 10–4:30. Closed Mon.*

Farther down the street is another Colonial saltbox, the **Thomas Griswold House,** built in 1774, displaying clothing, furniture,
farm tools, books, and photographs of early residents. There's
also a restored blacksmith shop and Colonial garden. *171 Boston St., Guilford, tel. 203/453–3176 or 203/453–5452. Admis-*

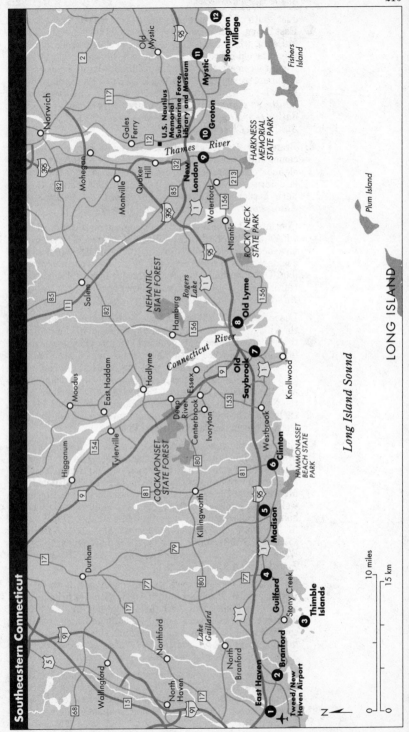

Southeastern Connecticut

- 1 East Haven
- Tweed/New Haven Airport
- 2 Branford
- 3 Thimble Islands
- 4 Guilford
- Stony Creek
- 5 Madison
- 6 Clinton
- 7 Old Saybrook
- 8 Old Lyme
- 9 New London
- 10 Groton
- U.S. Nautilus Memorial Submarine Force, Library and Museum
- 11 Mystic
- 12 Stonington Village

Long Island Sound

LONG ISLAND

Fishers Island

Plum Island

HARKNESS MEMORIAL STATE PARK

ROCKY NECK STATE PARK

NEHANTIC STATE FOREST

COCKAPONSET STATE FOREST

HAMMONASSET BEACH STATE PARK

Connecticut River

Thames River

Rogers Lake

Lake Gaillard

10 miles

15 km

N

sion: $1 adults, 50¢ children 12–18. Open mid-June–mid-Sept., Tues.–Sun. 11–4.

5 Continuing eastward to **Madison,** summertime traffic thickens as the crowds head for the sand and surf of **Hammonasset Beach State Park** (I–95, Exit 62, tel. 203/245–2785), the largest of the state's shoreline parks. The 2-mile beach along the eastern edge of town has facilities for swimming, camping, and picknicking. A large concession stand offers the usual beachfront food and beverages.

Back in town is the **Allis-Bushnell House and Museum,** built about 1785. Along with period rooms containing antique furnishings and costumes, you'll find an early doctor's office with period medical equipment. *853 Boston Post Rd. (I–95, Exit 61), Madison, tel. 203/245–4567 or 203/245–7891. Admission free. Open June–Labor Day, Wed.–Sun. 1–4.*

6 The Marquis de Lafayette stayed at the **Stanton House** in **Clinton,** in 1824, in a bed still displayed in its original surroundings. Built about 1790, the Stanton House was once a general store and now exhibits items it might have sold back then as well as a large collection of antique American and Staffordshire dinnerware. *63 E. Main St. (I–95, Exit 63), Clinton, tel. 203/669–2132. Admission free. Open June–Sept., Tues.–Sun. 2–5, and by appt.*

7 Located on the western side of the mouth of the Connecticut River, **Old Saybrook** was once a lively shipbuilding and fishing town. Today the bustle comes mostly from its many summer vacationers.

The Georgian-style **General William Hart House,** once the residence of a prosperous merchant and politician, was built about 1767. One of its eight corner fireplaces is decorated with Sadler and Green transfer-print tiles that illustrate Aesop's fables. *350 Main St. (I–95, Exit 67 or Rte. 9, Exit 2), Old Saybrook, tel. 203/388–2622. Admission free (donation suggested). Open late May–Sept., Fri.–Sun. 12:30–4.*

8 On the other side of the river mouth is **Old Lyme,** renowned among art lovers throughout the world. Central to its reputation is the **Florence Griswold Museum,** the former home of a great patron of the arts. Built in 1817, the mansion housed an art colony that included Willard Metcalfe, Clark Voorhees, and Childe Hassam. Many of their works are still on display here, along with early furnishings and decorative items. *96 Lyme St. (I–95, Exit 70, 1 block west), Old Lyme, tel. 203/434–5542. Admission: $2 adults. Open June–Oct., Tues.–Sat. 10–5, Sun. 1–5; Nov.–May, Wed.–Sun. 1–5. Closed Jan. 1, Easter, Dec. 25.*

A few steps away is the **Lyme Academy of Fine Arts,** housed in a Federal-style former private home built in 1817. Today it's a popular gallery featuring works by contemporary artists. *84 Lyme St., Old Lyme, tel. 203/434–5232. Admission free. Open weekdays 9–5, weekends by appt.*

9 **New London** is widely known as the home of the **U.S. Coast Guard Academy.** The 100-acre cluster of traditional redbrick buildings includes a museum and visitors' pavilion with a gift shop. When the three-masted training bark the USCGC *Eagle* is in port, you may board from Friday to Sunday, noon to 5 PM. *I–95, Exit 83 (1 mi north), New London, tel. 203/444–8270.*

Admission free. Academy open daily. Museum open week-days, also weekends May–Oct. Visitors' pavilion open May–Oct., daily 9–5.

Across from the academy entrance, step back in time at the **Lyman Allyn Art Museum,** with its small, selective collection of art and antiques—including an impressive array of dolls, doll-houses, and toys—dating from the 18th and 19th centuries. *625 Williams St., New London, tel. 203/443–2545. Admission free ($3 suggested donation). Open Tues.–Sat. 11–5, Sun. 1–5. Closed major holidays.*

Just off Williams Street is the **Thames Science Center,** a regional science museum with a permanent "Time and the River" exhibit and changing presentations focusing on the river basin, such as "Birds of the Basin." *Gallows La. (I–95, Exit 83), New London, tel. 203/442–0391. Admission: $2 adults, $1 children. Open Mon.–Sat. 9–5, Sun. 1–5. Closed major holidays.*

The **Joshua Hempstead House,** built in 1678, is the oldest house in New London; today it showcases early American furnishings. Nearly a century later, Nathaniel Hempstead built the nearby cut-stone house and its outdoor stone beehive bake oven, where occasional demonstrations of open-hearth cooking are given. *11 Hempstead St. (I–95, Exit 84S, 83N), New London, tel. 203/443–7949 or 203/247–8996. Admission: $2 adults, $1 senior citizens, 50¢ children 5–18. Open mid-May–mid-Oct., Tues.–Sun. 1–5.*

Nathan Hale Schoolhouse, where the state's Revolutionary War hero taught prior to his military service, is located at the foot of Captain's Walk, the pedestrians-only main street in the heart of town. *Captain's Walk, New London. No phone. Admission free. Open mid-June–Aug., weekdays 10–3.*

Other highlights of **Captain's Walk** are a beautifully restored 19th-century train station designed by H. H. Richardson, and the **Shaw Mansion,** a stone residence with unique, paneled-cement fireplace walls. Built in 1756, it was visited during the Revolutionary War by Washington and Lafayette, to the delight of the Shaw family, whose furnishings and portraits abound. *305 Bank St., New London, tel. 203/443–1209. Admission: $2 adults, $1.50 senior citizens, 50¢ children 6–12. Open Wed.–Fri. 1–4, Sat. 10–4. Closed major holidays.*

The **Monte Cristo Cottage,** in the downtown area, was the boy-hood home of the playwright Eugene O'Neill and was named for his actor-father's greatest role, as the literary count. The setting figures in two of O'Neill's landmark plays, *Ah, Wilderness!* and *Long Day's Journey into Night. 325 Pequot Ave., New London, tel. 203/443–0051. Admission: $3 adults, $1 students and children. Open Apr.–mid-Dec., weekdays 1–4.*

During the summer, sightseers turn into beachgoers at **Ocean Beach Park,** a 3-mile strip of shoreline that offers a choice of ocean or saltwater pool. Children have their own pool and playground, complete with triple water slide. There's also miniature golf, a picnic area, mechanical rides, a games arcade, food concessions, and a sit-down dining area. *Foot of Ocean Beach, New London, tel. 203/447–3031 or 800/962–0284 in CT. Admission: $1 adults, 50¢ children 5–16. Open Memorial Day weekend–Labor Day, daily 9 AM–10 PM.*

10 After crossing the river to **Groton,** you're in submarine country. There's no escaping the impact of the **U.S. submarine base** on the area. Just outside the entrance to the base is the **U.S. Nautilus Memorial/Submarine Force Library and Museum.** The world's first nuclear-powered submarine, the *Nautilus*, launched from Groton in 1954, is now permanently berthed here and welcomes you aboard. The adjacent library-museum contains submarine memorabilia, artifacts, and displays, including working periscopes and controls. *Rte. 12 (I–95, Exit 86), Groton, tel. 203/449–3174. Admission free. Open Apr. 15– Oct. 14, Wed.–Mon. 9–5; Oct. 15–Apr. 14, Wed.–Mon. 9–3:30. Closed 3rd week of Mar., 1st week of June, 3rd week of Sept., 2nd week of Dec., Jan. 1, Thanksgiving, Dec. 25.*

The best way to see the subs is by boat. The *River Queen II* conducts sightseeing and sunset cruises past the *Nautilus;* the sub base; the *Eagle* across the river when it's in home port; the Coast Guard Academy; a panoply of local craft; and whatever other ships are at berth. Evenings get a little jazzier with dinner and Dixieland as part of the scene. *193 Thames St. (departs from Harbour Inn), tel. 203/445–9516. Harbor tour fare: $6 adults, $3.50 children. Tours: Memorial Day weekend–mid-June, mid-Sept.–Columbus Day, weekends 11:15–3; mid-June–Labor Day, daily 10–3.*

Project Oceanology offers another way to explore the wonders of the briny deep aboard the **Enviro-Lab,** a 50-foot oceanographic research vessel. It's a great way to discover more about marine life, navigation, seawater, and the sea bottom during a 2½-hour cruise that takes you past lighthouses, islands, and submarines. *Bldg. 29, Avery Point, Groton, tel. 203/445–9007. Admission: $11 adults, $9 children. Cruises late June–Labor Day, Sun.–Fri. 10 and 1, Sat. 9, noon, and 3; Sept.–early Oct., weekends 10 and 1.*

Ft. Griswold State Park (Monument St. and Park Ave., Groton, I–95, Exit 85, tel. 203/445–1729) was the site of the massacre of American defenders by Benedict Arnold's British troops in 1781. Battle emplacements and historic displays commemorate the battle; from the top of the memorial tower you get a sweeping view of the shoreline. **Ebenezer Avery House,** a center-chimney Colonial home built by one of the great local Revolutionary War heroes, has a restored kitchen and a weaving room that are particularly well furnished. *Ft. Griswold, Groton (I–95, Exit 85), tel. 203/446–9257. Admission free. Open Memorial Day– Labor Day, weekends 1–5.*

11 A few miles down I–95 or Route 1 will take you from state-of-the-art marine biology to **Mystic's** earlier perspective on the seven seas. Some people think the name of the town is **The Mystic Seaport,** and it very well might be, given the lure of the museum that goes by that name. It is the nation's largest maritime museum, and its 17 riverfront acres feature authentic 19th-century sailing vessels you can board; a maritime village with historic homes; working craftspeople who give demonstrations; steamboat cruises; and small boat rentals. There are seasonal special events, shops, restaurants, and art exhibits. *50 Greenmanville Ave. (I–95, Exit 90, Rte. 27), Mystic, tel. 203/572–0711. Admission: $14 adults, $7.95 children 5–18. Open May–June and Sept.–Oct., daily 9–5; July–Aug., daily 9–8; Nov.–Apr., daily 9–4. Closed Dec. 25.*

At the same I–95 exit, you're steps away from **Olde Mistick Village,** a recreation of what an American village might have looked like about 1720. It truly is picturesque, but it's also quite commercial, with as much emphasis on the stores selling crafts, clothing, souvenirs, and food, as on the country church and old barn. *Coogan Blvd. (I–95, Exit 90), Mystic, tel. 203/536–4941. Admission free. Open Mon.–Sat. 10–5:30, Sun. noon–5:30, weekdays until 8 in summer.*

Within strolling distance is the **Mystic Marinelife Aquarium** with more than 6,000 specimens and 49 live exhibits of sea life. Seal Island, a 2½-acre outdoor exhibit, features seals and sea lions from around the world. Dolphins and sea lions perform every hour on the half hour at the marine theater. *55 Coogan Blvd. (I–95, Exit 90), Mystic, tel. 203/536–3323. Admission: $7.50 adults, $4.50 children 5–17. Open July–Labor Day, daily 9–5:30; Labor Day–June, daily 9–4:40. Closed Jan. 1, Thanksgiving, Dec. 25.*

Also in the cluster of attractions in this area is **Whitehall,** a country mansion, dating to the 1770s, that has been restored with authentic furnishings. The kitchen contains a rare brick "trimer arch" supporting the hearthstone of the fireplace in the room directly above. *Rte. 27 (I–95, Exit 90), Mystic, tel. 203/536–2428. Admission: $2 adults, 50¢ children 6–12. Open May–Oct., Tues.–Sun. 2–4.*

Take Route 27 south along the Mystic River and you'll come to Main Street. Cross over to West Main Street and you're in an area of remarkably well-preserved, beautiful 19th-century houses.

12 Back on I–95, head east again to **Stonington Village,** a few miles south of the highway. Explore the historic buildings that surround the green and continue down Water Street to the **Old Lighthouse Museum** at the very tip. The granite building with its octagonal-tower lighthouse was the first government-operated facility of its kind in the state. Built in 1823, it was moved to higher ground in 1840. Today you'll find a wealth of displays related to shipping, whaling, and early village life. Climb to the top of the tower for a spectacular view of the Sound. *7 Water St. (I–95, Exit 91), Stonington Village, tel. 203/535–1440. Admission: $2 adults, $1 children 6–12. Open May–Oct., Tues.–Sun. 11:30–4:30.*

Within the same borough are the **Stonington Vineyards,** a small coastal winery that has grown premium vinifera and French hybrid grape varieties since 1979. Tour the winery, stroll through the vineyard, and taste samples of the wines on sale. *Taugwonk Rd. (I–95, Exit 91), Stonington Village, tel. 203/535–1222. Admission free. Open daily 11–5.*

Just before you reach the Rhode Island border on I–95, you come to the town of **North Stonington** and the **Crosswoods Vineyards,** a modern winery with 35 acres of vineyards on a plateau overlooking the waters of Long Island Sound. *75 Chester Main Rd. (I–95, Exit 92), North Stonington, tel. 203/535–2205. Admission free. Open daily noon–4:30, weekends only in winter.*

Shopping

While New London has typical concentrations of shopping centers, downtown Mystic boasts a more interesting collection of shops, many of them offering traditional resort items; out near the Aquarium are Olde Mistick Village and the Mystic Factory Outlets (Coogan Blvd., tel. 203/443–4788), nearly two dozen stores offering discounts on famous-name clothing and other merchandise.

Art **Trade Winds Gallery** (20 W. Main St., Mystic, tel. 203/536–0119) shows rare prints and antique maps.

Gifts **Franklin's General Store** (Olde Mystick Village, tel. 203/536–1038) carries New England products, including Vermont maple syrup and Vermont cheddar, and an assortment of pottery.

Records **Mystic Disc** (10 Steamboat Wharf, Mystic, tel. 203/536–1312) has the look of a hole-in-the-wall operation and stocks out-of-print albums; musicians stop by here between gigs.

Toys **The Toy Soldier** (Olde Mystick Village, tel. 203/536–1554) shows and sells both miniature soldiers and dolls.

Sports and Outdoor Activities

Biking **Haley Farm** (Brook St., off Rte. 215, Groton) offers an 8-mile bike trail that winds through shoreline farm property.

Fishing Party fishing boats (or head boats or open boats) take passengers for half-day, full-day, and some overnight trips at fees from $20 to $35 per person; tuna-fishing trips may cost as much as $100 a day. Open-boat providers include **Niantic Beach Marina** (Niantic, tel. 203/443–3662 or 203/739–9296), **Mijoy Dock** (Waterford, tel. 203/443–0663), and **Hel-Cat Dock** (Groton, tel. 203/535–2066 or 203/535–3200).

Private charter boats, whose rentals range from $275 to $375 for a half day, to $450 and up for a full day, are available from **Boats, Inc., Dock** (Waterford, tel. 203/442–9959), **Niantic Fisheries** (Waterford, tel. 203/739–7419), **City Pier** (New London, tel. 203/767–0495 or 203/443–8331), and **Brewer Yacht Yard** (Mystic, tel. 203/536–3259).

Water Sports Surfboards and sailboards can be rented from **Action Sports** (324 W. Main St., Branford, tel. 203/481–5511), **Sunset Bay Surf Shop** (192 Boston Post Rd., Westbrook, tel. 203/669–7873), **Freedom Sailboards** (375 Middlesex Tpke., Old Saybrook, tel. 203/388–0322), **Sailways** (2 Pearl St., Mystic, tel. 203/572–0727), and **Ocean Flyer Wind Surfing** (Rte. 1, Pawcatuck, tel. 203/599–5694).

Boats can be rented or chartered from **Sea Sprite Charters** (113 Harbor Pkwy., Clinton, tel. 203/669–9613), **Colvin Yachts** (Hammock Dock Rd., Westbrook–Old Saybrook, tel. 203/399–9300), **Cardinal Cove Marina** (Rte. 1, Mystic, tel. 203/535–0060), **Shaffer's Boat Livery** (Mason's Island Rd., Mystic, tel. 203/536–8713), and **Dodson Boat Yard** (184 Water St., Stonington, tel. 203/535–1507).

State Parks

Harkness Memorial State Park (Rte. 213, Waterford, tel. 203/443–5725). This former summer estate of the Harkness family contains formal gardens, picnic areas, a beach for strolling and fishing (not swimming), in addition to the Italian villa-style mansion, Eolia. Come for the summer music festival in July and August.

Beaches

Rocky Neck State Park (Rte. 156, Niantic, I–95, Exit 72, tel. 203/739–5471). This mile-long crescent beach is one of the finest saltwater bathing sites in the state. Facilities include family campgrounds, picnicking sites and shelter, food concessions, fishing, and public bath houses.

Ocean Beach Park (Ocean Ave., New London, I–95, Exit 82A N/83S, tel. 203/447–3031 or 800/962–0284 in CT). Swim in the waters of Long Island Sound or in the Olympic-size outdoor pool with a triple water slide. The children have their own pool and playground, and everyone can enjoy the amusement park, miniature golf, arcade, boardwalk, picnic area, food concessions, and restaurant with an ocean view.

Dining and Lodging

The following dining price categories have been used: *Very Expensive*, over $25; *Expensive*, $20–$25; *Moderate*, $12–$20; *Inexpensive*, under $12.

The following lodging price categories have been used: *Very Expensive*, over $100; *Expensive*, $75–$100; *Moderate*, $50–$75; *Inexpensive*, under $50.

Groton
Lodging

Thames Harbour Inn. Located right on the bank of the Thames River, the inn offers boat dockage and fishing for guests. And it's within minutes of all the attractions in the Groton–New London area. Spacious rooms with modern furnishings all have refrigerators. *193 Thames St., 06340, tel. 203/445–8111. 5 rooms, 20 full efficiencies, 1 suite. AE, DC, MC, V. Moderate–Expensive.*

Guilford
Dining

Schooners. A time-honored, shore-dinner atmosphere pervades this spanking new waterside replacement of a neighborhood establishment. The menu combines familiar favorites with special new twists: The chowder is brimful of baby shrimp as well as plump clams. Grilled specialties include fillet of salmon and an ample tuna steak. In general, portions here are enormous and sharing is judicious. *506 Whitfield St., tel. 203/453–2566. No reservations. Dress: casual. AE, MC, V. Inexpensive–Moderate.*

Mystic
Dining

FloodTide. This gracious establishment, part of The Inn at Mystic, offers several dining options. One dining room overlooking the harbor serves guest breakfasts and afternoon tea. The lounge, where complimentary hors d'oeuvres are served at cocktail hour, opens onto a breezy deck and outdoor pool. The formal main dining rooms emphasize tableside preparation of such specialties as Caesar salad, chateaubriand, or bananas Foster (bananas flamed with liqueurs and served over vanilla ice cream). *Junction Rtes. 1 and 27, tel. 203/536–8140. Reservations advised. Dress: neat but casual. AE, D, DC, MC, V. Closed Dec. 25. Very Expensive.*

Lodging

The Inn at Mystic. To reach the winding driveway of the inn, follow signs to the "Mystic Motor Inn." The parking lot gives a breathtaking view of the harbor, and from the lot you can walk to the motor inn, the east wing, and the FloodTide restaurant. Up the hill you'll find the Corinthian-columned main inn and the gate house. Guest rooms are furnished in traditional Colonial style, some with four-poster or canopy beds. The best views are in the old mansion called the main inn. Rooms in the gate house are secluded and have a Jacuzzi and wet bar. *Junction Rtes. 1 and 27, 06355, tel. 203/536–9604 or 800/237–2415. 68 rooms. Facilities: restaurant, private dock with canoes and sailboats, outdoor pool and hot spa, landscaped walking trail. AE, D, DC, MC, V. Expensive–Very Expensive.*

The Taber Inn. This small compound is made up of the motor inn, Guest House, Town House, Country House, and Farmhouse. The most basic, least expensive rooms are in the motor inn; the fanciest and most expensive are the two-bedroom duplex apartments in the Town House. All rooms are furnished with Colonial reproductions. *29 Williams Ave. (Rte. 1), 06355, tel. 203/536–4904. 32 rooms. Facilities: cable TV, telephones, Jacuzzis in some rooms, tennis privileges at nearby Williams Beach. MC, V. Moderate–Very Expensive.*

Harbour Inne & Cottage. This 1950s-style bungalow and neighboring cottage right on the water provide accommodation for a small number of guests for short- or long-term stays. The compact bedrooms, simply furnished with modern maple beds, dressers, and chairs, embrace a nautical theme. A great location for bird-watching, paddling off to the harbor, or strolling into downtown. *Edgemont St., 06355, tel. 203/572–9253. 4 rooms, 3-room cottage with kitchen. Facilities: air-conditioning, cable TV, rowboats and canoes for rent, picnic facilities. Pets allowed. No credit cards. Inexpensive–Moderate.*

The Whaler's Inn. In the heart of downtown, this conglomeration of white clapboard buildings has provided guest accommodations since Civil War days. The inn is comprised of the original Victorian guest house, the sprawling main building, and the motor court across the parking lot. Decor is modern with nautical touches; there are some canopy beds, but mostly it's department-store maple. *20 E. Main St., 06355, tel. 203/536–1506 or 800/243–2588 outside CT. 45 rooms. Facilities: 2 restaurants, cable TV, telephones, minifridges in some rooms, courtesy car to airport and train station. AE, D, DC, MC, V. Inexpensive–Moderate.*

New London
Lodging

Radisson Hotel. The downtown location makes it convenient to Captain's Walk, I–95, and the Amtrak station. Rooms have nondescript modern furnishings but are quiet and spacious. *35 Gov. Winthrop Blvd. (I–95, Exit 83/86S), 06320, tel. 203/443–7000 or 800/333–3333. 114 rooms, 4 suites. Facilities: restaurant, lounge, exercise room, Jacuzzi, indoor pool. AE, DC, MC, V. Expensive–Very Expensive.*

Holiday Inn. You can't miss the bright neon sign on I–95. This link in the Holiday Inn chain is typical, with well-furnished rooms that offer no surprises. *Frontage Rd. (I–95, Exit 82A N/83S), 06320, tel. 203/442–0631. 135 rooms. Facilities: restaurant, lounge, health club, outdoor pool. AE, D, DC, MC, V. Expensive.*

North Stonington
Dining
★

Randall's Ordinary. Authentic Colonial dishes are prepared at the open hearth of this house, built in about 1685. "Ordinary" refers to the original town ordinance that made it possible for this site to provide food and lodging; the victuals served today in its small, intimate, low-ceiling dining rooms are anything but ordinary. Though the menu changes seasonally, you'll probably find Nantucket scallops, lightly breaded and sautéed in butter, with scallions, garlic, and paprika, prepared on a hanging skillet. Try the spider bread, a crisp cornbread named for the footed cast-iron pan in which it's cooked. For dessert, the Thomas Jefferson bread pudding is laced with brandy. *Rte. 2, tel. 203/599-4540. Reservations required for dinner. Dress: neat but casual. AE, MC, V. Very Expensive.*

Lodging **Randall's Ordinary.** This inn is famed for its open-hearth cooking. The original structure, the John Randall House, provides lodging on the second floor. The Jacob Terpenning Barn (built in 1819, moved from upstate New York in 1989, and renovated) now offers accommodation, in wonderfully irregular rooms. Most have fireplaces, and all are furnished in an authentic, early Colonial manner, with canopy beds, four-poster, trundle beds, and simple chairs and tables. The lack of carpets and scarcity of pictures on the walls make the guest rooms somewhat cheerless, despite the occasional antique knickknacks. *Rte. 2, Box 243, 06359, tel. 203/599-4540. 12 rooms. Facilities: whirlpool bath, shower, TVs, and telephones in barn rooms. AE, MC, V. Rates include Continental breakfast. Expensive.*

★ **Antiques and Accommodations.** The English influence is evident in the Georgian formality of this Victorian country home, built about 1861. Exquisite furniture and accessories, all for sale, are found throughout the common rooms and guest rooms of the main building. The 1820 house in the rear contains similarly furnished two- and three-bedroom suites. Breakfast, served by candlelight at the formal dining table, includes seasonal fruits, local eggs, and home-baked goods. Aromatic candles and fresh flowers create a warm and inviting atmosphere. *32 Main St., 06359, tel. 203/535-1736. 4 rooms, 3 with bath; 2 suites. Facilities: cable TV on main floor and in 1820 house. No smoking in main house. AE, MC, V. Rates include full breakfast. Moderate-Expensive.*

Old Lyme **Old Lyme Inn.** From farmhouse to glitzy Italian restaurant to
Lodging gracious dining and lodging establishment, this gray clapboard 1850s farmhouse has come a long way to its present welcoming state. The innkeeper has applied her antiques-collector's eye to the decor and filled the spacious bedrooms with a harmonious assortment of period-style and modern furnishings. Some of her collection is also on display in the bright and airy common rooms and in the popular restaurant, on the ground floor. *Box 787B, 06371, tel. 203/434-2600. 5 rooms, 8 suites. Facilities: restaurant, complimentary Continental breakfast, air-conditioning, telephones, clock radios. Pets allowed. AE, D, DC, MC, V. Closed first 2 weeks in Jan. Expensive-Very Expensive.*

Bee & Thistle Inn. Behind a weathered stone wall along a broad avenue in the historic district, this two-story, 1725 frame Colonial building provides superior hospitality in its cozy bedrooms and comfortable common rooms, as well as in its dining room. The Colonial ambience is cleverly wrought through a mixture of authentic period pieces and tasteful modern evocations. Canopy and four-poster beds are swathed with old quilts, afghans, and plump pillows. Delicious scents emanate from the fresh and dried flowers and the generous offerings of bath salts and scented soaps. Be sure to try the late afternoon high tea. *100 Old Lyme St., 06371, tel. 203/434-1667. 11 rooms, 9 with bath; cottage. Facilities: restaurant, air-conditioning,*

*clock radios, Continental breakfast in cottage. AE, DC, MC,
V. Closed first 2 weeks in Jan. Moderate–Very Expensive.*

Old Saybrook **Saybrook Point Inn.** Although called an inn, this establishment,
Lodging opened in 1989, feels more like a small hotel. Rooms are furnished with British traditional reproduction pieces, floral-
print bedspreads, and impressionist- and classical-style art.
The health club and indoor and outdoor pools overlook the inn's
marina and the Connecticut River. *2 Bridge St., Old Saybrook,
06475, tel. 203/395–2000. 62 rooms, including 7 suites, all with
bath. Facilities: restaurant, meeting rooms, marina, spa,
health club, indoor and outdoor pools, Jacuzzi. AE, D, DC,
MC, V. Very Expensive.*

Stonington **Harbor View.** Chef Bill Geary continues a 19-year tradition of
Dining fine French cuisine in romantic dining rooms with crisp blue
linens and candlelit tables. The large, old-fashioned taproom in
front offers a contrast, with its bare wood floor and kegs hung
from the ceiling. Specialties include *homard Melanie* (pan-
roasted lobster with bourbon and chervil butter) and *ris de
veau Guesclin* (braised veal sweetbreads with wild mushrooms
in a puff-pastry shell). *60 Water St. (Cannon Sq.), tel. 203/535–
2720. Reservations advised. Dress: neat but casual. AE, DC,
MC, V. Closed Dec. 25. Moderate–Expensive.*
Skipper's Dock. This seafood restaurant is located on the dock
behind the parking lot of the Harbor View and is run by the
same management. Surrounded by its nautical artifacts, you
might well choose the kettle of fisherman's stew Portuguese
(clams, mussels, shrimp, native fish, and chourico sausage in
broth with tomato and peppers). On the weekend, prime rib is
served in two generous sizes. *66 Water St. (on the pier), tel. 203/
535–2000. No reservations. Dress: casual. AE, DC, MC, V.
Closed Jan.–mid-Mar., Dec. 25. Moderate–Expensive.*

Lodging **Lasbury's Guest House.** On a quiet side street, overlooking a
salt marsh to the rear, sits a frame house with a small, red,
Colonial building a few steps behind it. A nautical theme, along
with framed posters for the annual Stonington Fair, provides
the decoration in these neat, trim surroundings. A Continental
breakfast is delivered to each room in a tiny basket. *24 Orchard
St., 06378, tel. 203/535–2681. 3 rooms, 2 with bath. No credit
cards. Moderate.*
Sea Breeze Motel. Behind its vibrant, mustard-and-white
exterior are basic, modern rooms, each with two double beds,
simple contemporary furnishings, and a stall shower in the
bathroom. *Rte. 1, 06378, tel. 203/535–2843. 25 rooms. Facilities: cable TV. AE, MC, V. Inexpensive.*

Westbrook **Talcott House.** This 1890 cedar-shingle beach cottage is now an
Lodging attractive shoreline B&B with a spacious main salon offering an
expansive ocean view. Bedrooms feature polished wood floors
topped with a scattering of bright carpets, some brass beds,
hobnail spreads, and stencilling atop pale painted walls.
Continental breakfast includes homemade muffins, breads,
and tarts. *161 Seaside Ave., Box 1016, 06498, tel. 203/399–
5020. 7 rooms, 4 with bath. Facilities: complimentary Continental breakfast, fans available. MC, V. Moderate–Expensive.*

The Arts

Connecticut College's **Palmer Auditorium** (Mohegan Ave., New London, tel. 203/439–2787) presents both dance and theater programs.

Eastern Connecticut Symphony Orchestra (tel. 203/443–2876) performs at the **Garde Arts Center** (325 Captain's Walk, New London, tel. 203/444–6766).

Puppet House Theatre (128 Thimble Island Rd., Stony Creek, tel. 203/773–8080) has a lively season of comedy, drama, and musical productions by three companies.

Nightlife

Bank St. Cafe (639 Bank St., New London, tel. 203/444–7932) bills itself as the top live blues club on the East Coast, with music every Friday and Saturday, as well as occasional Tuesday and Sunday sessions.

El 'n' Gee Club (86 Golden St., New London, tel. 203/443–9227) has different programs nightly—heavy metal, reggae, local bands, and occasionally nationally known acts.

Rhode Island's South County

When the principal interstate traffic shifted from the coastal Route 1 to the new I–95, coastal Rhode Island was left behind in time, largely escaping the advance of malls and tract housing developments that has overtaken other, more accessible, areas. More popular with visitors today than in recent years, the region is still undervisited compared to other parts of New England; its vast stretches of sandy beaches, wilderness, and interesting historic sites escape the crush of tourists. With 19 preserves, state parks, beaches, and forest areas, including Charlestown's Burlingame State Park, Ninigret Park, and the Trustom Pond Wildlife Refuge, South County is a region that respects the concept of wilderness.

Numbers in the margin correspond to points of interest on the Rhode Island Coast map.

❶ **Watch Hill** is a pretty Victorian-era resort town, with miles of beautiful beaches, a number of Native American settlements, and an active fishing port; it's a good place to shop for jewelry, summer clothing, and antiques. To reach Watch Hill, drive south on Route 1A to Watch Hill Road. At the end of Watch Hill Road, turn onto Everett Avenue, which becomes Westerly Road. Take Westerly to Plimpton Street, Plimpton to Bay Street, and you will encounter Watch Hill at its most scenic in the westward views of Watch Hill Cove.

On Bay Street you'll be greeted by a **statue of Ninigret,** a chief of the Rhode Island branch of the Niantics, first appearing in Colonial history in 1637. The model for this 19th-century statue was part of Buffalo Bill Cody's Wild West Review, on tour at the time in Paris.

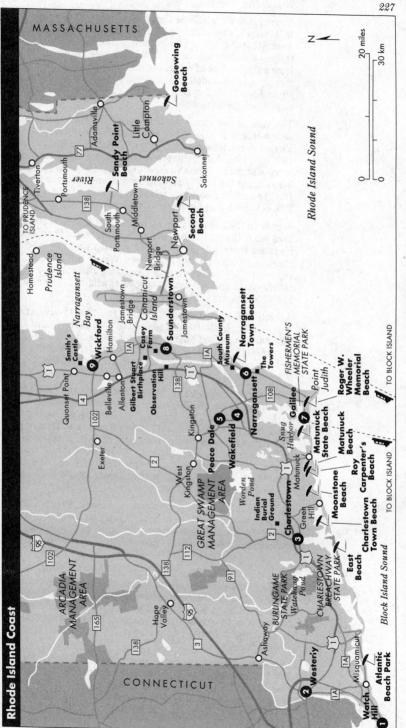

Rhode Island Coast

MASSACHUSETTS

CONNECTICUT

Rhode Island Sound

Block Island Sound

Narragansett Bay

Sakonnet River

N

20 miles
30 km

Goosewing Beach
Little Compton
Adamsville
Compton
Sandy Point Beach
Sakonnet
Tiverton
Portsmouth
Second Beach
South Portsmouth
Middletown
Newport
Newport Bridge
Homestead
TO PRUDENCE ISLAND
Prudence Island
Conanicut Island
Jamestown Bridge
Jamestown
Saundertown
Narragansett Town Beach
South County Museum
The Towers
Wickford
Smith's Castle
Hamilton
Casey Farm
Gilbert Stuart Birthplace
Observation Hill
Belleville
Allenton
Quonset Point
Narragansett
FISHERMEN'S MEMORIAL STATE PARK
Point Judith
Roger W. Wheeler Memorial Beach
Galilee
Snug Harbor
TO BLOCK ISLAND
Exeter
Kingston
West Kingston
Peace Dale
Wakefield
Matunuck State Beach
Matunuck Beach
Roy Carpenter's Beach
GREAT SWAMP MANAGEMENT AREA
Indian Burial Ground
Worden Pond
Moonstone Beach
Charlestown
Green Hill
Charlestown Town Beach
East Beach
Matunuck
TO BLOCK ISLAND
ARCADIA MANAGEMENT AREA
BURLINGAME STATE PARK
Watchaug Pond
CHARLESTOWN BREACHWAY STATE PARK
Hope Valley
Ashaway
Westerly
Watch Hill
Misquamicut
Atlantic Beach Park
TO BLOCK ISLAND

Nearby, the **Flying Horse Carousel,** the oldest merry-go-round in America, was built by the Charles W. F. Dare Co. of New York in about 1867. The horses, suspended from a center frame, swinging out when in motion, are each hand-carved from a single piece of wood, and embellished with real tails and manes, leather saddles, and agate eyes. *Bay St. Ride: 25¢. Open June 15–Labor Day, weekdays 1–9, weekends and holidays 11–9. Children only.*

The view of the sunset alone is worth the hike up the hill to **Ocean House** (2 Bluff Ave., tel. 401/348–8161), one of several Victorian-era hotels in this part of Watch Hill. Built in about 1868 by George Nash, this is one of the grand hotels that helped bring Watch Hill fame as a resort in the 19th century. If you're here during the hotel's short season, from late June to Labor Day, you might have a bite to eat or a drink on the magnificent 200-foot porch that faces the Atlantic.

A walk to the end of Bay Street and a left into Fort Road will take you in the direction of the path (at the end of Fort Road) to **Napatree Point,** one of the best long beach walks in the entire state. A sandy spit lying between Watch Hill's Little Narragansett Bay and the ocean, Napatree Point is a protected conservation area with many species of wildlife. Be careful not to disturb the area above the sand.

A stroll back up Fort Road to Larking Road and then southwest down Light House Road leads to the **U.S. Coast Guard Light Station.** Though you can't venture inside the station, on a clear day this is the place to go for the best view of the exclusive Fisher's Island. *Lighthouse Rd., Watch Hill, tel. 401/596–1182. Open daily 8–4.*

2 Drive north on Watch Hill Road to Route 1A, and head east to Winnipaug Road and **Westerly.** In the heart of town, **Wilcox Park,** designed in 1898 by Warren Manning, an associate of Frederick Law Olmsted and Calvert Vaux, is an 18-acre park with a garden for the visually impaired and handicapped. Signs in Braille identify the plantings of carnations, mint, chives, thyme, bay leaves, and coconut, apple, lemon, and rose-scented geraniums—to touch, smell, and taste. *71½ High St., Westerly, tel. 401/348–8362.*

Drive south on Winnipaug Road to **Atlantic Beach Park** at Misquamicut, a mile-long beach featuring an amusement park, a giant waterslide, a carousel, a miniature golf course, a roller rink, and fast-food stands. *Atlantic Ave., Westerly, tel. 401/ 322–0504. Open daily 9–8. Closed Sept.–May.*

3 Drive north along Winnipaug Road to Route 1A. Follow Route 1A (here it's called Shore Road) west to the intersections of Routes 1 and 2 to reach **Charlestown,** a resort town filled with summer cottages. **Kimball Wildlife Refuge,** a parklike Audubon refuge, is on the south side of Watchaug Pond, west of Charlestown. *Prosser Trail, Charlestown, tel. 401/231–6444. Open daily dawn–dusk.*

Drive east on Routes 1 and 2 to the entrance of **Ninigret National Wildlife Refuge,** a wildlife sanctuary maintained by the U.S. Fish and Wildlife Service. This 172-acre park includes picnic grounds, ball fields, a 10-speed bike path, and the Frosty Drew Nature Center. *Charlestown, tel. 401/364–9124. Open daily dawn–dusk.*

A few minutes northwest, on Kings Factory Road, you'll find **Burlingame State Park** (tel. 401/322–7337 or 401/322–7994), a 2,100-acre park offering freshwater swimming, camping, and picnic areas, as well as boating and fishing on Watchaug Pond.

Return to the intersection of Kings Factory Road and Route 1/1A. Drive east on Route 1A to Fort Neck Road, and drive south, back into Charlestown proper. **Fort Ninigret** is the remains of an earthwork fort built by Dutch traders during the early 1600s.

Return to Route 1. Make a U-turn after the Cross Mills exit, and drive north to Lewis Trail on Route 2/112. Charlestown retains much of the history of the Narragansett Indians, natives to the area. The **Indian Church** is the last of three Christian Indian Churches built in Rhode Island.

Drive south on Route 2/112, to Narrow Lane. About 1 mile southeast you'll find the **Indian Burial Ground,** the resting place of sachems, and families of the Narragansett tribe.

A 15-minute drive east on Route 1 brings you to **South Kingstown,** a large area made up of many small villages, including Green Hill, Matunuck, Snug Harbor, Wakefield, Peacedale, Rocky Brook, and West Kingston. The University of Rhode Island is here, as is rowdy Matunuck Beach (*see* Beaches, *below*). South Kingstown is a good place to spend a warm summer day—or a crisp fall afternoon.

❹ Five miles to the northeast is the village of **Wakefield,** where the old **Washington County Jail,** built in 1792, now houses the Pettaquamscutt Historical Society. Here you can see jail cells and rooms from the Colonial period, a Colonial garden, and changing exhibits that depict South County life during the last 300 years. *1348 Kingstown Rd., tel. 401/783–1328. Open May–Oct., Tues., Thurs., and Sat. 1–4.*

Drive north on Kingstown Road to Curtis Corner Road. Turn left here and then left again on Asa Pond Road. In the village of **❺** **Peace Dale,** the Winding Creek Trail (tel. 401/789–9331, ext. 245), a barrier-free nature trail, is specially equipped for the handicapped and elderly. The trail features ponds, swamps, a fishing pier, and many types of flora and fauna.

Head north on Route 108 to Route 138. Turn left onto Route 1. As you leave South Kingstown, you may want to pause to climb the 100-foot, open-air, wood **Observation Tower,** at the top of McSparren Hill. Your reward: a beautiful panoramic view of the Rhode Island coastline.

Travel east on Route 1 to Route 1A (called Kingstown Road here), and continue on to **Sprague Park** at the intersection of **❻** Kingstown Road and Strathmore Street in **Narrangansett,** the dining and lodging hub of the South County. Convenient to both Newport and the Block Island Ferry, it makes a logical home base for a tour of Rhode Island.

The section of Narragansett known as **Narragansett Pier** was a posh resort at the end of the 19th century, when it was linked by rail with New York and Boston and the wealthy streamed in from those cities and beyond. The town was also a major stop on the steamboat line that ran between New York and Newport. Wealthy Newporters might have taken the steamboat to Nar-

ragansett for luncheon at the Narragansett Casino, a portion of
which still stands, now known in Narragansett as The Towers.

Time Out   The locals claim there's no better breakfast than at **Dad's Place**
(142 Boon St., Narragansett, tel. 401/783-6420). The eggs
Benedict are legendary.

At Sprague Park you can see the **Narragansett Indian Monument.** Donated to the town by the sculptor Peter Toth, the 23-
foot monument weighs 10,000 pounds and is made from a single
piece of wood, the trunk of a giant Douglas fir. To create the
sculpture, Toth worked with hammer and chisel 12 hours a day
for two months, then applied 100 coats of preservative.

Head east on Route 1A (called Narragansett Avenue here), to
Beach Street. Turn right on Beach Street to Central Street,
and head east to Ocean Road. Turn right on Ocean Road. For a
sense of what Narragansett looked like at the height of the
Victorian era, visit **The Towers** (tel. 401/783-7121). This turret
structure is the last remaining section of the Narragansett Pier
Casino after a fire in September 1900. The massive building
arching over the roadway, designed by McKim, Mead, and
White in 1885, functioned as a hub of social activity in the late
1800s. The Towers now houses the Narragansett Chamber of
Commerce.

Drive south to the end of Ocean Road to find beautiful beaches
and the **Point Judith Lighthouse.** A beautiful ocean vista awaits
travelers who make it to land's end at this point. *1460 Ocean
Rd., tel. 401/789-0444. Open during daylight hours.*

Travel north on Ocean Road to Route 108 (called Point Judith
Road here), and turn left onto the Galilee Escape Road. Anoth-
er left onto Great Island Road brings you into the bustling fish-
❼ ing village of **Galilee.** One of the busiest ports on the East
Coast, the village has several excellent seafood restaurants.
The Southland Ferry (tel. 401/783-2954) leaves from Galilee on
a 1¾-hour tour of Point Judith, Galilee, and Jerusalem; or the
Super Squirrel II (tel. 401/783-8513) can take you on a whale-
watching expedition. This is also a good place to catch the Block
Island ferry, run by the Interstate Navigation Company (Galilee State Pier, Point Judith, tel. 401/783-4613).

Travel east on the Galilee Escape Road to Route 108, also called
Point Judith Road. Take Route 108 north to Route 1A, and head
northeast. On your way out of Narragansett, just after the
Narragansett Pavilion on the left side of the road, you'll see the
entrance to the **South County Museum.** On the grounds of
Canonchet Farm, the museum features reconstructions of
many typical New England buildings. Exhibits include a general store, a cobbler's shop, a tack shop, a children's nursery, and
a print shop. The museum hosts many special events throughout its season. *Canonchet Farm, tel. 401/783-5400. Admission: $2.50 adults, $1.50 children 6–16. Open June–Aug.,
Wed.–Sun. 10–4; May, Sept., Oct., weekends 10–4.*

Following Route 1A north will take you to **North Kingstown,**
"plantation country," the site of many farms dating to the Colonial era, some of which can be visited. Like South Kingstown,
North Kingstown is made up of many villages, including
Saunderstown, Hamilton, Allenton, Belleville, Quonset Point,

Davisville, and the charming Wickford, a favorite spot for shoppers.

8 In **Saunderstown** the **Silas Casey Farm** still functions much as it has since the 18th century. Home to the Casey family (prominent in military and political affairs), it was also the home of Thomas Lincoln Case, engineer of the Washington Monument. The farmhouse contains original furniture, prints, paintings, and political and military documents from the 18th to 20th centuries. The 360-acre farm is surrounded by nearly 30 miles of stone walls and has many barns; it was the site of Revolutionary War activity. *Boston Neck Rd., Rte. 1A, Saunderstown, tel. 401/294–9182. Admission: $3. Open June–Oct., Tues.– Thurs. 1–5, Sun. 1–5.*

Head north on Route 1A to Gilbert Stuart Road, turn left, and follow the signs for 2 miles down pleasant country roads to reach the **Gilbert Stuart Birthplace.** Built in 1751, the home of America's foremost portraitist of George Washington has been completely restored. The adjacent 18th-century snuff mill was the first in America. *Tel. 401/294–3001. Admission: $1.50 adults, 50¢ children. Open Mar.–Nov., Sat.–Thurs. 11–5.*

9 Continue north on Route 1A to the Colonial village of **Wickford,** a part of the town of North Kingstown, which has attractive 18th- and 19th-century homes and interesting shops. Turn right onto Main Street and left onto Church Lane to reach the **Old Narragansett Church,** one of the oldest Episcopal churches in America. *Tel. 401/294–4357. Open July–Aug., Fri. 11–5, Sat. 10–5, Sun. 11–5.*

Time Out | **Wickford Gourmet Foods** (21 W. Main St., tel. 401/295–8190) provides homemade and specialty foods to eat in the comfortable loft, outside on the patio, or to take for a picnic. It's only a short walk down historic Brown Street to the Municipal Wharf, where beaches and grass provide a lovely view of the harbor and its fishing activities.

Drive north through the village of Wickford to the intersection of Routes 1A and 1; take Route 1 north and turn right onto Richard Smith Drive. **Smith's Castle,** built in 1678 by Richard Smith Jr., was the site of many orations by Roger Williams, Rhode Island's most famous historical figure. *41 Richard Smith Dr., tel. 401/294–3521. Admission: $2 adults, 50¢ children. Open May 1–Oct., Thurs.–Sat. 10–4, Sun. 1–5.*

Shopping

Antiques | **Book and Tackle Shop** (7 Bay St., Watch Hill, tel. 401/596– 0700). The dealer buys, sells, and appraises old and rare books, prints, autographs, and photographs.

Dove and Distaff Antiques (365 Main St., Wakefield, tel. 401/ 783–5714). This is a good spot for early American furniture and accessories; restoration and refinishing and an upholstery and drapery workshop are available.

Fox Run Country Antiques (Jct. Rtes. 1 and 2, Crossland Park, Charlestown, tel. 401/364–3160 or 401/377–2581). In business for more than 20 years, this shop sells old jewelry, lighting devices, orientalia, country primitives, and a large selection of china and glassware.

Wickford Antiques Center I (16 Main St., tel. 401/295–2966) features wooden kitchen utensils and crocks, country furniture, china, glass, linens, and jewelry.

Wickford Antiques Center II (93 Brown St., tel. 401/295–2966) sells antique furniture from many periods.

Art Galleries **Artists' Gallery of Wickford** (5 Main St., tel. 401/294–6280). This small, friendly gallery shows the work of regional artists, some of whom are always on hand to share a cup of tea and talk about their work.

Hera Gallery (Rte. 1A, Main St., Wakefield, tel. 401/789–1488). Established as a women's art cooperative in 1974, Hera exhibits the work of emerging local artists, often dealing with ethnic or other provocative themes.

Crafts **Askham and Telham Inc.** (12 Main St., Wickford, tel. 401/295–0891). Needlepoint pillows, antique prints, fabric-bound books, and Shaker boxes are just a few of the elegant gifts and home furnishings you'll find here.

The Fantastic Umbrella Factory (Rte. 1A, Charlestown, tel. 401/364–6616). Three rustic shops built around a spectacular wild garden in which peacocks, pheasants, and chickens parade, the factory sells its own hardy perennials and unusual day lilies, and sells greeting cards, kites, and an interesting assortment of other wares. An outdoor café serves organic food in the summer.

Puffins of Watch Hill (84 Bay St., Watch Hill, tel. 401/596–1140) offers Halcyon Days enamels, Perthshire paperweights, Arthurcourt Designs, Seagull pewter, garden statuary and fountains, and handcrafted jewelry and gifts.

Sports and Outdoor Activities

Canoeing Many small rivers and ponds in the South County are perfect spots for canoeing. **Quaker Lane Bait Shop** (4019 Quaker La., North Kingstown, tel. 401/294–9642) has information as well as rentals.

Fishing Bait and tackle shops in the area include **Ocean House Marina** (12 Town Dock Rd., Charlestown, tel. 401/364–6040), **Quaker Lane Bait Shop** (4019 Quaker Ln., North Kingstown, tel. 401/294–9642), and **Wickford Bait and Tackle** (1 Phillips St., Wickford, tel. 401/295–8845).

Charters (Snug Harbor, Gooseneck Rd., South Kingstown, tel. 401/783–7766) can put you in touch with captains who skipper charters.

Hiking The **Rhode Island Audubon Society** (40 Bowen St., Providence, tel. 401/521–1670) offers interesting hikes and field expeditions. The **Sierra Club** (3 Joy St., Boston, MA 02114, tel. 617/227–5339) and the **Appalachian Mountain Club** (5 Joy St., Boston, MA 02114, tel. 617/523–0636) both have active groups in Rhode Island. For hiking, think of South Kingstown's Great Swamp.

Water Sports **Ocean House Marina, Inc.** (12 Town Dock Rd., Charlestown, tel. 401/364–6060), rents 14-foot motorboats and daysailers. **Narragansett Surf & Sports** (Pier Village, Narragansett, tel. 401/789–2323) rents sailboards, surfboards, and diving equipment. **Windsurfing of Watch Hill** (3 Bay St., tel. 401/596–0079) rents sailboards and gives lessons.

Beaches

The south coast of Rhode Island boasts mile after mile of beautiful ocean beaches, many of which are open to the public. The beaches are sandy, for the most part, and their water is clear and clean—in some places, the water takes on the turquoise color of the Caribbean Sea.

Westerly   **Atlantic State Beach at Misquamicut.** A haven for young people, the crowds throng to this lively, friendly beach in the summertime.

Charlestown   **Charlestown Town Beach** (Charlestown Beach Rd.). Don't slide down the sand dunes, covered with tall, rustling sea grass— they are fragile! The waves here can be high, the water turquoise and warm.

East Beach (East Beach Rd.). Two miles of dunes, backed by the crystal-clear waters of Ninigret Pond, make this beach a treasure, especially for the adventurous beachgoer who is willing to hike a distance from the car.

South Kingstown   **East Matunuck State Beach** (Succotash Rd.). This beach, also called Daniel O'Brien State Beach, is popular with the college crowd for its white sand, picnic areas, and bathhouse.

Matunuck Beach (Matunuck Beach Rd.). Unpredictable, high waves make this beach a good spot for surfing and raft-riding.

Moonstone Beach (Moonstone Beach Rd.). This beach is part wildlife refuge, part "clothes optional" bathing area. It is a beautiful beach, although public access is being increasingly restricted in deference to the wildlife refuge.

Roy Carpenter's Beach (Matunuck Beach Rd.). Quiet and out of the way, this beach seems private and secluded, yet there's food and drink within walking distance.

Narragansett   **Narragansett Town Beach** (Rte. 1A). This in-town beach has a boardwalk, good surf, and is within walking distance of many Narragansett hotels and guest houses. Its pavilion has changing rooms, showers, and concessions.

Roger W. Wheeler State Beach (Cove Wood Dr.). Picnic areas, a playground, mild surf, and swimming lessons make this beach a good place for families with young children. It's near the fishing port of Galilee.

Scarborough State Beach (Ocean Dr.). With high surf, a bathhouse, and concessions, this beach becomes crowded with teenagers on weekends. *Rhode Island Monthly* says: "Big hair, hard muscles, and more mousse and mascara than Factor 15. Definitely not for the timid or self-conscious."

Dining and Lodging

Rhode Island is home to much traditional regional fare. Johnnycakes are a sort of corn cake cooked on a griddle, and the native clam, the quahog (pronounced KO-hog) is served in chowder, stuffed clams, fried clams, and even clam pie. Particularly popular are "shore dinners," which include clam chowder, steamers, clam cakes, baked sausage, corn-on-the-cob, lobster, watermelon, and Indian pudding (a steamed pudding made with cornmeal and molasses). Dinners in Rhode Island tend to be early affairs; don't be surprised to find many restaurants, especially in the smaller towns, closed by 8 PM. Casual wear is the rule in the restaurants and dining rooms of South County.

The following dining price categories have been used: *Expensive*, over $20; *Moderate*, $10–$20; *Inexpensive*, under $10.

Bed and Breakfast of Rhode Island, Inc. (Box 3291, Newport 02840, tel. 401/849–1298) provides information on bed-and-breakfast arrangements in the state. The following lodging price categories have been used: *Expensive*, over $100; *Moderate*, $60–$100; *Inexpensive*, under $60. Throughout the state a 5% hotel tax plus the 7% sales tax will be added to lodging bills.

Narragansett
Dining

Basil's Restaurant. Within walking distance of the Towers, Basil's presents French and Continental cuisine in an intimate setting. Dark, floral wallpaper and fresh flowers decorate the small dining room, which seats 30. The specialty is milk-fed baby veal topped with a light cream and mushroom sauce; fine fresh fish dishes, mussels brunoise, and duck à l'orange are also featured. The desserts are homemade. *22 Kingstown Rd., tel. 401/789–3743. Reservations advised. AE, MC, V. No lunch. Closed Mon., Tues. Expensive.*

Coast Guard House. Frequently cited by those who know it as a favorite locale for a romantic dinner, the restaurant occupies an 1888 building by McKim, Mead, and White that overlooks Narragansett Bay. Dinner entrées feature seafood, pasta, poultry, veal, steak, and lamb. Friday and Saturday nights see entertainment in the Oak Room and a DJ in the upstairs lounge. *40 Ocean Rd., tel. 401/789–0700. Reservations accepted for 8 or more. AE, DC, MC, V. Closed Dec. 25. Expensive.*

Spain Restaurant. Rhode Island's only true Spanish restaurant is in a somewhat unlikely setting—on the ground floor of the modern, very American, Village Inn hotel. The interior, though, is appropriately dark and atmospheric, the air pungent with garlic and spices. Enjoy such appetizers as shrimp in garlic sauce, clams marinara, clams Casino, stuffed mushrooms, and Spanish sausages; the main courses are variations on lobster, steak, paella and mariscada, fresh fish, chops, and poultry. *Village Inn, 1 Beach St., tel. 401/783–9770. Reservations advised on Sat. AE, DC, MC, V. Expensive.*

Aunt Carrie's. This tremendously popular, family-owned place has been serving up traditional Rhode Island shore dinners, clam cakes and chowder, seafood, and meat dinners for more than 60 years—and there's a children's menu. At the height of the season you may find a line; one alternative is to order from the takeout window and picnic on the grass nearby. Try the enormous but light clam cakes; for the more adventurous, there's the squid burger, served on homemade bread. Indian pudding à la mode is a favorite dessert. *Rte. 108 and Ocean Rd., Point Judith, tel. 401/783–7930. Closed Labor Day–Memorial Day. Moderate.*

★ **Champlin's Seafood.** Come here for the best fried scallops in the South County, or perhaps the world. Other possibilities are bright-red boiled lobster, fried oysters, a seafood platter, and the snail salad. Take a seat out on the oceanfront deck and let the sea breezes waft over you and your meal. *Port of Galilee,*

Narragansett, tel. 401/783-3152. No reservations. MC, V. Closed weekdays Apr.–May, Nov.–Dec.; closed Jan.–Mar. Moderate.

George's of Galilee. The lines around the building on summer Saturday nights baffle local residents, who speculate that it might be because of the location at the end of a spit of land in a busy fishing harbor. They insist that it's certainly not the atmosphere (frantic and noisy) or the food (much better, they say, elsewhere in Galilee). Yet it's hard to argue with success, and George's has been a "must" for tourists since 1948. The restaurant offers several chowders and hosts barbecues on the beach on summer weekends. *Port of Galilee, Narragansett, tel. 401/783-2306. No reservations. MC, V. Open weekends only, Nov.–Feb. Moderate.*

Lodging **Stone Lea.** The spacious house, more than 100 years old and
★ filled with antiques collected by the owners, is a bed-and-breakfast that has the feel of an inn. Guest rooms have panoramic ocean views, the most striking in rooms 1 and 7; number 5 has a sitting room attached. *40 Newton Ave., 02882, tel. 401/783-9546. 7 rooms. Facilities: lounge with pool table, player piano. MC, V, with 3½% processing fee. Closed Thanksgiving, Dec. 25. Expensive.*

South Kingstown **Larchwood Inn.** The owners call this "a country inn with a
Dining Scotish flavor." More than 150 years old, the original building is set in a grove of larch trees. Ask for a table near the fireplace in winter, and try for a patio spot under the larch trees in summer. On the menu are halibut stuffed with scallops; and seafood, chicken, beef, and veal preparations. *521 Main St., Wakefield, tel. 401/783-5454. Reservations advised. AE, DC, MC, V. No lunch Sun. Closed Dec. 25. Expensive.*

★ **South Shore Grill.** The restaurant has a wood-fired grill and waterfront views: One wall, overlooking the Wakefield Marina, is all windows. Favorites on the constantly changing menu include roasted Santa Fe Game Hen marinated in lime juice, tequila, and fresh coriander and grilled jumbo scallops with fresh ginger. *210 Salt Pond Rd., Wakefield, tel. 401/782-4780. Reservations advised. AE, MC, V. Closed Feb. Expensive.*

Lodging **Admiral Dewey Inn.** Listed on the National Register of Historic Places, the building was constructed as a seaside hotel in 1898 and more recently stood unused until new owners, who live on the premises, began its restoration. The 10 rooms are furnished with Victorian antiques. The inn is in a summer community just across the road from Matunuck Beach. *668 Matunuck Beach Rd., 02881, tel. 401/783-2090. 10 rooms. MC, V. Rates include Continental breakfast. Moderate.*

Watch Hill **Olympia Tea Room.** Step back in time to a small restaurant first
Dining opened in 1916, where the soda fountain has a long marble counter and there are varnished wood booths. If you feel up to it, order a marshmallow sundae—or an orangeade. For dinner there's ginger chicken or and mussels steamed in white wine. On the dessert menu, the "world famous Avondale swan" is a fantasy of ice cream, whipped cream, chocolate sauce, and puff pastry. *30 Bay St., tel. 401/348-8211. BYOB. No reservations. AE, MC, V. Expensive.*

Lodging **Ocean House.** The grand old lady may appear a bit down at the heels, yet hers is one of the best seaside porches in New England. The casual, relaxing, quiet place has a reassuring if faded elegance. The furniture could be called "maple eclectic," with oldish mattresses, blankets, and sheets, yet those considerations pale next to the beautiful ocean view (ask for a good one). The Ocean House serves three meals a day, two of which are included in the price of the room. A large porch offers great sunset views, and a set of splintery stairs leads to an excellent private beach. *2 Bluff Ave., 02891, tel. 401/348–8161. 59 rooms. Facilities: restaurant, cocktail lounge, private beach. Children over 2 welcome. MC, V. Closed Sept.–June. Rates are MAP. Expensive.*

Westerly
Dining
★
Shelter Harbor Inn. Originally a farm established in the early 1800s, the property is now a comfortable, unpretentious country inn with a sun porch and an outdoor terrace for unwinding. The frequently changing menu might include smoked scallops and capellini; peppered salmon with lime ginger vinaigrette; and pecan-crusted duck breast. The wine list is extensive, and a bowl of warm, buttery Indian pudding makes a solid finish to any dinner. Those who stay the night can look forward to ginger-blueberry pancakes in the morning. *Rte. 1, tel. 401/322–8883. Reservations advised. AE, DC, MC, V. Expensive.*

Lodging
★
Shelter Harbor Inn. Set in a fairly quiet rural area not far from the beach, this place is perfect for a romantic weekend getaway, ruled by simple luxury, comfort, and privacy. The original house, built in the 1800s, has been extensively renovated, as have several outbuildings. Several rooms have both a working fireplace and a deck, and there's another deck, with a barbecue and a hot tub, on the roof. While the owner does not now live at the inn, you may find him mowing the front lawn. *Rte. 1, 02892, tel. 401/322–8883. 24 rooms. Facilities: restaurant, lighted paddle-tennis court, croquet court, hot tub, barbecue, van service to beach. AE, DC, MC, V. Moderate–Expensive.*

The Arts

Center for the Arts (116 High St., Westerly, tel. 401/348–5000), housed in a historic building, offers concerts, exhibits, and theater productions.

Colonial Theatre (1 Granite St., Westerly, tel. 401/596–0810), the town's only professional theater, presents musicals, comedies, and dramas throughout the year.

South County Players Children's Theater (High St., Wakefield, tel. 401/783–7202) gives performances by children for children in Father Greenan Hall of St. Francis Church.

Theatre-by-the-Sea (Cards Pond Rd., off Rte. 1, Matunuck, tel. 401/782–8587 or 800/782–8587 outside RI), built in 1933 and listed on the National Register of Historic Places, has had a major restoration. The barn-style summer theater presents musicals and children's plays.

Nightlife

Windjammer (Atlantic Ave., Westerly, tel. 401/322–0271) offers oceanfront dining and dancing to rock bands in a room that holds 1,500.

The Coast: Newport

Perched gloriously on the southern tip of Aquidneck Island and bounded on three sides by water, Newport is one of the great sailing cities of the world and the host to world-class jazz, blues, and classical music festivals. Newport's first age of prosperity was in the late 1700s, when it was a major port city almost on a par with Boston and New York; many homes and shops built in that era still stand in the Colonial section of the city. In the 19th century Newport became a summer playground for the wealthiest families in America. Each new home constructed on Bellevue Avenue was grander than the one built just before it, until the acme of extravagance was reached with Cornelius Vanderbilt II's home, the Breakers.

Newport on a summer afternoon can be exasperating, its streets jammed with visitors and the traffic slowed by the procession of sightseeing buses. Yet the quality of Newport's arts festivals persuades many people to brave the crowds. In fall, winter, and spring, visitors enjoy the sights of Newport without the crowds. Newport is a walker's city; whether or not you arrive with a car, in most cases you will want to tour on foot.

Getting Around Local bus service is provided by **Rhode Island Public Transit Authority** (tel. 401/847–0209) in the Newport area.

Guided Tours **Old Colony & Newport Railway** follows an 8-mile route along Narragansett Bay from Newport to Portsmouth's Green Animals Topiary Gardens. The round-trip takes a little over three hours, with a 1¼-hour stop at the garden. *19 America's Cup Ave., tel. 401/624–6951. Admission: $6 adults, $3 children 2–14, $5 senior citizens, $15 families, $9 First Class. Group rates available on request. Departs early May–July 4, Sun. 12:30; Labor Day–Jan. 1, weekends 12:30.*

The Spirit of Newport (tel. 401/849–3575) gives one-hour minicruises of Newport harbor and Narragansett Bay, departing from the Treadway Inn on America's Cup Avenue every 90 minutes.

Walking Tours The **Newport Freedom Trail** makes a loop through the downtown area, beginning at the Historical Society on Touro Street and finishing at the Automobile Museum.

Newport Historical Society (82 Touro Street, tel. 401/846–0813) sponsors walking tours on Friday and Saturday in summer.

Colonial Newport

Numbers in the margin correspond to points of interest on the Newport map.

A walk around **Colonial Newport,** which should give you a good idea of what the town was like at the time of the Revolutionary War, begins at **Hunter House** on Washington Street. Notice the carved pineapple over the doorway of this beautiful Colonial home of 1748; throughout Colonial America the pineapple was a symbol of hospitality from the days when a seaman's wife placed a fresh pineapple at the front door to announce that her husband had returned from the sea. Notice the elliptical arch (a typical Newport architectural detail) in the central hall. In the northeast parlor, notice the cherubs carved over the cupboard.

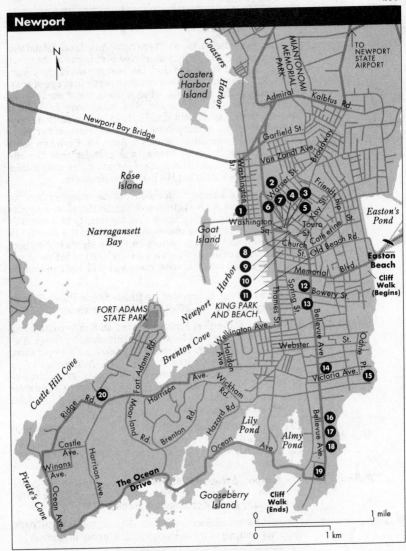

Newport

The Astors'
Beechwood, **17**

Belcourt Castle, **19**

The Breakers, **15**

Brick Market, **3**

Chateau-sur-mer, **14**

Common Burial
Ground, **2**

The Elms, **13**

Friends Meeting
House, **7**

Hammersmith
Farm, **20**

Hunter House, **1**

Kingscote, **12**

Marble House, **18**

Newport Historical
Society, **9**

Old Colony House, **4**

Redwood Library, **11**

Rosecliff, **16**

Touro Synagogue, **8**

Trinity Church, **10**

Wanton-Lyman-
Hazard House, **5**

White Horse Tavern, **6**

Much of the house is furnished with pieces made by Newport craftsmen Townsend and Goddard. *54 Washington St., tel. 401/ 847–1000. Admission: $6 adults, $3.50 children 6–11. Group rates and student group rates available. Open Apr.–Oct., daily 10–5.*

2 Walk north on Washington Street to Walnut Street and east on Walnut to Farewell Street to the 18th-century **Common Burial Ground.** The tombstones offer interesting examples of Colonial stonecarving, much of it the work of John Stevens.

3 Walk south on Farewell Street to Thames Street (pronounced *Thaymz*), the main street of Colonial Newport. Continue south on Thames Street to Washington Square. The **Brick Market,** built in 1760, was designed by Peter Harrison, who was also responsible for the Touro Synagogue and the Redwood Library. From 1793 to 1799 it was used as a theater, and if you look closely at the east wall, you'll find a trace of one of the theatrical scenes—a seascape of ships. In later years the building was used as a town hall. Restored to its original appearance in the 1920s, the building now houses shops. *Washington Sq. Open summer, Mon.–Sat. 10–9, Sun. noon–9; winter, Mon.–Sat. 10–5, Sun. noon–5.*

4 Facing the Market on Washington Square is the **Old Colony House,** built in 1739. The headquarters of the Colonial and state governments, it was from the balcony of this building that the succession of George III was announced and the Declaration of Independence was read to Newporters. George Washington met General Rochambeau here. *Washington Sq., tel. 401/846– 2980. In summer, tours available Mon.–Sat. 9–4.*

5 Walk northeast from Washington Square on Broadway to reach Newport's oldest house, the **Wanton-Lyman-Hazard House,** which displays a "two-room" plan typical of the time. It also has a Colonial garden, and there are demonstrations of 18th-century cooking. *17 Broadway, tel. 401/846–0813. Admission: $2 adults. Open mid-June–Aug., Tues.–Sat. 10–5.*

6 Walk west on Broadway and north on Farewell Street to Marlborough Street and the **White Horse Tavern** (tel. 401/849– 3600). In operation since 1687, The White Horse claims to be the oldest tavern in America. Its low, dark-beam ceiling, cavernous fireplaces, uneven plank floors, and cozy, yet elegant tables epitomize Newport's Colonial charm.

7 Also on this corner stands the **Friends Meeting House.** Built in 1699, this is the oldest Quaker meeting house in America. With its wide-plank floors, simple benches, balcony, and beam ceiling (considered lofty by Colonial standards), this two-story, shingle structure reflects the elegance, quiet reserve, and steadfast faith of Colonial Quakers. Though normally the building may be toured in summer months, it has been undergoing extensive repairs and at press time had not yet reopened. *29 Farewell St., tel. 401/846–0813.*

8 Walk south again on Farewell Street to Washington Square, then south across the square to Touro Street. Walk east on Touro Street to the oldest surviving synagogue in the country, **Touro Synagogue,** designed by Peter Harrison and dedicated in 1763. Very simple on the outside, the building's interior is elaborate. Notice the way its design combines the ornate columns and moldings of the Georgian style with Jewish ritualistic requirements. *85 Touro St., tel. 401/847-4794. Open Sun.-Fri. 10-5 in summer, Sun. 1-3 the rest of the year, and by appointment.*

9 At 82 Touro Street you'll find the headquarters of the **Newport Historical Society,** the departure point for walking tours of Newport. The building is also a museum featuring a large collection of Newport memorabilia, furniture, and maritime items. *82 Touro St., tel. 401/846-0813. Admission free. Open Tues.-Fri. 9:30-4:30.*

10 Walk south of Washington Square, down Division Street, to the corner of Spring and Church streets. Here you'll find **Trinity Church,** a Colonial beauty built in 1724. A special feature of the interior is the three-tiered wineglass pulpit, the only one of its kind in America. *Queen Anne Sq., tel. 401/846-0660. Open daily 10-4.*

11 For the last stop on our tour of Colonial Newport, walk east along Church Street to the beginning of Bellevue Avenue and the **Redwood Library,** built in 1748—the oldest library in continuous use in the United States. Another magnificent example of the architecture of Peter Harrison, the building, although made of wood, was designed to look like a Roman temple, the original exterior paint mixed with sand to resemble stone. The library houses a wonderful collection of paintings by the important early American artists Gilbert Stuart, Rembrandt Peale, and others. *50 Bellevue Ave., tel. 401/847-0292. Admission free. Open July-Aug., Mon.-Sat. 9:30-5; Sept.-June, Mon.-Sat. 9:30-5:30.*

At the **Newport Art Museum and Art Association,** permanent and changing exhibits of historic contemporary art of Rhode Island and New England are offered. Notice the building's stick-style Victorian architecture, courtesy of designer Richard Morris Hunt. *76 Bellevue Ave., tel. 401/847-0179. Admission: $2 adults, $1 senior citizens and students, free for children under 18. Open Tues.-Sat. 10-5, Sun. 1-5.*

Newport Mansions

We turn now to **Gilded Age Newport,** which is largely seen in the splendid mansions of the turn of the century. Contrary to our earlier caution about driving in Newport, you may find a car useful here in covering the considerable distances between the grand homes, for you'll have plenty of walking to do inside the mansions themselves. If you're eager to do some walking, however, a 3-mile **Cliff Walk,** which begins at Easton's Beach and runs along Newport's cliffs, offers a water level view of many mansions.

It is hard to imagine the sums of money possessed by the wealthy elite who made Newport their summer playground in the late 1800s and early 1900s. The "cottages" they built are almost obscenely grand, laden with ornate rococo detail and designed with a determined one-upmanship.

Six Newport mansions are maintained by the Preservation Society of Newport County (tel. 401/847-1000). A combination ticket—available at any of the society's properties—gives you a discount on individual admission prices. Each mansion provides a guided tour that lasts about one hour.

⑫ We begin at **Kingscote,** just west of Bellevue Avenue, on Bowery Street. Built in 1840 for George Noble Jones, a Savannah, Georgia, plantation owner, this mansion serves to remind us that Newport was popular with Southerners before the Civil War. Today it is furnished with antique furniture, glass, and Oriental art. It also has a number of Tiffany windows. *Bowery St., off Bellevue Ave. Admission: $6 adults, $3 children 6–11. Group rates and student group rates available. Open Apr.– Oct., daily 10–5. Closed in winter.*

Back on Bellevue Avenue, the **International Tennis Hall of Fame** and the **Tennis Museum,** housed in a magnificent building by Stanford White, features photographs and other memorabilia of more than a century of tennis history. The first National Tennis Championships were held here in 1881. *Newport Casino, 194 Bellevue Ave., tel. 401/849–3990. Admission: $4 adults, $2 children 6–12, $10 family. Open May–Sept., daily 11–5; Oct.–Apr., daily 11–4.*

⑬ Continue on Bellevue Avenue to **The Elms,** one of Newport's most graceful mansions. The Elms pays homage to the classical design, broad lawn, fountains, and formal gardens of the Château d'Asnières near Paris; it was built for Edward Julius Berwind, a bituminous-coal baron, at the turn of the century. *Bellevue Ave. Admission: $6 adults, $3 children 6–11. Group rates and student group rates available. Open Apr.–Oct., daily 10–4; Nov.–Mar., weekends 10–4.*

⑭ A few blocks south is **Chateau-sur-Mer,** the first of Bellevue Avenue's stone mansions. Built in 1852 and enlarged by Richard Morris Hunt for William S. Wetmore, a China trade tycoon, the mansion houses a toy collection. Compared to the more opulent homes built during the 1890s, this one seems rather modest today. A December visit will find the home decorated for a Victorian Christmas. *Bellevue Ave. Admission: $6 adults, $3 children 6–11. Group rates and student group rates available. Open Apr.–Oct., daily 10–5; Nov.–Mar., weekends 10–4.*

⑮ Turn left on Victoria Avenue and continue to Ochre Point Avenue and **The Breakers.** It's easy to understand why it took more than 2,500 workmen two years to create this structure, the most magnificent of the Newport mansions. Built in 1893 for Cornelius Vanderbilt II and his small family, The Breakers has 70 rooms and required 40 servants to keep it running. Just a few of the marvels within the four-story limestone villa are a gold-ceiling music room, a blue marble fireplace, rose alabaster pillars in the dining room, and a porch whose mosaic ceiling took Italian craftsmen six months, lying on their backs, to install. If it were possible to build The Breakers today, according to recent estimates, it could cost $400 million. *Ochre Point Ave. Admission: $7.50 adults, $3.50 children 6–11. Group rates and student group rates available. Open daily 10–5. Closed Nov.– Mar.*

⑯ Return to Bellevue Avenue and continue south to **Rosecliff.** Built for Mrs. Hermann Oelrichs, this romantic mansion was completed in 1902. Modeled after the Grand Trianon at Versailles, the 40-room home includes the Court of Love (inspired by a similar room at Versailles) and a heart-shape staircase designed by Stanford White. It has appeared in several movies, including *The Great Gatsby. Bellevue Ave. Admission: $6* *adults, $3 children 6–11. Group rates and student group rates available. Open daily 10–5. Closed Nov.–Mar.*

⓱ Farther down Bellevue Avenue is **The Astors' Beechwood,** where a succession of actors, dressed in period costume, play the parts of members of the Astor family (including Mrs. Astor, the belle of New York and Newport society), servants, and household guests. The guides involve visitors in much banter, such as noticing a woman's knee-length skirt and asking, "Do your clothes have a shrinkage problem?" If you'd enjoy a touch of time travel, by all means look in. *580 Bellevue Ave., tel. 401/846–3772. Admission: $7 adults, $5.50 senior citizens and children 6–12, $30 families (2 adults and up to 4 children). Call for group rates. Open May–Dec., daily 10–5; Jan.–Apr., Fri.–Sun. 10–5.*

Continue down Bellevue Avenue, and on your left will be
⓲ **Marble House,** with its extravagant gold ballroom, the gift of William Vanderbilt to his wife, Alva, in 1892. Alva divorced William in 1895, and married Oliver Perry Belmont to become the lady of Belcourt Castle (just down the road). When Oliver died in 1908, she returned to Marble House. Mrs. Belmont was involved with the suffragist movement and spent much of her time campaigning for women's rights. In the kitchen you'll see plates marked "Votes for Women." The lovely Chinese teahouse behind the estate was built in 1913 by Mrs. Belmont. *Bellevue Ave. Admission: $6 adults, $3 children 6–11. Group rates and student group rates available. Open Apr.–Oct., daily 10–5; Nov.–Mar., weekends 10–4.*

⓳ Farther along the avenue is **Belcourt Castle,** designed by Richard Morris Hunt, and based on Louis XIII's hunting lodge. The castle contains an enormous collection of European and Oriental treasures. Sip tea and admire the stained glass and carved wood, and don't miss the Golden Coronation Coach. *Bellevue Ave., tel. 401/846–0669 or 401/849–1566. Admission: $6 adults, $5 senior citizens, $2.50 children 6–12. Open daily 10–5. Closed Jan. 26–Mar. 31.*

⓴ Take Ocean Drive all the way along the coast to **Hammersmith Farm,** the childhood summer home of Jacqueline Bouvier Kennedy Onassis, the site of her wedding to John F. Kennedy, and a summer White House during the Kennedy Administration. It is also the only working farm in Newport. Loaded with Bouvier and Kennedy memorabilia, the house is so comfortable that it seems as though its owners have just stepped out of the room. The elaborate gardens were designed by Frederick Law Olmsted, and there are breathtaking views of the ocean. *Ocean Dr., near Ft. Adams, tel. 401/846–7346. Admission: $6 adults, $3 children. Open daily 10–5, summer until 7. Closed mid-Nov.–Mar.*

Continue around the point to Fort Adams and the **Museum of Yachting.** Here are four galleries of pictures: Mansions and Yachts; Small Craft; America's Cup; and the Hall of Fame for Single-handed Sailors. *Ft. Adams, Ocean Dr., tel. 401/847–1018. Admission: $2 adults, $1 senior citizens, children under 12 free. Open mid-May–Oct., Tues.–Sun. 10–5.*

It's less than 10 miles from Newport to **Portsmouth,** traveling north on Route 138. Situated on the Sakonnet River on the east side of Aquidneck Island, Portsmouth has seen much development in recent years, a departure from its somewhat rural past.

Turn east from Route 138 onto Sandy Point Avenue to reach **Sandy Point Beach,** where the calm surf of the Sakonnet River creates a choice spot for families and beginning windsurfers.

Leaving the beach area, continue north on Route 138, then head west and look out for the "Green Animals" signs that direct you to a **topiary garden** filled with plants sculpted to look like an elephant, a bear, a giraffe, and other animals, all set on a lovely sloping lawn that descends to Narragansett Bay. *Cory's La., tel. 401/847–1000. Admission: $6 adults, $3.50 children 6–22. Group rates and student group rates available. Open May–Oct., daily 10–5.*

Route 138 a few miles farther north will take you across the bridge over the Sakonnet River. Continue on Route 24 a couple of miles to I–195, which will take you to Cape Cod; if you want to end the tour here, you can keep on Route 24 all the way to Boston, a little less than an hour away (*see* Tour 1, Boston to Bar Harbor).

Shopping

Many of Newport's arts and antiques shops can be found on Thames Street or near the waterfront, and others are located on Spring Street, Franklin Street, and at Bowen's and Bannister's wharves. The Brick Market area—between Thames Street and America's Cup Avenue—has more than 50 shops.

Antiques **Aardvark Antiques** (475 Thames St., tel. 401/849–7233) has architectural pieces: mantels, doors, garden ornaments, and stained glass.

Black Sheep Antiques (54 Spring St., tel. 401/846–6810) stocks an unusual combination of antiques and collectibles. You may find period glassware, quilts, linens, baskets, furniture, and lots of nautical antiques.

Full Swing (474 Thames St., tel. 401/849–9494) has collectibles from the 1920s through the 1950s: odd lamps, ashtrays, books, dishes, strange furniture, and vintage fabrics.

John Gidley House (22 Franklin St., tel. 401/846–8303) features Continental furnishings from the 18th and 19th centuries. The store's own chandeliers and marble are a reminder of what Newport was like in the Gilded Age.

The Old Fashion Shop (38 Pelham St., tel. 401/847–2692) sells American furniture and accessories, including elegant china, kitchenware, quilts, and glass—and Oriental objects.

Art **The Liberty Tree** (128 Spring St., tel. 401/847–5925) has contemporary folk art, furniture, carvings, and paintings.

MacDowell Pottery (220 Spring St., tel. 401/846–6313) is a studio/shop where you can not only purchase the wares of many New England potters, but also see a potter's wheel in use.

Native American Trading Company: Indian Territory (138–140 Spring St., tel. 401/846–8465) sells paintings and artifacts.

Thames Glass (688 Thames St., tel. 401/846–0576) sells delicate and dramatic blown-glass gifts, designed by Matthew

Buechner and handmade in the adjacent studio. Don't miss the selection of slightly imperfect items.

William Vareika Fine Arts (212 Bellevue Ave., tel. 401/849–6149) exhibits and sells American paintings and prints from the 18th, 19th, and 20th centuries, and offers appraisal and consulting services.

Crafts **Tropea-Puerini** (492 Thames St., tel. 401/846–3344) calls itself the Alternative Bridal Registry and offers interesting pottery, sculpture, jewelry, and other crafts.

Flags **Ebenezer Flagg Co.** (corner of Spring and Touro Sts., tel. 401/846–1891) offers a large selection of flags, banners, and wind socks, as well as in-shop manufacturing and custom design.

Gourmet Food **Crest Farm** (43 Memorial Blvd., tel. 401/846–3416) is the place to go for fabulous gourmet foods, decadent pastries, and aromatic coffee to take out.

Home Furnishings **Rue de France** (78 Thames St., tel. 401/846–3636) specializes in French lace: curtains, pillows, and table linens.

Sports and Outdoor Activities

Biking **Ten Speed Spokes** (18 Elm St., tel. 401/847–5609) has bikes; **Newport Rent-a-Ped** (2 Washington St., tel. 401/846–7788) has mopeds.

Boating **Old Port Marine Services** (Sayer's Wharf, tel. 401/847–9109) offers harbor tours, daily and weekly yacht charters, and rides on a harbor ferry. **Sight Sailing of Newport** (Bowen's Wharf, tel. 401/849–3333) organizes two-hour sailing tours of Newport Harbor in a six-passenger sailboat with a U.S. Coast Guard–licensed captain.

Fishing No license is required for saltwater fishing, although anglers should check with local bait shops for minimum size requirements. Charter fishing boats depart daily from Newport, from the spring through the fall. Contact **Black Horse Fishing Charter** (Long Wharf Moorings, tel. 401/841–8848).

Beaches

Easton's Beach (Memorial Blvd.), also known as First Beach, is popular for its carousel for the kids and miniature golf.

Fort Adams State Park (Ocean Dr.), a small beach with a picnic area and lifeguards during the summer, has beautiful views of Newport Harbor.

King Park (Wellington Ave.), with lifeguards patrolling during the summer, is a haven for scuba divers.

Dining and Lodging

Newport Dining The following dining price categories have been used: *Expensive*, over $20; *Moderate*, $10–$20; *Inexpensive*, under $10. Casual wear is the rule in the restaurants of Newport except as noted.

American **The Black Pearl.** At this popular waterfront restaurant with a nautical decor, diners choose between the tavern and the more formal Commodore's Room. The latter offers such appetizers as black and blue tuna with red pepper sauce; and oysters warmed with truffles and cream. Sample entrées on a recent menu were swordfish with Dutch pepper butter; salmon with mustard dill hollandaise; and duck breast with green peppercorn sauce. *Bannister's Wharf, tel. 401/846-5264. Reservations advised. Jacket required. AE, DC, MC, V. Expensive.*

Clarke Cooke House. Formal dining occurs on the upper level of this restaurant; the timber-ceiling room has water views, dark-green latticework, richly patterned pillows, and wood model hulls, which combine to pay homage to Colonial, nautical, and Gilded Era Newport. The first two levels feature less formal dining in pleasant, airy, white-beamed sections with large windows facing the bustling pedestrian traffic of the wharf. The lamb and the game on the menu are raised here on the farm, and the vegetables are grown locally as well. Chicken breast stuffed with lobster in a lobster sauce; and sole poached in Chardonnay with asparagus are typical offerings at dinner. *Bannister's Wharf, tel. 401/849-2900. Reservations advised; required in summer. Jacket required. AE, MC, V. Expensive.*

Star Clipper Dinner Train. This four-course, 22-mile journey along Narragansett Bay features such delicacies as prime rib or swordfish, while providing fine water views and murder-mystery entertainment on Friday. Make reservations well in advance for the three-hour trip. *19 America's Cup Ave., tel. 401/849-7550. Reservations required. MC, V. Expensive.*

Brick Alley Pub. Low ceilings, small tables, plants, and American memorabilia give this place a friendly atmosphere. An extensive menu includes fresh fish, chowder, steaks, and homemade pasta. *140 Thames St., tel. 401/849-6334. Reservations advised. AE, MC, V. Moderate.*

Wave Cafe. Come here for fresh-roasted coffee, fresh-baked muffins, and such homemade Italian food as mile-high eggplant parmigiana and all sorts of pizza. The restaurant is crowded and tables here are small—if you're trying to juggle a lunch plate and a newspaper, you may have a little trouble—but the food is memorable. *580 Thames St., tel. 401/846-6060. No reservations. MC, V. BYOB. No dinner Mon. Moderate.*

Franklin Spa. Omelets and a thick, hearty beef stew are two attractions of this neighborhood luncheonette that looks as though it's been preserved in a 1950s time capsule. *229 Spring St., tel. 401/847-3540. No reservations. No credit cards. Inexpensive.*

Gary's Handy Lunch. Come to this fisherman's hangout—its long counter lined with chrome stools—for homemade soup, BLT sandwiches, and delicious fresh-brewed coffee. *462 Thames St., tel. 401/847-9480. No reservations. No credit cards. No dinner. Inexpensive.*

Continental ★ **White Horse Tavern.** One of the nation's oldest operating taverns, the White Horse offers a setting conducive to intimate dining. Lobster and beef Wellington are standard entrées. *Corner of Marlborough and Farewell Sts., tel. 401/849-3600. Reservations required. Jacket required. AE, DC, MC, V. No lunch Tues. Expensive.*

French **La Petite Auberge.** This romantic Colonial home offers exquisite French cuisine in intimate rooms with lace cloths on the tables and Napoleonic prints on the walls; in summer, you can dine on the patio. The owner-chef (once the maitre d' for General de Gaulle) prepares such delicacies as trout with almonds, duck flambée with orange sauce, and medallions of beef with goose liver pâté. *19 Charles St., tel. 401/849–6669. Reservations advised. AE, MC, V. Expensive*

Le Bistro. This chic haven on Newport's busy waterfront produces French nouvelle cuisine in a friendly, informal atmosphere. The third floor offers the best harbor views as you enjoy such specialties as grilled duck with figs, fillet of sole meuniere, and roast rack of lamb. The less expensive luncheon menu features soups, fancy sandwiches, salads, and pizza. *Bowen's Wharf, tel. 401/849–7778. Reservations advised. AE, DC, MC, V. Expensive.*

Italian **Puerini's.** The aroma of garlic and basil greet you as soon as you enter this friendly neighborhood restaurant with soft pink walls covered with black-and-white photographs of Italy and lace curtains on the windows. The long and intriguing menu presents such selections as green noodles with chicken in marsala wine sauce; tortellini with seafood; and cavatelli in four cheeses. *24 Memorial Blvd., tel. 401/847–5506. No reservations. No smoking. No credit cards. BYOB. No lunch. Closed Sun. in winter. Moderate.*

Seafood **Anthony's Seafood & Shore Dinner Hall.** The large, light room with the panoramic views of Newport Harbor is a cafeteria-style restaurant serving lobsters, fried clams, fish-and-chips, and other seafood at reasonable prices. Families find the atmosphere congenial. The adjoining seafood shop has local specialties. *Lower Thames St., at Waites Wharf, tel. 401/848–5058. No reservations. MC, V. Closed Oct.–Nov., Mon.–Wed; Dec.–Mar. Moderate.*

Salas'. Movie posters, red-and-white plastic tablecloths, and lines of waiting customers create a lively, good-natured waterfront dining spot. Pastas, lobster, clams, and corn-on-the-cob are the principal fare. Spaghetti and macaroni are served by the ¼, ½, and full pound. *341 Thames St., tel. 401/846–8772. No reservations. AE, V. Moderate.*

Newport Lodging The following lodging price categories have been used: *Expensive*, over $100; *Moderate*, $60–$100; *Inexpensive*, under $60.

The Inntowne. Accommodations are more modest than those of The Inn at Castle Hill (below), which is under the same management and which sends travelers here when it is fully booked. Guests use a private beach at Castle Hill, and tea is served in the afternoon. *6 Mary St., 02840, tel. 401/846–9200. 26 rooms, 25 with bath. AE, MC, V. Closed Dec. 24–25. Rates include Continental breakfast. Expensive.*

Cliffside Inn. Near Newport's Cliff Walk and downtown, on a quiet, tree-lined street, this elegant 1880 Victorian home offers a somewhat formal atmosphere of grandeur and comfort. The wide front porch has a view of the lawn, the foyer is welcoming and dramatic, and the tastefully appointed rooms—filled with Victorian antiques and some with bay windows—are light and airy. *2 Seaview Ave., 02840, tel. 401/847–1811. 11 rooms. Facilities: porch, meeting area. No smoking. AE, MC, V. Moderate–Expensive.*

The Francis Malbone House. The design of this stately 1760 house is attributed to the architect responsible for the Touro Synagogue and the Redwood Library. Centrally located on Thames Street, the house, with its whitewashed brick walls, provides a quiet and elegant shelter from Newport's bustling activities. Beautifully restored, the inn is furnished in modern and reproduction furniture. *392 Thames St., 02840, tel. 401/*

846–0392. 8 rooms, 1 suite. Facilities: most rooms have working fireplaces. AE, MC, V. Rates include Continental breakfast. Moderate–Expensive.

The Inn at Castle Hill. Perched on an oceanside cliff, this rambling inn was built as a summer home in 1874, and much of the original furniture remains. Bookings well in advance are necessary here. Watch out—there's a big difference between the rooms with private bath and those that share a bath. *Ocean Dr., 02840, tel. 401/849–3800. 10 rooms, 7 with bath. Facilities: 3 private beaches. AE, MC, V. Closed Dec. 24–25. Rates include Continental breakfast. Moderate–Expensive.*

★ **Ivy Lodge.** The only bed-and-breakfast in the mansion district has the look of a large Victorian home with a wraparound porch. Inside you'll find a 33-foot gothic paneled oak entry with a three-story turned baluster staircase. A fire burns brightly on fall and winter afternoons in the huge brick fireplace built in the shape of a Moorish arch. Rooms are spacious and very private. *12 Clay St., 02840, tel. 401/849–6865. 10 rooms, 8 with bath. MC, V. Rates include Continental breakfast. Moderate–Expensive.*

Victorian Ladies. This bed-and-breakfast is sumptuously decorated with Victorian antiques and is within walking distance of Newport's shops. While the thoroughfare has a fair amount of traffic, the house's insulation muffles the sound significantly. *63 Memorial Blvd., 02840, tel. 401/849–9960. 9 rooms with bath. Facilities: off-street parking. MC, V. Closed Jan. Moderate–Expensive.*

The Marriott. The luxury hotel on the harbor at Long Wharf has an elegant atrium lobby with marble floors and a gazebo. Rooms, bordering the atrium or overlooking the skyline or the water, are decorated in mauve and seafoam, with either a king-size bed or two double beds. *25 America's Cup Ave., 02840, tel. 401/849–1000 or 800/228–9290. 310 rooms, 7 suites. Facilities: restaurant, cocktail lounge, disco, pool, sauna, 4 racquetball courts, health club, Jacuzzi, conference rooms. AE, DC, MC, V. Moderate.*

Sheraton Islander Inn. This resort hotel, set on its own private island, has an impressive view of the harbor and Colonial Newport. Approximately 80% of the rooms have water views. Standard rooms have blond furniture and are decorated in seafoam and peach; seafoam and mauve is the scheme in the good-size Captain's Quarters and the suites. *Goat Island 02840, tel. 401/849–2600 or 800/325–3535. 250 rooms. Facilities: 4 restaurants, indoor pool, outdoor saltwater pool, health center, sauna, beauty salon, 2 racquetball courts, marina, conference rooms. AE, DC, MC, V. Moderate.*

Nightlife

The Ark (348 Thames St., tel. 401/849–3808) features jazz on Sunday.

Blue Pelican (40 W. Broadway, tel. 401/847–5675) is popular for live jazz, rhythm and blues, folk, and rock music.

Clark Cooke House (Bannister's Wharf, tel. 401/849–2900) has a piano bar upstairs, disco and swing downstairs.

Club Thames (337 America's Cup Ave., tel. 401/849–9840) plays high-energy dance music and videos.

Thackaberry's of Newport (212 Thames St., tel. 401/849–1110) presents live jazz and rhythm and blues on the second floor most evenings.

Viking Hotel (1 Bellevue Ave., tel. 401/847–3300) offers mainstream jazz on Sunday afternoon.

Cape Cod

Separated from the Massachusetts "mainland" by the 17.4-mile Cape Cod Canal, the Cape is always likened in shape to an outstretched arm bent at the elbow, its fist turned back at Provincetown toward the mainland. It's 90 miles from end to end, with 15 towns, each broken up into villages. The term *Upper Cape* refers to the towns of Bourne, Falmouth, Mashpee, and Sandwich; *Mid-Cape*, to Barnstable, Yarmouth, and Dennis; and *Lower Cape*, to Harwich, Chatham, Brewster, Orleans, Eastham, Wellfleet, Truro, and Provincetown.

The Cape is for relaxing—swimming and sunning, fishing and boating, playing golf and tennis, attending the theater and hunting antiques. Despite summer crowds and overdevelopment, much remains unspoiled. Visitors continue to enjoy the Cape's charming old New England villages of weathered shingle houses and white steepled churches as well as its pine woods, grassy marshes, and rolling dunes.

From Newport, Routes 138 and 24 lead northeast to I–195, which goes east toward Cape Cod. There are a few sights of interest along the way in Fall River and New Bedford, Massachusetts, but both are now industrial urban areas of little scenic value; most travelers will probably want to shoot on the 30 miles or so to I–495, the highway to the Cape. I–495 connects to Route 6, the main road running the length of the Cape. In summer, try to avoid arriving at the bridges in late afternoon, especially on holidays: All the major roads are heavily congested eastbound on Friday night and westbound on Sunday afternoon.

The **Cape Area Transportation System** (tel. 800/352–7155) provides bus service between Hyannis and Woods Hole. **Plymouth & Brockton Street Railway** (tel. 508/746–0378 or 800/328–9997 in MA) has service from Boston and Logan Airport, as well as between Sagamore and Provincetown, with stops at many towns in between.

Guided Tours   One-hour tours of Hyannis Port Harbor, including a view of the Kennedy compound, are offered by **Hy-Line**; sunset cruises also available. *Ocean St. Dock, Pier 1, Hyannis, tel. 508/778–2600. Cost: $7 adults, $3 children under 12 with adults, children under 3 free. Tours mid-May–mid-Oct.*

Cape Cod Canal Cruises (two or three hours, narrated) leave from Onset, just east of the bridges onto the Cape. A Sunday jazz cruise, sunset cocktail cruises, and evening dance cruises are available. *Onset Bay Town Pier, tel. 508/295–3883. Cost: $6–$8 adults, $3–$4 children 6–12; $1 senior citizen discount Mon. and Fri. Tours May–mid-Oct.*

Cape Cod Scenic Railroad runs 1¾-hour excursions between Sagamore and Hyannis with stops at Sandwich and the Canal. The train passes ponds, cranberry bogs, and marshes. *Main and Center Sts., Hyannis, tel. 508/866–4526. Cost: $10.50* *adults, $6.50 children 3–12. Several departures a day (no serv- ice Mon. or Fri.) in each direction mid-June–Columbus Day.*

Art's Dune Tours (tel. 508/487–1950 or 1050) has been offering narrated tours through the National Seashore and dunes around Provincetown since 1946.

Southeastern Massachusetts

Fall River is hardly an inspiring town in terms of scenery—in- dustrial docks and enormous factories recall the city's past as a major textile center in the 19th and 20th centuries. It also served as a port, however, and today the most interesting site is **Battleship Cove,** down beside the Taunton River in the shad- ow of the I–195 bridge. The cove harbors several museums and the 35,000-ton battleship USS *Massachusetts,* the battleship USS *Joseph P. Kennedy, Jr.,* and a World War II attack sub, the USS *Lionfish. Battleship Cove, tel. 508/678–1905. Admis- sion: $8 adults, $4 children 6–14, $6 senior citizens. Open daily 9–5. Closed Thanksgiving, Christmas, New Year's Day.*

Near the ships, the **Marine Museum at Fall River** celebrates the age of sail and steamship travel, especially the lavishly fitted ships of the Old Fall River Line, which operated until 1937 be- tween New England and New York City. The museum also con- tains the largest existing model of the *Titanic*—a 28-foot, 1-ton representation that was used in the 1952 movie by Twentieth Century Fox. *70 Water St., tel. 508/674–3533. Admission: $3 adults, $2 children 6–14, $3 senior citizens. Open weekdays 9– 4:30, weekends and holidays 10–5. Closed Thanksgiving, Christmas, New Year's Day.*

In the same riverside location, the **Fall River Heritage State Park** tells the story of Fall River's industrial past, focusing on the city's textile mills and their workers. *200 Davol St. W, tel. 508/675–5759. Admission free. Open early May–early Oct., daily 9–8; Nov.–May, Tues.–Sun. 9–4:30. Closed Thanks- giving, Christmas, New Year's Day.*

Route I–195 links Fall River to **New Bedford,** home of the larg- est fishing fleet on the East Coast. The historic district near the water is a delight; it was here that Herman Melville set his famous whaling novel, *Moby-Dick.* The **New Bedford Whaling Museum,** established in 1902, is the largest American museum devoted to the history of the whaling era, which lasted some 200 years in New Bedford. A 22-minute film depicting an actual whaling chase is shown twice daily July–August, once on week- ends the rest of the year. *18 Johnny Cake Hill, tel. 508/997– 0046. Admission: $3.50 adults, $2.50 children 6–14, $3 senior citizens. Open Sept.–June, Mon.–Sat. 9–5, Sun. 1–5; July– Aug., Mon.–Sat. 9–5, Sun. 11–5. Closed Thanksgiving, Christmas, New Year's Day.*

In the 1880s New Bedford was also an international leader in the art-glass movement. The **New Bedford Glass Museum** con- tains a collection of 2,000 objects of glass, silver, and porce- lain—most of them made locally. *50 N. 2nd St., tel. 508/994– 0115. Admission: $2 adults, 50¢ children 6–12, $1.50 senior cit- izens. Open mid-Apr.–Dec. 1, Mon.–Sat. 10–5; Dec. 2–mid- Apr., Tues.–Sat. 10–4.*

The **New Bedford Preservation Society** publishes a series of excellent walking tours of the city's restored area. These and other brochures are available at the Visitor's Center (47 N. 2nd St., tel. 508/991–6200). Melville fans may want to stop by **Seaman's Bethel** (15 Johnny Cake Hill, New Bedford, tel. 508/992–3295), a small chapel featured in *Moby-Dick*.

Time Out In the middle of the restored historic downtown area, **Free-stones** (41 William St., tel. 508/993–7477) is a large, attractive restaurant set in a refurbished bank, originally built in 1877. Stop here for a lunch of seafood, pasta, sandwiches, or salads.

Cape Cod

Numbers in the margin correspond to points of interest on the Cape Cod map.

Route 6, the Mid-Cape Highway, passes through the relatively unpopulated center of the Cape, characterized by a landscape of scrub pine and oak. Paralleling Route 6 but following the north coast is Route 6A, the Old King's Highway, in most sections a winding country road that passes through some of the Cape's best-preserved old New England towns. The south shore of the Cape, traced by Route 28, is heavily populated and the major center for tourism, encompassing Falmouth, Hyannis, and Chatham.

1 At the Cape's extreme southwest corner is **Woods Hole,** where ferries depart for Martha's Vineyard. An international center for marine research, it is home to the Woods Hole Oceanographic Institute (WHOI), whose staff led the successful search for the *Titanic* in 1986; the Marine Biological Laboratories (MBL); and the National Marine Fisheries Service, among other scientific institutions.

The Fisheries Service has a public **Aquarium** with two harbor seals in summer, tanks displaying regional fish and shellfish, plus hands-on tanks and microscopes for children. *Cnr. Albatross and Water Sts., Woods Hole, tel. 508/548–7684. Admission free. Open mid-June–mid-Sept., daily 10–4; mid-Sept.–mid-June, weekdays 9–4.*

The **Marine Biological Laboratory** (tel. 508/548–3705, ext. 423; call for reservations and meeting instructions) offers 1½-hour tours of its facilities, led by retired scientists, on weekdays during the summer.

A guided walking tour of the quaint village is conducted one afternoon a week in July and August by the **Woods Hole Historical Collection** (Bradley House Museum, 573 Woods Hole Rd., tel. 508/548–7270). Before leaving Woods Hole, stop at **Nobska Light** for a great view out to sea.

2 The village green in **Falmouth** was used as a military training field in the 18th century. Today it is the center of a considerable shopping district, flanked by attractive old homes, some fine inns, and the **Congregational Church,** with a bell made by Paul Revere.

The Falmouth Historical Society conducts free, docent-guided walking tours of the town in season. It also maintains two museums. The 1790 **Julia Wood House** has fascinating architectural details (wide-board floors, leaded-glass windows, Colonial kitchen with wide hearth), plus embroideries, baby shoes and clothes, toys and dolls, and furniture. The **Conant House** next door, a 1794 half-Cape, has military memorabilia, whaling items, scrimshaw, sailors' valentines, silver, glass, and china. *Palmer Ave. at the Village Green, Falmouth, tel. 508/548–4857. Admission: $2 adults, 50¢ children. Open mid-June–mid-Sept., weekdays 2–5; other times by appointment.*

Also in Falmouth is the **Ashumet Holly and Wildlife Sanctuary,** a 45-acre tract of woods, ponds, meadows, and hiking trails supervised by the Massachusetts Audubon Society. The 1,000 holly trees include American, Oriental, and European varieties. *Ashumet Rd., off Rte. 151, Falmouth, tel. 508/563–6390. Admission: $3 adults, $2 children and senior citizens. Open daily sunrise–sunset.*

❸ **Hyannis,** with its busy downtown, is the Cape's year-round commercial hub. The **John F. Kennedy Memorial Museum** is scheduled to open here in May. Collections of photographs, videos, papers, and artifacts from the presidential years will focus on JFK's ties to the Cape. *397 Main St., tel. 508/775–2201. Admission free.*

The **John F. Kennedy Memorial,** on Ocean Street overlooking Lewis Bay, is a plaque and fountain pool in memory of the pres-
❹ ident who spent his summers nearby. **Hyannis Port** is the site of the **Kennedy family compound;** although tourists are not allowed onto the compound, sightseeing buses often tie up traffic in the area.

The proliferation of motels, restaurants, and antiques shops continues past Hyannis on the south shore but thins out some-
❺ what as you go east. At **Harwich Port,** a right turn onto Harbor Road will take you past scenic **Wychmere Harbor.**

❻ **Chatham** is a seaside town that is relatively free of the development and commercialism found elsewhere on the Cape. Its attractive Main Street, lined with boutiques and crafts and antiques shops, is a pleasure to wander.

The view from **Chatham Light** is spectacular—a great vantage point to view the "Chatham Break" of 1987, when a fierce storm blasted a channel through a barrier beach off the coast. South of Chatham lies **Monomoy Island,** which was split in two by a similar break in 1958. A fragile barrier-beach area with dunes, it is protected as the **Monomoy National Wildlife Refuge.** The island provides nesting grounds and resting places for 285 bird species.

From Chatham, Route 28 curves north and joins Routes 6 and
❼ 6A at **Orleans,** the busy commercial center of the Lower Cape. A left turn at the Main Street traffic light will take you to Rock Harbor Road, a winding street lined with gray-shingled Cape houses, white picket fences, and neat gardens; at the end is the harbor.

❽ The north-shore segment of this tour begins at **Sagamore,** where you'll find a large Christmas Tree Shop and a factory-outlet mall. At **Pairpoint Glass** you can watch richly colored lead crystal being hand-blown in the factory, as it has been for 150 years. The shop sells finished wares, including ornamental cup plates. *Rte. 6A, Sagamore, tel. 508/888–2344. Open daily 9–6; demonstrations weekdays 10–4.*

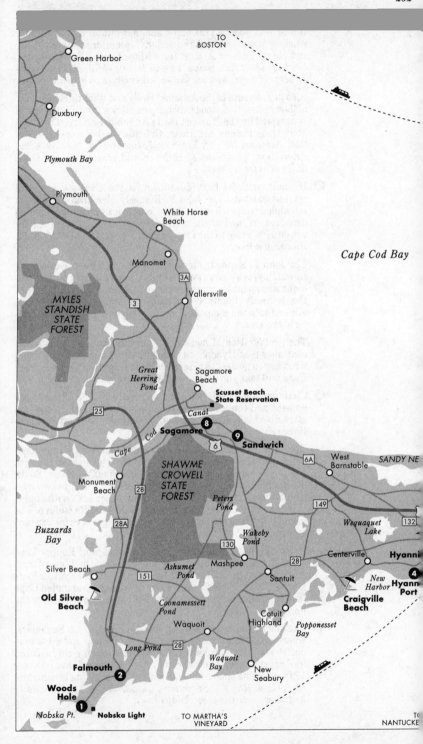

TO BOSTON

Green Harbor

Duxbury

Plymouth Bay

Plymouth

White Horse
Beach

Manomet

Cape Cod Bay

[3A]

Vallersville

MYLES
STANDISH
STATE
FOREST

[3]

*Great
Herring
Pond*

Sagamore
Beach

**Scusset Beach
State Reservation**

[25]

Cod Canal

Sagamore ❽

❾ **Sandwich**

[6]

Cape

SHAWME
CROWELL
STATE
FOREST

[6A]

West
Barnstable

SANDY NE

Monument
Beach

[28]

*Peters
Pond*

[149]

[132]

*Wequaquet
Lake*

[28A]

*Buzzards
Bay*

[130]

*Wakeby
Pond*

Centerville

Hyanni

Silver Beach

[151]

*Ashumet
Pond*

Mashpee

[28]

Santuit

New
Harbor

❹

**Hyann
Port**

**Old Silver
Beach**

*Coonamessett
Pond*

Cotuit
Highland

*Poppnesset
Bay*

**Craigville
Beach**

Waquoit

[28]

Long Pond

*Waquoit
Bay*

New
Seabury

Falmouth ❷

**Woods
Hole**

Nobska Pt. ■ **Nobska Light**

TO MARTHA'S
VINEYARD

❶

T
NANTUCKE

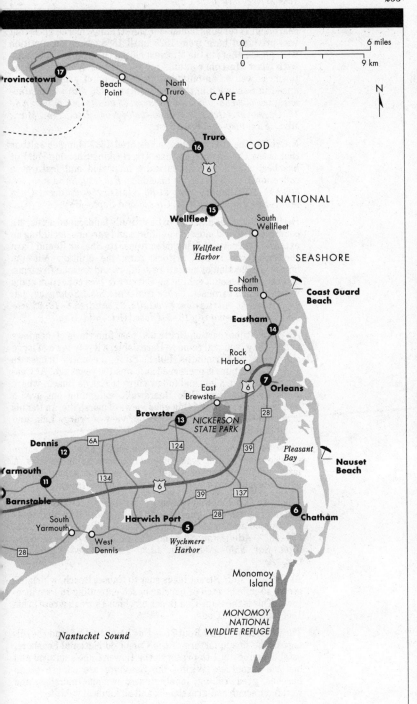

0   6 miles
0   9 km

N

Provincetown **17**
Beach Point
North Truro
CAPE

Truro **16**
6

COD

NATIONAL

Wellfleet **15**
South Wellfleet

Wellfleet Harbor

SEASHORE

North Eastham
Coast Guard Beach

Eastham **14**

Rock Harbor
East Brewster
6   Orleans **7**

Brewster **13**   *NICKERSON STATE PARK*
28

Dennis **12**
6A
124
39
Pleasant Bay
Nauset Beach

Yarmouth **11**
134
39
137

Barnstable
6
28

South Yarmouth
West Dennis
Harwich Port **5**
28
Chatham **6**

28
Wychmere Harbor

Monomoy Island

Nantucket Sound

MONOMOY NATIONAL WILDLIFE REFUGE

9 **Sandwich** is the oldest town on the Cape and one of the most charming. It remains famous for the striking colored glass that was produced here from 1825 until 1888, when competition with glassmakers in the Midwest closed the factory. The **Sandwich Glass Museum** contains relics of the early history of the town, as well as an outstanding collection of glassware produced in Sandwich in the 19th century. *129 Main St., Sandwich, tel. 508/888–0251. Admission: $3 adults, 50¢ children 6– 12. Open Apr.–Oct., daily 9:30–4:30; Nov., Dec., Feb., Mar., Wed.–Sun. 9:30–4. Closed Jan.*

Nearby is the **Hoxie House,** a restored 1637 shingled saltbox that is the Cape's oldest house. Overlooking Shawme Pond, it has been furnished authentically in period and features a collection of antique textile machines. *Rte. 130, Sandwich, tel. 508/888–1173. Admission: $1.50 adults, 75¢ children. Open Mon.–Sat. 10–5, Sun. 1–5. Closed mid-Sept.–May.*

Heritage Plantation, set on 76 beautifully landscaped acres, is a complex of several museum buildings and gardens, including an extensive collection of rhododendrons. Its Shaker Round Barn showcases classic and historic cars; the Military Museum houses a collection of miniature soldiers and antique firearms; and the art museum exhibits a Currier & Ives collection and a working 1912 carousel. *Grove and Pine Sts., Sandwich, tel. 508/888–3300. Admission: $7 adults, $3 children 6–12, $6 senior citizens. Open daily 10–5. Closed Oct.–mid-May.*

10 As you continue east on Route 6A, past fine views of meadows and the bay, you will come to **Barnstable,** a lovely town of large **11** old homes. In **Yarmouth, Hallet's Store,** a country drugstore and soda fountain, is preserved as it was 100 years ago. At Centre Street, take a left and follow signs to Gray's Beach, where you'll find the **Bass Hole Boardwalk,** extending out over a **12** marshy creek and providing good views of marsh life. In **Dennis** is **Scargo Hill,** offering a spectacular view of Scargo Lake and Cape Cod Bay.

13 **Brewster,** in the early 1800s the terminus of a packet cargo service from Boston, was home to many seafaring families. A large number of mansions built for sea captains remains today, and quite a few have been turned into bed-and-breakfasts.

The **Cape Cod Museum of Natural History** has environmental and marine exhibits, guided field walks, and self-guided trails through 80 acres rich in wildlife. *Rte. 6A, Brewster, tel. 508/ 896–3867. Admission: $2.50 adults, $1.50 children 6–14. Open Mon.–Sat. 9:30–4:30, Sun. 12:30–4:30. Closed Mon. mid-Oct.–Apr.*

At **Orleans,** Main Street leads east to **Nauset Beach,** which begins a 40-mile stretch of barrier beach extending to Provincetown. This is the Cape Cod Beach of which Thoreau wrote in his 1865 classic *Cape Cod.*

14 Three miles north on Route 6 is **Eastham.** Just beyond the village is the headquarters of the **Cape Cod National Seashore,** established in 1961 to preserve the Lower Cape's natural and historic resources. Within the Seashore are superb ocean beaches; great rolling, lonely dunes; swamps, marshes, and wetlands; scrub and grasslands; and all kinds of wildlife.

The **Salt Pond Visitor Center** in Eastham has displays, literature racks, and an auditorium for nature films. *Off Rte. 6,* *tel. 508/255–3421. Open Mar.–Jan. 1, daily 9–4:30; Jan., weekends 9–4:30; July–Aug., daily 9–6.*

Roads and bicycle trails lead to the **Coast Guard Beach** area and the **Nauset Beach Lighthouse.** During the season, park guides lead daily nature walks and lectures.

Five miles farther on Route 6 is the **Marconi Station,** with a model of the first transatlantic wireless station erected on the U.S. mainland. From here, Guglielmo Marconi sent an early wireless message to Europe on January 18, 1903. *South Wellfleet, tel. 508/349–3785. Open year-round, weekdays 9–4:30; Jan.–Feb., weekends 9–4:30.*

⑮ Wellfleet was once the location of a large oyster industry and, along with Truro to the north, a Colonial whaling and codfishing port. It is one of the more tastefully developed Cape resort towns, with a number of fine restaurants, historic homes, and art galleries.

⑯ Truro is popular with artists and writers. The most prominent painter to have lived here was Edward Hopper, who found the Cape light ideal for his austere brand of realism. About 4 miles up Route 6, follow signs to the **Pilgrim Heights Area.** The early history of the region—which the *Mayflower* explored for weeks before settling in Plymouth—is shown in displays at the shelter. A walking trail leads to the spring where the Pilgrims stopped to refill their casks.

Continue on Route 6 to reach the National Seashore's **Province Lands Area.** This area comprises Race Point and Herring Cove beaches; bike, horse, and nature trails; and a picnic area. *Visitor Center, tel. 508/487–1256. Open Apr.–Nov., daily 9–4:30; July–Aug., daily 9–6.*

⑰ Provincetown, called P-town locally, offers spectacular beaches and dunes, as well as first-rate shops and galleries. Portuguese and American fishermen mix with painters, poets, writers, whale-watchers from Boston or the Midwest, and, in high season, flamboyant gays and cross-dressers from everywhere. During the early 1900s Provincetown became known as Greenwich Village North, and long before the 1960s, local bohemians were shocking the more staid members of Provincetown society. Inexpensive summer lodgings close to the beaches attracted young rebels and artists, including John Reed, Mabel Dodge, Sinclair Lewis, and Eugene O'Neill. Some of O'Neill's early plays were presented first in Provincetown.

The Historical Society puts out a series of walking-tour pamphlets, available for less than $1 each at many shops in town, with maps and information on the history of many buildings and the famous folk who have occupied them.

Provincetown's main tourist attraction is the **Pilgrim Monument,** on a hill above the town center, commemorating the landing of the Pilgrims in 1620. From atop the 252-foot-high granite tower there's a panoramic view of the entire Cape. At the base a historical museum has a diorama of the *Mayflower* and exhibits on whaling, shipwrecks, scrimshaw, and more. A three-year exhibit of artifacts recovered from the early 1700s shipwreck of the *Whydah* opened in the spring of 1991; an extra charge applies to this exhibit. *Tel. 508/487–1310. Admission: $3 adults, $1 children. Open July–Sept., daily 9–9; Oct.–June, daily 9–4.*

Upon leaving the Cape, you may want to continue on up to Boston, where you can pick up Tour 1, Boston to Bar Harbor. Route 6 will return you to the Cape Cod Canal, from where you can drive north to Boston on either I–495 or the more leisurely Route 3 along the South Shore.

Shopping

Shopping Districts **Provincetown** has a long history as an art colony and remains an important art center, with many fine galleries and exhibitions of Cape and non-Cape artists. Write for a free "Provincetown Gallery Guide" (Provincetown Gallery Guild, Box 242, Provincetown 02657).

Wellfleet has emerged as a vibrant center for art and crafts as well, without Provincetown's crowds. Write for a free walking map of Wellfleet's art galleries and restaurants (Wellfleet Art Galleries Assn., Box 916, Wellfleet 02667).

Hyannis's Main Street—the Cape's largest—is lined with book shops, gift shops, jewelers, clothing stores, summer wear and T-shirt shops, and ice-cream and candy stores, plus minigolf courses and fun eating places. The orientation is youthful, but everyone enjoys watching the summer parade.

Chatham's Main Street is a pretty shopping area, with generally more upscale and conservative merchandise than Hyannis offers. Here you'll find galleries, crafts and clothing stores, and a few good antiques shops.

Falmouth and **Orleans** also have a large number of shops.

Shopping Malls **Cape Cod Mall** (Rtes. 132 & 28, Hyannis, tel. 508/771–0200), the Cape's largest, is where everyone congregates on rainy days. Its 90 shops include Jordan Marsh, Filene's, Woolworth, three restaurants, and many food shops.

Falmouth Mall (Rte. 28, Falmouth, tel. 508/540–8329) has Bradlees, T. J. Maxx, and 30 other shops.

Outlet Stores Fall River is a haven for those who enjoy the bargain hunt of outlet stores. More than 100 small outlets are housed in several old mills in the district north of downtown. Most are listed in a brochure available from the **Fall River Factory Outlet District Association** (Box 2877, 02722, tel. 508/678–6033).

Cape Cod Factory Outlet Mall (Factory Outlet Rd., Exit 1 off Rte. 6, Sagamore, tel. 508/888–8417) has more than 30 outlets.

Flea Market **The Wellfleet Drive-In Theatre** (Rte. 6, Eastham-Wellfleet line, tel. 508/349–2520) is the site of a giant flea market (mid-Apr.–fall, 8–4 weekends and Mon. holidays; July–Aug., also Wed. and Thurs.). There's a snack bar and playground.

Pick-your-own Farm **Tony Andrews Farm and Produce Stand** (398 Old Meeting House Rd., East Falmouth, tel. 508/548–5257) lets you pick your own strawberries (mornings from mid-June), as well as peas, beans, and tomatoes (late June–late Aug.).

Specialty Stores **Carriage House Antiques** (3425 Rte. 6A, Brewster, tel. 508/
Antiques 896–6570) has museum-quality 18th- and 19th-century marine antiques and American furniture, country pine, pottery, china, botanical prints, paintings, antique toy soldiers, and guns.

Eldred's (Rte. 6A, Box 796, East Dennis 02641, tel. 508/385–3116) has year-round auctions featuring such top-quality antiques as marine art; Oriental, American, and European art; Americana; and estate jewelry.

Eldred Wheeler (866 Main St., Box 90, Osterville 02655, tel. 508/428–9049 or 508/428–7093) is well known for handcrafting fine 18th-century furniture reproductions.

H. Richard Strand (Town Hall Sq., Sandwich, tel. 508/888–3230), in an 1800 home, displays an eclectic collection of very fine pre-1840 and Victorian antique furniture, paintings, American glass, and more.

Kingsland Manor (Rte. 6A, West Brewster, tel. 508/385–9741) is like a fairyland, with ivy covering the facade, fountains in the courtyard, and everything "from tin to Tiffany" from end to end.

Remembrances of Things Past (376 Commercial St., Province-town, tel. 508/487–9443) deals in jewelry, photographs, neon, and other articles from the 1920s to the 1960s.

Art **Blue Heron Gallery** (Bank St., Wellfleet, tel. 508/349–6724) is one of the Cape's best, with representational contemporary art by regional and nationally recognized artists.

Cummaquid Fine Arts (4275 Rte. 6A, Cummaquid, tel. 508/362–2593) has works by Cape Cod and New England artists, plus decorative antiques, beautifully displayed in an old home.

Hearle Gallery (488 Main St., Chatham, tel. 508/945–2406) offers fine original oil, watercolor, and acrylic East Coast representational art.

Long Point Gallery (492 Commercial St., Provincetown, tel. 508/487–1795) is a collective of several well-established artists, including Robert Motherwell.

Crafts **The Blacks Handweaving Shop** (597 Rte. 6A, West Barnstable, tel. 508/362–3955), in a barn-like building with the looms upstairs, makes and sells beautiful shawls, scarfs, throws, and more in traditional and jacquard weaves.

Scargo Pottery (off Rte 6A, Dennis, tel. 508/385–3894) has been a Cape favorite since 1953. The setting is a pine forest, where the potter Harry Holl's unusual wares—such as his signature castle birdfeeders—are displayed on tree stumps and hanging from branches. More pottery and the workshop and kiln are indoors.

The Spectrum (Rte. 6A, Brewster, tel. 508/385–3322; 342 Main St., Hyannis, tel. 508/771–4554) showcases imaginative American arts and crafts, including pottery, jewelry, stained glass, art glass, and more. **Sydenstricker Galleries** (Rte. 6A, Brewster, tel. 508/385–3272) features glassware handcrafted by a unique process, which you can watch in progress at the studio on the premises.

Tree's Place (Rte. 6A at Rte. 28, Orleans, tel. 508/255–1330), one of the Cape's most original shops, has handcrafted kaleidoscopes, art glass, hand-painted porcelain and pottery, hand-blown stemware, wood boxes, Russian lacquer boxes, imported tiles, and jewelry.

Jewelry **September Morn** (385 Commerical St., Provincetown, tel. 508/487–9092) sells fine estate jewelry, plus art glass and antique Oriental art.

Sports and Outdoor Activities

Biking Bicycling is a very satisfying way of getting around the Cape, for the terrain is fairly flat and there are several bike trails.

Rentals are available at **All Cape Sales** (mopeds also; 627 Main St., West Yarmouth, tel. 508/771–8100), **Arnolds** (329 Commercial St., Provincetown, tel. 508/487–0844), **Bill's Bike Shop** (847 E. Main St., Falmouth, tel. 508/548–7979), **Cascade Motor Lodge** (201 Main St., Hyannis, tel. 508/775–9717), **P&M Cycles** (29 Main St., Buzzards Bay, tel. 508/759–2830), **Rail Trail Bike Rentals** (302 Underpass Rd., Brewster, tel. 508/896–2361), and **The Little Capistrano** (across from Salt Pond Visitor Center, Eastham, tel. 508/255–6515).

Cape Cod Rail Trail, the paved right-of-way of the old Penn Central Railroad, is the Cape's premier bike path. Running 20 miles, from Dennis to Eastham, it passes salt marshes, cranberry bogs, and ponds, and cuts through Nickerson State Park. The terrain is easy to moderate. The Butterworth Company (476 Main St., Harwich Port 02646, tel. 508/432–8200) sells a guide to the trail for $2.50.

On either side of the **Cape Cod Canal** is an easy 7-mile straight trail, offering a view of the bridges and canal traffic.

The **Shining Sea Bikeway** is a nice-and-easy 5-mile coastal route between Locust Street, Falmouth, and the Woods Hole ferry parking lot.

The Cape Cod National Seashore maintains three bicycle trails. (A brochure with maps is available at visitor centers.) **Nauset Trail** is 1.6 miles, from Salt Pond Visitor Center in Eastham to Coast Guard Beach. **Head of the Meadow Trail** is 2 miles of easy cycling between sand dunes and salt marshes from High Head Road, off Route 6A in North Truro, to the Head of the Meadow Beach parking lot. **Province Lands Trail** is a 5¼-mile loop off the Beech Forest parking lot on Race Point Road in Provincetown, with spurs to Herring Cove, Race Point, and Bennett Pond.

Camping There are many private campgrounds throughout the Cape, except within the National Seashore, where camping is not permitted. **Nickerson State Park** is a favorite tenting spot for its setting and wildlife. **Shawme Crowell State Forest** has tent, trailer, and motor home sites on 1,200 acres (*see* National and State Parks, *below*).

Fishing Charter boats and party boats (per-head fees, rather than charters' group rates) take you offshore for tuna, mako and blue sharks, swordfish, and marlin. There are also hundreds of freshwater ponds, including Mare's Pond in Falmouth and Mashpee-Wakeby Pond in Mashpee. A license is needed for freshwater fishing and is available at tackle shops, such as **Eastman's Sport & Tackle** (145 Main St., Falmouth, tel. 508/548–6900) and **Truman's** (Rte. 28 in West Yarmouth, tel. 508/771–3470), which rent gear.

Rental boats (and usually gear) are available from **Flyer's** (131A Commercial St., Provincetown, tel. 508/487–0898) and **Cape Cod Boats** (power and sail boats and canoes; Rte. 28 at Bass River Bridge, West Dennis, tel. 508/394–9268).

Deep-sea fishing trips are operated on a walk-on basis by **Hy-Line** (Ocean St. Dock, Hyannis, tel. 508/778–2600); **Cap'n Bill**

& **Cee Jay** (MacMillan Pier, Provincetown, tel. 508/487–4330 or 2353); and **Patriot Party Boats, Inc.** (Falmouth Harbor, tel. 508/ 548–2826), which also offers sailing and sightseeing excursions.

Golf The Cape's mild climate makes golf possible year-round on most of its 20 public courses, though January and February do get nippy. **Ocean Edge Golf Course** (1 Villagers Rd., Rte. 6A, Brewster, tel. 508/896–5911) is the top championship course, 18 holes. The semiprivate **Country Club of New Seabury** (Great Neck Rd., Mashpee, tel. 508/477–9110) has 36 excellent holes.

Other fine courses: **Captain's Course** (1000 Freeman's Way, Brewster, tel. 508/896–5100), 18 holes; **Cranberry Valley Golf Course** (Oak St., Harwich, tel. 508/430–7560), 18 holes; and **Chatham Bars Inn** (Chatham, tel. 508/945–0096), 9 holes—a good beginner's course.

Horseback Riding **Nelson's Riding Stable** (Race Point Rd., Provincetown, tel. 508/ 487–0034) is located by the **Province Lands Horse Trails,** three two-hour trails to the beaches through or past dunes, cranberries, forests, and ponds. Other stables: **Deer Meadow Riding Stables** (rides through conservation land; Rte. 137, East Harwich, tel. 508/432–6580), **Provincetown Horse and Carriage** (dune and beach rides; tel. 508/487–1112), and **Haland Stables** (Rte. 28A, West Falmouth, tel. 508/540–2552).

Nature Tours From June to mid-December, the **Massachusetts Audubon Society** (contact Wellfleet Bay Wildlife Sanctuary, Box 236, South Wellfleet 02663, tel. 508/349–2615) sponsors year-round, naturalist-led wildlife tours of Nauset Marsh and half- or full-day tours to Monomoy Island, plus canoe trips, bird and insect walks, hikes, and more.

Sailing and Water Sports **Arey's Pond Boat Yard** (off Rte. 28, Orleans, tel. 508/255–0994) has a sailing school with individual and class lessons. **Flyer's** in Provincetown (*see* Fishing, *above*) rents sailboats, sailboards, Sunfish, outboards, and rowboats, and teaches sailing. **Cape Watersports** (tel. 508/432–7079) has locations on several beaches for sailboat and sailboard rentals and lessons.

Tennis **Bissell's Tennis Courts** (Bradford St. at Herring Cove Beach Rd. near the Provincetown Inn, tel. 508/487–9512) has five clay courts and offers lessons. **Mid-Cape Racquet Club** (193 White's Path, South Yarmouth, tel. 508/394–3511) has one outdoor and nine indoor tennis courts, two racquetball, and two squash; plus whirlpool, steam, and sauna. **Manning's Tennis** (292 Rte. 28, West Harwich, tel. 508/432–3958) has four championship all-weather courts in a pine grove, and gives lessons. High schools and towns have public courts.

Whale-watching Provincetown is the main center on the Cape for whale-watching. Several operators offer 3- to 4-hour whale-watch tours from April through October, with morning, afternoon, or sunset sailings. Tickets are available at booths on MacMillan Wharf.

Dolphin Fleet tours are accompanied by scientists who provide commentary while collecting data on the whale population they've been monitoring for years. *Tel. 508/255–3857 or 800/ 826–9300 in MA. Open 7 AM–9 PM, 9 AM–1 PM in winter.*

Out of Barnstable Harbor, there's **Hyannis Whale Watcher Cruises,** offering a fully narrated cruise on Cape Cod Bay as well as a food and beverage service. Charters are available. *Tel. 508/775–1622 or 508/362–6088. Open 7 AM–9 PM; tours Apr.– Nov.*

Beaches

Beaches fronting on Cape Cod Bay generally have cold water, carried down from Maine and Canada, and gentle waves. Southside beaches, on Nantucket Sound, have rolling surf and are warmer, because of the Gulf Stream. Open-ocean beaches on the Cape Cod National Seashore have serious surf. Parking lots fill up by 10 AM or so. Those beaches not restricted to residents charge (sometimes hefty) parking-lot fees; for weekly or seasonal passes, contact the local town hall.

All of the Atlantic Ocean beaches on the National Seashore are superior—wide, long, sandy, dune-backed, with great views. They're also contiguous: you can walk from Eastham to Provincetown almost without leaving sand. All have lifeguards and rest rooms; none has food.

Craigville Beach, a long, wide strip of beach near Hyannis, is extremely popular, especially with the roving and volleyball-playing young (hence the nickname "Muscle Beach"). It has lifeguards and a bathhouse, and food shops across the road.

Old Silver Beach in North Falmouth is especially good for small children because a sandbar keeps it shallow at one end and makes tidal pools with crabs and minnows. There are rest rooms, a snack bar, and showers.

Sandy Neck Beach (tel. 508/362–8300) in West Barnstable, a 6-mile barrier beach between the bay and marshland, is one of the Cape's most beautiful with a wide swath of pebbly sand backed by grassy dunes extending forever in both directions.

National and State Parks

Cape Cod National Seashore (*see* Exploring Cape Cod, *above*).

Nickerson State Park (Rte. 6A, Box 787, Brewster 02631, tel. 508/896–3491; map available on-site) has more than 1,700 acres of forest with five freshwater kettle ponds; four are stocked year-round with trout for fishing. Other recreational options are biking, canoeing, sailing, motorboating, bird-watching, and ice-fishing, skating, and cross-country skiing in winter.

Scusset Beach Reservation, attracting primarily RV campers, consists of 450 acres near the canal, with a beach on the bay. Its pier is a popular fishing spot; other activities include biking, hiking, picnicking, and swimming. *Box 1292, Buzzard's Bay 02532, tel. 508/888–0859. Rates: $16 per night with electric hookup; $12 without. No reservations.*

Shawme Crowell State Forest (Rte. 130, Sandwich, tel. 508/888–0351) is 742 acres near the canal. Activities include camping, biking, hiking, and horseback riding.

Dining

Hearty New England cooking—meat-and-potatoes fare—is the overwhelming cuisine of choice on the Cape, along with the ubiquitous New England clam chowder and fresh fish and seafood. Extraordinary gourmet restaurants can be found, along with occasional ethnic specialties, such as the Portuguese kale soup or linguica. In the off season many Cape restaurants advertise early-bird specials (reduced prices in the early evening), and Sunday brunch often has musical accompaniment.

Fried clams appear on many menus on Cape Cod, where clam chowder is another specialty. Eating seafood "in the rough" (from paper plates in shacklike wooden buildings dominated by deep-fryers) is a revered local custom.

Brewster has become a focus on the Cape for gourmet restaurants.

The following dining price categories have been used: *Very Expensive*, over $40; *Expensive*, $25–$40; *Moderate*, $12–$25; *Inexpensive*, under $12.

Upper Cape **Amigo's.** This busy restaurant, its rough barn-board and plaster walls brightened with Mexican art and Tiffany lamps, serves good traditional Mexican fare as well as "gringo food" and such nightly specials as Cajun or blackened fish. *Tataket Sq., Rte. 28, Falmouth, tel. 508/548–8510. Reservations required for 6 or more. Dress: casual. MC, V. Moderate.*

★ **The Bridge.** The several small dining rooms have recessed lighting, art on the walls, and linen tablecloths. The Yankee pot roast is the star of the eclectic menu, which also features *bijoux de la mer* (lobster, scallops, and shrimp with lemon and tarragon on spinach pasta with a smoky mushroom-cream sauce). *Rte. 6A, Sagamore, tel. 508/888–8144. Weekend reservations advised in season. Dress: casual. MC, V. Moderate.*

Coonamessett Inn. Built in 1796, this elegant inn has lots of old-fashioned charm. The theme of the main dining room is the paintings by Ralph Cahoon; his signature hot-air balloons recreated in copper and enamel add a touch of whimsy to an otherwise subdued and romantic room. The regional American menu focuses on fresh fish and seafood, such as lobster pie—crunchy chunks baked with a light breading and cream, butter, and sherry. *Jones Rd., Falmouth, tel. 508/548–2300. Reservations advised. Dress: neat but casual. AE, DC, MC, V. Closed Mon. Jan.–Mar. Moderate.*

★ **Dan'l Webster Inn.** The Colonial New England patina of this inn belies its construction in 1971. The glassed-in conservatory features luxuriant greenery; the main dining room has a traditional Colonial look. The mostly regional American menu emphasizes seafood, such as lobster meat sautéed with chanterelle mushrooms in Fontina sauce on pasta. Hearty and elegant breakfasts and Sunday brunches are served. *149 Main St., Sandwich, tel. 508/888–3622. Reservations advised. Dress: neat but casual. AE, MC, V. Moderate.*

The Flume. This clean, plain fish house, decorated only with a few Native American artifacts and crafts (the owner is a Wampanoag chief), offers a small menu of straightforward food guaranteed to satisfy. The chowder is outstanding, perhaps the Cape's best. Other specialties are fried smelts, fried clams, Indian pudding, and in summer, fresh broiled fish. *Lake Ave. (Rte. 130), Mashpee, tel. 508/477–1456. Reservations advised weekends. Dress: casual. MC, V. June–Aug. closed Tues.; Sept.–May closed Mon., Tues., weekday lunch. Closed Thanksgiving–Jan. 1. Moderate.*

Mid-Cape
★ **Anthony's Cummaquid Inn.** The main dining room is spacious and genteel, with huge windows that reveal a water view of great beauty. Complemented by an impressive wine list, the traditional New England menu features an exceptional roast beef *au jus* and a baked fillet of sole rolled and stuffed with bread crumbs and lobster and topped with Newburg sauce. *Rte. 6A, Yarmouth Port, tel. 508/362–4501. Reservations advised. Jacket advised. AE, MC, V. No lunch. Expensive–Very Expensive.*

Cranberry Moose. Past the landscaped courtyard of this 18th-century cottage is a series of attractive dining rooms in different styles, accented with large floral displays. The new American cuisine emphasizes a clean taste, with light use of cream and butter, as in medallions of duck breast on a bed of wild mushrooms with blackberry sauce. The wine list features more than 125 choices. *43 Main St., Yarmouth Port, tel. 508/362–3501. Reservations advised. Jacket advised at dinner. AE, DC, MC, V. Closed Mon.–Tues. Jan.–Mar. Moderate–Expensive.*

Il Maestro. Behind the brick-and-glass front is regional Italian cuisine as good as you'll find on the Cape. The specialty of the house is veal, such as *braciolettine*—rolled veal stuffed with prosciutto and imported cheeses, sautéed in lemon and wine, and topped with mushroom Marsala sauce. The interior is spare, with dark green walls and paintings of Tuscan villas. *1870 W. Main St., Hyannis, tel. 508/775–1168. Reservations required. Dress: casual. AE, MC, V. No lunch. Moderate–Expensive.*

★ **The Paddock.** Long the benchmark of consistent quality dining, this formal restaurant is decorated in Victorian style—from the dark, clubby bar to the airy summer-porch area filled with green wicker and potted plants. The main dining room blends dark beams, frosted-glass dividers, sporting art, and banquettes. The wine list is extensive. The Continental-American menu emphasizes seafood and beef. Steak *au poivre* is popular. *W. Main St. Rotary (next to Melody Tent), Hyannis, tel. 508/775–7677. Reservations advised. Jacket advised. AE, DC, MC, V. Closed mid-Nov.–Apr. Moderate–Expensive.*

★ **Red Pheasant Inn.** The main dining room is pleasantly intimate and rustic, with stripped pine floors, exposed beams, and two fireplaces. The cuisine is American regional, with a French twist in the sauces. The large menu always features lamb, plus seafood and sweetbreads, duck, venison, or pheasant. *905 Main St. (Rte. 6A), Dennis, tel. 508/385–2133. Reservations advised. Dress: jacket optional. AE, MC, V. No lunch. Moderate–Expensive.*

Inaho. A welcome addition to the ethnic diversity of restaurants on the Cape is this little storefront place done up with such authentic details as screens and a sushi bar. Traditional Japanese fare, such as tempura, teriyaki, and *shabu-shabu*—beef cooked at table in hot broth—is served. *569 Main St., Hyannis Oaks Village, Hyannis, tel. 508/771–9255. Reservations accepted. Dress: casual. MC, V. No lunch. Moderate.*

★ **Up the Creek.** This casual spot with a busy hum about it serves fine food at very good prices. House specialties include seafood strudel—two pastries filled with lobster, shrimp, crab, cheese—and baked stuffed lobster. *36 Old Colony Rd., Hyannis, tel. 508/771–7866. Reservations advised. Dress: casual. AE, DC, MC, V. Moderate.*

★ **The Regatta of Cotuit.** A sister restaurant to the Regatta in Falmouth, the Cotuit Regatta is set in a restored 18th-century home. Its intimate dining rooms—dressed in Venetian mirrors, Chippendale furniture, Oriental carpeting—are romantically lighted. A specialty of the Continental and American menu is grilled foods, as well as pâtés of rabbit, veal, or venison. Boneless sliced rack of lamb with Cabernet sauce is outstanding. *Rte. 28, Cotuit, tel. 508/428–5715. Reservations advised. Dress: neat but casual. MC, V. No lunch. Closed Mon.–Wed. Jan.–Mar. Moderate.*

Three Thirty One Main. Also called Penguins Go Pasta—note the penguins in the bar—this sophisticated Northern Italian restaurant focuses on seafood and homemade pastas. A signature dish is the veal chops Pasetto, stuffed with prosciutto and Fontina, lightly breaded, pan-fried, and served with a sauce of shallots, capers, prosciutto, and fresh tomatoes. On the walls, mirrors alternate with warm wood paneling and exposed brick. *331 Main St., Hyannis, tel. 508/775–2023. Reservations advised. Dress: neat but casual. AE, DC, MC, V. No lunch. Moderate.*

★ **Fiddlebee's.** At this casual eating place, three levels of dining areas are arranged around a central well that, on the first floor, opens on a dance floor that's well patronized at night. The preparation is rather uneven, but the menu does have something for everyone: blackened chicken breast, Rio Grande Tex-Mex chili (a special), quiche, and basic burgers. *North St., Hyannis, tel. 508/771–6032. No reservations. Dress: casual. AE, MC, V. Inexpensive.*

Baxter's Fish N' Chips. On busy Lewis Bay, Baxter's gets a lot of back-in boaters at its picnic tables for possibly the best fried clams on the Cape, as well as other fried, baked, and broiled fresh fish and seafood (plus burgers, chicken, and Cajun steak). *Pleasant St., Hyannis, tel. 508/775–4490. No reservations. Dress: casual. No credit cards. Closed Mon.; Oct.–Apr. Inexpensive.*

Lower Cape **Chillingsworth.** The Cape's best restaurant, this elegant spot,
★ decorated in Louis XV furnishings, offers award-winning French and nouvelle cuisine and an outstanding wine cellar. The frequently changing dinner menu is a five-course prix-fixe and features such entrées as venison with celery root purée and fried pumpkin; or sweetbreads and foie gras with wild mushrooms and ham, asparagus, and smoky sauce. *Rte. 6A, Brewster, tel. 508/896–3640. Reservations required at dinner (seatings), advised at lunch. Jacket and tie required at dinner. AE, MC, V. Closed Mon. Memorial Day–Nov.; Mon.–Thurs. off-season. Very Expensive.*

High Brewster. A romantic country inn overlooking a pond, this restored sea captain's house offers seasonal four-course prix-fixe menus; a fall menu might include pumpkin-and-sage bisque and tenderloin medallions with chives and cheese glaze. In winter à-la-carte ordering is possible from the American regional menu. *964 Satucket Rd., Brewster, tel. 508/896–3636. Reservations required. Dress: neat but casual. MC, V. No lunch. Often closed Mon.–Wed. mid-Sept.–mid-June. Expensive.*

★ **Ciro and Sal's.** After 30 years, this stage-set Italian restaurant—raffia-covered Chianti bottles hanging from the rafters, walls of plaster and brick, strains of Italian opera in the air—plays out its role with the confidence of years on the boards. Scampi alla Griglia is grilled shrimp in lemon, parsley, garlic, butter, leeks, and shallots; veal and pasta dishes are specialties. *4 Kiley Court, Provincetown, tel. 508/487–0049. Reservations required summer, Sat. nights. Dress: casual. MC, V. Closed Mon.–Thurs. Christmas–Memorial Day. Moderate–Expensive.*

Captain Linnell House. Framed by huge trees, this neoclassical structure looks like an antebellum mansion. Inside are small dining rooms: one with a Normandy fireplace, exposed beams, and white plaster; another with a pecan-paneled fireplace, oil lamps, Aubusson rug, and rosette ceiling. Wild mushroom sauté is a striking dish with wine, butter, carrots, celery, and tomato topped with watercress, croutons, and puff pastry. *137 Skaket Beach Rd., Orleans, tel. 508/255–3400. Reservations required in season. Dress: casual. MC, V. No lunch. Moderate.*

Land Ho. Walk in, grab a newspaper from the lending rack, take a seat, and relax—for 20 years Land Ho has been making sure folks feel right at home. This casual spot serves kale soup that has been noted by *Gourmet* magazine, plus burgers, hearty sandwiches, grilled fish in summer, and very good chicken wings, chowder, and fish-and-chips. *Rte. 6A, Orleans, tel. 508/255–5165. No reservations. Dress: casual. MC, V. Inexpensive.*

Lodging

In summer lodgings should be booked as far in advance as possible—several months for the most popular cottages and bed-and-breakfasts. Assistance with last-minute reservations is available at the **Cape Cod Chamber of Commerce information booths** at Bourne, Sagamore, and West Barnstable. Off-season rates are much reduced, and service may be more personalized.

B&B reservations services include **House Guests Cape Cod** (Box 1881, Orleans 02653, tel. 800/666–4678) and **Bed and Breakfast Cape Cod** (Box 341, West Hyannis Port 02672, tel. 508/775–2772). **Provincetown Reservations System** (tel. 508/487–2400 or 800/648–0364) makes reservations year-round for accommodations, shows, restaurants, transportation, and more.

The following lodging price categories have been used: *Very Expensive*, over $150; *Expensive*, $95–$150; *Moderate*, $70–$95; *Inexpensive*, under $70.

Upper Cape
★ **Coonamessett Inn.** This classic inn provides fine dining and gracious accommodations in a tranquil country setting. One- or two-bedroom suites are located in five buildings arranged around a landscaped lawn that spills down to a scenic wooded pond. Rooms are casually decorated, with bleached wood or pine paneling, New England antiques or reproductions, upholstered chairs, couches, color TV, and phones. *Jones Rd. and Gifford St., Box 707, Falmouth 02541, tel. 508/548–2300. 24 suites, 1 cottage. Facilities: 2 restaurants, clothing shop. AE, DC, MC, V. Expensive.*

★ **Mostly Hall.** Set in a landscaped, park-like yard far back from the street, this 1849 house is imposing, with a wraparound porch and a dramatic cupola. Accommodations are in large corner rooms, with large shuttered windows giving leafy views, reading areas, antique pieces and reproduction canopied queen beds, pretty floral wallpapers, and Oriental accent rugs. A full breakfast is served on the porch or in the beautifully furnished parlor. *27 Main St., Falmouth 02540, tel. 508/548–3786. 6 rooms. Facilities: bicycles, central phone and TV, lending library, lawn games. No smoking. No credit cards. Closed Jan.–mid-Feb. Rates include full breakfast. Moderate– Expensive.*

The Village Inn At Sandwich. Recently renovated, this grand Federal-style home built in the 1830s is filled with beautiful furniture designed and hand-crafted by the owner. Rooms are tastefully decorated with elegant wallpaper, down comforters, and ceiling fans. Rocking chairs on the wraparound porch offer pleasant views of the neighborhood. *Box 951, 4 Jarves St., Sandwich 02563, tel. 508/833–0363 or 800/922–9989. 6 rooms. Facilities: Complimentary breakfast. No smoking. AE, MC, V. Closed Jan.–Mar. Moderate–Expensive.*

Earl of Sandwich Motor Manor. Single-story Tudor-style buildings form a U around a wooded lawn, with areas for croquet and horseshoes. The newer buildings (1981–1983) have air-conditioning, unlike the main building (1963). The rooms are comfortable—warmly paneled walls, exposed beams on white ceilings, olive leatherette wing chairs, Oriental throw rugs on slate or carpeted floors—and a good size, with large Tudor-style windows, small tiled baths, and telephones. *378 Rte. 6A, East Sandwich 02537, tel. 508/888–1415. 24 rooms. Facilities: complimentary Continental breakfast, minirefrigerators. AE, MC, V. Inexpensive–Moderate.*

Mid-Cape

★ **Ashley Manor.** Offering a relaxed and homey atmosphere, this charming country inn dates back to 1699. Large, well-appointed rooms have private baths, working fireplaces, and pencil-post or canopy beds; the Garden Cottage has an efficiency kitchen. The sitting room offers a large fireplace, piano, antiques, Oriental rugs, handsome country furniture, and a view of the brick terrace and gardens. A full breakfast is served in the elegant dining room or on the terrace. *Box 856, 3660 Olde Kings Hwy., Barnstable 02630, tel. 508/362–8044. 5 rooms, 1 cottage. Facilities: tennis court, complimentary beverages and snacks, central phone. AE, MC, V. Expensive–Very Expensive.*

★ **The Inn at Fernbrook.** This exquisite Victorian home offers the refined elegance of an earlier era, and the serenity and ambience for which the Cape is famous. Its bright and spacious rooms have beautiful antiques, hardwood floors, Oriental carpets, sheer curtains, and softly printed wallpaper. Each room is quiet and unique; no two share the same wall. Most rooms have private baths and some have working fireplaces. The Marstons Room and the Cardinal Suite overlook the lovely Sweetheart Rose Garden, designed by Frederick Law Olmsted—designer of the Boston Public Garden and New York's Central Park. The gourmet full breakfast, including fresh squeezed juice and homemade breads, is served in the formal dining room. *481 Main St., Centerville 02632, tel. 508/775–4334. 6 rooms, 1 cottage. Facilities: porch, complimentary tea, espresso, or lemonade. AE, MC, V. Expensive–Very Expensive.*

★ **Tara Hyannis Hotel & Resort.** For its central-Cape location, beautiful landscaping, extensive services, and superior resort facilities, it's hard to beat the Tara. The lobby area is elegant, but room decor is a bit dull, with pale colors and standard contemporary hotel-style furnishings. Some rooms have new baths. Rooms overlooking the golf greens or the courtyard garden have the best views. *West End Circle, Hyannis 02601, tel. 508/775-7775 or 800/843-8272. 216 rooms, 8 suites. Facilities: restaurant, lounge, golf course, 2 putting greens, 2 lighted tennis courts, indoor and outdoor pools, health club, roman baths, steam room, sauna, aerobics classes, hair salon, gift shop, business services, room service until midnight. AE, D, DC, MC, V. Expensive–Very Expensive.*

Capt. Gosnold Village. An easy walk to the beach and town, this colony of motel rooms and cottages is ideal for families. Some units have been remodeled with walls painted in light and airy colors, and new kitchens, baths, and furniture. In others, walls are attractively paneled in knotty pine; floors are carpeted; furnishings are Colonial style, simple and pleasant. All units have TVs and heat; most have decks. Motel rooms have fridges and coffee makers. *Gosnold St., Box 544, Hyannis 02601, tel. 508/775-9111. 8 motel rooms, 12 efficiencies. Facilities: outdoor pool, basketball area, game nets, playground equipment, picnic areas, hibachis. AE, MC, V. Closed Nov.–mid-May. Inexpensive–Moderate.*

Lower Cape   **Augustus Snow House.** Luxury is the operative word at this inn, a Princess Anne Victorian with gabled dormers and wraparound veranda. Early evening wine and hot hors d'oeuvres are served in silver and crystal, accompanied by quiet classical music. The rooms are done in Victorian style, with reproduction furnishings and wallpapers and authentic period brass bathroom fixtures. All rooms have phone and TV. *528 Main St., Harwich Port 02646, tel. 508/430-0528. 5 rooms. AE, MC, V. Rates include full breakfast. Very Expensive.*

★ **Chatham Bars Inn.** An oceanfront resort in the old style, this Chatham landmark comprises the main building—with its grand lobby—and 26 one- to eight-bedroom cottages on 80 beautifully landscaped acres. The entire inn has been renovated. Some cottage rooms have working fireplaces. Many rooms have private ocean-view porches; all have phones and TVs, Colonial reproduction furnishings, upholstered armchairs, and wall-to-wall carpeting. Service is attentive and extensive. *Shore Rd., Chatham 02633, tel. 508/945-0096 or 800/527-4884. 152 rooms. Facilities: restaurant, lounge, bar, beach grill, private beach, 5 tennis courts, adjacent 9-hole golf course, heated outdoor pool, shuffleboard court, launch service to North Beach, children's programs (July and Aug.). AE, DC, MC, V. Rates are MAP in season. Very Expensive.*

★ **Captain's House Inn.** Finely preserved architectural details, superb taste in decorating, opulent home-baked goods, and an overall feeling of warmth and quiet comfort are just part of what makes this possibly the finest small inn on Cape Cod. Each room in the three inn buildings has its own personality. Some have fireplaces. The decor is mostly Williamsburg; rooms in the Carriage House have a more spare, modern look. *371 Old Harbor Rd., Chatham 02633, tel. 508/945-0127. 12 rooms, 2 suites. AE, MC, V. Rates include Continental breakfast, afternoon tea. No smoking in public areas. Closed mid-Nov.–mid-Feb. Expensive.*

Hargood House. This apartment complex on the water is a great option for longer stays and families. Most of the individually decorated units have decks and large water-view windows; all have kitchens and modern baths. Apartment 8 is on the water, with three glass walls, cathedral ceilings, and private deck. Rental is mostly by the week in season; nightly available off-season. *493 Commercial St., Provincetown 02657, tel. 508/487–1324. 20 apartments. Facilities: private beach, maid service in season, barbecue grills. AE, MC, V. Expensive.*

Nauset Knoll Motor Lodge. On a low rise overlooking Nauset Beach, two minutes' walk away, this row of adjoining Cape houses offers basic, ground-level motel rooms. Each is sparsely furnished but light and bright, with six-foot picture windows facing the ocean, tile baths, and color TV. Book well in advance. *Nauset Beach, East Orleans 02643, tel. 508/255–2364. 12 rooms. MC, V. Closed late Oct.–mid-Apr. Moderate.*

The Fairbanks Inn. Just one block from Provincetown's busy Commercial Street, this comfortable inn offers cozy rooms filled with delightful antiques, reproduction furnishings, and art. Charming rooms in the 200-year-old main house feature four-poster or canopy beds and Oriental rugs covering wide-plank floors; many have private baths and working fireplaces. The Carriage House rooms are the most modern and the East Wing rooms most plainly decorated. Breakfast is served on the glassed-in garden porch. *90 Bradford St., Provincetown 02675, tel. 508/487–0386. 14 rooms, 7 with bath. Facilities: sun deck, free parking, kitchens in some rooms. AE, MC, V. Inexpensive–Moderate.*

★ **Old Sea Pines Inn.** Fronted by a wraparound veranda overlooking a broad lawn, this inn evokes the feel of a summer estate. Guest rooms are decorated with antiques; many are very large. Some fireplaces are available—one in the best room, with an enclosed sun porch. Rooms in the newer, modern building, although less charming, are bright and cheery and offer new bathrooms and TVs. *2553 Main St. (Rte. 6A), Brewster 02631, tel. 508/896–6114. 19 rooms (5 share baths), 2 suites. Smoking discouraged. AE, DC, MC, V. Rates include full breakfast. Inexpensive–Moderate.*

The Holden Inn. Located in a quiet neighborhood untouched by the Cape's commercialism, this inn is comprised of two of Wellfleet's oldest sea captain's homes, and the Lodge behind them. The 24 cheerful rooms are plainly decorated with wicker, antiques, and sturdy furniture; the prettiest rooms are in the main inn. Rocking chairs on the main porch offer views across the tree-lined street to Wellfleet Bay; expansive Cape Cod Bay can be seen from the porch at the Lodge. *Box 816, Wellfleet 02667, tel. 508/349–3450. 24 rooms. Facilities: central phone. No pets. No credit cards. Closed late-fall–May. Inexpensive.*

The Arts

Theater Summer stock theater is popular throughout the Cape. The top venues are the **Cape Playhouse** (Rte. 6A, Dennis, tel. 508/385–3911), with a nine-week season of Broadway shows often featuring star performers; and the **Falmouth Playhouse** (off Rte. 151, North Falmouth, tel. 508/563–5922; June–early Oct.), offering Broadway shows and children's plays.

The **College Light Opera Company** (Highfield Theatre, Depot Ave. Ext., Falmouth, tel. 508/548–0668) features college music majors performing operetta and musical comedy late June through August.

Wellfleet Harbor Actors Theatre (Wellfleet, tel. 508/349–6835) offers a May-to-October season with more serious fare, from drama to satire.

Music   **Cape Cod Melody Tent** (W. Main St., Hyannis, tel. 508/775–9100; through Ticketron or Teletron, tel. 800/382–8080) presents such top performers as Kenny Rogers and the Glenn Miller Orchestra in theater-in-the-round under a tent, July to Labor Day.

The 90-member **Cape Cod Symphony** (Mattacheese Middle School, West Yarmouth, tel. 508/428–3577) gives regular and children's concerts, with guest artists, October through May.

The **Cape & Islands Chamber Music Festival** (Box 72, Yarmouth Port 02675, tel. 508/778–5277) presents three weeks of top-caliber performances and master classes in August.

Nightlife

Bars and Lounges   **Oliver's** restaurant (Rte. 6A, Yarmouth Port, tel. 508/362–6062) has live guitar music weekends in its lounge. **Guido Murphy's Café** (615 Main St., Hyannis, tel. 508/775–7242) has live music in the summertime, and the **Chatham Squire** (487 Main St., Chatham, tel. 508/945–0942), with four bars and live music on Friday, is a rollicking place drawing a young crowd.

Jazz   The **Asa Bearse House** restaurant (415 Main St., Hyannis, tel. 508/771–4131) has dancing under the stars in a glass-topped atrium, to a jazz quartet, most evenings.

Rock   **Kasbar** (Rte. 28, South Yarmouth, tel. 508/760–1616) is a large nightclub with dancing to mostly DJ music, plus nightly laser light shows. **Sundancer's** (116 Rte. 28, West Dennis, tel. 508/394–1600) offers dancing to some reggae and Motown, mostly DJ. The **Mill Hill Club** (164 Rte. 28, West Yarmouth, tel. 508/775–2580) has more live entertainment and some DJ, plus large-screen videos. **Fiddlebee's** (North St., Hyannis, tel. 508/771–6032) has dancing to live rock, jazz, and blues. **The Laurels**, at the Tara Hyannis Hotel & Resort (West End Circle, Hyannis, tel. 508/775–7775), has dancing to DJs or live music from big band to jazz to rock most nights.

Oldies   **Admiralty Resort** (Rte. 28, Falmouth, tel. 508/548–4240) has dancing to '50s and '60s music in its lounge most nights. **T-Birds** (at Dorsie's, 325 Rte. 28, West Yarmouth, tel. 508/771–5898) is a '50s and '60s dance emporium, with '50s decor and DJ music.

Country and Western   **Bud's Country Lounge** (3 Bearse's Way and Rte. 132, Hyannis, tel. 508/771–2505) has live entertainment most nights; **The Good Times** (Rte. 130, Sandwich, tel. 508/888–6655) and **Sou'wester** (Rte. 28, West Chatham, tel. 508/945–9705) are open on weekends.

Tour 4: Philadelphia and Historic Pennsylvania

Philadelphia calls itself "the Cradle of Liberty," and it has a pretty firm basis for its claim, with Independence Hall, the Liberty Bell, Betsy Ross's house, and sites associated with Benjamin Franklin scattered all around Center City. But Philadelphia, its map covered with ethnic neighborhoods, is more than a living history museum. The city of Benjamin Franklin is also the city of Bill Cosby, Arturo Toscanini and Fabian, Chubby Checker and Rocky Balboa.

Within a relatively short distance from the city are three other historic destinations. At Valley Forge, you can visit the site where General Washington and his troops survived a critical winterlong encampment while the British occupied Philadelphia in 1777–1778. Drive west to Lancaster County to learn about another kind of liberty—freedom from religious intolerance—in the country settled by German and Swiss members of the Mennonite and Amish religious sects, who still practice their traditional way of life there today. Drive an hour or so farther west, and you can tramp around the battleground at Gettysburg, site of one of the bloodiest battles of the Civil War.

All of this territory could be covered in four or five days, although such a cursory visit would neglect one of the chief pleasures of Lancaster County—a leisurely drive around soaking up its atmosphere. Travelers with limited time may choose to end the tour at Lancaster, or to skip the Valley Forge stop. Families traveling with children especially will want to devote at least a week to this itinerary, adding a detour to the amusements centered around Hershey.

Visitor Information

Philadelphia **National Park Service Visitor Center** (3rd and Chestnut Sts., tel. 215/597–8974).

Philadelphia Convention and Visitors Bureau (1515 Market St., Suite 2020, Philadelphia 19102, tel. 215/636–3300).

Philadelphia Visitors Center (16th St. and John F. Kennedy Blvd., tel. 215/636–1666).

Pennsylvania Division of Travel Marketing (453 Forum Bldg., Harrisburg 17120, tel. 717/787–5453 or 800/VISIT–PA).

Valley Forge **Valley Forge Convention and Visitors Bureau** (Box 311, Norristown, PA 19404, tel. 215/278–3558 or 800/441–3549).

Lancaster County **Pennsylvania Dutch Convention & Visitors Bureau** (Greenfield Rd. exit of U.S. 30 E, Dept. 2201, 501 Greenfield Rd., Lancaster 17601, tel. 717/299–8901 or 800/735–2629).

Mennonite Information Center (2209 Millstream Rd., Lancaster 17602, tel. 717/299–0954).

Gettysburg **Gettysburg Travel Council** (35 Carlisle St., 17325, tel. 717/334–6274).

Gettysburg-Adams County Area Chamber of Commerce (30 York St., Gettysburg 17325, tel. 717/334–8151).

Gettysburg Tour Center (778 Baltimore St., 17325, tel. 717/334–6296).

Festivals and Special Events

Jan. 1: Mummer's Parade sees some 30,000 sequined and feathered paraders—members of string bands, "fancies," "brigades," and comics—march north on Broad Street to City Hall.

May: Philadelphia Open House is a two-week period during which selected private homes, gardens, and historic buildings around the city open their doors to the public. Tel. 215/928–1188.

June: Mellon Jazz Festival presents the top names in jazz in a week-long series of concerts in West Fairmount Park, the Academy of Music, and other spots around the city. Tel. 215/893–1999.

June–Aug.: Philadelphia Orchestra's Summer Season holds free concerts Monday, Wednesday, and Thursday evenings at Mann Music Center in West Fairmount Park. Tel. 215/878–7707 or 215/567–0707.

Late June–early July: Gettysburg Civil War Heritage Days commemorates the Battle of Gettysburg with living history encampments, band concerts, and battle re-enactments.

July: Freedom Festival. The city celebrates the nation's birth with several days of parades (including the Mummers), hot-air-balloon races, a drum-and-bugle competition, Independence Day ceremonies at Independence Hall, and the Old City Outdoor Restaurant Festival. Tel. 215/636–1666.

Late Aug.: Philadelphia Folk Festival, America's oldest continuous folk festival, consists of three days of concerts and workshops at Old Pool Farm, Schwenksville. Tel. 215/242–0150.

Oct.: Super Sunday on Benjamin Franklin Parkway is Philadelphia's largest block party with food, entertainment, rides, and games, more than 400 exhibit booths and as many as 250,000 guests. Tel. 215/299–1044.

Mid-Nov.: Remembrance Day, the anniversary of Lincoln's Gettysburg Address, includes a parade and wreath-laying ceremony at Gettysburg National Cemetery.

Dec. 25: Washington Crossing the Delaware reenacts the historic event of Christmas Day 1776 at Washington Crossing. Tel. 215/493–4076.

What to See and Do with Children

Most attractions described below are described more fully in the tour that follows:

A favorite family vacation area, eastern Pennsylvania has enough historic sights to teach youngsters almost all they need to know about America's past. Begin in **Philadelphia** with the Independence Square historic district, then take in the museums along Benjamin Franklin Parkway, notably the hands-on exhibits at the Academy of Natural Sciences, the Franklin Institute Science Museum and Fels Planetarium, and the Please Touch Museum. Also along the parkway, stop by the Free Library, where the city's largest collection of children's books is offered in a made-for-kids setting. Penn's Landing gives kids a chance to climb aboard three very different ships, while the Philadelphia Zoological Gardens displays some 1,600 animals, several of which are housed in a special children's zoo. Younger kids may also enjoy a visit to Smith Playground (33rd and Oxford Sts., East Fairmount Park, tel. 215/765–4325; open Mon.–Sat.), with its swings, slides, pools, and a play mansion. For entertainment, there are performances at the Annenberg Center Theater for Children (37th and Walnut Sts., tel. 215/898–6791) in November, February, April, and May, or puppetry and magic shows at the Philadelphia Marionette Theater (Belmont Mansion Ave., West Fairmount Park, tel. 215/879–1213).

An hour's drive northeast from Philadelphia, **Sesame Place** is an amusement park, based on the popular public-television show, geared to children ages 3–13. *100 Sesame Rd., Langhorne, tel. 215/757–1100. Admission: $15.95 adults, $17.95 children 3–15, $10.95 senior citizens. Open May–mid-Sept., daily; mid-Sept.–mid-Oct., weekends only.*

In **Lancaster County,** glimpses of the Amish way of life make a lasting impression on older children, while even the younger ones get a kick out of the buggy rides at Bird-In-Hand, the various railroad museums around Strasburg, and the hands-on Amish World exhibits at People's Place, in Intercourse. Important people from Lancaster County history are represented at the National Wax Museum (2249 Lincoln Hwy. E, Lancaster, tel. 717/393–3679; admission $4.25 adults, $2.75 children 5–11). Kids may also enjoy the candy- and pretzel-making demonstrations at Lititz. Younger children will feel safe on the relatively tame rides at the Dutch Wonderland amusement park (U.S. 30, east of Lancaster, tel. 717/291–1888; admission $14.50; open Memorial Day–Labor Day, daily; Easter–Memorial Day and Labor Day–Oct. 31, weekends only.

Families should make time for the sidetrip to **Hershey,** home of Hershey's Chocolate World exhibits and Hersheypark amusement park, and near to the extensive caves of Indian Echo Caverns.

After touring the historic Civil War battlefield at **Gettysburg,** kids can bone up on their history at two wax museums—the National Civil War Wax Museum and the Hall of Presidents and First Ladies.

Arriving and Departing

By Plane **Philadelphia International Airport** (tel. 215/492–3181) is located in the southwest part of the city, 8 miles from downtown. It's served by American, Continental, Delta, TWA, Midway, Northwest, United, and USAir, as well as four international carriers: Air Jamaica (tel. 800/523–5585), British Airways (tel. 800/247–9297), Lufthansa (tel. 800/645–3880), and Swissair (tel. 800/221–4750). **Airport Express trains** run between the airport and downtown stations every 30 minutes 6 AM–midnight. The trip takes about 20 minutes and costs $4.75 ($5.75 if you buy your ticket on the train). Taxis to downtown cost about $18 plus tip. More than a dozen limo companies connect with Center City hotels and charge about $10 a head. Among them are **Deluxe Transportation** (tel. 215/463–8787) and **Limelight Limousine** (tel. 215/342–5557).

Harrisburg International Airport (tel. 717/948–3900) is served by American, Continental, Delta, Northwest, United, and USAir airlines.

By Car The main north–south highway through Philadelphia, the Delaware Expressway, is part of I–95, which stretches from Maine to Florida. To reach Center City heading southbound on I–95, take the Vine Street exit. From the east, the New Jersey Turnpike and I–295 access U.S. 30, which enters Philadelphia via the Benjamin Franklin Bridge. The main east–west freeway through the city is the Schuylkill Expressway (I–76).

The Schuylkill Expressway leads directly west from Philadelphia to Valley Forge. Take Exit 25 (Goddard Blvd.), drive on Route 363 to North Gulph Road, and follow signs to Valley Forge National Historical Park. The Schuylkill Expressway connects with the Pennsvylania Turnpike (which becomes I–76) at Valley Forge; take the turnpike west to Exit 22 to reach Pennsylvania Dutch country. To reach Gettysburg, get off the turnpike at the junction with Rte. 15, just south of Harrisburg; Rte. 15 leads about 40 miles south to Gettysburg. An alternative route to Gettysburg is to take Rte. 30 directly west from Lancaster, which is about an hour-and-a-half's drive.

By Train **Amtrak** trains stop at Philadelphia's 30th Street Station (30th and Market Sts., tel. 215/824–1600 or 800/872–7245). At 30th Street Station you can connect with Southeastern Pennsylvania Transportation Authority (SEPTA) commuter trains to two downtown stations—Suburban Station at 16th Street and John F. Kennedy Boulevard (near major hotels), and Market East Station at 10th and Market streets (near the historic district)—and to outlying areas.

Amtrak (tel. 215/824–1600 or 800/872–7245) has regular service from Philadelphia's 30th Street Station to Lancaster (53 McGovern Avenue). There is no service to Valley Forge or Gettysburg.

By Bus **Greyhound/Trailways** (tel. 215/931–4000) stops at the Philadelphia terminal (10th and Filbert Sts., just north of the Market East commuter rail station); at Lancaster's RCS Bus Terminal (22 West Clay St.), and at Gettysburg (45 N. Stratton St.). To reach Valley Forge, take the **SEPTA** (tel. 215/574–7800) no. 125 bus from 16th Street and John F. Kennedy Boulevard for King of Prussia Plaza; on weekdays, it continues on to Valley Forge National Historical Park. On Saturdays, transfer at the plaza to the no. 99 "Royersford" bus, which goes through the park.

NJ Transit (tel. 215/569–3752) stops at the Greyhound/Trailways terminal and offers service between Philadelphia, Atlantic City, and other New Jersey destinations.

Philadelphia

"On the whole I'd rather be in Philadelphia." W. C. Fields may have been joking when he wrote his epitaph, but if he were here today he could make the statement seriously. They no longer roll up the sidewalks at night in Philadelphia. An entertainment boom, a restaurant renaissance, and a cultural revival have helped transform the city.

Philadelphia's compact 2-square-mile downtown (William Penn's original city) is nestled between the Delaware and the Schuylkill rivers. Thanks to Penn's grid system of streets—laid out in 1681—the downtown area is easy to navigate. The traditional heart of the city is Broad and Market streets (Penn's

Center Square), where City Hall now stands. Market Street divides the city north and south; 130 S. 15th Street, for example, is in the second block south of Market. North–south streets are numbered, starting with Front (First) Street, at the Delaware River, and increasing to the west. Broad Street is equivalent to 14th Street. The Benjamin Franklin Parkway breaks the rigid grid pattern by leading out of Center City into Fairmount Park, which straddles the Schuylkill River and the Wissahickon Creek for 10 miles.

Philadelphia is a city of neighborhoods: Shoppers haggle over the price of tomatoes in South Philly's Italian Market; families picnic in the parks of Germantown; street vendors hawk soft pretzels in Logan; and all over town, kids play street games such as stickball, stepball, wireball, and chink. The downtown is comparatively safe during the day, but after dark, exercise caution, especially in areas like Market Street east of Broad Street, 13th Street, and the neighborhoods ringing the downtown.

Getting Around
By Car Parking in center city Philadelphia can be tough. A spot at a parking meter, if you're lucky enough to find one, costs 25¢ per 15 minutes. Parking garages charge up to $1.50 per 15 minutes.

By Subway The Broad Street Subway runs from Fern Rock Station in the northern part of the city to Pattison Avenue and the sports complex in South Philadelphia. The Market–Frankford Line runs across the city from the western suburb of Upper Darby to Frankford in the northeast. Both lines operate 24 hours a day. Base fare is $1.50; transfers cost 40¢ (exact change).

By Trolley With 10 routes, Philadelphia is one of the few U.S. cities that still operate trolleys. Route 23—the longest trolley ride in the nation—passes through some of the best neighborhoods and some of the worst on its 12½-mile, one-hour-plus run between South Philadelphia and Chestnut Hill. Base fare is $1.50; transfers cost 40¢ (exact change).

By Bus Bus routes extend throughout the city and into the suburbs. Base fare is $1.50; transfers cost 40¢ (exact change).

By Commuter Train All trains serve 30th Street Station (30th and Market Sts.), where they connect to Amtrak trains; Suburban Station (16th St. and John F. Kennedy Blvd., across from the Visitors Center); and the new Market East Station (10th and Market Sts.) beneath the Gallery at Market East shopping complex. Fares, which vary according to route and time of travel, range from $2 to $6.25 one way. These trains are your best bet for reaching Germantown, Chestnut Hill, and other suburbs. For information, call 215/574–7800.

By Taxi Cabs cost $2 for the flag throw and then $1.40–$2.30 per mile. They are plentiful during the day downtown—especially along Broad Street and near hotels and train stations. At night and outside Center City, taxis are scarce, so try calling for a cab. The main cab companies are **Yellow Cab** (tel. 215/922–8400), **United Cab** (tel. 215/625–2881), and **Quaker City Cab** (tel. 215/ 728–8000).

Orientation Tours **Gray Line Tours** (tel. 215/569–3666) offers a 5½-hour "Grand Combination" tour of historic and cultural areas, a three-hour Historic Tour, and a 2½-hour Cultural Tour of the Art Museum and Fairmount Park. Call ahead; at press time only group charters were being offered.

Fairmount Park Trolley Bus (tel. 215/636–1666) is planning a daily schedule of tours of the historic and cultural areas as well as the Fairmount Park mansions. You can buy your ticket at the Visitors Center (16th St. and Kennedy Blvd.) and get on and off all day at no additional charge. *Cost: about $14 adults, $6 children.*

ABC Bus and Walking Tours (tel. 215/677–2495) has six tours, including historic Philadelphia, the Italian Market, and Valley Forge. Reservations only.

Boat Tours **Spirit of Philadelphia** (tel. 215/923–1419) is a three-deck ship that leaves Pier 3, Delaware Avenue and Market Street, for lunch and dinner cruises.

R & S Harbor Tours (tel. 215/928–0972) offers hour-long narrated tours of the waterfront aboard a 65-foot sightseeing boat, the *Rainbow*, departing from Penn's Landing at Lombard Street. There is also a two-hour sunset cruise Saturday and Sunday.

A 93-foot Great Lakes steamer, the **Liberty Belle II** (tel. 215/824–0889) offers lunch, dinner, Sunday brunch, and moonlight cruises departing from Penn's Landing.

Walking Tours **Audio Walk and Tour** (tel. 215/925–1234) at the Norman Rockwell Museum, 6th and Sansom streets, rents go-at-your-own-pace tape tours of historic Philadelphia with accompanying map.

Centipede Tours (tel. 215/735–3123) uses guides in Colonial dress to lead groups on candlelit tours from the City Tavern at 2nd and Walnut streets, Thursday–Saturday 6:30 PM, May–October.

Foundation for Architecture Tours (tel. 215/569–3187) focus on architecture, organized either by neighborhood or by themes.

Carriage Rides Numerous horse-drawn carriages wend their way through the narrow streets of the historic area. A half dozen companies give narrated tours lasting anywhere from 15 minutes to an hour; the cost ranges from $10 to $50. Carriages line up on Chestnut and 5th streets near Independence Hall and at Head House Square, 2nd Street between Pine and Lombard streets, or you can reserve a carriage and be picked up anywhere downtown. Operators include **Ben Franklin Carriages** (tel. 215/923–8516), **Philadelphia Carriage Company** (tel. 215/922–6840), **76 Carriage Company** (tel. 215/923–8516), and **Society Hill Carriage Company** (tel. 215/627–6128).

Historic District

Numbers in the margin correspond to points of interest on the Philadelphia map.

❶ Start the tour at the **Visitor Center** (3rd and Chestnut Sts.). Operated by the National Park Service, the center has a large counter staffed by several park rangers who answer questions and distribute maps and brochures on Independence National Historical Park and other sites in the historic area. If you want to visit the Bishop White House and the Todd House (described below), pick up a ticket here for the obligatory free guided tour of the two houses. The main attraction at the visitor center itself is *Promise of Permanency*, a video-computer exhibit that

Academy of Natural
Sciences, **26**
Betsy Ross House, **9**
Bishop White
House, **13**
Carpenter's Hall, **2**
Christ Church Burial
Ground, **11**
Christ Church, **7**
City Hall, **19**
Elfreth's Alley, **8**
Fairmount Park, **31**
Franklin Institute, **27**
Franklin Court, **6**
Free Library of
Philadelphia, **25**
Graff House, **5**
Hill-Physick-Keith
House, **15**
Independence Hall, **3**
John Wanamaker
Store, **21**
Liberty Bell, **4**
Masonic Temple, **20**
Penn's Landing, **17**
Pennsylvania
Academy of the Fine
Arts, **23**
Philadelphia Museum
of Art, **30**
Philadelphia Visitors'
Center, **18**
Please Touch
Museum, **28**
Powel House, **16**
Reading Terminal
Market, **22**
Rodin Museum, **29**
Rosenbach Museum
and Library, **24**
Todd House, **14**
United States Mint, **10**
Visitor Center, **1**
Welcome Park, **12**

Philadelphia

gives Constitutional perspectives on contemporary issues such as gun control, drug testing, sex discrimination, and the national speed limit. Shown in two 300-seat auditoriums, the 28-minute movie *Independence*, directed by John Huston, dramatizes events surrounding the birth of the nation. The center's bookstore specializes in books about the Revolution, the Constitution, and Colonial times.

Directly across 3rd Street is the **First Bank of the United States** (not open to the public), the oldest bank building in the country and headquarters of the government's bank from 1797 to 1811. The mahogany pediment carving is one of the few remaining examples of 18th-century wood carving (it has withstood acid rain better than the bank's marble pillars). Next to the bank is a wrought-iron gateway topped by an eagle. Pass through it and you step out of modern-day Philadelphia and into Colonial America. A red-brick path alongside manicured lawns and ancient oaks and maples leads to the first group of historic buildings, Carpenter's Court, which includes **Carpenter's Hall.** Built in 1770, this was the headquarters of the Carpenters' Company, a carpenters guild that still owns and operates the building. In September 1774 the First Continental Congress convened here and addressed a declaration of rights and grievances to King George III. Re-creations of Colonial settings include original chairs and candle sconces and displays of 18th-century carpentry tools. *320 Chestnut St., tel. 215/597-8974. Admission free. Open Tues.–Sun. 10–4.*

Next door are two buildings of interest to military history buffs—the **Pemberton House** (the Army–Navy Museum) and **New Hall (the Marine Corps Memorial Museum),** with displays of historic weaponry and uniforms. *Chestnut St. east of 4th St., tel. 215/597-8974. Admission free. Open daily 9–5.*

Leave Carpenter's Court and continue west on the red-brick path across 4th Street to the **Second Bank of the United States.** Built in 1824 and modeled after the Parthenon, the Second Bank is an excellent example of Greek Revival architecture. Housed in the building are portraits of prominent Colonial Americans by noted artists such as Charles Willson Peale, William Rush, and Gilbert Stuart. *420 Chestnut St., tel. 215/597-8974. Admission free. Open daily 9–5.*

As you continue west on the red-brick path, you pass **Library Hall,** the library of the American Philosophical Society. A research library for historians, it contains such artifacts as a copy of the Declaration of Independence handwritten by Thomas Jefferson, William Penn's 1701 Charter of Privileges, and Benjamin Franklin's will. *105 S. 5th St., tel. 215/440-3400. Admission free. Open weekdays 9–4:45.*

Crossing 5th Street, you arrive at **Independence Square,** where, on July 8, 1776, the Declaration of Independence was first read in public. Although the square is not as imposing today, you can still imagine the impact that this setting had on the Colonials. The first building on your right, directly across fromn Library Hall, is **Philosophical Hall** (104 S. 5th St., tel. 215/627-0706), the headquarters of the American Philosophical Society, founded by Benjamin Franklin in 1743 to promote "useful knowledge." The membership, which is limited to 500 Americans and 100 foreigners, has included Washington, Jefferson, Emerson, Darwin, Edison, Churchill, and Einstein.

The building (dating from 1785) is closed to the public except by appointment.

❸ Next is **Independence Hall,** the scene of many early events in the nation's history. It opened in 1732 as the State House for the Colony of Pennsylvania, and the Second Continental Congress convened here on May 10, 1775. In June 1775, George Washington accepted appointment as general of the Continental Army. On July 4, 1776, the Declaration of Independence was adopted. The Articles of Confederation were signed here in 1778 and the Constitution was formally adopted on September 17, 1787. The site of these events was the first-floor Assembly Room, which has been painstakingly restored. Note the inkstand used for signing the Declaration and the Constitution, and the chair from which Washington presided over the Constitutional Convention. Also on the first floor is the Pennsylvania Supreme Court chamber, with judge's bench, jury box, and prisoner's dock. The 100-foot Long Room on the second floor was the site of banquets, receptions, balls, and suppers. The east wing of the building is Old City Hall, home of the U.S. Supreme Court from 1791 to 1800. Free tours start there every 15 to 20 minutes; admission is first come, first served. The tour lasts 35 minutes, but you may have to wait in line up to an hour from early May to Labor Day. *Chestnut St. between 5th and 6th Sts., tel. 215/597–8974. Admission free (all visitors take the tour). Open mid-Sept.–late June, daily 9–5; early July–early Sept., daily 9–8.*

The west wing of Independence Hall is **Congress Hall,** formerly the Philadelphia County Courthouse and the meeting place of the U.S. Congress from 1790 to 1800. On the first floor is the House of Representatives, where President John Adams was inaugurated in 1797. On the second floor is the Senate chamber, where George Washington was inaugurated for his second term in 1793. Both chambers have been authentically restored. *6th and Chestnut Sts., tel. 215/597–8974. Admission free. Open daily 9–5.*

❹ North of Independence Hall, one block up the mall, is Philadelphia's best-known symbol, the **Liberty Bell.** Ordered in 1751 and originally cast in England, the bell cracked during testing and was recast in Philadelphia by Pass and Stow in 1753. To keep it from falling into British hands during the Revolution—they would have melted it down for ammunition—the bell was spirited away by horse and wagon to Allentown 60 miles north. The subject of much legend, the bell may have cracked when tolled at the funeral of Chief Justice John Marshall in 1835. It was repaired but cracked again in 1846 and then forever silenced. You can touch the 2,080-pound bell and read its biblical inscription, "Proclaim liberty throughout all the land unto all the inhabitants thereof." After being housed in Independence Hall for more than 200 years, the bell was moved to a glass-enclosed pavilion for the 1976 Bicentennial, where it is on view 24 hours a day. *Market St. between 5th and 6th Sts.*

❺ At the soutwest corner of Market Street and 7th Street is a reconstruction of the **Graff House,** where Thomas Jefferson wrote the rough draft of the Declaration of Independence in June 1776. Jefferson rented rooms from bricklayer Jacob Graff. The bedroom and parlor in which he lived that summer have been re-created with period furnishings. The first floor has a Jefferson exhibit and a seven-minute film, *The Extraordinary*

Citizen. The display on the Declaration of Independence shows changes Jefferson made in the writing. *7th and Market Sts., tel. 215/597–8974. Admission free. Open daily 9–5.*

Time Out On 5th Street across from the Liberty Bell Pavilion is the **Bourse,** Philadelphia's former stock exchange and now a festive complex of shops, offices, and eateries. The third floor has a dozen restaurants, including a salad bar, a deli, a pastry shop, a Chinese fast-food restaurant, and an American restaurant. You can eat your food at a table overlooking the Grand Hall of this magnificently restored 1895 building, or in the outdoor café.

6 Now walk east to 316 Market Street, the entrance to **Franklin Court.** First notice the post office, the only one in the country where employees wear Colonial dress. Letters mailed here are hand-stamped with the cancellation "B. Free Franklin." Pass through the archway and you'll see a steel-girder superstructure in the shape of Franklin's last house, which stood on the site. Down the long ramp is an underground museum, which has displays and a 20-minute film on Franklin's life and achievements. Beside the post office are four other restored homes once owned by Franklin. No. 318 contains architectural and archaeological displays of the houses themselves and artifacts found in the court. No. 320–322 was the print shop and office of the Colonial newspaper, *The Aurora,* published by Franklin's grandson Benjamin Franklin Bache. *314–322 Market St. (or enter from Chestnut St. walkway), tel. 215/597–2760. Admission free. Open mid-Sept.–late June, daily 9–5; early July–early Sept., daily 10–6.*

When you leave the underground museum, you'll be facing the entrance of the **Philadelphia Maritime Museum.** It displays three main exhibits: "The Titanic and Her Era," "The Ironclad Intruder," and "Man and the Sea." *321 Chestnut St., tel. 215/925–5439. Admission: $2.50 adults, $1 children. Open Tues.–Sat. 10–5, Sun. 1–5.*

7 Walk east on Market Street and north on 2nd Street to **Christ Church,** where noted Colonials, including 15 signers of the Declaration, worshiped. The congregation was organized in 1695 on this site; the present church—a fine example of Georgian architecture—was completed in 1754. The bells and the steeple were financed by lotteries run by Benjamin Franklin. Brass plaques mark the pews of Washington, Robert Morris, Betsy Ross, and others. *2nd St. north of Market St., tel. 215/922–1695. Open Mon.–Sat. 9–5, Sun. 1–5. Services Sun. at 9 and 11.*

8 Continue north on 2nd Street past Arch Street to **Elfreth's Alley,** the oldest continuously occupied residential street in America, dating back to 1702. No. 126, a Colonial craftsman's home, has been restored with authentic furnishings and a Colonial kitchen. *Tel. 215/574–0560. Admission free. Open Mar.–Dec., daily 10–4; Jan. and Feb., weekends 10–4.*

Walk back to 2nd Street, turn right, and a few footsteps take you to the **Fireman's Hall Museum.** Housed in an authentic 1876 firehouse, the museum traces the history of firefighting, from the volunteer company founded in Philadelphia by Benjamin Franklin in 1736. *147 N. 2nd St., tel. 215/923–1438. Admission free. Open Tues.–Sat. 9–5.*

Walk south on 2nd Street and turn right to 239 Arch Street, the
Betsy Ross House. In this three-story brick house, seamstress
and upholsterer Betsy Ross supposedly sewed the first American flag. The eight-room house is crammed with artifacts such
as a family Bible and Betsy Ross's wardrobe and yardstick. *239
Arch St., tel. 215/627–5343. Admission free. Open May–Oct.,
Mon.–Sat. 10–6; Nov.–Apr., Mon.–Sat. 10–5.*

Continuing west on Arch Street, you'll see an eight-foot-high
bust of Benjamin Franklin made of 80,000 pennies donated by
Philadelphia schoolchildren and children of city firefighters.
On the southeast corner of Arch and 4th streets is the **Arch
Street Meeting House,** built in 1804 for the Philadelphia Yearly
Meeting of the Society of Friends (still used today, as some
13,000 Quakers congregate here for five days each March). A
small museum inside includes a 14-minute slide show on Wil-
liam Penn. *Tel. 215/627–2667. Open Mon.–Sat. 10–4; services
Thurs. at 10 and Sun. at 10:30.*

⑩ Across 4th Street, the **United States Mint** stands just two
blocks from the first U.S. mint, which opened in 1792. Built in
1969, this is the largest mint in the world. A self-guided tour
shows how blank discs are turned into U.S. coins. The David
Rittenhouse Room on the mezzanine level has a display of U.S.
gold coins. Seven Tiffany stained-glass mosaics depict coin
making in ancient Rome. A shop in the lobby sells special coins
and medals—in mint condition. *5th and Arch Sts., tel. 215/597–
7350. Admission free. Open Mon.–Sat. 9–4:30.*

⑪ Across Arch Street is the **Christ Church Burial Ground,** resting
place of five signers of the Declaration and other Colonial patriots. The best-known graves are those of Benjamin Franklin
and his wife, Deborah. According to local legend, throwing a
penny on Franklin's grave will bring you good luck. *Open daily
late spring, summer, and early fall 9:30–4:30, weather permitting.*

Society Hill

⑫ Starting from the Visitor Center, walk east to 2nd Street and
south to Sansom Street to see **Welcome Park,** site of the slate-
roof house where William Penn lived briefly and where he
granted the Charter of Privileges in 1701. (The *Welcome* was
the ship that transported Penn to America.) On a 60-foot-long
map of Penn's Philadelphia carved in the pavement in the park
sits a scale model of the Penn statue from atop City Hall.

Time Out Stop for a bite to eat or a drink at the historic **City Tavern** (2nd
and Walnut Sts.), where the fathers of our country hung out
and where waiters in Colonial dress now serve traditional
American dishes.

⑬ West on Walnut Street is the **Bishop White House,** home of
Bishop William White, rector of Christ Church, first Episcopal
bishop of Pennsylvania, chaplain to the Continental Congress,
and spiritual leader of Philadelphia for 60 years. Built in 1786,
this upper-class house has been restored to Colonial elegance.
*309 Walnut St., tel. 215/597–8974. Admission free, by tour only
(tickets at Visitor Center). Open daily 9:30–4:30.*

⑭ On the same block, the simply furnished **Todd House** stands in
direct contrast to the lavish Bishop White House. Built in 1775,

it has been restored to its appearance in the 1790s, when its best-known resident lived here. Dolley Payne Todd lost her husband, the lawyer John Todd, to the yellow-fever epidemic of 1793. She later married James Madison, who became the fourth president. *4th and Walnut Sts., tel. 215/597–8974. Admission free, by tour only (tickets at Visitor Center). Open daily 9:30–4:30.*

⑮ South on 4th Street is the 22-room **Hill-Physick-Keith House,** built in 1786. Philip Syng Physick, a leading physician in the days before anesthesia, is known as the "Father of American Surgery." While caring for victims of the yellow-fever epidemic of 1793, he contracted the disease himself. This is the only free-standing house left in Society Hill. On three sides is a garden filled with plants common in the 19th century. *321 S. 4th St., tel. 215/925–7866. Admission: $2 adults, 50¢ children. Open Tues.–Sat. 10–4, Sun. 1–4. Tours Tues.–Sat. 11, 1:30, and 3; Sun. 1:30 and 3.*

⑯ Go east to 3rd Street and then north to the **Powel House,** a brick Georgian house built in 1765 and purchased by Samuel Powel in 1769. Powel was the last mayor of Philadelphia under the Crown and the first in the new republic. The lavish house is furnished with 18th-century antiques and has such appointments as a mahogany staircase from Santo Domingo, a 1765 mahogany secretary, and a signed Gilbert Stuart portrait. *244 S. 3rd St., tel. 215/627–0364. Admission: $3 adults, $2 students with ID and senior citizens, 50¢ children under 12. Open Tues.–Sat. 10–4, Sun. 1–4.*

The Waterfront

⑰ **Penn's Landing,** the spot where William Penn stepped ashore in 1682, is the hub of a 37-acre riverside park from Market Street to Lombard Street. This ambitious effort to reclaim the Delaware River waterfront began in 1967, and today there are plans to add condominiums, offices, more recreation areas, hotels, and restaurants. The Great Plaza at Penn's Landing—an outdoor amphitheater—is often the scene of concerts, festivals, and other special events (call Penn's Landing Info-Line, tel. 215/923–4992). Walk along the waterfront and you'll see scores of pleasure boats moored at the marina, and cargo ships chugging up and down the Delaware. Three historic ships docked here are available for tours. At Spruce Street, you can visit the USS *Olympia,* Commodore George Dewey's flagship at the Battle of Manila in the Spanish-American War, and the World War II "guppy class" submarine USS *Becuna* (combined admission: $3 adults, $2 senior citizens, $1.50 children under 12; open daily 10–4, summer 10–5). A block north is the *Gazela of Philadelphia,* a Portuguese cod-fishing ship that is the oldest (built in 1883) and largest (177-foot) wooden square-rigger still sailing. *Tel. 215/923–9030. Admission free. Open Memorial Day–Labor Day, daily 10–6; rest of year, weekends noon–5.*

A few steps from the *Gazela* is the **Port of History Museum,** featuring ever-changing displays of fine art, crafts, and design. *Penn's Landing at Walnut St., tel. 215/925–3804. Admission: $2. Open Wed.–Sun. 10–4:30. Call for information on current exhibit.*

In the middle of Delaware Avenue are the tracks of the **Penn's Landing Trolley Company.** You can board an authentic turn-of-the-century trolley at Dock Street or Spruce Street for a 20-minute narrated round-trip along the Delaware River waterfront. *Tel. 215/627–0807. Fare: $1.50 adults, 75¢ children under 12, for an all-day pass. Runs 11–dusk weekends and holidays from mid-Apr. to late Nov.; also Thurs. and Fri. in July and Aug.*

City Hall and Environs

⓲ At the **Philadelphia Visitors Center,** you can get brochures about the city and surroundings and information about current events. Volunteers and staff members are on hand to answer your questions.*16th St. and John F. Kennedy Blvd., tel. 215/636–1666. Open daily 9–5, until 6 in summer.*

⓳ Walk east on Kennedy Boulevard to 15th Street for an incomparable, unobstructed view of **City Hall.** Topped by a newly restored 37-foot bronze statue of William Penn, the city's founder, City Hall stands 548 feet high and until 1987 was Philadelphia's tallest building. With 642 rooms, it is the largest city hall in the country and the tallest masonry-bearing building in the world: No steel structure supports it. It took 30 years to build (1871 to 1900) and cost the taxpayers more than $23 million. The observation deck—closed for the recent restoration but scheduled to be reopened in 1991—affords a 30-mile view of the city and surroundings. Start at the northeast corner and ascend one flight to the mayor's ornate reception room (Room 202) and the recently restored Conversation Hall (Room 201). Take a look, too, at the City Council Chambers (Room 400) and the Supreme Court of Pennsylvania. Municipal court sessions are open to the public. *Broad and Market Sts., tel. 215/686–1776; Mayor's Office of Information, Room 121, tel. 215/686–2250; 1-hr tours of City Hall weekdays at 12:30, tel. 215/568–3351. For additional information, call the office of Tours and Guides, tel. 215/686–2840.*

⓴ Leave City Hall by the northern exit and cross Kennedy Boulevard to the **Masonic Temple.** Philadelphia is the mother city of American Masonry, and the temple is home to the Grand Lodge of Free and Accepted Masons of Pennsylvania. The gavel used at the laying of the cornerstone in 1868 was the one that Brother George Washington used to lay the cornerstone of the U.S. Capitol. Designed by Brother James H. Windrim and built by Masons, the ornate interior consists of seven Lodge Halls built to represent seven styles of architecture: Corinthian, Ionic, Italian Renaissance, Norman, Gothic, Oriental, and Egyptian. The collection of Masonry items includes handwritten letters from Washington to brothers of the Grand Lodge and Benjamin Franklin's printing of the first book on Free Masonry published in America. *1 N. Broad St., tel. 215/988–1917. Free 45-min tours weekdays 10, 11, 1, 2, and 3; Sat. 10 and 11. Closed Sat. July and Aug.*

㉑ Just east of City Hall is the **John Wanamaker Store,** the grandest of Philadelphia's department stores. Designed by the Chicago firm of D. H. Burnham and Company, the building has a nine-story grand court with a 30,000-pipe organ—the largest ever built—and a 2,500-pound statue of an eagle, both remnants of the 1904 Louisiana Purchase Exposition in St. Louis. "Meet me at the Eagle" is a popular way for Philadelphians to arrange get-togethers. *13th and Market Sts., tel. 215/422–*

2000. Open Mon., Tues, Thurs.–Sat. 10–7, Wed. 10–9, Sun. noon–5. Organ performances at 11:15 and 5:15.

One block east, on 12th Street, is the **Philadelphia Saving Fund Society (PSFS) Building** (tel. 215/629–7000; open Mon.–Thurs. 9–3, Fri. 9–6), one of the city's first skyscrapers, built in 1930. Pay special attention to the enormous escalators and the main banking floor, two striking contrasts to the utilitarian approaches of architecture today. North on 12th Street, at Filbert Street, is the **Reading Terminal Market** (tel. 215/922–2317; open Mon.–Sat. 8–6 PM), a sprawling market located beneath the defunct Reading Railroad's 1891 train shed. No other place in the city offers a wider variety of eating places—a vegetarian restaurant, a gourmet ice cream store, a cookie shop, and a Philadelphia cheesesteak store. The entire building is a National Historic Landmark and the train shed is a National Engineering Landmark. The city's new convention center is being built above and behind the market, but pledges and legal guarantees are in place to preserve this Philadelphia treasure.

Return to City Hall and go north on Broad Street two blocks to the **Pennsylvania Academy of the Fine Arts,** a High Victorian Gothic building (1876) that's a work of art in itself. Designed by the noted, sometimes eccentric, Philadelphia architects Frank Furness and George Hewitt, the multicolored stone-and-brick exterior is an extravagant blend of columns, friezes, Art Deco, and Moorish flourishes. Inside, the oldest art institution in the United States (founded 1804) boasts a collection that ranges from Winslow Homer and Benjamin West to Andrew Wyeth and Red Grooms. *Broad and Cherry Sts., tel. 215/972–7600. Admission: $5 adults, $3 senior citizens, $2 students; free Sat. 10–1. Open Tues.–Sat. 10–5, Sun. 11–5.*

Back at City Hall, you have two options. Walk to 18th Street, head south, and you soon come upon **Rittenhouse Square** (between 18th and 19th Sts. at Walnut St.). Once grazing ground for cows and sheep, this is now Philadelphia's classiest park. Until 1950 town houses bordered the square, but they have now been replaced on three sides by swank apartment buildings and hotels. Go south on 19th Street and then west on Delancey Place to the **Rosenbach Museum and Library,** which has more than 130,000 manuscripts and 30,000 rare books. This 1863 three-floor town house is furnished with Persian rugs and 18th-century antiques by Chippendale, Adam, and Hepplewhite. The collection includes paintings by Canaletto, Sully, and Lawrence; drawings by Daumier, Fragonard, and Blake; book illustrations ranging from medieval illumination to Maurice Sendak; the first edition of Benjamin Franklin's *Poor Richard's Almanac;* and manuscripts of Chaucer's *Canterbury Tales* and James Joyce's *Ulysses. 2010 Delancey Pl., tel. 215/732–1600. Admission: $2.50 adults, $1.50 senior citizens and students. Open Tues.–Sun. 11–4. Guided 1-hr tour (come no later than 2:45). Closed Aug. and national holidays.*

Your other choice from City Hall is to head up the **Benjamin Franklin Parkway** to Fairmount Park, stopping off at a cluster of fine museums. The 250-foot-wide parkway, inspired by the Champs Élysées, was designed by French architect Jacques Greber and built in the 1920s. Adorned by fountains, statues, trees, and flags of every country, it is the route of most of the city's parades. Northwest on the parkway is **Logan Circle,** one of the four original squares William Penn laid out at the corners of a rectangle around Center Square, where City Hall now stands. (The others are Franklin Square to the northeast, Washington Square to the southeast, and Rittenhouse Square to the southwest.) The focal point of Logan Circle is the Swann Fountain of 1920, designed by Alexander Stirling Calder, son of Alexander Milne Calder, who did the William Penn statue atop City Hall. Walking counterclockwise around Logan Circle, you'll see twin marble Greek Revival buildings off to your right. The nearer is the city's Family Court; the other is the

㉕ Free Library of Philadelphia. Founded in 1891, this central library of the city's public library system has more than 1 million volumes. With its grand entrance hall, sweeping marble staircase, 30-foot ceilings, enormous reading rooms with long tables, and spiral staircases leading to balconies, this Greek Revival building looks the way libraries ought to look. The Newspaper Room stocks papers from all major U.S. and foreign cities and back issues on microfilm, some going all the way back to Colonial times. The Rare Book Room is a beautiful suite that has first editions of Dickens, ancient Sumerian clay tablets, illuminated medieval manuscripts, and more-modern manuscripts, including Poe's *Murders in the Rue Morgue* and "The Raven." *19th St. and Benjamin Franklin Pkwy., tel. 215/686–5322. Open Mon.–Wed. 9–9, Thurs. and Fri. 9–6, Sat. 9–5, Sun. 1–5. Closed Sun. June–Aug. Tours of Rare Book Room weekdays at 11.*

Time Out The rooftop cafeteria of the **Free Library** (19th St. and Benjamin Franklin Pkwy.) provides inexpensive meals at umbrellaed tables.

㉖ Cross Logan Circle to the **Academy of Natural Sciences,** America's first museum of natural history. Founded in 1812, the present building dates from 1868. The collection is famous for stuffed animals from around the world, displayed in 35 natural settings, and its dinosuar exhibits. *19th St. and Benjamin Franklin Pkwy., tel. 215/299–1020. Admission: $5.50 adults, $4.50 children. Open weekdays 10–4:30, weekends and holidays 10–5.*

From the Academy, walk west on Race Street to 20th Street

㉗ and the **Franklin Institute.** Founded to honor Benjamin Franklin, the institute is a science museum with an abundance of hands-on exhibits. You can sit in the cockpit of a T-33 jet trainer, trace the route of a corpuscle through the world's largest artificial heart (15,000 times life-size), and ride to nowhere on a 350-ton Baldwin steam locomotive. The Fels Planetarium features shows about the stars; the Futures Center explores such issues as space, computers, careers, energy, and health; the Omniverse Theater, with a 79-foot domed screen and high-tech sound system, transports you down ski slopes and up mountains. *20th St. and Benjamin Franklin Pkwy., tel. 215/448–1200. Admission: ticket packages range from $7 to $12.50. Open Sept.–June, weekdays 9:30–5.*

Winter Street bounds the Franklin Institute to the north. Take it west one block to 21st Street; cross it and turn left to the

㉘ **Please Touch Museum,** the only U.S. museum designed specifically for children seven and younger. (It also appeals to adults.) The premise here is hands-on, feet-on, try-on: Perform in a circus ring; pet small animals in the "Animals as Pets" exhibit;

dress up in costumes, wigs, and masks. *210 N. 21st St., tel. 215/963–0667. Admission: $5. Open daily 9–4:30.*

(29) Return to the parkway, cross to its north side, and walk northwest past the statue of *The Thinker* to the **Rodin Museum,** the best collection of Auguste Rodin's works outside France. Before entering, marvel at the *Gates of Hell,* a 21-foot-high sculpture with more than 100 human and animal figures. Inside are 124 sculptures by the French master, including *The Kiss, The Burghers of Calais, Eternal Springtime,* and hands and busts of his friends. *22nd St. and Benjamin Franklin Pkwy., tel. 215/787–5431. Donation requested. Open Tues.–Sun. 10–5.*

(30) Atop Faire Mount, the plateau at the end of Franklin Parkway, stands the **Philadelphia Museum of Art.** This mammoth building of Minnesota dolomite is modeled after ancient Greek temples but on a grander scale. Covering 10 acres, it has 200 galleries and a collection of over 300,000 works. You can enter the museum from the front or the rear; we recommend the front, where you can run up the 98 steps made famous in the movie *Rocky.* From the expansive terrace, look up to the pediment on your right at a group of 13 glazed, multicolored statues of classical gods, and then climb the last flight of steps and turn around to savor the view down the parkway. Once inside, you'll see the grand staircase and Saint-Gaudens's statue of *Diana.* Famous paintings in the collection include Van Eyck's *St. Francis Receiving the Stigmata,* Rubens's *Prometheus Bound,* Benjamin West's *Benjamin Franklin Drawing Electricity from the Sky,* Van Gogh's *Sunflowers,* Renoir's *The Bathers,* and Picasso's *Three Musicians.*Marcel Duchamps is a specialty of the house; the museum has the world's most extensive collection of his works. Another specialty is reconstructions of entire buildings: a 12th-century French cloister, a 16th-century Indian temple hall, a 16th-century Japanese Buddhist temple, a 17th-century Chinese palace hall, and a Japanese ceremonial tea house. Pick up a map of the museum at either of the two entrances, or choose from a variety of guided tours. *26th St. and Benjamin Franklin Pkwy., tel. 215/763–8100, 215/787–5488 for 24-hr taped message. Admission: $5 adults, $2.50 senior citizens, students, and children; free Sun. 10–1. Open Tues.–Sun. 10–5; closed on legal holidays.*

(31) Stretching from the edge of downtown to the city's northwest corner, **Fairmount Park** is the largest city park in the world, covering about 4,500 acres. The park encompasses beautiful natural areas—woodlands, meadows, rolling hills, two scenic waterways, and a forested 5½-mile gorge. It also contains tennis courts, ball fields, playgrounds, trails, exercise courses, several celebrated cultural institutions, and some fine early American country houses. More than 200 works of outdoor art—including statues by Frederic Remington, Jacques Lipchitz, and Auguste Rodin—are scattered throughout Fairmount Park. A car is the best way to explore the park; an excellent 25¢ map is available at Memorial Hall (on North Concourse Dr.) and most park mansions and sites. Fairmount Park Trolley Bus (tel. 215/636–1666) is planning a daily schedule of tours of the park mansions; buy your ticket ($14 adult, $6 children) at the Visitors Center (16th St. and Kennedy Blvd.) and get on and off all day at no additional charge.

Neighborhoods to Visit

Chinatown Centered on 10th and Race streets just two blocks north of Market Street, Chinatown serves as the residential and the commercial hub of the Chinese community. Along with more than 50 restaurants, Chinatown attractions include grocery stores, souvenir and gift shops, martial-arts studios, a fortune-cookie store, bilingual street signs, and red-and-green pagoda-style telephone booths.

University City University City, in West Philadelphia directly west of Center City across the Schuylkill River, has three college campuses—the University of Pennsylvania, Drexel University, and the Philadelphia College of Pharmacy and Science. It also has the University City Science Center (a leading think tank), a large and impressive collection of houses, and a variety of restaurants, movie theaters, stores, and bars catering to students and other residents. Prominent on your itinerary here should be the **University of Pennsylvania.** For a good look at the Ivy League campus stop at the **Information Center** at 34th and Walnut streets (tel. 215/898–1000), then follow **Locust Walk** between 33rd Street and 40th Street.

At 33rd and Spruce streets is the **University Museum,** one of the finest archaeological/anthropological museums in the world. The collection of more than a million objects, gathered largely during worldwide expeditions by University of Pennsylvania scholars, includes a 12-ton giant sphinx from Egypt, a crystal ball owned by China's dowager empress, the world's oldest writing—Sumerian cuneiform clay tablets—and the 4,500-year-old golden jewels from the royal tombs of Ur. *33rd and Spruce Sts., tel. 215/898–4000. Admission: $4 adults, $2 children and senior citizens. Open Tues.–Sat. 10–4:30, Sun. 1–5. Closed Sun. Memorial Day to Labor Day.*

Germantown and Chestnut Hill In the late 1600s, a group of 13 German families seeking religious freedom in the New World settled 6 miles northwest of Philadelphia in what is now Germantown. By the time of the Revolution, Germantown had become a bustling industrial town. In 1777, Colonial troops under George Washington attacked part of the British force here and fought the Battle of Germantown in various skirmishes.

You can reach Germantown from Center City via the no. 23 trolley, by the two Chestnut Hill SEPTA commuter trains, or by car. The best way to tour the area is by car. From City Hall, drive north on Broad Street for about 3½ miles to Pike Street (two blocks north of Erie Ave.). Turn left, go one block to Germantown Avenue, and turn right.

The **Germantown Historical Society,** with its historical and genealogical library and collections of industrial and decorative arts, serves as an orientation point for visiting all the Germantown houses. *5501 Germantown Ave., tel. 215/844–0514. Open Tues. and Thurs. 10–4, Sun. 1–5.*

If you have time for only one site in Germantown, make it **Cliveden.** Built in 1763 by Benjamin Chew, Germantown's most elaborate country house was occupied by the British during the Revolution. On October 4, 1777, Washington's unsuccessful attempt to dislodge the British resulted in his defeat at the Battle of Germantown. You can still see bullet marks on the outside

walls. *6401 Germantown Ave., tel. 215/848–1777. Open Tues.–
Sat. 10–4, Sun. 1–4.*

North of Germantown is the residential community of Mount
Airy, and north of that is Chestnut Hill, one of Philadelphia's
poshest neighborhoods. Chestnut Hill sights include **Pastorius
Park** at Lincoln Drive and Abington Avenue (one block west of
the 8100 block of Germantown Ave.) and 166-acre **Morris Arboretum** (Hillcrest Ave. between Germantown and Stenton
Aves., tel. 215/247–5777), an eclectic retreat with a formal rose
garden, English garden, Japanese garden, meadows, and
woodlands. The **Woodmere Art Museum** (9201 Germantown
Ave., tel. 215/247–0476) displays paintings, tapestries, sculpture, porcelains, ivories, Japanese rugs, and works by contemporary local artists.

Other Notable Sites

Atwater Kent Museum. Founded in 1938 and housed in an elegant 1826 Greek Revival building, the museum portrays Philadelphia history from the beginning to the present day. It
includes exhibits on municipal services such as police, fire, water, and gas; shipbuilding; model streets and railroads; and
maps showing the city's development. One gallery, "The City
Beneath Our Feet," has changing exhibits culled from the thousands of artifacts uncovered during 20th-century excavations.
Recent temporary exhibits have included "Tune In—Philadelphia Radio, 1820–1950." *15 S. 7th St., tel. 215/922–3031. Admission free. Open Tues.–Sat. 9:30–4:45.*

Poe House. Edgar Allan Poe lived here, the only one of his Philadelphia residences still standing, from 1843 to 1844. During
that time, some of his best-known short stories were published:
"The Telltale Heart," "The Black Cat," and "The Gold Bug."
You can tour the 19th-century three-story brick house; to evoke
the spirit of Poe, the National Park Service deliberately keeps
the house empty. The adjoining house has exhibits on Poe and
his family, his work habits, his literary contemporaries, and his
"statement of taste," an eight-minute slide show. The house
also has a small Poe library and a reading room. At night, a statue in the garden casts the eerie shadow of a raven across the
side of the house. *532 N. 7th St., tel. 215/597–8780. Admission
free. Open daily 9–5.*

Norman Rockwell Museum. The Curtis Publishing Company
Building, where Rockwell delivered his paintings to the editors
of the *Saturday Evening Post,* now has the world's largest collection of the artist's works. Displays include all 324 Rockwell
Post cover illustrations; lithographs, prints, collotypes, and
sketches; and a replica of his studio in Stockbridge, Massachusetts. A 10-minute video illustrates Rockwell's life. *6th and
Sansom Sts. (lower level), tel. 215/922–4345. Admission: $2
adults, children under 12 free when accompanied by an adult.
Open Mon.–Sat. 10–4, Sun. 11–4.*

The War Library and Museum. This is one of the premier collections of Civil War memorabilia in the Union. Artifacts include
two life masks of Abraham Lincoln, dress uniforms and swords
of Generals Grant and Meade, plus many other weapons, uniforms, and personal effects of Civil War officers and enlisted
men. The library has more than 12,000 volumes on the war.

*1805 Pine St., tel. 215/735–8196. Admission: $3. Open Mon.–
Sat. 10–4.*

Philadelphia Zoological Gardens. Opened in 1874, America's
first zoo displays 1,600 animals on 42 acres. Orangutans, gorillas, gibbons, mandrills, and lemurs romp in the World of Primates, a 1-acre outdoor jungle. The African Plain is the
stomping ground of giraffes, zebras, and rhinoceroses. Bear
Country offers up-close views of sloths, spectacled bears, and
polar bears diving off 12-foot cliffs. The George D. Widener Memorial Treehouse provides an animal's-eye view of a four-story
tropical tree. The Children's Zoo has pony rides, a petting
area, and a sea lion show. *34th St. and Girard Ave., tel. 215/
243–1100. Admission: $5.75 adults, $4.75 children 2–11 and
senior citizens, children under 2 free. Additional charge for
Treehouse. Open weekdays 9:30–5, weekends 9:30–6.*

Shopping

Pennsylvania's 6% sales tax does not apply to clothing, medicine, and food bought in stores. Downtown shopping hours are
generally 9:30 or 10 AM to 5 or 6 PM. Many stores close at 9 PM on
Wednesday. Most downtown stores are closed on Sunday, but
the Bourse and the Gallery are open from noon to 5.

The leading shopping area is **Walnut Street** between Broad
Street and Rittenhouse Square, and the intersecting streets
just north and south. These blocks are filled with boutiques,
art galleries, jewelers, fine clothing stores, and many other unusual shops.

The **Chestnut Street Transitway,** another shopping street, has
rare-book sellers, custom tailors, sporting-goods stores, pinball arcades, and discount drugstores. At 17th and Chestnut
streets you'll find **The Shops at Liberty Place,** the city's newest
shopping complex, with more than 60 stores and restaurants
arranged in two circular levels under a striking 90-foot glass
atrium. A block north of Chestnut Street is Philadelphia's landmark effort at urban renewal cum shopping, the **Gallery at
Market East** (tel. 215/925–7162), America's first enclosed
downtown shopping mall. The four-level glass-roofed structure
on Market Street from 8th Street to 11th Street contains 220
shops and restaurants and three department stores—Stern's
(tel. 215/922–3399), Strawbridge and Clothier (tel. 215/629–
6000), and J. C. Penney (tel. 215/238–9100). Next to the Gallery
on Market Street between 7th Street and 8th Street is a pricier
urban mall, **Market Place East** (tel. 215/592–8905). Saved from
the wrecker's ball at the eleventh hour, the former Lit Brothers Department Store is now an office building featuring a five-level atrium with space for 50 stores and restaurants.

Across the street from the Liberty Bell, the **Bourse** (5th St. between Market St. and Chestnut St., tel. 215/625–0300) has 50
stores and restaurants, including designer boutiques such as
Howard Heartsfield and Forgotten Woman. Even if the specialty stores are beyond your budget, the elegantly restored
1895 commodities exchange is worth a visit.

South Street, one of Philadelphia's few entertainment strips, is
also one of its major shopping areas. From Front Street to 8th
Street you'll find more than 180 unusual stores—New Wave

and high-fashion clothing, New Age books and health food, avant-garde art galleries—and 70 restaurants.

If you want local color, nothing compares with South Philadelphia's **Italian Market.** On both sides of 9th Street from Christian Street to Washington Street and spilling onto the surrounding streets, hundreds of outdoor stalls and indoor stores sell food, household items, clothing, shoes, and other goods. It's crowded and smelly, and the vendors can be less than hospitable—but the food is fresh and the prices are reasonable.

Department Stores The granddaddy of local department stores is **John Wanamaker** (tel. 215/422–2000), a landmark store that occupies the entire city block from 13th Street to Juniper Street and from Market Street to Chestnut Street. The store has fashion boutiques, designer shops for men, the Williamsburg and Baker furniture galleries, a travel agency, a ticket office, a watch-repair desk, a beauty salon, and a post office.

Strawbridge and Clothier (tel. 215/629–6000), whose main store is at 8th Street and Market Street in the Gallery, is the other leading department store. It was founded in 1868 and is still owned by the Clothier and Strawbridge families.

Antiques Pine Street from 9th Street to 12th Street is Philadelphia's **Antiques Row.** The three-block area has dozens of antiques stores and curio shops, many specializing in period furniture and Colonial heirlooms.

Freeman Fine Arts (1808 Chestnut St., tel. 215/563–9275) is one of the city's leading auction houses. Examine furniture, china, prints, and paintings on Monday and Tuesday; bid for them on Wednesday. Freeman's auctioned one of the original flyers on which the Declaration of Independence was printed and posted throughout the city. It went for $400,000.

Art For current shows in Philadelphia's numerous galleries, see listings in *Philadelphia* magazine or the Weekend section of the Friday *Philadelphia Inquirer.* Many galleries are located near Rittenhouse Square; others are on South Street or scattered about downtown.

Gross-McCleaf Gallery (127 S. 16th St., tel. 215/665–8138) shows works by prominent and emerging artists, with emphasis on Philadelphia painters, printmakers, and sculptors.
Newman Galleries (1625 Walnut St., tel. 215/563–1779) has a range of works, from 19th-century paintings to contemporary lithographs and sculpture. Strong on early 20th-century painters from the Bucks County area.
School Gallery of the Pennsylvania Academy of the Fine Arts (1301 Cherry St., tel. 215/569–2797) rotates exhibits of works by faculty, alumni, and students.
University of the Arts' Rosenwald-Wolf Gallery (333 S. Broad St., tel. 215/875–1116) displays works by faculty and local, national, and international artists. Student exhibits May through August.
Frank S. Schwarz and Son (1806 Chestnut St., tel. 215/563–4887) deals in 19th- and 20th-century American and European paintings, concentrating on Philadelphia artists of the past.

Books **Borders** (1727 Walnut St., tel. 215/568–7400) is the biggest, the friendliest, the best bookstore in Philadelphia. The 110,000 titles and more than half-million books are spread over a two-level, 17,000-foot selling floor. Each of the 50 staffers had to pass a literature test to be hired. Book lovers get to know each other at the second-floor espresso bar. Frequent lectures and readings; Saturday-morning children's programs at 11:30.

Robin's Bookstore (108 S. 13th St., tel. 215/735–9600) became famous in the 1960s as the city's counterculture bookstore. Robin's has an exceptional variety of hard-to-find intellectual titles, especially in literature, poetry, and minority studies. Frequent poetry readings and book signings by local authors are held.

University of Pennsylvania Bookstore (3729 Locust St., tel. 215/898–7595) stocks over 60,000 titles of both popular and scholarly volumes, especially strong in linguistics, anthropology, psychology, and sociology.

Women's and Men's Clothing **Destination Philadelphia** (Bourse Bldg., 21 S. 5th St., tel. 215/440–0233) is a clothing store where every item bears some form of Philadelphia logo or design—from a soft pretzel to a line drawing of Billy Penn. Sweatpants, sweatshirts, and more than 40 styles of T-shirts.

Jewelry **Jewelers' Row,** centered on Sansom Street between 7th Street and 8th Street, is one of the world's oldest and largest markets of precious stones: More than 350 retailers, wholesalers, and craftsmen operate here. The 700 block of Sansom Street is a brick-paved enclave occupied almost exclusively by jewelers.

Sports and Fitness

Bicycling A treat for bikers is to ride out on the east side of the Schuylkill River, cross Falls Bridge, and return on the west side of the river. The 8.2-mile loop takes about an hour of casually paced biking. *1 Boathouse Row, behind the Art Museum, tel. 215/225-3560. Cost for bike rental: $6/hr ($10 deposit and picture ID required). Weekdays 10:30–8, weekends 9–8. Closed in winter.*

Boating and Canoeing Paddle or row through Fairmount Park along the scenic Schuylkill River, but yield the right of way to Olympic-caliber scullers speeding by. Rent canoes or rowboats at the **Public Canoe House.** *Kelly Dr., just south of Strawberry Mansion Bridge, tel. 215/225–3560. Cost for canoes or rowboats: $10/hr with $10 deposit. Photo ID required. Open daily 10 AM–1 hour before dark, March–Nov.*

Hiking and Jogging Fairmount Park—especially along the river drives and Wissahickon Creek—is a natural for hikers and joggers. Starting in front of the Philadelphia Museum of Art, an 8.2-mile loop runs up one side of the Schuylkill, across Falls Bridge, and down the other side of the river back to the museum. Forbidden Drive along the Wissahickon offers more than 5 miles of scenic hiking or jogging on a dirt surface with no automobile traffic.

For organized hiking, check with the following organizations:

American Youth Hostels (tel. 215/925–6004).

Batona Hiking Club (tel. 215/635–0933). These organized hikes tend to be a little more strenuous than those of the other clubs.

The Department of Recreation **Wanderlust Hiking Club** (tel. 215/685–0151).

Horseback Riding Of the numerous bridle paths coursing through Philadelphia, the most popular are the trails of the Wissahickon in the northwest, in Pennypack Park in the northeast, and in Cobbs Creek Park in the southwest. Riding academies that offer instruction and rentals include **Cobbs Creek Riding Academy** (63rd and Catharine Sts., tel. 215/747–2300. Cost: $15/hr, weekends only; book ahead) and **Ashford Farms** (River Rd., Miquon, tel. 215/825–9838. Cost: trail rides $20/hr, lessons $20–$30).

Tennis Fairmount Park has more than 100 free public courts but at many, players must bring their own nets. Call the **Department of Recreation** (tel. 215/686–3600) for information.

Many indoor courts are located in the surrounding areas. The only one close to Center City, the **Robert P. Levy Tennis Pavilion,** has eight courts open weekdays 7 AM–midnight, weekends 8 AM–midnight (closed weekends July and Aug.). *3130 Walnut St., tel. 215/898–4741. One-time membership fee $30. Cost: $22–$26/hr.*

Spectator Sports

Tickets are available at Veterans Stadium or the Spectrum, at Ticketron outlets, at ticket agencies, and by mail and phone from the respective teams.

Baseball **Philadelphia Phillies** (Box 7575, 19101, tel. 215/463–1000) play at Veterans Stadium, Broad Street and Pattison Avenue, April–October.

Basketball **Philadelphia 76ers** (Box 25050, 19147, tel. 215/339–7676) play at the Spectrum, Broad Street and Pattison Avenue, October–April.

Bicycling One of the world's top four bicycling events, the **CoreStates Pro Cycling Championship** (tel. 215/636–1666), is held each June. The 156-mile race starts and finishes at Benjamin Franklin Parkway, with 10 loops including the infamous Manayunk "Wall."

Football **Philadelphia Eagles** (tel. 215/463–5500) play at Veterans Stadium, Broad Street and Pattison Avenue, August–December.

Hockey **Philadelphia Flyers** (tel. 215/755–9700) play at the Spectrum, Broad Street and Pattison Avenue, October–April.

Rowing The **Dad Vail Regatta** (tel. 215/248–2600), the largest collegiate rowing event in the country, is held on the Schuylkill River in Fairmont Park in May. Free shuttle buses from art museum.

Track and Field The **Penn Relays,** the world's largest and oldest amateur track meet, held the last week of April at the University of Pennsylvania's Franklin Field, features world-class performers in track and field. The **Philadelphia Distance Run,** the nation's top half marathon, takes place in September. The **Fairmount Park Marathon** is held each November. For more information on these events, call 215/685–0052. The **Broad Street Run** (tel. 215/686–3614), a 10-miler down Broad Street, is held in May.

Tennis The **U.S. Pro Indoor Tennis Championships** are held at the Spectrum (tel. 215/947–2530), usually in February. More than 60 of the world's top pros compete.

Dining

Since the "restaurant renaissance" of the early 1970s, Philadelphia has become a first-class restaurant city. There's no specific Philadelphia cuisine (unless you count soft pretzels, cheesesteaks, hoagies, and Tastykakes). The city does, however, have exemplary American and Continental cooking, and ethnic restaurants of almost all descriptions—Greek, Japanese, Middle Eastern, and Thai, among many others. Chinatown alone has more than 50 restaurants.

The following price categories have been used: *Very Expensive*, over $35; *Expensive*, $25–$35; *Moderate*, $15–$25; *Inexpensive*, under $15.

American-International
Very Expensive
★

The Fountain. Nestled in the lavish yet dignified lobby of the Four Seasons, the Fountain has the city's most varied and freshest selection of meals. Cream of celery soup, fresh seafood ravioli, and sautéed foie gras over asparagus are three enticing appetizers. Entrées are predominantly local and American dishes such as sautéed salmon fillet and roasted Pennsylvania pheasant with bacon-flavored cabbage. A special health menu offers foods low in cholesterol, calories, and sodium. Breads are superb but desserts are a trifle disappointing. *1 Logan Sq., tel. 215/963–1500. Reservations necessary. Dress: informal. AE, DC, MC, V.*

Moderate

Carolina's. Located a block from Rittenhouse Square, Carolina's seats 60 at vinyl-covered tables and bentwood chairs under a stamped tin ceiling. The large menu of sandwiches, pastas, salads, a dozen appetizers, and more than a dozen entrées changes daily. Most popular are veal loaf with mashed potatoes and Cobb salad (a deep-fried tortilla shell stuffed with chicken, avocado, blue cheese, black olives, tomato, and romaine). The pastry chef's specialties are Carolina's brownie sundae and Key lime pie. *261 S. 20th St., tel. 215/545–1000. Reservations suggested. Dress: informal. AE, DC, MC, V. No lunch Sat.*

Downey's. The mahogany bar was salvaged from a Dublin bank, artwork and memorabilia cover the walls, and owner Jack Downey's antique radio collection is on display. Although the food is routine Irish fare, a lively crowd is always on hand. Irish stew and Irish whiskey cake are favorites. Downey's is popular with local athletes, especially baseball and hockey players. It has an oyster bar and outdoor tables. *Front and South Sts., tel. 215/629–0525. Reservations suggested. Dress: informal. AE, DC, MC, V.*

Inexpensive

The Commissary. This gourmet cafeteria is the flagship of prominent Philadelphia restaurateur Steve Poses. To accompany omelets, soups, pastas, salads, and pastries, it offers a wide selection of coffees and wines. Low-fat, low-calorie items have been added to the menu, and food is available for takeout. *1710 Sansom St., tel. 215/569–2240. Dress: informal. AE, DC, MC, V.*

The Restaurant School. Here's the only place in Philadelphia where you can get haute cuisine and European service at a fraction of the normal price: A fixed price of $13.95 buys an appetizer and entrée. It is managed and staffed entirely by students attending the Restaurant School, an institution that has produced the chefs and owners of many Philadelphia restaurants. Although the menu includes some Continental (Italian and Hungarian) dishes, it is mainly French traditional, with a focus on sauces. Entrées change regularly, and may include sole Véronique garnished with white sauce and green grapes; or turkey rolled and stuffed with mushrooms and seasonings, and cut into medallions. Located in the Alison Mansion—a restored

1860 Victorian in West Philadelphia near the University of Pennsylvania, it seats 120 in an atrium setting with glass, trees, and plants. *4207 Walnut St., tel. 215/222–4200. Reservations two weeks in advance. Jacket and tie preferred. No pipes or cigars. AE, DC, MC, V. Closed Sun. and Mon.*

Silveri's. This Center City neighborhood bar serves restaurant-quality food. Glass-block windows and pastel colors make it open and airy. New owner Jim Colby still serves Ken Silveri's standards, including the award-winning "Buffalo wings" (chicken wings cooked in butter, vinegar, and Louisiana hot sauce) and has introduced grilled chicken burgers. Complementing the standard menu of omelets, pastas, sauces, and casseroles, a fancier tableside menu offers entrées such as baked ocean bass. *315 S. 13th St., tel. 215/545–5115. Dress: informal. MC, V.*

Cafés and Delis
Inexpensive

Corned Beef Academy. This is *the* place to go for corned beef. The chain of two boisterous modern delis has outstanding brisket and great pickles. Onion rings and french fries are popular. Beer is served at the 18th Street location only. *18th St. and J. F. Kennedy Blvd., tel. 215/568–9696; 400 Market St., tel. 215/922–2111. No credit cards. Closed weekends.*

★ **Reading Terminal Market.** A Philadelphia treasure, the Reading Terminal Market is a potpourri of 79 stalls, shops, lunch counters, and food emporiums in a one-square-block indoor farmers market. You can choose from numerous cuisines—Chinese, Greek, Mexican, Japanese, Middle Eastern, Italian, and Pennsylvania Dutch. Food options include Oriental salad bar, deli, hoagie shop, and a sushi bar. Lunch early to beat the rush. *12th and Arch Sts., tel. 215/922–2317. Open Mon.–Sat. 8 AM–6 PM. Closed Sun.*

Chinese
Expensive
★

Susanna Foo. Susanna's is the most expensive Chinese restaurant in Philadelphia, and one of the best. In a decidedly un-Chinese atmosphere—Tchaikovsky playing in the background and remnants from the steakhouse that used to occupy the building—Chef Foo presents an imaginative and varied menu. Entrées include steamed bass with scallion and ginger sauce, and shrimp with tomato, leek, and hot garlic. Skip the Western-style desserts in favor of the chocolate-dipped fortune cookies. *1512 Walnut St., tel. 215/545–2666. Reservations required. Dress: informal. AE, DC, MC, V. Closed Sun.*

Inexpensive
★

Joe's Peking Duck House. Not the best Chinese restaurant in Philadelphia but the best in Chinatown. With its friendly atmosphere and plain environment, it's like many of the other 50 or so Chinese restaurants around 10th and Race streets, but the quality is better. Joe's is known for Peking duck and barbecued pork. The Cantonese wonton soup is excellent. *925 Race St., tel. 215/922–3277. Reservations advised. Dress: informal. No credit cards.*

French
Very Expensive
★

La Truffe. La Truffe serves both rich classic and lighter modern French cuisine in a French country-inn atmosphere. Specialties include appetizer—*mille-feuille de pleurotte* (wild mushrooms in a puff pastry); entrée—*carré d'agneau au thym* (rack of lamb with thyme sauce); dessert—white chocolate mousse with fresh raspberry sauce. *10 S. Front St., tel. 215/925–5062. Reservations advised. Jacket and tie required. AE, DC, MC, V. Closed Sun.*

★ **Le Bec-Fin.** The most prestigious—and the most expensive—restaurant in Philadelphia, it's fit for a French king: apricot silk walls, crystal chandeliers, and gilt-framed mirrors. "The Fine Beak" (or more loosely "The Fine Palate") has won a zillion awards, including the Mobil Five Diamond rating in 1991 (one of only 13 restaurants in the country to do so), but at about $100 per meal it doesn't always measure up to expectations. Chef-owner Georges Perrier's five-course prix fixe dinner includes choice of appetizer, fish course, main course, sorbet and cheese, and dessert cart. A sample meal: *ravioli de crevettes dans son coulis de tomates* (ravioli of shrimps); *feuillet de St. Jacques* (Napoleon pastry with scallops in butter sauce); and *rable de lapin* (roast breast of rabbit with a rosemary sauce); it also has a *charrette de dessert*, a cart with 40 desserts. Characteristic of the restaurant is the plethora of desserts: They're included in the fixed price, and patrons pile them on their plates. A more reasonably priced alternative at Le Bec-Fin is the $31 prix fixe lunch, and downstairs Le Bar Lyonnais has an à la carte menu of light food from $5 to $12. *1523 Walnut St., tel. 215/567–1000. Reservations required. Jacket and tie advised. AE, DC, MC, V. Closed Sun.*

Expensive **Ciboulette.** It's no surprise that Ciboulette (French for chives) is as good as it is. Four years ago at the Fountain Restaurant in the Four Seasons (one of the best restaurants in town), the chef, the manager, and the sous chef left to create a restaurant of their own. Ciboulette's one small room (seating 35) was the lavish home of the original Le Bec-Fin and is now done in what one might call French Provincial Minimalist—bare, beige walls with blue trim, and art-deco sconces. For appetizer, try the marinade-of-three-fish salad (sea bass, salmon, and tuna) with coriander. Chef Bruce Lim is proud of his rack of lamb with mashed potatoes, thyme juice, and garlic sauce. The best desserts are nougat glace with peach and fruit sauce; and crème brulée. *1312 Spruce St., tel. 215/790–1210. Reservations advised. Jacket and tie preferred. AE. Closed Sun.*

Moderate **Odeon.** Among the trendiest new eateries in the city, Odeon is a posh restoration of a former flower shop, with large mirrors, green marble columns, and Art Deco sconces. The sautéed fresh goose liver in a syrupy glaze with a chestnut garnish makes a memorable first course. The sautéed crab cakes in a lemon-butter sauce is one of the specialties of the house. Recommended for dinner is the Szechuan-peppercorn–encrusted duck breast in star anise and tamari sauce. Desserts include hazelnut meringue layered with buttercream. At the bar a cruvinet serves 16 different wines by the glass. Try to sit at the balcony tables above the sweeping stairway or at the table by the window. *114 S. 12th St., tel. 215/922–5875. Reservations required on weekends. Dress: informal. AE, DC, MC, V. Closed Sun.*

Italian **Osteria Romana.** You'll pay more than you're used to for Italian
Expensive food, but Osteria Romana is worth it. The stucco walls are
★ trimmed in dark wood and the white tile floors are styled after a Roman *ristorante*. Pastas are ample enough for a relatively inexpensive entrée: Don't pass up the gnocchi. Top entrées include suckling pig; *fritto misto* (a mixture of squid, scallops, and shrimp in a delicate batter); and saltimbocca (veal, sage, and prosciutto in white wine with a dash of cream). Homemade gelato is the star dessert. *935 Ellsworth St., South Philadelphia, tel. 215/271–9191. Reservations advised. Dress: informal. AE, DC, MC, V. Closed Mon.*

Moderate **Victor Cafe.** At the Victor Cafe the waiters are opera singers
★ and the kitchen plays second fiddle to the music. The northern
Italian cuisine has improved now that the third generation of
the Di Stefano family has taken charge, but people still come
here more for the music and the atmosphere. Busts of classical
music composers adorn the shelves, and framed photos of opera
singers line the walls. *1303 Dickinson St., South Philadelphia,
tel. 215/468-3040. Weekends booked weeks in advance. Dress:
informal. AE, DC. Closed Mon.*

Inexpensive **Boccie Pizza.** Two sparkling wood-burning ovens in a refurbished warehouse near the University of Pennsylvania turn out
both traditional and "nouveau" pizzas. Design your own from
22 ingredients, or choose one from the menu, such as the Moroccan (topped with lamb strips, scallions, and garlic), or the
Hawaiian with a pesto base. Non-pizza entrées are also available. After the meal, you can play a game of boccie on the court
right in the middle of the restaurant. *4040 Locust St., tel. 215/
386-5500. Dress: informal. MC, V.*

Japanese **Tokio.** Decor here is Japanese minimalist: A toy Godzilla
Moderate guards the four tables and sushi bar; Japanese rock plays in the
★ background. Sushi and sashimi are attractively presented; try
one of the combination dishes, such as the one including octo-
pus, yellowtail, eel, and a ring of rice adorned with flying-fish
eggs. If you can't fathom raw fish, consider the sukiyaki or the
yosenabe—they're cooked on your table. *124 Lombard St., tel.
215/922-7181. Dress: informal. AE, MC, V.*

Mexican **Tequila's.** For appetizers, skip the *nachitos obligatorios* and try
Moderate one of the citric seviches (such as lobster stuffed in pineapple).
★ The best entrée is the Mayan red snapper *filetina*. Others to
sample are *chiles en nogada*—peppers filled with raisins, nuts,
and ground beef, and topped with a cream cheese sauce—and
the defatted duck baked in a ground squash seed sauce. The full
bar serves wines and a variety of Mexican beers. The walls
have photos of Pancho Villa and Emiliano Zapata and alcoves
contain Mexican glassware and ceramics. For dessert, many
favor the Chihuahua crepes with goat's-milk syrup. *1511 Locust St., tel. 215/546-0181. Dress: informal. AE, DC, MC, V.*

Middle Eastern **Marrakesh.** There are no utensils here, and diners sit on low
Moderate cushioned benches at hammered-brass tables. After you wash
★ your hands, you're served a prix fixe seven-course banquet: salads, *bastilla* (meat pie with chicken, almonds, and scrambled
eggs), chicken and lamb with honey and almonds, couscous
with vegetables, fresh fruit, baklava, and sweet mint tea. *517
S. Leithgow St., tel. 215/925-5929. Reservations required.
Dress: informal. No credit cards. Dinner only.*
The Middle East. More than just a restaurant, the Middle East
is a show. It has mirrors, Oriental rugs on the walls, and gilded
portraits worthy of a sultan's harem. You might see a hula danc-
er or a fire-eater, but the Middle East is famous for its belly
dancers. The owners, the Tayoun family, have filled the menu
with dishes from their ancestral Lebanon and other Middle
Eastern countries. Lamb is the staple—on the shank, braised
with tomatoes; in moussaka; on kebabs; and ground raw in
kibbie nayee (raw lamb and wheat germ), the national dish of
Lebanon. American food, including meatless Pritikin dishes, is
also available. *126 Chestnut St., tel. 215/922-1003. Reservations suggested. Dress: informal. AE, DC, MC, V.*

Seafood
Very Expensive

Old Original Bookbinder's. Bookbinder's, the most famous name in Philadelphia restaurants, is actually two separate restaurants with different owners in different parts of town. Though not owned by the original family, this was the site of the Bookbinders's first restaurant, opened in 1865. It's a favorite haunt of celebrities, politicians, and athletes—many of whom appear in photos on the walls. The seafood is well prepared but not necessarily the best you'll ever eat. "Bookie's" is often criticized for being overpriced (entrées range from $25 to $30) and touristy (it runs a gift shop with Bookbinder souvenirs). You can select a lobster from a tank and have it cooked to order. *125 Walnut St., tel. 215/925-7027. Reservations suggested. Dress: informal. AE, DC, MC, V.*

Expensive

Bookbinder's Seafood House. This Bookbinder's is owned by the original family. Seafood House, a tad less expensive than Old Original, has typical seafood restaurant decor such as stuffed swordfish mounted on the walls and fishermen's nets dangling from the ceiling. The menu features lobster Coleman (chunks of lobster baked in a Newburg sauce), crab imperial, fresh stone crabs, snapper soup, and baked crabs. *215 S. 15th St., Center City, tel. 215/545-1137. Reservations suggested. Dress: informal. AE, DC, MC, V.*

Moderate
★

Sansom Street Oyster House. This Philadelphia favorite serves first-rate raw oysters plus clams, fish, shellfish, and grilled and blackened dishes, as well as some nonseafood items like steak and chicken. It's an unpretentious place with dark wood paneling and uncovered tables. The family collection of more than 200 oyster plates covers the walls. For dessert, try the peanut butter pie with chocolate. *1516 Sansom St., tel. 215/567-7683. Reservations accepted only for parties of 5 or more. Dress: informal. AE, DC, MC, V. Closed Sun.*

Steaks
Expensive

The Saloon. Here's a steakhouse with Italian specialties. Everything it does is big: big pieces of meat, big drinks, big prices. Big money went into the antique turn-of-the-century decor—mahogany paneling, mirrors, and stained glass. For an appetizer, try the salad of radicchio with shiitake mushrooms, served warm. For an entrée, order the off-the-menu special risotto with abundant porcini mushrooms, or cannelloni filled with veal in one of the excellent tomato sauces. Desserts include lemon and berry tarts. *750 S. 7th St., South Philadelphia, tel. 215/627-1811. Reservations recommended. Dress: informal. AE. Closed Sun.*

Vietnamese
Inexpensive
★

Van's Garden. Hodgepodge decor includes flocked red and black wallpaper, linoleum floors, and blond wood wainscoting. A superb appetizer is grilled meatballs wrapped in rice paper, with carrots, radishes, cucumbers, noodles, and a thick brown bean sauce for dipping—a sort of Vietnamese hoagie. Among entrées, you can get 10 sweet-and-sour shrimp in a tempura-like batter. *121 N. 11th St., Chinatown, tel. 215/923-2439. Dress: informal. BYOB. No credit cards.*

Lodging

Philadelphia has no off-season rates, but most hotels offer weekend packages. The following price categories have been used: *Very Expensive*, over $140; *Expensive*, $100–$140; *Moderate*, $50–$100; *Inexpensive*, under $50.

Very Expensive   **Four Seasons.** If a director wanted a location for a romantic ho-
★   tel-room view in Philadelphia, he would choose a room here,
overlooking the fountains in Logan Circle and the Benjamin
Franklin Parkway. Built in 1983, the eight-story *U*-shaped hotel has block-long hallways that some guests don't like. Guest-
room furniture is Federal style, dark and stately. Philadelphia's most expensive hotel provides terry robes and a complimentary shoeshine; bidets, formerly in all the bathrooms,
are now available only upon request. *1 Logan Sq. (near major
museums), 19103, tel. 215/963–1500 or 800/332–3442. 371
rooms. Facilities: concierge service, 5 no-smoking floors, exercise room, dry sauna, massage, aerobics classes, indoor pool,
restaurant, indoor/outdoor café. AE, DC, MC, V.*

★   **Hotel Atop the Bellevue.** A Philadelphia institution for 80 years,
the elegant Bellevue hotel was reopened in 1989 on seven floors
in its original building. The Barrymore Room, topped by a
stained-glass 30-foot dome, and the seven-story Conservatory
atrium are just two of the hotel's lavish public areas. From the
champagne toast available at registration, to the telephones
and TVs in the bathrooms, the Bellevue has more luxurious
amenities than any other hotel in town. Rooms are large and
each has an entertainment center with color TV, stereo, and
VCR (choose from the concierge's library of 50 cassettes); magazine rack with current periodicals; minibar; and computer mo-
dem data port. Guests have free use of the Sporting Club, the
best health club in town. *Broad and Walnut Sts., 19102, tel.
215/893–1776 or 800/221–0833. 170 rooms. Facilities: concierge, restaurant, lounge, wine bar, health club, shops. AE,
DC, MC, V.*

The Rittenhouse. This luxury hotel takes full advantage of its
Rittenhouse Square location; many rooms and both restaurants
overlook the city's classiest park. The expansive white-marbled
lobby leads to the Mary Cassatt Tea Room and Lounge and a
cloistered garden. The 33-story building's sawtooth design
gives the guest rooms their unusual shapes, with nooks and alcoves. Each room has two TVs, three telephones, an entertainment center in an armoire, a fully-stocked minibar, and a king-
size bed. Ninth-floor rooms facing the square have the best
views. *210 West Rittenhouse Sq., 19103, tel. 215/546–9000 or
800/635–1042. 98 rooms, including 11 suites. Facilities: 2 restaurants, bar, concierge, health club, business center, 3 no-
smoking floors. AE, DC, MC, V.*

Ritz-Carlton. Ritzy it is: a "security" elevator from the arrival
lobby to the main lobby; mantelpieces from Italy; silk walls in
the bar; a million dollars' worth of art displayed throughout.
Opened in November 1990, the 15-story building is nestled between the twin blue towers of Liberty Place and adjacent to the
Shops at Liberty Place (more than 70 stores, boutiques, and
restaurants). All rooms have a silver-gray motif; most have
king-size beds, although rooms with oversize twins are available. All the typical luxury amenities are here: entertainment
center in armoire; honor bar; complimentary shoe shine; valet
laundry service; in-the-bathroom telephone, terry robes, hair
dryers, and scale. You'll also find a recent copy of *Philadelphia*
magazine and a *TV Guide* marked for the proper day with a
Ritz-Carlton bookmark listing the hotel's special services. *17th
and Chestnut Sts., 19103, tel. 215/563–1600 or 800/241–3333.
290 guest rooms. Facilities: restaurant, bar, lobby lounge, concierge, baby-sitting, health club. AE, DC, MC, V.*

Expensive **The Barclay.** There's something special about having Rittenhouse Square right outside your front door. The elegant, dark-paneled lobby leads to a registration area sparkling with a half-dozen crystal chandeliers and matching wall fixtures. The hotel was built in 1929 and renovated in 1981. The halls have hardwood floors and Oriental rugs. Half the rooms have four-poster beds—and many of those have canopies. Furniture is antique style throughout and in most rooms TV sets are concealed in classic armoires. *Rittenhouse Sq. E., 19103, tel. 215/545–0300 or 800/421–6662. 240 rooms. Facilities: concierge, restaurant, lounge. AE, DC, MC, V.*

Holiday Inn Independence Mall. "Independence Mall" in the name is no exaggeration: This is one of the hotels most convenient to the downtown historic area. To complement its location, all rooms are done in Colonial decor with Ethan Allen Georgetown furniture, including poster beds and wing chairs. *4th and Arch Sts., 19106, tel. 215/923–8660 or 800/HOLIDAY. 364 rooms, 7 suites. Facilities: outdoor pool, videogame room, lounge, restaurant. AE, DC, MC, V.*

The Warwick. The lobby, brightened by mirrors and 18-foot Palladian windows, hosts a constant stream of activity. The 400 rooms are partly hotel rooms and partly apartments, making for an interesting mix of guests in business suits and residents in shorts and sneakers. The spacious rooms were totally redecorated in 1988 in "English country style." Bathrooms are flowery and bright, each adorned with commissioned watercolor by local artist Joe Barker. Guests get free admission to posh Polo Bay Club, a nightclub. *17th and Locust Sts., 19103, tel. 215/735–6000 or 800/523–4210. 200 rooms. Facilities: restaurant/bar, coffee shop, business center. AE, DC, MC, V.*

Moderate **Chestnut Hill Hotel.** Here's a colonial inn in the heart of Chestnut Hill, adjacent to a farmers market and shopping complex. Built as a hotel in 1899, the four-story building was renovated in 1983. Ask to see the rooms first; they vary widely in size and ambience. Some have mahogany reproductions of 18th-century furniture, including four-poster beds. A packet of brochures in each room describes area shops and sights. *8229 Germantown Ave., 19118, tel. 215/242–5905. 28 rooms, including 3 suites. Facilities: 2 restaurants. AE, MC, V.*

Quality Inn Center City. If you're willing to stay a bit away from downtown but near the museums, you'll find a bargain here. The three-story, Y-shaped building underwent a $5 million renovation in 1984. Rooms are done in mauve and taupe with oak-finish furniture and individual climate control. The best view faces south toward the Benjamin Franklin Parkway, the Rodin Museum, and the downtown skyline. *501 N. 22nd St., 19130, tel. 215/568–8300. 278 rooms, including 4 suites. Facilities: restaurant, outdoor café, sports lounge, outdoor pool, free parking. AE, DC, MC, V.*

★ **Quality Inn Historic Downtown Suites.** Because of the out-of-the-way location, you get suite accommodations at hotel-room prices. It opened late 1985 in a historically certified 1890 building that was once the Bentwood Rocker Factory. Much of the original building was incorporated into the present decor, including exposed brick walls and overhead beams, which give rooms a rustic, homey atmosphere. Every suite has a kitchen. The environment is East meets West: Drexel Heritage furniture with Oriental prints and accent pieces. *1010 Race St., 19107, tel. 215/922–1730 or 800/221–2222. 96 suites. Facilities:*

lounge, limited free parking, free buffet breakfast. AE, DC, MC, V.

Society Hill Hotel. This 1832 former longshoreman's house is one of the smallest hotels in the city. Renovated in 1988, all 12 rooms are uniquely furnished with antiques, brass beds, and lamps. Fresh flowers adorn all rooms and breakfast (included in rate) is brought to your room with fresh-squeezed juice and hand-dipped chocolates. *301 Chestnut St., 19106, tel. 215/925-1394. 12 rooms, including 6 suites. Facilities: outdoor café, piano bar, restaurant. AE, DC, MC, V.*

Thomas Bond House. Spend the night in the heart of Olde City the way Philadelphians did 220 years ago. Built in 1769 by a prominent local physician, this four-story house recently underwent a faithful, meticulous restoration of everything from its molding and wall sconces to its millwork and flooring. All rooms have 18th-century features such as marble fireplaces and four-poster Thomasville beds. It doesn't get any more Colonial than this. Breakfast included in rate. *129 S. 2nd St., 19106, tel. 215/923-8523. 12 rooms, including 2 suites. Facilities: parlor, complimentary wet bar. AE, MC, V.*

Inexpensive
Chamounix Mansion. Here's the cheapest place to stay in Philadelphia—$9.50 a night plus $3 American Youth Hostel membership. Located on a wooded bluff overlooking the Schuylkill River (and, unfortunately, the Schuylkill Expressway), the city's only youth hostel feels like it's out in the country. This restored 1802 Quaker country estate is loaded with character. The entrance hall is lined with flags; period rooms have antiques; walls display old maps, sketches, and paintings. Drawbacks: dormitory-style living, shared baths, hard to find. *Chamounix Dr., 19131, tel. 215/878-3676. 6 rooms for 48 people, shared baths and kitchen. Facilities: game room, outdoor sports. No credit cards. Closed Dec. 15–Jan. 15.*

International House. This residence for students and professors from around the world is located on the University of Pennsylvania campus. Rooms are available only from the end of May to the end of August, however, and guests must have an affiliation with an educational institution. The high-rise building has an unusual poured-concrete, tiered design and an oddly barren atrium. Both the public areas and the rooms themselves have a rough-hewn, spartan feel. Single rooms share bath and living room; double rooms have 2 single beds and private bath. *3701 Chestnut St., 19104, tel. 215/387-5125. 379 rooms, but limited number available. Facilities: cafeteria, bar. MC, V.*

Bed-and-Breakfasts

Bed and Breakfast, Center City. It represents a dozen homes in the city, from a posh high rise on Rittenhouse Square to a restored town house just off the square. Prices range from $45 to $75, 20% deposit required for stays of more than one night. *1804 Pine St., Philadelphia 19103, tel. 215/735-1137. No credit cards.*

Bed and Breakfast Connections. Its selection of more than 50 host homes and inns includes a Colonial town house, an English Tudor mansion on Chestnut Hill, and an 18th-century farmhouse on the Main Line. Prices range from $30 to $125. *Box 21, Devon 19333, tel. 215/687-3565 or 800/448-3619. AE, MC, V.*

Bed and Breakfast—The Manor. This service has various locations throughout Philadelphia and surrounding areas, including Amish country. Most hosts supply transportation for a nominal fee. Some accommodate the handicapped. Prices range from $45 to $85. *Box 416, 830 Village Rd., Lampeter 17537, tel. 717/464–9564. MC, V.*

Bed and Breakfast of Philadelphia. This reservation service books over 100 host homes in Philadelphia, Valley Forge, Amish country, and New Hope. Options range from a Federal town house in the downtown historic area to a pre-Revolutionary farmhouse in Chester County and many suburban homes. Prices range from $35 to $150. *Box 252, Gradyville 19039, tel. 215/358–4747 or 800/733–4747. AE, MC, V.*

The Arts

For current productions and performances, check the "Guide to the Lively Arts" in the daily *Philadelphia Inquirer*, the "Weekend" section of the Friday *Inquirer*, the "Friday" section of the *Philadelphia Daily News*, and the Donnelley Directory Events Hotline (tel. 215/337–7777 ext. 2540). *Philadelphia Spotlite*, a free weekly guide listing plays, music, sports, and events, is available at the Visitors Center (16th St. and John F. Kennedy Blvd.). Check "UpStages" (tel. 215/567–0670) at the Visitors Center for tickets to some of the smaller productions and concerts around town, sometimes at a discount.

The major arts venues are:

Academy of Music (Broad and Locust Sts., tel. 215/893–1930) is home to the renowned **Philadelphia Orchestra** from September to May, the **Philly Pops** (tel. 215/735–7506) from October to May, the **Pennsylvania Ballet** (tel. 215/551–7014) October to April, and the **Opera Company of Philadelphia** (tel. 215/732–5814) between November and April. In May, there's a Gilbert and Sullivan operetta by the **Savoy Company** (tel. 215/735–7161), the oldest amateur G&S company in the country.

Annenberg Center (3680 Walnut St., tel. 215/898–6791) has four stages, from the 120-seat Studio to the 970-seat Zellerbach Theater. Something is going on almost all the time—with established stars like Liv Ullman and Jose Ferrer and oddball acts such as the Flying Karamazov Brothers and Avner the Eccentric. The **Philadelphia Dance Company** (Philadanco) performs here in spring and fall (tel. 215/387–8200).

Painted Bride Art Center (230 Vine St., Old City, tel. 215/925–9914), by day a contemporary art gallery, by night is a "multidisciplinary, multicultural performance center," featuring performance art; prose and poetry readings; folk, electronic, international, and new music; jazz, dance, and avant-garde theater.

Port of History Museum (Penn's Landing at Walnut St., tel 215/925–3804) features children's theater with the **American Theater Arts for Youth** (tel. 215/563–3501) and the classical music series **Music from Marlboro** (tel. 215/569–4690) from October to May.

Shubert Theater (250 S. Broad St., tel. 215/732–5446), part of the University of the Arts, is the stage for the **Pennsylvania Opera Theater** (tel. 215/440–9797) November to May and the **Pennsylvania Ballet** (tel. 215/551–7014) October to April, as well as musicals and dramas occasionally performed by touring companies.

Walnut Street Theater (9th and Walnut Sts., tel. 215/574–3550), founded in 1809, is the oldest English-speaking theater in continuous use in the United States. Musicals, comedy, and drama, as well as chamber music concerts, are staged in its lovely auditorium.

Theater   **Forrest Theater** (1114 Walnut St., tel. 215/923–1515) has major Broadway productions, recently *Cats, La Cage Aux Folles, Les Misérables,* and *Phantom of the Opera.*

Philadelphia Festival Theater for New Plays (3680 Walnut St., tel. 215/222–5000) draws national attention with new works by new playwrights. It runs from October through June.

Freedom Theater (1346 N. Broad St., tel. 215/765–2793) is the oldest and most active black theater in Philadelphia. It's quartered in the Heritage House, the former residence of the great American actor Edwin Forrest. Performances are held September through April.

Concerts   **All-Star Forum** (tel. 215/735–7506), presented by impresario Moe Septee, features classical music superstars such as Itzhak Perlman and Isaac Stern.

Film   **Ritz Five** (214 Walnut St., tel. 215/925–7900), the finest movie theater in town, shows avant-garde films and films from all over the world.

Roxy Screening Rooms (2023 Sansom St., tel. 215/561–0114) is an art house showing the intellectual and the esoteric.

Temple Cinematheque (1619 Walnut St., tel. 215/787–1529) is a favorite of film buffs who prefer old movies and foreign movies.

Nightlife

Nightlife in Philadelphia is far better than it used to be (when they supposedly rolled up the sidewalks at 8 o'clock). Today you can listen to a chanteuse in a chic basement nightclub; dance till 3 AM in a smoky bistro; and watch street jugglers, mimes, and magicians on a Society Hill corner. For current information, check the entertainment pages of the *Philadelphia Inquirer,* the *Philadelphia Daily News,* and *Philadelphia* magazine. You can also call radio station WRTI's "Jazz Line," an extensive, up-to-the-minute listing of music in town, at 215/787–5277. For information about Penn's Landing events call 215/923–4992.

Bars, Lounges, and   **Dirty Frank's** (347 S. 13th St., tel. 215/732–5010) is dirty,
Cabarets   cheap, and a Philadelphia classic, attracting students, artists, journalists, and resident characters around the horseshoe-shaped bar.

Top of Centre Square (15th and Market Sts., tel. 215/563–9494) offers the best view in town—41 stories high, right across from the statue of William Penn atop City Hall.

Woody's (202 S. 13th St., tel. 215/545–1893) is Philadelphia's most popular gay bar.

Comedy Clubs   **Bank Street Comedy Club** (31 Bank St., tel. 215/226–5781) presents local amateurs (Thursdays) and headliners from New York and Los Angeles Friday and Saturday.

Comedy Works (126 Chestnut St., tel. 215/922–5997) features top young comedians from both coasts Wednesday–Saturday.

Dancing and   **Chestnut Cabaret** (3801 Chestnut St., tel. 215/382–1201), lo-
Discos   cated near the University of Pennsylvania campus, is a concert hall/dance club featuring New Wave music, rhythm-and-blues,

reggae, alternative, heavy metal, and rock 'n' roll. The crowd is mostly in their 20s and early 30s.

Flanigan's (Abbott's Sq., 2nd and South Sts., tel. 215/928–9898), a huge, glittery night spot, is popular with young singles. Top-40 dance music and videos attract a mixed crowd to a large, modern, laser-lit dance floor.

Monte Carlo Living Room (2nd and South Sts., tel. 215/925–2220) is a quiet, intimate upscale room where customers in their 30s to 50s dance to Top-40 hits, European sounds, and South American music.

Polo Bay (Warwick Hotel, 17th and Locust Sts., tel. 215/546–8800), Philadelphia's premier upscale "meet market," has a small dance floor.

Quincy's (Adam's Mark Hotel, City Ave. and Monument Rd., tel. 215/581–5000) plays live rock 'n' roll or DJ'ed dance music in a re-created turn-of-the-century atmosphere.

Revival (22 S. 3rd St., tel. 215/627–4825) presents New Wave and contemporary music, performance art, fashion shows, theme nights, and rock videos.

Trocadero (1003 Arch St., tel. 215/592–TROC) is a spacious rock n' roll club in Chinatown that occupies a former burlesque house where W. C. Fields and Mae West performed. A lot of the old decor remains: Mirrors, pillars, and balconies surround a dance floor. The under-30 crowd dances to nationally known acts or DJs.

Jazz   **Cafe Borgia** (406 S. 2nd St., downstairs from Lautrec restaurant, tel. 215/574–0414) has local singers performing ballads, blues, and old songs in the Billie Holliday style.

Ortlieb's Jazz Haus (847 N. 3rd St., tel. 215/922–1035) plays good jazz in a 100-year-old bar.

Valley Forge

If you're interested in early American history, a visit to the monuments, markers, huts, and headquarters in Valley Forge National Historical Park, 18 miles from center city Philadelphia, is illuminating. You'll have to take the Schuylkill Expressway to Valley Forge anyway to pick up the Pennsylvania Turnpike west to Pennsylvania Dutch country, so consider stopping off for an hour or two to stroll around the park, and perhaps have a picnic at one of the park's three picnic sites.

Valley Forge National Historical Park preserves the moment in American history when George Washington's Continental Army endured the bitter winter of 1777–1778. Although the park's 3,500 acres of rolling hills offer serenity and quiet beauty, it is doubtful that Washington enjoyed any peaceful nights as he struggled with the morale problems that beset his troops. The army had just lost the battles of Brandywine, White Horse, and Germantown. While the British occupied Philadelphia, Washington's soldiers were forced to endure horrid conditions—blizzards that iced up the rivers, inadequate food and clothing, damp quarters, and disease. Many men deserted and although no battle was fought at Valley Forge, 2,000 American soldiers died.

But the troops won one victory that winter—a war of the will. The forces slowly regained strength and confidence under the leadership of Prussian drillmaster Friedrich von Steuben. In June 1778, Washington led his troops away from Valley Forge in search of the British. Fortified, the Continental Army was able to carry on the fight for five years more.

Numbers in the margin correspond to points of interest on the Valley Forge map.

❶ **Valley Forge National Historical Park,** administered by the National Park Service, is the site of the 1777–1778 winter encampment of General George Washington and the Continental Army. Stop first at the Visitor Center for a 15-minute orientation film, exhibits, and a map for a 10-mile, self-guided auto tour of the park attractions. Stops include reconstructed huts of the Muhlenberg Brigade, and the National Memorial Arch, which pays tribute to those soldiers who suffered through the infamous winter. Other sites include the bronze equestrian statue on the encampment of General Anthony Wayne and his Pennsylvania troops; Artillery Park, where the soldiers stored their cannons; and the Isaac Potts House, which served as Washington's headquarters. A park employee is stationed here to answer questions. From May through October, you can purchase an auto-tour cassette tape for $8 or rent a tape and player for $10. The park contains 6 miles of paved trails for jogging or bicycling, and hiking trails. Visitors can picnic at any of three designated areas. A leisurely visit to the park will take no more than half a day. *Rtes. 23 and 363, Box 953, Valley Forge, PA 19481, tel. 215/783–1077. Admission to Washington's headquarters: $1 adults 17–61. Open daily 8:30–5. Closed Christmas.*

The Valley Forge National Historical Park Bus Tour (tel. 215/783–5788) is a narrated minibus tour that originates from the park Visitor Center (Rtes. 23 and 363). Passengers can alight, visit sites, and reboard. Tours are scheduled from May through September; times vary. Tours cost $5.50 for adults, $4.50 children 5–16.

❷ The **Valley Forge Historical Society Museum** tells the Valley Forge story with military equipment and Colonial artifacts plus a large collection of items that belonged to Martha and George Washington. The nearby Chapel Cabin Shop sells homemade goodies such as Martha's 16-Bean Soup and blue-barb jam. *In the Washington Memorial Chapel on Rte. 23, tel. 215/783–0535. Admission: $3 family, $1.50 adults, $1 senior citizens, 50¢ children 2–12. Open Mon.–Sat. 9:30–4:30, Sun. 1–4:30. Closed Thanksgiving, Christmas, New Year's Day, and Easter.*

❸ **Mill Grove** was the first American home of Haitian-born artist and naturalist John James Audubon. Built in 1762, the house is now a museum furnished in the style of the early 1800s and displays Audubon's major works. The collection includes reproductions, original prints, his paintings of birds and wildlife, and the double-elephant folio of his *Birds of America*. The attic has been restored to a studio and taxidermy room. The Audubon Wildlife Sanctuary has 4 miles of marked hiking trails along Perkiomen Creek. *Audubon and Pawlings Rds., Box 25, Audubon, PA 19407, tel. 215/666–5593. Admission free. Museum open Tues.–Sat. 10–4, Sun. 1–4; grounds open Tues.–Sun. dawn–dusk. Closed Thanksgiving, Christmas, and New Year's Day.*

On the Horseshoe Trail, two miles west of Valley Forge park, is
❹ the **Wharton Esherick Museum,** the former home and studio of

Court and Plaza, **5**

Mill Grove, **3**

Valley Forge
Historical Society
Museum, **2**

Valley Forge National
Historical Park, **1**

Wharton Esherick
Museum, **4**

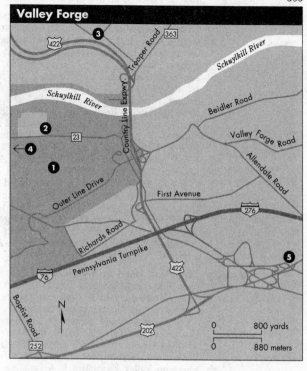

the "Dean of American Crafts." Best known for his sculptural furniture, Esherick shaped a new aesthetic in decorative arts by bridging art with furniture. The museum houses 200 samples of his work—paintings, woodcuts, furniture, and wood sculptures. The studio, in which everything from the light switches to the spiral staircase is hand-carved, is one of his monumental achievements. *Box 595, Paoli, PA 19301, tel. 215/ 644–5822. Admission: $5 adults, $3 children under 12. Open Sat. 10–5, Sun. 1–5 for hourly guided tours. Reservations required. Group tours weekdays. Closed Jan. and Feb.*

5 For lunch or an afternoon of browsing, head for the **Court and Plaza** at King of Prussia, one of the nation's largest shopping complexes. These two adjacent malls contain more than a dozen restaurants, 300 shops and boutiques, and a half-dozen major department stores, including Bloomingdale's and a stunning new branch of Philadelphia's own Strawbridge and Clothier. *Rte. 202 and N. Gulph Rd., tel. 215/265–5727. Open Mon.–Sat. 10–9:30, Sun. 11–5.*

Dining and Lodging

The following dining price categories have been used: *Expensive*, over $25; *Moderate*, $15–$25; *Inexpensive*, under $15.

The following lodging price categories have been used: *Very Expensive*, over $100; *Expensive*, $80–$100; *Moderate*, $65–$80; *Inexpensive*, under $65.

King of Prussia **Bocconcini.** Updated northern Italian specialties (angel hair
Dining pasta with goat cheese and sun-dried tomatoes; veal medallions
★ topped with lobster gratin) are served amid majestic marble
columns and hanging vines interlaced on cherrywood ceiling
beams. Panna Cotta, a cold cream soufflé, is the winning dessert. *Plaza Hotel at Valley Forge, N. Gulph Rd. and 1st Ave.,
tel. 215/265–1500. Reservations advised. Jackets required for
dinner, suggested for lunch. AE, DC, MC, V. Expensive.*

Kennedy Supplee Restaurant. New American cuisine is served
in the seven dining rooms of a circa 1852 Italian Renaissance
mansion overlooking Valley Forge National Historical Park.
*1100 W. Valley Forge Rd., tel. 215/337–3777. Reservations ad-
vised. Jackets required in The Carvery. AE, DC, MC, V. No
lunch weekends. Moderate–Expensive.*

Lily Langtry's. This lavishly appointed Victorian-era res-
taurant/cabaret serves American and Continental dishes, but
the campy Las Vegas–style entertainment—corny comedians,
scantily clad showgirls, and some fine singers, dancers, and ice
skaters—is the real draw here. *Sheraton Valley Forge Hotel,
N. Gulph Rd. and 1st Ave., tel. 215/337–LILY. Reservations
required. Jackets suggested. AE, DC, MC, V. Moderate.*

Lodging **The Plaza Hotel at Valley Forge.** The six-story Radisson,
opened in early 1988, and the Sheraton Valley Forge flank the
Valley Forge Convention Center and share several restaurants
and nightclubs. Contemporary rooms here are minisuites with
Jacuzzis for two and numerous telephones and TV sets. *N.
Gulph Rd. and 1st Ave., 19406, tel. 215/265–1500 or 800/333–
3333. 160 rooms. Facilities: restaurant, dinner theater, disco,
health club, outdoor pool. AE, DC, MC, V. Very Expensive.*

★ **Sheraton Valley Forge Hotel.** A bustling high rise caters to
groups and couples escaping to Jacuzzi-equipped fantasy
theme suites—a prehistoric cave, a wild-and-woolly jungle,
the outer-space-like "Outer Limits." *N. Gulph Rd. and 1st
Ave., 19406, tel. 215/337–2000 or 800/325–3535. 326 rooms, including 72 fantasy suites. Facilities: restaurants, dinner theater, disco, health club, outdoor pool. AE, DC, MC, V. Very
Expensive.*

Comfort Inn at Valley Forge. Spacious, modern rooms with
king-size beds, three phones, VCR, stocked refrigerators, and
remote control TV make this new five-story hotel a good buy.
*550 W. DeKalb Pike (Rt. 202N), 19406, tel. 215/962–0700 or
800/228–5150. 121 rooms. Facilities: complimentary Continental breakfast, dining area with microwave and frozen
foods. AE, DC, MC, V. Expensive.*

The Arts

Valley Forge Music Fair (tel. 215/644–5000) is a theater-in-the-
round presenting top names in entertainment, with recent performances by Diana Ross, the Pointer Sisters, and Chuck
Mangione.

The **People's Light and Theater Company** in nearby Malvern
(tel. 215/644–3500), a pioneer of the regional theater movement, offers classics and avant-garde productions throughout
the year.

Lancaster County

The plain and fancy live side by side in Lancaster County, some 65 miles west of Philadelphia. This is Pennsylvania Dutch Country, where horse-drawn buggies and horn-tooting cars jockey for position on picturesque country roads.

The tourists come to see the Old Order Amish, one of the most conservative of the Pennsylvania Dutch sects. Clinging to a centuries-old way of life, the Amish shun the amenities of modern civilization, using kerosene or gas lamps instead of electric lighting, horse-drawn buggies instead of automobiles. Ironically, in turning their backs on the modern world, they have attracted the world's attention.

This bucolic region can be hectic, especially on summer weekends and in October, when the fall foliage attracts crowds. Its main arteries, U.S. 30 and Route 340, are lined with souvenir shops and outlet stores. The farmers markets and family-style restaurants are often crowded with busloads of tourists. But there is still much charm here in the general stores, one-room schoolhouses, country lanes, and picture-perfect farms, many of which welcome overnight guests. There are pretzel factories to tour, quilts to buy, and a host of attractions for railroad buffs. The trick is to visit the top attractions and then get off the beaten path. If possible, plan your trip for early spring, fall, or Christmas season, when it is less crowded.

Note: Although many restaurants, shops, and farmers markets close Sunday for the Sabbath, commercial attractions are open.

Guided Tours **Amish Country Tours** (Rte. 340 between Bird-in-Hand and Intercourse, tel. 717/768–7063) has a variety of large bus or minivan tours. Most popular is the four-hour Amish farmlands trip.

Brunswick Tours (2034 Lincoln Hwy. E, tel. 717/397–7541) provides private guides who will tour with you in your car.

The Mennonite Information Center (2209 Millstream Rd., Lancaster, tel. 717/299–0954) has local Mennonite guides who will join you in your car.

Rutts Tours (3466 Old Philadelphia Pike, Intercourse, tel. 717/768–8238) has guides who will join you in your car.

For an aerial tour, try **Glick Aviation** at Smoketown Airport (Mabel Ave. off Rte. 340, Smoketown, tel. 717/394–6476). Fifteen-minute flights in a four-seater plane (pilot plus three) provide a splendid view of rolling farmlands.

You can rent or purchase a cassette tape for the self-guided **Auto Tape Tour of Pennsylvania Dutch Country.** Minimum driving time is 90 minutes. *Available at Dutch Wonderland (2249 U.S. 30E, Lancaster) and Holiday Inn East (521 Greenfield Rd., Lancaster).*

Tapetours, another self-guided auto tour, begins at the Pennsylvania Dutch Convention & Visitors Bureau on Greenfield Road. The 28 stops take about three hours. *Available from Brunswick Tours (see above).*

Numbers in the margin correspond to points of interest on the Lancaster County map.

From Philadelphia, take the Schuylkill Expressway (I–76) west to the Pennsylvania Turnpike. For a more scenic route, follow U.S. 30 (Lancaster Pike) west from Philadelphia. It's about 65 miles; allow 90 minutes. Exit 22 from the Pennsylvania Turnpike will get you onto Route 10, which you follow south to **People's Place**, a "people-to-people interpretation center" that provides an excellent introduction to the Amish, Mennonites, and Hutterites. A 30-minute multiscreen slide show titled "Who Are the Amish?" features close-ups of Amish life and perceptive narration. Geared toward children, **Amish World** is a hands-on exhibit on transportation, dress, schools, the effects of growing old, and mutual aid. Children can try on bonnets and play in the "feeling box." Don't miss the collection of wood sculptures by Aaron Zook. "Hazel's People," a feature film starring Geraldine Page and set in the Mennonite community, is shown Monday through Saturday from April through October at 6 PM; separate admission fee. *Rte. 340, Intercourse, tel. 717/768–7171. Admission: $4.25 adults, $2.10 children. Open Apr.–Oct., Mon.–Sat. 9:30–9; Nov.–Mar., Mon.–Sat. 9:30–5.*

Time Out To sample the local ice cream, order one of the 18 farm-fresh flavors at **Lapp Valley Farm**. It also sells homemade root beer and has animals to entertain the children. *Mentzer Rd., between New Holland and Intercourse (from Intercourse, follow Rte. 340 1 mi east, turn left on New Holland Rd., left on Peters Rd., and right on Mentzer Rd.), tel. 717/354–7988. Open weekdays noon–dark, Sat. 8 AM–7 PM, or later.*

Following Route 340 west past Bird-in-Hand will bring you to **Abe's Buggy Rides**. Abe chats about the Amish during a 2-mile spin down country roads in an Amish family carriage. *No phone. Price: $10 adults, $5 children 3–12. Open Mon.–Sat. 7 AM–dusk.*

Several furnished farmhouses offer a simulated, up-close look at how the Amish live. Note that these are commercial, not Amish-run, enterprises.

The Amish Homestead house and farm tour provides perhaps the most complete introduction to Amish life. You'll learn about Amish origins, worship, clothing, courtship, marriage and honeymoon rituals, the wearing of beards, and burial. The house and farm are occupied by an Amish and a Dunkard family and are in full operation. A 40-minute tour covers five rooms of the 1744 farmhouse and farm buildings. There are acres of growing crops and a vegetable garden. *2034 Lincoln Hwy. E (U.S. 30), Lancaster, tel. 717/392–0832. Admission: $4 adults, $2 children 6–11. Open daily 9–4, until 7 in summer.*

The Amish Farm and House offers 40-minute tours through a 10-room circa 1805 house furnished in the Old Order Amish style. A map guides visitors to the farmstead's animals, waterwheel, and barns. *2395 Lincoln Hwy. E (U.S. 30), Lancaster, tel. 717/394–6185. Admission: $4.25 adults, $2.50 children 5–11. Open daily 8:30–5, until 4 in winter, 6 in summer.*

Save an hour or two to explore the country roads on your own. Many Amish farms (they're the ones with windmills and green blinds) are clustered in the area between Ephrata and New Holland. Drive the side roads between routes 23 and 340; visit the roadside stands and farms where hand-painted signs entice you with quilts or farm-fresh produce and eggs. Drive in and

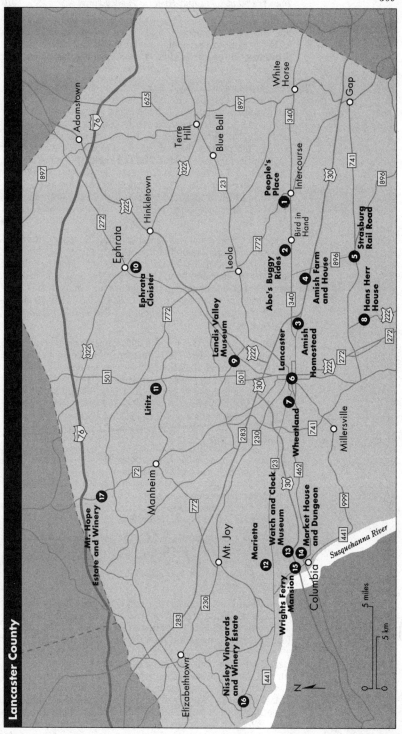

Lancaster County

Adamstown

625

897

76

897

Ephrata
272
Ephrata Cloister 10

322

Hinkletown
222

322

772

Terre Hill
322
Blue Ball
23

897

340

People's Place 1
Intercourse
Bird in Hand 2
Abe's Buggy Rides
340
Amish Farm and House 4
896

White Horse

Gap
741

896

Leola
772

501

Landis Valley Museum 9
222

501

Lancaster 6
30
501

Amish Homestead 3

222
272

Hans Herr House 8
222
272

Strasburg Rail Road 5

Lititz 11

Wheatland 7
741

Manheim
72

283
230

Millersville

Watch and Clock Museum 13
23
30

Marietta 12

Mt. Joy

772

462

Market House and Dungeon 14
Wrights Ferry Mansion 15
Columbia

30

999

441

Susquehanna River

283

Elizabethtown

230

441

Nissley Vineyards and Winery Estate 16

Mt. Hope Estate and Winery 17
76

N

0   5 miles
0   5 km

chat with the Amish—they always welcome polite inquiries.
For take-home goodies and gifts, stop at a farmers
market.Train lovers could easily spend an entire day in
Strasburg. To get from U.S. 30 to Strasburg, head south on
Route 896 and turn left on Route 741.

❺ The Strasburg Rail Road is a scenic 9-mile excursion from
Strasburg to Paradise on a rolling antique chartered in 1832 to
carry milk, mail, and coal. Passengers can chug along in the
open coach featured in *Hello Dolly.* Called America's oldest
short line, the wooden coaches are pulled by an iron steam locomotive. You can buy the makings for a picnic at the Strasburg
Country Store (Rtes. 896 and 741) and alight at Groff's Grove in
Paradise for a picnic lunch. *Rte. 741, Strasburg, tel. 717/687-
7522. Round-trip cost: $5.50 adults, $3 children 3–11. Open
mid-Mar.–Nov. and Dec. 26–31, daily; Dec. 1–24 and mid-
Jan.–mid-Mar., weekends only. Closed first two weeks of Jan.
Call for hours.*

Across the road from the Strasburg Rail Road, the **Railroad
Museum of Pennsylvania** features 13 colossal engines built between 1888 and 1930; 12 railroad cars including a Pullman
sleeper that operated from 1855 to 1906; sleighs; and railroad
memorabilia documenting the history of Pennsylvania railroading. *Rte. 741, Strasburg, tel. 717/687-8628. Admission: $5
adults, $3 children 6–17. Open Mon.–Sat. 9–5, Sun. noon–5.
Closed Mon. Nov.–Apr.*

On a smaller scale, antique and 20th-century model trains are
on display at the **Toy Train Museum,** the showplace for the
Train Collectors Association. There are four operating layouts
plus hundreds of locomotives and cars in display cases, nostalgia films, and many "push-me" buttons. *Paradise La., just
north of Rte. 741, Strasburg, tel. 717/687-8976. Admission: $3
adults, $1.50 children 5–12. Open May–Oct. and Christmas
week, daily 10–5; Apr. and Nov.–mid-Dec., weekends only.
Closed Jan.–Mar.*

Just down the road at the **Red Caboose Motel** R-5 cabooses have
been converted into motel units and a casual restaurant. **Ed's
Buggy Rides** depart from the motel for 20- to 30-minute horse-
drawn-carriage rides along scenic back roads. *Rte. 896, 1½ mi
south of U.S. 30, Strasburg, tel. 717/687-0360. Rides: $6
adults, $3 children 10 and under. Open daily 9–5.*

If you fancy fancy cars, **Gast Classic Motorcars Exhibit** has a
changing display of 50 antique, classic, sports, and celebrity
cars. *Rte. 896, Strasburg, tel. 717/687-9500. Admission: $6
adults, $3.50 children 7–12. Open May–Oct., daily 9–9; Nov.–
Apr, weekdays 9–5.*

Choo Choo Barn, Traintown, USA, is a family hobby that got
out of hand. What started in 1945 as a single train chugging
around the Groff family Christmas tree is now a 1,700-square-
foot display of Lancaster County in miniature with 13 O-gauge
electric trains and more than 130 animated figures and vehicles. Every five minutes a house catches on fire and fire engines
turn on their hoses to extinguish the blaze; flag bearers march
in a Memorial Day parade; animals perform in a three-ring circus. Periodically, the overhead lights dim and it is nighttime;
streetlights glow and locomotive headlights pierce the darkness. *Rte. 741, Strasburg, tel. 717/687-7911. Admission: $3*

adults, $1.50 children 5–12. Open Apr.–Oct., daily 10–5 (later in summer); Nov., Dec., weekends 10–5. Closed Jan.–Mar.

If you have another day to spend in Pennsylvania Dutch Country, tour the city of **Lancaster** and its surrounding attractions. **The Historic Lancaster Walking Tour,** a two-hour stroll through the heart of this charming old city, is conducted by costumed guides who impart lively anecdotes about local architecture and history. *Tours leave from S. Queen and Vine Sts., near Penn Sq., tel. 717/392–1776. Price: $4 adults, $3.50 senior citizens, $2 students. Tours Apr.–Oct., weekdays 10 and 1:30, Sat. 10, 11, 1:30, Sun. 1:30; Nov.–Mar. by reservation only.*

Built in 1742, **Central Market** is one of the oldest covered markets in the country. This is where the locals shop for fresh fruit and vegetables, meats (try the Lebanon bologna), and baked goods such as sticky buns and shoofly pie. You can pick up food for a picnic. *Penn Sq., tel. 717/291–4723. Open Tues. and Fri. 6–4:30, Sat. 6–1:30.*

The **Demuth Foundation** includes the restored 18th-century home, studio, and garden of Charles Demuth, one of America's first modernist artists. *114 E. King St., tel. 717/299–9940. Admission free. Open Mon.–Sat. 10–4, Sun. noon–3.*

The Old City Hall, reborn as the **Heritage Center Museum,** shows the work of Lancaster County artisans and craftsmen—clocks, furniture, homemade toys, *fraktur* (ornate paintings), and Pennsylvania long rifles. Some exhibits are on display permanently, while some exhibits change. *King and Queen Sts., tel. 717/299–6440. Donation requested. Open May–Nov., Tues.–Sat. 10–4; Dec., weekends only. Closed Jan.–Apr.*

Rock Ford Plantation and Kauffman Museum show antiques and folk art. The antiques are in a 1792 Georgian-style house once owned by Edward Hand, one of George Washington's generals; the Zoe and Henry Kauffman collection of pewter, brass, firearms, and furniture is displayed in the restored barn. *Lancaster County Park at 881 Rock Ford Rd., tel. 717/392–7223. Admission: $2.75 adults, $1 children 6–18. Guided 45-min tours. Open Apr.–Nov., Tues.–Sat. 10–4, Sun. noon–4. Closed Dec.–Mar.*

Wheatland was the home of the only president from Pennsylvania, James Buchanan. The restored 1828 Federal mansion displays the 15th president's furniture just as it was during his lifetime. A one-hour tour includes an entertaining profile of the only bachelor to occupy the White House. *1120 Marietta Ave. (Rte. 23), 1½ mi west of Lancaster, tel. 717/392–8721. Admission: $4 adults, $3.25 students, $1.75 children 6–12. Open Apr.–Nov., daily 10–4:15. The home is open for a Victorian Christmas exhibit the first 2 wks of Dec. Closed mid-Dec.–Mar.*

Artist Andrew Wyeth's ancestors were members of the Herr family and the **Hans Herr House** is the subject of several Wyeth paintings. Today, the house is owned by the Lancaster Mennonite Historical Society, which aims to correct misconceptions about the Mennonite religion with exhibits in its Visitors Center. Half-hour tours cover the grounds and the 1719 sandstone house, a former Mennonite meeting place. The house is considered the best example of medieval German architecture in North America. *1849 Hans Herr Dr., 5 mi south of Lancas-*

ter off U.S. 222, tel. 717/464–4438. *Admission: $3 adults, $1 children 7–12. Open Apr.–Dec., Mon.–Sat. 9–4. Closed Jan.– Mar.*

❾ Follow Oregon Pike (Rte. 272) north from Lancaster to the **Landis Valley Museum,** an outdoor museum of Pennsylvania/ German rural life and folk culture before 1900. Owned by brothers Henry and George Landis, the farm is now operated by the Pennsylvania Historical and Museum Commission. From May through October, you can visit over 15 historical buildings, from a farmstead to a country store, and see demonstrations of such skills as spinning and weaving, pottery making, and tinsmithing, the products of which are for sale in the Weathervane Shop. There are guided tours from November to April. *2451 Kissel Hill Rd. (just off Oregon Pike), Lancaster, tel. 717/569–0401. Admission: $5 adults, $4 senior citizens, $3 children. Open Tues.–Sat. 9–5, Sun. noon–5.*

❿ In the 1730s, a radical religious communal society took root in the town of Ephrata. A living example of William Penn's Holy Experiment, the monastic Protestants of the **Ephrata Cloister** lived an ascetic life of work, study, and prayer. They ate one meal a day of grain, fruit, and vegetables, and encouraged celibacy (the last sister died in 1813). The society was best known for a cappella singing, fraktur (ornate paintings), medieval German architecture, and its publishing center. Robed guides lead half-hour tours of three restored buildings; then visitors can tour the stable, print shop, and craft shop by themselves. *Rtes. 272 and 322, Ephrata, tel. 717/733–6600. Admission: $4 adults, $3 senior citizens, $2 children 6–17. Open Mon.–Sat. 9–5, Sun. noon–5.*

The **Green Dragon Farmers Market and Auction** is an old traditional agricultural market with a country carnival atmosphere. Each week livestock and agricultural commodities are auctioned in the morning. Local Amish and Mennonite farmers tend many of the 450 indoor and outdoor stalls selling meats, fruits, vegetables, fresh-baked pies, and dry goods. One of the state's largest farmer's markets (occupying 30 acres), it also has a flea market and an evening auction of small animals. Try the sticky buns at Rissler's Bakery and the sausage sandwiches at Newswanger's. *R.D. 4 just off Rte. 272, Ephrata, tel. 717/ 738–1117. Open Fri. 9 AM–10 PM.*

⓫ The town of **Lititz,** west of Ephrata, was founded by Moravians who settled in Pennsylvania to do missionary work among the Indians. It's a lovely town with a tree-shaded main street lined with 18th-century cottages and shops selling antiques, crafts, clothing, and gifts. Around the main square are the Moravian communal residences, a church dating from 1787, and a hospital that treated the wounded during the Revolutionary War. Pick up a Historical Foundation walking tour brochure at the General Sutter Inn (14 E. Main St./Rte. 501, tel. 717/626–2115).

At the nation's oldest pretzel bakery, the **Julius Sturgis Pretzel House,** you can see pretzels twisted by hand and baked in brick ovens the same way Julius Sturgis did it in 1861. At the end of the 20-minute guided tour, visitors can try their hand at the almost extinct art of pretzel twisting. *219 E. Main St., Lititz, tel. 717/626–4354. Admission: $1.50. Open Mon.–Sat. 9–4:30.*

The first thing you'll notice in Lititz is the smell of chocolate. It emanates from the **Wilbur Chocolate Company's Candy Ameri-**

cana Museum and Factory Candy Outlet (48 N. Broad St., Lititz, tel. 717/626–1131), which features a candy-making demonstration (with free samples) and a small museum of candy-related memorabilia. *Open Mon.–Sat. 10–5.*

Some visitors avoid the crowds and commercialism of eastern Lancaster County by staying in the sleepy towns along the Susquehanna River—Columbia, Marietta, Maytown, Bainbridge, Mount Joy, and Elizabethtown.

⑫ With architecture ranging from log cabins to more recent Federal and Victorian homes, 48% of the town of **Marietta** is listed on the National Historic Register. The restored river town, now seeing life as an artists' community, is perfect for strolling along, admiring the well-preserved facades and peeking into the art galleries and antiques shops.

⑬ In nearby Columbia, **The Watch and Clock Museum of the National Association of Watch and Clock Collectors** displays a large and varied collection of timepieces, specialized tools, and related items from the primitive to the modern. There's a 19th-century calendar clock, a German Black Forest organ clock with 94 pipes, and the show-stopper—the Engle Clock—an 1878 timepiece, which took clockmaker Stephen D. Engle 20 years to complete, intended to resemble the famous monument clock of Strasbourg, France. It has 48 moving figures. *514 Poplar St., Columbia, tel. 717/684–8261. Admission: $3 adults, $2.50 senior citizens, $1 children 6–17. Open Tues.–Sat. 9–4.*

⑭ The **Market House and Dungeon,** built in 1869, is one of the oldest continuously operating farmers markets in the state. You can buy handcrafted jewelry, baked goods, meat, fruits, and vegetables from local farms. The basement of the house used to be a dungeon; you can still see the ground-level windows through which prisoners were shoved down a chute into the darkness. *308 Locust St. (off of Rte. 441), Columbia, tel. 717/ 684–2468. Farmers market open Fri. 7–4, Sat. 7–1. Dungeon open Apr.–Oct., daily for self-guided tours.*

⑮ **Wrights Ferry Mansion** is the former residence of English Quaker Susanna Wright, a silkworm breeder known as the bluestocking of the Susquehanna. The 1738 stone house showcases Philadelphia William and Mary- and Queen Anne-style furniture and a great collection of English needlework, ceramics, and glass, all pre-dating 1750. *38 S. 2nd St., Columbia, tel. 717/684–4325. Admission: $3 adults, $1.50 students 6–18. Open May–Oct., Tues., Wed., Fri., Sat. 10–3.*

⑯ Two wineries operate in the western part of the county. At the 52-acre **Nissley Vineyards and Winery Estate,** you can review the grape-growing and wine-making process on a self-guided wine tasting tour. *Northwest of Columbia near Bainbridge, R.D. 1, tel. 717/426–3514. Admission free. Open Mon.–Sat. 10–5, Sun. 1–4.*

⑰ At the **Mt. Hope Estate and Winery,** you tour not vineyards but an elegant circa 1800 mansion with turrets, hand-painted 18-foot ceilings, Egyptian marble fireplaces, gold-leaf wallpaper, and crystal gas chandeliers. Tours are led by costumed guides and followed by a formal wine tasting of Mt. Hope Wines. There are lovely estate gardens for strolls. *North of Manheim on Rte. 72, ½ mi from Exit 20 of the Pennsylvania Tpke., tel. 717/665–*

7021. Admission: $4 adults, $1.50 children 5–11. Open July–mid-Oct., daily 10–5; mid-Oct.–June, Sat. 10–5, Sun. 11–5.

The **Pennsylvania Renaissance Faire** (tel. 717/665–7021) runs weekends from July to mid-October on the grounds of the Mt. Hope Estate and Winery. The winery is transformed into a 16th-century English village with human chess matches, jousting and fencing tournaments, street performances, craft demonstrations, jesters, and Shakespearean plays. *Admission: $13.95 adults, $4 children 5–11. Open July 4 weekend–Labor Day, Sat.–Mon. 11:30–7; Sept.–mid-Oct., weekends 10:30–6.*

If you've brought your children as far as Lancaster, you may want to continue north to **Hershey,** the "Chocolate Town" founded in 1903 by Milton S. Hershey where the street lights are shaped like giant Hershey Kisses. Take Route 283 northwest about 20 miles from Lancaster, then go north 10 miles on Route 743. The number one attraction is 87-acre **Hersheypark,** a dream come true for chocoholics who love rides. Who could resist a towering Hershey Kiss and a Hershey Bar that walks? In addition to the more than 50 rides, there are five theaters with musical performances, a wildlife park (ZooAmerica), and shopping in Tudor Square. *Rte. 743 and U.S. 422, Hershey, tel. 717/534–3900. Admission including ZooAmerica: $20.95 adults, $17.95 children 3–8. Reduced rates after 5 PM. Open Memorial Day–Labor Day, daily 10–10 (some earlier closings); in Sept. and May, weekends only.*

At **Hershey's Chocolate World,** an automated car takes you through the chocolate-making process, from a cacao plantation to a chocolate factory. *Park Blvd., Hershey, tel. 717/534–4900. Admission free. Open daily 9–4:45, until 6:45 in summer.*

Take Route 422 west from Hershey, where it quickly merges with U.S. 322 and soon arrives at **Indian Echo Caverns,** one of the largest caves in the northeastern United States. A 45-minute guided walking tour explores the underground wonderland. Bring a sweater; no strollers are allowed. *Off U.S. 322, Hummelstown, tel. 717/566–8131. Admission: $6 adults, $3 children 4–11. Open daily 9–6 in summer, shorter hours the rest of the year.*

Shopping

Crafts   Although craftspeople in the Lancaster County area produce fine handiwork, folk art, quilts, and needlework, much of the best work is sold to galleries nationwide and never shows up in local shops. Among the few places to see fine local crafts are the **Weathervane Shop** at the Landis Valley Museum (2451 Kissel Hill Rd., Lancaster, tel. 717/569–9312). Craftsmen sell the wares they make in on-site demonstrations—tin, pottery, leather, braided rugs, weaving, and chair-caning.

The **Tin Bin** (Landis Valley Rd. and Rte. 501, Neffsville, tel. 717/569–6210) features handmade tinware and pottery, and reproductions of 18th-century lighting devices. The **Artworks at Doneckers** (100 N. State St., Ephrata, tel. 717/733–7900) houses studios where you can watch painters, sculptors, and potters at work. There are also art, fine crafts, and antiques galleries. For antique quilts made in Lancaster County, try **Pandora's** (Rte. 340 just east of U.S. 30, Lancaster, tel. 717/299–5305, call ahead) or **Witmer's Quilt Shop** (1070 W. Main St.,

New Holland, tel. 717/656–3411). Though pricey, old quilts have proven to be good investments.

The Mennonite Central Committee operates **Selfhelp Crafts of the World Gifts and Tea Room** (Rte. 272 north, just north of the Cloister in Ephrata, tel. 717/738–1101). A job-creation program designed to aid developing countries, the store has more than 3,000 items—including jewelry, Indian brass, onyx, needlework, baskets, toys, handwoven Pakistani rugs, and odd musical instruments—from Bangladesh, Botswana, Brazil, and about 30 other countries. You can dig up some bargains; for example, a 100% alpaca sweater from Bolivia, usually about $300, was on sale for $69. Each week for breakfast and lunch the Tea Room features the cuisine of a different country.

Kitchen Kettle Village (Rte. 340, Intercourse, tel. 717/768–8261) consists of 28 shops showcasing local crafts, including decoy carving; furniture making; leather tooling; relish, jam, and jelly making; and tin punching. Sample the homemade fudge and funnel cakes. Closed Sunday.

Outlets   U.S. 30 is lined with outlets: Some are factory stores, which offer first-quality goods at large discounts; others call themselves outlets but don't have real bargains. It's a good idea to find out the retail prices of whatever you want before you leave home. With more than 90 stores, from Lenox to London Fog and the huge Reading China & Glass, **Rockvale Square Factory Outlet** (Rtes. 30 and 896) is the largest outlet center in Lancaster. It even has a shuttle bus that runs among the stores.

Antiques   On Sundays, antiques hunters frequent the huge antiques malls located on Route 272 between Adamstown and Denver, 2 miles east of Pennsylvania Turnpike Exit 21. As many as 5,000 dealers may turn up on summer festival Sundays. **Renninger's Antique and Collector's Market** (tel. 215/267–2177), **Barr's Auctions** (tel. 215/267–2861), and **Stoudt's Black Angus** (tel. 215/484–4385) all feature indoor and outdoor booths. Dealers display old books and prints, Victorian blouses, corner cupboards, pewter and local stoneware, and lots of furniture. Barr's is open on Saturdays, also. Several antiques cooperatives (Log Cabin Antique Center, Weaver's, Southpoint) also line the stretch.

Farmers Markets   Farmers markets offer the most unusual shopping experiences in the area. The **Central Market** in Lancaster and **Green Dragon Farmers Market and Auction** in Ephrata are the best; if you can't shop there, try **Bird-in-Hand Farmer's Market** (Rte. 340, Bird-in-Hand, tel. 717/393–9674), a conveniently located market with produce stands, baked goods, gift shops, and outlets. Open Wednesday, Friday, and Saturday. **Meadowbrook Farmer's Market** (Rte. 23, Leola, tel. 717/656–2226) is popular for its edible goodies as well as its flea-market items, crafts, collectibles, and country store. Open Friday and Saturday year-round, more days in summer.

Sports and Outdoor Activities

Ballooning   **Great Adventure Balloon Club** offers a bird's-eye view of Pennsylvania Dutch Country. As part of the crew, you help inflate the balloon, maneuver the controls, and land the craft in a farmer's field. You spend an hour airborne, about three hours total. A chase van drives you back to the starting point. *Rheems exit of Rte. 283, Mount Joy, tel. 717/653–2009. Price: $135 per per-*

son. *Open daily, weather permitting. One-day advance reservation required.*

Bicycling **New Horizon's Bicycle Adventures** (3495 Horizon Dr., Lancaster, tel. 717/285–7607) rents 15-speed mountain bikes. If you want to ride on your own, you can pick up bikes and maps with suggested routes or buy *Scenic Tours*, a book listing circular rides throughout Lancaster County. The book is available by mail for $9. There are also 12- to 44-mile guided tours past Amish farms and through covered bridges. A refreshment van follows; the agency will make lodging reservations and transfer your luggage.

Golf The **Lancaster Host Resort and Convention Center** (U.S. 30, Lancaster, tel. 717/299–5500) has 27 holes for regulation golf; carts are not required. *Greens fees: $26 for 18 holes until 2 PM, $13 after 2; $11.50 per person for a cart. Rental clubs available.*

Camping

The Pennsylvania Dutch Visitors Bureau has a complete list of area campgrounds. Some of the best include:

Mill Bridge Village and Campresort, which is attached to a restored 18th-century village. *½ mi south of U.S. 30 on Ronks Rd., tel. 717/687–8181. Snack shop, summer entertainment, free buggy rides, stream fishing.*

Muddy Run Park offers lovely campgrounds in the southern end of the county set among 700 acres of woodland and rolling fields which surround a 100-acre lake. Environmental programs include nature walks, bird-watching, and fly-fishing workshops. *172 Bethesda Church Rd. W, Holtwood, tel. 717/284–4325. Snack bar, general store, playground, boating, fishing.*

Spring Gulch Resort Campground is a glorious farmland and forest setting with 200 sites (pleasantly shaded) and rental cottages. A full schedule of weekend activities includes country dances and chicken barbecues. *Rte. 897 between Rtes. 340 and 322, New Holland, tel. 717/354–3100. Lake, indoor and outdoor pools for swimming, miniature golf, tennis and volleyball courts, fishing, game room, square dances, exercise classes.*

Dining and Lodging

Like the German cuisine that influenced it, Pennsylvania Dutch meals are hearty and are prepared with ingredients from local farms. To sample regional fare, eat at one of the several bustling restaurants in the area where diners sit with perhaps a dozen other people and the food is passed around in bowls family style. Meals are plentiful and basic—fried chicken, ham, roast beef, dried corn, buttered noodles, mashed potatoes, chowchow, bread, pepper cabbage, shoofly pie—and that's only a partial listing. Entrées are accompanied by traditional "sweets and sours," vegetable dishes made with a vinegar-and-sugar dressing. This is the way the Amish, who hate to throw things out, preserve leftover vegetables. Lancaster County has numerous smorgasbords and reasonably priced family restaurants along with a number of Continental and French restaurants in contemporary settings and quaint historic inns. Unless otherwise noted, liquor is served.

The following dining price categories have been used: *Very Expensive*, over $30; *Expensive*, $20–$30; *Moderate*, $10–$20; *Inexpensive*, under $10.

The following lodging price categories have been used: *Very Expensive*, over $100; *Expensive*, $80–$100; *Moderate*, $60–$80; *Inexpensive*, under $60.

Bird-in-Hand
Dining

Amish Barn Restaurant. Pennsylvania Dutch cuisine is served family style, which means generous helpings of meat and produce, breads, and home-baked pies. Apple dumplings are a specialty. You can choose from an à la carte menu or order a family-style meal. No liquor is served. *Rte. 340 between Bird-in-Hand and Intercourse, tel. 717/768–8886. Reservations advised on summer weekends. Dress: informal. AE, DC, MC, V. Open Apr.–Dec., daily; Jan.–Mar., Fri.–Sun. only. Moderate.*

★ **Bird-in-Hand Family Restaurant.** These family-owned, diner-style restaurants enjoy a good reputation for hearty Pennsylvania Dutch home cooking. The menu is à la carte. There is a lunch buffet weekdays at the Bird-in-Hand location. No liquor is served. *2760 Old Philadelphia Pike, Bird-in-Hand, tel. 717/768–8266; 1525 Manheim Pike, Lancaster, tel. 717/560–9302. Reservations not required. Dress: informal. No credit cards. Closed Sun. Inexpensive.*

Lodging

Village Inn of Bird-in-Hand. The Victorian flavor of this three-story country inn, built in 1850, is tempered by the modern comforts of down-filled bedding, cable TV, and phones. Continental breakfast, an evening snack, and a two-hour tour of the area are complimentary. *Box 253, 2695 Old Philadelphia Pike (Rte. 340), 17505, tel. 717/293–8369. 11 rooms, including 2 deluxe suites with Jacuzzis. Facilities: access to pool and tennis courts at nearby Bird-in-Hand Family Inn. AE, MC, V. Moderate–Very Expensive.*

Bird-in-Hand Family Inn. Plain, clean, comfortable rooms in a family-owned motel praised for its friendly staff. *Box B, 2740 Old Philadelphia Pike, 17505, tel. 717/768–8271 or 800/537–2535. 100 rooms. Facilities: restaurant, tennis courts, playground, indoor and outdoor pool. AE, DC, MC, V. Moderate.*

Churchtown
Lodging
★

Churchtown Inn. This restored 1735 fieldstone mansion, overlooking an Amish farm, has two beautiful Victorian parlors, a collection of handmade quilts and antique music boxes, and cozy, elegant bedrooms with pencil post canopies, brass, and high-back Victorian beds. The day dawns in the glass-enclosed garden room with a five-course breakfast including goodies such as Grand Marnier French toast, oatmeal and granola pancakes, and homemade coffee cake and ends in the parlor with an evening beverage hour, during which one of the innkeepers, a former music director, plays the piano and sings. Guests are invited to a nearby Amish home for Saturday dinner. Special-event weekends are held from mid-November through May, featuring road rallies, murder mysteries, barbecues, a formal Victorian costume ball, and professional concerts. *On Rte. 23 between Morgantown and New Holland, 5 mi from Pa. Turnpike Exit 22. Box 135, R.D. 3, Narvon 17555, tel. 215/445–7794. 8 rooms, 6 with private bath; carriage house. Children over 12 welcome. Two-night minimum stay on weekends, 3-night minimum on holiday weekends. MC, V. Inexpensive–Expensive.*

East Petersburg
Dining
★

Haydn Zug's offers American-Continental dining in an 1850s house with tasteful Williamsburg furnishings. Its specialties include rack of lamb, veal Vienna, crab cakes, and fresh fish. James Beard wrote about the cheesy chowder; *Bon Appetit* profiled the establishment. A tavern menu is also available. *Rte. 72 and State St., Lancaster, tel. 717/569–5746. Reservations advised. Dress: casual. AE, MC, V. Moderate–Expensive.*

Ephrata
Dining

The Restaurant at Doneckers. Classic and country French cuisine is served downstairs amid Colonial antiques and upstairs in a country garden. It is known for its chateaubriand for two, sautéed whole Dover sole, veal Oscar, and salmon. The service is fine; the wine cellar is extensive. From 4 to 10 its menu features lighter fare. Tuesday and Thursday nights the emphasis is on seafood. *333 N. State St., tel. 717/738–2421. Reservations advised. Dress: casual. AE, D, DC, MC, V. Closed Wed. Moderate–Expensive.*

Lodging

Guesthouses at Doneckers. Three turn-of-the-century homes have been tastefully furnished with French country antiques and decorated by hand-stenciling. They have light and airy rooms, five with Jacuzzis. Complimentary Continental-plus breakfast is served. *318–324 N. State St., 17522, tel. 717/733–8696. 19 rooms, 17 with private bath. The 1777 House, 6 blocks away, has 12 rooms with private bath, including 4 suites. AE, DC, MC, V. Moderate–Very Expensive.*

★

Smithton Inn. The B&B is in a historic former stagecoach inn with six lovingly furnished guest rooms and one four-room suite. The rooms have handmade antiques, fireplaces, and canopy beds. Two rooms with whirlpool; third floor has skylights, cathedral ceiling, Franklin stove fireplace. Nice touches abound: oversize goose-down pillows, nightshirts, magazines, and fresh flowers. Outside there's a lily pond, fountain, gazebo, and lovely garden. Full breakfast is included. *900 W. Main St., 17522, tel. 717/733–6094. 6 rooms. Well-behaved children and pets welcome by pre-arrangement. Two-night minimum stay on weekends and holidays. AE, MC, V. Moderate–Very Expensive.*

Hershey
Lodging

Hershey Lodge & Convention Center. This bustling, expansive, modern resort caters to families and has two casual restaurants where kids can be kids. *W. Chocolate Ave. and University Dr., 17033, tel. 717/533–3311 or 800/533–3131. 460 rooms. Facilities: 3 restaurants, indoor and outdoor pools, lighted tennis courts, chip-and-putt golf, bicycle rental, playground, nightclub with dance band, movie theater. AE, DC, MC, V. Very Expensive.*

Hotel Hershey. This gracious Spanish-style hotel surrounded by a golf course and a landscaped garden is a quiet and sophisticated resort with lots of options for recreation. The hotel is in the first phase of a needed facelift; ask for one of the recently renovated rooms—they've still got their Old World feel. Across the street from Hersheypark and popular with families, it's added a café for casual dining. AP, MAP, and EP available. *Box BB, 17033, tel. 717/533–2171 or 800/437–7439. 242 rooms. Facilities: formal restaurant, family buffet, indoor/outdoor pool, tennis, carriage rides, golf. AE, DC, MC, V. Very Expensive.*

Intercourse
Dining

Kling House. The Kling family home has been converted into a charming, casual restaurant featuring American cuisine at breakfast and lunch. Swordfish, teriyaki chicken, and snitz and knepp entrées come with complimentary appetizer of red-pepper jam and cream cheese with crackers. The soups are homemade, and the desserts are luscious. A children's menu is available. *Kitchen Kettle Village, Rtes. 340 and 772, tel. 717/ 768–8261. Reservations advised. Dress: casual. MC, V. Closed Sun. Dinner served Sat. nights only. Moderate.*

Stoltzfus Farm Restaurant. Homemade Pennsylvania Dutch foods, including meats butchered right on the farm, are served family style in a small country farmhouse. *Rte. 772 E, 1 block east of Rte. 340, tel. 717/768–8156. Reservations not required. Dress: casual. Closed Dec.–Mar.; open Apr., Oct., Nov., Sat. nights only. MC, V. Inexpensive.*

Lancaster Dining

Windows on Steinman Park. French-Continental cuisine is presented in elegant surroundings—lots of marble, fresh flowers, and huge windows overlooking an inviting redbrick courtyard. Its specialties include Caesar salad, Dover sole, and chateaubriand. A less pricey menu offers light Continental fare; there's piano music Tuesday through Saturday. *16–18 W. King St., tel. 717/295–1316. Reservations advised. Jackets required. AE, DC, MC, V. Closed Sat. lunch. Moderate–Very Expensive.*

Hoar House. Victorian decor and antiques set the mood for such Continental dishes as roast stuffed duckling with Grand Marnier sauce, veal Maryland, and baked seafood in phyllo topped with a mushroom and white wine sauce. A light menu has entrées from $8.95. The lounge has a disc jockey and a free buffet Friday and Saturday nights and live entertainment Sunday nights. *10 S. Prince St., tel. 717/397–0110. Reservations suggested. Dress: neat but casual. AE, MC, V. Closed Mon. Expensive.*

★ **The Log Cabin.** Steak, lamb chops, and seafood are prepared on a charcoal grill in this 1928 expanded log cabin which was a speakeasy during Prohibition. The atmosphere is elegant and the setting is embellished with an impressive art collection. *11 Lehoy Forest Dr. (off Rte. 272), Leola (5 mi north of Lancaster), tel. 717/626–1181. Jackets and reservations suggested. AE, MC, V. Expensive.*

Market Fare. The cuisine is American, and steaks, seafood, and veal are served in a cozy dining room with upholstered armchairs and 19th-century paintings. Steamed seafood in parchment, pasta with bay scallops, and pasta with crab and tomatoes are specialties. A light menu is also available. The café upstairs offers light breakfast, quick lunch, and carryout. *Market and Grant Sts. (across from the Central Market), tel. 717/299–7090. Reservations suggested. Dress: casual. AE, DC, MC, V. Expensive.*

Olde Greenfield Inn. Continental cuisine and a fine wine cellar form part of the attraction in this gracious 190-year-old restored farmhouse. House specialties include roast duckling with raspberry sauce, Cajun beef with shrimp, and jumbo lump crab cakes. Lighter entrées, like seafood crêpes, are also available. A piano player is in the lounge on weekends. Guests can dine on the patio. *595 Greenfield Rd., tel. 717/393–0668. Reservations suggested. Dress: casual. AE, MC, V. Closed Sun. night. Moderate–Expensive.*

Lancaster Dispensing Co. Fajitas, salads, sandwiches, and nachos are served until midnight in this stylish Victorian pub. The selection of imported beers is extensive. On the weekend, live music is played. *33–35 N. Market St., tel. 717/299–4602. No reservations. Dress: informal. AE, MC, V. Inexpensive.*

Lodging **Lancaster Host Resort and Conference Center.** This sprawling family resort was completely renovated in 1988, and now sports a striking marble lobby and comfortable, contemporary rooms with cherrywood furnishings, VCRs, bathrobes, and minibars. The golf course and grounds are beautifully landscaped. A camp program for children ages 1–12 takes place daily during the summer and on weekends throughout the year. A variety of packages are available. *2300 Lincoln Hwy. E (Rte. 30), 17602, tel. 717/299–5500 or 800/233–0121. 330 rooms. Facilities: 2 restaurants, indoor and outdoor pool, 27 holes of golf, 4 indoor and 8 outdoor tennis courts, game room, bike rental, miniature golf, DJ in lounge for dancing, piano bar. MAP and EP available. AE, DC, MC, V. Very Expensive.*

King's Cottage. This elegant Spanish mansion, which is on the National Register of Historic Places, has been transformed into a B&B furnished with antiques and 18th-century English reproductions. Full breakfast and afternoon tea are included. It's only two miles from the heart of downtown Lancaster. *1049 E. King St., 17602, tel. 717/397–1017. 7 rooms. Children over 12 only. Two-night minimum on weekends. MC, V. Moderate–Very Expensive.*

★ **Best Western Eden Resort Inn.** Spacious contemporary rooms (request a room at poolside) and attractive grounds contribute to a pleasant stay here. It has a stunning tropical indoor pool and whirlpool under a retractable roof. The award-winning chef in Arthur's is noted for seafood and pasta; the Sunday buffet brunch is excellent. There's fine dining in the skylit Eden courtyard; fun food is presented in Garfield's. Club Mirage has the latest dance music and videos; Encore provides live entertainment. *222 Eden Rd. (U.S. 30 and Rte. 272), 17601, tel. 717/569–6444 or 800/528–1234. 275 rooms and 40 residential-style Club Suites with full kitchens and fireplaces. Facilities: 2 movie theaters, indoor and outdoor pool, lighted tennis courts. AE, DC, MC, V. Expensive.*

Willow Valley Family Resort and Conference Center. This mom-and-pop operation has blossomed into a large and stylish family resort. The striking new skylit atrium lobby is surrounded by attractive rooms. There are moderately priced rooms, but the ones overlooking the atrium are the most attractive and most expensive. Since it is Mennonite owned, there is no liquor permitted on the premises. *2416 Willow St. Pike, 17602, tel. 717/464–2711 or 800/444–1714. 353 rooms. Facilities: 2 restaurants, 9-hole golf course, lighted tennis courts, small lake for fishing, adjacent gift mall, indoor and outdoor pools, whirlpool. AE, DC, MC, V. Expensive.*

CrestHil by Hilton. An new, elegant hotel popular with corporate travelers offers oversized rooms, many with cathedral ceilings and large desks. To keep prices down, Hilton scaled down the restaurant and eliminated room service. Reduced package plan with breakfast is a bargain on weekends. *101 Granite Run Dr., 17601, tel. 717/560–0880 or 800/HILTONS. 154 rooms. Facilities: restaurant, fitness center, indoor pool, whirlpool. AE, D, DC, MC, V. Moderate–Expensive.*

Olde Hickory Inn. A quiet one-story motel where many rooms open onto a spacious lawn with a pool, the Olde Hickory Inn sports attractive oak furnishings. The inn is across from the Landis Valley Museum. *2363 Oregon Pike, 17601, tel. 717/569–*

0477 or 800/255–6859. 83 rooms. Facilities: restaurant, out-door pool, volleyball, playground, access to Olde Hickory Rac-quet Club with 9-hole golf course, shops nearby. AE, DC, MC, V. Moderate.

Your Place Country Inn. This small, new hotel close to the out-lets and attractions has country furnishings handmade by Amish and local craftsmen. Continental breakfast is included. *2133 Lincoln Hwy. E, 17602, tel. 717/393–3413. 79 rooms. Fa-cilities: restaurant, outdoor pool. AE, D, MC, V. Moderate.*

Lititz **General Sutter Inn.** The oldest (1764) continuously run inn in
Lodging the state is a Victoriana lover's dream reminiscent of "Grand-ma's house." Its decor ranges from Pennsylvania folk art to Louis XIV sofas and marble-topped tables. Children are wel-come. *14 E. Main St. (Rte. 501), 17543, tel. 717/626–2115. 14 rooms, including 2 family suites. Facilities: dining room, cof-fee shop, cocktail lounge. AE, MC, V. Moderate–Expensive.*

★ **Swiss Woods.** Innkeepers Werner and Debrah Mosimann de-signed this Swiss-style chalet while they were still living in Werner's native Switzerland. They planted it on 30 acres in Lititz, just 20 minutes from Hershey, creating a comfortable, friendly, European-style bed-and-breakfast with light pine wood furnishings, a contemporary country decor, and goose-down comforters. Breakfast features such hearty fare as cream-dried beef and waffles or baked eggs and cheese and fresh baked breads—muffins, scones with homemade lemon curd, and Swiss pastries. The setting is sublime; the chalet is nestled on the edge of the woods overlooking Speedwell Forge Lake. From November to March, the Mosimanns serve dinners of Swiss fondues and raclettes to their house guests. *500 Blantz Rd., 17543, tel. 717/627–3358 or 800/594–8018. 6 rooms, 1 suite. Facilities: some rooms have Jacuzzis, canoeing, access to hik-ing, fishing, bird-watching, and biking. No smoking. Children welcome. Two-night minimum stay on weekends from Easter to Thanksgiving, 3-night minimum holiday weekends. MC, V. Moderate–Expensive.*

Marietta **Railroad House.** In a historic hotel on the east bank of the Sus-
Dining quehanna River, this restaurant has a split personality. Up-stairs, classic American cuisine reigns, with dishes such as veal marsala, veal Oscar, and filet mignon flavored with herbs from the on-premises garden; downstairs, a light tavern menu offers pasta, sandwiches, and smaller dinner entrèes. In warm weather, you can dine out on the patio in the garden. On Satur-day nights, the Victorian era is recreated with strolling min-strels. *W. Front and S. Perry Sts., tel. 717/426–4141. Reservations advised. Dress: casual. MC, V. Moderate–Ex-pensive.*

Lodging **Railroad House Bed & Breakfast.** Built in 1820 to service canal and river traffic, the Railroad House now welcomes guests to Victorian-style rooms refurbished with antiques and Oriental rugs. Full breakfast is served. *W. Front and S. Perry Sts., 17547, tel. 717/426–4141. 12 rooms, 8 with private bath, includ-ing 1 suite with kitchenette. Facilities: restaurant, tours of the area in a 19th-century surrey can be arranged. Children over 12 welcome. MC, V. Moderate.*

Mount Joy **Cameron Estate Inn.** American cuisine is presented with
Dining French service in a candlelit, Federal-style dining room of a country inn. Specialties include duckling in brandied peach sauce and crispy pecan-topped trout. *Donegal Springs Rd., tel.*

717/653–1773. Reservations required. Dress: casual, but no jeans. AE, DC, MC, V. Expensive.

★ **Groff's Farm.** Abe and Betty Groff's restaurant has received national attention for hearty Mennonite farm fare served in a restored 1756 farmhouse. Candlelight, fresh flowers, original Groff Farm country fabrics, and wall coverings contribute to the homey ambience. House specialties include chicken Stoltzfus, farm relishes, and cracker pudding. Dinner begins with chocolate cake. Lunch is à la carte, dinner à la carte or family style. *650 Pinkerton Rd., tel. 717/653–2048. Reservations required for dinner, suggested at lunch. Dinner seatings Tues.–Fri. at 5 and 7:30, Sat. 5 and 8. Dress: casual, but no shorts. D, DC, MC, V. Closed Sun. and Mon. Expensive.*

Bube's Brewery. The only intact, pre-Prohibition brewery in the United States contains a museum and three unique restaurants. **The Bottling Works** in the original bottling plant of the brewery serves steaks, light dinners, salads, burgers, and subs. *No reservations. Dress: informal.* **Alois's** offers prix fixe six-course international dinners in a Victorian hotel attached to the brewery. *Reservations required. Jacket and tie advised. Closed Mon.* **The Catacombs** serves traditional steak and seafood dishes in the brewery aging cellars 43 feet below street level. A feast master, with his wenches, presides over a medieval-style dinner on Sunday nights. Wine and ale flow, musicians entertain, and diners participate in the festivities. $30 per person. *Reservations required. Jackets preferred. An outdoor beer garden is open in summer. 102 N. Market St., tel. 717/653–2056. AE, MC, V. Inexpensive–Expensive.*

Lodging **Cameron Estate Inn.** This sprawling Federal red-brick mansion
★ set on 15 wooded acres was the summer home of Simon Cameron, Abraham Lincoln's first secretary of war. The rooms are equipped with Oriental rugs, antique and reproduction furniture, and canopy beds; seven have working fireplaces. The lovely porch overlooks the grounds. Continental breakfast is included. *Donegal Springs Rd., 17552, tel. 717/653–1773. 18 rooms, 16 with private bath. Facilities: restaurant, access to tennis courts and pool nearby. No children under 12. AE, DC, MC, V. Moderate–Very Expensive.*

Paradise **Miller's Smorgasbord.** Miller's presents a lavish spread with a
Dining good selection of Pennsylvania Dutch foods. Breakfast is sensa-
★ tional here with omelets, pancakes, and eggs cooked to order, fresh fruits, pastries, bacon, sausage, potatoes, and much more. It's one of the few area restaurants open on Sundays. *2811 Lincoln Hwy. E (U.S. 30), tel. 717/687–6621. Reservations for dinner only. Dress: casual. AE, MC, V. Breakfast weekends only Dec.–May. Moderate.*

Strasburg **Iron Horse Restaurant.** This charming, rustic, candlelit restau-
Dining rant is housed in the original 1780s Hotel Strasburg. Best bets are the catch-of-the-day, the daily veal special, the homemade breads, and, for dessert, the great, warm apple pie. There's live entertainment on weekends and an extensive wine list. *135 E. Main St. (Rte. 741), tel. 717/687–6362. Reservations suggested on weekends. Dress: casual. AE, MC, V. Closed Mon. Dec.–May. Expensive.*

Washington House Restaurant. This restaurant at the Historic Strasburg Inn offers fine candlelight dining in two Colonial-style dining rooms. The American menu features Cornish game hen, flounder stuffed with crabmeat, and filet Mignon. The lunch buffet is bountiful. *Rte. 896 (Historic Dr.), tel. 717/687–7691. Dress: casual. AE, DC, MC, V. Moderate.*

Lodging **Fulton Steamboat Inn.** At Lancaster's busiest intersection,
★ across from rows of outlet stores, sits a small lake, man-made waterfalls, piped-in sounds of a river, and a hotel that looks just like a steamboat. Named after the Lancaster native Robert Fulton, who built the first successful passenger steamer in the late 1700s, the hotel has three levels: The uppermost deck features whirlpool baths and private outdoor decks, the middle level has staterooms with two queen-size beds, and the bottom level has cabins with nautical themes and some bunk beds, making it a good choice for families with children. Rooms have Victorian-style furnishings, microwaves, remote control TV, and mini-refrigerators. The costumed staff look right at home in the Victorian lobby. Although the package offering two meals a day is economical, don't miss the local cooking at area restaurants. *Rtes. 30 and 896, Box 333, 17579, tel. 717/299–9990 or 800/922–9099 outside PA. 96 rooms. Facilities: restaurant, indoor pool, Jacuzzi, exercise room, game room. Two-night minimum stay on weekends, 3-night minimum on holidays. AE, MC, V. Expensive.*

Historic Strasburg Inn. The newly renovated, Colonial-style inn is set on 58 peaceful acres overlooking farmland. The rooms come with double beds only. Full breakfast is included. *Rte. 896 (Historic Dr.), 17579, tel. 717/687–7691 or 800/872–0201. 103 rooms. Pets allowed. Facilities: restaurant, tavern, outdoor pool, bicycles, volleyball. AE, D, DC, MC, V. Expensive.*

★ **Timberline Lodges.** Beautiful lodges nestled on a hillside put you close enough to Strasburg to hear the train whistles but far away enough to hear the birds. The lodges, which sleep from two to eight people, have stone fireplaces, balconies, TV, and furnished kitchens. *44 Summit Hill Dr., 17579, tel. 717/687–7472. 11 lodges and 5 motel units. Facilities: restaurant, outdoor pool, playground. Two-night minimum on weekends. AE, DC, MC, V. Motel moderate; lodge expensive.*

Strasburg Village Inn. This historic circa 1787 house has rooms elegantly appointed in the Williamsburg style. Most have canopy or poster beds; two have Jacuzzis. A sitting/reading room is on the second floor; an old-fashioned porch overlooks Main Street. Full breakfast in the adjacent ice cream parlor is included, except on Sunday, when it's Continental only. *1 W. Main St., 17579, tel. 717/687–0900 or 800/541–1055. 11 rooms. AE, MC, V. Moderate–Expensive.*

Hershey Farm. This continually expanding motel overlooks a picture-perfect pond and a farm. Ask for one of the large rooms in the new building. Breakfast is included, except Sundays. *Box 89 (Rte. 896), 17579, tel. 717/687–8635. 59 rooms, some no-smoking. Facilities: outdoor pool, family-style and smorgasbord restaurant, bakery, gift shops. D, MC, V. Moderate.*

Red Caboose Motel. The motel consists of 37 railroad cabooses that have been converted into a string of rooms: a unique place to stay, especially for railroad buffs. Half a caboose sleeps two; a family gets a whole car (one double bed, four bunks). TV sets are built into pot-bellied stoves. *Box 102, Paradise La. (off Rte. 741), 17579, tel. 717/687–6646. 40 units, including 8 efficiency suites. Facilities: restaurant, playground, buggy rides. AE, MC, V. Inexpensive.*

Wrightsville
Dining
★
Accomac Inn. A stone building with a magnificent Susquehanna River setting, the inn offers American cuisine with French flair. Tableside cooking is featured with dishes such as tenderloin flambéed with brandy, duck flambéed in orange Curaçao, and bananas Foster. Specialties include fresh rack of New Zealand lamb, veal, venison, and seafood. Queen Anne furnishings are reminiscent of Williamsburg; the wine list boasts 250 selections. *Across Susquehanna River from Marietta (take Rte. 30 west to Wrightsville exit, turn right and follow signs), tel. 717/252–1521. Reservations suggested. Jacket suggested. AE, D, DC, MC, V. Very Expensive.*

Farm Vacations

A number of farm families open their homes to visitors and allow them to observe, and even participate in, day-to-day farm life. Your hosts may teach you how to milk a cow and feed chickens. They serve you breakfast with their family, and invite you to church services. Make reservations weeks in advance: Most farms are heavily booked during the summer tourist season.

Jonde Lane Farm. Breakfast with the family is served every day but Sunday at this working dairy and poultry farm. There are four guest rooms including one family room, which can sleep up to seven people; two shared baths. Ponies, chickens, and cats are conspicuous. Guests can fish on the property. *1103 Auction Rd., Manheim 17545, tel. 717/665–4231. Open Easter–Thanksgiving. No credit cards. Inexpensive.*

Olde Fogie Farm. An organic farm specializing in asparagus, berries, lamb, and beef offers bed and breakfast in an old-frame home with an Amish cookstove, a petting farm, a goat to milk, a creek, and a pond. *R.D. 1, Box 166, Marietta 17547, tel. 717/426–3992. 2 rooms with shared bath, 2 efficiency apartments. No credit cards. Inexpensive.*

Rocky Acre Farm. Sleep in a 200-year-old stone farmhouse, which was once a stop on the Underground Railroad. This is a dairy farm with calves to feed, cows to milk, and dogs, kittens, roosters, and sheep—in the meadow, of course—to enjoy. Guests can go fishing and boating in the creek. A full hot breakfast is served daily. *1020 Pinkerton Rd., Mt. Joy 17552, tel. 717/653–4449. 5 rooms, 3 with bath, and 2 efficiency apartments. No credit cards. Inexpensive.*

Verdant View Farm. Don and Virginia Ranck's 1896 farmhouse sits on about 94 acres devoted to dairy and crop farming. Guests use five rooms on the second floor, one with a private bath. Hearty breakfasts are served in the family dining room every day but Sunday. *429 Strasburg Rd., Paradise 17562, tel. 717/687–7353. Closed Nov.–Easter. No credit cards. Inexpensive.*

The Arts

Theater **Dutch Apple Dinner Theater** (510 Centerville Rd. at U.S. 30, Lancaster, tel. 717/898–1900). A candlelight buffet plus Broadway musicals and comedies are the draws in this 300-seat theater.

The **Fulton Opera House** (12 N. Prince St., Lancaster, tel. 717/397–7425). This restored 19th-century Victorian theater offers a theater series, a series geared to families, and a music series with big band concerts and jazz as well as performances by the Lancaster Symphony Orchestra and the Lancaster Opera.

Sight & Sound Theatre (Rte. 896, Strasburg, tel. 717/687-7800) is a 400-seat, state-of-the-art theater—the largest Christian entertainment complex in the nation—presenting concerts and biblically-based theatrical productions with lavish costumes, special effects, and live animals.

Gettysburg

Cannons and monuments lining the roadside signal to visitors that they have arrived in historic Gettysburg, Pennsylvania, site of perhaps the most famous battle of the Civil War (or War Between the States, depending on from which side of the Mason-Dixon line you come). Here, for three days in July of 1863, Union and Confederate forces faced off in a bloody conflict that left some 50,000 casualties. The resulting Confederate defeat is regarded by many historians as the turning point of the war. Consecrating a national military cemetery on the site the following November, President Lincoln delivered a two-minute speech that has gone down in history.

Covering over 5,000 acres, the Gettysburg National Military Park contains more than 40 miles of scenic avenues winding around the landmarks of the battle. The National Cemetery in particular is a well-shaded spot for a lovely summer stroll. The tourist district in the southern end of town offers several museums and shops, and the historic downtown area contains more than 100 buildings restored to their original Civil War charm, plus a number of other historic sites. To skip from the Civil War era to the mid-20th century, the home of former President Dwight D. Eisenhower is right next to the park. The orchards of Adams County, just north of town, are especially beautiful to drive through in May.

If you are going to Gettysburg from the Harrisburg/Hershey area, take the Pennsylvania Turnpike (I-76) west to Route 15, which leads about 40 miles south to Gettysburg. From western Lancaster County, the most direct route is west on Route 30; once you've crossed the Susquehanna River, it's about 45 miles to Gettysburg. Parking in the downtown area can sometimes be a problem; the Race Horse Alley Parking Plaza off of Stratton Street, behind the Gettysburg Hotel, offers covered, lighted parking. Gettysburg's downtown area is served by a trolley. The fare is 50¢, paid to the trolley driver.

Guided Tours **Gettysburg Battlefield Bus Tours** (tel. 717/334-6296) offers narrated bus tours of the battlegrounds.

Eisenhower Farm Tour (tel. 717/334-1124) visits the President's homestead.

Gettysburg Railroad Steam Train (tel. 717/334-6932) is an 8-mile steam-train ride through the countryside, followed by a 12-mile guided bus tour of the scenic orchard area.

Association of Battlefield Guides (tel. 717/334-1124) arranges for licensed guides to drive you in your car through the battlefield.

Numbers in the margin correspond to points of interest on the Gettysburg map.

The Gettysburg National Military Park surrounds the town of Gettysburg, and at times the two are undistinguishable. To the south of town, you'll discover stone walls, rolling farmlands, and stately homes that were used as hospitals during the famous battle. Many of the oak trees along the roadway have stood for more than 150 years.

1 The main attraction is, obviously, **Gettysburg National Military Park.** Stop at the **Visitor Center** (Emmitsburg Rd., tel. 717/ 334–1124) to pick up an Auto Tour map that outlines an 18-mile driving tour to 16 marked historic sites, tracing the three-day battle in chronological order. Auto Tour Tapes, which can be bought or rented at the numerous tour centers, re-create the historic three-day battle with sound effects as you drive through the battlefield at your own pace. The center also offers the **Electric Map** presentation (admission $2, senior citizens $1.50), and across the parking lot is the **Cyclorama Center,** with its 360° canvas depicting the battle (tel. 717/334–1124; admission $2).

Highlights of the battlefield include the **Eternal Peace Light Memorial;** the view from the ridge at **Little Round Top;** the **Wheatfield,** site of a particularly bloody skirmish; the **Pennsylvania Memorial,** marking the site where Union artillery held the line on Cemetery Ridge; **Culp's Hill** (an optional 5-mile loop), with its observation tower and short walking trail; **High Water Mark,** site of the battle's climax, when some 7,000 Union soldiers repulsed the 12,000 Confederate soldiers of Pickett's Charge; and the **National Cemetery,** where President Lincoln delivered the Gettysburg Address on November 19, 1863.

2 Adjacent to the park to the west is the **Eisenhower National Historic Site,** a colonial-style farmhouse used as a retirement home by President Dwight D. Eisenhower. Shuttle buses take tours to the site from an information center on the lower level of the visitor center of the park (*see above*). *Tel. 717/334–1124. Admission: $2.25 adults, $1.25 senior citizens and children 13–16, 70¢ children 6–12. Closed Jan.*

3 Just west of the National Cemetery, the **National Civil War Wax Museum** is an audiovisual presentation that brings to life some 200 Civil War figures in 30 scenes, as well as a reenactment of the Battle of Gettysburg and an animated figure of Lincoln giving the Gettysburg Address. *Bus. Rte. 15, tel. 717/334–6245. Admission: $4.25 adults, $3.50 senior citizens, $2.50 children 13–17, $1.75 children 6–12. Open Mar. 1–weekend after Thanksgiving.*

4 To the north of the cemetery in the **Hall of Presidents and First Ladies,** a gallery displays wax reproductions of the presidents "narrating" the story of America. *789 Baltimore St., tel. 717/ 334–5717. Admission: $3.85 adults, $3.50 senior citizens, $2.20 children under 12. Open Mar.–Nov.*

5 The **Jennie Wade House,** directly north of the Hall of Presidents, is the carefully restored brick home of Jennie Wade, the only civilian to be killed in the battle of Gettysburg. *Baltimore St., tel. 717/334–4100. Admission: $3.85 adults, $3.50 senior citizens, $2.20 children under 12. Open Mar.–Nov.*

6 The heart of Gettysburg's historic downtown area is **Lincoln Square,** which you can reach by following Baltimore Street north of the park to York Street. On the south side of the square, the **Lincoln Room Museum** (tel. 717/334–8188; admission $3 adults, $2.50 senior citizens, $1.50 children 8–16; open

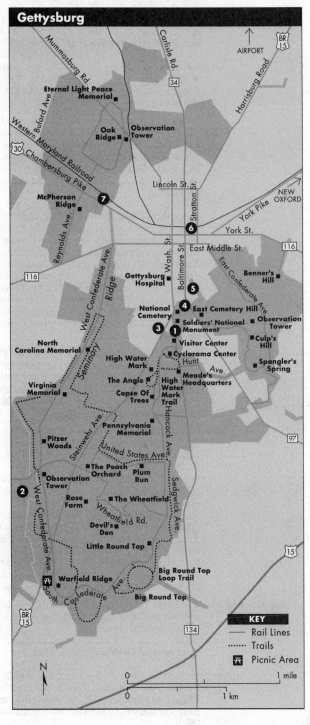

Gettysburg

Eisenhower National Historic Site, **2**

General Lee's Headquarters, **7**

Gettysburg National Military Park, **1**

Hall of Presidents and First Ladies, **4**

Jennie Wade House, **5**

Lincoln Square, **6**

National Civil War Wax Museum, **3**

Mummasburg Rd

Carlisle Rd

AIRPORT

BR 15

34

Harrisburg Road

Buford Ave.

Eternal Light Peace Memorial ■

Western Maryland Railroad

30

Chambersburg Pike

Oak Ridge ■

Observation Tower ■

Lincoln St.

Stratton St.

NEW OXFORD

McPherson Ridge ■

7

Lincoln St.

York Pike

6

York St.

116

Reynolds Ave.

Wash. St.

East Middle St.

116

West Confederate Ridge

Gettysburg Hospital ■

Baltimore St.

East Confederate Ave.

Benner's Hill ■

116

Seminary Ave.

National Cemetery

4

5

3

Soldiers' National Monument

East Cemetery Hill

Observation Tower ■

1

Visitor Center

Culp's Hill ■

North Carolina Memorial ■

High Water Mark

Cyclorama Center

Hunt Ave.

Spangler's Spring ■

Virginia Memorial ■

The Angle ■

High Water Mark Trail

Meade's Headquarters ■

Copse Of Trees ■

Pitzer Woods ■

Steinwehr Ave.

Pennsylvania Memorial ■

Hancock Ave.

97

United States Ave.

2

West Confederate Ave.

Observation Tower ■

The Peach Orchard ■

Plum Run ■

Sedgwick Ave.

Rose Farm ■

Wheatfield Rd.

The Wheatfield ■

Devil's Den ■

Little Round Top ■

15

Warfield Ridge ■

South Confederate Ave.

Big Round Top Loop Trail

Big Round Top

BR 15

134

N

KEY

— Rail Lines

······ Trails

🏕 Picnic Area

0   1 mile

0   1 km

Mar.–Nov.) is a historic old house where displays evoke the spirit of Lincoln. On the north side of the square, the recently restored **Gettysburg Hotel** (tel. 717/337–2000) was known as the vacation White House during the Eisenhower administration and hosted a number of other historic figures. In the brick wall of the People's Drug Store, facing York Street on Lincoln Square, look for a cannonball from the battle still embedded in the second story.

❼ Go west on York Street, which turns into Chambersburg Pike and takes you to **General Lee's Headquarters.** Used by Gen. Lee and his staff on the eve of July 1, 1863, this building houses one of the finest collections of Civil War relics. *Rte. 30W, tel. 717/ 334–3141. Admission free. Open Mar.–Nov.*

Shopping

Downtown, along Steinwehr Avenue and the streets radiating from Lincoln Square, you'll discover unique stores offering clothing, crafts, books, art, and hard-to-find items. In the tourist district near the park, you'll find **Old Gettysburg Village** (777 Baltimore St.), with its quaint shops including a fudge kitchen, doll shop, general store, and military art store. Homemade quilts and furniture, handcrafted by the local Amish community, can be found south of town. Stop at one of the many roadside markets north of Gettysburg, such as Sandoes Market, An Apple A Day, or Hollabaugh Brothers, for fresh fruits and vegetables at bargain prices.

Antiques **Mel's Antiques and Collectibles** (rear of 103 Carlisle St., tel. 717/334–9387; weekends only) has many bargains.
Arrow Horse International Market and Antiques (51 Chambersburg, tel. 717/337–2899) sells gifts, antiques, and baskets as well as vegetarian foods, fresh-baked breads, international groceries, and coffee beans.

Gifts **Codori's Bavarian Gift and Christmas Shop** (19 Barlow St., tel. 717/334–5019) offers German and Scandinavian gifts, music boxes, nutcrackers, nativities, collectible dolls, and Hummel figures.
Dalzell-Viking Factory Glass Outlet (646 York St., tel. 717/337–1677) sells handmade glassware, featuring exceptional colored glass.
Irish Brigade Gift Shop (504 Baltimore St., tel. 717/337–2519) is filled with a complete line of Irish jewelry, hand-blown crystal, Aran sweaters, linens, and china as well as Civil War–related items.
Gettysburg Crafts and Gifts (246 Steinwehr Ave., tel. 717/337–1300), located in a charming Victorian house, features Amish crafts, Civil War relics, baskets, and wreaths.

War Memorabilia **The Horse Soldier** (777 Baltimore St., tel. 717/334–0347) sells original military Americana, including guns, swords, documents, and photographs.

Sports and Outdoor Activities

Biking Marked bicycle routes offer a great way to discover the battlefield at your own pace. Bike rentals can be found at **Artillery Ridge Campground** (610 Taneytown Rd., tel. 717/334–1288) or **Blue and Gray Bike Rentals** (531B Baltimore St., tel. 717/334–2800).

Fishing	Inquire about seasons and licensing at area sporting good stores. **Granite Hill Campground** (3340 Fairfield Rd., tel. 717/642–8749 or 800/642–TENT) offers fishing in a 5-acre lake.
Golf	Area golf courses include **Cedar Ridge** (1225 Barlow Two Taverns Rd., tel. 717/359–4480), **Flatbush Golf Course, Inc.** (940 Littlestown Rd., Littlestown, tel. 717/359–7125); and **Mountain View Golf Resort** (Rte. 116W, Fairfield, tel. 717/642–5848).
Hiking/Walking	Hikers can pick up the Appalachian Trail at **Caledonia State Park,** about 15 miles west of Gettysburg, or **Pine Grove Furnace State Park,** about 25 miles north. A number of trails can be found on the Gettysburg Battlefield including: **The High Water Mark Trail** (1 mile, begins at the Cyclorama Center); the **Big Round Top Loop Trail** (1 mile); and paths winding through the enormous rocks, caves, and crevices that hid Confederate sharpshooters in **Devil's Den.** For a longer hike, inquire about the 9-mile **Billy Yank Trail** or the 3½-mile **Johnny Reb Trail.**
Horseback Riding	For trail riding across the battlefield, contact **Hickory Hollow Farm** (219 Crooked Creek Rd., tel. 717/334–0349) or **National Riding Stables** (610 Taneytown Rd., tel. 717/334–1288).
Skiing	Skiing during the winter months can be found at **Ski Liberty** (Rte. 116, Carroll Valley, tel. 717/642–8282).

Dining and Lodging

The following dining price categories have been used: *Moderate*, $15–25, and *Inexpensive*, under $15.

Bed-and-breakfasts with unique Civil War charm have joined the family-oriented motels throughout the Gettysburg area. Many are located within the town itself, but for added peace and quiet, you can find relaxing accommodations in historic homes or motels outside of town. Off-season rates begin the Sunday afterThanksgiving and end the first weekend of March.

The following lodging price categories have been used: *Expensive*, $80–$100; *Moderate*, $60–$80; and *Inexpensive*, under $60.

Gettysburg *Dining*	**Blue Parrot Bistro.** This cozy bar/restaurant near Lincoln Square offers an informal, intimate atmosphere, with a dinner menu including heart-healthy pastas. There's a piano player on Saturday nights. You can grab a quick lunch of soup or a deli combo from the counter bar. *35 Chambersburg St., tel. 717/337–3739. Dress: casual. MC, V. Moderate.*

Dobbin House Tavern. Built in 1776, this beautifully restored building in the tourist district features light, low-calorie, and char-broiled fare, with candlelit ambience at dinner. *89 Steinwehr Ave., tel. 717/334–2100. Dress: casual. AE, MC, V. Moderate.*

Farnsworth House Inn. The menu at this restored inn (*see* Lodging, *below*) harks back to Civil War–era dishes such as game pie, peanut soup, and spoon bread. *401 Baltimore St., tel. 717/334–8838. Dress: casual. AE, D, MC, V. Moderate.*

JD's Pub and Restaurant. Located on Lincoln Square, this lively restaurant offers a variety of dishes, from pastas and salads to seafood. *21 Lincoln Sq., tel. 717/334–7100. Dress: casual. AE, MC, V. Moderate.*

Stonehenge Restaurant and Big Boppers Lounge. Adjacent to the battlefield, this restaurant offers casual dining and weekend entertainment. Weekend buffets feature seafood; dinner specialties include chicken, pasta, and seafood. *985 Baltimore St., tel. 717/334–9227. Dress: casual. AE, MC, V. Moderate.*

Battle Theatre Cafeteria. This cafeteria-style restaurant across from the Visitor Center offers fast service and delicious country cooking—meat loaf, baked chicken, hot sandwiches, and daily soup specials. *Steinwehr Ave., tel. 717/334–7580. Dress: casual. No credit cards. Inexpensive.*

Dutch Cupboard Deli Delight. In the heart of the tourist district, this deli offers old-fashioned Dutch cooking, featuring soups, salads, and deli sandwiches. *523 Baltimore St., tel. 717/ 334–6227. Dress: casual. MC, V. Inexpensive.*

Lincoln Diner. You'll find the locals at this old-fashioned diner one block from Lincoln Square. Open 24 hours, it features fast service and Italian and Greek cooking. *32 Carlisle St., tel. 717/ 334–3900. Dress: casual. No credit cards. Inexpensive.*

Nature's Food and Restaurant. You can eat a healthy lunch or early supper at the counter of this health food store, which sells herb tea samplers and all-natural foods. *48 Baltimore St., tel. 717/334–7723. Dress: casual. MC, V. Inexpensive.*

Sunny Ray Family Restaurant. This restaurant, located on Route 30W, prepares food the old-fashioned way, including homemade soup and real mashed potatoes. There's a large salad bar, too. *90 Buford Ave., tel. 717/334–4816. Dress: casual. No credit cards. Inexpensive.*

Lodging   **Best Western Gettysburg Hotel 1797.** Built before the Civil War, this venerable stucco hotel with green-striped awnings was reconstructed from a burned-out shell and reopened in 1991. It's a cut above the motels and B&Bs that predominate in the area. *1 Lincoln Sq., 17325, tel. 717/337–2000. 83 rooms. Suites have whirlpool tubs and fireplaces; covered parking. D, MC, V. Expensive.*

The Brierfield Bed and Breakfast. Located conveniently near the major attractions, this restored 1878 house offers homey comfort, including well-furnished guest rooms and shady porches. *240 Baltimore St., 17325, tel. 717/334–8725. 1 room with bath, 2 rooms with shared bath. Continental breakfast included. No credit cards. Moderate.*

Farnsworth House Inn. This Civil War–period B&B is an elegant Victorian house complete with authentic bullet holes from the battle. Its restaurant (*see* Dining, *above*) serves authentic Civil War–era specialties. *401 Baltimore St., 17325, tel. 717/ 334–8838. 4 rooms. Full breakfast in garden included, restaurant. AE, D, MC, V. Moderate.*

The Little House Guest House. Originally a two-story Victorian carriage house, this small home-away-from-home with exposed brick walls and wooden beams includes a living room, upstairs bedroom, and kitchen, which can comfortably accommodate up to four people. *Rear 20 N. Washington St., 17325, tel. 717/334–4632 or 717/334–0664. AE, MC, V. Moderate.*

Ramada Inn. Located right down the road from the park, this outlet of the well-known chain is one of the larger Gettysburg motels and has a good menu of sports facilities: pool, saunas, fitness center, tennis, racquetball, miniature golf, and an exercise course. *2634 Emmitsburg Rd., 17325, tel. 717/334–8121. 203 rooms. Facilities: restaurant, lounge, pool, tennis, fitness center. AE, D, MC, V. Moderate.*

The Tannery Bed & Breakfast. Located in a residential area near major attractions, this Gothic-style Victorian home, built by a Civil War veteran in 1868, has shady porches and several common rooms where guests can relax. *449 Baltimore St., 17325, tel. 717/334–2454. 5 rooms. Continental breakfast included, off-street parking. MC, V. Moderate.*

American Youth Hostel—Gettysburg International. Dormitory-style lodging in bunk beds, this Civil War–era former hospital downtown gives an exceptional value; families or couples can opt for private accommodations. *27 Chambersburg St., 17325, tel. 717/334–1020. 60 beds. Kitchen, common room. Inexpensive.*

Blue Sky Motel. This family-owned motel 5 miles north of Gettysburg is on a main road, but the landscaping creates a quiet country atmosphere. Guest rooms are paneled in knotty pine. *2585 Biglerville Rd., 17325, tel. 717/677–7736. 16 rooms, 1 efficiency. Pool, picnic area. MC, V. Inexpensive.*

Colton Motel. Situated adjacent to the National Cemetery, museums, and restaurants, this low-slung motel offers neat wood-paneled guest rooms and conveniences such as in-room coffee. *232 Steinwehr Ave., 17325, tel. 717/334–5514. 26 rooms. Heated pool, off-street parking. AE, MC, V. Inexpensive.*

Home Sweet Home Motel. Located opposite the entrance to the Visitor Center, this *L*-shape brick motel offers a good view of the battlefield. *593 Steinwehr Ave., 17325, tel. 717/334–3916. 41 rooms. Off-street parking. MC, V. Inexpensive.*

Tour 5: Washington, D.C., and Historic Virginia

As All-American vacations go, this is as good as it gets. You start out in Washington, DC, the nation's capital and epicenter of political life, and then cross the Potomac to tour around the state of Virginia, with its wealth of restored Colonial settlements, Revolutionary War landmarks, Civil War battlefields, and Presidential homesteads (more U.S. Presidents have come from Virginia than from any other state). When this great living history lesson overwhelms, Virginia offers refuge in a vast official wilderness of mountains and forest in its extensive state and national parks.

If you have only a week to spend, you could begin with three or four days in Washington. Visit the Northern Virginia landmarks on your way out of town, then overnight in Richmond. From there, you have two choices. You can go east to the historic triangle of Williamsburg, Jamestown, and Yorktown for the final two or three days (this option is particularly good if you've got kids along) and return to Washington from there. Or you can go west, spending a day in Charlottesville, another day enjoying the spectacular scenery of Shenandoah National Park, and the final day heading back to DC with a stop at Manassas (Bull Run), the famous Civil War battlefield.

Two weeks would allow you to spend less time driving and more time exploring the entire state's history, combining the attractions in the eastern part of the state with those in the west. After visiting the early settlements in Williamsburg and Jamestown, a couple of days in the Charlottesville area will reveal more than ever how visionary Thomas Jefferson was. And after seeing the state's many restored plantations, it would be nice to have time to prowl around Loudon County's horse farms, the retreat of today's landowning aristocracy.

Visitor Information

Washington, DC **International Visitor Information Service** (733 15th St. NW, Suite 300, tel. 202/783–6540).

Washington Convention and Visitors Association (1212 New York Ave. NW, Washington, DC 20005, tel. 202/789–7000).

Washington, D.C. Convention and Visitors Association Tourist Information Center (1455 Pennsylvania Avenue, NW, tel. 202/789–7000; tel. 202/737–8866 for recorded announcement of upcoming events).

Virginia **Virginia Division of Tourism** (Old Bell Tower, Capitol grounds, 9th St., tel. 804/786–4484).

Virginia Travel Center (1629 K St. NW, Washington, DC, tel. 202/659–5523).

Northern Virginia **Alexandria Convention and Visitor's Bureau** (221 King St., tel. 703/838–4200).

Arlington County Visitor's Center (735 S. 18th St., tel. 703/358–5720 or 800/677–6267).

Fredericksburg Visitor's Center (706 Caroline St., tel. 703/373–1776).

Richmond **Metro Richmond Visitor's Center** (1700 Robin Hood Road, Exit 14 off Interstates 95 and 64, tel. 804/358–5511).

Historic Triangle **Williamsburg Area Tourism and Conference Bureau** (Drawer GB, 201 Penniman Rd., Williamsburg 23187, tel. 804/253–0192 or 800/368–6511).

Charlottesville and **Charlottesville/Albemarle Convention and Visitors' Bureau**
Shenandoah Valley (Rte. 20S, Box 161, Charlottesville, 22902, tel. 804/977–1783).

Front Royal/Warren County Chamber of Commerce (414 E. Main St., tel. 703/635–3185).

Shenandoah Valley Tourist Information Center (off I–81 at Exit 67, New Market, tel. 703/740–3132).

Historic Staunton Welcome Center (24 N. Coalter St., tel. 703/885–8097).

Festivals and Seasonal Events

Apr. 5–12: The National Cherry Blossom Festival's highlights are a VIP-led parade, a marathon run, a fashion show, and a Japanese Lantern Lighting ceremony. For parade information, tel. 202/728–1137. For general information, tel. 202/737–2599 or 202/619–7222.

May 24–25: Memorial Day Weekend leads off with a Sunday concert by the National Symphony Orchestra on the West Lawn of the U.S. Capitol; on the 25th, there's a wreath-laying ceremony at the Vietnam Veterans Memorial and a jazz festival in Old Town Alexandria.

June 5–7: The Alexandria Waterfront Festival activities include visiting tall ships, arts and crafts displays, a 10K run, and the blessing of the fleet. Tel. 703/549–8300.

June 24–28 and July 1–5: The Festival of American Folklife, sponsored by the Smithsonian and held on the Mall, celebrates the music, arts, crafts, and foods of various cultures. Tel. 202/357–2700.

July 4: The Independence Day Celebration includes a grand parade, a free jazz festival on Freedom Plaza, a free evening performance by the National Symphony Orchestra on the Capitol steps, and a fireworks display over the Washington Monument. Tel. 202/619–7222.

Dec.: Christmas celebrations include carol singing with the U.S. Marine Band, the Smithsonian Museum's annual display of Christmas trees, the Capitol Tree Lighting (done by the President himself), and the Pageant of Peace.

Mid-Dec.: Old Town Christmas Candlelight Tours visit historic Ramsay House, Gadsby's Tavern Museum, the Lee-Fendall House, and the Carlyle House in Old Town Alexandria. Tel. 703/838–4200.

What to See and Do with Children

Washington, DC, is a perennial favorite destination for families. The Smithsonian museums around the Mall invariably fascinate kids, especially the Air and Space Museum, the Discovery Room at the Museum of Natural History, and the Discovery Theater in the Arts and Industries Building (tel. 202/357–1500), which features plays, puppet shows, and storytellers October–June. After museum-going, a ride on the Mall's Carousel makes a good break for the younger ones. The

National Geographic Explorers Hall (17th and M Sts., tel. 202/
857–7588) is full of interactive exhibits on geography and science, and youngsters also enjoy the activity-packed Capital
Children's Museum (800 3rd St. NE, tel. 202/543–8600; admission: $5; open daily), and the Dolls' House and Toy Museum of
Washington (5236 44th St. NW, tel. 202/244–0024; admission:
$3 adults, $1 under 14; open Tues.–Sun.). The D.A.R. Museum
runs special tours for kids every other Sunday (call 202/879–
3239 for reservations). The National Aquarium and the National Zoo are sure-fire child-pleasers.

Richmond has its own hands-on Children's Museum (740 N. 6th
St., tel. 804/788–4949; admission: $3 adults, $2 children 2–12;
open Tues.–Sun.), as well as child-oriented exhibits in the Science Museum of Virginia (2500 W. Broad St., tel. 804/367–
1013; admission: $3.50 adults, $3 children 4–17). The **King's Dominion** entertainment complex (22 mi north of Richmond on I–
95, Doswell exit, tel. 804/876–5000; admission: $19.95; open
June–Aug. daily, Apr.–May and Sept.–Oct. weekends) has
more than 100 rides, including a stand-up roller coaster.

Three miles east of **Williamsburg,** the **Busch Gardens** theme
park (U.S. 60, tel. 804/253–3350; all-day admission $22.95;
open mid-May–Labor Day daily, Apr.–mid-May and Labor
Day–Oct. weekends only) has plenty of rides and entertainment, as well as environments evoking various European countries.

Charlottesville's Virginia Discovery Museum (East end of
Downtown Mall, tel. 804/977–1025; admission: $3 adults, $2
children; open Tues.–Sun.) offers kids lots of hands-on activities.

Arriving and Departing

By Plane   **National Airport,** in Virginia, 4 miles south of downtown Washington, is served by America West, American, Continental,
Delta, Midway, Midwest, Northwest, Pan American, Trump
Shuttle, TWA, United, and USAir. To reach downtown, you can
ride the **Metro** (National Airport station, on the Blue and Yellow lines); walk to the station or catch the free airport shuttle
that stops at each terminal. The ride downtown takes about 20
minutes and costs between $1 and $1.25, depending on the time
of day. **Washington Flyer** buses (tel. 703/685–1400) take 20 minutes and costs $7 ($12 round-trip). Many hotels have courtesy
vans as well. **Taxis** cost about $8 to downtown.

Dulles International Airport, a modern facility 26 miles west of
Washington, is served by Aeroflot, Air France, All Nippon,
American, Bahamasair, British Airways, Business Express,
Continental, Delta, Lufthansa, Mohawk, Northwest, Pan
American, Saudi Arabian, TWA, United, USAir, and Wings
Airways. **Washington Flyer** buses (tel. 703/685–1400) costs $14
for the hour-long ride ($22 round-trip). **Taxis** cost about $35 to
downtown.

A **Washington Flyer** inter-airport express between Dulles and
National takes 45 minutes and costs $14 ($26 round-trip).

Baltimore-Washington International (BWI) Airport in Mary-
land, about 25 miles northeast of Washington, is served by Air
Jamaica, America West, American, Continental, Cumberland,
Delta, Enterprise, Icelandair, KLM Royal Dutch, Mexicana,

Northwest, PanAm Express, TWA, United, and USAir. **Airport Connection** buses (tel. 301/441–2345) leave roughly every hour for downtown Washington, a 65-minute ride that costs $13 ($23 round-trip). **Amtrak** (tel. 800/USA–RAIL) and **MARC (Maryland Rail Commuter Service)** (tel. 800/325–RAIL) trains run between BWI and Washington's Union Station from around 6 AM to 11 PM (a free shuttle bus connect terminals to the BWI station). The cost for the 40-minute ride is $11 on an Amtrak train, $4.25 on a MARC train (weekdays only). **Taxis** cost about $36 to downtown.

Richmond International Airport, recently expanded, is served by 12 airlines, including USAir, the major regional carrier. A taxi ride downtown from the airport is $16–$18.

Charlottesville-Albemarle Airport is served by USAir, United Express, Alleghany, and T.W. Express.

By Train More than 50 trains a day arrive at Washington's restored **Union Station** on Capitol Hill (50 Massachusetts Ave. NE, tel. 202/ 484–7540 or 800/USA–RAIL). Washington is the last stop on Amtrak's Northeast Corridor line and is a major stop on most routes from the south and west. Metroliner trains travel between New York and Washington five times every weekday.

There are **Amtrak** stations in Alexandria (110 Callahan Dr.), Fredericksburg (Caroline St. and Lafayette Blvd.), Richmond (7519 Staples Mill Road), Williamsburg (468 N. Boundary St.), Charlottesville (810 W. Main St.), and Staunton (One Middlebrook Ave.).

By Bus **Greyhound/Trailways Bus Lines** stops in Washington, DC (1005 1st St. NE, tel. 301/565–2662), Fredericksburg (1400 Jefferson Davis Hwy., tel. 703/373–2103), Richmond (2910 N. Boulevard, tel.804/254–5910), Williamsburg (468 N. Boundary St., tel. 804/229–1460), Charlottesville (310 W. Main St., tel. 804/ 295–5131), and Staunton (100 S. New St., tel. 703/886–2424).

By Car **I-95** skirts Washington as part of the Beltway, the six- to eight-lane highway that encircles the city. The eastern half of the Beltway is **I-95**, the western half is **I-495**. If coming from the south, take I-95 to **I-395** and cross the 14th Street bridge to 14th Street in the District. From the north, stay on I-95 south before heading west on Route 50, the John Hanson Highway, which turns into New York Avenue. **I-66** approaches the city from the southwest; on weekdays from 6:30 to 9 AM cars traveling eastbound inside the Beltway (I-495) must have at least three people in them, and from 4 to 6:30 PM the same applies for westbound travel inside the Beltway. To reach downtown, take I-66 across the Theodore Roosevelt Bridge to Constitution Avenue. **I-270** approaches Washington from the northwest; to get downtown take 495 east to Connecticut Avenue south, towards Chevy Chase.

I–95 runs north–south from Washington, DC, through northern Virginia to Richmond, which is at the intersection of I–95 and I–64 east–west. I–64 runs southeast to the Historic Triangle or northwest through Charlottesville to the Shenandoah Valley. I–81 runs north–south the length of the Shenandoah Valley, just west of, and parallel to, the Skyline Drive, which runs through Shenandoah Valley National Park. I–66 passes through Front Royal to connect with Skyline Drive and I–81 at the northern end of the Valley; from there I–66 goes 90 miles east back to Washington.

Washington, D.C.

The Byzantine workings of the Federal government; the non-sensical, sound-bite-ready oratory of the well-groomed politician; murky foreign policy pronouncements issued from Foggy Bottom; and $600 toilet seats ordered by the Pentagon cause many Americans to cast a skeptical eye on anything that happens "inside the Beltway." Washingtonians take it all in stride, though, reminding themselves that, after all, those responsible for political hijinks don't come *from* Washington, they come *to* Washington. Besides, such ribbing is a small price to pay for living in a city whose charms extend far beyond the bureaucratic. World-class museums and art galleries (nearly all of them free), tree-shaded and flower-filled parks and gardens, bars and restaurants that benefit from a large and creative immigrant community, and nightlife that seems to get better with every passing year are as much a part of Washington as floor debates or filibusters.

George Washington himself selected in 1785 the exact site of the capital, a diamond-shaped, 100-square-mile plot that encompassed the confluence of the Potomac and Anacostia rivers, not far from the president's estate at Mount Vernon. To give the young city a bit of a head start, Washington included the already thriving tobacco ports of Alexandria, Virginia, and Georgetown, Maryland, in the District of Columbia. Charles Pierre L'Enfant, a young French engineer who had fought in the Revolution, offered his services in creating a capital "magnificent enough to grace a great nation." His 1791 plan owes much to Versailles, with ceremonial circles and squares, a grid pattern of streets, and broad diagonal avenues. At first the town grew so slowly that when Charles Dickens visited Washington in 1842 what he saw were "spacious avenues that begin in nothing and lead nowhere; streets a mile long that only want houses, roads, and inhabitants; public buildings that need but a public to be complete and ornaments of great thoroughfares which need only great thoroughfares to ornament." It took the Civil War—and every war thereafter—to energize the city, by attracting thousands of new residents and spurring building booms that extended the capital in all directions. Memorials to famous Americans like Lincoln and Jefferson were built in the first decades of the 20th century, along with the massive Federal Triangle.

The District is divided into four sections: northwest, northeast, southwest, and southeast; the Capitol Building serves as the center of the north/south and east/west axes. North Capitol and South Capitol streets divide the city into east and west; the Mall and East Capitol Street divide the city into north and south. Streets that run north to south are numbered; those that extend east to west are lettered from A to I and K to W, the letter J having been skipped. (Note that I Street is often written as "Eye Street.") Make sure you have a destination's complete address, including the quadrant designation. Addresses in Washington are coded to the intersections they're closest to. For example, 1785 Massachusetts Ave. NW is between 17th and 18th Streets; 600 5th St. NW is at the corner of 5th and F, the sixth letter of the alphabet.

Getting Around
By Subway

Metro trains run 5:30 AM–midnight, Monday–Friday; 8 AM–midnight Saturdays; 10 AM–midnight Sundays. The base fare is $1; the actual price you pay depends on the time of day and the distance traveled. Children under five ride free, with a maximum of two children per paying adult. Computerized **Farecard machines** in Metro stations dispense paper Farecards, which you insert into the turnstile to enter the platform. Hang onto the card—you'll need it to exit at your destination. An $8 **Metro Family/Tourist Pass** entitles a family of four to one day of unlimited subway and bus travel any Saturday, Sunday, or holiday (except July 4). Passes are available at Metro Sales Outlets (including the Metro Center station) and at many hotels.

By Bus

WMATA's red, white, and blue **Metrobuses** crisscross the city and nearby suburbs, with some routes running 24 hours a day. All bus rides within the District are $1. Free transfers, good for two hours, are available on buses and in Metro stations. Bus-to-bus transfers are accepted at designated Metrobus transfer points. Rail-to-bus transfers must be picked up before boarding the train; there are no bus-to-rail transfers.

By Car

A car can be a drawback in Washington. Traffic is horrendous and parking lots downtown are expensive, charging as much as $4 an hour and up to $13 a day. Since the city's most popular sights are within a short walk of a Metro station anyway, it's best to leave your car at the hotel, or in one of the free parking areas south of the Lincoln Memorial on Ohio Drive and West Basin Drive in West Potomac Park.

By Taxi

Taxis in the District are not metered; they operate instead on a curious zone system. Ask the cabdriver ahead of time how much the fare will be. The basic single rate for traveling within one zone is $3. There is an extra $1.25 charge for each additional passenger and a $1 surcharge during the 4 to 6:30 PM rush hour. Bulky suitcases larger than three cubic feet are charged at a higher rate and a $1.50 surcharge is tacked on when you phone for a cab. Two major companies serving the District are **Capitol Cab** (tel. 202/546–2400) and **Diamond Cab** (tel. 202/387–6200).

Guided Tours
Orientation Tours

Tourmobile (tel. 202/554–7950 or 202/554–5100) buses, authorized by the National Park Service, stop at 18 historic sites between the Capitol and Arlington Cemetery; the route includes the White House and the museums on the Mall. Tickets are $8 for adults, $4 for children 3–11.

Old Town Trolley Tours (tel. 202/269–3020) take in the main downtown sights and also foray into Georgetown and the upper northwest, stopping at out-of-the-way attractions like the Washington Cathedral. Tickets are $14 for adults, $5 for children 5 to 12, and free for the under 5 set.

Gray Line Tours (tel. 301/386–8300) runs a four-hour motorcoach tour of Washington, Embassy Row, and Arlington National Cemetery, as well as tours of Mount Vernon and Alexandria.

VIP tours of government buildings—including the Archives, the Capitol, the FBI Building, the Supreme Court, and the White House—can be arranged through your representative's or senator's office. Only limited numbers are available, so contact your representative up to six months in advance of your trip.

Scandal Tours (tel. 202/387–2253). This outrageous tour concentrates on Washington's seamier side with a 90-minute trip past scandalous locales. Costumed look-alikes ride on the bus and act out the scandals. The cost is $27 per person. Reservations required.

Boat Tours **Spirit of Washington** (Pier 4, 6th and Water Sts. SW, tel. 202/554–8000 or 202/554–1542), moored at the heart of Washington's waterfront, gives visitors a waterborne view of some of the area's attractions. A sister ship, the **Spirit of Mt. Vernon,** sails a 4-hour cruise to George Washington's plantation home mid-March–early October, Tuesday–Sunday.

Walking Tours **Black History National Recreation Trail** designates a group of sites within historic neighborhoods illustrating aspects of African-American history in Washington, from slavery days to the New Deal. A brochure is available from the National Park Service (Box 37127, Washington, DC 20013–7127, tel. 202/208–4747).

Construction Watch and Site Seeing (tel. 202/272–2448), sponsored by the National Building Museum, are architecturally oriented walking tours each spring and fall. Tickets range from $9 for Construction Watch tours to $60 for Site Seeing tours, which include bus transportation and a box lunch.

Pacesetter Productions (tel. 301/961–3529) has four self-guided walking tours on cassette. Two concentrate on Georgetown, one covers the Dupont Circle/Embassy Row area, and one the White House neighborhood. The 50-minute **"TapeWalks"** are available at bookstores and museum gift shops in Washington for $11.95 each.

Smithsonian Resident Associate Program (tel. 202/357–3030) offers walking and bus tours of neighborhoods in Washington and communities outside the city. Many tours are themed and include sites that illustrate, for example, Art Deco influences, African-American architecture, or railroad history.

Personal Guides **Guide Service of Washington** (tel. 202/628–2842). This company provides a licensed guide to accompany you in your car, van, or bus. The cost for an English-speaking guide is $88 for a four-hour tour; $131 for an eight-hour tour. Guides are available for tours in any of 20 languages.

The Mall

Numbers in the margin correspond to points of interest on the Washington, DC, map.

The Mall is the heart of nearly every visitor's trip to Washington. With nine diverse museums ringing the expanse of green, it's the closest thing the capital has to a theme park (unless you count the Federal government itself, which has uncharitably been called "Disneyland on the Potomac"). As at a theme park, you may have to stand in an occasional line, but unlike the amusements at Disneyland almost everything you'll see here is free.

Don't expect to see it all in one day, though. The Smithsonian Institution is the largest museum complex in the world. If you can, devote at least two days to the Mall. Do the north side one day and the south the next, or visit museums the first day, art galleries the second.

The best place to start an exploration of the museums on the Mall is in front of the first one constructed, the **Smithsonian Institution Building.** British scientist James Smithson left his entire fortune to the United States, "to found at Washington, under the name of the Smithsonian Institution, an establishment for the increase and diffusion of knowledge among men." In 1838 the United States received $515,169 worth of gold sovereigns, and the red sandstone, Norman-style headquarters building on Jefferson Drive was completed in 1855. Known as "the Castle," the building was designed by James Renwick, the architect of St. Patrick's Cathedral in New York City. The statue in front of the Castle's entrance is not of Smithson but of Joseph Henry, the scientist who served as the Institution's first secretary. Smithson's body was brought to America in 1904 and is entombed in a small room to the left of the Castle's Mall entrance.

To get your bearings or to get help deciding which Mall attractions you want to devote your time to, visit the **Smithsonian Information Center** in the Castle. *1000 Jefferson Dr. SW, tel. 202/ 357–2700. Open daily 9–5:30.*

This tour circles the Mall counterclockwise. Start by walking east on Jefferson Drive to the **Arts and Industries Building,** originally called the United States National Museum, built to house a wealth of artifacts donated to the federal government after the 1876 Centennial exposition in Philadelphia. Today the museum exhibits an extensive collection of American Victoriana: carriages, tools, furnishings, printing presses, even a steam locomotive, many of them from the original Philadelphia Centennial. In 1991 the Smithsonian opened the Experimental Gallery in the south quadrant of the Arts and Industries Building, a laboratory that allows museum curators to experiment not so much with what should be displayed but how to display it. Up to four exhibits are presented at any one time, with museum professionals assessing visitor reaction. *900 Jefferson Dr. SW, tel. 202/357–2700. Open daily 10–5:30.*

In front of the Arts and Industries Building is a **carousel** that is popular with young and old alike. In warmer months it operates between 10 and 5:30 (75¢ a ride).

The **Hirshhorn Museum,** the next building to the east on Jefferson Drive, contrasts totally with the gay Victoriana of the Arts and Industries Building. Dubbed "the Doughnut on the Mall," the reinforced-concrete building designed by Gordon Bunshaft is a fitting home for contemporary—and sometimes controversial—art. Opened in 1974, the museum manages a collection of 4,000 paintings and drawings and 2,000 sculptures donated by Joseph H. Hirshhorn, a Latvian-born immigrant who made his fortune in this country running uranium mines. American artists such as Eakins, Pollock, Rothko, and Stella are represented, as are modern European and Latin masters, including Francis Bacon, Magritte, and Miró. The Hirshhorn's impressive sculpture collection is arranged in the open spaces between the museum's concrete piers and across Jefferson Drive in the sunken **Sculpture Garden.** Rodin's *The Burghers of Calais* is a highlight. *Independence Ave. at 7th St. SW, tel. 202/357–2700.*

Open daily 10–5:30. Extended spring/summer hours determined annually. Sculpture garden open daily 7:30–dusk.

4 Cross 7th Street to get to the **National Air and Space Museum.** Opened in 1976, Air and Space is the most visited museum in the world, attracting 12 million people each year. Twenty-three galleries tell the story of aviation, from man's earliest attempts at flight to his travels beyond our solar system. Suspended from the ceiling like plastic models in a child's room are dozens of aircraft, including the actual "Wright Flyer" that Wilbur Wright piloted over the sands of Kitty Hawk, North Carolina; Charles Lindbergh's "Spirit of St. Louis"; the X-1 rocket plane in which Chuck Yeager broke the sound barrier; and the X-15, the fastest plane ever built. Other highlights include a back-up model of the Skylab orbital workshop that visitors can walk through; the Voyager airplane that Dick Rutan and Jeana Yeager flew non-stop around the world; and the USS Enterprise model used in the "Star Trek" TV show. Visitors can also touch a piece of the moon: a 4-billion-year-old slice of rock collected by Apollo 17 astronauts. Don't let long lines deter you from seeing the IMAX films shown in the museum's **Langley Theater**—including *The Dream is Alive, To Fly!, On the Wing,* and *The Blue Planet.* Buy your tickets ($2.75 for adults; $1.75 for children, students, and senior citizens) as soon as you arrive, then look around the museum. *Jefferson Dr. at Sixth St. SW, tel. 202/357–2700. Open daily 10–5:30. Specially priced double features are often shown in the Langley Theater after the museum has closed. For information, call 202/357–1686.*

Time Out Located in the eastern end of the National Air and Space Museum, **The Wright Place** is a table-service restaurant that takes reservations (tel. 202/371–8777), and the **Flight Line** is a self-service cafeteria. They each have a large selection of foods, but at peak times lines can be long.

After touring the Air and Space Museum, walk east on Jefferson Drive toward the Capitol. The open space on the periphery of the Mall bounded by 3rd and 4th streets and Independence Avenue and Jefferson Drive SW will be filled with the Smithsonian's **National Museum of the American Indian** scheduled to open in 1998.

Walk north on 4th or 3rd Street, and look to the left for a good view of the Mall. Cross Madison Drive to get to the two buildings of the **National Gallery of Art,** one of the world's foremost
5 collections of paintings, sculptures, and graphics. Its permanent collection includes works from the 13th to the 20th century, including *The Adoration of the Magi* by Fra Angelico and Fra Filippo Lippi, *The Alba Madonna* by Raphael, Botticelli's *Adoration of the Magi, Ginevra de'Benci* (the only painting by da Vinci outside of Europe), *Daniel in the Lions' Den* by Rubens, and a self-portrait by Rembrandt, and works by Impressionist painters such as Degas, Monet, Renoir, and Mary Cassatt. Although an underground moving walkway connects the National Gallery's two buildings, to appreciate architect I.M. Pei's impressive, angular **east building,** enter it from outside (exit the west building through its eastern doors, and cross 4th St.). The galleries here generally display modern art, though the east building also serves as a home for major temporary exhibitions that span years and artistic styles. *Madison Dr. and 4th St. NW, tel. 202/737–4215. Open Mon.–Sat. 10–5;*

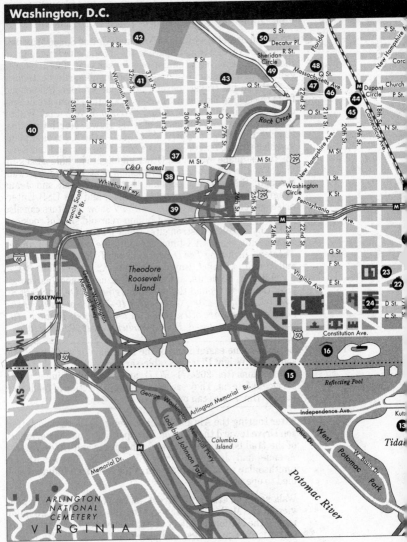

Washington, D.C.

Anderson House, **47**

Arthur M. Sackler Gallery, **10**

Arts and Industries Building, **2**

Barney Studio House, **49**

Bureau of Engraving and Printing, **8**

C & O Canal, **38**

Corcoran Gallery of Art, **22**

Decatur House, **19**

Department of the Interior, **24**

Dumbarton Oaks, **42**

Dumbarton House, **43**

Dupont Circle, **44**

Folger Shakespeare Library, **28**

Ford's Theater, **32**

Freer Gallery of Art, **9**

Georgetown University, **40**

Heurich Mansion, **45**

Hirshhorn Museum, **3**

J. Edgar Hoover Federal Bureau of Investigation Building, **35**

Jefferson Memorial, **14**

Library of Congress, **27**

Lincoln Memorial, **15**

Martin Luther King Library, **31**

National Archives, **36**

National Gallery of Art, **5**

National Aquarium, **33**

National Air and Space Museum, **4**

National Museum of American History, **7**	Old Post Office Building, **34**	Supreme Court Building, **29**	Washington Monument, **12**
National Museum of Natural History, **6**	Old Patent Office Building, **30**	The Capitol, **26**	Washington Harbour, **39**
National Museum of African Art, **11**	Phillips Collection, **48**	Tidal Basin, **13**	White House, **17**
Octagon House, **23**	Renwick Gallery, **21**	Tudor Place, **41**	Woodrow Wilson House, **50**
Old Stone House, **37**	Smithsonian Institution Building, **1**	Union Station, **25**	
Old Executive Office Building, **20**	St. John's Episcopal Church, **18**	Vietnam Veterans Memorial, **16**	
		Walsh-McLean House, **46**	

Sun. 11–6. Extended summer hours are determined annually. Tape-recorded tour available for $3.50 at ground floor sales area.

Time Out On the concourse level between the east and west buildings of the National Gallery you'll find a **buffet** serving a wide variety of soups, sandwiches, salads, hot entrees, and desserts, and the **Cascade Cafe,** where a soothing waterfall splashes against the glass-covered wall.

Between 7th and 9th streets is the **National Sculpture Garden/ Ice Rink** (tel. 202/371–5340). In the winter skates are rented out for use on the circular rink. Ice cream and other refreshments are available at the green building during the summer.

6 The **National Museum of Natural History** is a museum's museum, filled with bones, fossils, stuffed animals, and other natural delights. The first-floor hall under the rotunda is dominated by a stuffed, eight-ton, 13-foot African bull elephant, one of the largest specimens ever found. Off to the right is the popular Dinosaur Hall, with fossilized skeletons on display. In the west wing are displays on birds, mammals, and sea life. Many of the preserved specimens are from the collection of animals bagged by Teddy Roosevelt on his trips to Africa. Not everything in the museum is dead, though. The sea-life display features a living coral reef, complete with fish, plants, and simulated waves. The highlight of the second floor is the mineral and gem collection, second in value only to the crown jewels of Great Britain. It includes the Hope diamond, a blue gem found in India and reputed to carry a curse (though Smithsonian guides are quick to pooh-pooh this notion). *Madison Dr. between 9th and 12th Sts. NW, tel. 202/357–2700. Open daily 10–5:30. Extended summer hours determined annually.*

7 The **National Museum of American History**—the next building to the west, toward the Washington Monument—helps the Smithsonian live up to its nickname as "the Nation's attic." This is the museum that displayed Muhammed Ali's boxing gloves, the Fonz's leather jacket, and the Bunkers' living room furniture from "All in the Family." The exhibits on the first floor emphasize the history of science and technology; the second floor is devoted to U.S. social and political history; and the third floor has installations on ceramics, money, graphic arts, musical instruments, photography, and news reporting. The gowns of the seven most recent first ladies—Jacqueline Kennedy through Barbara Bush—are on display in the second-floor Ceremonial Court, which also features jewels, china, and other artifacts from the White House. *Madison Ave. between 12th and 14th Sts. NW, tel. 202/357–2700. Open daily 10–5:30.*

To continue the loop of the Mall, head south on 14th Street. From here you'll be able to view the length of the Mall from its western end, this time seeing the Capitol from afar. Instead of turning east on Jefferson Drive, continue south on 14th Street. On the right you'll pass a turreted, castle-like structure called the **Auditor's Building.** Built in 1879, it was the first building dedicated exclusively to the work of printing America's money. In 1914 the money-making operation was moved one block **8** south to the **Bureau of Engraving and Printing.** All the paper currency in the United States, as well as stamps, military certificates, and presidential invitations, is printed in this huge building. Despite the fact that there are no free samples, the 20-minute, self-guided tour of the Bureau—which takes visitors past presses that turn out some $40 million a day—is one of the city's most popular. *14th and C Sts. SW, tel. 202/447-0193. Open weekdays 9–2.*

Return up 14th Street and turn east onto Independence Avenue. Continuing down Independence Avenue back toward the Capitol, you'll walk between the two buildings of the **Department of Agriculture.** The cornices on the north side of this white-marble building feature depictions of forests and of grains, flowers, and fruits. A few steps farther up Independence Avenue, across 12th Street, is the **Freer Gallery of Art,** a gift from Detroit industrialist Charles L. Freer, who retired in 1900 and devoted the rest of his life to collecting Asian treasures. Nearing the end of an extensive renovation, the Freer is scheduled to reopen in late 1992 or early 1993. Its collection includes more than 26,000 works of art from the Far and Near East, including Asian porcelains, Japanese screens, Chinese paintings and bronzes, and Egyptian gold pieces.

Just beyond the Freer turn left off of Independence Avenue into the **Enid Haupt Memorial Garden.** This four-acre Victorian-style garden is built largely on the rooftops of the Smithsonian's two newest museums, the Arthur M. Sackler Gallery and the National Museum of African Art, both of which opened in 1987 and sit underground like inverted pyramids.

When Charles Freer endowed the gallery that bears his name, he insisted on a few conditions: objects in the collection could not be loaned out, nor could objects from outside the collections be put on display. Because of these restrictions it was necessary to build a second, complementary, Oriental art museum. The result was the **Arthur M. Sackler Gallery,** named after a wealthy medical researcher and publisher who began collecting Asian art as a student. Articles in the permanent collection include Chinese ritual bronzes, jade ornaments from the third millenium BC, Persian manuscripts, and Indian paintings in gold, silver, lapis lazuli, and malachite. *1050 Independence Ave. SW, tel. 202/357-2700. Open daily 10–5:30.*

The other half of the Smithsonian's new underground museum complex is the **National Museum of African Art.** (Before it was moved here in 1987, the collection was housed in a Capitol Hill town house that once belonged to ex-slave Frederick Douglass.) Dedicated to the collection, exhibition, and study of the traditional arts of sub-Saharan Africa, the museum displays artifacts representative of some 900 cultures. The permanent collection includes masks, carvings, textiles, and jewelry, all made from materials such as wood, fiber, bronze, ivory, and fired clay. *950 Independence Ave. SW, tel. 202/357-2700. Open daily 10–5:30.*

The Monuments

We'll start in front of the tallest of them all, the **Washington Monument.** Located at the western end of the Mall, the Washington Monument punctuates the capital like a huge exclamation point. Congress first authorized a monument to General Washington in 1783. In his 1791 plan for the city, Pierre L'Enfant selected a site (the point where a line drawn west from the Capitol crossed one drawn south from the White House), but because of the marshy conditions of L'Enfant's original site, the position of the monument was shifted to firmer ground 100 yards southeast. The cornerstone was laid in 1848 with the same Masonic trowel Washington himself had used to lay the Capitol's cornerstone 55 years earlier. A lack of funds and the onset of the Civil War kept the monument at a fraction of its final height, about a third of the way up: Although all of the marble in the obelisk came from the same Maryland quarry, that used for the second phase of construction came from a different stratum and is of a slightly different shade. In 1876 Congress finally appropriated $200,000 to finish the monument, and the Army Corps of Engineers took over construction, simplifying Robert Mill's original elaborately decorated design. Work was finally completed in December 1884, when the monument was topped with a 7½-pound piece of aluminum, then one of the most expensive metals in the world. At 555 feet 5 inches, the Washington Monument is the world's tallest masonry structure. The view from the top takes in most of the District and parts of Maryland and Virginia. Visitors are no longer permitted to climb the 898 steps leading to the top, but on Saturdays there are walk-down tours, with a Park Service guide. There is usually a wait to take the minute-long elevator ride up the monument's shaft. If the line goes all the way around the monument, you'll be waiting anywhere from 40 minutes to an hour. *Constitution Ave. at 15th St. NW, tel. 202/426–6840. Open Apr.–Labor Day, daily 8 AM–midnight; Sept.–Mar., daily 9–5.*

After your ascent and descent, walk on the path that leads south from the monument and cross Independence Avenue at 15th Street. Walk south, carefully cross Maine Avenue at the

13 light, and walk down to the **Tidal Basin.** This placid pond was part of the Potomac until 1882, when portions of the river were filled in to improve navigation. Paddleboats have been a fixture on the Tidal Basin for years. You can rent one at the boathouse on the east side of the basin, southwest of the Bureau of Engraving. *Tel. 202/484–0206. Rentals cost $7 an hour, $1.75 each additional quarter hour. Children under 16 must be accompanied by an adult. Open daily 10–6, weather permitting.*

Continue down the path that skirts the Tidal Basin and cross

14 the Outlet Bridge to get to the **Jefferson Memorial,** the southernmost of the major monuments in the District, positioned directly south of the White House. Jefferson had always admired the Pantheon in Rome—the rotundas he designed for the University of Virginia and his own Monticello were inspired by the dome of the Pantheon—so architect John Russell Pope drew from the same source when he designed this memorial to our third president. Dedicated in 1943, it houses a statue of Jefferson. Its walls are lined with inscriptions based on his writings. *Tidal Basin, south bank, tel. 202/426–6821. Open daily 8–midnight.*

Continue along the sidewalk that hugs the Tidal Basin. Once you cross the Inlet Bridge, you have a choice: You can walk to the left, along the Potomac, or continue along the Tidal Basin to the right. The latter route is somewhat more scenic, especially when the cherry trees are in bloom. The first batch of these trees arrived from Japan in 1909. The trees were infected with insects and fungus, however, and the Department of Agriculture ordered them destroyed. A diplomatic crisis was averted when the United States politely asked the Japanese for another batch, and in 1912 Mrs. William Howard Taft planted the first tree. The second was planted by the wife of the Japanese ambassador.

West Potomac Park, the green expanse to the west of the Tidal Basin, will change over the next few years as the $47.2 million Franklin Delano Roosevelt Memorial is constructed. When it's completed in 1995 the memorial will comprise a long sequence of walkways and shaded, exterior "rooms" containing sculptures and inscriptions about the 32nd president.

Walk northwest along West Basin Drive, then cut across to Ohio Drive. Cross Independence Avenue at the light; the traffic here can be dangerous.

🟡 The **Lincoln Memorial** is considered by many to be the most inspiring monument in the city. When it was first built in 1922, detractors thought it inappropriate that the humble Lincoln be honored with what amounts to a modified but nonetheless rather grandiose Greek temple. The 36 Doric columns represent the 36 states in the Union at the time of Lincoln's death; the names of the states appear on the frieze above the columns. Above the frieze are the names of the 48 states in the Union when the memorial was dedicated. Daniel Chester French's somber 19-foot-high statue of the seated president is in the center of the memorial and gazes out over the Reflecting Pool. Inscribed on the south wall is the Gettysburg Address, and on the north wall is Lincoln's second inaugural address. On the south wall is an angel of truth freeing a slave; the unity of North and South are depicted on the opposite wall. The memorial served as a fitting backdrop for Martin Luther King's "I have a dream" speech in 1963. Be sure to walk around the marble platform to the rear of the memorial for a clear view over the Arlington Memorial Bridge into Arlington National Cemetery. *West end of Mall, tel. 202/426–6895. Open 24 hours a day; staffed daily 8 AM–midnight.*

🟡 Walk down the steps of the Lincoln Memorial and to the left to get to the **Vietnam Veterans Memorial** and **Constitution Gardens.** The stark design of Maya Ying Lin, a 21-year-old Yale architecture student, was selected in a 1981 competition. Upon its completion in 1982, the memorial was decried by some veterans as a "black gash of shame." With the addition of Frederick Hart's statue of three soldiers and a flagpole just south of the Wall, most critics were won over. The Wall is one of the most visited sites in Washington, its black granite panels reflecting the sky, the trees, and the faces of those looking for the names of friends or relatives who died in the war. The names of more than 58,000 Americans are etched on the face of the memorial in the order of their deaths. Directories at the entrance and exit to the Wall list the names in alphabetical order. (Last year it was discovered that due to a clerical error the names of some two dozen living vets are carved into the stone as well.) For help in finding a specific name, ask a ranger at the blue-and-white hut near the entrance. *Constitution Gardens, 23rd St. and Constitution Ave. NW, tel. 202/634–1568. Open 24 hours a day; staffed 8 AM–midnight.*

A memorial to veterans of the Korean War is planned for a grove of trees known as Ash Woods near Independence Avenue and the Lincoln Memorial reflecting pool. When completed in

1993, it will consist of a column of American soldiers marching toward a flag pole. After years of debate over its design and necessity, the Vietnam Womens Memorial—in honor of the women who served in that conflict—is scheduled to be dedicated in 1993. The monument—a bronze figure of a female soldier standing on a marble pad equipped with nozzles that continuously blow a soft mist—sits in Constitution Gardens, southeast of the Vietnam Veterans Memorial.

The White House

In a city full of immediately recognizable images, perhaps none is more familiar than the **White House,** 1600 Pennsylvania Avenue. Irishman James Hoban's plan, based on the Georgian design of Leinster Hall near Dublin and of other Irish country homes, was selected in a contest, in 1792. The building wasn't ready for its first occupant until 1800. Completed in 1829, it has undergone many structural changes since then: Thomas Jefferson, who had entered his own design in the contest under an assumed name, added terraces to the east and west wings. Andrew Jackson installed running water. James Garfield put in the first elevator. Between 1948 and 1952, Harry Truman had the entire structure gutted and restored, adding a second-story porch to the south portico. Most recently, George Bush installed a horseshoe pit.

Tuesday through Saturday morning, from 10 AM to noon, selected public rooms on the ground floor and first floor of the 132-room mansion are open to visitors. Expect a long line. Most of the year you can simply join the line that forms along the east fence of the White House. Between Memorial Day and Labor Day, however, you'll need tickets to tour the mansion; a blue-and-green ticket booth on the **Ellipse** just south of the White House is open 8 AM–noon, Tuesday–Saturday, dispensing tickets on a first-come, first-served basis. (Tickets are often gone by 9 AM.)

You'll enter the White House through the East Wing lobby on the ground floor, walking past the Jacqueline Kennedy Rose Garden. Your first stop is the large white-and-gold **East Room,** the site of presidential news conferences. The Federal-style **Green Room,** named for the moss-green watered silk that covers its walls, is used for informal receptions and "photo opportunities" with foreign heads of state. The elliptical **Blue Room,** the most formal space in the White House, is furnished with a gilded Empire-style settee and chairs. Another well-known elliptical room, the president's **Oval Office** (not on the tour), is in the semidetached West Wing of the White House, along with other executive offices. The **Red Room** is decorated as an American Empire–style parlor of the early 19th century. The **State Dining Room,** second in size only to the East Room, is dominated by G.P.A. Healy's portrait of Abraham Lincoln, painted after the president's death. The stone mantel is inscribed with a quotation from one of John Adams's letters: "I pray heaven to bestow the best of blessings on this house and all that shall hereafter inhabit it. May none but honest and wise men ever rule under this roof." *1600 Pennsylvania Ave. NW, tel. 202/ 456–7041 (recorded information) or 202/472–3669. Open Tues.–Sat. 10 AM–noon.*

Lafayette Square, bordered by Pennsylvania Avenue, Madison Place, H Street, and Jackson Place, is an intimate oasis in the midst of downtown Washington. Soldiers camped in the square during the War of 1812 and the Civil War, turning it at both times into a muddy pit. Today, protesters set their placards up in Lafayette Square, jockeying for positions that face the White House. Standing in the center of the park—and dominating the square—is a large **statue of Andrew Jackson,** erected in 1853 and cast from bronze cannon that Jackson had captured during the War of 1812. Jackson's is the only statue of an American in the park; the others are of foreign-born soldiers who helped in America's fight for independence. In the southeast corner is the park's namesake, the **Marquis de Lafayette,** the young French nobleman who came to America to fight in the Revolution.

⑱ On H Street, across from the square, is the golden-domed **St. John's Episcopal Church,** the so-called "Church of the Presidents." Every president since Madison has visited the church, and many worshiped here on a regular basis. Built in 1816, the church was designed by Benjamin Latrobe, who worked on both the Capitol and the White House. Not far from the center of the church is pew 54, where visiting presidents are seated. The kneelers of many of the pews are embroidered with the presidential seal and the names of several chief executives. *16th and H Sts. NW, tel. 202/ 347–8766. Open Mon.–Sat. 8–4. Tours after 11 AM Sun. service and by appointment.*

Across 16th Street stands the **Hay-Adams Hotel,** a favorite with Washington insiders and visiting celebrities. It takes its name from a double house, owned by Lincoln biographer John Hay and historian Henry Adams, that stood on this spot. The **⑲** redbrick, Federal-style **Decatur House** on the corner of H Street and Jackson Place was built for naval hero Stephen Decatur and his wife Susan in 1819. Later occupants included Henry Clay and Martin Van Buren. The first floor is furnished as it was in Decatur's time. The second floor is furnished in the Victorian style favored by the Beale family, who owned it until 1956. *748 Jackson Pl. NW, tel. 202/842–0920. Open Tues.–Fri. 10–2, weekends noon–4. Admission: $3 adults, $1.50 senior citizens and students under 18, free to children under 5 and National Trust members. Tours on the hour and half hour.*

Head south on Jackson Place. Many of the row houses on this stretch date from the pre–Civil War or Victorian periods; even the more modern additions, though—such as those at 718 and 726—are designed in a style that blends with their more historic neighbors.

⑳ Directly across Pennsylvania Avenue, to the right of the White House, is the **Old Executive Office Building,** built between 1871 and 1888 to house the War, Navy, and State departments. The granite edifice may look like a wedding cake, but its high ceilings and spacious offices make it popular with occupants, who currently include the vice president, the Office of Management and Budget, the National Security Council, and other agencies of the executive branch. It was here that Secretary of State Cordell Hull met with Japanese diplomats after the bombing of Pearl Harbor, and it was here that Oliver North and Fawn Hall shredded Iran-Contra documents.

The green canopy at 1651 Pennsylvania Avenue marks the entrance to **Blair House,** the residence used by heads of state visiting Washington. Harry S. Truman lived here from 1948 to 1952, while the White House was undergoing renovation.

Continue west on Pennsylvania Avenue. At the end of the block, with the motto "Dedicated to Art" engraved above the entrance, is the **Renwick Gallery,** designed by Smithsonian Castle architect James Renwick in 1859 to house the art collection of Washington merchant and banker William Wilson Corcoran. Corcoran's collection quickly outgrew the building and in 1897 was moved to a new gallery a few blocks south on 17th Street (described below). After a stint as the U.S. Court of Claims, this building was opened as the Smithsonian's museum of American decorative arts in 1972. The collection covers a wide range of disciplines and styles; special exhibits have included such items as blown glass, Shaker furniture, and contemporary crafts. *Pennsylvania Ave. and 17th St. NW, tel. 202/357–2700. Open daily 10–5:30.*

Head south on 17th Street to New York Avenue to see the **Corcoran Gallery of Art,** one of the few large museums in Washington outside the Smithsonian family. The Beaux Arts–style building, its copper roof green with age, was designed by Ernest Flagg and completed in 1897. The gallery's permanent collection numbers more than 11,000 works, including paintings by the first great American portraitists John Copley, Gilbert Stuart, and Rembrandt Peale. The Hudson River School is represented by such works as *Mount Corcoran* by Albert Bierstadt and Frederic Church's *Niagara*. There are also portraits by Sargent, Eakins, and Mary Cassatt. European artwork is included in the Walker Collection (late 19th- and early 20th-century paintings, including works by Gustave Courbet, Monet, Pissarro, and Renoir) and the Clark Collection (Dutch, Flemish, and French Romantic paintings, and the recently restored entire 18th-century Grand Salon of the Hotel d'Orsay in Paris). Also be sure to see Samuel Morse's *The Old House of Representatives* and Hiram Powers's *The Greek Slave*, which scandalized Victorian society. *17th St. and New York Ave. NW, tel. 202/638–1439 (recording), 202/638–3211. Open Tues.–Sun. 10–4:30, Thurs. 10–9. Closed Mon., Christmas, and New Year's Day. Suggested donation: $3 adults, $2 students and senior citizens.*

A block up New York Avenue, at the corner of 18th Street, is the **Octagon House,** built in 1801 for John Tayloe III, a wealthy Virginia plantation owner. Designed by William Thornton, the Octagon House actually has only six sides, not eight. Thornton chose the unusual shape to conform to the acute angle formed by L'Enfant's intersection of New York Avenue and 18th Street. After the White House was burned in 1814 the Tayloes invited James and Dolley Madison to stay in the Octagon House. It was in a second-floor study that the Treaty of Ghent, ending the War of 1812, was signed. Exhibits relating to architecture, decorative arts, and Washington history are mounted in the upstairs galleries. *1799 New York Ave. NW, tel. 202/638–3105. Open Tues.–Fri. 10–4, weekends noon–4. Closed Christmas and New Year's Day. Suggested donation: $2 adults, $1.50 senior citizens, $1 children.*

A block south on 18th Street is the **Department of the Interior** building. While the outside of the building is somewhat plain, its hallways feature heroic oil paintings of dam construction, panning for gold, and cattle drives. Visit the charming, if dated, **Department of the Interior Museum** on the first floor. The Indian Craft Shop across the hall from the museum sells Native American pottery, dolls, carvings, jewelry, baskets, and books. *C and E Sts. between 18th and 19th Sts. NW, tel. 202/208–4743. Open weekdays 8–4.*

Capitol Hill

The people who live and work on "the Hill" do so in the shadow of the edifice that lends the neighborhood its name: the gleaming white Capitol building. More than just the center of government, however, the Hill also includes charming residential blocks lined with Victorian row houses and a fine assortment of restaurants, bars, and shops.

25 Start your exploration of the Hill inside the cavernous main hall of **Union Station,** which sits on Massachusetts Avenue north of the Capitol. Chicago architect and commission member Daniel H. Burnham patterned the station, opened in 1908, after the Roman Baths of Diocletian. In its heyday, during World War II, more than 200,000 people swarmed through the station daily. By the '60s, however, the decline in train travel had turned the station into an expensive white-marble elephant. The Union Station you see today is the result of a restoration completed in 1988, bringing in shops, restaurants, and a nine-screen movie theater. The jewel of the structure remains its meticulously restored main waiting room. With its 96-foot-high coffered ceiling gilded with eight pounds of gold leaf, it is one of the city's great spaces and is used for inaugural balls and other festive events. *Group tours available by appointment (tel. 202/289–1908).*

As you walk out Union Station's front doors, glance to the right. At the end of a long succession of archways is the Washington **City Post Office,** also designed by Daniel Burnham and completed in 1914. Nostalgic odes to the noble mail carrier are inscribed on the exterior of the marble building. The Post Office is currently being renovated, scheduled to open in late 1993 as the **National Postal History and Philatelic Museum,** the 14th Smithsonian museum in Washington.

Head south, away from Union Station, cross Massachusetts Avenue, and walk down Delaware Avenue. On the left you'll pass the **Russell Senate Office Building.** Completed in 1909, this was the first of the senate office buildings. Beyond it are the Dirksen and Hart office buildings.

26 Cross Constitution Avenue and enter the **Capitol** grounds, landscaped in the late-19th century by Frederick Law Olmsted, Sr., who, along with Calvert Vaux, created New York City's Central Park. On these 68 acres you will find both the tamest squirrels in the city and the highest concentration of television news correspondents, jockeying for a good position in front of the Capitol for their "stand-ups."

The Capitol design was the result of a competition held in 1792; the winner was William Thornton, a physician and amateur architect from the West Indies. With its central rotunda and dome, Thornton's Capitol is reminiscent of Rome's Pantheon. The cornerstone was laid by George Washington in a Masonic ceremony on September 18, 1793, and in November 1800, both the Senate and the House of Representatives moved down from Philadelphia to occupy the first completed section. The Congress House grew slowly and suffered a grave setback on August 24, 1814, when British troops set fire to it. Architect Benjamin Henry Latrobe supervised the rebuilding of the Capitol, adding such American touches as the corn-cob-and-tobacco-leaf capitals to columns in the east entrance to the Senate wing. He was followed by Boston-born Charles Bulfinch, and in 1826 the Capitol, its low wooden dome sheathed in copper, was finally finished. North and south wings were added in the 1850s and '60s, and in 1855, to keep the scale correct, work began on a taller, cast-iron dome. President Lincoln was criticized for continuing this expensive project while the country was in the throes of the bloody Civil War, but he called the construction "a sign we intend the Union shall go on."

Guided tours of the Capitol usually start beneath the dome in the Rotunda, but if there's a crowd you may have to wait in a line that forms at the top of the center steps on the east side. If you want to forgo the tour, which is brief but informative, you may look around on your own. Enter through one of the lower doors to the right or left of the main steps. Start your exploration under Constantino Brumidi's *Apotheosis of Washington*, the fresco in the center of the dome. Twenty-six people have lain in state in the Rotunda, including nine presidents, from Abraham Lincoln to Lyndon Baines Johnson.

South of the Rotunda is Statuary Hall, once the legislative chamber of the House of Representatives. The room has an interesting architectural feature that maddened early legislators: A slight whisper uttered on one side of the hall can be heard on the other. (Don't be disappointed if this parlor trick doesn't work when you're visiting the Capitol; sometimes the hall is just too noisy.) To the north, on the Senate side, you can visit the chamber once used by the Supreme Court as well as the splendid Old Senate Chamber, both of which have been restored.

If you want to watch some of the legislative action in the **House** or **Senate chambers** while you're on the Hill you'll have to get a gallery pass from the office of your representative or senator. (To find out where those offices are, ask any Capitol police officer, or dial 202/224–3121.) You may be disappointed by watching from the gallery. Most of the day-to-day business is conducted in the various legislative committees, many of which meet in the Congressional office buildings. The *Washington Post's* daily "Today in Congress" lists when and where the committees are meeting. To get to a house or senate office building, go to the Capitol's basement and ride the miniature subway used by legislators. *East end of the Mall, tel. 202/224–3121. For guide service, tel. 202/225–6827. Open daily 9–4:30; summer hours determined annually.*

Time Out   A meal at a **Capitol cafeteria** may give you a glimpse of a well-known politician or two. A public dining room on the first floor, Senate-side, is open from 7:30 AM to 4:30 PM when Congress is in session, 7:30 to 3:30 at other times. A favorite with legislators is the Senate bean soup, made and served every day since 1901 (no one is sure exactly why, though the menu, which you can take with you, outlines a few popular theories).

Across Maryland Avenue is the **United States Botanic Gardens,** a peaceful, plant-filled oasis between Capitol Hill and the Mall. The conservatory includes a cactus house, a fern house, and a subtropical house filled with orchids. Seasonal displays include blooming plants at Easter, chrysanthemums in the fall, and Christmas greens and poinsettias in December and January. Brochures just inside the doorway offer helpful gardening tips. *1st St. and Maryland Ave. SW, tel. 202/225–8333. Open Jun.– Aug. daily 9–9; Sept.–May daily 9–5.*

Walk east on Independence Avenue past the **Rayburn, Longworth,** and **Cannon House office buildings.** At Independence Avenue and 1st Street SE is the green-domed **Jefferson Building** of the **Library of Congress.** When it was completed, in 1897, some detractors felt its Italian-Renaissance design was a bit too florid. It is certainly decorative, with busts of Dante, Goethe, Hawthorne, and other great writers perched above its entryway. *The Court of Neptune,* Roland Hinton Perry's fountain at the base of the front steps, rivals some of Rome's best fountains. The **Adams Building,** on 2nd Street behind the Jefferson, was added in 1939. A third structure, the **James Madison Building,** opened in 1980, is just south of the Jefferson Building. The Library of Congress today holds some 90 million items, of which 30 million are books. *Jefferson Building, 1st St. and Independence Ave. SE, tel. 202/707–5458. Open weekdays 8:30–9:30, weekends 8:30–6.*

Behind the Jefferson Building stands the **Folger Shakespeare Library.** The Folger Library's collection of works by and about Shakespeare and his times is second to none. The white-marble Art Deco building, designed by architect Paul Philippe Cret, is decorated with scenes from the Bard's plays. Inside is a reproduction of an inn-yard theater that is home to the acclaimed Shakespeare Theatre at the Folger. A gallery, designed in the manner of an Elizabethan Great Hall, hosts rotating exhibits from the library's collection. *201 E. Capitol St. SE, tel. 202/ 544–4600. Open Mon.–Sat. 10–4.*

Walk back down East Capitol Street and turn right onto 1st Street. The stolid **Supreme Court Building** faces 1st Street here. The justices arrived in Washington in 1800 along with the rest of the government but were for years shunted around various rooms in the Capitol; for a while they even met in a tavern. It wasn't until 1935 that the Court got its own building, this white-marble temple with twin rows of Corinthian columns, designed by Cass Gilbert. The Supreme Court convenes on the first Monday in October and remains in session until it has heard all of its cases and handed down all its decisions (usually the end of July). For two weeks of each month (Monday through Wednesday), the justices hear oral arguments in the velvet-swathed court chamber. Visitors who want to listen can choose from two lines. One is a "three-to-five-minute" line, which shuttles visitors through, giving them a quick impression of the court at work. The other is for those who'd like to stay for the whole show. If you choose the latter, it's best to be in line by 8:30 AM. *1st and E. Capitol Sts. NE, tel. 202/479–3000. Open Mon.–Fri. 9–4:30.*

Old Downtown and Federal Triangle

Nowhere have the city's imperfections been more visible than on L'Enfant's grand thoroughfare, Pennsylvania Avenue. By the early '60s it had become a national disgrace, the dilapidated buildings that lined it home to pawn shops and cheap souvenir stores. Washington's downtown—once within the diamond formed by Massachusetts, Louisiana, Pennsylvania, and New York avenues—had its problems, too. But in recent years developers have rediscovered "old downtown," and buildings are now being torn down or remodeled at an amazing pace. After several false starts Pennsylvania Avenue is shining once again.

30 Right by the Gallery Place metro stop, at 8th and G streets, is the **Old Patent Office Building,** which was designed by Washington Monument architect Robert Mills. When the huge Greek-Revival quadrangle was completed in 1867 it was the largest building in the country. Many of its rooms housed glass display cabinets filled with the models inventors were required to submit with their patent applications. During the Civil War, the Patent Office, like many other buildings in the city, was turned into a hospital. Among those caring for the wounded here were Clara Barton and Walt Whitman.

Today the Old Patent Office contains two Smithsonian museums. The **National Museum of American Art** holds displays of early American art and art of the West, works by the American Impressionists, including John Henry Twachtman and Childe Hassam, massive landscapes by Albert Bierstadt and Thomas Moran, and modern art by Edward Hopper, Jasper Johns, Robert Rauschenberg, Milton Avery, Kenneth Noland, and others. *8th and G Sts. NW, tel. 202/357-2700. Open daily 10-5:30. Closed Christmas.*

You can enter the **National Portrait Gallery** from any floor of the National Museum of American Art or walk through the courtyard between the two wings. Highlights include the third-floor Civil War exhibition, the Hall of Presidents on the second floor, and items from *Time* magazine's "Person of the Year" collection. *8th and F Sts. NW, tel. 202/357-2700. Open daily 10-5:30. Closed Christmas.*

Time Out   The **Patent Pending** restaurant, between the two museums, serves an ample selection of salads, sandwiches, hot entrées, and other treats. Tables and chairs in the large museum courtyard make sitting outside the thing to do when the weather is pleasant.

31 The squat black building at 9th and G streets is the **Martin Luther King Library,** designed by Mies van der Rohe. A mural on the first floor depicts events in the life of the Nobel-prize winning civil rights activist. *801 G St. NW, tel. 202/727-1111. Open Mon.-Thurs. 9-9, Fri.-Sat. 9-5:30, Sun. 1-5.*

32 Turn left onto 10th Street and walk down to **Ford's Theater.** In 1861 Baltimore theater impresario John T. Ford leased the First Baptist Church building that stood on this site and turned it into a successful music hall. The building burned down late in 1862, and Ford rebuilt it. The events of April 14, 1865, would shock the nation and close the theater. On that night, during a production of *Our American Cousin,* John Wilkes Booth entered the presidential box and assassinated Abraham Lincoln.

Ford's Theater was remodeled as a Lincoln museum in 1932 and was restored to its 1865 appearance in 1968. The basement museum displays artifacts such as Booth's pistol and the clothes Lincoln was wearing when he was shot. *511 10th St. NW, tel. 202/426–6924. Open daily 9–5. Theater closed when rehearsals or matinees are in progress (generally Thurs. and weekends); Lincoln Museum in basement remains open at these times. Closed Christmas.*

The stricken president was carried across the street to the house of tailor William Petersen. Lincoln died in the **Petersen House** the next morning. *516 10th St. NW, tel. 202/426–6830. Open daily 9–5. Closed Christmas.*

Freedom Plaza, bounded by 13th, 14th, and E streets and Pennsylvania Avenue, is inlaid with a detail from L'Enfant's original 1791 plan for the Federal City. To compare L'Enfant's vision with today's reality, stand in the middle of the map's Pennsylvania Avenue and look west.

Near the plaza, the ornate Beaux Arts **Willard Hotel** on the corner of 14th Street and Pennsylvania Avenue was built in 1901. An earlier Willard Hotel on this spot was the place to stay in Washington; Abraham Lincoln stayed there while waiting to move into the nearby White House, and Julia Ward Howe wrote *The Battle Hymn of the Republic* after gazing down from her window to see Union troops drilling on Pennsylvania Avenue. It's said the term "lobbyist" was coined to describe the favor seekers who would buttonhole President Ulysses S. Grant in the hotel's public rooms. The second Willard, with its mansard roof dotted with circular windows, was designed by Henry Hardenbergh, architect of New York's Plaza Hotel. After being closed for almost 20 years, in 1986 it reopened amid much fanfare, after an ambitious restoration.

To the south of Freedom Plaza is **Federal Triangle,** the mass of government buildings constructed from 1929 to 1938 between 15th Street, Pennsylvania Avenue, and Constitution Avenue. A uniform classical architectural style, with Italianate red-tile roofs and interior plazas reminiscent of the Louvre, was chosen for the building project. The base of Federal Triangle, and the first part completed, is the **Department of Commerce** building, between 14th and 15th streets, which opened in 1932. In addition to the Commerce Department, the building houses the

㉝ National Aquarium. Established in 1873, it's the oldest public aquarium in the United States. Displays feature tropical and freshwater fish, moray eels, frogs, turtles, piranhas, even sharks. A "touch tank" allows visitors to handle sea creatures such as crabs and oysters. *14th St. and Constitution Ave., tel. 202/377–2825. Open daily 9–5. Admission: $2 adults, 75¢ children 3–12 and senior citizens. Sharks are fed Mon., Wed., and Sat. at 2; piranhas Tues., Thurs., and Sun. at 2.*

㉞ Across 12th Street is the Romanesque **Old Post Office Building.** When it was completed, in 1899, it was the largest government building in the District. In 1984 the public areas in the restored Old Post Office Pavilion—an assortment of shops and restaurants inside the airy central courtyard—were opened. Park Service rangers who work at the Old Post Office consider a trip to the observation deck in the **clock tower** to be one of Washington's best-kept secrets. *Pennsylvania Ave. and 12th St. NW, tower tel. 202/523–5691, pavilion tel. 202/289–4224. Tower* *open mid-Apr.–mid-Sept., daily 8 AM–11 PM; mid-Sept.–mid-Apr., daily 10–5:40.*

Continuing down Pennsylvania Avenue, the next big building on the right is the **Department of Justice.** Like the rest of Federal Triangle, it boasts some Art Deco features, including the cylindrical aluminum torches outside the doorways, adorned with bas-relief figures of bison, dolphins, and birds.

㉟ Across from Justice is the **J. Edgar Hoover Federal Bureau of Investigation Building.** A hulking presence on the avenue, it was decried from its birth in 1974 as hideous. Even Hoover himself is said to have called it the "ugliest building I've ever seen." The tour of the building remains one of the most popular tourist activities in the city. Exhibits outline famous past cases and illustrate the Bureau's fight against organized crime, terrorism, bank robbery, espionage, and extortion. The tour ends with a live-ammo firearms demonstration. *10th St. and Pennsylvania Ave. NW (tour entrance on E St. NW), tel. 202/324–3447. Tours weekdays 8:45–4:15. At peak times, there may be an hour wait for the tour.*

㊱ The classical **National Archives** building is located at the corner of 9th Street or 7th Street and Pennsylvania Avenue. The Declaration of Independence, the Constitution, and the Bill of Rights are on display in the Rotunda of the Archives building, in a case made of bulletproof glass, illuminated with green light, and filled with helium gas (to protect the irreplaceable documents). *Constitution Ave. between 7th and 9th Sts. NW, tel. 202/501–5000. Open Apr.–Labor Day, daily 10–9; Sept.–Mar., daily 10–5:30. Behind-the-scenes tours by reservation weekdays at 10:15 and 1:15, tel. 202/501–5205 well in advance.*

Georgetown

Long before the District of Columbia was formed, Georgetown, Washington's oldest neighborhood, was a separate city that boasted a harbor full of ships and warehouses filled with tobacco. Washington has filled in around Georgetown over the years, but the former tobacco port retains an air of aloofness. Its narrow streets, which refuse to conform to Pierre L'Enfant's plan for the Federal City, make up the capital's wealthiest neighborhood and are the nucleus of its nightlife.

㊲ Start your exploration of Georgetown in front of the **Old Stone House** (M St. between 30th and 31st Sts.), thought to be Washington's only surviving pre-Revolutionary building, built in 1764. Five of the house's rooms are furnished with the sort of sturdy beds, spinning wheels, and simple tables associated with middle-class Colonial America. *3051 M St. NW, tel. 202/426–6851. Open Wed.–Sun. 8–4:30.*

As you walk south on Thomas Jefferson Street, you'll pass over **㊳** the **Chesapeake & Ohio Canal,** intended to link the Potomac with the Ohio River across the Appalachians. Work started on the C & O Canal in 1828, and when it opened in 1850, its 74 locks linked Georgetown with Cumberland, Maryland, 184 miles to the northwest. Today the canal is a part of the National Park system, and walkers follow the towpath once used by mules while canoers paddle the canal's calm waters. Between April and October you can go on a leisurely, mule-drawn trip aboard *The Georgetown* canal barge. Tickets are available across the canal, in the **Foundry Mall** (1055 Thomas Jefferson St. NW, tel. 202/472–4376). The mall gets its name from an old foundry that overlooked the canal at 30th Street. Around the turn of the century it was turned into a veterinary hospital that cared for mules working on the canal. Today it's a restaurant.

39 Continue south, across K Street, and into **Washington Harbour,** a glittering, postmodern riverfront development designed by Arthur Cotton Moore that includes restaurants, offices, apartments, and upscale shops. The plazas around its large central fountain and gardens are dotted with the eerily realistic sculptures of J. Seward Johnson, Jr. From the edge of Washington Harbour you can see the Watergate complex and Kennedy Center to the east.

Time Out   If the breeze off the river has given you an appetite, stop at **Artie's Harbour Deli Cafe** for a sandwich. For dessert, select from the **Café Rosé's** waistline-threatening selection of authentic Viennese pastries. Both are in the Washington Harbour complex.

Georgetown's **K Street** is lined with the offices of architects, ad agencies, and public relations companies. In many of these offices you can hear the rumble of cars on the Whitehurst Freeway, the elevated road above K Street that leads to the Francis Scott Key Memorial Bridge. Walking up **Wisconsin Avenue** you'll again cross the C & O Canal via the only bridge that remains from the 19th century. The intersection of Wisconsin Avenue and M Street is the heart of boisterous Georgetown. This spot—under the gleaming, golden dome of Riggs Bank on the northeast corner—is mobbed every weekend. Turning left on **M Street** you'll come to the entrance to **Georgetown Park** (3222 M St. NW), a multilevel shopping extravaganza. A stroll up either M Street or Wisconsin Avenue will take you past a dizzying array of merchandise.

The heights of Georgetown to the north above N Street contrast with the busy jumble of the old waterfront. To reach the higher ground you can walk up M Street past the old brick streetcar barn at No. 3600 (now a block of offices), turn right, and climb the 75 steps that figured prominently in the eerie climax of the movie *The Exorcist.* If you would prefer a less demanding climb, walk up 34th Street instead.

40 The sounds of traffic diminish the farther north one walks from the bustle of M Street. To the west is **Georgetown University,** the oldest Jesuit school in the country. It was founded in 1789 by John Carroll, first American bishop and first archbishop of Baltimore. About 12,000 students attend Georgetown, known now as much for its perennially successful basketball team as for its fine programs in law, medicine, and the liberal arts.

Architecture buffs, especially those interested in Federal and Victorian houses, enjoy wandering along the red-brick sidewalks of upper Georgetown. The group of five Federal houses between 3339 and 3327 N Street are known collectively as **Cox's Row,** after John Cox, a former mayor of Georgetown, who built them in 1817. The flat-fronted, red-brick Federal house at **3307 N Street** was the home of then-Senator John F. Kennedy and his family before the White House beckoned. Turn left onto Potomac and walk a block up to O Street, which still has two leftovers from an earlier age: cobblestones and streetcar tracks.

St. John's Church (3240 O St. NW, tel. 202/338–1796) was built in 1809 and is attributed to Dr. William Thornton, architect of the Capitol.

Georgetown's largest estates sit farther north, commanding fine views of Rock Creek to the east and of the old tobacco town spread out near the river below. Make your way to Q Street between 31st and 32nd streets. Through the trees to the north, at the top of a sloping lawn, you'll see the neoclassical yellow stucco **Tudor Place,** designed by Capitol architect William Thornton and completed in 1816. The house was built for Thomas Peter, son of Georgetown's first mayor, and his wife Martha Custis, Martha Washington's granddaughter. On a house tour you'll see chairs that belonged to George Washington, Francis Scott Key's desk, and spurs of members of the Peter family who were killed in the Civil War. *1644 31st St. NW, tel. 202/965–0400. Tours Tues.–Sat. 10, 11:30, 1, and 2:30. Admission: $5. Reservations required.*

Dumbarton Oaks—not to be confused with the nearby Dumbarton House—is on 32nd Street, north of R Street. Harvard University maintains world-renowned collections of Byzantine and pre-Columbian art here. In 1944 representatives of the United States, Great Britain, China, and the Soviet Union met in the music room to lay the groundwork for the United Nations. Dumbarton Oaks' 10 acres of formal gardens are one of the loveliest spots in all of Washington (enter via R St.). *Art collections: 1703 32nd St. NW, tel. 202/338–8278 (recorded information) or 202/342–3200. Open Tues.–Sun. 2–5. Suggested donation for art collections: $1. Gardens: 31st and R Sts. NW. Open Apr. 1–Oct. 31, daily 2–6. Admission: $2 adults, $1 senior citizens and children, senior citizens free on Wed.; Nov. 1– Mar. 31, daily 2–5. Admission: free. Both gardens and collections are closed on national holidays and Christmas Eve.*

A few steps east of 28th Street on Q Street is **Dumbarton House,** the headquarters of the National Society of the Colonial Dames of America. Its symmetry and the two distinctive bow wings on the north side make Dumbarton a distinctive example of Federal architecture. Dolley Madison is said to have stopped here when fleeing Washington in 1814. Eight rooms inside have been restored to their Colonial splendor. The house is currently closed for renovation that's expected to be finished in the spring of 1993. *2715 Q St. NW, tel. 703/556–0881.*

Dupont Circle

Three of Washington's main thoroughfares intersect at **Dupont Circle:** Connecticut, New Hampshire, and Massachusetts avenues. With a handsome small park and a splashing fountain in the center, Dupont Circle is more than a deserted island around which traffic flows, making it an exception among Washington circles. The activity on the circle spills over into the surrounding streets, one of the liveliest, most vibrant neighborhoods in Washington.

Cross the traffic circle carefully and head south on New Hampshire Avenue. A block down on the left is the impressive **Heurich Mansion.** This severe, Romanesque Revival mansion was the home of Christian Heurich, a German orphan who made his fortune in this country in the beer business. After Heurich's widow died, in 1955, the house was turned over to the

Historical Society of Washington, D.C. Today it serves as the group's headquarters and houses its voluminous archives. The interior is an eclectic Victorian treasure trove filled with plaster detailing, carved wooden doors, and painted ceilings. *1307 Connecticut Ave. NW, tel. 202/785–2068. Open Wed.–Sat. noon–4. Admission: $3 adults, $1.50 senior citizens, students through 12th grade free.*

Time Out   Various branches of **Pan Asian Noodles & Grill** (2020 P St. NW) have been spreading through Washington lately (they're up to three now), but luckily the quality hasn't been compromised. Reasonably priced noodle dishes from around the Orient (thus *Pan* Asian) are the specialty.

46 At the corner of Massachusetts Avenue and 21st Street is the opulent **Walsh-McLean House.** Tom McLean was an Irishman who made a fortune with a Colorado gold mine and came to Washington to show his wealth. His daughter, Evalyn Walsh-McLean, the last private owner of the Hope diamond (now in the Smithsonian's Museum of Natural History), was one of the city's leading hostesses. Today the house is used as an embassy by the Indonesian government.

47 Head west on Massachusetts Avenue. The palatial home at No. 2118 is **Anderson House,** originally owned by diplomat Larz Anderson and his heiress wife, Isabel. They filled their residence, which was constructed in 1905, with the booty of their travels, including choir stalls from an Italian Renaissance church, Flemish tapestries, and a large—if spotty—collection of Asian art. All this remains in the house, for visitors to see. The building also serves as the headquarters of the **Society of the Cincinnati,** the oldest patriotic organization in the country, formed in 1783 by a group of officers who had served with George Washington during the Revolutionary War. Many of the displays in the society's museum focus on the Colonial period and the Revolutionary War. *2118 Massachusetts Ave. NW, tel. 202/785–2040. Open Tues.–Sat. 1–4.*

Across the street at 2121 Massachusetts Avenue is the **Cosmos Club,** founded in 1878 and perhaps the most exclusive private club in the city. Different rooms in the club celebrate members who have won Nobel prizes or appeared on postage stamps. The formerly men-only club started accepting women in 1988.

48 Washington has many museums that are the legacy of one great patron, but the **Phillips Collection,** at 21st and Q streets, is among the most beloved. In 1918 Duncan Phillips, grandson of a founder of the Jones and Laughlin Steel Company, started to collect art for what would become the first permanent museum of modern art in the country. Holdings include works by Braque, Cézanne, Klee, Matisse, John Henry Twachtman, and the largest museum collection in the country of the work of Pierre Bonnard. The collection's best-known paintings include Renoir's *Luncheon of the Boating Party, Repentant Peters* by both Goya *and* El Greco, Degas's *Dancers at the Bar,* Van Gogh's *Entrance to the Public Garden at Arles,* and Cézanne's self-portrait. *1600–1612 21st St. NW, tel. 202/387–2151. Open Tues.–Sat. 10–5, Sun. 2–7. Goh Annex closes Sun. at 5. Tours Wed. and Sat. at 2. Gallery talks 1st and 3rd Thurs. at 12:30. Suggested donation: $5 adults, $2.50 students and senior citizens.*

49 The Mediterranean-style **Barney Studio House** at 2306 Massachusetts Avenue was built by Alice Pike Barney, a Cincinnati heiress who early on developed a love of art, artists, and the bohemian lifestyle. The renovated home is part of the Smithsonian's National Museum of American Art and contains paintings by Barney and her friends, as well as a collection of furniture, rugs, and other antiques. *2306 Massachusetts Ave. NW, tel. 202/357–3111. Tours for groups of 5 or more by appointment only; Wed. and Thurs. at 11 and 1 and second and fourth Sun. of each month at 1.*

Continue west on Massachusetts Avenue. The **Cameroon Embassy** is housed in the mansion at 2349 Massachusetts Avenue. This fanciful castle, with its conical tower, bronze weathervane, and intricate detailing around the windows and balconies, is the westernmost of the Beaux Arts–style mansions built along Massachusetts Avenue in the late 19th and early 20th centuries.

50 Turn right on S Street to the **Woodrow Wilson House.** President Wilson and his second wife, Edith Bolling Wilson, retired in 1920 to this Georgian Revival house. The house also contains memorabilia related to the history of the short-lived League of Nations, which Wilson championed. *2340 S St. NW, tel. 202/ 387–4062. Open Tues.–Sun. 10–4. Closed major holidays. Admission: $4 adults, $2.50 senior citizens, children under 7 free.*

S Street is an informal dividing line between the Dupont Circle area to the south and the exclusive **Kalorama** neighborhood to the north. The name for this peaceful, tree-filled enclave is Greek for "beautiful view." Walk north on 23rd Street until it dead-ends at the Tudor mansion at 2221 **Kalorama Road.** This imposing house was built in 1911 for mining millionaire W.W. Lawrence, but since 1936 it has been the residence of the French ambassador.

Walk west on Kalorama Road, then turn right on Kalorama Circle. At the bottom of the circle you can look down over **Rock Creek Park.** The 1,800 acres of park on either side of Rock Creek have provided a cool oasis for Washington residents since Congress set them aside in 1890. There's a lot to enjoy here. Thirty picnic areas are scattered throughout the park. Bicycle routes and hiking and equestrian trails wend through the groves of dogwoods, beeches, oaks, and cedar. Rangers at the **Nature Center and Planetarium** (south of Military Rd. at 5000 Glover Rd. NW, tel. 202/426–6829) will acquaint you with the park and advise you of scheduled activities. Highlights include: **Pierce Mill,** a restored 19th-century gristmill powered by the falling water of Rock Creek (tel. 202/426–6908); **Fort Reno,** one of the original ring of forts that guarded Washington during the Civil War; and the **Rock Creek Golf Course,** an 18-hole public course. *Between 16th St. and Connecticut Ave. NW, tel. 202/ 426–6829 for park activities, 202/882–7332 for golf course. Park open daylight hours only; hours for individual sites vary.*

Other Sites of Interest

Frederick Douglass National Historic Site. Cedar Hill, the Anacostia home of noted abolitionist Frederick Douglass, was the first place designated by Congress as a Black National Historic Site. Douglass, an ex-slave who delivered fiery abolitionist speeches at home and abroad, was 60 when he moved here, in 1877. He lived at Cedar Hill until his death, in 1895. The house has a wonderful view of the Federal City, across the Anacostia, and contains many of Douglass's personal belongings. A short film on Douglass's life is shown at a nearby visitors center. *1411 W St. SE, tel. 202/426–5961. Open fall and winter, daily 9–4; spring and summer, daily 9–5. Tours given on the hour. Metro stop, Anacostia.*

The National Zoo. Created by an Act of Congress in 1889, the 160-acre zoo was designed by landscape architect Frederick Law Olmsted. The zoo's most famous residents are Hsing-Hsing and Ling-Ling, gifts from China in 1972 and the only giant pandas in the United States. Other exotic residents include red pandas, Pere David's deer, golden lion tamarins, pygmy hippopotamuses, and the only Komodo dragons in the country. Innovative compounds show many animals in naturalistic settings, including the Great Flight Cage, a walk-in aviary in which birds fly unrestricted. Amazonia, an ambitious display re-creating the complete ecosystem of a South American rainforest, is scheduled to open in the spring of 1992. *3001 Connecticut Ave. NW, tel. 202/673–4717. Open daily except Christmas, May 1–Sept. 15: grounds 8 AM–8 PM, animal buildings 8–6; Sept. 16–Apr. 30: grounds 8–6, animal buildings 9–6. Admission free. Limited paid parking is available.*

Washington National Cathedral. Construction of this stunning Gothic church—the sixth largest cathedral in the world—started in 1907 and was finished on September 30, 1990, when the cathedral was consecrated. Like its 14th-century counterparts, Washington's Cathedral Church of St. Peter and St. Paul has flying buttresses, naves, transepts, and barrel vaults that were built stone by stone. It is adorned with fanciful gargoyles created by skilled stone carvers. The tomb of Woodrow Wilson, the only president buried in Washington, is on the south side of the nave. The expansive view of the city from the Pilgrim Gallery is exceptional. The cathedral is under the governance of the Episcopal church but has played host to services of many denominations. *Wisconsin and Massachusetts Aves. NW, tel. 202/537–6200. Open fall, winter, and spring, daily 10–4:30; May 1–Labor Day, weekdays 10–9, weekends 10–4:30. Sunday services at 8, 9, 10, and 11; evensong at 4 PM. Tours Mon.–Sat. 10–3:15, Sun. 12:45–2. Tour information tel. 202/537–6207.*

Shopping

Shopping Districts   **Georgetown** remains Washington's favorite shopping area. Though it is not on a subway line, and parking is impossible, people still flock here. The attraction (aside from the lively street scene) is the profusion of specialty shops, antiques dealers, craft shops, and high-style clothing boutiques. The hub of Georgetown is the intersection of Wisconsin Avenue and M Street, with most of the stores lying to the west on M Street and to the north on Wisconsin. That intersection is also the location of **Georgetown Park** (tel. 202/342–8180, 8192), a three-level mall that looks like a Victorian ice cream parlor.

Dupont Circle has some of the same flavor as Georgetown, a lively mix of shops and restaurants, with most of the action on the major artery of Connecticut Avenue.

The city's department stores can be found in the "new" downtown, which is still being built. Its fulcrum is **Metro Center,** which spans 11th and 12th streets NW along G Street. The tri-level downtown mall **The Shops at National Place** (13th and F Sts. NW, tel. 202/783–9090) is oriented primarily to younger consumers; it's a good place to drop off teenagers weary of the Smithsonian and more in the mood to buy compact discs or T-shirts.

Although Washington doesn't have anything on the order of Boston's Faneuil Hall, it does have **The Pavilion at the Old Post Office** (12th St. NW and Pennsylvania Ave., tel. 202/289–4224), a renovated 19th-century building with 21 small shops.

Renovated **Union Station,** at Massachusetts Avenue NE, near North Capitol Street, is now both a working train station and a mall with three levels of stores, including one level of food stands. Union Station is full of trendy clothing boutiques.

The final major shopping district is on the outskirts of the city, straddling the Maryland border–the **Mazza Gallerie** (5300 Wisconsin Ave. NW, tel. 202/966–6114), a four-level mall anchored by the ritzy Neiman Marcus department store. Three other department stores are close by: Lord & Taylor, Woodward & Lothrop, and Saks Fifth Avenue. The neighborhood also contains an eclectic array of upscale shops. Newly opened across from Mazza Gallerie is **Chevy Chase Pavilion** (5335 Wisconsin Ave. NW, tel. 202/686–5335), a conglomeration of women's clothing stores and various specialty shops.

In the **Adams-Morgan** neighborhood, scattered among the dozens of Latin, Ethiopian, and Caribbean restaurants, are a score of the city's most eccentric shops—trendy gift shops, left-leaning bookstores, vintage clothing, boutiques selling objets d'art (or at least objets), and used furniture that sometimes approaches the antique.

Department Stores **Hecht's** (12th and G Sts. NW, tel. 202/628–6661) new downtown store is bright and spacious, and its sensible groupings and attractive displays of merchandise make shopping relatively easy on the feet and the eyes. The clothes sold here are a mix of conservative and trendy lines.

Lord & Taylor (5255 Western Ave., tel. 202/362–9600) lets other stores be all things to all people, while it focuses on nonutilitarian housewares and classic clothing by such American designers as Anne Klein and Ralph Lauren.

Neiman Marcus (Mazza Gallerie, tel. 202/966–9700) caters to the customer who values quality above all. The expensive but carefully selected merchandise includes couture clothes, furs, precious jewelry, crystal, and silver.

Saks Fifth Avenue (5555 Wisconsin Ave., tel. 301/657–9000) offers a wide selection of European and American couture clothes; other attractions are the shoe, jewelry, fur, and lingerie departments.

Woodward & Lothrop (11th and F Sts. NW, tel. 202/347–5300), the largest of the downtown stores, has eight floors of merchandise that can accommodate just about any need or whim. There is also a branch across the border in Maryland at Wisconsin and Western avenues (tel. 301/654–7600).

Sports and Fitness

Bicycling   Numerous trails in the District and the surrounding areas are well-maintained and clearly marked. Most of the paths described below in the section on jogging—the Mall, the C & O Canal, the Mount Vernon Trail, and Rock Creek Park—are also well-suited for use by bikers. **The Greater Washington Bicycle Atlas,** published by the American Youth Hostels Association, is available for $10 at most Washington area bookstores or from the Washington Area Bicyclist Association (1015 31st St. NW, 20007, tel. 202/944–8567).

Bicycles can be rented at **Big Wheel Bikes** (1034 33rd St. NW, Georgetown, tel. 202/337–254; and 315 7th St. SE, tel. 202/543–1600); **Fletcher's Boat House** (C & O Canal Towpath, near Reservoir Rd. NW, tel. 202/244–0461); **Metropolis Bike & Scooter** (709 8th St. SE, Capitol Hill, tel. 202/543–8900); **Proteus Bicycle Shop** (2422 18th St. NW, Adams-Morgan, tel. 202/332–6666); **Thompson's Boat House** (Virginia Ave. and Rock Creek Park, behind Kennedy Center, tel. 202/333–4861); and **Tow Path Cycle** (823 S. Washington St., Alexandria, VA, tel. 703/549–5368).

Boating   There are several places to rent boats along the Potomac River north and south of the city. Two boat houses are **Fletcher's Boat House** (tel. 202/244–0461), about two miles north of Georgetown on the C & O Canal, which rents rowboats and canoes for use in the canal; and **Thompson's Boat House** (tel. 202/333–9543), at Virginia Avenue and Rock Creek Parkway behind the Kennedy Center, which rents canoes, rowboats, rowing shells, and sailboards.

Paddle boats are available on the east side of the **Tidal Basin** in front of the Jefferson Memorial.

If you're interested in **sailing,** the **Washington Sailing Marina** (tel. 703/548–9027), just south of National Airport on the George Washington Parkway, and the **Bell Haven Marina** (tel. 703/768–0018), just south of Old Town Alexandria on the George Washington Parkway, rent Sunfish, Windsurfers, and larger boats to those qualified to charter.

Health Clubs   A number of downtown hotels are associated with the **fitness center at the ANA Hotel,** where celebrities like Cybill Sheperd, Holly Hunter, and Arnold Schwarzennegger come to sweat (ANA Hotel, 2401 M St. NW, tel. 202/457–5070).

The even fancier three-level **fitness center at the Four Seasons,** however, has complimentary juice and mineral water, movie rentals, and fitness gear use (Four Seasons Hotel, 2800 Pennsylvania Ave. NW, tel. 202/944–2022).

The **National Capital YMCA** (1711 Rhode Island Ave. NW, tel. 202/862–9622) offers just about everything a body could want, from basketball, weights, racquetball, and swimming to exercise equipment. Usage fees run from $5 to $15 a day depending on the time. Members of out-of-town Ys are welcome; simply show your membership card.

Horseback Riding   **Rock Creek Park Equestrian Center** (Military Rd. and Glover Rd. NW, tel. 202/362–0117) is open all year; the hours vary according to season.

Ice Skating   The **Sculpture Garden Outdoor Rink** (Constitution Ave. between 7th and 9th Sts. NW, tel. 202/371–5343) appears each winter with the cold weather. **Pershing Park Ice Rink** (Pennsylvania Ave. between 14th and 15th Sts. NW, tel. 202/737–6938) is also popular. Skates can be rented at both locations.

Jogging A word of caution: Joggers unfamiliar with the city should not go out at night, and, even in daylight, it's best to run in pairs if you venture beyond the most public areas and the more heavily used sections of the trails.

The Mall. The 4.5-mile loop around the Capitol and past the Smithsonian museums, the Washington Monument, the Reflecting Pool, and the Lincoln Memorial is the most popular of all Washington running trails. If you're looking for a longer run, you can veer south of the Mall on either side of the Tidal Basin and head for the Jefferson Memorial and East Potomac Park, the site of many races.

The Mount Vernon Trail. Just across the Potomac in Virginia, the 3.5-mile northern section begins near the pedestrian causeway leading to Theodore Roosevelt Island (directly across the river from the Kennedy Center), goes past National Airport and on to Old Town Alexandria. The longer southern section of the trail (approximately nine miles) takes you along the coast of the Potomac from Alexandria all the way to George Washington's home, Mount Vernon.

Rock Creek Park. The most popular run in the park is a trail along the creek extending from Georgetown to the National Zoo (about a 4-mile loop).

The C & O Canal. A pancake-flat gravel trail leads from Georgetown through wooded areas along the Potomac and northward into Maryland. The most popular loop is from a point just north of Key Bridge in Georgetown to Fletcher's Boat House (approximately 4 miles round-trip).

Tennis **Hains Point** (East Potomac Park, tel. 202/554–5962) has outdoor courts as well as courts under a bubble for wintertime play. Fees run from $11 to $23 an hour depending on the time and season. The **Washington Tennis Center** (16th and Kennedy Sts. NW, tel. 202/722–5949) has clay and hard courts. Fees range from $15 to $20 an hour depending on the time.

Spectator Sports

Tickets for all Capital Centre, Patriot Centre, and Baltimore Arena events can be purchased through **TicketCenter** (tel. 202/432–0200 in D.C., tel 202/481–6000 in Baltimore, or tel. 800/448–9009 in other areas).

Basketball The **Washington Bullets'** home games are held at the Capital Centre in Landover, Maryland, just outside the Beltway. Their schedule runs from September to April. For tickets, tel. 800/448–9009.

Georgetown University's Hoyas play at the Capital Centre (tel. 301/350–3400).

Football Since 1966, all **Redskins** games at the 55,750-seat Robert F. Kennedy Stadium on the eastern edge of Capitol Hill have been sold out to season-ticket holders. Tickets are occasionally advertised in the classified section of the Sunday *Post*, but expect to pay considerably more than face value.

Ice Hockey The **Washington Capitals'** season runs from October through April. Home games are played at the Capital Centre. For tickets call 301/350–3400 or TicketCenter at 800/448–9009.

Lacrosse The **Washington Waves** play in the Capital Centre from January through March. For tickets call 301/432–0200 or TicketCenter at 800/448–9009.

Soccer The Washington Stars and the Maryland Bays have merged into one team, called the **Maryland Bays,** with half their games to be played at Cedar Lane Park in Columbia, MD, and the other half to be played at RFK Stadium. For ticket and schedule information, call 301/206–2500. The **Washington Diplomats** play a season from April to August at Robert F. Kennedy Stadium (tel. 202/547–9077). Tickets for either team—$8 for adults—can also be purchased through TicketCenter (tel. 800/448–9009).

Dining

Although the turnover is rapid, Washington's restaurants are getting better and better. In the last few years Italian restaurants have come to rival French establishments, which for a long time set the standard in fine dining. There has also been an explosion of the kind of cooking usually called New American. Despite the dearth of ethnic neighborhoods in Washington, you *can* find almost any type of food here, from Nepalese to Salvadoran to Ethiopian.

The following dining price categories have been used: *Very Expensive*, over $35; *Expensive*, $25–$35; *Moderate*, $15–$25; *Inexpensive*, under $15.

Adams-Morgan
American

Belmont Kitchen. This popular neighborhood spot specializes in upside-down pizzas and simple, well-prepared grilled fish and meats. A low-calorie three-course dinner is always on the menu. Parking in Adams-Morgan is always difficult. *2400 18th St. NW, tel. 202/667–1200. Reservations advised. Dress: casual. DC, MC, V. Moderate.*

Ethiopian

Meskerem. Among Adams-Morgan's many Ethiopian restaurants, Meskerem is distinctive for its bright, appealingly decorated dining room. Another attractive feature: The restaurant has a balcony where you can eat Ethiopian-style—seated on the floor on leather cushions, with large woven baskets for tables. There is no silverware; instead, the food is scooped up with *injera*, a spongy flat bread on which the meal is presented. The country's main dish is the *watt*, or stew, which may be made with chicken, lamb, beef, or shrimp in either a spicy or a mild sauce. Several vegetarian watts are also available. *2434 18th St. NW, tel. 202/462–4100. Reservations advised. Dress: casual but neat. AE, DC, MC, V. Closed lunch Mon.–Thurs. Inexpensive.*

French

La Fourchette. Most of the menu consists of daily specials, but you can pretty much count on finding bouillabaisse and rabbit on the list. The most popular entrées on the regular menu are the hearty veal and lamb shanks. La Fourchette also looks the way a bistro should, with an exposed brick wall, tin ceiling, bentwood chairs, and quasi–post-impressionist murals. *2429 18th St. NW, tel. 202/332–3077. Reservations advised. Dress: casual but neat. AE, DC, MC, V. Closed lunch Sat. and Sun. Moderate.*

Washington D.C. Dining and Lodging

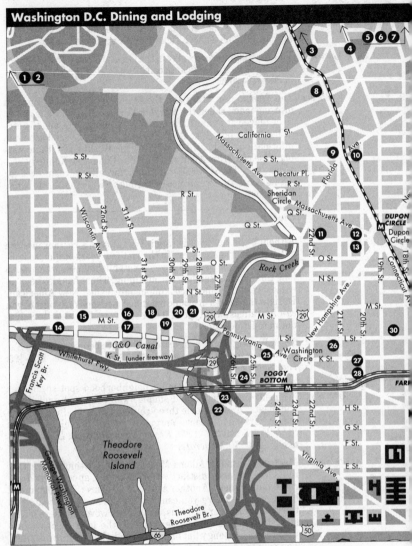

Dining

America, **45**
American Café, **16**
Austin Grill, **1**
Bamiyan, **14**
Belmont Kitchen, **6**
Bistro Français, **17**
Duke Zeibert's, **29**

Foggy Bottom
Café, **24**
Galileo, **26**
Georgetown Seafood
Grill, **18**
Geppetto, **20**
Jean-Louis at the
Watergate Hotel, **22**
La Colline, **44**

La Fourchette, **7**
Las Pampas, **15**
Marrakesh, **41**
Meskerem, **5**
The Monocle, **46**
Obelisk, **12**
Prime Rib, **27**
Primi Piatti, **28**

Sala Thai, **13**
Skewers, **34**
Sushi-Ko, **2**
Twenty-One
Federal, **31**

Lodging

Bellevue Hotel, **43**

Braxton Hotel, **36**

Four Seasons
Hotel, **21**

Georgetown Marbury
Hotel, **19**

Hay-Adams Hotel, **37**

Holiday Inn
Governor's House, **35**

Hotel Anthony, **30**

Hotel Tabard Inn, **33**

Howard Johnson
Kennedy Center, **23**

J. W. Marriott, **39**

Kalorama Guest
House, **4**

Mayflower Hotel, **32**

Morrison-Clark
Inn Hotel, **40**

Normandy Inn, **8**

Omni Shoreham
Hotel, **3**

Omni Georgetown, **11**

Phoenix Park
Hotel, **42**

Quality Hotel
Central, **9**

The Washington
Hilton and
Towers, **10**

Watergate Hotel, **22**

The Willard Inter-
Continental, **38**

Wyndham Bristol
Hotel, **25**

Capitol Hill
American

The Monocle. The bar at the Monocle is probably the closest thing on the Hill to the smoke-filled political hangout from the movies; management keeps members of Congress informed on when it's time to vote. Although nobody really goes to The Monocle for the food, the cooking, American cuisine with a Continental touch, is quite good. Seafood is a specialty; try the crabcakes, and take advantage of the lobster specials. *107 D St. NE, tel. 202/546–4488. Reservations advised. Jacket and tie advised. AE, DC, MC, V. Closed Sat. lunch and Sun. Expensive.*

America. Located in Union Station in the west front (in what was, before the remodeling, the men's room), this space has been transformed into a lively and attractive bar and restaurant, with WPA-style murals, Western landscapes, and aluminum outlines of states. The menu is enormous, with offerings ranging from Kansas City steaks to Minnesota scrambled eggs, New Orleans muffalata sandwiches to San Diego fish tacos. The kitchen has its successes and failures—a good general rule is "the simpler the better." *Union Station, 50 Massachusetts Ave. NE, tel. 202/682–9555. Reservations advised. Dress: casual but neat. AE, DC, MC, V. Parking validated in Union Station lot. Moderate.*

French
★

La Colline. For the past nine years, Robert Gréault has worked to make La Colline into one of the city's best French restaurants. The menu changes daily, and it seems always to strike the perfect balance between innovation and tradition. The emphasis is on seafood, with offerings ranging from simple grilled preparations to fricassees and gratins with imaginative sauces. The non-seafood menu usually offers duck with an orange or cassis sauce and veal with chanterelles. Desserts are superb, as is the wine list. *400 N. Capitol St., tel. 202/737–0400. Reservations required. Jacket and tie advised. AE, DC, MC, V. Closed lunch Sat. and Sun. Free parking in underground lot. Expensive.*

Downtown
American
★

Prime Rib. Despite its name, the Prime Rib now devotes half its menu to fish and shellfish, some of it shipped express from Florida. The most popular of the seafood dishes is the imperial crab, made only of jumbo lump-crabmeat. The aged beef from Chicago includes a steak au poivre in addition to New York strip, porterhouse, filet mignon, and the restaurant's namesake, for which you might need to reserve ahead. Black walls, leather chairs, and leopardskin print rugs give the restaurant a timeless sophistication. *2020 K St. NW, tel. 202/466–8811. Reservations advised. Jacket and tie required. AE, DC, MC, V. Closed Sat. lunch and Sun. Very Expensive.*

Duke Zeibert's. At lunch, this 450-seat restaurant is filled with regulars who come to talk sports with Duke and eat heartily from a menu that essentially hasn't changed in 39 years— boiled beef and chicken in a pot, deli sandwiches, and specials like corned beef and cabbage. At dinner, couples and families replace the deal makers. In the evening the signature chicken and beef in a pot are still available, but the menu leans more toward broiler items like lamb chops and sirloin, not to mention the famous prime rib and crab cakes. *1050 Connecticut Ave. NW (on mezzanine of Washington Square Building), tel. 202/ 466–3730. Reservations required. Jacket and tie advised. AE, DC, MC, V. Closed lunch Sun. Closed Sun. during July and Aug. Validated parking at Washington Square lot. Expensive.*

Foggy Bottom Café. For a hungry theatergoer who doesn't

want to eat at the Kennedy Center's overcrowded restaurants, this small, pleasant eatery in the River Inn is a good alternative for either a snack—a hamburger, sandwich, or salad—or a full meal. Though the entrée list is not extensive, it is diverse, with Oriental, Southwestern, and Middle Eastern traditions represented. The most popular items are the shrimp and vegetable tempura, the barbecued spareribs, and the fresh salmon. *924 25th St. NW, tel. 202/338–8707. Reservations required. Dress: casual but neat. AE, DC, MC, V. Moderate.*

French **Jean-Louis at the Watergate Hotel.** A showcase for the cooking
★ of Jean-Louis Palladin, this small restaurant is often cited as one of the best in the United States. The contemporary French fare is based on regional American ingredients—crawfish from Louisiana, wild mushrooms from Oregon, game from Texas— combined in innovative ways. There are two limited-choice fixed-price dinners: five courses for $75 or six courses for $90. There is also a pre-theater menu of four courses for $38. Corn soup with oysters and lobster quenelles is a signature offering. The wine cellar is said to be the largest on the East Coast. *2650 Virginia Ave. NW (downstairs in the Watergate Hotel), tel. 202/298–4488. Reservations required. Jacket and tie required. AE, DC, MC, V. Closed lunch, Sun., and the last 2 weeks in Aug. Validated parking. Very Expensive.*

Italian **Galileo.** The menu changes daily, but there is always risotto; a
★ long list of grilled fish; a game bird, such as quail, guinea hen, or woodcock; and one or two beef or veal dishes. Preparations are generally simple and authentic. For example, the veal may be served with mushroom-and-rosemary sauce, the beef with tomato sauce and polenta. Everything is made in house, from the breadsticks to the mozzarella, and it all tastes terrific. *1110 21st St. NW, tel 202/293–7191. Reservations advised. Jacket and tie advised. AE, DC, MC, V. Closed Sat. and Sun. lunch. Valet parking at dinner. Very Expensive.*

Primi Piatti. Aside from the manic exuberance of the dining room, diners come here for dishes that are both authentically Italian, and light and healthful. There's a wood-burning grill, on which several kinds of fish are cooked each day, as well as lamb and veal chops. Meat is also done to a succulent turn on the rotisserie. Pastas, made in house, are outstanding, as are the pizzas, which come with such contemporary twists as sun-dried tomatoes. *2013 I St. NW, tel. 202/223–3600. Reservations accepted only during certain hours. Jacket and tie suggested. AE, DC, MC, V. Closed Sat. lunch and Sun. Moderate.*

Moroccan **Marrakesh.** A knock on the carved wooden door summons a
★ caftanned figure, who ushers you past a splashing fountain into the dining room, where you are seated on a couch piled with pillows in front of a low table. The menu offers a fixed-price, seven-course feast shared by everyone at your table and eaten without silverware. The second course, b'stella, is a pigeon-stuffed pie (Marrakesh substitutes chicken) that is one of the glories of Moroccan cuisine. Belly dancers put on a nightly show. *617 New York Ave. NW, tel. 202/393–9393. Reservations required. Jacket and tie advised. No credit cards. Closed lunch. Valet parking. Moderate.*

New American **Twenty-One Federal.** Offering New American cuisine in a so-
★ phisticated setting, Twenty-One Federal is one of the city's hottest restaurants. The menu changes seasonally but always includes a spit-roasted chicken; lamb, pheasant, and rabbit are

also prepared on the rotisserie. The New England–born chef has a way with seafood, as exemplified in his grilled oysters and pancetta. Meat eaters will find such dishes as beef in a marrow-shallot crust, and a lamb plate that includes a rack chop, a loin stuffed with veal, and a grilled, butterflied slice of leg. The large dining room is decorated primarily in black and gray, with marble tiles and brass gridwork adding a touch of class. *1736 L St. NW, tel. 202/331–9771. Reservations advised. Jacket and tie advised. AE, DC, MC, V. Closed Sat. lunch and Sun. Free valet parking at dinner. Very Expensive.*

Dupont Circle **Obelisk.** One of the most exciting new restaurants in Washing-
Italian ton, Obelisk serves eclectic Italian cuisine, with a small, fixed-
★ price menu that includes both traditional dishes and the chef's imaginative innovations. The meat is likely to be lamb, with garlic and sage or perhaps anchovies; fish might be a pompano stuffed with bay leaves; a typical poultry selection is the hardly typical pigeon with chanterelles. In winter there is lasagne, but what lasagne—layered with wild mushrooms or with arti-chokes and sweetbreads. The minimally decorated dining room is tiny, with tables closely spaced, but with food like this, who needs conversation? *2029 P St. NW, tel. 202/872–1180. Reservations advised. Dress: casual but neat. AE, MC, V, and personal checks. Dinner only. Closed Sun. and the last 2 weeks of Aug. Expensive.*

Middle Eastern **Skewers.** Depending on your point of view, Skewers is an American restaurant with a strong Middle Eastern influence or an avant-garde Middle Eastern restaurant. In either case, it offers fresh, flavorful meals at reasonable prices. The specialty is kebabs. The lamb with eggplant and the chicken with roasted pepper are the most popular, but filet mignon and shrimp are equally tasty. Skewers's decor uses a few lengths of shimmering cloth to create an Arabian Nights fantasy. *1633 P St. NW, tel. 202/387–7400. Reservations advised on weekends. Dress: casual. AE, DC, MC, V. Moderate.*

Thai **Sala Thai.** You can order the food as spicy as you wish, but the chef is interested in flavor, not fire. Among the subtly seasoned offerings are *panang goong* (shrimp in curry-peanut sauce), chicken sautéed with ginger and pineapple, and flounder with a choice of four sauces. The *Pad Thai* P Street is an exceptional treatment of that signature dish, which consists of noodles with shrimp and bean sprouts in a peanut sauce. Sala Thai is decorated in the currently fashionable minimalist style, but colored lights take the harsh edges off its industrial look. *2016 P St. NW, tel. 202/872–1144. Reservations accepted. Dress: casual but neat. AE, DC, MC, V. Closed Sun. lunch. Inexpensive.*

Georgetown **Bamiyan.** Afghani food is quite appealing, unusual enough to
Afghani be interesting but not so strange as to be intimidating. Bamiyan is arguably the best Afghanian restaurant in the area, even though it does look like a motel that has seen better days. Kebabs—of chicken, beef, or lamb—are succulent. More adventurous souls should try the *quabili palow* (lamb with saffron rice, carrots, and raisins) or the *aushak* (dumplings with scallions, meat sauce, and yogurt). For a side vegetable, order the sautéed pumpkin; it will make you forget every other winter squash dish you've ever had. *3320 M St. NW, tel. 202/338–1896. Reservations accepted. Dress: casual. AE, MC, V. Closed lunch. Moderate.*

American **Georgetown Seafood Grill.** This restaurant has an appropriately weathered visage—old tilework and exposed brick decorated with nautical photographs—and its menu casts a wide net. There are four or five kinds of oysters at the raw bar, plus clams, spiced shrimp, and crab claws. Crab cakes are made with jumbo lump-meat and no filler, and soft shell crabs are served in season. On weekends you can order steamed lobsters, and each night you can choose among about seven fish specials—everything from fried catfish to broiled red snapper with macadamia pesto. *3063 M St. NW, tel. 202/333-7038. Reservations accepted for large parties. Dress: casual but neat. AE, DC, MC, V. Expensive.*

American Café. Serving fresh, healthy food—but not health food—at affordable prices in a casual but sophisticated environment, the American Café empire now numbers 15 restaurants in the Washington area. Sandwiches, such as the namesake roast beef on a humongous croissant, are still the mainstay of the café, with salads and nibbles rounding off the regular menu. But the list of specials, which changes every two weeks, offers intriguing possibilities for those wanting a larger meal. There's always a fresh fish, a seafood pie, a chicken dish, and barbecued ribs. Weekend brunches offer temptations like strawberry-banana-nut waffles and stuffed French toast. *1211 Wisconsin Ave. NW, tel. 202/944-9464 (also at 227 Massachusetts Ave. NE, tel. 202/547-8500; 1331 Pennsylvania Ave. NW, tel. 202/833-3434; 1200 19th St. NW, tel. 202/223-2121; and 5252 Wisconsin Ave. NW, tel. 202/363-5400). Reservations accepted only for large parties. Dress: casual. AE, DC, MC, V. Inexpensive.*

Argentinian **Las Pampas.** This Argentinian restaurant serves what many
★ think is the best steak in town. The beef, which is fresh, not aged, is cooked over a special grill that simulates charcoal heat; the result is a firm-textured steak with a crusty surface and a juicy interior. The preferred choice is the churrasco, a special Argentinian cut. Other options from the limited regular menu are a whole boneless chicken that is first roasted then grilled; and a combination plate of chicken, short ribs, and sausage. Daily specials usually include seafood, lamb, or chicken, and a pasta. Aside from a couple of wall hangings, Las Pampas is decorated in international nondescript. *3291 M St. NW, tel. 202/333-5151. Reservations advised. Dress: casual but neat. AE, DC, MC, V. Closed Sat. lunch, Sun., and first week of Aug. Moderate.*

French **Bistro Français.** A longtime fixture on M Street, this French country restaurant is a favorite among the city's chefs. Two big draws are the Minute Steak Maitre d'Hotel, a sirloin with herb butter, accompanied by french fries, and the rotisserie chicken. The Bistro also does well with the more complicated dishes it offers as daily specials, such as supreme of salmon with cauliflower mousse and beurre blanc. The café side includes sandwiches and omelettes in addition to the entrées. *3128 M St. NW, tel. 202/338-3830. Reservations advised. Dress: casual but neat. AE, DC, MC, V. Moderate.*

Italian **Geppetto.** People still wait in line for pizza at Geppetto—either a thick- or a thin-crust version. There's also a white pizza (cheese, garlic, and shallot; no tomato sauce) and a geppino, which is essentially a pizza sandwich. Geppetto also serves homemade pastas, several veal and chicken entrées, and a half dozen sandwiches. Decorated with puppets and cuckoo clocks, this is a good restaurant for children. *2917 M St. NW, tel. 202/ 333–2602. No reservations. Dress: casual. AE, DC, MC, V. Inexpensive.*

Japanese **Sushi-Ko.** In addition to the à la carte items and assortments of sushi and sashimi, the menu includes seafood and vegetable tempuras, fish teriyaki, and udonsuki (noodles with seafood and vegetables). Those looking for more exotic fare will find it on the back of the menu—printed in Japanese, but your waiter can be prevailed upon to translate. *2309 Wisconsin Ave. NW, tel. 202/333–4187. Reservations advised. Dress: casual but neat. AE, MC, V. Closed Mon. and weekend lunch. Moderate.*

Tex-Mex **Austin Grill.** This small, lively spot in upper Georgetown de-
★ serves its popularity. There's a food-smoker out back, where ribs are prepared for dinner. The mesquite grill is always in operation, turning out fajitas and grilled fish and providing the starting point for what the Austin claims is the best chili in town. With its multicolored booths, the restaurant looks like a post-modern diner. *2404 Wisconsin Ave. NW, tel. 202/337–8080. No reservations. Dress: casual. AE, MC, V. Closed Mon. lunch. Inexpensive.*

Lodging

The nation's capital has been riding a hotel boom for more than a decade, so visitors can expect variety as well as quantity, but reservations are still crucial. If you're interested in visiting Washington at a calmer time—and if you can stand tropical weather—come in July or August, during the Congressional recess. You may not spot many VIPs, but hotels will have more rooms to offer. Many Washington hotels, particularly those downtown, offer special reduced rates and package deals year-round.

To find reasonably priced accommodations in small guest houses and private homes, contact either of the following bed-and-breakfast services: **Bed 'n' Breakfast Ltd. of Washington, D.C.** (Box 12011, Washington, DC 20005, tel. 202/328–3510) or **Bed and Breakfast League, Ltd.** (3639 Van Ness St., Washington, DC 20008, tel. 202/363–7767).

The following lodging price categories have been used: *Very Expensive,* over $190; *Expensive,* $130–$190; *Moderate,* $100–$130; *Inexpensive,* under $100.

Capitol Hill **Phoenix Park Hotel.** Just steps from Union Station and only four blocks from the Capitol, this high-rise hotel has an Irish club theme and is the home of the Dubliner, one of Washington's best bars. Guest rooms are bright, traditionally furnished, and quiet. Penthouse suites have fireplaces. *520 North Capitol St. NW, 20001, tel. 202/638–6900 or 800/824–5419. 88 rooms, including 6 suites. Facilities: 2 restaurants, valet parking. AE, DC, MC, V. Expensive.*
Bellevue Hotel. In business for 61 years, the Bellevue is a charming and comfortable hotel. The public rooms have balconies and are modeled after great halls in manor houses of yore. Accommodations here are standard modest-hotel fare, but the staff is friendly. The location is convenient, near Union Station and the Mall. *15 E St. NW, 20001, tel. 202/638–0900 or 800/327–6667. 140 rooms, including 2 suites. Facilities: restaurant,*

bar, library, free overnight parking. AE, DC, MC, V. Moderate.

Downtown ★ **Hay-Adams Hotel.** Built in 1927, the Hay-Adams sits upon the site of houses owned by John Hay and Henry Adams, social and political paragons in turn-of-the-century Washington. In its early days the hotel housed Charles Lindbergh and Amelia Earhart; now, corporate executives and lawyers occupy its rooms during the week, and couples and families come on weekends. Italian Renaissance in design, the hotel looks like a mansion in disguise. The guest rooms are the most brightly colored in the city, decorated in 20 different English–country-house schemes. Rooms on the south side have a view of the White House. The hotel's afternoon tea is renowned. *One Lafayette Square, 20006, tel. 202/638–6600 or 800/424–5054. 143 rooms, including 23 suites. Facilities: 3 restaurants, bar, valet parking. AE, DC, MC, V. Very Expensive.*

J.W. Marriott. Opened in 1984, this large, glossy hotel is in a prime location close to the White House and next door to the National Theater. The Marriott usually lodges an equal mix of people traveling for business and pleasure. Rooms are furnished in hotel moderne and quiet colors. Guests have indoor access to the National Press Building and the shops and restaurants of National Place. *1331 Pennsylvania Ave. NW, 20004, tel. 202/393–2000 or 800/228–9290. 773 rooms, including 41 suites. Facilities: 4 restaurants, bar, health club, indoor pool, valet parking. AE, DC, MC, V. Very Expensive.*

★ **The Willard Inter-Continental.** The Willard, whose present building dates from 1901, welcomed every American president from Franklin Pierce in 1853 to Dwight Eisenhower in the 1950s. The new Willard is a faithful renovation, presenting an opulent, beaux-arts feast to the eye. Even D.C. residents drop in to stroll the famous "Peacock Alley," which runs between the front and back entrances. Rooms are furnished with mahogany Queen Anne reproductions; all have minibar. The sixth floor, which was designed with the help of the Secret Service and the State Department, has lodged 20 heads of state. Two restaurants, the Occidental and the Willard Room, have won nationwide acclaim. *1401 Pennsylvania Ave. NW, 20004, tel. 202/628–9100 or 800/327–0200. 365 rooms, including 37 suites. Facilities: 3 restaurants, 2 bars, valet, handicapped rooms, parking. AE, DC, MC, V. Very Expensive.*

Mayflower, A Stouffer Hotel. The Mayflower was opened in 1925 for Calvin Coolidge's inaugural and continues to be a central part of Washington life. Guests come from all walks of life; 8% of them are foreign. The recently renovated, ornate lobby gleams with gilded trim and cherubs supporting electrified candelabra. About half the hotel's rooms have been restored with custom-designed furniture, warmly colored fabrics, full marble bathrooms, and indirect lighting. The renovation is scheduled to be completed by July of 1992. *1127 Connecticut Ave. NW, 20036, tel. 202/347–3000 or 800/468–3571. 724 rooms, including 83 suites. Facilities: 2 restaurants, bar, shops, access to National Capital YMCA, parking at nearby garage. AE, DC, MC, V. Expensive.*

★ **Morrison-Clark Inn Hotel.** Victorian with an airy, modern twist, this unusual historic inn was created by merging two 1864 town houses. Appended to one of the houses is a 1917 Chinese Chippendale porch; Oriental touches echo throughout the public rooms, which also boast marble fireplaces and 14-foot–

high gilded mirrors. Antique-filled rooms—some with bay windows, fireplaces, or access to a porch—have different personalities. A new addition contains 42 rooms in the neoclassical style. Country rooms are plainly furnished with pine, wicker, and rattan. A complimentary Continental breakfast is served. Take a cab to the hotel after dark. *Massachusetts Ave. and 11th St. NW, 20001, tel. 202/898–1200 or 800/332–7898. 54 rooms, including 14 suites. Facilities: restaurant, valet parking. AE, DC, MC, V. Expensive.*

Holiday Inn Governor's House. A deluxe Holiday Inn with a sweeping staircase in the lobby, this hotel is close to the White House and Dupont Circle. All guest rooms were refurbished in the spring of 1990. The staff is friendly. *1615 Rhode Island Ave. NW, 20036, tel. 202/296–2100 or 800/821–4367. 152 rooms, including 9 suites; 36 rooms have kitchenettes. Facilities: restaurant, bar, outdoor pool, access to health club, parking. AE, DC, MC, V. Moderate.*

Hotel Anthony. A good value, this small hotel has a courteous staff, offers the basics in the midst of the K and L streets business district, and is close to the White House. Some rooms have a full kitchen, some a wet bar; king, queen, or extra-long double beds are available. *1823 L St. NW, 20036, tel. 202/223–4320 or 800/424–2970. 99 rooms. Facilities: 2 restaurants, access to health club, parking. AE, DC, MC, V. Moderate.*

Braxton Hotel. Billed as Washington's newest small hotel, the Braxton offers budget basics in a central location. The newly refurbished rooms in this older building have stucco walls and are small but quiet and clean. Take a cab to the hotel after dark. *1440 Rhode Island Ave. NW, 20005, tel. 202/232–7800. 62 rooms. AE, MC, V. Inexpensive.*

Dupont Circle
★ **The Washington Hilton and Towers.** At any moment, you could run into a leading actor, a cabinet official, six busloads of teenagers from Utah, 500 visiting heart surgeons, or Supreme Court Justice Sandra Day O'Connor, who is among the notables who have played tennis here. Though this Hilton specializes in large groups, individual travelers who like to be where the action is also check in. The light-filled, pastel-colored guest rooms are furnished in hotel moderne and have marble bathrooms. In back of the hotel is a miniresort with a café. The hotel is a short walk from the shops and restaurants of Dupont Circle, Embassy Row, the National Zoo, and the Adams-Morgan neighborhood. *1919 Connecticut Ave. NW, 20009, tel. 202/483–3000 or 800/445–8667. 1,150 rooms, including 88 suites. Facilities: 3 restaurants (one seasonal), 2 bars, 3 lighted tennis courts, outdoor pool, whirlpool, weight-training equipment, pro shop, valet parking. AE, DC, MC, V. Expensive.*

Omni Georgetown. Although this hotel is not actually Georgetown, it is conveniently located on P Street near Dupont Circle. Its most striking feature is the size of the guest rooms, among the largest of any hotel in the city. Each of the standard rooms has a king or two queen-size beds, a sofa and chairs, a large writing desk, three telephones, and bathrooms equipped with hair dryers. *2121 P St. NW, 20037, tel. 202/293–3100 or 800/843–6664. 288 rooms, including 65 suites. Facilities: restaurant, bar, outdoor pool, exercise room, business center, valet parking. AE, DC, MC, V. Moderate.*

★ **Hotel Tabard Inn.** Three Victorian town houses were linked 70 years ago to form an inn, and the establishment is still welcoming guests. Named after the hostelry of Chaucer's Canterbury

Tales, the hotel is furnished throughout with broken-in Victorian and American Empire antiques. Rooms have phone but no TV. There is no room service, but the Tabard Inn Restaurant serves breakfast, lunch, and dinner. Reserve at least two weeks in advance. *1739 N St. NW, 20036, tel. 202/785–1277. 40 rooms, 23 with private bath. Facilities: restaurant. MC, V. Inexpensive.*

Quality Hotel Central. This high-rise just up the street from Dupont Circle is one of the city's best values. Rooms are clean, quiet, and decorated with light colors and blond wood. Rooms on the western and southern sides have good views. *1900 Connecticut Ave. NW, 20009, tel. 202/332–9300 or 800/842–4211. 149 rooms. Facilities: restaurant, outdoor pool, access to health club, free parking. AE, DC, MC, V. Inexpensive.*

Georgetown

★ **Four Seasons Hotel.** A polished staff is at your service the moment you approach the doors of this contemporary hotel conveniently situated between Georgetown and Foggy Bottom. The Four Seasons is a gathering place for Washington's elite. Rooms, all of which have a minibar, are traditionally furnished in light colors. The quieter rooms face the courtyard; others have a view of the C & O Canal. The restaurant, Aux Beaux Champs, is highly esteemed by locals. The Four Seasons is also home to the private nightclub Desiree and perhaps the poshest health club of any hotel in America. *2800 Pennsylvania Ave., NW, 20007, tel. 202/342–0444 or 800/332–3442. 197 rooms, including 30 suites. Facilities: 2 restaurants, bar, nightclub, health club with pool, multilingual staff, valet parking. AE, DC, MC, V. Very Expensive.*

★ **Georgetown Marbury Hotel.** A small, red-brick colonial-style hotel, the Marbury is popular with Europeans, sports figures, and devotees of Georgetown. Extensive renovation is in progress; guests who value total quiet may want to request one of the 40 rooms underground. Other rooms have views of the C&O Canal or busy M Street. Rooms have low ceilings and country cotton prints. *3000 M St. NW, 20007, tel. 202/726–5000 or 800/368–5922. 164 rooms, including 9 suites. Facilities: 2 restaurants, 2 bars, outdoor pool, access to health club, valet parking. AE, DC, MC, V. Moderate.*

Upper Connecticut Avenue

Omni Shoreham Hotel. Resembling an old-time resort, this grand, 1930s Art Deco–Renaissance hotel overlooks Rock Creek Park. In back is the pool, where you can look out to a sweeping lawn and woods beyond. Adding to the tropical-resort atmosphere are mock bamboo furnishings in the entrance area and doormen wearing pith helmets during the warmer months. The rooms are large and light-filled. Some have fireplaces; half overlook the park. The loyal staff takes your stay personally. The Omni is close to Adams-Morgan, Dupont Circle, and the National Zoo. *2500 Calvert St. NW, 20008, tel. 202/234–0700 or 800/834–6664. 770 rooms, including 50 suites. Facilities: 2 restaurants, bar, snack counter, cabaret, outdoor pool, 3 lighted tennis courts, fitness center, parking. AE, DC, MC, V. Expensive.*

★ **Kalorama Guest House.** Really great-grandma's house in disguise, this inn consists of four turn-of-the-century town houses: three on a quiet street in the Adams-Morgan neighborhood and one in residential Woodley Park. The Kalorama's comfortable atmosphere is created by dark wood on the walls; hand-me-down antique oak furniture; traditional, slightly worn upholstery; brass or antique wooden bedsteads; and calico curtains at the windows. The coffee pot is always on, the staff is knowledgeable and friendly, and guests have the run of each house. Complimentary breakfast is served. Rooms range from large to tiny; none have phone or TV. *1854 Mintwood Pl. NW, 20009, tel. 202/667–6369; and 2700 Cathedral Ave. NW, 20008, tel. 202/328–0860. 50 rooms, including 5 suites; 30 with private bath. AE, DC, MC, V. Inexpensive.*

★ **Normandy Inn.** A small, European-style hotel on a quiet street in the exclusive embassy area of Connecticut Avenue, the Normandy is near some of the most expensive residential real estate in Washington. The rooms are standard and functional, but comfortable. A complimentary Continental breakfast is served. *2118 Wyoming Ave. NW, 20008, tel. 202/483–1350 or 800/424–3729. 75 rooms, including 10 suites. Facilities: parking. AE, MC, V. Inexpensive.*

West End/ Foggy Bottom   **Watergate Hotel.** The internationally famous Watergate, its distinctive sawtooth design a landmark along the Potomac, completed a $14 million renovation in 1988 and is now offering guests a taste of old-English gentility. Scenic murals and a portrait of Queen Elizabeth contribute to the effect. The rooms here are among the largest in Washington; many have balconies, and most have striking river views. Part of the exclusive Watergate apartment-and-commercial complex, the hotel is next door to the Kennedy Center and a short walk from Georgetown. *2650 Virginia Ave. NW, 20037, tel. 202/965–2300 or 800/424–2736. 237 rooms, including 160 suites. Facilities: 2 restaurants, 2 bars, health club, indoor pool, limo to Capitol Hill or downtown Mon.–Fri., valet parking. AE, DC, MC, V. Very Expensive.*

Wyndham Bristol Hotel. This hotel doesn't offer much in the way of views, but the location is excellent: midway between the White House and Georgetown, with the Kennedy Center just a few blocks away. The rooms here are quiet, although the building is bordered on two sides by major thoroughfares. A cabinet-full of Chinese porcelain greets guests on arrival in the small, quiet lobby. The rest of the hotel, created in 1984 from an apartment building, is English in decor; each room has a butler's table. *2430 Pennsylvania Ave. NW, 20037, tel. 202/955–6400, 800/822–4200, or in Canada 800/631–4200. 240 rooms, including 22 suites. Facilities: 2 restaurants, seasonal outdoor café, bar, access to health club, valet parking, garage. AE, DC, MC, V. Expensive.*

Howard Johnson Kennedy Center. This 10-story lodge offers HoJo reliability in a location close to the Kennedy Center, the Watergate complex, and Georgetown. Rooms are large and comfortable, and each has a refrigerator. *2601 Virginia Ave. NW, 20037, tel. 202/965–2700 or 800/654–2000. 192 rooms. Facilities: room service 6 AM–11 PM, restaurant, rooftop pool, free parking for cars only (no vans). AE, DC, MC, V. Inexpensive.*

The Arts

Friday's *Washington Post* "Weekend" section is the best guide to events for the weekend and the coming week. The *Post*'s daily "Guide to the Lively Arts" also outlines cultural events in the city. The *Washington Times* "Weekend" section comes out on Thursday. The free weekly *City Paper* hits the streets on Thursday and covers the entertainment scene well. You might

also consult the "City Lights" section in the monthly *Washingtonian* magazine.

Any search for cultured entertainment should start at the **John F. Kennedy Center for the Performing Arts** (New Hampshire Ave. and Rock Creek Parkway NW). America's national cultural center has a little of everything. The Kennedy Center is actually four stages under one roof: the **Concert Hall**, home park of the National Symphony Orchestra; the 2,200-seat **Opera House**, the setting for ballet, modern dance, grand opera, and large-scale musicals; the **Eisenhower Theater**, usually used for drama; and the **Terrace Theater**, an intimate space designed by Philip Johnson that showcases experimental works and chamber groups. For information call 202/467–4600 or 800/444–1324.

Tickets Tickets to most events are available by calling or visiting each venue's box office.

Metro Center TicketPlace sells half-price, day-of-performance tickets for selected shows; a "menu board" lists available performances. Only cash is accepted for same-day tickets; cash and credit cards may be used for full-price, advance tickets. *12th and F Sts. NW, tel. 202/TICKETS. Open Tues–Fri. noon–4, Sat. 11–5. Tickets for Sun. performances sold on Sat.*

TicketCenter (tel. 202/432–0200 or 800/448–9009) takes phone charges for events around the city. You can purchase TicketCenter tickets in person at all Hecht Company department stores. No refunds, exchanges, or cancellations.

Theater **Arena Stage** (6th St. and Maine Ave. SW, tel. 202/488–3300), the city's most respected resident company (now in its 41st season), presents a wide-ranging season in its three theaters: the theater-in-the-round Arena, the proscenium Kreeger, and the cabaret-style Old Vat Room.

Ford's Theatre (511 10th St. NW, tel. 202/347–4833), looking much the way it did when President Lincoln was shot, hosts mainly musicals, many with family appeal. Dickens's *A Christmas Carol* is presented each winter.

National Theatre (1321 E St. NW, tel. 202/628–6161), rebuilt four times, has operated in the same location since 1835. It presents pre- and post-Broadway shows.

Shakespeare Theatre at the Folger (201 East Capitol St. SE, tel. 202/546–4000) presents four plays—three by the Bard and another classic from his era—annually in this replica of an Elizabethan inn-yard theater.

Music **The National Symphony Orchestra** (tel. 202/416–8100), under conductor Mstislav Rostropovich, plays at the Kennedy Center September–June, and during the summer at Wolf Trap.

Wolf Trap Farm Park (1551 Trap Rd., Vienna, VA, tel. 703/255–1860), just off the Dulles Toll Road, about one-half hour from downtown, is a national park dedicated to the performing arts. On its grounds is the **Filene Center** (tel. 703/255–1868), an outdoor theater that is the scene of pop, jazz, opera, ballet, and dance performances each June through September. The rest of the year, the intimate, indoor **Barns at Wolf Trap** (tel. 703/938–2404) hosts folk and acoustic acts.

Choral and church groups frequently perform in the impressive settings of the **Washington Cathedral** (tel. 202/537–6200) and the **National Shrine of the Immaculate Conception** (tel. 202/526–8300).

Opera **Mount Vernon College** (2100 Foxhall Rd. NW, tel. 202/331–3467) offers rarely produced chamber operas each fall and spring.
Summer Opera Theater Company (Hartke Theater, Catholic University, tel. 202/526–1669) mounts two fully staged productions each July and August.
Washington Opera (tel. 202/416–7800 or 800/87–OPERA) performs seven operas November–March at the Kennedy Center.

Dance **Dance Place** (3225 8th St. NE, tel. 202/269–1600) studio theater hosts a wide assortment of modern and ethnic dance.
Joy of Motion (1643 Connecticut Ave. NW, tel. 202/387–0911) is the home of several area troupes.
Mount Vernon College (2100 Foxhall Rd. NW, tel. 202/331–3467), an emerging center for dance in Washington, presents eight dance companies a year.
Washington Ballet (tel. 202/362–3606) performs in October, February, and May selections from the works of such choreographers as George Balanchine and Paul Taylor, mainly at the Kennedy Center. Each December, the Washington Ballet presents *The Nutcracker*.

Film Several Washington theaters screen revivals and foreign, independent, and avant-garde films.

The American Film Institute (Kennedy Center, tel. 202/785–4600, 4601) screens more than 700 different movies annually—including contemporary and classic foreign and American films.
The Biograph (2819 M St. NW, recorded information tel. 202/333–2696) presents a mixture of first-run and repertory domestic and foreign films that are out of the mainstream.
Filmfest DC, an annual citywide festival of international cinema, takes place in late April and early May. For information, write Box 21396, Washington, DC 20009 or call 202/727–2396.
The Key (1222 Wisconsin Ave. NW, tel. 202/333–5100) is a four-screen theater specializing in foreign films.

Nightlife

Many night spots are clustered in a few key areas: Georgetown, Capitol Hill (Pennsylvania Ave. between 2nd and 4th Sts. SE), and downtown around the intersection of 19th and M streets NW, especially active during happy hour.

Bars and Lounges **Champions** (1206 Wisconsin Ave. NW, tel. 202/965–4005) is a sports lover's bar in Georgetown, with a big-screen TV and ballpark-style food.
15 Mins (1030 15th St. NW, tel. 202/408–1855) gathers a college-aged clientele to enjoy the funky decorations, tiny dance floor, progressive music, and black lights.
Food for Thought (1738 Connecticut Ave. NW, tel. 202/797–1095) is a Dupont Circle lounge and restaurant (vegetarian and organic meat) with a '60s coffeehouse feel. Nightly folk music completes the picture.
Gallagher's Pub (3319 Connecticut Ave. NW, tel. 202/686–9189) is a mildly Irish bar that's a restful haven for those eager to avoid the crush of Georgetown. Heartfelt acoustic music can be heard at the Sunday night open mike.
Hawk 'n' Dove (329 Pennsylvania Ave. SE, tel. 202/543–3300), a friendly neighborhood bar on Capitol Hill, is frequented by po-

litical types, lobbyists, and well-behaved Marines (from a near-by barracks).

Cabarets   **Chelsea's** (1055 Thomas Jefferson St. NW, tel. 202/298–8222 or 703/683–8330) presents the musical political satire of the Capitol Steps, a group of current and former Hill staffers, on Fridays and Saturdays.

d.c. space (433 7th St. NW, tel. 202/347–4960) offers dinner theater, poetry readings, film screenings, and other avant-garde events at this artists' hangout near the old Patent Office building.

Gross National Product (3135 K St. NW, tel. 202/783–7212) is an irreverent comedy troupe performing Saturdays at the Bayou in Georgetown.

Comedy Clubs   **Comedy Cafe** (1520 K St. NW, tel. 202/638–JOKE) presents local and national comics. Thursday is open-mike night; on Friday and Saturday, the pros take the stage.

Garvin's Comedy Clubs (1335 Greens Ct. NW, tel. 202/783–2442; also at Phillips Flagship Restaurant, 900 Water St. NW) serves jokes at various locations.

Music Clubs   **Afterwords** (1517 Connecticut Ave. NW, tel. 202/387–1462), shoehorned in a bookshop near Dupont Circle, presents folkish acts for browsing bohemian bookworms as well as patrons seated at a cozy in-store café.

Club Soda (3433 Connecticut Ave. NW, tel. 202/244–3189), despite its tiny room and dance floor, is one of the best places in town to hear cover bands perform consistently accurate oldies music Wednesday–Sunday.

Dylan's (3251 Prospect St. NW, tel. 202/337–0593), a Georgetown restaurant-cum-club, has different types of music every night, mostly in the light rock and acoustic folk categories.

9:30 Club (930 F St. NW, tel. 202/393–0930) books an eclectic mix of local, national, and international artists, most of whom play what used to be known as "new wave" music.

One Step Down (2517 Pennsylvania Ave. NW, tel. 202/331–8863) boasts the best jazz jukebox in town, talented local artists, the occasional national act, and many New York jazz masters. It's frayed and smoky, the way a jazz club should be.

Trumpets (1633 Q St. NW, tel. 202/232–4141) is a sleek mainstream jazz club featuring well-known artists on weekends, local talent during the week.

Dance Clubs   Hoofers who prefer "touch" dancing should call the recorded information line of the very active **Washington Area Swing Dance Committee** (tel. 301/779–0234). The group organizes monthly boogie woogie, jitterbug, and swing workshops and dances.

Chelsea's (1055 Thomas Jefferson St. NW, tel. 202/298–8222), an elegant Georgetown club near the C & O Canal, has hot Latin acts Thursday–Saturday, Persian music Wednesday and Sunday.

Club 2424 (2424 18th St. NW, tel. 202/328–7194) is a trendy Eurodisco featuring a thumping dance beat and DJs who "house" up the music.

The Ritz (919 E. St. NW, tel. 202/638–2582), in the shadow of the J. Edgar Hoover FBI Building, features five separate rooms of music, with DJs spinning everything from Top 40s and reggae in "Club Matisse" to house music in the upstairs "Freezone."

Northern Virginia

Much of this region has been subsumed into the official and residential life of Washington, DC, and has prospered as a result. The affluent and cosmopolitan Northern Virginians are somewhat estranged from the rest of the Commonwealth, yet they are proud of their distinction as Virginians. As their economy grows, they are protecting the historic treasures they hold in trust for the rest of the nation.

Old Town Alexandria remains apparently unsuburbanized; its hundreds of 18th- and 19th-century buildings are collectively listed in the National Register of Historic Places. Fredericksburg, only an hour from the nation's capital, seems much farther away: a quiet, well-preserved Southern town, with a 40-block National Historic District. But Fredericksburg was once the bloody scene of conflict in the Civil War.

Numbers in the margin correspond to points of interest on the Northern Virginia map.

❶ Cross Memorial Bridge from Washington to make the most impressive approach to **Arlington National Cemetery.** Directly behind you, on the Washington side, is the Lincoln Memorial; ahead, high atop a hill, is Robert E. Lee's Arlington House, and a little below it is the eternal flame that marks the grave of John F. Kennedy. All this is aligned with the bridge, and the effect of the arrangement is stunning.

In the cemetery are thousands of veterans buried beneath simple white headstones. The many famous Americans interred here include President Taft, Oliver Wendell Holmes, George C. Marshall, Joe Louis, and John and Robert Kennedy. In and around the Tomb of the Unknown Soldier are the graves of men killed in both world wars, Korea, and Vietnam. It is guarded constantly by members of the Old Guard: 1st Battalion (Reinforced), 3d Infantry. A changing-of-the-guard ceremony takes place every half-hour from 8 to 5, April–September, hourly the rest of the year. *Tel. 703/545–6700. Admission free. Open daily 8–5 Nov.–Mar., 8–7 rest of year.*

Within the cemetery is **Arlington House,** where Robert E. Lee lived for 30 years, until his job obliged him to leave the proximity of the Union capital. The Union confiscated the estate during the Civil War, when Arlington began to function as a cemetery. The massive house is of Greek Revival design, reminiscent of a temple, and is furnished in antiques and reproductions. The view of Washington from the portico is as gorgeous as the sight of the house from the bridge. *Tel. 703/557–0613. Admission free. Open daily 9:30–4:30 Oct.–Mar., 9:30–6 rest of year. Closed Christmas and New Year's.*

A narrated bus tour of Arlington National Cemetery, with stops at Arlington House, the Tomb of the Unknown Soldier, and the Kennedy graves, is given by Tourmobile (tel. 202/554–7950). Tours leave from the visitor center on the site starting at 8 AM. Cost: $2.50 adults, $1.25 children.

❷ Drive south on the George Washington Memorial Parkway to **Alexandria.** Established in 1749, this city once dwarfed Georgetown, which is just across the Potomac. That was before the Revolution; today Alexandria proudly maintains an identity separate from that of the federal capital.

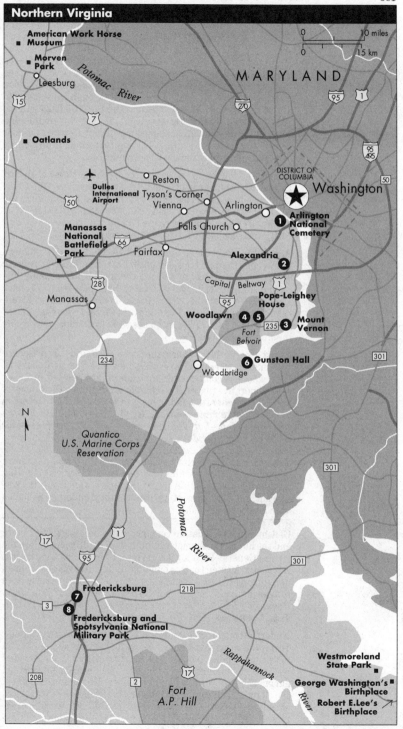

Northern Virginia

MARYLAND

American Work Horse Museum

Morven Park

Leesburg

Oatlands

Potomac River

Dulles International Airport

Reston

Tyson's Corner

Vienna

Falls Church

Arlington

DISTRICT OF COLUMBIA

Washington

Arlington National Cemetery ❶

Manassas National Battlefield Park

Fairfax

Alexandria ❷

Capital Beltway

Woodlawn ❹ ❺ ❸ Mount Vernon

Pope-Leighey House

Fort Belvoir

Manassas

Woodbridge

❻ Gunston Hall

N

Quantico U.S. Marine Corps Reservation

Potomac River

Fredericksburg ❼

❽ Fredericksburg and Spotsylvania National Military Park

Fort A.P. Hill

Rappahannock River

Westmoreland State Park

George Washington's Birthplace

Robert E. Lee's Birthplace

0   10 miles
0   15 km

The historic area is Old Town; its main arteries are Washington Street (the parkway as it passes through town) and King Street, which divide the town east–west and north–south, respectively. The shopping (art, antiques, and specialty) is of high quality, as are the sights. Most points of interest are on the east (Potomac) side of Washington Street. Visit them on foot if you are prepared to walk for 20 blocks or so. Guided walking tours of Alexandria from April through November begin at the Ramsay House Visitor's Center (221 King St., tel 703/838–4200). Parking is usually scarce, but the visitor's bureau will give you a 72-hour parking permit for the two-hour metered zones, along with a walking tour map. It also offers foreign translations and a video orientation.

Among the town's attractions is the **Boyhood Home of Robert E. Lee,** where he lived off and on for 13 years. The 1795 Georgian town house is furnished in antiques that reflect life in the 1820s. *607 Oronoco St., tel. 703/548–8454. Admission: $3 adults, $1.50 senior citizens, $1 children. Open Mon.–Sat. 10–4, Sun. noon–4. Closed Thanksgiving and Dec. 15–Feb. 1.*

Across the street is the **Lee-Fendall House,** built in 1785 by an in-law and lived in by Lees until 1903. The interior reflects styles from a variety of periods and includes Lee-family furnishings. Labor leader John L. Lewis lived here from 1937 until 1969. *614 Oronoco St., tel. 703/548–1789. Admission: $3 adults, $1 children. Open Tues.–Sat. 10–4, Sun. noon–4. Closed holidays and Mon. The Lee homes sometimes close for private functions; call ahead.*

Christ Church looks much the same as it did when George Washington worshiped here. His pew and that of Robert E. Lee, who was confirmed in the church, are marked by silver commemorative plates. The churchyard contains the graves of several Confederate dead, among others. *118 N. Washington St. at Cameron intersection, tel. 703/549–1450. Admission free. Open Mon.–Sat. 9–5, Sun. noon–4:30. Closed (except for services) major holidays.*

Time Out Take a break for a pint of Guinness or Harp and perhaps a ploughman's lunch (pickles and cheese) at **Murphy's** (713 King St., tel. 703/548–1717). At night this brick-walled pub and restaurant, on two floors of an 18th-century building, resounds with an Irish sing-along.

Gadsby's Tavern Museum comprises two buildings: the tavern and the hotel. The former was built in 1770, 22 years before the latter. General Washington reviewed his troops for the last time from the steps of this building. Lafayette was entertained here during his 1824 visit. The rooms in the tavern have been convincingly restored to their appearance in the 1790s. *134 N. Royal St., tel. 703/838–4242. Admission: $3 adults, $1 children. Open Tues.–Sat. 10–5, Sun. 1–5. Closed major holidays.*

Modern Alexandria is represented by the extremely popular **Torpedo Factory Art Center.** About 180 artists and craftsmen have their studios (with wares for sale) within this renovated waterfront building where torpedo parts were manufactured during the two world wars. The center also houses exhibits of the city's archaeology program (one of the nation's largest and oldest) and laboratories, where you can observe work in progress. *105 N. Union St., tel. 703/838–4565. Admission free. Cen-*

ter open daily 10–5. Closed Thanksgiving, Christmas, New Year's Day. Archaeology Section (tel. 703/838–4399) open Tues.–Thurs. 10–3, Fri.–Sat. 10–5, Sun. 1–5.

③ Nine miles south of Alexandria, via the Mount Vernon Memorial Highway (a continuation of the George Washington Parkway) is **Mount Vernon,** once George Washington's home and today the most visited house museum in the United States. About 30% of the furnishings are original; the rest are carefully selected and authenticated antiques.

Washington considered himself, first and foremost, a farmer. His farmhouse was a formal one, certainly, but none of the embellishments disguised the noble practicality of its purpose. In the ornate dining room, guests ate at simple trestle tables assembled from boards and sawhorses. More of a sage than an intellectual, he read mostly for practical reference; his enormous library of 900 volumes (now mostly dispersed) was composed largely of presents from the authors. The outbuildings, including kitchen and stable, have been precisely restored. A bit farther on are the graves of George and Martha Washington, laid to rest in the land they loved so well. *From DC, take any Virginia-side bridge to the George Washington Memorial Pkwy. (which becomes Mt. Vernon Memorial Hwy. to the south) and follow signs southward, tel. 703/780–2000. Admission: $5 adults, $4 senior citizens, $2 children under 12. Open daily 9–5 Mar.–Oct., 9–4 rest of year.*

④ Near Mount Vernon—on land given by Washington to his nephew Lawrence Lewis and step-daughter, Nelly Custis, as a wedding gift—is **Woodlawn.** Designed by the architect of the Capitol, William Thornton, to resemble Lewis's boyhood home, Kenmore, in Fredericksburg, it was begun in 1800, then furnished well but not lavishly, to accommodate and entertain a family of many children. Today, the formal gardens are well maintained and include a large collection of rare old-fashioned roses. *14 mi south of DC on U.S. 1, and 3 mi from Mount Vernon on the George Washington Memorial Pkwy., tel. 703/780–4000. Admission: $5 adults, $3.50 senior citizens and students. Open daily 9:30–4:30. Closed Thanksgiving, Christmas, and New Year's Day.*

⑤ Also on the grounds of Woodlawn is the **Pope-Leighey House,** designed by Frank Lloyd Wright and built in 1940. It has no Washington-family connection; it is here because when highway construction augured its destruction on its original site nearby, the National Trust stepped in and moved it to Woodlawn, where it makes a nice contrast to the Federal mansion. The longer you look around and the more that is explained, the more of its peculiar beauty is revealed. It does not appeal to every taste, but it *is* an architectural education. *Tel. 703/780–4000. Admission: $5 adults, $3.50 senior citizens and students. Open Mar.–Dec., daily 9:30–4:30; Jan. and Feb., weekends only. Combined ticket to Woodlawn and Pope-Leighey House: $8 adults, $6 senior citizens and students.*

⑥ Unlike Mount Vernon, **Gunston Hall,** 15 miles away in Lorton, is rarely crowded with visitors. This was the home of a lesser-known George: George Mason, father of the Bill of Rights. He was one of the framers of the Constitution, then refused to sign it because it did not prohibit slavery, adequately restrain the powers of the federal government, or include a bill of rights.

The interior of the house, with its carved woodwork in styles ranging from Chinese to Gothic, has been meticulously restored, using paints made from the original recipes and with carefully carved replacements for the intricate mahogany medallions in the moldings. The grounds—with formal gardens featuring large boxwood hedges—may look familiar, since the last scene in the 1987 movie *Broadcast News* was filmed here, by the gazebo. *U.S. 1S to VA 242S, tel. 703/550–9220. Admission: $4 adults, $3 senior citizens, $1 children. Open daily 9:30–5. Closed Christmas.*

❼ Fifty miles south of Washington on I–95 is **Fredericksburg,** which rivals Alexandria and Mount Vernon for Washington-family associations. The first president lived at nearby Ferry Farm (across the Rappahannock River) between the ages of six and 16 and later bought a house for his mother here, near his sister and brother. **U.S. Tours** (tel. 703/373–8440) offers a guided bus tour of Fredericksburg ($10 per person) that departs from the Visitor's Center.

Washington's only sister, Betty, married her cousin Fielding Lewis in 1750, and they built **Kenmore** a few years later. The plain exterior belies the lavish interior; these have been called some of the most beautiful rooms in America. The plaster moldings in the ceilings are even more ornate than Mount Vernon's. Of equal elegance are the furnishings, including a large standing clock that belonged to Betty's mother, Mary. In the reconstructed kitchen next door you can enjoy tea and a fresh facsimile of Mary Washington's gingerbread after the tour. *1201 Washington Ave., tel. 703/373–3381. Admission: $4 adults, $2 children. Open Mar.–Nov., daily 9–5; Dec.–Feb., daily 10–4. Closed Christmas Eve and Day, and New Year's Eve and Day.*

In 1760, George Washington's brother Charles built as his home what became the **Rising Sun Tavern,** a watering hole for such pre-Revolutionary patriots as the Lee brothers, Patrick Henry, Washington, and Jefferson. A "wench" in period costume leads the tour without stepping out of character. From her perspective you watch the activity—day and night, upstairs and down—at this busy institution. In the tap room, you are served spiced tea. *1306 Caroline St., tel. 703/371–1494. Admission: $2.50 adults, 50¢ children. Open Mar.–Nov., daily 9–5; Dec.–Feb., daily 10–4. Closed Thanksgiving, Christmas Eve and Day, and New Year's Eve and Day.*

On Charles Street is the modest white **Home of Mary Washington.** George purchased it for her in 1772, and she spent the last 17 years of her life here, tending the charming garden where her boxwood still flourishes and where many a bride and groom now come to exchange their vows. *Charles and Lewis Sts., tel. 703/373–1569. Admission: $2.50 adults, 50¢ children. Open Mar.–Nov., daily 9–5; Dec.–Feb., daily 10–4. Closed Thanksgiving, Christmas Eve and Day, and New Year's Eve and Day.*

Dr. Mercer might have been more careful than most other Colonial physicians, yet his methods will make you cringe. At his **Apothecary Shop,** a costumed hostess will explicitly describe amputations and cataract operations. You will also hear about therapeutic bleeding and see the gruesome devices used in Colonial dentistry. This is an informative if slightly nauseating look at life two centuries ago. *Caroline and Amelia Sts.,* *tel. 703/371–3486. Admission: $2.50 adults, 50¢ students. Open Mar.–Nov., daily 9–5; Dec.–Feb., daily 10–4. Closed Thanksgiving, Christmas Eve and Day, and New Year's Eve and Day.*

The **James Monroe Museum and Memorial Library** is the tiny one-story building where the man who was to be the fifth president of the United States practiced law from 1787 to 1789. In this building are many of Monroe's possessions, collected and preserved by his family until this century, including the desk on which Monroe signed the doctrine named for him. *908 Charles St., tel. 703/373–8426. Admission: $2.50 adults, 50¢ children. Open daily 9–5. Closed Thanksgiving, Christmas Eve and Day, and New Year's Eve and Day.*

Time Out   Stop for a gourmet sandwich or some quiche at the **Made in Virginia Store Deli** (807 Caroline St., tel. 703/371–2030). Do not skip the rich desserts.

Four nearby Civil War battlefields—Fredericksburg, Chancellorsville, the Wilderness, and Spotsylvania Courthouse—constitute the **Fredericksburg and Spotsylvania National Military Park**. All are within 17 miles of Fredericksburg. At the in-town visitor's center for the park, there's a slide show about the battles and there are two floors of exhibits. On the fields, signs and exhibits point out moments in the battles. *1013 Lafayette Blvd. (U.S. 1), tel. 703/373–4461. Admission free. Open daily 9–5, but hours vary seasonally. Closed Christmas and New Year's.*

Sports and Outdoor Activities

Bicycling   The **Mount Vernon Bicycle Trail** (tel. 703/285–2598) is 19 miles of asphalt along the shore of the Potomac and through Alexandria. For a free map of Arlington County's Bikeway System, call 703/528–2941. The **Fredericksburg Visitor's Center** (tel. 703/373–1776) has mapped out rides of 3, 9, and 20 miles that take in the historical and natural beauty of the town.

Dining and Lodging

The following dining price categories have been used: *Very Expensive*, over $30; *Expensive*, $20–$30; *Moderate*, $10–$20; *Inexpensive*, under $10.

The following lodging price categories have been used: *Very Expensive*, over $120; *Expensive*, $90–$120; *Moderate*, $50–$90; *Inexpensive*, under $50.

Alexandria   **Gadsby's Tavern.** Located in Old Town, this tavern will take you
Dining   back 200 years with its decor, cuisine, and unique entertainment. While you dine, John Douglas Hall, in the costume and character of an 18th-century gentleman, performs on the lute and chats about the latest news and gossip of Colonial Virginia. The tavern, built in 1792, was a favorite of George Washington's, and he is remembered today on the menu with George Washington's Favorite Duck: cornbread-stuffed roast duck with fruit-and-madeira sauce. Other special offerings are Colonial Game Pye, of lamb, pork, and rabbit; Sally Lunn bread; and rich English trifle. Upstairs is a museum showing authentic table settings and the section of the tavern that was once a hotel.

138 N. Royal St., tel. 703/548–1288. Dress: informal. Reservations advised. AE, DC, MC, V. Moderate.

★ **Taverna Cretekou.** Whitewashed stucco walls and brightly colored macramé tapestries bring the Mediterranean to the center of Old Town. In the warm months, you can dine in the canopied garden. The Lamb Exohikon—lamb baked in a pastry shell—and the swordfish kabob are especially good. All wines served are Greek. *818 King St., tel. 703/548–8688. Dress: informal. Reservations advised. AE, DC, MC, V. Closed Mon. Moderate.*

Lodging **Holiday Inn—Old Town.** This luxury hotel in 1988 completed a $4 million refurbishment. The rooms are decorated in Federal style, with such high-tech touches as "executive phones" with computer-modem capabilities. Bathrooms have marble tubs and floors. *480 King St., 22314, tel. 703/549–6080 or 800/465–4329. 227 rooms. Facilities: indoor pool and sauna, restaurant, disco. AE, D, DC, MC, V. Very Expensive.*

★ **Morrison House.** This small, luxurious hotel in Old Town is decorated in Federal style throughout, complete with four-poster beds. Afternoon tea is served as it must have been 200 years ago. *116 S. Alfred St., 22314, tel. 703/838–8000. 45 rooms, including 3 suites. Facilities: 24-hr butler and room service, French restaurant. AE, DC, MC, V. Very Expensive.*

Arlington **Tivoli.** This popular, upscale Northern Italian spot on the third
Dining floor of an office building on top of the Rosslyn Metro station opened in 1982. The restaurant sparkles with glass and mirrors and lots of green plants. White linen, peach napkins, and lambs from Murano add to the modern look, and the food's a treat as well. Everyone loves the linguine Saracena, done in a cream sauce with mussels, clams, and calamari; the medallions of veal with porcini; and the swordfish with black olives and rosemary. There's free parking after 5, when the office building empties. *1700 N. Moore St., tel. 703/524–8900. Jacket required. Reservations advised. AE, DC, MC, V. Expensive–Very Expensive.*

Cafe Dalat. Photos and silkscreens of Vietnamese scenery decorate this restaurant, which caters to the area's large Vietnamese population. Try the Fairy Combination, crispy noodles with chicken, scallops, shrimp, and mixed vegetables; beef wrapped in grape leaves; or any fish dish. Portions are generous. *3143 Wilson Blvd., tel. 703/276–0935. Dress: informal. Reservations not needed. No credit cards. Inexpensive.*

Lodging **Holiday Inn–National Airport.** A basic high-rise Holiday Inn off the highway, with modern, cheerful decor and a convenient location a mile from the airport. *1489 Jefferson Davis Hwy., 22202, tel. 703/521–1600 or 800/465–4329. 306 rooms, including 11 suites. Facilities: outdoor pool, restaurant bar; adjacent to racquetball club. AE, D, DC, MC, V. Very Expensive.*

Marriott Crystal Gateway. This modern, elegant hotel caters to the business traveler and the tourist who wants to be pampered. Its two towers rise 17 stories above the highway. Inside, there's black marble, blond wood, Oriental touches, and lots of greenery. Rooms are modern. *1700 Jefferson Davis Hwy., 22202, tel. 703/920–3230 or 800/228–9290. 702 rooms, including 110 suites. Facilities: indoor/outdoor pools; health spa with whirlpool, sauna, and exercise rooms; 4 restaurants and lounges; nightclub. AE, DC, MC, V. Very Expensive.*

Fredericksburg **P.K.'s.** This is a conventional and comfortable surf-and-turf
Dining restaurant with a 19th-century atmosphere. *2051 Plank Rd.*

(Rte. 3), tel. 703/371–3344. Dress: informal. Reservations not needed. AE, D, DC, MC, V. Moderate.

Ristorante Renato. This unlikely Italian restaurant in the center of a Colonial town has a strong if coventional menu. Romeo and Juliet is a dish of veal and chicken covered with mozzarella and swimming in white-wine sauce; the Shrimp Scampi Napoli has a butter-lemon sauce. *Williams and Prince Edward Sts., tel. 703/371–8228. Dress: informal. Reservations advised on weekends. AE, MC, V. Moderate.*

Lodging **Best Western–Johnny Appleseed.** This family-oriented two-story motel is five minutes from the battlefields. Rooms are motel basic; queen-size beds are available. *543 Warrenton Rd. (U.S. 17 at Jct. I–95), 22405, tel. 703/373–0000 or 800/528–1234. 90 units, including 1 suite and 4 efficiencies. Facilities: outdoor pool, playground, nature trail, volleyball, restaurant, free HBO. AE, D, DC, MC, V. Inexpensive.*

Hampton Inn. A cheerful and comfortable new motel on the interstate, near the historic district. *2310 Plank Rd., 22401, tel. 703/371–0330 or 800/426–7866. 166 rooms, including king suites with whirlpools. Facilities: outdoor pool. AE, D, DC, MC, V. Inexpensive.*

The Arts and Nightlife

The Arts The **Harris Theater** at George Mason University (tel. 703/323–2075) is the scene of acclaimed student drama. The **Lazy Susan Dinner Theater** (tel. 703/550–7384) has a varied program all year long.

Nightlife In Arlington, **Whitey's** (tel. 703/525–9825) is a crowded, noisy,
Bluegrass and irresistible dive with a loyal following of diverse ages and backgrounds.

Irish and Folk **Murphy's Grand Irish Pub** in Alexandria (tel. 703/548–1717) has a fire blazing in winter and boisterous entertainment all year.

Jazz Upstairs at Alexandria's **Two Nineteen** (tel. 703/549–1141) there's jazz, or hang out in the sports bar in the basement.

Richmond

At the fall line of the James River, 71 miles southeast of Charlottesville, is the capital of the Commonwealth: Richmond. Discovered in 1607, it replaced Williamsburg as the capital in 1779 and became the capital of the Confederate States in 1861.

Richmond's historical significance alone makes it an important place to visit; moreover, it is a metropolis surprisingly lively and sophisticated for its size (the population is under a quarter of a million—second in Virginia to the bustling Norfolk–Virginia Beach–Hampton Roads complex). Following years of urban decay, this pinnacle of the Old South is prospering anew. Long a center for shipping and banking, it has fostered high-technology and the heavier industries in order to flourish. The results can be seen in an array of distinctive neighborhoods.

Monument Avenue is a wide thoroughfare lined with stately houses, divided by a verdant median, and punctuated by statues of Civil War heroes. Two of the major streets retain their traditional identifications: Main with banks and Grace with shops. Shockoe Slip is several blocks of warehouses converted into a fashionable shopping-and-entertainment zone on Cary Street, between 12th and 15th streets. The James Center, adjoining Shockoe, is an even newer (1987) complex of shops, office buildings, and restaurants. The Fan District—so called because its streets fan out to the west from Laurel Street—is bordered by Monument Avenue on the north, Main Street on the south, and The Boulevard on the west. This treasury of restored turn-of-the-century town houses has been the "hip" neighborhood for several decades. It may, in time, be succeeded as such by venerable Church Hill to the east (the area around St. John's Church, at 25th and Broad Sts.), which is still more fashionable than safe after dark.

Guided Tours On weekends, the **Cultural Link Trolley,** leaving from the Science Museum, makes a continuous 55-minute loop, stopping at 34 cultural and historic landmarks. You can pace yourself, getting on and off when and where you like. *Tel. 804/358–GRTC. Cost per day: $5 adults, $2.50 children, under 5 free. Runs Sat. 10–5, Sun. 12:30–5.*

Historic Richmond Foundation (tel. 804/780–0107) gives various bus and walking tours, as does **Winning Tours** (tel. 804/358–6666).

Heritage Cruise Line (tel. 804/222–5700) offers lunch and dinner voyages on the James River on a three-deck, air-conditioned paddle wheeler replica from April through October. **Historic Richmond Foundation** (tel. 804/780–0107) offers specialized scenic-tour and dining cruises.

Numbers in the margin correspond with points of interest on the Richmond map.

Start downtown at the **Court End** district, the heart of old Richmond, which includes seven national historic landmarks, three museums, and 11 other buildings on the National Register of Historic Places—all within eight blocks. At any one of the museums you will receive a self-guided walking tour with the purchase of a discount block ticket ($9 adults, $8.50 senior citizens, $4 children 7–12), good for all admission fees.

❶ The first museum, the **John Marshall House,** was built in 1790 by the Chief Justice of the Supreme Court, who was also secretary of state and ambassador to France. It is now fully restored and furnished with a convincing mix of period pieces and heirlooms. *9th and Marshall Sts., tel. 804/648–7998. Admission: $3 adults, $2.50 senior citizens, $1.25 children. Open Tues.–Sat. 10–5, Sun. 1–5. Closed major holidays.*

❷ The **Valentine Museum,** in the former home of sculptor Edward Valentine, is devoted to the life and history of Richmond. Exhibits include Early American clothing and toys. The building will remain open throughout its current extensive restoration, which is fascinating to observe in progress. *1015 E. Clay St., tel. 804/649–0711. Admission: $3.50 adults, $3 senior citizens, $2.75 students, $1.50 children. Open Memorial Day–Labor Day, Mon.–Thurs. 10–7, Fri.–Sun. 10–5; Labor Day–Memorial Day, Mon.–Sat. 10–5, Sun. noon–5.*

❸ The **Museum and White House of the Confederacy** are better seen in that order. The former offers elaborate permanent exhibitions on the Civil War era. The "world's largest collection of Confederate memorabilia" features such relics as the sword

The Piedmont

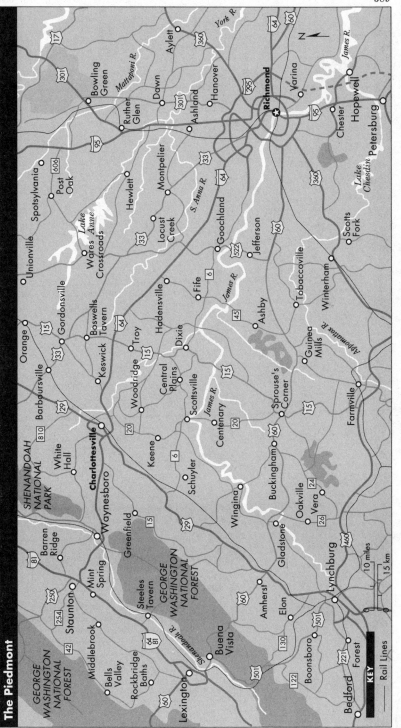

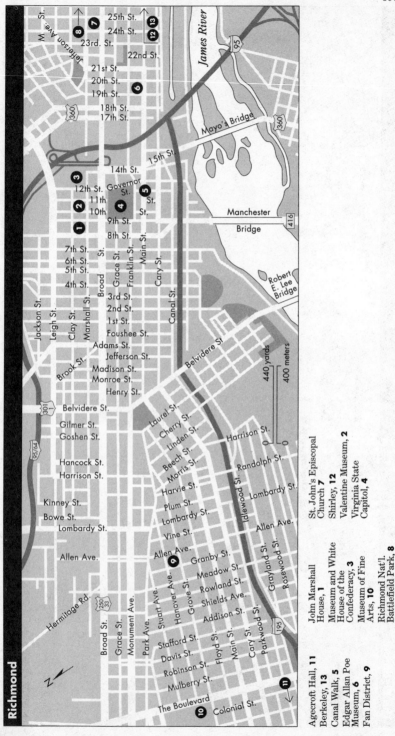

Richmond

James River

95

360

Mayo's Bridge

Manchester Bridge

416

Robert E. Lee Bridge

Jefferson Ave. W

25th St.
24th St.
23rd. St.
22nd St.
21st St.
20th St.
19th St.
18th St.
17th St.

15th St.

14th St.
12th St.
11th St.
10th St.
9th St.
8th St.
7th St.
6th St.
5th St.
4th St.
3rd St.
2nd St.
1st St.
Foushee St.
Adams St.
Jefferson St.
Madison St.
Monroe St.
Henry St.

Governor St.

Broad St.
Grace St.
Franklin St.
Main St.
Cary St.
Canal St.

Jackson St.
Leigh St.
Clay St.
Marshall St.

Brook St.

360

301

95/64

Belvidere St.
Gilmer St.
Goshen St.
Hancock St.
Harrison St.
Kinney St.
Bowe St.
Lombardy St.
Allen Ave.

Laurel St.
Cherry St.
Linden St.
Beech St.
Morris St.
Harvie St.
Plum St.
Lombardy St.
Vine St.
Allen Ave.
Granby St.
Meadow St.
Rowland St.
Shields Ave.
Addison St.

Belvidere St.

Harrison St.

Randolph St.

Lombardy St.

Idlewood St.

Allen Ave.

Grayland St.
Rosewood St.

95

440 yards
400 meters

Hermitage Rd.

250
33

Broad St.
Grace St.
Monument Ave.
Park Ave.
Stuart Ave.
Hanover Ave.
Grove St.
Stafford St.
Davis St.
Robinson St.
Mulberry St.

The Boulevard
Colonial St.

Main St.
Floyd St.
Cary St.
Parkwood St.

N

Agecroft Hall, 11
Berkeley, 13
Canal Walk, 5
Edgar Allan Poe
Museum, 6
Fan District, 9

John Marshall
House, 1
Museum and White
House of the
Confederacy, 3
Museum of Fine
Arts, 10
Richmond Nat'l.
Battlefield Park, 8

St. John's Episcopal
Church 7
Shirley, 12
Valentine Museum, 2
Virginia State
Capitol, 4

8 · 7 · 12 · 13 · 6 · 3 · 2 · 1 · 4 · 5 · 9 · 11 · 10

General Lee wore for the surrender at Appomattox. At the White House, next door, preservationists have painstakingly re-created the interior as it was during the Civil War, when Jefferson Davis lived here. *1201 E. Clay St., tel. 804/649–1861. Admission to both sites (1 site): $7 ($4) adults, $5 ($3.50) senior citizens, $3.50 ($2.25) children 7–12, under 7 free. Open Mon.– Sat. 10–5, Sun. 1–5. Closed holidays.*

❹ The **Virginia State Capitol** was designed by Thomas Jefferson in 1785. Inside is a wealth of sculpture, including busts of each of the eight presidents Virginia has given the nation; also the famous life-size, and lifelike, statue of George Washington by Houdon. In the old Hall of the House of Delegates, Robert E. Lee accepted the command of the Confederate forces in Virginia. Also on the grounds is the Old Bell Tower, where you can get travel information about the whole state. *Capitol Sq., tel. 804/ 786–4344. Admission free. Open daily 9–5 Apr.–Nov.; Mon.– Sat. 9–5, Sun. 1–5 rest of year. Closed Thanksgiving, Christmas, and New Year's Day.*

Across 9th Street from Capital Square is **St. Paul's Church,** where Jefferson Davis, president of the Confederacy, was at Sunday worship in 1865 when he received word from Lee that his Confederates could no longer hold Richmond.

❺ The **Canal Walk** starts south of the Capitol at 12th and Main and follows the locks of the James River–Kanawha Canal, proposed by George Washington. At 12th and Byrd, under the archway, watch a free slide show (daily 9–5) about the history of the canal. Follow the river to **Brown's Island,** across from the ruins of the Tredegar Iron Works. The island, terminus of the scenic walk, boasts a heliport and some unique sculptures, and hosts concerts in season.

❻ Leaving downtown Richmond, follow Main Street east to the Church Hill Historic District and the **Edgar Allan Poe Museum,** inside the Old Stone House. Poe never lived in the house (built in 1737) that his disciples have turned into a shrine, with some of his possessions on display. The Raven Room is hung with illustrations inspired by his most famous poem. *1914 E. Main St., tel. 804/648–5523. Admission: $4 adults, $3 senior citizens, $2 students. Open Tues.–Sat. 10–4, Sun. and Mon. 1:30–4. Closed Christmas.*

❼ Three blocks north is Broad Street, leading east to **St. John's Episcopal Church.** For security reasons, the rebellious Second Virginia Convention met here, instead of at Williamsburg, and on March 23, 1775, Patrick Henry delivered at this church the speech in which he insisted: "Give me liberty or give me death!" *25th and Broad Sts., tel. 804/648–5015. Admission: $2 adults, $1.50 senior citizens, $1 children. Open Mon.–Sat. 10–3:30, Sun. 1–3:30. Closed Easter, Christmas Eve and Day, and New Year's Eve and Day.*

❽ At the eastern end of Broad Street is the visitor center for the **Richmond National Battlefield Park,** the launching point for tours of the Richmond and other Civil War battlefields in the surrounding countryside. Here you can watch a movie about the city during the war and a slide show about the battlefields, then pick up a map to use on your self-guided tour. *3215 E. Broad St., tel. 804/226–1981. Admission free. Open daily 9–5. Closed Christmas and New Year's Day.*

Returning west on Broad Street, turn south on The Boulevard, along the edge of the **Fan District,** and you'll come to the **Virginia Museum of Fine Arts,** with major collections from Paul Mellon and Sydney Lewis. The museum's most startling exhibits have to be Duane Hanson's true-to-life wax figures: With their contemporary, unglamorous attire, and provocative poses they fool visitors all the time. But the paintings by Goya, Renoir, Monet, and van Gogh are quite real, and so are the African masks, Roman statuary, Oriental icons, and five Fabergé eggs. *Boulevard and Grove Ave., tel. 804/367–0844. $2 donation suggested. Open Tues.–Sat. 11–5 (Thurs. until 10), Sun. 1–5. Closed July 4, Thanksgiving, Christmas, and New Year's Day.*

Just west of the Fan District, in the Windsor Farms neighborhood, is **Agecroft Hall,** built in the 15th century in Lancashire and transported here in 1925. Set amid gardens, it contains an extensive assortment of Tudor and early Stuart furniture and art plus a few priceless anomalies, such as a Ming vase. *4305 Sulgrave Rd., tel. 804/353–4241. Admission: $3 adults, $2.50 senior citizens, $1.50 students. Open Tues.–Sat. 10–4, Sun. 2–5. Closed major holidays.*

From here, travelers can continue on to the Historic Triangle of Williamsburg, Jamestown, and Yorktown, or can choose to go west on I–64 to Charlottesville and the Shenandoah Valley. Those who are going to Williamsburg may either take I–64 east (the fastest route) or take the slower route on VA 5 east, which includes an intersting detour to two historic plantation houses less than half an hour from Richmond. The most impressive fact about **Shirley** is that the same family, the Carters, have lived here for 10 generations. Their claim to the land goes back to 1660, when it was settled by a relative, Edward Hill. The house was built in 1723; Robert E. Lee's mother was born here. Your first view of the elegant Georgian manor is a dramatic one: the house stands at the end of an allée lined by towering Lombardy poplars. Inside, the impressive hall staircase rises for three stories without any visible support. *VA 5E to Rte. 608, tel. 804/ 829–5121. Admission: $6 adults, $5 senior citizens, $4 students under 22, $3 children under 13. Open daily 9–5. Closed Christmas.*

Continue east a bit on VA 5 for **Berkeley.** It is said that the first Thanksgiving was celebrated not in Massachusetts but here, on December 4, 1619. The plantation was later the home of U.S. president William Henry Harrison. The Georgian brick house, built in 1726, is furnished with period antiques, not original pieces. The gardens are in excellent condition, particularly the boxwood hedges. There is a restaurant on the premises, with seating indoors and out. *VA 5E, then follow signs, tel. 804/829– 6018. Admission: $7 adults, $4 teenagers, $3 children, $6.30 senior citizens. Open daily 8–5. Closed Christmas.*

Shopping

In general, banks are open weekdays 9–3, Saturdays 9–noon. Shops open at 10 AM Monday–Saturday, noon on Sunday. Malls stay open until 9 PM Monday–Saturday, 6 PM Sunday; downtown stores close at 5:30.

6th Street Marketplace, as you might guess, is between 5th and 7th—also between Grace and Leigh. Here you'll find more than

50 specialty shops, chain stores, and eateries. Next door is **Thalhimers,** the best-known department store in Virginia.

Shockoe Slip (E. Cary St., between 12th and 15th Sts.), in the cobblestoned tobacco warehouse district of the 18th and 19th centuries, has boutiques and branches of such upscale stores as **Beecroft & Bull** and **The Toymaker of Williamsburg.**

At the **Farmers Market** (17th and Main Sts.) fresh produce is sold directly by the farmers. Nearby are boutiques, art galleries, and antiques shops, many in converted warehouses and factories.

Participant Sports

Within Richmond and the three suburban counties, there are open to the public—for free or at a nominal charge—405 tennis courts, 45 swimming pools, 20 golf courses, and seven miles of fitness trails. The following are just a few of the facilities available; the Visitor's Center (tel. 804/358–5511) and Division of Tourism (tel. 804/786–4484) have complete listings.

Golf **The Crossings** (tel. 804/266–2254), 20 minutes north of downtown in Glen Allen at the intersection of I–95 and I–295, has an 18-hole course open to the public.

Jogging There is a **running track** in the park around the Randolph pool (on Idlewood St.) and a **fitness track** in Byrd Park (off The Boulevard).

Rafting From April through October, the **Richmond Raft Co.** (tel. 804/ 222–7238) offers guided white-water rafting through the heart of the city on the James River (Class 3 and 4 rapids), float trips upriver, and overnight camping/rafting trips.

Swimming Among the city-run outdoor pools—open only in summer—are the **Randolph pool** (on Idlewood Ave.), which has a little park with a running track and tennis and basketball courts, and the **Bell Meade pool** (off Jefferson Davis Hwy.); call the City Dept. of Recreation and Parks for more information, tel. 804/780–5930. The **YWCA** (6 N. 5th St., tel. 804/643–6761) has an indoor pool that is open to members of any YWCA and guests of certain Richmond hotels.

Tennis **Byrd Park** (off The Boulevard) has lighted courts.

Dining

The following dining price categories have been used: *Very Expensive,* over $30; *Expensive,* $20–$30; *Moderate,* $10–$20; *Inexpensive,* under $10.

Very Expensive **La Petite France.** The atmosphere is formal, with emerald
Classic French green walls and tuxedoed waiters. The traditional food and service set the standard for Richmond's best. Specialties include Dover sole amandine and chateaubriand. *2912 Maywill St., tel. 804/353–8729. Jacket and tie required. Reservations advised. AE, DC, MC, V. Closed Sun. and Mon.*

Expensive **Millie's.** You'd pass right by this small unprepossessing brick
International building if you weren't in the know. It's a '40s atmosphere with
★ a counter and booths with juke boxes. The California chef-owners serve such entrées as Thai-style spicy shrimp with asparagus and shiitake mushrooms, and Virginia free-range veal with

sun-dried tomatoes and Shenandoah chèvre. *2603 East Main St., tel. 804/643–5512. Dress: informal. No reservations. MC, V.*

Nouvelle Cuisine **Mr. Patrick Henry's.** Two 1858 houses were restored and joined to make this restaurant and inn (upstairs there are three suites with kitchenettes and fireplaces). The dining room is Colonial in atmosphere, with antiques and fireplaces; there's also an English-style pub in the basement and a garden café. Especially popular dishes are the crisp roasted duck with crushed-plum sauce, and the crabcakes. *2300 E. Broad St., tel. 804/644–1322. Dress: informal. Reservations advised. AE, DC, MC, V. No dinner Sun.*

Inexpensive– **Bottoms Up.** This new pizza place in a three-cornered old build-
Moderate ing in Shockoe Bottom now serves full meals (they also deliver).
American The black-and-white tile floor, exposed brick, and long mahogany bar add to the appeal. *1700 Dock St., tel. 804/644–4400. Dress: informal. Reservations advised. MC, V.*

Inexpensive **Joe's Inn.** Spaghetti—especially spaghetti á la Greek, with feta
American and provolone cheese baked on top—is the specialty, but try the sandwiches, too. The regulars, who predominate at this local hangout in the Fan District, make outsiders feel right at home. *205 N. Shields Ave., tel. 804/355–2282. Dress: informal. Reservations not needed. AE, MC, V.*

Lodging

The following lodging price categories have been used: *Very Expensive*, over $120; *Expensive*, $90–$120; and *Moderate*, $50–$90.

Very Expensive **Jefferson Sheraton Hotel.** A regal, 26-step staircase reputedly
★ used as a model for the one in the movie *Gone With the Wind* graces the lobby of this famous old downtown hotel. Built in 1895, it is a National Historic Landmark that has been restored to its former glory by Sheraton. Guests are given passes to the YMCA spa across the street. *Franklin and Adams Sts., 23220, tel. 804/788–8000 or 800/343–6320. 273 rooms, including 26 suites. Facilities: 3 restaurants, lounges. AE, D, DC, MC, V.*
Omni Richmond. This luxury hotel in the James Center Complex opened in 1987. Rooms are furnished in contemporary style, and the lobby is homey despite the Italian marble. *100 S. 12th St., 23219, tel. 804/344–7000 or 800/843–6664. 375 rooms. Facilities: indoor/outdoor pool; sun deck; health club with racquetball, squash courts, indoor track, Nautilus, whirlpool, saunas; 3 restaurants; bar. AE, D, DC, MC, V.*

Expensive **The Berkeley Hotel.** Right in Shockoe slip, this new, small hotel caters to businesspeople and those who want to be in the thick of things. The owner's early map collection decorates the public rooms, adding to the Colonial atmosphere. Eleven rooms have balconies. *1200 E. Cary St., tel. 804/780–1300, fax 804/343–1885. 55 rooms. Facilities: restaurant, 3 meeting rooms, free use of pool and fitness center at Capital Club, free valet parking. AE, D, DC, MC, V.*
Richmond Marriott. The lobby of this luxury hotel near the 6th Street Marketplace has a marble floor and crystal chandeliers; rooms are furnished in a contemporary style. Concierge service is offered. *500 E. Broad St., 23219, tel. 804/643–3400 or 800/228–9290. 400 rooms. Facilities: 3 restaurants, nightclub,*

indoor pool, exercise room, tanning parlor. *AE, D, DC, MC, V.*

Moderate–Expensive **Linden Row.** Seven Federal row houses connected by a gallery in back are a charming new addition to the hotel scene. Built 1847–53, they're furnished in a mix of Empire and Victorian antiques and reproductions, and the high-ceiling rooms are larger than usual. *100 E. Franklin St., tel. 804/783–7000 or 800/348–7424, fax 804/648–7504. 69 rooms. Facilities: restaurant, meeting room, use of YMCA, free valet parking, complimentary Continental breakfast, wine and cheese. AE, DC, MC, V.*

Moderate **Days Inn North.** This three-story motel is located 2 miles from downtown. *1600 Robin Hood Rd., 23220, tel. 804/353–1287. 87 rooms. Facilities: restaurant, bar, outdoor pool. AE, D, DC, MC, V.*

The Arts

The campus of Virginia Commonwealth University is usually teeming with artistic activity. Events here and throughout the city are listed in the *Times-Dispatch* and the *News-Leader*.

Theater **Barksdale Theatre,** in historic Hanover Tavern (tel. 804/537–5333), built in 1723, was the first dinner theater in the country, founded in 1953. Performances are given Wednesday through Saturday. Touring companies are often featured at the **Carpenter Center** (tel. 804/782–3900), a restored 1928 motion-picture palace. A unique Moorish-style auditorium called **The Mosque** (tel. 804/780–4213), at Main and Laurel streets, is worth a peek even when the stage is dark. The **Swift Mill Creek Playhouse** (tel. 804/748–4411) is a dinner theater set in a 17th-century gristmill. The Virginia Museum of Fine Arts maintains an equity theater, **Theatre Virginia** (tel. 804/367–0831).

Music The **Richmond Symphony** (tel. 804/788–1212), more than 30 years old, often features internationally known guest performers. Members of the orchestra perform as **The Sinfonia** for concerts of chamber music; and with popular guest artists, the versatile orchestra plays as **The Richmond Pops.**

Dance There are two professional ballet companies in town: the **Richmond Ballet** (tel. 804/359–0906) and the more experimental **Concert Ballet of Virginia** (tel. 804/780–1279).

Nightlife

Comedy The **Richmond Comedy Club** (1218 E. Cary St., tel. 804/745–3166) is modeled on successful establishments in New York and Los Angeles.

Folk At **The Jade Elephant** (909 W. Grace St., tel. 804/353–9674) you can enjoy cheap, well-made drinks while you listen to performers who usually appear solo.

Jazz **Benjamin's** (2053 W. Broad St., tel. 804/355–3667) is a favorite with younger Richmonders.

Bogart's (203 N. Lombardy St., tel. 804/353–9280) is a cozy club.

Rock   **The Flood Zone** (18th and Main Sts., tel. 804/644–0935) is a converted recording studio where you can listen and dance to live music, or listen and watch from the balcony.

The Historic Triangle

The Historic Triangle comprises Williamsburg, Jamestown, and Yorktown, sites that figure crucially in the pre-independent history of the United States. Williamsburg, once the capital of a colony that extended into present-day Minnesota, is now most famous for its Historic Area, restored to 18th-century perfection. Jamestown is where the English first settled successfully in North America; it is no longer an inhabited town. Yorktown, the site of the last major battle of the War of Independence, remains a living—albeit minuscule—community. About an hour's drive southeast of Richmond, via I-64, the three historic towns themselves are linked by the scenic, 23-mile-long Colonial Parkway.

Numbers in the margin correspond to points of interest on the Williamsburg and Environs map.

❶   Begin at **Colonial Williamsburg**, which is a marvel. The Historic Area comprises 173 acres of restored buildings populated by costumed interpreters and craftspeople. In the various shops you can observe coopers, milliners, wigmakers, and other tradesmen at their tasks, and their wares are for sale nearby. The taverns serve period-style food and beverages.

Begin at the visitor center, where you buy your tickets. Here you can watch an introductory movie, starring Jack Lord (of "Hawaii Five-O" fame) as an apocryphal patriot in the early 1770s. *I-64 Exit 56, tel. 804/229-1000. Admission: The Patriot's Pass ($26 adults, $12.50 children) is good for a year and admits the bearer to every Colonial Williamsburg–run site, including Bassett Hall and Carter's Grove Plantation. A range of less expensive tickets is available for those who haven't the time or inclination to see every site. Tickets are also sold at the courthouse in the Historic Area. In winter, some of the sites close down on a rotating basis; Carter's Grove closes in Jan. and Feb.; otherwise, every attraction except DeWitt Wallace (whose hours change frequently) is open daily. For a Vacation Planner, write Colonial Williamsburg, Box C, Williamsburg, VA 23187 (tel. 800/447-8679).*

A good three or four days can be spent in Colonial Williamsburg alone—there's so much to see and do. Be sure to allow enough time, because this place is too good to rush through. You have to tour the Historic Area on foot, but in case you get tired, shuttle buses follow a route along the perimeter of the area and will take you to and from the visitor center. There are some 25 attractions on and off broad, mile-long Duke of Gloucester Street, which serves as the spine of the whole area; you should start at its east end, which is closest to the visitor center and includes the building that made the town so important.

At the east end of Duke of Gloucester is the **Capitol**, where you can take an informative tour that explains the earliest stages in the development of American democracy from its English parliamentary roots. Here the pre-Revolutionary House of Burgesses, made up of the rising gentry, challenged the bigger landowners who sat on the royally appointed Council, an almost

Williamsburg and Environs

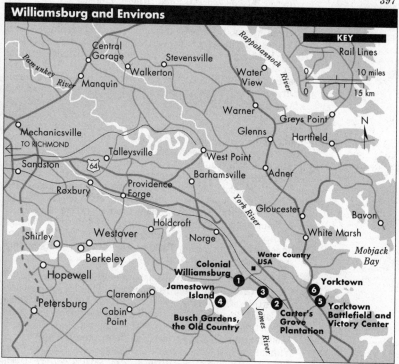

medieval institution. It was the House that eventually arrived at the resolutions that amounted to rebellion. In the courtroom you will hear the harsh Georgian sentences meted out: for instance, petty theft was a capital crime. Note this official building's ornate interior, characteristic of aristocratic Virginia—a marked contrast to the plain town meeting halls in New England, where other Founding Fathers were governing themselves.

The **Governor's Palace,** at the center of Duke of Gloucester Street, was completed in 1720 for Alexander Spotswood, and after the Revolution it housed the Commonwealth's first two governors, Patrick Henry and Thomas Jefferson. It burned in 1781; a 20th-century reconstruction stands on the original foundation. Little inside is original, but the antiques are matched to an extraordinary inventory of 16,000 items. The lavish decorations include 800 guns and swords arrayed on the walls and ceilings of several rooms.

Anchoring the west end of the street is the **Wren Building,** part of the campus of the College of William and Mary, the second-oldest college in the United States (founded in 1693). This building, erected in 1695, was based on the work of Sir Christopher Wren, the London architect for whom it was named—and who never made it to the Colonies. The professors' Common Room suggests Oxford and Cambridge, which were models for this institution. Jefferson studied and later taught law here—to James Monroe, among others.

Sharing the limelight with the handsome public buildings, restored homes, tidy reconstructed shops, and costumed interpreters are three very personal legacies from some modern-day benefactors of this historic town. The Public Hospital serves as Colonial disguise for the relatively new **DeWitt Wallace Decorative Arts Gallery** on Francis Street, where furniture, textiles, prints, metals, and ceramics from England and America are on display. The collection includes a famous full-length portrait of Washington by Charles Willson Peale. The **Abby Aldrich Rockefeller Folk Art Center,** a mile away on South England Street (a good time to take the shuttle bus), is a showcase for American "decorative usefulwares," such as toys, furniture, weathervanes, and quilts, along with folk paintings and sculptures. This is a populist complement to the exquisite DeWitt Wallace. Eclectic and precious furnishings make **Bassett Hall** a most personal house museum. Mr. and Mrs. John D. Rockefeller, Jr., who bankrolled the restoration of Colonial Williamsburg, beginning in the 1920s, lived in this two-story 18th-century house among Chinese, American, and English antiques. The 19th-century Turkish prayer rugs are outstanding specimens.

② About six miles east of Williamsburg on U.S. 60 is the palatial **Carter's Grove Plantation.** The house, built in 1750, is more luxurious than others of the period, since it was built as a showcase by Carter Burwell, whose grandfather King Carter had made his fortune elsewhere among the family's vast holdings. Though atypical, it is perfectly authentic and the epitome of Williamsburg in all its educational glamour. *Tel. 804/229–1000. Admission included in Patriot's Pass; separately, $7. Open daily 9–5. Closed Jan., Feb., first 2 weeks in Dec.*

③ For sheer contrast, you might stop at **Busch Gardens,** three miles east of Williamsburg on U.S. 60. This 360-acre, razzle-dazzle family entertainment park features water and other rides, shows, and eight European hamlets (*see* What to See and Do with Children, at the beginning of this chapter, *above*).

④ Nine miles west of Williamsburg on the Colonial Parkway is **Jamestown Island,** the site, in 1607, of the first permanent English settlement in North America. All that is left of the city is its foundations and the ruins of a 1639 tower—now part of the Memorial Church, built on the site of the original. The island is ringed by a five-mile nature drive. There are guided tours daily during the summer and on weekends in the spring. *Tel. 804/ 229–1733. Cost: $5 per car, $2 per pedestrian or cyclist. Open daily 9–6:30 June–Labor Day, 9–5 rest of year. Closed Christmas.*

As you leave the island (which is linked by a small isthmus to the rest of Virginia), stop at **Glass House Point,** at the park entrance, to observe a demonstration of glass-blowing, an unsuccessful business venture of the early colonists.

Adjacent to Jamestown Island is **Jamestown Settlement,** a living-history museum formerly known as Jamestown Festival Park. A version of the early fort has been built, and within it "colonists" cook, make armor, and tell of a hard life under thatched roofs and between walls of wattle and daub. In the Indian Village, enter a wigwam and watch a costumed interpreter make tools and pottery. Stroll to the pier and inspect reproductions of the boats in which the settlers arrived. *Be-*

tween Rte. 31 and Colonial Pkwy., tel. 804/229–1607. Admission: $6.50 adults, $3 children. Open daily 9–7 June 15–Aug. 15, 9–5 rest of year. Closed Christmas and New Year's Day.

5 Fourteen miles east of Williamsburg on the Parkway is **Yorktown Battlefield.** In the visitor center here is a museum with George Washington's original field tent, pitched and furnished as it was during the fighting. You can see the battlefield by self-guided auto tour, stopping at the signs. For $2 the gift shop will rent you a cassette player with a taped tour to hear as you drive around. *Tel. 804/898–3400. Admission free. Visitor center open daily 8:30–5:30, with extended hours in the spring, summer, and fall. Closed Christmas.*

On the western edge of the battlefield is the **Yorktown Victory Center,** where you will find a Continental Army encampment, with tents and a covered wagon. Costumed soldier-interpreters will try to enlist you and then answer your questions. Indoor sight-and-sound presentations are arranged along a street of a generalized 18th-century town. *Exit Colonial Pkwy. at VA 238, tel. 804/887–1776. Admission: $5 adults, $2.50 children. Open daily 9–7 June 15–Aug. 15, 9–5 rest of year. Closed Christmas and New Year's Day.*

6 Follow Route 238 into **Yorktown,** whose Main Street is a picturesque array of preserved 18th-century buildings, many still in use. **Moore House,** where the terms of surrender were negotiated, and **Nelson House,** the residence of a Virginia governor and signer of the Declaration of Independence, are open for tours in summer. On adjacent Church Street is **Grace Church,** built in 1697 and still an active Episcopal congregation. In rustic quarters on the York is **Yorktown Watermen's Museum,** exhibiting artifacts of Chesapeake fishermen. *309 Water St., tel. 804/887–2641. Admission: $2 adults, 50¢ children. Open Tues.–Sat. 10–4, Sun. 1–4. Closed Jan.–Mar.*

From Yorktown, return to Richmond on I–64. If you want to go on to Charlottesville and the Shenandoah Valley, circle around Richmond on I–295 and continue west on I–64 to Charlottesville. If you want to return to Washington instead, it's about an hour-and-a-half drive north on I–95.

Sports and Outdoor Activities

Bicycling Colonial Williamsburg ticketholders can rent bicycles at the Lodge on South England Street; everyone else can try **Bikesmith** (tel. 804/229–9858) on York Street. A 20-mile route is mapped out in the pamphlet "Biking through America's Historic Triangle," available at bike shops.

Golf **Colonial Williamsburg** (tel. 804/220–7696) operates two courses, nine- and 18-hole. **Kingsmill Resort** (tel. 804/253–3906), near Busch Gardens, has two courses.

Tennis In Williamsburg, **Colonial Williamsburg** (tel. 804/220–7794) has six courts, **Kingsmill** (tel. 804/253–3945) has 10 clay and two hard courts open to the public, and there are public courts at **Kiwanis Park** on Longhill Road and at Quarterpath Park on Pocahontas Street.

Dining and Lodging

The following dining price categoies have been used: *Very Expensive*, over $30; *Expensive*, $20–$30; *Moderate*, $10–$20; *Inexpensive*, under $10.

The following lodging price categories have been used: *Very Expensive*, over $120; *Expensive*, $90–$120; *Moderate*, $50–$90; *Inexpensive*, under $50.

Williamsburg
Dining
★ **The Regency Room.** This Continental restaurant in the Williamsburg Inn is the place to dine if you're looking for an elegant atmosphere, attentive service, and excellent cuisine. Crystal chandeliers, Oriental silkscreen prints, and full silver service set the tone. Specialties include rack of lamb, carved at the table; lobster bisque; and rich ice cream desserts. *S. Francis St., tel. 804/229–1000. Tie and jacket required for dinner and Sun. brunch; informal for breakfast and lunch. Reservations advised. AE, MC, V. Very Expensive.*

★ **The Trellis.** Although it's in an old Colonial building, the hardwood floors, ceramic tiles, and green plants evoke the feeling of being in a country inn in the Napa Valley. There are five small, cozy dining rooms, one overlooking historic Duke of Gloucester Street. The wine vault has 8,000 bottles, most from California vineyards, a few from Virginia. Try the grilled swordfish served with crispy fried leeks and sautéed onions, and Death by Chocolate dessert, seven layers of chocolate topped with cream sauce. *Merchant Sq., tel. 804/229–8610. Dress: informal. Reservations advised. AE, MC, V. Expensive.*

Lodging
★ **The Williamsburg Inn.** Adjacent to the Historic Area, and owned and operated by Colonial Williamsburg, the inn is the grand hotel of Williamsburg. Built in 1932, it is decorated in luxurious English Regency style throughout. The surrounding Colonial houses, also part of the inn, are decorated in Federalist style but with modern kitchens and baths. The Tazewell Club—a $5-million facility with full fitness offerings as well as conference rooms and executive suites—is available to guests of any of the Colonial Williamsburg operated properties. *136 E. Francis St., 23185, tel. 804/229–1000 or 800/447–8679. 232 rooms, 150 in inn, 82 in Colonial houses. Facilities: outdoor pool, golf, tennis, health club, restaurant, lounge, tavern. AE, MC, V. Very Expensive.*

The Motor House. This newly renovated motel—another official Colonial Williamsburg hostelry—is on the grounds of the visitor center. Rooms are in separate buildings set in a pine grove. All inn facilities are open to motel guests. *Information Center Dr., 23187, tel. 804/229–1000 or 800/447–8679. 219 rooms. Facilities: 2 pools, miniature golf, putting green, tennis, playground, cafeteria, restaurant. AE, MC, V. Expensive.*

Heritage Inn. This is a charming and comfortable inn one mile from the Historic Area. The three-story building is about 25 years old and decorated inside and out in Colonial style. *1324 Richmond Rd., 23185, tel. 804/229–6220 or 800/782–3800. 54 rooms. Facilities: outdoor pool with patio, restaurant. AE, DC, MC, V. Moderate.*

Bassett Motel. Three blocks from the Historic Area, this single-story brick property is quiet, well run, and family oriented. *800 York St. (U.S. 60), 23185, tel. 804/229–5175. 18 rooms. MC, V. Inexpensive.*

Yorktown
Dining

Nick's Seafood Pavilion. This riverside eatery has a wide selection of fresh seafood—including seafood shish kebab (lobster, shrimp, scallops, tomatoes, peppers, mushrooms, and onion, served with pilaf and topped with brown butter) and a buttery lobster pilaf—along with Chinese dishes and a fine baklava. *Water St., tel. 804/887–5269. Dress: informal. Reservations advised. AE, DC, MC, V. Expensive.*

The Arts and Nightlife

The Arts
A variety of popular song and dance shows (country, gospel, opera, German folk) are held in several theaters at **Busch Gardens,** and the 5,000-seat Royal Palace Theater there features famous pop stars of every kind. The 10,000-seat W&M Hall at the **College of William and Mary** is also the scene of concerts by well-known artists on tour, where student drama (tel. 804/221–4000) also goes on during the school year.

Nightlife
J.B.'s Lounge at the Fort Magruder Inn near Williamsburg (tel. 804/220–2250) has a bar with some rock music and a transient crowd.

Charlottesville and the Shenandoah Valley

Charlottesville is at the heart of "Mr. Jefferson's Country," as the locals proudly call it. The influence of the Sage of Monticello is inescapable anywhere in the Commonwealth (and far beyond its borders), but around here, in Albemarle County and in Orange County to the north, it is downright palpable. Also here are sites associated with other giants among his contemporaries and with crucial events in American history.

Since Jefferson founded the University of Virginia in 1819, this area has been a cultural center. The countryside has been discovered by an array of celebrities, including Jessica Lange and Sissy Spacek, who have settled here in recent years. A growing community of writers and artists is making this affluent area the "Santa Fe of the East Coast": a colony of the intellectual and the fashionable in a historic and remote setting.

The Shenandoah Valley is best known for its rugged beauty and rural charm, yet its cities and towns have much to offer in the way of history and culture. Staunton preserves the birthplace of Woodrow Wilson, the 28th president of the United States and the latest of eight from Virginia.

Numbers in the margin correspond to points of interest on the Shenandoah Valley and the Highlands map.

❶ Start in **Charlottesville** at the Visitors Center, where you can get oriented. The people here are glad to answer your questions about attractions and accommodations in the area and the whole state. A free extensive permanent exhibition, "Thomas Jefferson at Monticello," provides background on the house and its legendary occupant. On display are artifacts recovered during recent archaeological excavations. Do not miss it, before or after Monticello; it will make the experience at least twice as rich, since there is so much that is not explained on the tour. *Rte. 20S from Charlottesville (Monticello exit off I–64),*

Shenandoah Valley and the Highlands

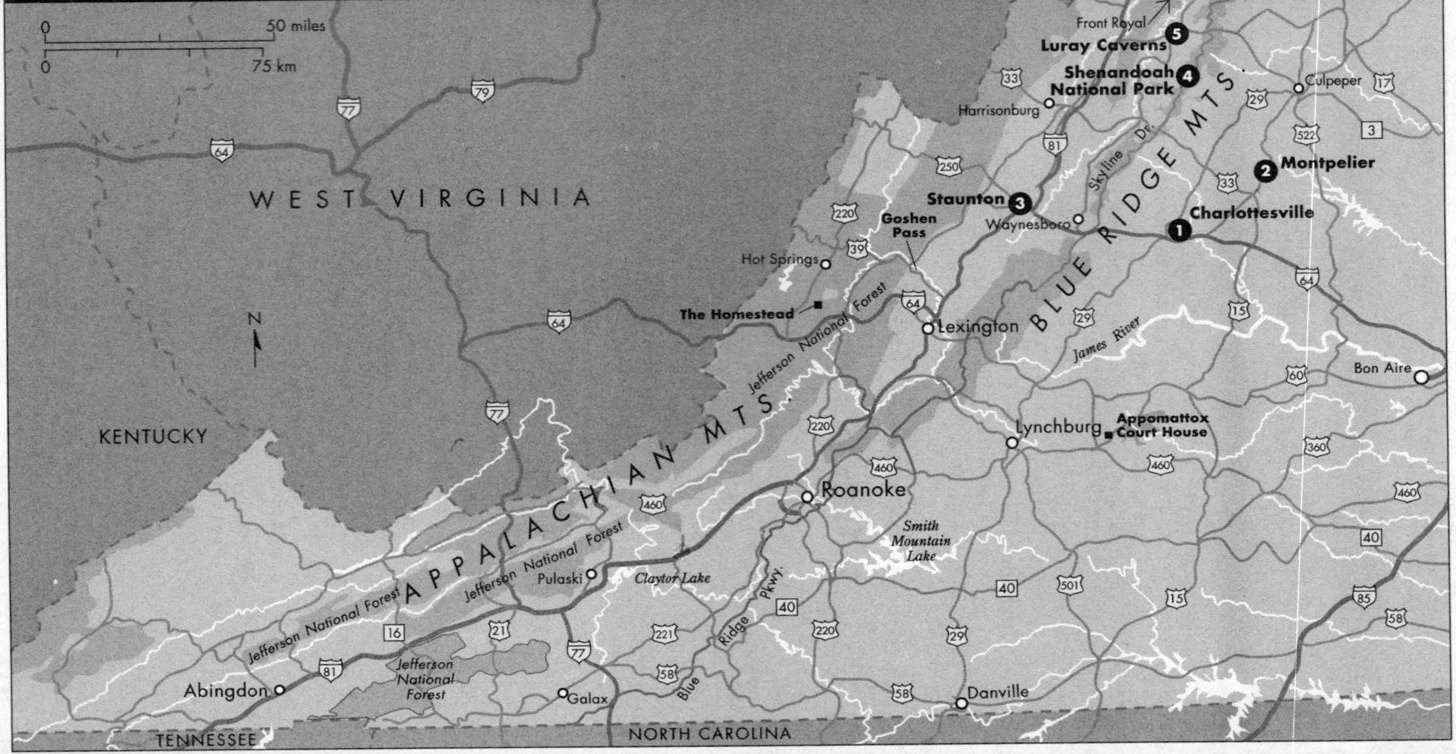

WEST VIRGINIA

KENTUCKY

NORTH CAROLINA

TENNESSEE

BLUE RIDGE MTS

APPALACHIAN MTS

Jefferson National Forest

Jefferson National Forest

Jefferson National Forest

Culpeper

Montpelier **2**

Charlottesville **1**

Bon Aire

Front Royal

Luray Caverns **5**

Shenandoah National Park **4**

Skyline Dr.

Harrisonburg

Staunton **3**

Waynesboro

Lexington

Goshen Pass

Hot Springs

The Homestead

Lynchburg

Appomattox Court House

Danville

Roanoke

Smith Mountain Lake

Blue Ridge Pkwy.

Clayton Lake

Pulaski

Galax

Abingdon

James River

James

50 miles

75 km

N

tel. 804/977–1783. Open weekdays 9–5 (until 5:30 Mar.–Oct.). Closed Christmas Day.

There's not really a whole lot to see in Charlottesville itself, though the visitor center does have a walking-tour map of the downtown historic district and a complete list of crafts and antiques shops, of which the city has a nice supply. The main shopping area is the Downtown Mall, spread along six blocks of Main Street. Fountains, outdoor restaurants, and restored buildings line the street, which has been bricked over and restricted to pedestrians. At the west end of town is the **University of Virginia,** one of the most distinguished institutions of higher education in the nation. It was founded and designed by Thomas Jefferson, who called himself its "father" in his own epitaph. Experts polled during the U.S. Bicentennial named his campus "the proudest achievement of American architecture in the past 200 years." You will be struck by the innovative beauty of the "academical village": it is subtle—almost delicate—and totally practical. Students vie for rooms in the original pavilions that flank the Lawn, a graduated expanse that flows down from the Rotunda, a half-scale replica of the Pantheon in Rome. Behind the pavilions are gardens and landscaping laced with serpentine walls. To arrange a free one-hour tour, call 804/924–3239.

Time Out Have lunch with UVA students at one of their haunts: **Martha's Café** (11 Elliewood Ave., tel. 804/971–7530). Try the enchiladas or a vegetarian entrée. In warm weather, ask for a table on the patio, where the plantings are lush and appealing.

Monticello is the most famous of Jefferson's homes, and his lasting monument to himself—an ingenious masterpiece created over more than 40 years. Not typical of any style, it is characteristic of Jefferson, who made a statement with every detail: the staircases are narrow and hidden because he considered them unsightly and wasteful of space, and contrary to plantation tradition, his outbuildings are in the back, not on the east side, where his guests arrived. In these respects, as in its overall conception, Monticello was a subversive structure, a classical repudiation of the prevalent English Georgian style and the colonial mentality behind it.

As if to reflect this revolutionary aspect, a concave mirror in the entrance hall presents you with your own image upside down. Throughout the house are Jefferson's inventions, including a seven-day clock and a "polygraph," a two-pen contraption with which he could make a copy of his correspondence as he wrote it. The Thomas Jefferson Center for Historic Plants features interpretive gardens, exhibits, and a sales area. The tour guides are happy to answer questions, but they have to move you through quickly since there is always another group waiting. It is impossible to see everything in one visit. *On Rte. 53 (off Rte. 20), 2 mi southeast of Charlottesville, tel. 804/295–8181 or 295–2657. Admission: $7 adults, $6 senior citizens, $3 children. Open daily 9–4:30 Nov.–Feb., 8–5 rest of year. Closed Christmas.*

Like its grand neighbor, modest **Ash Lawn–Highland** is marked by the personality of its owner. This is no longer the simple farmhouse built for James Monroe, who lived in the small L-shaped single story at the rear. A subsequent owner added the more prominent two-story section. Yet the furnishings are mostly original, and it is not hard to imagine Monroe here at his beloved retreat. The small rooms are crowded with presents from notable contemporaries and with souvenirs from his time as envoy to France. Such coziness befits the fifth president, the first from the middle class. Today Ash Lawn is a working plantation where spectacular peacocks roam the grounds. *On Rte. 795 (off Rte. 53), 2 mi past Monticello, tel. 804/293-9539. Admission: $6 adults, $5.50 senior citizens, $2 children. Open daily 9-6 Mar.- Oct., 10-5 rest of year. Closed Thanksgiving, Christmas, and New Year's Day.*

Because of its proximity to Monticello and Ash Lawn, **The Historic Michie Tavern** also has become a popular attraction. Most of the complex was constructed in 1784 at Earlysville, 17 miles away, and moved here piece by piece in 1927. Costumed hostesses lead you into a series of rooms, where you hear recorded interpretations of the interiors. A visit here is not as entertaining or educational as the tour of the Rising Sun Tavern in Fredericksburg (*see* Exploring Northern Virginia, *above*): the narration is less informative, and the conditions are too tidy. The restaurant serves mediocre "Colonial" fare (fried chicken) for lunch. The old gristmill has a gift shop. *On Rte. 53 near Monticello, tel. 804/977-1234. Admission: $5 adults; $4.50 senior citizens, students, and the military; $1 children under 12. Open daily 9-5. Closed Christmas and New Year's Day.*

About an hour north of Charlottesville is another presidential residence, recently opened to the public. Originally the home of James Madison, **Montpelier** in its present condition has more to do with its 20th-century owners, the du Pont family, who enlarged and redecorated it. This dual legacy poses a dilemma in the restoration, since the house only vaguely resembles itself in Madison's day. Markings on walls, floors, and ceilings show the locations of underlying door and window frames, etc., as a preliminary step to future restoration work. The process of restoration is slow, to the credit of the painstaking preservationists of the National Trust. In the meantime, it takes your imagination and your guide's eloquent narration to appreciate the history of this mostly empty house. The house can be seen only on a 1½- to 2-hour guided tour, which begins with a slide show on the history of the house, then takes you on a shuttlebus tour of the farm and paddock area, followed by a tour of the mansion and another slide show, free time to wander the delightful grounds and gardens, and a shuttle-bus tour of the cemetery where James, Dolley, and other Madisons are buried. *On Rte. 20, outside the town of Orange, tel. 703/672-2728 or 672-2206. Admission: $6 adults; $5 senior citizens; $1 children 6-12, under 6 free. Open daily 10-4. Closed major holidays.*

Waynesboro, 28 miles west of "Mr. Jefferson's Country" on I-64, is the southern terminus of the Skyline Parkway, which some travelers may want to drive north on from here. Those with a bit more time for historic exploring, however, will find two interesting attractions 11 miles to the west of Waynesboro in **Staunton** (pronounced "Stan-ton"), a town with a distinguished past. It was once the seat of vast Augusta County—formed in 1738 and encompassing present-day West Virginia, Kentucky, Ohio, and Indiana—and was briefly the capital of Virginia (the general assembly fled here from the British in 1781). The **Historic Staunton Foundation** (tel. 703/885-7676) offers free one-hour guided tours of the town every Saturday morning at 11, Memorial Day through October, departing from the Woodrow Wilson Birthplace (24 N. Coalter St.). A brochure is available for a self-guided tour.

In the **Woodrow Wilson House,** the president was born in 1856. The house has been restored, with period antiques and some original pieces, to reflect its time as the residence of an antebellum Presbyterian minister (which is what Woodrow's father was). Wilson's presidential limousine, a 1919 Pierce-Arrow sedan, is on display in the garage. *24 N. Coalter St., next door to the Welcome Center (I–81 to I–64 at Exit 57), tel. 703/885– 0897. Admission: $3.50 adults, $3 senior citizens, $1 children. Open 9–6 daily Memorial Day–Labor Day, 9–5 Mar.–Memorial Day and Labor Day–Dec., 9–5 Mon.–Sat. rest of the year. Closed Thanksgiving, Christmas, and New Year's Day.*

Just outside town is the new **Museum of American Frontier Culture,** an outdoor living museum that shows the beginnings of agrarian life in America. Four 18th-century farmsteads have been created from original buildings brought from Northern Ireland, England, Germany, and upland Virginia. The attention to authenticity and detail is painstaking. For instance, master craftsmen were brought in from Ulster to thatch the roofs on farm buildings that were transported here from County Tyrone. Livestock have been backbred and ancient seeds germinated in order to create an environment accurate in all respects. *230 Frontier Dr., off I–81 at Exit 57 to Rte. 250W, tel. 703/332–7850. Admission: $4 adults, $3.60 senior citizens, $2 children. Open daily 9–8 Memorial Day–Labor Day, 9–5 rest of year. Closed Christmas and New Year's Day.*

From Waynesboro, the **Skyline Drive** winds 105.4 scenic miles north over the mountains. It must be admitted that the justifiable fame of the Skyline Drive has its drawbacks. The holiday and weekend crowds in high season—spring or fall—can slow traffic (already held to a maximum speed of 35 mph) to a crawl and put enormous strain on the few lodges, campsites, and eating places along the way. But for those seeking easily accessible wilderness and stunning views, there are few routes that can compete with this one. The Drive runs through the length ④ of the **Shenandoah National Park** and affords spectacular vistas of the Shenandoah Valley to the west and the rolling country of the Piedmont to the east. Hundreds of miles of hiking trails (including a section of the Appalachian Trail), canoeing on the Shenandoah River, and trout fishing in the rushing streams provide many incentives for the action-minded, and the rangers supervise a variety of activities (outlined in the *Shenandoah Overlook,* a free newspaper you can pick up as you enter the park). It's better to choose another route in the winter; most facilities are closed from November through April, and parts of the Drive itself can be closed due to treacherous conditions. So come during the fine weather, but bring a sweater—temperatures can be brisk. *For information, contact the Park Superintendent, Box 348, Rte. 4, Luray 22835, tel. 703/999–2229. Admission to the park and the Drive: $5 per car; $2 per person on foot, bicycle, or motorcycle.*

You'll also want that sweater for one not-to-be-missed detour: ⑤ **Luray Caverns,** the largest in the state and only nine miles west of the Drive. For millions of years the water has seeped through the limestone and clay to create a variety of suggestive rock and mineral formations. The world's only "Stalacpipe Organ" is composed of stalactites hanging from the ceiling (stalagmites rise from the floor), which are tuned to concert pitch and tapped by rubber-tipped plungers under the organist's control. A one-hour tour starts every 20 minutes. *West on Rte. 211 from Skyline Dr., tel. 703/743-6551. Admission: $9 adults, $8 senior citizens, $4.50 children. Open daily 9-7 June 15-Labor Day, 9-6 Mar. 15-June 15 and after Labor Day to Nov. 14, 9-4 rest of year.*

At the northern end of the Drive, at **Front Royal**, get onto I-66 to return to Washington.

About 35 miles east of Front Royal, you can turn north on U.S. 15 for a drive around Virginia horse country. Touring the well-tended countryside is a pleasure; its history is detailed in exhibits at the **Loudoun County Museum and Visitors Center** in Leesburg (16 W. Loudoun St., tel. 703/777-0519). **Oatlands,** six miles south of Leesburg on U.S. 15, is a former 5,000-acre plantation built by a great-grandson of the famous King Carter. In 1827, a stately portico was added to the original 1803 manor house. The house has been beautifully restored, and the manicured fields that remain host a variety of public and private equestrian events from spring to fall—including April's popular Loudoun Hunt Point-to-Point, a steeplechase that brings out the whole community for picnics on blankets and tailgates, and Draft Horse and Mule Day in late summer, when competing teams flex their muscles in pulling contests and craftspeople spread out their wares for an all-day fair. *Tel. 703/777-3174. Admission: $5 adults, $4 students and senior citizens, children under 12 free weekdays. Other charges apply for special events. Open Mon.-Sat. 10-5, Sun. 1-5. Closed from just before Christmas until mid-Mar.*

A mile north of Leesburg is **Morven Park,** a mansion open to the public, as well as a stronghold of horsedom: The **Westmoreland Davis Equestrian Institute** (a private riding school), the **Winmill Carriage Museum** (boasting over 100 horse-drawn vehicles), and the **Museum of Hounds and Hunting** make their home on this 1,200-acre estate. The price of admission includes entrance to 16 rooms in the mansion and the two museums. *Rte. 7 north from Leesburg, then follow signs, tel. 703/777-2414. Admission: $4 adults, $3.75 senior citizens, $2 children. Open Tues.-Sat. 10-5, Sun. 1-5 Memorial Day-Labor Day. Closed mid-Oct.-first week in May, weekends only at other times (call ahead).*

This may be Thoroughbred country, but the workhorse gets his day in the sun at Paeonian Springs's **American Work Horse Museum,** where two enormous live Clydesdales greet visitors. Here, the exhibits point out this unsung hero's contributions to the growth of our nation. *Rte. 7 west from Leesburg to Rte. 662, tel. 703/338-6290. Admission free. Open Wed. 9-5 Apr.-Oct., other times by appointment.*

On your way back to Washington on I-66, you can stop off at another major Civil War battlefield: **Manassas National Battlefield Park.** The self-guided tour begins at the visitor center, which offers exhibits and audiovisual presentations that greatly enhance the visit. Here the Confederacy won two important victories—and Stonewall Jackson won his famous nickname. Turn off at Route 234; the visitor center is half a mile north on the right. *Tel. 703/754-7107. Admission: $1 adults, children under 16 and senior citizens free. The visitor center is open daily 8:30-6 in summer, 8:30-5 rest of year; the park is open until dusk.*

From Manassas, it's about a 25-mile drive back into Washington.

Shopping

Paula Lewis (4th and Jefferson Sts., in Historic Court Square, 2 blocks north of Main St., Charlottesville, tel. 804/295-6244) specializes in handmade quilts from across the country.

Lewis Glaser Quill Pens (1700 Sourwood Pl., in the Hollymead neighborhood of Charlottesville, tel. 804/293-8531 or 800/446-6732) sells feather pens and pewter inkwells of the kind it has made for the U.S. Supreme Court and the British royal family.

Sports and Outdoor Activities

Canoeing Canoe rentals are available through **Front Royal Canoe** (Rte. 340, near Front Royal, tel. 703/635-5440), **Downriver Canoe Company** (Rte. 613, near Front Royal, tel. 703/635-5526), and **Shenandoah River Outfitters** (Rte. 684, near Luray, tel. 703/743-4159).

Fishing To take advantage of the trout that abound in Shenandoah National Park—in some 50 streams—obtain a five-day Virginia fishing license, which is available in season (early April through mid-October) at concession stands along Skyline Drive.

Golf **McIntire Park Golf Course** (Charlottesville, tel. 804/977-4111) and **Pen Park Golf Course** (Charlottesville, tel. 804/977-0615) offer nine holes each. **Caverns Country Club Resort** (Rte. 211 in Luray, tel. 703/743-6551) has a par-72 18-hole course along the river. **Greene Hills Golf Club** (Rte. 33 in Stanardsville, tel. 804/985-7328) has an 18-hole course open to the public.

Hiking There are 500 miles of trails through the **Shenandoah National Park.** The more popular trails are described in the guidebook available at the visitor centers.

Tennis **The Boar's Head Inn** in Charlottesville (*see* Lodging, *below*) offers tennis to nonguests as well as guests. **Caverns Country Club Resort** (Rte. 211 in Luray, tel. 703/743-6551) has four courts. There are **public courts** in Charlottesville at the intersection of 250 Bypass and McIntire Road and in Pen Park at Park Street and Rio Road (tel. 804/977-0615).

Spectator Sports

The **University of Virginia** is nationally or regionally ranked in several varsity sports. In season, you can watch the Cavaliers play first-rate ACC basketball in University Hall. There's also football at Scott Stadium, plus baseball, soccer, lacrosse, and more. Check *The Cavalier Daily* for listings.

In June and August, **jousting tournaments** are held at the Natural Chimneys area in Mt. Solon, north of Staunton and east of

I–81. The day's entertainment also includes a parade and crafts exhibitions. *Tel. 703/350–2510. Park admission: $4 per car.*

Thirty minutes northwest of Front Royal, in West Virginia, is the **Charles Town Race Track** (tel. 304/725–7001), where thoroughbred racing goes on year-round, every day except Tuesday and Thursday.

Dining and Lodging

The following dining price categories have been used: *Very Expensive,* over $30; *Expensive,* $20–$30; *Moderate,* $10–$20; *Inexpensive,* under $10.

A B&B service for the area is **Guesthouse Bed & Breakfast, Inc.** (Box 5737, Charlottesville 22905, tel. 804/979–7264 or 804/979–8327). To see about staying in a private home or old, reconverted inn, contact the **Shenandoah Valley Bed & Breakfast Reservations Service** (Box 305, Broadway, VA 22815, tel. 703/896–9702).

The following lodging price categories have been used: *Very Expensive,* over $120; *Expensive,* $90–$120; *Moderate,* $50–$90; *Inexpensive,* under $50.

Charlottesville
Dining
★

C&O Restaurant. A boarded-up storefront hung with an illuminated Pepsi sign conceals one of the best restaurants in town. Downstairs is a lively bistro serving pâtés, cheeses, and light meals. The stark white formal dining room upstairs features excellent regional French cuisine. Recommended are the coquilles St. Jacques—steamed scallops served in a sauce made of grapefruit juice, cream, and Dijon mustard—and, for an appetizer, the terrine de campagne, a pâté of veal, venison, and pork. The wine list includes 300 varieties. *515 E. Water St., tel. 804/971–7044. Upstairs, tie and jacket required; downstairs, informal. Reservations advised. Seatings at 6:30 and 9:30 for dining room. MC, V. Upstairs closed Sun. Very Expensive.*

The Galerie. Set amid woods and cornfields seven miles from town is an elegant restaurant reminiscent of a French country inn. Specialties include Norwegian salmon with raspberry and lime sauce; duckling braised in port wine and shallot sauce; and rich desserts like *vacherin glacé*—layers of grilled meringue and French vanilla ice cream topped with unsweetened whipped cream and chestnut sauce. The wine list includes 190 varieties. *Rte. 250W, tel. 804/823–5883. Tie and jacket required. Reservations advised. MC, V. Closed Mon. and Tues. Very Expensive.*

Old Mill Room. In a onetime gristmill (built in 1834), prints and posters of the mill, a fireplace, and wrought-iron chandeliers set the mood as waiters and waitresses in Colonial dress serve such offerings as prime rib and veal Oscar—veal topped with crabmeat, asparagus spears, and béarnaise sauce. Light meals are served in the Tavern downstairs. *In the Boar's Head Inn, U.S. 250W (3 mi from town), tel. 804/296–2181. Jacket required. Reservations advised. AE, DC, MC, V. Expensive.*

★ **Eastern Standard.** Here's another restaurant with a formal dining room upstairs and a bistro downstairs. Dining room specialties include rainbow trout stuffed with shiitake mushrooms, wild rice, and fontina cheese; oysters cooked in a champagne and caviar sauce; and loin of lamb with mint pesto. Curries and stirfried Asian dishes are also offered. The bistro is crowded and lively, with taped music, primarily jazz and rock. It serves pastas and light meals. *West End, Downtown Mall, tel. 804/ 295–8668. Dress: informal. Reservations advised for dining room. AE, MC, V. Dinner only. Upstairs closed Sun. Expensive.*

The Hardware Store. Deli sandwiches, burgers, salads, seafood, and ice cream from the soda fountain are the specialties in this former Victorian hardware shop. The store was built in 1890, and some of the original wood paneling and brick walls remain. There's outdoor dining in the warm months. *316 E. Main St., tel. 804/977–1518. Dress: informal. Reservations not needed. MC, V. Closed Sun. No dinner Mon. Moderate.*

Crozet Pizza. Twelve miles west of Charlottesville, you'll find some of Virginia's best pizza. There are 18 different toppings to choose from, including snow peas and asparagus spears. On weekends take-out must be ordered hours in advance. *Rte. 240, Crozet, tel. 804/823–2132. Dress: informal. Reservations not needed. No credit cards. Closed Sun. and Mon. Moderate.*

Lodging **Boar's Head Inn.** At this luxurious, quiet resort on two small lakes, rooms and suites are simple but elegant, furnished mostly with antiques. Some suites have fireplaces, some are efficiencies, and some rooms have king- or queen-size beds. *U.S. 250 (3 mi from town), Box 5307, Charlottesville 22905, tel. 804/ 296–2181. 175 rooms, 11 suites. Facilities: 5 restaurants (see Dining, above); complete health club, with 3 pools, squash and racquetball courts, tennis; biking; fishing; hot-air balloon rides. AE, DC, MC, V. Very Expensive.*

Omni Charlottesville. A recent addition to the luxury chain, this attractive hotel looms over the Downtown Mall. The decor is a mixture of modern and Colonial. *235 W. Main St., 22901, tel. 804/971–5500 or 800/843–6664. 209 rooms. Facilities: multilevel restaurant, bilevel lounge with live entertainment, atrium lobby lounge, indoor/outdoor pools, fitness center with saunas, whirlpool, exercise room. AE, DC, MC, V. Very Expensive.*

200 South Street Inn. Two historic houses, one of them a former brothel, have been combined and restored to create this old-fashioned inn in the historic district. Furnishings throughout are English and Belgian antiques. Many rooms have private sitting rooms, fireplaces, and whirlpools. *200 South St., 22901, tel. 804/979–0200. 20 rooms, all with private bath and canopy beds. AE, MC, V. Very Expensive.*

Sheraton Charlottesville. An elegant hotel a mile from town, near the university. *2350 Seminole Trail (U.S. 29, 3 mi north of jct. Rte. 250 Bypass), 22901, tel. 804/973–2121. 252 rooms. Facilities: indoor/outdoor pools, 2 tennis courts, jogging trails, 2 restaurants, lounge. AE, D, DC, MC, V. Expensive.*

Best Western–Cavalier Inn. Next to the university and an easy drive to Monticello. *105 Emmet St., 22905, tel. 804/296–8111 or 800/528–1234. 118 rooms. Facilities: outdoor pool, restaurant and lounge, cable TV. AE, D, DC, MC, V. Moderate.*

★ **English Inn.** This inn is a motel treatment of the bed-and-breakfast theme on a large but comfortable scale, located near the university. Continental breakfast is served in a 150-year-old, transplanted Tudor-style dining room with fireplace. There's an attractive three-story atrium lobby with cascading plants. Suites feature king-size beds and reproduction antiques; the other rooms have modern furnishings. *2000 Morton Dr. (jct. U.S. 29 and Rte. 250 Bypass), 22901, tel. 804/971–*

9900. 88 rooms, including 21 king suites with sitting room and wet bar. Facilities: large indoor pool, sauna, exercise equipment, restaurant lounge, cable TV. AE, DC, MC, V. Moderate.
Econo Lodge. Basic chain lodgings next to the university. *400 Emmet St., 22903, tel. 804/296–2104. 60 rooms. Facilities: outdoor pool. AE, D, DC, MC, V. Inexpensive.*

Orange **Mayhurst.** This old Victorian building is a cozy and comfortable
Lodging B&B about a half-hour northeast of Monticello, surrounded by
★ 36 acres of woods and hiking trails. It was built in 1859 by the
grandnephew of James Madison. All the rooms are decorated
with early Victorian antiques. Afternoon tea is served. *Box 707 (U.S. 15), Orange 22960, tel. 703/672–5597. 6 rooms with private bath, and a guesthouse. Facilities: pond for fishing and swimming. MC, V. Very Expensive.*

Staunton **Rowe's Family Restaurant.** This homey restaurant, with a
Dining bright and comfortable dining room filled with booths, has
been operated by the same family since 1947. Homemade baked
goods are outstanding. Specialties include Virginia ham,
steak, and chicken. *I–81 Exit 57, tel. 703/886–1833. Dress: informal. Reservations not needed. D, MC, V. Inexpensive.*

Lodging **Belle Grae Inn.** At this restored Victorian mansion, built in
1870, many rooms are furnished with rocking chairs and canopied or brass beds. Free breakfast and afternoon tea are
served. *515 W. Frederick St., 24401, tel. 703/886–5151. 12 rooms. Adults only. Facilities: bistro with live music Wed.–Sat., candlelight dinner in inn, light fare in garden restaurant. AE, DC, MC, V. Moderate.*
★ **Frederick House.** Three restored town houses dating to 1810
make up this inn in the center of the historic district. All the
rooms are decorated with antiques. Adjacent is a pub and restaurant. No smoking on the premises. *18 E. Frederick St., 24401, tel. 703/885–4220. 11 rooms; each with bath, cable TV, phones. AE, D, DC, MC, V. Moderate.*

The Arts

Dance, music, and theater events of every kind take place all
year at the **University of Virginia.** Check *The Cavalier Daily* for
details. The **McGuffey Art Center** (201 2nd St. NW, tel. 804/
295–7973), housed in a converted school building, contains the
studios of painters and sculptors, and is also the scene of musical and theatrical performances.

Nightlife

Folk **Miller's** (109 W. Main St., Downtown Mall, tel. 804/971–8511) is
a large and comfortable bar that also hosts jazz musicians.

Singles Postgraduate students are strongly represented at the bar at
Eastern Standard (Downtown Mall, tel. 804/295–8668).

Tour 6: The Southeast Coast to Orlando

Sandwiched between the amusement parks of Myrtle Beach, South Carolina, and the world's greatest amusement park, Walt Disney World in Orlando, Florida, is a stretch of Atlantic Ocean coast that seems made for pure pleasure. Three of the South's most gracious historic cities, Charleston, Savannah, and St. Augustine, preside grandly over their no-longer-bustling waterfronts, like belles whose beauty has grown quieter but no less lovely with age. South Carolina's Grand Strand and Florida's Jacksonville and Daytona areas boast mile after mile of fabulous beaches, each with their own distinctive type of sand, shells, and sun-worshippers. Between Charleston and Jacksonville, however, the coast is ragged, fringed with inlets and islands, some of which have been developed tastefully, some less tastefully, and others left windswept and wild.

This tour is a logical choice for families, but with Disney World beckoning at the end, parents will want to pick and choose only a few stops en route. On the other hand, travelers without children may want to begin the tour with the civilities of Charleston, relax for a while at a resort island along the road south, and complete the journey at Jacksonville or St. Augustine—though even adults unaccompanied by a child have certainly been known to enjoy themselves in Orlando. Because Interstate 95 runs almost the entire length of this tour, it's easy to tailor the tour to your own interests and schedule; simply return to I-95, bypass any number of sights, and pick up the tour farther south wherever you wish.

Tourist Information

South Carolina **Beaufort County Chamber of Commerce** (Box 910, 1006 Bay St., Beaufort 29901–0910, tel. 803/524–3163).

Charleston Visitor Information Center (375 Meeting St., tel. 803/853–8000).

Hilton Head Island Visitors & Convention Bureau (Box 5647, Hilton Head Island 29938, tel. 803/785–3673).

Georgetown County Chamber of Commerce and Information Center (U.S. 17, Georgetown 29442, tel. 803/546–8436).

Myrtle Beach Area Convention Bureau (710 21st. Ave. N., Ste. J, Myrtle Beach, SC 29577, tel. 803/448–1629 or for literature only, 800/356–3016).

Georgia **Jekyll Island Convention and Visitors Bureau** (901 Jekyll Island Causeway, Jekyll Island 31520, tel. 912/635–3636).

National Park Service (Cumberland Island National Seashore, Box 806, St. Mary's 31558, tel. 912/882–4335).

Savannah Area Convention and Visitors Bureau (222 W. Oglethorpe Ave., Savannah 31499, tel. 800/444–2427).

St. Simons Island Chamber of Commerce (Neptune Park, St. Simons Island 31522, tel. 912/638–9014).

Florida **Amelia Island-Fernandina Beach Chamber of Commerce** (102 Centre St., tel. 904/261–3248).

Destination Daytona! (126 E. Orange Ave., tel. 904/255–0415 or 800/854–1234).

Jacksonville and Its Beaches Convention & Visitors Bureau (6 E. Bay St., Suite 200, tel. 904/353–9736).

Kissimmee/St. Cloud Convention and Visitors' Bureau (1925 E. Irlo Bronson Memorial Hwy., Kissimmee 32742, tel. 407/847–5000, 800/432–9199 in FL, 800/327–9159 outside FL).

Orlando Visitor Information Center (8445 International Dr., Orlando 32819, tel. 407/363–5800).

St. Augustine Visitor Information Center (10 Castillo Dr., tel. 904/824–3334).

Festivals and Seasonal Events

Early Feb.–late Feb.: Speed Weeks is a three-week celebration of auto racing that culminates in the famous Daytona 500 in Daytona Beach. Contact Daytona International Speedway, Drawer S, Daytona Beach 32015, tel. 904/253–6711.

Mar.: SpringFest on Hilton Head Island features concerts, plays, films, art shows, theater—along with sporting events, food fairs, and minitournaments. Contact SpringFest, Box 5278-D, Hilton Head Island, SC 29938, tel. 803/842–3378.

Mid-March–mid-April: Festival of Houses in Charleston features tours of private homes, gardens, and churches, along with symphony galas, plantation oyster roasts, candlelight tours, and more. Contact Historic Charleston Foundation, 51 Meeting St., Charleston 29401, tel. 803/723–1623.

Late May–early June: Spoleto Festival USA, one of the world's greatest celebrations of the arts, fills Charleston with performances of opera, dance, theater, symphonic and chamber music performances, jazz, and the visual arts. Contact Spoleto Festival USA, Box 704, Charleston, SC 29402, tel. 803/722–2764.

Mid-May–early June: Piccolo Spoleto Festival, the spirited companion festival of Charleston's Spoleto Festival USA, showcases local and regional talent in every artistic discipline from jazz to puppetry. Contact the Office of Cultural Affairs, Piccolo Spoleto Festival, 133 Church St., Charleston 29401, tel. 803/724–7305.

June: Sun Fun Festival ushers in the summer on the Grand Strand, South Carolina.

Mid-July: Beaufort Water Festival in Beaufort, South Carolina, is a popular outdoor festival.

Aug.: Beach Music Festival is held on Jekyll Island, Georgia, and **Sea Island Festival** competes on nearby St. Simons Island.

Oct.: Oktoberfest is a major annual event in Savannah, Georgia.

Early Oct.: Moja Arts Festival celebrates the heritage of the African continent with arts events at sites throughout Charleston's historic district. Tel. 803/724–7305.

Oct.: Jacksonville Jazz Festival is a three-day event featuring jazz superstars, performances, arts and crafts, food, and the Great American Jazz Piano Competition. Tel. 904/353–7770.

What to See and Do with Children

Most of the attractions described below are described more fully in the tour that follows.

Among the many amusements in **Myrtle Beach,** kids especially enjoy the Myrtle Beach Pavilion and Amusement Park, Myrtle Waves Water Park (U.S. 17 Bypass and 10th Ave., N. Myrtle Beach, tel. 803/448–1026; open Memorial Day–Labor Day daily, May and Sept. weekends only), and the Myrtle Beach Grand Prix (U.S. 17 Bus. S, Surfside, across from Air Force base, tel. 803/238–2421; and Windy Hill, U.S. 17N, N. Myrtle Beach, tel. 803/272–6010; both open Mar.–Oct. daily) with its go-carts, bumper boats, and kiddie cars.

Families interested in staying at one of the barrier islands along the coast often choose **Hilton Head Island,** in South Carolina, because so many of its hotels and resorts offer youth programs, or **St. Simons Island,** Georgia, where Neptune Park offers some commercial amusements. **Hunting Island State Park** has playgrounds and is a fine family picnicking site.

The main attractions of Charleston and Savannah may be too staid for some youngsters, but families can still find diversions in these historic cities. Best bets for the **Charleston** area include the American Military Museum, the hands-on Discover Me Room at the Charleston Museum, and Herbie's Antique Car Museum (2140 Van Buren Rd., N. Charleston, tel. 803/747–7207; admission: $4, under 12 free), as well as the boat ride to Fort Sumter. West across the Ashley River is the Charles Towne Landing Animal Forest; a short drive north on U.S. 17 takes you to Palmetto Islands County Park (Long Point Rd., tel. 803/884–0832; admission: $1; open daily), with it Big Toy playground, a two-acre pond, a canoe trail, an observation tower, and marsh boardwalks. To keep children amused in **Savannah,** try the Science Museum and its planetarium (4405 Paulsen St., tel. 912/355–6705; admission: $2.50 adults, $1.50 children 12 and under; open Tues.–Sun.) or the excursion to Tybee Island, with its lighthouse, and the two forts along the way, Fort Pulaski and Fort Jackson. Girl Scouts and Brownies should appreciate the Juliette Gordon Low Girl Scout National Center, and young nature lovers can be taken to the Oatland Island Education Center (711 Sandtown Rd., tel. 912/897–3773; open weekdays), a 175-acre coastal forest preserve only 15 minutes from downtown Savannah.

Florida's northeastern beach towns have more to offer the younger set. **Jacksonville** has a fine zoo (I–95 north to Hecksher Dr. E., tel. 904/757–4463; admission: $4 adults, $2.50 children 3–18), and just south of St. Augustine on Highway A1A is **Marineland** (tel. 904/471–1111; admission: $12 adults, $7 children 3–11), with its lovable dolphins, sea lions, and seals. In **Daytona Beach,** there's the Castle Adventure fun park (200 Hagen Terr., on U.S. 92, tel. 904/238–3887; admission: $7 adults, $6 children), where you can play miniature golf, wander through a giant maze, and explore waterfalls, caves, and lush tropical landscaping. **Cocoa Beach** is a prime attraction, with Spaceport USA.

Walt Disney World in itself is an overwhelming reason to bring kids to **Orlando,** but families will also enjoy Sea World, Universal Studios Florida, and a number of other family amusements that have been developed in the area.

Arriving and Departing

By Plane The tour's starting point can be reached directly from the **Myrtle Beach Jetport,** served by American, American's American Eagle affiliate; Delta and its Atlantic Southeast Airlines affiliate; and USAir.

Charleston International Airport, in North Charleston, is on I–26, 12 miles west of downtown Charleston, and is served by American, Bankair, Delta, United, and USAir. Taxis to downtown Charleston average $13, plus tip. By car, take I–26S to its terminus, at U.S. 17, near the heart of the city.

Savannah International Airport, 8 miles west of downtown, is served by American, Continental, Delta, United, and USAir. Vans operated by **McCalls Coastal Express** (tel. 912/966–5364) leave the airport daily 6 AM–10 PM destined for downtown locations. The trip takes 20–30 minutes, and the one-way fare is $12. Taxi fare from the airport to downtown hotels is $15 for one person, $3 for each additional person. Cars should drive south on Dean Forest Drive to I–16, then east on I–16 into downtown Savannah. **Hilton Head Helicopters** (tel. 803/681–9120) offers shuttle service from Savannah's airport to Hilton Head Island.

More than 21 scheduled airlines and more than 30 charters operate in and out of **Orlando International Airport,** with direct service to more than 100 U.S. cities. A public bus runs between the airport and the downtown terminal of Tri-County Transit Authority (1200 W. South St., Orlando, tel. 407/841–8240; fare 75¢). **Mears Transportation Group** (tel. 407/423–5566) sends 11-passenger vans to Disney World and along Rte. 192 every 30 minutes; prices begin at $13 adults, $8 children 4–11. **Town & Country Limo** (tel. 407/828–3035) and **First Class Transportation** (tel. 407/578–0022) also offer limousine service. Taxis are the fastest way to travel (25–30 minutes to hotels), but will cost about $25–$35 plus tip.

By Train **Amtrak** (tel. 800/USA–RAIL) has regular service along the Eastern Seaboard, with daily stops in North Charleston (4565 Gaynor Ave., tel. 800/872–7245), Savannah (2611 Seaboard Coastline Dr., tel. 912/234–2611), Jacksonville, Sanford (23 miles from Orlando, 600 Persimmon Blvd. for the Auto Train), Orlando (1400 Sligh Blvd.), and Kissimmee (416 Pleasant St.).

By Bus **Greyhound/Trailways** has stations in North Charleston (3610 Dorchester Rd., tel. 803/722–7721), Savannah (610 W. Oglethorpe Avenue, tel. 912/233–7723), Jacksonville (tel. 904/356–5521), St. Augustine (tel. 904/829–6401), Daytona Beach (tel. 904/255–7076), and Orlando (300 W. Amelia St., tel. 407/843–7720).

By Car This tour's starting point, the Grand Strand of South Carolina, can be reached from all directions via Interstates 20, 26, 40, 77, 85, and 95, which connect with U.S. 17, the major north–south coastal route through the Strand and on to Charleston. Some 50 miles southwest of Charleston, U.S. 17 feeds into with I–95, the interstate highway that traces the coast on through Georgia and Florida as far south as Miami. Various state roads, bridges, and ferries lead from I–95 east to the resort towns and islands along the coast. Beginning at the northeast corner of Florida, on Amelia Island, Route A1A (given various names in each locality) is a slower and more scenic drive right along the coast. At Daytona, angle southwest on I-4 to Orlando.

Myrtle Beach and the Grand Strand

The Grand Strand, a resort area along the South Carolina coast, is one of the Eastern Seaboard's megafamily-vacation centers and the state's top tourist area. The main attraction, of course, is the broad, beckoning beach—55 miles of it, stretching from the North Carolina border south to Georgetown, with its hub at Myrtle Beach, whose population of 26,000 increases to about 350,000 in summer. It is here that you find the amusement parks and other children's activities that make the area so popular for family vacations, as well as most of the nightlife that keeps parents and teenagers happy after beach hours. North of Myrtle Beach, in the North Strand, there is Little River, with a thriving fishing and charter boat industry, and the several communities—each with its own small-town flavor—that make up North Myrtle Beach. In the South Strand, Surfside Beach and Garden City are family retreats of year-round and summer homes and condominiums. Farther south are Murrells Inlet, once a pirate's haven and now a popular fishing port, and Pawleys Island, one of the East Coast's oldest resorts. Historic Georgetown, the state's third-oldest city, forms the Strand's southern tip.

Numbers in the margin correspond to points of interest on the South Carolina Coast map.

❶ Our tour begins in **Myrtle Beach.** At the **Myrtle Beach Pavilion and Amusement Park,** you'll find activities for all ages and interests: thrill and kiddie rides, including the Carolinas' largest flume, plus video games, a teen nightclub, specialty shops, antique cars, and sidewalk cafés. *Ninth Ave. N and Ocean Blvd., tel. 803/626–5024. Fees for individual attractions; family discount book available. Open late May–Sept., daily 1 PM–midnight; Oct.–mid-May, weekends 1 PM–midnight.*

Nearby, at the **Guinness World Records Museum,** fantastic human and natural phenomena spring to life through videotapes, replicas, and other displays. *911 N. Ocean Blvd., tel. 803/448–4611. Admission: $3.95 adults; $2.95 children 7–12, under 7 free. Open mid-Mar.–early Oct., daily 10 AM–midnight.*

More of the unusual awaits at **Ripleys Believe It or Not Museum.** Among the more than 750 exhibits is an eight-foot, 11-inch wax replica of the world's tallest man. *901 N. Ocean Blvd., tel. 803/448–2331. Admission: $5.25 adults; $3.25 children 6–12, under 6 free. Open Apr.–Nov., daily 10 AM–10 PM. Closed Jan.–Feb.*

Drama, sound, and animation highlight religious, historical, and entertainment sections in the **Myrtle Beach National Wax Museum.** *1000 N. Ocean Blvd., tel. 803/448–9921. Admission: $4.50 adults; $2 children 6–12, under 6 free. Open Feb.–mid-Oct., daily 9 AM–9 PM. Closed rest of year.*

When your family's appetite for more raucous amusements has been sated, it's time to head out of town. Going south on Kings **❷** Highway, you'll come to **Murrells Inlet,** a picturesque little fish-

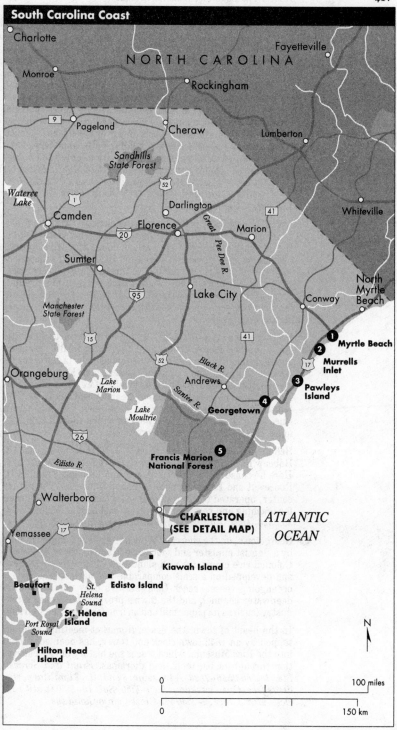

South Carolina Coast

ing village that boasts some of the most popular seafood restaurants on the Grand Strand. It's also a great place for chartering a fishing boat or joining a half- or full-day group excursion. Three miles south, on the grounds of a Colonial rice plantation, is the largest outdoor collection of American sculpture, with works by such American artists as Frederic Remington and Daniel Chester French. **Brookgreen Gardens** was begun in 1931 by railroad magnate/philanthropist Archer Huntington and his wife, Anna, herself a sculptor. Today, more than 400 works are set amid beautifully landscaped grounds, with avenues of live oaks, reflecting pools, and over 2,000 plant species. Also on the 9,000-acre site is a wildlife park, an aviary, a cypress swamp, nature trails, and an education center. It's a lovely, soothing place for a picnic. *18 mi south of Myrtle Beach off U.S. 17, tel. 803/237–4218. Admission: $5 adults; $2 children 6–12, under 6 free. Tape tours, $2.50 extra. Open daily 9:30– 4:45 except Christmas.*

Across the highway is **Huntington Beach State Park,** the 2,500-acre former estate of the Huntingtons. The park's focal point is the Moorish-style "castle" Atalaya, once the Huntingtons' home, now open to visitors in season. In addition to the splendid beach, there is surf fishing, nature trails, an interpretive center, a salt-marsh boardwalk, picnic areas, a playground, concessions, and a campground. *Tel. 803/237–4440. Admission free; parking fee in peak months; incidentals fees. Open daily during daylight hours.*

❸ Farther south is one of the first summer resorts on the Atlantic coast, **Pawleys Island.** Prior to the Civil War, wealthy planters and their families summered here to avoid malaria and other fevers that infested the swampy coastal region. Four miles long and a half-mile wide, it's made up mostly of weathered old summer cottages nestled in groves of oleander and oak trees. The famed Pawleys Island hammocks have been handmade here since 1880. In several shops, you can watch them being fashioned of rope and cord by local craftsfolk.

Bellefield Nature Center, south on U.S. 17, is at the entrance of Hobcaw Barony, the vast estate of the late Bernard M. Baruch. Here he consulted with such guests as President Franklin D. Roosevelt and Prime Minister Winston Churchill. The nature center, operated by the Belle W. Baruch Foundation, is used for teaching and research in forestry and marine biology. *Tel. 803/546–4623. Admission free. Open weekdays 10–5, Sat. 1–5.*

❹ **Georgetown,** on the shores of Winyah Bay, was founded in 1729 by a Baptist minister and soon became the center of America's Colonial rice empire. A rich plantation culture took root here and developed on a scale comparable to Charleston's. Today, oceangoing vessels reach Georgetown's busy port through a deepwater channel, and the town's prosperity is based on industry (such as its paper mill and an iron foundry) and tourism.

In the heart of town, the graceful market-meeting building, topped by an 1842 town clock and tower, has been converted into the **Rice Museum,** which traces the history of rice cultivation through maps, tools, and dioramas. *Front and Screven Sts., tel. 803/546–7423. Admission: $2 adults, $1 military, students free. Open weekdays 9:30–4:30, Sat. 10–4:30 (until 1 PM Oct.–Mar.), Sun. 2–4:30 PM. Closed major holidays.*

Nearby, **Prince George Winyah Episcopal Church,** named after King George II, still serves the congregation established in 1721. It was built in 1737 with bricks brought over from Mother England. *Broad and Highmarket Sts., tel. 803/546–4358. Donation suggested. Visitors welcome weekdays 8–4.*

Overlooking the Sampit River from a high bluff is the **Harold Kaminski House** (ca. 1760). It's especially notable for its collections of regional antiques and furnishings, and for its Chippendale and Duncan Phyfe furniture, Royal Doulton vases, and silver. *1003 Front St., tel. 803/546–7706. Admission: $4 adults; $3 senior citizens; $2 children 12–16, under 12 free. Open weekdays 10–5, tours hourly. Closed holidays, 2 weeks at Christmas.*

Twelve miles south of Georgetown, **Hopsewee Plantation,** surrounded by moss-draped live oaks, magnolias, and tree-size camellias, overlooks the North Santee River. The mansion is notable for its fine Georgian staircase and hand-carved Adam candlelight moldings. *U.S. 17, tel. 803/546–7891. Admission: $5 adults; $1 children 6–18, under 6 free. Open Mar.–Oct., Tues.–Fri. 10–5, other times by appointment. Grounds only, including nature trail, $1 per car.*

Hampton Plantation State Park, at the edge of the Francis Marion National Forest, preserves the home of Archibald Rutledge, poet laureate of South Carolina for 39 years until his death in 1973. The 18th-century plantation house is an excellent example of a Low Country mansion. The exterior has been restored; cutaway sections in the finely crafted interior show the changes made through the centuries. The grounds are landscaped, and picnic areas are available. *Off U.S. 17, tel. 803/546–9361. Admission: $1 adults; 50¢ children 6–18, under 6 free. Grounds free; open Thurs.–Mon. 9–6. House open Sat. 10–3, Sun. noon–3.*

❺ **Francis Marion National Forest,** about 40 miles north of Charleston via U.S. 52, comprises 250,000 acres of swamps, vast oaks and pines, and little lakes thought to have been formed by meteors—a good place for picnicking, camping, boating, and swimming (tel. 803/336–3248 or 803/887–3311). At the park's **Rembert Dennis Wildlife Center** (off U.S. 52 in Bonneau, tel. 803/825–3387), deer, wild turkey, and striped bass are reared and studied.

Shopping

Malls   **Myrtle Square Mall** (2502 N. Kings Hwy., Myrtle Beach, tel. 803/448–2513) is an upscale complex with 71 stores and restaurants, and a 250-seat Food Court. **Briarcliffe Mall** (10177 N. Kings Hwy., Myrtle Beach, tel. 803/272–4040) has 100 specialty shops, JC Penney, and K-mart.

Discount Outlets   Off-price shopping outlets abound in the Grand Strand. **Waccamaw Pottery and Outlet Park** (U.S. 501 at the Waterway, Myrtle Beach, tel. 803/236–0797) is one of the nation's largest. In several buildings, over three miles of shelves are stocked with china, glassware, wicker, brass and pewter, and countless other items. Outlet Park has about 50 factory outlets with clothing, furniture, books, jewelry, and more. Open Monday through Saturday 9–10. The **Hathaway Factory Outlet** (tel. 803/236–4200), across from Waccamaw, offers menswear by Christian Dior, Ralph Lauren, and Jack Nicklaus and women's wear by White Stag and Geoffrey Beene, among others.

Specialty Stores **The Hammock Shops at Pawleys Island** (tel. 803/237–8448) is a handsome complex of 17 boutiques and gift shops built with old brick brought from England as ballast. In one shop, summer visitors can see rope hammocks being made. Other wares include jewelry, toys, antiques, and designer fashions.

Beaches

All the Grand Strand beaches are family oriented, and almost all are public. The widest expanses are in North Myrtle Beach, where the sand stretches for up to an eighth of a mile from the dunes to the water at low tide. Vacationers seeking a quieter day head for the South Strand communities of Surfside Beach and Garden City, or historic Pawleys Island.

Participant Sports

Fishing Because offshore waters along the Grand Strand are warmed by the Gulf Stream, fishing is usually good from early spring through December. Anglers can walk out over the Atlantic from 10 piers and jetties to try for amberjack, sea trout, and king mackerel. Surfcasters may snare bluefish, whiting, flounder, pompano, and channel bass. In the South Strand, salt marshes, inlets, and tidal creeks yield flounder, blues, croakers, spots, shrimp, clams, oysters, and blue-claw crabs. Some conveniently located marinas that offer both half- and full-day fishing and sightseeing trips are **Capt. Dick's** (U.S. 17 Bus., Murrells Inlet, tel. 803/651–3676), and **Hurricane Fleet, Vereen's Marina** (U.S. 17N at 11th Ave. N, N. Myrtle Beach, tel. 803/249–3571).

The annual **Grand Strand Fishing Rodeo** (Apr.–Oct.) features a "fish of the month" contest, with prizes for the largest catch of a designated species. The October **Arthur Smith King Mackerel Tournament** offers more than $350,000 in prizes and attracts nearly 900 boats and 5,000 anglers.

Golf The Grand Strand—known as the World's Golf Capital—has 65 public courses. Many are championship layouts by top designers. All share meticulously manicured greens, lush fairways, and challenging hazards. Spring and fall are the busiest seasons because of warm temperatures and off-season rates. An organization called **Golf Holiday** (tel. 803/448–5942), whose members include hotels, motels, condominiums, and golf courses along the Grand Strand, offers many package plans throughout the year.

Popular courses include: in Myrtle Beach, **Arcadian Shores Golf Club** (tel. 803/449–5217) and **Dunes Golf and Beach Club** (tel. 803/449–5236); in North Myrtle Beach, **Gator Hole** (tel. 803/249–3543), **Oyster Bay Golf Links** (tel. 803/272–6399), and **Robbers Roost Golf Club** (tel. 803/249–1471); and at Calabash, **Marsh Harbor Golf Links** (tel. 803/249–3449).

Scuba Diving In summer, a large variety of warm-water tropical fish find their way to the area from the Gulf Stream. Off the coast of Little River, rock and coral ledges teem with coral, sea fans, sponges, reef fish, anemones, urchins, arrow crabs, and stone crabs. Several outlying shipwrecks are home to schools of spadefish, amberjack, grouper, and barracuda. Instruction and equipment rentals are available from **The Hurricane Fleet** (Vereen's Marina, U.S. 17N, N. Myrtle Beach, tel. 803/249–3571).

Tennis There are over 150 courts throughout the Grand Strand. Facilities include hotel and resort courts, as well as free municipal courts in Myrtle Beach, North Myrtle Beach, and Surfside Beach. Among tennis clubs offering court time, rental equipment, and instruction are **Myrtle Beach Racquet Club** (tel. 803/449–4031), **Myrtle Beach Tennis and Swim Club** (tel. 803/449–4486), and Surfside Beach's **Grand Strand Tennis Club** (tel. 803/650–3330).

Water Sports Surfboards, Hobie Cats, Jet Skis, Windsurfers, and sailboats are available for rent at **Downwind Sails** (Ocean Blvd. at 29th Ave. S, Myrtle Beach, tel. 803/448–7245).

Dining and Lodging

A wealth of seafood, fresh from inlets, rivers, and ocean, graces the tables of coastal South Carolina. Enjoy it in lavish portions, garnished with hush puppies, cole slaw, and fresh vegetables, in many family-style restaurants. The following dining price categories have been used: *Very Expensive*, over $25; *Expensive*, $15–$25; *Moderate*, $7–$15; *Inexpensive*, under $7.

Among other lodgings options, condominiums are popular on the Grand Strand, combining spaciousness and modern amenities and appealing especially to families. You can choose among cottages, villas, and hotel-style high-rise units. Maid service is frequently available. For the free directories *Grand Hotel and Motel Accommodations* and *Grand Condominium and Cottage Accommodations*, write the Myrtle Beach Area Convention Bureau (710 21st Ave. N, Ste. J, Myrtle Beach, SC 29577, tel. 803/448–1629 or 800/356–3016).

Attractive package plans are available between Labor Day and spring break. The following lodging price categories have been used: *Very Expensive*, over $100; *Expensive*, $65–$100; *Moderate*, $45–$65; *Inexpensive*, under $45.

Georgetown **Rice Paddy.** This cozy seafood restaurant is apt to be crowded
Dining at lunch, when local business folk flock in for homemade vegeta-
★ ble soup, garden-fresh salads, and sandwiches. Dinner is more relaxed, and the menu showcases broiled fresh seafood. Crabmeat casserole is a tasty specialty. So is veal scaloppine. *408 Duke St., tel. 803/546–2021. Dress: informal. Reservations not required. AE, MC, V. Closed Sun. Moderate.*

Lodging **Carolinian Inn** (formerly Best Western Carolinian). This conveniently located in-town motor inn has spacious rooms with reproduction period furnishings. *706 Church St., 29440, tel. 803/546–5191 or 800/722–4667. 89 rooms. Facilities: pool, cable TV/movies, restaurant, lounge. AE, DC, MC, V. Expensive.*

Murrells Inlet **Planter's Back Porch.** Sip cool drinks in the spring house of a
Dining turn-of-the-century farmhouse, then have dinner in a garden
★ setting reminiscent of a 19th-century Southern plantation. Black wrought-iron chandeliers are suspended from high white ceiling beams, and hanging baskets of greenery decorate white latticework archways separating the fireplace-centered main

dining room and the airy, glass-enclosed porch. You can't go wrong with baked whole flounder, panned lump crabmeat, or the hearty Inlet Dinner showcasing several fresh daily catches. *U.S. 17 and Wachesaw Rd., tel. 803/651–5263 or 651–5544. Dress: informal. Reservations not required. AE, MC, V. Closed Dec.–mid-Feb. Moderate.*

Myrtle Beach
Dining

Slug's Rib. A Carolinas institution, this immensely popular restaurant has a welcoming contemporary setting, with outdoor lounge overlooking the Intracoastal Waterway. It features only aged prime rib. There is also a children's menu. *9713 N. Kings Hwy., tel. 803/449–6419. Dress: informal. No reservations. AE, DC, MC, V. Moderate–Expensive.*

★ **Rice Planter's Restaurant.** Dine on fresh seafood, quail, or steaks grilled to order in a homey setting enhanced by Low Country antiques, rice-plantation tools and artifacts, and candlelight. Shrimp Creole is a house specialty; among the appetizers, don't miss the crab fingers! Bread and pecan pie are home-baked. *6707 N. Kings Hwy., tel. 803/449–3456 or 449–3457. Dress: informal. Reservations not required. AE, MC, V. Closed Dec. 25 and 26. Moderate.*

Sea Captain's House. At this picturesque seafood restaurant with a nautical decor, the best seats are in the windowed porch room, with its sweeping ocean views. The fireplace in the wood-paneled inside dining room casts a warm glow on cool off-season evenings. Menu highlights include she-crab soup, Low Country crab casserole, and avocado-seafood salad. Breads and desserts are home-baked. *3002 N. Ocean Blvd., tel. 803/448–8082. Also on U.S. 17 Bus., Murrells Inlet, tel. 803/651–2416. Both: Dress: informal. Reservations not required. AE, MC, V. Closed mid-Dec.–mid-Feb. Moderate.*

Southern Suppers. Here's hearty family dining in a cozy farmhouse filled with country primitive art; handmade quilts line the walls. The menu features an all-you-can-eat seafood buffet. You can also order down-home Southern specialties such as fried chicken, country-fried steak, and country ham with redeye gravy and grits. *U.S. 17S, midway between Myrtle Beach and Surfside Beach, tel. 803/238–4557. Dress: informal. Reservations not required. No liquor. MC, V. Closed Oct.–Feb. Moderate.*

Lodging
★

Myrtle Beach Hilton and Golf Club. This luxurious high-rise oceanfront property—part of the Arcadian Shores Golf Club—is highlighted by a dramatic 14-story atrium. Spacious, airy rooms, all with sea views, are decorated in chic plum, mauve, gray, and rose tones and accented by ultracontemporary lamps and accessories. Two newly redecorated executive floors offer two-phone rooms and other amenities. *701 Hilton Rd., Arcadian Shores 29577, tel. 803/449–5000 or 800/445–8667. 392 rooms. Facilities: 600-foot private beach, oceanfront pool, tennis, golf, restaurant, lounges, entertainment, shops, social program. AE, DC, MC, V. Very Expensive.*

Radisson Resort Hotel. The Grand Strand's newest luxury property, this 20-story glass-sheathed tower is part of the Kingston Plantation complex of shops, restaurants, hotels, and condominiums set amid 145 acres of oceanside woodlands. Guest rooms are highlighted by bleached-wood furnishings and attractive artwork. The balconied one-bedroom suites have kitchenettes. *9800 Lake Dr., 29577, tel. 803/449–0006 or 800/228–9822. 513 suites. Facilities: 2 restaurants and lounge; privileges at sports/fitness complex offering racquetball, ten-*

nis, squash, aerobics, exercise equipment, sauna, pools, whirlpool. AE, DC, MC, V. *Very Expensive.*

Best Western/The Landmark. The rooms in this high-rise oceanfront resort hotel are tastefully decorated in a modern style. Some have balconies and refrigerators. *1501 S. Ocean Blvd., 29577, tel. 803/448–9441 or 800/528–1234. 325 rooms. Facilities: pool, children's activity program, game room, dining rooms, lounges, nightclub, live nightly entertainment. AE, DC, MC, V. Expensive–Very Expensive.*

The Breakers Resort Hotel. The rooms in this oceanfront resort are airy and spacious, with contemporary decor. Many have balconies and refrigerators. *2006 N. Ocean Blvd., Box 485, 29578–0485, tel. 803/626–5000 or 800/845–0688. 247 rooms. Facilities: restaurant, 3 oceanfront pools, indoor and outdoor whirlpools, saunas, exercise room, restaurant, lounge, laundry, children's programs. AE, DC, MC, V. Expensive–Very Expensive.*

Sheraton Myrtle Beach Resort. All rooms and suites have recently been renewed to create a fresh, contemporary effect. Oceanfront Lounge, highlighted by tropical colors and rattan furnishings, is a lively evening gathering spot. *2701 S. Ocean Blvd., 29577, tel. 803/448–2518 or 800/325–2525. 219 units. Facilities: restaurant, seaside dining, deck, lounge, health club, arcade, gift shop, heated outdoor pool, indoor pool. Golf and tennis package plans. AE, DC, MC, V. Expensive–Very Expensive.*

Driftwood-on-the-Oceanfront. Under the same ownership for over 50 years, this facility is popular with families. Some rooms are oceanfront; all have recently been redecorated in sea, sky, or earth tones. *1600 N. Ocean Blvd., Box 275, 29578, tel. 803/ 448–1544. 90 rooms. Facilities: room refrigerators, 2 pools, laundry. AE, DC, MC, V. Expensive.*

Holiday Inn Oceanfront. This in-town oceanfront inn is right at the heart of the action. The spacious rooms have been newly redecorated in cool sea tones. After beach basking, you can prolong the mood in the inn's spacious, plant-bedecked indoor recreation center. *415 S. Ocean Blvd., 29577, tel. 803/448–4481 or 800/465–4329. 310 rooms. Facilities: oceanfront pool with bar, pool parties, heated indoor pool, snack bar, sauna, whirlpool, game room, restaurant, 2 lounges (1 with live entertainment). AE, DC, MC, V. Expensive.*

Comfort Inn. This new inn, 400 yards from the ocean, is clean, well furnished, and well maintained. *2801 S. Kings Hwy., 29577, tel. 803/626–4444 or 800/228–5150. 153 rooms. Facilities: 8 Jacuzzi suites, 6 kitchen suites, outdoor pool, health club with whirlpool and sauna, cable TV, restaurant, par-3 golf course adjacent. AE, DC, MC, V. Moderate–Expensive.*

Cherry Tree Inn. This rambling, low-rise oceanfront inn is in a quiet North Strand section and caters to families. It is furnished Scandinavian-style. *5400 N. Ocean Blvd., 29577, tel. 803/449–6425 or 800/845–2036. 57 rooms. Facilities: kitchens, cable TV, Jacuzzi, laundry, video games, heated pool (enclosed in winter). AE, MC, V. Moderate.*

North Myrtle Beach
Lodging

Economy Inn. This hotel, formerly an Econo-Lodge, is across from the airport and near Waccamaw Pottery. *3301 U.S. 17S, 29582, tel. 803/272–6191. 40 rooms. Facilities: pool, cribs, cable TV. AE, DC, MC, V. Inexpensive.*

Pawleys Island
Dining

Scarlett's. Tables are decked with white linen, crystal and silver sparkle against green walls in this open, plant-filled room overlooking a lake where swans and ducks drift lazily by. Director Gerald Collins and chef Paul Brown focus on classic Southern cuisine highlighted by South Carolina seafood, poultry, and produce. Specialties include Carolina mountain trout stuffed with lump crabmeat and chopped herbed mushrooms, and chicken breast Rochambeau, sauteed and served over Holland rusk with artichoke hearts, sliced ham, and broiled tomatoes in a marchand de vin brown sauce. Desserts include sweet-potato pecan pie with chocolate chips, and Nanny's Lane cake—a pecan, raisin, and pineapple concoction frosted with bourbon-tinged seven-minute icing. *U.S. 17 on mainland, 2 miles north of Pawley's Island at Litchfield by the Sea Resort and Country Club, tel. 803/237–3000. Dress: informal. Reservations suggested. AE, MC, V. Moderate–Expensive.*

Lodging **Litchfield by the Sea Resort and Country Club.** Contemporary gray-blue wood suite units on stilts, a 10-minute walk from the beach, nestle amid 4,500-acre gardenlike grounds, which include three private golf clubs open to guests. *U.S. 17, 2 miles north of Pawley's Island, tel. 803/237–3000 or 800/845–1897. 97 suites. Facilities: exercise room, whirlpool, sauna, racquetball court, indoor-outdoor pools, 17 tennis courts, conference center. AE, MC, V. Moderate–Expensive.*

Ramada Inn Seagull. This is a very well-maintained inn on a golf course (excellent golf packages are available). The rooms are spacious, bright, and airy. *U.S. 17S, Box 2217, 29585, tel. 803/237–4261 or 800/272–6232. 99 rooms. Facilities: pool, dining room, lounge with entertainment, in-room movies. AE, DC, MC, V. Moderate.*

Nightlife

Myrtle Beach **Sandals,** at the Sands Ocean Club (tel. 803/449–7055), is an intimate lounge with live entertainment. **Coquina Club,** at the Best Western Landmark Resort Hotel (tel. 803/448–9441), features beach-music bands. **Studebaker's** (tel. 803/626–3855 or 803/448–9747) is one of the area's hot night spots, with live beach music. At The Breakers Hotel, **Top of the Green Lounge and Sidewalk Cafe** (tel. 803/626–5000) is a popular spot, with nightly dancing and entertainment.

Murrells Inlet **Drunken Jack's** (tel. 803/651–2044 or 803/651–3232) is a popular restaurant with a lounge overlooking the docks and fishing fleets.

North Myrtle Beach The lounge at **Holiday Inn on the Ocean** (tel. 803/272–6153) showcases live bands.

Surfside Beach **Carolina Opry** offers music, comedy, and a variety show to combine the flavor of the Grand Ole Opry with a dash of Broadway. Entertainment for the whole family. *301 U.S. 17S, Surfside Beach, tel. 803/238–8888. Tickets: $12 adults, $6 children under 12. Show at 8 PM, days vary with season. Closed Jan.*

Charleston

At first glimpse, Charleston resembles an 18th-century etching come to life. Its low-profile skyline is punctuated with the spires and steeples of 181 churches, representing 25 denominations that have sought out Charleston as a haven (it was known for having the most liberal provisions for religious freedom of the 13 original colonies). Parts of the city appear stopped in time. Block after block of old downtown structures have been preserved and restored for both residential and commercial use. After three centuries of epidemics, earthquakes, fires, and hurricanes, Charleston has prevailed, and it is today one of the South's best-preserved cities.

Along the Battery, on the point of a narrow peninsula bounded by the Ashley and Cooper rivers, handsome mansions surrounded by gardens face the harbor. Called the "Charleston style," this distinctive look is reminiscent of the West Indies, and for good reason. Before coming to the Carolinas in the late 17th century, many early British colonists had first settled on Barbados and other Caribbean islands. In that warm and humid climate they had built homes with high ceilings and rooms opening onto broad piazzas at each level to catch welcome sea breezes. In Charleston, the settlers adapted these designs for other practical reasons. One new twist—building narrow two- to four-story houses (called single houses) at right angles to the street—emerged partly because of the British Crown's policy of taxing buildings according to frontage length. To save money (as well as to catch the prevailing winds), shrewd Charlestonians faced their houses to the side.

This lovely city, with its vibrant cultural life, is guarded by a string of semitropical coastal islands that contain some of the nation's finest resorts—Kiawah, Seabrook, and Isle of Palms—all connected to the South Carolina mainland by bridge or causeway, so that it is fairly easy to spend a day or two sightseeing in Charleston while staying at an island resort.

Getting Around Fares within the city average $2–$3 per trip. Companies in-
By Taxi clude Everready Cab Co. (tel.803/722–8383), Yellow Cab (tel. 803/577–6565), Safety Cab (tel. 803/722–4066), and Airport Limo-Taxi (tel. 803/572–5083).

By Bus Regular bus service within the city is provided by **SCE&G** (South Carolina Electric and Gas Company). The cost is 50¢; at nonpeak hours (9:30–3:30), senior citizens and disabled persons pay 25¢. Exact change is needed, and free transfers are available. SCE&G also operates the **DASH** (Downtown Area Shuttle) trolley service on weekdays in the main downtown areas. The fare is 50¢; $1 for an all-day pass. For schedule information, call 803/724–7368 (DASH) or 803/745–7928 or 803/747–0922 (regular service).

Guided Tours **Adventure Sightseeing** (tel. 803/762–0088), **Carolina Low-Coun-try Tours** (tel. 803/797–1045), and **Gateway to Historic Charles-ton** (tel. 803/722–3969) offer van or motor-coach tours of the historic district. **Gray Line** (tel. 803/722–1112) offers similar motor-coach tours, plus seasonal tours to gardens and planta-tions. **Livin' in the Past** (tel. 803/723–0933) offers historically oriented van and minibus tours of the city and the plantations.

Doin' Charles Towne Tours, St. Helena's Point (tel. 803/763–1233), and **Charleston Carriage Co.** (tel. 803/577–0042) rent self-paced cassette tours of the historic district.

For personal guides, contact **Associated Guides of Historic Charleston** (tel. 803/724–6419); **Charleston Guide Service** (tel. 803/724–5367); **Parker Limousine Service** (tel. 803/723–7601), which offers chauffeur-driven luxury limousine tours; or **Tours of Historic Charleston** (tel. 803/722–3405).

Carriage Tours **Charleston Carriage Co.** (tel. 803/577–0042) offers 40- to 50-minute horse-drawn carriage tours through the historic district. **Old South Carriage Co.** (tel. 803/723–9712) has similar tours, but conducted by guides in Confederate uniforms. **Palmetto Carriage Works** (tel. 803/723–8145) offers one-hour horse- and mule-drawn carriage tours of the historic district.

Walking Tours Guided walking tours are given by **Charleston Carriage Co.** (tel. 803/577–0042) and **Charleston Tea Party Walking Tour** (tel. 803/577–5896; includes tea in a private garden).

Boat Tours **Charles Towne Princess Gray Line Water Tours** (tel. 803/722–1112) and **Charleston Harbor Tour** (tel. 803/722–1691) offer nonstop harbor tours. **Fort Sumter Tours** (tel. 803/722–1691) includes a stop at Fort Sumter in its harbor tour. It also offers Starlight Dinner Cruises aboard a luxury yacht.

Numbers in the margin correspond to points of interest on the Charleston map.

Marion Square Area

❶ For a good overview of the city before you begin touring, drop by the **Visitor Information Center,** where there's free parking (for two hours; 50¢ per hour thereafter) and you can view *Forever Charleston,* a 20-minute film. *375 Meeting St., tel. 803/853–8000. Admission: $2 adults; $1.50 senior citizens; $1 children 6–12, under 6 free. Shown daily 9–5 on the half-hour.*

❷ Walk up Meeting Street to Wragg Street and take a right to reach the 1817 **Aiken-Rhett Mansion.** Furnished in a variety of 19th-century styles, with a heavy, ornate look overall, the house was the headquarters of Confederate General P.G.T. Beauregard during the Civil War. *48 Elizabeth St., tel. 803/722–2996. Admission: $4 adults; $3.60 senior citizens; $2 children 3–12, under 3 free. Open Mon.–Sat. 10–5, Sun. 1–5.*

❸ Back on Meeting Street, housed in a $6-million contemporary complex, is the oldest city museum in the United States. The **Charleston Museum,** founded in 1773, is one of the Southeast's major museums and is especially strong on South Carolina decorative arts. The 500,000 items in the collection—in addition to Charleston silver, fashions, toys, snuff boxes, etc.—include objects relating to natural history, archaeology, and ornithology. *360 Meeting St., tel. 803/722–2996. Admission: $4 adults; $3.60 senior citizens; $2 children 3–12, under 3 free. Open Mon.–Sat. 9–5, Sun. 1–5. Three historic homes—the Joseph Manigault House, the Aiken-Rhett Mansion, and the Heyward-Washington House—are part of the museum, and a combination ticket can be bought for $10.*

❹ Across John Street is one of Charleston's fine house museums, and a National Historic Landmark, the **Joseph Manigault Mansion.** An outstanding example of Adam-style architecture, it was designed by Charleston architect Gabriel Manigault in 1803 and is noted for its carved-wood mantels and elaborate plasterwork. Furnishings are British, French, and Charleston antiques, including rare tricolor Wedgwood pieces. *350 Meeting St., tel. 803/722–2996. Admission: $4 adults; $3.60 senior citizens; $2 children 3–12, under 3 free (for combination ticket see Charleston Museum, above). Open Mon.–Sat. 10–5, Sun. 1–5.*

Aiken-Rhett
Mansion, **2**

American Military
Museum, **22**

Calhoun Mansion, **26**

Charleston Museum, **3**

Circular
Congregational
Church, **14**

City Hall, **20**

College of
Charleston, **7**

Congregation Beth
Elohim, **8**

Dock Street
Theatre, **18**

Edmonston-Alston
House, **27**

Emanuel African
Methodist Episcopal
Church, **6**

Exchange
Bldg./Provost
Dungeon, **23**

French Huguenot
Church, **19**

Gibbes Museum of
Art, **11**

Heyward-Washington
House, **24**

Joseph Manigault
Mansion, **4**

Market Hall, **9**

Nathaniel Russell
House, **25**

Old Citadel Bldg., **5**

Old City Market, **10**

Old Powder
Magazine, **15**

St. John's Lutheran
Church, **13**

St. Michael's Episcopal
Church, **21**

St. Philip's Episcopal
Church, **17**

Thomas Elfe
Workshop, **16**

Unitarian Church, **12**

Visitor Info. Center, **1**

White Point
Gardens, **28**

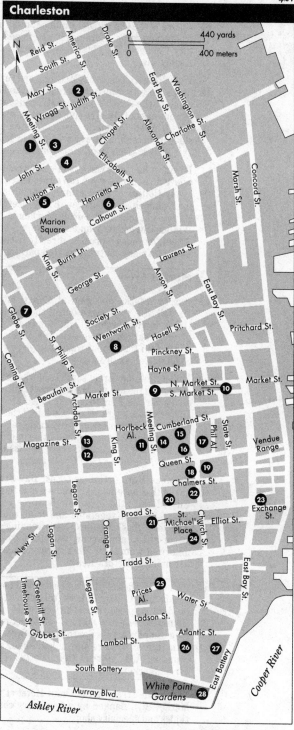

Charleston

⑤ Walk down Meeting Street to Marion Square. Facing the square is the **Old Citadel Building,** built in 1822 to house state troops and arms. Here began the famed South Carolina Military College—The Citadel—now located on the banks of the Ashley River.

⑥ Walk down a block, cross Meeting, and turn east to 110 Calhoun Street to visit **Emanuel African Methodist Episcopal Church,** home of the South's oldest AME congregation, which had its beginnings in 1818. The church was closed in 1822 when authorities learned Denmark Vesey used the sanctuary to plan his slave insurrection. It was reopened in 1865 at the present site. *Tel. 803/722-2561 in advance for tour. Open daily 9-4.*

⑦ If you've left your car at the visitor center, return now to retrieve it. From here you can either take an excursion to see the lovely **College of Charleston** (founded in 1770 as the nation's first municipal college, with a graceful main building constructed in 1828 after a design by famed Philadelphia architect William Strickland) and/or make a shopping tour of King Street, or you can proceed directly to the market area, where there are many centrally located parking garages.

Market Area

⑧ Our tour picks up again at **Congregation Beth Elohim** (90 Hassell St.), considered one of the nation's finest examples of Greek Revival architecture. It was constructed in 1840 to replace an earlier temple—the birthplace of American Reform Judaism in 1824—that was destroyed by fire. Visitors are welcome weekdays 10 AM–noon.

⑨ Follow Meeting Street south to Market Street, and at the intersection on the left you'll see **Market Hall.** Built in 1841 and modeled after the Temple of Nike in Athens, the hall is a National Historic Landmark. Here you'll find the **Confederate Museum,** where the Daughters of the Confederacy preserve and display flags, uniforms, swords, and other memorabilia. *188 Meeting St., tel. 803/723-1541. Museum admission: $1 adults; 25¢ children 6-12, under 6 free. Hours vary.*

⑩ Between Market Hall and East Bay Street is a series of low sheds that once housed produce and fish markets. Called **Old City Market,** the area now features restaurants and shops. There are still vegetable and fruit vendors here, too, along with local "basket ladies" busy weaving and selling distinctive sweet-grass, pine-straw, and palmetto-leaf baskets—a craft inherited from their West African ancestors—which are fast becoming collectors' items.

Time Out Pick up batches of Charleston's famed benne (sesame) seed wafers at **Olde Colony Bakery** (tel. 803/722-2147) in the open-air market. Choose from 13 gourmet food stands in **The Gourmetisserie** (tel. 803/722-4455) in the Market Square shopping complex across South Market Street. Or indulge the urge to munch on oysters on the half-shell, steamed mussels, and clams at **A.W. Shucks** (tel. 803/723-1151) in nearby State Street Market.

Across the street is the **Omni Hotel at Charleston Place** (130 Market St.), flanked by a four-story complex of upscale boutiques and specialty shops.

⑪ Heading south on Meeting Street, we come to the **Gibbes Museum of Art.** Its collection of American art includes notable 18th- and 19th-century portraits of Carolinians and an outstanding group of more than 300 miniature portraits. Don't miss the miniature rooms—intricately detailed with fabrics and furnishings and nicely displayed in shadow boxes inset in dark-paneled walls—or the Tiffany-style stained-glass dome in the rotunda's 30-foot ceiling. *135 Meeting St., tel. 803/722-2706. Admission: $2 adults, $1 senior citizens and college students, 50¢ children under 18. Open Tues.–Sat. 10–5, Sun. and Mon. 1–5.*

⑫ For a little detour, head south on Meeting Street to Queen Street, then west to Archdale. At no. 8 is the **Unitarian Church,** built in 1774. The building was remodeled in the mid-19th century after plans inspired by the Chapel of Henry VII in Westminster Abbey, including the addition of an unusual Gothic fan-tracery ceiling. *No regular visiting hours. Call 803/723-4617 10–noon weekdays in winter, Mon. and Fri. only in summer, to see whether someone can unlock the church.*

⑬ At the corner of Clifford and Archdale streets is the Greek Revival–style **St. John's Lutheran Church,** built in 1817. Notice the fine craftsmanship in the delicate wrought-iron gates and fence. Organ aficionados may be interested in the 1823 Thomas Hall organ case. The church is open weekdays 9–1 (tel. 803/723-2426 before arrival). Back at Meeting Street, across from ⑭ the Gibbes is the unusual **Circular Congregational Church.** Legend has it that its corners were rounded off so the devil would have no place to hide. The inside of this Romanesque-style church is simple but pretty, with a beamed, vaulted ceiling. It is open weekdays 9–1.

⑮ On Cumberland Street, one of Charleston's few remaining cobblestone thoroughfares, is the **Old Powder Magazine,** built in 1713, used as a powder storehouse during the Revolutionary War, and now a museum with costumes, furniture, armor, and other artifacts from 18th-century Charleston. *79 Cumberland St., tel. 803/722-3767. Admission: $1 adults, 50¢ students. Open weekdays 9:30–4.*

⑯ It's a few steps down Church Street to the **Thomas Elfe Workshop,** the home and workplace of one of the city's famed early furniture makers. Inside this restored miniature "single house," original and replica Elfe furniture is on display. *54 Queen St., tel. 803/722-2130. Admission: $3. Tours weekdays 10–4:30, Sat. 10–noon. Closed Sun., holidays.*

⑰ At 146 Church Street is graceful **St. Philip's Episcopal Church.** The late-Georgian–style structure, the second on the site, was completed in 1838. In its serene graveyard are buried some legendary native sons, including statesman John C. Calhoun and DuBose Heyward, the author of *Porgy.*

⑱ The **Dock Street Theatre,** across Queen Street, was built on the site of one of the nation's first playhouses. It combines the reconstructed early Georgian playhouse and the preserved Old Planter's Hotel (ca. 1809). *135 Church St., tel. 803/723-5648. Open weekdays noon–6 for tours ($1).*

⑲ At 110 Church Street is the Gothic-style **French Huguenot Church,** the only U.S. church still adhering to the original Huguenot liturgy. A French-liturgy service is held each spring.

Tel. 803/722–4385. Donations accepted. Open to visitors weekdays 10–12:30 and 2–4. Closed weekends, holidays, Jan.

Four Corners to the Battery

The intersection of Meeting and Broad streets is known as the Four Corners of Law, because structures here represent federal, state, city, and religious jurisdiction. The County Court House and the U.S. Post Office and Federal Court occupy two corners.

(20) The Council Chamber of the graceful 1801 **City Hall,** on the northeast corner, has interesting historical displays as well as fine portraits, including John Trumbull's famed 1791 portrait of George Washington and Samuel F. B. Morse's likeness of James Monroe. *Admission free. Open weekdays 9–5. Closed holidays.*

(21) On the last corner is **St. Michael's Episcopal Church,** modeled after London's St. Martin's-in-the-Fields. Completed in 1761, this is Charleston's oldest surviving church. Climb the 186-foot steeple for a panoramic view. *Open Mon., Tues., Thurs., Fri. 9–4:30; Wed. 9–3:30; Sat. 9–noon.*

(22) From the Four Corners, head down Broad Street toward the Cooper River. The **American Military Museum** displays hundreds of uniforms and artifacts from all branches of service, dating from the Revolutionary War. *115 Church St., tel. 803/ 723–9620. Admission: $2 adults, $1 children under 12, military in uniform no charge. Open Mon.–Sat. 10–6, Sun. 1–6.*

(23) At the corner of East Bay Street stands the **Exchange Building/Provost Dungeon.** The building itself was originally a customs house. The dungeon was used by the British to confine prisoners during the Revolutionary War; today, a tableau of lifelike wax figures recalls this era. *East Bay and Broad Sts., tel. 803/792–5020. Admission: $2.50 adults; $2 senior citizens; $1 children 6–11, under 6 free. Open Mon.–Sat. 9:30–5, Sun. 1–5. Closed major holidays.*

(24) Returning to Church Street and continuing south, you'll come to the **Heyward-Washington House.** Built in 1772 by rice king Daniel Heyward, it was the residence of President George Washington during his 1791 visit. The mansion is notable for fine period furnishings by such local craftsmen as Thomas Elfe and includes Charleston's only restored 18th-century kitchen open to visitors. *87 Church St., tel. 803/722–2996. Admission: $4 adults; $3.60 senior citizens; $2 children 3–12, under 3 free. Combination ticket with Manigault House, Charleston Museum, and Aiken-Rhett Mansion: $10. Open Mon.–Sat. 10–5, Sun. 1–5.*

(25) At 51 Meeting Street is the **Nathaniel Russell House,** headquarters of the Historic Charleston Foundation. Built in 1808, it is one of the nation's finest examples of Adam architecture. The interior is notable for its ornate detailing, its lavish period furnishings, and a "flying" circular staircase that spirals three stories with no apparent support. *Tel. 803/723–3646 or 803/ 722–3405. Admission: $4, children under 6 free. Open Mon.– Sat. 10–5, Sun. 2–5. A combination ticket with the Edmonston-Alston House can be purchased at either location for $6.*

Continuing south, you'll come into an area where somewhat
26 more lavish mansions reflect a later era. The **Calhoun Mansion**,
at 16 Meeting Street, is opulent by Charleston standards, an
interesting reflection of Victorian taste. Built in 1876, it's notable for ornate plasterwork, fine wood moldings, and a 75-foot
domed ceiling. *Tel. 803/722–8205 or 577–9863. Admission: $5
adults; $4.50 senior citizens over 62; $3 children 6–13, under 6
free. Open daily 10–4, other times by appointment.*

27 The **Edmonston-Alston House**, at 21 East Battery, is an imposing 1828 Greek Revival structure with a commanding view of
Charleston harbor. It is tastefully furnished with antiques,
portraits, Piranesi prints, silver, and fine china. *Tel. 803/722–
7171 or 803/556–6020. Admission: $4, children under 6 free. A
combination ticket with the Nathaniel Russell House can be
purchased at either location for $6. Open Mon.–Sat. 10–5,
Sun. 1:30–5.*

28 After all this serious sightseeing, relax in **White Point Gardens**,
on Battery Point, facing the harbor. It's a tranquil spot, shaded
by palmettos and graceful oaks.

Excursions from Charleston

Across the Cooper River Bridges, via U.S. 17, is the town of
Mt. Pleasant. Here, along Shem Creek, where the area's fishing fleet brings in fresh daily catches, seafood restaurants attract visitors and locals alike. Mt. Pleasant is home to **Patriots
Point**, the world's largest naval and maritime museum.
Berthed here are famed aircraft carrier *Yorktown*, nuclear
merchant ship *Savannah*, vintage World War II submarine
Clamagore, cutter *Ingham*, and destroyer *Laffey*. Missiles,
airplanes, and weapons are also displayed. Tours are offered in
all vessels, and the film *The Fighting Lady* is shown regularly
aboard the *Yorktown*. *Tel. 803/884–2727 or 800/327–5723. Admission: $8 adults; $7 senior citizens and military in uniform;
$4 children 6–11, under 6 free. Open Apr.–Oct., daily 9–6; 9–5
rest of year.*

From the docks here, Fort Sumter Tours' boats leave for 2¼-
hour cruises that include an hour-long stop at **Fort Sumter National Monument.** (The company also has boats leaving from
the Municipal Marina, on Charleston's west side.) This is the
only way to get there, as the fort is on a manmade island in
the harbor. *Tel. 803/722–1691. Cost: $8 adults; $4 children 6–
11, under 6 free. Tours depart daily from Charleston at 9:30,
noon, and 2:30; from Patriots Point at 10:45, 1:30, and 4; from
Mount Pleasant at 1 Easter weekend and June 15–Labor Day.
Schedule varies rest of year. Call for information. Closed
Christmas.*

It was at Fort Sumter that the first shot of the Civil War was
fired, when Confederate forces at Fort Johnson (now defunct)
across the way opened fire on April 12, 1861. After a 34-hour
bombardment, Union forces surrendered and Confederate
troops occupied Sumter, which became a symbol of Southern
resistance. The Confederacy managed to hold the fort—despite almost continual bombardment—for nearly four years,
and when it was finally evacuated, Fort Sumter was a heap of
rubble. Today National Park Service rangers conduct free
guided tours of the restored structure, which includes a muse-

um (also free) with historical displays and dioramas. *Tel. 803/883-3123.*

On U.S. 17, about eight miles northeast of Charleston, is the 1681 **Boone Hall Plantation,** approached via one of the South's most majestic avenues of oaks. The primary attraction is the grounds, with formal azalea and camellia gardens, as well as the original slave quarters—the only "slave street" still intact in the Southeast—and cotton-gin house. Visitors may also tour the first floor of the classic columned mansion, which was built in 1935 incorporating woodwork and flooring from the original house. *Tel. 803/884-4371. Admission: $6 adults; $5 senior citizens over 55; $2 children 6-12, under 6 free. Open Apr.-Labor Day, Mon.-Sat. 8:30-6:30, Sun. 1-5; rest of year, Mon.-Sat. 9-5, Sun. 1-4. Closed holidays.*

Cross the Ashley River Bridge out of Charleston and take SC 171 north to reach **Charles Towne Landing State Park,** commemorating the site of the original Charleston settlement, begun in 1670. There's a reconstructed village and fortifications, English park gardens with bicycle trails and walkways, and a replica 17th-century vessel moored in the creek. In the animal park roam species native to the region for three centuries. A pavilion includes exhibits and a film about the region. Bicycle and kayak rentals and cassette and tram tours are available. *1500 Old Towne Rd., tel. 803/556-4450. Admission: $5 adults; $2.50 senior citizens over 65 and children 6-14, under 6 free; Open June-Labor Day, daily 9-6; rest of the year, daily 9-5. Closed Dec. 24-25.*

Nine miles west of Charleston via the Ashley River Road (SC 61) is **Drayton Hall,** built between 1738 and 1742. A National Historic Landmark, it is considered the nation's finest example of Georgian Palladian architecture. The mansion is the only plantation house on the Ashley River to have survived the Civil War intact and serves as an invaluable lesson in history as well as architecture. It has been left unfurnished to highlight the original plaster moldings, opulent hand-carved woodwork, and other ornamental details. *Tel. 803/766-0188. Admission: $6 adults; $3 children 6-18, under 6 free. Guided tours Mar.-Oct., daily 10-5; Nov.-Feb., daily 10-3. Closed major holidays.*

A mile or so farther on SC 61 is **Magnolia Plantation and Gardens.** The 50-acre informal gardens, begun in 1686, boast one of the continent's largest collections of azaleas and camellias and were proclaimed the "most beautiful garden in the world" by John Galsworthy. Nature lovers may canoe through the 125-acre Waterfowl Refuge, explore the 30-acre swamp garden along boardwalks and bridges, or walk or bicycle over 500 acres of wildlife trails. Tours of the manor house, built during the Reconstruction period, depict plantation life. Several nights weekly the gardens are open for strolls along lighted paths. There is also a petting zoo and a mini-horse ranch. *Tel. 803/571-1266. Admission: $7 adults; $6.50 senior citizens; $5 teens; $3 children 4-12, under 4 free. House tours $4 extra. Mar. 15-May 15, all prices $1 additional. Open daily 8-5.*

Middleton Place, four miles farther north on SC 61, has the nation's oldest landscaped gardens, dating from 1741. Design highlights of the magnificent gardens—ablaze with camellias, magnolias, azaleas, roses, and flowers of all seasons—are the floral *allées,* terraced lawns, and ornamental lakes. Much of the mansion was destroyed during the Civil War, but the south wing has been restored and houses impressive collections of silver, furniture, paintings, and historic documents. The stableyard is a living outdoor museum: here craftsfolk, using authentic tools and equipment, demonstrate spinning, blacksmithing, and other domestic skills from the plantation era. Farm animals, peacocks, and other creatures roam free. Rides in a vintage horse-drawn wagon are offered. *Tel. 803/556–6020. Gardens and stableyard open daily 9–5. Admission: $8 adults; $4 children 4–12, under 4 free. Prices slightly higher mid-Mar.–mid-June. House tours Tues.–Sun. 10–4:30, Mon. 1:30–4:30; $4 extra.*

The picturesque town of **Summerville,** about 25 miles northwest of Charleston via I–26 (Exit 199), is a pleasant place for a drive or stroll. Built by wealthy planters as an escape from hot-weather malaria, it's a treasure trove of mid-19th-century and Victorian buildings—many of which are listed in the National Register of Historic Places—with colorful gardens of camellias, azaleas, and wisteria. Streets often curve around tall pines, since a local ordinance prohibits cutting them down. This is a good place for a bit of antiquing in attractive shops.

Last but not least, about 24 miles north of Charleston via U.S. 52 is **Cypress Gardens,** a swamp garden created from what was once the freshwater reserve of a vast rice plantation. Explore the inky waters by boat, or walk along paths lined with moss-draped cypress trees, azaleas, camellias, daffodils, wisteria, and dogwood. Peak season is late March into April. *Tel. 803/553–0515. Admission (not including boat ride) Feb. 15–Apr. 30: $6 adults; $5 senior citizens; $3 children 6–16, under 6 free. Rest of year, $1 less and boat ride included in admission cost. Open daily 9–5.*

Shopping

Most downtown Charleston shops and department stores are open from 9 or 10 AM to 5 PM. The malls are open Monday–Saturday 10–9, Sunday 1–6. The sales tax is 5%.

Shopping Districts One of the most interesting shopping experiences awaiting visitors to Charleston is the colorful produce market in the two-block **Old City Market** at East Bay and Market streets. Adjacent to it is the **open-air flea market,** with crafts, antiques, and memorabilia. A portion of the Old City Market where cotton was once auctioned, now called **The Market,** has been converted into a complex of specialty shops and restaurants. Other such complexes in the area are **Rainbow Market** (in two interconnected 150-year-old buildings), **Market Square,** and **State Street Market.** Over two dozen upscale boutiques are clustered in a luxurious complex adjoining the Omni Hotel called **The Shops at Charleston Place.** Some of Charleston's oldest and finest shops are on the main downtown thoroughfare, **King Street.**

Antiques Charleston is one of the South's major cities for antiques shopping. King Street is the center. **Coles & Company** (84 Wentworth St., tel. 803/723–2142) is a direct importer of 18th- and 19th-century English antiques. **Livingston Antiques,** dealers in 18th- and 19th-century English and Continental furniture, clocks, and bric-a-brac, has two locations: a large one west of the Ashley (2137 Savannah Hwy., tel. 803/556–3502) and a smaller one in the historic district (163 King St., tel. 803/723–9697). **Vendue House Antiques** (9 Queen St., tel. 803/577–5462) sells 18th- and 19th-century English antiques and distinctive objets d'art.

Art Galleries The **Birds I View Gallery** (119-A Church St., tel. 803/723–1276) sells bird paintings and prints by Anne Worsham Richardson. The **Elizabeth O'Neill Verner Studio & Museum** (79 Church St., tel. 803/722–4246) is located in a 17th-century house where the late artist, one of Charleston's most distinguished, had her studio. The studio is now open to the public, as is a gallery of her pastels and etchings. Prints of her work are on sale at adjacent **Tradd Street Press** (38 Tradd St., tel. 803/722–4246). The **Virginia Fouché Bolton Art Gallery** (127 Meeting St., tel. 803/577–9351, or 869–2372) has original paintings and limited-edition lithographs of Charleston scenes.

Gift Shops **Charleston Collections** (142 E. Bay St., tel. 803/722–7267, the Straw Market, Kiawah Island Resort, tel. 803/768–7487, and Bohicket Marina Village, between Kiawah and Seabrook resorts, tel. 803/768–9101) has Charleston chimes, prints, and candies, T-shirts, and more.

Ben Silver (in The Shops at Charleston Place) is the premier purveyor of blazer buttons, with over 800 designs struck from hand-engraved dies, including college, monogram, British regimental, and specialty motifs. (Ben Silver also sells British neckties, embroidered polo shirts, and blazers.)

Period Reproductions **Historic Charleston Reproductions** (105 Broad St., tel. 803/723–8292) has superb reproductions of Charleston furniture and accessories, all authorized by the Historic Charleston Foundation. Royalties from sales contribute to restoration projects. At the **Thomas Elfe Workshop** (54 Queen St., tel. 803/722–2130), you'll find excellent 18th-century reproductions and objets d'art, Charleston rice beds, handmade mirrors, and Charleston pieces in silverplate, pewter, or porcelain. At the **Old Charleston Joggling Board Co** (tel. 803/723–4331), these Low Country oddities can be purchased.

Sports and Outdoor Activities

Bicycling The **historic district** is level and compact, ideal for bicycling, and many city parks have biking trails. **Palmetto Islands County Park** also has trails. Bikes can be rented at **The Bicycle Shop** (tel. 803/722–8168), which offers a self-guided tour of the district; and at the **Charleston Carriage Co.** (tel. 803/577–0042), which also rents tandem bikes. **Pedal Carriage Co.** (tel. 803/722–3880) rents a sort of pedal "surrey with the fringe on top" for two riders (plus two children) and offers a 40-minute self-guided tour of the historic district; it also rents one-speed balloon-tire bikes.

Boardsailing Instructions are provided by **Sailsports** in Mt. Pleasant (tel. 803/881–4056) and **Time Out Sailing**, Lakewood Dr. at the Charleston marina (tel. 803/577–5979).

Fishing Fresh- and saltwater fishing is excellent along 90 miles of coastline. Surf fishing is permitted on many beaches, including Palmetto Islands County Park's. Charter fishing boats offering partial- or full-day sails to individuals include **Blue Water Sportfishing Charter**, Charleston-Awendaw area (tel. 803/884–0868). **Bohicket Yacht Charters** on Seabrook Island (tel. 803/

768–7294) arranges charters for groups of four to six for full- or half-day sportfishing, shark fishing, flat-bottom-boat marsh fishing, shrimping, crabbing, shelling, and nature-observing expeditions.

Golf Public courses include **Charleston Municipal** (tel. 803/795–6517), **Patriots Point** (tel. 803/881–0042), **Plantation Pines** (9 holes; tel. 803/599–2009), and **Shadowmoss** (tel. 803/556–8251). **Kiawah Island** (tel. 803/768–2121) and **Wild Dunes** (tel. 803/886–6000) offer golf to nonguests on a space-available basis.

Jogging Jogging paths wind through **Palmetto Islands County Park,** and **Hampton Park** has a fitness trail.

Miniature Golf There are also three 18-hole **Putt-Putt Golf Courses** (tel. 803/797–7874) in the area and 36 holes of miniature golf at **Classic Golf** (tel. 803/881–9614).

Sailing Boats can be rented and yachts chartered from **Bohicket Yacht Charters** on Seabrook Island (tel. 803/768–7294).

Tennis Courts are open to the public at **Farmfield Tennis Courts** (tel. 803/724–7402), **Shadowmoss** (tel. 803/556–8251), **Kiawah Island** (tel. 803/768–2121), and **Wild Dunes** (tel. 803/886–6000).

Beaches

South Carolina's climate allows swimming from April through October. There are public beaches at **Beachwater Park,** on Kiawah Island; **Folly Beach County Park** and **Folly Beach,** on Folly Island; **Isle of Palms;** and **Sullivan's Island.** Resorts with extensive private beaches are **Fairfield Ocean Ridge,** on Edisto Island; **Kiawah Island Resort; Seabrook Island;** and **Wild Dunes Resort,** on the Isle of Palms. This is definitely not a "swingles" area; all public and private beaches are family oriented.

Dining

Known for its Low Country specialties—she-crab soup, sautéed shrimp and grits, and variations on pecan pie—Charleston is also a hotbed of new American cuisine. Its chefs are busy creating marriages of the classical and the contemporary, of down-home cooking and haute cuisine. The following dining price categories have been used: *Expensive,* over $30; *Moderate,* $20–$30; *Inexpensive,* under $20.

Expensive **Louis's Charleston Grill.** When owner-chef Louis Osteen took
Low Country over the former Shaftesbury Room in the Omni, he created an
★ elegant low-key ambience, with historic photographs of old Charleston on mahogany-panel walls and wrought-iron chandeliers reflected in gleaming crystal and china. The food is "local, not too fancy," and entrées might include scallops pan-seared with corn sauce; pan-fried littleneck clams with green-onion pasta and garlic sauce; dessert might be buttermilk tart with raspberries. *Omni Hotel at Charleston Place, 130 Market St., tel. 803/577–4522. Jacket advised. Reservations advised. AE, MC, V. No lunch.*

Moderate **82 Queen.** This popular restaurant, part of a complex of pink
American stucco buildings dating to the mid-1800s, is the unofficial head-
★ quarters for many of the city's annual events; during Spoleto, musicians perform in the courtyard garden. At the outdoor raw bar, tourists can meet and mingle with the locals. Low Country

favorites such as crab cakes are served with basil tartar sauce. The traditional commingles with innovations such as scallops simmered in leek sauce over spinach fettuccine, garnished with toasted pine nuts. Ask about the homemade relishes, particularly the garden salsa. For dessert, the Death by Chocolate is exceptional. *82 Queen St., tel. 803/723–7591. Dress: informal. Reservations preferred for dinner. AE, DC, MC, V.*

Low Country **Carolina's.** European chic with its black lacquer, white, and peach decor, Carolina's is the brainchild of German restaurateurs Franz Meier and Chris Weihs. Many come here for the "appeteasers" and the late-night (until 1 AM) offerings, which include everything from baby back smoked ribs to pasta with crawfish and tasso (spiced ham) in cream sauce. Dinner entrées are selections from the grill: Carolina quail with goat cheese, sun-dried tomatoes, and basil; salmon with cilantro, ginger, and lime butter; and lamb loin with jalapeño chutney. *10 Exchange St., tel. 803/724–3800. Dress: informal. Reservations suggested. AE, MC, V. Dinner only. Closed Sun.*

The Moultrie Tavern. This reconverted brick warehouse, dating from 1833, is filled with artifacts and artwork from the Civil War era. Chef/owner Robert Bohrn, who greets guests in a Confederate uniform, is a historian and unearths his own relics. The fife-and-drum music plays continuously and the food and spirits are authentically 1860s. Try an early Southern specialty: baked oyster and sausage pie with puff pastry. *18 Vendue Range, tel. 803/723–1862. Dress: informal. Dinner reservations recommended. AE, MC, V. Closed Sat. lunch and Sun.*

Seafood **Barbadoes Room.** This large, airy plant- and light-filled space has a sophisticated island look and a view out to a cheery courtyard garden. Entrées include sautéed jumbo shrimp and scallops served with creamy wild mushroom sauce on a bed of fresh spinach; linguini with an assortment of fresh shellfish in a light saffron sauce; and grilled breast of duck served with tarragon pear sauce. There's an elegant and extensive Southern-style breakfast menu and a popular Sunday brunch. *115 Meeting St., in the Mills House Hotel, tel. 803/577–2400. Jacket and tie suggested at dinner. Reservations required for Sun. and holiday brunch, suggested for dinner in season. AE, DC, MC, V.*

Queen Street Seafood Inn. Surrounded by a white picket fence, it was converted from a two-story residence, c. 1880. Classical music is played and there is dining in the courtyard, weather permitting. The rooms are intimate, with period furnishings and decor—Victorian black and pink upstairs, lighter and softer downstairs. Chef Wade Tholen's Low Country specialties include grouper fillet lightly rolled in fresh chives, tarragon, and cracked black pepper, then grilled with lemon butter; angelhair pasta tossed with baby shrimp, shirred lean ham, and garden peas in a basil cream sauce; and snapper Legare sauteed with capers, shallots, and freshly squeezed lemon juice. The peach crisp is a dense, moist, cinnamony delight, served hot with vanilla ice cream. The kitchen is very accommodating to those on restricted diets. *68 Queen St., tel. 803/723–7700. Jacket and tie optional. Reservations recommended. AE, DC, MC, V.*

Inexpensive **California Dreaming.** The floor-to-ceiling windows of this
American heavy-volume restaurant, in an impressive stone fort on the Ashley River, look out at night on the lights of the harbor. The

crowds come for the great view, low prices, and bountiful platters of food, such as Texas smoked ribs, barbecued chicken, prime rib, and catch of the day. To make the wait bearable, go to the bar for a frothy frozen margarita. *1 Ashley Pointe Dr. (5 min from downtown), tel. 803/766–1644. Dress: informal. No reservations. AE, MC, V.*

Greek **Athens.** Located just six minutes from downtown, a sojourn here is like a Greek holiday. The *bouzouki* music is straight from the *Plaka* in Athens. George Koutsogiannaks, one of three owners, is the vocalist on tape. The *kalamari lemonato* (baby squid in lemon) is like that served in the *tavernas* on the isle of Hydra. Traditional dishes moussaka and pasticcio are mainstays, but in keeping with current health trends, the freshest of seafood appears on the special board and a vegetarian plate with eggplant, pita, feta cheese, stuffed grape leaves, and *spanakopita* (spinach pie) has been added. The homemade Greek pizza with 12 different spices is Charleston's best. *325 Folly Rd., Cross Creek Shopping Center, James Island, tel. 803/795–0957. MC, V. Closed Sun. lunch.*

Low Country/ **Magnolias.** This popular place, in an 1823 warehouse on the site
Southern of the old customs house, is cherished by Charlestonians and
★ visitors alike. The magnolia theme is seen throughout, and a custom-built circular bar overlooks the dining room. Specialties include grilled dolphin fillet topped with creamed crabmeat and fresh herbs. Even a predictable New York strip steak is distinctive, served with sweet local onion chutney and new-potato hash browns. Equally innovative appetizers include seared yellow grits cakes with white chicken gravy and Cajun ham, and cheese ravioli with creamed shrimp, sea scallops, and fresh dill. An expensive wine list includes some California vintages created especially for Magnolias. *185 E. Bay St., tel. 803/577–7771. Dress: informal. Reservations advised. AE, MC, V.*

Seafood **Shem Creek Bar & Grill.** This pleasant dockside spot is perennially popular for its oyster bar and light fare (Mon.–Wed. until 10 PM, Thurs.–Sun. until 1 AM). There's also a wide variety of seafood entrées, including a steam pot—lobsters, clams, oysters, and sausages with melted lemon butter or hot cocktail sauce—big enough for two. *508 Mill St., Mt. Pleasant, tel. 803/ 884–8102. Dress: informal. No reservations. AE, MC, V.*

Lodging

Hotels and inns on the peninsula are generally more expensive. Also, rates tend to increase during the Spring Festival of Houses (mid-March to mid-April) and the Spoleto Festival USA (late May to early June); at those times, reservations are essential. During Visitors' Appreciation Days, from mid-November to mid-February, discounts of up to 50% may apply. For a Courtesy Discount Card, write to the **Charleston Trident Convention and Visitors Bureau** (Box 975, Charleston 29402, tel. 803/577–2510).

Three organizations offer rooms in homes, cottages, and carriage houses: **Charleston East Bed and Breakfast League** (1031 Tall Pine Rd., Mt. Pleasant 29464, tel. 803/884–8208), **Charleston Society Bed & Breakfast** (84 Murray Blvd., Charleston 29401, tel. 803/723–4948), and **Historic Charleston Bed and Breakfast** (43 Legare St., Charleston 29402, tel. 803/722–

6606). Those interested in renting condominiums or houses on the beach on the Isle of Palms—some with private pools and tennis courts—might contact **Island Realty** (Box 157, Isle of Palms 29451, tel. 803/886–8144 or 800/845–2546).

The following price categories have been used: *Very Expensive*, over $150; *Expensive*, $90–$150; *Moderate*, $50–$90; *Inexpensive*, under $50.

Hotels and Motels
Very Expensive

Best Western King Charles Inn. This inn in the historic district has spacious rooms furnished with period reproductions. *237 Meeting St., 29401, tel. 803/723–7451 or 800/528–1234. 91 rooms. Facilities: pool, dining room, lounge. AE, DC, MC, V.*

Hawthorn Suites at the Market. Charleston's newest luxury hotel, its traditionally inspired architecture highlighted by a restored entrance portico from an 1874 bank, also incorporates a refurbished 1866 firehouse, now a meetings facility. Its three luxuriant gardens, named for 18th-century French botanist André Michaux, are planted with indigenous shrubs, trees, and flowers. The spacious suites, all decorated with 18th-century reproductions and canopied beds, include full kitchens or wet bars with microwave ovens and refrigerators. *181 Church St., 29401, tel. 803/577–2644 or 800/527–1133. 17 rooms, 164 suites. Facilities: business services, concierge, fitness center, pool, whirlpool, video library, complimentary breakfast and afternoon refreshments, 6 meeting rooms, valet parking. AE, D, DC, MC, V.*

★ **Mills House Hotel.** Antique furnishings and period decor give great charm to this luxurious Holiday Inn property, a reconstruction of a historic hostelry on its original site in the historic district. There's a lounge with live entertainment, and excellent dining in the Barbadoes Room (*see* Dining, *above*). *115 Meeting St., 29401, tel. 803/577–2400 or 800/465–4329. 215 rooms. Facilities: pool. AE, DC, MC, V.*

★ **Omni Hotel at Charleston Place.** Among the city's most luxurious hotels, this graceful, low-rise structure in the historic district is flanked by upscale boutiques and specialty shops (*see* Shopping, *above*). The lobby features a magnificent hand-blown Venetian glass chandelier, an Italian marble floor, and antiques from Sotheby's. Rooms are furnished with period reproductions. *130 Market St., 29401, tel. 803/722–4900 or 800/843–6664. 443 units, including 46 suites. Facilities: fitness center with heated pool, sauna, whirlpool, Nautilus; concierge floor with complimentary food and drink service; 2 restaurants including Louis's Charleston Grill; lounges with entertainment. AE, DC, MC, V.*

Expensive

Sheraton Charleston Hotel. Some rooms and suites in this 13-story hotel outside the historic district overlook the Ashley River. Spacious rooms and suites are highlighted with Queen Anne furnishings, and there's concierge service. Live entertainment and dancing contribute to the lounge's local popularity. *170 Lockwood Dr., 29403, tel. 803/723–3000 or 800/325–3535. 337 rooms. Facilities: 4 lighted tennis courts, pool, jogging track, coffee shop, dining room. AE, DC, MC, V.*

Moderate–Expensive

Holiday Inn Charleston/Mt. Pleasant. Just over the Cooper River Bridge, a 10-minute drive from the downtown historic district, is this new full-service hotel. Everything has been graciously done: brass lamps, crystal chandeliers, Queen Anne–style furniture. Two suites have Jacuzzis. "High-tech suites" offer PC cable hookups, large working areas, glossy ultramodern furniture, and refrigerators. *250 U.S. 17 Bypass, Mt. Pleasant 29464, tel. 803/884–6000 or 800/465–4329. 158 rooms. Facilities: outdoor pool, sauna, exercise room, cable TV/movies, meeting facilities and ballroom, concierge floor, laundry, restaurant, raw bar, lounge with DJ. AE, DC, MC, V.*

Moderate
★ **Days Inn Historic District.** This inn is well located and attractively furnished. *155 Meeting St., 29401, tel. 803/722–8411 or 800/325–2525. 124 units. Facilities: pool, dining room. AE, DC, MC, V.*

Inexpensive **Econo-Travel Motor Hotel.** This budget-chain unit is eight miles from downtown. Contemporary-style rooms are spacious and well maintained. *4725 Arco La., N. Charleston 29405, tel. 803/747–3672 or 800/446–6900. 48 rooms. Facilities: cable TV/ free movies. Senior citizen, military/government discounts. AE, DC, MC, V.*

Hampton Inn Charleston Airport. This economy arm of Holiday Inns offers lower rates with full service amenities. Rooms are decorated in contemporary style. *4701 Arco La., N. Charleston 29418, tel. 803/554–7154 or 800/426–7866. 125 rooms. Facilities: pool, cable TV/free movies, suite for small meetings. AE, DC, MC, V.*

Motel 6. This well-maintained motor inn, part of a budget chain, is 10 miles from the downtown historic district. The decor is cheerful, colorful, and contemporary. *2551 Ashley Phosphate Rd., N. Charleston, 29418, tel. 803/572–6590. 126 rooms. Facilities: pool, cable TV/movies. DC, MC, V.*

Inns and Guest Houses
The charms of historic Charleston can be enhanced by a stay at one of its many inns, most housed in restored structures in the historic district. Some are reminiscent of European inns; one is tastefully contemporary, tucked away on the grounds of a famous garden estate. For complete listings, consult the "Charleston Area Visitors Guide," published by the Charleston Trident Convention & Visitors Bureau (Box 975, Charleston 29402, tel. 803/577–2510).

Expensive–Very Expensive
The Anchorage Inn. This intimate harborside inn, furnished with antiques and period reproductions, is near Charleston's waterfront park. Guests are served a complimentary evening tea and a hearty complete breakfast. *26 Vendue La., 29401, tel. 803/723–8300 or 800/421–2952. 19 rooms. Facilities: library, free parking, turn-down service. AE, D, DC, MC, V.*

Indigo Inn. All the rooms here focus on the picturesque interior courtyard and are furnished with 18th-century antiques and reproductions. The trademark "hunt breakfast" consists of homemade breads, ham biscuits, fruit, and coffee. There are six slightly more expensive suites—one with a Jacuzzi—in the nearby **Jasmine House,** a pre–Civil War Greek Revival structure. These have high ceilings, fireplaces, and Oriental rugs. *1 Maiden La., 29401, tel. 803/577–5900 or 800/845–7639. 40 rooms. AE, MC, V.*

★ **The John Rutledge House Inn.** This 1763 house, built by John Rutledge, one of the signers of the U.S. Constitution, was opened in 1989 as a luxury inn. Ornate ironwork on the facade features a palmetto tree and eagle motif, signifying Rutledge's service to both his state and his nation. Complimentary wine and tea are served in the ballroom, and complimentary Continental breakfast and newspapers are delivered to rooms each morning. Two charming period carriage houses also accommodate guests. *116 Broad St., tel. 803/723–7999 or 800/476–9741. 11 rooms in mansion, 4 in each carriage house. Facilities: free parking. AE, MC, V.*

★ **Vendue Inn.** Near the waterfront, this European-style inn in a renovated 1828 warehouse offers antiques-furnished public areas and guest rooms, with canopied four-poster beds and Oriental rugs. The adjacent **Vendue West**, in a restored 1800 house, has deluxe suites with fireplaces, wet bars, Jacuzzis, and marble baths. Complimentary wine and cheese are served afternoons in the courtyard, accompanied by a piano. Concierge service is offered, and there is a restaurant, Chouinards. *19 Vendue Range, 29401, tel. 803/577–7970 or 800/845–7900. 33 rooms and suites. AE, MC, V.*

Expensive **Battery Carriage House.** This small luxury guest house—one of Charleston's first inns—has handsomely furnished rooms with period furniture and kitchenettes. *20 S. Battery St., 29401, tel. 803/720–2603. 4 rooms. Facilities: pool. AE, MC, V.*

Lodge Alley Inn. All of the various accommodations here are luxuriously appointed in traditional Charleston fashion with Oriental carpets and period reproduction furnishings. Room refrigerators are stocked with complimentary wine. The French Quarter Restaurant features a grand rotisserie. Adjacent is a lounge with an ornate bar. *195 E. Bay St., 29401, tel. 803/722–1611 or 800/845–1004. 34 rooms, 37 suites with kitchens, one 2-bedroom penthouse. AE, MC, V.*

Meeting Street Inn. The rooms in this handsome 1870 structure are furnished in period. Each has a reproduction four-poster rice bed, and all open onto a piazza. Guests mingle in the courtyard garden for complimentary afternoon champagne and for evening cocktails and chamber music. *173 Meeting St., 29401, tel. 803/723–1882 or 800/842–8022. 54 rooms. Facilities: whirlpool, boardroom suite for meetings. AE, MC, V.*

★ **Planters Inn.** Rooms and suites here are beautifully appointed with opulent fabrics and furnishings, including mahogany four-poster beds and marble baths. There's a concierge and 24-hour room service. *112 N. Market St., 29401, tel. 803/722–2345 or 800/845–7082. 41 rooms and suites. AE, DC, MC, V.*

★ **Middleton Inn and Conference Center.** This contemporary-style lodge with sumptuously furnished rooms is located on the grounds of Middleton Place Plantation. Floor-to-ceiling windows are hung with wooden shutters, and working fireplaces are serviced by tools forged by the estate's blacksmith. There is a cafe. *Ashley River Rd. (U.S. 61), Middleton Place, 29407, tel. 803/556–0500 or 800/543–4774. 55 rooms. Facilities: pool, tennis courts. AE, MC, V.*

Resort Islands Though all of these resorts fall into the Very Expensive category, a wide variety of packages makes them more affordable. Peak-season rates (during spring and summer vacations) range from $100 to $250 per day, double occupancy. Costs often drop considerably off-season.

★ **Kiawah Island Resort.** Choose from 150 inn rooms, 48 suites, and 500 completely equipped one- to four-bedroom villas in two luxurious resort villages on 10,000 wooded acres. There are 10 miles of fine broad beaches, four championship golf courses, two complete tennis centers, jeep and water safaris, land sailing, canoeing, surfcasting, fishing, and children's programs. There's also a general store and shops. Dining options are many and varied: Low Country specialties in the Jasmine Porch and

Veranda, Indigo House; Continental cuisine in the Charleston Gallery; lagoonside dining at the Park Cafe; casual dining in the Sand Wedge, Sundancers, Jonah's. *On Kiawah Island, 21 mi from Charleston (take U.S. 17S to Main Rd., take left and follow signs), Box 12910, Charleston 29412, tel. 803/768–2121 or 800/654–2924 nationwide, 800/845–2471 in SC. AE, DC, MC, V. Very Expensive.*

Seabrook Island Resort. There are 360 completely equipped one- to three-bedroom villas, cottages, and beach houses. Beach Club and Island Club, open to all guests, are centers for dining and leisure activities. Amenities include championship golf, tennis and equestrian centers, bicycling, water sports, pools, children's programs. *On Seabrook Island, 23 mi from Charleston (take U.S. 17S to SC 171S to SC 700, then follow signs), Box 32099, Charleston 29417, tel. 803/768–1000 or 800/ 845–5531. AE, DC, MC, V. Very Expensive.*

Wild Dunes. This lavish, 1,500-acre resort has 360 villa accommodations, each with a fully equipped kitchen and washer and dryer. There are two widely acclaimed championship golf courses, a racquet club, a yacht harbor on the Intracoastal Waterway, bicycling, nature trails, surfcasting, water sports, and children's programs. Guests enjoy beef specialties at The Club House and fresh seafoods at The Island House, where all dishes are created by a French master chef. There's a lounge with live entertainment. *On the Isle of Palms, 12 mi northeast of Charleston (take U.S. 17 to SC 703), Box 1410, Charleston 29402, tel. 803/886–6000 or 800/845–8880 nationwide. AE, DC, MC, V. Very Expensive.*

The Arts

Pick up the comprehensive Schedule of Events at the Visitors Information Center (85 Calhoun St.) or at area hotels, inns, and restaurants. For an advance copy, contact **Charleston Trident Convention and Visitors Bureau** (Box 975, Charleston 29402, tel. 803/577–2510). Also see "Tips for Tourists" each Saturday in *The News & Courier/The Evening Post.* And the weekend ARTSline (tel. 803/723–2787) gives information on arts events for the week.

Arts Festivals **Spoleto Festival USA.** Founded by renowned maestro Gian Carlo Menotti in 1977, Spoleto has become one of the world's greatest celebrations of the arts. For two weeks, from late May to early June, opera, dance, theater, symphonic and chamber music performances, jazz, and the visual arts are showcased in concert halls, theaters, parks, churches, streets, and gardens throughout the city. For information: Spoleto Festival USA (Box 704, Charleston, SC 29402, tel. 803/722–2764).

Piccolo Spoleto Festival. The spirited companion festival of Spoleto Festival USA showcases the best in local and regional talent from every artistic discipline. There are about 700 events—from jazz performances to puppet shows—held at 60 sites in 17 days, from mid-May through early June, and most performances are free. For a program, available May 1 each year, contact the Office of Cultural Affairs, Piccolo Spoleto Festival (133 Church St., Charleston 29401, tel. 803/724–7305).

Moja Arts Festival. Theater, dance, and music performances, art shows, films, lectures, and tours celebrating the rich heritage of the African continent are held at sites throughout the historic district the first two weeks in October. For information: The Office of Cultural Affairs (133 Church St., Charleston 29401, tel. 803/724–7305).

Concerts The College of Charleston has a free **Monday Night Recital Series** (tel. 803/792–8228). The **Charleston Symphony Orchestra** (tel. 803/723–7528) presents its Classics Concerts Series at Gaillard Municipal Auditorium (77 Calhoun St., tel. 803/577–4500). Its Brass Quintet plays at the Charleston Museum Auditorium (360 Meeting St., tel. 803/722–2996) and the Garden Theatre (371 King St., tel. 803/722–6230). Its Woodwind Quintet also performs at the Charleston Museum Auditorium, and its chamber music series is held at various locations throughout the city.

Dance The **Charleston Ballet Theatre** (tel. 803/723–7334) and the **Charleston Civic Ballet** (tel. 803/722–8779 or 577–4502) perform at Gaillard Municipal Auditorium. The **Robert Ivey Ballet Company** (tel. 803/556–1343), a student group at the College of Charleston, gives a fall and spring program of jazz, classical, and modern dance at the Simons Center for the Arts.

Theater The **Footlight Players,** the **East Cooper Theater,** and the **Young Charleston Theatre Co.** stage performances at the Dock Street Theatre. The East Cooper Theatre also stages some performances at the Garden Theatre.

Nightlife

Beach Bar **Windjammer** (tel. 803/886–8596), on the Isle of Palms, is an oceanfront spot featuring live rock music.

Dance Clubs In the market area, there's **Fannigans** (tel. 803/722–6916), where a DJ spins Top-40 hits and the best of beach music; **Juke Box** (tel. 803/723–3431), with a DJ, '50s and '60s music, and a '50s look (waitresses wear cheerleader outfits); and **Myskyns** (tel. 803/577–5595), with live rock, reggae, R&B, or other bands most nights and an 8-by-10 video screen.

Jazz Club **Coconut Club,** in the Old Seaman's Chapel (32 N. Market St., tel. 803/723–3614), features live jazz Thursday through Saturday night in a quiet atmosphere that actually allows conversation. Light appetizers are served, and there's a 1:30 Gospel brunch on Sunday.

Dinner Cruises For an evening of dining and dancing afloat on the luxury yacht *Spirit of Charleston*, call 803/722–2628. *The Southern Star*, a reconverted paddlewheeler, also has dinner cruises and sails from the Ripley Light Marina near California Dreaming. Call Bill Miller, 803/722–6182. *The Pride* operates from the same dock and is an 84-foot gaff-topsail schooner available for daily harbor excursions and cruises to Savannah, Georgia. Phone Capt. Bob, 803/795–1180.

The Coast to Hilton Head

The road southwest from Charleston takes you past a deeply indented coast with some marvelous barrier islands. Farther west is Beaufort, a gracious antebellum town with a compact historic district preserving lavish 18th- and 19th-century homes. Anchoring the southern tip of South Carolina's coastline is 42-square-mile Hilton Head Island, home to some of the nation's finest and most luxurious resort developments. Hilton Head Island's casual pace, broad beaches, wide-ranging activities, and genteel good life make it one of the East Coast's most popular vacation getaways.

Heading west from Charleston on Route 17, turn south on Route 20 to reach **Kiawah Island,** a resort island that has excellent shelling. To pick some beautiful shells, go to **Beachwalker Park** at the west end of the island.

Continue south on Route 17 to Route 174 and follow that road east to the ocean to reach **Edisto Island** ("ED-is-toh"), settled in 1690 and once a notable center for cultivation of silky Sea Island cotton. Here, magnificent stands of age-old oaks festooned with Spanish moss border quiet streams and side roads. Wild turkeys roam freely in open grasslands. Trawlers dock at rickety piers in an antiquated fishing village that looks like a monochromatic etching in early morning mists. Some of its elaborate mansions have been restored; others brood in disrepair. About the only contemporary touches on the island are a few cottages in a popular state park and modern villas in Fairfield Ocean Ridge Resort. Most of the island's inhabitants are descendants of former slaves, and they preserve many aspects of their African heritage, such as painting doorways and window sills bright blue to ward off evil spirits.

Edisto Beach State Park, one of the state's most popular, offers three miles of beach with excellent shelling. There are cabins by the marsh and campsites by the ocean. The cabins are basic but clean, and offer full housekeeping facilities. *For information and reservations, contact: Superintendent, Edisto Beach State Park, 8377 State Cabin Rd., Edisto Island 29438, tel. 803/869–2156 or 803/869–3396.*

Return to Route 17 and continue about 40 miles southwest to Route 21, which takes you 18 miles south to the waterfront city of **Beaufort.** Established in 1710, Beaufort achieved immense prosperity toward the close of the 18th century when Sea Island cotton was introduced as a money crop. Many of the lavish houses that the wealthy landowners and merchants built—with wide balconies, high ceilings, and luxurious appointments—today remain, a legacy of an elegant and gracious era. Self-guided walking or driving tours are available through the **Beaufort County Chamber of Commerce** (1006 Bay St., tel. 803/524–3163).

Across the street from the Chamber of Commerce is the handsome **George Elliott House,** which served as a Union hospital during the Civil War. It was built in 1840 in Greek Revival style, with leaded-glass fanlights, pine floors, and rococo ceilings. The furnishings include some fine early Victorian pieces. *1001 Bay St., tel. 803/524–8450. Admission: $3 adults, $2 children. Open weekdays 11–3, Sun. 1–3.*

Nearby, the **John Mark Verdier House,** an Adam-style structure built around 1790 and headquarters for Union forces during the war, has been restored and furnished as it would have been between 1790 and the visit of Lafayette in 1825. Guided tours are available. *801 Bay St., tel. 803/524–6334. Admission:*

$3 adults, $2 children under 15. Open Feb.–mid-Dec., Tues.–Sat. 11–4. Closed rest of year and Thanksgiving.

Built in 1795 and remodeled in 1852, the Gothic-style arsenal was home of the Beaufort Volunteer Artillery. It now houses the **Beaufort Museum,** with prehistoric relics, Indian pottery, Revolutionary and Civil War exhibits, and decorative arts. *713 Craven St., tel. 803/525-7471. Donations requested. Open weekdays 10 AM–noon and 2–5 PM, Sat. 10 AM–noon. Closed Sun., holidays.*

St. Helena's Episcopal Church, dating from 1724, was also touched by the Civil War: It was turned into a hospital and gravestones were brought inside to serve as operating tables. *501 Church St., tel. 803/524-3163. Donations appreciated. Visitors welcome Mon.–Sat. 9–4.*

Part of the 304-acre Historic Beaufort District, **Old Point** includes many private antebellum homes not open to visitors. Some may be open during the annual Fall House Tour, a mid-October weekend, and the Spring Tour of Homes and Gardens, in April or May. The rest of the year, you'll have to content yourself with appreciating the fine exteriors.

Pause in the **Henry C. Chambers Waterfront Park** to rest and survey the scene. Its seven landscaped acres along the Beaufort River, part of the Intracoastal Waterway, include a seawall promenade, a crafts market, gardens, and a marina.

Just south of Beaufort is **Parris Island,** home of the U.S. Marine Corps Recruit Depot, where visitors are welcome to observe recruit training. Guided tours are available. Also on the base, the **War Memorial Building Museum** features a collection of vintage uniforms, photographs, special exhibits, and weapons. On the grounds is a replica of the Iwo Jima flag-raising monument. *Museum: Tel. 803/525-2951. Admission free. Open daily 10–4:30. Closed major holidays.*

Nine miles southeast of Beaufort via U.S. 21 is **St. Helena Island,** site of the **Penn School Historic District** and the **York W. Bailey Museum.** The institution was established in the middle of the Civil War as the South's first school for freed slaves. Today, the center works to promote community services. The museum (formerly Dr. Bailey's clinic) has displays reflecting the heritage of sea island blacks. *Land's End Rd., St. Helena Village, tel. 803/838-2432. Suggested donation: $1 adults, 50¢ children 12 and under. Open weekdays 9–5.*

Nine miles farther east via U.S. 21 is **Hunting Island,** a secluded domain of ocean beaches, semitropical woodlands, and the photogenic 140-foot-high **Hunting Island Lighthouse,** built in 1859 and abandoned in 1933. If you want to make the effort to climb the spiral staircase—all 181 steps—you'll be rewarded with sweeping vistas of the island, ocean, and marshland. The 5,000-acre barrier island is a popular state park offering three miles of broad swimming beach, hiking, nature trails, and surf, inlet, and lagoon fishing. *Nominal admission per car in summer. For cabin reservations, write Hunting Island State Park, Rte. 1, Box 668, Frogmore 29920, tel. 803/838-2011.*

From Beaufort, drive on Route 170 across Port Royal Sound to Route 278, which leads south and then east across to **Hilton Head Island.** Named after English sea captain William Hilton, who claimed it for England in 1663, the island was settled by planters in the 1700s and flourished until the Civil War. Thereafter, the economy declined and the island languished until Charles E. Fraser, a visionary South Carolina attorney, began developing the Sea Pines resort in 1956. Sea Pines's emphasis on preserving the integrity of the island's ecology has set the tone for resorts that have followed. Lined by towering pines, wind-sculpted live oaks, and palmetto trees, Hilton Head's 12 miles of beaches are a major attraction of this semitropical barrier island; its oak and pine woodlands, meandering lagoons, and temperate ocean climate provide an incomparable environment for golfing, tennis, water sports, beachcombing, and sea splashing.

Choice stretches of the island are occupied by various resorts, or "plantations," among them Sea Pines, Shipyard, Palmetto Dunes, Port Royal, and Hilton Head. In these resorts, accommodations range from rental vacation villas and lavish private homes to luxury hotels. The resorts are also private residential communities, although many have restaurants, marinas, shopping areas, and/or recreational facilities that are open to the public. All are secured, and visitors cannot tour the residential areas unless arrangements are made at the visitor or security office near the main gate of each plantation.

In the south of the island, at the **Newhall Audubon Preserve,** you'll find unusual native plant life identified and tagged in a pristine 50-acre site. There are trails, a self-guided tour, and plant walks seasonally. *Palmetto Bay Rd., tel. 803/671–2008. Admission free. Open daily during daylight hours.*

Also in the south, and part of the Sea Pines resort, is the **Sea Pines Forest Preserve,** a 605-acre public wilderness tract. There are seven miles of walking trails, a well-stocked fishing pond, a waterfowl pond, and a 3,400-year-old Indian shell ring. Both guided and self-guided tours are available. *Tel. 803/671–7170. $3 per-car fee for nonguests. Open daily 7 AM–9:30 PM. Closed during the Heritage Golf Classic in Apr.*

On Hilton Head Plantation, you might stop to note the earthwork fortifications that mark the site of **Fort Mitchell,** built in 1812 on a bluff overlooking Skull Creek as part of a large system across the island's northern end.

Beach walks are conducted daily in season by the Environmental Museum of Hilton Head for a nominal fee (tel. 803/842–9197; the museum itself is years away from opening).

Off the island, there's the **Waddell Mariculture Research and Development Center,** three miles west. Here methods of raising seafood commercially are studied, and visitors are invited to tour its 24 ponds and the research building to see work in progress. *Sawmill Creek Rd., near U.S. 278–SC 46 intersection, tel. 803/681–8800. Admission free. Tours weekdays at 10 AM and by appointment.*

From Hilton Head Island, you can visit remote **Daufuskie Island** by boat. It was the setting for Pat Conroy's novel *The Water Is Wide,* which was made into the movie *Conrack.* Most inhabitants, descendants of former slaves, live on small farms. Remnants of churches, homes, and schools scattered among the live oaks, pines, palmettos, and semitropical shrubs serve as reminders of antebellum times, when the island was well populated and prosperous. Two major developments are under way.

Boats offering excursions to the island from various marinas in Hilton Head include *The Adventure* in Shelter Cove Harbor (tel. 803/681–8222) and *The Gypsy* in Harbour Town Marina (tel. 803/842–4155).

Shopping

Malls   Major Hilton Head Island shopping sites include **Pinelawn Mall** (U.S. 278 at Matthews Dr., tel. 803/681–8907 or 681–9807), with 33 shops and six restaurants; and **Coligny Plaza** (Coligny Circle, tel. 803/842–6050), with 60-plus shops, restaurants, food stands, a movie theater, and a supermarket.

Antiques   **Christina's Antiques Et Cetera** (Hilton Head Plaza, tel. 803/686–3333) features Oriental and European antiques and New Guinea primitives. **Den of Antiquity** (20 mi north of Hilton Head on U.S. 170, in Beaufort, tel. 803/842–6711), the area's largest antiques shop, carries a wide assortment of Low Country and nautical pieces. **Harbour Town Antiques** (at Harbour Town, Hilton Head, tel. 803/671–5999) has an impressive collection of American and English furniture, plus unusual pieces of Oriental and English porcelain.

Art Galleries   In Hilton Head, the **Red Piano Art Gallery** (220 Cordillo Pkwy., tel. 803/785–2318) showcases works by island artists and craftsfolk. In Beaufort, the **Rhett Gallery** (809 Bay St., tel. 803/524–3339) sells Low Country art by Nancy Ricker Rhett, William Means Rhett, Stephen Elliott Webb, and James Moore Rhett.

Jewelry   On Hilton Head, **The Bird's Nest** (Coligny Plaza, tel. 803/785–3737) sells locally made shell and sand-dollar jewelry. **The Goldsmith Shop** (3 Lagoon Rd., tel. 803/785–2538) features classic jewelry, island charms, custom designs, and repairs. **Touch of Turquoise** (The Market on Palmetto Bay Rd., tel. 803/842–3880) sells authentic Indian jewelry, sand-dollar pendants, and more. In Beaufort, **The Craftseller** (210 Scott St., tel. 803/525–6104) showcases jewelry and other items by Southern craftsfolk.

Sports and Outdoor Activities

Bicycling   There are pathways in several areas of Hilton Head Island (many in the resorts), and pedaling is popular along the firmly packed beach. Bicycles can be rented at most hotels and resorts. One of the oldest rental shops here is **Harbour Town Bicycles** (Graves Plaza, Hwy. 278, tel. 803/785–3546; Sea Pines Plantation, tel. 803/671–7300) and **Palmetto Dunes Resort** (tel. 803/671–5386).

Fishing   On Hilton Head, you can pick oysters, dig for clams, or cast for shrimp. Each year a billfishing tournament and two king mackerel tournaments attract anglers to the island.

Golf   Many golf courses on Hilton Head Island are ranked among the world's top 100. Several resort courses are open for public play, including two at the residential Hilton Head Plantation. Each April, Sea Pines's Harbour Town course is the site of the MCI Heritage Golf Classic, drawing top PGA stars.

Horseback Riding   Many trails wind through woods and nature preserves. There are five fully equipped stables in the Hilton Head area: **Lawton Fields Stable** in Sea Pines (tel. 803/671–2586), **Moss Creek Plan-**

tation **Equestrian Center** (tel. 803/785–4488), **Rose Hill Plantation Stables** (tel. 803/757–3082), **Sandy Creek Stables** near Spanish Wells (tel. 803/681–4610), and **Seabrook Farm Stables** in Hilton Head Plantation (tel. 803/681–5415).

Tennis There are more than 300 courts on Hilton Head. Three resorts—**Sea Pines** (tel. 803/785–3333), **Shipyard Plantation** (tel. 803/785–2313), and **Port Royal** (tel. 803/681–3322)—are rated among the top 50 tennis destinations in the United States. Racquet clubs that welcome guest play on clay, composition, hard-surface, synthetic, and even a few grass courts include **Port Royal Tennis Club** (tel. 803/681–3322), **Rod Laver Tennis** at Palmetto Dunes (tel. 803/785–1152), **Sea Pines Racquet Club** (tel. 803/671–2494), and **Van der Meer Tennis Center** (tel. 803/785–8388 or 800/845–6138). Each April, top professional women's stars participate in the Family Circle Magazine Cup Tennis Tournament at Sea Pines Racquet Club.

Windsurfing Lessons and rentals are available from **Windsurfing Hilton Head** at Sea Pines Resort's South Beach Marina (tel. 803/671–2643) and at Shelter Cove Plaza (tel. 803/686–6996).

Spectator Sports

Polo There are matches every other Sunday during spring and fall at **Rose Hill Plantation** (tel. 803/842–2828).

Beaches

On Hilton Head Island, the ocean side features wide stretches of gently sloping white sand, extending for the island's entire 12-mile length. Many spots remain secluded and uncrowded. Although resort beaches are reserved for guests and residents, there are about 35 public beach entrances from Folly Field to South Forest Beach near Sea Pines. Two main parking areas are at Coligny Circle, near the Holiday Inn, and on Folly Field Road, off U.S. 278 near the Hilton Head Island Beach and Tennis Resort. Signs along U.S. 278 point the way to Bradley, Burkes, and Singleton beaches, where parking space is limited.

Hunting Island State Park has three miles of broad swimming beaches. **Edisto Beach State Park** on Edisto Island also has nearly three miles of public beach.

Dining and Lodging

The following dining price categories have been used: *Very Expensive*, over $25; *Expensive*, $15–$25; *Moderate*, $7–$15; *Inexpensive*, under $7.

There are four major resorts on Hilton Head. **Sea Pines,** the oldest and best-known of Hilton Head's resorts, occupies 4,500 choice, thickly wooded acres. Its three championship golf courses include renowned Harbour Town Links, designed by Pete Dye and Jack Nicklaus and one of the top 20 U.S. courses. There's a fine beach, two racquet clubs, riding stables, two shopping plazas, and a 500-acre forest preserve. Accommodations are in luxurious homes and villas fronting the ocean or the golf courses. **Shipyard Plantation** has the Marriott hotel and a wide array of villa condominiums, most overlooking an excellent golf facility with three championship nines. There's a rac-quiet club and a small beach club. **Palmetto Dunes Resort** is home of the renowned Rod Laver Tennis Center and has a good stretch of beach and three championship golf courses. In addition to its two hotels (the Hyatt Regency and the Mariner's Inn), there are several luxury rental villa complexes overlooking the ocean. **Port Royal Plantation** has three championship golf courses, which have hosted PGA events, and its racquet club offers play on clay, hard, and grass courts. Besides the Westin, there are also a few rental homes and a limited selection of villas.

Not all lodgings are located within the resorts, however. **Hilton Head Central Reservations** (Box 5312, Hilton Head Island, 29938, tel. 800/845-7018) is a good source of detailed information about various island resorts and properties. It represents almost every hotel, motel, and condominium rental agency on the island.

Rates can drop appreciably in the off-season (on Hilton Head Island, Nov.–Mar.), and package plans are available year-round. The following lodging price categories have been used: *Very Expensive*, over $145; *Expensive*, $95–$145; *Moderate*, $55–$95; *Inexpensive*, under $50.

Beaufort **The Anchorage House.** The pre-Revolutionary ambience of this
Dining 1765 structure is enhanced by period furnishings, candlelight, and gleaming silver and crystal. Sherry-laced she-crab soup, crabmeat casserole, and other Low Country specialties share the menu with such Continental selections as veal piccata and steak *au poivre*. *1103 Bay St., tel. 803/524-9392. Jackets suggested at dinner. Reservations suggested. AE, DC, MC, V. Closed Sun., major holidays. Moderate–Expensive.*

Lodging **Best Western Sea Island Inn.** At this well-maintained resort inn in the downtown historic district, rooms feature period decor. *1015 Bay St., Box 532, 29902, tel. 803/524-4121 or 800/528-1234. 43 rooms. Facilities: pool, cable TV, restaurant, lounge. AE, DC, MC, V. Moderate.*
Holiday Inn of Beaufort. This motor inn is conveniently located for visitors to Parris Island or the Marine Corps Air Station. *U.S. 21 and Lovejoy St., Box 1008, 29902, tel. 803/524-2144 or 800/465-4329. 152 rooms. Facilities: heated pool, tennis, cable TV/movies, restaurant, lounge with live entertainment. AE, DC, MC, V. Moderate.*

Edisto Island **Fairfield Ocean Ridge Resort.** This is a good choice for vaca-
Lodging tioners seeking to combine all the resort amenities with a get-away-from-it-all setting. There are accommodations in well-furnished two- and three-bedroom villa units tastefully decorated in contemporary style. *1 King Cotton Rd., Box 27, 29438, tel. 803/869-2561. 100 units. Facilities: pool, wading pool, beach, marina, fishing, tennis, golf, miniature golf, social and recreational programs, children's activities, nature trails, playground, restaurant, lounge, AE, DC, MC, V. Moderate–Expensive.*

Fripp Island **Fripp Island Resort.** The resort encompasses the entire island,
Lodging and access is limited to guests only. The two- and three-bedroom villas are contemporary in decor. *19 mi south of Beaufort via U.S. 21, 1 Tarpon Blvd., 29920, tel. 803/838-2441 or 800/845-4100. 133 units. Facilities: pools, tennis courts, championship golf course, full-service marina with rental boats, bi-*

cycle and jogging trails, laundry, children's program, 3 restaurants. AE, MC, V. Moderate–Expensive.

Hilton Head Island
Dining

Harbourmaster's. With sweeping views of the harbor, this spacious, multilevel dining room offers such Continental dishes as chateaubriand and New Zealand rack of lamb laced with a brandy demiglaze. Service is deft. *In Shelter Cove Marina, off U.S. 278, across from Palmetto Dunes, tel. 803/785–3030. Jacket required at dinner. Reservations required. AE, DC, MC, V. Closed Sun. and for about a month in winter. Very Expensive.*

★ **The Barony.** An intimate series of softly lighted seating areas with "upscale country French" decor range off the main dining room, which is centered with a display of drop-dead desserts, marzipan flowers, and exotic cheeses and breads, spotlighted by a crystal chandelier. There's glittering crystal and silver, and a quartet of tuxedoed waiters for every table. In addition to the regular Low Country and Continental entrées, elegant low-calorie menus are offered, such as chilled coconut-and-pineapple soup, asparagus salad with quail eggs, sorbet, poached fillet of Dover sole with seafood mousse, and macédoine of fresh fruits with raspberry sauce. *The Westin Resort, Hilton Head Island (formerly Hotel Inter-Continental), 135 S. Port Royal Dr., tel. 803/681–4000. Jacket and tie required. Reservations suggested. AE, DC, MC, V. Closed Mon. Expensive–Very Expensive.*

Fulvio's. A rather elegant, formal atmosphere, reinforced by deft service, prevails in this popular dining room. The menu emphasizes Italian specialties, such as a hearty and luscious *cioppino di frutti di mare*—a tomato-based stew of shellfish and vegetables. *New Orleans Rd. and U.S. 278, in Shipyard Center, tel. 803/681–6001. AE, DC, MC, V. Closed Sun., holidays, first 2 wks in Jan. Dinner only. Expensive.*

Hemingway's. This oceanfront seafood restaurant serves pompano *en papillote*, trout amandine with herbed lemon-butter sauce, fresh grilled seafoods, and steaks, in a relaxed, Key West–type atmosphere. *Hyatt Regency Hilton Head, in Palmetto Dunes Resort, tel. 803/785–1234. Dress: informal. Reservations suggested. AE, DC, MC, V. Moderate.*

Hudson's Seafood House on the Docks. This huge, airy, family-owned restaurant has its own fishing fleet; catches are rushed straight from the boats to the kitchens. The dining room always seems full, but service is quick and friendly and diners never feel rushed. There's a separate oyster bar, as well as an adjacent family-style restaurant, The Landing. *1 Hudson Rd., on the docks, tel. 803/681–2773. The Landing, tel. 803/681–3363. Dress: informal. No reservations. AE, MC, V. Moderate.*

Old Fort Pub. Tucked away in a quiet site overlooking Skull Creek, this rustic restaurant specializes in such Low Country dishes as oyster pie, oysters wrapped in Smithfield ham, Savannah chicken-fried steak with onion gravy, and hoppin' john. *In Hilton Head Plantation, tel. 803/681–2386. Dress: informal. No reservations. AE, DC, MC, V. No lunch Sun. Moderate.*

Lodging

Hyatt Regency Hilton Head. At this newly renovated oceanside hotel, the largest on the island, guest rooms have been lavishly redecorated. Some have balconies. The Hyatt has a concierge floor and extensive meeting space and services, making it especially appealing to groups. A good array of vacation packages attracts families as well. *U.S. 278, in Palmetto Dunes Resort,*

Box 6167, 29938, tel. 803/785–1234 or 800/233–1234. 505 rooms. Facilities: pools, health club, sailboats, cable TV/movies, coffee shop, dining rooms, lounges, entertainment, dancing. Guests have privileges at 3 18-hole championship golf courses and 25 hard, grass, and clay tennis courts at Palmetto Dunes, plus its 3 mi of private beach. AE, DC, MC, V. Very Expensive.

★ **The Westin Resort, Hilton Head Island** (formerly Hotel Inter-Continental Hilton Head). Among the island's newest luxury properties, this horseshoe-shaped hotel sprawls in a lushly landscaped oceanside setting. The expansive guest rooms, most with ocean view, are furnished in a pleasing mix of period reproduction and contemporary furnishings. All have comfortable seating areas and desks. Public areas display museum-quality Oriental porcelains, screens, paintings, and furnishings. The Barony restaurant (*see* Dining, *above*) is one of the island's finest. With vast meeting spaces and an emphasis on upscale amenities, the Westin caters to the upscale business traveler and middle-aged or older affluent vacationers. Not that families aren't warmly welcomed, but the atmosphere is a bit more formal than elsewhere on the island. *At Port Royal Resort, 135 S. Port Royal Dr., 29928, tel. 803/681–4000 or 800/228–3000. 412 rooms. Facilities: pool and ocean swimming, water sports, health club, restaurants, lounge with live entertainment, pianist in elegant lobby lounge. AE, DC, MC, V. Very Expensive.*

Mariner's Inn–A Clarion Hotel. There's a Caribbean-island feel to this five-story resort hotel set in an enclave. The grounds are beautifully landscaped. All oceanside, the rooms are spacious and colorfully decorated in a modern style. Kitchenettes make this a great favorite with families and honeymooners. *In Palmetto Dunes Resort, 23 Ocean La., Box 6165, 29938, tel. 803/842–8000 or 800/221–2222. 324 rooms. Facilities: pool, health club, sauna, whirlpool, volleyball, canoeing, fishing, biking, sailing, restaurant, full resort privileges of Palmetto Dunes. AE, DC, MC, V. Expensive–Very Expensive.*

Marriott's Hilton Head Resort. This oceanside hotel has spacious rooms with informally elegant tropical decor and ocean, garden, or forest views. The lobby is highlighted by a dramatic five-story atrium. Pathways wind amid lagoons and gardens to a wide, sandy private beach. The resort caters to groups from 50 to 1,500; its luxuriant garden setting, water sports, and fitness center make it a favorite with family vacationers as well. *130 Shipyard Dr., Shipyard Plantation, 29928, tel. 803/842–2400 or 800/228–9290. 338 rooms and suites. Facilities: pool, exercise rooms, sauna, rental catamarans, restaurants, privileges at nearby golf and tennis clubs. AE, DC, MC, V. Expensive–Very Expensive.*

Holiday Inn Oceanfront Resort. This handsome high-rise motor hotel is located on a broad, quiet stretch of beach. The rooms are spacious and well furnished in a contemporary style. This hotel is very popular with families and smaller groups, and it's easily accessible from the main business area. *S. Forest Beach Dr., Box 5728, 29938, tel. 803/785–5126 or 800/465–4329. 249 rooms. Facilities: outdoor pool, poolside bar, restaurant, lounge with entertainment, golf, tennis, marina privileges. AE, DC, MC, V. Expensive.*

Red Roof Inn. This two-story inn at the center of the island is especially popular with families. It's a short drive to the public beaches. *5 Regency Pkwy. (U.S. 278), 29928, tel. 803/686–6808*

otters, snowy egrets, great blue herons, ibis, wood storks, and more than 300 other species of birds. In the forests are armadillos, wild horses, deer, raccoons, and an assortment of reptiles.

After the ancient Guale Indians came 16th-century Spanish missionaries, 18th-century English soldiers, and 19th-century planters. During the 1880s, Thomas Carnegie of Pittsburgh built several lavish homes here, but the island remained largely as nature created it. In the early 1970s, the federal government established the Cumberland Island National Seashore and opened this natural treasure to the public.

The only public access to Cumberland Island is by a 45-minute ride on *The Cumberland Queen*, a reservations-only, 150-passenger ferry based near the National Park Service Information Center at the docks at St. Mary's on the mainland. Ferry bookings are very heavy during summer, but cancellations and no-shows often make last-minute space available. *Contact National Park Service, Cumberland Island National Seashore, Box 806, St. Mary's 31558, tel. 912/882–4335. Ferry departs St. Mary's 9 and 11:45 AM; departs Cumberland 10:15 AM and 4:45 PM. Mid-May–Labor Day runs daily; Labor Day–mid-May runs Thurs.–Mon.*

From the Park Service docks at the island's southern end, you can follow wooded nature trails, swim and sun on 18 miles of undeveloped beaches, go fishing and bird-watching, and view the ruins of Carnegie's great estate, **Dungeness.** You can also join history and nature walks led by Park Service rangers. There is no transportation on the island, so the length of your explorations will be determined by your own interests and energy. Bear in mind that summers are hot and humid, and that you must bring your own food, soft drinks, sunscreen, and a reliable insect repellent. All trash items must be transported back to the mainland by campers and picnickers. *Nothing can be purchased on the island.*

Sports and Outdoor Activities

Golf　Jekyll's 63 holes of golf include three 18-hole courses (tel. 912/635–2368) with a main clubhouse on Capt. Wylly Road and a 9-hole course (tel. 912/635–2170) on Beachview Drive.

Tennis　Nine courts on Jeykll Island include J.P. Morgan's indoor court (tel. 912/635–2600).

Water Park　**Summer Waves,** an 11-acre water park, opened in June 1988, has an 18,000-square-foot wave pool; eight water slides; a children's activity pool with 2 slides; and a 1,000-foot river for tubing and rafting. *210 Riverview Dr., Jekyll Island, tel. 912/635–2074. Admission: $7.95 adults, $5.95 children 4–8. Open daily 10–6.*

Camping

Sea Camp. A five-minute walk from the *Cumberland Queen* dock, Sea Camp offers rest rooms and showers adjacent to campsites. The beach is just beyond the dunes. Experienced campers will want to hike 3–10 miles to several areas where cold-water spigots are the only amenities. *Contact National Park Service, Cumberland Island National Seashore, Box 806, St. Mary's 31558, tel. 912/882–4335.*

Dining and Lodging

The following dining price categories have been used: *Expensive*, over $30; *Moderate*, $15–$30; *Inexpensive*, under $15.

The following lodging price categories have been used: *Very Expensive*, over $100; *Expensive*, $75–$100; *Moderate*, $50–$75; *Inexpensive*, under $50.

Cumberland Island
Lodging

Greyfield Inn. The island's only hotel lodgings are in a turn-of-the-century Carnegie family home. Greyfield's public areas are filled with family mementos, furnishings, and portraits (you may feel as though you've stepped into one of Agatha Christie's mysterious Cornwall manors). Prices include all meals, sales tax, mandatory gratuity, and pickup and drop off by the inn's ferry at Fernandina Beach, Florida. *Drawer B, Fernandina Beach, FL 32034, tel. 904/261–6408. 9 rooms. MC, V. Very Expensive.*

The Charter House. The accommodations of the 120-room motel are spartan but air-conditioned. It is located 2 miles from the Cumberland ferry dock. The on-site restaurant serves reasonably priced breakfasts, lunches, and dinners and presents live evening entertainment in the lounge. *2710 Osborne St., St. Mary's 31588, tel. 800/768–6250. Facilities: restaurant, lounge, pool. AE, DC, MC, V. Inexpensive.*

Jekyll Island
Dining

The Grand Dining Room. In the Jekyll Island Club Hotel the dining room sparkles with silver and crystal. What sets the meals apart from the ordinary are the sauces that flavor the dishes of fresh seafood, beef, veal, and chicken. *371 Riverview Dr., tel. 912/635–2600, ext. 1002. Jacket requested at dinner. Reservations recommended. AE, DC, MC, V. Expensive.*

The Wharf. Opened in 1989 as the Golden Isles' only over-the-water dining experience, this restaurant provides a saltwater marsh view from its dock location. Fresh seafood is featured nightly in the dining room and screened-porch raw bar. Cocktails are served in the lounge. *1 Pier Rd., tel. 912/635–3800. Dress: casual. AE, MC, V. Inexpensive.*

Lodging

Jekyll Island Club Hotel. Built in 1887, the four-story clubhouse, with wraparound verandas, towers, and turrets, once served as dining area, social center, and guest accommodations for some of the wealthiest families in the United States. In 1985, a group of Georgia businessmen spent $17 million restoring it to a splendor that would astonish even the Astors and Vanderbilts. The guest rooms and suites are custom-decorated with mahogany beds, armoires, and plush sofas and chairs. Some have flowery views of the Intracoastal Waterway, and several suites have Jacuzzis. The adjacent Sans Souci Apartments, former "bachelor quarters" built in 1886 by J.P. Morgan and William Rockefeller, have been converted into guest rooms. The hotel is operated as a Radisson Hotels resort. *371 Riverview Dr., Jekyll Island 31520, tel. 912/635–2600 or 800/333–3333. 134 rooms. Facilities: restaurant, outdoor pool, gift shops, croquet lawn, free shuttle to nearby beaches, tennis courts. AE, DC, MC, V. Expensive–Very Expensive.*

Jekyll Inn. This is the largest facility on the island. Located on a landscaped 15-acre site, these oceanfront units, including some villas with kitchenettes, also underwent a $2.5 million renovation. Rooms were redecorated with new lighting and carpeting, and saunas and Jacuzzis in some bathrooms. Island decor was added to the second-floor Ocean View lounge. *975 Beachview*

Dr., Jekyll Island 31520, tel. 912/635–2531 or 800/528–1234. 264 rooms. Facilities: restaurant, large pool, playground. AE, DC, MC, V. Moderate–Very Expensive.

Holiday Inn Beach Resort. Nestled amid natural dunes and oaks in a secluded oceanfront setting, this hotel has a private beach, but its rooms with balconies still don't have an ocean view. Its recreational activities include outdoor pool and playground, tennis courts, and 63 holes of golf. *200 S. Beachview Dr., Jekyll Island 31520, tel. 912/635–3311 or 800-HOLIDAY. 205 rooms. Facilities: restaurant, lounge with live entertainment, satellite cinema, some in-room saunas and whirlpools, bike rentals. AE, DC, MC, V. Moderate–Expensive.*

Sea Island
Dining and Lodging

The Cloister Hotel. Like a person of some years, the Cloister has its eccentricities. Guest rooms were only recently equipped with TVs. Credit cards are not honored, but personal checks are accepted. Gentlemen must cover their arms in the dining rooms, even at breakfast. And for the most part, nouvelle cuisine, new American cuisine, and other culinary trends of the '80s have yet to breach the hotel's traditional menus. Guests lodge in spacious, comfortably appointed rooms and suites in the Spanish Mediterranean main hotel and in beachside cottages and villas. For recreation, there's a choice of golf, tennis, swimming in pools or at the beach, skeet shooting, horseback riding, sailing, biking, lawn games, surf and deep-sea fishing. After dinner, a big-band orchestra plays for dancing in the lounge. A complete spa facility opened in 1989 features a fully equipped workout room, daily aerobics classes, facials and massages, and other beauty treatments. *The Cloister, Sea Island 31561, tel. 912/638–3611, reservations 800/SEA–ISLAND. 264 rooms, 450 cottages, 44 condos. Facilities: shuttle service to and from Jacksonville, Savannah, and Brunswick airports. Full American Plan. No credit cards, but personal checks are accepted. Very Expensive.*

St. Simon's Island
Dining

Blanche's Courtyard. Located in the village, this lively restaurant/nightclub is gussied up in "Bayou Victorian" dress, with lots of antiques and nostalgic memorabilia. True to its bayou decor, the menu features Cajun-style seafood as well as your basic steak and chicken. A ragtime band plays for dancers on the weekends. *440 Kings Way, tel. 912/638–3030. Dress: informal. Reservations accepted. AE, DC, MC, V. Moderate.*

Emmeline & Hessie. A large dining room and bar offer patrons a spectacular view of the marina and marshes. Specialties are seafood, steak, and lobster. There's also a bakery, a deli, and a seafood market on the premises. There's usually a line here, but it's well worth the wait to watch the sun set over the marshes as you dine. During the summer months, live bands play on the outdoor terrace. *Golden Isles Marina, tel. 912/638–9084. Dress: informal. Reservations accepted for dinner only. AE, MC, V. Moderate.*

Alfonza's Olde Plantation Supper Club. Seafood, superb steaks, and plantation fried chicken are served in a gracious and relaxed environment. The club also has a cocktail lounge. *Harrington La., tel. 912/638–9883. Dress: informal. Reservations recommended. MC, V. Inexpensive–Moderate.*

The Crab Trap. One of the island's most popular spots, the Crab Trap offers a variety of fried and broiled fresh seafood, oysters on the half shell, clam chowder, heaps of batter fries, and hush puppies. The atmosphere is rustic-casual—there's a hole in the middle of every table to deposit corn cobs and shrimp shells.

1209 Ocean Blvd., tel. 912/638–3552. Dress: informal. No reservations. Inexpensive–Moderate.

Spanky's. This trendy restaurant and bar in the Golden Isles Marina is popular for hamburgers, pizza, salads, sandwiches, seafood, beer, and cocktails. The panoramic view is also a drawing point. *225 Marina Dr., tel. 912/638–0918. Dress: informal. No reservations. AE, MC, V. Inexpensive–Moderate.*

Lodging **The King and Prince Hotel and Villas.** This hotel facing the beach stepped into the deluxe resort category with a recently completed, multimillion-dollar modernization and expansion. Guest rooms are spacious, and villas offer from two to three bedrooms. *Box 798, 201 Arnold Rd., St. Simons Island 31522, tel. 912/638–3631 or 800/342–0212. 130 rooms, 50 villas. Facilities: restaurant, lounge, indoor/outdoor pool, tennis, golf, bike rentals. AE, DC, MC, V. Very Expensive.*

Sea Palms Golf and Tennis Resort. A contemporary resort complex with fully furnished, ultramodern villas nestles on an 800-acre site. *5445 Frederica Rd., St. Simons Island 31522, tel. 912/638–3351. 263 rooms. Facilities: 2 pools, health club, 27-hole golf course, tennis, children's recreation programs. AE, DC, MC, V. Expensive–Very Expensive.*

Days Inn of America. This new facility opened in 1989 on an inland stretch of the island's main thoroughfare. Each room has built-in microwaves and refrigerators. Continental breakfast is included in the cost. *1700 Frederica Rd., St. Simons Island 31522, tel. 912/634–0660. 101 rooms. Facilities: pool, color cable TV. AE, MC, V. Moderate.*

Queen's Court. This family-oriented complex in the village has clean, modest rooms, some with kitchenettes. The grounds are beautiful. *437 Kings Way, St. Simons Island 31522, tel. 912/638–8459. 23 rooms. Facilities: color cable TV, shower baths, pool. MC, V. Moderate.*

Little St. Simon's Island
Dining and Lodging
River Lodge and Cedar House. Up to 24 guests can be accommodated in the lodge and house. Each has four bedrooms with twin or king-size beds, private baths, sitting rooms, and screened porches. Older hunting lodges have some private and some shared baths. None of the rooms are air-conditioned, but ceiling fans make sleeping comfortable. The rates include all meals and dinner wines (cocktails available at additional cost). Meals, often featuring fresh fish, pecan pie, and home-baked breads, are served family-style in the lodge dining room. *Box 1078, Little St. Simons Island 31522, tel. 912/638–7472. Facilities: stables, pool, beach, transportation from St. Simons Island, transportation on the island, fishing boats, interpretive guides. Minimum two-night reservations. MC, V. Very Expensive.*

Northeast Florida

When Orlando's new cinema industry scouts for filming locations, it can find almost any setting it needs in Northeast Florida. Towering, tortured live oaks, plantations, and antebellum-style architecture symbolize the Old South, and the mossy marshes of Silver Springs and the St. Johns River look today as they did generations ago when Tarzan movies were filmed in the jungles here. Jacksonville is a modern metropolis abounding with skyscrapers. And the beaches, spreading in shimmering, sandy glory south from Fernandina, vary in likeness from the stony shores of the North Sea to the deep, hot sands of the Caribbean. Beaches in northeastern Florida are the most varied in the state, ranging from the rocky moonscape of Washington Oaks State Park, just below St. Augustine, to the slick sands of Daytona.

Numbers in the margin correspond to points of interest on the Northeast Florida map.

The 300-year-old seaport town of **Fernandina Beach** lies on the ❶ northern tip of **Amelia Island,** across the border from St. Marys, Georgia. Once an important political and commercial stronghold and now merely a quaint haven for in-the-know tourists, Fernandina Beach offers a wide range of accommodations from bed-and-breakfasts to Amelia Island Plantation, a sprawling landmark resort. The town's 30-block historic district includes the old cemetery where names on gravestones reveal the waves of immigrants who settled here: Spanish, French, Minorcan, Portuguese, and English. In **Old Town** you'll see some of the nation's finest examples of Queen Anne, Victorian, and Italianate mansions dating back to the town's glory days of the mid-19th century. Begin your self-guided walking or driving tour of the historic district with a visit to the old railroad depot, originally a stopping point on the first cross-state railroad. Now the **Amelia Island-Fernandina Beach Chamber of Commerce,** this is a good place to pick up leaflets and information on the area. *102 Centre St., tel. 904/261-3248. Open weekdays 9–5.*

Follow Centre Street (which turns into Atlantic Ave.) for about 8 blocks to **St. Peter's Episcopal Church.** Founded in 1859, the church once served as a school for freed slaves. Continuing on Atlantic, you will reach the bridge. From here you can see the **Amelia Lighthouse,** built in 1839. It's a great background for photos, but is not open to the public.

A couple of blocks farther is the **Fort Clinch State Park,** home to one of the best-preserved and most complete brick forts. Built around the rim of Florida and the Gulf states, the fort served to protect against further British intrusion after the War of 1812 and was occupied in 1847 by the Confederacy; a year later it was retaken by the north. During the Spanish-American War it was reactivated for a brief time but for the most part was not used. Today the park offers camping, nature trails, carriage rides, swimming, surf fishing, picnicking, and living history reenactments showing life in the garrison at the time of the Civil War. *Tel. 904/261-4212. Admission: FL residents, $1 driver plus 50¢ per passenger; out-of-state, $2 driver plus $1 per passenger. Open daily 8 AM–sunset.*

Time Out **The Palace Saloon** (117 Centre St., tel. 904/261-6320) is the state's oldest continuously operating watering hole, still sporting swinging doors straight out of Dodge City. Stop in for a cold drink and a bowl of boiled shrimp. The menu is limited, but the place is unpretentious, comfortable, and as genuine as a silver dollar.

To continue south, take Route A1A, called the **Buccaneer Trail,** through marshlands and beaches. After you've crossed the Nassau Sound, A1A will take you to **Little Talbot Island State Park**—a gorgeous stretch of sand dunes, endless beaches, and golden marshes that hum with birds and bugs. Come to picnic,

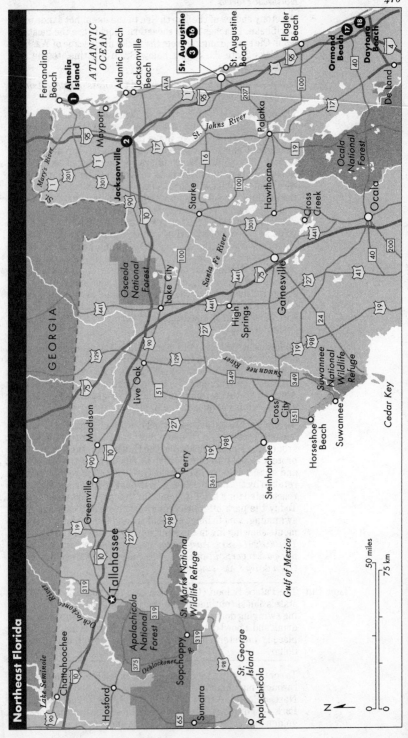

fish, swim, snorkel, or camp. *Tel. 904/251–3231. Admission: FL residents, $1 driver plus 50¢ per person; out-of-state, $2/car and driver plus $1 per person. Open daily 8 AM–sunset.*

Drive southwest on A1A for about 5 miles to Fort George Island, where signs will lead you to the **Kingsley Plantation.** Built by an eccentric slave trader, the Kingsley dates to 1792 and is the oldest remaining plantation in the state. Slave quarters, as well as the modest Kingsley home, are open to the public. *Tel. 904/251–3122. Admission: $1 adults, children under 6 free. Open daily 8–5. Guided tours Mon.–Thurs. 9:30, 11, 1:30, and 3.*

Three miles east of A1A is **Mayport,** where there's a ferry across the St. John's River. Mayport, dating back more than 300 years, is one of the oldest fishing villages in the United States. Today it's home to a large commercial shrimp boat fleet and is the Navy's fourth largest home port. *Ferry tel. 904/246–2922. Ferry admission: $1.50 per car, 10¢ pedestrians. Ferry runs daily 6:20 AM–10 PM, every ½ hour. Naval station tel. 904/241–NAVY. Admission free. Open Sat. 10–4:30, Sun. 1–4:30.*

Jacksonville's sensational beaches spread south from Mayport, but casual tourists can miss the boundaries between, as well as the distinctions among, the beaches. **Atlantic Beach** was a Henry Flagler project, developed in 1901 with the building of a hotel. A condo now stands on the site of the once-grand Atlantic Beach Hotel, built in 1929. Neighboring **Neptune Beach** is a quiet bedroom community, while **Jacksonville Beach** is a solid resort community, with new beach hotels replacing the original 350-guest resort hotel that burned in 1890. **Ponte Vedra Beach,** now the home of the Tournament Players Club and American Tennis Professionals, has been popular with golfers since 1922 when the National Lead Company built a 9-hole course for its workers to play.

One of the oldest cities in Florida, in area the largest city in the United States, and an underrated tourist destination, ❷ **Jacksonville** continues its battle against the stench of the sulfur pulp mill that keeps many travelers speeding straight on through. Improvements have been made, and winds shift, so if you stay you may be pleasantly surprised.

Stop off in Jacksonville and savor remnants of the Old South that continue to flavor the city, and the sense of subtropical paradise for which Florida is famous. Because the city was settled around the St. John's River, many attractions are on or near one riverbank or the other. To avoid crossing back and forth, you may want to sit down with a map and plan your trip carefully. Some attractions can be reached by water taxi (fare $3 round-trip adult, $2 senior citizens; water taxis run every 15 minutes), but for others, a car is necessary.

On the south side of the river, the **Jacksonville Art Museum** brings together contemporary and classic arts. Especially noteworthy are the Koger collection of Oriental porcelains and the pre-Columbian collection of rare artifacts. Special exhibits, film and lecture series, and workshops make this destination worthy of more than one visit. Travel by car. *4160 Boulevard Center Dr., tel. 904/398–8336. Admission free. Open Tues., Wed., Fri. 10–4, Thurs. 10–10, weekends 1–5. Closed Mon.*

The **Cummer Gallery of Art,** situated on the northwest side of the river, amidst leafy formal gardens, occupies a former baron's estate home. The permanent collection of more than 2,000 items includes one of the nation's largest troves of early Meissen porcelain as well as the works of some impressive Old Masters. Travel by car. *829 Riverside Ave., tel. 904/356–6857. Admission free. Open Tues.–Fri. 10–4, Sat. noon–5, Sun. 2–5. Closed Mon.*

Jacksonville's Museum of Science and History (originally the Children's Museum) presents hands-on exhibits, live animals, temporary displays, and a planetarium with free astronomy programs. Devote an entire day to this museum, and lunch in the cafe. Located downtown on the south bank, the museum can be reached by water taxi. *Riverwalk, downtown, tel. 904/ 396–7062. Admission: $5 adults, $3 senior citizens, $3 children, children under 4 free. Open Mon.–Thurs. 10–5, Fri. and Sat. 10–6, Sun. noon–6.*

The **Alexander Brest Museum,** located on the campus of Jacksonville University, has a small but important collection of Stueben glass, Boehm porcelain, ivories, and pre-Columbian artifacts. The home of composer Frederick Delius is also on the campus and is open for tours, upon request. Travel by car. *2800 University Blvd. N., east bank of the St. Johns River, tel. 904/ 744–3950, ext. 3374. Admission free. Open weekdays 9–4, Sat. 1–4 during school year. Closed holidays.*

Take State Route 10 east from the city; about 2 miles before you get to A1A, turn north on Girven Road; follow signs to the replica of **Fort Caroline National Monument.** The original fort was built in the 1560s by French Huguenots who were later slaughtered by the Spanish. The site, which is the scene of the first major clash between European powers for control of what would become the United States, maintains the memory of a brief French presence in this area. Today, it's a sunny place to picnic (bring your own food and drink), stretch your legs, and explore a small museum. *12713 Fort Caroline Rd., tel. 904/641– 7111. Admission free. Museum open daily 9–5. Closed Christmas, New Year's.*

❸ To reach **St. Augustine,** take U.S. 1 south from Jacksonville and head straight for the **Visitor Information Center** (10 Castillo Dr., tel. 904/824–3334), where you'll find loads of brochures, maps, and information about the nation's oldest city.

Numbers in the margin correspond to points of interest on the St. Augustine map.

❹ The massive **Castillo de San Marcos National Monument** hunkers over Matanzas Bay, and looks every century of its 300 years. Park rangers provide an introductory narration, after which you're on your own. This is a wonderful fort to explore, complete with moat, turrets, and 16-foot-thick walls. The fort was constructed of coquina, a soft limestone made of broken shells and coral, and it took 25 years to build it. Garrison rooms depict the life of the era, and special artillery demonstrations are held periodically on the gun deck. *1 Castillo Dr., tel. 904/ 829–6506. Admission: $1 adults, children under 16 and senior citizens free. Open daily 9–5:15.*

❺ The **City Gate,** at the top of St. George Street, is a relic from the days when the Castillo's moat ran westward to the river and the

Basilica Cathedral, **7**

Castillo de San Marcos National Monument, **4**

City Gate, **5**

Flagler College, **13**

Flagler Memorial Presbyterian Church, **14**

Fountain of Youth, **15**

Lightner Museum, **12**

Mission of Nombre de Dios, **16**

Museum Theatre, **6**

Oldest House, **11**

Oldest Store Museum, **10**

Plaza de la Constitution, **8**

Ximenez-Fatio House, **9**

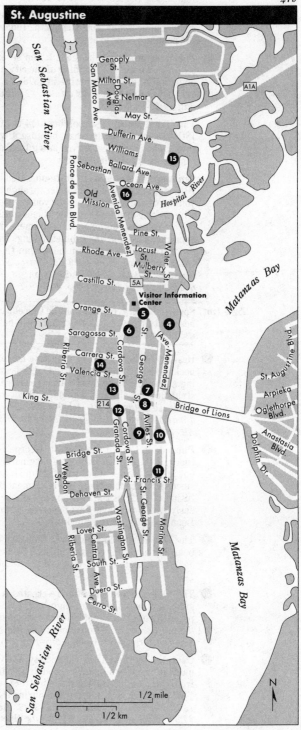

St. Augustine

Cubo Defense Line (defensive wall) protected the settlement against approaches from the north. Today it is the entrance to the popular restored area.

⑥ The **Museum Theatre** screens a film several times daily. One tells the story of the founding of the city in 1565, and the other depicts life in St. Augustine in 1576. *5 Cordova St., tel. 904/824–0339. Admission: $3 adults, $1 children under 15. Open daily 9:30–5:30.*

The **Oldest Wooden Schoolhouse** (14 St. George St.) is a tiny 18th-century structure that, because it was the closest structure to the city gates, served as a guardhouse and sentry shelter during the Seminole Wars.

San Augustin Antiguo is a state-operated living-history village with eight sites; you can wander through the narrow streets at your own pace. Along your way you may see a Colonial soldier's wife cooking over an open fire; a blacksmith building his shop (a historic reconstruction); and craftsmen busy at candle dipping, spinning, weaving, and cabinetmaking. They are all making reproductions that will be used within the restored area. *Entrance at Triay House, 29 St. George St., near the Old City Gate, tel. 904/825–6830. Admission: $3.50 adults, $2 students 6–18; $8 family ticket. Open daily 9–5.*

Time Out | **Spanish Bakery,** behind Casa de Calcedo on St. George Street, has meat turnovers, cookies, and fresh-baked bread made from a Colonial recipe.

⑦ **Basilica Cathedral of St. Augustine** has parish records dating back to 1594, the oldest written records in the country. Following a fire in 1887, extensive changes were made to the current structure, which dates from 1797. It was remodeled in the mid-1960s. *40 Cathedral Pl., tel. 904/824–2806. Admission free, but donations requested. Open weekdays 5:30–5, weekends 5:30 AM–7 PM.*

⑧ **Plaza de la Constitución,** at St. George Street and Cathedral Place, is the central area of the original settlement. It was laid out in 1598 by decree of King Philip II, and little has changed since. At its center there is a monument to the Spanish constitution of 1812; at the east end is a public market dating from early American days. Just beyond is a statue of Juan Ponce de León, who discovered Florida in 1513.

⑨ The **Ximenez-Fatio House** was built in 1797, and it became a boarding house for tourists in 1885. *20 Aviles St., tel. 904/829–3575. Admission free. Open Mar. 1–Aug. 31, Sun.–Thurs. 1–4.*

⑩ The **Oldest Store Museum** re-creates a turn-of-the-century general store. There are high-button shoes, lace-up corsets, patent drugs, and confectionery specialties. *4 Artillery La., tel. 904/829–9729. Admission: $3 adults, $2.50 senior citizens, $1.50 children 6–12. Open Mon.–Sat. 9–5, Sun. noon–5.*

⑪ Operated by the Historical Society, the **Oldest House** reflects much of the city's history through its changes and additions, from the coquina walls built soon after the town was burned in 1702 to the house's enlargement during the British occupation. *14 St. Francis St., tel. 904/824–2872. Admission: $5 adults, $4.50 senior citizens, $2.50 students. Open daily 9–5.*

⑫ The **Lightner Museum** is housed in one of two posh hotels built in 1888 by railroad magnate Henry Flagler, who wanted to create an American Riviera. The museum contains a collection of ornate antique music boxes (ask about demonstrations!), and the Lightner Antique Mall perches on three levels of what was the hotel's grandiose indoor pool. *75 King St., tel. 904/824–2874. Admission to museum: $4 adults, $1 students, children under 12 free. Museum open daily 9–5; mall open Tues.–Sun. 10–4.*

⑬ Across from the Lightner Museum, **Flagler College** occupies the second of Flagler's hotels. The riveting structure is replete with towers, turrets, and arcades decorated by Louis Comfort Tiffany. The front courtyard is open to the public.

⑭ At Valencia and Sevilla streets, behind Flagler College, the **Flagler Memorial Presbyterian Church,** which Flagler built in 1889, is a splendid Venetian Renaissance structure. The dome towers more than 100 feet, and it is topped by a 20-foot Greek cross. *Open Mon.–Sat. 9–5.*

⑮ The **Fountain of Youth** salutes Ponce de León. In the complex there is a springhouse, an explorer's globe, a planetarium, and an Indian village. *155 Magnolia Ave., tel. 904/829–3168. Admission: $3.50 adults, $2.50 senior citizens, $1.50 children 6–12, children under 6 free. Open daily 9–5.*

⑯ The **Mission of Nombre de Dios** commemorates the site where America's first Christian mass was celebrated. A 208-foot stainless-steel cross marks the spot where the mission's first cross was planted. *San Marco Ave. and Old Mission Rd., tel. 904/824–2809. Admission free, but donations requested. Open daily 7 AM–8 PM summer; 8–6 winter.*

Numbers in the margin correspond to points of interest on the Northeast Florida map.

As you venture along the Intracoastal Waterway, take note of the different names assigned to the passage. In the Daytona area, some fifty miles farther south (take I–95, Rte. 1, or A1A, depending on how fast you want to go), it's called the Halifax River, though it is not actually a river, but a tidal waterway that flows between the mainland and the barrier islands. **Dixie Queen Riverboat Cruises** (tel. 904/255–1997 or 800/329–6225) runs lunch, brunch, dinner, and specialty cruises throughout the Daytona Beach area.

A good place to begin touring Daytona environs is along a segment of Old Dixie Highway. From I–95 north of Ormond Beach, take Exit 90 and travel east. The first left off Old Dixie Highway (Kings Highway) will take you to the entrance of **Bulow Plantation Ruins State Historic Site,** built in 1821. From the entrance, a winding dirt road cuts through tangled vegetation and leads to a picnic area and day-use facilities facing Bulow Creek. All that remains of the plantation are the massive ruins of the sugar mill, which may be reached either by auto or bicycle along a one-way loop road, or on foot via a scenic walking trail from the picnic area. *Tel. 904/439–2219. Admission: $1 per car. Open daily 9–5.*

Continue southeast on Old Dixie Highway through a tunnel of vine-laced oaks and cabbage palms. Next stop is **Tomoka State Park,** site of a Timucuan Indian settlement discovered in 1605 by Spanish explorer Alvaro Mexia. Wooded campsites, bicycle and walking paths, and guided canoe tours on the Tomoka and Halifax rivers are the main attractions. *North Beach St., Ormond Beach, tel. 904/677–3931. Admission: June 1–Dec. 31, $8 per day; Jan. 1–May 31, $17 per day; electricity, $2 per day. Open daily 8 AM–sunset.*

17 Time moves forward and the canopy begins to thin as you travel east on Old Dixie Highway to **Ormond Beach.** Auto racing was born on this hard-packed beach back in 1902, when R. E. Olds and Alexander Winton staged the first race. **Birthplace of Speed Antique Car Show and Swap Meet** is an annual event, attracting enthusiasts from across the nation. Sportsmen and socialites flocked to Ormond Beach each winter and made the massive Ormond Hotel their headquarters. The grand old wooden hotel (built in 1888 to pamper Flagler's East Coast Railway passengers) still stands watch on the east bank of the Halifax, but it is now vacant and no longer entertains guests.

Across the street from the hotel is **The Casements,** the restored winter retreat of John D. Rockefeller, now serving as a cultural center and museum. The estate and its formal gardens, on the National Register of Historic Places, are the setting for an annual lineup of special events and exhibits. Tours of the estate also are offered. *25 Riverside Dr., Ormond Beach, tel. 904/673–4701. Admission free; donations accepted. Open weekdays 9–5, Sat. 9–noon.*

From the Casements go two blocks east to the **Birthplace of Speed Museum.** Devoted to the most exciting moments in America's long love affair with the automobile, the museum exhibits a replica of the Stanley Steamer, old Model T and Model A Fords, and a wealth of auto racing memorabilia, including a commemoration to auto-aero pioneer Glenn Curtis. *160 E. Granada Blvd., Ormond Beach, tel. 904/672–5657. Admission: $1 adults, 50¢ children under 12. Hours vary depending on race events.*

Take A1A about 8 miles south to Beach Street, on the mainland. In the old downtown section is the **Halifax Historical Society Museum.** Photographs, Indian artifacts, and war memorabilia relevant to this area's fascinating, varied past are on display here. You can also shop for gifts and antiques. *252 S. Beach St., tel. 904/255–6976. Admission free. Open Tues.–Sat. 10–4.*

Pick up Volusia Avenue and drive west to Nova Road. Go two blocks south and follow signs to Museum Boulevard and the **Museum of Arts and Sciences.** This competent little museum has two blockbuster features: One is a large collection of pre-Castro Cuban art; the other is a complete and eye-popping skeleton of a giant sloth. The sloth remains—found near here—are the most complete skeleton of its kind ever found in North America. *1040 Museum Blvd., tel. 904/255–0285. Admission: $2 adults, 50¢ children, students, senior citizens, and members; Wed. and Fri. free. Open Tues.–Fri. 9–4, weekends noon–5.*

18 To reach the famous beaches of **Daytona Beach** go east to A1A and follow signs to beach ramps, which lie for miles both north and south. During spring break, race weeks, and summer holidays, expect heavy traffic along this strip of garishly painted beach motels and tacky souvenir shops.

Several miles south of the Marriott, on A1A, is **Ponce Inlet,** which is frequented by locals and visitors who are familiar with the area. A manicured drive winds through low-growing shrubs and windblown scrub oaks to parking and picnic areas. Boardwalks traverse the delicate dunes and provide easy access to the wide beach. Marking this prime spot is a bright red century-old lighthouse, now a historic monument and museum. *Token admission. Open daily 10–5.*

Time Out **Lighthouse Landing** (4931 S. Peninsula Dr., tel. 904/761–1821), only yards from the historic light, is a good place for sipping cocktails and watching the sunset.

From Daytona, I–4 leads southwest straight to Orlando, the final destination of this tour. If you're not in a hurry, though, and especially if you've got kids in tow, continue south another 50 miles along the Atlantic coast (take either I–95 or Rte. 1) to **Cocoa Beach,** where you can visit the **Kennedy Space Center Spaceport USA.** Free museum exhibits and films are featured, as well as guided bus tours and an IMAX theater film presentation, *The Dream Is Alive,* narrated by Walter Cronkite. The film alone is worth the trip. *Visitors' Center, tel. 407/452–2121. Bus tours: $4 adults, $1.75 children 3–12. IMAX theater admission: $2.75 adults, $1.75 children 3–12. Open daily 9–7. Closed Christmas.*

Shopping

For specialty shops, roam around **Jacksonville Landing,** downtown at the Main Street Bridge.

Brand-name items are sold at discount prices at the **Daytona Beach Outlet Mall** (2400 S. Ridgewood Ave., South Daytona, tel. 904/756–8700). Daytona's **Flea Market** is one of the South's largest (I–4 at U.S. 92).

Participant Sports

Boating Boats for the Tomoka River are offered by **Daytona Recreation-**
Rentals **al Sales & Rentals** (Ormond Beach, tel. 904/672–5631). **Club Nauticos** rents boats to members and nonmembers (Amelia Island, tel. 904/261–7328; Daytona Beach, tel. 904/252–7272; Jacksonville, tel. 904/825–4848; Jacksonville Beach, tel. 904/241–2628). Other rentals are available from **The Boat Club** (Daytona Beach, tel. 904/258–2991).

Fishing You can deep-sea troll in the Atlantic for blue and white marlin, sailfish, dolphin, king mackerel, tuna, and wahoo. Grouper, red snapper, and amberjack are deep-sea bottom-fishing prizes. Surf casting is popular for pompano, bluefish, flounder, and sea bass. From fishing piers, anglers pull in sheepshead, mackerel, trout, and tarpon. Most Atlantic beach communities have a lighted pier with a bait-and-tackle shop and rest rooms. **Jacksonville Beach Fishing Pier** extends 1,200 feet into the Atlantic, and the cost for fishing is $3 for adults, $1.50 for children and senior citizens, or 50¢ for watching.

Deep-sea fishing charters are provided by **Critter Fleet Marina,** (Daytona Beach, tel. 904/767–7676 or 800/338–0850 in FL); **Cindy Jay Charters** (Ponce Inlet, tel. 904/788–3469); **Cape Marina** (800 Scallop Dr., Port Canaveral, tel. 407/783–8410); **Miss**

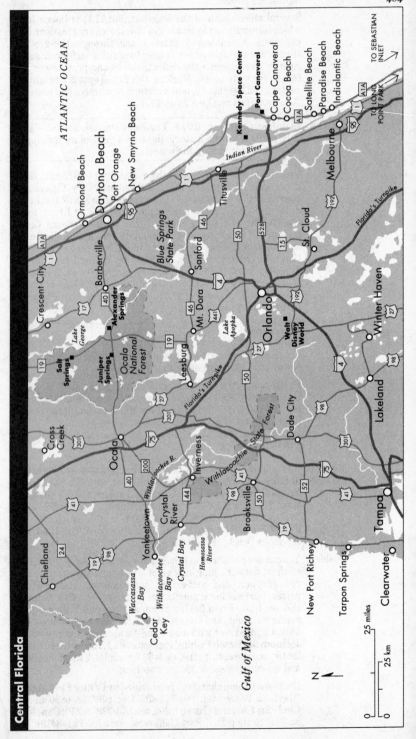

Central Florida

ATLANTIC OCEAN

Crescent City
Ormond Beach
Daytona Beach
Port Orange
New Smyrna Beach
Barberville
Alexander Springs
Blue Springs State Park
Sanford
Titusville
Kennedy Space Center
Port Canaveral
Cape Canaveral
Cocoa Beach
Satellite Beach
Paradise Beach
Indialantic Beach
Melbourne

Indian River

TO SEBASTIAN INLET

TO LONG POINT PARK

Lake George
Salt Springs
Juniper Springs
Ocala National Forest
Mt. Dora
Leesburg
Lake Apopka
Orlando
Walt Disney World
St. Cloud
Winter Haven
Lakeland

Cross Creek
Ocala
Withlacoochee R.
Inverness
Withlacoochee State Forest
Dade City

Chiefland
Waccasassa Bay
Cedar Key
Withlacoochee Bay
Crystal Bay
Yankeetown
Crystal River
Homosassa River
Brooksville
New Port Richey
Tarpon Springs
Clearwater
Tampa

Gulf of Mexico

Florida's Turnpike

N

0   25 miles
0   25 km

Cape Canaveral (630 Glen Cheek Dr., Port Canaveral, tel. 407/ 783–5274); **Pelican Princess** (665 Glen Cheek Dr., Port Canaveral, tel. 407/784–3474). For sportfishing, charter the *Sea Love II* (St. Augustine, tel. 904/824–3328) or contact **Critter Fleet Marina** (Daytona Beach, tel. 904/767–7676).

Golf In Daytona Beach, the **Indigo Lakes Course** (tel. 904/258–6333) is now developing a headquarters course and golfing community for the LPGA (tel. 904/254–8800). The **Tournament Players Club at Sawgrass** (tel. 904/285–2261) in Ponte Vedra is home to the championship of that name; **Spruce Creek Golf & Country Club** (tel. 904/756–6114), near Daytona, has 18 holes of championship golf and its own fly-in runway for private planes.

At **Amelia Island Plantation** (tel. 904/261–6161), three stunning oceanfront holes are true "links" in the old Scottish golf tradition.

Cocoa Beach Municipal Golf Course (5000 Tom Warriner Blvd., Cocoa Beach, tel. 407/783–5351) has a 6,968-yard course.

Tennis Resorts especially well known for their tennis programs include **Amelia Island Plantation** (tel. 904/261–6161), site of the nationally televised WTA Championships; the **St. Augustine Beach and Tennis Resort** (tel. 904/471–9111); **Ponce de Leon Lodge and Country Club** (tel. 904/824–2821); the **Ponte Vedra Club** (tel. 904/285–6911); and the **Marriott at Sawgrass** (tel. 904/ 285–7777).

Water Sports Rentals Jetskiing, boardsailing, waterskiing, sailing, and powerboating are popular pastimes on the Atlantic Intracoastal Waterway. Most larger beachfront hotels offer equipment for rent. Other sources for renting sailboards, surfboards, or boogie boards include **The Surf Station** (1002 Anastasia Blvd., St. Augustine Beach, tel. 904/471–9463); **Aloha Sports** (100 N. Atlantic Ave., Daytona Beach, tel. 904/257–3843); **Sandy Point Sailboards** (1114 Riverside Dr., Holly Hill, tel. 904/255–4977), or **The Water Works** (1891 E. Merritt Island Causeway, Rte. 520, Merritt Island, tel. 407/452–2007).

For jet ski rentals try **J&J** (841 Ballough Rd., Daytona Beach, tel. 904/255–1917) or **Jet Ski Headquarters** (3537 Halifax Dr., Port Orange, tel. 904/788–4143).

Diving/Snorkeling Scuba equipment, trips, refills, and lessons are available from **Adventure Diving** (3127 S. Ridgewood Ave., S. Daytona, tel. 904/788–8050).

Beaches

Amelia Island's lower half is mostly covered by the Amelia Island Plantation resort. However, on the island's extreme southern tip you can go horseback riding along the wide, almost deserted beaches.

Atlantic Beach, north of Neptune Beach, is the other favored surfing area. Around the popular Sea Turtle Inn, you'll find catamaran rentals and instruction. Five areas have lifeguards on duty in the summer 10–6.

Daytona, which bills itself as the "World's Most Famous Beach," permits cars to drive right up to your beachsite, spread out a blanket, and have all your belongings at hand; this is especially convenient for elderly or handicapped beachgoers.

Flagler Beach is a vast, windswept swath of sand with easy access.

Fort Clinch State Park, on Amelia Island's northern tip, includes a municipal beach and pier. That's where Fernandina Beach's city beaches are, meaning you pay a state-park entrance fee to reach them. But the beaches are broad and lovely, and there is parking right on the beach, bathhouses, picnic areas, and all the facilities of the park itself, including the fort.

Jacksonville Beach is the liveliest of the long line of Jacksonville Beaches. Young people flock to the beach, where there are all sorts of games to play and also beach concessions, rental shops, and a fishing pier.

Kathryn Abbey Hanna Park, near Mayport, is the Jacksonville area's showplace park, drawing families and singles alike. It offers beaches, showers, and snack bars that operate April–Labor Day.

Neptune Beach, adjoining Jacksonville Beach to the north, is more residential and offers easy access to quieter beaches. Surfers take to the waves, and consider it one of the area's two best surfing sites.

St. Augustine has 43 miles of wide, white, level beaches. The young gravitate toward the public beaches at St. Augustine Beach and Vilano Beach, while families prefer the Anastasia State Recreation Area. All three are accessible via Route A1A: Vilano Beach is to the north, across North River, and Anastasia State Park and St. Augustine Beach are both on Anastasia Island, across the Bridge of Lions.

Spectator Sports

Auto Racing The massive **Daytona International Speedway** on U.S. 92 (Daytona Beach's major east–west artery) is home of year-round auto and motorcycle racing including the annual Daytona 500 in February and Pepsi 400 in July. Twenty-minute narrated tours of the historic track are offered daily 9–5 except on race days. For racing schedules, call 904/254–2700.

Golf The Tournament Players Championship is a March event at the **Tournament Players Club** (near Sawgrass in Ponte Vedra Beach, tel. 904/285–7888), which is national headquarters of the PGA Tour.

Greyhound Races During the summer, you can bet on the dogs every night but Sunday at the **Daytona Beach Kennel Club** (on U.S. 92 near the International Speedway, tel. 904/252–6484).

Greyhounds race year-round in the Jacksonville area, with seasons split among three tracks: **Jacksonville Kennel Club,** May–September (1440 N. McDuff Ave., tel. 904/646–0001); **Orange Park Kennel Club,** November–April (U.S. 17, about ½ mi south of I–295, tel. 904/646–0001); and **St. John's Greyhound Park,** March and April (7 miles south of I–95 on U.S. 1, tel. 904/646–0001).

Tennis The top-rated Women's Tennis Association Championships is held in April, and the Men's All-American Tennis Championship in September, both at **Amelia Island Plantation** (Amelia Island, tel. 904/277–5145).

Dining and Lodging

The following dining price categories have been used: *Very Expensive*, over $60; *Expensive*, $40–$60; *Moderate*, $20–$40; *Inexpensive*, under $20.

As a general rule, the closer you are to the center of action in the coastal resorts, the more you'll pay. The following lodging price categories have been used: *Very Expensive*, over $120; *Expensive*, $90–$120; *Moderate*, $50–$90; *Inexpensive*, under $50.

Amelia Island
Lodging
★

Amelia Island Plantation. One of the first "environmentally sensitive" resorts, Amelia Island's grounds ramble through ancient live-oak forests and behind some of the highest dunes in the state. A warm sense of community prevails; some homes are occupied year-round, and accommodations range from home and condo rentals to rooms in a full-service hotel. The resort is best known for its golf and tennis programs, but hiking and biking trails thread through the 1,300 acres. Restaurants range from casual to ultra elegant. *3000 First Coast Hwy., 32034, tel. 904/261–6161 or 800/874–6878 outside FL. 125 rooms in the inn; 475 villa apartments; home rentals by arrangement. Facilities: private indoor pools in honeymoon villas, water sports, 25 tennis courts, golf courses, fishing, racquetball, fitness center, instruction, pro shops, children's activities, restaurants, shopping, entertainment. AE, DC, MC, V. Expensive.*

Cocoa Beach
Dining

Bernard's Surf. Don't come to Bernard's for the view; there are no windows in the two main dining rooms. Come for steaks and local fish and a few unusual dishes like alligator and buffalo. A specialty is Doc Stahl's Skillet, a combination of shrimp, crabmeat, mushrooms, and wild rice sautéed and served in the skillet. *2 S. Atlantic Ave., tel. 407/783–2401. Dress: casual. Reservations advised. Closed Christmas. AE, DC, MC, V. Moderate.*

Gatsby's Food and Spirits. This casual waterfront spot serves up prime rib, steaks, and seafood. Early-bird special dinner prices are in effect between 4:30 and 6:30. *480 W. Cocoa Beach Causeway, tel. 407/783–2380. Dress: casual. Reservations advised. AE, DC, MC, V. Moderate.*

Mango Tree Restaurant. Candles, fresh flowers, white linen tablecloths, rattan basket chairs, and eggshell-color walls adorned with tropical watercolors by local artists set a romantic mood at the Mango Tree. The intimate dining room overlooks a garden aviary that is home to exotic doves and pheasants. Try the grouper broiled and topped with scallops, shrimp, and hollandaise sauce. *Cottage Row, 118 N. Atlantic Ave., tel. 407/799–0513. Dress: casual. Reservations advised. AE, MC, V. Moderate.*

Alma's Italian Restaurant. Five crowded, noisy dining rooms keep the waitresses busy. The specialties of the house are veal marsala and more than 200 imported and domestic wines. *306 N. Orlando Ave., tel. 407/783–1981. Dress: casual. Reservations advised. AE, DC, MC, V. Inexpensive.*

Lodging

Holiday Inn Cocoa Beach Resort. When two separate beach hotels were redesigned and a promenade park landscaped between them, the Holiday Inn Cocoa Beach Resort was born. It features plush modern public rooms, an Olympic-size heated pool, tennis courts, and private access to the beach. You can choose from a wide selection of accommodations—standard, king, and oceanfront suites; villas; and bilevel lofts—all with in-room movies. Free aerobic workouts are offered, as are planned activities for children. *1300 N. Atlantic Ave., Cocoa Beach 32931, tel. 407/783–2271. 500 rooms. AE, DC, MC, V. Very Expensive.*

Crossway Inn. Located across the street from the ocean and within walking distance of at least 16 restaurants, this is a convenient lodging. You can choose from standard double rooms, minisuites, or fully equipped efficiencies—all are clean, comfortable, and decorated in tropical colors. Amenities include a lighted volleyball court, 15-foot "mallet pool" court (you sink the 8-ball with a croquet mallet), children's playground, and an airy Key West–style lounge with rattan furnishings and hand-painted tropical murals. *3901 N. Atlantic Ave., Cocoa Beach 32931, tel. 407/783–2221, 800/247–2221 in FL, 800/327–2224 outside FL. 94 units. AE, DC, MC, V. Inexpensive–Moderate.*

Pelican Landing Resort On the Ocean. This recently refurbished, two-story beachfront motel conveys a friendly family atmosphere with its oceanfront views and screened porches (available in units 1 and 6). A microwave in each room, boardwalks to the beach, picnic tables, and a gas grill round out the amenities. *1201 S. Atlantic Ave., Cocoa Beach 32931, tel. 407/783–7197. 11 units. MC, V. Inexpensive–Moderate.*

Daytona Beach
Dining

Gene's Steak House. This family-operated restaurant, located west of town, in the middle of nowhere, has long upheld its reputation as the place for steaks. The wine list is one of the state's most comprehensive, and there are seafood specialties, but it's basically a meat-and-potatoes paradise for power beef-eaters. *U.S. 92, 4.5 mi west of the I–95/I–4 interchange, tel. 904/255–2059. Dress: neat but casual. Reservations advised. Closed Mon. AE, DC, MC, V. Expensive.*

★ **Top of Daytona.** Especially dazzling at sundown, this 29th-floor supper club has a 360° view of the beach, Intracoastal, and the city. It's a project of television personality and cookbook author Sophie Kay, who is famous for her shrimp dishes, chicken inventions, and delicate veal recipes. *2625 S. Atlantic Ave., tel. 904/767–5791. Jacket and tie suggested. Reservations advised. AE, DC, MC, V. Moderate.*

Cap'n Coty's. Locally popular, this seafood and steak center, with a cozy bar, is known for its eye-popping, 70-item Sunday brunch. Ask about the daily specials, which depend on the day's catch. *333 Beville Rd., S. Daytona, tel. 904/761–1333; other location is at 601 W. Granada Blvd., Ormond Beach, tel. 904/672–2601. Dress: casual. AE, DC, MC, V. Inexpensive.*

Lodging

Captain's Quarters Inn. It may look like just another mid-rise hotel, but inside, this is a home away from home with an antique desk, Victorian love seat, and tropical greenery set in the lobby of this beachfront inn. Fresh-baked goodies and coffee are served in The Galley, which overlooks the ocean and looks like grandma's kitchen with a few extra tables and chairs. Each guest suite features rich oak furnishings, a complete kitchen, and private balcony. *3711 S. Atlantic Ave., Daytona Beach Shores 32127, tel. 904/767–3119. 25 suites. Facilities: pool, sunbathing deck. AE, MC, V. Expensive.*

Daytona Beach Hilton. A towering landmark, this Hilton is situated on a 22-mile beach. Most rooms have balconies; some have a kitchenette, patio, or terrace. Convenient touches include an extra lavatory in every room, hair dryer, lighted makeup mirror, and a bar with refrigerator. *2637 S. Atlantic Ave., 32018, tel. 904/767–7350 or 800/525–7350. 214 rooms. Facilities: heated pool, children's pool, putting green, exercise room, sauna, game room, playground, gift shop, laundry. AE, DC, MC, V. Expensive.*

★ **Daytona Beach Marriott.** The location is a bombshell: The Ocean Center is in one direction and the best of the beach, boardwalk, and band shell is in the other. Fresh and flowery pastels set a buoyant tone for a beach vacation and every room views the ocean. *100 N. Atlantic Ave., 32118, tel. 904/254–8200. 402 rooms. Facilities: indoor-outdoor pool, 2 whirlpools, children's pool and playground, poolside bar, 2 restaurants, 30 specialty shops. AE, DC, MC, V. Expensive.*

Howard Johnson Hotel. Straight out of the glamour films of the 1930s, this 14-story hotel on the beach is an oldie that has been brought back to the splendor of its Deco years. Kitchenette suites are available. *600 N. Atlantic Ave., 32018, tel. 904/255–4471 or 800/767–4471. 323 rooms. Facilities: heated pool, golf privileges, restaurant, lounge with live entertainment and dancing. AE, DC, MC, V. Moderate.*

★ **Indigo Lakes Resort & Conference Center.** Home of the Ladies Professional Golf Association, this sprawling inland resort offers sports galore. The championship golf course measures 7,123 yards and has the largest greens in the state. Rooms are light and lavish in Florida tones. *U.S. 92 and I–95, Box 10859, 32120, tel. 904/258–6333, 800/223–4161 in FL, 800/874–9918 outside FL. 212 rooms, 64 condo suites. Facilities: Olympic-size pool, racquetball, tennis, golf, archery, pro shops, restaurant, courtesy transportation to airport and around resort, in-room coffee, no-smoking and handicapped-equipped rooms available. AE, MC, V. Moderate.*

Perry's Ocean-Edge. Long regarded as a family resort, Perry's enjoys one of the highest percentages of repeat visitors in the state. Spacious grounds are set with picnic tables. Free homemade doughnuts and coffee—a breakfast ritual here—are served in the lush solarium, a good way to get acquainted. *2209 S. Atlantic Ave., 32118, tel. 904/255–0581, 800/342–0102 in FL, 800/447–0002 outside FL. 204 rooms. Facilities: heated indoor pool, whirlpools, golf privileges, planned activities, café open for breakfast and lunch, shops. AE, DC, MC, V. Moderate.*

Aku Tiki Inn. Located right on the beach, the family-owned inn has a Polynesian theme inside and out. You can bake by the large heated pool or snooze under a shady tree on the spacious grounds. *2225 S. Atlantic Ave., 32118, tel. 904/252–9631, 800/ AKU–TIKI, or 800/528–1234. 132 rooms, some with efficiencies. Facilities: pool, shuffleboard, game room, restaurant, 2 lounges with live entertainment, pool bar, gift shop, laundry. AE, DC, MC, V. Inexpensive–Moderate.*

Flagler Beach
Dining
★

Topaz Café. An unexpected treasure on a quiet stretch of the beach highway, this intimate restaurant is operated by two sisters who do all their own cooking and baking: vegetables are bright and appealing and meats and fish are artistically presented. The menu changes weekly. Though the selection is limited, there are always enough choices, including a vegetarian entrée. The decor is a whimsical combination of enamel-top tables, unmatched settings and linens, and wildflowers. *1224 S. Ocean Shore Blvd., tel. 904/439–3275. Dress: neat but casual.*

Reservations advised. Closed Sun.–Mon. Lunch Fri. only. MC, V. Moderate.

Lodging **Topaz Motel/Hotel.** This lovingly restored 1920s beach house is
★ lavishly furnished in museum-quality Victoriana. It's a popular
beachfront honeymoon hideaway—romantic and undiscov-
ered. *1224 S. A1A, 32136, tel. 904/439–3301. 48 units, including efficiencies. Facilities: pool, restaurant, laundry. MC, V.
Moderate.*

Flagler Beach Motel. If you yearn for the mom-and-pop motels
of old Florida, at 1950s prices, this is it in plain vanilla. It's on a
quiet stretch of beach, away from the Daytona crowds, and
dressed with old-fashioned informality and friendliness. *1820
Ocean Shore Blvd., 32136, tel. 904/439–2340. 23 units, including efficiencies, cottages, and apartments. Facilities: pool,
shuffleboard, cable TV. MC, V. Inexpensive.*

Jacksonville/ **Cafe on the Square.** This 1920 building, the oldest on San Marco
Jacksonville Beach Square, is an unpretentious place for an after-theater meal,
Dining tête-à-tête dining, or Sunday brunch. Dine indoors or out and
choose from a menu ranging from steak sandwiches to quiche,
marinated chicken, or pasta—all choices with a Continental
flair. *1974 San Marco Blvd., Jacksonville, tel. 904/399–4848.
Dress: casual. Reservations accepted Mon.–Thurs. No lunch.
AE, MC, V. Moderate.*

Crustaceans. With the Intracoastal in the background, hearty
hard-shell crabs or juicy grilled fillet will taste all the better.
The menu also offers steak and homemade bakery specialties.
It's especially festive on summer weekends when there's live
entertainment. *2321 Beach Blvd., Jacksonville Beach, tel. 904/
241–8238. Dress: casual. Reservations advised. No lunch. AE,
MC, V. Moderate.*

Ragtime. A New Orleans theme threads through everything
from the Sunday jazz brunch to the beignets. It's loud,
crowded, and alive with a sophisticated young bunch. If you
aren't into Creole and Cajun classics, have a simple po-boy
sandwich or fish sizzled on the grill. *207 Atlantic Blvd., Atlantic Beach, tel. 904/241–7877. Dress: casual. No reservations.
AE, DC, MC, V. Moderate.*

Angelo's. A cozy, inelegant, hospitable family spot where you
can dive into mountainous portions of southern Italian standards, including a socko eggplant parmigiana. House specials
change daily. *2111 University Blvd. N., Jacksonville, tel. 904/
743–3400. Dress: casual. AE, DC, MC, V. Inexpensive.*

Beach Road Chicken Dinner. If down-home chicken, potatoes,
and biscuits are your comfort food, this is the place. It's the
best of basic roadside diner stuff at Depression-era prices. Eat
in or take out. *4132 Atlantic Blvd., Atlantic Beach, tel. 904/
398–7980. Dress: casual. No credit cards. Inexpensive.*

Crawdaddy's. Take it Cajun or cool, this riverfront fish shack is
the place for seafood, jambalaya, and country chicken. Dig into
the house specialty, catfish—all you can eat—then dance to a
fe-do-do beat. Sunday brunch served. *1643 Prudential Dr.
(just off I–10 at I–95), Jacksonville, tel. 904/396–3546. Dress:
casual. AE, DC, MC, V. Inexpensive.*

★ **Homestead.** A down-home place with several dining rooms, a
huge fireplace, and country cooking, this restaurant specializes in skillet-fried chicken, which comes with rice and gravy.
Chicken and dumplings, deep-fried chicken gizzards, buttermilk biscuits, and strawberry shortcake also draw in the locals.
1712 Beach Blvd., Jacksonville Beach, tel. 904/249–5240.

Dress: informal. Reservations accepted for parties of 6 or more. AE, MC, V. Inexpensive.

The Tree Steakhouse. You select your steak and watch the staff cook it over a charcoal fire. Charbroiled chicken is also on the list, and there are several seafood dishes, too. The atmosphere is low-key and casual. *942 Arlington Rd., in Arlington Plaza, Jacksonville, tel. 904/725–0066. Jacket required. No reservations. AE, DC, MC, V. Inexpensive.*

Lodging **Jacksonville Omni Hotel.** The city's newest hotel is a 16-story, ultramodern facility with a splashy lobby atrium and large, stylish guest rooms. All rooms have either a king-size or two double beds. You'll feel pampered anywhere in the hotel, but the extra frills are to be found in the two floors of the concierge level. *245 Water St., Jacksonville 32202, tel. 904/355–6664. 354 rooms. Facilities: heated pool, restaurant, lounge, exercise room, no-smoking rooms, cable TV. AE, DC, MC, V. Expensive.*

Marina Hotel at St. Johns Place. This five-story luxury hotel, connected to the Riverwalk complex, has modern rooms with either a king-size or two double beds. It's located right in the center of things, and the hotel bustles with activity inside and out. Rooms overlooking the St. Johns River command the highest prices. *1515 Prudential Dr., Jacksonville 32207, tel. 904/ 396–5100. 350 rooms, 18 suites. Facilities: pool, 2 lighted tennis courts, 2 restaurants, lounge, shopping arcade, privileges at Downtown Athletic Club, no-smoking rooms, facilities for handicapped persons. AE, DC, MC, V. Expensive.*

Comfort Suites Hotel. Located in bustling Baymeadows, central to the currently "in" restaurants, nightclubs, and shops, this all-suites hotel is an unbeatable value. Suites, which are decorated in breezy, radiant Florida hues, include refrigerators, remote control TV, and sofa sleepers. Microwaves and VCRs come with master suites. Daily Continental breakfast and cocktail hour during the week are included in rates. *8333 Dix Ellis Trail, Jacksonville 32256, tel. 904/739–1155. 128 suites. Facilities: outdoor pool, heated spa, laundry. AE, DC, MC, V. Moderate.*

House on Cherry St. This early 20th-century treasure is furnished with pewter, Oriental rugs, woven coverlets, and other remnants of a rich past. Carol Anderson welcomes her guests to her riverside home with wine and hors d'oeuvres and serves full breakfast every morning. Walk to the parks and gardens of the chic Avondale district. Call for restrictions. *1844 Cherry St., Jacksonville 32205, tel. 904/384–1999. 4 rooms with private bath. Facilities: free use of bicycles. MC, V. Moderate.*

Sea Turtle Inn. Every room in this inn has a view of the Atlantic. Let the staff arrange special outings for you: golf, deep-sea fishing, or a visit to a Nautilus fitness center. You'll be welcomed each evening with a complimentary cocktail reception, and in the morning you'll be awakened with hot coffee and a newspaper. *One Ocean Blvd., Atlantic Beach 32233, tel. 904/ 249–7402. 198 rooms. Facilities: oceanfront pool with cabana bar, restaurant, lounge with live entertainment, room service, free airport shuttle. AE, DC, MC, V. Moderate.*

New Smyrna Beach **The Skyline.** Watch private airplanes land and take off at the
Dining New Smyrna Beach airport as you dine on secretly seasoned Tony Barbera steaks, veal, shrimp, chicken, and fish. A tray will be brought for your selection: order steaks by the ounce, cut to order if you wish. House specialties include the *zuppa di*

pesce, served in a crock; fresh homemade pastas; and a New England clam chowder that took first place in the 1988 Chowder Debate. The building, once an officers club for American and RAF pilots, is filled with aeronautical nostalgia. *2004 N. Dixie Freeway, tel. 904/428–5325. Dress: neat but casual; no jeans or T-shirts. Reservations advised. No lunch. AE, MC, V. Moderate.*

Riverview Charlie's. Look out over the Intracoastal Waterway while you choose from a menu loaded with local and imported fish, all available broiled, blackened, or grilled. The shore platters are piled high; landlubbers can choose steaks and chicken dishes instead. *101 Flagler Ave., tel. 904/428–1865. Dress: neat but casual. Reservations advised. AE, DC, MC, V. Moderate–Inexpensive.*

Blackbeard's Inn. An array of seafood comes in fresh from the nearby docks. It's hard to beat the shrimp Louie, which is served at lunchtime, the stuffed grouper, or mountainous combo platters, but the inn is also known for its prime beef and barbecues. *701 N. Dixie Hwy., tel. in Daytona, 904/788–9476; outside Daytona, 904/427–0414. Dress: casual. No reservations except for parties of 15 or more. No lunch weekends. AE, DC, MC, V. Inexpensive.*

Franco's. Begun as a pizza joint in 1983, Franco's has become a high-voltage Italian specialty house. Light concoctions include spinach or broccoli pies, pasta salads, and what could possibly be the best Greek salad you've ever had. There's a long list of fish, Italian classics, including a captivating zucchini parmigiana, seven styles of veal, and gourmet pizzas. *1518 S. Dixie Freeway (U.S. 1, ½ mi south of S.R. 44), tel. 904/423–3600. Dress: casual. Reservations advised. No lunch Sun. MC, V. Inexpensive.*

Goodrich Seafood & Restaurant. For those who like mullet, this is a piscatorial Shangri-la. Gorge on steamed oysters, fried fish, hush puppies, clams, shrimp, and chowders. Fresh and frozen seafood is also sold over the counter. *253 River Dr., tel. 904/345–3397. Dress: casual. Reservations required for all-you-can-eat buffet (Sept.–May). Closed Sun. No credit cards. Inexpensive.*

Lodging **Riverview Hotel.** A landmark since 1886, this was once a bridge tender's home. Verandas look over the Intracoastal, dunes, and marshes, while inside, Haitian prints and wicker furniture add to a feeling of island getaway. Complimentary Continental breakfast is served in your room, on the balcony, or poolside. *103 Flagler Ave., 32169, tel. 904/428–5858. 18 rooms with private bath. Facilities: restaurant, pool. AE, MC, V. Moderate.*

Sea Woods Resort Community. Get the best of the beach plus 50 acres of rolling dunes and hammocks. A true community of homes, condos, and villas, this has a rhythm of doing, going, and playing. Most people rent by the week, month, or season, but nightly rates are available. *4400 S. Atlantic Ave., 32169, tel. 904/423–7796 or 800/826–8614. 180 units. Facilities: racquetball, tennis, Nautilus fitness center, outdoor heated pool, planned activities in winter. No credit cards. Moderate.*

Ocean Air Motel. One of those modest little "finds," this motel is operated by a caring British couple who, in the English manner, groom the grounds as carefully as they do the neat and commodious rooms. It's only a five-minute walk from the beach. *1161 N. Dixie Freeway, 32069, tel. 904/428–4728. 14* *rooms. Facilities: pool, picnic tables. AE, DC, MC, V. Inexpensive.*

Ormond Beach **Shogun II.** The largest of this area's Japanese steak and sea-
Dining food houses, this is the place for flashy tableside food preparation, a sushi bar, and a tropical bar. It's a fun, family place; call
ahead if you want to celebrate a special occasion in traditional
Japanese style. The steak and shrimp are stellar, but the lobster and chicken are also tempting. *630 S. Atlantic Ave. (A1A),
in the Ellinor Village Shopping Center, tel. 904/673–1110.
Dress: casual. AE, MC, V. Inexpensive.*

Ponte Vedra Beach **The Augustine Room.** For a very special night out, come here
Dining not just to dine but for a look at the Marriott Sawgrass's emerald exterior and grounds filled with lagoons and waterfalls.
Gaze at pleasing original paintings and enjoy the fresh flowers
on your table while pondering a menu of fine steaks, native seafood, and veal specialties. The wine list is one of the area's most
comprehensive. *1000 TPC Blvd., tel. 904/285–7777. Jacket and
tie required. Reservations advised. Closed Sun. AE, MC, V.
Very Expensive.*

Lodging **The Lodge at Ponte Vedra Beach.** The look of this plush new resort is Mediterranean villa grand luxe, aimed at serving an
elite clientele whose passions are golf and tennis. The PGA
Tour, Tournament Players Club, and Association of Tennis Professionals are based here. Rooms, designed with a country-
French flair, have private balconies and cozy window seats. *607
Ponte Vedra Blvd., 32080, tel. 904/273–9500. 42 rooms, 24
suites, some with private whirlpool and fireplace. Facilities: 54
holes of golf, water sports, deep-sea fishing, horseback riding,
two beachside pools with bar and grill, exercise room, restaurant, lounge. AE, DC, MC, V. Very Expensive.*
Marriott at Sawgrass. A tropical design is conveyed throughout
this luxury hotel. Pick a room with a fireplace or private balcony. Fine details, from the private lounge and special services
on the concierge level to the mood set by the lagoon and waterfall in the complex, enhance this resort. *1000 TPC Blvd., 32082,
tel. 904/285–7777. 512 units. Facilities: 5 pools, children's program and pool, lighted tennis courts, 99 holes of golf and complete golf program, bicycling, croquet, boating, exercise
facilities, restaurants, valet, gift shop, private beach privileges. AE, MC, V. Very Expensive.*

St. Augustine **Columbia.** An heir to the cherished reputation of the original
Dining Columbia founded in Tampa in 1905, this one serves time-hon-
★ ored dishes including *arroz con pollo* (chicken with rice), filet
salteado, shrimp and scallops Marbella, and a fragrant, fla-
grant paella. The Fiesta Brunch on Sunday is a Spanish gala. *98
St. George St., tel. 904/824–3341 or in FL 800/227–1905. Dress:
neat but casual. Reservations advised. AE, MC, V. Moderate.*
La Parisienne. Tiny and attentive, pleasantly lusty in its approach to honest bistro cuisine, this little place is a true find—
and weekend brunches are available, too. Save room for the
pastries. *60 Hypolita St., tel. 904/829–0055. Dress: neat but
casual. Reservations required at dinner. Closed Mon. MC, V.
Moderate.*
Le Pavilion. The Continental approach spills over from France
to Germany with a wow of a schnitzel with spätzle. Hearty
soups and good breads make a budget meal, or you can splurge
on the rack of lamb or escargot. *45 San Marco St., tel. 904/824–*

6202. Dress: neat but casual. Reservations advised; required for 6 or more. DC, MC, V. Moderate.

★ **Raintree.** The oldest home in this part of the city, this building has been lovingly restored. The buttery breads and pastries are baked on the premises. Try the brandied pepper steak or the Maine lobster special. The Raintree's Madrigal or Champagne dinners are especially fun. The wine list is impressive, and there are two dozen beers to choose from. Courtesy pickup is available from any lodging in the city. *102 San Marco Ave., tel. 904/824-7211. Dress: neat but casual. Reservations advised. No lunch. DC, MC, V. Moderate.*

Santa Maria. This ramshackle landmark, run by the same family since the 1950s, perches over the water beside the colorful city marina. Seafood is the focus, but there are also steaks, chicken, prime rib, and a children's menu. Have drinks first in the salty lounge or feed the fish from the open-air porch. *135 Avenida Menendez, tel. 904/829-6578. Dress: casual. AE, DC, MC, V. Inexpensive-Moderate. AE, DC, MC, V.*

Zaharias. The room is big, busy, and buzzing with openhanded hospitality. Serve yourself from an enormous buffet instead of, or in addition to, ordering from the menu. Greek and Italian specialties include homemade pizza, a big gyro dinner served with a side order of spaghetti, shish kebab, steaks, seafood, and sandwiches. *3945 A1AS, tel. 904/471-4799. Dress: casual. AE, MC, V. Inexpensive.*

Lodging **Sheraton Palm Coast.** This is a bright, nautical-style resort ho-
★ tel near the beach, and easily accessed by the nearby newly built bridge. Rooms have private patios that overlook the Intracoastal. *300 Club House Dr., 32137, tel. 904/445-3000 or 800/325-3535. 154 rooms. Facilities: 2 heated pools, children's pool, marina, 16 tennis courts, 3 championship golf courses, whirlpool, exercise equipment, sauna, restaurant, bar, shops, refrigerators, free transportation around resort and to beach. AE, DC, MC, V. Very Expensive.*

★ **Casa Solana.** A hushed air of yesteryear hangs over this gracious, antiques-filled, 225-year-old home where you'll be welcomed like an old friend. Complimentary sherry and chocolates and a breakfast of fresh fruits and homemade specialties further convey the mellow but comfortable tone of this inn. *21 Aviles St., 32084, tel. 904/824-3555. 4 suites. Facilities: bicycles. AE, MC, V. Expensive.*

★ **Colony's Ponce de Leon Golf and Conference Resort.** Pick your site to loll in the sun from the 350 lavishly landscaped subtropical acres or seek the shade of century-old live oaks in spacious contrast to the narrow streets and crowding of the old city. Insiders reserve well in advance to stay here for special events occurring in and around the area. *4000 U.S. 1N, 32085, tel. 904/824-2821 or in FL 800/228-2821. 200 rooms, 25 condos. Facilities: pool, tennis, 18-hole championship golf course, 18-hole poolside putting course, volleyball, horseshoes, restaurant. AE, DC, MC, V. Expensive.*

★ **Kenwood Inn.** For more than a century this stately Victorian inn has been welcoming wayfarers, and the Constant family continues the tradition. Located in the heart of the historic district, the inn is within walking distance of restaurants and sightseeing. A Continental breakfast of home-baked cakes and breads is included. Call for restrictions. *38 Marine St., 32084, tel. 904/824-2116. 10 rooms, 4 suites. Facilities: walled-in* *courtyard with pool, fish pond, street parking and off-street parking 1 block away. MC, V. Moderate.*

The Old Powder House Inn. Part of an 1899 Flagler development of winter cottages for the rich, this inn stands on the site of an 18th-century Spanish gunpowder magazine. Imaginative decor makes every room, from "Granny's Attic" to "Queen Anne's Lace," unique. Try the two-night package, which includes a romantic room, full breakfast and afternoon tea daily, wine and hors d'oeuvres nightly, and a moonlight carriage ride with champagne. *38 Cordova St., 32085, tel. 904/824–4149. 6 rooms. Facilities: bicycles. MC, V. Moderate.*

Beacher's Lodge. An all-suites hotel on the dazzling white beach of Anastasia Island provides complimentary coffee, juice, newspaper, and a glimpse of the sun rising over the Atlantic. *6970 A1AS, 32086, tel. 904/471–8849 or 800/527–8849. 132 suites. Facilities: pool, fully equipped kitchen, laundry. MC, V. Inexpensive–Moderate.*

Carriage Way Bed and Breakfast. A Victorian mansion grandly restored in 1984, this B&B is within walking distance of restaurants and historic sites. Innkeepers Karen Burkley-Kovacik and husband Frank see to welcoming touches such as fresh flowers and home-baked breads. Special-occasion breakfasts, flowers, picnic lunches or romantic dinners, or a simple family supper can be arranged with advance notice. *70 Cuna St., 32084, tel. 904/829–2467. 7 rooms. Facilities: bicycles. MC, V. Inexpensive–Moderate.*

St. Francis Inn. If only the walls could whisper, this late-18th-century house would tell tales of slave uprisings, buried doubloons, and Confederate spies. The inn, which was a boarding house a century ago, now offers rooms, suites, an apartment, and a cottage. Rates include Continental breakfast. *279 St. George St., 32084, tel. 904/824–6068. Facilities: pool, some fireplaces, bicycles. MC, V. Inexpensive–Moderate.*

The Arts and Nightlife

The Arts Broadway touring shows, top-name entertainers, and other major events are booked at the **Florida Theater Performing Arts Center** (128 E. Forsyth St., Jacksonville, tel. 904/355–5661), the **Jacksonville Civic Auditorium** (300 Water St., Jacksonville, tel. 904/360–3900), and **The Ocean Center** (101 N. Atlantic Ave., Daytona Beach, tel. 904/254–4545 or 800/858–6444 in FL).

The **Jacksonville Symphony Orchestra** (tel. 904/354–5479) presents a variety of concerts and hosts visiting artists.

Seaside Music Theater (901 6th St., Holly Hill, tel. 904/252–3394) presents professional musicals January–March and June–August.

Alhambra Dinner Theater (12000 Beach Blvd., Jacksonville, tel. 904/641–1212) offers professional theater and competent menus that change with each play.

Nightlife **Finky's** (640 N. Grandview, Daytona Beach, tel. 904/255–5059)
Bars and brings in name entertainers you've seen on the Nashville Net-
Nightclubs work and MTV. **Waves** in the Daytona Beach Marriott (100 N. Atlantic Ave., tel. 904/254–8200) is the area's hot, upscale place to drink, dance, and nosh while you listen to Top 40 and mellow standards. **Ocean Pier** (1200 Main St., Daytona Beach,

tel. 904/253–1212), located on the ocean, has four bars and one of the biggest dance floors in town.

In St. Augustine, **Richard's Jazz Restaurant** (77 San Marco Ave., tel. 904/829–9910), **Scarlett O'Hara's** (70 Hypolita St., tel. 904/824–6535), the **White Lion** (20 Cuna St., tel. 904/829–2388), and **Trade Winds** (Charlotte St., tel. 904/829–9336) offer live music from bluegrass to classic rock. Call for information on specific performances.

In Cocoa Beach, **Coconuts** (2 Minuteman Causeway, tel. 407/784–1422) and **Plum's Lounge/Holiday Inn Cocoa Beach** (1300 N. Atlantic Ave., tel. 407/783–2271) feature dancing and live entertainment nightly.

Disney World and the Orlando Area

Orlando, a high-profile city of fast growth boosted by a robust business climate and thriving tourist trade, seems to be an area touched by pixie dust. A magical city. But it was not always that way.

Upon its incorporation in 1875, Orlando had less than 100 residents. The town had no seaport or major waterway. There was no railroad to spur its growth. There was little to stimulate or sustain any prosperity. But Orlando had a sunny year-round climate. And it had something else—a location in the very center of what would become one of the fastest-growing states in the country. The population of the greater metropolitan area is now approaching one million, and various surveys cite the greater Orlando area as among the fastest growing in the country.

Orlando is best known as the world's number one tourist destination. Disneyland had long been a successful staple in California when Disney decided, in the early 1960s, to build another theme park in the eastern United States. By 1963, Florida was chosen as the best state. Orlando was chosen for a variety of reasons, including its transportation system and its large amounts of open, available land. Eventually, a huge tract of 28,000 acres was bought. On November 16, 1965, Walt Disney outlined his master plan. The first phase was the Magic Kingdom and a vacation complex, which opened in 1971. On October 1, 1982, Epcot Center opened its gates and was an immediate success. Almost 23 million visitors passed through its gates the very first year. Walt Disney World added the 135-acre Disney-MGM Studios Theme Park in 1989.

In its graceful and quiet past Orlando enjoyed a small-town pace that earned it the title of "The City Beautiful." The city today is far more metropolitan, even cosmopolitan, but much of the original charm remains. Many residents have homes near the hundreds of clear spring-fed lakes, far from the south Orlando-based tourist corridor. The aroma here is often that of orange blossoms and citrus trees. The city has retained its parklike atmosphere.

Getting Around
Orlando

The most important artery in the Orlando area is **Interstate 4** (**I–4**). Be aware that I–4 is considered an east-west expressway in our national road system, but in the Orlando area, I–4 actually runs north-south: when the signs say east, you are often going north, and when the signs say west, you are often going south. Another main drag is **International Drive,** which has several major hotels, restaurants, and shopping centers. You can get onto International Drive from I-4 Exits 28, 29, and 30B. The other main road, **Irlo Bronson Memorial Highway (U.S. 192),** cuts across I-4 at Exits 25A and 25B.

Taxi fares start at $2.45 and cost $1.30 for each mile thereafter. Call Yellow Cab Co. (tel. 407/699-9999) or Town and Country Cab (tel. 407/828-3035).

Walt Disney World Walt Disney World has its own complete transportation system, but because the property is so extensive, the system can be a bit confusing, even for an experienced visitor. Best-known is the elevated monorail, which connects Walt Disney World's biggest resorts and attractions. There are also extensive bus, motor-launch, and ferry systems. If you are staying at an on-site resort or if you hold a combination Magic Kingdom-Epcot Center ticket, transportation is free. If not, you can buy unlimited transportation within Walt Disney World for $2.50 a day. The central connecting station for the monorail, buses, and ferries is called the **Transportation and Ticket Center** (TTC).

If you arrive at either the Magic Kingdom, Epcot, or Disney-MGM by car, there is a $4 parking charge. If you're staying at a Disney World hotel, show your guest ID for free parking. Remember or write down *exactly* where you park in the sea of automobiles. Trams make frequent trips between the parking areas and the front gate.

Walt Disney World

Admission tickets are sold for two age groups—adult, meaning everyone aged 10 and older, and children aged 3-9. Children under age 3 get in free. Various tickets or passports specify how many days you can visit the parks, or which specific parks you can visit. Here is a list of prices; they are subject to change, so call for confirmation.

One-day ticket	$33 adults, $26 children
Four-day passport	$111 adults, $88 children
Five-day passport	$145 adults, $116 children
Six-day passport	$150 adults, $120 children
Annual Pass (new)	$180 adults, $155 children*
Annual Pass (renewal)	$160 adults, $135 children*
Annual Pass (charter renewal)	$140 adults, $115 children*
River Country, one day	$11.75 adults, $9.25 children; *$10.75/$8.25*
River Country, two days	$17.75 adults, $13.75 children; *$16.75/$12.75*
River Country, annual pass	$50 adults and children

Combined River Country/Discovery Island, one day	$15 adults, $11 children; *$14/$10*
Discovery Island, one day	$8 adults, $4.50 children
Typhoon Lagoon, one day	$18.25 adults, $14.50 children; *$16.25/$13*
Typhoon Lagoon, annual pass	$79.50 adults and children
Pleasure Island, one day	$9.95 adults and children
Pleasure Island, annual pass	$24.95 adults and children

*An additional $15 (adults) and $11 (children) entitles pass-holders to unlimited use of River Country and Discovery Island for the duration of their annual passes.

Italics indicate prices for visitors staying in a Disney World resort or in a resort in the WDW Village Hotel Plaza.

Each time you use a Passport, the entry date is stamped on it; the remaining days may be used any time in the future. If you buy a one-day ticket and later decide to extend your visit, you can get full credit for it toward the purchase of any Passport. Exchanges can be made at City Hall in the Magic Kingdom, at Earth Station in Epcot, or at Guest Relations at Disney-MGM. Do this before leaving the park; once you've left, the ticket is worthless.

Tickets and Passports to Walt Disney World and Epcot Center may be purchased at admission booths at the TTC, in on-site or Hotel Plaza resorts (if you're a registered guest), or at the Walt Disney World kiosk on the second floor of the main terminal at Orlando International Airport. If you want to buy tickets before you arrive in Orlando, send a check or money order to Admissions, Walt Disney World, Box 10000, Lake Buena Vista, 32830. Allow four to six weeks for the order to be processed.

If you want to leave the Magic Kingdom or Epcot Center and return on the same day, be sure to have your hand stamped on the way out. You'll need your ticket *and* the hand stamp to be readmitted.

Hours vary widely throughout the year. During the summer, the Magic Kingdom is open until midnight, Epcot Center is open to 11 PM, and Disney-MGM is open to 9 PM. At other times of year, Epcot Center and Disney-MGM are open until 8 PM, and the Magic Kingdom to 6 PM, with Main Street remaining open until 7. Each park usually opens at 9 AM, although you can enter the grounds up to an hour earlier.

Magic Kingdom You'll first see Town Square. City Hall is on your left. The railroad station is directly behind you. Sprawling before you is Main Street—a shop-filled boulevard with Victorian-style stores, and dining spots. Walk two blocks along Main Street and you'll enter Central Plaza, with **Cinderella Castle** rising directly in front of you. This is the hub of the Kingdom; seven "lands" radiate out from it.

Walt Disney World

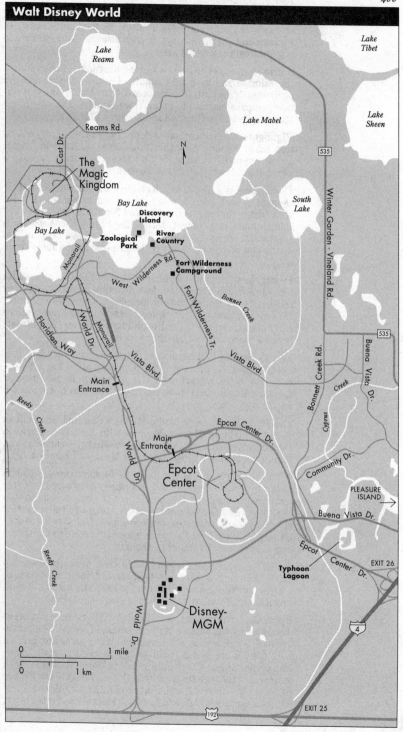

Lake Reams

Lake Tibet

Lake Mabel

Lake Sheen

Reams Rd.

535

Cast Dr.

The Magic Kingdom

Bay Lake

Discovery Island

Zoological Park

River Country

South Lake

Winter Garden - Vineland Rd.

Bay Lake

Fort Wilderness Campground

Monorail

West Wilderness Rd.

Fort Wilderness Tr.

Bonnet Creek

Floridian Way

World Dr.

Monorail

Vista Blvd.

Vista Blvd.

Bonnett Creek Rd.

Cypress Creek

535

Buena Vista Dr.

Main Entrance

Reedy Creek

World Dr.

Main Entrance

Epcot Center Dr.

Epcot Center

Community Dr.

PLEASURE ISLAND →

Buena Vista Dr.

Reedy Creek

World Dr.

Epcot Center Dr.

EXIT 26

Typhoon Lagoon

Disney-MGM

4

0   1 mile

0   1 km

192

EXIT 25

This is as good a place as any to see the daily parade at 3 PM. All Disney's characters are featured in the 20-minute show. In summer and during holidays, there's also an Electrical Parade of giant floats at 9 and 11 PM.

A great way to get an overview of the Kingdom is to hop aboard the railroad and take a 14-minute, 1½-mile ride around the perimeter of the park. You can board at the Victorian-style station you pass beneath to enter Town Square. The only other stations are at Frontierland and Mickey's Starland.

Highlights of **Adventureland** include: *Jungle Cruise*, a boat trip that takes visitors along the Nile, across an Amazon jungle, and so on; and *Pirates of the Caribbean*, a journey through a world of pirate strongholds and treasure-filled dungeons.

Fantasyland is a land in which children are very much in their element. There are a few traditional amusement-park rides with Disney themes, such as the *Mad Tea Party*, where teacups spin around a large teapot, *Dumbo the Flying Elephant*, and a spectacular merry-go-round. The popular *20,000 Leagues Under the Sea* is an underwater cruise inspired by the Jules Verne novel.

Frontierland replicates a gold-rush town of the Southwest. Its top ride is *Big Thunder Mountain Railroad*, a scream-inducing roller coaster. Entertainment includes *Country Bear Jamboree* and the *Diamond Horseshow Jamboree* (make reservations early in the morning at the Hospitality House on Main Street, because there are only five shows daily).

Liberty Square is a small land adjoining and blending into Frontierland. Its theme is Colonial history and it has a few decent but tame attractions. The exception is the popular *Haunted Mansion;* its spine-tingling effects may be too intense for the very young.

The newest of Disney's lands, **Mickey's Starland** was built in 1988 to celebrate Mickey Mouse's 60th birthday. Here, in Duckburg, visitors can view some of Mickey's cartoons and films, visit Mickey's house, and meet Mickey for some photos.

"Fun in the Future" is the motto of **Tomorrowland,** which is slated for a makeover by 1996. Its rides are mostly lackluster compared to others in the park; about the only reason to stop here at present is *Space Mountain*, a space-age roller coaster ride in the dark, with everyone screaming. Children 7 and over also enjoy *Grand Prix Raceway*, where they can drive mini race cars to speeds up to 7 miles per hour.

Epcot Center   As you enter Epcot Center, you'll pass beneath **Spaceship Earth,** a 17-story sphere. Inside Spaceship Earth, visitors take a highly praised journey through the dramatic history of communications, from cave drawings to space-age technology.

Epcot Center is divided almost equally into two distinct areas separated by the 40-acre World Showcase Lagoon. The northern half, which is where the main admission gates are, is filled with the Future World pavilions, sponsored by major American corporations. The southern half is World Showcase, with an entrance through International Gateway next to the France pavilion. Stop first at Earth Station to pick up a guidebook and entertainment schedule and to make reservations for the busy, full-service restaurants here. (Guests who are staying in on-site properties can make their reservations ahead of time.)

Future World explores technological concepts, such as energy and communications, in entertaining ways. Future World's highlights include *Horizons*, with its robotic-staffed farms, ocean colonies, and space cities; *Journey Into Imagination*, a tour of the creative process, where teenagers especially enjoy *Captain EO*, a $17-million, 3-D film starring singer Michael Jackson; and the new *The Living Seas* attraction, which takes visitors on a gondola ride beneath the sea for a dynamic close-up look at marine life in a six-million-gallon aquarium more than four fathoms deep.

World Showcase is a series of pavilions in which various nations portray their cultures through a combination of films, exhibits, and seemingly endless shops. Bring a hearty appetite, because ethnic cuisines are featured in each of the 11 foreign pavilions. Most of the nations have done an imaginative and painstaking job of re-creating scale models of their best-known monuments, such as the Eiffel Tower in France, a Mayan temple in Mexico, and a majestic pagoda in Japan. Unlike Future World and the Magic Kingdom, the Showcase doesn't offer amusement-park-type rides (except for tame boat rides in Mexico and Norway). The focal point of World Showcase, on the opposite side of the lagoon from Future World, is the host pavilion, the *American Adventure*. The pavilions of the other countries fan out from the right and left of American Adventure, encircling the lagoon. Going clockwise from the left as you enter World Showcase from Future World are the pavilions of Mexico, Norway, People's Republic of China, Germany, Italy, the United States, Japan, Morocco, France, United Kingdom, and Canada. One film should not be missed; the China pavilion's CircleVision presentation on the landscape of China, taking viewers on a fantastic journey from inner Mongolia to the Tibetan mountains, along the Great Wall, and into Beijing.

Disney-MGM Studios Theme Park   Those who want a close-up, behind-the-scenes look at a real studio can take the 2-hour **Backstage Studio Tour,** which consists of a tram ride and a walking tour, and the **Animation Tour,** which takes visitors step-by-step through the process by looking over the artists' shoulders from a raised, glass-enclosed walkway. **Epic Stunt Spectacular** is a live show with real stunt performers. **The Great Movie Ride** begins tamely, like the Magic Kingdom's Pirates of the Caribbean, but soon the guide begins interacting with the Audio-Animatronics characters, and the action picks up to the delight of the younger children. A play area is known as the **Honey, I Shrunk the Kids Adventure Zone.**

Star Tours is one of Disney's more recent simulator thrill rides. Created under the direction of George Lucas, the five 40-seat theaters become spaceships, and you are off to the moon of Endor. Be forewarned: the ride is rough.

Scheduled to open this year is the **Muppet Studios,** which will include a 3-D movie.

Typhoon Lagoon   This 50-acre aquatic entertainment complex features the largest water-slide mountain in the world. The mountain is just under 100 feet high, with nine water slides shooting down it into white-water rivers and swirling pools. There are huge wave-making lagoons for swimming and surfing. The water park also includes a Swiss Family Robinson–type tropical island covered with lush greenery, where guests can play at being shipwrecked. A saltwater pool contains a coral reef where snorkelers come mask-to-face with all sorts of Caribbean sea creatures, such as groupers, parrotfish, and even baby sharks. *Tel. 407/560–4142.*

River Country In the backwoods setting of the Fort Wilderness Campground Resort, kids can slide, splash, and swim about in an aquatic playground, complete with white water inner-tubing channels and corkscrew water slides that splash down into a 300,000 gallon pond. The pool is heated during the winter, so kids can take a dip here year-round. During the summer, River Country can get very congested, so it's best to come late in the afternoon. *Tel. 407/824–2760.*

Discovery Island Covered with exotic flora, small, furry animals, and colorful birdlife, this little island makes a great escape from the manmade tourist attractions of Walt Disney World. Visitors listen to nature as they stroll along winding pathways and across footbridges. Keep an eye out for the Galapagos tortoises, trumpeter swans, scarlet ibis, and bald eagles. Tickets are sold at Fort Wilderness's River Country, at the TTC, at guest service desks in the Disney resorts, and on the island itself. You can get there by watercraft from the Magic Kingdom, Contemporary Resort, Polynesian Village, Grand Floridian, and River Country in Fort Wilderness. *Tel. 407/824–2875.*

The Orlando Area

Numbers in the margin correspond to points of interest on the Orlando Area map.

① **Central Florida Zoological Park.** A 110-acre zoo. *U.S. 17–92, 1 mi east of I–4 and 4 mi west of Sanford, tel. 407/323–4450. Admission: $5 adults, $2 children 3–12. Open daily 9–5.*

② **Mystery Fun House.** Magic mirrors, moving floors, laughing doors, barrels that roll, a shooting arcade—all are favorites with children, though the price is high for not much more than a few minutes' entertainment. *5767 Major Blvd., off Kirkman Rd. near International Dr., tel. 407/351–3355. Admission: $7.95 adults, children under 4 free; $4.95 for Starbase Omega, a laser tag game. Open daily 10 AM–midnight.*

③ **Universal Studios Florida.** The largest working film studio outside Hollywood, Universal opened its doors to tours in the summer of 1990. The tour is patterned after the one at the highly successful attraction in Los Angeles, except the Florida tours have been developed to integrate the tour more fully with studio production facilities, allowing visitors an interactive behind-the-scenes look at movie and TV production. Visitors view live shows, participate in movie-themed attractions, and tour back-lot sets. The tour showcases the special-effects magic of creative consultant Steven Spielberg and the animation wizardry of Hanna-Barbera. A **Hard Rock Cafe** is on the premises. *Get off I–4 at Exit 30B and follow the signs. Tel. 407/363–8000. One-day admission: $29 adults, $23 children 3–11; two-day admission: $49 adults, $39 children 3–11. Hours vary seasonally.*

④ **Wet 'n Wild.** Water slides, flumes, lazy rivers, and other water-related activities for swimmers and sunbathers. *6200 In-*

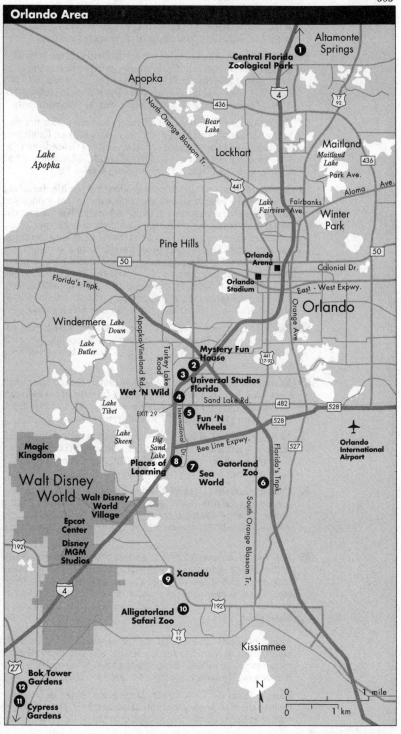

Orlando Area

Altamonte Springs

Central Florida Zoological Park ①

Apopka

436

I 4

17 92

Bear Lake

North Orange Blossom Tr.

Lockhart

Maitland

Maitland Lake

436

Park Ave.

Aloma Ave.

Fairbanks Ave.

Lake Apopka

Lake Fairview

Winter Park

441

Pine Hills

50

Orlando Arena

Colonial Dr.

50

Florida's Tnpk.

Orlando Stadium

East - West Expwy.

Orlando

Orange Ave.

Windermere

Lake Down

Lake Butler

Apopka-Vineland Rd.

Turkey Lake Road

Mystery Fun House

② ③ Universal Studios Florida

441 17-92

Wet 'N Wild ④

Sand Lake Rd.

482

528

528

527

Orlando International Airport

Lake Tibet

EXIT 29

⑤ Fun 'N Wheels

International Dr.

Lake Sheen

Big Sand Lake

Bee Line Expwy.

Magic Kingdom

Places of Learning ⑧ ⑦ Sea World

Gatorland Zoo

⑥

Florida's Tnpk.

South Orange Blossom Tr.

Walt Disney World

Walt Disney World Village

Epcot Center

Disney MGM Studios

192

I 4

⑨ Xanadu

Alligatorland Safari Zoo ⑩

192

17 92

Kissimmee

N

0   1 mile

0   1 km

27

Bok Tower Gardens

⑫

⑪ Cypress Gardens

ternational Dr., Orlando, tel. 407/351–WILD or 800/992–WILD. Admission: $17.95 adults, $15.95 children 3–12, $8.45 adults 55 and over. Open daily 10–6, except in winter.

⑤ Fun 'n Wheels. An expensive but active family theme park with go-cart tracks, rides, minigolf course, bumper boats, and cars. *6739 Sand Lake Rd. at International Dr., Orlando, tel. 407/351–5651. General admission free. Open Sun. 10 AM–11 PM, Mon.–Thurs. 4–11, Fri. 4–midnight, Sat. 10 AM–midnight.*

⑥ Gatorland Zoo. Thousands of alligators and crocodiles sleeping in the sun are viewed from a walkway. Also snakes, flamingos, monkeys, and other Florida critters. *South of Orlando on U.S. 17–92 near Kissimmee, tel. 407/857–3845. Admission: $7.95 adults, $4.95 children 3–11. Open daily 8 AM–6 PM.*

⑦ Sea World. A major theme park celebrating sea life, including popular Baby Shamu and an awesome exhibit that guides you through a shark tank on a moving sidewalk. Marine animals perform in seven major shows. The park also has penguins, tropical fish, otter habitats, walrus training exhibits, botanical gardens, and other educational diversions in a setting more tranquil than that of most theme parks. *Located 10 mi south of Orlando at the intersection of I–4 and the Bee Line Expressway, 7007 Sea World Dr., Orlando, tel. 407/351–3600 or 800/327–2420. Admission: $25.50 adults, $21.70 children 3–9. Open daily 9–8, with extended summer and holiday hours.*

⑧ Places of Learning. Great selection of children's books and educational games. Recommended for the nonbookish, too. *6825 Academic Dr., Orlando, tel. 407/345–1038. Admission free. Open daily 9–6.*

⑨ Xanadu. A dome-shaped home showcasing technological and electronic devices. Guided tours daily. *Located at the intersection of U.S. 192 and Rte. 535, Kissimmee, tel. 407/396–1992. Admission: $5.95 adults, $4.95 children 3–12.*

⑩ Alligatorland Safari Zoo. More than 1,600 exotic animals and birds in a natural setting. *U.S. 192 between Kissimmee and Walt Disney World, tel. 407/396–1012. Admission: $5 adults, $3.95 children 4–11. Open daily 8:30–dusk.*

⑪ Cypress Gardens. Central Florida's original theme park features exotic flowers, waterskiing shows, and bird and alligator shows. *East of Winter Haven off Rte. 540, tel. 813/324–2111. Admission: $18.95 adults, $12.95 children 3–9. Open daily 9–6.*

⑫ Bok Tower Gardens. A 128-acre garden with pine forests, shady paths, and a bell tower that rings daily at 3 PM. *Between Haines City and Lake Wales off U.S. 27, tel. 813/676–1408. Admission: $3 per person, children under 12 free. Open daily 8–5.*

Shopping

Altamonte Mall. The largest mall in central Florida includes Sears, Maison Blanche, Jordan Marsh, and Burdine's department stores, as well as 165 specialty shops. *½ mi east of I–4 on Rte. 436 in Altamonte Springs, tel. 407/830–4400.*

Florida Mall. This is a newer, large-scale center in Orlando, close to the Walt Disney World tourism corridor. More than 160 stores in three distinctive shopping areas—Victorian, Mediterranean, and Art Deco. *Corner Sand Lake Rd. (Rte. 482) and S. Orange Blossom Trail, near International Dr., tel. 407/ 851-6255.*

Flea World. Flea markets are scattered across the Orlando area, but this is the largest and most popular. Well over 1,500 booths, some air-conditioned, offer arts and crafts, auto parts, citrus produce, and so on. *Hwy. 17-92 between Orlando and Sanford, tel. 407/645-1792.*

Park Avenue. This is the place to go for fashionable, upscale shopping in Winter Park. The shops range from the Ralph Lauren Polo Shop to small antiques shops.

Mercado Mediterranean Village. Visitors wander along brick streets and browse through more than 50 specialty shops in the atmosphere of a Mediterranean village. Free entertainment nightly. Exotic foods are all under one roof at the International Food Pavilion. *8445 International Dr., tel. 407/345-9337.*

Participant Sports

Bicycling   The most scenic bike riding in Orlando is on the property of Walt Disney World. Bikes are available for rent at **Caribbean Beach Resort** (tel. 407/934-3400), **Fort Wilderness Bike Barn** (tel. 407/824-2742), and **Walt Disney World Village Villa Center** (tel. 407/824-6947). Bike rental is $3 an hour, $7 per day.

Golf   **Golfpac** (Box 940490, Maitland 32794, tel. 407/660-8559) packages golf vacations and prearranges tee times at over 30 courses around Orlando.

Many resort hotels let nonguests use their golf facilities. Some hotels are affiliated with a particular country club and offer preferred rates. Be sure to call in advance to reserve tee times. The following places are open to the public:

Poinciana Golf & Racquet Club (500 Cypress Pkwy., tel. 407/ 933-5300) has a par-72 course about 18 miles southeast of Walt Disney World.
Walt Disney World's three championship courses—all played by the PGA Tour—are among the busiest and most expensive in the region. Greens fees are $70 and $32 after 3 PM.
Grenelefe Golf and Tennis Resort (3200 Rte. 546, Haines City, tel. 813/422-7511, 800/237-9546, or 800/282-7875 in FL), about 45 minutes from Orlando, has three 18-hole courses over gentle hills.
Orange Lake Country Club (8505 W. U.S. 192, Kissimmee, tel. 407/239-0000) offers three nine-hole courses and is about five minutes from Walt Disney World's main entrance.
Other challenging courses open to the public are: **Marriott's Orlando World Center** (1 World Center Dr., Orlando, tel. 407/239-4200 or 800/228-9290, 6,265 yards); **Cypress Creek Country Club** (5353 Vineland Rd., Orlando, tel. 407/425-2319, 6,952 yards); **Hunter's Creek Golf Course** (14401 Sports Club Way, Orlando, tel. 407/240-4653, 7,432 yards); **Wedgefield Golf and Country Club** (20550 Maxim Parkway, Orlando, tel. 407/568-2116, 6,378 yards); **MetroWest Country Club** (2100 S. Hiawassee Rd., Orlando, tel. 407/297-0052, 7,051 yards).

Horseback Riding   **Grand Equestrian Center** (tel. 407/239-4608) offers hunter, jumper, and dressage private lessons, as well as trail rides. **Fort Wilderness Campground** (tel. 407/824-2803) in Walt Disney World offers tame trail rides through the backwoods and along lakesides. **Poinciana Horse World** (tel. 407/847–4343) takes visitors for hour-long rides along old logging trails near Kissimmee.

Jogging Walt Disney World has several scenic jogging trails. Pick up jogging maps at any Disney resort. **Fort Wilderness** (tel. 407/824–2900) has a 2.3-mile jogging course, with numerous exercise stations along the way.

Tennis **Disney Inn** (tel. 407/824–1469) has two courts; **Village Clubhouse** (tel. 407/828–3741) has three; the **Dolphin** and **Swan** (tel. 407/934–6000) share eight; the **Grand Floridian** (tel. 407/824–2438) has two composition courts; the **Yacht and Beach Club** (tel. 407/934–8000) has two; **Fort Wilderness Campground** (tel. 407/824–2900) has two (first come, first served); and the **Contemporary Resort** (tel. 407/824–3578) has six. All courts are lighted and open until 10 PM. Racquets may be rented by the hour.

Orange Lake Country Club (8505 W. U.S. 192, Kissimmee, tel. 407/239–2255) has 16 all-weather courts, 10 of them lighted.

Orlando Tennis Center (649 W. Livingston St., tel. 407/246–2162) has 16 lighted courts (nine clay, seven hard), two racquetball courts, and four tennis pros.

Water Sports Marinas at **Caribbean Beach Resort, Contemporary Resort, Fort Wilderness, Polynesian Village,** and **Yacht and Beach Club, Walt Disney World Village** rent Sunfish, catamarans, motor-powered pontoon boats, pedal boats, and Water Sprites for the 450-acre Bay Lake, the adjoining 200-acres of the Seven Seas Lagoon, Club Lake, Lake Buena Vista, and Buena Vista Lagoon. The Polynesian Village marina rents outrigger canoes. Fort Wilderness rents canoes. For waterskiing ($65 per hour) reservations, phone 407/824–1000.

Airboat Rentals (4266 Vine St., Kissimmee, tel. 407/847–3672) rents airboats ($20 per hour) and canoes for use on Shingle Creek, with views of giant cypress trees and Spanish moss.

Ski Holidays (13323 Lake Bryan Dr., tel. 407/239–4444) has waterskiing, jetskiing, and parasailing on a private lake next to Walt Disney World. Boat rental: $60 per hour. Also available: wave runners, jet boats, and jetskis. To get there take I–4 to the Lake Buena Vista exit, turn south on Route 535 toward Kissimmee. Turn left onto a private dirt road about 300 yards down on the left.

Spectator Sports

Basketball **Orlando Magic** (Box 76, Orlando 32802, tel. 407/839–3900) joined the National Basketball Association in the 1989–90 season. The team plays in the new, 15,077-seat Orlando Arena. *Admission: $8–$28. Off I–4 at Amelia; the arena is 2 blocks west of the interstate.*

Dining

The following dining price categories have been used: *Very Expensive,* over $40; *Expensive,* $30–$40; *Moderate,* $20–$30; *Inexpensive,* under $20.

In Epcot Center World Showcase offers some of the finest dining not only in Walt Disney World but in the entire Orlando area. The problem is that the restaurants are often crowded and difficult to book. Though the top-of-the-line restaurants are expensive, most have limited-selection children's menus with drastically lower prices, so bringing the kids along to dinner won't break the bank. Casual dress is expected in all the restaurants, even the finest.

Unless you are staying at one of the Walt Disney World hotels, you cannot reserve in advance of the day on which you wish to eat, and you must reserve in person—either at each restaurant or at Earth Station at the base of Spaceship Earth. There you will find a bank of computer screens called WorldKey Information where you can stand in line to place your reservation (the lines form very early—on busy days, most top restaurants are filled within an hour of Epcot's opening time). On the far side of Future World, just before the bridge to World Showcase, is an outdoor kiosk with five WorldKey terminals that few people notice; there is another WorldKey kiosk on the far side of the Port of Entry gift shop, near the boat dock for the water taxi to the Moroccan pavilion.

If you are a guest at an on-site Walt Disney World resort or at one of the Walt Disney World Village hotels, avoid the battle of the WorldKey by booking a table by phone (tel. 407/824–4000) either one or two days in advance between noon and 9 PM. When you get to the restaurant for your meal, be sure to have your resort identification card.

Epcot restaurants accept American Express, Visa, and Mastercard; if you're a guest of a Disney hotel, you can charge the tab to your room.

British **Rose and Crown.** This is a very popular, friendly British pub, where you can knock off a pint of crisp Bass ale or blood-thickening Guinness stout with a few morsels of Stilton cheese. "Wenches" serve up simple pub fare, such as steak-and-kidney pie, beef tenderloin, and fish and chips. The Rose and Crown sits on the shore of the lagoon, so on warm days it's nice to lunch on the patio at the water's edge. *Moderate.*

French **Bistro de Paris.** Located on the second floor of the French pavilion, above Chefs de France (*see below*), this is a relatively quiet and charming spot for lunch or dinner. The bistro specializes in regional cooking from southern France. A favorite is steamed filet of fresh grouper with tomato, mushrooms, fresh herbs, and white wine sauce, served with rice pilaf. Wines are moderately priced and available by the glass. *Expensive.*

★ **Chefs de France.** Three of France's most famous culinary artists—Paul Bocuse, Gaston Lenôtre, and Roger Vergé—created the menu here and carefully trained the chefs. Some of their most popular classic dishes are roast duck with prunes and wine sauce; beef filet with fresh ground pepper, raisins, and Armagnac sauce; and filet of grouper topped with salmon-vegetable mousse and baked in puff pastry. *Expensive.*

German **Biergarten.** This popular spot boasts Oktoberfest 365 days a year. Visitors sit at long communal tables and are served hearty German fare by waitresses in typical Bavarian garb; performers yodel, sing, and dance to the rhythms of an oompah band. The atmosphere is usually cheerful—some would say raucous. *Moderate.*

Italian   **L'Originale Alfredo di Roma Ristorante.** This is a World Show-case hot spot, with some of the finest food in Walt Disney World. During dinner, waiters skip around singing Italian songs and bellowing arias. The restaurant is named for the man who invented the now-classic fettuccine Alfredo, a pasta served with a sauce of cream, butter, and loads of freshly grated Parmesan cheese. Another popular dish is *lo Chef Consiglia* (the chef's selections), which consists of an appetizer of spaghetti or fettuccine, a mixed green salad, and a chicken or veal entrée. The most popular veal dish is *piccata di vitello*—veal thinly sliced and panfried with lemon and white wine. *Expensive.*

Japanese   **Mitsukoshi.** This isn't just a restaurant, it's a complex of dining areas on the second floor above the Mitsukoshi Department Store. Each of the five dining rooms (on your left as you enter) has tables equipped with a grill on which chefs prepare meats and fish with acrobatic precision. *Moderate.*

Mexican   **San Angel Inn.** The lush, tropical surroundings—cool, dark, almost surreal—make this one of the most exotic restaurants in Disney World. Tables are candlelit, and the restaurant is open to the pavilion, where musicians play guitars or marimbas. One of the specialties is *langosta Baja California*—Baja lobster meat, sautéed with tomatoes, onions, olives, Mexican peppers, and white wine, and baked in its shell. Try the margaritas, and, for dessert, don't miss the chocolate Kahlúa mousse pie. *Moderate.*

Moroccan   **Restaurant Marrakesh.** Belly dancers and a three-piece Moroccan band may make you feel as though you have stumbled onto the set of *Casablanca.* The food is mildly spicy and relatively inexpensive. At lunch, you may want to try the national dish of Morocco, *couscous*, served with garden vegetables. For dinner, try the *bastila*, an appetizer of sweet and spicy pork between many layers of thin pastry, with almonds, saffron, and cinnamon. *Moderate.*

Norwegian   **Restaurant Akershus.** Norway's tradition of seafood and cold meat dishes is highlighted at the restaurant's *koldtbord*, or Norwegian buffet. The first trip is for appetizers, usually herring prepared in a number of ways. On your next trip choose cold seafood items—try gravlaks, salmon cured with salt, sugar, and dill. Pick up cold salads and meats on your next trip, and then you fill up with hot dishes on your fourth trip, usually a choice of lamb, veal, and venison. Desserts include cloudberries, delicate, seasonal fruits that grow on the tundra. *Moderate.*

The Walt Disney World Area *American*   **Empress Lilly.** Disney's 220-foot, 19th-century Mississippi-style riverboat is a popular tourist dining spot at the far end of Walt Disney World Shopping Village, right on Buena Vista Lagoon. This replica of an elegant old-fashioned Victorian showboat, complete with brass lamps, burgundy velvet love seats, and mahogany wood, has several restaurants and lounges. Beef is served in the *Steerman's Quarters* and seafood in *Fisherman's Deck;* only 5% of their tables are open for reservations, two days in advance, and visitors without reservations should arrive early. The food is as predictable as it is expensive, but dining here can be an enjoyable experience for large families or groups who do not want to feel inhibited by a stuffy atmosphere. The third restaurant on the showboat is the *Empress Room,* a plush, Victorian dining room featuring such specialties as duck, pheasant, venison, and various seafood dishes, though the food is unlikely to live up to your expectations. *Steerman's Quarters and Fisherman's Deck: Walt Disney World Shopping Village, tel. 407/828–3900. Dress: casual. Only a few reservations accepted. AE, DC, MC, V. Moderate. Empress Room: Jacket required. Reservations required, up to a month in advance. AE, DC, MC, V. Expensive.*

★ **Chatham's Place.** In this elegant, simple, unpretentious restaurant the Chatham brothers show their skills with such entrées as black grouper with pecan butter, spaghetti à la Grecque, and duck breast, grilled to crispy perfection. It's a small space, and the office building exterior belies what's inside, but this is arguably one of Orlando's best. *7575 Dr. Phillips Blvd., Orlando, tel. 407/345–2992. Dress: informal. Reservations advised. MC, V. Moderate–Expensive.*

Hard Rock Cafe Orlando. The guitar-shaped structure is at Universal Studios Florida with an entrance from the studio or off the street. Hamburgers, barbecue, and sandwiches are served to the sound of rock music amidst rock memorabilia. *Universal Studios Florida, 5401 S. Kirkman Rd., tel. 407/363–ROLL. Dress: casual. No reservations. AE, MC, V. Inexpensive.*

Chinese **Ming Court.** This is no take-out Chinese, but truly fine Oriental-style dining. Try the jumbo shrimp in lobster sauce flavored with crushed black beans, or the Hunan *kung pao* chicken with peanuts, cashews, and walnuts. Glass walls allow you to look out on the pond and floating gardens. *9188 International Dr., Orlando, tel. 407/351–9988. Dress: casual. Reservations advised. AE, DC, MC, V. Moderate.*

Continental **Dux.** In the Peabody Hotel's gourmet restaurant, some creations are innovative, such as the grilled quail with poached quail eggs, served with wild rice in a carrot terrine nest. Others are a trifle self-conscious, like the avocado with sautéed salmon, artichoke chips, and champagne caviar sauce. For an entrée, consider the baked Florida lobster with chanterelle mushrooms, spinach, and champagne sauce. The selection of California wines is outstanding. *Peabody Hotel, 9801 International Dr., Orlando, tel. 407/352–4000. Jacket required. Reservations strongly recommended. AE, DC, MC, V. Expensive.*

Indian **Darbar.** This lavishly decorated dining room features northern Indian cuisine. In addition to curries and pilafs, Darbar specializes in tandoori cooking—barbecuing with mesquite charcoal in a clay oven. Meats and vegetables are marinated in special sauces overnight and cooked to perfection. *7600 Dr. Phillips Blvd., Orlando, tel. 407/345–8128. Take Sand Lake Blvd. (exit 29 off I–4) and head west to the Marketplace Shopping Center. Dress: casual. Reservations advised on weekends. AE, DC, MC, V. Moderate.*

Italian **Christini's.** For traditional Italian cuisine, this is Orlando's fin-
★ est. The restaurant is not about to win any awards for decor, but the food couldn't be fresher and the service couldn't be more efficient. The restaurant makes its own pastas daily and serves them with herbs, vegetables, and freshly grated Parmesan. Specialties include fresh fish; a fish soup with lobster, shrimp, and clams; and veal chops with fresh sage. *Intersection of Sand Lake Rd. and Dr. Phillips Blvd., in the Marketplace Shopping Center, tel. 407/345–8770. Jacket required. Reservations recommended. AE, DC, MC, V. Expensive.*

Japanese   **Ran-Getsu.** The best Japanese food in town is served in this
★   palatial setting. The atmosphere may seem a bit self-conscious—an American's idea of the Orient—but the food is fresh
and carefully prepared. Sit at the curved, dragon's tail-shaped
sushi bar for the Matsu platter—an assortment of *nigiri-* and
maki-style sushis—or, if you are with a group, sit Japanese
style at tables overlooking a carp-filled pond and decorative
gardens. Specialties are sukiyaki and *shabu-shabu* (thinly
sliced beef in a boiling seasoned broth, served with vegetables
and prepared at your table). *8400 International Dr., Orlando,
tel. 407/345-0044. Dress: casual. Reservations accepted. AE,
DC, MC, V. Moderate.*

Kosher   **Palm Terrace.** This is a kosher restaurant supervised by a rabbi
of the Orthodox Union. Diners who are not guests at the Hyatt
Orlando pay a fixed price of $38 (half-price half portions for
children 3–12) for Shabbos meals. Meals must be prepaid on
Friday, and reservations are required one-half hour before
candle-lighting. Kosher breakfast and lunch items are available next door at the Marketplace Deli from 6 to 1 AM. *Hyatt
Orlando, 6375 Irlo Bronson Memorial Hwy., Kissimmee, tel.
407/396-1234. Dress: casual. Reservations required. AE, DC,
MC, V. Moderate.*

Middle Eastern   **Phoenician.** *Hummus, baba ghanouj,* and *lebneh* are just some
of the exotic dishes at this small café serving authentic Mediterranean and Middle Eastern cuisine. The best bet is to order
a tableful of appetizers, *meza,* and sample as many as possible.
*7600 Dr. Phillips Blvd., Suite 142, Orlando, tel. 407/345-1001.
Dress: casual. No reservations. AE, MC, V. Inexpensive.*

Seafood   **Hemingway's.** Located by the pool at the Hyatt Regency Grand
Cypress, this restaurant serves all sorts of sea creatures, from
conch, scallops, and squid to grouper, pompano, and monkfish.
In addition to the regular menu, Hemingway's also has what is
called a "Cuisine Naturelle" menu, featuring dishes that are
low in fat, calories, sodium, and cholesterol. *Hyatt Regency
Grand Cypress Resort, 1 Grand Cypress Blvd., Orlando, tel.
407/239-1234. Dress: casual. Reservations suggested. AE,
DC, MC, V. Moderate–Expensive.*

Thai   **Siam Orchid.** Another in the trend of elegant Oriental restaurants offering fine dining, Siam Orchid is in a gorgeous structure and is a bit off the more beaten path of International
Drive. Waitresses, in the attire of their homeland, serve authentic Thai cuisine. Some standouts are the Siam wings appetizer—stuffed chicken wings—and *pla lad prig* (a whole fish,
deep-fried and covered with a sauce of red chili, bell peppers,
and garlic). *7575 Republic Dr., Orlando, tel. 407/351-3935.
Dress: casual. AE, DC, MC, V. Moderate.*

24 Hours   **Beeline Diner.** This is a slick 1950s-style diner that's always
open. It is in the Peabody Hotel, so it's not exactly cheap, but
the salads, sandwiches, and griddle foods are tops. A good bet
for breakfast or a late-night snack. *Peabody Hotel, 9801 International Dr., Orlando, tel. 407/352-4000. Dress casual. AE,
DC, MC, V. Moderate.*

The Orlando Area   **Jordan's Grove.** This old house was built in 1912 and now holds
American   one of Orlando's most popular restaurants. The menu changes
daily and the prix fixe includes choice of soup or salad, appetizer, entrée with vegetables, and dessert. An à la carte

menu was recently added. The changing menu allows for some creative flexing in the kitchen, and few people leave unsatisfied. Wine is the only alcoholic beverage served. The list is small but well-planned, featuring mostly American wines from smaller estates. *1300 S. Orlando Ave. (U.S. 17–92), Maitland, tel. 407/628–0020. Dress: casual. Reservations advised. AE, DC, MC, V. Moderate–Expensive.*

Chinese **4, 5, 6.** Pedestrian surroundings don't hide well-prepared and well-served traditional dishes, such as steamed sea bass and chicken with snow peas that are served in Chinatown-fashion by cart-pushing waiters. *657 N. Primrose Dr., Orlando, tel. 407/898–1899. Dress: casual. Reservations advised on weekends. Open weekends to 2 AM. AE, DC, MC, V. Inexpensive.*

Continental **Chalet Suzanne.** If you are returning from a day at Cypress
★ Gardens, consider dining at this award-winning family-owned country inn and restaurant. It looks like a small Swiss village—right in the middle of Florida's orange groves. For an appetizer, try broiled grapefruit. Recommended among the seven entreés are chicken Suzanne, shrimp curry, lobster Newburg, shad roe, and filet mignon. Crêpes Suzanne are a good bet for dessert. This unlikely back-road country inn should provide one of the most memorable dining experiences one can have in Orlando. *U.S. 27 north of Lake Wales, about 10 mi past Cypress Gardens turnoff, tel. 813/676–6011. Jacket required. Reservations advised. Closed Mon. during summer. AE, DC, MC, V. Expensive.*

Sweet Basil. Standing apart from other fast-food restaurants, Sweet Basil has a creative cuisine designed to take a little time. Red snapper Provençale and chicken diavolo are standouts. Specialty of the house is the painted desserts. Cheesecakes and pies are served on a vanilla sauce painted with chocolate sauce and raspberry coulis. *1009 W. Vine St., Kissimmee, tel. 407/846–1116. Dress: casual. Reservations accepted. AE, MC, V. Moderate.*

Cuban **Romeros.** Cuban cuisine is a Florida staple, and Romeros is one of the best places to try it. Black bean soup, dirty rice, chicken with yellow rice, and minced meat are just a few of the specialties of this cuisine. *870 Sermoran Blvd., Casselberry, tel. 407/767–9677. Dress: casual. No reservations. MC, V. Inexpensive.*

French **Le Coq au Vin.** The atmosphere here is "Mobile Home Mod-
★ ern," but the traditional French fare is first class and it's a place few tourists know about. Owners Louis Perrotte and his wife, Magdalena (the hostess), give the place its warmth and personality. The specialties include homemade chicken liver pâté, fresh rainbow trout with champagne, and roast Long Island duckling with green peppercorn sauce. For dessert, try the *crème brûlée. 4800 S. Orange Ave., Orlando, tel. 407/851–6980. Dress: casual. Reservations suggested. AE, DC, MC, V. Moderate.*

Mexican **Border Cantina.** A new addition to Park Avenue, Border Cantina is trendy Tex-Mex. If you can forgive the pink walls and neon lights in this third-floor restaurant, you won't have any complaints about the food. The Border does fajitas better than you'll find in most places, and the salsa is a fresh, chunky mix that will suit all tastes. *329 Park Ave. S, Winter Park, tel. 407/*

740–7227. Dress: casual. Reservations accepted for parties of 8 or more. AE, MC, V. Inexpensive–Moderate.

★ **Bee Line Mexican Restaurant.** It looks like another hole-in-the-wall eatery, but the burritos, taco salads, meat *chalupas*, and chili rellenos are among the best in the area. *4542 Hoffner Rd., Orlando (near the airport), tel. 407/857–0566. Dress: casual. No reservations. No credit cards, but checks are accepted. Inexpensive.*

Pizza **Johnny's Pizza Palace.** Red leather booths are the setting for crisp pizza and a two-crust pie that Chicagoans call a stuffed pizza. Pasta and sandwiches are also on the menu. *4909 Lake Underhill Rd., Orlando, tel. 407/277–3452. Dress: casual. Reservations not necessary. MC, V. Inexpensive.*

Seafood **Gary's Duck Inn.** This long-time Orlando favorite is known for its knotty-pine nautical motif and its fresh shrimp, crab, and fish dishes. This was the model for a seafood chain known as Red Lobster. *3974 S. Orange Blossom Trail, Orlando, tel. 407/843–0270. Dress: casual. Reservations accepted. AE, DC, MC, V. Moderate.*

Steak **Cattle Ranch.** If you're hungry and looking for a big, thick, juicy, down-home American steak, then steer for the Cattle Ranch. It's cheap and, if you're insanely hungry, it's free—just take "The 6-pound Challenge," in which you're given 75 minutes to eat an entire six-pound steak dinner, including salad, potato, and bread. If you can do it, you won't have to pay a dime. If you can't, it will cost you just over $30. There is nothing fancy about this cowboy cafeteria except the steaks that come off the burning orangewood fire. And you won't see another tourist for miles around. *6129 Old Winter Garden Rd., Orlando (5 blocks west of Kirkman Rd.), tel. 407/298–7334. Dress: casual. No reservations. Closed Sun. and Mon. AE, MC, V. Inexpensive.*

Lodging

If you are coming to Orlando for only a few days and are interested solely in the Magic Kingdom, Epcot Center, and the other Disney attractions, the resorts on Disney property may be right for you. Built with families in mind, rooms in the on-site resorts are large and can as a rule accommodate up to five persons. They offer cable TV with the Disney Channel and a channel providing the latest updates on special daily events, and the hotels stage many of their own special events. As a Disney guest, you get first rights to tee-off times at the busy golf courses, and you are able to call in advance to make reservations at the restaurants in Epcot Center. As an on-site guest, you also get a transportation pass. The Grand Floridian, Contemporary, and Polynesian Village resorts have their own monorail stops; four other hotels built around a 50-acre lagoon—the Swan, the Dophin, the Yacht Club, and the Beach Club—are linked with Epcot by a dazzling boardwalk filled with entertainment, restaurants, and shopping.

Besides the resorts that are actually inside Walt Disney World, the seven hotels at Lake Buena Vista's Hotel Plaza are also popular. They are "official" Walt Disney World Hotels and offer many of the same incentives, although they are not owned by Disney.

On the negative side, hotels with comparable facilities tend to cost more on Disney property than off it. By staying at a Disney hotel you get discounts on multiple-day passports, but whatever small savings you may realize will be undercut by the higher cost of staying in an on-site property. If you plan to visit other attractions in the Orlando area, you should at least consider staying somewhere besides the Disney properties. "Maingate resorts" are in an area full of large hotels that are not affiliated with Walt Disney World but are clustered around its northernmost entrance, just off I-4. These hotels are mostly resort hotels on sprawling properties, catering to Disney World vacationers. The International Drive area, referred to by locals as "I Drive" and formally labeled "Florida Center," is a main drag for all sorts of hotels, restaurants, and shopping malls. As you head north along The Drive, the hotels get cheaper, the restaurants turn into fast-food joints, and malls translate into factory outlets. The U.S. 192 strip, generally known as Kissimmee, is an avenue crammed with bargain-basement motels and hotels, inexpensive restaurants, fast-food chains, nickel-and-dime attractions, gas stations, and minimarts.

All on-site accommodations—both in Walt Disney World and in Lake Buena Vista Village—may be booked through the Walt Disney World Central Reservations Office (Box 10100, Suite 300, Lake Buena Vista 32830, tel. 407/W-DISNEY) or, if you're calling for same-day reservations, the individual phone numbers listed in reviews below. Land/air packages, with accommodations both on and off Disney property, can be booked through **Disney Reservation Service** (tel. 800/828-0228).

The following lodging price categories have been used: *Very Expensive*, over $150; *Expensive*, $120-$150; *Moderate*, $65-$120; *Inexpensive*, under $65. Rates usually include the price of two children under 18.

Walt Disney World   **Contemporary Resort Hotel.** This high rise in the heart of Walt Disney World has a slick, space-age impersonality. It seems to be crowded with children and conventioneers, yet it is also the center of action, with entertainment, shops, and restaurants bustling under the 15-story atrium. The futuristic monorail running right through the lobby contributes to the stark, modernistic mood. *Tel. 407/824-1000. 1,052 rooms. AE, MC, V. Very Expensive.*

Disney Inn. Anyone who wants to get away from the crowds will appreciate this hotel, the smallest and quietest resort among the on-site hotels. The golf is world class, but since its name change (from the Golf Resort) the inn has also been discovered by couples who want some quiet time (with or without children). Rooms with a view of the golf fairways are particularly pleasant. *Tel. 407/824-2200. 288 rooms. AE, MC, V. Very Expensive.*

★ **Grand Floridian Beach Resort.** This Palm Beach-style coastal hot spot offers old-fashioned character with all the conveniences of a modern hotel. The gabled red roof, brick chimneys, and long ambling verandahs were built with loving attention to detail. As might be expected from a beach resort, there are all sorts of water sports at the marina. The Floridian also has its own monorail stop that links it to the TTC. *900 rooms, including 69 concierge rooms and 12 suites. AE, MC, V. Very Expensive.*

Polynesian Village Resort. This resort is the most popular, particularly with families and couples. It has a relaxed environment with low, tropical buildings and walking paths along the Seven Seas Lagoon. Everything at The Poly, as it's called, has a South Pacific slant to it. The focal point of the resort is the Great Ceremonial House, where visitors check in. The atrium sets the tone, with its lush tropical atmosphere complete with volcanic rock fountains, blooming orchids, and coconut palms—the whole bit. Stretching from the main building are 11 two- and three-story "longhouses," each of which carries the name of some exotic Pacific Island. All rooms offer two queen-size beds and a small sleeper sofa, and accommodate up to five people. Except for some second-floor rooms, all have a balcony or patio. Rooms overlooking the lagoon are the priciest, but they are also the most peaceful and include a host of upgraded amenities and services that make them among the most sought after in Disney World. Recreational activities center around the hotel's large sandy beach and marina, where you can rent boats for sailing, waterskiing, and fishing. The two pools can be overrun by children; you may want to go to the beach for a dip instead. *Tel. 407/824-2000. 855 rooms. AE, MC, V. Very Expensive.*

Walt Disney World Dolphin. This unforgettable Disney landmark features two 55-foot sea creatures at both ends of the 14-story rectangular main section; its 27-story pyramid, makes this the tallest structure in Walt Disney World. Seashell fountains with cascading waterfalls and large dolphin statues adorn this monstrous building. Seven restaurants surround the shell-shaped pool. The exterior is painted with a giant mural of banana leaves in coral and green. The rooms are furnished colorfully; the 12th through 18th floors are Tower Floors and offer special services. Hotel facilities include multilingual concierge service, health club, game room, eight tennis courts, shops, youth hotel, beauty salon, car rental, airlines desk, and swimming in regular pools, a grotto, or a lake with a white-sand beach. *1500 Epcot Resort Blvd., Lake Buena Vista 32830, tel. 407/934-4000 or 800/325-3535. 1,509 rooms. AE, DC, MC, V. Very Expensive.*

Walt Disney World Swan. Connected by a covered causeway to the Dolphin, the Swan is 12 stories high with two seven-story wings. Two 45-foot swans grace the rooftop, and the exterior of the hotel is painted in waves of aquamarine and coral. Rooms are decorated in a blend of coral, peach, teal, and yellow floral and geometric patterns. Amenities include a stocked refrigerator, youth hotel, three restaurants, two lounges, health club, heated pool, tropical grotto, white-sand beach, eight lighted tennis courts, and shops. *1200 Epcot Resort Blvd., Lake Buena Vista 32830, tel. 407/934-3000 or 800/248-SWAN or 800/228-3000. 713 rooms; 45 concierge rooms on 11th and 12th floors. AE, DC, MC, V. Very Expensive.*

The Disney Yacht Club. This five-story, oyster-gray clapboard resort on the lagoon was built to resemble a New England seaside summer cottage of the late 1800s. A lighthouse on the pier and evergreens carry out the themed landscaping. A replica of a 1902 yacht is available for evening cocktail cruises. The resort has restaurants and shops and shares a water recreation area with the Beach Club (*see below*). *634 rooms. AE, DC, MC, V. Expensive.*

The Disney Beach Club. Like an old seaside hotel of the late 1800s, the Beach Club has colorful blue-and-white stick architecture, an entrance flanked with palm trees, and an ornamented gateway bridge. The distinctive walkway also leads past a croquet lawn to beachside cabanas on a white-sand shore. The Beach Club has its own shops and restaurants, and it shares the commons with the Yacht Club. *580 rooms. AE, DC, MC, V. Expensive.*

Disney's Village Resort. Here you can choose among five clusters of villas, each with its own character and ambience. Though they are not quite as plush as rooms in the resort hotels, they are more spacious. Since the villas are not on the monorail, transportation to the parks can be slow, but you have immediate access to golf, fishing, shopping, and an active nightlife. **One- and two-bedroom villas** have complete living facilities with equipped kitchens; the one-bedroom villas accommodate up to four people, and the two-bedroom units accommodate up to six. **Club Suite Villas** are the smallest of the villas—they're the only ones with no kitchens—and are also the least expensive. Their size and ambience reflect the needs of business people attending meetings at the nearby Conference Center. There are a few Deluxe Club Suites that sleep six and have Jacuzzis. **Three-Bedroom Villas** are isolated within a peaceful, heavily wooded area, and are curious villas that stand on stilts. Predictably, this out-of-the-way little forest retreat is popular among young couples. All "tree houses" accommodate six and have a kitchen and breakfast bar, as well as two bathrooms and a utility room with a washer/dryer. *Tel. 407/827–1100. 60 3-bedroom units; 139 1-bedroom units; 151 2-bedroom units; 61 Club Suite units. Two outdoor pools; some two-bedroom units are surrounded by the Lake Buena Vista Golf Course. Villa check-in at entrance to Village Resort reception center. AE, MC, V. Expensive–Very Expensive.*

The Caribbean Beach Resort. Like the Polynesian Village Resort, the Caribbean Beach Resort is made up of villages—Aruba, Barbados, Jamaica, Martinique, and Trinidad—all two-story buildings on a 42-acre tropical lake. Each village has its own pool and stretch of white-sand beach. Bridges over the lake connect the mainland with Parrot Cay, a one-acre island featuring footpaths, bike paths, and children's play areas. There is a 500-seat food court and an adjoining 200-seat lounge. Check-in is at the Custom House, off Buena Vista Drive. *Tel. 407/934–3400. 1,200 1-bedroom units. AE, MC, V. Moderate.*

Fort Wilderness. If you want to rough it, stay among 730 acres of woodland, streams, small lakes, and plenty of water activities along the southeastern edge of Bay Lake, at the northern edge of Walt Disney World property. You can rent a 42-foot-long trailer (accommodating up to six) or a 35-foot trailer (accommodating up to four). Both types have one bedroom, a bath, a full kitchen, air-conditioning, heat, and daily housekeeping services. The trailer sites are spread over 80 forested acres. For those who are more serious about getting in touch with the great outdoors, there are campsites spread across 21 areas. Some are for visitors' own trailers, complete with electrical outlets, outdoor charcoal grills, private picnic tables, water, and waste disposal; there are also tent sites with water and electricity but not sewage. *Tel. 407/824–2900. Trailers, Moderate; campsites, Inexpensive.*

Lake Buena Vista Village

Buena Vista Palace and Palace Suites Resort at Walt Disney World Village. This is the largest of the Hotel Plaza resorts, with one of its towers soaring 27 stories. When you enter its lobby, the hotel seems smaller and quieter than its bold, modern exterior and sprawling parking lots might suggest. Don't be fooled. You have entered on the third floor; when you head down to the ground level, you'll see just how large this place truly is. Resort facilities include a health club, three heated pools, four tennis courts, game room, shops, and 10 restaurants and lounges. *1900 Lake Buena Vista Dr., Lake Buena Vista 32830, tel. 407/827–2727 or 800/327–2990, in FL 800/432–2920. 11,029 rooms. AE, DC, MC, V. Expensive–Very Expensive.*

Guest Quarters. This hotel has suites that consist of a comfortable living room area and a separate bedroom with two double beds or a king-size bed. With a sofa bed in the living room, a suite can accommodate up to six people, but certainly not all comfortably. The arrangement is convenient for small families who want to avoid the hassle of cots and the expense of two separate rooms. Each unit has a TV in each room (plus a small one in the bathroom!), a stocked refrigerator, a wet bar, a coffee maker and, on request, a microwave oven. The hotel attracts a quiet, family-oriented crowd. Facilities include a whirlpool spa, heated pools, two tennis courts, a game room, and a children's play area. *2305 Hotel Plaza Blvd., Lake Buena Vista 32830, tel. 407/934–1000 or 800/424–2900. 229 units. AE, DC, MC, V. Expensive–Very Expensive.*

★ **Hilton at Walt Disney World Village.** The Hilton is generally considered the top hotel in the Village. It is also one of the most expensive. In contrast to the lackluster facade, the interiors are richly decorated with brass and glass and softened with tasteful carpets. Guest rooms sparkle. Rooms are not huge, but they are cozy and contemporary, with high-tech amenities. The Hilton provides a service that many parents will consider indispensable—a **Youth Hotel** for children aged 4–12, with a supervised playroom, a large-screen TV, a six-bed dormitory, and scheduled meals. Other facilities include two pools, a health club, two lighted tennis courts, and several outdoor and indoor bars and restaurants. *1751 Hotel Plaza Blvd., Lake Buena Vista 32830, tel. 407/827–4000 or 800/445–8667. 813 rooms. Youth Hotel open daily 4:30 PM–midnight, cost $4/hr. AE, MC, V. Expensive–Very Expensive.*

Royal Plaza. From the lobby, this hotel seems a bit dated in comparison with the slick, modern hotels in the neighborhood. But the extremely casual, fun-loving atmosphere makes it popular with families who have young children and teenagers. The rooms are generous in size, the best ones overlooking the pool. The hotel has several restaurants and bars, shops, four lighted tennis courts, a sauna, pool, and putting green. *1905 Hotel Plaza Blvd., Lake Buena Vista 32830, tel. 407/828–2828 or 800/248–7890. 397 rooms. AE, DC, MC, V. Expensive–Very Expensive.*

Howard Johnson, Lake Buena Vista. The hotel is popular with young couples and senior citizens. The price and the upgraded, 24-hour Howard Johnson's restaurant make up for the rather plain appearance. There are two heated pools, a wading pool, and a game room. *1805 Hotel Plaza Blvd., Lake Buena Vista 32830, tel. 407/828–8888 or 800/654–2000, 800/FLORIDA in FL, 800/822–3950 in NY. 323 rooms. AE, DC, MC, V. Moderate–Very Expensive.*

Travelodge Hotel Walt Disney World Village. The hotel was recently refurbished, so the lobby and rooms are stylishly decorated, but other than having minibars, the rooms are unexceptional. The pool, playground, and game room are popular with kids; the nightclub on the 18th floor has a beautiful view of Disney World. *2000 Hotel Plaza Blvd., Lake Buena Vista 32830, tel. 407/828–2424, 800/423–1022 in FL, 800/348–3765 outside FL. 325 rooms. AE, DC, MC, V. Expensive.*

Grosvenor Resort. This attractive hotel, the former Americana Dutch Resort, is probably the best deal in the neighborhood. Furnished in British-colonial style, public areas are spacious, with high molded ceilings and columns, warm cheerful colors, and plenty of natural light. Recreational facilities include two heated pools; two lighted tennis courts; racquetball, shuffleboard, basketball and volleyball courts; a children's playground; and a game room. Rooms are average in size, but colorfully decorated, with a refrigerator/bar and a VCR. *1850 Hotel Plaza Blvd., Lake Buena Vista 32830, tel. 407/828–4444 or 800/624–4109. 629 rooms. AE, DC, MC, V. Moderate–Expensive.*

Maingate Resorts **Grand Cypress Resort.** If you were to ask someone familiar with
★ the Orlando area which resort is the most spectacular, few would hesitate to name the Grand Cypress. The resort property is so extensive—over 1,500 acres—that guests need a trolley system to get around. There is virtually every activity you can imagine at a resort: a dozen tennis courts, boats of all shapes and varieties, scenic bicycling and jogging trails, a full health club, dozens of horses, a 600,000-gallon, triple-level swimming pool fed by 12 cascading waterfalls, a 45-acre Audubon nature reserve, 45 holes of Jack Nicklaus-designed golf, and a golfing academy for a high-tech analysis of your game. This huge resort has just one drawback: the king-size conventions that it commonly attracts. *1 Grand Cypress Blvd., Orlando 32819, tel. 407/239–1234 or 800/233–1234. 750 rooms. AE, DC, MC, V. Very Expensive.*

Vistana Resort. Anyone interested in tennis should consider staying at this peaceful time-share resort spread over 50 beautifully landscaped acres. It is also popular with families or groups who are willing to share a spacious, tastefully decorated villa or town house, each with at least two bedrooms and all the facilities of home—a full kitchen, living room, a washer/dryer, and so on. Each condominium-like unit can accommodate up to six or eight people. The 14 tennis courts can be used without charge. Other facilities include five heated outdoor pools and a full health club. *8800 Vistana Centre Dr., Orlando 32821, tel. 407/239–3100 or 800/877–8787. 722 units. AE, DC, MC, V. Very Expensive.*

Hyatt Orlando Hotel. This is another very large hotel, but without the extensive resort facilities. Instead of a single towering building, the hotel consists of nine two-story buildings in four clusters. Each cluster is a community with its own pool, Jacuzzi, park, and playground at its center. The rooms are spacious but otherwise unmemorable. The lobby and convention center are in a building at the center of the clusters. The lobby is vast and mall-like, with numerous shops and restaurants. There are a few tennis courts, but not much else in the way of recreation. *6375 W. Irlo Bronson Memorial Hwy., Kissimmee 34746, tel. 407/396–1234, 800/331–2003 in FL, 800/544–7178 outside FL. 924 rooms. AE, DC, MC, V. Moderate.*

Ramada Resort Maingate at the Parkway. The Ramada may offer the best deal in the neighborhood—a more attractive setting at more competitive prices. It has three lighted tennis courts, a pool with a waterfall, a few shops and restaurants, and a delicatessen for picnickers. The rooms, like the rest of the hotel grounds, are spacious and bright, decked out in tropical and pastel colors. *2900 Parkway Blvd., Kissimmee 32746, tel. 407/396–7000, 800/255–3939 in FL, 800/634–4774 outside FL. 716 rooms. AE, DC, MC, V. Moderate.*

Knight's Inn Orlando Maingate West. There's a good selection of rooms here for a budget motel, including rooms with two double beds and efficiency apartments. No-smoking rooms are available, and there is a pool. *7475 W. Irlo Bronson Hwy., Kissimmee 32746, tel. 407/396–4200. 120 units. AE, DC, MC, V. Inexpensive.*

International Drive
★ **Peabody Orlando.** From afar, the Peabody looks like a high-rise office building. Don't let its austere exterior scare you away. Once inside, you will discover a very impressive, handsomely designed hotel. The Peabody's lobby has rich marble floors and fountains, and the entire hotel is decorated with modern art, giving it much color and flare. The rooms with the best views face Walt Disney World and a sea of orange trees that extends as far as the eye can see. The Peabody Club on the top three floors offers special concierge service. The Peabody has two fine restaurants, a pool, a health club, and four lighted tennis courts. *9801 International Dr., Orlando 32819, tel. 407/352–4000 or 800/PEABODY. 891 rooms. AE, DC, MC, V. Expensive–Very Expensive.*

★ **Sonesta Villa Resort Hotel.** The Sonesta, located off I–4 near International Drive, is a string of multi-unit town houses on a lakefront. Following the lead of the all-suite hotels, the Sonesta "villas" consist of small apartments, some of which are bilevel with a fully equipped kitchenette, dining room/living room area, small patio, and bedroom. The units are comfortable and homey, each with its private, ground-floor entrance. Outdoor facilities include tennis courts, mini health club, pool, and whirlpools convenient to each villa. Guests can sail and waterski on the lake or sunbathe on a sandy beach. There is a restaurant and bar, but the only action is the nightly outdoor barbecue buffet. *10000 Turkey Lake Rd., Orlando 32819, tel. 407/352–8051 or 800/343–7170. 384 units. AE, DC, MC, V. Expensive.*

Stouffer Orlando Resort. This first-rate resort, originally the Wyndham Hotel Sea World, is directly across the street from Sea World. It's a bulky, 10-story building with what is billed as the largest atrium lobby in the world. Facilities include six lighted tennis courts, a pool, a Nautilus fitness center, a whirlpool, a child-care center, a game room, and access to an 18-hole golf course. Guest rooms are all large and spacious. The most expensive rooms face the atrium, but be warned that the music and party sounds of conventioneers often rise through the atrium. *6677 Sea Harbor Dr., Orlando 32821, tel. 407/351–5555, 800/327–6677, or 800/HOTELS–1. 778 rooms. AE, DC, MC, V. Expensive.*

Embassy Suites Hotel at Plaza International. All suites have a bedroom and a full living room equipped with wet bar, refrigerator, desk, pull-out sofa, and two TVs. It is a comfortable and economical arrangement, somewhat less expensive than a single room in the top-notch hotels. Because the bedroom can be closed off, it is ideal for small families. The core of the hotel is a wide atrium, much cozier than the atrium at the Stouffer. The hotel has both an indoor and an outdoor pool, an exercise room with Jacuzzi, sauna, steam room, and game room. *8250 Jamai-*

can Court, Orlando 32819, tel. 407/345–8250 or 800/327–9797. 246 rooms. AE, DC, MC, V. Moderate–Expensive.

Orlando Heritage Inn. If you are looking for a simple, small hotel with reasonable rates but plenty of deliberate charm, the Heritage is the place to stay. Located next to the towering Peabody, this inn creates the atmosphere of Victorian-style Florida, complete with reproduction turn-of-the-century furnishings, rows of French windows and brass lamps, and a smattering of genuine 19th-century antiques. The guest rooms are decorated with a Colonial accent—lace curtains on double French doors, folk-art prints on the walls, and quilted bed covers. The hotel has a pool, a small saloon-type lounge, and a dinner theater. The staff is strong on Southern hospitality. *9861 International Dr., Orlando 32819, tel. 407/352–0008, 800/282–1890 in FL, 800/447–1890 outside FL. 150 rooms. AE, DC, MC, V. Moderate.*

Radisson Inn and Aquatic Center. Radisson is a big, modern, moderately priced hotel offering comfortable rooms (the best ones face the pool), but what makes it truly special are its outstanding athletic facilities: a fine outdoor pool; an indoor Aquatic Center with an Olympic-size swimming and diving pool; a complete Nautilus center; tennis, raquetball, and handball courts; a jogging track; aerobics and swimmercise classes; and access to a local country club for golf. *8444 International Dr., Orlando 32819, tel. 407/345–0505 or 800/333–3333. 300 rooms. AE, DC, MC, V. Moderate.*

U.S. 192 Area **The Residence Inn.** Of the all-suite hotels on U.S. 192, this one is probably the best. It consists of a row of four-unit town houses with private stairway entrances to each suite. Some rooms overlook an attractive lake, where visitors can sail, waterski, jet ski, and fish. Forty of the units are penthouses, and the others are studio apartments; all have complete kitchens and even fireplaces. Regular studio suites accommodate two people; double suites accommodate up to four. Both Continental breakfast and a grocery shopping service are complimentary. There is no charge for additional guests, so you can squeeze in the whole family at no extra cost. *4786 W. Irlo Bronson Memorial Hwy., Kissimmee 32746, tel. 407/396–2056, 800/648–7408 in FL, 800/468–3027 outside FL. 160 units. AE, DC, MC, V. Moderate–Expensive.*

Radisson Inn Maingate. Located just a few minutes from the Magic Kingdom's front door, the building is very sleek and modern with cheerful guest rooms, large bathrooms, and plenty of extras for the price. Facilities include a pool, a whirlpool, two lighted tennis courts, and a jogging trail. *7501 W. Irlo Bronson Memorial Hwy., Kissimmee 32746, tel. 407/396–1400 or 800/333–3333. 580 rooms. AE, DC, MC, V. Moderate.*

★ **Casa Rosa Inn.** For simple motel living—no screaming kids or loud music, please—this is your place. The pink, Spanish-style motel does not have much in the way of facilities other than a little pool and free in-room movies, but it is a good, serviceable place to hang your hat. *4600 W. Irlo Bronson Memorial Hwy., Kissimmee 32746, tel. 407/396–2020 or 800/432–0665. 54 rooms. AE, MC, V. Inexpensive.*

Nightlife

Walt Disney World **Top of the World.** This is Disney's sophisticated nighttime entertainment spot, located on the top floor of the Contemporary

Resort. A single price includes the show and dinner; tax, gratuity, and alcoholic drinks are extra. Men must wear a jacket. *Contemporary Resort, tel. 407/W–DISNEY. Reservations necessary months in advance. Admission: $42.50 adults, $19.50 children 3–11. Seatings at 6 and 9:15.*

Polynesian Revue and Mickey's Tropical Revue. At the Polynesian Village Resort, there's an outdoor barbecue and a tropical luau, complete with fire jugglers and hula drum dancers, as well as an earlier show for children called Mickey's Tropical Revue. *Polynesian Village Resort, tel. 407/W–DISNEY. Reservations necessary, usually months in advance. Polynesian Review: $29 adults, $23 juniors 12–20, and $15 children 3–11. Seatings at 6:45 and 9:30. Mickey's Tropical Revue: $25 adults, $20 juniors, $11 children. Seating at 4:30.*

Hoop-Dee-Doo Revue. This family entertainment dinner show may be corny, but it is also rollicking. The chow consists of barbecued ribs, fried chicken, corn on the cob, strawberry shortcake, and all the fixins'. *Fort Wilderness Resort, tel. 407/W–DISNEY or for same day reservations, 407/824–2748. Reservations necessary, sometimes months in advance. Admission: $32 adults, $24 juniors 12–20, $16 children 3–11. Seatings at 5, 7:30, and 10 PM.*

Pleasure Island. There is a single admission charge to this nightlife entertainment complex, which features a comedy club, teenage dance center, rock-and-roller skating-rink disco, numerous restaurants, lounges, shops, and even a 10-screen theater complex. *Pleasure Island, tel. 407/934–7781. Reservations not necessary. Admission: $9.95 after 7 PM or $12 with Pleasure Island/AMC combined ticket.*

IllumiNations. Epcot Center's grand finale is a spectacular laser show that takes place along the shores of the World Showcase lagoon, every night just before Epcot closes.

The Orlando Area Dinner Shows

Arabian Nights. This attraction inside an Arabian Palace (home to eight breeds of horses from around the world) features 60 performing horses, music, special effects, a chariot race, and a four-course dinner. Low-cholesterol meals may be ordered when making reservations. *6225 W. Irlo Bronson Memorial Hwy. (U.S. 192), Kissimmee, tel. in Orlando 407/239–9223, in Kissimmee 407/396–7400 or 800/533–6116, in Canada 800/533–3615. Reservations required. Admission: $27.97 adults, $16.95 children 3–11. AE, DC, MC, V.*

Mardi Gras. This recently expanded, jazzy, New Orleans–style show is the best of Orlando's dinner attractions. A New Orleans jazz band plays during dinner, followed by a one-hour cabaret with colorful song-and-dance routines to rhythms of the Caribbean, Latin America, and Dixieland jazz. *At the Mercado Mediterranean Village, 8445 International Dr., Orlando, tel. 407/351–5151 or 800/347–5151. Reservations required. Admission: $27.95 adults, $19.95 children 3–11. AE, D, DC, MC, V.*

Fort Liberty. This dinner show whisks you out to the Wild West for a mixed bag of real Native American dances, foot-stompin' sing-alongs, and acrobatics. The chow is what you might expect to eat with John Wayne out on the prairie. Fort Liberty is a stockade filled with Western-themed gifts and souvenirs, and a Brave Warrior Wax Museum ($4 adults, $2 children 2–11). There's also a lunchtime performance. *5260 Irlo Bronson Me-*

morial Hwy. (U.S. 192), Kissimmee, tel. 407/351–5151 or 800/ 847–8181. Reservations required. Admission: $26.95 adults, $18.95 children 3–11. AE, DC, MC, V.

King Henry's Feast. Set in a Tudor-style building, the entertainment includes dancers, jesters, jugglers, magicians, and singers who encourage audience participation as King Henry celebrates his birthday and begins a quest for his seventh bride. Saucy wenches, who refer to customers as "me lords" and "me ladies," serve potato-leek soup, salad, chicken and ribs, and all the beer, wine, and soft drinks you can guzzle. Bar drinks are extra. *8984 International Dr., Orlando, tel. 407/ 351–5151 or 800/347–8181. Reservations required. Admission: $26.95 adults, $18.95 children 3–11. AE, D, DC, MC, V.*

Medieval Times. In a huge, modern-medieval manor, visitors enjoy a four-course dinner while watching the struggle of good and evil in a tournament of games, sword fights, and jousting matches, including no less than 30 charging horses and a cast of 75 knights, nobles, and maidens. *4510 W. Irlo Bronson Memorial Hwy. (U.S. 192), Kissimmee, tel. 407/239–0214 or 407/396– 1518, in FL 800/432–0768, outside FL 800/327– 4024. Reservations required. Admission: $26 adults, $18 children. AE, MC, V.*

Mark Two. This is the only true dinner theater in Orlando, with full Broadway musicals, such as *Oklahoma!, My Fair Lady, West Side Story* and *South Pacific,* staged through most of the year. A buffet and full-service cocktail bar open for business about two hours before the show. *Edgewater Center, 3376 Edgewater Dr., Orlando (from I-4, take Exit 44 and go west), tel. 407/843–6275. Reservations advised. Admission: $24–$28 adults, $19–$23 children 12 and under. Closed Mon. AE, MC, V.*

Church Street Station This downtown Orlando attraction is a complete entertainment experience. Widely popular among both tourists and locals, it single-handedly began Orlando's metamorphosis from a sleepy town, to the nighttime hot spot it now boasts to be and is on its way to becoming. You can spend an evening in part of the complex, or you can wander from area to area, soaking up the peculiar characteristics of each. For a single admission price of $14.95 adults or $9.95 children 4–12, you're permitted to wander freely; food and drink cost extra and are not cheap, but they add to the fun. Popular spots include: **Rosie O'Grady's Good Time Emporium,** a turn-of-the-century saloon with a Dixieland band, can-can dancers, and vaudeville singers; **Apple Annie's Courtyard,** a relatively quiet nook featuring live folk and bluegrass music; **Lili Marlene's Aviator's Pub and Restaurant,** a relaxed, wood-paneled pub that serves the finest dining on Church Street—mostly steaks, ribs, and seafood; **Phileas Phogg's Balloon Works,** a very popular disco filled with young singles; **Orchid Garden,** a striking Victorian arcade where visitors sit, drink, and listen to first-rate bands pounding out popular tunes from the 1950s to the '80s; and **Cheyenne Saloon and Opera House,** a former triple-level opera house where a seven-piece country-and-western band darn near brings the house down.

Church Street Exchange. The newest addition to the complex, near Church Street Station, is a razzle-dazzle marketplace filled with more than 50 specialty shops and restaurants on the first two floors. *129 W. Church St., Orlando, tel. 407/422-2434. Reservations not necessary. AE, MC, V.*

Bars and Clubs **Little Darlin's Rock n' Roll Palace** is a 1950s and '60s nostalgia nightclub with an orchestra-pit dance floor and a huge bandstand stage featuring famous old rock bands that still tour, such as The Drifters, Platters, and Bo Diddley. The crowd is a mix of young and old, singles and couples. *Old Town, 5770 Spacecoast Pkwy., tel. 407/396-6499 or 407/827-6169. Open noon-2 AM. Admission: $8.50, children under 3 free. AE, MC, V.*

Giraffe Lounge, located inside the Royal Plaza hotel, Lake Buena Vista (World Village), is a small but flashy disco that's usually densely packed on weekends. *Hotel Royal Plaza, Walt Disney World Village, tel. 407/828-2828. Open 4 PM-3 AM. No cover. AE, DC, MC, V.*

The Laughing Kookaburra has live band music nightly and a serious singles crowd of all ages. The dance floor can get very crowded—a plus for some, a minus for others. *Buena Vista Palace Hotel, Walt Disney World Village, tel. 407/827-3520. Open 4 PM-3 AM. No cover. AE, DC, MC, V.*

Bennigan's, a young singles' spot, draws crowds in the early evening; happy hours are 4-7 PM and 11 PM-2 AM. It caters mostly to nontourists who work in the area. *6324 International Dr., Orlando, tel. 407/351-4436. Open 11 AM-2 AM.*

J.J. Whispers is a trendy singles disco, equally popular with the over-30 set, who listen to music from the 1940s, '50s, and '60s in the Showroom. It is also home to Bonkerz!, a comedy club. *5100 Adanson St., Orlando 32804, tel. 407/629-4779. Take I-4 to Lee Rd. exit, go west ½-mi on Lee Rd., make sharp left-hand turn at Adanson St. Cover charge: $5 and up; $10 and up for Bonkerz, tel. 407/629-2665. AE, MC, V.*

Sullivan's Trailways Lounge is a country-and-western dance hall with the largest dance floor in Florida. Big name performers entertain on occasion; local bands play Tuesday-Saturday. *1108 S. Orange Blossom Trail (U.S. 441), tel. 407/843-2934. Bands play 8 PM-2 AM. Cover charge: $2 and up.*

Tour 7: Nashville to New Orleans

The spine of this tour is the Natchez Trace Parkway, a historic highway that has been meticulously landscaped and will eventually run all the way from Nashville, Tennessee, to Natchez, Mississippi. Early settlers, traders, and adventurers rambled down the Trace on their way to port on the Mississippi River; today travelers enjoy its billboard-free scenery thickly planted with cypress and dogwood, detouring from the parkway frequently to visit Civil War battlefields, antebellum mansions, and lush state parks.

Nashville is perhaps best known today as the capital of country music, although it's much more sophisticated and charming than that reputation suggests. At the other end of the drive is the famous jazz city New Orleans, renowned also for Creole cuisine, French Quarter bohemians, voodoo, and Mardi Gras celebrations. Nashville is a quintessentially American city; New Orleans is in many ways more European than American. The cities in between—Jackson, Natchez, Vicksburg, Baton Rouge—are about as Deep South as you can get, steeped in Delta charm.

This tour describes a long diagonal cutting across Tennessee, a corner of Alabama, and the length of Mississippi. From there, it's a straight drive south to Baton Rouge, then an eastward swing around Lake Pontchartrain to New Orleans. A comfortable drive with few stops could take you in one day from Nashville to Jackson, and another day to New Orleans, but many optional detours are described en route. Nashville deserves at least two days of sightseeing; Jackson a full day; and New Orleans at least three days. If you want to take several plantation tours, allow extra time for Vicksburg, Natchez (especially during Pilgrimage weeks in March and October), and the River Road drive from Baton Rouge to New Orleans. Travelers who have an interest in history may want to spend a full 10 days on this tour, devoting extra time to the Civil War sites in Shiloh, Corinth, and Vicksburg.

At the end of this tour, you can pick up Tour 8, which will take you east along the Gulf Coast and then south to Orlando, Florida.

Tourist Information

Tennessee **Nashville Area Chamber of Commerce** (161 4th Ave. N, tel. 615/259-3900).

Visitor Information Center (I-65 and James Robertson Pkwy., Exit 85, tel. 615/242-5606).

Mississippi **Corinth/Alcorn Area Chamber of Commerce** (810 Tate St., Corinth 38834, tel. 601/287-5269).

Jackson Convention and Visitors Bureau (Box 1450, Jackson 39205, tel. 601/960-1891).

Jackson Visitor Information Center (at entrance to Mississippi Agriculture and Forestry Museum, 1150 Lakeland Dr. east of I-55, tel. 601/960-1800).

Natchez Trace Parkway Visitor Center (Rte. 1, NT-143, Tupelo 38801; on the Natchez Trace Pkwy., milepost 266, tel. 601/845-1572).

Natchez-Adams County Chamber of Commerce (300 N. Commerce, Natchez 39120, tel. 601/445–4611).

Tupelo Convention and Visitors Bureau (712 E. President St., Box 1485, Tupelo 38801, tel. 601/841–6521).

Louisiana **Louisiana Visitor Information Center** (Louisiana State Capitol, State Capitol Dr., Baton Rouge, tel. 504/342–7317, 800/33–GUMBO outside LA, or 504/342–8119 in LA).

The Greater New Orleans Tourist and Convention Commission (1520 Sugar Bowl Dr., New Orleans, LA 70112).

Festivals and Seasonal Events

Feb.: Mardi Gras is New Orleans's biggest annual parade and party. Make reservations well in advance.

Mar.: Natchez Pilgrimage opens up antebellum houses to tours in Natchez, Mississippi (contact Pilgrimage Tours, Box 347, Natchez 39120, tel. 601/446–6631 or 800/647–6742). Similar house tours take place in Vicksburg and Port Gibson.

Apr.: New Orleans Jazz and Heritage Festival and **French Quarter Festival** keep things hopping in New Orleans.

Early June: Summer Lights is Nashville's prime music and arts festival, showcasing top names and newcomers in pop, rock, jazz, country, classical, and reggae on five outdoor stages downtown. Contact Metro Nashville Arts Commission, 111 Fourth Ave. S, 37201, tel. 615/259–6374.

June: International Country Music Fan Fair follows Summer Lights in Nashville, with more than 35 hours of musical events. Contact Fan Fair, 2804 Opryland Dr., 37214, tel. 615/889–7503.

Late Aug.–early Sept.: Tennessee Walking Horse National Celebration draws visitors, horses, and riders from all over the land to Shelbyville, Tennessee. Information: Box 1010, Shelbyville 37160, tel. 615/684–5915.

Sept.: Tennessee State Fair is held in Nashville.

Oct.: Mississippi State Fair is held in Jackson. **Natchez Pilgrimage** tours (*see* March, *above*) return to antebellum mansions in Natchez.

What to See and Do with Children

Nashville's main attractions for youngsters are country-music-related: the Opryland theme park, the Music Valley Wax Museum of the Stars, and the outrageous stars' cars featured at many country-music museums. **Wave Country** (Two Rivers Pkwy., off Briley Pkwy., tel. 615/885–1052; admission $4 adults, $3 children; open Memorial Day–Labor Day, daily) is a water park near Opryland. The **Cumberland Museum and Science Center** (800 Ridley Blvd., tel. 615/862–5174; admission $5 adults, $4 children; open Tues.–Sun.)has interactive exhibits and a planetarium. In nearby Murfreesboro, **Children's Discovery House** (503 N. Maple St., tel. 615/890–2300; admission $3 adults, $2 children; open Tues.–Sun.) is a youngster's dream, with bubble blowers on the front lawn, colored chalk by the sidewalks, dress-up clothes, a play store and play hospital, a nature collection, and more.

In Mississippi, various Civil War sites, most notably **Corinth** and **Vicksburg,** will absorb kids who like history. **Tupelo** interests children with its Elvis Presley birthplace, chapel, museum, and park. **Jackson** has a **Zoological Park** (2918 W. Capitol St., tel. 601/960–1575 or 601/960–1576; admission $2 adults, $1 children; open daily) featuring animals in natural settings, including many endangered species. While younger children may get bored visiting the antebellum mansions, **Natchez** also offers the **Grand Village of the Natchez Indians** (400 Jefferson Davis Blvd., tel. 601/445–6502; admission free; open daily), an archaeological park and museum depicting the culture of the Natchez Indians; there are also Indian mounds at **Bynum Mounds** and **Emerald Mound.**

In **Baton Rouge,** kids may enjoy a ride on the *Samuel Clemens Riverboat,* or a visit to the **Lousiana Arts & Science Center Riverside Museum** with its Egyptian tomb, restored cars, and Discovery Depot for kids. While Plantation Country house tours may not appeal to every youngster, **St. Francisville's** "haunted house," **the Myrtles,** often is a hit.

New Orleans has lots to offer familes. The **Audubon Zoo** is excellent; **Aquarium of the Americas** in Riverfront Park is a new attraction that kids will love; and **City Park** has an amusement park with a turn-of-the-century carousel and miniature train. Rides on the **St. Charles Streetcar** and various **riverboats** (the *Natchez,* tel. 504/586–8777, or the *Cotton Blossom,* tel. 504/586–8777) are a kick for kids. The **Musée Conti Wax Museum** and the **Voodoo Museum,** both in the French Quarter, appeal to young people who appreciate the ghoulish. **Ripley's Believe It or Not Museum** (501 Bourbon St., tel. 504/529–5131; admission $5 adults, $3 children; open daily) exhibits oddities from Robert Ripley's collections.

Arriving and Departing

By Plane **Nashville Metropolitan Airport,** approximately eight miles from downtown, is served by American, American Eagle, Comair, Delta, Northwest, Southwest, TWA, United, and USAir. Airport limousine service (tel. 615/367–2305) to and from downtown is $8 for the first person and $4 for each additional person. To reach downtown by **car,** take I–40W.

Baton Rouge Metropolitan Airport (tel. 504/355–0333), 12 miles north of downtown, is served by American, Continental, Delta, L'Express, and Northwest.

New Orleans International Airport (Moisant Field), located 15 miles west of New Orleans in Kenner, is served by American, Continental, Delta, Midway, Northwest, Royale, Southwest, TWA, United, and USAir. Foreign carriers serving the city include Aviateca, Lacsa, Sahsa, and Taca. **Buses** operated by Louisiana Transit (tel. 504/737–9611) run every 22 minutes between the airport and Elk Place in the Central Business District (CBD), 6 AM–6:20 PM; the $1.10 trip takes about an hour. **Rhodes Transportation** (tel. 504/469–4555) vans leave the airport every 5–10 minutes, 24 hours a day, for the 20- to 30-minute trip into town. The fare is $7 per person. **Taxi** fare is $18 for up to three passengers, and $6 for each additional person. **Driving** from Kenner into New Orleans is via Airline Highway (U.S. 61) or I–10. Hertz, Avis, Budget, and other major car-rental agencies have outlets at the airport.

By Train **Amtrak** (tel. 800/USA–RAIL) trains pull into New Orleans's Union Passenger Terminal (1001 Loyola Ave., tel. 504/528–1610).There is no service to the other towns on this tour.

By Bus **Greyhound-Trailways** has stations in Nashville (8th Ave. S and McGavock St., tel. 615/256–6141), Tupelo (201 Commerce St., tel. 601/842–4557), Corinth (204 U.S. 72E, tel. 601/287–1466), Jackson (201 S. Jefferson St., tel. 601/353–6342), Natchez (103 Lower Woodville Rd., tel. 601/445–5291), Baton Rouge (1253 Florida Blvd., tel. 504/343–4891), and New Orleans (1001 Loyola Ave., tel. 504/525–9371 or 800/237–8211).

By Car Nashville sits at the intersection of a number of interstate highways: I–65 north into Kentucky and south into Alabama; I–24 leads northwest into Kentucky and southeast into Georgia; I–40 east to North Carolina and west to Arkansas. To pick up the Natchez Trace Parkway, go south 40 miles on I–65 and then take Rte. 50 west 30 miles to the parkway; or go west on I–40 to TN 22, and drive south to Corinth, Mississippi, from where you can take U.S. 72 east to the parkway.

The Natchez Trace Parkway is incomplete at Jackson, connected by I–55 and I–20, which run through the city. At Natchez, where the parkway ends, get on U.S. 61 and go 85 miles south to Baton Rouge. I–10 is the direct route to New Orleans from Baton Rouge, but a combination of LA 1, 18, and 44 is a more scenic drive along the banks of the Mississippi River into New Orleans.

From New Orleans, I–10 runs east–west, connecting with northward I–55 to the west of New Orleans, and northeastward I–59 just north and east of New Orleans.

By Boat The **Delta Queen Steamboat Co.** (tel. 504/586–0631) offers four-night paddlewheeler cruises between St. Louis and Nashville, with stops along the way.

Nashville

Heralded as the Country Music Capital and birthplace of the "Nashville Sound," Tennessee's fast-growing capital city is also a leading center of higher education, appropriately known as the Athens of the South. Both labels fit. Far from developing a case of civic schizophrenia at such contrasting roles, Nashville has prospered from them both, becoming one of the middle South's liveliest and most vibrant cities in the process.

Much of Nashville's role as a cultural leader, enhanced by the presence of the new performing arts center, derives from the many colleges, universities, and technical and trade schools located here. Several, including Vanderbilt University, have national or international reputations, and many have private art galleries. As ancient Athens was the "School of Hellas," so Nashville fills this role in the contemporary South.

As every fan knows, it was Nashville's "Grand Ole Opry" radio program, which began as station WSM's "Barn Dance" in 1925, that launched the amazing country music boom. The Opry performs in a sleek $15 million Opry House now, but it's still as gleeful and down-home informal as it was when it held forth in the old Ryman Auditorium. Joining the Opry in Nashville are dozens of country music attractions—some large, some small, many begun by or memorials to individual stars.

Getting Around It helps to remember that the river horizontally bisects the central city. Numbered avenues, running north–south, are west of and parallel to the river; numbered streets are east of the river and parallel to it.

By Bus **Metropolitan Transit Authority (MTA)** buses (tel. 615/242–4433) serve the entire county 4 AM–11:15 PM. Fare is 75¢ (exact change required). For disabled persons, a van is available for downtown transport (tel. 615/351–RIDE).

By Trolley **Nashville Trolley Co.** (tel. 615/242–4433) offers rides in the downtown area. The fare is 25¢ (exact change).

By Taxi The fare is a basic $1.50, plus 10¢ for each quarter-mile. It's best to phone for service: **Checker Cab** (tel. 615/254–5031), **Nashville Cab** (tel. 615/242–7070), **Yellow Cab** (tel. 615/256–0101).

Guided Tours Standard tours include drives past stars' homes and visits to
Orientation the Grand Ole Opry, Music Row, and historic structures. Companies includes **American Sightseeing** (tel. 615/256–1200 or 800/826–6456), **Gray Line** (tel. 615/883–5555 or 800/251–1864), **Grand Ole Opry Tours** (tel. 615/889–9490).

Special-interest **Country & Western Round-Up Tours** (tel. 615/883–5555) offers a daily Twitty City/Johnny Cash Special motorcoach tour. **Johnny Walker Tours** (tel. 615/834–8585 or 800/722–1524) has an evening Music Village Nightlife Tour. **Stardust Tours** (tel. 615/244–2335) offers a daily Music Village Sunset Tour. **Nissan** (tel. 615/459–1400) offers free tours by appointment of its vast, supermodern Smyrna auto plant on Tuesday and Thursday.

Boat Tours **Belle Carol Riverboat Co.** (tel. 615/244–3430 or 800/342–2355) offers Cumberland River sightseeing, luncheon, and dinner cruises from the Nashville Old Steamboat Dock. From its dock, **Opryland USA** (tel. 615/889–6611) offers daytime cruises and evening dinner cruises aboard its four-deck *General Jackson* showboat.

Downtown

Numbers in the margin correspond to points of interest on the Downtown Nashville and Nashville maps.

Although considerably smaller, the Cumberland River has been as important to Nashville as the Mississippi has been to Memphis. That this is still true can be seen by any visitor to **❶ Riverfront Park** at First Avenue and Broadway, a welcoming green enclave on the west bank of the Cumberland, with an expansive view of the busy barge traffic on the river. The park serves as a popular venue for summer concerts and picnics, as well as a docking spot for riverboat excursions (*see* Guided **❷** Tours, *above*). North on First Avenue is **Fort Nashborough**. High on the limestone bluffs overlooking the river that brought them to this place, the first settlers built a crude log fort in 1779 as protection and shelter. Today it has been painstakingly recreated to serve as a monument to their courage, and in five log cabins costumed interpreters evoke the indomitable spirit of the American age of settlement. *Tel. 615/255–8192. Admission: $2 adults, $1 children. Open Tues.–Sat. 9–4. Closed major holidays.*

By the early 19th century, logs had given way to brick and marble. Downtown was thriving, and today it thrives anew, thanks

Barbara Mandrell
Country, **12**

Belmont Mansion, **23**

Belle Meade
Mansion, **21**

Boxcar Willie's/Cars of
the Stars, **17**

Car Collectors Hall of
Fame, **14**

Cheekwood, **22**

Country Music Hall of
Fame and Museum, **10**

Country Music Wax
Museum and Mall, **15**

Downtown
Presbyterian
Church, **4**

Fort Nashborough, **2**

Hank Williams Jr.
Museum, **13**

The Hermitage, **25**

Historic 2nd Ave. Bus.
District, **3**

House of Cash, **26**

Jim Reeves
Museum, **19**

Music Valley Wax
Museum of the
Stars, **18**

Opryland USA, **16**

Parthenon, **20**

Riverfront Park, **1**

Ryman Auditorium
and Museum, **9**

State Capitol, **7**

Studio B, **11**

Tennessee Performing
Arts Center, **6**

Tennessee State
Museum, **5**

Travellers' Rest, **24**

Twitty City/Music
Village USA, **27**

War Memorial Bldg., **8**

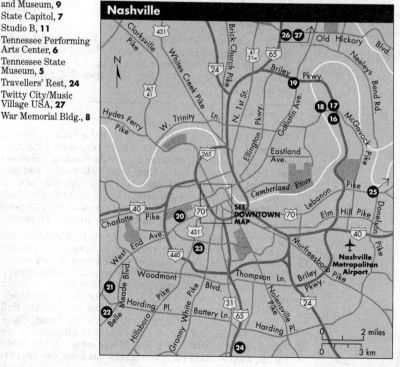

Downtown Nashville

Nashville

to an extensive preservation program. From Fort Nashborough, turn left onto Church Street and you'll be in the heart
③ of the **Historic Second Avenue Business District,** where 19th-century buildings have been handsomely restored to house offices, restaurants, boutiques, and residences.

Continue west on Church Street, which between Fourth and Eighth avenues is cobblestoned and tree-lined, retaining a picturesque quality reminiscent of a European town. At the corner
④ of Fifth is the **Downtown Presbyterian Church,** an Egyptian Revival tabernacle (c. 1851) designed by noted Philadelphia architect William Strickland.

Strolling north on Fifth Avenue, you'll come to one of the city's finest contemporary structures: the James K. Polk Office
⑤ Building, home to the impressive **Tennessee State Museum.** Here over 6,000 artifacts are displayed in settings that explore life in Tennessee. Included are a log cabin, an exhibition of Indian life, and a demonstration of bygone printing techniques.
⑥ (Also part of the complex is the **Tennessee Performing Arts Center.**) *505 Deaderick St., tel. 615/741-2692. Admission free. Open Mon.-Sat. 10-5, Sun. 1-5. Closed New Year's Day, Easter, Thanksgiving, Christmas.*

Walking west along Charlotte Avenue, you'll come to the Greek
⑦ Revival **State Capitol,** also designed by Strickland, who was so impressed with his creation that he requested—and received—entombment behind one of the building's walls. On the grounds—guarded by statues of such Tennessee heros as Andrew Jackson—are buried the 11th U.S. president, James K. Polk, and his wife. *Tel. 615/741-3011 (Education Dept.). Open for free tours weekdays, 9-4, Sat. 10-5, Sun. 1-5. Closed major holidays.*

⑧ On the corner of Seventh and Union is the **War Memorial Building,** built to honor the state's World War I dead and now housing a collection of military memorabilia. *Tel. 615/741-5383. Admission free. Open Mon.-Sat. 10-5, Sun. 1-5. Closed major holidays.*

Music Row

The leap from state capital to music capital is not as great as it may seem. If you're walking, you might head down Fifth Avenue
⑨ to pass recently renovated **Ryman Auditorium and Museum,** home of the Grand Ole Opry from 1943 to 1974 and now open for tours—a shrine for die-hard Opry fans. *116 Opry Pl. (Fifth Ave. N, between Broadway and Commerce Sts.), tel. 615/254-1445. Admission: $2 adults; $1 children 6-12, under 6 free. Open daily 8:30-4:30. Closed Thanksgiving, Christmas.*

By car, take the Demonbreun exit off I-40 to Music Row, the heart of Nashville's recording industry and a center for country
⑩ music attractions. The ample free parking next to the **Country Music Hall of Fame and Museum** is convenient to all the country attractions clustered nearby and is another reason to begin your Music Row tour at Nashville's premier country music museum. Costumes, instruments, film, photos, insights: the Hall of Fame has it all (including Elvis Presley's "solid gold" Cadillac). A ticket for the Hall of Fame includes admission to the
⑪ legendary RCA **Studio B** a few blocks away. Elvis, Dolly Parton, and countless others once recorded here; now the stu-

dio is a hands-on exhibit area showing how records are produced. *4 Music Sq. E, tel. 615/256–1639. Admission: $6.50 ad-
ults, $1.75 children 6–11, under 6 free. Open June–Aug., daily
8–8; Sept.–May, daily 9–5. Closed New Year's Day, Thanksgiving, Christmas.*

Those inspired by their visit to Studio B might stop by the **Recording Studios of America** (1510 Division St., tel. 615/254–
1282) to record, at nominal cost, a demo tape of their own. The
studio is part of **Barbara Mandrell Country,** an intimate look at
the career and family life of that superstar (including a replica
of her bedroom). *Tel. 615/242–7800. Admission: $6 adults,
$2.25 children, under 5 free. Open Sept.–May, daily 9–5;
June–Aug., daily 8–8.*

The car seems to be as much a country music icon as the guitar,
a fact underlined by two museums on Demonbreun Street. At
the **Hank Williams Jr. Museum,** family memorabilia includes
Hank Sr.'s '52 Cadillac and Hank Jr.'s '58 pink Cadillac. *1524
Demonbreun St., tel. 615/726–2962. Admission: $4 adults,
children under 16 free with an adult. Open Mar.–Sept., daily 8
AM–9 PM; Oct.–Feb., daily 8–3.*

A few doors away, the **Car Collectors Hall of Fame** displays
another of Elvis's Cadillacs (alongside one of George's), Webb
Pierce's startling "silver dollar car," and 50 other flashy vehicles with country provenances. *1534 Demonbreun St., tel. 615/
255–6804. Admission: $4.85 adults, $3.25 children 6–11, under 6 free. Open Sept.–May, daily 9–5; June–Aug., daily 8–8.*

In the same block, you'll find the guitars: At the **Country Music
Wax Museum and Mall** are over 60 figures of country stars,
complete with original stage costumes, and musical instruments. *118 16th Ave. S, tel. 615/256–2490. Admission: $4 ad-
ults, $3.50 over 55, $1.75 children 6–12, under 6 free.*

In the same building is Waylon Jenning's private collection of
six automobiles, including the General Lee used in the TV series, "The Dukes of Hazard." *Admission: $3 adults, $2.50 over
55, $1.75 children. Open May–Aug., daily 9–9; Sept.–Apr.,
daily 9–5.*

Opryland

Country music lovers may continue their pilgrimage at
Opryland USA, an attraction-filled show park just 15 minutes
from downtown via Briley Parkway. The complex was created
in part because the enormously popular Grand Ole Opry—65
years old and still going strong—had outgrown its old stomping grounds, the Ryman. Each weekend, top stars perform at
the nation's oldest continuous radio show, in the world's largest
broadcast studio (it seats 4,424). There are special matinees in
summer. *To avoid disappointment, purchase tickets in advance. Request a ticket-order form from Grand Ole Opry, 2808
Opryland Dr., 37214, tel. 615/889–3060. Admission: reserved
seats $14 evenings, $11.85 matinees; upper balcony $11.85 eve-
nings, $9.70 matinees.*

The show park also offers more than a dozen live shows ranging
from bluegrass bands to huge stage productions, and there are
22 thrilling rides, including brand-new Chaos, a $7-million in-
door thriller combining a roller-coaster ride and spectacular
audio-visual effects. The **Roy Acuff Musical Collection and Mu-**

seum (tel. 615/889–6700) contains memorabilia, including many guns and fiddles, of the "king of country music." **Minnie Pearl's Museum,** relocated to the same building in 1989, provides a nostalgic tour of the performer's life. Admission to the museums in Opryland Plaza is free; hours vary widely, so it's best to inquire locally. The *General Jackson,* Opryland's new showboat, offers several cruises daily with a musical revue while you dine (tel. 615/889–6611). There's also dining at food stands or full-service restaurants, and shopping for trinkets or treasures. *Tel. 615/ 889–6700. Admission: $21.50 one-day, $26.88 two-day, $64.60 3-day passport, including Grand Ole Opry matinee, daytime cruise, performance in Acuff Theatre (adjacent to Opry). Children under 4 free. Open late Mar.–May, Sept., Oct., weekends; late May–Labor Day, daily 9–9. Closed Nov.–late Mar. Hours vary widely but are generally weekdays 9–6, weekends 9–9; call to be sure.*

Several shows produced at Opryland USA and other Nashville sites—including *Hee Haw* (June and October only) and TNN cable programs—are open to visitors, and most are free. *Call TNN Viewer Services at 615/883–7000 for schedules and to make reservations.*

⑰ Just north of Opryland USA is **Boxcar Willie's Railroad Museum,** with displays depicting the life and travels of this Opry performer and "world's most famous hobo." In the same building is the inevitable **Cars of the Stars,** where classic cars share center stage with those of such country notables as Randy Travis, Dolly Parton, and Roy Acuff (about 45 cars in all). *2611 McGavock Pike, tel. 615/885–7400. Admission (Willie's/Cars/ both): $2/$3.50/$4.50 adults; $1.50/$3/$4 senior citizens; $1/ $1.50/$2 children 6–12, under 6 free. Both open Memorial Day–Labor Day, daily 8 AM–9 PM; rest of the year, daily 9–5. Closed Thanksgiving, Christmas.*

⑱ Next door is **Music Valley Wax Museum of the Stars,** with lifesize wax figures of more country stars, and outside is the **Sidewalk of the Stars,** Nashville's version of Graumann's Chinese, with the footprints, handprints, and signatures of over 200 country music performers. (Fame is also written in cement at the Fountain Square shopping complex's lakeside **Star Walk,** where 50 Grammy winners' pawprints are displayed on pedestals at hip level so you can compare yours with theirs without bending, while reading the stars' personally engraved messages—*see* Shopping, *below*). *2515 McGavock Pike, tel. 615/ 883–3612. Admission: $4 adults, $3 senior citizens, $2 children. Open Memorial Day–Labor Day, daily 8 AM–10 PM; rest of the year, daily 9–5.*

⑲ Fans of Gentleman Jim Reeves will not want to miss the collection of memorabilia at the **Jim Reeves Museum,** in an attractive 1794 house. This place continues the tradition of up close and personal à la Barbara Mandrell: Jim's bedroom furniture is on display, too. *1023 Joyce Lane (off Briley), tel. 615/226–2062. Admission: $4 adults; $3 over 64, $2 children 6–12, under 6 free. Open daily 9–5. Closed New Year's Day, Thanksgiving, Christmas.*

Farther Afield

Apart from the many educational and cultural institutions that lend credence to Nashville's Athens of the South sobriquet are the gracious estates that form a necklace of emerald green around the city. To get into the spirit, begin your tour at Centennial Park's **Parthenon,** an exact copy of the Athenian original right down to the Elgin Marbles. Newly renovated, including the addition of a huge statue of Athena, the Parthenon houses an art gallery with changing exhibits. *Tel. 615/259-6358. Admission: $2.50 adults, $1.25 senior citizens and children 6–17, under 6 free. Open Tues.–Sat. 9–4:30 (until 8 on Thurs.), Sun. 1–4:30.*

21 **Belle Meade Mansion** is a stunning Greek Revival house, the centerpiece of a 5,300-acre estate that was one of the nation's first and finest thoroughbred breeding farms. It was also the site of the famous Iroquois, the oldest amateur steeplechase in America, which is still run each May but in nearby Percy Warner Park. A Victorian carriage museum continues the equine theme. *110 Leake Ave. (from Centennial Park, head west on West End Ave. and follow the signs for Belle Meade—not to be confused with Belle Meade Blvd.), tel. 615/356–0501. Admission: $4 adults, $3.50 children 13–18, $2 ages 7–12; under 6 free. Open Mon.–Sat. 9–5, Sun. 1–5.*

22 The Georgian-style mansion at nearby **Cheekwood** (take Harding Rd. east, turn right on to Belle Meade Blvd., and look for a sign) is now a fine arts center, and the surrounding 55-acre **Tennessee Botanical Gardens** showcases herbs, roses, irises, daffodils, and area wildflowers. Greenhouses, streams, and pools make this a delightful spot for a picnic. *Forrest Park Dr., tel. 615/356–8000. Admission: $4 adults; $3 senior citizens and college students with ID, $1 children 7–18, under 6 free. Open Mon.–Sat. 9–5, Sun. 1–5. Closed New Year's Day, Thanksgiving, Dec. 24–25, 31.*

23 **Belmont Mansion,** now on the campus of Belmont College, was the home of Adelicia Acklen, Nashville's answer to Scarlett O'Hara, who married "once for money, once for love, and once for the hell of it." This outstanding Italianate villa of the 1850s is a Victorian gem right down to its cast-iron gazebos. *Take Belle Meade Blvd. north from Cheekwood. Turn right on to West End Ave., then right on to Blakemore, which becomes Wedgewood. Turn right on to Magnolia Blvd., first left, then follow signs. Corner of Acklen Ave. and Belmont Blvd., tel. 615/269–9537. Admission: $3 adults, $1 children 6–12, under 6 free. Open Tues.–Sat. 10–4, also Mon., Jun–Aug. Closed major holidays.*

24 From here, take I–65 south to the first of two Harding Place exits to **Travellers' Rest,** the early 19th-century clapboard home of pioneer landowner John Overton. Following the fortunes of Overton, the law partner, mentor, campaign manager, and lifelong friend of Andrew Jackson, whose own home is nearby, the house metamorphosed from a 1799 four-room cottage to a 12-room mansion with Federal and Greek Revival additions. *636 Farrell Pkwy., tel. 615/832–2962. Admission: $4 adults, $1 children 6–18, under 5 free. Open June–Aug., Mon.–Sat. 9–5, Sun. 1–5; Sept.–May, Mon.–Sat. 9–4, Sun. 1–4. Closed New Year's Day, Thanksgiving, Christmas.*

25 Forming the eastern end of this semicircle of homes is **The Hermitage,** 12 miles east of Nashville (I–40E to Old Hickory Blvd. exit), where the life and times of Tennessee's beloved Old Hickory are reflected with great care. Andrew Jackson built this mansion on 600 acres for his wife, Rachel, and both are entombed here. The **Andrew Jackson Center,** a 28,000-sq.-ft. museum, visitor, and education center, opened in 1989, contains many Jackson artifacts never before exhibited. A 16-minute film, "Old Hickory," is shown in its auditorium; the structure also includes Rachel's Garden Cafe and a museum store. Tours take you through the mansion, furnished with many original pieces. Across the road stands **Tulip Grove,** built by Mrs. Jackson's nephew, and **The Hermitage Church,** fondly known as "Rachel's Church." *4580 Rachel's La., Hermitage, tel. 615/889–2941. Admission (includes Tulip Grove and church): $7 adults; $6.50 senior citizens, $3.50 children 6–13, under 6 free. Open daily 9–5. Closed major holidays.*

In Hendersonville, 20 miles northeast of downtown Nashville (eight miles from The Hermitage), there are yet more shrines **26** to country music notables. The **House of Cash** displays possessions and memorabilia of the "Man in Black," a legend in his own time, including some superb Frederic Remington bronzes. *700 Johnny Cash Pkwy., tel. 615/824–5110. Admission: $6 adults; $4 senior citizens; $1 children 6–12, under 6 free. Open Apr.–Oct., Mon.–Sat. 9–4:30.*

27 **Twitty City/Music Village USA** is not only the home of superstar Conway Twitty but also a 15-acre entertainment complex with live shows, shops, restaurants, and museums highlighting the life and times of such entertainers as Bill Monroe, Ferlin Husky, and Marty Robbins. *Music Village Blvd., Hendersonville, tel. 615/822–6650. Admission: $8 adults; $4.50 children 6–15, under 6 free. Open daily 9–5; Thanksgiving–Dec. weekdays 5–9, weekends 5–10.*

South to the Natchez Trace

The most direct route from Nashville to the Natchez Trace Parkway is south 40 miles on I–65 to TN 50, then 30 miles west, through Columbia, to the beginning of the parkway. The two following routes, however, offer some fun alternatives.

One option is to drive about 15 miles southeast of Nashville on I–24 to **Murfreesboro,** which calls itself the Antique Center of the South. Pick up a free antiques shopping guide at Cannonsburgh Pioneer Village, a living museum of 19th-century life in the South (tel. 615/890–0355). Then continue on I–24 another 45 miles to **Manchester,** where you can visit **Old Stone Fort State Park** (U.S. 41, tel. 615/728–0751). There's a walled structure here that's believed to have been built at least 2,000 years ago. The scenic 600-acre site, on bluffs overlooking Duck River, is laced with waterfalls and has a visitor center, a nine-hole golf course, and campsites. From Manchester, take TN55 southwest to **Lynchburg,** home to the Jack Daniels Distillery, where you can observe every step of the sour-mash-whiskey-making art. *¼ mi northeast of Lynchburg on TN 55, tel. 615/759–4221. Guided tours daily 8–4. Closed major holidays.*

Also in Lynchburg, **Miss Mary Bobo's Boarding House** is a Tennessee institution. Diners flock to the big two-story 1867 white frame house with a white picket fence to feast family-style at tables groaning with fried chicken, roast beef, fried catfish, stuffed vegetables and sliced tomatoes fresh from the gardens out back, corn on the cob, homemade biscuits, cornbread, pecan pie, lemon icebox pie, fruit cobblers, and strawberry short-

cake. ½ block from the Public Square, Lynchburg, tel. 615/759–7394. Reservations required, at least a week in advance in summer. Lunch only, served at 1 PM, Mon.–Sat. Closed major holidays. Fixed price is $9 adults, $4 children under 12.

From Lynchburg, follow TN 50 southwest 13 miles to Fayetteville, where you can pick up U.S. 64 west to the Natchez Trace Parkway.

The other optional route from Nashville is west on I–40. Go north on TN 13 to Hurricane Mills to visit the Loretta Lynn Ranch, the singer's personal museum housed in an old restored gristmill. Narrated hayride tours of the 3,500-acre ranch are offered during the summer; you can also tour her stately antebellum home. *Tel. 615/296–7700. Admission: $3 adults; $1 children 6–12, under 6 free. Open Apr. 15–Oct. 31, daily 8–5.*

Continue on I–40 through the Natchez Trace State Park, then pick up Route 22 south to **Shiloh National Military Park,** site of one of the Civil War's grimmest and most decisive battles. At the visitor center, you'll see a film explaining the battle's strategy, along with a display of Civil War relics. A self-guided auto tour leads past markers explaining monuments and battle sites. Almost 4,000 soldiers, many unidentified, are buried here in the national cemetery. *Tel. 901/689–5275. Visitor center open daily 8–6 June–Aug., 8–5 rest of year. Closed Christmas. Admission: $1 adults, children under 12 and senior citizens free.*

Route 22 continues into Corinth, Mississippi, from where you can take Route 72 east 32 miles to get on the parkway.

Shopping

Church Street is Nashville's major downtown shopping area; there you'll find department stores, smaller chain stores, and numerous boutiques. **Fountain Square** (2244 Metro Center Blvd., tel. 615/256–7467) is a complex of 35 shops, a food court, pushcart vendors in season, and Star Walk—all ranged round a 48-acre lake. There is free live entertainment nightly, from classical music to mime to dance.

Antiques
In Nashville, browse for distinctive 18th- and 19th-century English antiques and art objects at **Madison Antique Mall** (404 Gallatin Rd. S, tel. 615/865–4677), **Nashville Antique Mall** (657 Wedgewood Ave., tel. 615/256–1465), and **Smorgasbord Antique Mall** (4144-B Lebanon Rd., tel. 615/883–5789).

Arts and Crafts
You'll find works of major regional artists at **Ambiance Art Gallery** (2137 Bandywood Dr., tel. 615/385–3161) and **Cumberland Gallery** (4107 Hillsboro Circle, tel. 615/297–0296). For pottery and ceramics, seek out **Forrest Valley Galleries,** a working studio (2218 Eighth Ave. S, tel. 615/356–2484).

Country-and-Western Wear
Stores geared to the latest look in country clothing include **Boot Country** (2412 Music Valley Dr., tel. 615/883–2661), **Loretta Lynn's Western Stores** (120 16th Ave. S, tel. 615/889–5582; 435 Donelson Pike, tel. 615/889–5582), and the **Nashville Cowboy** (118 16th Ave. S, tel. 615/242–9497; 1516 Demonbreun St., tel. 615/256–2429).

Records and Tapes
Fans can find good selections of records and tapes at **Conway's Twitty Bird Record Shop** (1530 Demonbreun St., tel. 615/242–2466), **Ernest Tubb Record Shops** (2414 Music Valley Dr., tel.

615/889–2474; 417 Broadway, tel. 615/255–7503), and **The Great Escape** (1925 Broadway, tel. 615/327–0646; 139 Gallatin Rd. N, Madison, tel. 615/865–8052).

Sports and Outdoor Activities

Golf
: Among courses open to the public year-round are **Harpeth Hills** (tel. 615/373–8202), **Hermitage Golf Course** (tel. 615/847–4001), and **Rhodes Golf Course** (9 holes; tel. 615/242–2336). Hermitage is the site each April of the LPGA Sara Lee Classic.

Horseback Riding
: You can jog or canter on gentle steeds at **Riverwood Recreation Plantation and Riding Academy** (tel. 615/262–1794), and **Ramblin' Breeze Ranch** (tel. 615/876–1029).

Ice Skating
: From September through April, there's indoor skating at **Sportsplex** (tel. 615/862–8480), in Centennial Park.

Jogging
: Favorite sites include **Centennial Park**, the **Vanderbilt University running track**, and **Percy Warner Park**. The 1,700-plus-member running club Nashville Striders (tel. 615/254–0631) can recommend choice spots and will provide information on many summer races.

Mini-golf
: Enjoy this uniquely American family sport at **Grand Old Golf** (tel. 615/871–4701), across the street from the Opryland Hotel.

Tennis
: Several municipal tennis facilities offer good play. **Centennial Sportsplex Tennis Center** (tel. 615/862–8480) has grass and clay outdoor courts plus indoor courts.

Dining

If you expect Nashville dining to be all cornbread, turnip greens, and grits, you're in for a staggering surprise. You will find some of Tennessee's most sophisticated restaurants, with service that is as polished as any you'll find in cities twice the size.

The following dining price categories have been used: *Expensive*, over $30; *Moderate*, $12–$30; *Inexpensive*, under $12.

Expensive
American
: **Belle Meade Brasserie.** Mark Rubin and Robert Siegel have created a comfortable suburban restaurant and a menu filled with surprises—corn fritters and pepper jelly, angel-hair pasta with Cajun popcorn (crayfish), hickory-grilled pork loin with corn-chili relish, and shrimp and scallops served on a bed of black linguine. Desserts are just as compelling, including a knockout chocolate-walnut praline cake. *101 Page Rd., tel. 615/356–5450. Dress: informal. AE, DC, MC, V. Closed Sun.*

The Merchants. A $3.2 million renovation of a historic property in downtown Nashville, this former hotel provides three levels of dining and an appealing outdoor patio. Specialties include deep-fried alligator bits, the freshest seafoods, and meats grilled over native hardwoods. The menu changes to lighter fare in summer and all rolls, pastas, and pastries are made fresh daily. Save room for the Key lime pie. *401 Broadway, tel. 615/254–1892. Dress: informal. Reservations recommended. AE, DC, MC, V.*

Classic French
★
: **Julian's Restaurant Français.** If you can't travel to the City of Light, dine at Julian's instead, for here, in the intimate rooms of a turn-of-the-century town house, chef Sylvain Le Coguic serves some of the best French cuisine this side of Paris. His

creations include sautéed veal sweetbreads in Sauternes sauce with fresh wild mushrooms, and grilled breast of duckling in tart cherry sauce. *2412 West End Ave., tel. 615/327–2412. Jacket and tie suggested. Reservations suggested. AE, DC, MC, V. Closed Sun.*

Continental

Arthur's. This restaurant has relocated to the renovated Union Station, where an upscale hotel has taken the place of the train terminal. The five-course meals are still dazzling, and the ambience is as romantic as ever. Be sure to save room for dessert, especially the Crown Royal Cake, a fruit-and-nut cake created for HRH, The Princess Royal, when she visited Nashville for the Royal Chase. The decor is lush, with lace curtains, velveteen-upholstered chairs, white linen, and fine silver service. *In Union Station. 1001 Broadway, tel. 615/255–1494. Jacket and tie suggested. Reservations suggested. AE, DC, MC, V. Dinner only weekends.*

Mère Bulles, The Wine Bar and Restaurant. There's an aura of casual elegance in this locally popular restaurant with brass-trimmed mahogany bar and changing artworks decorating mellow, exposed brick walls. Guests can enjoy tapas and drinks in the cozy lounge, then move into one of three intimate dining areas with views of the river. There's live entertainment nightly, usually jazz or folk music. Specialties include veal saltimbocca stuffed with honey-cured ham and Swiss cheese, and topped with chef Chris's special sauces; pesto Mère Bulles—shrimp and scallops with walnut-pesto sauce served on a bed of shell pasta. There are 50 wines by the glass and a stock of over 170 selections by the bottle. *152 2nd Ave. N, tel. 615/256–1946. Jacket and tie suggested. Reservations accepted. AE, DC, MC, V.*

The Wild Boar. Chef Siegfried Eisenberger and local restaurateur Mario Ferrari have pooled their enormous talents to create The Wild Boar. The restaurant emphasizes game, in classic Continental style. The menu also features trout, lobster, duck, and beef dishes, with several that are prepared at tableside. The atmosphere is all starched-linen formality; this is definitely for the big night out. *2014 Broadway, tel. 615/329–1313. Jacket and tie recommended. AE, DC, MC, V. Closed Sun. and Mon.*

Northern Italian

Mario's Ristorante Italiano. Owner Mario Ferrari is the genius behind this Nashville institution. Country music stars, visiting celebrities, and local society come here to see and be seen. The atmosphere is elegant, with lots of brass and an impressive wine collection on view, yet it's never stuffy. Pastas created by Chef Sandro Bozzatto are memorable, the seafood and veal—such as the *saltimbocca*, veal medallions with mozzarella, prosciutto, mushrooms, and fresh sage—are equally palate-pleasing. *2005 Broadway, tel. 615/327–3232. Jacket required. Reservations required, 2–3 days ahead on weekends. AE, DC, MC, V. Closed Sun.*

Moderate
American

F. Scott's. At this elegant café and wine bar, Nashville artist Paul Harmon's bright avant-garde paintings stand out on the steel-gray-and-mauve walls. Chef Anita Hartel's creations include pasta with chicken and artichokes in a cream sauce, and braised lamb with mint sauce. F. Scott's has one of the largest wine lists in Nashville, with many fine wines available by the glass. *2220 Bandywood Dr., tel. 615/269–5861. Dress: informal. Reservations accepted. AE, MC, V.*

Continental **Maude's Courtyard.** "Meet me at Maude's" is more than an advertising slogan—it's a way of life in Nashville. Owner Morton Howell III encourages his chefs to add personal flair to every dish. Some examples: lobster pasta with artichoke hearts, superb seafood gumbo—a true Louisiana recipe, scampi and scallops brochette, and veal florentine. A covered courtyard with a fountain and several fireplaces throughout the restaurant allow guests to choose their own ambience. Sundays, there's live jazz by the Bourbon Street Trio. *1911 Broadway, tel. 615/320-0543. Dress: informal. Reservations recommended. AE, DC, MC, V. No lunch Sat.; Sun., brunch only.*

106 Club. A white baby grand and a bar of shiny black enamel and glass brick set the atmosphere in this intimate, Art Deco dining room in suburban Belle Meade. The cuisine is a mix of California nouvelle—such as veal medallions with litchi nuts, strawberries, and pistachios sautéed in a light sauce made from nuts and berries—and international favorites. The pasta primavera is one of the best in town. In the evening, the outdoor patio is a good place to relax with one of 106's rich desserts and listen to old and new melodies on the baby grand. *106 Harding Pl. tel. 615/356-1300. Jacket and tie suggested. Reservations suggested. AE, DC, MC, V.*

Inexpensive **Cakewalk Restaurant.** The first things to catch your eye at this
Mixed Menu cozy bistro are the intriguing paintings by local artists on the turquoise walls. The eclectic cuisine is equally imaginative, blending the best of nouvelle California, a bit of Southwestern, and a dash of Cajun/Creole, with some down-home American specialties thrown in for fun. Desserts are outstanding—especially the Kahlua cake, a four-layer chocolate cake laced with liqueur. *3001 West End Ave., tel. 615/320-7778. Dress: informal. Reservations recommended for dinner. DC, MC, V.*

Southern **Loveless Cafe.** An experience in true down-home Southern
★ cooking. Don't come for the decor—which is also down-home, including red-and-white-checked tablecloths—but, rather, for the feather-light homemade biscuits and preserves, country ham and red-eye gravy, and fried chicken. *8400 Hwy. 100, tel. 615/646-9700. Dress: informal. Reservations suggested, especially on weekends. No credit cards. Closed Mon.*

Lodging

Nashville offers a very impressive selection of hotel, motel, and all-suite accommodations in all price categories and levels of luxury. Although some establishments increase rates slightly during the peak summer travel season, most maintain the same rates year-round. Some downtown luxury hotels offer special weekend rates to attract guests to otherwise vacant rooms.

For information on B&Bs in the area, contact **Bed & Breakfast of Middle Tennessee** (Box 40804, Nashville 37204, tel. 615/297-0883). **Bed & Breakfast Host Homes of Tennessee** (Box 110227, Nashville, TN 37222, tel. 615/331-5244) has listings for homes here and throughout the state.

The following lodging price categories have been used: *Very Expensive,* over $130; *Expensive,* $79–$130; *Moderate,* $50–$79, *Inexpensive,* under $50.

Very Expensive **Hotel Watauga House.** This downtown, vintage 1902 structure has been restored to its original Victorian grandeur. The suites, all with kitchenettes, are decorated in period. *222 Polk Ave., 37203, tel. 615/252–2500. 24 suites. Facilities: hot tub, sauna, party rooms. AE, MC, V.*

Hyatt Regency Nashville. Downtown near the State Capitol, this 28-story tower has Hyatt's signature vast, skylighted atrium lobby awash with greenery, along with the glassed-in elevators that still seem to fascinate all but the most blasé occupants. Rooms are extra spacious and contemporary in decor. The hotel is topped by Nashville's only revolving rooftop restaurant. *623 Union St., 37219, tel. 615/259–1234 or 800/233–1234. 476 rooms, including 32 suites. Facilities: cable TV/movies, restaurant, coffee shop, lounge, recreational privileges at Y. AE, DC, MC, V.*

★ **Opryland Hotel.** Adjacent to Opryland, this massive hostelry has recently almost doubled in size. Even if you don't stay here, come out to take a look—it's an attraction in its own right. The two-acre glass-walled Conservatory is a lush enclave of tropical vegetation, streams, waterfalls, statuary, and fountains. Just added is the Cascades, another skylighted interior space with streams, waterfalls, and a half-acre lake. The hotel claims to have more meeting space than any other in the nation. The culinary staff is directed by a member of the U.S. Culinary Olympics Team. *2800 Opryland Dr., 37214, tel. 615/883–2211. 1,891 rooms, including suites. Facilities: 3 restaurants, coffee shop, 5 lounges, heated pool, wading pool, lighted tennis (fee). AE, DC, MC, V.*

★ **Park Suite Nashville Hotel.** Near the airport and Opryland is this hotel of all suites, ranged around a nine-story parklike atrium lobby with live plants, meandering watercourses, and tropical birds. Suites are comfortably furnished in tasteful contemporary style; each has a wet bar, a refrigerator, and two color TVs. *10 Century Blvd., 37214, tel. 615/871–0033 or 800/432–7272. 294 suites. Facilities: cable TV/movies, indoor pool, whirlpool, sauna, exercise room, free full buffet breakfast, dining room, lounge. AE, DC, MC, V.*

Stouffer Nashville Hotel. This luxurious new ultracontemporary high-rise hotel adjoins Nashville Convention Center and is also connected to the new Church Street Centre Mall with fine shops, restaurants, and entertainment. Spacious rooms are highlighted by period reproduction furnishings. Executive Club concierge floors offer extra privacy and personal services. *611 Commerce St., 37203, tel. 615/255–8400 or 800/468–3571. 673 units, including 34 suites, 46 Club level rooms. Facilities: spa, indoor pool, whirlpool, sauna, exercise facilities, cable TV, restaurant, coffee shop, lounge, garage, airport transportation. AE, DC, MC, V.*

Expensive ★ **Courtyard by Marriott–Airport.** This handsome new low-rise motor inn with a sunny, gardenlike courtyard offers some amenities you'd expect in higher-priced hotels: spacious rooms, king-size beds, oversize work desks, and hot-water dispensers for in-room coffee. *2508 Elm Hill Pike, 37214, tel. 615/883–9500 or 800/321–2211. 145 rooms, including 12 suites. Facilities: cable TV/movies, restaurant, lounge, indoor pool, sauna, whirlpool, exercise room. AE, DC, MC, V.*

Holiday Inn–Briley Parkway. To while away your time between flights or Opryland visits, there's the trademark Holidome Indoor Recreation Center, with pool, sauna, whirlpool, game room, table tennis, pool tables, and putting green. Business travelers will appreciate the conference center and spacious, well-lighted guest rooms. *2200 Elm Hill Pike at Briley Pkwy., 37210, tel. 615/883–9770 or 800/465–4329. 385 rooms, including 4 suites. Facilities: cable TV, restaurant, lounge, coin laundry. AE, DC, MC, V.*

Ramada Inn Across from Opryland. This contemporary-style, well-maintained new low-rise motor inn has the closest location to the theme park other than the Opryland Hotel. *2401 Music Valley Dr., 37214, tel. 615/889–0800 or 800/272–6232. 308 rooms, including 7 suites. Facilities: cable TV/movies, rental refrigerators, indoor pool, sauna, whirlpool, dining room, lounge. AE, DC, MC, V.*

Moderate **Best Western at Opryland.** Conveniently located near Opryland and other attractions, this chain unit offers rooms that are comfortable and bright. *2600 Music Valley Dr., 37214, tel. 615/889–8235 or 800/528–1234. 212 rooms. Facilities: cable TV/movies, pool, restaurant, coffee shop, lounge. AE, DC, MC, V.*

Comfort Inn Hermitage. Near the Hermitage, this inn offers first-rate accommodations, some with water beds or whirlpool baths. *5768 Old Hickory Blvd., 37076, tel. 615/889–5060 or 800/228–5150. 106 rooms, including 7 suites. Facilities: pool, cable TV/movies. AE, DC, MC, V.*

★ **Hampton Inn Vanderbilt.** Near the Vanderbilt University campus, this inn is new, clean, and contemporary. The rooms are colorful and spacious. A multipurpose hospitality suite has a conference table, chairs, and an audiovisual unit for meeting and business groups. *1919 West End Ave., 37203, tel. 615/329–1144 or 800/426–7866. 163 rooms. Facilities: cable TV/free movies, pool. AE, DC, MC, V.*

La Quinta Motor Inn. The rooms here are especially spacious and well lighted, with a large working area and oversize bed. King Plus rooms have a full-length mirror and an ottoman. *2001 Metrocenter Blvd., 37227-0001. (1 mi north of downtown), tel. 615/259–2130 or 800/531–5900. 121 rooms. Facilities: cable TV, pool. AE, DC, MC, V.*

The Arts

For a complete listing of weekly events, consult the Visitor Information Center or the local newspapers. For information on concerts and special events, call WSM Radio's entertainment line (tel. 615/889–9595) or TV Channel 5's hot line (Thurs.; tel. 615/248–5200). Ticketmaster (tel. 615/741–2787) has information on events at various Nashville venues.

Concerts Country music takes center stage at the 4,424-seat **Grand Ole Opry Auditorium** (tel. 615/889–3060). The Nashville Symphony Orchestra's classical and pops series and concerts by out-of-town groups are staged at **Andrew Jackson Hall** (tel. Ticketmaster at 615/741–2787), part of the Tennessee Performing Arts Center (TPAC). Chamber concerts take place at TPAC's **James K. Polk Theater** (tel. 615/741–7975). Some rock and country music events are held at the **Nashville Municipal Auditorium** (tel. 615/862–6395). The **Starwood Amphitheatre** (tel. 615/641–7500) is the site of rock, pop, country, and jazz concerts, musicals, and special events; it's also the summer home of the Nashville Symphony. Vanderbilt University stages music, dance, and drama productions (many free) at its **Blair School of Music** (tel. 615/322–7651).

Festivals   **Summer Lights.** The first weekend each June, more than half a million visitors attend Nashville's unique music and arts festival, showcasing top names and newcomers in pop, rock, jazz, country, classical, and reggae on five outdoor stages downtown. Visual arts are exhibited in warehouses and storefronts along First and Second avenues. Local cuisine is available from street vendors or sidewalk cafés, and street entertainers fill the Family Arts Arcade. Most events are free. *Contact: Metro Nashville Arts Commission, 111 Fourth Ave. S, 37201, tel. 615/259–6374.*

International Country Music Fan Fair. For six days following Summer Lights, this celebration is staged at the Tennessee State Fairgrounds, Vanderbilt University's Dudley Field, and Opryland USA. There are more than 35 hours of musical events, autograph sessions with country music stars, and the Grand Masters Fiddling championship. *Contact: Fan Fair, 2804 Opryland Dr., 37214, tel. 615/889–7503.*

Theater   **James K. Polk Theater** hosts touring Broadway shows and local theatrical performances. For theater-in-the-round, there's the **Andrew Johnson Theater.** The **Academy Theatre** (tel. 615/254–9103) hosts children's theater performances. **Chaffin's Barn,** 8204 Hwy. 100 (tel. 615/822–1800), offers dinner theater year-round, and a live country show is staged here daily Memorial Day–Labor Day.

Nightlife

Revues   **Ernest Tubb Midnight Jamboree** (2414 Music Valley Dr., tel. 615/889–2474) presents a live midnight radio show with performances by new talent as well as Opry stars, usually including Ernest himself.

Nightclubs   **Boots Randolph's** (209 Printers Alley, between Third and Fourth Aves., tel. 615/256–5500) is one of the city's landmark night spots, a sophisticated supper club featuring Boots—"Mr. Yakkety Sax" in the showroom.
McGavocks Place II Nightclub (Sheraton Music City Hotel, 777 McGavock Pike, tel. 615/885–2200) offers dancing to live bands or recorded music with a DJ and music videos in a turn-of-the-century atmosphere.
Monroe's Bluegrass Country (2620 Music Valley Dr., tel. 615/885–0777) dinner club features top-name country and bluegrass entertainers, with plenty of room for dancing. The legendary Bill Monroe appears frequently.
Nashville Palace (2400 Music Valley Dr., tel. 615/885–1540) presents live country entertainment, highlighted by popular Music City entertainers and rising talent.
Stock Yard Bull Pen Lounge (901 Second Ave. N and Stock Yard Blvd., tel. 615/255–6464) has a popular steak-and-seafood restaurant and lounge with live entertainment upstairs; downstairs, the Bull Pen features dancin', pickin', and singin' as many of Nashville's big names show up for performances—both scheduled and unscheduled.

The Natchez Trace

The Natchez Trace Parkway is what God meant highways to be. Flower-sprigged and forested, it is a long thin parkway running from Nashville to Natchez, crossing the early paths worn by Choctaw and Chickasaw Indians, flatboatmen, outlaws, itinerant preachers, postriders, soldiers, and settlers. Landscaped by the National Park Service, the Trace is meticulously manicured to show off the straightest pines and spookiest cypresses, to alternate peaceful vistas of reeds and still waters with dense woodlands where the dogwood stars shine. The Trace grows increasingly wild and mysterious as it nears Natchez; the cutthroats and murderers who frequented the early trails come unwanted to mind.

When completed, the Trace will be 449 miles long, with 313 miles in Mississippi. There are no billboards along its route, and commercial vehicles are forbidden to use it. Park rangers are serious about the 50 mph speed limit; you'll probably get acquainted with one if you drive any faster.

Numbers in the margin correspond to points of interest on the Natchez Trace map.

❶ Named for J.P. Coleman, Mississippi's governor from 1955 to 1959, **J.P. Coleman State Park** vies with Tishomingo State Park for the title of most spectacular Mississippi state park. There are wooded campsites for tents and RVs, and 10 secluded cabins, some of them old and rustic (no air-conditioning); others from the 1970s with fireplaces and central air and heat. Rooms at the balconied lodge overlook the shale beaches of serene Pickwick Lake. Visitors explore nature trails, rent canoes and boats, fish, swim, waterski, drink beer, or play canasta under the oaks and virgin pines. *Rte. 5, Box 503, Iuka 38852 (13 mi north of Iuka off U.S. 25), tel. 601/423–6515.*

❷ **Tishomingo State Park** lies in the Appalachian foothills, making its terrain unique in Mississippi. If you're feeling peppy, a 13-mile nature trail winds through a canyon along steep hills by waterfalls, granite outcrops, and a swinging bridge; otherwise, take the winding roads through forests so leafy they can hide the brightest day in shadow. Eight-mile canoe trips and float trips are offered from mid-March to October. Around Haynes Lake are primitive campsites, hookups, and five rustic cabins to rent. Bring your own provisions. *Rte. 1, Box 310, Dennis 38838 (15 mi south of Iuka, and 3 mi north of Dennis off U.S. 25), tel. 601/438–6914.*

❸ West of the parkway 32 miles on U.S. 72, **Corinth** is a town of special interest for Civil War enthusiasts. The Battles of Shiloh and Corinth are commemorated with markers and displays throughout the area. Corinth was settled just seven years before the war and assumed military importance because of its two railroad lines. In April 1862, after the bloody battle of Shiloh, near Shiloh Church in Tennessee, 21 miles to the north, the Confederates turned Corinth into a vast medical center. In May 1862, the Confederates, under General P.G.T. Beauregard, were forced to withdraw further; their retreat involved the most ingenious hoax of the war: To fool the Federal forces, campfires were lighted, dummy cannoneers were placed at fake cannons, empty trains were cheered as if they brought reinforcements, and buglers moved along the deserted works, play-

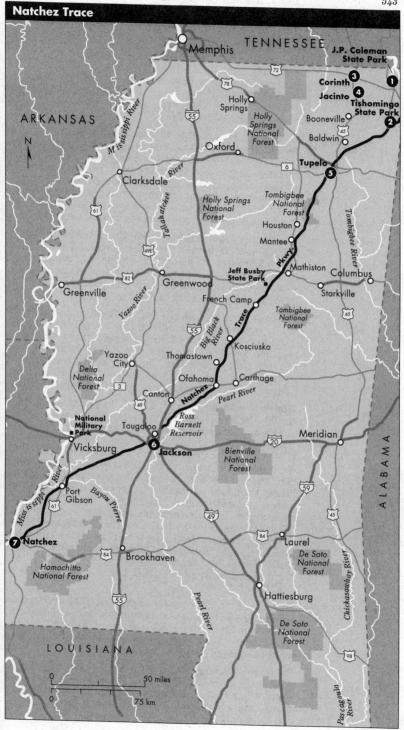

Natchez Trace

ing taps. Union forces occupied the town and, in October 1862, a Confederate attempt to recapture the town—the Battle of Corinth—failed.

To visit all of Corinth's Civil War sites, follow the street markers, using the self-guided tour brochure available free at the **Northeast Mississippi Museum**. *Fourth St., at Washington St., tel. 601/287–2231. Admission: $1.50 adults, 50¢ children. Open Feb.–Dec., Sun.–Wed., Fri., and Sat. daily 1–4. Closed Thurs. and the month of Jan.*

Go south 10 miles on U.S. 45, then east 8 miles on MS 356 to **Jacinto**, a ghost town with a restored Federal-style courthouse (1854) surrounded by pre-1870 buildings that are slowly being restored. Jacinto also has nature trails that lead to mineral springs, and a swinging bridge. A new recreational park provides hookups for eight campers, a playground, and a picnic area with grills. *On MS 356, tel. 601/287–4296. Admission free. Open Tues.–Sun. 1–5, other times by appointment.*

The **Natchez Trace Parkway Visitor Center** (milepost 266, tel. 601/845–1572) is located five miles north of Tupelo on the Trace. The Visitor Center offers exhibits, a 12-minute film, a hands-on area for children, and the *Official Map and Guide*, which opens to a four-foot length to give detailed, mile-by-mile information from Nashville to Natchez.

The largest city in north Mississippi, **Tupelo** (named after the tupelo gum tree), was founded in 1859 and is a city of accomplishment. Progressive leaders have successfully lured business and industry to an area that only 30 years ago was predominantly agricultural. The arts flourish here, and the medical center is the largest in the state. The scenic hill country provides beautiful places to camp, swim, fish, jog, and bike.

Why do so many tourists flock here? Because this is a city of destiny: the birthplace of Elvis Presley, the one-and-only king of rock and roll. **Elvis Presley's birthplace**, a tiny, two-room "shotgun" house, was built by his father, Vernon Presley, for $180. Elvis Aaron Presley was born here on January 8, 1935. The home has been restored and furnished much as it was when the Presleys lived in it. The house is now surrounded by **Elvis Presley Park**, land purchased with proceeds from Elvis's 1956 concert at the Mississippi-Alabama Fair. The park includes a swimming pool, tennis courts, playground, and a gift shop (for Elvis souvenirs) in the Youth Center. The **Elvis Presley Memorial Chapel**, suggested by the singer in 1971 as a place for his fans to meditate, was dedicated in 1979, two years after Presley's death. *Off Old Hwy. 78, at 306 Elvis Presley Dr., tel. 601/841–1245. Admission: $1 adults, 50¢ children. Open Mon.–Sat. 9–5:30, Sun. 1–5.*

Five miles north of the Presley birthplace is **Elvis Presley Lake and Campground** where you can swim, ski, sun, and fish—and think about Elvis. *Off Canal St. extended, tel. 601/841–1304. Primitive and full-service campsites. Separate fees for swimming, camping, fishing, and boat launching.*

The **Tupelo Museum** displays further Presley memorabilia along with other exhibits, including a turn-of-the-century Western Union office, a working sorghum mill, a train depot and caboose, and an old-time country store. *Located in James J. Ballard Park, off MS 6W, tel. 601/841–6438. Admission: $1* *adults; 50¢ children 3–11, under 3 free. Open Tues.–Fri. 10–4, weekends 1–5.*

Once you've satisfied your Elvis mania, turn your thoughts to the Civil War Battle of Tupelo. In 1864, Union General A. J. Smith marched 14,000 troops against Nathan Bedford Forrest's forces near Tupelo. Smith's goal was to end the constant Southern harrassment of supply lines to Sherman's army besieging Atlanta. The battle, on July 14, 1864, was the last major battle in Mississippi and one of the bloodiest. A **National Battlefield** site on West Main Street (MS 6), inside the city limits, commemorates the battle with monuments and displays.

From Tupelo, the trip to Jackson takes three hours if you don't stop. It can easily take an entire day, however, if you stop to read the brown wooden markers, explore nature trails, and admire the neat fields, trees, and wildflower meadows.

Bynum Mounds (milepost 232.4) are ceremonial hills that were constructed between 100 BC and AD 200 by prehistoric people. Exhibits describe their daily existence.

Jeff Busby State Park (milepost 193.9) was named for the Mississippi congressman who introduced legislation creating the Natchez Trace Parkway. The park includes an overlook at one of the state's highest points (603 feet) and a 20-minute nature trail that identifies native plants and describes their use by pioneers. Campers may wish to spend the night. For more information contact the State Parks (Box 20305, Jackson 39209).

The **Little Mountain Service Station** is located at the campground entrance. This privately owned station is the only place to fuel up right on the parkway.

At **French Camp** (milepost 180.7), where Frenchman Louis LeFleur established a stand (or inn) in 1812, you can watch sorghum molasses being made on Saturdays in late September and October.

At **Beaver Creek** (milepost 145.1) a short (5- to 10-minute), self-guided nature trail explains beavers' habits.

Cypress Swamp (milepost 122.0), a pleasure today, was once a treacherous, mosquito-infested morass for early travelers. A 20-minute self-guided nature walk takes you through the gloom of a tupelo/bald cypress swamp.

The **Ridgeland Crafts Center** displays and sells high quality crafts in a dogtrot log cabin. Members of the Craftsman's Guild of Mississippi have created Choctaw Indian baskets of seamless doubleweave, splint baskets of Mississippi white oak, wooden plates and utensils, handwoven and handscreened clothing, pottery, pewter jewelry, and sturdy, whimsical wooden toys. The Center sponsors free demonstrations (usually on weekends) of basketweaving, Indian dances and games, bread baking in an outdoor stone oven, and glassblowing. *Natchez Trace at Ridgeland (milepost 102.4) tel. 601/856–7456. Restrooms, picnic tables, water fountain. Admission free. Open daily 9–5.*

The parkway is incomplete from milepost 101.5 to 87.0. I–55, I–20, and I–220 are connecting routes. To reach Jackson, follow I–55 south from the Trace.

❻ At its spangled edges, **Jackson** has little to distinguish it, but the state capital becomes increasingly original toward its shady heart. The downtown area has many small museums and most of the city's notable architecture.

The city is named for Andrew Jackson, who was popular with Mississippians long before he became president. As Major General Jackson, he helped negotiate the Treaty of Doak's Stand by which the Choctaw Indians ceded large chunks of Mississippi to the United States, on October 18, 1820. The City of Jackson is the county seat of Hinds County, named for another negotiator, Major General Thomas Hinds, an enterprising and daring hero of the Battle of New Orleans in the War of 1812.

The **Jackson Visitor Information Center** is a small log cabin with anachronistic plate glass windows and a good stock of brochures. *At the Mississippi Agriculture and Forestry Museum, 1150 Lakeland Dr., east of I–55, tel. 601/960–1800. Open weekdays 8:30–5.*

The **Agriculture and Forestry Museum** looks like an old farm marooned in the midst of expanding suburbs, but the city was actually here first. The 10 farm buildings were brought here to stand exactly as they once did in Jefferson Davis County, Mississippi. They are still surrounded by a working farm with fields of corn and cotton, and pastures for sheep, goats, and horses. A crossroads town, similar to small Mississippi towns in the 1920s, has also been assembled. Work goes on in a blacksmith's shop and a cotton gin, meetings are held in the old Masonic Lodge, and the 1897 Epiphany Episcopal church building can be rented for weddings. The General Store sells soft drinks, snacks, and souvenirs. A complete tour of the museum will take about 90 minutes. *1150 Lakeland Dr., Tour Coordinator, Box 1609, Jackson 39215, tel. 601/354–6113. Admission: $3 adults; $1 children 6–18, under 6 free. Open Tues.–Sat. 9–5, Sun. 1–5. Summer hours: Tues.–Sat. 10–7, Sun. 1–5.*

The **Old Capitol Building** sits serenely on Capitol Green, with the **War Memorial Building** (1940) to the north and the **Mississippi Archives Building** (1971) to the south. Begun in 1833 and completed in 1840, the Old Capitol, with its simple columns and elegant proportions, is an excellent example of Greek Revival architecture. The building was restored in 1959–61 for use as the **State Historical Museum.** Capitol Green is a leafy reminder of the checkerboard pattern of alternating squares of buildings and parks recommended by President Thomas Jefferson and proposed for Jackson by Peter A. Vandorn. Vandorn submitted a map and plan for the new city in April 1822. The Vandorn map and other exhibits depicting Mississippi's history are on display in the museum. *100 North State St., tel. 601/354–6222. Admission free. Guided tours available. Open weekdays 8–5, Sat. 9:30–4:30, Sun. 12:30–4:30.*

The **Spengler's Corner Building** (101 N. State St.) is one of Jackson's oldest commercial structures. In 1840 Joseph Spengler opened a tavern here that was popular with legislators, but when the New Capitol was built, the inn closed. Many other businesses occupied the building, which was restored as a law office in 1976. Adjoining it to the north are attractive late 19th- and early 20th-century buildings, with the stucco and bay windows making them primarily Victorian-Italianate in style.

The old **Central Fire Station** (201 N. President St.) is a three-story brick structure completed in 1905; it served as Central

Station No. 1 until 1975. The Jackson Chamber of Commerce restored it in 1978.

City Hall (203 S. President St.) is a white Greek Revival building that has served continuously as Jackson's center of government since its opening in 1847. A Masonic Hall originally occupied the third floor. During the Civil War, City Hall was used as a hospital. Look into the tiny City Council chamber with its black and white floors and heavy red velvet curtains. On the west side of the building is the formal Josh Halbert Garden, with a statue of Andrew Jackson designed in 1968.

In the **Mississippi Arts Center** you will find the **Mississippi Museum of Art** and the **Impressions Gallery.** The museum has changing exhibits and a permanent collection of regional paintings. In the high-tech, hands-on Impressions Gallery, you can create music by walking through beams of light, wave your arms to send colors rippling from your shadow, and more—all in the name of education and art. *201 E. Pascagoula St., tel. 601/960–1515. Admission: $2 adults, $1 children. The Impressions Gallery is free. Museum open Tues.–Fri 10–5, weekends noon–4. Closed Mon.*

Davis Planetarium is the largest planetarium in the Southeast and one of the world's best-equipped, but its shows vary wildly in quality. Seek local guidance or reviews in the *Clarion-Ledger* newspaper. *201 E. Pascagoula St., tel. 601/960–1550. Admission: $3 adults, $2 children 12 and under, $2 senior citizens. Closed Mon.*

The **U.S. Federal Courthouse** (245 E. Capitol St.) is a good example in concrete and sandstone of the streamlined Art Deco style that was popular between the world wars, a time when many Jackson buildings were constructed. This building was completed in 1934 and served as Jackson's post office and as a federal court building until 1988, when a new post office was built. The motifs of eagles, stars, and geometric designs on the exterior are repeated throughout the interior and on the free-standing aluminum light fixtures around the building.

St. Andrew's Episcopal Cathedral (305 E. Capitol St.) offers free musical programs at noon each Wednesday (except in the summer), followed by sandwiches at a nominal fee. The original building is an important example of Gothic Revival architecture enhanced by fine stained glass windows.

The Lamar Life Building, adjacent to St. Andrew's, was designed to complement the cathedral. Although it has lost the alligators that once flanked its doors, it still exhibits other Gothic designs and a crenellated clock tower. The president of Lamar Life during the building's construction (1924–25) was C.W. Welty, father of Eudora Welty, Pulitzer Prize–winning author and lifelong Jackson resident.

The **Mississippi Governor's Mansion** has been continuously in use as the official home of the state's first family since its completion in 1841. At that time, Jackson was a tiny city and this grand Greek Revival dwelling was an optimistic statement. General Sherman presumably lived here during his occupation of Jackson in 1863. The original building was carefully restored in the 1970s and furnished with museum-quality antiques that the state could never have afforded in the 1800s. Invest 30 minutes in the lively tours, strong on legend as well as fact. *300 E. Capitol St., tel. 601/350–3175. Admission free. Tours Tues.–Fri. 9:30–11:30.*

Smith Park is the only public square that remains from the 1822 checkerboard plan of the city. It is the center of the Smith Park Historic District. The park was a grazing area for animals until 1884, when James Smith of Glasgow, Scotland, a former Jacksonian, donated $100 to fence and beautify it, and the park was named for him. It is the setting for a famous short story, "The Winds," by Eudora Welty. The park hosts frequent concerts, festivals, picnics, and art exhibits. A popular "Fridays in Smith Park" program offers noontime entertainment in April and October.

The **Cathedral of St. Peter the Apostle** (203 N. West St.), built 1897–1900, is the third building of the congregation, which organized in 1846. Their first building was burned by Federal troops in 1863, as were many others in the city. Their second church, now in the very center of the downtown area, at the site of the present rectory (123 N. West St.), was criticized for its remoteness from town.

Across Yazoo Street from Smith Park is a Greek Revival building with graceful columns. Constructed of slave-made brick in 1843–44, this simple, elegant structure housed the First Baptist Church until 1893, then a Methodist church, followed by the Central Church of Christ. After several years as an apartment house, it became an office building in 1959, and it now belongs once more to the Methodists.

The **Galloway House** (304 N. Congress St.) is a two-story house built in the Victorian "Second Empire" style. Completed in 1889, this house was built for Methodist Bishop Charles Galloway, a distinguished churchman of international renown. In 1983 it was renovated for use as a law office.

The **New Capitol** sits in Beaux Arts splendor at the junction of Mississippi and North Congress streets, its dome surmounted by a gold-plated copper eagle with a 15-foot wingspan. Completed in 1903 at a cost of $1 million, the Capitol enjoyed a $19-million renovation from 1979 to 1983. It was designed by the German architect Theodore C. Link, who was strongly influenced by the national capitol in Washington, DC. Elaborate architectural details inside the building include a Tiffany window. Ride up in the ornate brass-and-wood elevator if the grand staircase outside daunts you. *High St., tel. 601/359–3114. Admission free. Open weekdays 8–5, Sat. 10–4, Sun. 1–4. Guided tours: weekdays 9, 10, 11, 1:30, 2:30, 3:30.*

Eudora Welty Library (300 N. State St.), the largest public library in Mississippi, is named in honor of the city's famed short-story writer and novelist (*The Ponder Heart, Losing Battles, The Optimist's Daughter*). The library opened in 1986; it has a 42-foot-long circulation desk, handcrafted of African rosewood and curly maple by local craftsman Fletcher Cox. It houses the Mississippi Writer's Room exhibit on Miss Welty, William Faulkner, Tennessee Williams, Margaret Walker Alexander, Ellen Douglas, and many others. *300 N. State St., tel. 601/968–5811. Open Mon.–Thurs. 10–9, Fri. and Sat. 10–6, and (Sept.–May) Sun. 1–5.*

A few Victorian homes stand on North State Street between College Street and Fortification Street, the survivors of the many large houses that lined this street in its heyday as Jackson's best address. The **Morris House** (505 N. State St.) is a Classic Revival house built about 1900. The **Virden-Patton House** (512 N. State St.), built about 1849, was undamaged in the Civil War, suggesting that Union officers may have used it as headquarters. The **Millsaps-Buie House** (628 N. State St.), built in 1888, has been restored as a bed-and-breakfast inn (*see* Lodging, *below*). It was built by Major Reuben Webster Millsaps, the founder of Millsaps College in Jackson. Two doors north is the **Garner Green House** (1910), with an imposing portico of Corinthian columns. This house was moved across the street from its original location and restored in 1988 to become an office building. **Greenbrook Flowers** (c. 1895–97; 705 N. State St.) occupies the former St. Andrew's Episcopal rectory; it has been greatly altered.

Time Out | **Kitchen Delights** (709 Poplar Blvd., tel. 601/353–FOOD) offers takeout food as appealing as its tomato-red building—plate lunches such as tarragon chicken breast over rice and salads such as fresh tomato and mozzarella with basil. Other specialties are crawfish and crabmeat quiche (in season), fresh-baked breads, and raisin-walnut cookies.

The **Manship House** was built about 1857 by Charles H. Manship, the Jackson mayor who surrendered the city to General William Tecumseh Sherman on July 16, 1863. The museum is a careful restoration of a small Gothic Revival–style home with examples of wood graining painted by Manship himself. *420 E. Fortification St. (enter parking area from Congress St.), tel. 601/961–4724. Admission free. Tours: Tues.–Fri. 9–4, weekends 1–4. Closed Mon.*

C.W. Welty and his wife Chestina built the house at **741 North Congress Street** in 1907. Their daughter Eudora was born here in 1909 in the master bedroom on the second floor. Welty used images of this house and neighborhood in many of her literary works, including *The Golden Apples*. It has been restored for use as a law office.

The **Smith Robertson Museum,** the state's only Afro-American museum, has displays that focus on black life in Mississippi throughout its history. The building, which was the first public school for black children in Jackson, has been creatively adapted for use as a museum and meeting place. *528 Bloom St., tel. 601/969–9638. Admission: $1.50 adults, 50¢ children. Open weekdays 9–5, Sat. 9–noon, Sun. 2–5.*

Jackson's oldest house, **The Oaks,** was built by James Hervey Boyd, mayor of Jackson between 1853 and 1858. *823 N. Jefferson St., tel. 601/353–9339. Admission: $1.50. Open Tues.–Sat. 10–4, Sun. 2–4. Closed Mon.*

Jackson is a city of neat, tree-shaded neighborhoods, excellent for walking, jogging, or "Sunday driving," especially the **Belhaven area** bounded by Riverside Drive, I–55, Fortification Street, and North State Street. **Carlisle, Poplar, Peachtree,** and **Fairview streets** are distinguished by fine homes.

Leaving Jackson, follow I–20 westward. You can either pick up the Trace again just past Clinton, or you can drive another 30 miles or so to reach **Vicksburg,** an important Civil War site. **Vicksburg Historic Tours** (1104 Monroe St., Vicksburg 39180, tel. 601/638–8888) gives morning bus tours daily, which cover the Vicksburg National Military Park, the USS *Cairo,* and antebellum homes throughout the city. Afternoon tours, offered Monday through Saturday, drive through the city visiting antebellum homes.

Near the site of present-day Vicksburg, the Spanish established Fort Nogales in 1790. Vicksburg itself began as a mission founded by the Reverend Newitt Vick in 1814. He chose a spot high on the bluffs above a bend in the Mississippi River, a location that would have important consequences for the young city during the War Between the States, when the Confederacy and the Union vied for control of this strategic location. U.S. Grant's men doggedly slogged through canals and bayous in five futile attempts to capture the city, which was called the Gibraltar of the Confederacy because of its almost impregnable defenses. Then, in a series of raids and battles, Grant laid waste the area between Vicksburg and Jackson to the east and Port Gibson to the south. Grant's attacks on Vicksburg were repulsed once again; he then laid siege to the city for 47 days. On July 4, 1863, the city surrendered, giving the Union control of the river and sounding the death knell for the Confederacy.

The suffering at Vicksburg was profound. The land was devastated; today's green and serene countryside was a region of blasted trees and blackened hills. Vicksburg's **National Military Park** marks the spot where the town was under siege. Battle positions are marked, and monuments line the 16-mile drive through the park. The Visitor Center offers orientation programs and exhibits. A guided tour is a good investment, should time and money ($15 for two hours) permit. The self-guided driving tour is well marked, however, and a cassette tape may be rented for $4.50. *Entrance and Visitor Center located on Clay St. (U.S. 80), 1 mi from I–20, Exit 4B, tel. 601/636–0583. 18-min film shown on the hour and half-hour. Admission: $3 per car load. Open daily 8–5; summer 8–6. Closed Christmas Day.*

The Union gunboat, the **USS *Cairo,*** was the first ironclad ever sunk by an electrically-detonated mine. It has been raised from the Yazoo River and restored. A small museum adjacent to it displays Civil War artifacts recovered from the *Cairo. 3201 Clay St., Vicksburg Military Park, tel. 601/636–2199. Admission free. Open daily 9–5, summer 9–6.*

The Vanishing Glory is a multimedia, 15-projector show portraying the sights and sounds of Vicksburg under siege. *Waterfront Theatre, 500 Grove St., tel. 601/634–1863. Admission: $3.50 adults, $2 students. Open daily 10–8.*

Vicksburg's historic homes may have cannonballs imbedded in their walls, but they have been beautifully restored. Worth a visit are **Cedar Grove** (2200 Oak St.), **Balfour House** (Crawford and Cherry Sts.), and the **Martha Vick House** (1300 Grove St.).

A riverboat ride on ***The Spirit of Vicksburg*** will show you the Confederate gun emplacements, the remains of the steamboat *Sprague,* and activity in the port. *Foot of Clay St., tel. 601/634–6059. Admission: $5.50 adults, $2.50 children under 12. 1½-, 2- and 3-hr cruises offered daily. Sightseeing, dinner, and dance cruises.*

In 1894 Coca-Cola was first bottled at the **Biedenharn Candy Company,** which is now a Coke museum. *1107 Washington St., tel. 601/638–6514. Admission: $1.75 adults, $1.25 children under 12. Open Mon.–Sat. 9–5, Sun. 1:30–4:30.*

To return to the Trace, you can either retrace your drive on I–20 or head south on Rte. 61 from Vicksburg about 25 miles to Port Gibson.

If you elect to follow the parkway all the way from Clinton on, you'll pass through **Rocky Springs** (milepost 54.8), a stop for post riders during the early 1800s. General Grant's army camped here on its march to Jackson and Vicksburg during the Civil War. You can camp here, too. It's a first-come, first-served race, especially on weekends, but at least you needn't worry about Confederate sharpshooters. Overhung by ancient trees, the stream ripples and sings like mountain waters. Trails meander through the woods and up a steep hill to a tiny old cemetery and **Rocky Springs Methodist Church** (1837), where services are still held on Sundays.

At milepost 41.5 is a portion of the **Old Trace,** a short section of the original Indian Trace of loess soil (easily eroded and compacted earth). You can park and walk along it for a short way.

Port Gibson is the earliest town to grow up along the Trace that is still in existence. On Church Street is the much-photographed **First Presbyterian Church** (1859), its spire topped by a 12-foot hand pointing heavenward. The church chandeliers came from the old steamboat *Robert E. Lee.* Among the churches and houses along Church Street that have been recently restored are **Gage House** (602 Church St.), 1830, with double galleries and a handsome brick dependency; **Temple Gemiluth Chassed** (706 Church St.), 1892, a synagogue with Moorish Byzantine architecture unique in Mississippi; **St. James Episcopal Church** (808 Church St.), c. 1897, a high Victorian Gothic structure designed by a Boston architect, thus reflecting Massachusetts architecture; **Port Gibson Methodist Church** (901 Church St.), 1860, Romanesque Revival in style; the **Hughes Home** (907 Church St.), 1825, once owned by Henry Hughes, author of the first sociology textbook, and once the residence of black poet Irvin Russell; and **St. Joseph's Catholic Church** (909 Church St.), 1850, Gothic in style, with pointed arches and buttresses. The **Disharoon House** (1002 Church St.), 1830s, one of the finest in Claiborne County, is a 2½-story house with double galleries that have Tuscan colonnettes. **Oak Square** (1207 Church St.), 1850–1906, is now a bed-and-breakfast inn (*see* Lodging, *below*). The Chamber of Commerce is housed in a small 1805 home built by Port Gibson's founder and moved to this site in 1980.

Unless you're a brave and lucky navigator, you'll need a map from the Port Gibson Chamber of Commerce to negotiate the winding roads that plunge through dense forests to historic sites around the city.

Grand Gulf Military Monument commemorates the once-thriving town of Grand Gulf that was left in ruins by Federal gunboats during the Civil War. On a steep hill, the old town site has become a museum with an 1863 cannon, a collection of carriages, an 1820s dogtrot cabin, an old Catholic church, and a Spanish house from the 1790s. *North of Port Gibson off U.S. 61. Rte. 2, Box 389, Port Gibson 39150. Admission: $1.50 adults,*

75¢ children. Open Mon.–Sat. 8–noon and 1–5, Sun. 9–noon and 1–6.

Time Out   Handmade bonnets swing in the breeze on the porch of **The Old Country Store** (U.S. 61, south of Lorman, tel. 601/437–3661), which has been in business since 1890. Its longleaf-pine flooring is jammed with display cases, most installed when the store was built, and you can buy souvenirs, soft drinks, and snacks, including mellow hoop cheese sliced with an antique cutter.

Ask directions at the Old Country Store to the restored **Rodney Presbyterian Church** (about 12 miles southwest of Lorman). The town of **Rodney,** once home to wealthy plantation owners and river merchants, became a ghost town when the Mississippi River shifted its course. Your visit to Rodney will be enhanced by reading Eudora Welty's powerful essay "Some Notes on River Country" and her short story "At the Landing."

Northwest of Lorman, on MS 552, are 23 vine-clad columns that are the romantic ruins of **Windsor,** a huge Greek Revival mansion that was built in 1861 and burned down in 1890.

Just off the Trace near milepost 20 is **Springfield,** a plantation home built in Jefferson County in 1791. Tradition says Andrew Jackson married Rachel Donelson Robards here soon after the house was completed. *Rte. 1, Box 201, Fayette 39069, west of Natchez Trace on MS 553, tel. 601/786–3802. Admission: $4 adults, $2 children under 12. Open spring and summer, daily 10–8; fall, daily 10–6; winter, daily 10:30–5:30.*

Emerald Mound (milepost 10.3) is the second largest Indian mound in the country, covering almost eight acres. It was built around 1300 for religious ceremonies practiced by ancestors of the Natchez Indians. It's a good place to picnic, view a sunset, fly a kite, and let your children run loose.

The Parkway abruptly ends, putting you on U.S. 61 as you near Natchez. Here is the little town of **Washington,** with the buildings of **Historic Jefferson College** meticulously restored. Washington was the capital of the Mississippi Territory from 1802 to 1817, and Jefferson College was chartered in 1802 as the territory's first educational institution. Here Aaron Burr, who served as Thomas Jefferson's vice president, was arraigned for treason, under an oak tree, which still stands. Burr was lionized by Natchez society while he awaited trial. *U.S. 61 at Natchez, tel. 601/442–2901. Admission free. Buildings open Mon.–Sat. 9–5, Sun. 1–5.*

7 **Natchez** is named for the mound-building, sun-worshiping Natchez Indians who lived here, undisturbed, in small villages before the French built Fort Rosalie in 1716. Later the city came under British rule (1763–1779), and the district known today as **Natchez-under-the-Hill** grew up at the Mississippi River landing beneath the bluff. The Spanish took control in 1795; they left their mark on the city by establishing straight streets—which intersect at right angles, atop the bluff—and green parkland that overlooks the river. The United States claimed Natchez by treaty in 1795. The city gave its name to the Natchez Trace and prospered as travelers heading for Nashville passed through with money in their pockets and a willingness to spend it on a rowdy good time.

The real glory days came between 1819 and 1860, when cotton plantations and the bustling river port poured riches into Natchez. Wealthy planters built stylish town houses and ringed the city with opulent plantation homes. Because the city had little military significance, it survived the Civil War almost untouched, but its economy was wrecked. The city entered a decline that actually saved its architectural treasures. No one could afford to tear houses down or even to remodel them. In 1932, the women of Natchez originated the idea of a pilgrimage, which would raise money for preservation. The Natchez Pilgrimage is now held twice a year, three weeks in October and four weeks in March and April. Many houses are open only during Pilgrimage weeks, when crowds flock to see them, but others are open year-round. **Pilgrimage Tours, Inc.** tours 13 antebellum homes year-round and 25 or 30 homes during Pilgrimage. At their headquarters, you can purchase *Natchez: Walking Guide to the Old Town* ($4.95) and *The Great Houses of Natchez* ($35), a coffee-table tome with color photographs and a reliable text; too heavy to carry on a walking tour but a good souvenir. *Canal St. at State St., Box 347, Natchez 39120, tel. 601/446–6631 or 800/647–6742 out-of-state. AE, MC, V. Open daily 8:30–5:30.*

Carriage rides are a fun way to see downtown Natchez. Tours begin at Natchez Pilgrimage Tour Headquarters (Canal St. at State St.) or the Eola Hotel (110 N. Pearl St.). A tour lasts about 30 minutes and costs $7 per person.

Rosalie (1823) established the ideal form of the "Southern mansion" with its white columns, hipped roof, and red bricks. Furnishings purchased for the house in 1858 include a famous Belter parlor set. *100 Orleans St., tel. 601/445–4555. Admission: $4 adults, $2 children over 10. Open daily 9–5.*

Magnolia Hall (c. 1858) was shelled by the Union gunboat *Essex* during the Civil War. The shell reportedly exploded in a soup tureen, scalding several diners. The Greek Revival mansion has scored stucco walls and fluted columns topped with curving Ionic capitals. Note the plaster magnolia blossoms on the parlor ceiling. *215 S. Pearl St., tel. 601/442–7259. Admission: $4 adults, $2 children. Overnight lodgings. Daily tours 9–5.*

Dunleith (1856) stands like a Greek temple on a knoll surrounded by 40 acres of green pastures and wooded bayous (with the culture shock of a Wal-Mart department store across the way). The Greek Revival mansion is completely encircled by 26 columns, each two stories high. It has extensive gardens and restored outbuildings. It was also used as a backdrop for scenes in the film *Huckleberry Finn* (the 1970 version) and *Showboat* (the 1950s version). *84 Homochitto St., tel. 601/446–8500. Bed-and-breakfast inn, tel. 601/446–6631 or 800/647–6742. Admission: $4 adults, $2 children. Open Mon.–Sat. 9–5:30, Sun. 12:30–5:30.*

Longwood (1860–61) is the largest octagonal house in the United States. When the Civil War broke out, Northern workers fled to their homes, preventing the immensely wealthy Dr. Haller Nutt from completing the mansion. Hoping to finish the house at the war's end, Nutt moved his family into the basement, but he died in 1864. Still unfinished, Longwood is now a museum for the Pilgrimage Garden Club. *140 Lower Woodville*

Rd., tel. 601/442–5193. Admission: $4 adults, $2 children. Open daily 9–5.

During Pilgrimage you can tour only those homes that are open on a given day. To the list above try to add **Mount Repose** (Pine Ridge Rd.), **Hawthorne** (Lower Woodville Rd.), **Fair Oaks** (U.S. 61S), **The Parsonage** (305 S. Broadway), and **Elmscourt** (John R. Junkin Dr.).

From Natchez, take Rte. 61 on south to Baton Rouge, a drive of 85 miles.

Shopping

Jackson
Antiques **Bobbie King's** (Woodland Hills Shopping Center, Old Canton Rd. at Duling Ave., tel. 601/362–9803) specializes in heirloom textiles and exhibits them in lavish displays with one-of-a-kind accessories to wear or with which to decorate your home. **Cottage Antiques** (4074 N. State St., tel. 601/362–6510; closed Sat.) carries fine American antiques, accessories, and textiles. **C.W. Fewel III & Co., Antiquarians** (840 N. State St., tel. 601/355–5375) specializes in fine 18th- and 19th-century furnishings and accessories.

Books Books by Mississippi authors and about Mississippi are available from knowledgeable booksellers at **Lemuria** (202 Banner Hall, tel. 601/366–7619). **Choctaw Books** (406 Manship St., tel. 601/352–7281) stocks first editions of Southern writers' works.

Gifts **The Everyday Gourmet** (2905 Old Canton Rd., tel. 601/362–0723) stocks state products, including pecan pie, bread, and biscuit mixes; muscadine jelly; jams and chutneys; cookbooks; fine ceramic tableware; and a complete stock of kitchenware and gourmet foods.

Sports and Outdoor Activities

Golf **Lefleur's Bluff State Park**, 18 holes (Highland Dr., Jackson, tel. 601/960–1436).

Jogging In Jackson: Jog on paths that curve under tall pines and stretch down to a sunny meadow in **Parham Bridges Park** (5055 Old Canton Rd.).

In Natchez: An asphalt road runs about one-and-a-half miles through **Duncan Park** (Duncan St. at Auburn Ave.).

Tennis In Jackson: **Tennis Center South** (2827 Oak Forest Dr., off McDowell Rd., tel. 601/960–1712) and **Parham Bridges Park** (5055 Old Canton Rd., tel. 601/956–1105).

In Natchez: There are courts in **Duncan Park** (Duncan St. at Auburn Ave.).

Dining and Lodging

In Tupelo, Jackson, and Natchez you can find everything from caviar to chitlins. Fine food often comes in casual surroundings. Jackson boasts several elegant restaurants, and Natchez offers plantation breakfasts in antebellum opulence. Tupelo specializes in down-home cooking. If you're eating on the run, Jackson's County Line Road east of I–55 and the East Frontage Roads along I–55N are jammed with fast food joints. Blue plate dinners of fresh Mississippi vegetables are a widely available alternative.

The following dining price categories have been used: *Very Expensive*, over $20; *Expensive*, $15–$20; *Moderate*, $10–$15; *Inexpensive*, under $10.

Jackson has the area's greatest choice of lodgings, but bed-and-breakfasters may be more interested in Natchez, with its number of plantation homes open to guests. **Natchez Pilgrimage Tours** (Canal St. at State St., Box 347, Natchez 39120, tel. 800/647–6742) can answer questions and handle reservations. Contact **Creative Travel** (Canal St. Depot, Natchez 39120, tel. 601/442–3762) about stays in private homes, which are less expensive than the mansions.

The following lodging price categories have been used: *Very Expensive*, over $70; *Expensive*, $50–$70; *Moderate*, $30–$50; *Inexpensive*, under $30.

Jackson
Dining

400 East Capitol. This elegant restaurant occupies a historic building that has been carefully restored on the outside and beautifully adapted for business use within. Signature dishes are regional: Mississippi farm-raised rabbit, quail salad, angel-hair pasta with shrimp. All are subtly seasoned and sauced, and artistically presented. Desserts are rich confections such as Linzer torte or Chocolate Paradise laced with crème Anglais and chocolate sauce. This is food for a special occasion; give yourself plenty of time to enjoy. *400 East Capitol St., tel. 601/355–9671. Jacket and tie recommended. Reservations recommended for lunch and dinner. AE, MC, V. Very Expensive.*

Hal and Mal's Restaurant and Oyster Bar. This vast warehouse has been converted with the help of neon, 1930s antiques and memorabilia, and terrific entertainment. A mixed crowd of artistic, business, and collegiate types comes to this trendy spot for such specialties as grilled fresh fish, grilled chicken, and oyster po'boys. *200 S. Commerce St., tel. 601/948–0888. Dress: casual. Reservations recommended for dinner. MC, V. Closed Sun. Moderate.*

The Mayflower. A perfect 1930s period piece with black and white tile floors, straight-back booths, and formica-topped coffee counter, this café specializes in Greek salads, fresh fish sautéed in lemon butter, and people-watching till all hours. *123 W. Capitol St., tel. 601/355–4122. Dress: casual. No reservations. MC, V. Moderate.*

The Palette. This restaurant, in a gallery in the Mississippi Arts Center, is one of the state's finest lunch spots. Everybody likes the large, light-filled spaces, the art on the white walls, the friendly bustle of the arts community and businesspeople, the piano music, and most of all the carefully prepared and beautifully presented creations of chef Jim Hudson. You may find Mississippi catfish sautéed in pecan butter; fresh vegetable lasagne; or chicken with penne in garlic brie sauce; but the delicacies change frequently. *201 E. Pascagoula St., tel. 601/960–2003. Dress: casual. MC, V. Closed Mon. Inexpensive–Moderate.*

Gridley's. Mexican tile tables and floors enhance small, sunny dining areas. Eat pancakes as big as a plate ($1 each) for breakfast, and spicy barbecued pork and ribs anytime else. *1428 Old Square Rd., tel. 601/362–8600. Dress: casual. No reservations. AE, MC, V. Inexpensive.*

The People's Cafe. Crammed with artsy memorabilia, this tiny café packs in Jackson's downtown crowd with its amazing lunch buffet. The country cooking on Monday and Wednesday is better than Mom's or almost anybody's; Tuesday, Italian specialities; Thursday, Mexican; and Friday, seafood. All are served with fresh local vegetables and homemade breads, soups, and desserts. A Jackson tradition, the People's Cafe is now run by a fine chef who not only upgrades Mississippi blue-plate fare to gourmet standards, but also takes time to make friends of his customers. *232 W. Capitol St., tel. 601/353–7100. Dress: casual. No reservations. MC, V. No dinner. Inexpensive.*

Lodging **Millsaps-Buie House.** This Queen Anne–style home, with its corner turret and tall-columned porch, was built in 1888 for Jackson financier and philanthropist Major Reuben Webster Millsaps, founder of Millsaps College in Jackson; it is listed on the National Register of Historic Places. Restored as a B&B in 1987, its guest rooms are individually decorated with antiques. An attentive staff serves morning coffee and pastries in your room or in the Victorian dining room. *628 N. State St., 39202, tel. 601/352–0221. 11 rooms, each with telephone and private bath. AE, DC, MC, V. Expensive–Very Expensive.*

Holiday Inn Downtown. This convention hotel with cheerful guest rooms (those on the east side overlook the Cathedral of St. Peter the Apostle and Smith Park) has a convenient downtown location. *200 E. Amite St., 39201, tel. 601/969–5100 or 800/ HOLIDAY. 358 rooms. Facilities: restaurant, pool, lounge. AE, DC, MC, V. Expensive.*

Ramada Renaissance Hotel. This new high-rise convention motel is sleekly contemporary. *1001 County Line Rd., 39211, tel. 601/957–2800 or 800/272–6232. 300 rooms. Facilities: airport courtesy van, restaurant, lobby bar. AE, DC, MC, V. Expensive.*

Edison Walthall Hotel. The cornerstone and huge brass mailbox near the elevators are almost all that remain of the original Walthall Hotel. The dismal motel that occupied the site next to it was transformed into the new hotel. The marble floors, gleaming brass, a panelled library/writing room, and cozy bar almost fool you into thinking this is a restoration. *225 E. Capitol St., 39201, tel. 601/948–6161 or 800/228–9822. AE, DC, MC, V. 211 rooms. Facilities: pool, Jacuzzi, transportation to airport. Moderate–Expensive.*

Natchez Dining **Cock of the Walk.** The famous original of a regional franchise, this shanty overlooking the Mississippi River specializes in fried catfish fillets, fried dill pickles, hush puppies, mustard greens, and coleslaw. Waiters in red long john shirts serve cornbread to the constant strum of banjos. *15 Silver St., Natchez-Under-the-Hill, tel. 601/446–8920. Dress: casual. AE, MC, V. Moderate.*

Natchez Landing. The porch tables provide a view of the Mississippi River, which is at its very best when both the *Delta Queen* and *Mississippi Queen* steamboats dock. Specialties are barbecue (pork ribs, chicken, beef) and fried and grilled catfish. *11 Silver St., Natchez-Under-the-Hill, tel. 601/442–6639. Dress: casual. AE, MC, V. Closed Sun. Moderate.*

Ramada Hilltop Motel Restaurant. Don't be discouraged by this motel setting; the spacious dining room has a beautiful view. Try the noon buffet or the oyster soup and prime rib on Wednesday night. *130 John R. Junkin Dr., tel. 601/446–6311. Jacket and tie required. Reservations recommended at night. AE, MC, V. Moderate.*

Scrooge's. This old storefront once housed the studio of Norman of Natchez (a well-known local photographer) and the Tango Tearoom, where locals learned to dance for a quarter. The restaurant has a pub atmosphere downstairs and a more subdued intimate ambience upstairs. The menu includes red beans and rice, and mesquite-grilled chicken or shrimp with angelhair pasta. *315 Main St., tel. 601/446–9922. Dress: casual. AE, MC, V. Moderate.*

Annex Tea Room. The tearoom is airy, and bright with Natchez chitchat and gossip. Specialties are chicken salad, gumbo, sandwiches on homemade bread, and homebaked cakes and pies. *209 Franklin St., tel. 601/446–6544. Dress: casual. Reservations for groups only. MC, V. Closed Sun. Inexpensive.*

The Fare. The red, white, and blue color scheme of this Victorian café creates a carnival air. The menu includes homemade soups, sandwiches, beignets (French doughnuts), and café au lait. *109 N. Pearl St., tel. 601/442–5299. Dress: casual. No reservations. MC, V. Inexpensive.*

The Parlor. This parlor is a comfortable mishmash of unmatching tables and chairs, racks of magazines, jazz posters, and an enclosed patio with picnic tables and umbrellas. Mexican food is a specialty (the fajitas are fresh); so is grilled catfish with vegetables and seafood pasta. *116 S. Canal St., tel. 601/446–8511. Dress: casual. Reservations recommended. AE, MC, V. Closed Sun. Inexpensive.*

Lodging **The Burn.** This elegant 1832 mansion offers a seated plantation breakfast, private tour of the home, and swimming pool. *712 N. Union St., 39120, tel. 601/445–8566 or 601/442–1344. 6 bedrooms, all with private baths. AE, MC, V. Very Expensive.*

Monmouth. This plantation mansion (c. 1818) was owned by Mississippi governor John A. Quitman from 1826 until his death in 1858. Guest rooms are decorated with tester beds and antiques. The grounds are tastefully landscaped, with a New Orleans–style courtyard, a pond, and a gazebo. Plantation breakfast and a tour of home included. *36 Melrose, 39120, tel. 800/828–4531. 4 bedrooms, 1 suite in main house; 5 bedrooms in servants' quarters; 4 in garden cottages. AE, MC, V. Expensive–Very Expensive.*

Dunleith. Stately, colonnaded Dunleith is the most popular bed-and-breakfast inn in Natchez. The inn reserves a wing for overnight guests and serves them breakfast in their rooms or across the herb garden in the former poultry house. A Southern breakfast and a tour of the house are included. *84 Homochitto St., 39120, tel. 601/446–6631. 12 guest rooms with private bath. AE, MC, V. Moderate–Very Expensive.*

Eola Hotel. This beautifully restored 1920s hotel has a tiny formal lobby and small guest rooms with antique reproduction furniture. Request rooms in the Eola guest house across the street if you want more space, some antiques, and a balcony. Its restaurant was once a liability but is now under new management. *110 N. Pearl St., 39120, tel. 601/445–6000 or 800/821–3721. 122 rooms. AE, DC, MC, V. Moderate.*

Ramada Hilltop. The typical motel decor is forgotten if your room overlooks the Mississippi River. *130 John R. Junkin Dr., 39120, tel. 601/446–6311 or 800/272–6232. AE, DC, MC, V. Moderate.*

Port Gibson **Oak Square.** Constructed around 1850, this home, with its nu-
Lodging merous outbuildings and lovely gardens, occupies an entire block on historic Church Street. Now a bed-and-breakfast inn,

it offers a full southern breakfast. *1207 Church Street, Port Gibson 39130, tel. 601/437–4350. 8 rooms. AE, MC, V. Expensive–Very Expensive.*

Tupelo
Dining

Chez Bernard. In a new brick building with white columns, classic French cuisine is prepared by a Swiss chef who was formerly with the Drake Hotel in New York. The dining room, with natural moldings, a brick wine rack, green marbleized wallpaper, and European paintings, is lighted by 8-foot French windows and a crystal chandelier. To begin, you might try the Parma ham with melon or the pâté in pastry; then there's sliced duck breast in a Pinot noir sauce or a delicate fillet of sole *bonne femme*. *150 S. Industrial Rd., tel. 601/841–0777. Jacket required. Reservations required at dinner. AE, MC, V. Closed Sat. lunch and Sun. Very Expensive.*

Jefferson Place. This austere 19th-century house is lively inside, with red-checked tablecloths and bric-a-brac. The place is popular with the college crowd; short orders and steaks are the specialties. *823 Jefferson St., tel. 601/844–8696. Dress: casual. AE, MC, V. Closed Sun. Expensive.*

Papa Vanelli's Pizzaria. Family pictures and scenes of Greece decorate the walls of this comfortably nondescript restaurant where tables wear traditional red-and-white checkered tablecloths. Specialties (all homemade) include pizza with 10 toppings, lasagna, moussaka, manicotti, and Greek salad. Vanelli's own bakery produces breads, strudels, and pastries. *120 N. Gloster, tel. 601/844–4410. Dress: casual. AE, D, MC, V. Inexpensive.*

Lodging

Executive Inn. Guest rooms in this large, contemporary hotel are plain and functional, yet new and clean. *1011 N. Gloster, 38801, tel. 601/841–2222. 119 rooms. Facilities: indoor pool, whirlpool, sauna, cable TV. AE, DC, MC, V. Moderate–Expensive.*

Ramada Inn. This modern three-story hotel caters to business travelers and conventions as well as families. Dancing nightly (except Sunday) in Bogart's Lounge. Breakfast and lunch buffets are served. *854 N. Gloster, 38801, tel. 601/844–4111 or 800/272–6232. 230 rooms, 10 executive suites. Facilities: outdoor pool, in-room movies. AE, DC, MC, V. Moderate.*

Best Western Trace Inn. This old, rustic inn on 15 acres near the Natchez Trace offers neat rooms and friendly service. *3400 W. Main St., 38801, tel. 601/842–5555. 165 rooms. Facilities: in-room movies, playground, pool, restaurant, courtesy car. AE, MC, V. Inexpensive–Moderate.*

Vicksburg
Dining

Delta Point. This large, elegant restaurant sits high on the bluff, and its picture windows provide excellent views of the Mississippi River. Service is impeccable, the menu varied and ambitious, and the food sometimes erratic. China, crystal, and flowers contribute to the gracious mood. Specialties are beef tenderloin stuffed with marinated Bing cherries; shrimp and fettuccine; and cherries jubilee and bananas Foster. *4155 Washington St., tel. 601/636–5317. Jacket and tie required. Reservations recommended. Sun. brunch. AE, DC, MC, V. Expensive.*

Maxwell's. This candlelit place looks neither tacky nor chic; however, its food is consistently well prepared. It serves a homestyle noon buffet (baked ham and raisin sauce; chicken livers with mushrooms) and goes fancy at night with such specialties as oysters Rockefeller, stuffed mushrooms, fresh redfish with shrimp sauce, and prime rib. Live entertainment. *4207 Clay St., tel. 601/636–1344 or 601/636–9656. Dress: casual. Reservations recommended. Closed Sun. AE, MC, V. Expensive.*

Lodging **Anchuca.** Guests stay in the slave quarters or a turn-of-the-century cottage of this antebellum mansion. Rooms are decorated in period antiques and fabrics. A plantation breakfast and house tour are included. *1010 1st East St., 39180, tel. 601/ 636–4931 or 800/262–4822. 9 rooms, each with private bath. Facilities: pool, hot tub. AE, MC, V. Very Expensive.*

Cedar Grove. Guest rooms are furnished with antiques in this 1840 Greek Revival mansion. Service is erratic, staff noisy, but the gaslit surroundings more than make up for lapses. Plantation breakfast and tour of home included. *2300 Washington, tel. 601/636–2800, 800/448–2820, or 800/862–1300 in MS. Facilities: pool. AE, MC, V. Very Expensive.*

Duff Green Mansion. This 1856 mansion was used as a hospital during the Civil War. Each guest room is individually decorated with antiques, including half-tester beds. A large, Southern-style breakfast and a tour of the home are included. *1114 1st East St., 39180, tel. 601/638–6662. 5 rooms, 1 suite, all with private baths. Facilities: pool. AE, MC, V. Very Expensive.*

Comfort Inn. Functional, clean rooms in a new motel. *I–20 Frontage Road S., 39180, tel. 601/634–8607 or 800/228–5150. 50 rooms. Facilities: pool, exercise room, whirlpool, sauna. AE, DC, MC, V. Inexpensive–Moderate.*

Nightlife

Jackson **Hal and Mal's** (200 S. Commerce St., tel. 601/948–0888) is the city's most popular night spot. There's live entertainment at **The Dock** (Main Harbor Marina at Ross Barnett Reservoir, tel. 601/856–7765) Thursday–Sunday as people step off their boats to dine, drink, and listen to the rock and roll and rhythm and blues. The restaurant, which sits on a pier, generally attracts a young crowd, but draws an older one on Sundays.

Poet's (1855 Lakeland Dr., tel. 601/982–9711) presents food, drink, and a jazz trio in an old-fashioned atmosphere, created by antiques, old signs, pressed tin ceiling, and wooden floors.

Shucker's (1216½ N. State St., tel. 601/353–7536) is a tiny room with neon lights, pool table, and outdoor deck. Blues and classic rock are performed by local bands on Friday and Saturday; drinks, po'boys, and oysters are served.

Natchez **The River City Cafe and Lounge,** at the Briars, is a rustic pavilion on the highest point of the Mississippi River between St. Louis and New Orleans. The lounge is ideal for drinks at sunset.

Pearl Street Cellar (211 N. Pearl St., tel. 601/446–5022) is popular with the young set, but draws a mixed crowd when its bar hosts a jazz combo.

Under-the-Hill Saloon (33 Silver St., tel. 601/446–8023) features live entertainment on weekends in one of the few original buildings left in Natchez-Under-the-Hill.

Vicksburg **Maxwell's** (4207 Clay St., tel. 601/636–1344 or 601/636–9656) offers live entertainment in its lounge. **Miller's Still,** in the Velchoff Corner Restaurant (1101 Washington St., tel. 601/

638–8661), opens at 11 AM Mon.–Sat. and at 4 PM Sun., with live entertainment Thurs.–Sat.

Baton Rouge and Plantation Country

Legend has it that in 1699 French explorers observed that a red stick planted in the ground on a high bluff overlooking the Mississippi served as a boundary between two Indian tribes. Sieur d'Iberville, leader of the expedition, noted *le baton rouge*—the red stick—in his journal, and *voila!* Baton Rouge.

This state capital is the city from which Huey P. Long ruled the state and also the site of his assassination. Even today, more than half a century after Long's death, legends abound of the colorful, cunning, and controversial governor and U.S. senator.

The parishes to the north of Baton Rouge are quiet and bucolic, with gently rolling hills, high bluffs, and historic districts. John James Audubon lived in West Feliciana Parish in 1821, tutoring local children and painting 80 of his famous bird studies. In both terrain and traits, this region is more akin to North Louisiana than to South Louisiana—which is to say, the area is very Southern.

Louisiana is graced with many stately mansions. But the area designated Plantation Country begins with a reservoir of fine old homes north of Baton Rouge that cascades all the way down the Great River Road to New Orleans.

Numbers in the margin correspond to points of interest on the Baton Rouge and Plantation Country map.

❶ Soon after you cross the border between Mississippi and Louisiana, about 60 miles south of Natchez on U.S. 61, is **St. Francisville,** which has been described as a town two miles long and two yards wide. Much of the long, skinny town is listed on the National Register of Historic Places. Stop by the **West Feliciana Historical Society Information Center** for advice and information. *364 Ferdinand St., St. Francisville, tel. 504/635–6330. Open Mon.–Sat. 9–4, Sun. 1–4.*

Allow plenty of time for your visit to **Rosedown Plantation and Gardens.** This house and its surroundings bring on a bad attack of hyperbole. Suffice it to say that the opulent house dates from 1835, is beautifully restored, and nestles in 28 acres of exquisite formal gardens. *LA 10, just off U.S. 61, tel. 504/635–3332. Admission: $5 to the house and gardens, $3 for the gardens only. Open Mar.–Oct., daily 9–5; Nov.–Feb., daily 10–4. Closed Christmas Eve and Christmas Day.*

A few miles south of St. Francisville, off U.S. 61, you'll find the 100-acre **Audubon State Commemorative Area,** where Audubon did a major portion of his "Birds of America" studies. The three-story Oakley Plantation House on the grounds is where Audubon tutored the young Eliza Pirrie. *LA 956, tel. 504/635–3739. Admission to the park and plantation: $2. Grounds open Apr. 1–Sept. 30, daily 9–7; Oct. 1–Mar. 31, daily 9–5. Oakley open daily 9–5. Closed Christmas, Thanksgiving, and New Year's Day.*

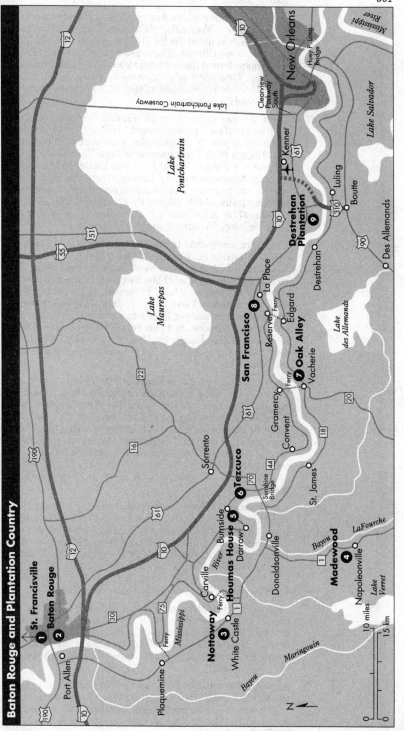

Baton Rouge and Plantation Country

The Myrtles bills itself as America's Most Haunted House and hosts Mystery Weekends, Halloween Tours, and such. The Myrtles is best noted for its 110-foot gallery with Wedgwood blue cast-iron grillwork. The house was built around 1796, and has elegant formal parlors with rich molding and faux marble paneling. *5 mi north of St. Francisville on U.S. 61, tel. 504/ 635-6277. Admission: $4.50 adults, $2.50 children. Open daily 9-5. Closed Christmas.*

There are two routes from St. Francisville to Baton Rouge. Civil War buffs will probably want to follow U.S. 61 to the capital; 10 miles past St. Francisville, you can stop off to visit the **Port Hudson State Commemorative Area.** The 650-acre park is the site of a fiercely fought Civil War battle, and the longest siege in American military history. There are high viewing towers, gun trenches, and, on a more peaceful note, seven miles of hiking trails. *756 W. Plains-Port Hudson Rd. (U.S. 61), tel. 504/654-3775. Admission $2. Open Wed.-Sun. 9-5. Closed Thanksgiving, Christmas, and New Year's Day.*

For a more scenic drive to Baton Rouge, board the ferry ($1 per car) just outside St. Francisville for a breezy ride across the Mississippi. Pick up LA 1 in New Roads and head south. You'll be driving right alongside **False River,** which was an abandoned riverbed that became a lake. In contrast to the muddy Mississippi, the waters of False River are dark blue. This is an excellent fishing area, and you'll see long piers and fishing boats tied up all along the route. Just past Port Allen, pick up I-10 for the bridge into Baton Rouge. Or, if you want to skip Baton Rouge, continue on LA 1, the Great River Road between Baton Rouge and New Orleans.

❷ Start your tour of **Baton Rouge** at the Visitors Information Center in the lobby of the **State Capitol Building.** Armed with maps and brochures, you can take a tour of the first floor, which includes the spot where Huey Long was shot. This building is America's tallest state capitol, standing 34 stories tall. There is an observation deck on the 27th floor that affords a spectacular view of the Mississippi River and the city. *State Capitol Dr., tel. 504/342-7317. Admission free. Open daily 8-4:30; last tour at 4 PM. Closed Thanksgiving, Christmas, New Year's, and Mardi Gras.*

A museum in the **Pentagon Barracks** has exhibits that acquaint visitors with the Capitol complex. The barracks were originally built in 1823-24 to quarter U.S. Army personnel, and when Louisiana State University moved from Pineville to Baton Rouge in 1869, it was located in these buildings. *Riverside North on the State Capitol grounds, tel. 504/342-1866. Admission free. Open Tues.-Sat. 10-4, Sun. 1-4. Closed Christmas, Thanksgiving, New Year's Day, Easter, and Mardi Gras.*

Only one battle of the American Revolution was fought outside the 13 original colonies, and it was fought on these capitol grounds. At press time, one of the historic buildings, the **Old Arsenal Museum** (tel. 504/387-2464), a heavy-duty structure dating from about 1835, was being restored. It's scheduled to open in late 1991.

Although the restored **Old State Capitol** contains no exhibits, the building itself is worth seeing. When it was completed in 1849 it was to some a masterpiece, to others a monstrosity. In any case, the Gothic Revival castlelike structure stands on a bluff; its name is on the list of National Historic Landmarks. At press time plans had been announced for a museum of Louisiana politics in the old building, and parts of it will be closed while work is in progress. *150 North Blvd., tel. 504/342–8211. Admission free. Open Tues.–Sat. 9:30–4.*

Across the street from the Old State Capitol is the **Louisiana Arts & Science Center Riverside Museum,** housed in an old railroad station. There is a fine arts museum with changing exhibits, an Egyptian tomb exhibit, restored trains from the 1890s to the 1950s, and a Discovery Depot with a children's art gallery and workshop. *100 S. River Rd., tel. 504/344–9463. Admission: $1.50 adults; 75¢ students, senior citizens, and children 6–12; children under 6 free. Museum does not charge admission on Sat. 10–noon. Open Tues.–Fri. 10–3, Sat. 10–4, Sun. 1–4. Closed Thanksgiving, Christmas, New Year's Day, and Mardi Gras.*

The *Samuel Clemens Riverboat* gives one-hour narrated tours of Baton Rouge harbor and evening supper cruises. *Departures from Florida Blvd. at the River, tel. 504/381–9606. Admission: $5 adults, $3 children under 12. 1-hr tours 10 AM, noon, and 2 PM; Apr.–Aug., daily; Sept.–Nov. and Mar., Wed.–Sun.; call for schedule Dec.–Feb. Closed Thanksgiving and Christmas.*

The **Louisiana Arts & Science Center** is in the restored Old Governor's Mansion, which was built in 1930 during Huey Long's administration. Rooms in the antiques-filled house are dedicated to the memories of Louisiana governors. *502 North Blvd., tel. 504/344–9463. Admission: $1.50 adults; 75¢ students, senior citizens, and children 6–12. Open Sat. 10–4, Sun. 1–4. Closed Thanksgiving, Christmas, New Year's, and Mardi Gras.*

Time Out At the **Blackforest** (321 North Blvd., tel. 504/334–0059) you can get German food, deli sandwiches, plate lunches, and imported beer.

About 1½ miles from the center of town, **Magnolia Mound Plantation** is an early 19th-century raised cottage furnished with American Federal antiques and Louisiana artifacts. On Tuesday, Thursday, and Saturday from October through April cooking demonstrations are conducted in the outbuildings. *2161 Nicholson Dr., tel. 504/343–4955. Admission: $3.50 adults, $2.50 senior citizens, $1.50 students, 75¢ children. Open Tues.–Sat. 10–4, Sun. 1–4. Closed Thanksgiving, Christmas, New Year's Day, Easter, and Mardi Gras.*

Continuing south on Nicholson Drive you'll come to **Louisiana State University.** LSU was founded in Pineville in 1860 as the Louisiana State Seminary of Learning and Military Academy. Its president was William Tecumseh Sherman, who resigned when war broke out and four years later made his famous march through Georgia. The 200-acre campus has several museums of interest, as well as Indian Mounds that are of particular interest to archaeologists and archaeology buffs.

Baton Rouge's other major institution of higher learning is **Southern University,** about five miles north of town on U.S. 61. Founded in 1880, Southern U. is the nation's largest predominantly black university.

3 Sixteen miles south of Baton Rouge on LA 1 is **Nottoway,** the South's largest plantation home, built in 1859 by famed architect Henry Howard. The Greek Revival/Italianate mansion has 64 rooms filled with antiques and is especially noted for its white ballroom, which has original crystal chandeliers and hand-carved Corinthian columns. Several of the rooms are open for overnighters. Before you leave the lush grounds of Nottoway, walk across the road and go up on the levee for a splendid view of Old Man River. *LA 1, 2 mi north of White Castle, tel. 504/545–2730. Admission: $8 adults, $3 children under 12. Open daily 9–5. Closed Christmas Day.*

4 Henry Howard was also the architect for **Madewood,** a magnificent 21-room Greek Revival mansion with double galleries and white columns. *A Woman Called Moses,* starring Cicely Tyson, was filmed in the house. This, too, is an elegant antebellum bed-and-breakfast. *LA 308, 15 mi south of Donaldsonville, tel. 504/524–1988. Admission: $5 adults, $4 students, $3 children under 12; 10% discount for senior citizens. Open daily 10–5. Closed Christmas and Thanksgiving.*

5 On the East Bank of the River, docents in antebellum garb guide you through **Houmas House,** a Greek Revival masterpiece famed for its three-story spiral staircase. *Hush Hush, Sweet Charlotte,* with Bette Davis and Olivia de Haviland, was filmed here, as was the pilot for the TV series "Longstreet." *LA 942, ½ mi off LA 44 in Burnside, tel. 504/522–2262. Admission: $6.50 adults, $4.50 ages 13–17, $3.25 children 6–12. Open Feb.–Oct., daily 10–5; Nov.–Jan., daily 10–4. Closed Thanksgiving, Christmas Day, and New Year's Day.*

6 Built in 1835, **Tezcuco** is a graceful raised cottage with delicate wrought-iron galleries, ornate friezes, an antiques shop, and overnight cottages. *LA 44, about 7 mi above Sunshine Bridge, tel. 504/562–3929. Admission: $5 adults, $2.50 children 4–12, $3.50 students and senior citizens. Open Mar.–Oct., daily 10–5; Nov.–Feb., daily 10–4. Closed Thanksgiving, Christmas, and New Year's Day.*

7 **Oak Alley** is also a movie star, having served as the setting for the Don Johnson–Cybil Shepherd TV remake of *The Long Hot Summer.* The house dates from 1839, and the 28 gnarled and arching live oaks trees that give the house its name were planted in the early 1700s. There is a splendid view of those trees from the upper gallery. *LA 18, 6 mi upriver of the Gramercy-Vacherie ferry, tel. 504/523–4351. Admission: $6 adults, $3 ages 3–13. Open Mar.–Oct., daily 9:30–5:30; Nov.–Feb., daily 9–5. Closed Christmas, Thanksgiving, and New Year's Day.*

8 **San Francisco,** completed in 1856, is an elaborate "Steamboat Gothic" house noted for its ornate millwork and ceiling frescoes. *LA 44 near Reserve, tel. 504/535–2341. Admission: $5.50 adults, $3.75 students, $2.50 children 6–11. Open daily 10–4. Closed Thanksgiving, Christmas, New Year's Day, Mardi Gras, and Easter.*

9 **Destrehan Plantation** is the oldest plantation left intact in the lower Mississippi Valley. The simple West Indies–style house, dating from 1787, is typical of the homes built by the earliest planters in the region. *9999 River Rd., tel. 504/764–9315. Admission: $5 adults, $4 students and senior citizens, $3 children*

6–11. Open daily 9:30–4. Closed Thanksgiving, Christmas, New Year's Day, Mardi Gras, and Easter.

Destrehan is about an hour's drive from New Orleans, and U.S. 61 will take you right into the city.

Sports and Outdoor Activities

Golf   Baton Rouge boasts three 18-hole championship golf courses that are open to the public: **Santa Maria Golf Course** (19301 Old Perkins Rd., tel. 504/292–9667); **Howell Park** (5511 Winbourne Ave., Baton Rouge, tel. 504/357–9292); and **Webb Park** (1351 Country Club Dr., Baton Rouge, tel. 504/383–4919). St. Francisville has a new 18-hole Arnold Palmer course that visitors are welcome to play (**The Bluffs,** LA 965, six miles east of U.S. 61, tel. 504/634–5222).

Hiking   There are seven miles of hiking trails in the **Port Hudson State Commemorative Area** (756 W. Plains-Port Hudson Rd. [Hwy 61], tel. 504/654–3775).

Swimming   **Blue Bayou Water Park** (18142 Perkins Rd. off I–10, Baton Rouge, tel. 504/753–3333) splashed on the scene in 1990 with a wave pool and all sorts of flumes, sleds, and slides—including a corkscrew critter called the Serpentine, a Lazy River, and a 7-story Tower slide. For the little ones there's a 7,000-square-foot Pollywog pool. There's also a restaurant and a fast-food facility. *Admission: $11.95 for anyone over 4 feet, $9.95 for anyone under 4 feet. Open mid-May–Labor Day; hours vary.*

Tennis   You can lob and volley at **City Park** (1440 City Park Ave., Baton Rouge, tel. 504/344–4501 or 923–2792); **Highland Road Park** (Highland and Amiss Rd., Baton Rouge, tel. 504/766–0247); and **Independence Park** (549 Lobdell Ave., Baton Rouge, tel. 504/923–1792).

Dining and Lodging

Cajun is *the* way to go here. Dine and dance at the new Mulate's in Baton Rouge, or try the po'boys at The Cabin in Burnside.

The following dining price categories have been used: *Very Expensive,* over $35; *Expensive,* $25–$35; *Moderate,* $15–$20; *Inexpensive,* under $15.

Staying on the plantation is your best bet for lodging in South Louisiana, but if you are stuck in the city or are budget conscious, you'll have no problem finding suitable accommodations.

The following lodging price categories have been used: *Very Expensive,* over $120; *Expensive,* $90–$120; *Moderate,* $50–$90; *Inexpensive,* under $50.

Baton Rouge   **Chalet Brandt.** Swiss-born Charles Brandt has created an Al-
Dining   pine house that lacks only the Alps. The elegant dining rooms gleam with brass and china collectibles from around the globe, and many of the edibles are also imported. Brandt's motto is "Continental cuisine with Louisianians in mind." There is a changing menu that might include fresh poached Norwegian salmon with mousseline sauce; veal tournedos topped with foie gras, truffles, and madeira sauce; or speckled trout with crawfish Cardinale sauce. *7655 Old Hammond Hwy. tel. 504/927–*

6040. Jacket and tie required. Reservations suggested. AE, DC, MC, V. Expensive.

Mike Anderson's. Former LSU football player Mike Anderson believes in serving up enormous portions and almost single-handedly supports the folks who manufacture doggie bags. His rustic, barnlike restaurant features the freshest of Louisiana seafood, with specialties like trout Norman (fried trout filet with crabmeat au gratin). Don't pass up the fried onion rings. Lowly cole slaw is elevated here to heavenly realms. *1031 W. Lee Dr., tel. 504/766-7823. Dress: casual. AE, MC, V. Closed Thanksgiving, Christmas, New Year's Day, Easter. Inexpensive.*

★ **Mulate's.** A rustic place with cypress beams, red-checkered cloths, and artwork by Cajun artist George Rodrigue, Mulate's offers shrimp and oyster en brochette, a Super Seafood Platter, and live Cajun music every night. *8322 Bluebonnet Rd., tel. 504/767-4794 or 800/634-9880. Dress: casual. AE, MC, V. Inexpensive.*

Lodging **Crown Sterling Suites.** Built in 1985 as an Embassy Suites Hotel, this centrally located property has a southwestern motif. Each two-room suite, with complexions of peaches and greens, has a galley kitchen with microwave, and custom-made mahogany furniture. The complimentary full breakfast is cooked to order. *4914 Constitution Ave., 70808, tel. 504/924-6566 or 800/ EMBASSY. 224 suites. Facilities: free airport shuttle, cable TV, lounge, coffee shop, restaurant, free parking, handicapped facilities, laundry, indoor pool, sauna, steam room. AE, DC, MC, V. Expensive.*

Baton Rouge Hilton. This Hilton bills itself as a city resort hotel and boasts that it's the only capital city hotel with 24-hour room service. Centrally located at I–10 and College Drive, the tall, skinny white high rise offers a no-smoking floor and half a floor with facilities for the handicapped. There are traditional furnishings throughout, in hues of plum and blue. *5500 Hilton Ave., 70808, tel. 504/924-5000, 800/621-5116, or 800/221-2584 in LA. 305 rooms. Facilities: free airport shuttle, cable TV, lounge, coffee shop, restaurant, concierge, free parking, laundry, lighted tennis courts, sauna, health club, jogging track. AE, DC, MC, V. Moderate-Expensive.*

★ **Marriott's Residence Inn.** One- and two-bedroom suites with dens, dining rooms, wood-burning fireplaces, and kitchens equipped with everything right down to popcorn poppers. The two-bedroom suites come with Jacuzzis. There are traditional furnishings in the centrally located hotel, which opened in 1984. *5522 Corporate Blvd., 70808, tel. 504/927-5630 or 800/ 331-3131. 80 suites. Facilities: cable TV, concierge, free parking, handicap facilities, laundry service, spa/health club, outdoor pool. AE, DC, MC, V. Moderate.*

Burnside **The Cabin.** This rustic 150-year-old slave cabin-cum-restaurant
Dining has yellowed newspapers covering the walls and ancient tools
★ dangling here and there. Crawfish stew and crawfish étouffée are featured, but there are po'boys, steaks, and burgers, too. *Junction of LA 44 and 22, tel. 504/473-3007. Dress: casual. AE, MC, V. Closed Christmas, Thanksgiving, New Year's. Moderate.*

Napoleonville **Madewood.** Expect gracious Southern hospitality in this an-
Lodging tiques-filled Greek Revival mansion, which is both elegant and cozy. The $159 price for a room in the main house includes not

only breakfast but wine and cheeses in the parlor, followed by a candlelit gourmet dinner in the stately dining room. There are also suites in restored outbuildings on the plantation grounds ($89 per couple including Continental breakfast, $159 for full breakfast and dinner). *New Orleans Office: 420 Julia St., New Orleans 70130, tel. 504/524–1988 or 800/375–7151 in LA. Napoleonville Office: Rte. 2, Box 478, Napoleonville 70390, tel. 504/369–7151. All rooms with private bath. AE, V. Closed Christmas and Thanksgiving. Expensive.*

White Castle **Nottoway.** A massive Italianate mansion with 64 rooms filled
Lodging with antique treasures, this is reputed to be one of the most stunning B&Bs in the nation. Thirteen of its elegant rooms are let to overnight guests, who are welcomed with complimentary sherry upon arrival. Your first breakfast of croissants, juice, and coffee is served in your room; second breakfast is a full feast in the Magnolia Room. *2 mi north of White Castle on LA 1, White Castle 70788, tel. 504/545–2730. All rooms have private bath. AE, DC, MC, V. Closed Christmas Day. Expensive–Very Expensive.*

The Arts

The **Baton Rouge Little Theatre** (7155 Florida Blvd., tel. 504/924–6496) has been presenting musicals, comedies, and dramas for more than 40 years.

Guest soloists perform frequently with the **Baton Rouge Symphony Orchestra** (Centroplex Theatre for the Performing Arts, tel. 504/387–6166). LSU's annual **Festival of Contemporary Music** (tel. 504/388–5118), which takes place in February, is more than 40 years old.

Nightlife

Baton Rouge The new **Mulate's** (8322 Bluebonnet Rd., tel. 504/767–4794) in
Cajun Clubs Baton Rouge is a chip off the famed old Breaux Bridge block.

Country/Western The **Texas Club** (456 N. Donmoor Ave., tel. 504/926–0867) is the hot spot for top-name country artists.

Bars and An LSU crowd congregates at the **Bayou** (124 W. Chimes St.,
Nightclubs tel. 504/346–1765), where there is occasional live music Saturday night. The **Bengal** (2286 Highland Rd., tel. 504/387–5571) draws a young disco crowd to its dance floor, game room, and patio. Live bands and DJs alternate at **Sports Illustrated Bar** (1176 Bob Pettit Blvd., tel. 504/766–6794). The young and not so young dance in a tropical setting at **TD's** (Baton Rouge Hilton Hotel, tel. 504/924–5000). An older, upscale crowd collects at the **Quarternote Lounge** (3827 S. Sherwood Forest Blvd., tel. 504/291–0312). The **Ascot Club** (711 Jefferson Hwy., Goodwood Shopping Village, suite 4A, tel. 504/924–4540) and **ZeeZee Gardens** (2904 Perkins Rd., tel. 504/346–1291) are both restaurants with lively bars. And there's Dixieland at **Rick's Cafe Americain** (2363 College Dr., tel. 504/924–9042).

Comedy Clubs Nationally known comics appear at the Baton Rouge outlet of the **Funny Bone** (4715 Bennington Dr., tel 504/928–9996). The cover charge varies according to the celebrity on stage.

New Orleans

The jewel in the South Louisiana crown is New Orleans, home of the splashiest festival in all of North America—Mardi Gras. When Rhett Butler took Scarlett O'Hara to New Orleans on their honeymoon, the city was scarred by war, carpetbaggers were looting the town, and decent folk feared for their lives. But gone with the wind the city wasn't. Captain Butler and his bride were entertained at a continuous round of lavish parties, suppers, and plays.

Since the 1980s, New Orleans, like most cities, has had its problems with crime and a depressed economy. But its reputation as a good-time town has remained intact. Despite its problems, New Orleans is forever finding something to celebrate. As well as world-famous Mardi Gras, new festivals crop up at the drop of a Panama hat. The city's most famous party place is the French Quarter. Also called the Vieux Carré (Old Square), the Quarter is the original colony, founded in 1718 by French Creoles. As you explore its famous restaurants, antiques shops, and jazz haunts, try to imagine a handful of determined early 18th-century settlers living in crude palmetto huts, battling swamps, floods, hurricanes, and yellow fever. Two cataclysmic fires in the late 18th century virtually leveled the town. The Old Ursuline Convent on Chartres Street is the only remaining original French Colonial structure. Survival was a struggle for the Creoles, and the sobriquet "The City That Care Forgot" stems from a determination not only to live life but to celebrate it, come what may.

Necessity may be the mother of invention, but it was the Father of Waters that forced Crescent City denizens to devise a new vocabulary for dealing with directions. The Mississippi River moves in mysterious waves, looping around the city and wreaking havoc with ordinary directions. New Orleanians, ever resourceful, refer instead to lakeside (toward Lake Pontchartrain), riverside (toward the Mississippi), upriver (also called uptown), and downriver (downtown).

Getting Around The French Quarter, laid out in a perfect grid pattern, covers about a square mile and is best explored on foot. In the early 19th century, the American Sector was just upriver of the French Quarter, so street names change as you cross Canal Street from the French Quarter: Bourbon Street to Carondelet Street, Royal Street to St. Charles Avenue, and so on.

The Central Business District (CBD) cuts a wide swath between Uptown and Downtown, with Canal Street the official dividing line. Bordered by Canal Street, the river, Howard Avenue, and Loyola Avenue, the CBD has the city's newest high-tech convention hotels, along with ritzy new shopping malls, age-old department stores, foreign agencies, fast-food chains, monuments, and the monumental Superdome.

Nestled in between St. Charles Avenue, Louisiana Avenue, Jackson Avenue, and Magazine Street is the Garden District, so named because the Americans who built their estates upriver surrounded their homes with lavish lawns, forgoing the Creoles' preference for secluded courtyards.

By Bus Buses require 60¢ exact change (except for the CBD shuttle, which is 30¢). Transfers are 5¢ extra. The CBD shuttle bus op-

erates weekdays from 6:30 AM to 6 PM, and the Vieux Carré
shuttle operates weekdays from 5 AM to 7:23 PM. **Easy Rider,** a
shuttle bus between the Riverwalk and the New Orleans Convention Center complex, charges 25¢ and connects with other
bus routes.

By Streetcar The **St. Charles Streetcar,** New Orleans's moving Historic
Landmark, clangs up St. Charles Avenue through the Garden
District, past the Audubon Zoo and other Uptown sights. The
streetcar can be boarded in the CBD at Canal and Carondelet
Streets (60¢ exact change). The streetcar operates daily, every
5 minutes 7:30 AM–6 PM, every 15–20 minutes 6 PM–midnight,
and hourly midnight–7 AM. The **Riverfront Streetcar** rolls along
the river between Esplanade Avenue and the Robin Street
Wharf. The fare is 60¢ (exact change), and it operates weekdays 6 AM–midnight; weekends 8 AM–midnight.

By Taxi Taxi fares start at $1.10, adding 20¢ for each fifth of a mile or 40
seconds of waiting time.

By Ferry A free ferry crosses the Mississippi from the Canal Street
Wharf to Algiers, leaving the pier every 25 minutes.

Guided Tours **Gray Line** buses (tel. 504/587–0861) run a two-hour tour of New
Orientation Orleans's major sights. **Tours by Isabelle** (tel. 504/367–3963)
uses air-conditioned, 14-passenger vans for a more personal-
ized and multilingual three-hour tool around town. Both companies provide hotel pickup, and reservations can be made
through your hotel.

Free **tours** of the French Quarter and the Garden District (although you must hand over 60¢ for the streetcar fare for the
last) are given by park rangers. Reservations are necessary for
the cemetery and Garden District tours. *Walks begin at the
Folklife & Visitor Center, 916–18 N. Peters St., in the French
Market, tel. 504/589–2636.*

Special-interest **Let's Go Antiquing** (tel. 504/899–3027) takes you under the
wing of a knowledgeable guide to the city's antiques shops.
Specialty Tours (tel. 504/861–2921) tailors tours to your taste,
covering everything from architecture to voodoo. Statistics for
the **Superdome** (tel. 504/587–3810) are staggering and you can
learn all about the huge facility during daily tours. On the flat-
boats of **Honey Island Swamp Tours** (tel. 504/641–1769), steered
by a professional wetland ecologist, you can tour one of the
country's best-preserved river swamps. **Tours by Isabelle** (tel.
504/367–3963) takes you to the bayous for a visit with a Cajun
alligator hunter. **Acadian-Creole Tours** (tel. 504/524–1700 or
504/524–1800) travels to a famous old sugar plantation. **Preservation Resource Center** (tel. 504/581–7032) occasionally conducts two-hour architectural tours of the CBD. **Le 'Ob's Tours**
(tel. 504/288–3478) runs a daily black-heritage/city tour highlighting sites and history important to the African-American
experience.

The French Quarter and Central Business District

*Numbers in the margin correspond to points of interest on the
French Quarter and Central Business District map.*

Tucked in between Canal Street, Esplanade Avenue, Rampart
Street, and the Mississippi River, the Vieux Carré is a carefully preserved historic district. But the Quarter is also home

to some 7,000 residents, some of the most famous of the French Creole restaurants, and many a jazz club. An eclectic crowd, which includes some of the world's best jazz musicians, ambles in and out of small two- and three-story frame, old-brick, and pastel-painted stucco buildings. Baskets of splashy subtropical plants dangle from the eaves of buildings with filigreed galleries, dollops of gingerbread, and dormer windows. Built flush with the *banquettes* (sidewalks), the houses, most of which date from the early to mid-19th century, front secluded courtyards awash with greenery and brilliant blossoms.

❶ Make your first stop the **New Orleans Welcome Center** (529 St. Ann St.), for free maps, brochures, and friendly advice. The ❷ Welcome Center is in the heart of **Jackson Square,** near a large equestrian statue of General Andrew Jackson, for whom the square is named. Jackson Square was known as Place d'Armes to the Creoles; it was renamed in the mid-19th century for the man who defeated the British in the Battle of New Orleans. Place d'Armes was the center of all Colonial life, home to parading militia, religious ceremonies, social gatherings, food vendors, entertainers, and pirates. The square remains a social hub today. Pirate attire is not uncommon in the colorful crowd that flocks to the square. The only thing missing is the militia.

❸ **St. Louis Cathedral,** soaring above the earthly activity taking place right in its front yard, is a quiet reminder of the spiritual life of New Orleans citizens. The present church dates from 1794, and it was restored in 1849. Tours are conducted daily except during services.

Alongside the church are **Pirate's Alley** and **Père Antoine's Alley.** Those cracked-flagstone passageways seem redolent of infamous plots and pirate intrigue—but, alas, the streets were laid long after Jean Lafitte and his Baratarian band had vanished. William Faulkner wrote his first novel, *A Soldier's Pay,* while living at 624 **Pirate's Alley.**

❹ The church is flanked by two buildings of the **Louisiana State Museum.** As you face the church, the **Cabildo** is on the left, the **Presbytere** on the right. Transfer papers for the Louisiana Purchase of 1803 were signed on the second floor of the Cabildo. It now holds historic documents, works of art, and artifacts pertinent to the region, including a death mask of Napoleon, who was a hero for many a New Orleanian. A four-alarm fire in 1988 damaged the roof and top floor of the Cabildo. The structure is expected to be renovated entirely by mid-1992.

The Presbytere was built as a home for priests of the church, but was never used for this purpose. Like the Cabildo, it is also a museum, with changing exhibits. The odd-shaped structure in the arcade of the Presbytere is a Confederate submarine. Hours and admission charges for the Cabildo and Presbytere are the same. *Jackson Sq., tel. 504/568–6968. Admission: $3 adults; $1.50 students and senior citizens (children under 13 free). Open Wed.–Sun. 10–5. Closed holidays.*

You can see what life was like for upscale 19th-century Creole apartment dwellers on a guided tour in the **1850s House.** Located in the lower Pontalba Buildings (lower because it's on the downriver side of the square), the building contains period furnishings, antique dolls, and evidence of cushy Creole living. It, too, is part of the Louisiana State Museum complex. *525 St. Ann St., Jackson Sq., tel. 504/568–6968. Admission: $3 adults,*

*$1.50 students and senior citizens (children under 13 free).
Open Wed.–Sun. 10–5. Closed legal holidays.*

The **Pontalba Buildings** that line Jackson Square on St. Ann
and St. Peter streets are among the oldest apartment houses in
the country. Built between 1849 and 1851, they were constructed under the supervision of the baroness Micaela Pontalba, who occasionally lent the laborers a helping hand.

The promenade of **Washington Artillery Park,** across Decatur
Street, affords a splendid perspective of the square on one side
and Old Man River rolling along on the other. On the **Moon
Walk** promenade, across the tracks from the park, you can sit
on a bench or stroll down the steps to the water's edge.

Washington Artillery Park is anchored on the upriver side by
the **Jackson Brewery and Millhouse,** and downriver by the
French Market. Jax Beer used to be brewed in the brewery, and
the market is on the site of a late 17th-century Indian trading
post. Both are now filled with boutiques and restaurants. Toward Canal Street on Decatur Street is the Jackson Brewery
Corporation's latest addition, **The Marketplace,** on Decatur
Street, home of yet more restaurants and retail outlets.

⑤ Café du Monde in the French Market, a 24-hour haven for café
au lait and *beignets* (square, puffy, holeless doughnuts sprinkled with powdered sugar), is a traditional last stop after a
night out on the town, and a New Orleans institution.

Make a right and continue down Decatur Street to Esplanade
Avenue. *This area on the fringe of the Quarter should be
avoided at night,* but you'll be safe during the day when you vis-
⑥ it the Jazz and Mardi Gras Exhibits in the **Old U.S. Mint.** This
was the first branch of the U.S. Mint, and it turned out money
hand over fist from 1838 until Something (the Civil War)
stopped it in 1861. It's now a part of the Louisiana State Museum. **A Streetcar Named Desire,** one of the cars from the old Desire line, is in mint condition and on display behind the
building. *400 Esplanade Ave., tel. 504/568–6968. Admission:
$3 adults; $2 students and senior citizens, children under 12
free. Open Wed.–Fri. 10–5. Closed Mardi Gras, Thanksgiving,
Christmas, and New Year's Day.*

Speaking of streetcars, the upriver trip is now a breeze since
the Riverfront Streetcar began rolling. The streetcar rumbles
right along the river from Esplanade Avenue all the way up to
the Robin Street Wharf, where the *Mississippi Queen* and the
Delta Queen dock.

After viewing the mint, make a left; after one block, turn left
⑦ again at Chartres Street and walk three blocks to **The Old Ursuline Convent** (1114 Chartres St.). Erected in 1749 by order of
Louis XV, it is the only building remaining from the original
colony. The Sisters of Ursula, who arrived in New Orleans in
1727, occupied the building from 1749 to 1824. It is now an ar-
chival and research center for the archdiocese and is not open to
the public.

The Greek Revival raised cottage across the street is the
⑧ Beauregard-Keyes House. General P.G.T. Beauregard, the man
who ordered the first shot at Fort Sumter, lived in the house
after the Civil War. In the mid-1940s the house was bought by
novelist Frances Parkinson Keyes (author of *Dinner at
Antoine's*), whose office was in the slave quarters. Costumed

New Orleans

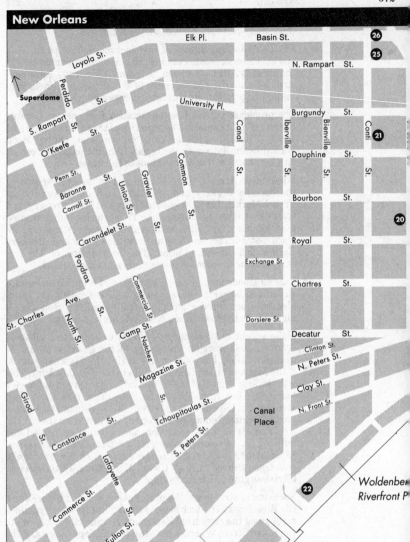

Aquarium of the Americas, **22**

Beauregard-Keyes House, **8**

Café du Monde, **5**

Cornstalk Fence, **11**

First Skyscraper, **15**

Gallier House, **9**

Hermann-Grima House, **20**

Historic New Orleans Collection, **17**

Jackson Square, **2**

LaBranche House, **14**

Lafitte's Blacksmith Shop, **10**

Louis Armstrong Park, **23**

Louisiana State Museum, **4**

Madame John's Legacy, **13**

Musée Conti, **21**

Napoleon House, **19**

New Orleans Pharmacy Museum, **18**

New Orleans Welcome Center, **1**

Old Ursuline Convent, **7**

Old U.S. Mint, **6**

Our Lady of Guadalupe, **25**

Preservation Hall, **16**

St. Louis Cathedral, **3**

St. Louis Cemetery No. 1, **26**

Theatre for the Performing Arts, **24**

Voodoo Museum, **12**

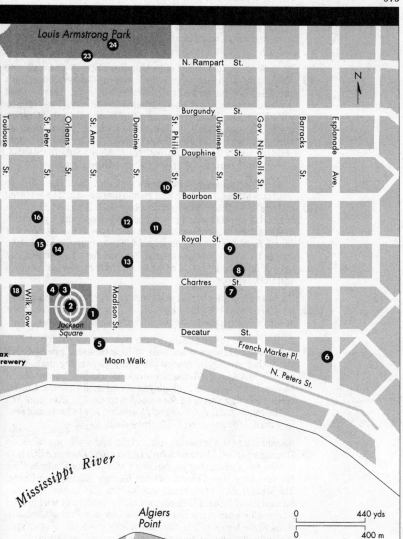

573

docents will tell you all about the dwelling and its dwellers. *1113 Chartres St., tel. 504/523–7257. Admission: $4 adults, $2 senior citizens and students, $1 children under 12. Open Mon.– Sat. 10–3. Closed Christmas, Thanksgiving, and Mardi Gras.*

⑨ At the corner turn right onto Ursulines Street and walk one block to Royal Street, where you'll find the **Gallier House.** Built about 1857 by famed architect James Gallier, Jr., this is one of the best-researched house museums in the city. The Galliers were Irish, but this is a fine example of how well-heeled Creoles lived. *1118-32 Royal St., tel. 504/523–6722. Admission: $4 adults, $3 senior citizens, AAA members, and students, $2.25 children under 12, $9 families. Tours Mon.–Sat. 10:30–3:45. Closed Thanksgiving, Christmas, and Mardi Gras.*

⑩ Back on Ursulines Street, turn right and walk one block to Bourbon Street, turn left, and go one more block. The tattered cottage is **Lafitte's Blacksmith Shop** (941 Bourbon St.). The house dates to 1772, and it is typical of houses built by the earliest settlers. According to a cherished legend, the cottage was once a front for freebooter Jean Lafitte's smuggling and slave trade. Today it's a neighborhood bar, and for a long time it has been a favorite haunt of artists and writers, the well-known and the never-known.

⑪ Go down St. Philip Street one block and turn right for a look at the **Cornstalk Fence** (915 Royal St.). Morning glories and ears of corn are intricately intertwined in the cast-iron fence.

⑫ At the corner of Royal Street turn right onto Dumaine Street. The **Voodoo Museum** is an "only in New Orleans" phenomenon and either spooky or campy (or both), depending upon what spirits move you. Remembrances of voodoo queen Marie Laveau are prominently displayed, along with altars, artifacts, and everything you need for a voodoo to-do. *724 Dumaine St., tel. 504/523–7685. Admission: $5 adults, $4 students and senior citizens; $3 children 6–12. Open daily 10–6.*

⑬ As you leave the museum, turn right and walk one block on Dumaine Street. **Madame John's Legacy** (632 Dumaine St.) is so named for a character in the short story "Tite Poulette," by 19th-century New Orleans writer George Washington Cable. The West Indies–style house was built in 1788 on the site of the birthplace of Renato Beluche, a Lafitte lieutenant who helped Andrew Jackson in the Battle of New Orleans. Part of the Louisiana State Museum (tel. 504/568–6968), the house is open sporadically, depending upon the state's financial situation.

⑭ Go back to Royal Street, turn left and walk two blocks past the quiet, green **Cathedral Garden,** which is at the rear of St. Louis Cathedral. One block more will bring you to St. Peter Street and the most-photographed building in the city. The **LaBranche House** (740 Royal St.), dating from about 1840, wraps around the corner of Royal Street and runs halfway down St. Peter Street. Its filigreed double galleries are cast iron with an oak-leaf-and-acorn motif.

⑮ Directly across the street is the **First Skyscraper** (640 St. Peter St.). Built between 1795 and 1811, it was a three-story high rise; rumor has it that the fourth floor was added later so that it might retain its towering title. Behind weathered walls is **⑯** **Preservation Hall** (726 St. Peter St.), home of the world's best traditional and Dixieland jazz (*see* Nightlife, *below*).

17 Continue on Royal Street one block to the **Historic New Orleans Collection.** The **Merieult House** was one of the few buildings to survive the fire of 1794, and it now contains an extensive collection of documents and research materials pertaining to the city. Exhibits in the **Williams Gallery** on the ground floor can be seen for free, and for a nominal fee you can take a guided tour and hear the legends of the historic house. *533 Royal St., tel. 504/523–4662. Admission: $2. Open Tues.–Sat. 10–4:30. Closed Christmas, Thanksgiving, Mardi Gras, and New Year's Day.*

18 Turn left and then right onto Toulouse Street, walk toward the river, and turn right onto Chartres Street. The **New Orleans Pharmacy Museum** is a musty old place where Louis Dufilho had his pharmacy in 1823. It's full of ancient and mysterious medicinal items, and there is an Italian marble fountain used by 19th-century soda jerks. *514 Chartres St., tel. 504/524–9077. Admission: $1. Open Tues.–Sun. 10–5. Closed Mon.*

19 At the corner of Chartres and St. Louis streets is the **Napoleon House** (500 Chartres St.), a long-time favorite haunt of artists and writers. The bar fairly oozes atmosphere from every splinter, with peeling sepia walls, Napoleonic memorabilia, and taped classical music to back up your libation. It is entirely possible—and this is a proven fact—to laze away an entire afternoon sitting by an open door and watch rain splatter down on the pavement (*see* Dining, *below*).

20 If you can wrench yourself away, turn right at the corner and walk along St. Louis Street past Antoine's Restaurant and go one more block to the **Hermann-Grima House.** Guides will steer you through the American-style town house, built in 1831, and on winter Thursdays you can get a taste of Creole during cooking demonstrations. *820 St. Louis St., tel. 504/525–5661. Admission: $4 adults, $3.50 AAA members, $3 senior citizens and students, children under 8 free. Open Mon.–Sat. 10–4. Closed Thanksgiving, Christmas, and Mardi Gras.*

21 Turn left as you leave the house, left again on Dauphine Street, and then right on Conti Street to reach the **Musée Conti Wax Museum.** The museum waxes lifelike on Louisiana legends, among them Andrew Jackson, Jean Lafitte, Marie Laveau, and Governor Edwin Edwards. *917 Conti St., tel. 504/525–2605. Admission: $4.95 plus tax adults, $3 children 6–12. Open daily 10–5:30. Closed Christmas and Mardi Gras.*

22 At the end of Canal Street is the **Aquarium of the Americas,** whose spectacular design lets viewers feel part of the watery world by offering close-up encounters with the 7,000 aquatic creatures in 60 separate displays in four major environments. The beautifully landscaped 16-acre **Woldenberg Riverfront Park** around the aquarium is a tranquil spot with an excellent view of the river. *Foot of Canal St., tel. 504/595–FISH. Admission: $7.50 adults, $6 senior citizens, $4 children. Open daily except Christmas, 9:30–5.*

Time Out   Nearby **Arnaud's Grill** (813 Bienville St., tel. 504/523–5433) has mosaic-tile floors, ceiling fans, and a player piano as the backdrop for its mixed drinks.

We'll now take a look at some of the attractions on unattractive, run-down Rampart Street, but we'll do so with a warning: The section of the street between St. Peter and Canal streets is relatively safe during daylight hours, but *should be avoided at night. Avoid the section between St. Peter Street and Esplanade Avenue day* and *night.*

At St. Ann Street, a large arch hovers over the entrance to **㉓㉔ Louis Armstrong Park,** which is named for native son Louis "Satchmo" Armstrong. Inside the park are the **Municipal Auditorium** and the **Theatre for the Performing Arts.** The auditorium is on the site of Congo Square, scene of 18th- and 19th-century slave gatherings. Congo Square is believed to have been the birthplace of jazz, with the voodoo Afro-Caribbean rhythms of the slaves' songs and chants influencing the new music. Large crowds attend the opera and ballet at the theater, and many a Carnival ball is still held at the auditorium. *Do not venture into the park alone, even in the daytime.*

㉕ **Our Lady of Guadalupe Catholic Church** (411 N. Rampart St.) was dedicated in 1827, when it was known as the Mortuary Chapel. It was originally used only for funerals, usually for victims of yellow fever and cholera. This church is home to one of the city's legends, St. Expedite. The story is that a statue was delivered to the church in a crate marked simply "Expedite." It was expeditiously mounted, and it can be seen to the right as you enter the church.

㉖ Just behind the church on Basin Street is **St. Louis Cemetery No. 1,** between St. Louis and Conti streets. This is New Orleans's oldest City of the Dead, so called because the stark white above-ground tombs resemble tiny houses. The cemetery dates from 1789, and well-worn paths lead through a maze of tombs and mausoleums, many with the same ornate grilles and ironwork as the houses where live folks live. Many a well-known early New Orleanian is buried here, and voodoo doings mark the tomb believed to be that of Marie Laveau. (Some say she is buried in St. Louis Cemetery No. 2.) *Warning: The cemetery is adjacent to a crime-ridden housing project, and you should not visit it alone. Go on a group tour, which can be arranged through an agency (see* Guided Tours, *above).*

Audubon Park and Zoo

Rolled out across St. Charles Avenue from Tulane and Loyola universities is **Audubon Park and Zoo.** You can board the **St. Charles Streetcar** at Poydras Street and St. Charles Avenue to tool off Uptown. The Friends of the Zoo operate a free shuttle that boards in front of Tulane every 15 to 20 minutes for a ride to the zoo, which lies on the 58 acres of the park nearest the river. It is entirely possible to while away an entire day exploring Audubon Zoo. A wooden walkway strings through the zoo, and a miniature train rings around a part of it. More than 1,500 animals roam free in natural habitats, such as the **Australian exhibit,** where kangaroos hop-nob with wallabies, and the **Louisiana Swamp exhibit,** where alligators bask on the bayou. A special treat is the feeding of the sea lions, which is marked by a great deal of flapping about and barking. The **Wisner Children's Village** has a petting zoo and elephant and camel rides. *Tel. 504/861–2537. Admission: $6.50 adults, $2.75 senior citizens and children 2–12. Open weekdays 9:30–5; weekends (winter) 9:30–5, during daylight savings time 9:30–6. Closed Thanksgiving, Christmas, and Mardi Gras.*

The 400-acre Audubon Park, with live oaks and lush tropical plants, was once part of the plantation of Etienne de Bore and his son-in-law Pierre Foucher. In 1795, de Bore figured out how to granulate sugar for commercial purposes, thereby revolutionizing the sugar industry.

In addition to the 18-hole golf course, there is a two-mile jogging track with 18 exercise stations along the way, a **stable** that offers guided trail rides, and 10 tennis courts. The park is also eminently suitable for lolling about under a tree and doing nothing. Note, however, that you should stay *out* of the park after dark.

Around Town

City Park Avenue, Bayou St. John, Robert E. Lee Boulevard, and Orleans Avenue embrace the 1,500 luxuriant acres of **City Park,** which can be reached via the Esplanade or the City Park bus. You can spend a great deal of time simply admiring the lagoons and majestic live oaks, whose gnarled branches bow and scrape to Mother Earth, but there is plenty to keep you busy if you are not an idler. There are four 18-hole golf courses, a double-deck driving range, 39 lighted courts in the Wisner Tennis Center, Botanical Gardens, baseball diamonds, and stables. At the casino on Dreyfous Avenue you can rent **bikes, boats,** and **canoes**—or just have a bite to eat—and at the amusement park, you can ride the turn-of-the-century carousel and miniature train. **Storyland** offers puppet shows, talking storybooks, storybook exhibits, and storytelling—hence its name. Unfortunately, it is no fairy tale that City Park is *not safe at night.*

The **New Orleans Museum of Art** (NOMA), located in the park, displays from its collections Italian paintings from the 13th to 18th centuries, 20th-century European and American paintings and sculptures, Chinese jades, and the Imperial Treasures by Peter Carl Fabergé. *Lelong Ave., City Park, tel. 504/488–2631. Open Tues.–Sun. 10–5. Admission: $3 adults, $1.50 senior citizens and children 3–17; admission free on Thurs. Closed Thanksgiving, Christmas, Mardi Gras.*

To reach the **Pitot House** from NOMA, walk along Lelong Avenue, cross over the Bayou St. John Bridge, and make a right turn on Moss Street. Continue following Moss Street as it winds alongside the bayou, and look for the house on your left. The West Indies–style house was built in the late 18th century and bought in 1810 by New Orleans mayor James Pitot. It is furnished with Louisiana and other American 19th-century antiques. *1440 Moss St., tel. 504/482–0312. Admission: $3 adults, $1 children under 12. Open Wed.–Sat. 10–3. Closed Thanksgiving, Christmas, New Year's Day, Mardi Gras.*

Longue Vue House & Gardens sits right on the border between Orleans and Jefferson parishes, about a $5 cab ride from the Quarter. To describe this mansion, the word "opulent" immediately comes to mind. The house is furnished with elegant antiques and sits on eight acres of landscaped gardens. Yes, opulent is the word. *7 Bamboo Rd., tel. 504/488–5488. Admission: $5 adults, $3 students and children. Open Tues.–Fri. 10–4:30, weekends 1–5. Closed Mon., Thanksgiving, Christmas, New Year's, Mardi Gras, July 4th.*

Shopping

The French Quarter is the place to search for antiques shops, art galleries, designer boutiques, bookstores, and all sorts of shops in all sorts of edifices. Among **Canal Place**'s (333 Canal St.) lofty tenants you'll find Saks Fifth Avenue, Laura Ashley, Gucci, Charles Jourdan, and Benetton. **Riverwalk** (1 Poydras St.) is a long, tunnellike marketplace brightened by over 200 splashy shops, restaurants, food courts, and huge windows overlooking the Mississippi. The tony **New Orleans Centre,** between The Hyatt Regency Hotel and the Superdome on Poydras St., boasts more than 100 occupants, including Macy's and Lord & Taylor. Along six miles of **Magazine Street** are Victorian houses and small cottages filled with antiques and collectibles. Stop at the New Orleans Welcome Center for a copy of the shopper's guide published by the Magazine Street Merchants Association. Turn-of-the-century Creole cottages cradle everything from toy shops to designer boutiques and delis in the **Riverbend** (Maple St. and Carrollton Ave.). At **Uptown Square** (200 Broadway), boutiques and restaurants surround—guess what?—a square. Macy's and Mervyn's are among the 155 shops in Metairie's glittering three-level **Esplanade Mall** (1401 W. Esplanade Ave.).

Antiques   **As You Like It** (3025 Magazine St., tel. 504/897–6915) carries obsolete patterns in silver and silverplate. **Mid-America Shop** (3128 Magazine St., tel. 504/895–4226) offers crystal and Depression glass.

Shoulder to shoulder along **Royal Street** are some of the finest—and oldest—antiques stores in New Orleans. Among them are: **French Antique Shop** (225 Royal St., tel. 504/524–9861); **Manheim Galleries** (403–409 Royal St., tel. 504/568–1901); **Moss Antiques** (411 Royal St., tel. 504/522–3981); **M.S. Rau, Inc.** (630 Royal St., tel. 504/523–5660); **Royal Antiques** (307–309 Royal St., tel. 504/524–7033); and **Waldhorn Company** (343 Royal St., tel. 504/581–6379).

Art   The French Quarter is known for its many art galleries, most of which are located on Royal Street: **Bergen Galleries** (730 Royal St., tel. 504/523–7882) offers posters and collectibles by local artists; **The Black Art Collection** (738 Royal St., tel. 504/529–3080) displays and sells works by local and national black artists; **Dyansen Gallery** (433 Royal St., tel. 504/523–2902) features the work of modern and contemporary artists; **Kurt E. Schon, Ltd.,** (523 Royal St., tel. 504/523–5902) has classic paintings from the 17th through the 20th centuries; **Merrill B. Domas American Indian Art** (824 Chartres St., tel. 504/586–0479) offers antique and contemporary art and crafts by North American Indian artists; **Southern Expressions** (521 St. Anne St. at Jackson Sq., tel. 504/525–4530) shows the work of regional artists.

Food to Go   **Bayou to Go** (New Orleans International Airport, Concourse C, tel 504/468–8040) has a full line of Louisiana food products, including fresh, frozen, and cooked seafood packed to check or carry on the plane. For the best pralines in town, try **Old Town Praline Shop** (627 Royal St., tel. 504/525–1413).

Jazz Records   Chances are you'll find the hard-to-find vintage stuff at **Record Ron's** (1129 Decatur St. and 407 Decatur St., tel. 504/524–9444).

Masks **Hidden Images** (523 Dumaine St., tel. 504/524–8730) has a whole store full of handmade leather, feather, and frilly Mardi Gras masks. For exotic handmade masks to decorate your face or your wall, try **Rumors** (513 Royal St., tel. 504/525–0292).

Sports and Fitness

Biking In the French Quarter, Bourbon and Royal streets are closed to all but pedalers and pedestrians. Rentals are available at **Bicycle Michael's** (618 Frenchmen St., tel. 504/945–9505; $3.50 hour, $12.50 day).

Golf There are four 18-hole golf courses in City Park, plus a double-decker driving range. You can rent clubs, handcarts, and electric carts at the **Main Clubhouse** (1040 Filmore Dr., tel. 504/283–3458). To rent clubs and tee off on Audubon Park's luscious links, check into **Audubon Park's Clubhouse** (473 Walnut St., tel. 504/865–8260). The **Joe Bartholomew Municipal Golf Course** (6514 Congress Dr., tel. 504/288–0928) has an 18-hole course in Pontchartrain Park.

Tennis There are 39 courts in the **City Park Wisner Tennis Center** (1 Dreyfous Ave. in City Park, tel. 504/483–9383). **Audubon Park** (tel. 504/895–1042) has 10 courts near Tchoupitoulas Street. **Pontchartrain Park Tennis Center** (5104 Hayne Blvd., tel. 504/283–9734) lets you lob on 10 courts, and there are 11 courts at the Hilton's **River Center Tennis & Racquetball Club** (2 Poydras St., tel. 504/587–7242).

Spectator Sports

Basketball The **Sugar Bowl Basketball Classic** is played in the Superdome the week preceding the annual football classic.

Football The **New Orleans Saints** play NFL games in the Superdome (tel. 504/522–2600). The annual **Sugar Bowl Football Classic** (tel. 504/525–8573) is played in the Dome on New Year's Day, and in late November the **Bayou Classic** (tel. 504/587–3663) pits Southern University against Grambling University.

Dining

New Orleans usually means excellent dining. The Big Easy is recognized almost as much for hot and spicy culinary delights as it is for hot and steamy jazz. Louisiana styles of cooking are becoming increasingly popular worldwide—but what is a fad elsewhere is a tradition here.

Apart from K-Paul's and Galatoire's, where people stand in line to be served on a first-come basis, you are strongly advised to make reservations and to book well in advance for weekends, particularly during holiday periods or conventions.

The following terms will appear frequently throughout this section:

andouille (an-*dooey*)—Cajun sausage made with pork blade meat, onion, smoked flavorings, and garlic.
boudin (boo-*dan*)—hot, spicy pork with onions, rice, and herbs stuffed in sausage casing.
bananas Foster—a dessert of bananas sautéed with butter, brown sugar, and cinnamon, flambéed in white rum and banana liqueur, and served on ice cream.

barbecue shrimp—large shrimp baked in the shell, covered with butter, rosemary, herbs, and spices. They are not barbecued at all.

court bouillon (coo–bee–*yon*)—a thick, hearty soup made with a roux, vegetables, and fish, and served over rice.

crawfish (pronounced as spelled)—also known as "mud-bugs," because they live in the mud of freshwater streams. They resemble miniature lobsters and are served in a great variety of ways.

étouffée (ay-too-*fay*)—crawfish étouffée is made with a butter and flour roux of celery and onion, then cooked for a short period of time and served over rice. Shrimp étouffée is heartier, made with an oil and flour roux or tomato paste, celery, onion, bell pepper, tomatoes, and chicken stock, cooked for approximately an hour and served over rice.

filé (fee-*lay*)—ground sassafras, used to season gumbo and many other Creole specialties.

grillades (gree-*yads*)—bite-size pieces of veal rounds or beef chuck, braised in red wine, beef stock, garlic, herbs, and seasoning, served for brunch with grits and with rice for dinner.

gumbo—a hearty soup prepared in a variety of combinations (okra gumbo, shrimp gumbo, chicken gumbo, to name a few).

jambalaya (jum-bo-*lie*-yah)—a spicy rice dish cooked with stock and chopped seasoning, and made with any number of ingredients including sausage, shrimp, ham, and chicken.

muffuletta—a large, round loaf of bread filled with cheese, ham, and salami smothered in a heavy, garlicky olive salad.

rémoulade—a cold dressing that accompanies shrimp (sometimes crabmeat) over shredded lettuce, made of mayonnaise and Creole mustard, oil and vinegar, horseradish, paprika, celery, and green onion.

praline (praw-*leen*)—candy patty most commonly made from sugar, water or butter, and pecans. There are many different flavors and kinds.

Cajun cuisine is rarely served in its purest form in New Orleans; rather it is often blended with Creole to create what's known as "New Orleans–style" cooking. There is a difference, though, between the two: Creole is distinguished by its rich and heavy sauces; Cajun, by its tendency to be spicy and hot.

The following dining price categories have been used: *Very Expensive*, over $35; *Expensive*, $25–$35; *Moderate*, $15–$25; *Inexpensive*, under $15.

Louisiana Cuisine
Cajun-inspired

K-Paul's Louisiana Kitchen. National celebrity chef Paul Prudhomme made blackened redfish so famous that a fishing ban was levied and restaurateurs can no longer acquire the fish. K-Paul's now serves blackened yellowfin tuna. Strangers often must share tables, and the "no reservations" policy makes for long lines outside. But K-Paul's is a shrine to the popular concept of New Orleans Cajun cooking. *416 Chartres St., French Quarter, tel. 504/942–7500. Dress: casual. No reservations. AE. Closed Sat. and Sun. Expensive.*

★ **Bayona.** "New World" is the label chef Susan Spicer (formerly at The Bistro) applies to her cooking style. It's as good a name as any for such dishes as phyllo-pastry turnovers filled with spicy crawfish tails; fresh salmon filet in white-wine sauce with sauerkraut; grilled duck breast with pepper-jelly glaze; and shrimp with coriander sauce. The chef herself supervised the renovation of the early 19th-century Creole cottage, now fairly glowing with flower arrangements, elegant photographs, and trompe l'oeil murals suggesting Mediterranean landscapes. In good weather drinks and meals are served in a rear patio overflowing with tropical greenery. *430 Dauphine St., French Quarter, tel. 504/525–4455. Jackets suggested. Reservations strongly advised. AE, DC, MC, V. Moderate–Expensive.*

Classic Creole **Arnaud's.** Beveled glass, ceiling fans, and tile floors cast an ★ aura of traditional Southern dining. The lively Sunday jazz brunch is a classic New Orleans experience. Pompano *en croûte*, veal Wohl, and filet Charlemond topped with two sauces are savory entrée selections, and there is little on the menu here that isn't excellent. *813 Bienville St., French Quarter, tel. 504/523–5433. Jackets required. Reservations required. AE, MC, V. Expensive.*

★ **Galatoire's.** Operated by the fourth generation, Galatoire's is a tradition in New Orleans. Creole specialties, moderately priced by New Orleans standards, are served in a large, brightly lit room with mirrors on all sides. Lunch is served all afternoon, and you can avoid the long lines by arriving after 1:30 PM. An extensive menu offers every imaginable Creole dish. Seafood is the most diverse category, but there is also a fine lineup of steaks, sweetbreads, and chicken dishes. *209 Bourbon St., French Quarter, tel. 504/525–2021. Jacket and tie required after 5 and all day Sun. No reservations. No credit cards. Closed Mon. Moderate.*

Tujague's. In the city's second-oldest eatery, one of the dining rooms is decorated with memorabilia relating to Madame Begue, the late and legendary restaurateur who had an establishment housed on the same spot many long years ago. The six-course dinner menu always includes shrimp remoulade, soup, boiled beef brisket, a choice of three entrées, vegetables, and bread pudding. *823 Decatur St., French Quarter, tel. 504/525–8676. Dress: casual. Reservations advised for dinner. AE, MC, V. Moderate.*

French Creole **Antoine's.** Established in 1840, Antoine's is the oldest res- ★ taurant in the United States under continuous family ownership. You can best appreciate this fine old restaurant if you are accompanied by a regular. Oysters Rockefeller originated here, as did pompano *en papillote* and puffed-up soufflé potatoes. *Tournedos marchand de vin* is a legend in its own wine. Be sure and tour the restaurant after dinner. *713 St. Louis St., French Quarter, tel. 504/581–4422. Jacket required for dinner. Reservations advised on weekends. AE, DC, MC, V. Very Expensive.*

Brennan's. Opened in 1946, Brennan's is one of the city's premier dining establishments. Breakfast at Brennan's is a tradition unto itself. The extensive menu includes rich, creamy eggs Benedict, Sardou, and Houssarde. The traditional breakfast dessert is bananas Foster, flamed with liqueur in a tableside ritual. The oysters tournedos Chanteclair, three prime cuts, each with a different sauce, represents one of the restaurant's strong suits: excellent French sauces with a Creole stamp. Brennan's also serves brunch on weekends. *417 Royal St., French Quarter, tel. 504/525–9711. Jacket required at dinner. Reservations advised. AE, DC, MC, V. Very Expensive.*

★ **Commander's Palace.** Housed in a renovated Victorian mansion, this elegant restaurant offers the best sampling of old Creole cooking prepared with a combination of American and French styles. Entrée selections include veal chop

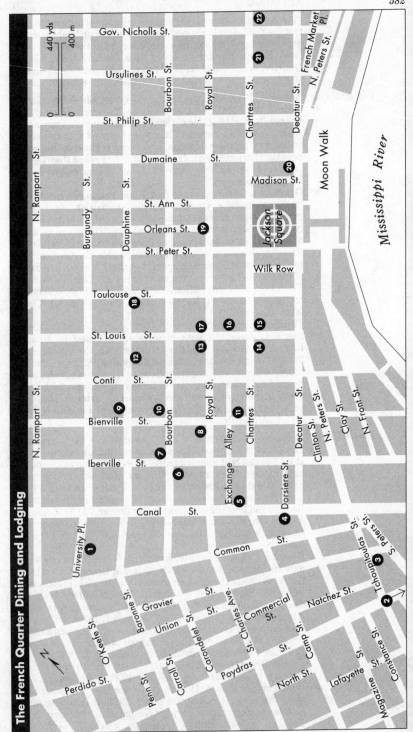

582

The French Quarter Dining and Lodging

Gov. Nicholls St.

Ursulines St.

Bourbon St.

Royal St.

Chartres St.

Decatur St.

French Market Pl.

N. Peters St.

St. Philip St.

N. Rampart St.

Burgundy St.

Dauphine St.

Dumaine St.

Madison St.

Moon Walk

Mississippi River

St. Ann St.

Orleans St.

Jackson Square

St. Peter St.

Wilk Row

Toulouse St.

St. Louis St.

Conti St.

Royal St.

Chartres St.

Decatur St.

Clinton St.

N. Peters St.

Clay St.

N. Front St.

Bienville St.

Bourbon St.

Iberville St.

Exchange Alley

Dorsiere St.

Canal St.

University Pl.

Common St.

Gravier St.

O'Keefe St.

Baronne St.

Carondelet St.

St. Charles Ave.

Commercial St.

Camp St.

Tchoupitoulas St.

S. Peters St.

Natchez St.

Union St.

Carroll St.

Penn St.

Perdido St.

Poydras St.

North St.

Lafayette St.

Magazine St.

Constance St.

N

440 yds
400 m

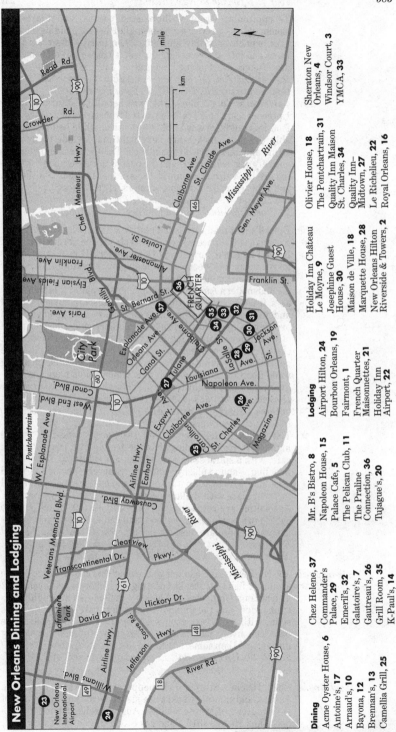

New Orleans Dining and Lodging

Dining
Acme Oyster House, 6
Antoine's, 17
Arnaud's, 10
Bayona, 12
Breman's, 13
Camellia Grill, 14

Chez Helene, 37
Commander's Palace, 29
Emeril's, 32
Galatoire's, 7
Gautreau's, 26
Grill Room, 35
K-Paul's, 14

Mr. B's Bistro, 8
Napoleon House, 15
Palace Cafe, 5
The Pelican Club, 11
The Praline Connection, 36
Tujague's, 20

Lodging
Airport Hilton, 24
Bourbon Orleans, 19
Fairmont, 1
French Quarter Maisonnettes, 21
Holiday Inn Airport, 22

Holiday Inn Château Le Moyne, 9
Josephine Guest House, 30
Maison de Ville, 18
Marquette House, 28
New Orleans Hilton Riverside & Towers, 2

Olivier House, 18
The Pontchartrain, 31
Quality Inn Maison St. Charles, 34
Quality Inn–Midtown, 27
Le Richelieu, 22
Royal Orleans, 16

Sheraton New Orleans, 4
Windsor Court, 3
YMCA, 33

583

Tchoupitoulas, trout with roasted pecans, and tournedos. Commander's serves a one-of-a-kind bread pudding soufflé. Jazz brunch Saturday and Sunday, a festive affair with balloons and lots of Creole egg dishes, is best enjoyed in the Garden Room overlooking the patio. *1403 Washington Ave., Garden District, tel. 504/899–8221. Jackets required. Reservations required. AE, DC, MC, V. Very Expensive.*

★ **Gautreau's.** This is one of the most popular restaurants in the Uptown area: a small café converted from an old pharmacy. The food is straightforward but imaginative, while being comfortably Creole. Lunches are very light and include many good soups and salads with the entrées. The dinner menu consists entirely of specials; perhaps the best of those regularly appearing are the various manifestations of filet mignon, but the fish and veal are also consistent winners. *1728 Soniat St., Uptown, tel. 504/899–7397. Dress: casual. Reservations advised. MC, V. Closed for lunch; closed for dinner Sun. Moderate.*

Avant-garde **Emeril's.** For many seasoned restaurant goers in New Orleans,
★ Emeril's is the pace-setter for Creole cuisine. Proprietor-chef Emeril Lagasse, formerly at Commander's Palace, opened this large, noisy and decidedly contemporary restaurant in early 1990 with an ambitious menu that gives equal emphasis to Creole and modern American cooking. On the plate, this translates as a fresh corn crepe topped with Louisiana caviar, grilled andouille sausage in the chef's own sauce, a sauté of crawfish over jambalaya cakes, fresh fruit cobblers, and a cornucopia of other creative dishes. You can grab a stool at a food bar and get close-up views of the chef at work. The looks of the place are appropriately avant-garde—brick and glass walls, gleaming wood floors, burnished-aluminum lamps, and a huge abstract-expressionist oil painting. *800 Tchoupitoulas St., Warehouse District, tel. 504/528–9393. Jackets suggested. Advance reservations strongly advised. AE, DC, MC, V. Closed Sun., no lunch Sat. Expensive.*

★ **The Palace Cafe,** a split-level two-story restaurant in the historic Werlein Building, has the feeling of a large Parisian café, with a spiral staircase, a black-and-white tile floor, wood paneling, and splashy murals. Starters include grilled andouille with sweet potato cakes, and oyster shooters (served in a shot glass with shallots, lemon, and cracked-pepper sauce). Specialties are rotisserie chicken basted in garlic oil, superb catfish in a pecan crust, seafood, and game. Wait till you see the separate chocolate-dessert listing. *605 Canal St., Central Business District, tel. 504/523–1661. Dress: casual but neat. No reservations. AE, DC, MC, V. Moderate.*

Creole-inspired **Mr. B's Bistro.** You can tell you're near this classy bistro by the
★ aroma of fish and steaks roasting on hickory and pecan logs. The shrimp Chippewa and hickory-grilled fish are highly recommended, and the gumbo ya-ya is first-rate. The wine list is solid, with some very good wines by the glass available at the bar. The lively jazz brunch offers New Orleans classic egg dishes, and then some. *201 Royal St., French Quarter, tel. 504/ 523–2078. Dress: casual. Reservations advised. AE, MC, V. Sun. brunch. Moderate.*

Soul Creole **Chez Helene.** Stuffed bell peppers, fried chicken, Creole gumbo, and smothered okra are just some of the fine recipes of Helene Howard, whose nephew, Austin Leslie, opened the second Chez Helene (316 Chartres St. in the de la Poste Hotel,

French Quarter, tel. 504/525–6130). The soul and Cajun specialties are marked by spiciness and fresh herbs—no bottled, dried, or dehydrated condiments. The Creole jambalaya and crawfish étouffée are among the city's simplest and best; the fresh corn bread is a joy. *1540 N. Robertson St., Mid-City, tel. 504/947–1206. Dress: casual. Reservations accepted. AE, MC, V. Moderate.*

★ **The Praline Connection.** Down-home cooking in the Southern-Creole style is the forte of this laid-back and likable restaurant where the food is the no-nonsense kind that has fueled generations of Southern families. The fried or stewed chicken, smothered pork chops, barbecued ribs, and collard greens are definitively done. And the soulful filé gumbo, crowder peas, bread pudding, and sweet-potato pie are among the best in town. Add to all this some of the lowest prices anywhere, a congenial service staff, and a neat-as-a-pin dining room and the sum is a fine place to spend an hour or two. *542 Frenchmen St., Faubourg Marigny, tel. 504/943–3934. Dress: casual. No reservations. AE, MC, V. Inexpensive.*

International Cuisines
Continental

★ **Grill Room.** Among locals, this is one of the most highly celebrated of the newer hotel dining rooms. The opulence begins with a Lalique crystal table at the entrance and continues with an array of original art. Chef John Carey calls the cuisine New American, although there are strong Continental overtones. Especially recommended are the steamed halibut on Swiss mâche with Beluga caviar, and the saddle of red deer with red currant sauce. There is a grill here (as the name suggests) over which much good fish is prepared. The wine cellar was assembled with the rich collections of two local claret fans; it is not only mind-boggling but fairly priced, too. *Windsor Court Hotel, 300 Gravier St., Central Business District, tel. 504/522–1992. Dress: casual. Reservations advised. AE, MC, V. Very Expensive.*

★ **The Pelican Club.** Sassy New York flourishes are found throughout the menu of this smartly decorated but eminently comfortable place in the heart of the French Quarter. Still, evidence of chef Richard Hughes's South Louisiana origins also keeps popping up. Hughes spent seven years in Manhattan as the top chef of the acclaimed Memphis. In three handsome dining rooms inside a balconied old town house, he turns out a stew of shellfish that's a clever improvisation of both San Francisco's cioppino and Louisiana's bouillabaisse. A touch of saffron in his jambalaya of chicken, sausage, and shellfish makes it a cousin of Spain's paella. Closer to home are red snapper stuffed with crabmeat; a bisque of bourbon, crab, and corn; and a crème brûlée in the grandest French-Creole tradition. Each of the dining rooms, hung with consignment art from local galleries, has its own ambience. *615 Bienville St., French Quarter, tel. 504/523–1504. Jacket suggested. Reservations advised. AE, MC, V. No lunch weekends. Expensive–Very Expensive.*

Back to Basics
Seafood

★ **Acme Oyster House.** The granddaddy of local oyster bars, the Acme has a big old marble counter at which you stand and eat dozen after dozen of oysters, opened before your eyes by old pros. Next to that is another bar where you get your beer, the preferred drink with cold oysters. You order your sandwiches from the cooking station, where you can see them frying the oysters. The wait can be aggravating if it's a crowded day, but it's worth it. A recent addition is a very limited salad bar. You can eat oysters on the half shell at a table, but this isn't the style of the natives. *724 Iberville St., French Quarter, tel. 504/522–5973. Dress: casual. No reservations. AE, MC, V. Closes Sun. at 7 AM. Inexpensive.*

Grills and Coffee Shops ★ **Camellia Grill.** This is the class act among lunch counters, with linen napkins and a maître d'. The omelets are the best in town. Especially good is the ham, cheese, and onion—huge and fluffy. Good red beans and rice on Monday. Great hamburgers, pecan pie, cheesecake, and banana-cream pie. The chocolate freezes here are also popular. Dining here is entertaining, mainly due to the somewhat theatrical waiters. Expect long lines on weekends for breakfast. *626 S. Carrollton Ave., Uptown, tel. 504/866–9573. Dress: casual. No reservations. No credit cards. Inexpensive–Moderate.*

★ **Napoleon House.** The tables in the front room of this ancient bar open on to the street, and there's a charming courtyard in the back. The very limited menu offers several po' boys, appetizers, a salad bar for lunch weekdays, and a few desserts. But people come here for the muffuletta, one of the best in town. The popular drink is still the Pimm's cup, cool and light with a slice of cucumber. The classical music and mellow ambience make this an alluring spot for repose. Very popular with locals. *500 Chartres St., French Quarter, tel. 504/524–9752. Dress: casual. AE, MC, V. Closes Sun. at 6 PM. Inexpensive.*

Lodging

Visitors to New Orleans have a wide variety of accommodations to choose from: posh high-rise hotels, antiques-filled antebellum homes, Creole cottages, or old slave quarters. Try to reserve well in advance, especially during Mardi Gras or other seasonal events. Frequently, hotels offer special packages at reduced rates, but during Mardi Gras almost every accommodation raises its rates higher than listed here.

The following lodging price categories have been used: *Very Expensive,* over $120; *Expensive,* $90–$120; *Moderate,* $50–$90; *Inexpensive,* under $50.

Hotels Central Business District ★ **Fairmont Hotel.** The Fairmont is one of the oldest grand hotels in America. The red and gold Victorian splendor of the massive lobby evokes a more elegant and gracious era. The hotel is composed of three separate buildings. The Baronne and University sections have spacious rooms. Rooms in the Shell section are smaller and were completely redone in 1989; there is no elevator service in this building. Special touches in every room include four down pillows, electric shoe-buffers, and bathroom scales. Impressive murals depicting life in the South enliven the walls of the famed Sazerac Bar; the herbs used in the restaurants are grown on the roof and delivered to the kitchens within 20 minutes of being cut. The Sazerac Restaurant has had a face-lift that removed the old world ambience and replaced it with a contemporary look. *University Pl., 70140, tel. 504/529–7111 or 800/527–4727. 685 rooms, 50 suites. Facilities: 4 restaurants with bars, outdoor pool, 2 lighted tennis courts, lobby pastry shop, valet parking. AE, DC, MC, V. Very Expensive.*

★ **Windsor Court Hotel.** Exquisite, gracious, elegant, eminently civilized—these words are frequently used to describe Windsor Court, but all fail to capture its wonderful quality. Le Salon's scrumptious high tea is served each afternoon in the lobby. Plush carpeting, canopy and four-poster beds, stocked wet bars, marble vanities, oversize mirrors, dressing areas—all contribute to the elegance and luxury of the Windsor Court. The hotel is located across from the Rivergate and four blocks from the French Quarter. In 1990 the hotel and its fine Grill Room restaurant received the AAA 5 Diamond award. *300 Gravier St., 70140, tel. 504/523–6000 or 800/262–2662. 58 rooms, 266 suites. Facilities: 2 restaurants, lounge, outdoor pool, health club, Jacuzzi, steambath, sauna, valet laundry, parking. AE, DC, MC, V. Very Expensive.*

New Orleans Hilton & Towers. It's located on the banks of the Mississippi, with Riverwalk sprawled out around it and the New Orleans Convention Center just down the street. Pete Fountain's Club is here. The River Center Tennis & Racquetball Club is a handy spot for working off all the calories you'll consume at Winston's. VIPs check into the Tower suites, where a concierge looks after things, but the best views of the river are in the appropriately named Riverside section. *Poydras St. at the Mississippi River, 70130, tel. 504/561–0500 or 800–HILTONS. 1,602 rooms, 86 suites. Facilities: 5 restaurants, 6 lounges, 2 outdoor pools, tennis and racquetball club, golf clinic, business center. AE, DC, MC, V. Moderate–Very Expensive.*

★ **Sheraton New Orleans.** On Canal Street, across from the French Quarter, the Sheraton has a lobby that is large and user-friendly. A tropical atmosphere permeates its Gazebo Lounge, which features jazz nightly. Café Promenade encircles the second level. Executive rooms on the top floors come with many special amenities. The year 1991 saw the completion of a multimillion-dollar renovation that added a health club, two restaurants, and a conference center, and redecorated all the guest rooms. Expect top-quality service. *500 Canal St., 70130, tel. 504/525–2500 or 800/325–3535. 1,200 rooms, 84 suites. Facilities: restaurant, lounge, outdoor pool with restaurant, video checkout, no-smoking rooms, valet service, and parking. AE, DC, MC, V. Moderate–Very Expensive.*

Quality Inn—Midtown. Too far to walk but only a short drive from the French Quarter. *3900 Tulane Ave., 70119, tel. 504/486–5541 or 800/228–5151. 102 rooms. Facilities: restaurant, lounge, outdoor pool, whirlpool, no-smoking rooms, airport shuttle, free parking. AE, DC, MC, V. Moderate.*

French Quarter
★ **Bourbon Orleans.** The splendid lobby of this historic hotel is done in white marble with crystal chandeliers and a grand piano. A magnificent spiral staircase leads to the 1815 Orleans Ballroom, which was the site of innumerable masquerade and quadroon balls. The large guest rooms have Queen Anne furnishings; bathrooms are fitted with telephones and mini-TVs. Even-numbered rooms face a beautiful courtyard, but you can still hear the Bourbon Street noise. The suites are bilevel and have two entrances. *717 Orleans St., 70116, tel. 504/523–2222 or 800/521–5338. 164 rooms, 47 suites. Facilities: restaurant, lounge, outdoor pool, valet service, parking. AE, DC, MC, V. Very Expensive.*

★ **Hotel Maison de Ville.** This small, romantic hotel lies in seclusion amid the hustle and bustle of the French Quarter. Tapestry-covered chairs, a fire burning in the sitting room, and antiques-furnished rooms all contribute to a 19th-century atmosphere. Some rooms are in former slave quarters in the courtyard; others are on the upper floors of the main house. The complimentary Continental breakfast is served with a rose on a silver tray. Other meals can be enjoyed at Le Bistro. Visitors who seek a special hideaway will love the Audubon housekeeping cottages—in a private, enclosed area, with statuary and individual patios—two blocks from the hotel. *727 Toulouse St., 70130, tel. 504/561–5858 or 800/634–1600. 14 rooms, 2 suites, 7 cottages. Facilities: restaurant, pool, valet service, parking. AE, MC, V. Expensive–Very Expensive.*

★ **Royal Orleans Hotel (Omni).** This elegant, white-marble hotel, built in 1960 re-creates an aura that reigned in New Orleans more than a century ago. Rooms, though not exceptionally large, are well appointed with marble baths (telephone in each) and more marble on dressers and tabletops. Balcony rooms cost the most. The well-known Rib Room Restaurant makes its home on the lobby level. *621 St. Louis St., 70140, tel. 504/529–5333 or 800/THE–OMNI. 350 rooms, 16 suites. Facilities: 2 restaurants, 3 lounges, rooftop pool, exercise room, valet service, parking. AE, DC, MC, V. Expensive–Very Expensive.*

Le Richelieu. Here the friendly, personal atmosphere of a small hotel is combined with amenities usually associated with a luxury high rise—all at a moderate rate. Some rooms have mirrored walls and walk-in closets, many have refrigerators, and all have brass ceiling fans. Luxury suites (like the one Paul McCartney stayed in) are also available. An intimate bar and café off the courtyard has tables on the terrace by the pool. *1234 Chartres St., 70116, tel. 504/529–2492 or 800/535–9653. 69 rooms, 17 suites. Facilities: restaurant, lounge, outdoor pool, valet service, free parking. AE, DC, MC, V. Moderate–Very Expensive.*

Olivier House. The entrance of this small hotel, in two 1836 town houses, contains an enormous carved mirror and chandeliers that are original to the house. Room design and decor vary; some rooms have lofts, many have complete kitchens; gas-burning fireplaces are found throughout. Most rooms are a comfortable mixture of antiques and traditional decor; some have a tropical feeling, with wicker furnishings and sunny colors. Pets are welcome. Noisy birds inhabit the three pretty courtyards filled with tropical plants. Don't expect a spic-and-span luxury hotel; in this family-owned and operated charmer, the homey, casual atmosphere is the thing. Popular with Europeans and with theater (and opera) people. *828 Toulouse St., 70112, tel. 504/525–8456. 40 rooms. Facilities: pool. AE, DC, MC, V. Moderate–Very Expensive.*

★ **Holiday Inn Château Le Moyne.** Old World atmosphere and decor; 8 suites located in slave quarters off a tropical courtyard. *301 Dauphine St., 70112, tel. 504/581–1303 or 800/HOLIDAY. 160 rooms, 11 suites. Facilities: restaurant, lounge, outdoor pool, valet parking. AE, DC, MC, V. Moderate–Expensive.*

★ **French Quarter Maisonnettes.** All the maisonnettes (some with two and three rooms) open directly onto a private flagstone courtyard. Functional furnishings, private baths, and TVs are included; private phones are not available. Children over 12 and well-trained pets are welcomed. *1130 Chartres St., 70116, tel. 504/524–9918. 1 room, 7 suites. No credit cards. Closed July. Inexpensive.*

Garden District/
Uptown
★
The Pontchartrain Hotel. Maintaining the grand tradition is the hallmark of this quiet, elegant European-style hotel that has reigned on St. Charles Avenue for more than 60 years. From the canopied entrance to the white-gloved elevator operator, the hotel's commitment to quality, service, and taste

comes through clearly. Accommodations range from lavish, sun-filled suites to small, darkish rooms with shower baths. The internationally known Caribbean Room restaurant provides memorable dining. *2031 St. Charles Ave., 70140, tel. 504/ 524–0581 or 800/952–8092. 50 rooms, 25 suites. Facilities: 2 restaurants, piano bar, concierge, limousine, valet service, parking. AE, DC, MC, V. Moderate–Very Expensive.*

★ **The Josephine Guest House.** In this restored Italianate mansion, built in 1870, French antiques fill the rooms, and Oriental rugs cover gleaming hardwood floors. Four rooms and a parlor are in the main house; there are two smaller but spacious rooms in the garçonnière (quarters where the original owners' sons stayed). The bathrooms are impressive in both size and decor. A complimentary Creole breakfast of fresh-squeezed orange juice, café au lait, and homemade biscuits can be brought to your room (Wedgwood china on a silver tray) or served on the secluded patio. Phones can be installed in rooms upon request. *1450 Josephine St., 70130, 1 block from St. Charles Ave., tel. 504/524–6361. 6 rooms. AE, DC, MC, V. Moderate.*

★ **Quality Inn Maison St. Charles.** This lovely property in five historic buildings along St. Charles Avenue is the home of Patout's fine restaurant. *1319 St. Charles Ave., 70130, tel. 504/ 522–0187 or 800/228–5151. 121 rooms, 11 suites. Facilities: lounge, outdoor pool, whirlpool, no-smoking rooms, valet parking. AE, DC, MC, V. Moderate.*

Kenner/Airport **New Orleans Airport Hilton & Conference Center.** This moderately new facility (opened in January 1989) is directly opposite the New Orleans International Airport. *901 Airline Hwy., Kenner 70062, tel. 504/469–5000 or 800/HILTON. 315 rooms. Facilities: restaurant, lounge, outdoor pool, tennis court, fitness center, business center, valet service, airport shuttle. AE, DC, MC, V. Moderate–Expensive.*

Holiday Inn–Airport Holidome. Many of the rooms here face the dome-covered pool area. *I–10 and Williams Blvd., Kenner 70062, tel. 504/467–5611 or 800/HOLIDAY. 301 rooms, 1 suite, Facilities: restaurant, lounge, indoor pool, exercise room, sauna, Jacuzzi, airport shuttle, free parking. AE, DC, MC, V. Moderate.*

Bed-and-Breakfasts **New Orleans Bed & Breakfast.** Among 300 properties citywide are private homes, apartments, and condos. Prices range from $35 to $150. *Contact Sarah-Margaret Brown, Box 8163, New Orleans 70182, tel. 504/838–0073. AE, MC, V. Inexpensive–Very Expensive.*

Bed & Breakfast, Inc.—Reservations Service. This service offers a variety of accommodations in all areas of New Orleans. Some homes are 19th-century, others are contemporary. Guest cottages, rooms, and suites are also available. Prices range from $40 to $110. *Write or call Hazel Boyce, 1360 Moss St., Box 52257, New Orleans 70152, tel. 504/525–4640 or 800/228–9711– Dial Tone–184. No credit cards. Inexpensive–Expensive.*

Hostels **International Center YMCA.** Accommodations are for both men and women. Rooms in Pratt Building are newer and have TVs. Hint for Mardi Gras: 20 of these rooms face St. Charles Avenue or Lee Circle and provide excellent parade views. There are bathrooms and showers on each floor. *936 St. Charles Ave., 70130, tel. 504/568–9622. 150 rooms, no private baths. Facilities: restaurant, gym, weight room, track, indoor pool, parking. MC, V. Inexpensive.*

Marquette House, New Orleans International Hostel. This is the fourth-largest youth hostel in the country, run by Steve and Alma Cross. It is located in a 100-year-old lower Garden District home, one block from St. Charles Avenue and the streetcar. There are bunk beds in dorms, and private rooms with double beds also available. *2253 Carondelet St., 70130, tel. 504/ 523–3014. 80 beds, 5 private rooms, no private baths. Facilities: 2 lounge areas with TV (1 no-smoking), 2 equipped community kitchens, dining room, coin-operated laundry, lockers, garden patio with picnic tables. AE, MC, V. Inexpensive.*

The Arts

Comprehensive listings of events can be found in the weekly newspaper *Gambit*, which is distributed free at newsstands, supermarkets, and bookstores. The Friday edition of the daily *Times-Picayune* carries a "Lagniappe" tabloid that lists weekend events. The monthly *New Orleans Magazine* also has a Calendar section. Credit-card purchases of tickets for events at the Saenger Performing Arts Center, the Orpheum Theater, and UNO Lakefront Arena can be made through TicketMaster (tel. 504/888–8181).

Theater The avant-garde, the off-beat, and the satirical are among the theatrical offerings at **Contemporary Arts Center** (900 Camp St., tel. 504/523–1216). At **Le Petit Théâtre du Vieux Carré** (616 St. Peter St., tel. 504/522–2081), classics, contemporary drama, children's theater, and musicals are presented. Touring Broadway shows, dance companies, and top-name talent appear at the **Saenger Performing Arts Center** (143 N. Rampart St., tel. 504/524–2490).

Concerts Free jazz concerts are held on weekends in **Dutch Alley.** Pick up a schedule at the information kiosk (French Market at St. Philip St., tel. 504/522–2621). The New Orleans Symphony performs at the **Orpheum Theatre** (129 University Pl., tel. 504/525–0500), which also presents jazz and pop concerts.

Nightlife

Jazz was born in New Orleans, and the music refuses to be confined to nighttime. Weekend jazz brunches are enormously popular and are featured all over town. But a stroll down Bourbon Street will give you a taste of the city's eclectic rhythms. You'll hear Cajun, gutbucket, R&B, rock, ragtime, New Wave, and you name it, and you'll hear it almost around the clock. During the annual Jazz and Heritage Festival, held from the last weekend in April through the first weekend in May, musicians pour in from all over the world to mix it up with local talent, and the music never misses a beat.

New Orleans is a 24-hour town, meaning that there are no legal closing times and it ain't over till it's over. Closing times, especially on Bourbon Street, depend on how business is. Your best bet is to call and ask before tooling out to bar-hop at 2 AM. It is also a superb idea to call and ask about current credit-card policy, cover, and minimum.

Gambit, the free weekly newspaper, has a complete listing of who's doing what where. Things can change between press and performance times, so if there's an artist you're especially eager to hear, it's wise to call and confirm before turning up.

Jazz Aboard the *Creole Queen* (Poydras St. Wharf, tel. 504/529–4567) you'll cruise on the river with Andrew Hall's Society Jazz Band and there's a buffet to boot. If you've an ounce of romance racing through your veins, do it.

There's live music five nights a week (Wed.–Sun.) at the **Palm Court Jazz Cafe** (1204 Decatur St., tel. 504/525–0200). Traditional jazz is the rule, with blues thrown in on Wednesday. The fine Creole and international kitchen stays open until the music stops.

Pete Fountain's (2 Poydras St., tel. 504/523–4374) is a New Orleans legend with his clarinet and his band that plays in a plush 500-seat room on the third floor of the Hilton Hotel. This is Pete's home base, and the man's on the stand Tuesday, Wednesday, Friday, and Saturday when he's in town. But he makes frequent appearances around the country, so it's wise to call first.

Speaking of legends, the old-time jazz greats lay out the best traditional jazz in the world in a musty, funky hall that's short on comfort, long on talent. **Preservation Hall** (726 St. Peter St., day tel. 504/522–2238, night tel. 504/523–8939) is *the* place for traditional jazz, and it costs you a mere $3 at the door. You may have to stand in line to get in, but it will help if you get there around 7:30.

Dixieland is the name of the tune at the **Seaport Cafe & Bar** (424 Bourbon St., tel. 504/568–0981). You can dine on seafood and Cajun dishes while sitting on a balcony and watching the movable feast down on "the Street."

There's yet more Dixieland Friday and Saturday nights at **Fritzel's** (733 Bourbon St., tel. 561–0432) Clarinet player Chris Burke and his New Orleans Band come on around 10 PM and jazz things up till . . .

Rambling, rustic, and raucous **Snug Harbor** (626 Frenchmen St., tel. 504/949–0696) is where greybeards and undergrads get a big bang out of the likes of the Dirty Dozen, Charmaine Neville, the David Torkanowsky Trio, and Maria Muldaur.

R&B, Cajun, Industrial-strength rock rolls out of the sound system at the
Rock, New Wave **Hard Rock Cafe** (418 N. Peters, tel. 504/529–5617). Hard Rock Hurricanes are dispensed at a guitar-shaped bar, and the place is filled with rock 'n' roll memorabilia. Hamburgers, salads, and steaks are served.

The college crowd raises the rafters at **Jimmy's Music Club** (8200 Willow St., tel. 504/861–8200). The music, by national as well as local groups, is rock, New Wave, reggae, R&B . . . whatever.

Benny's Bar (938 Valence, tel. 504/895–9405) is a laid-back lair for blues and reggae. There's never a cover here.

An institution, **Tipitina's** (501 Napoleon Ave., tel. 504/897–3943) is sort of a microcosm of the Jazz Fest, featuring progressive jazz, reggae, R&B, rock, New Wave, and blues. Its name comes from a song by Professor Longhair, who was posthumously awarded a Grammy for Best Traditional Blues Recording, and the place is dedicated to his memory. Funky, mellow, loaded with laid-back locals. $3–$10 cover.

Bars One of the world's best-known bars and home of the Hurricane (a sweetly potent concoction of rum and fruit juices) is **Pat O'Brien's** (718 St. Peter St., tel. 504/525–4823). There are three bars, including a lively piano bar and a large courtyard bar, and mobs of collegians and tourists line up to get in. Very lively, very loud, very late.

Dancing **Forty-one Forty-one** (4141 St. Charles Ave., tel. 504/897–0781) is a stylish bastion for disco dancing and mingling singles.

Two-stepping to a Cajun band is billed as the "spécialité de la maison," but the **Maple Leaf Bar** (8316 Oak St., tel. 504/866–9359) moves with rock, R&B, reggae, and gospel as well. (Cajun nights *are* special.) There's a $2–$5 cover, depending on what's up.

If you're into heavy-duty dancing to Top-40s discs, check out **Club Galleria West** (The Galleria, 1 Galleria Blvd., Metairie, tel. 504/836–5055). The glitzy disco draws a loyal crowd of young locals.

Tour 8: New Orleans to Orlando

Most Americans know all about New Orleans—home of Dixieland jazz, Mardi Gras, and Cajun cooking—and Orlando, home of Mickey Mouse and theme parks galore. But the road that lies between these great tourism magnets is not so well traveled, and it should be. This long drive along the Gulf of Mexico offers an authentic taste of the Deep South, with its antebellum mansions, blooming azaleas, and live oaks festooned with Spanish moss. History here is multilayered, in towns where local Indians, Spaniards, French, and British all ruled in their time, not to mention the secessionists of the Confederacy. Travelers with a taste for busy modern beach resorts will find them—the fine, sparkling white sand along the Gulf makes incredibly beautiful beaches—but there are also islands, forests, and wildlife refuges where the undergrowth is lush and the silence complete. For sports enthusiasts, there are several excellent golf courses and tennis resorts, and anything that happens on water happens here, from surfboarding and scuba diving to fishing off the end of a pier or casting a line from a deep-sea charter boat.

With so much to see in New Orleans and Orlando, most travelers will spend only a limited amount of time on the drive in between. This entire route could be covered in two days, taking I-10 from downtown New Orleans straight east across Mississippi, Alabama, and Florida, and picking up I-75 east of Tallahassee for the final shoot south to Orlando. But the interstate scenery can get monotonous, so break up your trip with some interesting stops along the way—or better yet, choose a stretch of this trip where you can switch over for a while to one of the smaller parallel highways that hug the Gulf coast. On the interstate, you'll feel as if you could be anywhere in America, but get off it and you'll definitely know you're in the South.

Tourist Information

Mississippi **Mississippi Gulf Coast Convention and Visitors Bureau** (Box 6128, Gulfport 39506, tel. 601/896–6699 or 800/237–9493).

Alabama **Alabama Gulf Coast Convention and Visitors Bureau** (Hwy. 59, 3150 Gulf Shores Pkwy., Drawer 457, Gulf Shores 36542, tel. 205/968–7511).

Mobile Chamber of Commerce (451 Government St., Mobile, tel. 205/433–6951). **Fort Condé,** the official visitor center for Mobile (150 S. Royal St., tel. 205/434–7304 or 800/252–3862).

Orange Beach Chamber of Commerce (Hwy. 182, Drawer 399, Orange Beach 36561, tel. 205/981–8000).

Florida **Destin Chamber of Commerce** (Stahlman Ave., tel. 904/837–
Panhandle 6241).

Fort Walton Beach Chamber of Commerce (34 Miracle Strip Pkwy., U.S. 98, tel. 904/244–8191).

Panama City Beach Visitors & Convention Bureau (12015 W. Front Beach Rd., tel. 800/PCBeach).

Pensacola Convention & Visitor Information Center (1401 E. Gregory St., tel. 904/434–1234 or 800/343–4321).

Tallahassee to **Apalachicola Chamber of Commerce** (128 Market St., tel. 904/
Gainesville 653–9419).

Gainesville Chamber of Commerce (300 E. University Ave., tel. 904/336–7100).

Ocala-Marion County Chamber of Commerce (110 E. Silver Springs Blvd., tel. 904/629–8051).

Tallahassee Area Convention and Visitor Bureau (200 W. College Ave., tel. 904/681–9200 or 800/628–2866).

Festivals and Seasonal Events

Feb.: **Mardi Gras** is celebrated with parades and merrymaking not only in New Orleans but also in Mobile, Alabama.

Feb.: **Olustee Battle Festival** in Lake City, Florida, the second largest Civil War reenactment in the nation after Gettysburg, features a memorial service, crafts and food festival, 10K run, and parade. Box 1847, Lake City FL 32056, tel. 904/755–5666.

Mar.: **Historic Mobile Homes Tour,** opens to visitors 36 houses, from 19th-century Federal-style town houses to Creole cottages and antebellum plantation homes. Contact Historic Mobile Homes Tours, Box 2187, Mobile, AL 36652, or call 205/433–0259.

Mar.-Apr.: **Azalea Trail Festival** in Mobile, Alabama, follows 37 well-marked miles in and around the city, showing off azaleas at their best. Throughout the preceding week, scores of special events celebrate the yearly blossoming.

Mid-Mar.–Mid-Apr.: **Springtime Tallahassee** is a major cultural, sporting, and culinary event in the Florida state capital. Tel. 904/224–5012.

Apr.: **Spring Pilgrimages** in 11 Mississippi Gulf coast communities tour historic homes.

June: **Blessing of the Fleet, Shrimp Festival**, and **Fais Do Do** are three colorful celebrations held in Biloxi, Mississippi.

Mid-June: **Fiesta of Five Flags** in Pensacola, Florida, celebrates de Luna's landing with dancing and reenactments of the event. Tel. 904/433–6512.

Early–mid-June: **Billy Bowlegs Festival** in Fort Walton Beach, Florida, is a week of entertaining activities in memory of a pirate who ruled the area in the late 1700s. Tel. 904/244–8191.

Oct.: **Destin Seafood Festival** is a two-day affair in Destin, Florida, where you can sample smoked amberjack, fried mullet, or shark kabobs. Tel. 904/837–6241.

Early Nov.: **Florida Seafood Festival** is Apalachicola's celebration of its seafood staple with oyster-shucking-and-consumption contests and parades. Tel. 904/653–8051.

Dec.: **Christmas on the Water** greets the season in Biloxi, Mississippi.

What to See and Do with Children

This is an excellent trip to make with youngsters, not only because it ends up in **Orlando,** Florida, home of Disney World and many other theme parks, but also because there's a string of commercial amusement parks all along the Gulf Coast. **Gulfport**, Mississippi, has two: Funtime USA (1300 Beach Blvd., tel. 601/896–7315), with water slides, a playground, bumper boats and cars, and arcade games, and Marine Life (east of junction U.S. 49–U.S. 90., tel. 601/896–3981), with its performing dolphins, sea lions, and macaws. **Gulf Shores,** Alabama, has Romar Miniature Golf (Beach Rd. E, tel. 205/981–4418) and Waterville USA (AL 59, tel. 205/948–2106; open Memorial Day–Labor Day), with its wave pool, water slides, rides, miniature golf, and video-game arcade. **Pensacola,** Florida, offers Fast Eddie's Fun Center (W St. at Michigan, Pensacola, tel. 904/433–7735), which has kiddie rides, a video room, air hockey, and basketball, and across the bay in **Gulf Breeze** is a 30-acre zoo (5701 Gulf Breeze Pkwy., tel. 904/932–2229). **Fort Walton Beach** claims the Island Golf Center (1306 Miracle Strip Pkwy., Fort Walton Beach, tel. 904/244–1612), which has minigolf, a nine-hole par-3 course, video arcade, and pool tables. In **Destin,** kids can ride go-carts at The Track (1125 U.S. 98, tel. 904/654–4668) or splash in water rides at the Big Kahuna (U.S. 98, tel. 904/837–4061). **Panama City Beach** offers water rides at Shipwreck Island (12000 U.S. 98W, tel. 904/234–2282), a roller coaster and other thrill rides at Miracle Strip Amusement Park (12000 U.S. 98W, tel. 904/234–5810), performing sea animals at Gulf World (15412 Front Beach Rd., tel. 904/234–5271), and performing reptiles at Snake-A-Torium (9008 Front Beach Rd., tel. 904/234–3311).

Plentiful beaches and ubiquitous boat tours give kids a chance to enjoy the Gulf of Mexico first-hand. The Marine Education Center in **Biloxi,** the Gulfarium in **Fort Walton Beach,** and the Museum of the Sea and Indian in **Destin,** all described more fully in the tour below, give a closer look at the creatures of the deep.

Kids who are interested in war history may enjoy visits to the following sites described in the tour: the USS *Alabama,* anchored just east of **Mobile;** the National Museum of Naval Aviation in **Pensacola;** and the Air Force Armament Museum in **Fort Walton Beach.** In **Gainesville,** the Fred Bear Museum (Fred Bear Dr. at Archer Rd., tel. 904/376–2411; open Wed.–Sun.) displays archery artifacts dating to the Stone Age, and a wealth of natural history exhibits. In **Tallahassee,** the Tallahassee Junior Museum (3945 Museum Dr., tel. 904/576–1636; admission: $4 adults, $3 senior citizens, $2 children 4–15, under 4 free; open Tues.–Sat. 9–5, Sun. 12:30–5) features a collection of old cars and carriages, a red caboose, nature trails, a snake exhibit, and a restored plantation home.

Arriving and Departing

By Plane Most travelers will arrive by air in New Orleans or Orlando. There are also regional airports in Gulfport-Biloxi, Mobile, Pensacola, Tallahassee, and Gainesville.

By Train Amtrak (tel. 800/USA–RAIL) serves New Orleans (1001 Loyola Ave., tel. 504/528–1610) with The Crescent service to New York, and Orlando with service that stops either at Sanford (the Autotrain, 600 Persimmon Blvd.), Orlando (1400 Sligh Blvd.), or Kissimmee (416 Pleasant St.). The Gulf Coast has no rail service, but Amtrak trains do stop in Waldo (near Gainesville) and Ocala.

By Bus Greyhound/Trailways has stations in New Orleans (1001 Loyola Ave., tel. 504/525–9371); Bay St. Louis (512 Ulman Ave., tel.

601/467–4272); Gulfport (11205 25th Ave., tel. 601/863–1022); Biloxi (502 W. Railroad Ave., tel. 601/436–4335); Mobile (201 Government St., tel. 205/432–1861); Pensacola (505 W. Burgess Rd., tel. 904/476–4800); Tallahassee (tel. 904/222–4240); Gainesville (tel. 904/376–5252); and Orlando (300 W. Amelia St., tel. 407/843–7720).

By Car From New Orleans, take I–10 east across Mississippi and Alabama, or, just after crossing the Mississippi/Louisiana border, pick up U.S. 90, which runs along the Mississippi Gulf coast and on to Mobile. East from Mobile, the coastal alternative to I–10 is U.S. 98, all the way into Florida until just south of Tallahassee. After Tallahassee, the route described in this tour sticks to the interstates: I–10 east to Lake City, then I–75 through Gainesville and Ocala to the Sunshine Parkway toll road, which you pick up at Wildwood. The turnpike continues southeast to Orlando.

The Mississippi Gulf Coast

The Mississippi Gulf Coast runs along U.S. 90 from Alabama to Louisiana. The traveler seeking a boisterous good time will find it in the restaurants, bars, hotels, motels, and souvenir shops that jostle for space along U.S. 90's busy four lanes.

Don't let the clamor of this neon strip hide the coast's quieter treasures: the ancient land, sculpted by wind and water, continually changing; serene beachfront houses set on green and shady lawns; the teeming wildlife of the Mississippi Sound and its adjacent bayous and marshes; the unspoiled natural beauty of the seven barrier islands that separate the Gulf of Mexico from the Mississippi Sound. On a clear day, if you have good eyesight or a good imagination, you can see these islands. Their names (from east to west) are Petit Bois (anglicized as "Petty Boy"), Horn, East and West Ship, and Cat. Two others, Round and Deer, lie within the Mississippi Sound. The islands are constantly shifting as the tides and prevailing winds work on their fragile sands.

During the 1700s France, England, and Spain ruled the area, according to their fortunes in international wars. Street names, family names, and traditions still reflect this colorful heritage. In the late 19th and early 20th centuries, the coast became a fashionable vacation spot for wealthy New Orleanians and Delta planters eager to escape yellow fever epidemics. Elegant hotels, imposing beachfront mansions, and smaller summer homes sprang up. Edgewater Plaza shopping mall now stands on the site of the queen of the early hotels, the Edgewater Gulf, which in its heyday had its own stop on the L & N Railroad. Today the homes that have endured the vagaries of time and hurricanes stand along the beach—brave and beautiful survivors.

Take your cue from the natives and ignore any urge to swim in the sound. It's too murky (at best). Instead, admire the stately live oaks and accept the salutes of crabs. Go floundering and spear your supper. Above all, slow down. On the Mississippi Coast only the traffic on U.S. 90 moves quickly.

Numbers in the margin correspond to points of interest on the Mississippi Coast map.

Driving east on I–10 from New Orleans, soon after you cross the Mississippi state line turn onto Rte. 607, which soon becomes U.S. 90, the main local highway for this strip of Gulf Coast. From here it's only a few miles to **Waveland,** which boasts the best beach in Mississippi (E. Beach Boulevard, 2 miles south of U.S. 90). Take a beach walk or drive through Buccaneer State Park's mossy live oaks to enjoy the splendid, unimpeded view of sparkling waters.

Continue east on U.S. 90 through Bay St. Louis to **Pass Christian** (Chris-chi-ANN). Here sailboat racing began in the South, and here the second yacht club in the country was formed (it still exists today). Louisiana landowner Zachary Taylor was at the yacht club when he was persuaded to run for the presidency. In 1913, President Woodrow Wilson and his family spent a Christmas vacation here, but his Dixie White House, the Herndon Home, was destroyed by Camille.

The highway runs eastward, between stately homes on the north and shimmering water on the south, toward Long Beach and **Gulfport.** If you have time for only one activity on the coast, make it a getaway to **Ship Island** on the passenger ferry from the Gulfport Harbor. At **Ship Island** a U.S. Park Ranger will guide you through Fort Massachusetts, built in 1859 and used by Federal troops to blockade the sound during the Civil War. The rangers will treat you to tales of the island's colorful past, including the story of the *filles aux casquettes*—young women sent by the French government as brides for the lonely early colonists. Each girl (*fille*) carried a small hope chest (*casquette*). If you bring your own casquette filled with a picnic lunch, you can skip the snack bar and head straight for the surf on the island's southern shore. Spend the day sunning, swimming in the clear green water, and beachcombing for treasures washed up by the surf. You'll feel a world away (just remember to return on the last boat). *Ticket office at Gulfport Harbor in the Joseph T. Jones Memorial Park, just east of the intersection of U.S. 49 and U.S. 90, tel. 601/864–1014. Cost (round-trip): $11 adults, $5 children 3–10. 1–3 trips daily, Mar.–Oct.*

Another option from the Port of Gulfport is a gambling cruise aboard the ***Southern Elegance,*** a posh version of Biloxi's gambling ship, which includes a dinner buffet, live entertainment, gaming in the casino for adults, and supervised activities and a video arcade for youngsters. *US 90, tel. 800/441–7447. Tickets $29–$49, plus tax.*

Four miles east of Gulfport is **Beauvoir,** the antebellum beachfront mansion that was the last home of Jefferson Davis. Here the president of the Confederacy wrote his memoirs and his book *The Rise and Fall of the Confederate Government.* This National Historic Landmark is maintained much as it was when Davis lived here. The serene, raised cottage-style house, with its sweeping front stairs, is flanked by pavilions and set on a broad lawn shaded by ancient live oaks. A Confederate cemetery on the grounds includes the Tomb of the Unknown Soldier of the Confederacy. *On U.S. 90 between Biloxi and Gulfport, tel. 601/388–1313. Admission: $4 adults, $2 children, $3 senior citizens. Open daily 9–5. Closed Christmas Day.*

Continue east on U.S. 90 to **Biloxi,** practicing the correct pronunciation, "Bi-LUX-i," as you go. Biloxi is the oldest continuous settlement on the Gulf Coast and the second largest city in

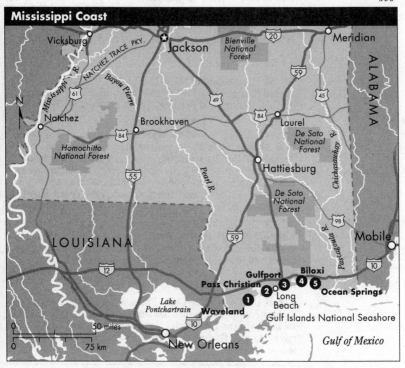

Mississippi Coast

Mississippi. When Pierre LeMoyne Sieur D'Iberville met the Indians who called themselves Biloxi, or "first people," he gave their name to the area and to the bay. The French constructed Fort Louis here; it served as the capital of the Louisiana Territory from 1720 to 1722, when the capital was moved to New Orleans.

Biloxi's landmark 65-foot **lighthouse** on U.S. 90 was erected in 1848. During the Civil War, Federal forces, operating from Ship Island, blockaded the Mississippi Sound and cut Biloxi off from much-needed supplies. When the Yankees demanded that Biloxi submit or starve, the reply was that the Union would have to "blockade the mullet" first. Ever since, mullet has been known as "Biloxi bacon" and honored with its own festival each October. (You may want to try it if you've eaten your fill of delicate redfish, fresh crabmeat, plump Gulf oysters, and tender shrimp.) The city defended itself with what appeared to be a formidable cannon array near the lighthouse but what was actually only two cannons and many logs painted black! *U.S. 90. Admission: $1 adults, 50¢ children under 12. Open Wed.–Sun. 10–6:30. Closed Oct.–Apr. 1.*

The lighthouse is the starting point for the **Biloxi Tour Train,** which bumps you past historic mansions and shrimp trawlers, new banks and old restaurants. *U.S. 90 at Porter Ave. Admission: $1.50 adults, $1 children. Six tours daily, Mar. 1–Labor Day.*

Biloxi's **Small Craft Harbor,** off U.S. 90 on the sound, captures the atmosphere of a lazy fishing village. Catch the **Sailfish**

Shrimp Tour boat here to experience 80 minutes as a shrimper. Cast your nets upon the waters and let the crew identify your catch, however bizarre, for you. *1500 E. Beach Blvd., tel. 601/ 374–5718. Admission: $6 adults, $5 children. Runs begin at 10 AM daily; call for schedule.*

At the intersection of the I-10 loop and U.S. 90 you can hop aboard the good ship *L.A. Cruise* for an afternoon or evening of gaming, dining, and dancing. *Tel. 800/752–1778. Tickets: $29 day; $39 night, plus tax.*

At the foot of the Biloxi–Ocean Springs Bridge, on the south, is **Gulf Marine State Park,** jutting over the water on wooden decks. Through its telescopes you can glimpse **Deer Island** 12 miles away or watch gulls and pelicans, sailboats and sailboards. This is a great spot for fishing, 24 hours a day. Bait and tackle are sold here and fishing poles may be rented daily 9–5. *Just south of U.S. 90 at the west end of the Biloxi–Ocean Springs Bridge. Open daily.*

Adjacent to Gulf Marine State Park is the **Marine Education Center,** featuring live exhibits of Gulf Coast animals and a spectacular 40,000-gallon aquarium. *1650 E. Beach Blvd., Biloxi, tel. 601/374–5550. Admission: $2 adults, $1 children and senior citizens. Open Mon.–Sat. 9–4.*

Across U.S. 90 is **Point Cadet Plaza,** a waterfront complex now under development, which has a marina and a seafood industry museum. In the 1880s Point Cadet was home to European emmigrants who flocked to Biloxi to work in the seafood canneries.

Time Out Mary Mahoney's **Old French House Restaurant** (138 Rue Magnolia, tel. 601/374–0163) is in a renovated 1737 mansion with several elegant, though expensive, dining rooms and enclosed patios. Come for drinks in the Old Slave Quarter Lounge (11 AM–11 PM) and for Le Café's beignets, coffee, gumbo, and po'boys served 24 hours a day (there's take-out, too).

❺ Cross the Biloxi–Ocean Springs bridge to **Ocean Springs.** Here, in 1699, the French commander Pierre LeMoyne Sieur D'Iberville established Fort Maurepas to shore up France's claim to the central part of North America. This first colony was temporary, but is fondly remembered by Ocean Springs in its annual spring festival celebrating D'Iberville's landing. Magnificent oaks shade the sleepy town center, a pleasant area of small shops to explore on foot.

Ocean Springs is famous as the home of Walter Anderson (1903–1965), an artist of genius and grand eccentricity who enjoyed an ecstatic communion with nature, which he revealed in thousands of drawings and watercolors, most of them kept secret until his death. You can discover his work at the **Walter Anderson Museum of Art,** to which murals from the **Anderson Cottage** were moved, and the adjoining **Old Community Center.** Anderson painted the intricate murals in the Community Center for a fee of $1; they are appraised at $1 million. *510 Washington Ave., tel. 601/872–3164. Admission: $3 adults, $1 children 12 and under. Open Tues.–Sat. 10–5, Sun. 1–5.*

The nearby **Shearwater Pottery and Showroom** offers a wide selection of original and reproduction Anderson family hand-thrown and cast pottery. Visitors can watch the pottery being made in the workshop. *102 Shearwater Dr., tel. 601/875–7320. Showroom open Mon.–Sat. 9–5:30, Sun. 1–5:30. Workshop open weekdays 9–noon and 1–4.*

A brochure from the **Ocean Springs Chamber of Commerce** (tel. 601/875–4424) will guide you on a driving tour of the D'Iberville Trail, shaded by moss-draped trees and bordered by summer houses.

Gulf Islands National Seashore—which includes Ship, Horn, and Petit Bois Islands—has its headquarters on Ocean Springs's Davis Bayou. In the summer you can explore the marshes by boat with a U.S. Park Ranger as your guide. When heat and humidity allow, picnic here and explore the nature trails. *3500 Park Rd., Ocean Springs, tel. 601/875–9057. Ranger boat tours begin at 6:30 PM Thurs.–Sun.; rangers start taking reservations at 6 PM (limit of 20 people).*

Either I–10 or U.S. 90 will take you the next 50 miles or so east to Mobile.

Shopping

Gifts At **Ballard's Pewter** (1110 Government St., Ocean Springs, tel. 601/875–7550) you can find necklaces and earrings made from sand dollars and crabs, or have the pewtersmith fashion a "bespoke" (custom-made) piece.

Outfit yourself at **Realizations** (1000 Washington St., Ocean Springs, tel. 601/875–0503) in T-shirts, skirts, blouses, and dresses silk-screened with Walter Anderson's swirling block print designs. Books, reproductions, and posters of the artist's work are also available. Next door is **Gayle Clarke Artisans** (tel. 601/875–3900), where you can purchase crafts, blown glass, pottery, and handmade jewelry—including dragonfly necklaces.

Beaches

Twenty-six miles of man-made beach extend from Biloxi to Pass Christian. Toward the west the beaches become less commercialized and crowded; **Waveland's** is the best of all. Tan, sail, jet-ski, or beachcomb, but *don't* swim; it's shallow and not clean.

Participant Sports

Boating Sailboats, sailboards, jet skis, and catamarans may be rented from the many vendors who station themselves along the beach. You can also rent 14-foot motorboats at **End of the Wharf** (1020 E. Beach Blvd., Biloxi), just behind Fisherman's Wharf Restaurant.

Camping From U.S. 90 in Waveland, turn south on Nicholson and follow the signs to **Buccaneer State Park** (tel. 601/467–3822), which conceals 129 campsites in a grove of live oaks streaming with moss. An Olympic-size wave pool may lure you from the nature trail and picnic sites. There are no cabins, but toilet and shower facilities are available.

Gulf Islands National Seashore (*see above*) offers campsites for trailers and RV's.

Fishing and Crabbing For **floundering** you'll need nighttime, a light, and a gig. Head for the sound, roll up your jeans, and spear your supper! A chicken neck and a string will put you in the **crabbing** business at any public pier. If you want to be lazy, substitute a crab trap for the string.

Charter boats for half-day and full-day **deep-sea fishing** can be found at marinas and harbors all along the Gulf Coast. Prices range upward from $30 per person, averaging $55; group rates are usually available. The Mississippi Gulf Coast Convention and Visitors Bureau (tel. 601/388–8000) can assist you.

Golf The coast's climate allows for year-round golfing, and many golf packages are offered by hotels and motels. **Diamondhead's Pine and Cardinal courses** (7600 Country Club Circle, Bay St. Louis, tel. 601/255–2525) offer 36 challenging wooded holes, ringed by the large, elegant houses and condominiums of Diamondhead resort community.

Hickory Hill Country Club and Golf Course (900 Hickory Hill Dr., Gautier, tel. 601/497–5575, ext. 204) offers visitors fairways lined with whispering pines, tall oaks, magnolias, and dogwoods. Flowers surround the teeing areas.

Pine Island Golf Course (Gulf Park Estates 2¼ mi east of Ocean Springs, 3 mi south of U.S. 90, tel. 601/875–1674), designed by Pete Dye, spans three islands, and its abundant wildlife, beautiful setting, and club house can console you for any bogeys.

Windance Country Club (94 Champion Circle, Gulfport, tel. 601/832–4871) has a public golf course ranked among the top 100 in the United States by *Golf Digest*.

Dining and Lodging

Fresh Gulf seafood, particularly redfish, flounder, and speckled trout dishes, stars in coast restaurants. Soft-shell crab is a coast specialty, and crab claws are a traditional appetizer. Coast natives are fond of quaffing Barq's root beer with their seafood.

The following dining price categories have been used: *Very Expensive*, over $20; *Expensive*, $15–$20; *Moderate*, $10–$15; *Inexpensive*, $5–$10.

The following lodging price categories have been used: *Very Expensive*, over $70; *Expensive*, $50–$70; *Moderate*, $30–$50; *Inexpensive*, $20–$30.

Bay St. Louis
Lodging **Diamondhead Inn.** This standard-issue motel attracts golfers who play the nearby Diamondhead Pine and Cardinal courses (*see* Participant Sports, *above*). The wooden walks and balconies are nicked by cleats; some walls are scarred, presumably by golfers' rages or rowdies. Each room has a balcony and kitchenette (actually just a fridge for beer). *4300 Aloha Circle, Bay St. Louis 39520, tel. 601/255–1421 or outside MS 800/647–9550. 67 rooms. Facilities: yacht club, marina, tennis courts, 36-hole golf course, stable, and a nearby 3,500-ft lighted airstrip. AE, MC, V. Expensive.*

Biloxi
Dining **Fisherman's Wharf.** A neighboring shrimp factory perfumes the parking lot here, but race inside to fresher air and views of oyster shuckers at work on the pier. Crabmeat salad for lunch; broiled catch-of-the-day for dinner; and always, the only des-

sert, the mysterious Fisherman's Wharf pie. *1020 E. Beach Blvd., tel. 601/436–4513. Dress: informal. Reservations recommended. AE, MC, V. Expensive.*

Baricev's. The restaurant's large, plain dining room is enhanced by display cases of shrimp, fish, and oysters heaped on ice, and by sweeping views of the ocean where the creatures so recently cavorted. Fried soft-shell crab, a specialty, is succulent inside a thick, flaky crust. If you scorn "fry," other specialties are snapper Baricev, rolled in seasoned cracker crumbs and broiled in olive oil; and oysters Baricev, a casserole of plump oysters, green onions, garlic, cheese, and olive oil. Baricev's is Yugoslavian, but the hearty gumbo bespeaks a proper French *roux. 633 Central Beach Blvd., tel. 601/435–3626. Dress: informal. No reservations. AE, DC, MC, V. Moderate.*

McElroy's Harbor House Seafood Restaurant. Biloxi natives and real shrimpers eat hearty breakfasts, lunches, and dinners here in functional surroundings. Notable are the po'boys, oysters on the half shell, broiled stuffed flounder, and stuffed crabs. You can also try "Biloxi bacon." *Biloxi Small Craft Harbor, tel. 601/435–5001. Dress: informal. AE. DC, MC, V. Inexpensive.*

Ole Biloxi Schooner. Coast residents flock to this family-run restaurant on Biloxi's serene back bay. It's tiny—little more than a shack—but the food is good, especially the gumbo and the po'boys, which come "dressed" and wrapped in paper. *159 E. Howard, tel. 601/374–8071. Dress: informal. No credit cards. Inexpensive.*

Lodging **Mississippi Beach Resort Hotel.** Formerly the Biloxi Hilton, this high-rise hotel with its flanking motellike wings, gains distinction from tropical plantings. Rooms can be tired and musty. *3580 W. Beach Blvd., Biloxi 39531, tel. 601/388–7000. 450 rooms. Facilities: lounge with entertainment, 6 lighted tennis courts, championship golf course, pool, 2 playgrounds, game room. AE, MC, V. Expensive–Very Expensive.*

Royal d'Iberville Hotel. This hotel has gone upscale since a recent decoration that left the spacious rooms bright with chintz. Furniture is hotel-functional; the large public areas are comfortably contemporary. *1980 W. Beach Blvd., Biloxi 39530, tel. 601/388–6610, 800/647–3955, 800/222–3906 in MS. 264 rooms. Facilities: beachfront lounge, entertainment, 2 swimming pools, restaurants, children's playground, tennis, golf, meeting facilities, suites, babysitting. AE, DC, MC, V. Expensive–Very Expensive.*

Beachwater Inn. Set among live oaks that contrast with its contemporary lines, this family-owned motel attracts repeat customers. Its owners are experts on coast attractions and events. The rooms are fresh and neat, though not elegant. *1678 W. Beach Blvd., Biloxi 39530, tel. 601/432–1984. 31 rooms, some with cooking nooks and porches; beach views. Facilities: tree deck, baby-sitting, pool, golf packages, deep-sea fishing, and activity director. No restaurant. AE, MC, V. Rates depend on season. Moderate.*

Gulfport **Vrazel's.** In 1969, Hurricane Camille blew away the restaurant
Dining that had long stood here; the brick building that replaced it gets its charm from soft lighting and dining nooks with large windows facing the beach. Added attractions include the red snapper, Gulf trout, flounder, and shrimp prepared every which way: étouffée, au gratin à la Cajun, amandine, à la

Vrazel, blackened, Pontchartrain, meuniere. Snapper Lenwood is a specialty, teaming broiled snapper with crabmeat and crawfish in a Cajun-style sauce. For the best of land and sea, try veal Aaron (crabmeat, mushrooms, and lemon sauce combined with tender veal medallions). *3206 W. Beach Blvd. (U.S. 90), tel. 601/863–2229. Jacket and tie required. Dinner reservations recommended. AE, MC, V. Moderate.*

Lil Ray's, Etc. The tacky coast decor here includes running lights and other nautical trappings. But for giant po'boys (9″ or 14″ long) on thick French bread, the only place as good as this Lil Ray's in Gulfport is the original Lil Ray's in Waveland *(see Waveland Dining, below)*. Try fried soft-shell crabs or fried oysters your first time round. Regulars wolf down enormous seafood platters (stuffed crab and fried catfish, shrimp, and oysters) and mountains of boiled shrimp, crabs, and crawfish in season. The gumbo is excellent. *U.S. 49 across from Norwood Village Shopping Center, tel. 601/831–1160 or 601/831–1161. Dress: informal. No reservations. MC, V. Closed Sun. Inexpensive.*

Long Beach Dining

Chappy's. Special occasion dining for Coast residents often means a visit to this pleasant restaurant with its twinkling white lights outside, its black-clad waiters inside. Specialties include rich gumbo, redfish pan-fried Cajun style, and barbecued shrimp. The fish, fresh from the Gulf, is cooked by Chappy himself. *624 E. Beach, tel. 601/865–9755. Dress: dressy for the Coast, informal by world standards. Reservations recommended. AE, MC, V. Expensive.*

Ocean Springs Dining

Germaine's. Formerly Trilby's, this little house surrounded by live oaks has served many a great meal to its faithful clientele. The atmosphere is reminiscent of New Orleans, with unadorned wooden floors, walls decked in local art-for-sale, fireplaces, and attentive service. Specialties include mushrooms le marin, crabmeat au gratin, trout desoto, veal Angela, and chicken Chardonnay. *U.S. 90E, tel. 601/875–4426. Jacket and tie required. Reservations recommended. AE, DC, MC, V. Expensive.*

Jocelyn's Restaurant. Jocelyn scandalized Mississippians when she left Trilby's kitchen *(see above)*, but they love her cooking just as much in this old frame house. This is as good as Coast seafood gets. The specialty is the day's catch of flounder, trout, and redfish subtly seasoned and served with garnishes as bright and original as modern art. Chicken pot pie is another (surprising) specialty. *U.S. 90E, opposite Eastover Bank, tel. 601/875–1925. Dress: a fine line between jacket and tie and informal, depending on your mood. Reservations recommended. No credit cards. Expensive.*

La Casa de Elva. Pink stucco and round arches say Mexico, but the wooded views say Gulf Coast at this large restaurant that's open for lunch and dinner. Specialties include marinated shrimp stuffed with cheese and jalapeño, wrapped in bacon and broiled under a cheese topping; shrimp baked in a delicate butter-citrus sauce with cilantro; and traditional Mexican dishes like boneless breast of chicken baked in an *achiote* sauce and beef strips in *ranchero picante* salsa. There's a piano bar until midnight, with dancing. *U.S. 90, 1 mi. east of Biloxi–Ocean Springs Bridge, tel. 601/875–0144. Dress: casual. Reservations not required. MC, V. Inexpensive.*

Waveland **Lil Ray's.** The appointments in the *original* Lil Ray's are lim-
Dining ited to trestle tables and benches. This is a place to dream about
when you're hungry for seafood platters and po'boys. The menu
is the same as Lil Ray's in Gulfport (*see* Gulfport Dining,
above). A waitress, asked by a customer for a diet drink, said it
best: "Mister, this ain't no diet place." *1015 U.S. 90, tel. 601/
467–4566. Dress: informal. Reservations not required. MC, V.
Inexpensive.*

Nightlife

David M's (857 Beach Blvd., Biloxi, tel. 601/374–8832) includes
five bars and restaurants that offer varied entertainment: music of the '60s and '70s, dancing on a black-marble dance floor,
and relaxing in a large hot tub. There's also a barefoot bar at
the end of a pier (in case you wish to arrive by boat).

Steep yourself in antebellum splendor at **Mary Mahoney's Irish
Pub** adjacent to the Old French House (*see* Time Out, *above*), or
tip a frosty beer with the locals in the fishhouse-plain bar at
Baricev's (*see* Biloxi Dining, *above*). Swim up to barstools in the
pool for summer drinks at the **Mississippi Beach Resort Hotel**
(*see* Biloxi Lodging, *above*).

Mobile and the Gulf Coast

Mobile, one of the oldest cities in Alabama, is perhaps the most
graceful. Its main thoroughfare, Government Street, is bordered with live oaks, and many antebellum buildings survive as
a bridge with a treasured past. The city is also rich in azaleas—a feature that is highlighted each spring with the Azalea
Trail Festival. Nearby is Bellingrath Gardens, one of the most
spectacular public gardens in the country.

The area of the Gulf Coast around Gulf Shores, to the south of
Mobile, encompasses about 50 miles of pure white sand beach,
including a former peninsula called Pleasure Island and Dauphin Island to the west. Though hotels and condominiums take
up a good deal of the beachfront, some of it remains public.
Here you'll find small-town Southern beach life, with excellent
deep-sea fishing, as well as freshwater fishing in the bays and
bayous, plus water sports of all types.

*Numbers in the margin correspond to points of interest on the
Mobile and the Gulf Coast map.*

❶ The busy port city of **Mobile,** on the western bank of the Mobile
River and at the top of Mobile Bay, overlaps past and present.
Despite a raking-over by Hurricane Frederick in 1979, gracious old mansions, iron-grillwork balconies, and lovely gardens abound. Many businesses in town are conducted from
buildings that predate the Civil War.

Fort Condé was the name the French gave the site in 1711;
around it blossomed the first white settlement in what is now
Alabama. For eight years it was the capital of the French colonial empire, and it remained under French control until 1763,
long after the capital had moved to New Orleans. This French
connection survives in the area's cuisine, which is strongly Cre-
ole-flavored and rivals New Orleans in fieriness.

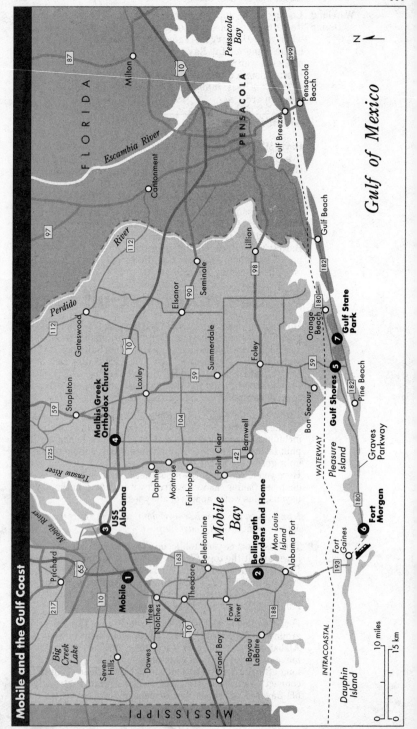

Mobile and the Gulf Coast

606

Fort Condé, too, survives, thanks to a $2.2-million restoration, which preserved it when its remains were discovered—150 years after the fort was destroyed—during construction of the I-10 interchange (an I-10 tunnel now runs under the fort). A reconstructed portion houses the visitor center for the city, as well as a museum and several re-created rooms. Costumed guides interpret and enlighten. *150 S. Royal St., tel. 205/434-7304. Admission free. Open daily 8–5. Closed Christmas and Mardi Gras.*

Mobile today is noted for its tree-lined boulevards fanning out from **Bienville Square,** at the center of the city. Once upon a time, the square was a showplace, where the town's finest dressers would stroll beneath the live oaks and listen to bands playing on the ornate wrought-iron, gazebo-style bandstand. On special occasions—unfortunately few and far between these days—bands play again. One such occasion is the September Celebration, when weekend musical celebrations fill the air.

The city's main thoroughfare is Government Street. From here, signs lead to **Oakleigh,** a gorgeous white antebellum mansion with a stairway circling under ancient live oaks to a small portico. The high-ceilinged half-timber house was built between 1833 and 1838 and is typical of the most expensive dwellings of its day. Fine period furniture, portraits, silver, jewelry, kitchen implements, toys, and more are displayed throughout. Tickets can be purchased next door at the **Cox-Deasy House,** another antebellum home that is not quite as old as Oakleigh (1850) and by no means as grand. It is, rather, a cottage, built for middle-class folk, and is furnished in simple 19th-century pieces. *350 Oakleigh Place, tel. 205/432–1281. Admission: $4 adults, $3 over 65, $2 college students with ID, $1 children 6–18, under 6 free. Open Mon.–Sat. 10–4, Sun. 2–4. Guided tours conducted every half-hour. Closed major holidays and Christmas week.*

❷ Less than 20 miles south of Mobile off I-10 (turn south onto Bellingrath Rd. at the town of Theodore) is **Bellingrath Gardens and Home,** site of one of the world's most magnificent azalea gardens. Here, set amid a 905-acre semitropical landscape, are some 65 spectacular acres of gardens. Showtime for its azaleas is spring, when some 250,000 plantings of 200 different species are ablaze with color. But Bellingrath is a year-round wonder. In summer, 2,500 rosebushes are in bloom; in autumn, 60,000 chrysanthemum plants; in winter, fields of poinsettias. And countless other species and varieties of flowering plants spring up along a river or stream or around a lake populated by ducks and swans. The gardens are also a sanctuary to over 200 species of birds. Coca-Cola bottling pioneer Walter D. Bellingrath began the nucleus of the gardens in 1917, when he and his wife bought a large tract as a fishing camp. Their travels, however, prompted them to create, instead, a garden rivaling some they had seen in Europe, and before long they opened it to the public. Today their brick home on the property is also open to visitors and offers one of the finest collections of antiques in the Southeast. Along with furniture, Meissen porcelain figurines, Dresden china, and other objets d'art amassed by Mrs. Bellingrath is the world's largest collection of Boehm porcelain birds. *Tel. 205/973–2217. Admission: gardens, $5 adults, $2.50 children 6–11, under 6 free; combination admission with house $11.25 adults, $8.75 children 6–11, $6.25 under*

6. *$6.25 home only. Gardens open daily 7 AM–sunset; house open daily 8 AM–1 hr before sunset. Closed Christmas.*

From Mobile, there are two ways to reach **Pleasure Island,** a 30-mile region for romping along the Gulf of Mexico. One is to take a scenic drive south along Rte. 163, perhaps stopping off at Bellingrath Gardens, and cross over the bridge to Dauphin Island, where you catch the **Mobile Bay Ferry** (tel. 904/434–7345 or 800/634–4027) for the 30-minute trip over to Fort Morgan, at the tip of Pleasure Island. This coastal route is shorter in mileage, though probably not in time. The other approach—the one our tour follows—is via U.S. 90E through the Bankhead Tunnel, then south on AL 59.

③ On the way, stop to pay a call aboard the USS *Alabama,* anchored in Mobile Bay just east of Mobile off I–10. Public subscription saved the mighty gray battleship from being scrapped ignominiously after her heroic World War II service, which ranged from Scapa Flow to the South Pacific. A tour of the ship gives a fascinating look into the life of a 2,500-member crew. Anchored next to the battleship is the submarine USS *Drum,* another active battle weapon during World War II, also open to visitors. Other exhibits in the 100-acre Battleship Park include a B–52 bomber called *Calamity Jane* and a P–51 Mustang fighter plane. *Battleship Pkwy., tel. 205/433–2703. Admission: $5 age 12 and up; $2.50 ages 6–11, under 6 free. Parking fee: $1. Open 8 AM–sunset. Closed Christmas.*

④ Twelve miles east of Mobile, on U.S. 90, just off I–10, is the **Malbis Greek Orthodox Church,** a replica of a beautiful Byzantine church in Athens, Greece. It was built in 1965, at a cost of more than $1 million, as a memorial to the faith of a Greek immigrant and former monk, Jason Malbis, who founded the community but died before his dream for a cathedral could be realized. The marble for the interior was imported from the same quarries that provided stone for the Parthenon, and a master painter was brought over from Greece to paint murals on the walls and the 75-foot dome of the rotunda. The stained-glass windows are stunning. *County Route 27, tel. 205/626–3050. Admission free. Tours daily 9 AM–noon, 2–5 PM.*

⑤ When you're ready for some sun and surf, take AL 59 south to the end. At AL 182, head west. A block later, turn right for a circular drive next to the **Gulf Shores** public beach area, crowded with Alabama high school and college students at spring break and everyone in summer. There's ample free parking—though the traffic is bumper-to-bumper at peak times—and the beach is as white as snow.

⑥ At the western tip of Pleasure Island, 20 miles from Gulf Shores at the end of AL 180, is **Fort Morgan,** built in the early 1800s to guard the entrance to Mobile Bay. The fort saw fiery action during the Battle of Mobile Bay in 1864: Confederate torpedoes sank the ironclad *Tecumseh,* on which Admiral David Farragut gave his famous command "Damn the torpedoes! Full speed ahead!" The original outer walls still stand; inside, a museum chronicles the fort's history and displays artifacts from Indian days through World War II, with an emphasis on the Civil War. *Mobile Point, tel. 205/540–7125. Admission: $2 adults; $1 over 61 and children 6–18, under 6 free. Open daily 9–5. Closed major holidays.*

❼ Five miles east of Gulf Shores on AL 182 is **Gulf State Park,** which covers more than 6,000 acres of Pleasure Island. Along with 2½ miles of pure white beaches and glimmering dunes, the park also has two freshwater lakes with canoeing and fishing, plus biking, hiking, and jogging trails through pine forests. There is a large beach pavilion with a snack bar, rest rooms, and showers, and nearby is a concrete fishing pier that juts 825 feet into the Gulf. There is also a resort inn and convention center, 468 campsites, and 21 cottages, plus tennis courts and an 18-hole golf course. *For information, write Gulf State Park, Rte. 2, Box 9, Gulf Shores 36542. Tel.: cabins and bike, canoe, and motorless flat-bottom fishing boat rentals, 205/968–7544; camping, 205/968–6353; resort inn, 205/968–7531. Open year-round.*

Those with more time might explore the eastern shore of Mobile Bay—Spanish Fort, Daphne, and Fairhope—which has a laid-back atmosphere of yesteryear: live oaks laced with Spanish moss; sprawling clapboard houses with wide porches overlooking the lazy, dark water of the bay; and interesting watering holes where local artists and writers meet informally. At Point Clear, south of Fairhope, is the Victorian-style Marriott's Grand Hotel, host for the past 143 years to the vacationing wealthy.

Shopping

Mobile   The **Bel Air Mall** (one block east of I–65 Beltline off Airport Blvd., tel. 205/478–1893) has some 175 stores under one roof, including JC Penney and Sears, plus a food court. **Springdale Mall-Plaza** (Airport Blvd. and I–65, tel. 205/471–1945), anchored by Gayfer's, McRae's, and Montgomery Ward, recently expanded and now has more than 100 stores.

Antiques   At **Allen's Antiques & Collectibles** (121 Telegraph Rd., in Chickasaw, just north of Mobile, tel. 205/452–0717), the specialty is wicker. **Al Atchison Courtyard Antiques** (601 Government St., tel. 205/438–9421 or 205/432–8423), one of the largest antiques dealers in the South, is packed with antique brass beds and other American and European antique furniture.

Gulf Shores   **Riviera Centre** (AL 59 S, Foley, AL, tel. 205/943–8888), a handsome complex of factory-direct stores, offers savings of up to 75% off regular retail prices. Stores include West Point Pepperell, L'Eggs Hanes Bali, Judy Bond, J. G. Hook, Dansk, Danskin, Calvin Klein, Liz Claiborne, American Tourister, Polo/Ralph Lauren, Manhattan, Bass Shoes, Pfaltzgraff, and other top names.

Participant Sports

Biking   **Gulf State Park** (tel. 205/948–7275) in Gulf Shores has biking trails through pine forests and rents bicycles. **Island Recreation Services** (tel. 205/948–7334) in Gulf Shores rents bikes, mopeds, and water-sports equipment (*see* Water Sports, *below*).

Canoeing   **Sunshine Canoe Rentals** (tel. 205/344–8664) runs canoe trips at Escatawpa River, 15 miles west of Mobile. The river has no rapids but makes for pleasant, leisurely travel past lots of white sandbars.

Fishing The freshwater and saltwater fishing in the Gulf area is excellent. **Gulf State Park** has fishing from an 825-foot pier and rents flat-bottom boats for lake fishing. Deep-sea fishing from charter boats is very popular; in Gulf Shores, you can sign on board the *Marina Queen* (tel. 205/981–8499) for a full- or half-day fishing expedition; Orange Beach has 40 boats to choose from, including the 98-foot *Moreno Queen* (tel. 205/981–8499) and the 48-foot *Island Lady* (tel. 205/981–4510). Catches from these deep-sea expeditions include king mackerel, amberjack, tuna, white marlin, blue marlin, grouper, bonito, sailfish, and red snapper. Nonresidents 16 or over may not fish anywhere in Alabama without a valid fishing license; for information, call 205/242–3260.

Golf A good public 18-hole course in Mobile is the **Spring Hill College Golf Course** (tel. 205/343–2356); the 18-hole **Azalea City Golf Club** (tel. 205/342–4221) is rather flat and not a great challenge. **Gulf Shores Golf Club** (tel. 205/968–7366) has an 18-hole, 72-par championship course. The 18-hole course at the **Gulf State Park Resort** (tel. 205/948–4653) is one of the most beautiful, with moss-hung live oaks and giant magnolia trees. The newest links in the area, **Lakeview Golf Club** (off AL 59 on Rte. 20 south of Foley, tel. 205/943–4653), has 27 holes and six lakes and is well sand-trapped. Only 25 minutes from Gulf Shores, on the Beach Road East in Florida, is **Perdido Bay Resort** (tel. 904/492–1223), the home of October's Pensacola Open.

Horseback Riding **Horseback Beach Rides** (tel. 205/943–6674) offers guided group rides along country trails or along the beach at Gulf Shores.

Sailing Sailboats that can be rented with captain include the *Cyrus King* (at **Island Sailing Center**, tel. 205/968–6775) and the *Daedalus* (tel. 205/986–7018) in Gulf Shores. **Island Recreation Services** (tel. 205/948–7334) in Gulf Shores; and **Land 'N' Sea** (tel. 205/943–3600) in Foley, rent sailboats without captain.

Water Sports **Fun Marina** (tel. 205/981–8587) in Orange Beach rents Jet Skis, pontoon boats, and 16-foot bay-fishing boats. In Gulf Shores, **Island Recreation Services** (tel. 205/948–7334) rents boogie boards, body boards, surf boats, and sailboats.

Dining and Lodging

In Mobile and throughout the Gulf area, the specialty is fresh seafood, often prepared in Creole style, with peppery spices, crabmeat dressing, and sometimes a tomato-based sauce. Mobile, in fact, prides itself on being the only city in Alabama with a cuisine of its own, whose precedence (in time, at least) over New Orleans's it has been claiming for years. The basis of the claim is history: The founders of Mobile, French explorers Bienville and Iberville, came here first, then moved west to New Orleans.

The following dining price categories have been used: *Expensive*, over $25; *Moderate*, $15–$25; *Inexpensive*, under $15.

The following lodging price categories have been used: *Very Expensive*, over $95; *Expensive*, $70–$95; *Moderate*, $50–$70; *Inexpensive*, under $50.

Mobile **Carlucci's.** Word of mouth is fast spreading the fame of this
Dining restaurant in an ancient town house in downtown Mobile. You
★ have to search for the place—the sign is so small, it looks like a

lawyer's shingle. Inside, it's quietly elegant. The menu show-cases an imaginative mélange of Creole and Italian specialties. In the upstairs bistro, top-notch jazz performers entertain ($5 cover charge). *358 Dauphin St., tel. 205/433–7955. Jacket and tie requested. Reservations suggested. AE, DC, MC, V. Closed Sun. Expensive*

La Louisiana. This antiques-filled old house on the outskirts is a delightful setting in which to dine. The seafood is fresh, prepared with a touch of French Creole. Shrimp dishes are heavy with cream sauces unless you order them lightly fried. The seafood gumbo is made the Mobile way: heavy on shrimp, oysters, and okra. *2400 Airport Blvd., tel. 205/476–8130. Jacket and tie requested. Reservations preferred. AE, MC, V. Closed Sun. Dinner only. Expensive.*

★ **The Pillars.** Sitting amid fine antiques from the 18th and 19th centuries in a huge old mansion with wide porches overlooking the live oaks in the yard, it is easy to imagine oneself in another time, listening to the latest news from the battlefront at Vicksburg or Shiloh. The beautifully cooked snapper with a white-wine-and-cream sauce and the snapper with crabmeat and a pecan Creole sauce are delicious. The lamb chops are cut thick and cooked just the way you like them over a charcoal grill. *1757 Government St., tel. 205/478–6341. Dress: jacket and tie suggested. Reservations preferred. AE, DC, MC, V. Closed Sun. Dinner only. Expensive.*

The Malaga Restaurant. This is a small, intimate restaurant in the former carriage house of The Malaga Inn (*see* Lodging, *below*). At the end of one of its two rooms, a set of French doors lets in lots of light and a view out to the pool, landscaped with banana trees and other tropical plants. The walls are a mixture of old brick and a cream-and-green floral-print wallpaper. The menu is a mix of Creole-style seafood and Continental dishes. One of the most popular choices is snapper Brennan—fresh Gulf snapper served with a sauce of crabmeat, mushrooms, wine, and other delights. Continental choices include chateau-briand and steak Diane. *359 Church St., tel. 205/433–5858. Dress: casual. Reservations preferred for dinner. AE, DC, MC, V. Moderate*

Rousso's Restaurant. A local favorite, with a nautical look created by lots of fishnets and scenes of ships at sea, Rousso's is known for its crab claws, fried in a light batter and served with a catsup-horseradish sauce. *166 S. Royal St., tel. 205/433–3322. Dress: casual. Reservations accepted. AE, DC, MC, V. Closed Sun. Moderate.*

Wintzell's Oyster House. Opened in 1938, this is a place to see and be seen. All the local celebrities (not to mention a movie or TV star or two) eat here—especially at the raw bar. Every piece of space on the walls and ceilings is covered with Wintzell's favorite sayings and photographs of celebrities and political figures. The seafood is fresh from the Gulf, fried or broiled—perfectly complemented by good draft beer. *605 Dauphin St., tel. 205/433–1004. Dress: casual. No reservations. AE, DC, MC, V. Closed Sun. Inexpensive.*

Lodging **Stouffer's Riverview Plaza.** A stylish new contemporary struc-
★ ture, the 28-story Riverview offers panoramic views of the Mobile River and downtown Mobile. The lobby and guest rooms are decorated in a contemporary style. *64 S. Water St., 36602, tel. 205/438–4000 or 800/468–3571. 365 rooms, 10 suites. Fa-*

cilities: outdoor pool, sauna, whirlpool, deli, lounge, restaurant. AE, DC, MC, V. Very Expensive.

★ **Radisson Admiral Semmes Hotel.** An old hotel that was renovated several years ago, this is a favorite with local politicians. It is also popular with party-goers, particularly during Mardi Gras, because of its excellent location directly on the parade route. Rooms are furnished in Queen Anne and Chippendale styles. *251 Government St., Box 1209, 36633, tel. 205/432–8000 or 800/333–3333. 147 rooms, 22 suites. Facilities: cable TV/free movies, outdoor pool, Jacuzzi, Oliver's Restaurant (specializing in Cajun, Creole cuisines), Admiral's Corner Lounge, privileges at Y. AE, DC, MC, V. Expensive.*

Ramada Resort and Conference Center. This glass-and-brick hotel, with a four-story main section and a two-story wing, is known for having the most "happening" bar in town. Suites are large, and all rooms are decorated in a contemporary style. *600 S. Beltline Hwy. 36608, tel. 205/344–8030 or 800/272–6232. 230 rooms, 6 suites. Facilities: cable TV/free movies, heated indoor pool with Jacuzzi, outdoor pool, Nautilus room, putting green, lighted tennis court, restaurant, lounge, bar, 8 meeting rooms. AE, DC, MC, V. Expensive.*

★ **The Malaga Inn.** A delightful, romantic getaway place, The Malaga comprises two town houses built by a wealthy landowner in 1862. The lobby is furnished with 19th-century antiques and opens onto a tropically landscaped central courtyard with a fountain. The rooms are large, airy, and furnished with massive antiques. Ask for the front suite, with 14-foot ceilings and crimson velveteen wallpaper. *359 Church St., 36602, tel. 205/ 438–4701. 40 rooms. Facilities: cable TV, outdoor pool, restaurant (see Dining, above), lounge. AE, DC, MC, V. Inexpensive–Moderate.*

Gulf Shores Area
Dining

Original Oyster House. A rustic but very clean, plant-filled restaurant overlooking the bayou, this has become a Gulf Shores tradition. Oysters on the half-shell, fresh out of nearby Perdido Bay, are the specialty of the house. The Cajun-style gumbo— a concoction of crab claws, shrimp, amberjack, grouper, redfish, okra and other vegetables, and Cajun spices—has won 20 major awards. *Bayou Village Shopping Ctr., AL 59, Gulf Shores, tel. 205/948–2445. Dress: casual. No reservations. AE, DC, MC, V. Moderate–Expensive.*

★ **Voyagers.** Roses in crystal vases and Art Deco touches set the tone for this airy, elegant dining room. Two-level seating allows beach or poolside views from every table. The specialties include trout with roasted pecans in Creole meunière sauce and soft-shell crab topped with Creole sauce Choron. Follow up with fried-apple beignet topped with French vanilla sauce or crepe soufflé praline. Service is deft, sophisticated, and there's an extensive wine selection. *Perdido Beach Hilton, Hwy. 182, Orange Beach, tel. 205/981–9811. Dress: jacket and tie suggested. Reservations advised. AE, DC, MC, V. Moderate–Expensive.*

Dempsey's Restaurant. The setting is tropical, enhanced by a 20-foot waterfall, at this lakeside dining room. Cajun seafood specialties are arranged temptingly at the all-you-can-eat dinner buffet that includes such seafood dishes as stuffed jumbo shrimp. There's also nightly blues and a small dance floor. *AL 182, Romar Beach, tel. 205/981–6800. Dress: casual. No reservations. AE, DC, MC, V. Inexpensive.*

Hazel's Family Restaurant. Former Alabama Governor Fob

James, a resident of Gulf Shores, says Hazel's has "the best biscuits in the state." The plain but tasteful family-style restaurant serves a good, hearty breakfast, soup-and-salad lunches, and adequate buffet dinners featuring such seafood dishes as flounder Florentine or crab-stuffed broiled snapper. *Gulf View Square Shopping Ctr., Romar Beach, tel. 205/981–4628. Dress: casual. No reservations. AE, MC, V. Inexpensive.*

Pompano's. All seats at this hotel restaurant have a view of the Gulf; one of the four high-ceilinged rooms has two glass walls. Furnishings are blond wood with green upholstery, gray tablecloths, and maroon napkins. The specialty is local seafood, served in a "coastal tradition." The Captain's Platter features Gulf jumbo shrimp, oysters, flounder, and bay scallops, all fried in a light batter. *Quality Inn Beachside, W. Beach Blvd., Gulf Shores, tel. 205/948–6874. Dress: casual. No reservations. AE, DC, MC, V. Inexpensive.*

★ **Zeke's Landing Restaurant and Oyster Bar.** Overlooking the restaurant's marina on Cotton Bayou, the large rooms are highlighted by bleached woods, black lacquer, and brass. Service is deft, unhurried, and unfailingly friendly. There's an excellent, modestly priced selection of fried or grilled seafood, steaks, garden salads, and sandwiches, such as the seafood melt—crab and shrimp with Cheddar-cheese sauce over an open-faced English muffin. All entrées come with freshly baked bread, soup or salad, and a choice of potato. *Beach Hwy. 180, Orange Beach, 4 mi west of Perdido Beach Hilton, tel. 205/ 981–4001. Open daily for lunch and dinner; weekend brunch. Dress: casual. No reservations. AE, DC, MC, V. Inexpensive.*

Lodging **Perdido Beach Hilton.** The eight- and nine-story towers are
★ Mediterranean stucco and red tile. The lobby is tiled in terracotta and decorated with mosaics by Venetian artists and a brass sculpture of gulls in flight. Rooms are furnished in luxurious Mediterranean style, and all have a beach view and balcony. *AL 182E, Box 400, Orange Beach 36561, tel. 205/981– 9811 or 800/634–8001. 345 units, including 16 suites. Facilities: heated indoor/outdoor pool, whirlpool, sauna, exercise room overlooking beach, 4 lighted tennis courts, pool bar, café, restaurant. AE, DC, MC, V. Very Expensive.*

Gulf Shores Holiday Inn. This four-story beachfront hotel has Gulf-front, poolside, and king-size leisure rooms in a contemporary style. *E. Beach Blvd., Box 417, Gulf Shores 36542, tel. 205/968– 6191 or 800/465–4329. 118 rooms. Facilities: cable TV/ free movies, outdoor pool, poolside, 2 lighted tennis courts, restaurant, lounge, 3 meeting rooms. AE, DC, MC, V. Expensive–Very Expensive.*

Quality Inn Beachside. This spacious motel is made up of two buildings, one five years old (three stories) and a new one (six stories). All the guest rooms are modern, decorated in pastels, with private balconies; most face the Gulf; half have kitchens. In the Art Deco–style atrium lobby, with glass-brick walls, is a 70-foot swimming pool and a waterfall. Glass-walled elevators rise six stories. *921 W. Gulf Shores Blvd., Box 1013, Gulf Shores 36542, tel. 205/948–6874 or 800/228–5151. 158 rooms. Facilities: cable TV, exercise room, large hot tub, outdoor pool, pool bar, piano bar, Pompano's restaurant (see Dining, above), deli. AE, DC, MC, V. Expensive–Very Expensive.*

Lighthouse. This complex of five two- to four-story buildings, surrounded by brightly colored exotic flowers, is set on a 580-foot private beach. The waterfront rooms have private balconies, and some units have kitchens. All have contemporary furnishings. *E. Beach Blvd., Box 233, Gulf Shores 36542, tel. 205/948–6188. 124 rooms. Facilities: cable TV/movies, 2 outdoor pools (1 heated, with large Jacuzzi). AE, DC, MC, V. Moderate–Expensive.*

Beachport Motel. Across the street from Gulf Shores beach, this four-story hotel has some rooms (20) with kitchenettes. *201 E. Beach Blvd., Box 955, Gulf Shores 36542, tel. 205/948–6844. 52 rooms. Facilities: cable TV, restaurant, lounge with live music and dance floor. AE, DC, MC, V. Moderate.*

Port of Call. At this three-story facility across the highway from Gulf Shores beach, suites have full kitchens and separate living rooms. Some units have balconies. *W. Beach Blvd., Box 978, Gulf Shores 36542, tel. 205/948–7739. 18 suites, 3 efficiencies. Facilities: cable TV, outdoor pool, coin laundry. MC, V. Inexpensive–Moderate.*

Point Clear
Dining and Lodging
★

Marriott's Grand Hotel. Nestled amid 550 acres of beautifully landscaped grounds, the "Grand" has been a cherished tradition since 1847. Extensively refurbished by Marriott, it is one of the South's premier resorts. Its two-story cypress–paneled and beamed lobby evokes an aura of traditional elegance. Spacious rooms and cottages are also traditionally furnished. *On Mobile Bay, US Scenic 98, Point Clear 36564, tel. 205/928–9201 or 800/228–9290. 308 units, including some suites, 2 rooms with refrigerators. Facilities: cable TV, movies, pool, beach, sauna and whirlpool, marina with rental boats, sailing, charter fishing, social program, complimentary Grand Fun Camp for youngsters Mon.–Sat., rental bicycles, playground, 10 tennis courts, 36 holes golf, horseback riding, 3 dining rooms, including award-winning Magnolia Room, coffee shop, lounge with entertainment. AE, DC, MC, V. Very Expensive.*

Nightlife

Adam's (Airport Blvd.–Beltline Hwy., tel. 205/344–8030), at Mobile's Ramada Inn Airport, is popular among younger partygoers who enjoy loud, fast music. There's live entertainment in **Admiral's Corner** at the Radisson Admiral Semmes Hotel (251 Government St., tel. 205/432–8000) and live entertainment and dancing in the **Jubilation** lounge of the Holiday Inn (I–10 and U.S. 90, tel. 205/666–5600).

On the Alabama–Florida line is the **Flora-Bama Lounge** (Beach Rd., tel. 205/981–8555), with country-and-western music performed by a local band and vocalist. It's the place where Mobile native Jimmy Buffet got his start to stardom.

At **Shirley & Wayne's** (AL 182, Romar Beach, tel. 205/981–4818), Wayne Perdew and his band play swing and country Monday–Saturday nights while you dine and/or dance.

The Panhandle

Because there are no everglades or palm trees here, some call northwest Florida "the other Florida." Magnolias, live oaks, and loblolly pines flourish, just as they do in other parts of the Deep South. When the season winds down in south Florida, it picks up here (beginning in May). Also known as the Panhandle—because of the region's long, narrow shape—northwest

Florida is nestled between the Apalachicola River, the Gulf of Mexico, and the Alabama state line.

By the mid-1950s, the 100-mile stretch along the Panhandle coast between Pensacola and Panama City was dubbed the "Miracle Strip" because of the dramatic rise in property values of this beachfront land that in the 1940s sold for less than $100 an acre. Today, property fetches millions. But the movers and shakers of the area felt this sobriquet fell short of conveying the richness of the region, with its forever-green sparkling waters, swamps, bayous, and Gulf beaches where the sugar-white quartz-crystal sand crunches underfoot like snow on a sub-zero night. And so the term "Emerald Coast" was coined.

This little green corner of Florida that snuggles up to Alabama is a land of superlatives: It has the biggest military installation in the Western Hemisphere (Eglin Air Force Base); the oldest city in the state (Pensacola, claiming a founding date of 1559); and the most prolific fishing village in the world (Destin). Thanks to restrictions against commercial development imposed by Eglin AFB and the Gulf Islands National Seashore, the Emerald Coast has been able to maintain several hundred linear miles of unspoiled beaches.

Numbers in the margin correspond to points of interest on the Panhandle map.

❶ **Pensacola,** with its antebellum homes and historic landmarks, is a good place to start your trek through northwest Florida. Spanish conquistadors, under the command of Don Tristan de Luna, made landfall on the shores of Pensacola Bay in 1559, but, discouraged by a succession of destructive tropical storms and dissension in the ranks, De Luna abandoned the settlement two years after its founding. In 1698, the Spanish once again established a fort at the site. During the early 18th century, control jockeyed back and forth between the Spanish, the French, and the British and ultimately, in 1819, landed in the hands of the United States. During the Civil War, Pensacola came under the governance of the Confederate States of America, so by the time the 20th century rolled around, the flags of five different nations had flown over this fine, old southern city; hence its nickname, the City of Five Flags.

Today, historic Pensacola consists of three distinct districts— Seville, Palafox, and North Hill—though they are easy to explore as a unit. Stroll down streets mapped out by the British and renamed by the Spanish, such as Cervantes, Palafox, Intendencia, and Tarragona. Be warned, though, that it is best to stick to the beaten path; Pensacola is a port town and can get rough around the edges, especially at night.

The best way to orient yourself is to stop at the **Pensacola Convention & Visitors Information Center** (1401 E. Gregory St., tel. 904/434–1234 or 800/874–1234). Located at the foot of the Three-Mile Bridge over Pensacola Bay, it's easy to find. You can pick up maps of the self-guided historic district tours and other information.

Approaching from the east, the first historic district you reach is **Seville**—the site of Pensacola's first permanent Spanish colonial settlement. Its center is Seville Square, a live oak-shaded park bounded by Alcaniz, Adams, Zaragoza, and Government streets. Park your car and roam these brick streets past honey-

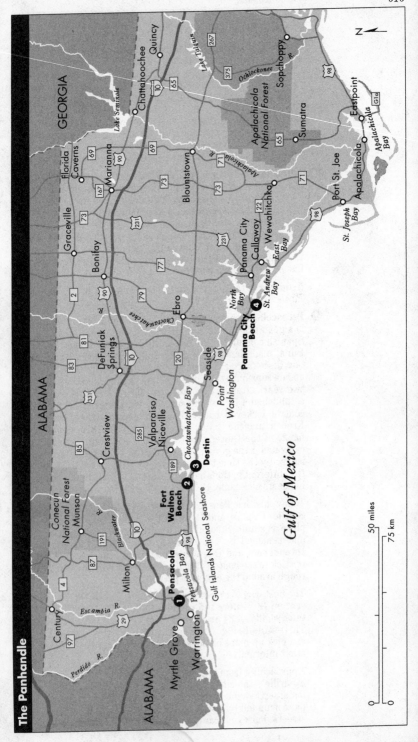

The Panhandle

616

GEORGIA

ALABAMA

Quincy

Chattahoochee

Lake Seminole

Lake Talquin

Ochlockonee R.

Sopchoppy

Apalachicola National Forest

Florida Caverns

Marianna

Graceville

Bonifay

Blountstown

Apalachicola R.

Sumatra

Eastpoint

Apalachicola

Apalachicola Bay

DeFuniak Springs

Ebro

Panama City

Callaway

Wewahitchka

Port St. Joe

St. Joseph Bay

East Bay

Crestview

Valparaiso/ Niceville

Choctawhatchee Bay

Seaside

Point Washington

Panama City Beach

North Bay

St. Andrew Bay

Munson

Conecuh National Forest

Destin

Fort Walton Beach

Blackwater R.

Milton

Pensacola

Pensacola Bay

Gulf Islands National Seashore

Century

Escambia R.

Myrtle Grove

Warrington

Perdido R.

Choctawhatchee R.

ALABAMA

Gulf of Mexico

N

50 miles

75 km

moon cottages and bay-front homes. Many of the buildings have been restored and converted into restaurants, commercial offices, and shops where you can buy anything from wind socks to designer clothes.

Continue west to Palafox Street, the main stem of the **Palafox Historic District.** This was the commercial and government hub of old Pensacola. On Palafox Place, note the Spanish Renaissance-style Saenger Theater, Pensacola's old movie palace; and the Bear Block, a former wholesale grocery with wrought-iron balconies that are a legacy from Pensacola's Creole past. Though the San Carlos Hotel has been closed for many years, in its heyday the Mediterranean-style building at Palafox and Garden streets was the proper place for business tycoons and military officers to savor their cigars and brandies and where Pensacola's elite dined after the theater and introduced their daughters to society. Nearby, on Palafox between Government and Zaragoza streets, is a statue of Andrew Jackson that commemorates the formal transfer of Florida from Spain to the United States in 1821.

Palafox Street also funnels into the **North Hill Preservation District,** where Pensacola's affluent families, many made rich during the turn-of-the-century timber boom, built their homes on ground where British and Spanish fortresses once stood. To this day residents occasionally unearth cannonballs while digging in their gardens. North Hill occupies 50 blocks that consist of more than 500 homes in Queen Anne, neoclassical, Tudor Revival, and Mediterranean architectural styles. Take a drive through this community, but remember these are private residences not open to the public. Places of general interest in the district include the 1902 Spanish mission-style Christ Episcopal Church; Lee Square, where a 50-foot-high obelisk stands as Pensacola's tribute to the Old Confederacy; and Fort George, an undeveloped parcel of land at the site of the largest of three forts built by the British in 1778.

From the North Hill district, go south on Palafox Street to Zaragoza Street to reach the **Historic Pensacola Village,** a cluster of museums between Adams and Tarragona. The **Museum of Industry,** housed in a late 19th-century warehouse, hosts permanent exhibits dedicated to the lumber, maritime, and shipping industries—once mainstays of Pensacola's economy. A reproduction of a 19th-century streetscape is displayed in the **Museum of Commerce,** while the city's historical archives are kept in the **Pensacola Historical Museum**—what was once Old Christ Church, one of Florida's oldest churches. Also in the village are the **Julee Cottage Museum of Black History, Dorr House, Lavalle House,** and **Quina House.** *Pensacola Village Information Center, tel. 904/444–8905. Open Mon.–Sat. 10–4:30; Pensacola Historical Museum, tel. 904/433–1559. Open Mon.– Sat. 9–4:30. Admission: free.*

In the days of the horse-drawn paddy wagon the two-story mission revival building housing the **Pensacola Museum of Art** served as the city jail. *407 S. Jefferson St., tel. 904/432–5682. Admission free. Open Tues.–Fri. 10–5, Sat. 10–4.*

Pensacola's 1908 old City Hall has been refurbished and reopened as the **T. T. Wentworth Jr. Florida State Museum.** The Wentworth displays some 150,000 artifacts ranging from Civil War weaponry to bottle caps. Representing more than 80 years of collecting, the assemblage is worth over $5 million. *333 S. Jefferson St., tel. 904/444-8905. Admission: $5 adults, $4.50 senior citizens, $2 children over 4. Open Mon.–Sat. 10–4:30.*

From the port, take Palafox Street to U.S. 98 (Garden St.) to reach the **Pensacola Naval Air Station** (tel. 904/452-2311). Established in 1914, it is the nation's oldest such facility. On display in the **National Museum of Naval Aviation** are more than 100 aircraft that have played an important role in naval aviation history. Among them are the NC-4, which in 1919 became the first plane to cross the Atlantic by air; the famous World War II fighter, the F6F *Hellcat;* and the *Skylab Command Module.* Thirty-minute films on aeronautical topics are shown, June–August. Call for details. The National Park Service-protected **Fort Barrancas,** established during the Civil War, is also located at the NAS. Nearby are picnic tables and a half-mile woodland nature trail. *Navy Blvd. (off U.S. 98), tel. 904/452-3604. Admission free. Open daily 9–5.*

Travelers with limited time may want to take I–10 east, whizzing across the Panhandle and through Tallahassee to pick up I–75 south to Orlando. Others have two choices: drive directly to Fort Walton Beach on U.S. 98 (about an hour's drive), or mosey along eastward on **Santa Rosa Island,** a spit of duneland that juts out into the turquoise and jade waters of the Gulf of Mexico. Take U.S. 98 over the 3-mile-long Pensacola Bay Bridge and then cross a second bridge to Santa Rosa Island, where Route 399 can be a scenic drive if the day is clear; otherwise, it's a study in gray. This barrier reef offers more than seascapes and water sports: It's also a must-see for bird-watchers. Since 1971 more than 280 species of birds from the common loon to the majestic osprey have been spotted here. At Santa Rosa Island's western tip is **Fort Pickens National Park,** where there are a museum, nature exhibits, aquariums, and a campground with more than 180 campsites, many with electrical hookups. Fort Pickens's most famous resident was Apache Indian chief Geronimo. Legend has it that he became a fairly likable fellow before he was transferred to Oklahoma's Fort Sill for his final incarceration. *Ranger station at Fort Pickens Rd., tel. 904/934-2635. Admission: $3 per car. Open daily 8:30–4.*

② From the east end of Santa Rosa Island, cross over the Navarre Bridge to U.S. 98, which will take you to **Fort Walton Beach,** the Emerald Coast's largest city and the hub of its vacation activity, with shops and restaurants galore. The city dates from the Civil War years when patriots loyal to the Confederate cause organized Walton's Guard (named in honor of Colonel George Walton, one-time acting territorial governor of West Florida) and made camp on Santa Rosa Sound, the site that would come later to be known as Camp Walton. In 1940, fewer than 90 people lived in Fort Walton Beach, but thanks to the development of Eglin Field during World War II, and New Deal money spent for new roads and bridges, within a decade the city became a boom town. Today, the military is Fort Walton Beach's main source of income, but tourism runs it a close second.

Eglin Air Force Base encompasses 728 square miles of land, has 10 auxiliary fields, including Hurlburt and Duke fields, and a total of 21 runways. Jimmie Doolittle's Tokyo Raiders trained here, as did the Son Tay Raiders, a group that made a daring attempt to rescue American POWs from a North Vietnamese prison camp in 1970. Tours leave from the officers club at the base. The main gate is on U.S. 98 northeast of Fort Walton Beach. Tour tickets, which are free, may be picked up at the **Niceville/Valparaiso Chamber of Commerce,** or from the museum (*see below*). *Tel. 904/678–2323. Tours Jan.–Mar. and June–Aug., Mon., Wed., Fri. 9:30–noon.*

Just outside Eglin's main gate on U.S. 98, is the **Air Force Armament Museum,** with an uncluttered display of more than 5,000 articles of Air Force armaments from World Wars I and II, and the Korean and Vietnam wars. Included are uniforms, engines, weapons, aircraft, and flight simulators; larger craft such as transport planes and swept-wing jets are exhibited on the grounds outside the museum. A 32-minute movie about Eglin's history and its role in the development of armaments is presented continuously throughout the day. *Rte. 85, Eglin Air Force Base, tel. 904/882–4062. Admission free. Open daily 9:30–4:30.*

Artifacts reflecting the cultural, artistic, technological, and spiritual achievements of the many prehistoric peoples who have inhabited northwest Florida during the past 10,000 years are on exhibit at the **Indian Temple Mound Museum.** Of special interest are the funerary masks and weaponry of these pre-Columbian tribes. The museum is adjacent to the 600-year-old National Historic Landmark Temple Mound, which is a large earthwork built over saltwater. *139 Miracle Strip Pkwy. (U.S. 98), tel. 904/243–6521. Open Sept.–May, Mon.–Sat. 11–4; June–Aug., Mon. to Sat. 9–4. Admission: 75¢ adults, children 12 and under free.*

A 2-mile jaunt east on U.S. 98 will bring you to the **Gulfarium**—a great way to spend a few hours when bad weather drives you off the beach. The Gulfarium's main attraction is its "Living Sea" presentation, in a 60,000-gallon tank, that simulates conditions on the ocean bottom. There are performances by trained porpoises, sea lion shows, and marine life exhibits featuring seals, otters, and penguins. There's also an extensive gift shop where you can buy anything from conch shells and sand-dollar earrings to children's beach toys. *U.S. 98E, tel. 904/244–5169. Admission: $10 adults, $6 children 4–11, children under 3 free. Open May–Sept., daily 9–6; Oct.–Apr., daily 9–4.*

③ Drive across the causeway between the Gulf and Choctawhatcee Bay to **Destin.** A fishing village since the mid-1830s, Destin was calm until the strait connecting the bay with the gulf was bridged in 1935. Then, recreational anglers discovered its white sands, blue-green waters, and the abundance of some of the most sought-after sport fish in the world. More billfish are hauled in around Destin each year than from all other Gulf fishing ports combined. But you don't have to be the rod-and-reel type to love Destin. You could stay in Destin for a month and still not try every gourmet restaurant in the area. There's also plenty to entertain the sand-pail set as well as seniors who ask for nothing more than a chance to sprawl in the sun and soak up its rays.

The Destin Fishing Museum has a dry aquarium where lighting and sound effects create the sensation of being underwater. You can get the feeling of walking on a sandy bottom that's dotted with sponges while viewing the species of fish indigenous to the Gulf of Mexico. *35 U.S. 98E, tel. 904/654–1011. Admission: $1 adults, children under 12 free. Open Wed.–Sun. noon–4.*

Drive east on U.S. 98 for about 8 miles to the **Museum of the Sea and Indian,** where there are exhibits on marine life in the Gulf of Mexico as well as the seven seas of the world. Artifacts from both North and South American Indian tribes also are displayed here. *4801 Beach Hwy. (off U.S. 98), tel. 904/837–6625. Admission: $3.75 adults, $2 children. Open summer, daily 8–7; winter, daily 9–4.*

In the **Eden State Gardens,** 25 miles east of Destin on U.S. 98, an antebellum mansion, with colonnaded porticoes and upstairs galleries that wrap the entire house, is set amid an arcade of moss-draped live oaks and is open to the public for touring. Furnishings in the spacious rooms date from several periods as far back as the 17th century. The surrounding gardens are beautiful year-round, but they're nothing short of spectacular in mid-March when the azaleas and dogwoods are in full bloom. *County Rte. 395, Point Washington, tel. 904/231–4214. Admission to gardens free; mansion tour $1. Open daily 8 AM–sunset. Mansion tours Thurs.–Mon. 9–4 (hourly).*

About halfway between Destin and Panama City is **Seaside,** a modern resort town built as a Florida version of Cape Cod. "A new town with the old ways," Seaside, with its Victorian fretwork, white picket fences, and captain's walks, is contrived. But the pastel paint jobs, latticework, and Adirondack chairs also make this community stunning. Open-air markets for shoppers and old-fashioned ice-cream parlors for the kids add up to a memorable way to spend a tranquil afternoon. *County Rte. 30A (off U.S. 98), 25 mi east of Destin, tel. 904/231–4224.*

4 An hour's drive east of Destin lies another vacation spot with mass appeal, **Panama City Beach,** about 5 miles south and to the west of Panama City proper. In spite of shoulder-to-shoulder condominiums, motels, and amusement parks that make it seem like one big carnival ground, Panama City Beach has a natural beauty that excuses its overcommercialization. The incredible white sands, navigable waterways, and plentiful marine life that attracted Spanish conquistadors and gave sustenance to the settlers early on, are a lure to today's family-vacation industry. Peak season for Panama City is June–September, and during spring break.

Time Out   **Pineapple Willie's** (Beach Blvd. at Thomas Dr., tel. 904/235–0928) brings together the best elements of a discotheque and a Wild West saloon, and caters to the 25- to 40-year-old crowd. If you feel overwhelmed by the live entertainment, you can escape to the serenity of a seaside deck.

At the eastern tip of Panama City Beach is the **St. Andrews State Recreation Area,** which comprises 1,038 acres of beaches, pinewoods, and marshes. There are complete camping facilities here, as well as ample opportunities to swim, pier fish, or hike the dunes over clearly marked nature trails. You can board a ferry to **Shell Island**—a barrier island in the Gulf of Mexico that offers some of the best shelling north of Sanibel Island.

About 40 miles southeast of Panama City Beach on U.S. 98 at **Port St. Joe** is the spot where Florida's first constitution was drafted in 1838. Most of the old town, including the original hall, is gone—wiped out by hurricanes—but the exhibits in the **Constitution Convention State Museum** recall the event. There are also provisions for camping and picnicking in a small park surrounding the museum. *200 Island Memorial Way, tel. 904/ 229-8029. Admission: 50¢ per person, children under 6 free. Open Thurs.-Mon. 9-5. Closed noon-1.*

Shopping

Harbourtown Shopping Village (913 Gulf Breeze Pkwy., Gulf Breeze, no phone) has trendy shops and the ambience of a wharfside New England village. There are four department stores in the **Santa Rosa Mall** (300 Mary Esther Cut-off, Mary Esther, tel. 904/244-2172), as well as 118 other shops and 15 bistro-style eateries. Stores in the **Manufacturer's Outlet Centers** (127 U.S. 98W, Fort Walton Beach, and 105 W. 23rd St., Panama City, no phone) offer well-known brands of clothing and accessories at a substantial discount. **The Market at Sandestin** (5494 U.S. 98E, tel. 904/654-5588) has 27 upscale shops that peddle such wares as gourmet chocolates and designer clothes in an elegant minimall with boardwalks. **The Panama City Mall** (U.S. 231 and Rte. 77, Panama City, tel. 904/ 785-9587) has a mix of more than 100 franchise shops and national chain stores.

Participant Sports

Biking Some of the nation's best bike paths run through northwest Florida's woods and dunelands, particularly on Santa Rosa Island where you can pedal for 50 miles and never lose sight of the ocean. Routes through Eglin AFB Reservation present cyclists with a few challenges. Biking here requires a $3 permit, which may be obtained at **Jackson Guard Forestry** (tel. 904/882-4164). Rentals are available from **Bob's Bicycle Center** (Fort Walton Beach, tel. 904/243-5856) and at **The Wheel Works** (Fort Walton Beach, tel. 904/244-5252).

Boating You can rent powerboats for fishing, skiing, and snorkeling at **Club Nautico** (320 U.S. 98E, Destin, tel. 904/837-6811, and U.S. 98E, Santa Rosa Beach, tel. 904/267-8123). Pontoon-boat rentals for the more laid-back water enthusiast are available at **Consigned RV's** (101 W. Miracle Strip Pkwy., Fort Walton Beach, tel. 904/243-4488).

Diving In the Panama City Beach area, investigate the wreckage of sunken tanker ships, tugboats, and cargo vessels. For snorkelers and beginning divers, the jetties of St. Andrews State Recreation Area, where there is no boat traffic, are safe. Wreck dives are offered by **Diver's Den** (3603 Thomas Dr., tel. 904/234-8717) or **Panama City Dive Center** (4823 Thomas Dr., tel. 904/235-3390). In the Destin-Fort Walton Beach area, you can arrange for diving instruction and excursions through **Aquanaut Scuba Center, Inc.** (24 U.S. 98W, Destin, tel. 904/ 837-0359) or **The Scuba Shop** (348 Miracle Strip Pkwy., Fort Walton Beach, tel. 904/243-1600).

Fishing Northwest Florida's fishing options range from fishing for pompano, snapper, marlin, and grouper—in the saltwater of the Gulf of Mexico—to angling for bass, catfish, and bluegill in the freshwaters of the region. All fisherfolk, except Florida residents 65 years or older, children under 16, and anyone fishing from a licensed charter boat, must have fishing licenses, which are available at tackle shops, and hardware and sporting-goods stores where fishing tackle is sold. You can buy bait and tackle at **Stewart's Outdoor Sports** (4 Eglin Pkwy., Fort Walton Beach, tel. 904/243–9443; 1025 Palm Plaza, Niceville, tel. 904/678–4804), at **Panama City Beach Pier Tackle Shop** (16101 U.S. 98W, Panama City, tel. 904/235–2576), or at **Penny's Sporting Goods** (1800 Pace Blvd., Pensacola, tel. 904/438–9633). If your idea of fishing is to drop a line off the end of a pier, you can fish from **Old Pensacola Bay Bridge** or from the 3,000-foot-long **Destin Catwalk**, along the East Pass Bridge. For $2 adults, $1.50 children, $1 observer, you can also fish from Panama City Beach's **city pier.**

Deep-Sea Fishing Charters When planning an excursion, be advised that rates for renting deep-sea fishing boats are usually quoted by the day (about $550) or half day (about $350). This is an immensely popular pastime on the Emerald Coast, so there are boat charters aplenty. Among them are **Miller's Charter Services/Barbi-Anne** (off U.S. 98 on the docks next to A.J.'s Restaurant, Destin, tel. 904/837–6059), **East Pass Charters** (at East Pass Marina, U.S. 98E, Destin, tel. 904/837–1918), **Paper Tiger** (U.S. 98E, Destin, tel. 904/654–5860), **Lafitte Cove Marina** (1010 Ft. Pickens Rd., Pensacola Beach, tel. 904/932–9241), **The Moorings Marina** (655 Pensacola Beach Blvd., Pensacola Beach, tel. 904/932–0305), and **Holiday Lodge Marina** (6400 U.S. 98W, Panama City Beach, tel. 904/235–2809).

Party boats that carry as many as 100 passengers at $35–$40 per head are the cheapest way to go, offering everything from half-day fishing excursions to dinner cruises. The old standbys are *Capt. Anderson's* (Captain Anderson Pier, 5558 N. Lagoon Dr., Panama City Beach, tel. 904/234–3435) and *Her Majesty II* or *Emmanuel* (U.S. 98E, Destin, tel. 904/837–6313).

Golf **Perdido Bay Golf & Country Club** (1 Doug Ford Dr., Pensacola, tel. 904/492–1223) has an 18-hole layout with four sets of tees, making it virtually four different courses. **Tiger Point Golf & Country Club** (1255 Country Club Rd., Gulf Breeze, tel. 904/932–1333) offers 36 holes of golf overlooking the natural wonderland of Santa Rosa Sound. **The Club at Hidden Creek** (3070 PGA Blvd., Gulf Breeze, tel. 904/939–4604) has 18 holes that wind through woods of hickory, magnolia, oak, and pine. Ranked among the Southeast's top 50, the 18-hole course at the **Shalimar Pointe Golf & Country Club** (2 Country Club Dr., Shalimar, tel. 904/651–1416) presents a professional challenge, but is forgiving enough for players of all levels. Long, well-groomed fairways rank the 18-hole **Fort Walton Beach golf course** (Rte. 189, Fort Walton Beach, tel. 904/862–3314) one of the state's finest municipal routes. **Indian Bayou Golf & Country Club's** (Airport Rd. off U.S. 98, Destin, tel. 904/837–6192) bunkered, undulating greens make this 7,000-yard course one of the most interesting on the Emerald Coast. **Baytowne Golf Club** (Emerald Coast Pkwy., Destin, tel. 904/267–8155) at the Sandestin Beach Resort is gentler than its sister course, the sticky **Sandestin Links** (Emerald Coast Pkwy., Destin, tel. 904/267–8144), but is no pushover. Tight fairways, cavernous sand traps, and water hazards make the 18-hole course at **Santa Rosa Golf & Beach Club** (County Rte. 30A, Santa Rosa Beach, tel. 904/267–2229) provoking yet memorable. Water, water everywhere and island fairways make the **Lagoon Legend** (100

Delwood Beach Rd., Panama City Beach, tel. 904/234–3307), at Marriott's Bay Point, northwest Florida's answer to the Blue Monster at Doral. Bruce Devlin and Bob von Hagge designed this one to punish the big boys; its complement, the **Club Meadows** (100 Delwood Beach Rd., Panama City Beach, tel. 904/234–3307) course, is kinder and gentler.

Sailing   **Hobie Shop** (12705 Front Beach Rd., Panama City Beach, tel. 904/234–0023) rents Hobie Cats and Windsurfers. Sailing instruction as well as rentals are offered by **Friendship Charter Sailing** (404 U.S. 98, Destin, tel. 904/837–2694). **S & S Sailing** (1350 Miracle Strip Pkwy., Fort Walton Beach, tel. 904/243–5696) operates a sailing school as well as a charter service. Renting sailboats, jet skis, or catamarans from **Bonifay Water Sports** (460 Pensacola Beach Blvd., Pensacola Beach, tel. 904/932–0633) includes safety and sailing instructions. Hobie Cats, Sunfish, jet skis, Windsurfers, and surfboards are available at **Key Sailing** (400 Quietwater Beach Blvd., Pensacola Beach, tel. 904/932–5520).

Tennis   At **Marriott's Bay Point Resort**'s (100 Delwood Beach Rd., Panama City Beach, tel. 904/234–3307) tennis center there are 12 Har-Tru clay tennis courts. **Sandestin Resort** (U.S. 98E, Destin, tel. 904/267–8000), one of the nation's five-star tennis resorts, has 16 courts with grass, hard, or Rubico surfaces. **Destin Racquet & Fitness Center** (995 Airport Rd., Destin, tel. 904/837–7300) boasts 6 courts. The **Municipal Tennis Center** (45 W. Audrey, Fort Walton Beach, tel. 904/243–8789) has 12 lighted Laykold courts and four practice walls. You can play tennis day or night on nine courts at the **Ft. Walton Racquet Club** (23 Hurlburt Field Rd., Fort Walton Beach, tel. 904/862–2023). Tennis courts are available in more than 30 locations in the Pensacola area, among them the **Pensacola Racquet Club** (3450 Wimbledon Dr., Pensacola, tel. 904/434–2434).

Beaches

Crystal Beach Wayside Park (tel. 904/837–6447). With something to appeal to just about everyone, this Gulf-side sanctuary is located just 5 miles east of Destin and is protected on each side by undeveloped state-owned land.

Eglin Reservation Beach (no phone). Situated on 5 miles of undeveloped military land and located about 3 miles west of the Brooks Bridge in Fort Walton Beach, this beach is a favorite haunt of local teenagers and young singles.

Grayton Beach State Recreation Area (tel. 904/231–4210). Sandwiched between Santa Rosa Beach and Grayton Beach, this is one of the most scenic spots along the Gulf Coast. Located about 30 miles east of Destin on Rte. 30A, this recreation area offers blue-green waters, white-sand beaches, salt marshes, and swimming, snorkeling, and campground facilities.

Gulf Island National Seashore (tel. 904/934–2631). This 150-mile stretch of pristine coastline runs all the way from Gulfport, Mississippi, to Destin. Managed by the National Park Service, these beach and recreational spots include the **Fort Pickens Area**, at the west end of Santa Rosa Island; the **Santa Rosa Day Use Area**, 10 miles east of Pensacola Beach; and **Johnson's Beach** on Perdido Key, about 20 miles northwest of

Pensacola's historic districts. Check with the National Park Service for any restrictions that might apply.

John C. Beasley State Park (no phone). Located on Okaloosa Island, this is Fort Walton Beach's seaside playground. A boardwalk leads to the beach where you'll find covered picnic tables, changing rooms, and freshwater showers. Lifeguards are on duty during the summer. In the winter, the desolate, nostalgic quality is peaceful.

Panama City Beaches (tel. 800/PC–BEACH). These public beaches along the Miracle Strip combine with the plethora of video-game arcades, miniature golf courses, sidewalk cafés, souvenir shops, and shopping centers to lure people of all ages.

Pensacola Beach (tel. 904/932–2258). To get to Pensacola Beach, which is 5 miles south of Pensacola, take U.S. 98 to Gulf Breeze, then cross the Bob Sikes Bridge over to Santa Rosa Island. Beachcombers and sunbathers, sailboarders and sailors keep things going at a fever pitch in and out of the water. In season, no particular demographic group has a lock on Pensacola Beach. Off season, conventioneers keep things hopping.

St. Andrews State Park (tel. 904/234–2522). On the eastern tip of Panama City Beach, this is Florida's most visited park. An artificial reef creates a calm, shallow play area that is perfect for young children.

Dining and Lodging

The following dining price categories have been used: *Very Expensive*, over $60; *Expensive*, $40–$60; *Moderate*, $20–$40; *Inexpensive*, under $20.

For lodging, the rule of thumb is: The closer you are to the water, the more you can expect to pay. If you're planning a lengthy stay, a condominium rental is a good idea. Most accept walk-ins, but to be on the safe side, reserve a spot through a property management service.

The following lodging price categories have been used: *Very Expensive*, over $120; *Expensive*, $90–$120; *Moderate*, $50–$90; *Inexpensive*, under $50.

Destin
Dining
★

Flamingo Cafe. Two types of atmosphere are presented at the Flamingo Cafe: the black, white, and pink color scheme, with waiters and waitresses dressed in tuxedos with pink bow ties, shouting nouveau; and the airy, seaside setting embraced by the panoramic view of Destin harbor seen from every seat in the house, or from a table on the full-length porch outside. Chef specialties include veal *Magenta* (baby white veal sautéed with lobster and shrimp, finished with raspberry beurre blanc and garlic butter) and grouper Flamingo (broiled with butter, Madeira wine, and bread crumbs, topped off with sautéed mushrooms and artichoke hearts in lemon-butter sauce). *414 U.S. 98E, tel. 904/837–0961. Jacket advised. Reservations advised. No lunch. AE, DC, MC, V. Inexpensive–Moderate.*

Vaccaro's. Black ashtrays and gray napkins on pink tablecloths cap off the art deco appointments in this restaurant's striking interior. The mostly Italian menu features a variety of selections, from pizza made with sun-dried tomatoes, roasted shallots, and mushrooms to *pollo saltimbocca* (sautéed breast of chicken with prosciutto, mozzarella, and tomato sauce). Join the happy hour festivities on the rooftop deck and watch the sun set over Destin harbor. *Morena Plaza, U.S. 98, tel. 904/ 654–5722. Jacket advised. Reservations accepted. No lunch. AE, DC, MC, V. Inexpensive–Moderate.*

Captain Dave's on the Gulf. This beachfront restaurant comprises three dining rooms: a central room with a glass dome overlooking the Gulf; a sports room filled with bats, helmets, jerseys, autographed baseballs, and photographs of professional atheletes; and finally, a more intimate dining area with small dim lights and potted plants. The hearty menu offers seafood entrées such as fillet of snapper sprinkled with crabmeat and covered with shrimp sauce and Parmesan cheese; and a medley of broiled seafood served with celery, onions, bell peppers, tomatoes, and topped with black olives and mozzarella cheese. Children's plates are available. Dancing and live entertainment are featured in the downstairs lounge. *3796 Old Hwy. 98, tel. 904/837–2627. Dress: casual. No reservations. No lunch. AE, MC, V. Inexpensive.*

Lodging **Sandestin Beach Resort.** This 2,600-acre resort of villas, cottages, condominiums, and an inn seems to be a town unto itself. All rooms have a view, either of the Gulf, Choctawhatchee Bay, a golf course, lagoon, or bird sanctuary. This resort provides something for an assortment of tastes, from simple to extravagant, and offers special rates October–March. *Emerald Coast Pkwy., 32541, tel. 904/267–8000 or 800/277–0800. 175 rooms, 400 villas. Facilities: miles of private beach, several pools, 2 golf courses, 16 tennis courts, tennis and golf pro shops, marina, 5 restaurants, shopping mall. AE, DC, MC, V. Expensive–Very Expensive.*

Summer Breeze. White picket fences and porches or patios outside each unit make this condominium complex look like a summer place out of the Gay Nineties. One-bedroom suites have fully equipped kitchens and can sleep up to six people in queen-size beds, sleeper sofas, or bunks. It's halfway between Destin and Sandestin and is across from a roadside park that gives it the feel of privacy and seclusion. *3885 U.S. 98E, 32541, tel. 904/ 837–4853; 800/874–8914 or 800/336–4853. 35 units. Facilities: pool, outdoor Jacuzzi, barbecue. MC, V. Moderate.*

Village Inn. This Best Western property, only minutes away from the Gulf, was built in 1983 with families in mind. A variety of amenities, including entertainment, are provided to occupy each member of the family in some way. Rooms have serviceable dressers and queen- or king-size beds. Senior citizen discounts are available. *215 U.S. 98E, 32541, tel. 904/837–7413. 100 rooms. Facilities: pool, free HBO, 24-hr restaurant, lounge. AE, DC, MC, V. Moderate.*

Fort Walton Beach **Liollio's.** Spicy Greek seafood somehow doesn't seem right in a
Dining restaurant with an Italian name—unless it's Liollio's. Dishes
★ such as snapper seasoned with Greek spices, tomatoes, green peppers, onions, and garlic, or Athenian-style shrimp (shrimp broiled with spices in garlic butter and topped with Parmesan cheese) represent a couple of the interesting preparations that come out of this kitchen. Every table enjoys a view of Santa Rosa Island, and owner John Georgiades is always around to schmooze with customers. *14 Miracle Strip Pkwy., tel. 904/ 243–5011. Dress: casual. Reservations accepted. AE, DC, MC, V. Inexpensive–Moderate.*

Seagull. In addition to an unobstructed view of Brooks Bridge and the sound, this waterside restaurant has a 400-foot dock for its cruise-minded customers. Decorated with pictures from Fort Walton in the 1940s, and dimly lit, the Seagull is a comfortable place to dine. Choose between no-frills steak and prime rib or fancier fare such as fillet of snapper topped with almonds and Dijon mustard sauce. After the family business clears out, things liven up a bit when one of two bands provide live soft rock music. *U.S. 98E, by the Brooks Bridge, tel. 904/243–3413. Dress: casual. Reservations accepted. No lunch. AE, DC, MC, V. Inexpensive–Moderate.*

Lodging **Holiday Inn.** This U-shape hotel consists of a seven-story tower flanked on either side by three-story wings. Rooms feature pastel green-and-peach decor and have flowered bedspreads and complementing striped draperies and face either the Gulf or the pool, but even the poolside rooms have at least some view of the sea. There are four floors of suites in the middle tower, each with a spacious sitting area and access to an extensive veranda overlooking the Gulf. The lobby, with an upscale, contemporary design, boasts glass elevators, colored banners hanging from the ceiling, wicker furniture, and tiled floors. *1110 Santa Rosa Blvd., 32548, tel. 904/243–9181 or outside FL, 800/465–4329. 385 rooms. Facilities: 3 pools, 800-foot beach, tennis courts, exercise room, restaurants, lounge. AE, DC, MC, V. Moderate–Expensive.*

Ramada Beach Resort. The lobby and entrance presents a slick look: black marble and disco lights—what some locals feel is too much like the Las Vegas strip. Activity here centers around a pool with a five-story grotto and a swim-through waterfall, and along the 800-foot private beach. *U.S. 98E, 32548, tel. 904/243–9161, 800/874–8962 in FL, 800/2–RAMADA outside FL. 454 rooms. Facilities: pools, whirlpool, tennis courts, game room, exercise room, restaurants, lounges. AE, MC, V. Moderate–Expensive.*

Panama City Beach
Dining

Capt. Anderson's. Come early to watch the boats unload the catch of the day, and be among the first to line up for one of the 600 seats in this noted eatery. The atmosphere is nautical, with tables made of hatch covers. The Greek specialties aren't limited to feta cheese and shriveled olives; charcoal-broiled fish and steaks have a prominent place on the menu, too. *5551 N. Lagoon Dr., tel. 904/234–2225. Dress: casual. No reservations. AE, DC, MC, V. No lunch. Closed Sun. and Nov.–Jan. Inexpensive–Moderate.*

Boar's Head. An exterior that looks like an oversize thatch cottage sets the mood for dining in this ever-popular ersatz-rustic restaurant and tavern. Prime rib has been the number-one people-pleaser since the house opened in 1978, but broiled shrimp with crabmeat and vegetable stuffing, and native seafood sprinkled with spices and blackened in a white-hot skillet are popular, too. For starters, try escargot in mushroom caps or a shrimp bisque. There's a special menu for the junior appetite. *17290 Front Beach Rd., tel. 904/234–6628. Dress: casual. No reservations. No lunch. AE, DC, MC, V. Inexpensive–Moderate.*

Montego Bay. Queue up with vacationers and natives for a table at any one of the four restaurants in this local chain. Service is swift and the food's good. Some dishes, such as red beans and rice or oysters on the half shell, are no surprise. Others such as shrimp rolled in coconut and served with a honey mustard and orange marmalade sauce, or steak doused with Kentucky bourbon and presented with a bourbon marinade are real treats.

4920 Thomas Dr., tel. 904/234–8686; 9949 Thomas Dr., tel. 904/ 235–3585; The Shoppes at Edgewater, tel. 904/233–6033. 17118 Front Beach Rd., tel. 904/233–2900. Dress: casual. No reservations. MC, V. Inexpensive.

Lodging **Edgewater Beach Resort.** Luxurious one-, two-, or three-bed-
★ room units in beachside towers or golf-course villas are elegantly furnished with wicker and rattan and done in the seaside
colors of peach, aqua, and sand. The centerpiece of this resort
is a Polynesian-style lagoon pool with waterfalls, reflecting
ponds, footbridges, and more than 20,000 species of tropical
plants. *11212 U.S. 98A, 32407, tel. 904/235–4044 or 800/874–
8686 outside FL. Facilities: golf, 12 tennis courts, game rooms,
health club, shuffleboard, restaurants, lounge. MC, V. Expensive–Very Expensive.*

★ **Marriott's Bay Point Resort.** Sheer elegance is the hallmark of
this pink stucco jewel on the shores of Grand Lagoon. Wing
chairs, camel-back sofas, and Oriental-patterned carpets in the
common areas re-create the ambience of an English manor
house, which is sustained by the Queen Anne furnishings in the
guest rooms. Gulf view or golf view—take your pick. Kitchen-
equipped villas are a mere tee-shot away from the hotel. *100
Delwood Beach Rd., 32411, tel. 904/234–3307 or 800/874–7105
outside FL. 400 rooms, suites, or villas. Facilities: 5 pools, including indoor pool with Jacuzzi, 2 golf courses, 12 lighted
Har-Tru tennis courts, 145-slip marina, sailboat rentals, fishing charters, riverboat cruises, 5 restaurants, lounges. AE,
DC, MC, V. Moderate–Expensive.*

Miracle Mile Resort. A mile of beachfront is awash with hotels:
Sheraton, Gulfside, Sands, Barefoot Beach Inn. These older
properties target the family and convention trade. *9450 S.
Thomas Dr., 32407, tel. 904/234–3484, 800/342–8720 in FL,
800/874–6613 outside FL. 632 units. Facilities: pools, tennis
courts, restaurants, lounges. AE, DC, MC, V. Inexpensive–
Moderate.*

Pensacola **Cap'n Jim's.** Get a table by a picture window and gaze at Pensa-
Dining cola Bay while you savor a house special such as snapper
Chardonnay (served with lobster-based wine and cream sauce,
scallions, and mushrooms) or snapper Dean'o (broiled and
served with fresh tomatoes, spring onions, and lemon butter
sauce). *905 E. Gregory St., tel. 904/433–3562. Dress: casual.
Reservations advised. Closed Sun. AE, DC, MC, V. Inexpensive.*

★ **Jamie's.** This is one of a handful of Florida restaurants that are
members of the prestigious Master Chef's Institute. Dining
here is like spending the evening in the antiques-filled parlor of
a fine, old southern home. If a visit to Florida has you fished-
out, try the pâté du jour, followed with almond-coated breast of
chicken accompanied by a champagne cream sauce and seedless
grapes. The wine list boasts more than 200 labels. *424 E. Zaragoza St., tel. 904/434–2911. Jacket required at dinner.
Reservations advised. AE, MC, V. Inexpensive.*

McGuire's Irish Pub. Drink cherry beer brewed right on the
premises in copper and oaken casks, and eat your corned beef
and cabbage while an Irish tenor croons in the background. Located in an old firehouse, the pub is replete with antiques,
moose heads, Irish Tiffany lamps, and Erin-go-bragh memorabilia. More than 36,000 dollar bills signed and dated by the
pub's patrons flutter from the ceiling. McGuire's also has a
House Mug Club with more than 2,000 personalized mugs. The

waitresses are chatty and aim to please. Menu items run from kosher-style sandwiches to chili con carne to Boston cream pie. *600 E. Gregory St., tel. 904/433–6789. Dress: casual. No reservations. AE, DC, MC, V. Inexpensive.*

Perry's Seafood House & Gazebo Oyster Bar. This vintage 1858 house, known locally as "the big red house," was a residence, a tollhouse, and a fraternity house before Perry purchased it in 1968 and turned it into a restaurant. Native fish are broiled with Perry's secret sauce and garlic butter, or baked and topped with garlic sauce and lemon juice. The menu varies depending on weather conditions, fishing boat schedule, and what was caught that day. *2140 S. Barrancas Ave. tel., 904/434–2995. Dress: casual. No reservations. Closed Tues. AE, DC, MC, V. Inexpensive.*

Lodging **Perdido Sun.** This high rise is the perfect expression of Gulfside resort living. After a stay here, you'll know why the Spanish explorers of 300 years ago called the area the "Lost Paradise." One-, two-, or three-bedroom decorator-furnished units all have seaside balconies with spectacular views of the water. You can choose to make this your home away from home—accommodations include fully equipped kitchens—or you can pamper yourself with daily maid service. *13753 Perdido Key Dr., 32507, tel. 904/492–2390 or 800/227–2390 outside FL. 93 rooms. Facilities: glass-enclosed heated pool, outdoor pool, spa, health club, restaurant. MC, V. Expensive–VeryExpensive.*

Pensacola Hilton. The Hilton's lobby is in the renovated L & N train depot. Ticket and baggage counters are still intact and old railroad signs remind guests of the days when steam locomotives chugged up to these doors. The old train station connects via a canopied two-story galleria to a 15-story tower. Here's where the spittoons and hand trucks give way to upholstered furniture and deep-pile carpet; standard doubles are up-to-date and roomy. Bilevel penthouse suites have snazzy wet bars and whirlpool baths. The hotel is adjacent to the Pensacola Civic Center and only few blocks away from the historic districts. *200 E. Gregory St., 32590, tel. 904/433–3336 or 800/HILTONS. 212 rooms. Facilities: heated pool, restaurants, lounges, complimentary airport limo. AE, DC, MC, V. Moderate–Expensive.*

Holiday Inn/Pensacola Beach. This property enjoyed its finest hour during the filming of *Jaws II*, when the cast made this its headquarters. Inside, the lobby is simple, with potted plants, floral arrangements, and a coral–colored decor. Outside, the Holiday Inn has its own 1,500 feet of private beach. From the ninth-floor Penthouse Lounge, you can watch the goings-on in the Gulf, especially when the setting sun turns the western sky to lavender and orange. *165 Ft. Pickens Rd., Pensacola Beach, 32562, tel. 904/932–5361 or 800/HOLIDAY. 150 rooms. Facilities: heated pool, tennis courts, restaurant, lounge. AE, DC, MC, V. Moderate.*

★ **New World Inn.** This is Pensacola's little hotel, where celebrities who visit the city are likely to stay. Photos of dozens of the inn's famous guests (Lucille Ball, Shirley Jones, Charles Kuralt) hang behind the front desk in the lobby. The exquisite furnishings in the guest rooms take their inspiration from the five periods of Pensacola's past: French or Spanish provincial, early American, antebellum, or Queen Anne. The baths are handsomely appointed with brass fixtures and outfitted with oversize towels. *600 S. Palafox St., 32501, tel. 904/432–4111 or 800/258–1103 outside FL. 14 rooms, 2 suites. Facilities: restaurant, lounge. AE, DC, MC, V. Moderate.*

Ramada Inn North. All the guest rooms at this hotel have been renovated. Suites have game tables and entertainment centers; some have whirlpools. This Ramada is conveniently located close to the airport. *6550 Pensacola Blvd., 32505, tel. 904/477–0711 or 800/2–RAMADA outside FL. 106 rooms. Facilities: pool, restaurant, lounge, courtesy airport transportation, complimentary Continental breakfast. AE, DC, MC, V. Inexpensive.*

Seaside Dining
★

Bud & Alley's. This roadside restaurant grows its own herbs—rosemary, thyme, basil, fennel, and mint—in a garden visible from the restaurant. The inside room has a unique, down-to-earth feel, with hardwood floors, ceiling fans, and six-foot windows looking out onto the garden. There is also a screened-in porch area with a view of the Gulf. The Gorgonzola salad with sweet peppers is a delightful introduction to one of the entrées, perhaps the seared duck breast with caramelized garlic, wild mushrooms, and Cabernet sauce. *County Rte. 30A, tel. 904/231–5900. Dress: casual. Closed Tues. MC, V. Inexpensive.*

Lodging
★

Seaside. Two- to five-bedroom porticoed Victorian cottages are furnished right down to the vacuum cleaners. Although there's no air-conditioning, the Gulf breezes blowing off the water will cool rooms and remind you of the miles of unspoiled beaches so nearby. *County Rte. 30A, 32459, tel. 904/231–4224 or 800/635–0296 outside FL. 133 units. Facilities: pool, tennis court, croquet, badminton, bicycles, Hobie Cats, and beach equipment rentals. MC, V. Expensive.*

The Arts and Nightlife

The Arts

Broadway touring shows, top-name entertainers, and concert artists are booked into the **Marina Civic Center** (8 Harrison Ave., Panama City, tel. 904/769–1217) and the **Saenger Theatre** (118 S. Palafox St., Pensacola, tel. 904/438–2787).

Nightlife
Destin

Nightown (140 Palmetto St., tel. 904/837–6448) has a dance floor with laser lights and a New Orleans–style bar with live band music.

Fort Walton Beach

Catch the action at **Cash's Faux Pas Lounge** (106 Santa Rosa Blvd., tel. 904/244–2274) where anything goes. **Jamaica Joe's** (790 Santa Rosa Blvd., tel. 904/244–4137) features a dee-jay and drink specials that appeal to younger pub crawlers.

Panama City Beach

Pineapple Willie's (9900 Beach Blvd., tel. 904/235–0928) alternately features big-band and rock music and caters to the post-college crowd.

Pensacola

After dark, **McGuire's Irish Pub** (600 E. Gregory St., tel. 904/433–6789) welcomes anyone of legal drinking age, particularly those of Irish descent. **Mesquite Charlie's** (5901 N. W St., tel. 904/434–0498) offers good, ol' down-home pickin' and grinnin' with live entertainment. **Seville Quarter** (130 E. Government St., tel. 904/434–6211) with five bars featuring music from disco to Dixieland is this city's equivalent to the New Orleans French Quarter. **Trader Jon's** (511 Palafox St., tel. 904/438–3600) is officially recognized as the second home for Navy aviators as well as the preferred pub for all pilots. **Tickets** at the

Pensacola Hilton (200 E. Gregory St., tel. 904/433–3336) is the spot for those who dip when they dance but still like to boogie.

Tallahassee to Gainesville

Like the Panhandle to the west of it, this region of northern Florida is much more akin to the Deep South than to Miami and the rest of southern Florida. Tallahassee, the state capital, has its share of antebellum mansions, live oaks, and azaleas; it was the only Confederate state capital east of the Mississippi that was never captured by the Union forces. In Gainesville, home of the University of Florida Gators, football is serious business, while Ocala is prime territory for thoroughbred horse farms.

Besides two huge national forests, one by Apalachicola and the other next to Ocala, the area boasts some exotic outdoor attractions—deep springs, jungle-lined waterways, sinkholes, fern forests, even an eerie dried-up lake bed. The remains of early Indian and Spanish settlements, as well as Civil War battle sites, will intrigue history-lovers.

If you're taking the fast route across the state on I–10, you can still stop off in Tallahassee, then pick up I–75 through Gainesville and Ocala on your way to the Florida Turnpike to Orlando.

Numbers in the margin correspond with points of interest on the Northeast Florida map.

① From Port St. Joe, the last stop on the previous leg of this tour, it's about 25 miles east on U.S. 98 to **Apalachicola,** the state's most important oyster fishery. Visit the **Raney House,** circa 1850; **Trinity Episcopal Church,** built from prefabricated parts in 1838; and the **John Gorrie State Museum.** In this museum, the physician who is credited with inventing ice-making and air-conditioning is honored. Exhibits of early Apalachicola history are displayed here as well. *John Gorrie State Museum, Ave. C and Sixth St., tel. 904/653–9347. Admission: 50¢ adults, children under 6 free. Open Thurs.–Mon. 9–5.*

If hiking and the outdoors are an important part of your travels, explore **St. George Island State Park,** reached by a causeway from Eastpoint, where you can drive toward the sea along the narrow spit of land with its dunes, sea oats, and abundant bird life. *Tel. 904/927–2111. Admission: FL residents, $1/driver plus 50¢ per passenger; out-of-state, $2/driver plus $1 per passenger; children under 6 free. Open 8 AM–sunset.*

Spreading north of Apalachicola and west of Tallahassee is the **Apalachicola National Forest** where you can camp, hike, picnic, fish, or swim.

Drive east along the coast on Route 98; about 25 miles south of Tallahassee is the **St. Marks Wildlife Refuge and Lighthouse.** The once-powerful Fort San Marcos de Apalache was built here in 1639. Stones salvaged from the fort went into building the lighthouse, which is still in operation today. Exhibits are on display at the visitor center. *C.R. 59 (3 mi south of the Newport and U.S. 98 intersection) in St. Marks, tel. 904/925–6121. Admission: $3 per car. Refuge open sunrise–sunset; visitor center open weekdays 8–4:15, weekends 10–5.*

Route 363 branches north off Route 98 to Tallahassee; go west on Route 267 to visit one of the deepest springs in the world,

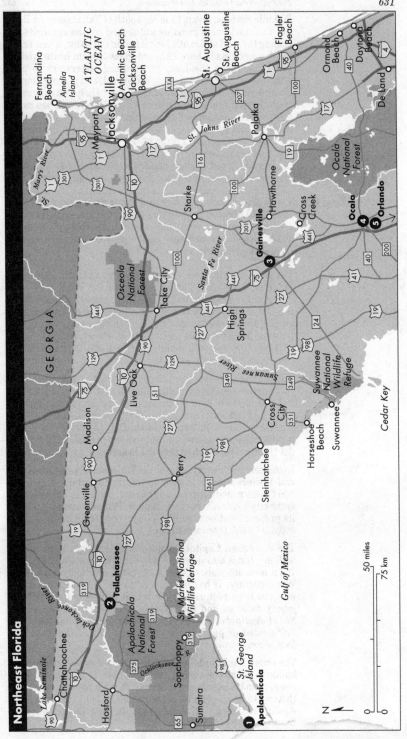

Northeast Florida

Wakulla Springs, about 15 miles south of Tallahassee on Route 61. The wilderness remains untouched by the centuries, retaining the wild and exotic look it had in the 1930s, when Tarzan movies were made here. Aboard glass-bottom boats, visitors probe deep into the lush, jungle-lined waterways to catch glimpses of alligators, snakes, waterfowl, and nesting limpkin. Nature guides are available at the lodge to help you explore the trails around the springs. More than 154 bird species can be spotted in a teeming wilderness that also hosts raccoon, gray squirrel, and an encyclopedia of southern flora. *1 Springs Dr., Wakulla Springs, tel. 904/222-7279. Admission: $1/driver plus 50¢ per passenger for FL residents; $2 driver plus $1 per passenger for out-of-state residents. Boat tours $4 adults, $2 children. Tours daily 9–5:30. Springs open daily 8 AM–sunset.*

Time Out The **Wakulla Springs Lodge and Conference Center** (tel. 904/224–5950), located on the grounds, serves three meals a day in a sunny, spartan room that seems little changed from the 1930s. Schedule lunch here to sample the famous bean soup, home-baked muffins, and a slab of pie.

In 1865, Confederate soldiers stood firm against a Yankee advance on St. Marks. The Rebs held, saving Tallahassee—the only southern capital east of the Mississippi that never fell to the Union. The **Natural Bridge Battlefield State Historic Site,** about 10 miles southeast of the capital, marks the victory, and is a good place for a hike and a picnic. *Natural Bridge Rd. (Rte. 354), off U.S. 363 in Woodville, tel. 904/488–3648. Admission free. Open daily 8 AM–sunset.*

Whether you're coming up from the coast or taking the fast route across the state on Interstate 10, stop off in the state capital, **Tallahassee,** with its canopies of ancient oaks and spring bowers of azaleas. Among the best canopied roads are St. Augustine, Miccosukee, Meridian, Old Bainbridge, and Centerville. Country stores and antebellum plantation homes still dot these roads, much as they did in earlier days.

In the heart of the city, stop at the **Tallahassee Area Convention and Visitors Bureau** to pick up information about the capital and the surrounding area. The bureau, housed in **The Columns,** is the city's oldest structure, built in 1833 and moved in 1970 to its present location. *200 W. College Ave., tel. 904/681–9200 or 800/628–2866. Open weekdays 8:30–5.*

The downtown **Capitol Complex area** is compact enough for walking, but is also served by a free, continuous shuttle trolley. It's a pleasant walk to the **Old Capitol,** originally a pre–Civil War structure. It has been added to and subtracted from but now has been restored to the way it looked in 1902, with its jaunty awnings and combination gas-electric lights. *Monroe St. at Apalachee Pkwy., tel. 904/487–1902. Admission free. Self-guided or guided tours weekdays 9–4:30, Sat. 10–4:30, Sun. noon–4:30.*

The **Union Bank Building,** built in 1833, is Florida's oldest bank building. Since the time it closed in 1843, it has played many roles, from ballet school to bakery. It's been restored to what is thought to be its original appearance as a bank. *Monroe St. at Apalachee Pkwy., tel. 904/487–3803. Admission free. Open Tues.–Fri. 10–1, weekends 1–4.*

At the **Museum of Florida History,** the long, intriguing story of the state's role in history—from prehistoric times of mastodons to the present, with the launching of space shuttles—is told in lucid and entertaining ways. *500 S. Bronough St., tel. 904/488-1673. Admission free. Open weekdays 9-4:30, Sat. 10-4:30, Sun. and holidays noon-4:30.*

On a clear day, from the 22nd floor of the **New Capitol,** you can catch a panoramic view of Tallahassee and its surrounding countryside. *Duvall St., tel. 904/488-6167. Admission free. Hourly tours of the New Capitol, weekdays 9-4, weekends 11-3.*

San Luis Archaeological and Historic Site focuses on the archaeology of 17th-century Spanish mission and Apalachee Indian townsites. In its heyday, in 1675, the Apalachee village here had a population of at least 1,400. Threatened by Creek Indians and British forces in 1704, the locals burned the village and fled. *2020 W. Mission Rd., tel. 904/487-3711. Admission free. 1-hr guided tours weekdays noon, Sat. 11 and 3, Sun. 2.*

A short drive north of Tallahassee, off U.S. 27 is **Lake Jackson,** a resource bass fishermen hold in reverence. Sightseers view, along the shores of the lake, Indian mounds and the ruins of an early-19th-century plantation built by Colonel Robert Butler, adjutant to General Andrew Jackson during the siege of New Orleans. *Indian Mound Rd., off U.S. 27, tel. 904/562-0042. Admission free. Open 8 AM-sunset.*

Five miles north of town on U.S. 319 is the magnificent **Maclay State Gardens.** In springtime the grounds are afire with azaleas, dogwood, and other showy or rare annuals, trees, and shrubs. Allow at least half a day for wandering the paths past the reflecting pool, into the tiny walled garden, and around the lakes and woodlands. The Maclay residence, furnished as it was in the 1920s, as well as picnic grounds, and swimming and boating facilities, are open to the public. *3540 Thomasville Rd. (1 mi north of I-10), tel. 904/487-4556. Admission: $1/driver plus 50¢ per passenger, May-Dec; $3 adults, $1.50 children 12 and under, Jan.-Apr. Open daily 8 AM-sunset.*

Lafayette Vineyards, a mile west of exit 31-A off I-10, is a gleaming, modern winery set among timeless vineyards. In 1812, these lands were granted by President Monroe to the Marquis de Lafayette in gratitude for his role in the American Revolution. French settlers planted the vines, and today award-winning wines catch the attention of oenophiles nationwide. Engage in the entertaining slide show, winery tour, and wine tastings (juice is also available). Wines are sold by the case or bottle at discount prices. *Tel. 904/878-9041 or 800/768-WINE. Admission free. Open Mon.-Sat. 10-6, Sun. noon-6.*

3 Continue east on I-10 to the junction with I-75, where you will head south. About 150 miles from Tallahassee lies **Gainesville,** home of the University of Florida and its beloved Gators football games. In addition to the excellent theater, concerts, film series, and other activities typical of campus life, tourists come to the Gainesville area for its strange geological features. The **Devil's Millhopper State Geological Site** is a botanical wonderland of exotic, subtropical ferns and trees, with a waterfall. The state geological site is situated in and around an enormous 1,100-foot-deep sinkhole. *Off U.S. 441 north of Gainesville, tel. 904/336-2008. Admission: $1 per car. Open daily 9 AM-sunset.*

The **Florida State Museum,** on the campus of the University of Florida, will be of interest to the entire family. Explore a replica Mayan palace, see a typical Timucuan household, and walk through a full-size replica of a Florida cave. There are outstanding collections from throughout Florida's history, so spend at least half a day here. *Museum Rd. at Newell Dr., tel. 904/392–1721. Admission free. Open Mon.–Sat. 9–5, Sun. and holidays 1–5; closed Christmas.*

About 11 miles south of Gainesville on U.S. 441 is the village of **Micanopy** (micka-*no*-pee), where Timucuan Indians settled. There was a Spanish mission here, but little remains from before white settlement, which began in 1821. Today, the streets are lined with antiques shops and live oaks. Browse the shops on the main street, or come in the fall for a major antiques event involving 200 dealers.

Paynes Prairie, situated between I–75 and U.S. 441 in Micanopy, is a strangely out-of-context site that attests to Florida's fragile, highly volatile ecology. Evidence of Indian habitation dated as early as 7,000 BC has been found on this 18,000-acre wilderness that was once a vast lake. Only a century ago, the lake drained so abruptly that thousands of beached fish died in the mud. The remains of a ferry, stranded here in the 1880s can still be seen. In recent years buffalo lived here; today persimmon trees, planted by settlers long ago, flourish, and wild cattle and horses roam. Swimming, boating, picnicking, and camping are permitted in the park. *Tel. 904/836–4281. Admission: $1 per car. Open daily 8 AM–sunset.*

At the **Marjorie Kinnan Rawlings State Historic Site,** readers of Rawlings novels (such as *The Yearling*) will feel her presence. A typewriter rusts on the ramshackle porch; the closet where she hid her booze during Prohibition yawns open; and clippings from her scrapbook reveal her legal battles and marital problems. Bring lunch and picnic in the shade of one of Rawlings's trees. Then visit her grave a few miles away at peaceful Island Grove. *S.R. 325 at Hawthorn, southeast of Gainesville, tel. 904/466–3672. Small admission fee. Open Thurs.–Mon. 10–11:30 and 1–4:30; closed Thanksgiving, Christmas, and New Year's day. Tours every half hour.*

❹ To reach **Ocala,** about 30 miles south of Gainesville, take any of three Ocala exits off I–75. The city is on State Route 40, an east-west artery that runs from Yankeetown on the Gulf of Mexico to Ormond Beach. Once known only as the home of Silver Springs and the Ocala National Forest, the city has become a center for thoroughbred breeding and training. Along with the horses have come a new generation of glitterati, with their private jets and massive estates surrounded by green grazing grasses and white fencing.

As Ocala matures from country to gentry, its tourist appeal becomes more upscale. Trendy hotels and inns now dot the city; restaurants serve more innovative, international fare; and the Appleton Museum of Art is turning into a complex for all the arts, including theater, dance, and music.

Silver Springs, the state's oldest attraction (established 1890), and listed on the National Register of Historic Landmarks, features the world's largest collection of artesian springs. Today, the park presents wild animal displays, glass-bottom boat tours in the Silver River, a jungle cruise on the Fort King Waterway, Jungle Safari, an antique and classic car museum, and walks through natural habitats. A multimillion-dollar project is recapturing the look and atmosphere of the 1890s. The attraction promises visitors a journey to the wild kingdom above and below the water. *Rte. 40, 1 mi east of Ocala, tel. 904/236–2121. Admission to all attractions: $19.95 adults, $14.95 children 3–10. Open daily 9–5.*

Next door is Silver Springs's **Wild Waters,** a water theme park with a giant wave pool and seven water-flume rides. *Admission: $8.95 adults, $7.95 children 3–11. Open late Mar.–June 7, daily 10–5; Aug., daily 10–7; Sept. 4–30, weekends only 10–5.*

Farther east on Route 40 is the entrance to **Ocala National Forest,** a 366,000-acre wilderness with lakes, springs, rivers, hiking trails, campgrounds, and historic sites. Area residents recall the filming of *The Yearling* at several sites within the forest. The **Visitor Information Center** (tel. 904/625–7470) on the left just over the bridge, is the site of old-fashioned sugar-cane grinding and cane-syrup making during the first two weeks of November each year. The syrup is bottled and sold on the premises. **S.R. 19** runs north and south through the Ocala National Forest, giving a nonstop view of stately pines and bold wildlife. Short side roads lead to parks, springs, picnic areas, and campgrounds.

Lake Waldena Resort & Campground (tel. 904/625–2851), several miles farther east into the national forest on Route 40, features a white-sand bathing beach and crystal-clear freshwater lake. Noncampers pay day-use fees for picnicking and access to the beach.

South of Route 40 (via Route 314-A) is **Moss Bluff,** on the Oklawaha River, which forms the southern boundary of Ocala National Forest. Three major recreational areas are found in the national forest: **Juniper Springs,** off Route 40, featuring a picturesque stone waterwheel house, campground, natural-spring swimming pool, and hiking and canoe trails; **Salt Springs,** off Route 40 (via Rte. 19 North), featuring a natural saltwater spring, where Atlantic blue crabs come to spawn each summer; and **Alexander Springs,** off Route 40 (via Rte. 445 South), featuring a swimming lake and campground.

From Ocala, it's about a half-hour's drive south on I–75 to the turnpike to **Orlando** (*see* Tour 6).

Participant Sports

Canoeing Float down sparkling clear spring "runs" that may be mere tunnels through tangled jungle growth. To canoe the Wakulla River near Tallahassee, contact **TNT Hideway** (St. Marks, tel. 904/925–6412); the 7-mile Juniper Springs run in the Ocala National Forest (tel. 904/625–2808); the Sante Fe River at High Springs (tel. 904/454–1853).

Golf The Central Classic is held yearly at **Killearn** (tel. 904/893–2186) in Tallahassee.

Ocala's **Golden Ocala Course** (tel. 904/622–0198) is rated among the state's top 25. Each of its holes is modeled after one of the world's most famous, from St. Andrews to Troon.

Horseback Riding Ocala's bluegrass horse country can be explored during trail rides organized by **Oakview Stable** (S.W. 27th Ave., behind the Paddock Mall, tel. 904/237–8844).

Dining and Lodging

The following dining price categories have been used: *Very Expensive*, over $60; *Expensive*, $40–$60; *Moderate*, $20–$40; *Inexpensive*, under $20.

The following lodging price categories have been used: *Very Expensive*, over $120; *Expensive*, $90–$120; *Moderate*, $50–$90; *Inexpensive*, under $50.

Gainesville
Dining

Sovereign. Crystal, candlelight, and a jazz pianist set a theme of restrained elegance in this 1878 carriage house. The veal specialties are notable, particularly the *saltimbocca* (veal sautéed with spinach and cheese). Duckling and rack of baby lamb are dependable choices as well. *12 S.E. Second Ave., tel. 904/378–6307. Jacket suggested. Reservations advised. AE, DC, MC, V. Expensive.*

Fiddler's. This rooftop restaurant is a celebration spot for locals and a dependable place for travelers who are looking for a good meal. The superb view, classic Continental cuisine, and mellow background music make for a relaxing evening. The pastries and breads are home-baked; lobster fra diablo is a specialty, and the Friday night seafood buffet should not be missed. *University Centre Hotel, 1535 S.W. Archer Rd., tel. 904/371–3333. Jacket and tie requested. Reservations advised. AE, DC, MC, V. Moderate.*

The Yearling. Marjorie Kinnan Rawlings would have been proud of this country restaurant with city savvy. On the menu are quail, frogs' legs, alligator, and "cooter"—the local name for turtle. For dessert, try the frozen lemon pie laced with Bacardi rum. *Rte. 3, Box 123, Hawthorne, tel. 904/466–3033. Dress: casual. Reservations accepted Tues.–Thurs. only; wait can be long on Sun. Closed Mon. AE, MC, V. Inexpensive.*

Lodging

Herlong Mansion. Adorned with old relics at every turn, this late-19th-century home screams out its antiquity. Continental breakfasts and evening cordials with petit fours, provided by caring hosts, strengthens the appeal. Although the nearest restaurants are in Gainesville, this inn has much to offer. There's no street address; just look for the big, brick house on the short main street of Micanopy. *Tel. 904/466–3322. 6 rooms. Facilities: library, parlor with TV. MC, V. Expensive.*

Holiday Inn University Center. An upbeat, casual look sets the scene for business, medical, and vacation travelers. It's downtown and near the university and football stadium, jogging paths, and tennis courts. *1250 W. University Ave., 32601, tel. 904/376–1661 or 800/HOLIDAY. 167 rooms. Facilities: rooftop pool, remote control TV, rental cars on property, restaurant, lounge, airport transportation. AE, DC, MC, V. Moderate.*

Residence Inn by Marriott. Studios and two-bedroom suites with kitchen and fireplace make a cozy pied-à-terre. Cocktails, Continental breakfast, and a daily paper are part of the hospitality. The central location is convenient for the university or business traveler. *4001 S.W. 13th St., (at U.S. 441 and S. R. 331), 32602, tel. 904/371–2101 or 800/331–3131. 80 suites. Facilities: pool, whirlpool, exercise equipment, restaurant,*

*lounge, microwave, laundry, free transport to airport or bus
station. AE, DC, MC, V. Moderate.*

Cabot Lodge. Included in the room rate is a Continental breakfast and a chummy two-hour cocktail reception. Spacious rooms
and a clublike ambience make this a favorite with business and
university travelers. *3726 S.W. 40th Blvd., 32608, tel. 904/375–
2400, 800/331–8215 in FL, 800/843–8735 outside FL. Facilities:
satellite TV. AE, DC, MC, V. Inexpensive.*

Ocala　**Ocala Hilton.** A winding, tree-lined boulevard leads to this
Lodging　nine-story pink tower, nestled in a forested patch of countryside just off I–75. The marble-floor lobby, with piano bar,
greets you before you enter your spacious guest room, decorated in deep, tropical hues. *3600 S.W. 36th Ave., 32674, tel.
904/854–1400. 200 rooms. Facilities: outdoor heated pool and
Jacuzzi, tennis courts, restaurant, pub, live entertainment.
AE, DC, MC, V. Expensive.*

Seven Sisters Inn. This showplace Queen Anne mansion is now a
bed and breakfast. Each room has been glowingly furnished
with period antiques; each has its own bath and some have a
fireplace. Rates include a gourmet breakfast. *820 S.E. Fort
King St., 32671, tel. 904/867–1170. 7 rooms; wicker-furnished
loft sleeps 4. Moderate. AE, MC, V.*

Tallahassee　**Andrew's 2nd Act.** Part of a smart complex in the heart of the
Dining　political district, this is classic cuisine: elegant and under-
★　stated. If you like pub hopping, there's Andrew's Upstairs, and
the Adams Street Cafe (also by Andrew) is next door. For dinner, the veal Oscar is flawless or choose a chef's special from
the chalkboard. You can't go wrong. *102 W. Jefferson St., tel.
904/222–2759. Jacket and tie suggested. Reservations advised.
AE, DC, MC, V. Expensive.*

Anthony's. Often confused with Andrew's, a different and
equally deserving restaurant, this is the locals' choice for un-
compromising Italian classics. Try one of the Italian-style
grouper or salmon dishes. *1950 Thomasville Rd., tel. 904/224–
1447. Dress: casual. Reservations advised. AE, MC, V. Moderate.*

Nicholson's Farmhouse. The name says a lot about this friendly, informal country place with its outside kitchen and grill. If
you've never tried amberjack, discover this unusual, meaty
fish—a specialty of the house. *Turn off Hwy. 27 to Hwy. 12 toward Quincy; follow signs, tel. 904/539–5931. Dress: casual.
Reservations advised. BYOB. Closed Sun.–Mon. MC, V. Moderate.*

★　**Barnacle Bill's.** Don't be put off by the slummy decor. The seafood selection is whale-size and it's steamed to succulent
perfection before your eyes, with fresh vegetables on the side.
This popular hangout is famous for pasta dishes and home-
smoked fish, too. Choose from complete weight-loss menus and
daily chalkboard specials. Children eat free on Sunday. The full
menu is available for carryout. *1830 N. Monroe St., tel. 904/
385–8734. Dress: casual. Reservations required for large
groups. AE, MC, V. Inexpensive.*

Lodging　**Governors Inn.** Only a block from the Capitol, this plushly re-
★　stored historic warehouse is abuzz during the week with politicians, press, and lobbyists. It's a perfect location for business
travelers involved with the state, and on weekends, for tourists
who want to tour the Old Capitol and other downtown sites.
Rooms are a rich blend of mahogany, brass, and classic prints.

The VIP treatment includes airport pickup, breakfast, cocktails, robes, shoe shine, and a daily paper. *209 S. Adams St., 32301, tel. 904/681–6855 or 800/342–7717 in FL. 41 units. Facilities: lounge. AE, DC, MC, V. Expensive.*

Las Casas. The quiet courtyard with its own pool and the darkly welcoming cantina where a complimentary Continental breakfast and evening cocktail are served convey the look of old Spain. Rooms are furnished in heavy Mediterranean style. *2801 N. Monroe St. 32303, tel. 904/386–8286 or 800/521–0948 in FL. 113 rooms. Facilities: heated pool. AE, DC, MC, V. Moderate.*

Tallahassee Hilton. Bustling and upscale, the hotel hosts heavy hitters from the worlds of politics and media who can walk from here to the Capitol. *101 S. Adams St., 32301, tel. 904/224–5000, or 800–HILTONS. 246 rooms. Facilities: pool, 2 restaurants, lobby bar, lounge with entertainment, gift shop, valet service. AE, DC, MC, V. Moderate.*

The Arts and Nightlife

The Arts   Tallahassee is the region's focal point for the arts. Broadway touring shows, top-name entertainers, and other major events are booked at the **Tallahassee-Leon County Civic Center** (Box 10604, Tallahassee, tel. 904/487–1691). **Florida State University School of Music** (tel. 904/644–4774), in Tallahassee, stages 350 concerts and recitals a year, and the **Florida State University** theater (tel. 904/644–6500) presents 15–20 plays a year. The **Tallahassee Symphony Orchestra** (tel. 904/224–0461) performs at Florida State University, September–April. The **Capitol City Band** (tel. 904/893–8303) has been brandishing its brass in Tallahassee since 1924. The **Monticello Opera House** (tel. 904/997–4242) presents operas in the restored gaslight-era playhouse, near Tallahassee.

Nightlife   In Tallahassee, stop by **Andrew's Upstairs** (228 S. Adams St., tel. 904/222–3446) to hear contemporary, jazz, and reggae music.

Tour 9: Chicago and the Upper Great Lakes

They aren't called the Great Lakes for nothing. Standing on the southern tip of Lake Michigan, surrounded by Chicago's dynamic skyscrapers, you gaze out upon water as far as the eye can see. Drive for hours north along the Wisconsin shore, well past Milwaukee, and you still haven't measured the lake's full length. Door County peninsula, the Midwest's charming version of Cape Cod, is only a small finger of land jutting into Lake Michigan. But angle across northern Wisconsin, or drive north through Michigan's rugged Upper Peninsula, and you'll eventually come upon an even bigger body of water: Lake Superior, the world's largest freshwater lake.

The scenery here is spectacular: thick forests, dramatic waterfalls, towering bluffs. Much is set aside in state and national parks, and the fishing, canoeing, and hiking is excellent. Attractions en route illustrate a rugged way of life—reconstructed forts and trading posts, lumberjack camps, copper mines, Indian mounds, wildlife zoos. Casual restaurants serve hearty portions of untrendy food, and hotels are more comfortable than glitzy. An antidote to all this is provided in Chicago, of course, with its bustling downtown, upscale shops, sophisticated cuisine, and world-class luxury hotels.

There are many options to this tour. You can drive around Lake Michigan alone, make a slightly wider circuit to visit the southern Lake Superior shore, or do the complete Circle Route around Lake Superior, a 1,300-mile-long drive. The distances to be covered are great, and even the shortest route will take at least five days. Allow two weeks if you plan to do the Circle Route. You will not want to stop at every town along the way, but do leave some time to explore one or two of the parks, for the real pleasures of the northwoods cannot be experienced from inside a car.

Visitor Information

Chicago **Chicago Office of Tourism** (806 N. Michigan Ave., Water Tower in the Park, Chicago 60611, tel. 312/280–5740 or 800/487–2446).

Chicago Tourist Information Center (Water Tower, 806 N. Michigan Ave., tel. 312/280–5740).

Wisconsin *Milwaukee and Cedarburg* **Greater Milwaukee Convention & Visitors Bureau** (510 W. Kilbourn Ave., 53203, tel. 414/273–7222 or 800/231–0903; taped message on area events, tel. 414/799–1177).

Milwaukee Visitor Information Center (Mitchell International Airport, tel. 414/747–4808).

Eastern Wisconsin **Door County Chamber of Commerce** (Box 406, Sturgeon Bay, 54235, tel. 414/743–4456 or 800/527–3529).

Green Bay Visitor & Convention Bureau (1901 Oneida St., 54307–0596, tel. 414/494–9507 or 800/236–3976).

Northern Wisconsin **Bayfield Chamber of Commerce** (42 Broad St., 54814, tel. 715/779–3335 or 800/447–4094).

Madeline Island Chamber of Commerce (Box 274, La Pointe 54850-0274, tel. 715/747–2801).

Superior Area Chamber of Commerce (305 E. Second St., 54880, tel. 715/392–2773 or 800/942–5313).

Minnesota **Duluth Convention and Visitors Bureau** (Endion Station, 100 Lake Place Dr., 55802, tel. 218/722–4011 or 800/438–5884).

Grand Marais Chamber of Commerce (Tip of the Arrowhead Visitor Information Center, Municipal Bldg., Grand Marais 55604, tel. 218/387–2524 or 800/622–4014).

Ontario **Public Affairs—Visitors and Convention Dept.** (520 Leith St., Thunder Bay, Ontario P7C 1M9, tel. 807/625–2149).

North of Superior Tourism (79 N. Court St., Thunder Bay, Ontario P7A 4T7, tel. 807/345–3322).

Ontario Ministry of Tourism and Recreation (77 Bloor St., W., 9th floor, Toronto, Ontario M7A 2R9, tel. 800/668–2746).

Michigan **Mackinac Island Chamber of Commerce** (Box 451, Mackinac Is-
Upper Peninsula land 49757, tel. 906/847–3783).

Mackinaw Area Tourist Bureau (708 S. Huron Ave., Mackinaw City 49701, tel. 616/436–5664 or 800/666–0160).

Sault Area Chamber of Commerce (2581 I-75 Business Spur, Sault Ste. Marie 49783, tel. 906/632–3301 or 800/647–2858).

Lower Peninsula **Grand Traverse Convention and Visitors Bureau** (415 Munson Ave., Suite 200, Traverse City 49684, tel. 616/947–1120 or 800/872–8377).

Holland Area Chamber of Commerce (272 E. 8th St., Holland 49422, tel. 616/392–2389).

Saugatuck–Douglas Chamber of Commerce (303 Butler St., Saugatuck 49453, tel. 616/857–5801).

Festivals and Seasonal Events

Early June: 57th Street Art Fair in Chicago (Ray School yard, 57th St., and Kimbark Ave.), one of the major juried art fairs in the Midwest, selects exhibitors from applicants from all over the country. Tel. 312/744–3315.

Mid-June: Chicago Blues Festival in Grant Park, a three-day, three-stage event featuring blues greats from Chicago and around the country.

Mid-June: Summerfest in Milwaukee, Wisconsin, is 10 days of jazz, country, and rock music on stages along the waterfront. Tel. 414/273–2680.

Late June—early Sept.: Ravinia Festival, Highland Park, hosts a variety of classical and popular musical artists in a pastoral setting north of Chicago. Tel. 312/728–4642.

Early July: Taste of Chicago (Columbus Dr. between Jackson and Randolph) feeds 4 million hungry visitors with specialties from scores of restaurants in the Chicago area.

Late July: Chicago to Mackinac Island Boat Race is run under the auspices of the Chicago Yacht Club. Monroe St. Harbor, tel. 312/861–7777.

Late Sept.–early Oct.: Oktoberfest brings out the best in beer and German specialties at the Berghoff Restaurant (17 W. Adams St., tel. 312/427–3170) and Chicago area pubs.

Late Oct.–early Nov.: Chicago International Film Festival brings outstanding new American and foreign films to the Music Box and Biograph theaters. Tel. 312/644–3400.

Thanksgiving Weekend: Chicago's Christmas tree lights up on Friday in the Daley Center Plaza (Washington St. between Dearborn and Clark Sts.). The **Christmas parade,** with balloons, floats, and Santa bringing up the rear, travels down Michigan Avenue on Saturday.

Late Nov–Dec.: Christmas Around the World display at Chicago's Museum of Science and Industry (57th St. and Lake Shore Dr., tel. 312/684–1414) features trees decorated in the traditional styles of more than 40 countries.

What to See and Do with Children

All along this tour there are opportunities to get out on the water in a boat, from sightseeing cruiseboats to canoes in wilderness parks. With so many big national and state parks in Wisconsin, Minnesota, and upper Michigan, families can spend a lot of time outdoors together, but many of them have only limited facilities—check in advance.

Kids usually love Chicago, with its combination of tall skyscapers, windy lakeshore, and great museums. Popular attractions include the **Field Museum of Natural History,** the **Chicago Academy of Sciences** in Lincoln Park, the **Adler Planetarium,** the interactive **Express-Ways Children's Museum** designed specifically for the very young, and one of the world's most fascinating places for youngsters, the **Museum of Science and Industry.** The **Lincoln Park Zoo** has a children's zoo and a Kids' Corner Discovery Place, and the **John G. Shedd Aquarium** has the fascinating Oceanarium. At the much larger **Brookfield Zoo,** in the western suburb of Brookfield, animals inhabit naturalistic settings. *By car, take I–290 (the Eisenhower Expressway) to First Ave., or take I–55 (the Stevenson Expressway) to First Ave. and follow the signs to the zoo. 8400 W. 31st St., Brookfield, tel. 708/485–0263. Admission: $2.75 adults, $1 children 3–11 and senior citizens; free Tues.*

Several Milwaukee museums have special exhibits geared toward youngsters, including: **Discovery World Museum, Milwaukee Public Museum's Wizard Wing, Milwaukee Public Library Discovery World Museum.** The **Milwaukee County Zoo** is also popular with children, and certain kids may also enjoy the brewery tours.

The resort town of **Minocqua,** Wisconsin, has lots for young people to do, as does **Mackinac Island,** Michigan. Though it verges on corniness, the Dutch town of **Holland,** Michigan, can be fun for children. In **Duluth,** Minnesota, the Lake Superior Zoological Gardens (72nd W and Grand Aves., tel. 218/624–1502) have more than 500 animals from throughout the world, as well as a children's zoo.

Kids have plenty of opportunities to learn about ships and fishing on this tour. **Manitowoc,** Wisconsin, has a great Maritime Museum, and nearby in **Two Rivers** is the Rogers Street Fishing Village, with artifacts recovered from shipwrecks among its displays. Cruises around the **Duluth–Superior** harbor give a close-up view of shipyards, grain elevators, huge docks, and the Aerial Lift Bridge. The Split Rock Lighthouse in **Two Har-**

bors, Minnesota, is another maritime treat. The twin **Sault Ste. Maries,** in Ontario and Michigan, offer a chance to view some spectacular locks on the St. Marys River. Complete the lesson with the Mackinac Maritime Park in **Mackinaw City,** Michigan, and the White River Light Station Musem in **Whitehall,** Michigan.

To bring history lessons alive, visit the **Grand Portage** National Monument, a reconstructed settlement in Arrowhead Minnesota, the reconstructed Fort William in **Thunder Bay,** or the restored forts in **Mackinaw City** and **Mackinac Island.** For kids who are interested in Native American culture, there are the Indian Mound Park in **Sheboygan,** Wisconsin, the **Oneida Nation Museum** in Green Bay, and the Chief Oshkosh Museum in **Egg Harbor.** Northern Wisconsin features a lumberjack museum in **Laona** and the Logging Museum in **Rhinelander.** Tours of copper mines are a hit on the **Keweenau Peninsula** of Michigan's Upper Peninsula. Young sports fan usually enjoy the **Green Bay Packer Hall of Fame.**

Arriving and Departing

By Plane Every national airline, most international airlines, and a number of regional carriers fly into **Chicago**'s three airports. **O'Hare International Airport,** one of the world's busiest, is some 20 miles from downtown, in the far northwestern corner of the city. There's a rapid transit station at O'Hare Airport (fare $1.25, travel time 40–60 minutes). **Continental Airport Express** (tel. 312/454–7799) coaches leave every 30 minutes for major downtown and Near North hotels every half hour; the trip takes an hour or longer, fare $12.50. **CW Limo** (tel. 312/493–2700) vans go every 45 minutes to Hyde Park and the South Side; travel time is about an hour, and the fare is $9.75. A **taxi** to downtown will cost about $28–$32 plus tip. If you're driving from O'Hare, follow the signs to I–90 east (the Kennedy Expressway), which merges with I–94, the Edens Expressway. Take the eastbound exit at Ohio Street to get to Near North, Washington or Madison Street exits for Downtown.

Midway Airport is on Chicago's Southwest Side, about 7 miles from downtown. **Continental Airport Express** (tel. 312/454–7799) coaches leave every 30 minutes for major downtown and Near North hotels every half hour; the trip takes half an hour, fare $9.50. **CW Limo** (tel. 312/493–2700) vans run five times daily, at Midway's traffic peaks; the fare is $8.50. A **taxi** to downtown will cost about $14 plus tip.

Meigs Field, on the lakefront just south of Downtown, serves commuter airlines.

Milwaukee's General Mitchell International Airport (tel. 414/747–5300), six miles from downtown, is served by American, American Eagle, American Trans Air, ComAir, Continental, Delta, Enterprise, Midstate, Midwest Express, Northwest, TWA, United, and USAir. City **buses** (tel. 414/344–6711) run to and from the airport 6 AM–6:45 PM; the fare is $1. **Taxis** take about 20 minutes and cost $13–$15. Limousine service to downtown hotels cost $6.50 per person. Courtesy cars to many major hotels can be called by direct phones at the airport.

By Car Travelers coming to Chicago from the east can pick up the Indiana Toll Road (I–80/90) westbound to the Chicago Skyway (also a toll road), which runs into the Dan Ryan Expressway (I–90/94). Travelers coming from the south should take I–57 northbound to the Dan Ryan Expressway. Travelers from the west may follow I–80 eastbound across Illinois to I–55, which is the major artery from the southwest. Those coming from areas due west of Chicago may prefer to pick up I–290 eastbound. Travelers from the north will need to be on I–90 or I–94, which merges to form the Kennedy Expressway.

I–94 runs from Chicago to Milwaukee (I–894 bypasses Milwaukee) and I–43 goes on up the Lake Michigan shore to Green Bay. U.S. 2 runs across northern Wisconsin and the Upper Peninsula of Michigan. U.S. 61 traces the Lake Superior shore from Duluth to Thunder Bay, Ontario, where you can pick up the Trans-Canada Highway (Route 17) to circle Lake Superior. I–75 runs south from the Canada border through Michigan; U.S. 31 traces Lake Michigan's eastern shore. Several smaller roads provide scenic drives along the coast, and a number of different routes can be taken, depending upon the length of time one wants to spend on the road—complete directions are given below.

By Train **Amtrak** (tel. 800/USA–RAIL) has stations in Chicago (Union Station, Jackson and Canal Sts., tel. 312/558–1075) and Milwaukee (433 W. St. Paul Ave., tel. 414/271-0840).

By Bus **Greyhound/Trailways** has several stations in Chicago: 630 W. Harrison St. (tel. 312/408–5971); on the South Side at the 95th Street and Dan Ryan Expressway CTA station; and on the northwest side at the Cumberland CTA station, 5800 North Cumberland Avenue, near O'Hare Airport. **Indian Trails, Inc.** (tel. 312/408–5971) service from Indiana and Michigan shares Greyhound's terminal facilities at Harrison Street and at 95th Street.

Greyhound also has service to Milwaukee (606 N. 7th Street, tel. 414/272–8900).

Chicago

Ask anyone who has never visited Chicago what images the city's name calls to mind, and you'll hear of gangsters and tommy guns; stockyards and packinghouses; and the Windy City—a grimy, smelly, industrial town whose climate is severe and whose denizens are rough-and-ready workingmen. Few non-Chicagoans know that the city's motto is *Urbs in Horto*, "City in a Garden," and first-time visitors are often astonished to find the elegant and sophisticated shops along Michigan Avenue's Magnificent Mile; the beauty of Grant Park's acres of blooms, sailboats gliding through the sparkling waters of Lake Michigan, and the lush green parkland along the lakefront; and the handsome and impressive buildings, old and new, designed by world-class architects.

This gracious and attractive city is the city most visitors see. The stockyards and packinghouses have been gone for 20 years; the sites of storied gangland raids and slayings are now parking lots; the steel mills have closed. But many corporate greats, including Quaker Oats, Helene Curtis, and Johnson Publishing, remain, and the financial district, home of the Chicago Board of Trade, the Chicago Board Options Exchange, the Midwest Stock Exchange, and international banking houses, bustles. In the last two decades the Sears tower, the Amoco Building, the John Hancock Building, The Associates Center, the NBC Building, Illinois Center, 333 West Wacker, the CNA Building, Lake Point Towers, and other structures have made the Chicago skyline one of the most exciting in the world. Cultural life flourishes, with lots of excellent little theaters, talented chefs, art galleries, opera, classical music, and jazz.

Leave downtown and the lakefront, and you soon encounter a city of neighborhoods with signs in Polish, Spanish, Chinese, Arabic, Hebrew, or Korean. The neighborhoods are the part of Chicago that a visitor rarely sees, yet they are the underpinning of the world-class city, and both must be experienced to understand the real Chicago.

Getting Around   Chicago's planners followed a grid pattern in laying out the city's streets. Madison Street is the baseline for streets and avenues that run north/south; house numbers start at 1 at the baseline and climb in each direction, generally by 100 a block. Even-numbered addresses are on the west side of the street, odd numbers on the east side. For streets that run east–west, State Street is the baseline; even-numbered addresses are on the north side of the street, odd numbers on the south side.

By Car   Chicago is not the best place to bring a car. There's heavy traffic, on-street parking is nearly impossible to find, parking lots are expensive, congestion creates frustrating delays, and other drivers may be impatient with those who are unfamiliar with the city and its roads.

By Train and Bus   The basic fare is $1.25 for rapid transit trains; this fare also applies to buses during morning and afternoon rush hours (at other times, the bus fare is $1). A roll of 10 tokens (which can be used for full fare on either buses or rapid transit trains) costs $9 and can be bought at currency exchanges, some rapid transit stations, and Jewel and Dominick's supermarkets. Transfers, which must be bought when you board the first bus or train, cost an extra 25¢. Children ages 7–11 travel for less than half fare (40¢ at this writing). Children under 7 travel free. Most, but not all, rapid transit lines operate 24 hours, but late-night travel is not recommended.

Buses generally run either south from the Loop or north from the Loop. Principal transfer points are on Michigan Avenue at the north side of Randolph Street for northbound buses, Adams and Wabash for westbound buses and the el, and State and Lake streets for southbound buses.

By Taxi   Chicago taxis are metered, with fares beginning at $1.20 for the first ⅛ mile and 20¢ for each additional ⅛ mile (or each minute of waiting time). A charge of 50¢ is made for each additional passenger between the ages of 12 and 65. A charge of 25¢ per bag may be levied when luggage is bulky. Taxi drivers expect a 15% tip. The principal taxi companies are American United Cab Co. (tel. 312/248–7600), Yellow Cab Co. (tel. 312/829–4222), and Checker Cab Co. (tel. 312/829–4222).

Guided Tours   May through September, the **Sunday Culture Bus** of the Chica-
Orientation Tours   go Transit Authority (tel. 312/664–7200) offers three low-cost 2- to 3-hour narrated tours: **The West tour** visits many of Chicago's ethnic neighborhoods; **the North tour** takes you through the upscale Lincoln Park area; **the South tour** goes to the Field Museum, the Planetarium, the Aquarium, the Muse-

um of Science and Industry, and the mansions of Hyde Park and Kenwood. You can leave a tour at any stop and pick up a later bus to continue the tour.

Chicago Motor Coach Co. (tel. 312/922–8919) runs narrated 1- to 3-hour double-decker bus tours of Chicago landmarks. **Gray Line** (tel. 312/346–9506) has sightseeing tours of downtown, Lincoln Park, Chinatown, and Hyde Park, lasting two to seven hours. **American Sightseeing** (tel. 312/427–3100) runs 2-hour tours of either the North (along State Street and North Michigan Avenue) or the South (financial district, Grant Park, the University of Chicago, the Museum of Science and Industry, and Jackson Park).

Wendella Sightseeing Boats (400 N. Michigan Ave., tel. 312/ 337–1446) traverse the Chicago River or Lake Michigan on 90- minute tours or 2-hour evening tours, May–September. **Mercury Skyline Cruises** (Wacker Drive at Michigan Avenue, tel. 312/332–1353) operates a 90-minute river and lake cruise, a two-hour sunset cruise, and a 1-hour evening lakefront cruise, and a 1-hour summer weekend Chicago River cruise. **Shoreline Marine** (tel. 708/673–3399) in summer has half-hour boat trips on Lake Michigan, leaving from the Adler Planetarium or the Shedd Aquarium; evening trips leave from Buckingham Fountain. **Interlude Enterprises** (tel. 312/641–1210) offers lunchtime cruises with an architectural narrative, leaving from the Wabash Avenue bridge.

Special-Interest Tours The **Chicago Architecture Foundation** gives tours, such as a walking tour of Loop architecture and tours of historic houses, on a regular daily or weekly schedule, depending on the season. Prices run about $5–$10 per person. For information, write or call the foundation at Glessner House (1800 S. Prairie Ave., tel. 312/326–1393), where the house tours begin, or at the Archicenter (330 S. Dearborn St., tel. 312/782–1776), where most other tours originate.

Friends of the Chicago River (407 S. Dearborn St., Chicago 60605, tel. 312/939–0490) offers walking tours along the river April–July, September, and October, Saturdays at 10 AM. The tours last two hours and cost $5.

Downtown and Downtown South

Numbers in the margin correspond to points of interest on the Chicago Downtown map.

Downtown Chicago is a city lover's delight. Here are the buildings by famous architects, the great American cultural institutions, and the canyons of commerce and finance that drive the pulse of the city. Downtown comprises the area south of the Chicago River, west of Lake Michigan, and north of the Congress Parkway/Eisenhower Expressway. Downtown Chicago's western boundary used to be the Chicago River, but the boundary continues to push westward.

We begin our tour on North Michigan Avenue at South Water Street. On the southwest corner of the intersection stands the elegant Art Deco **Carbide and Carbon Building** (233 N. Michigan), designed by the Burnham Brothers in 1929.

Walk south on Michigan to Randolph Street. On the northwest corner is the **Associates Center** (150 N. Michigan Ave.), with its

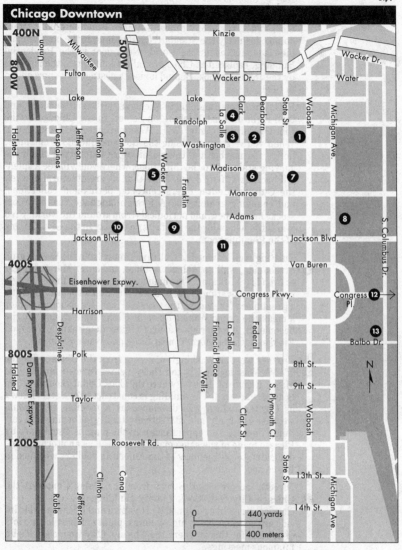

Chicago Downtown

Art Institute of Chicago, **8**

Buckingham Fountain, **12**

Carson Pirie Scott, **7**

Chicago Board of Trade, **11**

Chicago City Hall–Cook County Building, **3**

Chicago Mercantile Exchange, **5**

Daley Center, **2**

First National Bank Plaza, **6**

Grant Park, **13**

Marshall Field & Co., **1**

Sears Tower, **9**

State of Illinois Center, **4**

Union Station, **10**

distinctive diamond-shaped, angled face visible for miles. Two blocks east, the coolly graceful **Amoco Building** (200 E. Randolph), formerly the Standard Oil Building, is the largest marble-clad building in the world. Next door is the **Prudential Building,** replaced as Chicago's tallest building in the late '60s by the John Hancock. Behind it rises a postmodern spire added in 1990.

Return west on Randolph to Michigan, walk south a block, and turn right on East Washington Street, to the **Chicago Public Library Cultural Center** (78 E. Washington, tel. 312/269–2900). When you've stepped inside the Romanesque-style entrance, notice the marble and the mosaic work before you climb the curving stairway to the third floor, where you will see a splendid back-lit Tiffany dome. More than an architectural marvel, the Cultural Center offers concerts, permanent collections, and changing exhibitions. A foreign-language reading room stocks newspapers and periodicals from around the world. Civil War buffs will enjoy the artifacts on display in the Grand Army of the Republic room.

❶ Turn right on leaving the Cultural Center from the Washington Street side, walk to Wabash Avenue, and enter **Marshall Field & Co.** (111 N. State). This mammoth store, now undergoing a massive renovation, boasts some 500 departments, and it's a great place for a snack (the Crystal Palace ice cream parlor) or a meal (the grand Walnut Room or Hinky Dink Kenna's in the basement). Another spectacular Tiffany dome can be found on Field's southwest corner, near State and Washington.

❷ Further west on Washington, across from the **Chicago Temple** (77 W. Washington), is the **Daley Center** (named for the late Mayor Richard J. Daley), where the Cook County court system is headquartered. The building is constructed of a steel known as Cor-ten, which was developed as a medium that would weather naturally and attractively (and weathering has certainly improved its appearance). In the plaza is a sculpture by Picasso made of the same material, as well as an eternal flame dedicated to the memory of the American soldiers who died in Korea and Vietnam.

❸ Directly across Clark Street from the Daley Center is the **Chicago City Hall–Cook County Building,** a handsome neoclassical structure designed by Holabird and Roche in 1911. Inside are spacious halls, high ceilings, plenty of marble, and lots of hot air, for this is where the Chicago City Council holds its infamous meetings.

❹ Head north on Clark for a block and you'll reach the notorious **State of Illinois Center** (100 W. Randolph), designed by Helmut Jahn. Some people love it and some do not; the structure's sky blue, white, and red exterior colors have elicited such adjectives as "garish" and "tacky" from viewers. Its enormous interior atrium embraces a volume of 8 million cubic feet. For the first years after the building opened, the state-of-the-art heating and cooling system simply did not work. In summertime office workers equipped themselves with large fans and parasols to ward off the baking rays that shone relentlessly through the glass. In wintertime coats and mittens were required for sedentary workers. Ongoing repairs have mitigated some of the worst extremes, but the elevators, handsome as they are, often break down. On the northwest corner of Randolph and Clark stands *Monument to a Standing Beast*, a sculpture by Jean Dubuffet. Its curved shapes, in white with black traceries, set against the curving red, white, and blue of the center, merely add to the visual cacophony.

Head three blocks west to Wacker Drive and turn left to see the **Civic Opera House** (20 N. Wacker, tel. 312/346–0270), where Chicago's Lyric Opera gives its performances. The Civic Opera House is very grand indeed, with marble floors and pillars in the main hall, crystal chandeliers, and a marvelous sweeping staircase to the second floor.

❺ One block south you'll see the pale grape colored twin towers of the **Chicago Mercantile Exchange** (10 and 30 S. Wacker). The visitor's gallery of the Merc, open weekdays from 7:30 AM to 3:15 PM, looks down on the frenetic activity on the trading floor. Here is where hog belly futures (they have to do with the supermarket price of bacon), soybeans, and dollars are traded on national and international markets.

❻ Go east again on Madison to the **First National Bank Plaza**, which runs the length of the block from Dearborn to Clark. The Chagall mosaic known as *The Four Seasons* (1974) stands at the northeast end of the plaza, between Madison and Monroe on Dearborn. It is said that when Chagall arrived in Chicago to install the mosaic, he found it a more vigorous city than he had remembered, and he began immediately to modify the work to reflect the stronger and more vital elements he found around him.

❼ On the southeast corner of Madison and State streets stands **Carson Pirie Scott** (1 S. State), Chicago's "second" department store, known to architecture students as one of Louis Sullivan's outstanding works. The building illustrates the Chicago Window, a large fixed central window with smaller movable windows on each side. Notice also the fine exterior ornamentation at street level, particularly the exquisite work over the entrance on the southeast corner of Madison and State.

❽ From the south end of Carson's, head east on Monroe and south on Michigan to Adams Street and the imposing entrance to the marvelous **Art Institute of Chicago.** You'll recognize the Art Institute by its beloved guardian lions on each side of the entrance. The Art Institute has outstanding collections of Medieval and Renaissance paintings as well as Impressionist and Post-Impressionist works. Be sure to visit the Rubloff paperweight collection; a Chicago real estate magnate donated these shimmering, multicolored functional objects. And don't miss the Stock Exchange room, a splendid reconstruction of a part of the old Chicago Stock Exchange, which was demolished in 1972. If you have a youngster with you, make an early stop at the Children's Museum downstairs, where your child will be given a set of delightful Gallery Games. The museum store has an outstanding collection of art books, calendars, merchandise related to current exhibits, and an attractive selection of gift items. *S. Michigan at Adams, tel. 312/443–3600. Admission: $6 adults, $3 children and senior citizens, free Tues. Open weekdays 10:30–4:30 (Tues. until 8), Sat. 10–5, Sun. noon–5. Closed Christmas Day.*

Head one-and-a-half blocks west on Adams Street to visit the **Palmer House** (17 E. Monroe, tel. 312/726–7500), one of Chicago's grand old hotels. The ground-floor level is a shopping arcade with patterned marble floors and antique lighting fixtures, but it's the lobby—up one flight of stairs—that you must see: Richly carpeted, outfitted with fine furniture, and lavishly decorated (look at the ceiling murals).

On the next block of Adams, on your left, have a look at the westernmost building of the **Berghoff Restaurant** (17 W. Adams). Although at first glance it appears as though the front is masonry, it is in fact ornamental cast iron. The practice of using iron panels cast to imitate stone was common in the latter part of the 19th century (this building was constructed in 1872), but this building and the **Page Brothers Building** on State Street, built in the same year, are the only examples known to have survived.

On the corner of Dearborn and Adams stands the **Federal Center and Plaza.** The twin Federal Buildings, the Kluczyinski (219 S. Dearborn) and the Dirksen (230 S. Dearborn), built in 1964, are classic examples of the trademark Mies van der Rohe glass and steel box. In the plaza, on the southwest side of Dearborn and Adams, is the wonderful Calder stabile *Flamingo*, dedicated on the same day in 1974 as Calder's *Universe* at the Sears Tower. It is said that Calder had a grand day, riding through Chicago in a brightly colored circus bandwagon accompanied by calliopes, heading from one dedication to the other.

At La Salle, go one block south to the little two-block lane called Quincy Street. At its terminus on Franklin you will be ⑨ directly opposite the entrance to the **Sears Tower** (233 S. Wacker Dr.). A Skidmore, Owings & Merrill design of 1974, Sears Tower has 110 stories and is almost 1,500 feet tall. Although this is the world's tallest building, it certainly isn't the world's most livable one. Once inside, you'll probably be baffled by the escalators and elevators that stop on alternate floors (the elevators have double cars, one atop the other, so that when one car has stopped, say, at 22, the other is at 21). In high winds the building sways noticeably at the upper levels and, most alarming, in 1988 there were two occasions on which windows were blown out. On a clear day, however, the view from the Skydeck is unbeatable. (Check the visibility ratings at the security desk before you decide to ride up and take it in.)

⑩ Head west on Jackson Boulevard and across the river to Canal Street. The wonderful old (1917) **Union Station** (210 S. Canal) is everything a train station should be, with a 10-story dome over the main waiting room, a skylight, columns, and gilded statues.

⑪ We return east on Jackson to the Art Deco **Chicago Board of Trade** (141 W. Jackson), designed in 1930 by the firm of Holabird and Roche; at the top is a gilded statue of Ceres, the Greek goddess of grain, an apt overseer of the frenetic commodities trading that goes on within. The observation deck that overlooks the trading floor is open to the public weekdays 9 AM–2 PM. The lobby is well worth your attention.

Two blocks south on LaSalle is the striking building of 1985 by Skidmore, Owings & Merrill known as **One Financial Place** (440 S. La Salle), which has an exterior and interior of Italian red granite and marble. Among its striking features is the arched section that straddles the rushing traffic on the Congress Parkway/Eisenhower Expressway below. The building's tenants include the **Midwest Stock Exchange,** whose visitor's gallery is open weekdays 8:30–4.

Return to Jackson Boulevard and go east to the massive, darkly handsome **Monadnock Building** (53 W. Jackson), the tallest building ever constructed entirely of masonry. The problem with all-masonry buildings is that the higher they go, the thicker the walls at the base must be to support the upper stories, and the Monadnock's walls at the base are six feet thick.

Across Dearborn Street is the **Fisher Building** (343 S. Dearborn), designed by D. H. Burnham & Co. in 1896. This Gothic-style building, exquisitely ornamented in terra-cotta, is for some reason (perhaps because of favorable rents) the headquarters of dozens of arts and other not-for-profit organizations.

Taking up the entire block bounded by Jackson, State, Van Buren and Dearborn, the new **Harold Washington Library Center** is a postmodern homage to classical-style public buildings. It has some of the most spectacular terra-cotta work seen in Chicago since the 19th century: ears of corn, faces with puffed cheeks (representing the Windy City), and the logo of the Chicago Public Library are a few of the embellishments. During construction, the building looked so much like the vintage skyscrapers around it that visitors mistook it for a renovation project.

Return to Michigan Avenue and turn right past **Roosevelt University,** a massive building that houses the remarkable **Auditorium Theatre** (430 S. Michigan), built in 1889 by Dankmar Adler and Louis Sullivan. Head east on Congress to Columbus Drive ⑫ and, set in its own plaza, **Buckingham Fountain.** Between Memorial Day and Labor Day you can see it in all its glory, when it's elaborately illuminated at night.

Downtown South

The Downtown South area, bounded by Congress Parkway/Eisenhower Expressway on the north, Michigan Avenue on the east, Roosevelt Road on the south, and the Chicago River on the west, presents a striking and often fascinating contrast to the downtown area we have just visited. Once a thriving commercial area and the center of the printing trades in Chicago, it fell into disrepair as the printing industry moved south in search of lower costs. Sleazy bars, pawnbrokers, and pornographic shops filled the area, and homeless winos found a place to sleep at the Pacific Garden Mission (646 S. State). Then, about a decade ago, investors became interested in renovating the run-down yet sturdy loft and office buildings in the old printing district. Today the Printer's Row district is a thriving urban neighborhood enclave.

We'll begin our tour of Downtown South at the corner of Balbo and Michigan. East of the intersection is the heart of beautiful ⑬ **Grant Park.** On a hot summer night during the last week of August 1968, the park was filled with young people protesting the Vietnam War and events at the Democratic presidential nominating convention that was taking place at the Conrad Hilton Hotel down the street. Rioting broke out; heads were cracked, protesters were dragged away screaming, and Mayor Daley gave police the order to "shoot to kill." Later investigations into the events of that evening determined that a "police riot"—not the misbehavior of the protesters, who had been noisy but not physically abusive—was responsible for the violence that erupted.

The **Blackstone Hotel** (636 S. Michigan), on the northwest corner of the intersection, is rich with history. Presidential candidates have been selected here, and presidents have stayed here. Note the ornate little roofs that cap the first-floor windows. Inside, the elegant lobby has impressive chandeliers, sculptures, and handsome woodwork. Next door is the **Blackstone Theatre,** another vintage building, where Broadway-bound shows were once booked; the theater was recently acquired by De Paul University for its own use and that of local theater companies.

At the corner of Harrison and Dearborn streets, the pioneering **Printer's Row Restaurant** (550 S. Dearborn, tel. 312/461–0780) was one of the first upscale restaurants to open in this area, helping to spur redevelopment. It's a wonderful place to stop for an elegant (but not inexpensive) lunch during the week. A block south on Dearborn is the grand old **Franklin Building** (720 S. Dearborn), originally "The Franklin Co.: Designing, Engraving, Electrotyping" and now condominium apartments. Note the decorative tilework on the facade and the scene over the front door, representing the medieval birth of the printer's craft. Next door, **Sandmeyer's Bookstore** (714 S. Dearborn, tel. 312/922–2104; closed Mon.) has a fine selection of books about Chicago. In June this street is the locale of the Printer's Row Book Fair, a weekend event where dealers offer a wide variety of books and prints, demonstrations of the papermaking and bookbinding crafts are given, and street performers and food vendors add to the festivity.

Time Out For a quick pick-me-up, stop at the **Deli on Dearborn** (723 S. Dearborn) or at the **Moonraker Restaurant and Tavern** (733 S. Dearborn). In summer, you can sit outside at either establishment, although the cool interior of the Moonraker may be more welcome after a tramp through the city streets.

Cross Polk Street and turn left to see the recently restored **Dearborn Station** (47 W. Polk), designed in Romanesque-Revival style in 1885 by the New York architect Cyrus L. W. Eidlitz. Since its re-opening in 1985, Dearborn Station has been successful in attracting office tenants, less so in attracting retail tenants.

Two major residential developments played a large part in this neighborhood's rehabilitation. Walk east on Polk Street and then south on Plymouth Court to **Dearborn Park,** a tidy mix of high-rise, low-rise, and single-family units, built on the old railroad yards. West on Polk Street at Wells, turn left to reach the entrance to **River City** (800 S. Wells), a futuristic self-contained city within a city. Apartments, all with curving exterior walls (making it a bit difficult to place square or rectangular furniture), ring the circumference of the building.

Head back toward Grant Park; at State Street, go to your right to pick up 8th Street. Across Wabash stands the **Chicago Hilton and Towers** (720 S. Michigan, tel. 312/922–4400), with its opulent lobby tastefully done in shades of mauve and soft sea green. Notice the gilded horses that flank the main entrance on the inner wall and the sweeping stairway to your right off the main entrance that leads to the spectacular Grand Ballroom.

The Hilton's owners had been considering demolition, but spurred by signs of revitalization all around, they instead mounted a renovation of tremendous proportion. Now one of the most beautifully appointed hotels in the city, the Chicago Hilton and Towers once again attracts the business it needs to fill its thousands of rooms.

Hyde Park and Kenwood

Numbers in the margin correspond to points on the Hyde Park and Kenwood map.

Site of the World's Columbian Exposition of 1893, residence at the turn of the century of the meat-packing barons Swift and Armour, home of the University of Chicago, locale of five houses designed by Frank Lloyd Wright, and the nation's oldest stable racially integrated neighborhood (in the nation's most segregated city), Hyde Park and the adjoining Kenwood may be Chicago's most interesting community: important historically, intellectually, and culturally.

To reach Hyde Park, take the Jeffery Express southbound from the Loop (board it anywhere on State Street between Lake and Congress streets) and get off at 56th Street and Hyde Park Boulevard. Or you can take the Illinois Central Gulf (ICG) RR train from Randolph Street and Michigan Avenue; get off at the 55th Street stop and walk east through the underpass one block and south one block. By auto, take Lake Shore Drive south to the 57th Street exit, turn right at the first traffic light (Hyde Park Boulevard), and continue half a block west.

Our exploration of Hyde Park and Kenwood begins at 56th Street and Cornell Avenue. Walk half a block east on 56th Street to the **Windermere House** (1642 E. 56th St.), designed in 1920 by Rapp and Rapp, known generally for their movie palaces. It's the sole survivor of the many grand hotels built along the lakefront for the Columbian Exposition.

14 Across 56th Street is the **Museum of Science and Industry,** built for the Columbian Exposition as a Palace of Fine Arts. Here you can visit a U-505 submarine, descend into a coal mine, experience an auditory miracle in the whispering gallery, learn how telephones work, trace the history of computing and the development of computer hardware, explore spacecraft and man's history in space, visit Main Street of Yesterday, learn how the body works, and much more. Many of the exhibits are hands-on, and you could spend days here and still not see everything. The Omnimax Theater shows science and space-related films on a giant screen. *5700 S. Lake Shore Dr., tel. 312/684–1414. Admission: $5 adults, $2 children. Open Memorial Day–Labor Day, daily 9:30–5:30; Labor Day–Memorial Day, weekdays 9:30–4, weekends and holidays 9:30–5:30.*

Continue east to South Shore Drive to the **Promontory Apartments** (5530 S. South Shore Dr.), designed by Mies van der Rohe in 1949. The building was named for **Promontory Point,** which juts out into the lake just east of here; it's a favorite spot for picnics and frisbee, and it can be reached by an underpass just north of 55th Street at Lake Shore Drive.

Return west on 56th Street to Blackstone Street, where you can turn right to 55th Street. Between Blackstone and Dorchester is one of the fruits of this area's post-World War II ur-

654

Adler Planetarium, **17**
Field Museum of
Natural History, **19**
John G. Shedd
Aquarium, **18**
Museum of Science
and Industry, **14**
Quadrangle,
University of
Chicago, **15**
Robie House, **16**

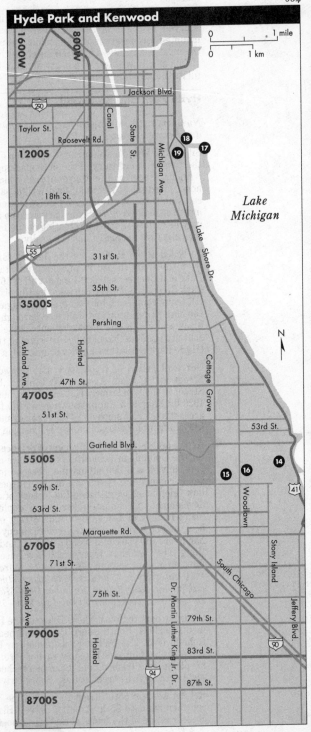

Hyde Park and Kenwood

ban renewal, **1400–1451 East 55th Street,** an apartment building
designed by I. M. Pei, as were the town houses that border it on
the north. Turn right and head up Blackstone, passing a variety of the Kenwood neighborhood's housing stock between 55th
and 51st streets. Although these houses command prices in the
hundreds of thousands of dollars today, they were originally
cottages for workingmen, conveniently located near the cable
car line that ran west on 55th Street. Go west on 52nd Street
four blocks to the **Heller House** (5132 S. Woodlawn), built by
Frank Lloyd Wright in 1897; note the plaster naiads cavorting
at the top.

Continue south on Woodlawn. On the east side of the street is
St. Thomas the Apostle Church and School (5467 S. Woodlawn),
built in 1922 and now a national landmark. Note its terra-cotta
ornamentation.

Time Out | **The Woodlawn Tap** (1172 E. 55th St.), or Jimmy's, is a neighbor-
hood institution, the sole bar on 55th Street to survive urban
renewal. Students hang out here, professors sometimes hold
classes here, and poetry-reading groups meet here. Despite
the sloping floors and the rather grimy demeanor, the beer is
cold and the food—standard tavern fare—is good.

Now we're in University of Chicago territory, full of students
and bookstores. Continue west to University Avenue and the
Lutheran School of Theology (1100 E. 55th St.). Built in 1968 by
the firm of Perkins and Will, the massive structure seems almost to float from its foundation, lightened by the transparen-
cy of its smoked-glass exteriors. Across the street is **Pierce
Hall** (5514 S. University), a student dormitory designed by
Harry Weese. Walk west on 55th Street to Ellis and the intimate **Court Theatre** (5535 S. Ellis, tel. 312/753–4472), a professional repertory company that specializes in revivals of the
classics. South on Ellis about half a block beyond 56th Street is
the Henry Moore sculpture *Nuclear Energy,* commemorating
the first controlled nuclear chain reaction, which took place below ground roughly where the sculpture stands. At the corner
of Ellis and 58th streets, the **University of Chicago Bookstore**
has, in addition to scholarly books, a large selection of general-
interest books, an outstanding collection of cookbooks, and
clothing, mugs, and other souvenir. *5750 S. Ellis, tel. 312/702–
8729. Open weekdays 9–5.*

Across Ellis Avenue stands the **University of Chicago Administration Building.** Just to the south is a small passageway to the
Quadrangle of the university. Here is a typical college campus,
green and grassy, with imposing neo-Gothic buildings all
around. Cross the Quadrangle, heading east, to the circular
drive. Bear left, then turn left at the intersecting road. Follow
this path north and you will pass a reflecting pool (Botany
Pond) before you exit through the wrought-iron gate.

Directly ahead, the **Joseph Regenstein Library** is framed in the
gate. The "Reg," the main library of the university, was designed by Skidmore, Owings, and Merrill and built in 1970.

Turn right on 57th Street and continue east. The massive building on the right-hand corner, **Mandel Hall** (5706 S. University,
tel. 312/702–8511; enter on 57th St.), which also houses the student union, is a gem of a concert hall that has been tastefully

restored. Peek in, if you can, for a glimpse of gold leaf and soft greens against the dark wood of the theater.

Continue east on 57th Street one block to Woodlawn and turn right, noting the stately brick mansions that line both sides of the street. Many of the buildings were built by the University of Chicago in the 1890s to provide housing for professors. Professors continue to live in several of them; others have been repurchased by the university for institutional use.

16 Continue south on Woodlawn to Frank Lloyd Wright's **Robie House.** Built in 1909, Robie House exemplifies the Prairie style. Its cantilevered roof offers privacy while allowing in the light. The house sits on a pedestal; Wright abhorred basements, thinking them unhealthful. You can enter Robie House and examine the interiors, including the built-in cupboards, the leaded-glass windows, and the spacious kitchen. Rescued by the university from the threat of demolition, the building now houses the University Alumni Office, and it is used for small official dinners and receptions. *5757 S. Woodlawn, tel. 312/702–8374. Free tours daily at noon.*

Cross Woodlawn and continue west on 58th Street, past the **Oriental Institute,** which focuses on the history, art, and archaeology of the ancient Near East. *1155 E. 58th St., tel. 312/702–1062 (312/702–9521 for recorded information). Admission free. Open Tues. and Thurs.–Sat. 10–4, Wed. 10–8:30, Sun. noon–4.*

Around the corner, on University, is the **Chicago Theological Seminary** (5757 S. University). Its basement accommodates the **Seminary Cooperative Bookstore** (tel. 312/752–4381), which has an extensive selection of books in the humanities. Defying all the rules of marketing, this store—which does not advertise, is not visible from the street, and has no parking—has more sales per square foot than any other bookstore in Chicago.

Continue south on University to the **Midway Plaisance.** Created for the World's Columbian Exposition, this green, hollowed-out strip of land was intended to replicate a Venetian canal. When the "canal" was filled with water, houses throughout the area were flooded as well, and the idea had to be abandoned.

Go east along the Plaisance one block and turn north on Woodlawn. On your right, set back on a grassy expanse, is the neo-Gothic **Rockefeller Memorial Chapel** (5850 S. Woodlawn, tel. 312/702–7000), designed by Bertram Goodhue and named in honor of the founder of the university. The interior has a stunning vaulted ceiling; hand-sewn banners decorate the walls.

On your way back to the starting point, walk up Dorchester street; at 5704 South Dorchester, an Italian-style villa, is one of the few survivors constructed before the Chicago Fire. Two additional houses that predate the fire are at 5642 and 5607 South Dorchester.

If you're returning to the Loop by car up Lake Shore Drive, you'll pass the low-rise, dark **McCormick Place Convention Hall** (2300 S. Lake Shore Dr.); opposite it, to your left, is the **McCormick Hotel.** Immediately north of the hotel, the low-rise **McCormick Place North** is the latest addition to the complex, its completion having been delayed by almost a year because of political machinations and scandals, in true Chicago style.

Coming up on the left, the building with the massive columns on an ancient Grecian model is **Soldier Field** (425 E. McFetridge Dr.), the home of the Chicago Bears. To the right, you can see

17 the dome of the **Adler Planetarium,** a museum with exhibits about the stars and the planets and a popular program of Sky Shows. *1300 S. Lake Shore Dr., tel. 312/322–0304 (general information), 312/322–0300 (Sky Show information), 312/322–0334 (information on the skies for the month). Admission free. Sky Show admission: $3 adults, $1.50 children 6–17. Open Mon.–Thurs. 9:30–4:30, Fri. 9:30–9, weekends 9:30–4:30.*

18 Straight ahead is the **John G. Shedd Aquarium,** with its dazzling new Oceanarium starring two beluga whales and several Pacific dolphins. Don't miss the sharks, tarpon, turtles, and myriads of smaller fish and other aquatic forms in the coral reef exhibit. Hundreds of other watery "cages" display fish from around the world, some bizarre and many fantastically beautiful. *1200 S. Lake Shore Dr., tel. 312/939–2426. Admission: $3 adults, $2 children and senior citizens. Open daily 9–5.*

Opposite the Shedd Aquarium, just north of Soldier Field on **19** the left, is the **Field Museum of Natural History,** one of the country's great natural history museums. You can hear songs and stories about Pawnee life while sitting in a reconstructed Pawnee earth lodge (built in conjunction with the Pawnee of Oklahoma) and touch tools and artifacts. You can return to ancient Egypt by visiting a reconstructed Mastaba tomb complex that houses Unis-ankh, the son of a fifth-dynasty pharaoh, along with 23 mummies and 1,400 rare artifacts. A gem room contains more than 500 gemstones and jewels. Place for Wonder, a three-room exhibit for children, lets youngsters handle everything on display, including a half-ton polar bear (named Earthquake Charlie), shells, animal skins, stuffed animals, clothing and toys from China, aromatic scent jars, and gourds. *Lake Shore Drive at E. Roosevelt Rd., tel. 312/922–9410. Admission: $10 families, $3 adults, $2 students and senior citizens; free Thurs. Open daily 9–5.*

As you round the curve past the Shedd Aquarium, look to your right for a view of the harbor. Off to the left looms the handsome, massive complex of the **Chicago Hilton and Towers** (720 S. Michigan), and soon thereafter the **Buckingham Fountain** will appear immediately to your left. To the far right, at the north and east, you can just see the ornate towers of **Navy Pier.**

River North

Numbers in the margin correspond to points of interest on the River North and Lincoln Park map.

Cross the Chicago River at Michigan Avenue. Flanking the avenue here are the **Tribune Tower** (435 N. Michigan Ave., tel. 312/222–3232), an ultra-traditional, crenellated Gothic skyscraper that is home to the *Chicago Tribune* newspaper. Look for chunks of other famous buildings (such as Westminster Abbey) embedded in the outside of the tower. The graceful **Wrigley Building** (400 N. Michigan Ave., tel. 312/923–8080), which is illuminated at night, is the corporate home of the Wrigley chewing gum empire.

This stretch of Michigan Avenue is Chicago's most glamorous shopping district, known as the Magnificent Mile (*see* Shopping, *below*). Walk north to Chicago Avenue to the distinctive 20 yellow stone **Water Tower**, a survivor of the Great Fire of 1871, now a tourist information center. **Pumping Station** (806 N. Michigan Ave., at the Water Tower, tel. 312/467–7114) shows *Here's Chicago!*, a multimedia show about the city. *Admission: $5.75 adults, $4.50 children.*

Walk west on Chicago Avenue, where the flavor of River North is more readily apparent. This neighborhood was a vigorous commerical, industrial, and warehouse district at the turn of the century. In the early 1970s economic conditions changed, and as factories moved away, the buildings fell into disrepair. But artists and craftspeople moved into River North, attracted by the space and the low rents, and as galleries and restaurants arose in the 1970s, developers began to renovate the solid, large red brick buildings. At La Salle Street you'll pass the **Moody Bible Institute** (820 N. La Salle, tel. 312/329–4000), a handsome, if massive, contemporary brick structure where students of various conservative Christian denominations study and prepare for religious careers. Three blocks further west, **The River North Concourse** (750 N. Orleans at Chicago Ave.) houses numerous art galleries along with a collection of stores and businesses. The striking lobby is done in exposed brick and glass block. On the ground floor is Gallery Vienna, specializing in furniture and decorative arts from turn-of-the-century Vienna. Others include the Brandywine Fantasy Gallery, which features American painting and "fantasy art," and Chiaroscuro, a gallery/shop with jewelry, clothing, furniture, and paper goods that could all be classified as objets d'art.

Time Out   **Cafe Tête-à-Tête**, on the second floor of 750 North Orleans, is a good spot for a croissant and espresso, a sandwich, or gelati and Viennese-style pastries. The art on the walls (from the building's various galleries) is for sale.

Just south of this shopping concourse is an area rich in art galleries, bounded by Huron, Superior, and Hudson streets and 21 known as **SuHu**—a double play on New York's SoHo. Don't be shy about walking in and browsing; a gallery's business is to sell the works it displays, so most galleries welcome interested visitors and, time permitting, the staff will discuss the art they are showing. While each gallery sets its own hours, most of them are open weekdays and Saturday 10–5 or 11–5 and are closed Sunday. For announcements of openings and other news of the art scene, write for the *Chicago Gallery News* (107 West Delaware Pl., Chicago, IL 60610).

For a change in atmosphere, head south on Franklin Street to Ontario Street, where an art deco–style building houses **Ditka's** (*see* Dining, *below*) and **City Lights** (223 W. Ontario, tel. 312/280–1790), a trendy sports-oriented restaurant and a nightclub owned in part by Mike Ditka, the coach of the sometime Superbowl champion Chicago Bears. Next door is the **Chicago Sports Hall of Fame**, housing a modest collection of memorabilia. *227 W. Ontario, tel. 312/915–4500. Admission: $3 adults, $2 senior citizens and children. Open Mon.–Sat. 10–4.*

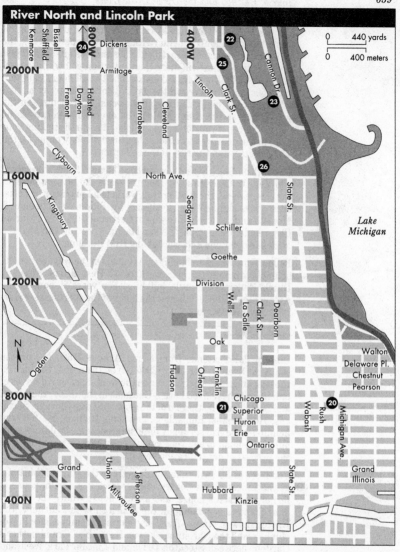

River North and Lincoln Park

Kenmore
Bissell
Sheffield

800W

Dickens

400W

Armitage

Lincoln

Cannon Dr.

Halsted
Dayton
Fremont

Clark St.

Larrabee

Cleveland

2000N

Clybourn

Kingsbury

1600N

North Ave.

Sedgwick

0   440 yards

0   400 meters

Schiller

State St.

Goethe

Lake
Michigan

1200N

Division

Wells

Clark St.
La Salle

Dearborn

N

Oak

Walton
Delaware Pl.
Chestnut
Pearson

Ogden

800N

Hudson

Orleans

Franklin

Chicago
Superior
Huron
Erie
Ontario

Wabash
Rush

Michigan Ave.

Grand

Union

Jefferson

Milwaukee

Hubbard

Kinzie

State St.

Grand
Illinois

400N

Chicago Academy of
Sciences, **25**
Chicago Historical
Society, **26**
DePaul University, **24**
Lincoln Park
Conservatory, **22**
Lincoln Park Zoo, **23**
SuHu, **21**
Water Tower, **20**

Proceed east on Ontario for another one-of-a-kind experience, the **Rock and Roll McDonald's** at Clark and Ontario. Though it has a standard McD's menu (with slightly higher prices), the profusion of rock and roll artifacts, '50s and '60s kitsch, and just plain bizarre items will more than entertain you while you savor your $2.30 Big Mac. Jukeboxes blast at all hours, and vintage '50s cars often crowd the parking lot on Saturday nights. It's one of the highest-grossing McDonald's franchises in the world, and so the company lets the operator decorate as he pleases. Even if you don't like the food, it's worth sticking your head in the door just to admire the Howdy Doody puppets, the '59 Corvette, and the rest of the collection.

Go south on Clark Street toward the Chicago River. Two recent additions to Chicago's architecture scene can be seen here; at the river's edge, the **Quaker Oats** world headquarters, in a massive, glass-skinned box designed by Skidmore, Owings & Merrill, and the circular towers of Bertrand Goldberg's **Marina City** residential complex. Near Marina City you can also see Mies van der Rohe's classic boxlike **IBM Building**.

Follow Kinzie back to Michigan Avenue. On the way, notice the splendid ornamental brickwork of **33 West Kinzie Street**, a Dutch Renaissance style building. For years it housed the Kinzie Steak House; it is now the home of the sportscaster Harry Caray's restaurant.

Lincoln Park

Lincoln Park extends from North Avenue (1600 N.) on the south to Diversey Parkway (2800 N.) on the north, the lake on the east and the Chicago River on the west. Successive waves of immigrants have lived here—Germans in the 1860s, then Irish and Scotch, and by the end of the century Poles, Slovaks, Serbians, Hungarians, Romanians, and some Italians. By 1960 the neighborhood had seriously deteriorated; some buildings were bulldozed in an urban renewal effort, others were restored as the process of gentrification began.

㉒ The No. 151 bus will take you directly to the start of this tour, at the **Lincoln Park Conservatory**, which has a palm house, a fernery, a cactus house, and a show house where the special annual shows are mounted: the azalea show in February, the Easter show in March–April, the chrysanthemum show in November, and the Christmas show in December. Grandmother's Garden, between Stockton Drive and Lincoln Park West and dating from 1893, is a collection of informal beds of perennials including hibiscus and chrysanthemums. A large outdoor garden has flowering plants. *2400 N. Stockton Dr., tel. 312/294–4770. Admission free. Open Sun.–Thurs. 10–6, Fri. 10–9. Hours vary during shows.*

㉓ **Lincoln Park Zoo** is perfect for those who want to visit a zoo and can't spend a lot of time getting there. The 35-acre zoo is noted especially for its Great Ape House: The 23 gorillas are thought to be the finest collection in the world. In addition to the reptile house, the large mammal house (elephants, giraffes, black rhinos), the monkey house, the bird house, the small mammal house, and a huge polar bear pool with two bears, the zoo has several rare and endangered species. To reach the zoo, take the northbound La Salle Street bus or the Sheridan Avenue (No.

151) bus. Metered parking is available. *2200 N. Cannon Dr., tel. 312/294–4660. Admission free. Open daily 9–5.*

Go west on Fullerton Parkway to **Lincoln Avenue,** a diagonal that creates a three-way intersection with Fullerton and Halsted Street. Like most urban strips (as opposed to suburban malls), this shopping strip tells a good deal about the neighborhood. Upscale and trendy without being avant-garde, it caters to well-educated, young and middle-aged professionals. You'd be hard pressed to find a drugstore or a shoemaker's shop on this strip. That might be inconvenient if you lived here, but it makes it all the more fun for browsing.

The **Biograph Theater** (2433 N. Lincoln, tel. 312/348–1350), where the gangster John Dillinger met his end at the hands of the FBI, is now on the National Register of Historic Places. The Biograph shows first-run movies with an emphasis, as you might expect from the neighborhood, on foreign and art films.

Time Out Hungry or not, you'll want to step inside the **Potbelly Sandwich Works** (2264 N. Lincoln, tel. 312/528–1405). The walls are decorated with old-fashioned signs, the tables are covered in tile. Vintage malted-milk machines whir behind the counter. A massive old Toledo scale sits against the wall. In the oaken loft is a player piano and a small potbellied stove. And the centerpiece of the restaurant is a huge potbellied stove that you'll have to walk around to get to the service counter.

⟨24⟩ Go south on Halsted one block, then west on Belden to the campus of **DePaul University,** on the north side of Belden between Sheffield and Halsted. As you walk through the entrance on Belden Street, you're on the grounds of the former McCormick Semnary, where antislavery groups met during the Civil War and Chicagoans sought refuge from the Great Fire in 1871. Note the elegant New England-style church on your right as you enter. The small street inside the U on your left is Chalmers Place. Enter the cul-de-sac, where the brick houses, more than 100 years old and once faculty residences at McCormick Seminary, are now privately owned. At the west end of the street is the Gothic seminary building. Continue south past the seminary, east on Chalmers Place, and south again to exit the university grounds where you entered on Belden.

Sheffield/De Paul, the western section of the neighborhood, includes some of Lincoln Park's most beautiful housing, as well as beautiful private gardens, a profusion of flowers and old, leafy trees. As you walk around, watch for the numbers designed in the half-moon leaded-glass windows that often cap the doorways of the neighborhood. Many of the numbers have no relation to the address of the building in which they are set. Renovators pay high prices for leaded-glass windows that fit the openings in their houses; the "misnumbered" windows once graced other homes. (The theft of leaded-glass windows was a serious crime problem in Lincoln Park a few years ago.)Turn right on Belden, go two blocks to Bissell, and walk south to the 2100 block. This street is noteworthy for the detailed stone and terra-cotta insets in many of the houses, especially the row at **2135–2127 North Bissell Street,** and for the elaborately carved cornices, window overhangs, and turrets on the buildings, typical of the Queen Anne style that you see throughout Sheffield/De Paul.

Turn right on Dickens Street and go west three blocks to Seminary. At **2018 North Seminary Avenue,** note the raised entryway; this is a one-and-a-half-story building, typical of an early style of construction known as Chicago cottage. Many buildings in the area have a steep flight of steps leading to the entry and a small story below, at ground level. Across the street are two buildings that predate the Chicago Fire—**2023 North Seminary Avenue** and **2029 North Seminary Avenue.** Go north on Seminary back to Belden and turn left. **1125 West Belden Avenue,** with its stately bays extending out over Clifton, has a familiar design feature: the ornate corner bay, supported by a single column. As you continue east on Belden, you'll find that the very contemporary poured-concrete buildings of the De Paul University campus to your left are an interesting juxtaposition.

Take Lincoln southeast to Armitage, turn left and continue to Clark to reach the imposing classical-style building that houses
❷❺ the **Chicago Academy of Sciences.** Despite its scholarly name, this is not an institution of higher learning but a museum specializing in the natural history of the Midwest. The permanent exhibits include dioramas showing the ecology of Chicago millions of years ago, before it was settled by man, and back-lit ceiling images of the nighttime sky as seen from Chicago. Special exhibits are mounted regularly. *2001 N. Clark, tel. 312/ 549–0343. Admission: $1 adults, 50¢ children and senior citizens, free Mon. Open daily 10–5.*

Follow Clark Street south to Wisconsin, turn west, and proceed to Lincoln Park West. This neighborhood, **Old Town Triangle,** is filled with courts and lanes that run for only a block or so. There are two marvelous frame houses at **1838 and 1836 North Lincoln Park West,** rare because of the restrictions on wood construction that went into effect following the Chicago Fire in 1871. Continue south, turn west on Menomonee and go one block to Sedgwick. Turn right onto the **1800 North Sedgwick Street** block and proceed about halfway up the block. On the right is a strip of houses that may be the most expensive in all of Chicago. Each was custom-designed for its owner, at an astronomical price, by a world-renowned architect. Such were the egos involved that the architects could agree on nothing, not style, not materials, not lot size, not even the heights of the buildings. While some of the structures might look good on another site, here they look like transplanted misfits, jammed in together.

❷❻ Walk east on Eugenie across Clark Avenue, to the **Chicago Historical Society.** A sparkling, all-glass addition to the front of the structure gives it a dramatically different appearance from the stately brick building you see from the westbound La Salle Street exit from Lake Shore Drive. The Historical Society's permanent exhibits include the much-loved diorama room that portrays scenes from Chicago's history, and the famous statue of Abraham Lincoln, whose nose gleams from having been rubbed by countless numbers of those children. The Society's Civil War exhibit, "A House Divided," shouldn't be missed by Civil War buffs. *1601 N. Clark, tel. 312/642–4600. Admission: $3 adults, $2 students and senior citizens, $1 children, free Mon. Open Mon.–Sat. 9:30–4:30, Sun. noon–5.*

The southbound Clark Street (No. 22) bus will return you to the near north or downtown.

Oak Park

Ernest Hemingway once called Oak Park—his birthplace and childhood home from 1899 to 1917—a town of "broad lawns and narrow minds." The ethnic and political leanings of this neighborhood have diversified since Hemingway played on its streets, however, as young professionals have moved in with their children in search of safer streets, better public schools, and easy access to the Loop. Oak Park is not only one of Chicago's oldest suburbs, but also features the world's largest collection of Prairie School buildings, an architectural style created by Frank Lloyd Wright. Prairie School houses hug the earth with their emphatic horizontal lines; inside, open spaces flow into each other, rather than being divided into individual rooms.

To get to the heart of Oak Park, take the Eisenhower Expressway (I–290) west to Harlem Avenue and exit to the left. Turn right at the top of the ramp, head north on Harlem Avenue to Chicago Avenue, turn right, and proceed to Forest Avenue.

On the southeast corner of Forest and Chicago avenues you'll see the **Frank Lloyd Wright Home and Studio.** In 1889, the 22-year-old Wright began building his own Shingle Style home—financed by a $5,000 loan from his then-employer and mentor, Louis Sullivan (of the noted firm Adler & Sullivan)—at the same time as he began to develop the Prairie School of architecture. Over the next 20 years, Wright expanded his business as well as his original modest cottage, establishing his own firm in 1894 and adding a studio in 1898. Wright's home, made of brick and dark shingles, is filled with natural wood furnishings and earth-tone spaces; Wright's determination to create an integrated environment prompted him to design the furniture as well. The leaded windows have colored art glass designs, and several rooms feature skylights or other indirect lighting. A spacious playroom on the second floor is built to a child's scale. The studio is made up of four spaces—an office, a large reception room, an octagonal library, and an octagonal drafting room that uses a chain harness system rather than traditional beams to support its balcony, roof, and walls. A testimony to Wright's somewhat eccentric regard for nature, the house was built around a tree that grew through the wall of a hallway and up through the ceiling; though the original tree died years ago, the restoration includes a replacement branch. *951 Chicago Ave., tel. 708/848–1500. Admission: Mar.–Oct., $5 adults, $3 senior citizens and children 10–18; Nov.–Feb., $4 adults, $2 senior citizens and children 10–18. Tours weekdays at 11 AM, 1 PM, and 3 PM, and continuously on weekends 11–4. Reservations required for groups of 10 or more. Closed Thanksgiving, Christmas, and New Year's Day.*

Several other examples of Wright's work are within easy walking or driving distance from his home and studio. Except for the Unity Temple, though, these are all private homes, so you'll have to be content with what you can view from the outside. One block left on Chicago Avenue takes you past **1019, 1027,** and **1031 Chicago Avenue.** Turn left on Marion Street and then left again on Superior Street to reach **1030 Superior Street.** Continue down Superior Street, turn right onto Forest Avenue, and take a look at **333, 318, 238,** and **210 Forest Avenue.** Head left for a detour to **6 Elizabeth Court.** Follow Forest Avenue a few blocks south to Lake Street and turn left. On the corner of Lake Street and Kenilworth Avenue is **Unity Temple** (875 Lake St., tel. 708/848–6225), built for a Unitarian congregation in 1905.

Hemingway fans may want to head back up Forest Avenue to Chicago Avenue. One block east and two blocks north brings you to **Ernest Hemingway's boyhood home** (600 N. Kenilworth). This gray stucco house is privately owned and not open to the public.

Maps, tour information, and recorded tours of other historic buildings in the River Forest/Oak Park area (including those by Prairie School architects E. E. Roberts and George Maher) are available through the **Oak Park Visitors Center** (158 N. Forest Ave., tel. 708/848–1500).

Shopping

There are far too many stores in Chicago to attempt a complete, fully descriptive listing here. The following pages offer a general overview of the more popular shopping areas and list some of the stores where certain items can be found. Most department stores, except those in Water Tower Place, are open Monday–Saturday 9:45–5:30 or 9:45–6, Thursday until 7. Sunday hours at Magnificent Mile department stores are usually noon–5. Loop department stores are closed Sunday except once a month (designated Super Sunday); the newspapers announce the specific day. Lord & Taylor and Marshall Field at the Water Tower are open Monday–Saturday 10–8 and Sunday noon–6.

Major Shopping Districts

The Loop, bordered by Lake Street on the north, Michigan Avenue on the east, Congress Street on the south, and Wells Street on the west, is the heart of Chicago business and finance. The city's two largest department stores, Marshall Field & Co. and Carson Pirie Scott, anchor the Loop's State Street–Wabash Avenue area, which has declined since the years when it was known as "State Street, that great street." Several Loop buildings, including the Stevens Building (17 N. State St.) and the Mallers Building (5 S. Wabash Ave.), contain groups of small shops on their upper floors, and there are a number of interesting specialty stores on the west end of the Loop.

The Magnificent Mile, Chicago's most glamorous shopping district, stretches along Michigan Avenue from the Chicago River (400 N.) to Oak Street (1000 N.). The street is lined on both sides with some of the most sophisticated names in retailing: Tiffany (715 N.), Gucci (900 N.), Chanel (990 N.), I. Magnin (830 N.), and Ralph Lauren (960 N.), to name just a few. Look on the Mag Mile for stores offering clothing, shoes, jewelry, and accessories, as well as for several art galleries. Michigan Avenue also features three "vertical malls": **Water Tower Place** (835 N. Michigan Ave.), anchored by Lord & Taylor and Marshall Field's; the sophisticated and expensive **Avenue Atrium** (900 N. Michigan Ave.), anchored by Bloomingdale's; and **Chicago Place** (700 N. Michigan Ave.), anchored by Saks Fifth Avenue.

Oak Street, between Michigan Avenue and Rush Street, is populated with stores selling designer clothing and European imports. Designers with Oak Street addresses include Giorgio

Armani (113 E. Oak St.), Gianni Versace (101 E. Oak St.), Sonia Rykiel (106 E. Oak St.), and Ultimo (114 E. Oak St.).

The upscale residential neighborhoods of **Lincoln Park and Lakeview** offer several worthwhile shopping strips. **Clark Street** between Armitage Avenue (2000 N.) and School Street (3300 N.) contains clothing boutiques, antiques stores, and some bookstores. **Broadway** between Diversey Avenue and Addison Street (3600 N.) also offers a variety of shops. The **Century Mall**, in a former movie palace at Clark Street, Broadway, and Diversey Parkway, houses a variety of national outlets and small specialty stores.

The **North Pier** development, on the Lake, at 435 E. Illinois St. is teeming with fascinating small shops, including a seashell store, a hologram showroom, and a shop that embroiders custom designs on T-shirts and jackets.

Contained by the Chicago River on the south and west, Clark Street on the east, and Oak Street on the north, **River North** boasts a profusion of art galleries, furnishing stores, and boutiques. The *Chicago Gallery News*, available from the tourist information center at the Water Tower (Michigan Ave. and Pearson St.), provides an up-to-date listing of current art gallery exhibits.

Department Stores　**Marshall Field & Co.** (111 N. State St., at the corner of Randolph St., tel. 312/781-1000). Founder Marshall Field's catchphrase was "Give the lady what she wants!" and, for many years both ladies and gentlemen have been able to find everything they want, from furs to riding boots to padded hangers, on one of Field's nine floors. It was recently acquired by Dayton-Hudson Corp., Minneapolis, but observers of the retail industry don't expect the new owners to tamper with this Chicago tradition.

Carson Pirie Scott (1 S. State St., tel. 312/641-7000). Second only to Field's for many years, Carson's was acquired recently by P.A. Bergner, a Milwaukee-based retail chain. At this writing, the fate of the State Street store is unknown.

Neiman Marcus (737 N. Michigan Ave., tel. 312/642-5900). Neiman's prices may be steep, but browsing here is fun. Be sure to take a look at the graceful four-story wood sculpture that rises between the escalators of this branch of the famous upscale Dallas department store.

Bloomingdale's (900 N. Michigan Ave., tel. 312/440-4460). Unlike both its Michigan Avenue neighbors and its New York City sibling, this branch of Bloomies, built in a clean, airy style, gives you plenty of elbow room to sift through its selection of designer labels.

Specialty Stores　**Kroch & Brentano** (29 S. Wabash St., tel. 312/332-7500). The
Books　most comprehensive branch of this local chain, the Wabash Street flagship store will special-order any book they don't have in stock. The lower level carries an impressive paperback department; upstairs is Kroch's extensive collection of hardcover books plus several sale tables.

Stuart Brent (670 N. Michigan Ave., tel. 312/337-6357). A Chicago literary landmark, Stuart Brent carries an extensive and tasteful, if sometimes quirky, collection of hardcover and paperback books, as well as a good selection of music and art books.

57th Street Books (1301 E. 57th St., tel. 312/684–1300). Wood floors, brick walls, and books from the popular to the esoteric distinguish this Hyde Park institution.

Rand McNally Map Stores (150 S. Wacker Dr., tel. 312/332–2009 and 444 N. Michigan Ave., tel. 312/321–1751). Maps for everywhere from Manhattan to the moon, as well as travel books and globes, are available in abundance here.

Savvy Traveller (upstairs at 50 E. Washington St., tel. 312/263–2100). Aside from a full range of travel books, the Savvy Traveller also carries a number of odds and ends that can come in handy on the road.

I Love a Mystery (55 E. Washington St., tel. 312/236–1338). This shop specializes in—you guessed it—mysteries.

Season to Taste (911 W. School St., tel. 312/327–0210). This homey shop has all manner of cookbooks, as well as an assortment of cooking videocassettes.

The Stars Our Destination (2942 N. Clark St., tel. 312/871–2722). Science fiction fans will find a large selection of their favorites, along with the latest news on local sci-fi happenings.

Le Grand Tour Bookstore (3229 N. Clark St., tel. 312/929–1836). Foreign-language books are the specialty here, but there's a large selection of English volumes and an eclectic assortment of periodicals, as well.

Powell's (1501 E. 57th St., tel. 312/955–7780). Powell's Hyde Park store has one of the largest and most diverse selections of used books in town.

Abraham Lincoln Bookstore (357 W. Chicago Ave., tel. 312/944–3085). Civil War buffs will want to visit this shop, which specializes in Lincolniana and Civil War books. Closed Sundays.

Gifts **C.D. Peacock** (101 S. State St., tel. 312/630–5700). This elegant store, which occupies the same city block as the Palmer House hotel, has been selling jewelry and silver to Chicago for more than 150 years.

The Sharper Image (55 W. Monroe St., tel. 312/263–4535) and **Hammacher Schlemmer** (618 N. Michigan Ave., tel. 312/664–9292). Both stores are great for browsing and can provide upscale gadgets and unusual gifts.

Kitchenware **Crate & Barrel** (101 N. Wabash Ave., tel. 312/372–0100, 646 N. Michigan Ave., tel. 312/787–5900. Warehouse store: 800 W. North Ave., tel. 312/787–4775). One of the first "lifestyle" cookware, glassware, and furniture stores, the Crate remains one of the best.

Williams Sonoma (17 E. Chestnut St., tel. 312/642–1593). The selection of kitchenware and cookbooks is excellent, and if you're there during an equipment demonstration you get to taste the results.

Music **Jazz Record Mart** (11 W. Grand Ave., tel. 312/222–1467). This specialty store stocks one of Chicago's largest collections of records, in addition to compact discs and tapes. Jazz and blues fanciers will be delighted to find many rare historic recordings and obscure imports at the Record Mart.

Sporting Goods **MC/Mages Sports** (620 N. LaSalle St., tel. 312/337–6151). Be sure to look at the "Wall of Fame" outside the store that shows the handprints of famous Chicago sports figures such as football's Jim McMahon, baseball's Ryne Sandberg, and hockey's Stan Mikita. Inside you will find six floors of reasonably priced sporting and camping equipment, shoes, and clothing.

Sportmart (3134 N. Clark St., tel. 312/871–8500 and 440 N. Orleans St., tel. 312/222–0900). These large emporia, one in Lakeview and the other in River North, offer low prices and good selections.

Eddie Bauer (123 N. Wabash Ave., tel. 312/263–6005). You'll find clothing for the outdoors and some camping equipment at this chain's Wabash Avenue store.

Erehwon Mountain Outfitters (644 N. Orleans St., tel. 312/337–6400). For hiking, camping, rock climbing, canoeing, and other rigorous outdoor pursuits, you can probably find clothing and equipment at Erehwon, which has a rough-hewn atmosphere and friendly salespeople.

Sports and Fitness

Bicycling The lakefront bicycle path extends some 20 miles along Chicago's lakefront, offering a variety of scenic views. Rent a bike for the day as you enter Lincoln Park at Fullerton or from Village Cycle Center (1337 N. Wells St., tel. 312/751–2488). There are many other scenic rides in the Chicago area. For information, contact the Chicagoland Bicycle Federation (Box 64396, Chicago, IL 60664, tel. 312/427–3325).

Ice Skating During the winter months there is ice skating at the Daley Bicentennial Plaza, Randolph Street at Lake Shore Drive. A small fee is charged, and skate rentals are available (tel. 312/294–4790).

Jogging The lakefront path accommodates both joggers and bicyclists, so you'll need to be attentive. Avoid jogging in areas where there are few other people and after dark. You can pick up the path at Oak Street Beach (across from the Drake Hotel), at Grand Avenue underneath Lake Shore Drive, or by going through Grant Park on Monroe Street or Jackson Boulevard until you reach the lakefront.

Beaches

Chicago has some 20 miles of lakefront, most of it sand or rock beach. Beaches are open to the public daily 9 AM–9:30 PM, Memorial Day to Labor Day; the water is too cold for swimming at other times of the year. Many beaches have changing facilities. **Oak Street Beach** (600-1600 N.) is probably Chicago's most popular, particularly in the 1000 North Area, where the shoreline curves. There are bathrooms here, but for changing facilities you'll have to make the walk to the North Avenue Beach bathhouse. **North Avenue Beach** (1600-2400 N.) tends to be more family oriented; its southern end features lively volleyball action during the summer and fall. **South Shore Country Club Beach** (7100 S.), Chicago's newest and one of the nicest beaches, is quite pretty and not overcrowded. Enter through the South Shore Country Club grounds at 71st Street and South Shore Drive.

Spectator Sports

Baseball   The **Chicago Cubs** (National League) play at Wrigley Field (1060 W. Addison St., tel. 312/404–2827). Wrigley Field is reached by the Howard St. el line; take the B train to Addison Street. Wrigley Field finally received lights in 1988, the last major-league ballpark in the nation to be lighted for night games, but the Cubs still play most of their home games during the day.

The **Chicago White Sox** (American League) play at their brand-new stadium (333 W. 35th St., tel. 312/924–1000 or 312/559–1212 for ticket information) across from Comiskey Park, which is being demolished. Take an A or B Dan Ryan el train to 35th Street.

Basketball   The **Chicago Bulls** play at the Chicago Stadium (1800 W. Madison St., tel. 312/943–5800). Avoid leaving the game early or wandering around this neighborhood at night.

Football   The **Chicago Bears** play at Soldier Field (425 E. McFetridge Dr., tel. 312/663–5100), just south of the Field Museum of Natural History. While subscription sales generally account for all tickets, you can sometimes buy the tickets of a subscriber who can't use them at the stadium shortly before game time. To reach Soldier Field, take the Jeffery Express (No. 6) bus to Roosevelt Road and Lake Shore Drive and follow the crowd.

Hockey   The **Chicago Blackhawks** play at the Chicago Stadium (1800 W. Madison St., tel. 312/733–5300). Again, avoid leaving the game early or wandering around the neighborhood at night.

Dining

Chicago's more than 7,000 restaurants range from those ranked among the best in the nation, and priced accordingly, to simple storefront ethnic eateries (the city has more than 80 Thai restaurants alone) and old-fashioned pubs that offer good food in unpretentious settings at modest prices. However you judge a city's restaurant scene—by ethnic diversity, breadth and depth of high-quality establishments, nationally prominent chefs—Chicago ranks as one of the nation's finest restaurant towns. A few of the more popular restaurants require that you book a week or two—some even five or six weeks—in advance, particularly for weekend evenings. Some of the trendier restaurants do not accept reservations; standing at the bar with the crowd until your table is ready is thought to be part of the experience.

The following dining price categories have been used: *Very Expensive*, over $45; *Expensive*, $30–$45; *Moderate*, $18–$30; *Inexpensive*, under $18.

Near North, River   **Ditka's.** Owned by the Chicago Bears' coach, Mike Ditka, this is
North, and   one of the top-grossing restaurants in the U.S. If you're a
Lincoln Park   sports fanatic, hanker for an excellent pork chop, and don't
American   really care about much else, this is your place. The cavernous, dimly lit main room packs in the fans whenever Bears games are televised. *223 W. Ontario, tel. 312/280–1790. AE, DC, MC, V. Reservations accepted. Expensive.*

★ **Gordon.** At Gordon the decor is rococo, with Oriental rugs, swag curtains, and dark wood. Consistently one of the most innovative contemporary restaurants in Chicago, Gordon's lighter new American cuisine features salsas and an extensive use of herbs in place of heavier cream-based sauces. Entrees have included seared tuna with red tomato and chive vinaigrette; roasted sweetbreads with chanterelle mushrooms, prosciutto, and Chardonnay; and grilled beef tenderloin with Cabernet-braised mushrooms and marjoram. *500 N. Clark St., tel. 312/ 467–9780. Jackets required. Reservations required. AE, DC, MC, V. Closed holidays. Expensive.*

Rue St. Clair. This restaurant bills itself as an American bistro, a good characterization. Pâté of the day rubs shoulders with gravlax and goat cheese on the appetizer menu; sandwiches include croque monsieur, eggs Benedict with hollandaise, Reuben, club, and hamburger. Steak *pommes frites*, classic French bistro fare, shares its place with seafood crepes, baked eggplant Parmigiana, and grilled brook trout. Toulouse-Lautrec posters and doors open on all sides create a casual atmosphere. *640 N. St. Clair St., tel. 312/787–6907. Lunch reservations advised. AE, DC, D, MC, V. Closed holidays. Moderate.*

Al's Italian Beef. This tiny spot on busy Ontario Street is one of the best in Chicago for those two local delicacies, "Italian beef" (thinly sliced, well-done beef, served on a bun with its juice and as many toppings—hot peppers, onions, ketchup, mustard— as you like), and the Chicago-style hot dog (hot dog with toppings in the same manner). Eat at one of the tiny, cramped tables or carry the food away. *169 W. Ontario St., tel. 312/943– 3222. No credit cards. Inexpensive.*

Billy Goat Tavern. A favorite hangout for reporters from the *Chicago Tribune*, this self-service bar and grill just across the street is columnist Mike Royko's second office. Don't come here if you're watching your cholesterol level: The famed "chizboogers" are held together with grease. *430 N. Michigan Ave. (lower level), tel. 312/222–1525. No credit cards. Inexpensive.*

★ **Ed Debevic's.** Half serious, half tongue-in-cheek, this imitation 1950s diner packs them in from morning till midnight. The signs are an important part of the decor: "If you don't like the way I do things—buy me out"; "If you're not served in 5 minutes—you'll get served in 8 or 9. Maybe 12 minutes. Relax." The menu features eight types of hamburger; a sandwich selection that includes tuna salad, chicken salad, chicken BLT, and Sloppy Joe; four chili preparations; five hot dog offerings; and a selection of "deluxe plates": meat loaf, pot roast, breaded pork loin, and chicken pot pie. Ed's has recently added more salads in a slight divergence from the diner motif. The banana cream pie, coconut cream pie, and pecan pie are homemade. *640 N. Wells St., tel. 312/664–1707. No reservations; the wait may be substantial. No credit cards. Closed some holidays. Inexpensive.*

American Eclectic **The Eccentric.** Restaurateur Richard Melman has teamed with talk-show star Oprah Winfrey to open this combination French café/Italian coffeehouse/English pub. The food is surprisingly good; don't miss the excellent steaks and chops, as well as Oprah's mashed potatoes with horseradish. For dessert, try the butterscotch or bittersweet chocolate pot de crème. *159 West Erie, tel. 312/787–8390. Reservations accepted for 6 or more. AE, DC, D, MC, V. No lunch weekends. Moderate–Expensive.*

Chicago Dining and Lodging (North)

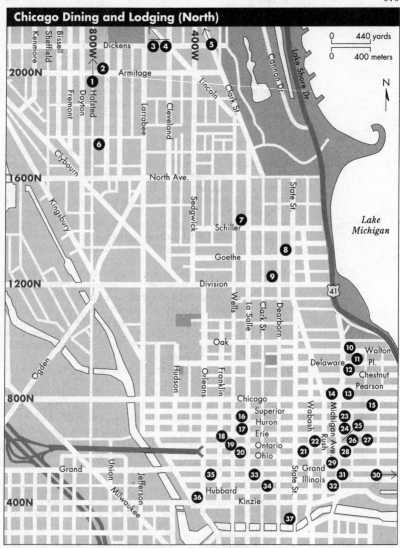

Dining

Al's Italian Beef, **20**
Ambria, **5**
Avanzare, **24**
The Berghoff, **44**
Billy Goat Tavern, **32**
Cafe Ba-Ba-Reebal, **2**
Courtyards of Plaka, **38**
Ditka's, **18**

The Eccentric, **17**
Ed Debevic's, **19**
Eli's The Place For Steak, **15**
The Everest Room, **45**
Frontera Grill, **34**
Gene & Georgetti, **35**
Gordon, **33**

Harold's Chicken Shack, **53**
Hatsuhana, **25**
House of Hunan, **29**
Klay Oven, **36**
La Tour, **14**
L'Escargot, **1, 23**
Lou Mitchell's, **39**
Mirador, **7**
Montana Street Cafe, **4**

Nick's Fishmarket, **41**
Old Carolina Crab House, **30**
Pizzeria Due, **22**
Pizzeria Uno, **21**
Prairie, **46**
Printer's Row, **47**
Rue St. Clair, **27**
Trattoria Gianni, **6**

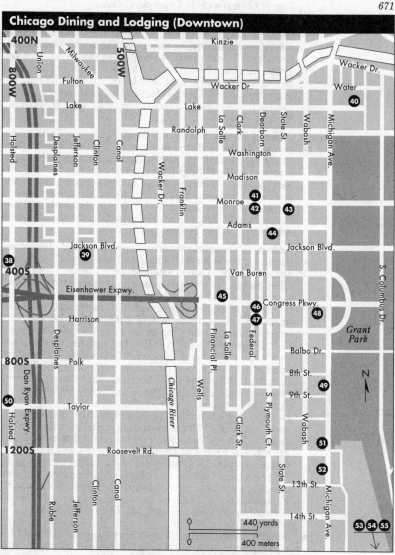

Chicago Dining and Lodging (Downtown)

Tuscany, **50**
University
Gardens, **54**
Vivere, **42**

Lodging
Avenue Motel, **51**
Chicago Hilton &
Towers, **48**
Claridge Hotel, **9**

Comfort Inn of Lincoln
Park, **3**
The Drake, **10**
Essex Inn, **49**
The Fairmont, **40**
Guest Quarters
Suites, **11**
Hotel Inter-
Continental
Chicago, **31**
Hotel Nikko, **37**

Inn of Chicago, **28**
La Salle Motor
Lodge, **16**
The Palmer House, **43**
Radisson Plaza
Ambassador West, **8**
Ramada Inn, **55**
The Raphael, **12**
The Richmont, **26**
Ritz-Carlton, **13**
Travel Inn, **52**

Montana Street Cafe. Although designed to look and feel like a classy neighborhood tavern, Montana Street Cafe has a more innovative and surprising menu than the average corner bar. Chef Barry Brooks's creations range from sandwiches such as a grilled ham and cheese filled with green onions and avocados on sourdough bread to light beer-batter chicken with red pepper jelly. *2464 N. Lincoln Ave., tel. 312/281-2407. Reservations advised. Closed lunch; Sun. AE, DC, D, MC, V. Moderate-Expensive.*

Chinese **House of Hunan.** The original Magnificent Mile Chinese res-
★   taurant, House of Hunan continues to please. The large, elegantly decorated dining area is appointed with porcelains and carvings. With offerings from the four principal Chinese culinary regions—Mandarin (from Beijing), Hunan, Szechuan, and Canton—the enormous menu offers a satisfying dinner to anyone who enjoys Chinese food. Spicy hot dishes are plentiful, but so are mild ones. *535 N. Michigan Ave., tel. 312/329-9494. AE, DC, D, MC, V. Moderate-Expensive.*

French **Ambria.** In the spacious atmosphere of a turn-of-the-century
★   mansion, Ambria serves the most contemporary of French food and light cuisine. Gabino Sotelino, one of Chicago's best chefs, offers menus that change seasonally; a recent spring-summer menu offered terrine of salmon and striped bass with melon, tricolored ravioli of lobster and wild mushroom in lobster broth, and roast tenderloin of baby lamb with eggplant wrapped in crisp potato and served with couscous. The assortment of cheeses, sherbets, fruits, and pastries includes a hot soufflé. At the same address is Un Grand Café, which offers wonderful bistro food at moderate prices. *2300 N. Lincoln Park West, tel. 312/472-5959. Dress: casual but neat. Reservations required. AE, DC, D, MC, V. Closed lunch; Sun.; holidays. Very Expensive.*

La Tour. One of Chicago's finest and most expensive restaurants, La Tour is a large room done in marble with tones of peach and green. Tuxedoed waiters serve you from an exquisite nouvelle French menu: foie gras, apples, and potatoes in puff pastry; raviolis of celery root with truffles and foie gras; and veal medallions with cucumbers, morels, and cream. Come here for an elegant, grand splurge. *Park Hyatt Hotel, 800 N. Michigan Ave., tel. 312/280-2230. Jacket required at dinner. Dinner reservations required. AE, DC, D, MC, V. Very Expensive.*

★   **Mirador.** Owned by Amy Morton Kerr (daughter of famed Chicago restaurateur Arnie Morton), Mirador offers wonderfully flavorful French country cooking in a funky, intimate environment. The menu changes weekly, sometimes daily, sometimes by the minute. Try the sweetbreads with greens if they're available, or the simple but compelling roast free-range chicken. *1400 N. Wells St., tel. 312/951-6441. Reservations advised. AE, MC, V. Closed lunch. Expensive.*

L'Escargot. This restaurant's two locations, on North Michigan and on North Halsted, are both simply decorated and comfortable. The French country cuisine emphasizes foods of the Loire region in summer and of Alsace in winter. Appetizers include marinated mushrooms, spinach timbale, and homemade sausage in puff pastry with warm lentil salad. Entrées have included bay scallops on a bed of linguini with tomato and vermouth sauce, fricassee of veal in Dijon mustard sauce, snails en casserole, and cassoulet. *L'Escargot on Michigan: Allerton*

Hotel, 701 N. Michigan Ave., tel. 312/337–1717. Reservations advised. AE, DC, MC, V. Closed holidays. Moderate–Expensive. L'Escargot on Halsted: 2925 N. Halsted Ave., tel. 312/525–5522. Reservations advised. AE, DC, D, MC, V. Closed lunch; Sun. Moderate.

Indian **Klay Oven.** Quite possibly unlike any Indian restaurant you've
★ ever seen, Klay Oven is a bold experiment in applying fine-dining standards to what is all too frequently represented as storefront food. Such offbeat treats as marinated prawns, mahimahi, rack of lamb, and pork ribs make their way onto the menu here, and all succeed admirably. *414 N. Orleans St., tel. 312/527–3999. Reservations accepted. AE, DC, MC, V. Moderate.*

Italian **Avanzare.** A handsome pair of marble, carpeted rooms, one
★ raised a few steps above the other, is dominated by traditional accents of brass, leather banquettes, and a full-length mirrored bar between the rooms. The main room tends to be quite noisy, the mezzanine somewhat less so. Avanzare offers a wide-ranging menu of pastas, unusual salads, and entrées. Try an appetizer of tuna carpaccio, paper-thin slices of raw tuna in soy sauce with avocado and sweet onions. Among the entrées, try one of the unusual game dishes, a tempting seafood special, or the unsurpassed veal chop. The freshness and quality of the ingredients shine through the preparations. *161 E. Huron St., tel. 312/337–8056. Reservations advised. AE, DC, D, MC, V. No lunch weekends. Expensive.*

Harry Caray's. Housed in the handsome old ornamented brick building that for years was the Kinzie Steak House, Harry Caray's is one of the new breed of "celebrity" restaurant. The interior has a long wood bar, tile flooring, and high tables covered with checkered cloth. Baseball memorabilia decorates the walls, and the food reflects Harry's own preferences: Steaks and chops share the bulk of the menu with traditional Italian preparations. Unlike the "name" owners of some celebrity restaurants, Harry really does stop by. Holy cow! *33 W. Kinzie St., tel. 312/465–9269. Lunch reservations advised; no reservations other times. AE, DC, D, MC, V. Moderate–Expensive.*

Trattoria Gianni. This Lincoln Park establishment successfully re-creates the homey atmosphere and skillful cooking common in Italian trattorias, though at a higher price. Appetizers are a standout: choose among three antipasto plates—hot, cold, or vegetarian—or crunchy deep-fried squid, zucchini strips, or mussels. Imaginative and usually well prepared pasta dishes include *rigatoni nocerina* (pasta tubes with cream, mushrooms, and sun-dried tomatoes), *farfalle contadina* (bow-tie macaroni with vegetables), and *gnocchi à la panna-pesto* (potato dumplings with cream-and-pesto sauce). Simple but satisfying entrées include grilled red snapper with herbs and olive oil, and charcoal-grilled cornish game hen. *1711 N. Halsted St., tel. 312/266–1976. Reservations advised. MC, V. Closed weekend lunch and Mon. Moderate–Expensive.*

Pizzeria Uno/Pizzeria Due. This is where Chicago deep-dish pizza got its start. Uno has been remodeled to resemble its franchised cousins in other cities, but its pizzas retain their light crust and distinctive taste. You'll usually have a shorter wait for a table at Pizzeria Due (same ownership and menu, different decor and longer hours), a block away. Some say Uno's pizza is better, but the product at both establishments is among the best in town. *Uno: 29 E. Ohio St, tel. 312/321–1000. Due:*

619 N. Wabash Ave., tel. 312/943-2400. No reservations, but phone-ahead orders are accepted weekdays only. AE, DC, D, MC, V. Inexpensive.

Japanese **Hatsuhana.** Hatsuhana has a long, angled sushi bar and wood
★ tables set on purple carpeting; its white stucco walls are hung with Japanese lanterns. Sushi and sashimi lovers have long esteemed this restaurant as the best in Chicago for these Japanese vinegared rice and raw fish delicacies. Specials have included steamed baby clams in sake, broiled king mackerel with soybean paste, and boiled snails in sweet sauce. *160 E. Ontario St., tel. 312/280-8287. Reservations advised. AE, DC, MC, V. Closed Sat. lunch; Sun.; holidays. Moderate–Expensive.*

Mexican **Frontera Grill.** Chef/owner Rick Bayless and his wife, Deann,
★ literally wrote the book on Mexican cuisine—*Authentic Mexican*—and that's what you'll find at this casual café, along with a tiled floor, bright colors, and Mexican folk art. They serve a sampling from charbroiled catfish, Yucatan style (with pickled red onions and *jicama* salad), to garlicky skewered tenderloin, Agauscalientes style (with poblano peppers, red onion, and bacon)! This place proves once and for all that Mexican cuisine is anythingbut limited and boring. Its more expensive sister restaurant next door, Topolobampo, is more formal and adventurous, but equally wonderful. *445 N. Clark St., tel. 312/661-1434. Reservations for parties of 6 or more only; expect a long wait. AE, DC, D, MC, V. Closed Sun. and Mon. Moderate.*

Seafood **The Old Carolina Crab House.** This waterside restaurant, with fishing tackle and pictures of fishermen covering the walls, is about as close as Chicago gets to that Southern-style "little crab house on the shore." Stop in for a laid-back dinner of steamed crab and beer. The hush puppies and greens are the best in town. *In the North Pier complex at 465 E. Illinois St., tel. 312/321-8400. Reservations accepted. AE, MC, V. Closed Mon. Moderate.*

Spanish **Cafe Ba-Ba-Reeba!** This large, open restaurant, with its prominent bar, is usually crowded with upscale young folk having a very good time. Choose among a large selection of cold and warm tapas, ranging from cannelloni stuffed with tuna, asparagus, and basil served with tomato basil sauce and white wine vinaigrette to veal with mushrooms, eggplant, and tomato with sherry sauce. The limited entrée menu includes two *paellas* (meat and seafood or seafood only, baked in rice) and two seafood casseroles. There are several desserts for those who have the room. *2024 N. Halsted St., tel. 312/935-5000. Limited reservations; the wait may be substantial. AE, DC, MC, V. Closed lunch; Sun.; holidays. Moderate.*

Steak **Eli's The Place for Steak.** Eli's developed its outstanding repu-
★ tation through an unflagging commitment to top-quality ingredients prepared precisely to customers' orders and generously served. Prime aged steaks are the specialty here, and you won't find better ones in Chicago. You'll also find a superb, thickly cut veal chop and a splendid calves' liver. For dessert, order Eli's renowned cheesecake, now sold nationally in countless varieties. *215 E. Chicago Ave., tel. 312/642-1393. Jacket required. Reservations required. AE, DC, D, MC, V. Closed weekend lunch; holidays. Expensive.*

★ **Gene & Georgetti.** Would you give your right arm for a good, old-fashioned piece of prime aged beef or a plate of spaghetti with meat sauce and mushrooms? If so, Gene & Georgetti is for you. Here is one restaurant that hasn't fallen prey to trendiness and does what it has always done as it has always done it, to the immense relief of its customers. Service may be brusque. *500 N. Franklin St., tel. 312/527–3718. Reservations recommended. AE, DC, MC, V. Closed Sun., some holidays. Expensive.*

Downtown **Prairie.** The interior is inspired by the work of Frank Lloyd
American Wright, and the food by the flavors of the Midwestern states. The result is a thoroughly well conceived American regional restaurant. Meats and game are solid choices, but don't overlook regional fish selections, especially the Lake Superior whitefish. *500 S. Dearborn St., tel. 312/663–1143. Reservations recommended. AE, DC, D, MC, V. Expensive.*

★ **Printer's Row.** The owner and chef, Michael Foley, opened this stylish restaurant when the historic Printer's Row district was just beginning its renaissance, and it has consistently been one of the most interesting and satisfying restaurants in Chicago, largely because Foley constantly refreshes his menu with new ideas. A current menu emphasizes game: braised pheasant with black currants, grilled mallard duck with radicchio and endive, cabbage, and venison sausage. There are several fish preparations and a ragout of sweetbreads with aromatic vegetables and orzo pasta. The decor features warm woods and brown tones that contrast pleasingly with the neutral walls and crisp white tablecloths. *550 S. Dearborn St., tel. 312/461–0780. Jacket advised. Reservations advised, required on weekends. AE, DC, D, MC, V. Closed Sat. lunch; Sun. Expensive.*

★ **Lou Mitchell's.** Be prepared to stand in line, and be assured that the wait is worth it. You're likely to be seated at a long communal table (smaller tables may require a longer wait). The waitresses have a rough and hearty style that gets everyone served promptly, if briskly. Fourteen omelets are the centerpiece of a menu that includes pancakes, French toast, and Belgian waffles for breakfast; sandwiches, salads, and a few hot plates for lunch. People flock to Lou Mitchell's because the ingredients are top-quality, everything is fresh, and everything is homemade—the Greek bread, the raisin toast, the orange marmalade, the pies, the pound cake, and the pudding with cream. *565 W. Jackson Blvd., tel. 312/939–3111. No reservations. No credit cards. Closed dinner; Sun.; holidays. Inexpensive.*

French **The Everest Room.** The Everest Room, in the La Salle Street
★ Club in the heart of the financial district, is arguably the best restaurant in Chicago. Chef Jean Joho has a personal approach that places dishes squarely in the classic French tradition yet appeals to contemporary tastes. Soups are prepared daily, as is a seasonal salad; another salad has garden vegetables and Illinois goat cheese sautéed in olive oil. Entrées change frequently; among recent offerings were fish fillet wrapped and roasted in potato with thyme; yellowfin tuna tournedos sautéed medium-rare with shallots and rice wine; and sautéed breast of squab with truffle coulis and Napa cabbage. An eight-course, fixed-price degustation menu is also available for a minimum of two diners. *440 S. La Salle St., tel. 312/663–8920. Jacket re-*

quired. *Reservations required. AE, DC, MC, V. Closed Mon. dinner; Sat. lunch; Sun., holidays. Very Expensive.*

German   **The Berghoff.** This Chicago institution has a splendid bar with Berghoff Beer on tap, oak paneling, a bustling beer hall ambience, and a huge dining room that is usually full, especially at midday. A menu of German classics (Wiener schnitzel, sauerbraten) is augmented by American favorites. The seeded rye bread is outstanding. *17 W. Adams St., tel. 312/427–3170. Reservations accepted for parties of 6 or more. AE, DC, MC, V. Closed Sun. Moderate.*

Greek   **Courtyards of Plaka.** With its salmon-color walls, red-tile floors, aquamarine bar, white-clothed tables, and live music, Courtyards of Plaka is one of the most sophisticated Greek restaurants in Chicago. Appetizers include the ubiquitous *saganaki* (fried cheese), *melizzanoszlata* (a purée of lightly spiced eggplant to be spread on Greek bread), and *taramosalata* (cod roe spread). Entrées include all of the standard Greek offerings, plus a variety of creative dishes not found elsewhere. *340 S. Halsted St., tel. 312/263–0767. Reservations not required. AE, DC, D, MC, V. Moderate.*

Italian   **Vivere.** The old Florentine Room, on the middle floor of the
★   venerable three-restaurant Italian Village, has been transformed into a palace of modern Italian dining. The decor alone is worth the visit: The designers have made sure there isn't an uninteresting view in the house. The menu takes traditional recipes and gives them a slight nouvelle spin and nearly everything works beautifully. *71 W. Monroe St., tel. 312/332–7005. Reservations recommended. AE, DC, MC, V. Closed Sun., Sat. lunch. Expensive.*

Tuscany. As the name suggests, this restaurant focuses on hearty flavors and simple preparations. The rotisserie-grilled chicken is especially good. The Taylor Street neighborhood, just west of the Loop, is a popular destination at lunchtime. *1014 W. Taylor St., tel. 312/829–1990. Reservations recommended. AE, MC, V. Moderate.*

Seafood   **Nick's Fishmarket.** This dark room, rich with leather and wood, adorned with sports paintings and fresh flowers on white linen tablecloths, has the feel of a traditional club. In addition to such standbys as sole, trout, and salmon, there are several preparations of fresh catfish, calamari, crab legs, scallops, frog legs, Hawaiian opakapaka, ahi, and abalone. Although the ingredients are fresh and top-quality, they are sometimes overcooked; ask for your fish underdone to insure moistness and tenderness. A porterhouse steak, a fillet, baby beef liver, and several pastas are available for diners who just won't eat fish. *1 First National Plaza, tel. 312/621–0200. Jacket and tie advised. Reservations advised. AE, DC, D, MC, V. Closed Sun.; Sat. lunch; holidays. Very Expensive.*

Hyde Park   **Harold's Chicken Shack.** The name says it all: This cramped
American   hole-in-the-wall carryout serves up perhaps the best fried chicken in the city, crisply coated on the outside and moist and tender within. Although the restaurant is part of a chain, Harold maintained control of all the branches and insisted that his techniques and recipes be followed everywhere. For an unusual snack treat, try the deep-fried gizzards in hot sauce (they can become an addiction). *1364 E. 53rd St., tel. 312/667–9835. No credit cards. Inexpensive.*

Middle Eastern **University Gardens.** Arabic music plays in the background and prayer rugs adorn the walls along with Arabic movie posters. Use the pita-pocket bread, baked here daily, to dip in hummos or to surround felafel, lettuce, and tomato for a Middle Eastern sandwich. For dinner, choose a kebab plate, the lamb shank braised with Middle Eastern spices, or the spinach stew with meat. Ask for an order of pickled vegetables; they are quite unlike what Americans think of as "pickles." *1373 E. 53rd St., tel. 312/684–6660. BYOB. No credit cards. Inexpensive.*

Lodging

Chicago is a convention town, and while the opening of several new hotels in recent years has made many new rooms available, the accommodations situation can be tight when major events are scheduled. Prospective visitors should make their plans and book lodging well in advance of a visit. Early action is even more essential when the location and price of accommodations are important considerations. Lower rates are often available, especially at the more expensive hotels, when there are no conventions around; weekend and other special packages, when available, can be real bargains.

The following price categories have been used: *Very Expensive*, over $180; *Expensive*, $135–$180; *Moderate*, $90–$135; *Inexpensive*, under $90.

Downtown **Chicago Hilton and Towers.** Built in 1927 at a cost of more than $30 million, this "grand hotel" was completely renovated in 1984–1986 at a cost of $185 million. Public areas are done in mauve and sea green, marble is used lavishly, and there are antiques and original artwork in the main lobby, the upper floor corridors, even the health club. Bathrooms are outfitted in Italian marble with brass fixtures. The state-of-the-art health club features a 60-foot heated swimming pool, Universal equipment, two whirlpools, men's and women's saunas, and massage service. Business guests will appreciate the up-to-date office technology. The more expensive Towers has its own registration desk and concierge, complimentary Continental breakfast and newspaper, a library with business periodicals, a VCR tape library, and a lounge with honor bar. *720 S. Michigan Ave., Chicago 60605, tel. 312/922–4400 or 800/445–8667; fax 312/922–5240. 1,543 rooms. Facilities: pool, health club, 5 restaurants, lounge, café, deli, valet and laundry service, free shopping and business-district bus shuttles. AE, DC, D, MC, V. Very Expensive.*

The Fairmont. One of Chicago's most attractive hotels, the Fairmont is a 45-story neoclassic structure of Spanish pink granite with copper roofs. Part of the Illinois Center complex (which also contains the Hyatt Regency Chicago and the Swissotel), it offers fine views of the lake and Grant Park. Rooms are furnished in either contemporary or period styles; antiques and original artwork are part of the decor in the public areas. Clever design places every room no more than four doors from an elevator. The rooms are spacious, the beds are extra long, the marble bathrooms have oversize tubs. *200 N. Columbus Dr., Chicago 60601, tel. 312/565–8000 or 800/527–4727; fax 312/856–1032. 694 rooms, 66 suites. Facilities: cabaret lounge, 2 restaurants, lobby tea lounge, use of nearby health club, valet and concierge service. AE, DC, D, MC, V. Very Expensive.*

The Palmer House. The Palmer House was built more than 100

years ago by the Chicago merchant Potter Palmer. Meant to be
opulent and luxurious, it accomplished its aim in its own time;
today it ranks with just a few other Chicago hotels in the elegance of its construction and its public areas. The street level,
with its marble floors and classic shops, is splendid, but you
must see the main lobby, up a flight of stairs: ceiling decorations consist of 21 paintings by Louis Rigal, furnishings are upholstered in velvet, moiré taffeta, and brocade, and there are
crystal light fixtures and custom-made carpeting. A decade-
long renovation, nearly complete, has modernized, upgraded,
and refurbished the guest rooms. A recently opened Executive
Fitness Center offers pool, whirlpool, steam room, sauna,
aerobics, massage, and exercise equipment. Other recent additions include a conference center and a business center. Two
rooms on each floor are designed for disabled guests. A "towers" hotel-within-a-hotel offers additional amenities. *17 E.
Monroe St., Chicago 60603, tel. 312/726–7500 or 800/445–8667;
fax 312/263–2556. 1,740 rooms, 88 suites. Facilities: pool, fitness center, 6 restaurants, 2 lounges, business center, no-
smoking floor, valet, concierge, laundry services, and parking. AE, DC, D, MC, V. Expensive.*

Essex Inn. Located just south of the "best" Downtown South
area, the Essex Inn offers good value. Although not glamorous,
the hotel is nicely situated opposite Grant Park, and its rooms
are pleasantly decorated. Conference facilities are available.
The hotel houses the 8th Street Deli, a spacious casual restaurant that offers unusually pleasing New York–style food. *800 S.
Michigan Ave., Chicago 60605, tel. 312/939–2800 or 800/621–
6909; fax 312/939–1605. 255 rooms. Facilities: restaurant,
lounge, outdoor pool, game room, valet service, free shuttle bus
to N. Michigan Ave. AE, DC, D, MC, V. Moderate.*

Avenue Motel. This no-frills hotel has drab public spaces but a
convenient location and pleasant rooms. Parking is included in
the very modest price. Weekend packages reduce the rate even
further. *1154 S. Michigan Ave., Chicago 60605, tel. 312/427–
8200 or 800/621–4196. 75 rooms. Facilities: restaurant, lounge,
valet, and concierge service. AE, DC, MC, V. Inexpensive.*

Travel Inn. The decor is in basic motel style, and the prices are
basic motel, too. All rooms have color TV, direct-dial telephones, and a hot pot for making instant coffee or tea. Parking
is included. The value is good, for the motel is a short walk from
the Field Museum of Natural History, the Adler Planetarium,
the Shedd Aquarium, and Soldier Field. *1240 S. Michigan
Ave., Chicago 60605, tel. 312/427–4111 or 800/255–3050. 60
rooms. Facilities: use of nearby health club. AE, DC, MC, V.
Inexpensive.*

Hyde Park **Ramada Inn.** Mauve and beige walls, marble-top coffee tables,
brass pieces, and a maroon and beige geometric carpet deco-
rate the entry of this modest hotel. Rooms are pleasantly done
but hardly breathtaking. As Hyde Park and Kenwood's only
first-class hotel, it can do less than it might and still attract
business. A recent renovation converted part of the hotel into a
conference center. *4900 S. Lake Shore Dr., Chicago 60615, tel.
312/288–5800 or 800/237–4933. 288 rooms. Facilities: restaurant, coffee shop, lounge, use of health club, outdoor pool, valet
and concierge service, conference center, free shuttle to downtown area. AE, DC, D, MC, V. Moderate.*

Near North **Guest Quarters Suites.** This pink marble postmodern tower
opened in 1990 and is one of several "all-suites" hotels near

Michigan Avenue. The two-room standard suite is snug, probably with no more floor space than one room at most hotels in the same price category, but families may prefer this setup, where parents can have a bedroom to themselves while children sleep on a sofa bed in the living room. (Children under age 18 sleep free in their parents' suite.) All rooms have a wet bar, a coffeemaker, TVs in both rooms, two telephones, and good-size bathrooms. *198 E. Delaware Pl., Chicago 60611, tel. 312/664–1100 or 800/424–2900; fax 312/664–9881. 345 suites. Facilities: 2 restaurants, bar and lounge, health club, concierge, valet parking. AE, DC, D, MC, V. Very Expensive.*

Hotel Inter-Continental Chicago. This luxury property is a recent renovation of the 1929 Medinah Athletic Club, which has had several incarnations as a hotel. The Michigan Avenue location is within walking distance of most tourist destinations. Unlike most grand hotels, this one has a low-ceiling lobby, done in dark green and dark wood, with an intimate bar to the left and a long lounge area to the right. Rooms are done in a 1920s neoclassical style, in beige and green; the furniture was designed specifically for the hotel. Bathrooms are roomy and nicely appointed. The "executive" level has a spectacular skylit lounge area with terrific views. The showpiece of the Inter-Continental is its Italianate Junior Olympic–size swimming pool with ornate gold and royal blue tiles. *505 N. Michigan Ave., Chicago, 60611, tel. 312/944–4100 or 800/327–0200; fax 312/944–3050. 338 rooms, 30 suites. Facilities: restaurant, bar, concierge, health club. AE, DC, D, MC, V. Very Expensive.*

★ **Hotel Nikko.** Hotel Nikko is one of Chicago's most beautiful hotels, with many exquisite pieces of Oriental art placed throughout. The low-rise main lobby is outfitted in polished granite, Japanese ash, and African mahogany; the south side of the lobby area is glassed-in, giving views of a traditional Japanese garden and a riverfront park beyond. The rooms, furnished either in contemporary or traditional Japanese decor, offer marble baths with separate dressing areas. Complimentary breakfast coffee is brought to your room. The three upper floors ("Nikko Floors") have their own check-in and checkout, a special concierge, and complimentary breakfast and hors d'oeuvres. Two Japanese suites offer a *tatami* sleeping room, large tub, and private rock gardens. The hotel features an executive health club and cardio-fitness center with sauna and massage. Business services include computers, telex and fax, secretarial services, a business library, and an executive lounge. Afternoon tea is served in a handsome lobby lounge; one restaurant is American, one Japanese. Guests may stroll the grounds and enjoy the landscaped rock gardens and terraced promenades. *320 N. Dearborn St., Chicago 60610, tel. 312/744–1900 or 800/645–5687; fax 312/527–2650. 425 rooms, 26 suites. Facilities: 2 restaurants, lounge, fitness center, valet parking, concierge, laundry. AE, DC, D, MC, V. Very Expensive.*

The Ritz-Carlton. Because the Ritz-Carlton Hotel occupies the floors above the Water Tower Place shops, you must ride an elevator to the 12th floor to reach the registration area (while your baggage is handled on the ground floor). The lobby is very grand: A great skylighted fountain is enhanced by bronze sculptures, and lavish plantings line a floor-to-ceiling window. Rooms are decorated with fine furniture; the amenities include three telephones (one in the bathroom), AM/FM clock radio, minibar, bathrobes, hair dryers and lighted makeup mirrors. On the floor below the registration floor, a health club maintains a swimming pool, whirlpool, exercise equipment, steam rooms, sauna, and massage. *160 E. Pearson St. (in Water Tower Pl.), Chicago 60611, tel. 312/266–1000 or 800/621–6906; fax 312/266– 9498. 433 rooms, 55 suites. Facilities: 3 restaurants, bar, indoor pool, health club, sauna, valet, laundry, concierge, valet parking and garage next door. AE, DC, D, MC, V. Very Expensive.*

Radisson Plaza Ambassador West. North State Parkway is one of Chicago's better kept secrets: The extension of bustling State Street in the Loop, it becomes a street of handsome old turn-of-the-century residences north of Rush Street. This is the site of the small, European-style Ambassador West, whose oak-paneled lobby is filled with art treasures. Included in the tariff are complimentary Continental breakfast, cocktails, and daily newspaper; nightly turndown service; and honor bar. Business-meeting rooms and related services are offered. Its sister hotel across the street, the Omni Ambassador East, is also good but even more expensive. *1300 N. State Pkwy., Chicago 60610, tel. 312/787–7900 or 800/333–3333. 217 rooms, 41 suites. Facilities: restaurant, two no-smoking floors, valet laundry, concierge, parking, airport transportation. AE, DC, MC, V. Expensive.*

★ **The Drake.** The Drake is perhaps the grandest of Chicago's traditional hotels. Designed and built by Ben Marshall after the style of Italian palaces of the Renaissance, the hotel opened in 1920 and was listed in the National Register of Historic Places in 1981. Situated at a bend in the Lake Michigan shoreline, the Drake offers splendid lake views from rooms on two sides. The hotel spans an entire city block on Michigan Avenue. The Drake's street-level arcade is an attractive enclosed shopping mall; the main lobby is lavishly carpeted, decorated with original art, chandeliered, and accented in oak throughout. In the middle of the lobby, a splendid marble fountain is surrounded by cherubs riding dolphins. Amenities include fresh fruit and flowers, afternoon ice delivery, bed turndown, and morning newspaper delivery. For business travelers, the Vista Executive Floor at the top of the hotel offers valet service, lounge, conference center, and complimentary breakfast and cocktails. Businesswomen can request one of the hotel's 34 Executive Business Women's Suites, whose foldaway beds permit easy conversion from bedroom into conference room. *140 E. Walton Pl., Chicago 60611, tel. 312/787–2200 or 800/553–7253; fax 312/ 787–1431. 535 rooms, 65 suites. Facilities: 3 restaurants, 2 lounges, laundry and valet service, secretarial service, wheelchairs, valet parking. AE, DC, D, MC, V. Expensive.*

★ **Claridge Hotel.** Nestled among Victorian houses on a tree-lined Near North street, this building of 1930s vintage was fully renovated in 1987. With 173 rooms on 13 floors, the hotel is intimate rather than bustling. Guest rooms are simply but tastefully furnished. Complimentary Continental breakfast is served, and a newspaper is provided. Two floors are designated for nonsmokers. *1244 N. Dearborn Pkwy., Chicago 60610, tel. 312/787–4980 or 800/245–1258; fax 312/266–0978. 173 rooms, 3 suites. Facilities: restaurant, bar, access to health club, valet parking, concierge and limousine service. AE, DC, D, MC, V. Moderate.*

Inn of Chicago. This hotel, opened some 60 years ago, recently became a Best Western property. After a three-year, $15 million renovation, Inn of Chicago is attractive and tasteful. Handicapped-equipped rooms are available, and the entrance is handicapped accessible. The hotel is not lavish, but neither are its prices, which are quite reasonable given its great location just east of Michigan Avenue. The top floor, once the Chicago Press Club, has been turned into business suites. *162 E. Ohio St., Chicago 60611, tel. 312/787–3100 or 800/528–1234. 358 rooms, 26 suites. Facilities: restaurant, lounge, valet laundry, access to health club. AE, DC, D, MC, V. Moderate.*

★ **The Raphael.** On one of the nicest Near North streets, east of Michigan Avenue and next to the John Hancock Center, the Raphael offers the same intimacy, the same European-style multilingual service, the same tastefully furnished and appointed rooms with color TV and refrigerator that other hotels provide—at half the price. True, there are no galleries of fine art or state-of-the-art business equipment. But for those who want the experience of a fine hotel at the price of a chain hotel, the Raphael is the place to come. *201 E. Delaware Pl., Chicago 60611, tel. 312/943–5000 or 800/821–5343; fax 312/943–9483. 175 rooms. Facilities: restaurant, lounge. AE, DC, D, MC, V. Moderate.*

★ **The Richmont.** One of a new breed of hotel, the Richmont is an intimate establishment in recently renovated quarters. Charming rather than luxurious, comfortably rather than elegantly appointed, it offers a lot at relatively reasonable prices. Continental breakfast is included. *162 E. Ontario St., Chicago 60611, tel. 312/787–3580 or 800/621–8055; fax 312/787–1299. 193 rooms, 13 suites. Facilities: restaurant, piano bar, access to health club, valet service, valet parking. AE, DC, D, MC, V. Moderate.*

Comfort Inn of Lincoln Park. A bit out of the way when your business or pleasure is Downtown or on the Magnificent Mile, this Comfort Inn is nonetheless pleasantly situated in a vintage building at the northern edge of the Lincoln Park neighborhood. As at all Comfort Inns, you can expect a complimentary Continental breakfast, color TV, and attractively clean rooms. Nothing fancy here, but neither is the price. *601 W. Diversey Ave., Chicago 60614, tel. 312/348–2810 or 800/221–2222; fax 312/348–1912. 74 rooms. Facilities: free parking. AE, DC, D, MC, V. Inexpensive.*

La Salle Motor Lodge. The rooms of this unusually nice establishment have been recently renovated, and the pleasant furnishings include color TV. Don't expect amenities here; what you will get is more than the minimum accommodation and a good location, five blocks west of the Magnificent Mile, at close to a minimum price. *720 N. La Salle St., Chicago 60610, tel. 312/664–8100. 71 rooms, 4 suites. Facilities: restaurant, free parking. AE, DC, D, MC, V. Inexpensive.*

Bed-and-Breakfasts An alternative to a hotel, particularly for those visiting such areas as Hyde Park or Lincoln Park, which are underserved by first-class hotels, is the bed-and-breakfast. Don't expect to save a great deal of money over the comparable level of accommodation at a hotel. **Bed and Breakfast Chicago** (Box 14088, Chicago 60614, tel. 312/951–0085) is the clearinghouse for more than 50 B & B establishments throughout the greater Chicago area.

The Arts

Chicago is a splendid city for the arts. In addition to dozens of classical music organizations, including a world-class symphony orchestra and opera company, there are hundreds of clubs featuring jazz, rock, folk, and country music; some 50 theaters; an outstanding dance company; and movie theaters that show everything from first-run features to avant-garde films. *The Reader* (available Thursday and Friday in Lincoln Park and Hyde Park) is your best guide to the entertainment scene. The *Chicago Tribune* and the *Chicago Sun-Times* on Friday are good sources of information on current shows and starting times.

Music **Auditorium Theatre** (70 E. Congress Pkwy., tel. 312/922–2110). Subscription concerts, recital series, and touring theater pieces are given throughout the year.

Orchestra Hall (220 S. Michigan Ave., tel. 312/435–8122). A variety of concerts and recitals are programmed during the year.

Mandel Hall (57th St. at University Ave., tel. 312/702–8068). Guest orchestras and performers are scheduled on a regular basis at this hall on the University of Chicago campus.

Chicago Children's Choir (tel. 312/324–8300). One of the country's premier children's choral groups performs during the Christmas season and in early June; other concerts are scheduled periodically.

Chicago Opera Theatre (2936 N. Southport Ave., tel. 312/663–0048). The Chicago Opera specializes in English-language productions of smaller works suited to the intimate setting of the comfortable church auditorium in which it performs.

Chicago Symphony (220 S. Michigan Ave., tel. 312/435–8122). The season at Symphony Hall extends from September through May, although subscribers take almost all the tickets; show up half and hour before a performance and you may find someone with an extra ticket to sell. Daniel Barenboim took over the baton from Sir Georg Solti in the 1991–1992 season. In the summer you can see and hear the Chicago Symphony at Ravinia Park in suburban Highland Park, a trip of about 25 miles from Chicago, accessible by train. For program, ticket, and travel information, tel. 312/728–4642.

Grant Park Symphony Orchestra (tel. 312/294–2420). Sponsored by the Chicago Park District, the Grant Park Symphony gives free concerts during the summer at the James C. Petrillo Bandshell in Grant Park.

Lyric Opera of Chicago (20 N. Wacker Dr., tel. 312/332–2244). The season at the Civic Opera House runs from September through January; the tickets are difficult to come by.

Music of the Baroque (tel. 312/663–1900). This nationally known, highly polished professional chorus and orchestra concentrates on the Baroque period. It schedules eight concerts a year, with performances at various locations.

William Ferris Chorale (tel. 312/922–2070). This distinguished choral ensemble focuses on 20th-century music.

Theater You can save money on seats at **Hot Tix** (24 S. State St.), where unsold tickets are available at half price (plus a small service charge) on the day of performance. You have to pay cash. The Hot Tix booth is open Monday noon–6, Tuesday–Friday 10–6, and Saturday 10–5; tickets for Sunday performances are sold on Saturday.

Body Politic/Victory Gardens (2257–61 N. Lincoln Ave., tel. 312/871–3000). These two venerable institutions have traditionally offered polished productions of both modern American plays and works of Shakespeare and Shaw. The Body Politic, however, recently underwent a change of artistic directors and may shift its focus.

City Lit Theater Company (Live Bait Theater, 3912 N. Clark St., tel. 312/271–1100). This imaginative troupe presents original scripts based on novels and other literary works. The hit of its 1989–1990 season was *The Good Times Are Killing Me*, an adaptation of cartoonist Lynda Barry's novel about growing up amid racial tension.

Court Theater (5535 S. Ellis Ave., tel. 312/753–4472). On the University of Chicago campus, the Court revives classic plays with varying success.

Goodman Theater (200 S. Columbus Dr., tel. 312/443–3800). One of the oldest and best theaters in Chicago, the Goodman is known for its polished performances of contemporary works starring well-known actors. Now situated behind the Art Institute, it may move into two former movie palaces in the north Loop.

Remains Theater (1800 N. Clybourn, tel. 312/335–9800). Remains specializes in original scripts by American writers, featuring gritty acting in the Steppenwolf tradition. Cofounder William Petersen turns up in the movies now and then.

Steppenwolf (1650 N. Halsted, tel. 312/335–1650). The nationally known Steppenwolf company brings a dark, brooding, Method-acting style to its consistently successful productions. Illustrious alumni include John Malkovich, Joan Allen, and Laurie Metcalf.

The Theatre Building (1225 W. Belmont Ave., tel. 312/327–5252). This rehabbed warehouse provides a permanent home for half a dozen small companies of local renown.

Dance **Ballet Chicago** (222 S. Riverside Plaza, tel. 312/993–7575) is the city's only resident classical ballet troupe, successor to the now-defunct Chicago City Ballet. The group is currently planning to conduct a spring season only.

Chicago's most notable success story in dance is the **Hubbard St. Dance Company** (tel. 312/663–0853), whose contemporary, jazzy vitality has made it extremely popular.

Film Many cinemas on the near north side offer first-run Hollywood movies on multiple screens, including **Chestnut Station** (830 N. Clark St., tel. 312/337–7301), **Water Tower Theater** (845 N. Michigan Ave., tel. 312/649–5790), **900 N. Michigan Theater** (tel. 312/787–1988), and **McClurg Court** (330 E. Ohio St., tel. 312/642–0723).

The **Esquire** (58 E. Oak St., tel. 312/280–0101), an Art Deco landmark, recently underwent a renovation that preserved its facade but divided it into four theaters.

A north-side first-run movie house of some historical interest is the **Biograph Theatre** (2433 N. Lincoln Ave., tel. 312/348–4123); gangster John Dillinger was shot in front of the Biograph by FBI agents in 1934.

The Film Center of the Art Institute (Columbus Dr. at Jackson Blvd., tel. 312/443–3737) specializes in unusual current films and revivals of rare classics. The program here changes almost daily, and filmmakers sometimes give lectures.

The Music Box Theatre (3733 N. Southport Ave., tel. 312/871–6604) is a small and lovingly restored 1920s movie palace. Programs at this richly decorated theater change nightly, except for special runs; the theatre shows a mix of classics and outstanding recent films, emphasizing independent filmmakers.

Nightlife

If you want to find "Rush Street," the famous Chicago bar scene, don't bother looking on Rush Street itself. Most of the nightlife is now located on Division Street between Clark and State streets, having been pushed north by office- and apartment development. This area is particularly festive on warm weekend nights, when the street adopts a carnival-like atmosphere. You can find a similar atmosphere in the establishments at the North Pier development (455 E. Illinois St.).

Singles Bars   Among the better-known singles bars are **Mother's** (26 W. Division St.), featured in the motion picture . . . *About Last Night;* **P.S. Chicago** (8 W. Division St.); and **Butch McGuire's** (20 W. Division St.). If you are in the mood for dancing, try **Eddie Rocket's** (9 W. Division St.).

Blues   **B.L.U.E.S.** (2519 N. Halsted St., tel. 312/528–1012). The best of Chicago's own musicians play here and attract a large, friendly crowd.

Blue Chicago (937 N. State St., tel. 312/642–6261). This large room has a good sound system and attracts a cosmopolitan, heterogeneous crowd. The same management runs **Blue Chicago on Clark** (536 N. Clark St., tel. 312/661–0100). Minimum.

Buddy Guy's Legends (754 S. Wabash Ave., tel. 312/427–0333). One of Chicago's own blues legends is part-owner of this converted double storefront in the south Loop. It's spacious, with good sound, good sight lines, and weekday sets that start at 8:30 PM. Cover charge varies.

Kingston Mines (2548 N. Halsted St., tel. 312/477–4646). One of the North Side's oldest spots, the Mines attracts large numbers of blues lovers and cruising singles, the first because of its continuous live weekend entertainment on two stages, the second because of its late closing (4 AM Friday, 5 AM Saturday).

Wise Fools Pub (2270 N. Lincoln Ave., tel. 312/929–1510). The intimate room is an old-time Lincoln Park spot that books name performers. Minimum Saturday.

Jazz   **Andy's** (11 E. Hubbard St., tel. 312/642–6805). Once just a big old friendly neighborhood bar in the shadow of the IBM Building, Andy's has become one of Chicago's best spots for serious jazz.

Gold Star Sardine Bar (680 N. Lake Shore Dr., tel. 312/664–4215). Housed in a splendid renovated building that once was the Chicago Furniture Mart, this tiny spot books top names that attract a trendy clientele. Minimum.

Jazz Showcase (636 S. Michigan Ave., tel. 312/427–4300). Nationally known acts perform in the once elegant but decaying setting of the Blackstone Hotel.

Pops for Champagne (2934 N. Sheffield Ave., tel. 312/472–1000). Despite the incongruous name, this is a good spot for serious jazz fans. Pops sports a popular champagne bar.

Rock   **Lounge Ax** (2438 N. Lincoln Ave., tel. 312/525–6620). A mix of local rock, folk, country, and reggae acts is presented here nightly.

Folk and Ethnic   **Earl's Pub** (2470 N. Lincoln Ave., tel. 312/929–0660). Famed in another incarnation as the Earl of Old Town, Earl still provides outstanding American folk music.

Dance Clubs   **Excalibur** (632 N. Dearborn St., tel. 312/266–1944). This River North brownstone hides a super-disco with multiple dance floors and bars, a game room, and a restaurant. Popular with young adults, it attracts a large suburban crowd on weekends. Open Friday till 2 AM, Saturday till 3 AM. No cover.

Gordon (500 N. Clark St., tel. 312/467–9780). Principally a fine restaurant, Gordon has a very good jazz combo that plays after 9 PM Saturday for dancing.

Neo (2350 N. Clark St., tel. 312/528–2622). Neo is loud but not way out. Open until 4 AM Friday, 5 AM Saturday.

Comedy Clubs   **Improvisations** (504 N. Wells St., tel. 312/782–6387). When you tire of the comedy here, you can munch dim sum in the attached restaurant. Cover charge and minimum.

Second City (1616 N. Wells St., tel. 312/337–3992). An institution for more than 20 years, Second City has spawned some of the hottest comedians around. Yet in recent years the once bitingly funny, loony improvisation has given way to a less imaginative and more raunchy style.

Zanies (1548 N. Wells St., tel. 312/337–4027). Perhaps Chicago's best stand-up comedy spot, Zanies books outstanding national talent. Reservations recommended.

Northeastern Illinois

I–94 provides the fastest route north out of Chicago to Milwaukee, Wisconsin, the next stop on this tour. Pick up the Kennedy Expressway (I–90/94) in downtown Chicago, and stay on I–94 (it becomes the Edens Expressway) when the two interstates diverge in north Chicago. Just past Glencoe, make sure you get on the Edens Spur (a toll road), which angles west to the junction with I–294. At the junction, I–94 goes straight north, becoming the Tri-State Tollway. The drive to Milwaukee should take about two hours.

An alternative route for travelers with more leisure is to get on Lake Shore Drive downtown and follow it north through some of Chicago's most affluent suburbs, along the Lake Mighigan shore. You'll drive past **Oak Street beach**, through **Lincoln Park**, then pass the campuses of **Loyola University** and then **Northwestern University** in Evanston. Past Evanston, in Wil-

Northeastern Illinois

WISCONSIN

10 miles

15 km

N

Channel Lake
Loon Lake
Grass Lake
Pistakee Lake
Zion
Old Mill Creek
Wadsworth
Fox Lake
Lake Villa
Druce Lake
Waukegan
Gurnee
McHenry
Volo
North Chicago
Ivanhoe
Lake Bluff
Libertyville
Wauconda
Lake Forest
Mundelein
Lake Michigan
Lake Zurich
Highwood
Barrington Hills
Buffalo Grove
Deerfield
Highland Park
Carpentersville
Northbrook
Glencoe
Dundee
Winnetka
Schaumburg
Arlington Heights
Kenilworth
Wilmette
Elgin
Mount Prospect
Glenview
Evanston
Des Plaines
Morton Grove
Skokie
Chicago-O'Hare International Airport
Park Ridge
West Chicago
Franklin Park
River Forest
CHICAGO
Wheaton
Villa Park
Lombard
Elmhurst
Oak Park
Glen Ellyn
Berwyn
Cicero
Warrenville
Chicago Midway Airport
Aurora
Downers Grove
Bedford Park
Darien
Burbank
Evergreen Park
Riverdale
Orland Park
Calumet City
Plainfield
Lockport
Marley
Homewood
Lansing
Joliet
Chicago Heights
Park Forest
INDIANA

mette, stay on what is now called Sheridan Road to go through Winnetka and Glencoe.

At the northern end of Glencoe, go west on Lake-Cook Road to the **Chicago Botanic Garden,** which covers 300 acres, has 15 separate gardens, among them a traditional rose garden, a three-island Japanese garden, a waterfall garden, a sensory garden for the visually impaired, an aquatic garden, a learning garden for the disabled, and a 3.8-acre fruit and vegetable garden whose yields are donated to area food kitchens. Ten greenhouses provide flowers all winter long. Special events and shows are scheduled most weekends, many of them sponsored by area plant societies. Major shows are the winter orchid show, an August bonsai show, a daffodil show, a cactus and succulent show, and Japan Fest in May. *Lake-Cook Rd., Glencoe, tel. 708/835–5440. Admission: $3 per car. Open daily 7 AM–sunset in summer, 8 PM–sunset in winter; closed Christmas Day.*

You can either pick up I–94 here (half a mile west of the gardens on Lake-Cook Road) or return to the lakeshore, continuing on Sheridan Road through Highland Park, Lake Forest, and Lake Bluff. Route 176 (Rockland Road) or Route 137 (Buckley Road) go west to I–94 from Lake Bluff.

Milwaukee

It was beer that made Milwaukee famous. Although the city's first brewers were English, by 1850 Milwaukee had a population of 20,061 and a dozen breweries, nearly all operated by Germans. Someone counted 255 saloons, 47 churches, and six temperance societies as well. Athough other industries have dethroned brewing as king in recent years, downtown Milwaukee still smells of malt and hops, and several lavish homes the early brewers built are now public museums. Two of the breweries, Miller and Pabst, are among the nation's largest. The city's beloved American League baseball team is named the Brewers. And not surprisingly, Milwaukee drinks more beer per capita than any other city in the nation.

Milwaukee's first settlers were Potawatomi Indians, who called the site the "Gathering Place by the Waters." The first European of record was a Northwest Fur Company agent named Jacques Vieau, who arrived in 1795 and built a cabin and trading post on the west bank of the Menominee River in what is now Mitchell Park. Most Indians were gone by the mid-1840s, but a few Potawatomi huts could still be found as late as 1854 in what is now downtown Milwaukee. The city's population in 1845 was about 10,000, more than half of German descent. Many Germans arrived in the 1850s, along with Italians, Poles, Scandinavians, Serbs, and Irish. By the last half of the 19th century, Milwaukee's German population was so large that the city was often called the German Athens. Only the Polish and Irish populations came close, and English was rarely heard in some neighborhoods, especially on the northwest side.

Milwaukee is Wisconsin's largest city, and thanks to the St. Lawrence Seaway it's an international seaport and the state's primary commercial and manufacturing center. Publishing has become a major business, and Milwaukee's graphic-arts field is considered outstanding. The city has 10 colleges and universities, including Marquette University and the University of Wisconsin–Milwaukee. Yet Milwaukee is not so much a large city as a large collection of neighborhoods with respect for small-town values. Streets are clean, homes are tidy, parks and green spaces abound. Modern steel and glass high rises occupy much of the downtown area, but the early heritage persists in the restored and well-kept 19th-century buildings that share the city skyline.

Milwaukeeans are proud of their festivals, their museums, their top-notch performing arts companies, their 137 parks, the Brewers, the lakefront, the zoo, and the horticultural domes in Mitchell Park. Milwaukeeans will readily admit their city doesn't dazzle like Houston, or charm you like San Francisco. And they don't mind. At the same time the city lacks the hard edge of a Detroit or a Chicago, and they don't mind that, either.

Getting Around   Lake Michigan is the city's eastern boundary, and Wisconsin Avenue is the main east–west thoroughfare. The Milwaukee River divides the downtown area into east and west sections. The East–West Expressway (I–94/I–794) is the dividing line between north and south. Streets are numbered in ascending order from the Milwaukee River west well into the suburbs to the Milwaukee County line.

By Bus   **Milwaukee County Transit System** (1942 N. 17th St., tel. 414/ 344–6711) operates buses 24 hours a day. The fare is $1; ages 6–11, 50¢. Exact fare required.

By Taxi   Taxis use a meter system. The fare is $2.50 for the first mile and $1.25 for each additional mile. Taxis can be ordered by phone or at taxi stands at most major hotels.

Guided Tours   **Emerald Isle Cruise Line** (tel. 414/786–6886) offers narrated
Boat Tours   waterfront tours May–November, departing from 333 N. Water Street several times daily.

Iroquois Harbor Cruises (tel. 414/332–4194) offers daily afternoon cruises of Milwaukee's harbor late June–Labor Day, departing from docks at the Clybourn Street bridge on the west bank of the Milwaukee River.

Lunch, brunch, dinner, and sightseeing cruises are offered daily mid-April–October by **Edelweiss Cruise Dining** (tel. 414/272– 3625). The boats leave from Riverfront Plaza at 3rd Street and Highland Avenue.

Numbers in the margin correspond to points of interest on the Milwaukee maps.

Downtown Milwaukee

1 On the east side of the river, start at the **Greater Milwaukee Convention & Visitors Bureau** at 510 W. Kilbourn Avenue to pick up maps, brochures, and listings of events.

2 The **Iron Block Building** at the corner of N. Water Street and E. Wisconsin Avenue is one of the few remaining iron-clad buildings in the United States. The metal facade was brought in by ship from an eastern foundry. Put up during the Civil War, the four-story building was recently restored to its original white color.

In the 1860s Milwaukee exported more wheat than any other port in the world, which gave impetus to building the **Grain Exchange Room** in the **Mackie Building** (1879). The carved likeness of Mercury, the Roman god of trade and commerce (and messenger to the gods), is wedged between the granite pillars flanking the entrance. The 10,000-square-foot trading room has three-story-high columns and painted ceiling panels that feature Wisconsin wildflowers. A mural depicts classical figures representing Trade, Industry, and Agriculture. The models for the women in the mural were Milwaukee society ladies. *225 E. Michigan Ave., tel. 414/272-6230. Admission free. Open weekdays 8:30-5.*

The Milwaukee Art Museum is in the lakefront War Memorial Center designed by Eero Saarinen. The museum's permanent collection is strong in European and American art of the 19th and 20th centuries, German Expressionism, and the Bradley collection of modern masters. There are works by Degas, Toulouse-Lautrec, Miró, Picasso, Georgia O'Keeffe, and Andy Warhol, along with designs by Frank Lloyd Wright. Programs include art films, lectures, and Sunday tours. The grounds offer an ideal view of Milwaukee's scenic lakefront. *750 N. Lincoln Memorial Dr., tel. 414/271-9508. Admission: $4 adults, $2 students, senior citizens over 59, and disabled. Children under 12 accompanied by an adult, free. Open Tues., Wed., Fri., and Sat. 10-5, Thurs. noon-9, Sun. noon-5; closed Mon., Jan. 1, Thanksgiving, Dec. 25.*

On your way back to the river, rest a moment at **Cathedral Square.** This quiet park (at E. Kilbourn Ave. and Jefferson St.) was built on the site of Milwaukee's first courthouse. **St. John's Cathedral,** across the street, was the first church built in Wisconsin specifically as a Roman Catholic cathedral. Dedicated in 1853, it is one of the city's oldest church buildings.

As you cross the river to the west side, notice that the east side and west side streets in this old section of town are not directly opposite each other and that the bridges across the Milwaukee River are built at an angle. This layout dates from the 1840s, when the area east of the river was called Juneautown and the region to the west was known as Kilbourntown. The rival communities had a fierce argument over which would pay for the bridges that connected them, and the antagonism was so intense that citizens venturing into rival territory carried white flags. The Great Bridge War was finally settled by the state legislature in 1845, but the streets on either side of the river never were aligned.

Both banks of the Milwaukee River are busy in summer, especially at noon, when downtown workers lunch in the nearby parks and public areas. It's a perfect place for people-watching and getting a sense of everyday Milwaukee. **Pere Marquette Park,** named for the venerable Father Jacques Marquette (who may have camped here in 1674) and situated next to the river at Old World 3rd Street and W. Kilbourn Avenue, is a pleasant place to spend a summertime noon hour.

Adjacent to the park is the **Milwaukee County Historical Center.** Housed in a graceful former bank building (circa 1913), the museum features early fire-fighting equipment, toys, fashions, and old-time doctor's office, an early drug store, and exhibits on military history and banking. Photographs and audiovisual

Milwaukee (Metropolitan Area)

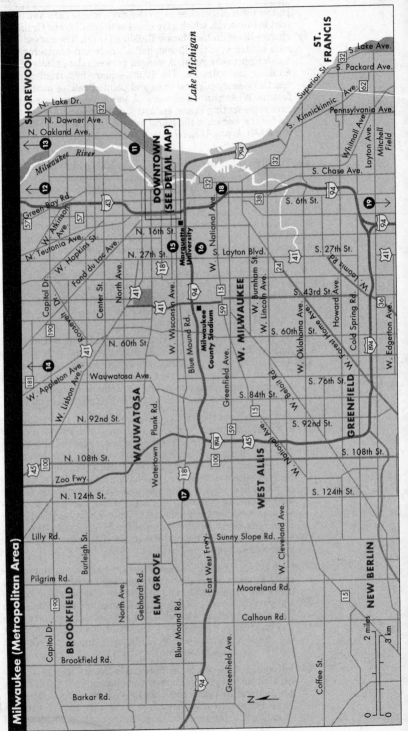

SHOREWOOD

ST. FRANCIS

Lake Michigan

N. Lake Dr.

S. Lake Ave.

S. Packard Ave.

Superior St.

S. Kinnickinnic Ave.

Pennsylvania Ave.

N. Downer Ave.

N. Oakland Ave.

13

Milwaukee River

11

DOWNTOWN (SEE DETAIL MAP)

794

Whitnall Ave.

Layton Ave.

Mitchell Field

12

Green Bay Rd.

43

32

S. Chase Ave.

57

W. Atkinson Ave.

57

N. Teutonia Ave.

W. Hopkins St.

N. 16th St.

N. National Ave.

18

32

38

S. 6th St.

94

19

94

15

Marquette University

16

S. Layton Blvd.

S. 27th St.

Loomis Rd.

41

Fond du Lac Ave.

N. 27th St.

18

41

W. Layton Blvd.

S. 43rd St.

24

41

190

Capitol Dr.

Hopkins Dr.

Center St.

North Ave.

41

94

15

W. Burnham St.

W. Lincoln Ave.

S. 60th St.

W. Oklahoma Ave.

Howard Ave.

Forest Home Ave.

Cold Spring Rd.

36

894

W. Edgerton Ave.

N. 60th St.

Milwaukee County Stadium

Blue Mound Rd.

59

Greenfield Ave.

W. MILWAUKEE

14

W. Appleton Ave.

41

Wauwatosa Ave.

S. 84th St.

W. Beloit Rd.

S. 76th St.

GREENFIELD

181

W. Lisbon Ave.

N. 92nd St.

WAUWATOSA

Plank Rd.

15

S. 92nd St.

45

100

N. 108th St.

59

894

100

S. 108th St.

45

100

Zoo Fwy.

Watertown Plank Rd.

18

WEST ALLIS

N. 124th St.

17

S. 124th St.

Lilly Rd.

Burleigh St.

ELM GROVE

Sunny Slope Rd.

W. National Ave.

W. Cleveland Ave.

Pilgrim Rd.

North Ave.

Gebhardi Rd.

East West Frwy.

Mooreland Rd.

15

NEW BERLIN

190

Capitol Dr.

BROOKFIELD

Brookfield Rd.

Blue Mound Rd.

Greenfield Ave.

Calhoun Rd.

Coffee St.

94

Barkar Rd.

N

2 miles

3 km

0

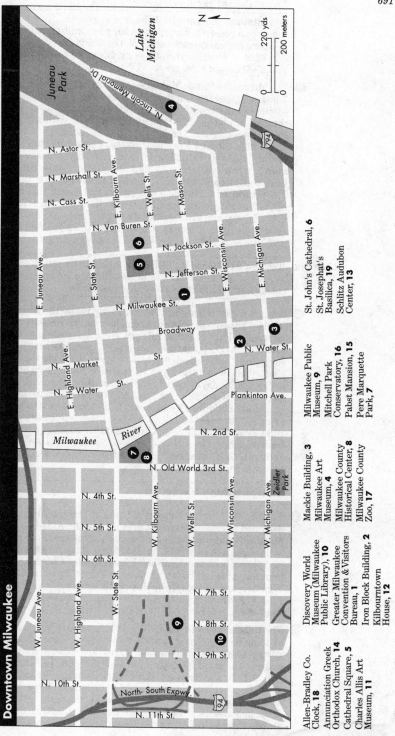

Downtown Milwaukee

Lake Michigan

Juneau Park

N. Lincoln Memorial Dr.

N. Astor St.
N. Marshall St.
N. Cass St.
N. Van Buren St.
E. Kilbourn Ave.
E. Wells St.
E. Mason St.
N. Jackson St.
N. Jefferson St.
E. Wisconsin Ave.
E. Michigan Ave.
N. Milwaukee St.
Broadway
N. Water St.
E. State St.
E. Juneau Ave.
N. Highland Ave.
N. Market St.
N. Water St.
Plankinton Ave.
Milwaukee River
N. 2nd St.
N. Old World 3rd St.
Zeidler Park
N. 4th St.
N. 5th St.
N. 6th St.
W. Kilbourn Ave.
W. Wells St.
W. Wisconsin Ave.
W. Michigan Ave.
W. State St.
W. Highland Ave.
W. Juneau Ave.
N. 7th St.
N. 8th St.
N. 9th St.
N. 10th St.
N. 11th St.
North-South Expwy.

220 yds
200 meters

Allen-Bradley Co. Clock, **18**
Annunciation Greek Orthodox Church, **14**
Cathedral Square, **5**
Charles Allis Art Museum, **11**

Discovery World Museum (Milwaukee Public Library), **10**
Greater Milwaukee Convention & Visitors Bureau, **1**
Iron Block Building, **2**
Kilbourntown House, **12**

Mackie Building, **3**
Milwaukee Art Museum, **4**
Milwaukee County Historical Center, **8**
Milwaukee County Zoo, **17**

Milwaukee Public Museum, **9**
Mitchell Park Conservatory, **16**
Pabst Mansion, **15**
Pere Marquette Park, **7**

St. John's Cathedral, **6**
St. Josephat's Basilica, **19**
Schlitz Audubon Center, **13**

presentations document Milwaukee's growth. The center zqhouses a research library containing naturalization records and genealogical resources. *910 N. Old World 3rd St., tel. 414/ 273–8288. Admission free. Open weekdays 9:30–5, Sat. 10–5, Sun. 1–5. Closed holidays.*

9 The **Milwaukee Public Museum,** at the corner of W. Wells and 7th streets, has the fourth largest collection of natural history exhibits in the country. The Streets of Old Milwaukee walk-through exhibit depicts the city in the 1890s, with a general store, corner saloon, and Milwaukee's earliest shops. There is also a walk-through European village, a two-story rain forest exhibit, and the Third Planet (complete with full-size dinosaurs), where visitors walk into the interior of the earth to learn about its history and the forces that continue to change it. The Wizard Wing has hands-on natural and human history exhibits for children and families. *800 W. Wells St., tel. 414/278–2702. Admission: $4.50 adults, $2.50 children 4–17, $10 family, disabled free. Open daily 9–5, Thanksgiving, Christmas, and New Year's Day 11–4. (Wizard Wing open daily 10–3.)*

Time Out **Wales on Wells** (1508 W. Wells St.), a Marquette campus favorite, is one of the best places in town for hamburgers, served chargrilled with sautéed onions, for just $1.39.

10 Anyone with a science bent will be intrigued by the **Discovery World—Museum of Science, Economics and Technology** in the Milwaukee Public Central Library. Here is a wide range of exhibits on magnets, motors, electricity, personal health, and computers that are designed to be touched; it also has the Great Electric Show and the Light Wave–Laser Beam Show on Saturday and Sunday. The gift shop is crammed with science goodies. *818 W. Wisconsin Ave., tel. 414/765–9966. Admission: $3 adults, $1 children 17 and under, children 5 and under free when accompanied by an adult. Great Electric Show and Light Wave-Laser Show, $2.50 adults, $1.25 students, children under 6 not admitted. Open Mon.–Sat. 9–5, Sun. 11–5, closed major holidays. Great Electric Show Sat. at 11 AM. Light Wave-Laser Show open weekends at 2:15.*

Metropolitan Milwaukee

11 The **Charles Allis Art Museum** occupies an elegant Tudor home designed in 1909 for the first president of the Allis-Chalmers Manufacturing Co. As you enter, look up at the three-tiered stained glass window by Louis Comfort Tiffany. The art exhibited throughout the furnished house includes Chinese porcelains dating from 300 BC, graphics by Dürer, Rembrandt, and Whistler, and landscapes by Homer, Gainsborough, and Corot. *1801 N. Prospect Ave., tel. 414/278–8295. Admission: $2. Open Wed.–Sun. 1–5, Wed. 7–9 PM; closed holidays.*

12 The **Kilbourntown House,** built in 1844, is an excellent example of temple-style Greek Revival architecture. Once slated for destruction, the building was saved and moved from Kilbourntown, one of the city's original settlements, to its present site in 1938. During restoration, three fireplaces were uncovered. Doric columns and exterior walls of hand-hewn beams and brick give the structure a feeling of strength, while the furnishings reflect the decor of its time. Displays include an outstanding collection of mid-19th-century furniture and decorative arts. Ice cream socials and other public events are often held on weekends. *4400 W. Estabrook Dr., tel. 414/273–8288. Admission free. Open late June–Labor Day, Tues., Thurs., and Sat. 10–5, Sun. 1–5.*

13 The **Schlitz Audubon Center** is a 225-acre wildlife area of forests, ponds, marshlands, and nature trails that was once the domain of the horses of the Joseph Schlitz Brewing Co. Popular with cross-country skiers in winter and bird-watchers year-round, this restful spot on the Lake Michigan shoreline is only minutes from downtown. The environmental-research and education center offers natural history exhibits and unadvertised drop-in nature programs on weekends during the summer. *1111 E. Brown Deer Rd., tel. 414/352–2880. Admission: $1.50 adults, 75¢ children under 12 and senior citizens over 65. Open Tues.–Sun. 9–5; closed Mon. and holidays.*

14 The **Annunciation Greek Orthodox Church** was Frank Lloyd Wright's last major work; the famed Wisconsin architect called it his "little jewel." As such, the blue-domed, saucer-shaped church has drawn visitors from all over the world since it opened in 1961. *9400 W. Congress St., tel. 414/461–9400. Tours by appointment, $1.*

15 The **Pabst Mansion,** built for the beer baron Captain Frederick Pabst, is one of Milwaukee's treasured landmarks and a prime example of how Milwaukee's early wealthy lived. Pabst, who came from Germany at age 12, was a Great Lakes sailor until he married into the Best brewing family. He became one of Milwaukee's leading and wealthiest citizens. His castle-like, Flemish Renaissance–style Pabst Mansion, built in 1893 for $225,000, has a tan pressed-brick exterior, decorated with carved stone and terra-cotta ornamentation. The house features carved cabinets and woodwork by the Matthews Brothers, ornamental iron work by Cyril Colnik, marble, tile, and stained glass, along with carved panels imported from a 17th-century Bavarian castle. Captain Pabst's study and a pavilion originally used at the Columbian Exposition in Chicago are a tribute to the buying power of the 1893 dollar. Friendly docents provide informative tours that take about 90 minutes. Holiday activities in December draw the largest crowds of the year. *2000 W. Wisconsin Ave., tel. 414/931–0808. Admission: $5 adults, $2.50 children 6–17, under 6 free. Open Mar. 15–Dec. 31, Mon.–Sat. 10–3:30, Sun. noon–3:30; Jan. 1–Mar. 14, Sat. 10–3:30, Sun. noon–3:30; closed major holidays and during October except for a special Halloween event.*

16 Ask for directions to the **Mitchell Park Conservatory** and you may get stares from lifelong Milwaukeeans. But ask about the "domes," and you'll get instant recognition. A unique horticultural structure, the Mitchell Park Conservatory consists of three massive glass domes housing tropical, arid, and seasonal plant and flower exhibits. The complex was built between 1959 and 1967. Each dome is 140 feet wide and 85 feet high, covering an area of 15,000 square feet. The displays of lilies at Easter and poinsettias at Christmas are spectacular. A map of the plantings and exhibits included with admission enables visitors to take a self-guided tour of the domes. *524 S. Layton Blvd., tel. 414/649–9800. Admission: $2.50 adults, $1 children 6–17. Open daily 9–5.*

⑰ The **Milwaukee County Zoo,** one of the finest in the world, houses about 4,000 wild animals and birds, including many endangered species. Within the zoo is a Children's Zoo (open Memorial Day to Labor Day) where youngsters can pet and feed baby and farm animals. Twenty-minute educational programs are presented several times daily, weather permitting. A schedule is provided with admission. You can take a narrated tour of the zoo aboard the Zoomobile, or enjoy a miniature train ride. Pony, camel, and elephant rides are offered. There are picnic areas and food services, and a three-mile cross-country ski trail. Rides are not included in the admission price. Allow four to six hours to see the entire zoo. *10001 W. Bluemound Rd., tel. 414/771–3040. Admission: $6 adults, $4 children 3– 12, $5 senior citizens. Parking: $4. Stroller and wheelchair rentals available. Open Memorial Day–Labor Day, Mon.–Sat. 9–5, Sun. and holidays 9–6; Sept.–May, daily 9–4:30.*

⑱ The **Allen-Bradley Co. clock** (1201 S. 2nd St.) is a Milwaukee landmark and, according to the *Guinness Book of World Records,* "the largest four-faced clock in the world." Each of its octagon-shape faces is nearly twice the area of London's Big Ben. It is actually four clocks, one in each side of the tower atop the Allen-Bradley Co. headquarters and research laboratory. The clock is some 300 feet above street level, and on a clear night the lighted faces can be seen nearly halfway across Lake Michigan. Ships sometimes use the clock as a navigational reference point.

⑲ **St. Josephat's Basilica** (2336 S. 6th St., tel. 414/645–5623), built at the turn of the century, is adorned with a remarkable collection of relics, portraits of Polish saints and leaders, stained glass, and wood carvings. Its dome, modeled after St. Peter's in Rome, is reputed to be one of the five largest in the world. Elevated to basilica status in 1929, it is the first Polish basilica in North America.

Brewery Tours

The **Miller Brewing Co.** (4251 W. State St., tel. 414/931–2337) gives free 1-hour tours on the hour Mon.–Sat. 10–3:30. **Pabst Brewery** (915 W. Juneau Ave., tel. 414/223–3709) has free 40-minute tours on the hour June–Aug., weekdays 10–3, Sat. 9–11 AM; Sept.–May, weekdays 10–3. **Sprecher Brewing Co.** (730 W. Ogden St., tel. 414/272–2337) permits self-guided tours Sat. 1–3.

Shopping

Using the downtown skywalk system, it's possible to browse in hundreds of stores over several blocks without once setting foot outside. Downtown Milwaukee's major shopping street is Wisconsin Avenue west of the Milwaukee River. The **Grand Avenue Mall** stretches east from Marshall Field's at the river to the Boston Store on Wisconsin Avenue. This four-block-long, multilevel shopping area, linked entirely by skywalks, features about 150 specialty shops and restaurants. Among the buildings in the center is the restored **Plankington Arcade,** a spacious skylighted promenade in the Old World tradition.

The redbrick-paved streets of **Old World 3rd Street,** running north from Wisconsin Avenue to Highland Avenue, are a throwback to the streets of Old Milwaukee. The heart of Milwaukee's old German business district, this neighborhood includes many ethnic stores and restaurants, and such Milwaukee landmarks as **Usinger's Famous Sausage** and the **Wisconsin Cheese Mart.** Many stores here are closed on Sundays.

East of the river, you'll find restored 19th-century shops and ethnic stores clustered near the Pfister Hotel and along **Jefferson Street** between East Mason and East Wells streets. **Donner Avenue** between East Webster and East Park streets is another popular east-side shopping location.

Shopping centers in the metropolitan area include **Bayshore** (5900 N. Port Washington Rd.), **Brookfield Square** (95 N. Moorland Rd.), **Capital Court** (5500 W. Capitol Dr.), **Mayfair** (2500 N. Mayfair Rd.), **Northridge** (7700 W. Brown Deer Rd.), **Point Loomis** (3555 S. 27th St.), **Southgate** (3333 S. 27th St.) and **South Ridge** (5300 S. 76th St.).

Food Gifts **Ambrosia Chocolate Co.** (6th St. and Highland Ave., tel. 414/271-5774), established by Otto Schoenleber in 1894, is called the world's biggest manufacturer of bulk chocolate. The largest selection of chocolate and candies in Wisconsin can be found at the company's outlet store here.

Royale Gourmet Products (1522 S. 84 St., West Allis, tel. 414/771-8448) is a "turn-of-the-century" candy shop. Watch them make fudge, chocolate-covered potato chips, and candies.

Usinger's Famous Sausage (1030 N. 3rd St., tel. 414/276-9100) sells more than 75 kinds of cold cuts and fine sausages. Gift boxes available.

West Allis Cheese and Sausage Shop (6832 W. Becher St., West Allis, tel. 414/543-4230) is a country-style store offering 40 Wisconsin cheeses and gift packages.

Wisconsin Cheese Mart, Inc. (215 W. Highland Ave. at Old World 3rd St., tel. 414/272-3544) offers Wisconsin cheese, honey, jellies, mustard, and other delicacies.

Clocks **Alpine Boutique & Christmas Chalet** (8400 W. Capitol Dr., tel. 414/461-3322) has a wide variety of Alpine items: beer steins, nutcrackers, cuckoo clocks, Christmas ornaments.

Outdoor Equipment **Laacke & Joys** (1433 N. Water St., tel. 414/271-7878) supplies outdoor clothing and equipment for skiing, camping, fishing, and specialized sports. The company manufactures Wildwood tents and canvas products.

Sports and Fitness

Beaches and Water Sports Lake Michigan is the place to swim, but be prepared: The midsummer water temperature is only in the 50s and 60s and the wind adds to the chill. Among the most popular beaches are **Bradford Beach** (2400 N. Lincoln Memorial Dr., tel. 414/961-9799), **Doctors Beach** (1870 E. Fox La. in Fox Point, tel. 414/352-9949), and **Grant Beach** (100 Hawthorne Ave., South Milwaukee, tel. 414/762-9907).

Bicycling A 76-mile bike trail encircles the city, and several bike tour maps have been produced by the Milwaukee County Department of Parks (tel. 414/257-6100).

Fishing Lake Michigan offers trout and salmon as big as 30 pounds. A Wisconsin fishing license and Great Lakes stamp are required. While some fishing is done from piers and breakwaters, anglers on boats equipped with the latest in fishing and electronic gear seem to land the big ones. **Associated Fishing Charters of Milwaukee** (tel. 414/258–1119) can help you hire licensed professional captains.

Jogging Most joggers use the city parks. The area along the lakefront off North Lincoln Memorial Drive just north of the Art Museum is a favorite of downtown joggers.

Spectator Sports

Baseball The **Milwaukee Brewers** play at County Stadium (201 S. 46th St., tel. 414/933–1818 for ticket information, 414/933–9000 for credit-card purchases).

Basketball The **Milwaukee Bucks** play their NBA home games at the Bradley Center (4th and State Sts., tel. 414/227–0500).

Football The **Green Bay Packers** play three home games each year at Milwaukee County Stadium (tel. 414/342–2717).

Dining

Milwaukee's culinary style was shaped to a great extent by the Germans who first settled here. Many restaurants—whether or not they are German—offer Wiener schnitzel or the meringue-based desserts called "schaumtortes." County Stadium, home of the Milwaukee Brewers, is not famous for hot dogs, but for bratwurst. And rye bread, sometimes crusted with coarse salt, is as common on Milwaukee tables as robins are on a spring lawn. The Poles were next to provide stock for Milwaukee's ethnic flavor. The city's South Side is dotted with shops that turn out fresh Polish sausage and restaurants that pride themselves on *pierogi*. Many other ethnic groups, including Italians, Serbs, Mexicans, Armenians, Chinese, Greeks, Russians, Norwegians, Swiss, and most recently, Southeast Asians, have also donated their specialties to Milwaukee's tradition of *gemütlichkeit*, or fellowship and good cheer, in German.

A word of caution to visitors ordering drinks: In Milwaukee, scotch and soda means scotch mixed with 7-Up. Ask for seltzer or club soda to avoid confusion with what the locals call sweet or white soda.

The following dining price categories have been used: *Very Expensive*, over $30; *Expensive*, $20–$30; *Moderate*, $10–$20; *Inexpensive*, under $10.

American **Jake's.** There are two locations for this long-time Milwaukee favorite. The restaurant earned its reputation with perfectly prepared steaks and heaps of French-fried onion rings. Other offerings, including both fish and duck, are also popular, and there is a first-rate California wine list, with many wines by the glass. *6030 W. North Ave., Wauwatosa, tel. 414/771–0550, and 21445 W. Capitol Dr., Brookfield, tel. 414/781–7995. No reservations. AE, MC, V. Moderate.*
Nance's. Featuring contemporary dining in the Historic Third Ward, this restaurant's eclectic menu features fresh fish, poultry, and meats. Milwaukeeans love the clam cakes and choco-

late pecan pie. The wine list is extensive. *316 N. Milwaukee St., tel. 414/271-3932. Dress: casual. AE, DC, V. Closed Sun. Moderate.*

Elsa's on the Park. Located across from Cathedral Square Park, this is a chic but casual place where talkative young professionals go to eat big, juicy hamburgers and pork chop sandwiches. The decor is crisply stylish with a gray, white, and black color scheme. *833 N. Jefferson St., tel. 414/765-0615. No credit cards. No lunch weekends. Inexpensive.*

Watts Tea Shop. A genteel spot for breakfast or lunch located above George Watts & Sons, Milwaukee's premier store for china, crystal, and silverware. It features simple breakfast, sandwiches, a juice bar, and special custard-filled sunshine cake. Ask for a table by the window. *761 N. Jefferson St., tel. 414/276-6352. Dress: casual. No shorts. AE, MC, V. Closed Sun. Inexpensive.*

Continental **The English Room.** Milwaukee's premier hotel restaurant, in
★ the Pfister Hotel, has a dark, Victorian elegance. Executive chef Edouard Becker has put together a specialty menu that includes roast rack of lamb Provençal, escalope of veal, and seafood dishes. The service is formal, with plenty of tableside cooking. The wine list is very good. *424 E. Wisconsin Ave., tel. 414/273-8222. Jacket required. Reservations advised. AE, DC, MC, V. No lunch Sat. and Sun. Very Expensive.*

★ **Grenadier's.** Knut Apitz, chef-owner of this fine restaurant, serves some of the most elegant food in Milwaukee. The menu includes imaginative dishes that combine classical European style with Oriental or Indian flavors. Changing "chef's choices" (such as tenderloin of veal with raspberry sauce and angelhair pasta) and nouvelle cuisine selections (such as turban of fresh sea scallops and Norwegian salmon on pesto sauce) transport diners into enviable indecision. There are three small rooms with an air of matter-of-fact refinement, and a handsome, darkly furnished piano bar with tables. *747 N. Broadway St., tel. 414/276-0747. Jackets required. Reservations advised. AE, DC, MC, V. No lunch Sat. Closed Sun. Very Expensive.*

John Byron's. A wonderful view of the lakefront can be enjoyed while dining on well-prepared American-European dishes. Located in the First Wisconsin Building, the dining room has a sophisticated, elegant feeling. The reasonably priced wine list is excellent, with an emphasis on California wine. *777 E. Michigan St., tel. 414/291-5220. Reservations recommended. AE, DC, MC, V. No lunch Sat. Closed Sun. Very Expensive.*

Sanford. Award-winning chef Sanford D'Amato and his wife Angie are at the helm of one of Milwaukee's best and busiest restaurants. The innovative French-New American menu changes daily. The 50-seat dining room is decorated in understated grey and black. For cozier seating ask for one of the booths. *1547 N. Jackson St., tel. 414/276-9608. Jackets required. Reservations essential. AE, MC, V. No lunch. Closed Sun. Very Expensive.*

★ **Mike and Anna's.** This small, trendy restaurant is located in a working-class neighborhood on Milwaukee's South Side. The changing board menu features excellent nouvelle-inspired selections like fresh king salmon with basil, tarragon, beurre-blanc sauce or roast duck breast with carmelized onions and lingonberry sauce. Be sure to ask for directions when making the reservation. *1978 S. 8th St., tel. 414/643–0072. Dress: casual. Reservations recommended. MC, V. No lunch. Expensive.*

Steven Wade's Cafe. Noted for creative, freshly prepared food, chef and co-owner Steven Wade Klindt operates his successful establishment in a former paint-and-wallpaper store in the southwestern suburb of New Berlin. The changing board-menu might include Norwegian salmon fillet poached with vanilla sauce or coconut curried lamb. *17001 W. Greenfield Ave., New Berlin, tel. 414/784–0774. Reservations required. AE, DC, MC, V. No lunch Sat. Closed Sun. Expensive.*

★ **Chip and Py's.** Recently moved to the northern suburb of Mequon, this upscale restaurant features light gray dual-level dining rooms, a huge fireplace, and contemporary art. The eclectic gourmet cuisine features chicken, beef, seafood, blackened redfish, and a number of dishes with a Thai influence reflecting Chef James Sugid's heritage. Best bets are escargot, Shrimp Siracha, and Cappucino Ice Cream Pie. Live jazz is offered Friday and Saturday. *1340 W. Town Square Rd., Mequon, tel. 414/241-9589. AE, DC, MC. V. No lunch Sun., no dinner Mon. Moderate.*

Delicatessen **Benjamin's Delicatessen and Restaurant.** You'll find a wide selection of tasty specialties such as matzo ball soup, corned beef sandwiches, and brisket of beef at this classic neighborhood deli. There are booths, tables, and a counter where the TV is usually tuned to the latest sporting event. *4156 N. Oakland Ave., Shorewood, tel. 414/332–7777. MC, V. Open 7 PM–8 PM daily. Inexpensive.*

German **Karl Ratzsch's Old World Restaurant.** People daunted by excess amounts of German food still visit Ratzsch's to enjoy the authentic German atmosphere at this family-owned restaurant. Specialties such as schnitzel à la Ratzsch, roast duckling, and sauerbraten are served by dirndl-skirted waitresses, while a string trio schmaltzes it up. The tables in the main dining room are crowded but near the music, and provide the best vantage point for viewing the murals, antler chandeliers, and antique beer steins. Upstairs is quieter and somewhat less crowded. A pleasant alternative to an almost unavoidably heavy meal is to sit at the bar for a German beer or a glass of wine from one of the city's finest wine cellars. *320 E. Mason St., tel. 414/276–2720. Reservations recommended. Sun. brunch. AE, DC, MC, V. No lunch Mon. Expensive.*

Polish **Crocus Restaurant and Cocktail Lounge.** Tucked away on
★ Milwaukee's South Side, this is a friendly neighborhood restaurant that serves homemade Polish food. The decor is accented with ethnic paintings and artifacts. Braised beef rollups, stuffed potato dumplings, pierogi, or the special Polish Plate are all good choices. Try one of the Polish beers. *1801 S. Muskego Ave., tel. 414/643–6383. No credit cards. No lunch weekends. Inexpensive.*

Serbian **Old Town Serbian Gourmet House.** It's fun to eat dinner here; strolling musicians and a hustle-bustle atmosphere provide the background for good ethnic cooking. Try *burek*, stuffed pastries the size of Frisbees, or Serbian shish kebab. The service can be somewhat harried on busy nights. *522 W. Lincoln Ave., tel. 414/672–0206. Reservations recommended. AE, MC, V. No lunch weekends. Closed Mon. Moderate.*

Three Brothers Bar & Restaurant. In an 1887 tavern, this is one of Milwaukee's revered ethnic restaurants. Chicken paprikash, roast lamb, Serbian salad, and homemade desserts are served at old metal kitchen tables. It's about 10 minutes from downtown on Milwaukee's near South Side. *2424 S. St. Clair St., tel. 414/481–7530. Reservations recommended. No credit cards. No lunch. Closed Mon. Moderate.*

Lodging

Bed & Breakfast of Milwaukee, Inc. keeps a list of more than 30 homes in the eastern half of Wisconsin, from downtown penthouses to charming country homes. Advance reservations are recommended, but it is sometimes possible to make them on shorter notice. When calling indicate your preferences regarding smoking, children, pets, allergies, etc. Bed & Breakfast of Milwaukee is a member of Bed & Breakfast World-Wide, a B&B network. *1916 W. Donges Bay Rd., Mequon, 53092, tel. 414/242–9680. AE, MC, V. All price ranges.*

The following lodging price categories have been used: *Very Expensive*, over $90; *Expensive*, $70–$90; *Moderate*, $40–$70; *Inexpensive*, under $40.

Downtown
Very Expensive

Marc Plaza. Crystal chandeliers, marble-based columns, and dark woodwork in the lobby give this gracious hotel built in 1929 a handsome appearance. The traditionally decorated rooms vary quite a bit in size. *509 W. Wisconsin Ave., 53203, tel. 414/271–7250 or 800/558–7708. Facilities: restaurants, indoor pool, sauna, shopping arcade. AE, DC, MC, V.*

★ **Pfister Hotel.** Many of the rooms in Milwaukee's grand old hotel, built in 1893, have been combined to make suites, with enlarged bathrooms. A collection of 19th-century art hangs in the elegant Victorian lobby. The rooms in the Tower, built in 1975, are decorated traditionally, in keeping with furnishings throughout the hotel. *424 E. Wisconsin Ave., 53202, tel. 414/273–8222. Facilities: indoor pool. AE, DC, MC, V.*

Wyndham Hotel. A 221-room hotel perched atop the Milwaukee Center. The opulent lobby is tiled with Italian marble; the rooms are traditionally styled with mahogany furniture. *139 E. Kilbourn Ave., 53202, tel. 414/276–8686. Facilities: health club, jogging track. AE, DC, MC, V.*

Moderate–Expensive

Astor Hotel. Only half of this 200-room hotel built in 1920 is available for transient guests. Located just a few blocks from Lake Michigan, it has the not unpleasant air of a hotel past its heyday. The large lobby has comfortable seating, a handsome grandfather's clock, and a display of photographs of illustrious people who have stayed here. Many of the rooms and studio apartments have been remodeled, but they still contain old bathroom fixtures. *924 E. Juneau Ave., 53202, tel. 414/271–4220. AE, DC, MC, V.*

Moderate

Howard Johnson Downtown. This 10-story downtown hotel provides basic accommodations; the west-side rooms are quietest. *611 W. Wisconsin Ave., 53203, tel. 414/273–2950. Facilities: outdoor pool, free valet parking, health club privileges, restaurant. AE, DC, MC, V.*

Ramada Inn Downtown. Rough knotty-pine paneling gives the lobby of this 152-room hotel a casual feeling. Rooms are clean and standard-looking. *633 W. Michigan St., 53203, tel. 414/272–8410. Facilities: outdoor pool, restaurant, valet service. AE, DC, MC, V.*

Away from Downtown
Expensive–Very Expensive

Embassy Suites Hotel. The atrium lobby and glass elevators give this 203-suite hotel in the western suburbs a big-city feeling. *1200 S. Moorland Rd., Brookfield 53005, tel. 414/782-2900. Facilities: indoor pool, sauna, steam room, whirlpool, exercise room, restaurant, game room. AE, DC, MC, V.*

Moderate–Expensive

The Grand Milwaukee Hotel. Across from Mitchell Field, this 510-room hotel is the largest in the state. *4747 S. Howell Ave., 53207, tel. 414/481-8000 or 800/558-3862. Facilities: indoor and outdoor pool, fitness center, indoor track, airport transportation. AE, DC, MC, V.*

Sheraton Mayfair. This 150-room high rise is convenient to the County Medical Complex, the Milwaukee County Zoo, and the Mayfair Shopping Mall. The rooms have a bright contemporary look, and the top floors offer fine views. *2303 N. Mayfair Rd., Wauwatosa 53226, tel. 414/257-3400. Facilities: indoor pool, sauna, restaurant. AE, DC, MC, V.*

Moderate

Best Western Midway Motor Lodge. The rooms are standard-looking and clean in this 125-room facility. The rooms on the west side have a view of the golf course. *1005 S. Moorland Rd., Brookfield 53005, tel. 414/786-9540. Facilities: pool, game room, restaurant, bar. AE, DC, MC, V.*

Dillon Inn. The lobby of this three-story brick motel, with a fireplace and hanging plants, is more homey than most. *11111 W. North Ave., Wauwatosa 53226, tel. 414/778-0333. Facilities: complimentary breakfast. AE, DC, MC, V.*

Leilani Motel. In an area west of Milwaukee that has gone from farmland to fast food in the last 15 years, this family-owned motel retains the flavor of the late 1950s. The 60 rooms are clean but outdated in appearance. The indoor pool is crystal clear and kept at 86 degrees all year long. *18615 W. Bluemound Rd., Brookfield 53005, tel. 414/786-7100. Facilities: playground, tennis courts, free Continental breakfast. AE, MC, V.*

The Arts

Milwaukee's theaters are in a two-block area bounded by the Milwaukee River, E. Wells Street, N. Water Street, and E. State Street. With the recent renovation of several fine old theaters and the completion of the Milwaukee Center, which houses three theaters, this area is becoming the cultural center of the city.

The calendar section of the monthly *Milwaukee Magazine* has the most complete listing of events. The Greater Milwaukee Calendar of Events, put out twice a month by the Greater Milwaukee Convention & Visitors Bureau, contains helpful information. Also check the Arts section of the Sunday Milwaukee *Journal*.

Milwaukee Tix Box Office (510 W. Kilbourn Ave., tel. 414/271-3335) carries tickets to most local arts groups' shows, seasonal events, and attractions, as well as all Ticketron events. *Open Tues.–Fri. 10–6, Sat. 11–3. MC, V accepted for non-Ticketron events.*

The new **Milwaukee Center** (108 E. Wells St., tel. 414/224-9490) has a 720-seat main auditorium, the 216-seat Stiemke Theater, and the 120-seat Stackner Cabaret. The **Milwaukee Repertory Theater**, one of the top resident theaters in the nation, performs here September–May. **The Milwaukee Chamber Theater** performs contemporary and classical works, with an emphasis on George Bernard Shaw, in the Stiemke Theater.

The **Performing Arts Center** (929 N. Water St.) is the home of the famous **Milwaukee Symphony Orchestra** (tel. 414/273–7206), performing September–June, and the **Milwaukee Ballet Company** (tel. 414/643–7677), which offers both classical and contemporary dance.

Pabst Theater (144 E. Wells St., tel. 414/278–3663), built by beer baron Frederick Pabst, is both a historic landmark and a center for theatrical productions, concerts, and dance by touring artists, Broadway productions, and local professional and amateur groups.

Riverside Theater (116 W. Wisconsin Ave., tel. 414/271–2000), Wisconsin's largest landmark theater, recently renovated, seats 2,500; it's a showplace for touring Broadway productions, symphony, pop, and country artists.

Theater **Next Act Theatre** (tel. 414/278–7780) is a critically acclaimed off-Broadway theatre company presenting current and classic offerings from Americam and European cultural centers. Performances are in Centennial Hall (733 N. 8th St.).

Theatre Tesseract (Lincoln Center for the Arts, 820 E. Knapp St., tel. 414/273–7529) strikes a unique balance between entertaining and thought-provoking drama, showcasing the works of respected American and European playwrights.

Theater X (158 N. Broadway Ave., tel. 414/278–0555). The *X* is for experimental, and this 20-year-old contemporary theater ensemble is devoted to the creation of new works. Their season runs from September to June.

Concerts **Bel Canto Chorus** (tel. 414/226–8800) is a distinguished oratorio chorus performing at locations throughout the city.

"Music Under the Stars" Programs (Washington Park Temple of Music, 1859 N. 40th St., tel. 414/278–4389) are free summer evenings of music featuring top-name soloists, Broadway musicals, and other entertainment.

Opera **Florentine Opera Co.** (tel. 414/273–1474), an outstanding regional company for over a half century, performs at various locations.

Skylight Comic Opera (Skylight Music Theater, 813 N. Jefferson St., tel. 414/271–8815) presents vivid productions ranging from Mozart to Gilbert and Sullivan.

Film **Oriental Landmark Theater** (2230 N. Farwell Ave., tel. 414/276–8711) screens foreign and hard-to-find films. This 1927 theater, with its East Indian–style decor, onion-shape domes, and terra-cotta lions, is worth seeing in itself.

Nightlife

Milwaukee isn't likely to be your first choice when you think of an exciting place to spend an evening. Yet the city offers a variety of nightlife in one of the country's safest downtown areas.

Bars and **Polaris** (333 W. Kilbourn Ave., tel. 414/276–1234) is Mil-
Nightclubs waukee's only revolving rooftop restaurant and lounge, atop the Hyatt Regency Hotel. Spectacular views of downtown and Lake Michigan.

Major Goolsby's (340 W. Kilbourn Ave., tel. 414/271–3414) is a great sports bar, with cocktails, soft drinks, burgers, and fries on the menu.

Safe House (779 N. Front St., tel. 414/271–2007) is one of the city's most unusual clubs. A James Bond decor makes this "spy hideout" a favorite. Enter through the "International Exports" office.

Von Trier (2235 N. Farwell Ave., tel. 414/272–1775) is a quiet watering hole with Black Forest decor, steins, and murals, and a large selection of imported beers.

Jazz Clubs In a cabaret setting, **The Cafe Melange** (720 N. 3rd St., tel. 414/291–9889), located in the run-down Hotel Wisconsin, stages excellent jazz entertainment six nights a week (on Monday only the bar is open). Music might include blues, swing, salsa, big band, or contemporary creations. There is a tiny dance floor. Reservations suggested.

The Estate (2423 N. Murray Ave. tel. 414/964–9923) is a cozy little jazz club where people go to hear progressive jazz four nights a week.

Up and Under Pub (1216 E. Brady St., tel. 414/276–2677) plays the blues Friday, Saturday, and Sunday nights.

Comedy **Comedy Sportz** (tel. 414/962–8888), performing both in Milwaukee (Kalt's Bar and Restaurant, 2856 N. Oakland Ave.) and Brookfield (Midway Motor Lodge, 1005 S. Moorland Rd.), features improvisational comedy teams competing against each other with a referee.

Door County and the Wisconsin Lakeshore

You're never far from water in the East Wisconsin Waters region. Wisconsin has more than 200 miles of Lake Michigan coastline, as well as scores of inland lakes and streams. In some places people still fish Lake Michigan for a living, and the water sets the tone for the lifestyle. Much of Wisconsin's industrial belt also lies along Lake Michigan, stretching from the Illinois border north to Green Bay. Leaving Milwaukee, we head north along the Lake Michigan shore.

Numbers in the margin correspond to points of interest on the Eastern Wisconsin map.

From Milwaukee, drive on I–43 north 15 miles and take county
❶ highway C west 3 miles into **Cedarburg.** The drive from Milwaukee takes about 25 minutes. When the first settlers saw what is now Cedarburg, Indians were still passing through on a trail between Milwaukee and Green Bay. By the 1830s most of the Indians were gone. Relics and mounds, some of them 1,500 years old, are still being found.

The source of Cedarburg's vigor from its birth was the creek that German and Irish immigrants found here. They built five dams and mills, and the life of the town flowed along the banks of Cedar Creek. The pioneer settlers carved their history in limestone. Two local quarries provided the Niagara limestone

Eastern Wisconsin

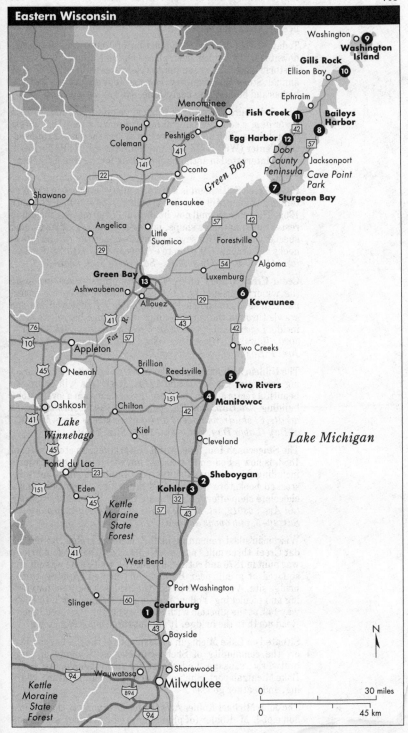

Washington
Washington Island **9**
Gills Rock
Ellison Bay **10**
Ephraim
Fish Creek 11
Menominee
Marinette
Egg Harbor 12
Baileys Harbor 8
Pound
Peshtigo
Coleman
Door County Peninsula
Jacksonport
Oconto
Cave Point Park
Shawano
Pensaukee
7
Sturgeon Bay
Angelica
Little Suamico
Forestville
Algoma
Luxemburg
Green Bay 13
Ashwaubenon
Allouez
Kewaunee 6
Appleton
Two Creeks
Neenah
Brillion
Reedsville
5 **Two Rivers**
Oshkosh
Chilton
4 **Manitowoc**
Lake Winnebago
Kiel
Cleveland
Lake Michigan
Fond du Lac
Sheboygan 2
Eden
Kohler 3
Kettle Moraine State Forest
West Bend
Port Washington
Slinger
Cedarburg 1
Bayside
Wauwatosa
Shorewood
Kettle Moraine State Forest
Milwaukee

Menominee
Marinette

Green Bay

N

0   30 miles

0   45 km

that was used to build many of the churches, homes, businesses, and shops still in use.

Today Cedarburg has a population of 10,000, and its entire downtown district has been placed on the National Register of Historic Places. The community celebrates its heritage with an annual Stone and Century Houses Tour of private historic homes and buildings in early June.

The Cedarburg Chamber of Commerce offers *A Walk Through Yesterday*, a self-guided walking and driving tour that covers 59 buildings. Pick up a tour booklet ($1) at the **Visitor Information Center** (W63 N645 Washington Ave., tel. 414/377–9620). Those interested in antiques should ask for the free list of dealers.

Cedar Creek Settlement is a historic village of shops in the Wittenberg Woolen Mill, which was built in 1864 and operated until 1969. The restored mill now holds over 35 businesses, including restaurants, antiques shops, pottery shops, art galleries, and specialty shops. With several levels, wooden floors, and lots of nooks and crannies, it's fun to explore. *N70 W6340 Bridge Rd., tel. 414/375–9390. Open Mon.–Sat. 10–5, Sun. noon–5.*

Cedar Creek Winery offers 45-minute guided tours including the winery museum and the cellars where the wine is fermented, aged, and bottled. Some guides will show you how one crawls through the tiny openings of the wine barrels to clean inside. *Lower level of the Cedar Creek Settlement, tel. 414/377–8020. Tours: $2. Open Mon.–Sat. 10–5, Sun. noon–5; closed Jan. 1, Easter, Thanksgiving, Dec. 25.*

The **Uihlein Antique Racing Car Museum** exhibits restored racing cars from the 1930s and 1940s. Race fans will enjoy the beautiful restorations; the museum is situated in a lovely stone building. *236 Hamilton Rd., tel. 414/375–4032. Admission: $3 adults, $1 children under 17 and senior citizens. Open Memorial Day–Labor Day, Wed.–Sat. 10–5, Sun. 1–5.*

The **Stagecoach Inn,** a beautiful restoration of a stone hotel of 1853, is now a bed-and-breakfast inn with twelve guest rooms including five whirlpool suites. The inn has a small but well-stocked bookstore for gifts and browsing, a cozy pub, and a chocolate shop offering handmade treats. *W61 N520 Washington Ave., 53012, tel. 414/375–0208. The shops are open Mon.–Sat. 10–5; pub opens at noon.*

Wisconsin's last remaining historic **covered bridge** crosses Cedar Creek three miles north of Cedarburg. The 120-foot bridge was built in 1876 and retired in 1962. Its white pine was cut and squared at a mill near Baraboo and hauled 75 miles to the bridge site. A small park beside the bridge is pleasant for viewing and picnicking. Follow Washington Avenue north to Highway 143; at the junction with Highway 60, take Covered Bridge Road north to the bridge. It's about three miles from town.

❷ Situated on Lake Michigan at the mouth of the Sheboygan River, the community of **Sheboygan** evokes thoughts of tasty bratwurst, sausage, and cheese for many people. An active Lake Michigan port, Sheboygan also turns out furniture, clothing, and leather goods.

The **John Michael Kohler Arts Center** incorporates the original home of J. M. Kohler (of plumbing-products fame), an Italianate villa built in 1882 and listed on the National Register of Historic Places. Exhibits of contemporary American art displayed include sculpture, crafts, and photography. There's a gift shop and sales gallery. *608 New York Ave., tel. 414/458–6144. Admission free. Open Mon. noon–5 and 7–9, Tues.–Sun. noon–5; closed holidays.*

The **Sheboygan County Museum's** collections are housed in a stately brick house (1850). Each room has a theme: musical instruments, toys, medicine, Indian artifacts, and country kitchen. There is also an 1862 log cabin and a barn with antique farm machinery. *3110 Erie Ave., tel. 414/458–1103. Admission: $2 adults, $1 children 7-12. Open Tues.–Sat. 10–5, Sun. 1–5; closed Mon. and Nov.–Mar.*

Indian Mound Park, situated on the south side, off Panther Avenue, has about a dozen burial mounds built in a variety of rare-animal effigies. They are believed to have been built by woodland Indians between AD 500 and 1,000. A hiking trail provides easy viewing. *Admission free.*

❸ Built to house employees of the Kohler Co. (manufacturers of plumbing products), the small, planned village of **Kohler,** two miles west of Sheboygan, surrounds the company's factories. The **Kohler Design Center,** a three-level exhibition hall, features a product pavilion, a designer showcase of 26 kitchen and bath interiors, a village museum, a ceramic art collection, and a multimedia theater. Waterfalls, working spas, and greenery share space with the "Great Wall of China," a three-story-high wall of bathroom fixtures in more colors and designs than you imagined possible. Factory tours can be arranged at the information desk. *101 Upper Rd., tel. 414/457–3699. Admission free. Open weekdays 9–5, weekends 10–4.*

Waelderhaus, a replica of the Kohler ancestral home in Bregenzerwald, Austria, contains original furnishings. Fascinating features include candle-reflected water-globe lighting fixtures, a tile stove, and secret hiding places for family valuables. *W. Riverside Dr., tel. 414/452–4079. Free guided tours daily at 2, 3, and 4; closed holidays.*

❹ The lakeshore community of **Manitowoc** is known as the Clipper City because of the hundreds of wooden ships local shipyards produced in the 19th-century. During World War II submarines and other warships were built here. Still an important Lake Michigan port, Manitowoc is home to a large sport fishing fleet.

Set on the banks of the Manitowoc River, the **Manitowoc Maritime Museum** is one of the largest marine museums on the Great Lakes. Exhibits depict the history of Manitowoc and Great Lakes shipping through models (some up to 12 feet long), artifacts from scrimshaw to ship engines and tools. The Richard Young Collection of ship models is outstanding. There is a full-size cross-section of the hull of a wooden sailing ship, with exhibits showing how it was built. The Port of Old Manitowoc exhibit includes three-story facades of businesses involved in 19th-century shipping. Several displays are dedicated to Manitowoc shipbuilding during World War II, and especially the 28 submarines built by local yards. The largest exhibit is the USS *Cobia,* a WW II submarine open for tours year-round. This may be the best maritime museum in the Great Lakes region. *75*

Maritime Dr., tel. 414/684–0218. Admission: $5.75 adults, $3.50 children under 13, $14.75 family. Open daily 9–5; closed holidays.

Pinecrest Historical Village is a pre-1900 village with more than 20 restored buildings relocated to a 40-acre site. There is a law office, school, operating blacksmith shop, sawmill, harness shop, and train depot with an 1887 engine. Special weekend events are scheduled during the summer. *927 Pinecrest La., 5 mi west on Hwy. JJ to Pinecrest La., tel. 414/684–5110. Admission: $4 adults, $2 children under 18. Open mid-May–Labor Day, daily 10–5; Labor Day–mid-Oct., Fri.–Sun. 10–4.*

The **Rahr-West Museum,** in a fine Victorian mansion (1891), exhibits 19th-century art and furniture as well as artifacts on the region's prehistoric Indians, and Chinese ivories, dolls, and porcelains. A modern exhibition wing presents changing art exhibits. *610 N. 8th St., tel. 414/683–4501. Admission free. Open weekdays 9–4:30, weekends 1–4; closed holidays.*

To shorten your tour, you may elect to head northwest from Manitowoc on U.S. 43 directly to Green Bay, about 35 miles away. To do so, however, would mean missing one of Wisconsin's prime vacationlands, Door County. Scenic **Route 42,** which runs along Lake Michigan most of the way between Manitowoc and Gill's Rock, at the tip of the Door County Peninsula, is a lovely drive any time of the year, but best in autumn.

⑤ Commercial fishermen still work on Lake Michigan in **Two Rivers,** the community where the American ice cream sundae was invented by a soda jerk in 1881. The **Rogers Street Fishing Village,** on the East Twin River, is a small museum that tells the story of commercial fishing over the past 150 years and displays artifacts recovered from shipwrecks. *2102 Jackson St., tel. 414/793–5905. Admission: $2.50 adults, $1 children. Open June–Aug., daily 10–4.*

⑥ In **Kewaunee,** the **Kewaunee County Jail Museum** comprises a jail, sheriff's office, and home built in 1876 and in use until 1969. Exhibits include antiques, artifacts, and memorabilia. There is a large basswood carving depicting Custer's Last Stand and life-size wood carvings of Father Marquette and Indians. *Courthouse Sq., corner Vliet and Dodge Sts., tel. 414/388–4906. Admission: $2 adults, $1 under 19. Open Memorial Day–Labor Day, daily 10:30–4:30.*

Jutting into Lake Michigan like the thumb on a mitten, **Door County** is a 70-mile-long, 13-mile-wide peninsula that is often called the Cape Cod of the Midwest. And not without reason; quaint coastal villages dot 250 miles of shoreline, with the waters of Green Bay on the west and Lake Michigan on the east. There are lighthouses, wide sand beaches, apple and cherry orchards, commercial fishermen, and offshore islands. Here, perhaps more than anywhere else in the state, one gets a true sense of Wisconsin's commercial, physical, and historical relationship to the Great Lakes.

Door County was named for a strait of water separating the peninsula from Washington Island—*Porte des Morts*, meaning Door of Death. The name was given by French explorers over 300 years ago because of accounts of a large party of Indians drowned in a sudden fierce storm in the "Door," where currents are often so strong that sailing vessels cannot make headway against it. Between 1837 and 1914, 24 vessels were lost in the *Porte des Morts* with another 40 lost on adjacent islands, reefs, and shoals, making the name doubly appropriate. During Lake Michigan's stormy autumn season, Great Lakes freighters often slip through the "Door" to seek shelter in the lee of Washington Island.

Nearly two million people flock to Door County each summer, with substantial numbers coming to view the brilliant colors in autumn. First-time visitors often make a circle tour via Highways 57 and 42. The Lake Michigan side of the peninsula is somewhat less settled and the landscape rougher. Depending on wind and weather conditions, it is not uncommon for the Lake Michigan side to be foggy and stormy, with rough seas, while just a few miles across the peninsula, the waters are calm, the skies blue and sunny.

No visit to Door County would be complete without sampling the region's famed fishboil, which originated more than 100 years ago. It is a simple but delicious meal that has reached legendary status in the Upper Great Lakes region. A huge caldron of water is brought to a boil over a wood fire. A basket of red potatoes is then cooked in the caldron, followed by a basket of whitefish steaks. At the moment the fish is cooked to perfection, kerosene is dumped on the fire, and the flames shoot high in the air. The intense heat causes the caldron to boil over, carrying away most of the fish oils and fat. The steaming whitefish is then served with melted butter, potatoes, cole slaw, and another Door County favorite, cherry pie. Door County's cherry orchards are extensive—the peninsula is carpeted in blossoms when the trees bloom in late May—and during the harvest between mid-July and early August, roadside stands throughout the county sell cherries, jams, jelly, and juice. You can pick your own cherries at many orchards at substantial savings.

7 **Sturgeon Bay,** with a population of about 9,000, is the region's largest community and the gateway to the peninsula. It is the sixth largest shipbuilding port in the nation, where Navy vessels, Great Lakes freighters, commercial fishing boats and luxury yachts have all been built.

Sunset Park, beside the Ship Canal in Sturgeon Bay, offers close views of shipbuilding operations and Great Lakes vessels in the shipyards. The Sturgeon Bay Marine Museum, in the former offices of the Roen Steamship Co., has displays on the history of shipbuilding and commercial fishing on the peninsula. Exhibits include a refurbished ship's pilothouse, antique engines, turn-of-the-century sailboats, and artifacts from sunken ships. *3rd Ave and Sunset Park, tel. 414/743–8139. Admission: $1 donation is suggested. Open Memorial Day–mid-Oct., weekdays 10–noon and 1:30–4.*

The **Door County Historical Museum** exhibits Indian relics, pioneer items, and an early firehouse. *18 N. 4th Ave., tel. 414/743–5809. Admission: donation. Open May–Oct., daily 10–5.*

The **Miller Art Center,** in the Door County Public Library, displays paintings and graphics by Door County and other midwestern artists, as well as changing exhibits. *107 S. 4th Ave., tel. 414/743–6578. Admission: free. Open Mon.–Thurs. 10–5 and 7–9, Fri. and Sat 10–5.*

❽ About four miles south of **Baileys Harbor,** on the Lake Mighigan side, you cross the 45th parallel, hafway between the Equator and North Pole. In Baileys Harbor, the **Ridges Sanctuary,** an 800-acre nature and wildlife area, has hiking trails. Guided tours are conducted in summer and early fall.

The Cana Island Lighthouse, one-quarter mile offshore and about four miles northeast of Baileys Harbor on Highway Q, was built in 1851; it is still in service. You can walk across a stone causeway to the island if the water is low; otherwise, you'll have to wade. **Northport,** at the tip of the peninsula, is the port of departure for the daily car ferries to Washington Island, six miles away. Passenger-only ferries to the island leave from nearby Gills Rock.

❾ **Northport,** at the tip of the peninsula, is the point of departure for the daily car ferries to **Washington Island,** six miles away. (Passenger-only ferries to the island leave from nearby Gills Rock.) Washington Island, with 600 inhabitants, is the oldest Icelandic settlement in the United States. Narrated tram tours aboard the **Washington Island Cherry Train** (tel. 414/847–2546) or the **Viking Tour Train** (tel. 414/854–2972) leave the ferry dock several times daily from Memorial Day to mid-October; purchase a combination tram-ferry ticket with the ferry line at Northport or Gills Rock. The island has nearly 100 miles of roads and is popular with bicyclists. You may take your own bicycle on the ferry or rent them from the ferry line at Gills Rock.

Jacobsen's Museum is a cedar log building that houses Indian artifacts, antiques, and rocks and fossils gathered on the island. *6 mi north of the ferry dock on Little Lake, tel. 414/847–2213. Admission: $1. Open mid-June–mid-Oct., daily 10–4:30.*

The Center for Creative Arts and Nature Study has exhibits devoted to island history from pre-historic times to colonization, nature displays, and exhibits of painting, photography, and crafts by island residents. *North of the harbor at Main and Jackson Harbor Rds., tel. 414/847-2025. Admission: $1 adults, under age 18 free. Open mid-June–Labor Day, daily 10:30–4:30.*

Ferries from Washington Island take visitors to remote **Rock Island State Park** (tel. 414/847–2235), a primitive park permitting only bicycling and backpacking. Rock Island was once the private estate of millionaire inventor Chester Thordarson, who built several striking stone buildings on the island. Exhibits are offered in the castle-like boathouse and Viking Hall.

❿ On the Green Bay side of the peninsula are the villages of Gills Rock, Ellison Bay, Sister Bay, Ephraim, Fish Creek, and Egg Harbor. New England-like in atmosphere and charm, they provide exceptional views of Green Bay where the sunsets can be breathtakingly beautiful. **Gills Rock,** a tiny commercial fishing village, is home to the Door County Maritime Museum, featuring commercial fishing history, artifacts, and nautical paintings. *12590 Hwy. 42, tel. 414/854–2860. Admission: donation. Open July and Aug., Mon.–Sat. 10–4, Sun. 1–4; June and Sept.–mid-Oct., weekends only.*

⓫ At **Peninsula State Park,** located in **Fish Creek,** you can tour in summer the 19th-century Eagle Bluff Lighthouse, which is still in use. The park is the state's busiest, drawing over a million visitors each year.

⑫ **Egg Harbor** is home to the **Chief Oshkosh Museum,** dedicated to the memory of Chief Roy Oshkosh (Tschekatchake mau ill), the last Chief of the Menominee Indians. Artifacts, craft work, and other items are exhibited. The **Cupola House,** built in 1871 is listed on the National Register of Historic Homes and features antiques, collectibles, and Amish quilts. Free concerts by the Birch Creek Music Academy are given in the Gazebo Wednesdays at 12:30 PM in summer.

Back on the mainland, at the head of Green Bay, the town of ⑬ **Green Bay** is Wisconsin's oldest city, although today it's best known for its football team. Permanent settlement dates from 1669 when Father Claude Allouez established a mission by the rapids of the Fox River at what is now the suburb of De Pere. Situated at the head of the strategic Fox-Wisconsin waterway, Green Bay under French control was an important outpost of fur trade and mission activity. British troops occupied the community and the French fort at the mouth of the river during the French and Indian War; the region remained under British dominance until the War of 1812. The United States did not gain control until 1816. Green Bay was a major lumbering and fishing center in the latter half of the 19th century and is today a manufacturing center for paper and related products. Using the St. Lawrence Seaway, ships of many nations call at Green Bay. A branch of the University of Wisconsin is here, and the city claims to be bowling capital of the world, with more alleys per capita than anywhere else.

Bay Beach Park has been a family amusement park for more than 60 years. Midway amusements, including rides on bumper cars, a miniature train, and children's rides, cost 10¢ each. *1313 Bay Beach Dr., on the Green Bay shore, tel. 414/448-3365. Open Memorial Day–Labor Day, daily 10–9; May and Sept., weekends 10–6.*

Bay Beach Wildlife Sanctuary is a 700-acre city park with a wildlife refuge and a nature education center. *Sanctuary Rd., across from the amusement park, tel. 414/497-6084. Admission free. Open mid-Apr.–mid-Sept., daily 8–8; mid-Sept.–mid-Apr., daily 8–5.*

The **Green Bay Packer Hall of Fame** tells the history of the National Football League's only city-owned team. Exhibits start with mementos from the days of Curly Lambeau, who founded the club with funds borrowed from a meat-packing firm. Films and videos of Packer game highlights are shown; the trophy from Super Bowl I is here. Of note are the Vince Lombardi collection and hands-on exhibits that allow you to throw a pass or kick a field goal. There is a gift shop with scads of green-and-gold Packer items for sale. *855 Lombardi Ave., across from Lambeau Field, tel. 414/499-4281. Admission: $5 adults, $4 over age 62, $3 ages 6–15. Open June–Aug., daily 9–6; Sept.–May, daily 10–5. Closed Dec. 25.*

Heritage Hill State Park, within the city, is not a typical state park, but a complex of furnished historical buildings grouped into theme areas. There is a 1762 fur trader's cabin, Tank Cottage (1776), the oldest standing home in Wisconsin, buildings from Fort Howard used during the 1830s, and a Belgian farmstead. A tiny bark chapel, representing the first missions in the region, shows the hardships of 17th-century Wisconsin life. *2640 S. Webster Ave., tel. 414/436–3010. Admission: $5 adults, $4 over 65, $2.75 under 17, $12.75 family. Open Memorial Day–Labor Day, Tues.–Sun. 10–5; May and Sept., weekends 10–5.*

Neville Public Museum has six galleries of art and science exhibits that illustrate Green Bay and Wisconsin history. Of special note are a silver monstrance used at the Green Bay mission in 1686 and the exhibit "On the Edge of the Inland Sea," which traces 13,000 years of northeast Wisconsin's geologic development. *210 Museum Pl., tel. 414/436–3767. Admission free. Open Tues.–Sat. 9–5, Sun. and Mon. noon–5.*

For those who wish to learn more about northeastern Wisconsin Indians, the **Oneida Nation Museum** traces the history of the Oneida Nation as it moved from New York to Wisconsin. Exhibits include a full-scale reconstruction of an Oneida longhouse. *5 mi west of Green Bay on Hwy. 54, then south 5 mi on Hwy. EE, tel. 414/896–2768. Admission: $1 adults, 50¢ under 18; Open May–Sept., Mon.–Sat. 9–5; Oct.–Apr., weekdays 9–5; closed holidays.*

National Railroad Museum has locomotives dating from 1910 and rolling stock from 1880. Exhibits include General Eisenhower's World War II staff train, Winston Churchill's traveling car, a "Big Boy" steam locomotive, and 40 locomotives and cars from the steam and diesel era. Admission includes a 1½-mile ride on an 1890s train complete with costumed guides and an occassional train robbery. *2285 S. Broadway, on the bank of the Fox River, tel. 414/435–7245. Admission: $5.50 adults, $4.75 over 62, $2.75 under 16, $15 family. Open May–Sept., daily 9–5.*

To make a shorter version of this tour, go north on U.S. 141 across the state border into Michigan, 155 miles to Covington, Michigan; another 50 miles north on U.S. 41 brings you to the Keweenau Peninsula (*see* Michigan's Upper Peninsula, *below*). To cut the tour even shorter, take U.S. 141 about 50 miles north from Green Bay to Marinette, cross the bridge to Menominee, Michigan, and follow Hwy. 35 northeast along the Lake Michigan shore 55 miles to Escanaba. From there, drive a scenic stretch of U.S. 2 for 130 miles to St. Ignace at the Straits of Mackinac (*see* Michigan's Upper Peninsula, *below*), where you can pick up the final segment of this tour.

Sports and Outdoor Activities

Beaches and Water Sports Lake Michigan's waters are cold, but its beaches are popular. **Kohler-Andrae State Park** (tel. 414/452–3457), seven miles south of Sheboygan, has two miles of beach. **Point Beach State Forest** (tel. 414/794–7480), six miles north of Two Rivers, has a large beach. Park sticker required at both. Farther north, **Kewaunee** and **Algoma** have small beaches.

Virtually every community in the Door County Peninsula has a beach. There are sand beaches at **Peninsula State Park** at Fish Creek (tel. 414/868–3258); **Whitefish Dunes State Park** near Sturgeon Bay (tel. 414/823–2400); and **Newport State Park**, near Ellison Bay (tel. 414/854–2500). Park stickers are required.

In Ephraim, on the northwest side of Door County, **Windsurf Door Co., Inc.** (9876 Water St., tel. 414/854–4071) rents sailboards.

Bicycling There are hundreds of miles of bicycle trails in city parks and arboretums, and much riding in state parks. Door County's **Peninsula State Park** has a trail from Fish Creek to Ephraim.

Fishing Some Lake Michigan trout and salmon fishing is done from docks and piers, but the really big fish are caught from well-equipped boats, whose skippers know the waters. Charter boats abound on the lakeshore, with over a hundred in **Manitowoc** and **Two Rivers.** The short-lived but frantic spring smelt run, where the tiny fish are dipped from the lake by the basketful, must be seen to be believed.

From late May through October, anglers comb **Door County**'s offshore waters in search of 10- to 25-pound chinook and coho salmon. Lake trout, brown, and rainbow trout are also plentiful from early spring through autumn. Charter fishing-boat operators who will take you after the big ones can be found in every community on the peninsula. All you'll need is a fishing license. Expect to pay $100 to $150 per person for a half-day charter for four. A report on Door County fishing conditions is available 24 hours a day by calling 414/743–7046.

Golf **Alpine Resort & Golf Club,** Egg Harbor (tel. 414/868–3000), 27
Door County holes; **Bay Ridge Golf Course,** Sister Bay (tel. 414/854–4085), 9 holes; **Cherry Hills Lodge and Golf Course,** Sturgeon Bay (tel. 414/743-4222 or 800/545-2307), 18 holes; **Maple Grove Golf Course,** Washington Island (tel. 414/847–2017); **Peninsula State Park Golf Course,** Ephraim (tel. 414/854–5791), 18 holes.

Green Bay **Brown County Golf Course** (897 Riverdale Dr., Oneida, tel. 414/497–1731), 18 holes; **Crystal Springs Golf Course** (2 mi northwest of Seymore on French Rd., tel. 414/833–6348), 18 holes; **Hilly Haven Ski and Golf** (6 mi southeast of De Pere on Hwy. PP, tel. 414/336–6204), 9 holes; **Mid Valley Golf Course** (Hwy. 41, De Pere, tel. 414/337–9594 or 766-5555), 18 holes; **Mystery Hills Golf Course** (3 mi east of De Pere on Hwy. G, tel. 414/336–6077), 27 holes; **Woodside Country Club** (530 Erie Rd., 1½ mi off I-41, tel. 414/468–5729), 18 holes.

Kohler **Blackwolf Run** at the American Club (1111 W. Riverside Dr., tel. 414/457–4446), 36 holes.

Manitowoc **Meadow Links Golf Course** (1540 Johnson Dr., tel. 414/682–6842), 18 holes; **Fairview Golf Club** (3659 Riverview Dr., Two Rivers, tel. 414/794–8726), 9 holes.

Sheboygan **Riverdale Country Club** (5008 S. 12th St., tel. 414/458–2561), 18 holes; **Sheboygan Town & Country Club** (W 1945 Hwy. J, tel. 414/467–2509), 27 holes.

Skiing **Hidden Valley** (13 mi north of Manitowoc, I–43 Exit 91 to Hwy. R, then 1 mi south, tel. 414/863–2713 or 682–5475) offers 3 runs, 2 rope tows, double chair, snowmaking; longest run 3,600 feet, vertical drop 200 feet. Rentals, repairs, instruction, chalet, bar/lounge, ski shop, snack bar. *Open Mon.–Wed. 4:30–10, Thurs.–Fri. 10–4, weekends 10–4:30; closed Dec. 24, 25, and 31.*

Potawatomi State Park (4 mi southwest of Sturgeon Bay off Hwy. 42/57 to Park Dr., tel. 414/743–8869) offers 3 runs, 2 rope tows, double chair, snowmaking; longest run 2,000 feet, vertical drop 120 feet. Cross-country skiing, instruction, chalet, snack bar, 2 warming shelters, winter camping. *Open weekends and holidays 10–4:30, Wed. 6–10.*

Spectator Sports

Football | The **Green Bay Packers** play half of their home football games at Lambeau Field, where the spirit of Vince Lombardi lives on. Tickets are sometimes available (tel. 414/494–2345).

Dining and Lodging

The following dining price categories have been used: *Very Expensive*, over $30; *Expensive*, $20–$30; *Moderate*, $10–$20; *Inexpensive*, under $10.

Door County is not the place to arrive without confirmed reservations, especially between June and October when even the state park campgrounds are filled. If you should find yourself without a place to stay, the **Door County Chamber of Commerce** has a 24-hour, computerized telephone information plaza at Highways 57 and 42, at the southern edge of Sturgeon Bay. You'll find pictures and descriptions of accommodations, a display to indicate which have space, and phone lines to motel, resort and campground offices throughout the county. The service is free.

Green Bay adds nearly 60,000 to its population on weekends when the Packers play at home, so if you plan to visit in autumn, check the NFL schedule in advance.

The following lodging price categories have been used: *Very Expensive*, over $90; *Expensive*, $70–$90; *Moderate*, $40–$70; *Inexpensive*, under $40.

Baileys Harbor | **Sandpiper.** A family restaurant featuring whitefish chowder,
Dining | homemade soups and desserts, broasted chicken, and fishboils. There are senior-citizens' and children's menus; beer is served. *Hwy. 57, north end of the village, tel. 414/839–2528. Dress: casual. MC, V. Closed Jan.–mid-Mar. Inexpensive.*

Lodging | **Gordon Lodge.** 40 rooms in cottage and motel accommodations,
★ | some with fireplaces, on Lake Michigan. *Box A, 54202, tel. 414/839–2331, 6 mi northwest on Hwy. Q. Facilities: outdoor pool, beach, putting green, 2 lighted tennis courts, rental bicycles and boats, marina, fishing, dining room, lounge. 3-day minimum stay summer weekends. MC, V. Closed mid-Oct.–mid-May. Expensive–Very Expensive.*

Cedarburg | **Barth's at the Bridge.** Early American decor and good soups,
Dining | salads, chicken, and seafood distinguish this restaurant with a children's menu and cocktail lounge. *N58 W6 194 Columbia Rd., tel. 414/377–0660. Reservations advised. AE, DC, MC, V. Closed Mon. and major holidays. Moderate.*
Victor's of Cedarburg. Sandwiches, stir-fries, chicken curry, hand-cut steaks, and a broiled fisherman platter are all part of Victor's eclectic menu. *W62 N547 Washington Ave. 414/375–1777. Reservations suggested. M, V. Sun. Brunch 10:30 AM–2 PM. Closed Mon. Moderate.*

Egg Harbor | **Landmark Resort.** 293 modern rooms with lake or wood view
Lodging | and pleasant public area with fireplace. *Box 260, 54209, tel.*
★ | *414/868–3205, 1 mi southwest on Hwy. G to Hillside Trail. Fa-*

cilities: indoor and outdoor pools, saunas, whirlpools, coin laundry, 5 tennis courts, exercise room, adjacent to 27-hole golf course, dining room, cocktail lounge. AE, MC, V. Expensive–Very Expensive.

Ellison Bay
Dining

The Viking. There are nightly outdoor fishboils, from late May through mid-October; the regular menu features sandwiches, steaks, and seafood. *Hwy. 42, center of town, tel. 414/854–2998. Dress: casual. Reservations suggested. AE, MC, V. Closed Easter, Thanksgiving, Dec. 25. Inexpensive–Moderate.*

Lodging

Grand View Motel. 30 rooms with spectacular view of Green Bay and village. *Box 30, 54210, tel. 414/854–5150, ¼ mi south on Hwy. 42. Facilities: bicycle rentals, ski and snowmobile trails, beaches, golf, restaurants nearby. AE, MC, V. Moderate.*

Ephraim
Lodging

The Edgewater Motel. 40 rooms overlooking waters of Green Bay. Three-day minimum stay from mid-June through Labor Day. *Box 143, 54211, tel. 414/854–2734, Hwy. 42, center of town. Facilities: outdoor pool, restaurant, beach, golf, boating nearby. AE, MC, V. Closed late Oct.–Apr. Moderate.*

Fish Creek
Dining
★

White Gull Inn. This 1896 country inn is noted for its fishboils, held Wednesday nights and weekends in summer, and Wednesday and Saturday evenings in winter. The regular menu features steaks and seafood. *On Main St., ¼ mi west of Hwy. 42, tel. 414/868–3517. Reservations recommended. AE, MC, V. Closed Thanksgiving, Dec. 23–25. Moderate–Expensive.*

Lodging

The Whistling Swan. 7 rooms with turn-of-the-century furnishings and modern conveniences. *Box 193, 54212, tel. 414/868–3442, on Main St., just west of Hwy. 42. Facilities: restaurant opposite, beach, golf, boating, skiing nearby. AE, MC, V. Moderate–Expensive.*
The Peninsula Motel. 17 rooms, including 3 two-bedroom units. *Box 246, 54212, tel. 414/868–3281, ¼ mi north at entrance to Peninsula State Park. Facilities: golf, beach, boating, restaurants nearby. MC, V. Moderate.*

Green Bay
Dining

Mariner Supper Club & Motel. The nightly specials here include prime rib, roast duck, and braised lamb. *2222 Riverside Dr., ½ mi north of Hwy. 172, tel. 414/437–7107. Dress: informal. AE, MC, V. No lunch weekends. Moderate.*
River Room. Overlooking the Fox River, this restaurant specializes in prime rib, seafood, and steaks. *In Holiday Inn City Centre, 200 Main St., tel. 414/437–5900. Dress: informal. AE, DC, MC, V. Moderate.*
Rock Garden Supper Club. Seafood, prime rib, and steak are favorites at this popular supper club and cocktail lounge. *1951 Bond St., tel. 414/497–4701. Dress: casual. AE, DC, MC, V. Inexpensive–Moderate.*
John Nero's. This family restaurant specializes in soups and pastries. *2130 Velp Ave., just west of U.S. 41, tel. 414/434–3400. Dress: casual. MC, V. Closed major holidays. Inexpensive.*

Lodging

Ramada Inn. 156 rooms. *2750 Ramada Way, 54304, tel. 414/499–0631, ½ mi southwest on U.S. 41 at Oneida St. exit. Facilities: indoor pool, sauna, whirlpool, putting green, coffee shop, restaurant, lounge. AE, DC, MC, V. Moderate.*
Best Western Downtowner Motel. 138 rooms. *321 S. Washington St., 54301, tel. 414/437–8771. Facilities: indoor pool, sauna,*

whirlpool, large recreation area, winter plug-ins, dining room, lounge, entertainment. AE, DC, MC, V. Inexpensive–Moderate.

Bay Motel. 55 rooms. *1301 S. Military Ave., 54304, tel. 414/ 494–3441, 3½ mi west on U.S. Business 41. Facilities: winter plug-ins, restaurant. AE, MC, V. Inexpensive.*

Exel Inn. 106 rooms, some no-smoking. *2870 Ramada Way, 53404, tel. 414/499–3599 or 800/356–8013, 6½ mi southwest on U.S. 41 at Oneida St. exit. Facilities: free satellite movies, restaurant adjacent. AE, MC, V. Inexpensive.*

Mariner Motel. 21 rooms with river view. *2222 Riverside Dr. on Hwy. 57, 54301, tel. 414/437–7107. Facilities: winter plug-in, restaurant. AE, MC, V. Inexpensive.*

Kohler
Dining
★

The Immigrant Room. Exceptional dining and service are offered at the American Club in one of Wisconsin's finest restaurants. There are six intimate, ethnic-theme dining rooms. *Highland Dr., tel. 414/457–8888. Jacket and tie required. Reservations recommended. AE, DC, MC, V. Dinner only; closed Easter, Dec. 25. Expensive.*

Lean Bean Restaurant. Part of the American Club Health Center, the Lean Bean overlooks a small lake, and has outdoor dining during the summer. *Highland Dr., tel. 414/457–4445. Dress: casual. Reservations recommended. AE, DC, MC, V. Closed Easter, Dec. 25. Inexpensive.*

Lodging
★

The American Club. This well-known resort is built around a recently renovated building listed in the National Register of Historic Places. The 165 large guest rooms feature whirlpools, and there are many sports facilities on the property. *Highland Dr., tel. 414/457–8000. Facilities: indoor pool, beach, sauna, golf, rental canoes and bicycles, 4 racquetball courts, 12 tennis courts (6 indoor), health club, tanning room, massage; dining room, restaurant, and coffee shop. AE, DC, MC, V. Expensive–Very Expensive.*

Manitowoc
Dining

The Breakwater. Good steaks and seafood are served in a nautical setting; the dining room has an outstanding harbor view. Cocktails, lounge. *In the Inn on Maritime Bay, 101 Maritime Dr., tel. 414/682–7000. Jacket and tie suggested. Reservations recommended. AE, DC, MC, V. Moderate–Expensive.*

The Penguin. One of the last true diners, with lots of neon on the outside and a good basic menu featuring big breakfasts, sandwiches, plate lunches, and dinners. *3900 Calcument Ave. (Highway 151), tel. 414/684–6403. Dress: casual. No credit cards. Inexpensive.*

Lodging

Holiday Inn. 204 rooms, some with balcony or patio overlooking an atrium, some for nonsmokers. *4601 Calmet Ave., 54220, tel. 414/682–6000 or 800/465–4329, junction of I–43 and U.S. 151. Facilities: indoor pool, whirlpool, sauna, dining room, lounge. AE, DC, MC, V. Moderate.*

Inn on Maritime Bay. 109 rooms, most with lake views; nautical themes in public areas. *101 Maritime Dr., 54220, tel. 414/682–7000. Facilities: indoor pool, sauna, whirlpool, lounge, restaurant. AE, DC, MC, V. Moderate.*

Budgetel Inn. 53 rooms. *908 Washington St., 54220, tel. 414/ 682–8271. Facilities: lounge, coffee shop adjoining. AE, DC, MC, V. Inexpensive.*

Sheboygan
Dining

City Streets. Steaks, seafood, and prime rib are served with a superb view of downtown Sheboygan and the Lake Michigan shoreline. *607 N. 8th St., tel. 414/457–9050. Dress: informal. Reservations recommended. MC, V. No lunch Sat.; closed Sun. Inexpensive–Moderate.*

Lodging **Budgetel Inn.** 97 rooms. *2932 Kohler Memorial Dr., 53081, tel. 414/457–2321, 1 mi east of I–43 at Hwy. 23 exit. Facilities: winter plug-ins, restaurant adjacent. AE, MC, V. Inexpensive.*
Parkway Motel. 32 rooms. *3900 Motel Rd., 53081, tel. 414/458–8333, on Hwy. V, just east of I–43 at exit 48. Facilities: winter plug-ins. AE, MC, V. Inexpensive.*

Sister Bay **Al Johnson's Swedish Restaurant.** Swedish specialties and decor
Dining distinguish this sod-roofed log building with goats on its roof in
★ summer. *Center of town on Hwy. 42, tel. 414/854–2626. Dress: casual. No reservations. AE, MC, V. Closed Thanksgiving, Dec. 25. Inexpensive–Moderate.*

Lodging **Open Hearth Lodge.** 30 rooms. *1109 S. Bay Shore Dr., 54234, tel. 414/854–4890, ¾ mi south on Hwy. 42. Facilities: indoor pool, whirlpool, snowmobile trails, skiing, beach, boating, golf nearby. AE, MC, V. Moderate.*

Sturgeon Bay **White Lace Inn.** The inn's 15 rooms are located in two Victorian
Lodging homes and a converted coach house. Some have fireplaces, 4 have whirlpool baths, and all are furnished with antiques and period pieces. *16 N. Fifth Ave., 54235, tel. 414/743–1105, 2 blocks north of business hwys. 42 and 57. MC, V. Expensive–Very Expensive.*
Best Western Maritime Inn. 91 large well-kept rooms. *1001 N. 14 Ave., 54235, tel. 414/743–7231, 1 mi north on business hwys. 42 and 57. Facilities: indoor pool, whirlpool. AE, DC, MC, V. Moderate.*

Two Rivers **Lighthouse on the Lake.** Steaks and seafood are featured in a
Dining dining room with a lake view. *In the Lighthouse Inn, 1515 Memorial Dr., tel. 414/793–4524. Dress: informal. Reservations recommended. AE, MC, V. Inexpensive–Moderate.*

Lodging **Lighthouse Inn.** 68 rooms, some with Lake Michigan view. Weekend packages available. *1515 Memorial Dr., 54241, tel. 414/739–4524. Facilities: indoor pool, sauna, whirlpool, lounge, restaurant, fishing, fish freezer. AE, MC, V. Inexpensive.*

The Arts

Sunset Concert Cruises aboard an excursion boat leave Sister Bay in July and August. *Concert Cruises, 10055-W. Hwy. 57, Sister Bay, 54234, tel. 414/854–2986.*

Northern Wisconsin

Northern Wisconsin is the land of endless green pine forests, sky-blue lakes, and crystal-clear streams. Here you can shoot the rapids in a whitewater raft, enjoy some of the best fishing anywhere, or discover a waterfall along a wilderness trail. It's hunting, fishing, and, in the winter, snowmobiling country. Families come back to the thousands of small lakeside resorts year after year. Northern Wisconsin is divided into two tourist regions—Northwoods and Indian Head Country.

When the 16th-century explorers and fur traders first saw Wisconsin's Northwoods, they found a region of glacial lakes and dense forests, with centuries-old white pines towering 100 to 130 feet above the forest floor. Following the Civil War, with the nation pushing westward and clamoring for building materials, lumbermen moved into the northern Wisconsin pinery. Early logging took place near the waterways and each spring rivers like the Wisconsin, Chippewa, and Black ran nearly solid with logs floating toward the Mississippi. The towns that sprang up around them were rip-roaring towns filled with saloons, bawdy houses, gamblers, fancy ladies, and others ready to take the lumberjack's money. But by the dawn of the 20th century, most of northern Wisconsin had been logged out and the lumberjacks moved on. Today, second-growth timber covers the scars of clear-cutting, but there are few trees in the Northwoods more than 100 years old.

While some logging continues (mainly for the manufacture of paper), the Northwoods today means recreation and tourism, and millions flock to the region's parks, forests, and sparkling waters each year to camp, fish, and enjoy the out-of-doors. Waterfalls are plentiful and the National Forests offer scenery, solitude, and the chance to get away from it all, be it for an hour or a week. From May through October, the highways are busy with campers and boaters heading northward on Friday evening, southward on Sunday. Snowmobilers repeat the pattern December through March. The November deer hunting seasons draws hundreds of thousands to the woods, but fishing remains the top sport; most sought after are Muskelunge (musky), walleye, bass, and northern pike. Fishing guides can be found in most communities, but they're usually booked well in advance; if your plans include serious fishing, make reservations early.

Indian Head Country stretches from Lake Superior's scenic shore to the Mississippi River. Here you can take a boat cruise through the international seaport of Superior, tour the beautiful Apostle Islands, and fish the waters of Gitche Gumee. The region has easily accessible waterfalls, including the fourth-highest falls east of the Rocky Mountains.

Numbers in the margin correspond to points of interest on the Northern Wisconsin map.

❶ About 45 miles north of Green Bay on U.S. 41 is **Peshtigo,** where, on October 8, 1871, a massive forest fire destroyed the commuity and some 1,280,000 acres of forest on both sides of Green Bay. So intense was the fire that the heat produced a fire storm. The death toll has been estimated at 1,200 to 1,300 people. It was the worst fire in the nation's history, but it was overshadowed by the great Chicago Fire, which occurred the same night. The **Peshtigo Fire Museum** contains a collection of miscellany, most having little to do with the fire, although there are a few artifacts that survived the conflagration. Adjacent is the **Oconto Cemetery,** which contains graves of the fire victims, and a monument marking the mass grave of unidentified dead. *Oconto Ave., tel. 715/582–3244. Admission: donation. Open June–early Oct., daily 9–5.*

Take Hwy. 64 west from Marinette, then go north on Hwy. 32 **❷** to **Laona.** The **Lumberjack Special and Camp Five Museum Complex** features steam-powered train rides aboard the Laona and Northern Railways' *Lumberjack Special* to the Camp Five complex. The logging museum includes blacksmith and harness

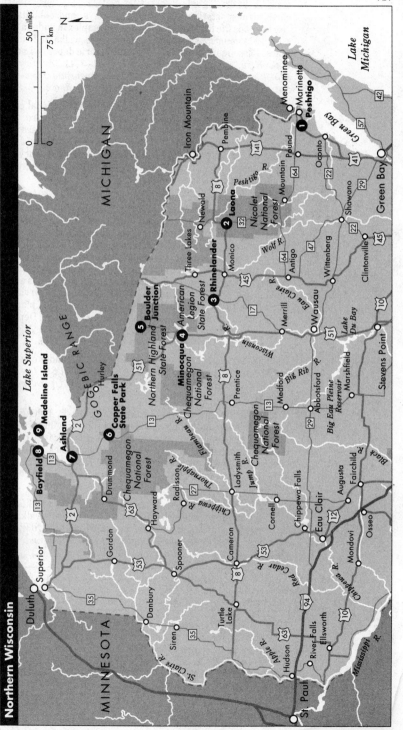

shops, transportation and logging displays, and exhibits on Northwoods life in lumbering days. The complex includes a vintage 1900 country store and offers nature walks and forest tours. Passengers board trains at the historic depot in Laona. *U.S. Hwy. 8 and Hwy. 32, tel. 715/674–3414. Admission: $10.50 adults, $4.25 children under 13. Open mid-June–last Sat. in Aug., Mon.–Sat.; trains at 11, noon, 1, and 2.*

❸ **Rhinelander** is the home of Hodag, a fearsome fictional creature from the 1880s created by the author Gene Shepard. The city's high school teams are named after the Hodag, as are several area businesses; a Hodag festival is held each July. Rhinelander was a major logging center in the 19th century; today its mainstays are paper manufacturing and tourism, with hundreds of lakes and resorts in the area.

The **Logging Museum** is a reproduction of a camp with bunkhouse, cook shack, blacksmith shop, sawmill, displays of logging equipment, and hundreds of artifacts and photos from lumbering days. It gives examples of the number and size of the huge logs taken from the forest, a remarkable feat considering that virtually all logging was done with hand tools. Nearby is one of Rhinelander's first public schools, furnished as it was in the days of the *McGuffey Reader*. Also on the grounds is a museum filled with memorabilia of the Civilian Conservation Corps, offering a fascinating account of the men who planted trees and built roads and parks here during the Great Depression. *Pioneer Park, Oneida Ave., tel. 715/369–5004. Admission: donation. Open mid-May–mid-Sept., daily 10–6.*

Rhinelander Paper Co. is one of the largest mills under one roof in the country; tours are offered. *515 Davenport St., tel. 715/369–4100. Admission free; no children under 12. Open June 1–Aug. 31, Tues.–Fri. at 10, 11, 1:30 and 2:30.*

❹ An all-year resort, **Minocqua** is known for musky fishing and boating in summer, skiing and snowmobiling in winter. **Circle M Corral** amusement and theme park features go-carts, bumper boats, miniature golf, kiddy rides, horseback riding, a shooting gallery, and video games. *10295 Hwy. 70 W, tel. 715/356–4441. Admission free; prices vary for rides and activity packages. Open May–mid-Oct., daily 9 AM–dusk.*

Jim Peck's Wildwood has more than 100 varieties of wildlife, including tame deer. There is a fishing pond and nature walk; visitors may pet animals. Boat rides are available. *Hwy. 70 W, tel. 715/356–5588. Admission: $5 adults, $3.75 children under 13. Open May 1–mid-Oct., daily 9–5:30.*

Time Out **The Peacock** (Hwy. 70 W at the bridge at St. Germain, 9 miles east of Minocqua, tel. 715/542–3483) is a great Northwoods bar, made of real logs, that serves sandwiches and dinner.

From Woodruff to Hurley, **U.S. 51** winds through some of Northwoods' most scenic country, peppered with small lakes. ❺ Detour north on country road M to **Boulder Junction,** which offers access to the woodlands and lakes of the Northern Highland–American Legion State Forest. Fishing for the elusive muskellunge is excellent around here. **Aqualand Wildlife Park** contains most species of the state's fish and wildlife, and visitors can feed many of the animals. There's a petting area for youngsters, as well as trout fishing and picnicking. *8 mi south-*

east on Hwy. K, tel. 715/385–2181. Admission: $4.75 adults, $3.75 children under 13. Open late May–Sept., daily 9–5:30.

If you're adventurous, discover one of the nearly inaccessible falls of the Montreal River in northern **Iron County.** Four of Wisconsin's highest waterfalls are on the Montreal and its west fork. Or explore the wild river setting of the Potato River Falls, which are just south of Gurney. (For a list of waterfalls and directions to them, contact **Iron County UWEX Office,** Courthouse, Hurley, 54535, tel. 715/561–2695). Follow Hwy. 77 west from Hurley to Mellen and **Copper Falls State Park,** which epitomizes the phrase "up north." Here Brownstone and Copper Falls plunge more than 30 feet into the Bad River gorge. Foot bridges and well-maintained trails give easy access to these spectacular cascades; there are camping and picnic areas. *Copper Falls State Park, Box 348, Mellen, tel. 715/274–5123. Park sticker required.*

Hurley is just across the state border from Michigan, and you could begin the Michigan leg of this tour here by driving 10 miles east on U.S. 2, then 52 miles on Hwy. 28 to Bruce Crossing, then another 58 miles north and east on Hwy. 26 to **Houghton** (*see* Michigan's Upper Peninsula, *below*). If you have a bit more time to spend in Wisconsin, however, take a detour to the scenic Bayfield Peninsula. Take either U.S. 2 from Hurley or Hwy. 13 north from Mellen to **Ashland,** gateway to the peninsula. Ashland was a lumbering and iron-mining center in the 19th century. The fur traders Radisson and Groseilliers spent the winter of 1659 here; the site is marked along Lake Superior at the western edge of the city. The iron-ore docks, huge trestle-like structures where railroad cars unloaded ore into lake boats, still stand. A brochure outlining a walking tour of Ashland's 2nd Street Historic District is available from the Ashland Chamber of Commerce.

Drive north on **Highway 13** for a scenic drive along the Chequamegon Bay–Lake Superior shoreline to **Bayfield.** Although Bayfield's population is less than 1,000, the community has some 50 buildings listed on the National Register of Historic Places, mansions made of the brownstone quarried here in the 19th century (the same brownstone used in the elegant town houses of Chicago and New York). The chamber of commerce offers a free brochure outlining a self-guided walking tour. The community draws many visitors from June through the Apple Festival in mid-October. The peninsula has attracted a variety of artists; there are art galleries, pottery studios, woodworking shops, and artists' studios open to visitors. A directory of artists is available at the chamber of commerce information center and at some local shops. There's also a guide to apple orchards that welcome visitors.

The **Apostle Islands National Lakeshore Visitors Center,** in the old Bayfield County Courthouse, has films and exhibits introducing tourists to the region and the National Lakeshore. The missionaries chose the name Apostle, thinking there were 12 islands. In reality, there are 22, ranging from less than an acre to more than 14,000 acres. Activities include hiking, boating, fishing, and primitive camping. There are naturalist programs on some islands in summer. *415 W. Washington St., tel. 715/779–3397. Admission free. Open June–Labor Day, daily 8–6; Sept.–Oct., daily 8–4:30, Nov.–May, weekdays 8–4:30.*

Apostle Islands Cruise Service offers narrated sightseeing cruises of many islands from mid-June to early October. Camper shuttle service to some islands is available. *City Dock at the end of Rittenhouse Ave., tel. 715/779-3925.*

The **Cooperage Museum** is Wisconsin's only working barrel factory; barrels for storing and shipping fish have been made here since the last century. Today you can watch a cooper assembling barrels around a huge open hearth. A slide presentation is shown when the cooper is not at work. There are also exhibits on commercial fishing and a gift shop. The site is listed on the National Register of Historic Places. *1 Washington Ave., tel. 715/779-3400. Admission free. Open Memorial Day-early Oct., daily 9:30-5:30.*

9 Because it is inhabited by approximately 175 people, **Madeline Island** is not part of the Apostle Islands National Lakeshore. The first French explorers reached this island—the largest of the Apostle Islands group—between 1618 and 1622. Trading posts were established by the French in 1693, by the British in 1793, and by the American Fur Trading Co. in 1816. The island has one settlement, the village of La Pointe, which serves the thousands of summer visitors. **Madeline Island Ferries** (tel. 715/747-2051) shuttle tourists and their autos between Bayfield and La Pointe from April to December, depending on the winter freeze. In winter residents drive back and forth across the bay on a marked and maintained ice road. There are 45 miles of roads on the island. Guides on **Madeline Island Bus Tours** (tel. 414/747-2051) will show you points of interest and explain the history of the islands in a one-hour tour aboard an air-conditioned bus. *Tours leave several times a day from the ferry landing in La Pointe from late June through early October.*

The **Madeline Island Historical Museum** (tel. 414/747-2415) is a small State Historical Society site consisting of a 19th-century fur company building, jail, barn, and sailor's home. Surrounded by a log stockade, the museum's exhibits provide excellent insight into early fishing, logging, and the fur trade. It's one of those museums that has a little of everything; tools, photos, religious artifacts, fishing gear, ship models, a lighthouse lens, even a glass-sided hearse on runners. *Near the ferry landing. Admission: $1.50 adults, $1.20 over 65, 50¢ under 18, $4 family. Open mid-June-early Oct., daily 10-5.*

Stop at the old **Indian Cemetery,** ½ mile from the ferry landing at the south edge of La Pointe near the marina. Some of the gravestones are 200 years old. Michael Cadotte, an 18th-century French trader who married the Indian woman after whom the island is named, is buried here.

Big Bay State Park has 60 campsites, picnic areas, five miles of hiking trails, and a mile-long sand beach. Swimmers be warned: Lake Superior's waters are extremely cold. At Big Bay Point there are picturesque sandstone bluffs and caves at the water's edge. *5 mi east on Hwy. H., tel. 715/747-6425. Admission: park sticker.*

The Town of La Pointe operates Big Bay Island Park, with 44 rustic campsites on the north side of Big Bay. Campsites are rented on a first-come basis; the park has a picnic area and sandy beaches.

Returning to Ashland, either drive east on U.S. 2 through Hurley into Michigan (see directions above) to complete the circuit around Lake Michigan, or head west on U.S. 2 to Superior, where you can explore the northwoods of Arrowhead Minnesota (*see* Arrowhead Minnesota, *below*). From Arrowhead, you can either head back toward Milwaukee and Chicago or complete the larger circuit around Lake Superior.

Sports and Outdoor Activities

Beaches and Water Sports With all the lakes and rivers in northern Wisconsin, beaches abound; you will be hard pressed to find a community, park, or resort that does not have one. One of the nicest is the 1½-mile sand beach at Big Bay State Park on Madeline Island.

Bicycling The **Bearskin Trail** is a 12-mile state trail that winds through the woods from Minocqua past lakes, bays, and remote forests to Bearskin Lake. The area, once the domain of the Indian, the logger, and the fur trader, retains much of its wilderness beauty. Trail fee.

Canoeing *Northwoods* The upper part of the **Peshtigo River** has some of the most difficult whitewater in the Midwest and requires considerable canoeing skill. The river widens and slows below Crivitz.

The **Brule River,** a boundary river between Wisconsin and Michigan, has long stretches of slow water and low-hazard rapids. There is potential hazard at the junction with the Michigamme; check local conditions.

The **Menominee River,** another river separating Wisconsin and Michigan, has stretches of fast water and difficult rapids. Parts of the upper river are extremely dangerous and should be run only by experts in decked boats.

Canoes can be rented locally from many sources; because of the difficult and sometimes dangerous nature of many Northwoods rivers, it is suggested you contact a local chamber of commerce or visitors bureau for additional information.

Indian Head Country The **St. Croix** is designated a National Scenic River, and contains low- to medium-hazard rapids. Below St. Croix Falls, the river is open to commercial traffic.

The rivers in Indian Head Country are generally not as wild as those in the Northwoods; however, it is suggested that you check local information before starting out.

Fishing

It really doesn't get much better than this. Virtually every tourism publication here has color photos of huge fish held high by grinning fishermen or small children. And they don't exaggerate; there's good fishing for almost every species found in Wisconsin. Fishing is serious business here; many motels and resorts include fish freezing as part of their service. Bait and tackle shops, resorts, and tourist agencies can help you get a fishing guide, which may well be worth the money if you're a serious fisherman.

Lake Superior Sport Fishing Charter Captains Association (Box 812, Superior, 54880, tel. 715/394–7716 or 800/223–2774, ext. 111) provides information on Lake Superior charterboat fishing.

Bayfield Trollers Association (Box 406, 54814, tel. 715/779-3330) will provide information on charter fishing in its area.

Golf

La Pointe **Madeline Island Golf Course** is an 18-hole course designed by Robert Trent-Jones (tel. 715/747-3212).

Minocqua **Jim Peck's Wildwood** (2 mi west on Hwy. 70, tel. 715/356-3477), 9 holes; **Pinewood Country Club** (Lakewood Rd., Harshaw, tel. 715/282-5500), 18 holes; **Trout Lake Golf and Country Club** (9 mi north of Woodruff on Hwy. 51, tel. 715/675-3044), 18 holes.

Skiing **Whitecap.** 33 runs, 2 rope tows, 4 double chairs, quad chair, snowmaking; longest run 5,000 feet, maximum vertical drop 400 feet. Rentals, repairs, instruction, chalet, ski shop, restaurant, snack bar, child care, cross-country skiing, ice fishing. Accommodations for 600 in 3 motels, condos, electrical hookups for campers. *11 mi west of Hurley on Hwy. 77, 3 mi west on Hwy. E, tel. 715/561-2227. Open daily 9-4.*

For information on cross-country skiing in national forests, contact **Chequamegon National Forest** (1170 4th Ave., Park Falls, 54552, tel. 715/762-2461), and **Nicolet National Forest** (68 S. Stevens St., Rhinelander, 54501, tel. 715/362-3415).

Dining and Lodging

Dining is an informal proposition up north, and dress is casual. Most restaurants offer hearty, stick-to-the ribs fare in prodigious amounts and the Friday night fish fry is universal. (Totally unscientific surveys indicate that places with stuffed fish and deer heads mounted on the back bar offer the best fish fries.)

The following dining price categories have been used: *Very Expensive*, over $30; *Expensive*, $20-$30; *Moderate*, $10-$20; *Inexpensive*, under $10.

Accommodations vary widely, probably more so than elsewhere in the state. Small lakeside family resorts with housekeeping cottages (complete with fishing boat) are the mainstay of the lodging industry, but usually require reservations well in advance. In recent years more and more luxury resorts have appeared, offering all the amenities you'll find in large cities, plus Northwoods scenery. Resort stays are generally a week or two, although off season some resorts welcome overnighters. Reservations are usually required months in advance.

The following lodging price categories have been used: *Very Expensive*, over $90; *Expensive*, $70-$90; *Moderate*, $40-$70; *Inexpensive*, under $40.

Ashland **Hotel Chequamegon.** 64 rooms in a new hotel with 19th-century
Lodging graciousness and decor. *101 W. Front St., 54806, tel. 715/682-9095. Facilities: indoor pool, sauna, whirlpool, dining room, cafe, coffee shop, lounge. AE, MC, V. Inexpensive-Moderate.*

Bayfield **Old Rittenhouse Inn.** Elegant six-course meals are served in
Dining this 1890s mansion. *301 Rittenhouse Ave., tel. 715/779-5111.*
★ *Jacket and tie required. Reservations recommended. MC, V. Closed Mon.-Thurs. Nov.-Apr. Expensive.*
Greunke's Inn. This restaurant built in the 1860s specializes in poached whitefish and whitefish livers, trout, steaks. *17*

Rittenhouse Ave., tel. 715/779–5480. MC, V. Closed Nov.–Mar. Inexpensive.

Pier Plaza Restaurant. The dining room has a lake view at this family restaurant that's especially good for breakfast. Try the Friday fish fry and box lunches, too. *Corner Rittenhouse and Front Sts., tel. 715/779–3330. MC, V. Closed Dec. 25. Inexpensive.*

Lodging **Old Rittenhouse Inn.** 21 rooms with fireplaces in an antique-
★ furnished 1890s mansion with all the modern conveniences. Make reservations well in advance. *301 Rittenhouse Ave., 54814, tel. 715/779–5111. MC, V. Moderate–Expensive.*

Bay Villa Motel. 25 rooms, many with a lake view. *Box 33, 54814, tel. 715/779–3252, ½ mi north on Hwy. 13. Facilities: cross-country and snowmobile trails. MC, V. Inexpensive.*

Harbor Edge Motel. 17 rooms opposite the ferry landing, some in a historic waterfront home. 33 Front St., 54814, tel. 715/779–3962. MC, V. Inexpensive.

Minocqua **Bosacki's Boathouse.** Overlooking Lake Minocqua, this north-
Dining woods restaurant offers light lunches and a dinner menu heavy on beef, chicken, and seafood; there is a separate children's menu. The cocktail lounge has a piano shaped like a boat. *Hwy. 51 at the bridge, tel. 715/356–5292. AE, MC, V. Inexpensive–Moderate.*

Paul Bunyan Lumberjack Meals. This family restaurant serves prime rib, chicken, spaghetti, and fish in a logging camplike setting. *On U.S. 51 between Minocqua and Woodruff, tel. 715/356–6270. Reservations recommended. MC, V. Closed Oct.–May 15. Inexpensive.*

Lodging **New Concord Inn.** This new motel with 53 rooms, 6 with private whirlpool, is located one block north of downtown across from Torpy Park. *320 Front St. (Hwy. 51), 54548, tel. 715/356–1800. Facilities: indoor pool, whirlpool, game room, lounge, rental boats, bicycles, and snowmobiles. AE, MC, V. Moderate.*

Lakeview Motor Lodge. There's a fireplace in the lobby, and several of the 33 comfortable rooms have lake views. *Box 575, 54548, tel. 715/356–5208, 311 Park St., adjacent to lake. Facilities: boat and snowmobile rental, winter plug-ins, lake swimming, fishing. AE, MC, V. Inexpensive–Moderate.*

Rhinelander **Pied Piper Supper Club.** This attractive contemporary dining
Dining room with views of the woods serves up steaks, chicken, and seafood. *Hwy. 8, east, tel. 715/369–2700. Reservations recommended. AE, DC, MC, V. Closed Easter, Thanksgiving, Dec. 24–25. Inexpensive–Moderate.*

Rhinelander Cafe and Pub. There's standard American fare and very good Greek specialties at this downtown restaurant and supper club owned by the same family since 1911. *33 N. Brown St., tel. 715/362–2918. Reservations recommended. MC, V. Inexpensive–Moderate.*

Lodging **Holiday Acres Resort.** 58 motor-lodge rooms and lakeshore cottages, some with fireplaces. *Box 460, 54501, tel. 715/369–1500, 4½ mi east on U.S. 8 and Hwy. 47, 2¼ mi north on Lake George Rd. Facilities: indoor pool, beach, rental boats, rental bicycles, 3 tennis courts, fishing, putting green, wind-surfing, waterskiing, dining room, coffee shop, lounge. MC, V. Closed mid-Mar.–mid-Apr. Moderate.*

Claridge Motor Inn. 80 well-kept rooms. *70 N. Stevens St., 54501, tel. 717/362–7100 or 800/528–1234. Facilities: indoor* *pool, whirlpool, winter plug-ins, restaurant, lounge. AE, DC, MC, V. Inexpensive–Moderate.*

Arrowhead Minnesota

North and east of Duluth, the Arrowhead region of Minnesota is one of the best-known sections of the state for outdoor vacations. The Boundary Waters Canoe Area and Lake Superior National Forest draw thousands of campers and canoeists each year. Scenic U.S. 61 hugs the Lake Superior shore from Duluth to the Canadian border, providing spectacular views of the lake and its rocky shoreline. Having left Lake Michigan and ventured this far up the Superior shore, you may want to complete the long Circle Drive around Lake Superior; brief directions for doing so are included below.

Numbers in the margin correspond to points of interest on the Arrowhead map.

❶ Situated 2,342 miles from the ocean, **Superior**, Wisconsin, is one of the farthest-inland seaports in the world. Along with its sister city of Duluth, Minnesota, it is one of the nation's busiest harbors, shipping millions of tons of iron ore and grain each year. Superior has 28 miles of shore lined with shipyards, grain elevators, heavy industry, and some of the world's largest docks. **Vista King and Queen Harbor Cruises** offer 2-hour narrated cruises of Superior-Duluth Harbor. *Depart from Barker's Island, 2 mi east od Superior on Hwy. 53 and U.S. 2, or Arena-Auditorium Dock at foot of W. 5th Ave. in Duluth; tel. 715/394–6846 or 218/722–6218. Fare: $6.95 adults, $3.25 children under 12. Departures May 1–mid-Oct., daily; call for times.*

The SS *Meteor,* built in 1896, is the sole survivor of 43 round-hulled Great Lakes freighters known as whalebacks built at Superior in the late 19th century. Guided tours take you through the ship from engine room to pilothouse. The vessel sailed until the late 1960s, and much of its equipment is intact. There is a museum and gift shop in the cargo hold. *Barker's Island, 2 mi east on Hwy. 53 and U.S. 2, tel. 715/392–5742. Admission: $3 adults, $2.50 over age 62 and under age 13, $10 family. Open Memorial Day–Labor Day, daily 10–5; Sept.–mid-Oct., weekends.*

Fairlawn Mansion and Museum, overlooking Barker's Island and Lake Superior, is a 42-room Victorian mansion, styled after a French chateau, that contains the collection of the Douglas County Historical Society. First-floor rooms have been restored to Victorian splendor; carved wood, marble fireplaces, decorative silver, brass, stained glass, and tile abound. The upper floors contain exhibits on Great Lakes shipping, Lake Superior Indians, and 19th-century fashions. *906 E. 2nd St., tel. 715/394–5712. Admission: $3 adults, $2 over 57 and under 19, $1 under 13. Open Memorial Day–Labor Day, daily 10–5; rest of the year, Tues.–Fri. 10–4, weekends noon–4. Closed Jan. 1, Thanksgiving, Labor Day.*

❷ With a population of 93,000, **Duluth** is Minnesota's fourth largest city. The man after whom Duluth is named, explorer Daniel de Greysolon, Sieur du Luth, stepped ashore here in 1679. Duluth became an important fur-trading center and jumping-off point to the west, but the traders came and went for nearly a

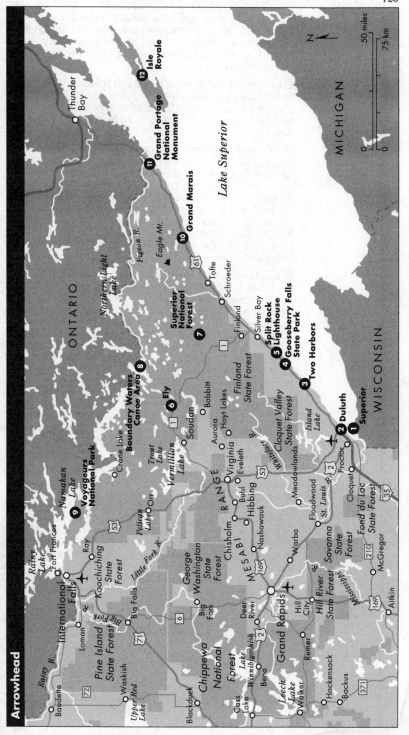

Arrowhead

century and permanent settlement did not begin until 1853. Minnesota Point, a narrow, seven-mile-long sand spit, creates a natural breakwater at the mouth of the harbor. The point has beaches, marinas, a seaplane base, and excellent views of the harbor and city.

The symbol of Duluth is the **Aerial Lift Bridge,** which connects the mainland with Minnesota Point at the mouth of the harbor. The 386-foot bridge must be raised to allow ships in and out of port, and the entire bridge floor can be lifted 138 feet in less than a minute.

The **Canal Park Marine Museum,** adjacent to the Aerial Lift Bridge, is Duluth's most popular waterfront attraction. Exhibits about the history of Lake Superior shipping and Duluth–Superior Harbor include models, shipwreck relics, films, and reconstructed ships' cabins. Located at the harbor entrance, the small museum and grounds offer close-up views of passing ships and the bridge rising. *1st Ave. at the foot of Main St., tel. 218/727–2497. Admission free. Open Memorial Day–Labor Day, daily 10 AM–9 PM; Apr. 1–Memorial Day and day after Labor Day–Nov., daily 10–6; Dec.–Mar., Fri.–Sun. 10–4:30.*

The **St. Louis County Heritage and Arts Center,** better known as the **Depot,** is located in the restored 1892 Duluth Union Depot and houses a wide array of cultural organizations. The **Depot Square** is a re-creation of 1910 Duluth, with an ice cream parlor, trolley rides, and a silent movie theater. The **St. Louis County Historical Museum** holds a replica of a fur-trading post, and the exhibits at the **A. M. Chisolm Museum** range from American pressed glass to antique dolls. The **Lake Superior Museum of Transportation** has hands-on train exhibits and the first locomotive in Minnesota. The depot—on the National Register of Historic Places—is also home to the **Duluth Ballet,** the **Duluth Art Institute,** the **Duluth Playhouse,** the **Duluth-Superior Orchestra,** and the **Matinee Musicale.** *506 W. Michigan St., tel. 218/727–8025. Admission: $4 adults, $3 senior citizens, $2 children 6–17, $11 family. Open May–mid-Oct., daily 10–5; mid-Oct.–Apr., Mon.–Sat. 10–5, Sun. 1–5.*

The elegance of Duluth at the turn of the century is revived at **Glensheen,** a restored 39-room Jacobean-style mansion furnished with period pieces and antiques, including some original furnishings. There are seven and one-half acres of grounds overlooking Lake Superior, and lovely formal gardens. The carriage house holds a collection of carriages and sleighs. *3300 London Rd., tel. 218/724–8864. Admission: $5.50 adults; $4.25 senior citizens and children 13–17, $2.50 children under 13. Guided tours May–Oct. Thurs.–Tues. 9–noon; Nov.–Apr., Mon., Tues., Thurs., Fri. at 1 and 2, weekends 1–3. Self-guided tours permitted 1–4 in summer. Closed Jan. 1, Easter, Thanksgiving, Dec. 25.*

The 16-mile **Skyline Parkway Drive** atop Duluth's 600-foot bluffs offers panoramic views of the city and harbor.

As you leave Duluth on U.S. 61, signs will urge you to leave the new highway and take "old" 61 along the lakeshore for 22 miles to Two Harbors. Do it! The scenic route goes through the tiny villages of French River and Knife River, where rivers cascade down from lakeshore bluffs to Lake Superior.

③ Two Harbors, the first of Minnesota's Lake Superior iron ports, earned its name from its twin harbors, Agate Bay and Burlington Bay. **Van Haven Lake Front Park** provides views of the giant loading docks on Agate Bay. The **Depot Museum,** run by the Lake County Historical Society, contains displays about railroading, logging, iron mining, commercial fishing, and Great Lakes shipping. Outdoor exhibits include the *Three Spot,* the first locomotive used in the area, and a Mallett, one of the world's most powerful steam locomotives. *Foot of Waterfront Dr., tel. 218/834–4898. Admission: $1.50 adults, 75¢ children 6–18. Open May–Oct. Sun.–Thurs. 9:30–6, Fri. and Sat. 9:30–8; Nov.–Apr. weekends 10–5.*

The Gooseberry River, which surges through the 1,600-acre **④ Gooseberry Falls State Park** on the shores of Lake Superior, has five waterfalls, two of which are more than 30 feet high. There are hiking trails, a park interpretive center, camping and picnic areas. *13 mi north of Two Rivers on U.S. 61, tel. 218/834–3855. Admission: $3.25 vehicle permit. Open daily 8 AM–10 PM.*

⑤ The 54-foot octagonal **Split Rock Lighthouse,** which still warns ships away from the dangerous cliffs that line the shore, is the most visited lighthouse on the Great Lakes. Built atop a 100-foot bluff in 1910, the light is 168 feet above the surface of Lake Superior. When the light was automated in 1961, the lighthouse, land, and other buildings became a state park. You can tour the light and tower, foghorn building, and keeper's quarters. An interpretive center has exhibits and videos on the construction of the lighthouse and its operation. *Split Rock Lighthouse State Park, 18 mi northwest of Two Harbors on U.S. 61, tel. 218/226–3065. Admission: $3.25 vehicle permit. Open May 15–Oct. 15, daily 9–5.*

⑥
⑦ A long detour northwest on Hwy. 1 will take you to **Ely,** the gateway community for **Superior National Forest** and the
⑧ Boundary Waters Canoe Area (BWCA). The 3-million-acre forest stretches for 150 miles along the Minnesota–Canada border; one million acres has been set aside as the BWCA, an area with several thousand lakes linked by short portages, and where motor boats are banned. The National Forest Information Center (118 S. 4th Ave., 218/365–6185) has information about travel in the BWCA and throughout the national forest. *Contact BWCA Reservations, Superior National Forest, Box 338, Duluth, 55801, tel. 218/720–5324 for permits to enter BWCA May–Sept.*

⑨ Dedicated in 1975, the 218,000-acre **Voyageurs National Park** commemorates the French-Canadian *voyageurs,* who were the backbone of the 17th–19th-century fur trade, paddling fur-laden canoes and carrying them on portages from lake to lake. The 30 major lakes in Voyageurs National Park form part of a water highway from Lake Superior to Lake of the Woods. Activities within the park include hiking, canoeing, guided boat tours, motorboating, fishing, cross-country skiing, and camping. Naturalist-led boat trips and hikes are offered during the summer. Park headquarters are located at South International Falls; the Rainy Lake Visitor Center is open year-round. *Admission free. For additional information contact Superintendent, Voyageurs National Park, Box 50, International Falls, 56649, tel. 218/283–9821.*

⑩ Back on the Lake Superior shore, **Grand Marais** is a village of 1,300 located at an excellent natural harbor. The Gunflint Trail, a hiking and cross-country ski trail that runs northwest to Saganaga Lake on the Canadian border, begins here. Nearby **Cascade Falls State Park** features a 50-foot-high waterfall.

⑪ Thirty-eight miles northeast on U.S. 61, the **Grand Portage National Monument** marks the site of the Grand Portage, the "great carrying place," a nine-mile trail that bypasses some 20 miles of waterfalls and rapids near the mouth of the Pigeon River on Lake Superior. The trail was first used and named by French fur traders and *voyageurs* in 1722 as a route into and out of the Canadian wilderness. In 1779 the Montreal-based North West Company made the site its inland headquarters and built a trading post here. A reconstructed stockade, Great Hall, kitchen, and other buildings re-create the setting of Minnesota's earliest settlement; craft demonstrations and interpretive programs are offered. Visitors may hike an eight-and-one-half-mile trail along the portage route. *Box 666, Grand Marais, 55604, tel. 218/387–2788. Admission: $1 adults, children under 16 and seniors free. Open mid-May–mid-Oct., daily 8–5.*

⑫ From Grand Portage, you can take a passenger ferry to **Isle Royale,** the largest island in Lake Superior, 45 miles long and 9 miles wide at its widest point. Isle Royale is a wilderness park inhabited by moose, wolves, beavers, red foxes, mink, and snowshoe hares. There are 166 miles of trails and many campgrounds; travel is on foot or by boat. A small marina and two lodges are open from May to October; reservations are required well in advance. All equipment must be backpacked in; all surface water must be boiled. The park is reached by boat or seaplane, for which reservations are also required. Boat service is available mid-May–October; the ferry takes 3 hours. Isle Royale is not a place where one drops in for a picnic; trips take advance planning. Those considering a visit are advised to obtain further information. *Superintendent, Isle Royale National Park, 87 N. Ripley St., Houghton 49931, tel. 906/482–0984. For ferry reservations, contact GPIR Transport Lines, 1332 London Road, Duluth 55805, tel. 218/728–1237.*

Lake Superior Circle Drive Some travelers may want to continue 470 miles through Ontario around Lake Superior, the world's largest freshwater lake. The scenery is breathtaking, and several wilderness parks along the route offer plenty of opportunities for hiking, canoeing, fishing, and camping. There are few towns equipped for overnight stops, however, so plan the trip carefully. **Thunder Bay,** 35 miles past Grand Portage on Highway 61, has a good supply of hotels and restaurants, and you can tour the reconstructed 19th-century Fort William. In Thunder Bay, you can pick up the Trans-Canada Highway (Rte. 17) which leads on east around the lake. The 178-mile stretch from Thunder Bay to **Marathon** provides outstanding views of Lake Superior and delightful northwoods vistas. Another 116 miles past Marathon is **Wawa** (pronounced just as it looks, it means "wild goose" in the Ojibwa tongue), another likely town for an overnight stop. Past Wawa, it's another 75 miles to **Sault Ste. Marie,** located directly across the St. Mary's River from its similarly named sister city in Michigan. A toll bridge connect the two Sault Ste. Maries—cross it and you can pick up the Michigan segment of the tour (*see* Michigan's Upper Peninsula, *below*).

To enter Canada, U.S. citizens need proof of citizenship: a passport, birth certificate or voter registration card will do. Naturalized U.S. citizens should have their naturalization papers. You will be required to go through Canadian Customs when you enter Canada and through U.S. Customs when you return to the United States. It is a quick and painless procedure in almost all cases.

Shopping

Fitger's on the Lake in Duluth is a shopping mall built in a refurbished 19th-century waterfront brewery that has more than 30 specialty shops and restaurants. *600 E. Superior St., tel. 218/722-8826. Open Mon.-Sat. 10-9, Sun. 11-5.*

Made in the Shade in Duluth offers a collection of crafts made by American artisans from Maine to California. There are hand-blown glass, leather, metal, and fiberwork items, toys, and hand-dipped candles. *600 W. Superior St., Duluth, tel. 218/722-1929. Open Mon.-Sat. 10-9, Sun. 11-5 in summer.*

The **Pioneer Crafts Co-op** near Two Harbors has a selection of handmade crafts and art produced by local and regional craftspeople. *4½ mi northwest of Two Harbors on U.S. 61, tel. 218/834-4175. Open Jan.-May, weekends 9-5; June-Sept., daily 9-7; Oct., daily 9-5; Nov.-Dec., Fri.-Sun. 9-5.*

Sports and Outdoor Activities

Beaches There is little swimming in Lake Superior, because the water is so very cold. Minnesota Point, the sand spit at the **Duluth** harbor entrance, has several unguarded sand beaches.

Bicycling The 22-mile **North Shore Bike Route** takes cyclists along old Route 61 between Duluth and Two Harbors and provides spectacular views of the Lake Superior shoreline.

Canoeing Minnesota's Arrowhead region contains some of the finest canoe waters in the nation, including the **Boundary Waters Canoe Area (BWCA)** and other sections of the **Superior National Forest, Voyageurs National Park,** and the **St. Croix National Scenic Waterway.** For canoe license information and a free, pocket-size map of canoe routes, contact the Outdoor Recreation Information Center (Box 40, 500 Lafayette Rd., St. Paul, MN 55146, tel. 612/296-4776 or 800/652-9747 in MN).

Fishing The waters up here are the big league of Midwest sport fishing. The thousands of lakes, streams, and rivers offer walleye, muskellunge, northern pike, bass, trout, and various species of panfish. Lake Superior offers a variety of fish including lake trout and Pacific salmon. "Big game" charter-boat operators are found in most Lake Superior ports, with more than a dozen operating out of Duluth. If you're fishing inland waters, resorts and bait and tackle shops can help you locate fishing hot spots or local guides.

The Twin Ports Fishing Guide contains information on fishing in the Duluth region, including charter fishing information, fish identification, and where and how to fish for various species. The Duluth Convention and Visitors Bureau distributes free copies.

Lake Superior Sport Fishing Charter Captains Association (Box 812, Superior 54880, tel. 715/394-7716 or 800/223-2774, ext. 111) provides information on Lake Superior charterboat fishing.

Skiing   **Chester Municipal Park** offers 3 runs and 1 rope tow; longest
Downhill   run 1,000 feet, vertical drop 160 feet. Services include children's programs, free ski lessons Jan.–Feb. *1 mi west of University of Minnesota–Duluth campus off Skyline Dr., tel. 218/ 723-3337. Open Tues., Thurs., and Fri. 5-9, weekends 11– 4:30.*

Spirit Mountain Ski Area has 14 runs, 4 chair lifts, 1 T-bar, 1 rope tow, and snowmaking; longest run 5,400 feet, vertical drop 700 feet. Services include cross-country skiing, equipment rental, instruction. *10 mi south of Duluth off I-35, Exit 249, tel. 800/247-0146. Open weekdays 10-9, weekends 9-9.*

Cross-country   The Arrowhead region offers excellent terrain for cross-country skiing; some of the state's finest trails are located here. For more information on cross-country trails, and a special publication issued each winter on cross-country skiing in Minnesota, contact DNR Trails and Waterways Unit (Box 52, 500 Lafayette Rd., St. Paul 55155, tel. 612/296-6699 or 800/652-9747 in MN).

The **North Shore Trail** runs 74 miles through the Lake Superior hills between Grand Marais and Little Marais. There are a number of lodges along the trail.

The **Gunflint Trail** runs north from Grand Marais and offers more than 100 miles of trails and a variety of terrain. Many trails loop through the Boundary Waters Canoe Area.

Grand Portage Ski Trail has 43 miles of maintained trails running north to near the Canadian border. The trails range from beginner to advanced levels.

Dining and Lodging

The selection of restaurants in this region is varied, but they are uniformly casual. Look for local fish specials, along with steaks, chicken, and prime rib.

The following dining price categories have been used: *Very Expensive*, over $20; *Expensive*, $12–$20; *Moderate*, $8–$12; *Inexpensive*, under $8.

Like most everything else in the northwoods, lodging is a fairly informal business. It runs the gamut from spartan fishing camps to full-service hotels, motels, and resorts.

The following lodging price categories have been used: *Very Expensive*, over $120; *Expensive*, $90–$120; *Moderate*, $50– $90; *Inexpensive*, under $50.

Duluth   **Pickwick Restaurant.** Owned and operated by the same family
Dining   since 1914, the Pickwick specializes in charbroiled steaks and seafood. There's a children's menu and a cocktail lounge. The contemporary dining room has views of Lake Superior. *508 E. Superior St., tel. 218/727-8901. Reservations suggested. AE, DC, MC, V. Closed Sun., major holidays. Inexpensive–Moderate.*

Coney Island Deluxe. At this casual spot, specialties include Coney Island sandwiches, gyro sandwiches, and other Greek delights. It's been a favorite with locals for nearly 50 years. *112 W. 1st St., tel. 218/722–2772. No credit cards. Inexpensive.*

Lodging **Fitger's Inn.** Part of a shopping area set in a refurbished brewery, this inn is listed in the National Register of Historic Places. It provides minisuites and elegant, spacious, individually styled rooms with period furnishings. Most rooms have a lake view. *600 E. Superior St., 55802, tel. 218/722–8826. 48 rooms. Facilities: restaurant, lounge, shopping mall and parking adjacent. AE, DC, MC, V. Expensive.*

Radisson Duluth. In downtown Duluth, the hotel overlooks the harbor and Lake Superior. The rooms, typically well kept and well furnished, have city or harbor views. *505 W. Superior St., 55802, tel. 218/727–8981. 268 rooms. Facilities: indoor pool, parking, restaurant. AE, DC, MC, V. Moderate–Expensive.*

Best Western Edgewater East Motel. Overlooking Lake Superior, this is the largest of the three Best Western inns in town. The rooms are light and airy, and many offer lake views. The moderate prices cover a large number of amenities. *2400 London Rd., 55812, tel. 218/728–3601. 119 rooms. Facilities: indoor pool, sauna, whirlpool, putting green, health club, playground, coin laundry, winter plug-ins. AE, DC, MC, V. Inexpensive–Moderate.*

Grand Marais **Birch Terrace Supper Club.** The specialties at this family-run
Dining restaurant in a restored 1899 home include ribs and fresh Lake Superior trout. The baked goods come straight from the restaurant kitchen. The lounge offers a lake view and cocktails. *½ mi east on U.S. 61, tel. 218/387–2215. Dinner reservations suggested. MC, V. Open Sun.–Thurs. 11:30–3 and 5–11; Fri., Sat. 5–11. May–mid-Oct. Inexpensive–Moderate.*

Superior **Constrom's Supper Club.** Prime rib and seafood are served at
Dining this restaurant owned by the same family for 30 years. *Tower and 33rd St., 2 mi south on Hwy. 35, tel. 715/392–2237. Reservations recommended. MC, V. Closed Mondays, July 4, Dec. 24–25. Moderate.*

The Shack Supper Club. American favorites such as steaks and ribs are the specialties here. *3301 Belknap St., 1½ mi west on U.S. 2, tel. 715/392–9836. DC, MC, V. Inexpensive–Moderate.*

Lodging **Barker's Island Inn.** Formerly the Country Hospitality Inn, this modern hotel has 115 rooms, all with water views. *300 Marina Dr., 54880, tel. 715/392–7152. 1½ mi east on U.S. 2, 53 and 35. Facilities: indoor pool, sauna, whirlpool, 3 lighted tennis courts, coin laundry, restaurant, lounge. AE, DC, MC, V. Moderate.*

Superior Inn. 72 rooms. *525 Hammond Ave., 54880, tel. 715/ 394–7706, 1 block south of U.S. 53 and the bridge. Facilities: indoor pool, sauna, whirlpool, winter plug-ins. AE, MC, V. Inexpensive.*

Michigan's Upper Peninsula

The Upper Peninsula, known as UP, is an area of state and national forests, copper and iron deposits, waterfalls (more than 150), old mining towns, and ski slopes. This is Big Snow Country, where well over 200 inches fall each year. Here, too, is the "Two-Hearted River" Ernest Hemingway wrote about. July and August are the big tourist months; nearly all attractions have limited hours in June and September, and most close by October 15. Snow is not uncommon in October.

If you're coming from Hurley, Wisconsin, take U.S. 2 east for 10 miles, then Hwy. 28 east for 52 miles, then Hwy. 26 north and east for 58 miles to reach the Keweenau (KEY-wa-naw) Peninsula. From Green Bay, Wisconsin, U.S. 141 leads north 155 miles to connect with U.S. 41 in Covington, Michigan; another 50 miles north on U.S. 41 brings you to the Keweenau.

Numbers in the margin correspond to points of interest on the Northwestern Michigan and Upper Peninsula map.

Curving into Lake Superior like a crooked finger, the **Keweenaw Peninsula** was the site of extensive copper mining from the 1840s to the 1960s. The deposits were exceptionally pure, and in its heyday Keweenaw produced a considerable part of the world's copper. The man-made Keweenaw Waterway, incorporating Portage Lake, cuts across the middle of the peninsula, providing shelter for storm-threatened vessels and enabling them to avoid the dangerous waters surrounding the peninsula.

The twin cities of Houghton and Hancock, the gateway to the Keweenaw, are connected by a double-deck lift bridge with a four-lane highway on the upper level and a railroad track on the lower level. **Houghton** is home to **Michigan Technical University**. The **E. A. Seaman Mineralogical Museum** (in the Electrical Energy Resources Center, tel. 906/487–2572) displays minerals native to the UP.

❷ The inland headquarters of **Isle Royale National Park** are also in Houghton. Isle Royale, the largest island in Lake Superior (45 miles long and 9 miles wide at its widest point), is a wilderness park inhabited by moose, wolves, beavers, red foxes, mink, and snowshoe hares. There are 166 miles of trails and many campgrounds; travel is on foot or by boat. A small marina and two lodges are open from May to October; reservations are required well in advance. Boat service is available mid-May–October, from Copper Harbor (4½ hours one way) or Houghton (6½ hours); plane service is available from Houghton mid-June to mid-September. Those considering a visit are advised to obtain further information. *Superintendent, Isle Royale National Park, 87 N. Ripley St., Houghton 49931, tel. 906/482–0984. For ferry reservations from Copper Harbor, contact Isle Royale Queen, Copper Harbor 49918, tel. 906/289–4437. For seaplane reservations, contact Isle Royale Seaplane Service, Box 371, Houghton 49931, tel. 906/482–8850.*

❸ In **Hancock**, the **Arcadian Copper Mine** has a ½-mile guided tour of workings no longer in operation. *1 mi east on Rte. M–26, tel. 906/482–7502. Admission: $4 adults, $2 children 6–12. Tours July and Aug., daily 9–6; June and Sept., daily 9–5.*

❹ The Victorian stone architecture in **Calumet** gives just a hint of the wealth in the copper towns during the boom days. At its peak, Calumet, whose population is 1,000 today, had more than 20 churches and a 37-room school. Much of the downtown area is listed on the National Register of Historic Places. The 1,000-seat **Calumet Theater**, built in 1910, was the stage for such stars as Lillian Russell, Sarah Bernhardt, William S. Hart, and Douglas Fairbanks Sr. Restored in 1974 at a cost of $200,000,

733

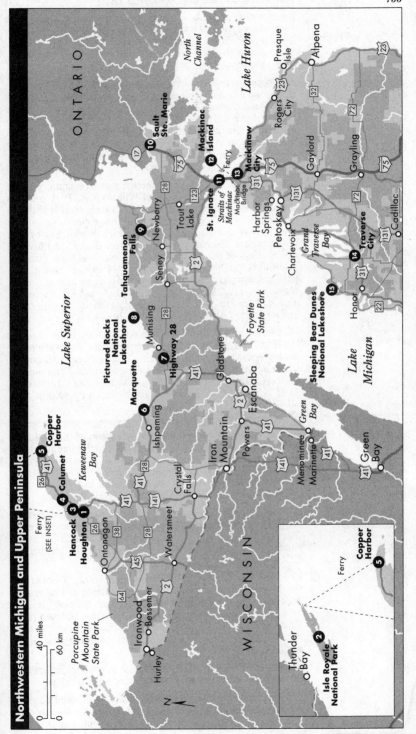

Northwestern Michigan and Upper Peninsula

Lake Superior

ONTARIO

Lake Huron

North Channel

Porcupine Mountain State Park

Houghton 1
Hancock 3
Calumet 4
Copper Harbor 5
Marquette 6
Highway 28 7
Pictured Rocks National Lakeshore 8
Tahquamenon Falls 9
Sault Ste. Marie 10
St. Ignace 11
Mackinac Island 12
Mackinaw City 13
Traverse City 14
Sleeping Bear Dunes National Lakeshore 15

Straits of Mackinac
Mackinac Bridge

WISCONSIN

Lake Michigan

Green Bay

Grand Traverse Bay

Fayette State Park

Keweenaw Bay

40 miles
60 km

N

Isle Royale National Park 2
Copper Harbor 5
Thunder Bay
Ferry

the theater presents performances and major community events throughout the year, including summer concerts by the Detroit Symphony. *340 6th St., tel. 906/337-2610. Admission: $2 adults, $1 students; under age 12 free. Tours late May–mid-Sept., weekdays 10-4:30.*

At **Coppertown USA,** a visitors center tells the story of the mines, towns, and people of the Keweenaw Peninsula. Exhibits of equipment trace the evolution of mining from ancient times through the boom days and the closing of the last working mine in 1968. A simulated mine affords a glimpse into the miner's world. *2 blocks west of U.S. 41, tel. 906/337-4354. Admission: $1.50 adults, 50¢ age 13 and under. Open mid-June–mid-Oct., Mon.–Sat. 10-8; closed holidays.*

❺ Copper Harbor is Michigan's northernmost community and a popular spot with campers. **Fort Wilkins State Park** contains the restored buildings of an Army post established in 1844 and abandoned in 1870. The complex also has copper mine shafts sunk in 1844 and the Copper Harbor Lighthouse. Audiovisual presentations and costumed interpreters depict the lifestyles and routines of the officers, enlisted men, and their families. Additional exhibits show the history of copper mining. The park has campgrounds and hiking trails. *3 mi east of Copper Harbor on U.S. 41, tel. 906/289-4215. $3 vehicle sticker required. Open June 1–Labor Day, daily 8 AM–10 PM; May 15-31 and day after Labor Day–Oct. 15, daily 8-5.*

Delaware Copper Mine Tours. Guided walking tours through the first level of a 142-year-old copper mine. There are tools, mining equipment, and old mining buildings, a small mining museum, children's petting zoo, and picnic areas. *12 mi south of Copper Harbor on U.S. 41, tel. 906/289-4688. Admission: $3.95 adults, $2.50 children 6-12. Tours every 20 min 10-5 mid-May–mid-Oct.*

Brockway Mountain Drive climbs more than 900 feet above Copper Harbor to provide magnificent views of the peninsula and Lake Superior; if the day is clear, look to the northwest and you might see Isle Royale as a dark smudge on the horizon. Constructed as a WPA project during the 1930s, the drive, which is regarded as one of the most scenic in Michigan, runs nine miles between Copper Harbor and Eagle Harbor.

Estivant Pines, a stand of virgin white pine on the outskirts of Copper Harbor, has trees more than 500 years old and over 100 feet tall. The largest, "Leaning Giant," measures 23 feet in circumference, making it one of the largest in the continental United States.

❻ Marquette was founded in 1849 as a shipping center for ore from the Marquette Iron Range. Northern Michigan University, which includes one of the nation's Olympic training sites, is here. The **Marquette County Historical Society Museum** (2 N. Front St., tel. 906/226-3571) has exhibits on pioneer life, mining, and lumbering, and supplies a map outlining a historical walking tour.

Presque Isle Park, on the city's Lake Superior shore, offers free picnicking, swimming, rock hunting, and a children's zoo.

The **Michigan Iron Industry Museum** has exhibits depicting the history of Michigan's iron ranges and the people who worked them. Along with displays of mining equipment, a mine tunnel has been re-created within the museum. *8 miles west of Marquette of Hwy 492 on Forge Rd., tel. 906/475-7857. Admission free. Open May–Oct., daily 9:30–4:30.*

7 Just east of Marquette, pick up **Highway 28** to Munising, an especially scenic drive that follows the Lake Superior shoreline for 42 miles. The rock formation known as **Miner's Castle,** the only significant one accessible on foot, is five miles northeast of Munising on Route H–13 and an easy walk from the parking lot at the end of the road. Picturesque Miner's Falls is easily reached nearby. Half a dozen or so waterfalls are in Munising itself.

Pictured Rocks Cruises takes visitors on three-hour, 37-mile cruises along the shore. *Municipal Pier, tel. 906/387–2379. Fare: $15 adults, $7 children 5–12. July and Aug., daily at 9, 11, 1, 3, and 5 June and Sept. 1–Oct. 10 at 10 and 2, weather permitting.*

8 Beyond Munising is the **Pictured Rocks National Lakeshore,** which extends 40 miles along Lake Superior from Munising to Grand Marais. Sandstone cliffs rising 200 feet above the lake have been carved by wind, waves, and ice into forms bearing such names as Miner's Castle, Battleship Rock, Indian Head, and Lover's Leap. Mineral seepage has painted the rocks red (iron), blue and green (copper), and white (limestone). Several drive-in campsites are along the shore. Visitors' centers near Munising Falls and Grand Marais are open in the summer. *Admission free. Open 24 hrs. Park headquarters on Sand Point Rd. near Munising (tel. 906/387–2607) open weekdays.*

9 If you're driving toward Sault Ste. Marie on Route 28, turn north on Route 123 to visit **Tahquamenon Falls,** one of the best known of the region's many waterfalls. These are the scene of the legends of Hiawatha. Sometimes called Little Niagara, the broad upper falls is among the largest east of the Mississippi. *Tahquamenon Falls State Park, east of Paradise on Rte. M–123. $3 vehicle permit required.*

10 Continue on Route 28 (or, if you're following the entire Circle Drive around Lake Superior, cross the toll bridge from Canada) to come to the oldest settlement in Michigan, **Sault Ste. Marie** (pronounced "Soo Saint Marie"). This site was visited by the French explorer Etienne Brule between 1618 and 1622 as he made his way along the St. Marys River, which connects Lake Superior and Lake Huron. In 1668 Jacques Marquette and Claude Dablon established a mission beside the rapids and named it in honor of the Virgin Mary. Its twin city, Sault Ste. Marie, Ontario, is across the river.

The half-mile-long rapids of the St. Marys was a barrier to Lake Superior navigation until 1855, when the first lock was completed. Today the U.S. Army Corps of Engineers operates the four parallel locks, the largest and busiest lock system in the world, raising and lowering ships the 21-foot difference between Lake Superior and Lake Huron. An adjoining park has three observation platforms allowing a close view of ships in the locks. A small museum displays exhibits and films on the locks and Great Lakes shipping. *Portage St. Admission free. Park open Apr. 1–Nov. 1, daily 6 AM–midnight; visitors center open mid-May–mid-Oct., daily 9–9.*

Soo Locks Boat Tours provides two-hour, 10-mile narrated cruises on the St. Marys. The boats traverse the waterfront, pass through the American locks, travel up the river, and return. *Depart from 500 E. Portage Ave. (tel. 906/632–2512) and 1157 E. Portage Ave. (tel. 906/632–6301). Fare: $11 adults, $8.50 age 13–18, $5.25 children 6–12. Tours May 15–Oct. 15, daily 9–7. MC, V.*

Soo Locks Train Tours run rubber-tired, glass-enclosed cars on 1½-hour narrated tours of points of interest in Sault Ste. Marie and cross the International Bridge for a brief stop in Sault Ste. Marie, Ontario. *315 W. Portage Ave. (across from Soo Locks), tel. 906/635–5912. Admission: $5 adults, $3 children 6–18. Departures every half-hour Memorial Day–Labor Day, daily 9 AM–7:30 PM.*

The **Museum Ship Valley Camp** is a retired 550-foot Great Lakes freighter permanently moored at the Soo and open for tours. The hold contains a maritime museum with aquariums, a recovered lifeboat from the Edmund Fitzgerald (which sank in Lake Superior in 1975), shipwreck exhibits, a marine hall of fame, theaters, and exhibits on Great Lakes history. The adjoining **Port Adventure** complex has gift shops, a picnic area, and a historic home. *Johnston and Water Sts., tel. 906/632–3658. Admission: $5.25 adults, $4.70 over age 62, $2.95 children 6–16. Open July 1–Aug. 31, daily 9–9; May 15–June 30 and Sept. 1–Oct. 15, daily 10–6. Last ticket sold hour before closing.*

The **Tower of History** is a modern 21-story observation tower. A small museum and a slide show on the history of Sault Ste. Marie and the Great Lakes are in the lobby; an elevator leads to the observation deck, which has views of the area. *326 E. Portage Ave., tel. 906/635–3050. Admission: $2.75 adults, $1.50 children 6–16. Open July 1–Aug. 31, daily 9–9; May 15–June 30 and Sept. 1–Aug. 15, daily 10–6. Last ticket sold hour before closing.*

Dating from 1671, when Père Marquette founded a mission ⓫ here, **St. Ignace** is the northern anchor of the **Mackinac Bridge,** known as Mighty Mac, which spans the Straits of Mackinac to connect the Upper and Lower peninsulas. (Though spelled differently, the straits, Mackinac Island, and Mackinaw City are all pronounced MACK-in-aw.) Completed in 1957, the bridge is five miles long, including approaches, making it one of the longest suspension bridges in the world. The main towers are 552 feet high and the bridge floor is 199 feet above water. The main suspension cables consist of 42,000 miles of wire. The toll for passenger cars is $1.50 each way. A Mackinac Bridge Walk is held each Labor Day morning, when the two east lanes are closed to auto traffic and as many as 40,000 people cross.

The *Chief Wawatam,* one of the last hand-fired railroad-car ferries on the Great Lakes, is docked here. The St. Ignace Area Chamber of Commerce distributes a free self-guided walking-driving tour.

The **Father Marquette National Memorial and Museum** is in the Marquette unit of **Straits State Park.** A simple contemporary structure contains a bronze plaque outlining some of the pioneer priest's achievements. An adjoining museum presents slides and films each half-hour and displays artifacts relating to mission activity and 19th-century St. Ignace. There are hiking trails and outstanding views of the straits and the bridge. The

park sector east of the bridge has campgrounds and a beach. ¼
mi west of I–75 at the bridge, tel. 906/643–8620. Admission to
monument and museum free; $3 vehicle permit required. Park
open daily 9 AM–8 PM, museum mid-June–late Sept., daily
10–5.

⑫ Mackinac Island, a small island—three miles by two—in the
east end of the straits, has high cliffs along the shore, with ra-
vines, natural bridges, caves, and strange rock formations
bearing names like Arch Rock and Sugar Loaf. No cars are
allowed (except for a public utilities truck, a fire truck, and an
ambulance), so transportation to the island is by ferryboat and
on it is by bicycle, carriage, or horse. The island actively pur-
sues tourist trade with gift and souvenir shops, tearooms and
restaurants. Aside from tourism, the chief industry is the concoction of Mackinac Island fudge, made in half a dozen shops
whose sweet aroma wafts about. Since nearly every one of the
700,000 tourists who visit the island each summer buys some,
they have become known as Fudgies. Most are day-trippers;
those who wish to stay overnight must make reservations well
in advance and pay premium prices. The island can be reached
by charter plane from St. Ignace (Great Lakes Air), or Pellston
(Michigan Airways), but most visitors use a ferryboat. Arnold
Transit (tel. 906/847–3351), Shepler's Mackinac Island Ferry
(tel. 616/436–5023), and Star Line Mackinac Island Passenger
Service (tel. 906/643–7635 or 616/436–5045) operate from both
Mackinaw City and St. Ignace. The trip takes 20 minutes.
Round-trip fare: $10.50 adults, $6.50 children 5–12; $4 for bi-
cycles. Mid-Apr.–Oct, every half-hour in summer. Arnold
Transit offers some service until the winter freeze.

Indians who lived here and used it as a burial ground called it
Michilimackinac, meaning "The Turtle"; early French and
British occupiers shortened and twisted the name to Mackinac.
Long a fur-trading post, the island became home to John Jacob
Astor's American Fur Company in 1815. Tourists began to ar-
rive as early as the mid-1850s, and the **Grand Hotel,** still stand-
ing, was built in 1887.

Old Fort Mackinac, on a bluff above the harbor, is preserved as
a living-history museum. It is now part of the state park, which
occupies about 80 percent of the island. **The State Park Visitor
Center,** where you obtain tickets and literature on the fort and
the island, is adjacent to the ferry docks. Then it's a short walk
up the hill to the fort and its 14 buildings, all dating from 1780 to
1885. Costumed guides conduct tours on the hour. There are
museum exhibits and demonstrations of blacksmithing, cooking, and spinning, along with military music and the firing of
musket and cannon. Admission includes several other nearby
historic buildings related to the fort, all within easy walking
distance: The **Beaumont Memorial,** dedicated to Dr. William
Beaumont, who pioneered studies of the human digestive system; the **Benjamin Blacksmith Shop; Biddle House,** said to be
the oldest house on the island; the **Indian Dormitory,** dating
from 1838; and **McGulpin House,** a French-style log house, possibly brought to the island from Fort Michilimackinac in 1780.
Lunches are available in the **Fort Tea Room** (additional charge)
overlooking the straits. *Old Fort Mackinac, tel. 906/847–3328.*
Admission: $6 adults, $3.50 children 6–12, $18.50 family.
Combination tickets with Fort Michilimackinac or Old Mill
Creek Historic Park at Mackinaw City: $11 adults, $6.50 chil-

dren 6–12. MC, V. Fort Mackinac open June 15–Labor Day, daily 9–6; reduced hours mid-May–mid-June and after Labor Day–mid-Oct. All other buildings open June 15–Labor Day, daily 11–5.

The Stuart House Museum was the original headquarters of Astor's fur company. Its **Agency House and Warehouse** contain company records, furniture dating from 1824, and exhibits on the fur trade. *Market St. Admission: $1. Open May–Oct., Mon.–Sat. and holidays, 11–5, Sun. 1–5.*

Route M–185 makes an eight-mile circle around the rim of the island, ideal for—and crowded with—bicycles. Island bicycle concessions rent by the hour or the day; several are near the ferry landing on Huron Street. **Mackinac Island Carriage Tours** cover the scenic and historic points of interest in 1¾-hour narrated tours. *Depart from Main St., in center of shopping district, tel. 906/847–3573. Fare: $10 adults, $6 age 4–11. Tours mid-June–Labor Day, daily 8:30–5; mid-May–mid-June, daily 8:30–4; after Labor Day–mid-Oct., daily 8:30–3.*

Marquette Park, which commemorates the work of the French priest, Père Marquette, has a statue of him that was dedicated in 1909. A reconstructed bark chapel is patterned after chapels built by the 17th-century missionaries. *Huron St., tel. 906/847–3328. Admission free.*

The **Grand Hotel** was built by the railroads that reached Mackinaw City, where there were no rooms for their passengers. The 286-room hotel has a porch reputed to be the world's longest, at 880 feet. The Grand is one of the few hotels that charge visitors just to look. For years tea and cookies were served to anyone in the lobby at 4 PM, but as the hotel's fame spread, gawkers gradually outnumbered paying guests. Today it costs $5 to stroll on the porch and wander into the elegant public spaces. Those not guests may buy meals in the dining rooms or dance in the Terrace Room; after 6 PM there is no entry charge, but there is a strict dress code—ties and jackets for men, dresses for women.

❸ Anchoring the southern end of the Mackinac Bridge, **Mackinaw City** is a bustling tourist community of 900 residents. It began life as a French fur-trading post; in 1715 it became Fort Michilimackinac, remaining under French rule until 1761, when the British took control of French possessions in the Great Lakes region. In 1780–1781 the British moved to nearby Mackinac Island, building their other fort there. Tours of Mackinaw City's carefully reconstructed **Colonial Fort Michilimackinac** begin at a visitors center where exhibits help put this fort and the one on the island into historical context. The reconstruction consists of stockade and blockhouses, water and land entrances, commanding officer's house, barracks, guardhouse, storehouses, trader's houses, St. Anne's Church, priest's house, blacksmith shop, and powder magazine. The fort's history is brought to life by museum displays, murals, cooking and blacksmithing demonstrations by costumed interpreters, the firing of musket and cannon, performances of Colonial music, and a sound-and-light show in the church. Summer visitors can view archaeological work. **Mackinac Maritime Park,** reached from the visitors center, contains the restored Old Mackinac Point Lighthouse (1829), a maritime museum with Great Lakes shipping artifacts, an aquarium, several old vessels, and examples of Mackinaw boats. The reconstructed 1775 sloop *Welcome*, which sank in a storm in 1781, is anchored at the City Marina on Main Street when not sailing, and is open to the public. *Foot of Mackinac Bridge, I–75 at Exit 339, tel. 616/436–5563. Admission includes Fort Michilimackinac, Mackinac Maritime Park, and sloop* Welcome *when in port: $6 adults, $3.50 children 6–12, $18.50 family. Combination ticket with Old Mill Creek State Historic Park: $9 adults, $5.50 children 6–12. MC, V.*

Old Mill Creek State Historic Park is the site of an 18th-century industrial complex; a sawmill built here in 1780 provided lumber for the construction of Fort Mackinac. Remnants of the complex were discovered in 1972. Now there is a working water mill, a mill dam, a museum, reconstructed buildings, and an interpretive nature trail. Visitors may watch archaeological work in progress in summer. Demonstrations by costumed guides supplement a slide show and exhibits at the visitors center. *3 mi south of Mackinaw City on Rte. M–23, tel. 616/436–7301. Admission: $4 adults, $2.50 children 6–12, $12.50 family. Combination ticket with Fort Michilimackinac: $9 adults, $5.50 children 6–12. Open June 15–Labor Day, daily 9–6, reduced hours mid-May–mid-June and after Labor Day–mid-Oct.*

Before the Mackinac Bridge came into being, the Upper Peninsula was extremely isolated. The **Mackinac Bridge Museum** depicts how the bridge has changed life in the region, using exhibits, artifacts, and a short film. *Central Ave., tel. 616/436–5534. Admission free. Open Apr. 1–Nov. 1, daily 7 AM–midnight.*

Sports and Outdoor Activities

Beaches and Water Sports
Upper Peninsula
Except in the shallowest of bays, there is little swimming in Lake Superior, for even at the height of summer the waters are dangerously cold. Some unguarded Lake Michigan beaches lie along U.S. 2 between St. Ignace and Naubinway. Upper Peninsula state parks that have swimming include: Brimley (tel. 906/248–3422); F. J. McLain (tel. 906/482–0278); and Twin Lakes (tel. 906/288–3321). *$3 vehicle sticker required.*

Fishing Panfish, trout, perch, walleye, bass, northern pike, and the elusive muskellunge abound. Inland waters are excellent, and fishing is good to excellent in many parks. If your quarry is lake trout and salmon, fishing off piers sometimes brings success, especially in spring. Charter operators are found in virtually all port cities.

Golf
Mackinac Island
Grand Hotel Golf Course (tel. 906/847–3331), 9 holes; **Wawashkamo** (tel. 906/847–3871), 9 holes.

Downhill Skiing **Marquette Mountain** (1 mi south of Marquette on County Rd. 553, tel. 906/225–1155) has 16 runs, 2 chair lifts, rope tow, and snowmaking; its longest run is 1½ miles, with a vertical drop of 600 feet. Instruction, equipment rental, ski shop, restaurant, lounge/bar, entertainment.

Cross-country Skiing Many downhill ski areas and resorts have marked, groomed trails, as do several state parks. **Fort Wilkins State Park,** Copper Harbor (tel. 906/289–4215); **F. J. McLain State Park,** Hancock (tel. 906/482–0278); and **Interlocken State Park,** Interlocken (tel. 616/276–9511) are popular cross-country ski areas.

Dining and Lodging

The following dining price categories have been used: *Very Expensive*, over $25; *Expensive*, $20–$25; *Moderate*, $12–$20; *Inexpensive*, under $12.

Reservations for Mackinac Island are an absolute necessity; make them as far in advance as possible, especially for July and August. To handle the overflow of tourists whose budgets preclude a night on Mackinac Island, Mackinaw City has a large number of lodging facilities for its size. Many motels and lodges are closed in winter, however.

The following lodging price categories have been used: *Very Expensive*, over $100; *Expensive*, $75–$100; *Moderate*, $50–$75; *Inexpensive*, under $50.

Copper Harbor
Dining

Harbor Haus. Michigan's northernmost restaurant has a dining room overlooking Lake Superior and the harbor. The menu offers fresh-caught Lake Superior whitefish and trout, plus German items like Sauerbraten and Wiener Schnitzel. *1 block off U.S. 41, tel. 906/289–4502. Dress: casual. DC, MC, V. Closed mid-Oct.–May 24. Inexpensive.*

Lodging

Keweenaw Mountain Lodge. The lodge consists of rustic duplex cabins and a modern motel set on a wooded hillside. Some cabins have fireplaces. The main lodge is of logs, with rustic public spaces. *Copper Harbor, 49918, tel. 906/289–4403. 1 mi south on U.S. 41. 41 rooms. Facilities: tennis court, 9-hole golf course (fee), cable TV, restaurant and lounge in main lodge. MC, V. Closed Oct. 16–May 14. Inexpensive–Moderate.*

Lake Fanny Hooe Resort. Some two-bedroom cottages and a modern motel with private balconies and kitchenettes are to be found at this establishment on the lakeshore. The decor is north-woods modern. Campground. *Box 31, Copper Harbor 49918, tel. 906/289–4451. 4 blocks east of U.S. 41 and Rte. M–26, then 2 blocks south on Manganese Rd. 14 rooms. Facilities: beach, sauna, playground, nature trails, coin laundry, dock fishing, rental boats, motors, and canoes, rental paddleboats. MC, V. Inexpensive.*

Houghton
Dining

Nelson's Summer Place. A rustic dining room overlooking Portage Lake, it serves seafood, including lake trout and whitefish, and steaks, chicken, and veal. Children's menu, cocktail lounge. *6 mi south on U.S. 41, Houghton, tel. 906/523–4848. Reservations suggested. Dress: casual. MC, V. Closed Nov.–Apr. Inexpensive–Moderate.*

Lodging

Best Western King's Inn. A modern, comfortable motel, with pleasant rooms, some with a view of the city and valley. *215 Shelden Ave., Houghton 49931, tel. 906/482–5000. 68 rooms. Facilities: indoor pool, sauna, whirlpool, winter plug-ins. AE, DC, MC, V. Inexpensive–Moderate.*

Mackinac Island
Dining
★

Cable Room. Elegant dining in a Victorian atmosphere in the Lake View Hotel and Conference Center. Seafood, beef, and chicken are featured. Children's menu. Cocktail lounge. The hotel's Hoban St. Cafe and the Pilot House restaurant are more casual. *Main St., tel. 906/847–3384. Reservations advised. Jacket and tie advised. AE, MC, V. Expensive.*

Carriage House. The glass-enclosed dining room in the Hotel Iroquois affords a view of the Straits of Mackinac. Seafood and beef and chicken dishes are featured. Children's menu. Cocktail lounge. *Main St., tel. 906/847–3321. Reservations advised. Jacket and tie advised. MC, V. Moderate–Expensive.*

Harbor View. This dining room in the Chippewa Hotel on the lakefront overlooks the harbor. Seafood, including Lake Huron whitefish, is featured, as are New York strip steak and other beef dishes. Sunday brunch in season. Children's menu. Cocktail lounge. *Main St., tel. 906/847–3341. Reservations suggested. Jacket and tie advised. AE, MC, V. Closed mid-Oct.– mid-May. Moderate.*

Horn's Gaslight Bar and Restaurant. Sandwiches, salads, and Mexican dishes are served in a room with a Gay '90s atmosphere. Cocktail lounge with entertainment afternoons and evenings. *Main St., tel. 906/847–6145. Reservations not required. Dress: casual. MC, V. Inexpensive.*

Lodging
★
Grand Hotel. Perched amid neatly manicured grounds on a hill overlooking the Straits of Mackinac, the gleaming white Grand expresses the elegance of a bygone era. Recently remodeled from top to bottom, it has luxurious rooms and suites that are decorated with period furnishings and antiques or are in modern style. Red-coated coachmen meet guests at the ferry landing. *Mackinac Island, 49757, tel. 906/847–3331. 317 rooms. Facilities: outdoor pool, sauna, whirlpool, playground, jogging/exercise trail, rental bicycles, golf (fee), 4 tennis courts, dining rooms, lounge, entertainment. MC, V. Closed Nov.– mid-May. Very Expensive.*

Lake View Hotel and Conference Center. This restored whiteframe hotel, built in 1862, has Victorian turrets and towers and a four-level porch; a new section has been added. Rooms have Victorian furnishings. Some whirlpool suites. *Main St., 49757, tel. 906/847–3384. 85 rooms. Facilities: indoor pool, sauna, whirlpool, dining room. Closed mid-Oct.–early May. Very Expensive.*

Island House. The island's oldest hotel, built in 1852, it has large porches, Victorian turrets and towers, and spacious grounds. Recently renovated, comfortable rooms display variety in decor. *Main St., 49757, tel. 906/847–3347. 95 rooms. Facilities: radios, rental bicycles, dining room, lounge, entertainment. MC, V. Closed mid-Oct.–mid-May. Expensive–Very Expensive.*

Mission Point Resort. A massive lobby, with heavy timbers, rustic woodwork, and fireplaces, sets the tone for this more recent hotel. Rooms range from modest to spacious, including 50 two-bedroom units. *Lake Shore Dr., Box 430, 49757, tel. 906/ 847–3312. 250 rooms. Facilities: outdoor pool, whirlpools, 3 tennis courts, exercise room, playground, rental bicycles, dining room, cocktail lounge. AE, D, MC, V. Closed mid-Oct.– May. Expensive–Very Expensive.*

Chippewa Hotel. This turn-of-the-century place has rooms ranging from modest to modern, many with a lake view. The decor leans toward Victorian. *Huron St., 49757, tel. 906/847– 3341. 75 rooms. Facilities: outdoor pool, rental TV, restaurant, lounge. AE, MC, V. Closed mid-Oct.–mid-May. Moderate–Very Expensive.*

Mackinaw City
Dining
The Admiral's Table. Located opposite the ferry docks, this restaurant features informal dining with a nautical theme and specializes in broiled whitefish and trout, fried perch, prime rib, and charbroiled steaks and chops. Children's and senior citizens' menu; cocktail lounge. *502 S. Huron St., tel. 616/436–5687.*

Open daily 7 AM–10PM, closed mid-Oct.–Memorial Day. AE, MC, V. Inexpenisve–Moderate.

Teysen's Cafeteria. Standing opposite the Mackinac Island ferryboat docks, this popular cafeteria has been operated by the same family since 1927. Native whitefish and chicken pot pie are specialties, and sandwiches and salads are offered. Friendly employees carry trays to your table. *416 S. Huron St., tel. 616/436–7011. No reservations. Dress: casual. Open May 1–Oct. 31, daily 7 AM–9 PM; June–Sept., daily 7AM–10 PM. AE, MC, V. Inexpensive.*

Lodging **Ramada Inn.** Standing near the Mackinac Bridge, the motel offers pleasant, comfortable rooms in the Ramada Inn style and is open year-round. *450 S. Nicolet St., 49701, tel. 616/436–5535 or 800/272–6232. ½ mi south of bridge at Exit 338 off I–75. 155 rooms. Facilities: indoor pool, sauna, whirlpool, recreation area, dining room and coffee shop. AE, DC, D, MC, V. Inexpensive–Moderate.*

Days Inn. Overlooking Lake Huron, the motel offers comfortable rooms and many amenities. Lakefront rooms have balconies and views of the Mackinac bridge. Honeymoon suites have in-room spas. *825 S. Huron St., 49701, tel. 616/436–5557 or 800/325–2525. 82 rooms. Facilities: indoor pool, sauna, whirlpool, puttinggreen, restaurant, lounge, shops. Closed Nov.–Mar. AE, D, MC, V. Inexpensive–Moderate.*

Affordable Inns of America. Formerly the Big Mac Motor Lodge, this pleasant family motel offers roomy accommodations at reasonable prices. Located three blocks from the Mackinac Island ferries and other attractions. *206 N. Nicolet St., 49701, tel. 616/436–8961 or 800/388–9508. 53 rooms. Facilities: indoor pool, whirlpool, cable TV, winter plug-ins; restaurant and cocktail lounge adjacent. AE, D, MC, V. Inexpensive–Moderate.*

Marquette **Northwoods Supper Club.** North-country dining is set in birch-
Dining and cedar-paneled rooms with fireplaces and views of the woods. The menu includes charbroiled steaks, prime rib, chicken, and seafood; some dishes are prepared at tableside. Sunday brunch and Tuesday-evening smorgasbord. Children's menu. Cocktail lounge. *3½ mi west on U.S. 41 and Rte. M–28, tel. 906/228–4343. Reservations suggested. Dress: casual. Open weekdays 11:30 AM–11 PM, Fri. and Sat. 11:30 AM–1 AM, Sun. 10:30 AM–10 PM; closed Dec. 24–26. AE, DC, MC, V. Inexpensive–Moderate.*

Vierling Saloon and Sample Room. This renovated 1883 saloon has an antique bar and local memorabilia. The menu features sandwiches, ribs, whitefish, and steaks; children's menu; cocktail lounge. *119 S. Front St., tel. 906/228–3533. Dress: casual. Closed Sun. and holidays. MC, V. Inexpensive.*

Lodging **Cedar Motor Inn.** A pleasant, comfortable motel offering clean rooms decorated in north-woods modern. *2523 U.S. 41 W., 49855, tel. 906/228–2280. 44 rooms. Facilities: indoor pool, sauna. AE, MC, V. Inexpensive.*

Tiroler Hof Motel. Set on spacious, wooded grounds overlooking Lake Superior, this two-story motel has anAustrian motiff that includes a small chapel in the woods. The rooms are spacious and well-kept. *2 mi southeast of US 41 at 150 Carp River Hill, 49855, tel. 906/226–7516. 44 rooms. Facilities: Coin laundry, sauna (fee), restaurant, cocktail lounge, nature trails. AE, MC, V. Inexpensive.*

Munising
Dining

DogPatch. This informal family restaurant serves such specials as "Earthquake McGoon's Rib-eye Steak Dinner" (charbroiled rib-eye, potatoes, salad, onion rings, rolls) and a "Li'l Abner" burger. Fish dishes include fresh Lake Superior trout. Children's menu. Cocktail lounge. *820 E. Superior St., tel. 906/387–9948. Reservations suggested. Dress: casual. Open Sun.-Thurs. 7 AM–10 PM, Fri.–Sat. 7 AM–11 PM; closed Dec. 25. MC, V. Inexpensive.*

Ziegert's Restaurant. A family restaurant, it serves breakfast until late afternoon. Specialties are whitefish and Lake Superior trout. Children's menu. Cocktail lounge. *Rte. M–28, tel. 906/387–4067. No reservations. Dress: casual. Open weekdays 6 AM–10 PM, weekends 6:30 AM–10 PM. DC, MC, V. Inexpensive.*

Lodging

Best Western of Munising. Munising's largest and newest motel has spacious, modern rooms. *Box 310, 49862, tel. 906/387–4864 or 800/528–1234. 3 mi east on Rte. M–28. 80 rooms. Facilities: indoor and outdoor pools, sauna, whirlpool, playground, game room, color TV, winter plug-ins, restaurant. AE, DC, MC, V. Inexpensive–Moderate.*

Sault Ste. Marie
Dining

Cafe du Voyageur. A family restaurant featuring seafood, including lake trout and whitefish, and beef and chicken, plus daily specials and homemade desserts. *205 W. Portage Ave., tel. 906/632–0228. Reservations not required. Dress: casual. AE, MC, V. Closed Sun., Thanksgiving, Dec. 25. Jan. 1–Mar. 1. Inexpensive–Moderate.*

Freighters Restaurant. The dining room overlooks the Soo Locks and specializes in prime rib, seafood, and Great Lakes fish. Children's menu and cocktail lounge. *240 W. Portage Ave. in the Ojibway Hotel, tel. 906/632–4211. Reservations suggested. Dress: casual. AE, DC, MC, V. Open 6 AM–10 PM. Moderate.*

Lodging

Best Western Colonial Inn. A family motel with clean, spacious rooms and modern decor, minutes away from downtown attractions. *Box 659, 49783, tel. 906/632–2170. ¼ mi northeast of downtown on Business I–75. 58 rooms. Facilities: indoor pool, sauna, indoor recreation area. AE, DC, MC, V. Inexpensive–Moderate.*

Ramada Inn. Comfortable rooms with modern decor—what you might expect from a Ramada. Some suites. *Ashmun St., 49783, tel. 906/635–1523. 1 mi northeast on Business I–75. 138 rooms. Facilities: indoor pool, saunas, whirlpool, restaurant, lounge. AE, DC, MC, V. Inexpensive–Moderate.*

St. Ignace
Dining

The Flame. Owned by the same family for 30 years, this restaurant features seafood and prime rib. There is a daily breakfast buffet, a children's menu, and a cocktail lounge with entertainment in summer. *U.S. 2 and Church St., tel. 906/643–8554. Reservations not required. Dress: casual. DC, MC, V. Inexpensive–Moderate.*

The Galley. A family restaurant overlooking Lake Huron and Mackinac Island, it has such seafood specials as broiled whitefish, trout, and deep-fried perch, along with beef and chicken dishes and homemade soups and salads. Children's menu. Cocktail lounge. *241 State St. at harbor, tel. 906/643–7960. Reservations not required. Dress: casual. MC, V. Inexpensive–Moderate.*

Driftwood Restaurant. Informal dining in a modern setting. The Driftwood's specialty is whitefish, a Great Lakes delicacy caught in nearby waters. Pizzas available until 2 AM. Children's menu, cocktail lounge. *590 State St., across from boat docks, tel. 906/643-9133. Reservations not required. Dress: casual. AE, MC, V. Inexpensive.*

Huron Landing. This pleasant harborfront restaurant and bar serves Italian food. The lounge is open until 1 AM. *441 N. State St., tel. 906/643-9613. AE, MC, V. Inexpensive.*

Lodging **Heritage Inn.** A two-story Colonial-style motel overlooking Lake Huron and Mackinac Island. The large, comfortable rooms have modern decor, refrigerators, and balconies on the lake. *1020 N. State St., 49781, 2¼ mi north of bridge on Business I-75, tel. 906/643-7581. 40 rooms. Facilities: indoor pool, beach, whirlpool, playground, fishing, picnic tables and grill. AE, DC, MC, V. Closed Nov. 1-Apr. 14. Moderate.*

Bavarian Haus Motel. A new motel with large, modern rooms done in Bavarian style, it overlooks Lake Huron and Mackinac Island; some rooms have balconies. *1067 N. State St., 49781, 3 mi north of bridge on Business I-75, tel. 906/643-7777 or 800/448-9189. 27 rooms. Facilities: indoor pool, whirlpool, fishing, cable TV; restaurant adjacent. AE, MC, V. Closed early Nov-mid-Apr. Moderate.*

Belle Isle Motel. Set on seven acres of landscaped grounds on a hill overlooking Lake Huron and Mackinac Island, this two-story motel has large, modern, well-kept rooms. *1030 N. State St., 49781, 2½ mi north of bridge on Business I-75, tel. 906/643-8060. 47 rooms. Facilities: indoor pool, whirlpool, playground, sauna deck and patio, picnic area, cable TV; restaurant adjacent. AE, DC, MC, V. Closed mid-Oct.-early May. Inexpensive-Moderate.*

Lake Michigan's Eastern Shore

From the Mackinac area, travelers have a number of options. I-75 leads to Detroit, a drive that takes about 6 hours. If you want to return to Chicago, you can take U.S. 31 to Petoskey, then follow U.S. 131 to Grand Rapids, from where I-196 swings around the southern tip of Lake Michigan to Chicago; it'll take about 5 hours to Grand Rapids, and another 3½ hours to Chicago. Or you can stay on U.S. 31 past Petoskey and follow the eastern shore of Lake Michigan, a more meandering route that will probably entail one more overnight stop.

Numbers in the margin correspond to points of interest on the Northwestern Michigan and Upper Peninsula map.

(14) Set at the southern end of Grand Traverse Bay, **Traverse City** is the center of a region with some 500 commercial orchards and is ranked as the world's largest producer of tart cherries. **Grand Traverse Bay** offers excellent small-boat sailing, and this entire corner of the Lower Peninsula offers excellent golf courses and ski resorts (*see* Sports and Outdoor Activities, *below*). **Clinch Park** has a small zoo with exhibits on the animals, birds, and fish native to Michigan—badger, gray wolf, lynx, buffalo, hawks, and owls, among others. A ministeam train carries visitors around the zoo. *West Bay, tel. 616/922-4094. Admission free. Train rides: $1.25 adults, 75¢ under 12. Zoo open Memorial Day-Labor Day, daily 9:30 AM-7:30 PM; Apr. 15-Memori-*

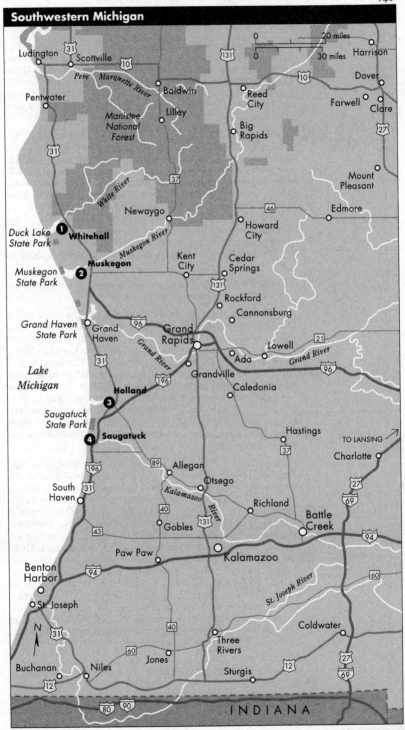

Southwestern Michigan

Ludington
Scottville
[31]
[10]
Pere Marquette River
Baldwin
Lilley
Pentwater
Manistee National Forest
[31]
White River
Newaygo
Muskegon River
1 Whitehall
Duck Lake State Park
Muskegon State Park
2 Muskegon
Kent City
Grand Haven State Park
Grand Haven
[96]
Grand River
Grand Rapids
[31]
Lake Michigan
Holland **3**
[196]
Grandville
Saugatuck State Park
Saugatuck **4**
[89]
Allegan
Otsego
Kalamazoo River
South Haven
[31]
[40]
[131]
Gobles
[43]
Paw Paw
Kalamazoo
Benton Harbor
[94]
St. Joseph
N
[31]
[40]
Buchanan
Niles
[60]
Jones
[12]
Three Rivers
[12]
Sturgis
[131]
Reed City
[10]
Big Rapids
Dover
Farwell
Clare
[27]
Mount Pleasant
[46]
Edmore
Howard City
Cedar Springs
[131]
Rockford
Cannonsburg
Lowell
[21]
Ada
Grand River
[96]
Caledonia
Hastings
[37]
TO LANSING
Charlotte
[27]
[69]
Richland
Battle Creek
[94]
St. Joseph River
Coldwater
[60]
[27]
[69]
[131]
Harrison
[131]

0   20 miles
0   30 miles

INDIANA
[80] [90]

*al Day and Labor Day–Oct. 31, daily 9:30–4:30. Train rides
daily 10–5 on same schedule.*

The **Con Foster Museum** focuses its exhibits and programs on
Grand Traverse history: Indians, blacksmithing, coopering,
harvesting maple syrup, lumbering, agriculture, and Great
Lakes shipping. *Clinch Park at 400 Boardman Ave., tel. 616/
922–4905. Admission: Memorial Day–Labor Day $1 adults,
50¢ children; free rest of year. Open Memorial Day–Labor
Day, daily 10–6; rest of the year, Tues.–Sat. 10–5.*

⑮ **Sleeping Bear Dunes National Lakeshore,** 25 miles west of Traverse City, has a 31-mile Lake Michigan shoreline and massive
sand dunes that tower nearly 500 feet above the water—said to
be the largest in the world outside the Sahara. The park has 35
miles of hiking trails and the 7.6-mile Pierce Stocking Scenic
Drive, which affords great views of the dunes and lake. More
than 50 species of animals, including white-tailed deer, red
fox, and bobcat, call the park home, as do more than 250 species
of birds. The park headquarters contains exhibits on regional
history and a slide program on the park. *Headquarters on Rte.
72, Empire, tel. 616/326–5134. Admission free. Open daily 9–
4:30.*

*Numbers in the margin correspond to points of interest on the
Southwestern Michigan map.*

Just above Manistee, U.S. 31 swings closer to the shore again,
then heads south through the **Manistee National Forest.** Twelve
miles past Ludington, at Pentwater, you may want to leave
U.S. 31 to drive on **Route BR–15,** which follows the Lake Michigan shoreline for about 25 miles to Montague. The next town on
① BR–15 is **Whitehall,** where you can visit the **White River Light
Station Museum.** In the lighthouse, built in 1875, a spiral
wrought-iron staircase leads to the museum rooms and a view
of Lake Michigan. Exhibits feature ship relics, charts, and
models. *6199 Murray Rd., Whitehall, tel. 616/894–8265, Open
Apr.–Sept. daily; Sept., weekends only. Call for schedule and
admission prices.*

Four miles past Whitehall, families may want to stop at **Deer
Park** (8 mi north of Muskegon, U.S. 31, tel. 616/766–3377, admission $6, open Memorial Day–Labor Day), an amusement
center with 16 rides, including roller coaster and water flume.
② **Muskegon,** once known as the Lumber Queen of the World, is
still the largest port on the eastern shore of Lake Michigan.
Muskegon State Park is at the north edge of the harbor entrance, **Pere Marquette Park** on the south. The **Muskegon Museum of Art** (296 W. Webster Ave., tel. 616/722–2600; admission
free; open Tues.–Sun.) features the works of such American
artists as Homer, Whistler, Hopper, and Wyeth. Six miles
south of town is another good stop for families, **Pleasure Island**
(1½ mi west of U.S. 31 on Pontaluna Rd., tel. 616/798–7857; admission $9.95 adults, $8.95 children 5–12, $7.95 children under
5; open Memorial Day–Labor Day), an aquatic amusement
park with pools, beaches, paddleboats, bumper boats, and water slides.

③ Thirty miles past Muskegon, U.S. 31 merges with I–196 in
Holland. Settled in 1847 by Dutch immigrants, Holland works
to retain its Dutch air, right down to daily street scrubbing and
millions of vibrantly-colored tulips. Attractions include the
DeKlomp Wooden Shoe and Delft Factory (Veldheer Tulip

Farm, 12755 Quincy at U.S. 31, tel. 616/399–1900); **Wooden Shoe Factory** (U.S. 31 at 16th St., tel. 616/396–6513); and the **Netherlands Museum** (12th St. and Central Ave., tel. 616/392–9084).

In the re-created **Dutch Village,** distinctive Dutch buildings, roofed with orange tiles, stand amid canals, bridges, and gardens. Live animals populate a farm. In warm weather brightly costumed girls perform klompen dances in their wooden shoes to the music of a huge Amsterdam street organ. The village has carving exhibits, windmills, shops, and a restaurant serving Dutch and American fare. *One mi north on U.S. 32, tel. 616/396–1475. Admission: $3 adults, $2 children under 12. Open July–Aug., daily 9–6; late Apr.–June and Sept.–mid-Oct., daily 9–4:30.*

On an island in the Black River is the municipal **Windmill Island** park, with canals, a working drawbridge, a miniature Dutch village called Little Netherlands, and tulip gardens surrounding a huge working windmill brought from Holland. *7th and Lincoln Sts., tel. 616/396–5433. Admission: $3.50 adults, $1.75 children under 13. Open May 1–Labor Day, daily; limited hours Labor Day–Oct. 31.*

Only a few miles past Holland, at the mouth of the Kalamazoo ❹ River, the small artists' colony of **Saugatuck** has become a trendy tourist spot with a turn-of-the-century feel. The boardwalk pier, one of the longest on the Great Lakes, overlooks a harbor with all manner of boats from yachts to dinghies. Rockhounds comb the beaches in search of so-called septarian nodules, which when halved and polished display an endless array of designs. Across the river is Saugatuck's sister city, **Douglas.**

You may want to get off I–196 past Saugatuck and drive on the more scenic lakeshore road, **Route A–2** to South Haven. From there it's another 70 miles or so to the Indiana border, and about an hour's drive through the industrial towns of Michigan City and Gary to Chicago.

Sports and Outdoor Activities

Beaches and Water Sports The beaches in the vicinity of Traverse City, including Clinch Park, are considered by some to be among the finest in Michigan. Traverse City State Park (tel. 616/947–7193) and Interlochen State Park (tel. 616/276–9511) have very good beaches.

Golf
Interlochen Interlochen (10586 U.S. 31, tel. 616/275–7311) has 18 holes available for play.

Traverse City **Cedar Hills** (4 mi west on Cedar Run Rd., tel. 616/947–8237), 9 holes; **Elmbrook** (420 Hammond Rd., tel. 616/946–9180), 18 holes; **Grand Traverse Resort** (6300 U.S. 31N, tel. 616/938–1620), 18 holes designed by Jack Nicklaus; **Green Hills** (2411 W. Silver Lake Rd., tel. 616/946–2975), 9 holes; **Mitchell Creek** (2846 3 Mile Rd., tel. 616/941–5200), 9 holes.

Holland **Crest View** (6279 96th Ave., Zeeland, tel. 616/875–8101), 18 holes; **Holland Country Club** (51 Country Club Rd., tel. 616/392–1844), 18 holes; **West Ottawa** (6045 136th St., tel. 616/399–1678), 18 holes; **Winding Creek** (8600 Ottogan St., tel. 616/396–4516), 18 holes.

Muskegon **Family Golf** (4200 Whitehall Rd., tel. 616/766–2217), 9 holes; **Fruitport** (6330 S. Harvey), 18 holes; **Chase Hammond** (2454 N. Putnam Rd., tel. 616/766–3035), 18 holes; **Lincoln** (4907 N. Whitehall Rd., tel. 616/766–2226), 18 holes; **Park View** (4600 S. Sheridan Dr., tel. 616/773–8814), 18 holes.

Saugatuck-Douglas **Clearbrook** (135th Ave., Saugatuck, tel. 616/857–2000), 18 holes; **West Shore** (14 Ferry St., Douglas, tel. 616/857–2500), 18 holes.

Downhill Skiing This region has some of the finest skiing in the Midwest. Phone ahead for schedules. For a report on snow conditions statewide, call 800/543–2937.

Boyne Highlands operates 17 runs, 7 chair lifts, a bar lift, 2 rope tows, and snowmaking; its longest run is one mile with a vertical drop of 520 feet. Instruction, equipment rental, ski shop, lodging, restaurant, lounge/bar, entertainment, heated outdoor pool. *Hedrick Rd., Harbor Springs, tel. 616/526–2171.*

Boyne Mountain has 18 runs, 11 chair lifts, rope tow, and snowmaking; its longest run is 1 mile, with a vertical drop of 450 feet. Services include instruction, equipment rental, ski shop, lodging, restaurant, lounge/bars, entertainment, heated outdoor pool. *Boyne Falls, 15 mi south of Petoskey on U.S. 131, tel. 615/549–2441 or 800/462–6963.*

Caberfae Ski Resort has 22 runs, 3 chair lifts, 5 T-bars, 3 rope tows, and snowmaking; its longest run is ½ mile, with a vertical drop of 470 feet. Instruction, equipment rental, ski shop, night skiing, lodge, restaurant, lounge/bar, entertainment. *Rte. M–55, 15 mi west of Cadillac, tel. 616/862–3301.*

Crystal Mountain Resort offers 22 runs, 3 chair lifts, rope tow, and snowmaking; its longest run is ½ mile, with a vertical drop of 375 feet. Instruction, equipment rental, ski shop, night skiing, lodging, restaurant, lounge/bar, entertainment, heated outdoor pool. *Rte. M–116 at Thompsonville, 36 mi northwest of Cadillac, tel. 616/378–2911 or 800/321–4637.*

The **Homestead** has 12 runs, 3 chair lifts, cable tow, and snowmaking; vertical drop is 375 feet. Instruction, equipment rental, ski shop, lodging, restaurant, lounge/bar, entertainment. *Glen Arbor, 8 mi north of Empire on Rte. M–22, tel. 616/334–5000.*

Nub's Nob Ski Area has 18 runs, 5 chair lifts, rope tow, and snowmaking; its longest run is ½ mile, with a vertical drop of 425 feet. Instruction, equipment rental, ski shop, restaurant, children's room, lounge/bar. *6 mi northeast of Harbor Springs on Rte. C–81, tel. 616/526–2131 or 800/878–6927.*

Petoskey Winter Sports Park has 1 run, rope tow, and snowmaking; length of run 460 feet, vertical drop 100 feet. Snack bar, sledding hills, skating rinks. *200 Division, Petoskey, tel. 616/347–4105.*

Schanty Creek-Schuss Mountain Resort has 28 runs, 6 chair lifts, 3 rope tows, and snowmaking; its longest run is 1 mile, with a vertical drop of 400 feet. Instruction, equipment rental, ski shop, lodging, restaurant, lounge/bar, indoor/outdoor heated pool. *Schuss Mountain Rd., Mancelona, U.S. 131 to Rte. M–88, 5 mi west of Mancelona, tel. 616/533–8621 or 800/748–0249.*

Sugar Loaf Resort has 20 runs, 6 chair lifts, a bar lift, and snowmaking; its longest run is 1 mile, with a vertical drop of 540 feet. Instruction, equipment rental, ski shop, lodging, restaurant, lounge/bar, entertainment, heated outdoor pool. *County Rd. 651, Cedar, 18 mi northwest of Traverse City, tel. 616/228–5461 or 800/748–0117.*

Dining and Lodging

The following dining price categories have been used: *Very Expensive*, over \$25; *Expensive*, \$20–\$25; *Moderate*, \$12–\$20; *Inexpensive*, under \$12.

The following lodging price categories have been used: *Very Expensive*, over \$100; *Expensive*, \$75–\$100; *Moderate*, \$50–\$75; *Inexpensive*, under \$50.

Holland
Dining

The Hatch. Specialties are prime rib, fresh seafood, steaks, and a garden-fresh salad bar. The dining room is casual, with contemporary nautical decor, and in summer there's a tropical outdoor patio bar. An indoor lounge features live entertainment Wednesday to Saturday. Sunday brunch served. *1870 Ottawa Beach Rd., tel. 616/399–9120. Reservations advised. Dress: casual. Open Mon.–Thurs. 11:30 AM–2 PM and 5:30–11 PM, Fri. and Sat. 11:30–11:30, Sun. 11:30 AM–7 PM; closed for lunch on Sat. and on Thanksgiving, Dec. 25, Jan. 1. AE, MC, V. Moderate.*

Dave's Garage. A restaurant aptly named for its automobile motif. The wide-ranging menu includes crab legs and other seafood, as well as steaks and prime rib. Cocktail lounge, imorted beer, fairly extensive wine list. *478 E. 16th St., tel. 616/392–3017. Reservations advised. Dress: casual. Open Mon.–Sat. 11 AM–2 PM and 4:45–10 PM. MC, V. Inexpensive–Moderate.*

Lodging

Point West Inn and Conference Center. Set on Lake Macatawa, the inn has luxurious rooms in modern decor, including suites and efficiency units and a four-bedroom cottage. Package plans. *2150 South Shore Dr., Macatawa, 49434, tel. 616/335–5894. 5 mi west, at west end of Lake Macatawa. 67 rooms. Facilities: pool, beach, 5 tennis courts, playground, dock (fee), paddleboat, sailboat, ski rental, restaurant, lounge. AE, DC, MC, V. Very Expensive.*

Budget Host Wooden Shoe Motel. A bright, sunny motel with some Dutch touches around the edges. No-smoking rooms and suites, package plans. *465 U.S. 31, 49423, tel. 616/392–8521 or 800/835–7427, ext. 630. U.S. 31 and 16th St. 29 rooms. Facilities: outdoor pool, satellite TV, tanning booth (fee), miniature golf (fee), restaurant. AE, DC, MC, V. Inexpensive.*

Comfort Inn. A newer motel with modern, comfortable, spacious rooms and public spaces. Some whirlpool rooms. Close to the Dutch Village and Windmill Island. *422 E. 32d St., 49423, tel. 616/392–1000 or 800/228–5150. 71 rooms. Facilities: outdoor pool and whirlpool, in-room movies; restaurant adjacent. AE, DC, MC, V. Inexpensive.*

Muskegon
Dining

Tohado House. The Victorian decor of this American restaurant blends in with the building, which dates to 1865. Specialties include steak, prime rib, and seafood. *450 W. Western Ave., tel. 616/726–4377. Closed Sun. and lunch Sat. AE, DC, MC, V. Moderate.*

Maxi's Restaurant and Nightspot. A daytime restaurant serving American and Mexican dishes becomes a popular night spot after 9 PM, with dancing Monday to Saturday. *576 Seminole Rd., tel. 616/733–3134. AE, MC, V. Closed Dec. 24 and 25. Inexpensive.*

Lodging **Muskegon Harbor Hilton.** A new hotel downtown near Muskegon Lake, it has spacious rooms with modern decor and comfortable appointments. *939 3rd St., 49440, tel. 616/722–0100 or 800/445–8667. 201 rooms. Facilities: indoor pool, sauna, whirlpool, steamroom, exercise room, parking ramp, restaurant, lounge. AE, DC, MC, V. Moderate–Expensive.*

Days Inn. There are two double beds in each room as well as modern, comfortable furnishings, touch-tone phones, and cable TV. *150 E. Seaway Dr., 49444, tel. 616/739–9429. 4½ mi south on I–96 and U.S. 31. 152 rooms. Facilities: indoor pool, 24-hr restaurant. AE, DC, MC, V. Inexpensive.*

Traverse City **Reflections Restaurant.** Sitting atop the Waterfront Inn, the
Dining dining room overlooks East Bay and Old Mission Peninsula. House specials are seafood (from both the East Coast and the Great Lakes), premium steaks, and prime rib. Raw-fish bar. Children's menu. Cocktail lounge with entertainment. Sunday brunch. *2061 U.S. 31 N. at Four Mile Rd., tel. 616/938– 2321. Reservations suggested. Dress: casual. Open daily 7 AM–3 PM and 5–10 PM; closed Dec. 24 and 25. AE, DC, MC, V. Moderate.*

D. J. Kelly's. A popular, casual restaurant with modern decor. Seafood and pasta highlight the menu, as well as fondues and veal, chicken, and beef dishes. Children's menu. Cocktail lounge. *120 Park St., tel. 616/941–4550. Reservations advised. Dress: casual. Open Mon.–Thurs. 11–10, Fri. and Sat. 11–11, Sun. 5–9; closed Thanksgiving, Dec. 25. AE, MC, V. Inexpensive–Moderate.*

Embers on the Bay. Modern, casual dining room overlooks Grand Traverse Bay. The house special is a one-pound porkchop dinner; also on the menu are seafood and beef dishes and daily early-bird specials. Children's menu. Cocktail lounge. *5 mi north of Traverse City at 5555 U.S. 31 N, in Acme, tel. 616/ 938–1300. Reservations advised. Dress: casual. Open Mon.– Thurs. 5–10 PM, Fri. and Sat. 5–11 PM, Sun. 10 AM–2 PM and 5–9 PM; closed Dec. 24 and 25. No dinner Nov. 1–Apr. 1. Sun. and Mon. AE, DC, MC, V. Inexpensive–Moderate.*

Lodging **Waterfront Inn.** The inn, on Grand Traverse Bay, has a 775-foot sand beach. All rooms have a view of the water; 56 are efficiencies with kitchenettes and dining tables. Weekend packages. *Box 1736, 49685, tel. 616/938–1100 or 800/678–4011. 2061 U.S. 31 N. at Four Mile Rd. 128 rooms. Facilities: indoor pool, whirlpool, sauna, sun deck, boat dock, restaurant, lounge, jet ski, surf jet, paddleboat rental. AE, DC, MC, V. Expensive– Very Expensive.*

Heritage Inn. The low white frame motel has a Colonial look; the spacious rooms have modern decor and most have two-person whirlpools. Some waterbeds. The pool/patio area is pleasantly secluded. *417 Munson Ave., 49684, tel. 616/947–9520. 39 rooms. Facilities: outdoor pool, exercise room, game room, tanning bed (fee), winter plug-ins. AE, MC, V. Expensive.*

Hampton Inn. A new motel set opposite a state park beach, with airy, comfortable rooms. *1000 U.S. 31 N, 49684, tel. 616/ 946–8900 or 800/426–7866. 4 mi east on U.S. 31 and Rte. M–72. 127 rooms. Facilities: indoor pool, whirlpool, free Continental breakfast, cable TV. AE, DC, MC, V. Moderate.*

Index

Acadia, ME, *103–109*
**Acadia National
  Park, ME,** *93,
  96–97, 103–107*
Bar Harbor Trolley
  tours, *104*
Cadillac Mountain,
  ME, *105*
camping, *107*
Hulls Cove approach,
  104
National Park Tours,
  104
Ocean Trail, *104*
outdoor activities,
  106–107
Sand Beach, *104*
sports, *106–107*
Thunder Hole, *104*
Alabama. *See also
  specific towns*
children, *596*
seasonal events, *595*
tourist information,
  594
Alexandria, VA,
  380–382
boyhood home of
  Robert E. Lee, *382*
Christ Church, *382*
dining, *382, 385–386*
Gadsby's Tavern
  Museum, *382*
Lee-Fendall House,
  382
lodging, *386*
shopping, *382*
Torpedo Factory Art
  Center, *382*
Amelia Island, FL,
  475, 485, 487
**American
  Automobile
  Association (AAA),**
  10
Amherst, MA, *185,
  189*
Amtrak, *10*
**Annandale, NY,
  Montgomery Place,**
  161
Apalachicola, FL,
  630
John Gorrie State
  Museum, *630*

Raney House, *630*
Trinity Episcopal
  Church, *630*
**Apalachicola
  National Forest, FL,**
  630
**Aqualand Wildlife
  Park, WI,** *718*
Aquariums
Aquarium of the
  Americas, LA, *575*
Gulfarium, FL, *619*
John G. Shedd
  Aquarium, IL, *657*
Marine Aquarium,
  McKown Point, ME,
  85
Mystic Marinelife
  Aquarium, CT, *220*
National Aquarium,
  Washington, D.C.,
  355
New England
  Aquarium, *27*
Woods Hole, MA, *250*
Arlington, VA
Arlington House, *380*
Arlington National
  Cemetery, *380*
dining, *386*
lodging, *386*
Arrowhead, MN,
  724–731
dining, *730–731*
Lake Superior circle
  drive, *728–729*
lodging, *730–731*
outdoor activities,
  729–730
scenic U.S. 61, *724,
  726*
shopping, *729*
sports, *729–730*
Ashland, WI, *719,
  722*
Atlantic Beach, FL,
  485
**Audubon, John
  James,** *304*
Audubon, PA, *304*
Auto club, *10*

Baileys Harbor, WI,
  708, 712
Baker Island, ME,

105–106
Bar Harbor, ME,
  103–104
arts, *109*
Bar Harbor Historical
  Society Museum,
  103–104
dining, *107–108*
lodging, *108*
nightlife, *109*
outdoor activities,
  106–107
shopping, *106*
sports, *106–107*
Barnstable, MA, *254,
  265*
**Bartholomew's
  Cobble, MA,** *170*
Bash Bish Falls, MA,
  170
Bass Harbor, ME,
  105
Bath, ME, *80, 84, 88*
Baton Rouge, LA,
  560–568
arts, *567*
Destrehan Plantation,
  564
dining, *563, 565–566*
Houmas House, *564*
lodging, *565–566*
Louisiana Arts &
  Science Center
  Riverside Museum,
  563
Louisiana State
  University, *563*
Madewood (mansion),
  564
Magnolia Mound
  Plantation, *563*
nightlife, *567*
Nottoway Plantation,
  564
Oak Alley, *564*
Old Arsenal Museum,
  562
Old State Capitol,
  562–563
outdoor activities, *565*
Pentagon Barracks,
  562
Samuel Clemens
  Riverboat, *563*
San Francisco (house),

564
Southern University,
  563
State Capitol
  Building, *562*
Tezcuco (cottage), *564*
Bay St. Louis, MS,
  602
Bayfield, WI, *719*
Apostle Island Cruise
  Service, *720*
Apostle Island
  National Lakeshore
  Visitors Center, *719*
Cooperage Museum,
  720
dining, *722–723*
historic homes, *719*
lodging, *723*
Beaches
Amelia Island, FL,
  485
Atlantic Beach, FL,
  485
Cape Cod, *254*
Charlestown, RI, *233*
Chicago, *667–668*
Daytona, FL, *482,
  485*
Door County, WI,
  710–711
Edisto Beach State
  Park, SC, *443*
Florida Panhandle,
  623–624
Fort Clinch State
  Park, FL, *486*
Golden Isles, GA,
  467
Grand Strand, SC,
  420
Gulf Islands National
  Seashore, MS, *601*
Gulf Shores public
  beach, AL, *608*
Hammonasset Beach
  State Park, CT, *217*
Hampton Beach, NH,
  63–64
Hilton Head Island,
  SC, *445, 447*
Huntington Beach
  State Park, SC, *418*
Jacksonville Beach,
  FL, *486*

Beaches *(continued)*
Jekyll Island, GA, *470*
Jenness Beach, NH, *64*
Kathryn Abbey Hanna Park, FL, *486*
Kennebunk Beach, ME, *76*
Kennebunkport, ME, *76*
Kiawah Island, SC, *443*
Little St. Simons, GA, *468–469*
Little Talbot Island State Park, FL, *475–476*
Long Sands Beach, ME, *76*
Myrtle Beach, SC, *420*
Napatree Point, Watch Hill, RI, *228*
Narragansett, RI, *230, 233*
Nauset Beach, MA, *254*
Neptune Beach, FL, *486*
New Hampshire, *67*
Newport, RI, *243, 244*
North Shore, MA, *55*
Ocean Beach State Park, New London, CT, *218, 222*
Ogunquit, ME, *76*
Panama City Beach, FL, *620*
Rocky Neck State Park, Niantic, CT, *222*
Sea Island, GA, *470*
South Carolina, *435*
South Kingstown, RI, *233*
St. Augustine, FL, *486*
St. Simons, GA, *468*
Traverse City, MI, *747*
Waveland, MS, *598*
Westerly, RI, *233*
Wisconsin Lakeshore, *710–711*
Beacon, NY, *158*
Bear Mountain, NY, *163*
Bear Mountain State Park, NY, *156–157*
Beaufort, SC, *443*
Beaufort Museum, *444*

dining, *448*
George Elliott House, *443*
Henry C. Chambers Waterfront Park, *444*
John Mark Verdier House, *443*
lodging, *448*
Old Point, *444*
St. Helena's Episcopal Church, *444*
Becket, MA, *183–184*
Bellefield Nature Center, SC, *418*
Berkeley Plantation, VA, *392*
The Berkshires, MA, *170–184*
arts, *183–184*
children, *112–113*
dining, *176–183*
lodging, *176–183*
nightlife, *184*
outdoor activities, *175–176*
shopping, *174–175*
sports, *175–176*
Biddeford, ME, *75*
Big Bay State Park, WI, *720*
Biloxi, MS
Biloxi Tour Train, *599*
dining, *600, 602–603*
Gulf Marine State Park, *600*
L.A. Cruise, *600*
lighthouse, *599*
lodging, *603*
Marine Education Center, *600*
Point Cadet Plaza, *600*
Sailfish Shrimp Tour, *600*
Small Craft Harbor, *599*
Bird-in-Hand, PA, *317*
Black history
African Meeting House, *22*
Black Heritage Trail, *22*
Black History National Recreation Trail, *339*
Frederick Douglass National Historic Site, *360–361*
Julee Cottage Museum of Black

History, *615*
King-Tisdell Cottage, *458*
Martin Luther King Library, *354*
Museum of Afro-American History, *22*
National Museum of African Art, *345*
Penn School Historic District, *444*
Smith Robertson Museum, *549*
York W. Bailey Museum, *444*
Blue Hill, ME, *96, 98–99, 103*
Boone Hall Plantation, SC, *432*
Boothbay Harbor, ME, *85*
boat trip, *86–87*
dining, *88*
lodging, *88*
Marine Aquarium, *85*
nightlife, *92*
Boothbay, ME, *80, 84–85, 88*
Boston, MA, *17–49*
Acorn Street, *22*
African Meeting House, *22*
arriving and departing, *16–17, 113–115, 199*
Arthur M. Sackler Museum, *33*
arts, *47–48*
Back Bay, *28–30*
Beacon Hill, *19–20*
Bed and Breakfast Associates Bay Colony, *43*
Black Heritage Trail, *22*
Boston Children's Museum, *27*
Boston Common, *19*
Boston Public Library, *29*
Boston Tea Party, *27*
Botanical Museum, *33*
Bunker Hill Monument, *25*
Busch-Reisinger Museum, *32*
Cambridge, *32–33*
Cambridge Discovery, *32*

Central Wharf, *27*
Charles Street, *22*
Charlestown, *24–25*
Charlestown Navy Yard, *24*
Chestnut Street, *22*
children, *15–16, 27*
Chinatown, *27–28*
Christian Science Church, *29–30*
churches, *19, 24, 25, 29*
Combat Zone, *26*
Computer Museum, *27*
Copley Place, *29*
Copley Square, *29*
Copp's Hill Burying Ground, *24*
dining, *22, 24, 26, 29, 30, 35–47*
Esplanade, *22–23*
Faneuil Hall, *26*
Fens, *31–32*
Fenway Park, *31*
financial district, *25–28*
Fogg Art Museum, *32*
getting around in, *17–18*
Gibson House, *28*
Globe Corner Bookstore, *25*
Harvard Square, *32*
Harvard University, *32–33*
Hayden Planetarium, *23*
Isabella Steward Gardner Museum, *31*
John Hancock Tower, *29*
Kenmore Square, *31*
King's Chapel, *25*
King's Chapel Burying Ground, *25*
lodging, *43–47*
Longfellow National Historic Site, *33*
Louisburg Square, *22*
Massachusetts Institute of Technology, *33*
Mt. Vernon Street, *22*
Mugar Omni Theater, *23*
Museum of Afro-American History, *22*
Museum of Fine Arts, *31*

Museum of Science, *23*
museums, *22, 23, 24,*
27, 28, 31, 32
New England
Aquarium, *27*
nightlife, *48–49*
North End, *23–24*
observatory, *29*
Old Granary Burial
Ground, *19*
Old North Church, *24*
Old South Meeting
House, *26*
Old State House, *26*
Park Street Church,
19
Park Street Station,
19
Paul Revere House, *24*
Paul Revere Mall, *24*
Peabody Museum of
Archaeology and
Ethnology, *33*
Prudential Center
Skywalk, *30*
Public Garden, *28*
Quincy Market, *26–27*
Radcliffe College, *33*
Rutland Square, *30*
shopping, *29, 34–35*
South End, *30*
sports, *31, 35*
St. Stephen's Church,
24
State House, *19*
Symphony Hall, *30*
Tenshin Garden, *31*
tourist information, *43*
tours, *18*
Trinity Church, *29*
Union Oyster House,
23
Union Park, *30*
USS *Constitution*, *24*
Boulder Junction,
WI, *718*
Branford, CT, *215*
Brewster, MA, *254,*
263, 267
Bridgeport CT
Barnum Museum, *204*
Beardsley Zoological
Gardens, *204*
Captain's Cove
Seaport, *204*
dining, *207*
Discovery Museum,
204
lodging, *207–209*
British travelers, *2–4*

Brookgreen Gardens,
SC, *418*
Brunswick, ME, *80,*
83
arts, *92*
Bowdoin College,
83–84
Bowdoin College
Museum of Art, *84*
dining, *89*
Peary-MacMillan
Arctic Museum, *84*
Burnside, LA, *566*
Bus travel, *10*
Busch Gardens
amusement park,
335, 398
Bynum Mounds, MS,
545

Calumet, MI, *732,*
734
Cambridge, MA,
32–33
Camden Hills State
Park, ME, *95*
Camden, ME, *92, 95*
arts, *103*
dining, *99*
lodging, *99–100*
outdoor activities,
97–98
shopping, *97*
Canaan, NY, *163*
Cape Cod, *248–268*
arriving and
departing, *199, 248,*
250
arts, *267–268*
beaches, *260*
bed-and-breakfasts,
264
children, *199*
dining, *260–264*
lodging, *264–267*
nightlife, *268*
outdoor activities,
258–260
seasonal events, *198*
shopping, *256–257*
sports, *258–260*
tourist information,
264
tours, *248–249*
Cape Cod Museum of
Natural History, *254*
Cape Cod National
Seashore, *254–255,*
260
Cape Elizabeth, ME,

87
Car rentals, *9–10*
Car travel, *9–10*
Carter's Grove
Plantation, VA, *398*
Cash machines, *11*
Castine, ME, *92,*
95–96, 100, 103
Cedarburg, WI,
702–704
Cedar Creek
Settlement, *704*
Cedar Creek Winery,
704
covered bridge, *704*
dining, *712*
historic houses, *704*
Stagecoach Inn, *704*
Stone and Century
House Tour, *704*
Uihlein Antique
Racing Car Museum,
704
tourist information,
704
Centerville, MA, *265*
Charlemont, MA, *174*
Charles Towne
Landing State Park,
SC, *432*
Charleston, SC,
424–442
Aiken-Rhett Mansion,
426
American Military
Museum, *430*
arts, *441–442*
Calhoun Mansion, *431*
Charleston Museum,
426
children, *414*
Circular
Congregational
Church, *429*
City Hall, *430*
College of Charleston,
428
Confederate Museum,
428
Congregation Beth
Elohim, *428*
dining, *428, 435–437*
Dock Street Theatre,
429
Edmonston-Alston
House, *431*
Emanuel African
Methodist Episcopal
Church, *428*
Exchange

Building/Provost
Dungeon, *430*
excursions from,
431–433
Four Corners to the
Battery, *430–431*
French Huguenot
Church, *429*
getting around in, *424*
Gibbes Museum of
Art, *429*
Heyward-Washington
House, *430*
Joseph Manigault
Mansion, *426*
lodging, *437–441*
Marion Square Area,
426–428
market area, *428*
Market Hall, *428*
Nathaniel Russell
House, *430*
nightlife, *442*
Old Citadel Building,
428
Old City Market, *428*
Old Powder Magazine,
429
resort islands,
440–441
shopping, *428,*
433–434
sports, *434–435*
St. John's Lutheran
Church, *429*
St. Michael's
Episcopal Church,
430
St. Philip's Episcopal
Church, *429*
Thomas Elfe
Workshop, *429*
tourist information,
426
tours, *424–425*
Unitarian Church, *429*
White Point Gardens,
431
Charlestown, RI,
228–229
Burlingame State
Park, *229*
Fort Ninigret, *229*
Indian Burial Ground,
229
Indian Church, *229*
Kimball Wildlife
Refuge, *228*
Ninigret National
Wildlife Refuge, *228*

Charlottesville, VA,
401–404
arts, *410*
children, *335*
dining, *403, 408–409*
downtown historic
district, *403*
Historic Michie
Tavern, *404*
lodging, *409–410*
Monticello, *403*
nightlife, *410*
shopping, *403, 407*
sports, *407–408*
tourist information,
401
University of Virginia,
403
Chatham, MA, *251,
266*
Chicago, *644–685*
Adler Planetarium,
657
Amoco Building, *648*
arriving and
departing, *643–644*
Art Institute of
Chicago, *649*
arts, *682–684*
Associates Center,
646–647
Auditorium Theatre,
651
beach, *667–668*
Berghoff Restaurant,
650
Biograph Theater, *661*
Blackstone Hotel, *652*
Blackstone Theatre,
652
Buckingham Fountain,
651
Carbide and Carbon
Building, *646*
Carson Pirie Scott
(department store),
649
Chicago Academy of
Sciences, *662*
Chicago Board of
Trade, *650*
Chicago City
Hall-Cook County
Building, *648*
Chicago Hilton and
Towers, *652*
Chicago Historical
Society, *662*
Chicago Mercantile
Exchange, *649*

Chicago Public
Library Cultural
Center, *648*
Chicago Sports Hall of
Fame, *658*
Chicago Temple, *648*
Chicago Theological
Seminary, *656*
children, *642*
Civic Opera House,
649
Court Theatre, *655*
Daley Center, *648*
dance, *683*
Dearborn Park, *652*
dining, *652, 655, 658,
661, 668–677*
downtown, *646–651*
downtown south,
651–653
Ernest Hemingway's
boyhood home, *664*
Federal Center and
Plaza, *650*
Field Museum of
Natural History, *657*
film, *683–684*
First National Bank
Plaza, *649*
Fisher Building, *651*
Frank Lloyd Wright
Home and Studio,
663
Franklin Building, *652*
getting around in, *645*
Grant Park, *651–652*
Harold Washington
Library Center, *651*
Heller House, *655*
historic houses,
654–656, 661–664
Hyde Park, *653–657*
IBM Building, *660*
John G. Shedd
Aquarium, *657*
Joseph Regenstein
Library, *655*
Kenwood, *653–657*
Lincoln Avenue, *661*
Lincoln Park, *660–662*
Lincoln Park
Conservatory, *660*
Lincoln Park Zoo, *660*
lodging, *677–681*
Lutheran School of
Theology, *655*
Mandel Hall, *655*
Marina City, *660*
Marshall Field & Co.,
648

McCormick Place
Convention Hall, *656*
Midway Plaisance, *656*
Midwest Stock
Exchange, *650*
Monadnock Building,
651
Moody Bible Institute,
658
Museum of Science
and Industry, *653*
music, *682*
Navy Pier, *657*
nightlife, *684–685*
Oak Park, *663–664*
Oak Park Visitors
Center, *664*
Old Town Triangle,
662
One Financial Place,
650
Oriental Institute, *656*
Page Brothers
Building, *650*
Palmer House, *649*
Pierce Hall, *655*
Promontory
Apartments, *653*
Promontory Point, *653*
Prudential Building,
648
Pumping Station, *658*
Quaker Oats world
headquarters, *660*
River City, *652*
River North, *657–660*
River North
Concourse, *658*
Robie House, *656*
Rock and Roll
McDonald's, *660*
Rockefeller Memorial
Chapel, *656*
Roosevelt University,
651
Sandmeyer's
Bookstore, *652*
Sears Tower, *650*
seasonal events,
641–642
Sheffield/De Paul
neighborhood, *661*
Soldier Field, *657*
sports, *667, 668*
St. Thomas the
Apostle Church and
School, *655*
State of Illinois
Center, *648–649*

SuHu district, *658*
theater, *682–683*
33 West Kinzie Street,
660
tourist information,
640
tours, *645–646*
Tribune Tower, *657*
Union Station, *650*
Unity Temple, *664*
University of Chicago,
655
University of Chicago
Administration
Building, *655*
University of Chicago
Bookstore, *655*
Water Tower, *658*
Windermere House,
653
Wrigley Building, *657*
Children, *4*
Alabama, *596*
Berkshires, MA,
112–113
Boston, MA, *15–16,
27*
Cape Cod, MA, *199*
Charleston, SC, *414*
Charlottesville, VA,
335
Chicago, IL, *642*
Connecticut, *198*
Florida, *414, 596*
Gettysburg, PA, *272*
Gulfport, MS, *595*
Hershey, PA, *272*
Hilton Head Island,
SC, *414*
Hudson Valley, NY,
112–113
Lancaster County,
PA, *272*
Louisiana, *526*
Maine, *16*
Massachusetts, *16,
112–113*
Michigan, *643*
Milwaukee, WI, *642*
Mississippi, *526, 596*
Myrtle Beach, SC,
414
Nashville, TN, *525*
New Hampshire, *16*
New Orleans, LA, *526*
New York City, *112*
Ontario, *643*
Orlando, FL, *595*
Philadelphia, PA,
271–272

Index 755

plane travel, *8*
Rhode Island, *198–199*
Richmond, VA, *335*
Savannah, GA, *414*
St. Simons Island, GA, *414*
Washington, D.C., *334–335*
Williamsburg, VA, *335*
Wisconsin, *642*
Churchtown, PA, *317*
Civil War
Battle of Shiloh, *542–543*
Battle of Tupelo, *545*
Confederate Museum, *428*
Corinth, MS, *542–543*
Ford's Theater, *354–355*
Fort Jackson, SC, *459–460*
Fort Morgan, LA, *608*
Fort Pulaski, SC, *459*
Fort Reno, *360*
Fort Sumter National Monument, SC, *431–432*
Fredericksburg and Spotsylvania National Military Park, VA, *385*
Gettysburg, PA, *325–331*
Manassas National Battlefield Park, VA, *406–407*
Museum and White House of the Confederacy, Richmond, VA, *388–391*
National Civil War Wax Museum, Gettysburg, PA, *326*
Natural Bridge Battlefield State Historic Site, FL, *632*
northern Virginia battlefields, *385*
Port Hudson State Commemorative Area, LA, *562*
Shiloh National Military Park, TN, *535*
Ship Island, MS, *598*

Vicksburg National Military Park, MS, *550*
Clinton, CT, *217*
Cocoa Beach, FL, *487–488*
Cold Spring, NY, *163–164*
Cold Spring-on-Hudson, NY, *158*
Colonial Williamsburg. *See* Williamsburg
Columbia, PA
Market House and Dungeon, *313*
Watch and Clock Museum of the National Association of Watch and Clock Collectors, *313*
Wrights Ferry Mansion, *313*
Connecticut. *See also specific towns*
children, *198*
arts, *226*
dining, *207–214, 222–226*
lodging, *207–214, 222–226*
nightlife, *226*
shopping, *206–207, 221*
sports, *207, 221*
tourist information, *197*
Constitution Island, NY, *157*
Coolidge, Calvin, *185*
Copper Falls State Park, WI, *719*
Copper Harbor, MI, *734*
Brockway Mountain Drive, *734*
Delaware Copper Mine Tours, *734*
dining, *740*
Estivant Pines, *734*
Fort Wilkins State Park, MI, *734*
lodging, *740*
Corinth, MS, *542–543*
Cos Cob, CT, *202*
Cotuit, MA, *263*
Cranberry Isles, ME, *105*

Crescent Beach State Park, ME, *87*
Cumberland Island, GA, *470–471*
Cypress Gardens, SC, *433*

Danvers, MA, *56*
Daufuskie Island, SC, *445*
Davis, Jefferson, *598*
Daytona Beach FL, *488–489*
Daytona, FL
beaches, *482, 485*
Birthplace of Speed Antique Car Show and Swap Meet, *482*
Birthplace of Speed Museum, *482*
Bulow Plantation Ruins State Historic Site, *481*
The Casements, *482*
dining, *483*
Halifax Historical Society Museum, *482*
Museum of Arts and Sciences, *482*
Ormond Beach, *482*
shopping, *483*
Deer Island, MS, *600*
Deer Isle, ME, *92, 96, 100–101*
Deerfield, MA, *190*
Dennis, MA, *254, 262*
Destin, FL, *619–620*
Destin Fishing Museum, *619–620*
dining, *624–625*
Eden State Gardens, *620*
lodging, *625*
Museum of the Sea and Indian, *620*
Seaside, *620*
Dickinson, Emily, *185*
Disabled travelers, *4–5*
plane travel, *9*
Disney World. *See also* Orlando, FL
Adventureland, *500*
Animation Tour, *501*
Backstage Studio, *501*
Cinderella's Castle, *498–500*
dining, *507–510*

Discovery Island, *502*
Disney-MGM Studios Theme Park, *501*
Epcot Center, *500–501*
Epic Stunt Spectacular, *501*
Fantasyland, *500*
Frontierland, *500*
Future World, *501*
getting around in, *497*
Great Movie Ride, *501*
Liberty Square, *500*
lodging, *512–515*
Magic Kingdom, *498–500*
Mickey's Starland, *500*
Muppet Studios, *501*
nightlife, *519–520*
River Country, *502*
Spaceship Earth, *500–501*
Star Tours, *501*
tickets, *497–498*
Tomorrowland, *500*
Typhoon Lagoon, *501*
World Showcase, *501*
Door County, WI, *706–715. See also specific towns*
arts, *715*
beaches, *710–711*
dining, *712–713*
lodging, *712–715*
sports, *710–712*
Douglas, MI, *747*
Douglass, Frederick, *360–361*
Dover, NH, *68*
Drayton Hall Plantation, SC, *432*
Duluth, MN, *725–726*
Aerial Lift Bridge, *726*
A. M. Chisolm Museum, *726*
Canal Park Marine Museum, *726*
Depot, *726*
Depot Square, *726*
dining, *730–731*
Glensheen, *726*
Lake Superior Museum of Transportation, *726*
lodging, *731*
shopping, *729*
Skyline Parkway Drive, *726*

Duluth, MN
(continued)
St. Louis County
Heritage and Arts
Center, *726*
St. Louis County
Historical Museum,
726
Durham, NH, *68*

Eagle Island, ME, *83*
East Haven, CT, *215*
East Orleans, MA,
267
East Petersburg, PA,
318
East Sandwich, MA,
265
Eastham, MA
Cape Cod National
Seashore, *254, 260*
Salt Pond Visitor
Center, *254*
**Edisto Beach State
Park, SC,** *443, 447*
Edisto Island, SC,
443, 448
Egg Harbor, WI
Chief Oshkosh
Museum, *709*
Cupola House, *709*
lodging, *712–713*
**Eglin Air Force
Base, FL,** *618–619*
**Eleanor Roosevelt
National Historic
Site,** *159*
Ellison Bay, WI, *713*
Ellsworth, ME, *106*
Ely, MN
Boundary Waters
Canoe Area, *727*
Superior National
Forest, *727*
Emerald Mound, MS,
552
Emergencies, *11*
Ephraim, WI, *713*
Ephrata, PA, *318*
Essex, MA, *53, 56*
Evanston, IL, *685*
Loyola University, *685*
Northwestern
University, *685*
Exeter, NH, *63*
dining, *63, 68–69*
Gilman Garrison
House, *63*
lodging, *69*
Phillips Exeter

Academy, *63*

Fairfield, CT
Birdcraft Museum, *204*
Connecticut Audubon
Society, *203*
lodging, *208*
Fall River, MA, *249*
Battleship Cove, *249*
Fall River Heritage
State Park, *249*
Marine Museum at
Fall River, *249*
Falmouth, MA, *250*
Ashumet Holly and
Wildlife Sanctuary,
251
Conant House, *251*
Congregational
Church, *250*
dining, *261*
Julia Wood House,
250–251
lodging, *264–265*
False River, LA, *562*
**Fernandina Beach,
FL,** *475*
Amelia Lighthouse,
475
Fort Clinch State
Park, *475*
Old Town, *475*
St. Peter's Episcopal
Church, *475*
Fish Creek, WI, *713*
Flagler Beach, FL,
489–490
Florida. *See also
specific towns*
arts, *495–496*
beaches, *484–485*
children, *414, 596*
dining, *487–495*
lodging, *487–495*
nightlife, *495–496*
seasonal events, *412,
595*
tourist information,
412, 594
Florida Panhandle,
614–630
arts, *629*
beach, *623–624*
dining, *624–629*
lodging, *624–629*
nightlife, *629*
shopping, *621*
sports, *621–623*
Foley, AL, *609*
Fort Clinch State

Park, FL, *486*
**Fort George Island,
FL,** *477*
Fort Morgan, LA,
608
Fort Pulaski, SC, *459*
**Fort Sumter National
Monument, SC,**
431–432
**Fort Walton Beach,
FL,** *618, 625–626*
**Francis Marion
National Forest, SC,**
419
Francisville, LA, *560*
Franklin, Benjamin,
25
Fredericksburg, VA,
384
Apothecary Shop, *384*
dining, *385, 386–387*
Home of Mary
Washington, *384*
James Monroe
Museum and
Memorial Library,
385
Kenmore, *384*
lodging, *387*
sports, *385*
Rising Sun Tavern,
384
Freeport, ME, *80, 83,
86, 89*
Fripp Island, SC, *448*

Gainesville, FL,
633–634
Devil's Millhopper
State Geological Site,
633
dining, *636*
Florida State
Museum, *634*
lodging, *636–637*
University of Florida,
634
Galilee, RI, *230*
Gardens
Bartholomew's
Cobble, MA, *170*
Bellingrath Gardens
and Home, AL, *607*
Bok Tower Gardens,
FL, *504*
Boston Public Garden,
28
Brookgreen Gardens,
SC, *418*
Chicago Botanic

Garden, *687*
Cypress Gardens, FL,
504
Cypress Gardens, SC,
433
Dumbarton Oaks,
Washington, D.C.,
358
Eden State Gardens,
FL, *620*
Enid Haupt Memorial
Garden, Washington,
D.C., *345*
Fuller Gardens, NH,
64
Maclay State Gardens,
FL, *633*
Magnolia Plantation
and Gardens, SC, *432*
Morris Arboretum,
Philadelphia, *288*
Tennessee Botanical
Gardens, *533*
Tenshin Garden, *31*
topiary, Newport, RI,
243
United States
Botanical Gardens,
Washington, D.C.,
353
Garrison, NY,
157–158
Boscobel (mansion),
158
dining, *164*
Garrison Art Center,
157
lodging, *164*
Georgetown, ME, *89*
Georgetown, SC,
418–419
dining, *421*
Harold Kaminski
House, *419*
lodging, *421*
Prince George Winyah
Episcopal Church,
419
Rice Museum, *418*
Georgia. *See also
specific towns*
seasonal events, *412*
tourist information,
412
Germantown, NY,
161
Gettysburg, PA,
325–331
children, *272*
dining, *329–330*

Eisenhower National
  Historic Site, *326*
General Lee's
  Headquarters, *328*
Gettysburg Hotel, *328*
Gettysburg National
  Military Park, *326*
Hall of Presidents and
  First Ladies, *326*
Jennie Wade House,
  326
Lincoln Room
  Museum, *326–328*
Lincoln Square, *326*
lodging, *330–331*
National Civil War
  Wax Museum, *326*
Old Gettysburg
  Village, *328*
shopping, *328*
special events, *271*
sports, *328–329*
tourist information,
  270
tours, *325*
Gills Rock, WI, *708*
Glencoe, IL, *687*
Gloucester, MA, *53,*
  56–57
Golden Isles, GA,
  467–474
beach, *467*
dining, *472–474*
lodging, *472–474*
Gooseberry Falls
  State Park, MN, *727*
Grand Marais, MN,
  728, 731
Grand Strand, SC,
  416
dining, *421–424*
lodging, *421–424*
nightlife, *424*
sports, *420–421*
Great Barrington,
  MA, *170, 176–177*
Great Island, NH, *65*
Green Bay, WI,
  709–710
Bay Beach Park, *709*
Bay Beach Wildlife
  Sanctuary, *709*
dining, *713*
Green Bay Packer
  Hall of Fame, *709*
lodging, *713–714*
National Railroad
  Museum, *710*
Neville Public
  Museum, *710*

Oneida Nation
  Museum, *710*
Greene, Nathaniel,
  454
Greenfield, MA,
  190–191
Greenwich, CT
Audubon Center, *200*
Bruce Museum, *200*
dining, *208–209*
lodging, *209*
Putnam Cottage,
  200–202
Greyhound/Trailway
  Lines, *10*
Groton, CT
boat tours, *219*
Ebenezer Avery
  House, *219*
Enviro-Lab, *219*
Ft. Griswold State
  Park, *219*
lodging, *222*
Nautilus Memorial/
  Submarine Force
  Library and
  Museum, *219*
Project Oceanology,
  219
U.S. submarine base,
  219
Guilford, CT, *215*
dining, *222*
Hyland House, *215*
Thomas Griswold
  House, *215*
Whitfield House
  Museum, *215*
Gulf Coast. *See also
  specific towns*
dining, *610–614*
lodging, *610–614*
nightlife, *614*
sports, *609–610*
Gulf Islands National
  Seashore, MS, *601*
Gulf Shores public
  beach, AL, *608*
Gulfport, MS, *598*
Beauvoir (mansion),
  598
children, *595*
dining, *603–604*
Southern Elegance
  (gambling ship), *598*

Hale, Nathan, *218*
Hampton Beach, NH,
  63–64, 69
Hampton Falls, NH

Applecrest Farm
  Orchards, *63*
dining, *69*
sports, *62–63*
Hampton, NH, *69*
Hampton Plantation
  State Park, SC, *419*
Hancock, MA, *177*
Hancock, ME, *108*
Hancock, MI, *732*
The Harpswells, ME,
  84
Harriman State
  Park, NY, *156–157*
Harwich Port, MA,
  266
Hawthorn, FL, *634*
Hemingway, Ernest,
  664
Hendersonville, TN,
  534
Heritage Hill State
  Park, WI, *709–710*
Hershey, PA, *314*
children, *272*
Hersheypark
  (amusement park),
  314
Hershey's Chocolate
  World, *314*
lodging, *318*
Hillsdale, NY, *164*
Hilton Head Island,
  SC, *444–445, 447*
children, *414*
dining, *447–450*
Fort Mitchell, *445*
lodging, *447–450*
Newhall Audubon
  Preserve, *445*
nightlife, *451*
resorts, *445, 447–448*
Sea Pines Forest
  Preserve, *445*
shopping, *446*
sports, *446–447*
Historic Deerfield,
  MA
Barnard Tavern, *185*
Deerfield Academy,
  185
historic homes, *185*
Historic houses
Annandale, NY, *161*
Baton Rouge, LA,
  560–564
Bayfield, WI, *719*
Beacon, NY, *158*
Beaufort, SC, *443,*
  444

The Berkshires, MA,
  172, 173
Boston, MA, *19–20,*
  24, 28, 33
Calumet, MI, *732*
Castine, ME, *95*
Charleston, SC, *426,*
  430, 431
Charlottesville, VA,
  403
Chicago, IL, *654–656,*
  661–664
Columbia, PA, *313*
Connecticut, *215, 217,*
  218, 219, 220
Cos Cob, CT, *202*
Destin, FL, *620*
Duluth, MN, *726*
Exeter, NH, *63*
Falmouth, MA,
  250–251
Fort George Island,
  FL, *477*
Garrison, NY, *158*
Georgetown, SC, *419*
Germantown, NY, *161*
Gettysburg, PA,
  326–328
Greenwich, CT,
  200–202
Hudson, NY, *162*
Hyde Park, NY, *160*
Jackson, MS, *547–549*
Kennebunk, ME, *74*
Kennebunkport, ME,
  74
Kinderhook, NY, *162*
Lancaster, PA, *311*
Lorman, MS, *551*
Marietta, PA, *313*
Milwaukee, WI, *692*
Mobile, AL, *607*
Nashville, TN, *533*
Natchez, MS, *553*
New Haven, CT, *206*
New Orleans, LA,
  570–575, 577
New York City, *126,*
  128
Newburyport, MA, *54*
Newport, RI, *237–243*
North Hampton, NH,
  64
Oatlands, VA, *406*
Orange, VA, *404*
Pemaquid Point, ME,
  85
Pensacola, FL, *617*
Philadelphia, PA,
  280–282, 287, 288

Historic Houses
(continued)
Pioneer Valley, MA,
185
Port Gibson, MS, *551*
Portland, ME, *80–81*
Portsmouth, NH, *64*
Poughkeepsie, NY,
158–159
Red Hook, NY, *160*
Richmond, VA,
388–392
Salem, MA, *52*
Sandwich, MA, *254*
Saunderstown, RI,
231
Savannah, GA,
454–458
Sheboygan, WI,
704–705
South Carolina,
432–433
South Norwalk, CT,
203
St. Augustine, FL,
480
Staatsburg, NY, *160*
Stroudwater Village,
ME, *82–83*
Tarrytown, NY, *155*
Vicksburg, MS, *550*
Virginia, *380,
382–384*
Washington, D.C.,
348–350, 355–360
Wickford, RI, *231*
Yonkers, NY, *153–155*
York Village, ME, *72*
Yorktown, VA, *399*
**Holbrook Island
Sanctuary, ME,** *98*
Holland, MI, *746–747*
DeKlomp Wooden
Shoe and Delft
Factory, *746*
dining, *749*
Dutch Village, *747*
lodging, *749*
Netherlands Museum,
747
Windmill Island park,
747
Wooden Shoe Factory,
747
Holyoke, MA
Children's Museum,
187
dining, *191*
Heritage Park
Railroad, *187*

Heritage State Park,
187
lodging, *191*
Volleyball Hall of
Fame, *187*
Home exchange, *6*
Hopper, Edward, *156*
**Hopsewee
Plantation, SC,** *419*
Houghton, MI, *732*
dining, *740*
E. A. Seaman
Mineralogical
Museum, *732*
lodging, *740*
Michigan Technical
University, *732*
Hudson, NY, *162*
Hudson Valley, NY,
153–169
arts, *169*
boat tours, *153*
children, *112–113*
nightlife, *169*
Hunting Island, SC,
444
**Hunting Island State
Park, SC,** *447*
Hurley, WI, *719*
Hyannis, MA
dining, *262, 263*
John F. Kennedy
Memorial, *251*
John F. Kennedy
Memorial Museum,
251
lodging, *265, 266*
Hyannis Port, MA,
51
Hyde Park, NY,
159–160
Culinary Institute of
America, *160*
dining, *164–165*
Franklin Delano
Roosevelt National
Historic Site, *159*
lodging, *165*
Vanderbilt Mansion,
160

Illinois. *See also
specific towns*
northeastern, *685*
seasonal events,
641–642
Insurance, *2*
British travelers, *3*
Intercourse, PA,
318–319

**Intracoastal
Waterway,** *481*
Ipswich, MA, *53*
Iron County, WI,
719
Irving, Washington,
155–156
Isle au Haut, ME,
93, 96–97, 101
**Isle Royale National
Park, MI,** *732*
Isles of Shoals, NH,
65–66
Islesboro, ME, *96,
101*
Islesford, ME, *105*
Islesford Historical
Museum, *105*

Jacinto, MS, *544*
Jackson, Andrew,
533–534
Jackson, MS,
545–549
Agriculture and
Forestry Museum,
546
Cathedral of St. Peter
the Apostle, *548*
Central Fire Station,
546–547
City Hall, *547*
Davis Planetarium,
547
dining, *549, 555–556*
Eudora Welty
Library, *548*
Galloway House, *548*
Garner Green House,
549
Greenbrook Flowers,
549
Lamar Life Building,
547
lodging, *556*
Manship House, *549*
Millsaps-Buie House,
549
Mississippi Archives
Building, *546*
Mississippi Arts
Center, *547*
Mississippi Governor's
Mansion, *547*
Morris House, *549*
neighborhoods, *549*
New Capitol, *548*
nightlife, *559*
The Oaks, *549*
Old Capitol Building,

546
St. Andrew's
Episcopal Cathedral,
547
741 North Congress
Street, *549*
shopping, *554*
Smith Park, *548*
Smith Robertson
Museum, *549*
Spengler's Corner
Building, *546*
sports, *554*
State Historical
Museum, *546*
tourist information,
546
U.S. Federal
Courthouse, *547*
Victorian homes,
548–549
Virden-Patton House,
549
War Memorial
Building, *546*
**Jacksonville Beach,
FL,** *477*
beach, *486*
dining, *490–491*
lodging, *491*
Jacksonville, FL,
477–478
Alexander Brest
Museum, *478*
Atlantic Beach, *477*
Cummer Gallery of
Art, *478*
dining, *490–491*
Fort Caroline National
Monument, *478*
Jacksonville Art
Museum, *477*
Jacksonville's Museum
of Science and
History, *478*
lodging, *491*
Neptune Beach, *477*
Ponte Vedra Beach,
477
shopping, *483*
**Jacob's Pillow Dance
Festival, MA,**
183–184
**Jamestown Island,
VA,** *398*
**Jamestown
Settlement, VA,**
398–399
**Jeff Busby State
Park, MS,** *545*

Jefferson, Thomas, *402*
Graff House, *279–280*
memorial, *346*
Monticello, *403*
University of Virginia, *403*
Jekyll Island, GA
beach, *470*
dining, *472*
Jekyll Island Club Historic District, *470*
Jekyll Shopping Center, *470*
lodging, *472–473*
sports, *471*
Jenness Beach, NH, *64*
J. P. Coleman State Park, MS, *542*

Kathryn Abbey Hanna Park, FL, *486*
Kennebunk Beach, ME, *76*
Kennebunk, ME, *74*
Brick Store Museum, *75*
dining, *77*
National Historic Register District, *75*
shopping, *75*
Kennebunkport, ME, *74*
beach, *76*
Cape Arundel, *74*
dining, *77*
Dock Square, *74*
lodging, *77–78*
Nott House, *74*
Seashore Trolley Museum, *74–75*
shopping, *75*
sports, *75*
Wedding Cake House, *74*
Kennedy, John F.
Georgetown home, *357*
Hammersmith Farm, *242*
Hyannis, MA, memorial, *251*
Hyannis Port, MA, home, *251*
Kewaunee, WI, *706*
Keweenaw Peninsula, MI, *732*
Kiawah Island, SC, *433*
Beachwalker Park, *433*
Kiawah Island Resort, *440–441*
Kinderhook, NY
Columbia County Museum and Library, *162*
dining, *165*
James Vanderpoel House, *162*
Lindenwald, *162*
lodging, *165–166*
King of Prussia, PA, *305–306*
King's Dominion entertainment complex, Richmond, VA, *335*
Kittery, ME, *71–72*
factory outlets, *71, 75*
Kohler, WI, *714*

Lake Jackson, FL, *633*
Lake Michigan, *744–750*
Lake Superior Circle Drive, *728–729*
Lancaster County, PA, *307–325.* See also Lancaster, PA
Abe's Buggy Rides, *308*
Amish Farm and House, *308*
arts, *324–325*
camping, *316*
children, *272*
dining, *307, 316–324*
Ephrata Cloister, *312*
farm vacations, *324*
Green Dragon Farmers Market and Auction, *312*
Indian Echo Caverns, *314*
Landis Valley Museum, *312*
Lapp Valley Farm, *308*
lodging, *316–324*
Mt. Hope Estate and Winery, *313*
Nissley Vineyards and Winery Estate, *313*
Pennsylvania Rennaissance Faire, *314*
shopping, *314*
sports, *315–316*
tourist information, *270, 308*
tours, *307*
Lancaster, PA. See also Lancaster County, PA
Central Market, *311*
Demuth Foundation, *311*
dining, *319–320*
Hans Herr House, *311*
Heritage Center Museum, *311*
lodging, *320–321*
Rock Ford Plantation and Kauffman Museum, *311*
Wheatland (mansion), *311*
Langhorne, PA, *272*
Laona, WI, *716–717*
Lee, Robert E., *380, 382*
Lee, MA, *172, 177–178*
Leesburg, VA
Morven Park, *406*
Museum of Hounds and Hunting, *406*
Westmoreland Davis Equestrian Institute, *406*
Winmill Carriage Museum, *406*
L'Enfant, Charles Pierre, *337*
Lenox, MA, *172*
Berkshire Scenic Railway, *172*
dining, *178, 180*
lodging, *178–180*
The Mount, *172*
Railway Museum, *172*
Tanglewood music festival, *172, 184*
Lincoln, Abraham, *347*
Lincolnville, ME, *101*
Lititz, PA, *312*
Julius Sturgis Pretzel House, *312*
lodging, *321*
Wilbur Chocolate Company's Candy American Museum and Factory Candy Outlet, *312–313*
Little St. Simon's Island, GA
beach, *468–469*
dining, *474*
lodging, *474*
Little Talbot Island State Park, FL, *475–476*
Long Beach, MS, *604*
Long Sands Beach, ME, *76*
Lorman, MS, *552*
Lorton, VA, *383–384*
Loudoun County, VA, *406*
Louisiana. See also specific towns
arriving and departing, *526–527*
children, *526*
seasonal events, *525*
tourist information, *525*
Low, Juliette Gordon, *546*
Luray Caverns, VA, *405–406*
Lynchburg, TN, *534*

Mackinac Island, MI, *737*
Agency House and Warehouse, *738*
dining, *740–741*
ferryboat, *737*
Grand Hotel, *737, 738*
lodging, *741*
Mackinac Island Carriage Tours, *738*
Marquette Park, *738*
Old Fort Mackinac, *737*
Stuart House Museum, *738*
Mackinaw City, MI, *738–739*
Colonial Fort Michilimackinac, *738*
dining, *741–742*
lodging, *742*
Mackinac Bridge Museum, *739*
Mackinac Maritime Park, *738–739*
Madeline Island, WI, *720*
Big Bay Island Park, *720*
Indian Cemetery, *720*

Madeline Island, WI
(continued)
Madeline Island
Historical Museum,
720
Madison, James, *404*
Madison, CT
Allis-Bushnell House
and Museum, *217*
Hammonasset Beach
State Park, *217*
**Magnolia Plantation
and Gardens, SC,**
432
Maine. *See also
specific towns*
arriving and
departing, *16–17*
arts, *92*
children, *16*
dining, *76–80*
festivals, *15*
lodging, *76–80*
sports, *87*
tourist information, *15*
**Manassas National
Battlefield Park,
VA,** *406–407*
Manchester, MA, *53*
Manchester, TN, *534*
**Manistee National
Forest, MI,** *746*
Manitowoc, WI,
705–706, 714
Marblehead, MA, *50,
57–58*
Marietta, PA, *313,
321*
**Marjorie Kinnan
Rawlings State
Historic Site,** *634*
Marquette, MI, *734*
Marquette County
Historical Society
Museum, *734*
Michigan Iron
Industry Museum,
734–735
Presque Isle Park,
734
Marquette, WI, *742*
Mashpee, MA, *261*
Massachusetts. *See
also specific towns*
arriving and depart-
ing, *16–17, 199*
children, *16, 112–113*
seasonal events, *15,
198*
tourist information,

14, 111, 198
Mayport, FL, *477*
Melville, Herman,
173
Micanopy, FL, *634*
Michigan. *See also
specific towns*
arriving and
departing, *643–644*
children, *643*
cruises, *735*
dining, *740–744*
lodging, *740–744*
sports, *739*
tourist information,
641
**Middleton Place
Plantation, SC,**
432–433
Milwaukee, WI,
687–702
Allen-Bradley Co.
clock, *694*
Annunciation Greek
Orthodox Church,
693
arts, *700–701*
breweries, *687*
Brewery Tours, *694*
Cathedral Square, *689*
children, *642*
dining, *692, 696–699*
Discovery
World–Museum of
Science, Economics
and Technology, *692*
downtown, *688–692*
getting around in, *688*
Iron Block Building,
688
Kilbourntown House,
692–693
lodging, *699–700*
Mackie Building, *689*
Milwaukee Art
Museum, *689*
Milwaukee County
Historical Center,
689–692
Milwaukee County
Zoo, *694*
Milwaukee Public
Museum, *692*
Mitchell Park
Conservatory, *693*
nightlife, *701–702*
Pabst Mansion, *693*
Pere Marquette Park,
689
St. John's Cathedral,

689
St. Josephat's
Basilica, *694*
Schlitz Audubon
Center, *693*
seasonal events,
641–642
shopping, *694–695*
sports, *695–696*
tourist information,
688
tours, *688*
Miner's Castle, MI,
735
Miner's Falls, MI,
735
Minnesota. *See also
specific towns*
arriving and
departing, *643–644*
dining, *730–731*
Lake Superior circle
drive, *728–729*
lodging, *730–731*
shopping, *729*
sports, *729–730*
tourist information,
641
Minocqua, WI, *718*
Circle M Corral
amusement park, *718*
dining, *718, 723*
Jim Peck's Wildwood,
718
lodging, *723*
Mississippi. *See also
specific towns*
arriving and
departing, *526–527*
children, *526, 596*
seasonal events, *525,
595*
tourist information,
524, 594
**Mississippi Gulf
Coast,** *597–605. See
also specific towns*
beach, *601*
dining, *602–605*
lodging, *602–605*
nightlife, *605*
shopping, *601*
sports, *601–602*
Mobile, AL, *605–606*
Bellingrath Gardens
and Home, *607*
Bienville Square, *607*
Cox-Deasy House, *607*
dining, *610–611*
Fort Condé, *606–607*

lodging, *611–612*
Malbis Greek Ortho-
dox Church, *608*
nightlife, *614*
Oakleigh (mansion),
607
seasonal events, *595*
shopping, *609*
sports, *609–610*
USS *Alabama,* *608*
Mobile Point, AL,
608
Mohawk Trail, *174*
**Monhegan Island,
ME,** *93*
**Monomoy Island,
MA,** *251*
Monomoy National
Wildlife Refuge, *251*
Monroe, James, *385,
403–404*
Morse, Samuel F. B.,
158
**Mount Desert Island,
ME,** *103*
arts, *109*
nightlife, *109*
**Mount Greylock
State Reservation,
MA,** *173*
Mount Joy, PA,
321–322
Mount Vernon, VA,
383, 385
Mt. Pleasant, SC, *431*
Munising, MI, *735,
743*
Murfreesboro, TN,
534
Murrells Inlet, SC,
416–417, 421–422
Muskegon, MI, *746,
749–750*
Myrtle Beach, SC
children, *414*
dining, *422*
Guinness World
Records Museum,
416
lodging, *422–423*
Myrtle Beach
National Wax
Museum, *416*
Myrtle Beach Pavilion
and Amusement
Park, *416*
nightlife, *424*
Ripleys Believe It or
Not Museum, *416*
shopping, *419–420*

sports, *420–421*
Mystic, CT, *219–220*
dining, *222*
lodging, *222*
Mystic Marinelife
  Aquarium, *220*
Mystic Seaport, *219*
Olde Mistick Village,
  220
shopping, *221*
Whitehall (museum),
  220

Napoleonville, LA,
  566–567
Narragansett, RI
beaches, *230*
dining, *230, 234–235*
lodging, *235*
Narragansett Indian
  Monument, *230*
Narragansett Pier,
  229–230
Point Judith
  Lighthouse, *230*
South County
  Museum, *230*
Sprague Park,
  229–230
The Towers, *230*
Nashville, TN,
  527–541
Andrew Jackson
  Center, *534*
arts, *540–541*
Belle Meade Mansion,
  533
Belmont Mansion, *533*
Boxcar Willie's
  Railroad Museum,
  532
Car Collectors Hall of
  Fame, *531*
Cars of the Stars, *532*
Cheekwood (arts
  center), *533*
children, *525*
Country Music Hall of
  Fame and Museum,
  530
Country Music Wax
  Museum and Mall,
  531
dining, *536–538*
downtown, *528–530*
Downtown
  Presbyterian Church,
  530
Fort Nashborough,
  528

getting around in, *528*
Hank Williams Jr.
  Museum, *531*
The Hermitage, *533*
The Hermitage
  Church, *534*
Historic Second
  Avenue Business
  District, *530*
Jim Reeves Museum,
  532
lodging, *538–540*
Minnie Pearl's
  Museum, *532*
Music Row, *530–531*
Music Valley Wax
  Museum of the Stars,
  532
nightlife, *541*
Opryland USA,
  531–532
Parthenon (museum),
  533
Recording Studios of
  America, *531*
Riverfront Park, *528*
Roy Acuff Musical
  Collection and
  Museum, *531–532*
Ryman Auditorium
  and Museum, *530*
shopping, *535–536*
Sidewalk of the Stars,
  532
sports, *536*
Star Walk, *532*
State Capitol, *530*
Tennessee Botanical
  Gardens, *533*
Tennessee Performing
  Arts Center, *530*
Tennessee State
  Museum, *530*
Travellers' Rest
  (mansion), *533*
Tulip Grove, *534*
War Memorial
  Building, *530*
Natchez, MS,
  552–554
carriage rides, *553*
dining, *556–557*
Dunleith (mansion),
  553
lodging, *557*
Longwood (mansion),
  553
Magnolia Hall, *553*
Natchez Pilgrimage,
  553, 554

Natchez-under-the-
  Hill, *552*
nightlife, *559*
Pilgrimage Tours, *553*
Rosalie (mansion), *553*
seasonal events, *525*
sports, *554*
Natchez Trace, *542*
Beaver Creek, *545*
Cypress Swamp, *545*
French Camp, *545*
Little Mountain
  Service Station, *545*
Ridgeland Crafts
  Center, *545*
National parks
Acadia National Park,
  ME, *93, 96–97, 103*
Cape Cod National
  Seashore, MA, *254,
  260*
Fort Pickens National
  Park, FL, *618*
Isle Royale National
  Park, MI, *732*
North Shore, MA, *55*
Shenandoah National
  Park, VA, *405*
Shiloh National
  Military Park, TN,
  535
Valley Forge National
  Historical Park, PA,
  303–304
Vicksburg National
  Military Park, MS,
  550
**National Park
  Service,** *2*
Native Americans
Indian Burial Ground,
  229
Indian Church, *229*
monument, *230*
**Natural Bridge
  Battlefield State
  Historic Site, FL,**
  632
Neptune Beach, FL,
  486
New Bedford, MA,
  249–250
dining, *250*
New Bedford Glass
  Museum, *249*
New Bedford
  Preservation Society,
  249–250
New Bedford Whaling
  Museum, *249*

New Castle, NH, *65*
Fort Constitution, *65*
New Hampshire,
  *62–71. See also
  specific towns*
arriving and
  departing, *16–17*
arts, *71*
beach, *67*
children, *16*
festivals, *15*
nightlife, *71*
sports, *67*
tourist information, *14*
New Haven, CT
Beinecke Rare Book
  Library, *205*
Black Rock Fort, *206*
Collection of Musical
  Instruments, *205*
dining, *205, 209–210*
East Rock Park, *206*
Ft. Nathan Hale, *206*
Harkness Tower,
  205–206
Lighthouse Point, *206*
lodging, *210–211*
New Haven Green, *206*
Pardee-Morris House,
  206
Peabody Museum of
  Natural History, *205*
Sterling Memorial
  Library, *205*
West Rock Nature
  Center, *206*
Yale Art Gallery, *205*
Yale Center for
  British Art, *205*
Yale University, *205*
New London, CT
Captain's Walk, *218*
Joshua Hempstead
  House, *218*
lodging, *218*
Lyman Allyn Art
  Museum, *218*
Monte Cristo Cottage,
  218
Nathan Hale
  Schoolhouse, *218*
Ocean Beach Park,
  218
Shaw Mansion, *218*
Thames Science
  Center, *218*
U.S. Coast Guard
  Academy, *217*
New Orleans,
  568–592

New Orleans
(continued)
arts, *590*
Audubon Park and
  Zoo, *576–577*
Beauregard-Keyes
  House, *571*
Café du Monde, *571*
Cathedral Garden, *574*
Central Business
  District, *569–576*
children, *526*
churches, *570, 576*
City Park, *577*
Cornstalk Fence, *574*
dining, *575, 579–586*
1850s House, *570*
First Skyscraper, *574*
French Market, *571*
French Quarter, *568,
  569–576*
Gallier House, *574*
getting around in,
  568–569
guided tours, *569*
Hermann-Grima
  House, *575*
historic houses,
  570–575, 577
Historic New Orleans
  Collection, *575*
Jackson Brewery and
  Millhouse, *571*
Jackson Square, *570*
LaBranche House, *574*
Lafitte's Blacksmith
  Shop, *574*
lodging, *586–590*
Longue Vue House
  and Gardens, *577*
Louis Armstrong
  Park, *576*
Louisiana State
  Museum, *570*
Madame John's
  Legacy, *574*
Merieult House, *575*
Moon Walk
  promenade, *571*
Municipal Auditorium,
  576
Musée Conti Wax
  Museum, *575*
museums, *570–575,
  577*
Napoleon House, *575*
New Orleans Museum
  of Art, *577*
New Orleans
  Pharmacy Museum,
  575
New Orleans Welcome
  Center, *570*
nightlife, *590–592*
Old Ursuline Convent,
  571
Old U.S. Mint, *571*
Our Lady of
  Guadalupe Catholic
  Church, *576*
Pirate's Alley, *570*
Pitot House, *577*
Pontalba Buildings,
  571
Père Antoine's Alley,
  570
Preservation Hall, *574*
seasonal events, *525*
shopping, *578–579*
sports, *579*
St. Louis Cathedral,
  570
St. Louis Cemetery
  No. 1, *576*
Storyland, *577*
Theatre for the
  Performing Arts, *576*
Voodoo Museum, *574*
Washington Artillery
  Park, *571*
Williams Gallery, *575*
Woldenberg River-
  front Park, *575*
**New Smyrna Beach,
  FL,** *491–492*
New York. *See also
  specific towns*
arriving and
  departing, *199*
tourist information,
  111
New York City,
  115–153
Alice Tully Hall, *122*
American Museum of
  Natural History, *123*
arriving and
  departing, *113–115*
arts, *148–151*
A&S Plaza, *122*
AT&T World
  Headquarters, *132*
Avery Fisher Hall,
  122
Battery Park, *130*
Battery Park City,
  131–132
bed-and-breakfasts,
  148
Bethesda Fountain,
  124
Bleecker Street, *128*
Brooklyn Bridge, *132*
Bryant Park, *120*
Bryant Park Half-
  Price Tickets, *120*
cabaret, *151*
Cathedral of St. John
  the Divine, *123*
Central Park,
  123–126
Central Park Zoo, *124*
children, *112*
Chinatown, *129*
Chrysler Building,
  121
churches, *117, 123,
  128, 129, 130, 131*
CitiCorp Center, *132*
City Hall, *132*
City Hall Park, *132*
Cloisters, *132–133*
Columbus Circle, *122*
concerts, *149–150*
Confucius Plaza, *129*
Cooper-Hewitt
  Museum, *125*
Dakota Apartments,
  122
dance performances,
  150
dining, *119, 126, 128,
  135–144*
discos and dance
  clubs, *152*
Eighth Street, *126*
El Museo del Barrio,
  125
Ellis Island, *130*
Empire State
  Building, *121*
F.A.O. Schwarz toy
  store, *124*
Federal Hall National
  Memorial, *131*
film, *150–151*
Ford Foundation
  Building, *121*
42nd Street, *120–121*
Fraunces Tavern, *130*
Frick Collection, *125*
Garment District, *122*
Gay Street, *126*
GE Building, *119*
getting around in, *116*
Gracie Mansion, *133*
Grand Army Plaza,
  123–124
Grand Central
  Terminal, *120–121*
Grant's Tomb, *123*
Greenwich Village,
  126–127
Grove Court (town
  houses), *128*
Guggenheim
  Bandshell, *122*
Guggenheim Museum,
  125
Hayden Planetarium,
  123
Herald Center, *122*
Herald Square, *122*
IBM Building, *133*
International Center
  of Photography, *125*
jazz clubs, *151–152*
Jefferson Market
  Library, *126*
Jewish Museum, *125*
Julliard School, *122*
Lincoln Center, *122*
Little Italy, *129*
lodging, *144–148*
Loeb Boathouse, *124*
Lord & Taylor, *121*
Lower Manhattan,
  130–132
MacDougal Alley, *126*
Macy's, *122*
The Mall, *124*
Metropolitan Museum
  of Art, *125*
Metropolitan Opera
  House, *122*
Mitzi E. Newhouse
  theater, *122*
Mott Street, *129*
Mulberry Street, *129*
Museum of the City of
  New York, *125*
Museum of Modern
  Art, *119*
Museum of Television
  and Radio, *119*
museums, *119, 122,
  123, 125–126*
National Academy of
  Design, *125*
New York Chinatown
  History Project, *129*
New York Convention
  and Visitors Bureau,
  122
New-York Historical
  Society, *122*
New York Public
  Library, *120, 121*
New York State
  Theater, *122*

New York Stock Exchange, *130–131*
nightlife, *151–153*
opera, *150*
Pierpont Morgan Library, *133*
Plaza Hotel, *124*
pop and rock clubs, *152*
Radio City Music Hall, *119*
Rockefeller Center, *117*
Roosevelt Island Aerial Tramway, *133*
Saks Fifth Avenue, *120*
San Gennaro Church, *129*
Seaport Harbor Line Cruise, *131*
seasonal events, *112*
Sheridan Square, *126–128*
shopping, *120, 133–135*
singles bars, *152–153*
SoHo, *128–129*
South Street Seaport Historic District, *131*
St. Luke's-in-the-Fields, *128*
St. Luke's Place, *128*
St. Patrick's Cathedral, *117*
St. Paul's Chapel, *131*
Staten Island Ferry Terminal, *130*
Statue of Liberty, *130*
Strawberry Fields, *122, 124*
Tavern on the Green, *122*
theater, *148–149*
theater tickets, *120, 149*
Tiffany & Co., *120*
Times Square, *120*
TKTS booth, *120, 149*
tours, *116–117*
Trinity Church, *130*
Umberto's Clam House, *129*
United Nations Headquarters, *121*
Upper East Side, *123–126*
Upper West Side, *122–123*
Vivian Beaumont

Theatre, *122*
Wall Street, *130*
Washington Square, *126*
Whitney Museum of American Art, *125*
Windows on the World, *131*
Woolworth Building, *132*
World Financial Center, *132*
World Trade Center, *131*
Newburyport, MA, *54*
Customs House, *54*
dining, *58*
lodging, *58–59*
Maritime Museum, *54*
Newcastle, ME, *90*
Newport, RI
arts, *237*
The Astors' Beechwood, *242*
beach, *243, 244*
Belcourt Castle, *242*
The Breakers, *241*
Brick Market, *239*
Chateau-sur-Mer, *241*
Cliff Walk, *240*
Colonial Newport, *237–240*
Common Burial Ground, *239*
dining, *244–246*
The Elms, *241*
Friends Meeting House, *239*
getting around in, *237*
Hammersmith Farm, *242*
Hunter House, *237–238*
International Tennis Hall of Fame, *241*
Kingscote, *241*
lodging, *246–247*
mansions, *240–243*
Marble House, *242*
Museum of Yachting, *242*
Newport Art Museum and Art Association, *240*
Newport Historical Society, *240*
nightlife, *247–248*
Old Colony House, *239*
Redwood Library, *240*

Rosecliff, *241*
Sandy Point Beach, *243*
shopping, *243–244*
Tennis Museum, *241*
topiary garden, *243*
Touro Synagogue, *239–240*
tours, *237*
Trinity Church, *240*
Wanton-Lyman-Hazard House, *239*
White Horse Tavern, *239*
North Adams, MA
Natural Bridge State Park, MA, *174*
Western Gateway Heritage State Park, *174*
North Brooklin, ME, *102*
North Hampton, NH, *64*
**North Kingstown, RI, 230–231*
North Myrtle Beach, SC, *423*
North Shore, MA, *49–62*
arts, *62*
beach, *55*
camping, *55*
dining, *55–62*
Halibut Point State Park, *55*
Harold Parker State Forest, *55*
lodging, *55–62*
national park, *55*
nightlife, *62*
Plum Island State Reservation, *55*
Salisbury Beach State Reservation, *55*
shopping, *54*
sports, *54–55*
state park, *55*
Willowdale State Forest, *55*
North Stonington, CT, *220*
Crosswoods Vineyards, *220*
dining, *223–224*
lodging, *224*
Northampton, MA, *185, 191–192*
Northeast Harbor, ME, *108–109*

Northport, WI, *708*
Norwalk, CT, *211–212*
Nyack, NY, *156*
Edward Hopper House, *156*

Oatlands Plantation, VA, *406*
Ocala, FL, *634*
lodging, *637*
sports, *635–636*
Wild Waters (water theme park), *635*
Ocala National Forest, FL, *635*
Ocean Springs, MS, *600*
D'Iberville Trail, *601*
dining, *604*
Ocean Springs Chamber of Commerce, *601*
Old Community Center, *600*
Shearwater Pottery and Showroom, *600–601*
Walter Anderson Museum of Art, *600*
Odiorne Point State Park, NH, *64*
Ogunquit, ME, *72–73*
arts, *80*
beach, *76*
dining, *78–79*
lodging, *79*
Museum of Art of Ogunquit, *72*
Perkins Cove, *73*
shopping, *75*
sports, *75*
Old Chatham, NY, *162*
Old Fort Mackinac, MI, *737*
Old Lyme, CT, *217*
Florence Griswold Museum, *217*
lodging, *224–225*
Lyme Academy of Fine Arts, *217*
Old Mill Creek State Historic Park, MI, *739*
Old Saybrook, CT, *217*
General William Hart House, *217*
lodging, *225*

Old Sturbridge Village, MA, *187–188*

Older travelers, *5–6*

Ontario. *See also specific towns*
arriving and departing, *643–644*
children, *643*
tourist information, *641*

Orange, VA, *404, 410*

Orlando, FL, *496–522. See also Disney World*
Alligatorland Safari Zoo, *504*
Bok Tower Gardens, *504*
Central Florida Zoological Park, *502*
children, *595*
Cypress Gardens, *504*
dining, *506–512*
Fun 'n Wheels, *504*
Gatorland Zoo, *504*
getting around in, *496–497*
lodging, *512–519*
Mystery Fun House, *502*
nightlife, *520–522*
Places of Learning, *504*
Sea World, *504*
shopping, *504–505*
sports, *505–506*
Universal Studios Florida, *502*
Wet 'n Wild, *502*
Xanadu (technology displays), *504*

Orleans, MA, *251*
dining, *264*
Nauset Beach, *254*

Ormond Beach, FL, *493*

Paeonian Springs, VA, *406*

Panama City Beach, FL
beach, *620*
dining, *620, 626–627*
lodging, *627*
St. Andrews State Recreation Area, *620*

Paoli, PA, *304–305*

Paradise, PA, *322*

Parris Island, SC,

444
War Memorial Building Museum, *444*

Pass Christian, MS, *598*

Pawleys Island, SC, *418, 420, 423–424*

Paynes Prairie, FL, *634*

Peace Dale, RI, *229*

Peaks Island, ME, *83, 90*

Peary, Admiral Robert E., *83–84*

Pemaquid Point, ME, *80, 85*

Peninsula State Park, WI, *708–709*

Pennsylvania. *See also specific towns*
arriving and departing, *272–273*

Penobscot Bay, *92–103*

Pensacola, FL, *615–618*
dining, *627–628*
Dorr House, *615*
Fort Barrancas, *618*
Gulfarium, *619*
Historic Pensacola Village, *615*
Indian Temple Mound Museum, *619*
Julee Cottage Museum of Black History, *615*
Lavalle House, *615*
lodging, *628–629*
Museum of Commerce, *615*
Museum of Industry, *615*
National Museum of Naval Aviation, *618*
North Hill Preservation District, *615*
Palafox Historic District, *615*
Pensacola Historical Museum, *615*
Pensacola Museum of Art, *615*
Pensacola Naval Air Station, *618*
Quina House, *615*
Seville historic district, *615–616*

T. T. Wentworth Jr. Florida State Museum, *615–618*
tourist information, *615*

Peshtigo, WI, *716*
Oconto Cemetery, *716*
Peshtigo Fire Museum, *716*

Philadelphia, *273–303*
Academy of Music, *301*
Academy of Natural Sciences, *285*
Annenberg Center, *301*
Arch Street Meeting House, *281*
arriving and departing, *272–273*
arts, *301–302*
Atwater Kent Museum, *288*
bed-and-breakfasts, *300–301*
Benjamin Franklin Parkway, *284*
Betsy Ross House, *281*
Bishop White House, *281*
Carpenter's Hall, *278*
carriage rides, *275*
Chestnut Hill, *288*
children, *271–272*
Chinatown, *287*
Christ Church, *280*
Christ Church Burial Ground, *281*
church, *280, 281*
City Hall, *283*
City Tavern, *281*
Cliveden (mansion), *287*
concerts, *301, 302*
Congress Hall, *279*
dining, *280, 285, 292–297*
Drexel University, *287*
Elfreth's Alley, *280*
Fairmount Park, *286*
film, *302*
Fireman's Hall Museum, *280*
First Bank of the United States, *278*
Franklin Court, *280*
Franklin Institute,

285
Free Library of Philadelphia, *285*
Gazela of Philadelphia, *282*
Germantown, *287–288*
Germantown Historical Society, *287*
getting around in, *273–275*
Graff House, *279–280*
Hill-Physick-Keith House, *282*
historic district, *275–281*
Independence Hall, *279*
Independence Square, *278*
John Wanamaker Store, *283*
Liberty Bell, *279*
Library Hall, *278*
lodging, *297–301*
Logan Circle, *284–285*
Masonic Temple, *283*
Morris Arboretum, *288*
museum, *278–282, 284–288*
New Hall Marine Corps Memorial Museum, *278*
nightlife, *302–303*
Norman Rockwell Museum, *288*
Painted Bride Art Center, *301*
Pastorius Park, *288*
Pemberton House, *278*
Penn's Landing, *282*
Penn's Landing Trolley Company, *282–283*
Pennsylvania Academy of the Fine Arts, *284*
Philadelphia College of Pharmacy and Science, *287*
Philadelphia Maritime Museum, *280*
Philadelphia Museum of Art, *286*
Philadelphia Saving Fund Society (PSFS) Building, *284*
Philadelphia Visitors Center, *283*

Philadelphia
Zoological Gardens,
289
Philosophical Hall, *278*
Please Touch
Museum, *285–286*
Poe House, *288*
Port of History
Museum, *282, 301*
Powel House, *282*
Reading Terminal
Market, *284*
Rittenhouse Square,
284
Rodin Museum, *286*
Rosenbach Museum
and Library, *284*
Second Bank of the
United States, *278*
shopping, *289–291*
Shubert Theater, *301*
Society Hill, *281–282*
special events, *271*
sports, *291–292*
theater, *302*
Todd House, *281–282*
tourist information,
270, 275–278
tours, *274–275*
United States Mint,
281
University City, *287*
University Museum,
287
University of
Pennsylvania, *287*
USS *Becuna*, *282*
USS *Olympia*, *282*
The War Library and
Museum, *288*
Waterfront, *282–283*
Welcome Park, *281*
Woodmere Art
Museum, *288*
Phippsburg, ME, *87*
**Pictured Rocks
National Lakeshore,
MI,** *735*
Pioneer Valley, MA,
184–185
arts, *194–195*
dining, *189–194*
lodging, *189–194*
nightlife, *195*
shopping, *188*
sports, *188–189*
Pittsfield, MA,
172–173
Berkshire
Athenaeum, *173*

Berkshire Museum,
172–173
dining, *180*
Hancock Shaker
Village, *173*
lodging, *180–181*
Plane travel, *6–9*
children, *8*
disabled travelers, *9*
luggage, *7–8*
smoking, *7*
Pleasure Island, AL,
608
Plum Island, MA, *54*
Poe, Edgar Allan,
288
Point Clear, AL, *614*
**Ponte Vedra Beach,
FL,** *493*
Port Clyde, ME, *92,
93*
Port Gibson, MS,
551, 557–558
Port St. Joe, FL,
620–621
Constitution
Convention State
Museum, *621*
Portland, ME, *80–82*
arts, *92*
boat trip, *86–87*
Casco Bay Lines, *83*
Custom House Wharf,
82
dining, *80, 85, 87,
90–91*
lodging, *91*
Mariner's Church, *82*
Neal Dow Memorial,
80–81
nightlife, *92*
Old Port Exchange, *82*
Portland Museum of
Art, *82*
shopping, *86*
Wadsworth
Longfellow House,
82
Portsmouth, NH, *64*
dining, *64, 69–70*
Folk Art Museum, *65*
John Paul Jones
House, *64*
lodging, *70–71*
Port of Portsmouth
Maritime Museum,
65
Portsmouth Historical
Society, *64*
Prescott Park, *65*

shopping, *66–67*
Strawbery Banke, *65*
Wentworth-Coolidge
Mansion, *64*
Portsmouth, RI,
242–243
Poughkeepsie, NY,
158–159
Clinton House, *159*
Glebe House, *159*
Locust Grove, *158*
Mid Hudson Arts and
Science Center
(MASC), *159*
Vassar College, *159*
Presley, Elvis, *544*
Prouts Neck, ME, *91*
Provincetown, MA,
255
arts, *255*
dining, *264*
lodging, *267, 268*
Pilgrim Monument,
255

Red Hook, NY, *161,
166*
Revere, Paul, *24, 25*
Revolutionary War
Battle of
Germantown, PA,
287
Boston, *18, 24–25, 26*
Constitution Island,
NY, *157*
Exchange
Building/Provost
Dungeon, SC, *430*
Fort Constitution,
NH, *65*
Ft. Griswold State
Park, CT, *219*
Old Powder Magazine,
SC, *429*
Siege of Savannah
site, *453*
Society of the
Cincinnati,
Washington, D.C.,
359
Stony Point
Battlefield Historic
Site, *156*
Valley Forge National
Historical Park, PA,
303–304
Yorktown Battlefield,
399
Yorktown Victory
Center, *399*

Rhinebeck, NY,
160–161, 167–168
Rhinelander, WI,
718, 723
Rhode Island. *See
also specific towns*
children, *198–199*
festival, *198*
lodging, *234*
seasonal events, *198*
tourist information,
197
Richmond, VA,
387–396
Agecroft Hall, *392*
arts, *395*
children, *335*
Court End district,
388
dining, *393–394*
Fan District, *388, 392*
John Marshall House,
388
King's Dominion
entertainment
complex, *335*
lodging, *394–395*
Museum and White
House of the
Confederacy,
388–391
nightlife, *395–396*
shopping, *388,
392–393*
sports, *393*
tours, *388*
Valentine Museum,
388
Virginia Museum of
Fine Arts, *392*
**Rock Island State
Park, WI,** *708*
Rockland, ME, *92,
93–95*
Samoset Resort, *93*
Shore Village
Museum, *95*
sports, *98*
William A.
Farnsworth Library
and Art Museum,
93
Rockport, MA, *53,
59–61*
Rockport, ME, *103*
Rockwell, Norman,
288
Rocky Springs, MS,
551
Rodney, MS, *552*

Rosedown Plantation and Gardens, LA, *560*

Royale, MN, *728*

Rye, NH, *64, 71*

Sagamore, MA, *251, 261*

St. Augustine, FL, *478*
Basilica Cathedral of St. Augustine, *480*
beach, *486*
Castillo de San Marcos National Monument, *478*
City Gate, *478–480*
dining, *480, 493–494*
Flagler College, *481*
Flagler Memorial Presbyterian Church, *481*
Fountain of Youth, *481*
Lightner Museum, *481*
lodging, *494–495*
Mission of Nombre di Dios, *481*
Museum Theatre, *480*
Oldest House, *480*
Oldest Store Museum, *480*
Oldest Wooden Schoolhouse, *480*
Plaza de la Constitution, *480*
San Augustin Antiguo, *480*
tourist information, *478*
Ximenez-Fatio House, *480*

St. Francisville, LA
Audubon State Commemorative Area, *560*
The Myrtles (haunted house), *562*

St. George Island State Park, FL, *630*

St. Helena Island, SC, *444*

St. Ignace, MI
dining, *743–744*
Father Marquette National Memorial and Museum, *736–737*
lodging, *744*
Mackinac Bridge, *736*

St. Marks Wildlife Refuge and Lighthouse, FL, *630*

St. Simons, GA
beach, *468*
children, *414*
Christ Episcopal Church, *468*
dining, *473–474*
Ft. Frederica National Monument, *468*
lodging, *474*
Museum of Coastal History, *468*
Neptune Park, *468*
Neptune Park Casino, *468*
St. Simons Lighthouse, *468*
village area, *468*

Salem, MA, *50–51*
dining, *61*
Essex Institute Museum Neighborhood, *52*
historic mansions, *52*
House of the Seven Gables, *52*
lodging, *61–62*
Peabody Museum, *52*
Pickering Wharf Antique Gallery, *54*
Pioneer Village and Forest River Park, *52*
Pyramid Books, *54*
Salem Maritime, *52*
Salem Witch Museum, *50*
Witch Dungeon Museum, *52*
Witch House, *52*

Salter's Island, SC, *459–460*

Sandwich, MA, *254*
dining, *261*
Heritage Plantation, *254*
Hoxie House, *254*
lodging, *265*
Sandwich Glass Museum, *254*

Santa Rosa Island, FL, *618*
Fort Pickens National Park, FL, *618*

Saugatuck, MI, *747*

Saugus, MA, *50*

Sault Ste. Marie, MI, *735–736*

dining, *743*
lodging, *743*
Museum Ship Valley Camp, *736*
Port Adventure, *736*
Soo Locks Boat Tours, *736*
Soo Locks Train Tours, *736*
Tower of History, *736*

Saunderstown, RI, *231*

Savannah, GA, *451–467*
Andrew Low House, *457*
Cathedral of St. John the Baptist, *456*
children, *414*
Chippewa Square, *456*
City Hall, *454*
Colonial Park Cemetery, *456*
dining, *454, 457, 461–464*
Emmet Park, *455*
Factors Walk, *454*
Forsyth Park, *458*
getting around in, *451–452*
Great Savannah Exposition, *453–454*
Green-Meldrim House, *457*
guided tours, *452*
Historic Landmark district, *451, 452–458*
Isaiah Davenport House, *455*
Johnson Square, *454*
Juliette Gordon Low House, *456*
King-Tisdell Cottage, *458*
Lafayette Square, *457*
lodging, *464–467*
Madison Square, *457*
Massie Heritage Interpretation Center, *458*
Monterey Square, *457*
nightlife, *467*
Oglethorpe Square, *456*
Oglethorpe's Bench, *454*
Olde Pink House, *455*
Owens-Thomas House, *455*

Reynolds Square, *455*
River Street, *454*
Riverfront Plaza, *455*
Scarbrough House, *454*
Ships of the Sea Museum, *455*
shopping, *457, 460–461*
Siege of Savannah site, *453*
sports, *461*
Telfair Mansion and Art Museum, *456*
Temple Mickve Israel, *458*
tourist information, *452–453*
Victorian District, *458*
Wesley Monumental, *458*
Wright Square, *456*

Scarborough Beach State Park, ME, *87*

Sea Island, GA
beach, *470*
Cloister Hotel, *470*
dining, *473*
lodging, *473*

Seabrook Island Resort, SC, *441*

Seabrook, NH, *62*

Searsport, ME, *95*

Seasonal events
Alabama, *595*
Cape Cod, *198*
Chicago, *641–642*
Florida, *412, 595*
Georgia, *412*
Gettysburg, PA, *271*
Illinois, *641–642*
Louisiana, *525*
Maine, *15*
Massachusetts, *15, 198*
Milwaukee, WI, *641–642*
Mississippi, *525, 595*
Mobile, AL, *595*
Natchez, MS, *525*
New Hampshire, *15*
New Orleans, *525*
New York City, *112*
Pennsylvania, *271*
Philadelphia, *271*
Rhode Island, *198*
South Carolina, *412*
Tallahassee, FL, *595*
Tennessee, *525*
Virginia, *334*
Washington, D.C., *334*

Sesame Place, Langhorne, PA, *272*

Shaker Museum, NY, *168*

Sheboygan, WI, *704–705*
dining, *714–715*
Indian Mound Park, *705*
John Michael Kohler Arts Center, *704–705*
Kohler Design Center, *705*
lodging, *715*
Sheboygan County Museum, *705*
Waelderhaus, *705*

Sheffield, MA, *170, 181*

Shelburne Falls, MA, *185*

Shell Island, FL, *620*

Shenandoah National Park, VA, *405*

Shenandoah Valley, VA, *401, 404–410*

Shiloh National Military Park, TN, *535*

Ship Island, MS, *598*

Shirley Plantation, VA, *392*

Silver Springs, FL, *634–635*

Sister Bay, WI, *715*

Skyline Drive, VA, *405*

Sleeping Bear Dunes National Lakeshore, MI, *746*

Somesville, ME, *105*

South Carolina. *See also specific towns*
beach, *435*
seasonal events, *412*
tourist information, *412*

South County, RI, *226–236*
arts, *236*
beaches, *233*
dining, *233–236*
lodging, *233–236*
nightlife, *236*
shopping, *231–232*
sports, *232–233*

South Egremont, MA, *170*

South Hadley, MA,

South Kingstown, RI, *229, 235*

South Norwalk, CT
commercial district, *203*
dining, *212*
Lockwood-Matthews Mansion Museum, *203*
Maritime Center, *202–203*
Mill Hill Historic Park, *203*

Southwest Harbor, ME, *105, 109*

Split Rock Lighthouse State Park, MN, *727*

Sports
Acadia National Park, ME, *106–107*
Bar Harbor, ME, *106–107*
The Berkshires, MA, *175–176*
Biddeford, ME, *75*
Boston, *31, 35*
Cape Cod, *258–260*
Charleston, SC, *434–435*
Charlottesville, VA, *407–408*
Chicago, *667, 668*
Door County, WI, *710–712*
Florida, northeastern, *483–484, 486*
Florida Panhandle, *621–623*
Gettysburg, PA, *328–329*
Grand Strand, SC, *420–421*
Gulf Coast, *609–610*
Hilton Head Island, SC, *446–447*
Kennebunkport, ME, *75*
Maine, *87*
Milwaukee, WI, *695–696*
Mississippi Gulf Coast, *601–602*
Mobile, AL, *609–610*
Myrtle Beach, SC, *420–421*
Nashville, TN, *536*
New Hampshire, *67*
New Orleans, *579*

North Shore, MA, *54–55*
Ocala, FL, *635–636*
Orlando, FL, *505–506*
Philadelphia, *291–292*
Pioneer Valley, MA, *188–189*
Richmond, VA, *393*
Savannah, GA, *461*
Shenandoah Valley, VA, *407–408*
South County, RI, *232–233*
Tallahassee, FL, *635–636*
Washington, D.C., *363–365*
Wells, ME, *75*
Wisconsin Lakeshore, *710–712*

Springfield, MA
Connecticut Valley Historical Museum, *187*
dining, *192–193*
George Walter Vincent Smith Art Museum, *187*
lodging, *193*
Museum of Fine Arts, *187*
Naismith Memorial Basketball Hall of Fame, *187*
Springfield Armory, *187*
Springfield Science Museum, *187*

Springfield Plantation, MS, *552*

Spruce Head, ME, *102*

Staatsburg, NY, *160*

Stamford, CT
dining, *212*
First Presbyterian Church, *202*
lodging, *212–213*
Stamford Museum and Nature Center, *202*
United House Wrecking (shopping), *202*
Whitney Museum of American Art, *202*

State parks
Bear Mountain State Park, NY, *156–157*
Big Bay State Park, WI, *720*

Burlingame State Park, RI, *229*
Camden Hills State Park, ME, *95*
Charles Towne Landing State Park, SC, *432*
Copper Falls State Park, WI, *719*
Crescent Beach State Park, ME, *87*
Edisto Beach State Park, SC, *443, 447*
Fall River Heritage State Park, CT, *249*
Fort Clinch State Park, FL, *475*
Fort Wilkins State Park, MI, *734*
Ft. Griswold State Park, CT, *219*
Gooseberry Falls State Park, MN, *727*
Gulf Marine State Park, MS, *600*
Gulf State Park, AL, *609*
Hammonasset Beach State Park, CT, *217*
Hampton Plantation State Park, SC, *419*
Harkness Memorial State Park, CT, *221–222*
Harriman State Park, NY, *156–157*
Heritage Hill State Park, WI, *709–710*
Heritage State Park, MA, *187*
Holbrook Island Sanctuary, ME, *98*
Hunting Island State Park, SC, *447*
Huntington Beach State Park, SC, *418*
Jeff Busby State Park, MS, *545*
J. P. Coleman State Park, MS, *542*
Little Talbot Island State Park, FL, *475–476*
Natural Bridge State Park, MA, *174*
Nickerson State Park, MA, *254*
North Shore, MA, *55*
Odiorne Point State Park, NH, *64*

State Parks
(continued)
Old Mill Creek State
Historic Park, MI,
739
Old Stone Fort State
Park, TN, *534*
Peninsula State Park,
WI, *708–709*
Popham Beach State
Park, ME, *87*
Reid State Park, ME,
87
Rock Island State
Park, WI, *708*
Rocky Neck State
Park, CT, *222*
Scarborough Beach
State Park, ME, *87*
Scusset Beach Reser-
vation, MA, *254*
Shawme Crowell State
Forest, MA, *254*
Sherwood Island State
Park, CT, *203*
Split Rock Lighthouse
State Park, MN, *727*
St. George Island
State Park, FL, *630*
Straits State Park,
MI, *736–737*
Tahquamenon Falls,
MI, *735*
Tishomingo State
Park, MS, *542*
Tomoka State Park,
FL, *481–482*
Wallis Sands State
Park, *64*
Western Gateway
Heritage State Park,
174
Wolfe's Neck Woods
State Park, ME, *87*
Staunton, VA,
404–405, 410
Stockbridge, MA,
170, 181–182
Stonington, ME, *96,*
97, 102
Stonington Village,
CT, *220*
Old Lighthouse
Museum, *220*
Stonington Vineyards,
220
Stony Point, NY, *156*
Straits State Park,
MI, *736–737*
Strasburg, PA, *310,*

322–323
Stratford, CT, *204*
Stroudwater Village,
ME, *82–83*
Stuart, Gilbert, *231*
Sturbridge, MA,
193–194
Sturgeon Bay, WI,
707, 715
Summerville, SC, *433*
Superior, MN, *731*
Superior, WI, *724*

Tahquamenon Falls,
MI, *735*
Tallahassee, FL,
632–633
arts, *638*
Capitol Complex area,
632
The Columns, *632*
dining, *637*
Lafayette Vineyards,
633
lodging, *637–638*
Maclay State Gardens,
FL, *633*
Museum of Florida
History, *633*
New Capitol, *633*
nightlife, *638*
Old Capitol, *632*
San Luis
Archaeological and
Historic Site, *633*
seasonal events, *595*
sports, *635–636*
tourist information,
632
Union Bank Building,
632
Tanglewood concert
series, *112, 172, 184*
Tarrytown, NY
dining, *169*
lodging, *169*
Lyndhurst, *155*
Old Dutch Church of
Sleepy Hollow,
155–156
Phillipsburg Manor
Upper Mills, *155*
Sunnyside, *155*
Tenants Harbor, ME,
93, 102
Tennessee. *See also*
specific towns
arriving and
departing, *526–527*
seasonal events, *525*

tourist information,
524
Thimble Islands, CT,
215
Thunder Bay,
Ontario, *728*
Tishomingo State
Park, MS, *542*
Tomoka State Park,
FL, *481–482*
Tour groups, 2. *See*
also specific
attractions
British travelers, *3–4*
Train travel, *10. See*
also specific
locations
Traverse City, MI,
744
beach, *747*
Clinch Park, *744*
Con Foster Museum,
746
dining, *750*
Grand Traverse Bay,
744
lodging, *750*
Truro, MA, *255*
Tupelo, MS, *544, 545,*
558
Two Harbors, MN,
727
Two Rivers, WI, *706,*
715
Tybee Island, GA,
458–459

U.S. Travel and
Tourism Adminis-
tration, *2*
Val-Kill, NY, *159*
Valley Forge, PA,
303–306
arts, *306*
dining, *305–306*
lodging, *305–306*
Valley Forge
Historical Society
Museum, *304*
Valley Forge National
Historical Park,
303–304
tourist information,
270
Van Buren, Martin,
162
Vicksburg, MS,
549–550
Biedenharn Candy

Company (Coke
museum), *551*
dining, *558–559*
historic homes, *550*
lodging, *559*
National Military
Park, *550*
nightlife, *559*
Spirit of Vicksburg
(riverboat), *550*
USS *Cairo,* 550
Vanishing Glory
multimedia show, *550*
Virginia, *380–410.*
See also specific
towns
arriving and
departing, *335–337*
arts, *382, 387*
dining, *385–387*
lodging, *385–387*
nightlife, *387*
seasonal events, *334*
touris information,
333
Voyageurs National
Park, MN, *727*

Wakefield, RI, *229*
Wakulla Springs, FL,
632
Wallis Sands State
Park, NH, *64*
Walt Disney World.
See Disney World
Washington, George
grave, *383*
monument, *345–346*
Mount Vernon, VA, *383*
Valley Forge National
Historical Park, PA,
303–304
Washington, D.C.,
337–379
Anderson House, *359*
arriving and
departing, *335–337*
Arthur M. Sackler
Gallery, *345*
arts, *376–378*
Arts and Industries
Building, *340*
Auditor's Building,
344
Barney Studio House,
360
bed-and-breakfast
services, *372*
Blair House, *350*
Bureau of Engraving

and Printing, 344–345

Cameroon Embassy, 360

Cannon House office building, 353

Capitol, 351–352

Capitol Hill, 351–356

cherry trees, 346–347

Chesapeake & Ohio Canal, 356–357

children, 334–335

churches, 349, 358, 361

City Post Office, 351

Constitution Gardens, 347

Corcoran Gallery of Art, 350

Cosmos Club, 359

Cox's Row, 357

Decatur House, 349

Department of Agriculture, 345

Department of Commerce, 355

Department of Justice, 356

Department of the Interior, 350–351

Department of the Interior Museum, 351

dining, 341, 344, 352, 354, 357, 359, 365–372

Dumbarton House, 358

Dumbarton Oaks, 358

Dupont Circle, 358–360

Ellipse, 348

Enid Haupt Memorial Garden, 345

Federal Triangle, 355–356

Folger Shakespeare Library, 353

Ford's Theater, 354–355

Fort Reno, 360

Foundry Mall, 357

Frederick Douglass National Historic Site, 360–361

Freedom Plaza, 355

Freer Gallery of Art, 345

Georgetown, 356–358

Georgetown University, 357

getting around in, 338

Hay-Adams Hotel, 349

Heurich Mansion, 358–359

Hirshhorn Museum, 340

House chambers, 352

J. Edgar Hoover Federal Bureau of Investigation Building, 356

Jefferson Memorial, 346

Kalorama neighborhood, 360

Lafayette Square, 349

Langley Theater, 341

Lincoln Memorial, 347

lodging, 372–376

Longworth office building, 353

Mall, 339–340

Martin Luther King Library, 354

monuments, 345–348

museums, 340–345, 350–351, 354–356, 359–361

National Air and Space Museum, 341

National Aquarium, 355

National Archives, 356

National Gallery of Art, 341

National Museum of African Art, 345

National Museum of American Art, 354

National Museum of American History, 344

National Museum of Natural History, 344

National Portrait Gallery, 354

National Postal History and Philatelic Museum, 351

National Sculpture Garden/Ice Rink, 344

National Zoo, 361

Nature Center and Planetarium, 360

nightlife, 378–379

Octagon House, 350

old downtown, 354–355

Old Executive Office Building, 349

Old Patent Office Building, 354

Old Post Office Building, 355

Old Stone House, 356

Petersen House, 355

Phillips Collection, 359

Pierce Mill, 360

Rayburn office building, 353

Renwick Gallery, 350

Rock Creek Golf Course, 360

Rock Creek Park, 360

Russell Senate Office Building, 353

St. John's Church, 358

St. John's Episcopal Church, 349

Sculpture Garden, 340

seasonal events, 334

Senate chambers, 352

shopping, 357, 361–362

Smithsonian Information Center, 340

Smithsonian Institution Building, 340

sports, 363–365

Supreme Court Building, 353

Tidal Basin, 346

tourist information, 333

tours, 338–339

Tudor Place, 358

Union Station, 351

United States Botanical Gardens, 353

Vietnam Veterans Memorial, 347

Walsh-McLean House, 359

Washington Harbour, 357

Washington Monument, 345–346

Washington National Cathedral, 361

West Potomac Park, 347

White House, 348

Willard Hotel, 355

Woodrow Wilson House, 360

Washington Island, WI, 708

Washington, MS, 552

Watch Hill, RI
dining, 235
Flying Horse Carousel, 228
lodging, 235–236
Napatree Point, 228
Ningret statue, 226
Ocean House, 228
U.S. Coast Guard Light Station, 228

Waterford, CT, 221–222

Waveland, MS, 605

Waynesboro, VA, 404

Wellfleet, MA, 255, 267

Wells, ME, 75

Welty, Eudora, 548–549

West Point, NY, 157, 169

West Stockbridge, MA, 182

Westbrook, CT, 225

Westerly, RI
Atlantic Beach Amusement Park, 228
dining, 236
lodging, 236
Wilcox Park, 228

Westport, CT
dining, 213–214
lodging, 214
Nature Center for Environmental Activities, 203
Sherwood Island State Park, 203

Wharton, Edith, 172

White Castle, LA, 567

Whitehall, MI
Deer Park (amusements), 746
White River Light Station Museum, 746

Wickford, RI, 231

Wild Dunes, SC, 441

Williamsburg, VA, 396–398
Abby Aldrich Rockefeller Folk Art Center, 398
arts, 401

Williamsburg, VA
(continued)
Bassett Hall, *398*
Busch Gardens
amusement park,
335, 398
Capitol, *396–397*
Carter's Grove
Plantation, *398*
children, *335*
DeWitt Wallace
Decorative Arts
Gallery, *398*
dining, *400*
Governor's Palace,
397
lodging, *400*
nightlife, *401*
sports, *399*
tourist information,
396
Wren Building, *397*

Williamstown, MA,
173
Chapin Library of
Rare Books and
Manuscripts,
173–174
dining, *182*
lodging, *183*
Sterling and Francine
Clark Art Institute,
173
Williams College,
173
Wilson, Woodrow,
405
Wiscasset, ME, *84*
Wisconsin. *See also
specific towns*
arriving and
departing, *643–644*
children, *642*
dining, *722–724*

fishing, *721–722*
lodging, *722–724*
scenic U.S. 51, *718*
sports, *721–722*
tourist information,
640
waterfalls, *719*
**Wisconsin
Lakeshore,** *702–715*
arts, *715*
beach, *710–711*
dining, *712–713*
lodging, *712–715*
sports, *710–711*
**Wolfe's Neck Woods
State Park, ME,** *87*
**Woodlawn
Plantation, VA,** *383*
Woods Hole, MA, *250*
Wright, Frank Lloyd,
383, 656, 663–664
Wrightsville, PA, *324*

**Wychmere Harbor,
MA,** *251*

Yarmouth, MA,
254
Yarmouth Port, MA,
262
Yonkers, NY,
153–155
The Yorks, ME, *72,
79*
Yorktown, VA
dining, *401*
Grace Church, *399*
Moore House, *399*
Nelson House, *399*
Yorktown Battlefield,
VA, *399*
Yorktown Victory
Center, *399*
Yorktown Watermen's
Museum, *399*

Personal Itinerary

Departure *Date*

Time

Transportation

Arrival *Date*   *Time*

Departure *Date*   *Time*

Transportation

Accommodations

Arrival *Date*   *Time*

Departure *Date*   *Time*

Transportation

Accommodations

Arrival *Date*   *Time*

Departure *Date*   *Time*

Transportation

Accommodations

Personal Itinerary

Arrival *Date*   *Time*

Departure *Date*   *Time*

Transportation

Accommodations

Arrival *Date*   *Time*

Departure *Date*   *Time*

Transportation

Accommodations

Arrival *Date*   *Time*

Departure *Date*   *Time*

Transportation

Accommodations

Arrival *Date*   *Time*

Departure *Date*   *Time*

Transportation

Accommodations

Addresses

Name	*Name*
Address	*Address*
Telephone	*Telephone*
Name	*Name*
Address	*Address*
Telephone	*Telephone*
Name	*Name*
Address	*Address*
Telephone	*Telephone*
Name	*Name*
Address	*Address*
Telephone	*Telephone*
Name	*Name*
Address	*Address*
Telephone	*Telephone*
Name	*Name*
Address	*Address*
Telephone	*Telephone*
Name	*Name*
Address	*Address*
Telephone	*Telephone*
Name	*Name*
Address	*Address*
Telephone	*Telephone*

Fodor's Travel Guides

U.S. Guides

Alaska
Arizona
Boston
California
Cape Cod, Martha's Vineyard, Nantucket
The Carolinas & the Georgia Coast
The Chesapeake Region
Chicago
Colorado
Disney World & the Orlando Area
Florida
Hawaii

Las Vegas, Reno, Tahoe
Los Angeles
Maine, Vermont, New Hampshire
Maui
Miami & the Keys
National Parks of the West
New England
New Mexico
New Orleans
New York City
New York City (Pocket Guide)

Pacific North Coast
Philadelphia & the Pennsylvania Dutch Country
Puerto Rico (Pocket Guide)
The Rockies
San Diego
San Francisco
San Francisco (Pocket Guide)
The South
Santa Fe, Taos, Albuquerque
Seattle & Vancouver

Texas
USA
The U. S. & British Virgin Islands
The Upper Great Lakes Region
Vacations in New York State
Vacations on the Jersey Shore
Virginia & Maryland
Waikiki
Washington, D.C.
Washington, D.C. (Pocket Guide)

Foreign Guides

Acapulco
Amsterdam
Australia
Austria
The Bahamas
The Bahamas (Pocket Guide)
Baja & Mexico's Pacific Coast Resorts
Barbados
Barcelona, Madrid, Seville
Belgium & Luxembourg
Berlin
Bermuda
Brazil
Budapest
Budget Europe
Canada
Canada's Atlantic Provinces

Cancun, Cozumel, Yucatan Peninsula
Caribbean
Central America
China
Czechoslovakia
Eastern Europe
Egypt
Europe
Europe's Great Cities
France
Germany
Great Britain
Greece
The Himalayan Countries
Holland
Hong Kong
India
Ireland
Israel
Italy

Italy 's Great Cities
Jamaica
Japan
Kenya, Tanzania, Seychelles
Korea
London
London (Pocket Guide)
London Companion
Mexico
Mexico City
Montreal & Quebec City
Morocco
New Zealand
Norway
Nova Scotia, New Brunswick, Prince Edward Island
Paris

Paris (Pocket Guide)
Portugal
Rome
Scandinavia
Scandinavian Cities
Scotland
Singapore
South America
South Pacific
Southeast Asia
Soviet Union
Spain
Sweden
Switzerland
Sydney
Thailand
Tokyo
Toronto
Turkey
Vienna & the Danube Valley
Yugoslavia

Wall Street Journal Guides to Business Travel

Europe | International Cities | Pacific Rim | USA & Canada

Special-Interest Guides

Bed & Breakfast and Country Inn Guides:
Mid-Atlantic Region
New England
The South
The West

Cruises and Ports of Call
Healthy Escapes
Fodor's Flashmaps New York

Fodor's Flashmaps Washington, D.C.
Shopping in Europe
Skiing in the USA & Canada

Smart Shopper's Guide to London
Sunday in New York
Touring Europe
Touring USA